EUROPE AND THE MEDITERRANEAN
• 1914 •

DREADNOUGHT

DREADNOUGHT

DREADNOUGHT

Britain, Germany,

and the Coming

of the Great War

ROBERT K. MASSIE

RANDOM HOUSE 🏠 NEW YORK

Library of Congress Cataloging-in-Publication Data

Massie, Robert K.
Dreadnought: Britain, Germany, and the coming of the great war/
by Robert K. Massie.—1st ed.
p.   cm.
Includes bibliographical references and index.
ISBN 0-394-52833-6
1. World War, 1914–1918—Causes.   2. William II, German Emperor, 1859–
1941   3. Edward VII, King of Great Britain, 1841–1910.   4. Germany—History—
William II, 1888–1918.   5. Great Britain—History—Edward VII, 1901–1910.   I. Title.
D517.M37   1991
940.3′11—dc20   91-52672

Manufactured in the United States of America
24689753
First Edition

Book design by Oksana Kushnir

For Kim Massie, Jack May, Charles Davis,
and Edmund Keeley
AMICIS A IUVENIBUS

And for Deborah

CONTENTS

TRAFALGAR

The supremacy of the British Navy was stamped indelibly on the history of the nineteenth century during a single terrible afternoon in October 1805. Between noon and four-thirty P.M. on October 21, in a light wind and rolling Atlantic swell off the coast of Spain, twenty-seven line-of-battle sailing ships commanded by Vice Admiral Lord Horatio Nelson annihilated a combined French and Spanish fleet of thirty-three ships-of-the-line under French Admiral Pierre Villeneuve. The battle took place in a small patch of ocean not more than two miles on each side, a few miles offshore between the port of Cádiz and the western end of the Strait of Gibraltar. The nearest map reference, a remote coastal bay, was to give the battle its name. The bay was called Trafalgar.

Nelson's victory that autumnal afternoon established a supremacy at sea which lasted a century and gave most of the world's great nations a period of relative calm known as the Pax Britannica. Both the naval supremacy and the peace endured while warships changed beyond recognition: wooden hulls were transformed to iron and steel; masts disappeared as sail gave way to steam; bottle-shaped, muzzle-loading guns were replaced by powerful, turret-mounted naval rifles of far greater range and accuracy. Something else remained constant as well: through all those years British seamen exuded a confidence *higher than arrogance, an assurance that was bred and passed along by the seventeen thousand men who served at Trafalgar in Nelson's oak-hulled leviathans.*

Trafalgar was fought because a mighty Continental state ruled by a conquerer, Napoleon Bonaparte, threatened the security and interests of England. The British Fleet attacked its enemy that day, bearing down on Villeneuve's worried captains with serene and implacable purpose, but the strategic role of the Royal Navy, then as always, was defensive. Historically, the mission of the British Fleet has been to protect the Home Islands from invasion and to guard the trade routes and colonies of the Empire. During the summer of 1805, the Emperor Napoleon assembled on the cliffs of Boulogne an army of 130,000 veterans to invade and subdue his English foe. The Emperor needed only a brief period of freedom of movement on the English Channel, time enough to transport his battalions across the twenty miles of water so that they could seize London and dictate peace. During their passage, the hundreds of flat-bottomed barges and small vessels collected along the coast to transport the army needed protection from the guns of the British Fleet. This protection could be provided only if Napoleon's own French Fleet, combined with the ships of France's reluctant ally, Spain, could at least briefly take control of the Channel. To block the Emperor's design and prevent the invasion of their homeland was the task of Britain's seamen.

They did so by performing one of the most remarkable feats of sustained seamanship in the annals of maritime history. Overwhelming as the victory at Trafalgar was, the battle was only the thunderous climax to an unparalleled nautical achievement. For two years before Trafalgar, the British Fleet remained continuously at sea off the coasts of Europe. Napoleon's fleet, broken into squadrons, was scattered in harbors from Brest on the Atlantic to Toulon in the Mediterranean. Britain's safety lay in preventing these squadrons from combining in sufficient numbers to force their way into the Channel and clear the way for passage of the Emperor's army into England. And so, for two years, the British Fleet watched and waited outside the ports of Europe; watching to see whether the enemy ships were raising sail and coming out, waiting to destroy them when they did. The blockade was maintained by fifty to sixty British ships-of-the-line, each vessel holding six hundred to nine hundred bored, lonely, hungry, weather-beaten men, lying at night in hammocks slung over their silent, waiting guns. For two years, the ships had been at sea, in the stifling heat and glassy calms of summer, in the gale winds, mountainous seas, and bitter cold of winter. They saw land rarely, touched it almost never. On the blockade, Nelson had spent two years without setting foot off the decks of his flagship, H.M.S. Victory. *For twenty-two months, Admiral Lord Cuthbert Collingwood, Nelson's second in command, had not heard the splash of his flagship's anchor. It was the blockade fleet and its success in stalemating the Emperor at Boulogne that Admiral Alfred Thayer Mahan described when he wrote: "those far distant, storm-beaten ships, upon which the Grand Army never looked, stood between it and the dominion of the world."*

Now, an angry, impatient Emperor had ordered his fleet to come out and sail for the Channel. The bulk of the fleet was at Cádiz, watched by an English fleet commanded by the idol of the British Navy and the hero of all England. Horatio Nelson was small, slight, and battered; one arm and one eye had already been given in the service of his country. He had other human frailties: he had abandoned his own wife to live openly with a lusty young woman, herself married to an elderly man who had given Nelson his unstinting friendship. Nelson disobeyed Admiralty orders when they did not suit him and he became seasick in bad weather. But his kindness and compassion already were legend, and his skill in battle has never been equalled. Every man in the British Fleet loved him and would follow wherever he led. Nelson's death at the moment of victory blurred triumph and tragedy. When the news reached England, the nation swayed dizzily between celebration and mourning.

Nelson's instructions, as the two fleets sailed slowly towards each other on a gentle morning breeze, were—as always—to attack. Recognizing that in the confusion of battle specific plans would go awry, he concluded his memorandum to his captains: "No captain can do very wrong who places his ship alongside that of an enemy." Implicit in this command was the assumption that any British ship could defeat any opposing enemy ship. Nelson's supreme confidence in British seamanship, British gunnery, and British courage was another legacy of Trafalgar.

Nelson divided his fleet into two divisions with himself in H.M.S. Victory *and Collingwood in H.M.S.* Royal Sovereign. *At the head of his division, Nelson steered his flagship straight at the center of the French line. At noon, the guns began to speak. Four hours of massive carnage were to follow. The lightness of the wind left the smoke of the cannonades hanging in thick curtains over the sea. Through these shrouds, ships would suddenly loom upon each other at close range, firing broadsides and then colliding, hugging each other in a hellish embrace. Cumbersome and slow, they drifted entangled while the men on one ship tried to kill the men on the other. At point-blank range of five yards, fifty guns would thunder and fifty heavy cannonballs would smash into the timbers of the adjacent ship. Huge masts* crashed to the deck, bringing down sails, spars, and lines across both ships and over the sides to trail in the water. On the main decks and in what remained of the rigging, marines fired muskets and cannon loaded with grape, sweeping the enemy's deck, covering it with rows of bodies, filling the scuppers with blood. Sometimes, when all the masts were down and the main deck empty, the men on the gun decks below continued oblivious, loading their cannon, running them out, depressing the muzzles to shoot through the hull or raising them to shoot through the upper decks of the opponent alongside. No matter how badly damaged their ships, Nelson's captains were relentless. Some British ships with masts down and rigging shot away still managed to rig temporary sails, gaining maneuverability to seek new enemies.

When the firing ceased about four-thirty P.M., eighteen enemy ships had struck their colors and a nineteenth had burned to the waterline and then exploded. Villeneuve himself was a prisoner, and later a suicide.

Trafalgar did not defeat Napoleon; ten more years were to pass before the Battle of Waterloo. But Trafalgar removed Napoleon's threat to seize the English Channel. Never again during those ten years did France or any other nation challenge Great Britain's dominion of the seas. And so it remained for one hundred years.

INTRODUCTION: SEA POWER

Thursday there had been great heat. Friday was worse. The breeze died, the air became moist and heavy. Flags hung limp and haze spread over the immense fleet anchored in the Solent. Only when the sun peeked through was it possible to see from shore the pale outline of what appeared to be an enormous city. One hundred and sixty-five warships of the British Navy lay in this protected body of water, three miles across from the sandy shores of the Hampshire plain to the wooded hills of the Isle of Wight. Five lines of black-hulled ships, thirty miles of warships, they carried forty thousand men and three thousand naval guns. It was the most powerful fleet assembled in the history of the world.

It was June 1897. Queen Victoria, seventy-eight, had reigned over Great Britain and its empire for sixty years and a Diamond Jubilee had been proclaimed. Saturday, June 26, was the review of the Royal Navy, the bulwark of Britain's security and the shield of her imperial power. Accordingly, the Admiralty had summoned the warships from Britain's home commands without withdrawing a single ship from the battle fleet in the Mediterranean or any of the squadrons on foreign stations. Twenty-two foreign navies had been invited and fourteen had accepted and sent ships.

The town of Portsmouth on the Solent, England's principal naval base since Tudor times, was crowded with sailors. Hundreds of British seamen came ashore every day from the fleet, along with foreign sailors from the foreign warships. The *Daily Mail* observed "black-browed little Spaniards, tall, dull-eyed Russians, and heavy-limbed Germans" browsing in the fruit stalls and tobacco shops. To amuse the sailors, the navy and the town organized garden parties, tours of the dockyard, sporting events, and a garden party for foreign seamen given by the Mayor. Naval planning, overwhelmed by numbers, went awry. "The victualing yard say they cannot possibly kill fast enough to supply the ships with fresh meat," an admiral ashore signalled the admirals afloat. "Suggest ships issue salt meat."

English men and women swarmed into Portsmouth. By Thursday night, all garrets were rented and people were sleeping on billiard tables and rows of chairs. It was difficult to sit and eat; every chair in every restaurant was coveted by a dozen hungry visitors. "Chief among the foreigners are Americans," noted the *Daily Chronicle.* "If they are not known by their accents, they are sure to disclose their nationality at mealtimes by rising without the slightest shame and prettily drinking the toast of 'The Queen!' . . . English folk would be shy of doing this except at a public dinner, but not so our cousins from over 'the Pond.' "

Every day, thousands of people paid a shilling to go out and see the fleet. Every available boat on the south coast of England—ocean liners, pleasure steamers, tugboats, steam launches and pinnaces, private yachts, watermen's boats, even clumsy Thames River barges—came up to Portsmouth piers to pick up spectators. Decorated with colored bunting and jammed with passengers, they steamed past the harbor mouth and the heavy stone forts guarding the anchorage and began the passage down the lines of warships. As the steamers passed, their wakes rocking the small navy boats set out from the warship hulls on booms, sailors and spectators waved and cheered each other. There were accidents: a black sailing schooner collided with a white steam yacht and lost her bowsprit; a launch ran into a small torpedo boat and the launch sank, but all her passengers were safely fished out of the water.

What the visitors saw, in the lines of black hulls, white superstructure, and yellow funnels, was British sea power. Farthest out from Portsmouth lay the Channel Squadron: eleven First-Class battleships, five First-Class cruisers, and thirteen Second-Class cruisers, with the flag of the Commander-in-Chief, Portsmouth, flying from H.M.S. *Renown.* This array of eleven battleships of the *Royal Sovereign* and *Majestic* classes, all under six years old, was unmatched for gunpower, armor, and speed. The next line contained thirty older

battleships and cruisers, the next thirty-eight small cruisers and torpedo boats, and the line nearest to Portsmouth forty-nine vessels, of
which thirty were new torpedo-boat destroyers.

The second line contained historic, but still serviceable, ships.
Here lay *Alexandra*, Admiral Sir Geoffrey Hornby's Mediterranean
Fleet flagship when he ran up to Constantinople in 1877 and trained
his guns on the Russian Army outside the city. Next to her was
Inflexible, which two decades before had been the world's mightiest
battleship. Her first captain, the famous Jacky Fisher, had used her
cannon to bombard Alexandria, opening the door to Britain's long
involvement in Egypt. *Inflexible* had recently been designated a
Second-Class battleship, but "even now," noted an observer, "the
muzzles of those four grim eighty ton guns peering from her turrets
could deal terrific blows." Ahead lay *Sans Pareil*, boasting a single
turret mounting two mammoth 110-ton guns, the largest of the
navy's weapons. Her presence could not help reminding spectators
of the Victorian Navy's greatest peacetime disaster: three years before her sister ship, *Victoria*, flagship of the Mediterranean Fleet,
had been rammed and sunk by *Camperdown* during maneuvers.

Beyond the farthest line of British battleships lay the foreign
warships. Visitors could stare at the big gray Italian battleship *Le-
panto*, the Japanese cruiser *Fuji*, built on the Thames, Norway's
black cruiser *Fritjhof*, and the modern French cruiser *Pothuau*,
whose bow sloped forward and down at a peculiar angle into the
sea. Interest centered on the Russian and American vessels, both
new. The *Rossiya* was the largest warship ever built in Russia.
Weighing 12,200 tons, she had three propellers and an advanced
engineering plant which could burn either coal or oil and drive the
ship at nineteen knots. The U.S.S. *Brooklyn*, an armored cruiser of
9,200 tons, was the pride of the United States Navy. She was the
most visually spectacular of the foreign ships; her sides, turrets, superstructure, and funnels were painted a gleaming white. British
observers with an eye to aesthetics declared the height of the tall,
thin funnels "by no means conducive to sightliness of appearance.
The effect is to dwarf the hull of the ship." For the Americans, it
was enough that the arrangement kept smoke off the decks and out
of the eyes of officers and seamen. The *Brooklyn* had other qualities
of interest to experts. Her decks, treated to be nonflammable, were
spongy and soft. "Will they stand the wear and tear?" the British
wondered (British decks were hard and combustible). The American ship used electricity to hoist shells from magazines to guns and
to rotate turrets. "We are at least seven or eight years behind,"
lamented the *Chronicle*. "Her equipment is so admirable that I

blush with shame that only one of our British men of war is fitted with electrical shell hoists." The deportment of the Americans attracted favorable comment: "The United States officers were exceptionally polite, never failing to raise their white-covered caps in greeting over the water."

Disappointment focussed on the next ship in line, a gray vessel with two red stripes around her funnel, S.M.S. *(Seine Majestät Schiff) König Wilhelm* (King William) of the Imperial German Navy. "Germany has sent us neither her newest nor her best," complained the *Daily Mail.* Indeed, the vessel, built as a battleship twenty-nine years before at Blackwell's Yard in England, had achieved fame primarily for ramming and sinking her sister *Grosser Kurfürst* (Great Elector). Recently, she had been stricken from the list of battleships and reclassified a First-Class cruiser. Kaiser William II cabled his brother, Rear Admiral Prince Henry of Prussia, who was aboard the *König Wilhelm,* "I deeply regret that I have no better ship to place at your disposal whilst other nations shine with their fine vessels. This is the result of those unpatriotic fellows [William was condemning the Reichstag] who opposed construction of the most necessary ships."

The British Empire, guarded by this fleet, was the largest in the history of the world. In 1897, the Empire comprised one quarter of the land surface of the globe and one quarter of the world's population: 11 million square miles, 372 million people. It was a cliché that "the sun never sets on the British Empire," but it remained, nevertheless, true. From Greenwich, the base from which the world reckoned time, the day moved westward to Gibraltar, Halifax, Ottawa, Vancouver, Wellington, Canberra, Hong Kong, Singapore, Rangoon, Calcutta, Bombay, Aden, Nairobi, Alexandria, and Malta. Within lay self-governing dominions ruled by parliaments, crown colonies, protectorates, and a unique empire within an empire, the brightest jewel in the imperial crown, the India of the Raj. The empire stretched over great land masses thinly (Canada, Australia) and densely (India) populated. It included tiny islands in the wastes of oceans: Bermuda in the North Atlantic; St. Helena, Ascension, and the Falklands in the South Atlantic; Pitcairn, Tonga, and Fiji in the Pacific. The Empire was a kaleidoscope of skin colors, a myriad of languages, dialects, religions, social customs, and political institutions.

All this had been won and was held by sea power.

Since the sixteenth century, when English mariners had an-

nexed Newfoundland and created England's first colony, the empire
had expanded. A single major defeat had marred the steady progression: between 1776 and 1881 the North American colonies had
successfully revolted and broken away. England bore this shock and
moved forward. Only a few years after the Treaty of Paris granted
American independence, Britain began two decades of war against
Napoleon Bonaparte. Once the Napoleonic Wars were over, with
the former Emperor confined on St. Helena, Britain became the
arbiter of affairs beyond the seas. Britons landed on the shores of
every ocean. They explored the continents; mountains, rivers, lakes,
and waterfalls were named for British explorers. Railroads were
laid, cities sprang up, governments were created, endorsed, or overthrown; by 1897 a multitude of kings, maharajahs, nawabs, nizams,
khedives, emirs, pashas, beys, and other chieftains sat on thrones
only at London's discretion. The British firmly believed they had
used their power benevolently. They had ended the slave trade,
policed and charted the oceans, and, believing in free trade, admitted all nations to the commerce they had opened.

In 1890, an American naval officer, more scholar than sea dog,
codified the Briton's intuitive sense of the relationship between sea
power, prosperity, and national greatness. In *The Influence of Sea
Power upon History*, Alfred Thayer Mahan traced the rise and fall
of maritime powers in the past and demonstrated that the state
which controlled the seas controlled its own fate; those which lacked
naval mastery were doomed to defeat or the second rank. Mahan,
using a graphic metaphor to make his point, said the sea "is . . . a
great highway, or better, perhaps . . . a wide common over which
men may pass in all directions, but on which some well-worn paths
show that controlling reasons have led them to choose certain lines
of travel rather than others. These lines of travel are called trade
routes; and the reasons which have determined them are to be
sought in the history of the world. . . . Both travel and traffic by
sea have always been cheaper than by land." From the metaphor
arose an imperative: to patrol the common, a policeman was
needed; to protect shipping and trade routes, maritime powers required navies.

The British Empire was a sea empire. More than half the
steamships plodding the oceans in 1897 flew the Red Ensign of the
British merchant navy. To service this huge tonnage, Britain had
girdled the globe with trading ports and coaling stations. The preeminent trade route, the Imperial lifeline, stretched to the east, through
the Mediterranean and Suez to India and China. Other sealanes
extended south to Capetown and west to Halifax, St. Johns, and

Montreal. There were fortresses to guard the strait at Gibraltar and Singapore and the narrow seas at Malta and Aden, but what made it all possible, the tie that held the empire together, was the navy. Wherever the Union Jack floated over battlements and warehouses, and the Red Ensign flew from the sterns of merchant steamers, there too was the White Ensign of the Royal Navy to protect, defend, deter, or enforce.

Without the navy, Britain was instantly vulnerable. The merchant steamers could be captured or driven from the seas, the fortresses besieged and taken, the colonies—deprived of reinforcement —stripped away. Without the navy, Britain itself, a small island state, dependent on imported food, possessing an insignificant army, could be in immediate peril of starvation or invasion. Bonaparte, waiting on the cliffs at Boulogne, had understood this. "Give me six hours' control of the Strait of Dover," he said, "and I will gain mastery of the world."

But with control of the seas, all was reversed. While Britain maintained naval supremacy, no Continental power, no matter how large or well-trained its army, could touch the British homeland. With naval supremacy, Britain acquired diplomatic freedom; British statesmen and diplomats could afford to stand back and regard with detachment the rivalries and hatreds which consumed the youth and treasuries of Continental powers facing each other across land frontiers.

Few European statesmen or military men understood Great Britain or the British Empire. They were puzzled when they studied the small island, with its ridiculous army, its aloof, almost patronizing manner, its pretension to be above the passions and squabbles which dominated their days. And yet, for all its smallness and seeming fragility, there Britain stood, serene, unchallengeable, with a range of action which was immense; which had in the past toppled Continental giants. Foreign military officers were particularly incredulous. With an army which was only an insignificant fraction of their own, Britain ruled a quarter of the globe. To German officers especially, representing the mightiest army in the world, it seemed absurd that Britain should claim to rule India's 300 million people with an army of seventy thousand. Yet, in India, Britain continued to rule.

If British naval supremacy had made it possible for the island kingdom to remain outside the web of Continental rivalries, Britain remained a European state. Political events on the great landmass across the twenty miles of water that separated Dover from Calais were of more importance to Britons than what happened in Brazil.

By 1897, Europe was divided into two alliance systems: Germany, Austria-Hungary, and Italy confronted France and Russia. England had taken no position and, under Lord Salisbury, her Prime Minister, did not intend to do so. This policy of aloofness Lord Salisbury had called "Splendid Isolation."

England's enemy since the Middle Ages had been France. Through the wars of the Plantagenets, against Louis XIV, Louis XV, and Napoleon, this had not changed. "France is, and always will remain, Britain's greatest danger," Lord Salisbury had said in 1867, and he clung to this view during his three terms as Prime Minister. France posed a multiple threat: to the British Isles directly across the Channel, and to the imperial lifeline as it passed through the Mediterranean. At a dozen spots around the globe, French and British colonies rubbed against each other uncomfortably.

Britain's other traditional enemy was Russia. Although the two nations had fought only once—and then awkwardly, in the Crimean War—the size and expansionist tendencies of the Russian Empire gave off a sense of menace. Russia might not reach the British Isles, but pushing down through Constantinople towards the Mediterranean, or thrusting over the roof of the world through the Khyber Pass onto the plains of India, or pressing from Manchuria against Britain's commercial monopoly in the Yangtze valley and South China, Russian policies seemed threatening. Britain's Director of Military Intelligence warned in 1887, "The countries with which we are most likely to go to war are France and Russia and the worst combination which we have any reason to dread is an alliance of France and Russia." In 1894, precisely such an alliance was signed and the dreaded became reality.

In the same month as the Diamond Jubilee Review, June 1897, two men were appointed to important offices in Berlin. Bernhard von Bülow, an ambitious career diplomat serving as German Ambassador to Italy, was promoted to State Secretary for Foreign Affairs—in effect Foreign Minister—of Imperial Germany. A week later, Rear Admiral Alfred Tirpitz, possessor of the most original mind and strongest will in the German Navy, became State Secretary of the Navy. Their assignments, although in different spheres, were linked. Kaiser William II wished his country, already the strongest in Europe, to advance beyond its Continental predominance to world power (Weltmacht). Bülow was to further this policy through diplomacy; Tirpitz was to provide the instrument by building a German battle fleet. William's interest in the sea and ships came in part from his English ancestry—his grandmother was Queen Victoria— but it had been profoundly stimulated by Mahan's book. "I am just now not reading but devouring Captain Mahan's book and am trying to learn it by heart," the young Kaiser wrote to a friend. "It is on board all my ships and [is] constantly quoted by my captains and officers."

Having grasped the importance of sea power and seeking to advance Germany's influence beyond Europe, William and his advisors confronted a dilemma: either Germany could accept British supremacy at sea and work within this framework, or it must challenge British supremacy and build a fleet powerful enough to wrest the trident away. Experience recommended the former course: in the 1880s, Germany had acquired colonies five times the size of the German Empire in Europe—and this had been done with British encouragement and assistance. The German merchant navy, the second-largest in the world, used British harbors and depended on British naval protection around the globe. German naval officers had grown up on British-built ships, burning British coal, using British techniques and tactics. British and German officers looked on each other as brothers. One choice, then, was to build on this relationship, reinforce and solidify it, looking to the day when Germany and Britain might act, in Europe and the world, in partnership, perhaps even in alliance.

The appointment of Admiral Tirpitz signalled that the opposite choice had been made. Why, the German Kaiser and millions of his people asked, should England, simply because it was an island and possessed an empire, claim to command the sea as a right? At any moment, the British Navy could blockade the German coast, bottle up German ships in harbor, and seize German colonies. Why should the German Empire exist on British sufferance? Why should German greatness come as a gift from another people?

Geography dictated confrontation. German merchant ships, leaving the Baltic or the North Sea harbors of Hamburg or Bremen, could reach the Atlantic and other oceans of the world only by steaming through the Channel or around the coast of Scotland. A German Navy strong enough to protect German merchant shipping in these waters and guarantee unimpeded passage to the oceans meant, in the last resort, a German fleet able to defeat the British Navy. This Great Britain would never permit, for it meant also a German fleet strong enough to screen an invasion of England, to sweep from the seas all British merchant shipping, to strip Britain of her colonies and empire. Thus, the goal of the German Navy—to protect German commerce on the high seas—was wholly incompatible with the interest of British security. What one power demanded, the other was unwilling to concede. The threat posed to German

security by the British Fleet, so British diplomats argued, was significantly less. Repeatedly, in the years ahead, British statesmen and
diplomats attempted to impress this point on their German counterparts; always the German reply was that German warships posed
little threat to Britain and that the German Empire had the same
right as the British Empire to build whatever warships it chose.

For a number of years, the Kaiser and his ministers, certain that
the most effective way of turning a neighbor into a friend was to
frighten him, cherished the belief that they could both build a powerful fleet *and* draw Great Britain into an alliance. The Kaiser believed—and Tirpitz said *he* believed—that once Britain saw and
accepted the formidable nature of the German Fleet, Britain would
respect Germany and offer friendship—a friendship in which Germany would become the dominant partner. This proved a catastrophic misunderstanding of the psychology of Britons, to whom
command of the sea remained a greater necessity than any Continental alliance.

As the century turned, the Diamond Jubilee and its great naval
review would be seen as the high-water mark of British naval supremacy. Soon, the strains on British power would begin to tell. The
empire was stretched too thin; even with the navy, Britain could not
meet its commitments. German shipbuilding would be met by British shipbuilding, but a change in British policy was necessary. Britain could not afford to be left to face single-handed a power which
dominated Europe and might acquire control of all the fleets of
Europe. To throw its weight against the dominance of one power or
group of powers which might threaten her existence had for centuries been the basic foreign policy of Great Britain. Now, as Britain
began to fear the German Fleet, it feared also that the greatest
military power in Europe would not aspire to become a great naval
power unless it wished to dominate the world.

And so Britain began to shift. Splendid Isolation was reexam-
ined. As the danger across the North Sea grew, enmities were composed, old frictions smoothed, new arrangements made. Britain
became, if not a full-fledged ally, at least a partner of her erstwhile
enemies, France and Russia. The alienation of Britain from Germany, the growing partnership between Britain and France and
Britain and Russia, were caused by fear of the German Fleet. "It
closed the ranks of the Entente," said Winston Churchill. "With
every rivet that von Tirpitz drove into his ships of war, he united
British opinion. . . . The hammers that clanged at Kiel and Wilhelmshaven were forging the coalition of nations by which Germany
was to be resisted and finally overthrown."

■ ■ ■

Saturday, dawn broke low and gray and heavy mists still hung over
the Solent. The sun rose at three forty-seven A.M., obscured by
masses of soft, gray clouds. The air was sultry. From shore, the lines
of ships could barely be discerned. The fleet became more visible at
eight A.M. when, on signal from the flagship, the whole of the lines
broke out in a rainbow of colors as each ship dressed itself in bunting from the bow, over the top of the masts, down to the stern. By
noon, the weather improved, as the sun burned off haze and mists.
A breeze blew out the flags and bunting, and covered the sea with
small whitecaps that changed in color and shade with every shadow
that crossed the surface of the water.

Through the morning, pleasure boats and sight-seeing craft had
swarmed through the lines. Then, near two P.M., as the hour of the
review approached, all private and commercial boats were shooed
away and the columns of warships lay in silence. Except for swooping gulls, snapping flags and bunting, the sunlight and shadows rippling over the water, there was no movement; it became a fleet of
ghostly mammoths, five walls of long, black hulls, standing majestically and silently on the pale-green water, stretching down the Solent as far as an eye could see.

Onshore, all was noise and tumult. The Southwest Railway
Company had promised to dispatch forty-six trains from Waterloo
Station to Portsmouth between the hours of six-thirty A.M. and nine-
thirty A.M. on Saturday morning. Trains ran every five minutes from
Waterloo, arriving in Portsmouth and pouring their human cargo,
slung with field glasses, cameras, and guidebooks, onto the cobble-
stones of the station square. From there, rivers of people flowed
through the town to piers and beaches. Every roof and window
looking out to sea was occupied; the piers, Southsea Beach, and
every little rise on the Hampshire plain were dense with spectators.

At twelve-twenty P.M. the first of two royal trains bearing the
reviewing party from Windsor Castle arrived at the Royal Quay in
Portsmouth Harbor. It carried the Dowager Empress Frederick of
Germany. Named Victoria after her mother, she was the Queen's
eldest child and the mother of the German Emperor, William II.
Her younger brother Arthur, Duke of Connaught, wearing the scarlet uniform of a colonel of the Scots Guards, gave her his arm and
conducted the Empress immediately on board the royal yacht, *Victoria and Albert,* which lay beside the quay. As she mounted the
gangplank, the gold and black German Imperial Standard soared up
the mainmast. Forty minutes later, a second royal train arrived and

the familiar rotund figure of Albert Edward, Prince of Wales, the central figure of the day's events, descended. The Prince would take the review while his mother, fatigued by her six-mile drive on Tuesday through the streets of London, surrounded by a million Britons cheering themselves voiceless, spent the day quietly at Windsor. With the Heir to the Throne were his wife Princess Alexandra, his brother, Alfred, Duke of Saxe-Coburg, and his son, George, Duke of York. The Prince was wearing the dark-blue and gold uniform of an Admiral of the Fleet. So was his brother, Alfred, who, until he had assumed the family duchy and moved to Germany in 1893, had been titled Duke of Edinburgh and had served as Commander-in-Chief of the British Mediterranean Fleet. Prince George, too, was in blue and gold and had earned his rank of Captain on active service. As the Prince and his party boarded the *Victoria and Albert* to join his sister for lunch, the Royal Standard of Great Britain ascended the mainmast to fly beside the German Imperial Standard, and the guns of Nelson's *Victory* boomed in salute.

At two P.M. precisely, the *Victoria and Albert* cast off her lines from the Portsmouth quay and her paddle wheels began to turn. Steaming out of the harbor, the royal yacht flew five huge flags, each the size of a baronial tapestry. Atop her foremast stood a dark-red banner with an anchor in yellow, the emblem of the Lords of the Admiralty. At the peak of her mainmast flew the Royal Standard of Great Britain, golden lions and silver unicorns on quartered fields of red and blue, and the German Imperial Standard, a black eagle on gold. At the mizzenmast floated the Union Jack and from the stern waved the White Ensign of the Royal Navy. Behind the yacht followed a procession of ships, large and small, carrying special guests. Immediately astern was the pale-green P & O line *Carthage,* her deck ablaze with the colorful uniforms and flashing jewels of foreign and Indian princes. Their guide was Captain Lord Charles Beresford, hero of the naval service. The Admiralty yacht *Enchantress* came next, bearing the Lords of the Admiralty and their guests. Next came the *Danube,* freighted with members of the House of Lords. She was followed by *Wildfire,* carrying the Colonial Secretary, Joseph Chamberlain, surrounded by the prime ministers and governors of the colonies and territories which made up the British Empire. Near the end, steaming very slowly "lest she tread on the toes of some of the little ones," came the huge Cunard liner *Campania,* biggest and fastest of Britain's transatlantic greyhounds, her immense bulk dwarfing even the battleships'. Steaming down from Southampton, where she had embarked 1,800 passengers—the members of the House of Commons and their friends and relations

—the *Campania* had followed in the wake of the much smaller *Danube,* carrying the Lords. At one point in this passage, John Burns, a Radical M.P., had quipped with a smile that if the *Campania*'s master would increase speed, many constitutional questions between Commons and Lords would be settled permanently. Last in line was the *Eldorado,* which bore the foreign ambassadors accredited to the Court of St. James's.

The fleet was ready. As soon as the boom of *Victory*'s signal cannon was heard announcing that the royal yacht was under way, a flag soared to the peak of *Renown*'s signal halyard: "Man ships!" In the days of sailing vessels, the result was the most dramatic of naval spectacles: seamen standing at regular intervals along every yardarm of the towering masts. Now masts and yards were gone, but the signal still created a memorable transformation. Great steel ships, previously grim and silent, now boiled with running men. Within a few minutes, lines of seamen stood motionless along the edge of every deck and on the tops of gun turrets and barbettes. Here and there, on the bridges and in the fighting tops, a splash of red showed where marine detachments were stationed.

As the royal yacht entered the lines, each warship boomed a salute and soon clouds of white smoke were drifting over the green water. (Sharp eyes noted an exception in the salutes from the French cruiser *Pothuau,* which was using the new smokeless powder.) Steaming slowly, the yacht came within easy hailing distance of the black behemoths. From the warships, it was easy to see the Prince of Wales surrounded by his party. His brother and his son stood beside him, and the Crown Prince of Japan and Sir Pertab Singh, huge jewels flashing in his silken turban, were nearby. Not far off was a mass of other officers, wearing scarlet, blue, and green tunics decorated with gold and silver. The ladies clustered around the German Empress and the Princess of Wales. Most were in yachting costumes of cream and navy blue, or sky blue and yellow, or maroon, or pale green. "No one looked better than the Countess of Warwick, in her dark blue alpaca, the neck of white embroidered batiste, the whole exquisitely fitting her beautiful figure," one correspondent described the Prince of Wales' former mistress.

As the royal yacht drew abreast each warship, officers and men removed their hats and shouted three cheers. If the ship carried a band, the band played "God Save the Queen." Observers noted pleasurably that the American sailors on board the *Brooklyn* cheered as lustily as any British crew and that the band on the deck of the *König Wilhelm* followed the anthem with a brisk playing of "Rule Britannia!"

While the Prince was inspecting the fleet, the lanes between the warships were kept clear of pleasure and spectator boats by naval tugs and patrol boats. But once *Victoria and Albert* had passed, an impudent maverick craft made a sudden appearance and began to race up and down the lines, weaving and darting between ships with astonishing speed and maneuverability. Patrol boats, attempting to overtake or intercept the intruder, failed. This strange craft, painted gray, shaped like a torpedo one hundred feet long and nine feet in beam, was *Turbina,* the world's fastest vessel, capable of thirty-four knots. Her performance was intended to persuade the navy to give up the heavy reciprocating steam engines which powered its warships and change to the steam turbine which sent *Turbina* knifing across the water. The boat's designer, Sir Charles Parsons, was on board, standing just aft of the tall midships funnel, which belched a flame at least as tall as the funnel itself. Racing among the towering men-of-war, defying authority, *Turbina* dramatically upset protocol. "Perhaps her lawlessness may be excused by the novelty and importance of the invention she embodies," grumbled *The Times.*

Finishing her tour of the lines at four P.M., *Victoria and Albert* drew abreast of the *Renown,* dropped her starboard anchor, and signalled all British and foreign flag officers to come on board to be received by the Prince of Wales. The admirals had been waiting in steam pinnaces and launches bobbing alongside their flagships, and when the signal came there was a race to the port gangway of the royal yacht. The behavior of the Russian admiral in this respect was much admired: disdaining to race, abjuring steam, he arrived in his barge pulled by the oars of sixteen sailors in white. While the guests were still on board, *Victoria and Albert* released a pigeon carrying a special message from the Prince to his mother at Windsor Castle: "Admirals just presented. Beautiful day, review unqualified success. The only thing to have made it perfect was the presence of the Queen."

At five, the visitors went down the gangway. *Victoria and Albert* pulled her anchor out of the Solent ooze, backed engines, and steamed away in the direction of Portsmouth. As she departed, another three cheers rolled out from the fleet. *Turbina* then made another surprise appearance. She had been lolling astern of a cruiser, but as the royal yacht got under way, *Turbina* fell in behind. At first she followed at moderate speed, but suddenly her propellers spun, she raised her bow, buried her stern in a mass of seething white foam, and blazed away on a tangent from the royal yacht. Leaving the fleet astern, the Prince of Wales ordered a welcome signal run up the halyard: "Splice the mainbrace!" and the Commander-in-Chief ordered every ship to distribute an extra tot of grog (rum and water) to every seaman.

Even as the Prince was receiving the admirals, menacing clouds were gathering on the southern horizon. As he left the fleet, the black hulls stood on black water with a bank of dark thunderheads towering overhead. Before *Victoria and Albert* reached Portsmouth Harbor, the sky was green and black and the first large raindrops had begun to fall. By the time the yacht was berthed alongside the quay, rain was lashing the decks with tropical violence. Lightning split the air with prolonged, crackling bolts of fire, and thunder rumbled like cannonade. Out in the fleet, curtains of rain blotted out the sight of ships in adjacent lines; decks and turrets became a tumult of dancing water. Ashore, where the drains were unequal to the deluge, great sheets of water lay on the Esplanade, and Southsea Common became a swamp. All shops were closed and crowds of people huddled under whatever shelter they could find. The thunderstorm, which lasted an hour, was one of the most severe ever recorded in southern England.

During the storm, it had seemed that the illumination of the fleet, the feature of the evening, would have to be cancelled. But at sunset only a canopy of heavy clouds darkened the twilight of the summer sky. To watchers on shore, the fleet was gradually fading into the deepening shadows. Then, at nine-fifteen, a signal cannon boomed. *Renown* suddenly jutted out, traced in fire, against the gloaming. A second later, every warship in the anchorage burst into outline, traced against the black sky by hundreds of electric lights. Strung the length of each ship, following the outlines of hull, bridge, funnels, masts, and turrets, the lights appeared as "lines of fire, which in the light haze which still hung above the water after the storm, took on the golden color of glowworm." Seasoned naval correspondents grew rhapsodic: The lights were "a myriad of brilliant beads," the ships "a fairy fleet festooned with chains of gold . . . lying on a phantom sea that sparkled and flashed back ripples of jewels." British flagships carried a large electrical display at their mastheads: a red cross on a white background announcing the presence of an admiral. Foreign ships created special effects. The *Rossiya* bore the Russian Imperial Double Eagle in lights. The *Brooklyn* spelled out electrically "v.r. [Victoria Regina] 1837–1897" along her armored side. Another *Brooklyn* feature was the fixing of the British and American flags floating at the top of her masts in the beam of powerful searchlights.

For almost three hours, this unique technological and imaginative accomplishment glimmered in the darkness. From shore and aboard the ships, people stared. Around ten P.M. the Prince and Princess of Wales came out again from Portsmouth in the small royal yacht *Alberta* to cruise through the fleet. The *Alberta* carried few lights and attracted little formal attention as she passed slowly down the stationary lines. At eleven-thirty, however, as the yacht departed, bands again played "God Save the Queen." Then, in a final salute to the Queen and her Heir, all the warships in the anchorage fired a royal salute. The ships were wreathed in curtains of smoke, illuminated by lurid red flashes from the guns. It was a spectacular climax: the continuous roar of a naval cannonade, tongues of bright flame leaping from multiple broadsides, smoke rolling in red clouds across the myriad of glowing electric lights.

The Prince returned to Portsmouth and the illuminations continued a little longer. Then, as the clock touched midnight, the flagship switched off and the rest of the fleet was plunged into darkness. From ashore, an observer standing on a hotel balcony recorded, "At the stroke of twelve, the golden, fairy fleet vanished. Was it a dream? Overhead the clouds pulled away and the stars twinkled above. The dim masthead riding light of countless vessels became visible. It had not vanished. The fleet was there."

PART I

THE
GERMAN
CHALLENGE

◆

CHAPTER 1

Victoria
and Bertie

◆

Queen Victoria was mostly German. Her father, Edward, Duke of Kent, fourth son of King George III, was a Hanoverian, a descendant of George Louis, Elector of Hanover, brought to England in 1714 and placed on the throne as King George I to ensure the Protestant succession. All of Queen Victoria's Hanoverian forebears—King George II, his son Frederick, Prince of Wales, and his son King George III—married German wives, reinforcing the German strain on her father's side. Queen Victoria's mother, Princess Victoria Mary Louisa of Saxe-Coburg, was German. Queen Victoria herself then redoubled the German fraction in the royal family by marrying her German cousin, Prince Albert of Saxe-Coburg, the son of her mother's older brother. The Queen's early environment was mostly German. Her governess was German; the cradle songs by which she was lulled to sleep were German; she heard nothing but German and spoke only that language until she was three. Her eager sympathy with most things German was due to her husband. "I have a feeling for our dear little Germany which I cannot describe," she said after visiting Prince Albert's birthplace.

The British monarchy, in the years before Victoria's accession, had come on hard times. Queen Victoria's immediate predecessors on the throne—George III, George IV, and William IV—have been described as "an imbecile, a profligate, and a buffoon." Victoria's father, the Duke of Kent, looked scarcely more promising. Retired from the British Army because of a taste for harsh discipline which had provoked a mutiny at Gibraltar, permanently in debt, a bachelor at forty-eight, he lived mostly abroad with his mistress of twenty-eight years, a French-Canadian woman named Madame de St. Laurent. Inspired in 1818 by an offer of an increased parliamentary subsidy if he would marry and produce a child, he ushered Madame de St. Laurent to the door and proposed to a thirty-year-old widow, Princess Victoria of Saxe-Coburg. They married and within ten months, on May 24, 1818, a daughter was born. Eight months later, the Duke of Kent, having made his contribution to English history, died of pneumonia.

The princess, second in line for the British throne, lived with her mother in practical, red-brick Kensington Palace, whence she journeyed from time to time to visit her aged uncle, King George IV. Early, she knew how to please. Climbing into the lap of the gouty, bewigged monarch, she would give him a beguiling smile and plant a whispery kiss on his dry, rouged cheek. "What would you like the band to play next?" the old gentleman once asked. "Oh, Uncle King, I should like them to play 'God Save the King,'" piped the child. "Tell me what you enjoyed most of your visit," King George said when it was time for her to go. "The drive with you," chimed little Princess Victoria.

She understood that she was different from other children. "You must not touch those, they are mine," she announced to a visiting child who was about to play with her toys. "And I may call you Jane, but you must not call me Victoria," she added for emphasis. An exasperated music teacher once presumed to lecture, "There is no royal road to music, Princess. You must practice like everyone else." Abruptly, Victoria closed the piano cover over the keys. "There! You see? There is no *must* about it!" When she was ten, she discovered and began to study a book of genealogical tables of the kings and queens of England. Startled, she turned to her governess and said, "I am nearer to the throne than I thought." When her governess nodded, Victoria's eyes filled with tears. Solemnly, she raised her right forefinger and made the famous declaration, "I will be good."

In 1830, when Victoria was eleven, the death of "Uncle King" brought the Princess even closer to the throne. The new King, her sixty-five-year-old uncle William, had sired ten children, all illegitimate; Victoria, accordingly, was Heir to the British Crown. King

William IV reigned for seven years, but at five A.M. on June 20, 1837, a group of gentlemen arrived at Kensington Palace, having come directly from Windsor Castle, where the King had just died. A sleepy young woman in a dressing gown, her hair still down her back, received them and they kneeled and kissed her hand. A reign of sixty-four years had begun. "I am very young," the new Queen wrote in her diary that night, "and perhaps in many, though not all things, inexperienced, but I am sure that few have more good will and more real desire to do what is fit and right that I have." The eighteen-year-old Queen, bubbling with youthful high spirits, provided a tonic for the British people, surfeited with foolish old men on the throne. On political matters, Victoria scrupulously followed the advice of her Prime Minister, Lord Melbourne. Their relationship was a blend of daughter and father, adoring younger woman and elegant, urbane older man—and sovereign and subject. The world thought Melbourne a cynic, but he charmed the Queen with his sophistication, his dry wit, and his deep devotion. She proclaimed him "the best-hearted, kindest, and most feeling man in the world," praise endorsed when her beloved spaniel, Dash, came up to lick Lord Melbourne's hand. "All dogs like me," the Prime Minister said, and shrugged, but the Queen would not believe it.

The vicissitudes of politics removed Lord Melbourne but, in 1839, Victoria herself chose the male counselor who was to have the greatest influence on her life. Her first cousin, Prince Albert of Saxe-Coburg, three months younger than Victoria, had grown up a serious, purposeful child. "I intend to train myself to be a good and useful man," he had written in his diary at age eleven. Victoria had first met her cousin before she came to the throne, when both were seventeen. "Albert's beauty is most striking," she told her diary. "His hair is about the same color as mine; his eyes are large and blue, and he has a beautiful nose and a very sweet mouth with fine teeth."

Subsequently, she noted further details: the "delicate moustachios and slight but very slight whiskers," the "beautiful figure, broad in the shoulders and a fine waist." Both knew that their elders hoped for a match. Still, the choice was up to her. She was almost ready to make that choice after watching him climbing the stairs at Windsor in October 1839. "It is with some emotion that I beheld Albert—who is beautiful," she told her diary. A few days later, she invited Albert to come to her private audience room, where she proposed. Albert consented and began the difficult task of becoming the husband of the Queen of England. When he suggested, before the marriage, that it would be nice to have a longer honeymoon than the two or three days set by the Queen, she reminded him, "You forget, my dearest Love, that I am the Sovereign and that business can stop and wait for nothing." The marriage ceremony took place at St. James's Chapel in London and the wedding night at Windsor. The following morning, the Queen rushed to her diary. Albert had played the piano while she lay on the sofa with a headache, but "ill or not I NEVER NEVER spent such an evening!!!. My DEAREST DEAR Albert sat on a footstool by my side and his excessive love and affection gave me feelings of heavenly love and happiness, I never could have *hoped* to have felt before!—really, how can I ever be thankful enough to have such a husband!"

In the early months of marriage, Albert's position was awkward. Victoria adored him and had insisted that the word "obey" remain in their marriage service, but, as he wrote to a friend, he remained "the husband, not the master of the house." His position improved when, nine months and eleven days after the wedding, he became a father as well as a husband. The child was a daughter, Victoria (called Vicky by the family), rather than the hoped-for Prince of Wales, but this disappointment was overcome eleven and a half months later when Prince Albert Edward (known as Bertie) arrived on November 20, 1840, at Buckingham Palace. The Prince was baptized at Windsor on January 25, 1842, in the presence of the Duke of Wellington and King Frederick William IV of Prussia, who bestowed on his godson the Prussian Order of the Black Eagle. After the ceremony, Victoria wrote: "We prayed that our little boy might become a true and virtuous Christian in every respect and *I* pray that he may become the image of his beloved father."

Bertie, installed in the nursery with an English and a German governess, began to speak bilingually; later, a visitor observed that the royal children "spoke German like their native tongue." Bertie's first words were mocked by his precocious older sister, and the Queen worried that her son "had been injured by being with the Princess Royal who was very clever and a child far above her age. She puts him down by a word or a look." Despite their squabbles, brother and sister were close.

Queen Victoria gave birth four times in her first four years of marriage, six times in her first eight years, nine times in all. Surprisingly in that era, all of her children lived to adulthood. She did not enjoy the process of childbearing. "What you say of the pride of giving life to an immortal soul is very fine, dear, but I own I cannot enter into that," she wrote eighteen years later when Vicky as Crown Princess of Prussia wrote rapturously about the birth of William, her own first child. "I think much more of our being like a cow or a dog at such moments when our poor nature becomes so very animal and unecstatic."

Prince Albert took primary charge of the children's education. His best pupil was his bright, adoring daughter Vicky; his most difficult the genial, stammering Prince of Wales. Albert decreed that Bertie could not be brought up as other boys—even other royal sons. The Heir to the Throne must waste none of his precious youth. Every day, every hour was planned. A platoon of tutors, carefully selected and rigidly monitored by Prince Albert, administered the program, while Prince Albert drafted the syllabi. Six days a week were crammed with Latin, French, German, algebra, geometry, and history. Bertie was required to write historical essays in German and French as well as in English. Meal hours (nine A.M., two P.M., and seven P.M.) and diets ("Luncheon: meat and vegetables, pudding best avoided") were established. Every night his tutors submitted a written report on his work. Unfortunately, the greater the effort invested, the smaller the apparent reward. Bertie did not learn; almost, it seemed, refused to learn. The result was redoubled effort, more syllabi, timetables more densely crammed—and a heavier flow of worried notes between tutors and royal parents. Bertie came to hate every book put in front of him. There were no other boys to play with. Prince Albert could find no hours in his son's schedule to be set aside for romping; besides, there was always the danger, even from titled boys, of contamination by frivolity. When, on the rarest occasions, boys from Eton were invited across the river to Windsor Castle to play with Bertie, Prince Albert was present to oversee and intimidate.

At the age of fifteen, Bertie was given a small allowance from which he was permitted to purchase his own ties and hats. The Queen used the occasion to deliver a lecture on dress: "Dress . . . [is] the one outward sign from which people in general judge upon the internal state of mind and feeling of a person. . . . We do not wish to control your own taste and fancies, which on the contrary, we wish you to indulge and develop, but we do *expect* that you will never wear anything extravagant or slang, not because we don't like it but because it would prove a want of self-respect and be an offence against decency, leading—as it has often done before in others —to an indifference to what is morally wrong." Prince Albert gave further advice two years later when Bertie reached seventeen and was appointed a Colonel in the British Army. "A gentleman," said Prince Albert, "does not indulge in careless, self-indulgent lounging ways, such as lolling in armchairs or on sofas, slouching in his gait," or standing about "with his hands in his pockets." "Satirical or ban-tering expressions" were considered vulgar and "a practical joke should never be permitted." In conversation, Bertie should be able to "take the lead and . . . find something to say beyond mere questions as to health and the weather." The supreme example, constantly placed before Bertie by the Queen, was his father. Repeatedly, Queen Victoria urged her children to emulate this matchless being. "You may well join us in thanking God for joining to us all your dearest, perfect Father," she wrote when Bertie was fifteen. *"None* of you can *ever* be proud enough of being *the child* of SUCH a Father who has not his *equal* in this world—so great, so good, so faultless. Try, all of you, to follow in his footsteps and don't be discouraged, for to be *really* in everything like him, *none* of you, I am sure, will ever be. Try, therefore, to be like him in *some* points and you will have *acquired a great deal."*

Bertie struggled to please, but usually disappointed. When he was seventeen, Queen Victoria wrote to Vicky, who had married Prince Frederick of Prussia, "I feel very sad about him. He is so idle and weak." Not long after, she complained again: "Oh dear, what would happen if I were to die next winter! One trembles to think of it. It is too awful a contemplation. . . . The greatest improvement will never make him fit for his position. His only safety—and the country's—is his implicit reliance in everything on dearest Papa, that perfection of human being!" Prince Albert, sending Bertie to visit Vicky in Berlin, tried to look on the bright side. "You will find Bertie grown up and improved," he wrote to his daughter. "Do not miss any opportunity of urging him to hard work. Our united effort must be directed to this end. Unfortunately, he takes no interest in anything but clothes, and again clothes. Even when out shooting, he is more occupied with his trousers than with the game." During this visit, Prince Albert wrote again, describing his son to his daughter: "Bertie has a remarkable social talent. He is lively, quick and sharp when his mind is set on anything, which is seldom. . . . But usually his intellect is of no more use than a pistol packed in the bottom of a trunk if one were attacked in the robber-infested Apennines."

At seventeen, in October 1859, the Prince of Wales began the first of four terms at the college of Christ Church, Oxford, where his efforts provoked his father to sigh, "Bertie's propensity is undescribable laziness. I never in my life met such a thorough and cunning lazybones." Even Bertie's dutiful handing over of his diary for inspection brought Albert's criticism of its lack of analysis and reflection. Gamely, Bertie apologized. "I am very sorry that you were not pleased with my journal as I took pains with it, but I see the justice of your remarks and will try to profit by them."

Bertie's first independent success came in North America. In July 1860, the Prince of Wales sailed on a tour of eastern Canada and the United States. At Niagara Falls, he stood on the Canadian side and saw the famous French acrobat Blondin cross from the American side on a tightrope, pushing a man in a wheelbarrow. Offered royal congratulations, Blondin proposed that the Prince come back with him in the wheelbarrow. Bertie eagerly accepted, but his advisors intervened and Blondin walked back across the falls on stilts. In the United States, then on the verge of civil war, the Heir to the British Throne traveled incognito as "Baron Renfrew." No one was fooled and in Philadelphia, which he declared the handsomest American city he had seen, the audience stood spontaneously and sang "God Save the Queen." He passed through Detroit, Chicago, St. Louis, Cincinnati, Pittsburgh, and Richmond, and in Washington was greeted by President Buchanan, who escorted him to Mount Vernon. In New York City, after a parade down Broadway, the Prince was the guest of honor at a ball at the Academy of Music. Two thousand uninvited guests pushed their way in with the result that just as Bertie arrived, the floor sagged three feet. He visited Boston, met Longfellow, Emerson, and Oliver Wendell Holmes, and sailed from Portland, Maine, at the end of October. The Queen was proud of his success and wrote to Vicky, "He was immensely popular everywhere and really deserves the highest praise."

To channel this new maturity, the Prince's parents decided that he should be married. Vicky eagerly undertook the assignment of Continental scout, compiling lists of eligible Protestant princesses who might meet her mother's specifications: "good looks, health, education, character, intellect, and a good disposition." Eventually, Vicky proposed a candidate: "She is a good deal taller than I am, has a lovely figure, but very thin, a complexion as beautiful as possible. Very fine, white, regular teeth and very fine large eyes . . . with extremely prettily marked eyebrows . . . as simple, natural, and unaffected as possible . . . graceful . . . bewitching . . . indescribably charming." Queen Victoria, impressed by this torrent of adjectives, pronounced the young woman "a pearl not to be lost."

The pearl was sixteen-year-old Princess Alexandra of Denmark, eldest daughter of Prince Christian of Schleswig-Holstein. A cousin of King Frederick VII of Denmark, Prince Christian had no money other than what he earned as an officer in the Danish Guards. He and his wife lived in an unpretentious house in Copenhagen with a front door opening directly onto a cobbled street. Nevertheless, despite modest circumstances, they managed to bring up

six children, four of whom were to sit upon thrones: his eldest son
Frederick as King Frederick VIII of Denmark, his daughter Alexandra as Queen of England, his son William as King George I of
Greece, and his daughter Dagmar as Empress Marie Feodorovna of
Russia. During their childhood, Alexandra and Dagmar (called Alix
and Minny), three years separated in age, were rarely apart. They
shared a small bedroom, studied English, German, and French side
by side, and learned music from their mother and gymnastics from
their father. In appearance and character, however, the two were
quite different. Princess Dagmar was short, dark, clever, quick-
witted, while Princess Alexandra, with her soft brown hair and deep
blue eyes, was affectionate with everyone, sleepily uninterested in
books and politics, and—as pronounced by Queen Victoria after
seeing a photograph—"outrageously beautiful."

Negotiations to acquire the Danish pearl began while the hus-
band-to-be spent the summer in an Irish training camp with the
Grenadier Guards. During this service, a group of sporting young
officers spirited a young woman named Nellie Clifden into Bertie's
bed. Nellie, who had known a whole regiment of officers, could not
help bragging about this particular conquest. In September, the
Prince departed for Germany and, in company with Vicky, traveled
incognito to meet Princess Alexandra "by chance" while strolling
through a church. Vicky reported the results to Windsor: "Alix has
made an impression on Bertie, though in his own funny and unde-
monstrative way. He said to me that he had never seen a young lady
who pleased him so much." For the moment, that was as far as the
Prince was willing to go. Prince Albert wrote sternly to his son,
stressing the importance of a marriage and the appeal of this exceptional candidate. Still, Bertie held back. The probable cause revealed itself in mid-November when rumors concerning Nellie
Clifden, swirling through the clubs of London, reached Prince Albert's ears. He wrote to Bertie "with a heavy heart on a subject
which has caused me the greatest pain I have yet felt in this life."
The malefactor confessed and his father forgave him, encouraging
him to "fight a valiant fight" and go ahead with an early marriage.
"You must not, you dare not, be lost. The consequences for this
country and for the world would be too dreadful!" Albert traveled
to Cambridge, where Bertie was enrolled at Trinity College, took a
long walk with his son, and came home pleased by Bertie's contri-
tion but physically exhausted. A few days later he wrote to his
daughter: "I am at a very low ebb. Much worry and great sorrow
(about which I beg you not to ask questions) have robbed me of
sleep during the past fortnight. In this shattered state I had a heavy

catarrh and for the past four days am suffering from headache and pains in my limbs which may develop into rheumatism."

In fact, Prince Albert had typhoid fever, the deadly killer of the nineteenth century. The Queen, in disbelieving horror, sat by Albert's bed while he wavered between clarity and delirium. In lucid moments, the two whispered to each other in German. On December 14, with the Queen kneeling beside him and the Prince of Wales standing at the end of the bed, Prince Albert died. He was forty-two; Victoria, now alone, was also forty-two. "He was my life," sobbed the Queen. "How am I alive . . . I who prayed daily that we might die together and I never survive him! I who felt when in those blessed Arms clasped and held tight in the sacred Hours at night— when the world seemed only to be ourselves and that nothing could part us! I felt so very secure."

The Queen was convinced that what she called "Bertie's fall" was at least in part responsible for Prince Albert's death. "Oh, that Boy—much as I pity, I never can or shall look at him without a shudder," she wrote to Vicky. Nevertheless, the wedding project was not cancelled, and Queen Victoria asked Vicky to explain to Alexandra's parents about Nellie Clifden: "that *wicked wretches* had led our poor innocent boy into a scrape which had caused his beloved father and myself the deepest pain . . . but that both of us had forgiven him the *one sad mistake* . . . and that I was very confident he would make a steady Husband. . . ."

In September Bertie met Alexandra at a palace in Belgium and there, walking in a garden, he proposed. He described the moment to his mother: "After a few commonplace remarks . . . I asked how she liked our country and if she would some day come to England and how long she would remain. She said she hoped some time. I said that I hoped she would remain always there and offered her my hand and my heart. She immediately said Yes. But I told her not to answer too quickly but to consider over it. She said she had long ago. I then asked her if she liked me. She said Yes. I then kissed her hand and she kissed me." Two days later, writing again to his mother, Bertie gave his feelings greater rein: "I frankly avow to you that I did not think it possible to love a person as I do her. She is so good and kind."

Alexandra came to England to become acquainted with the Queen while Bertie set off on a Mediterranean cruise with Vicky and her husband, Frederick of Prussia. By day, the seventeen-year-old Alexandra wrote letters to her twenty-two-year-old fiancé; at night she sat with Queen Victoria and listened to stories about Prince Albert. Her charm captivated the Queen, who wrote her ultimate approval in her diary: "How beloved Albert would have loved her!" The wedding took place at Windsor Castle on March 10, 1863. During a dinner earlier that week, the queen, "feeling desolate," remained in her rooms. But immediately before the meal, "dear, gentle Alix knocked at the door, peeped in, and came and knelt before me with that sweet, loving expression which spoke volumes. I was much moved and kissed her again." The day before the ceremony, Queen Victoria took the engaged couple to the Frogmore mausoleum, where Albert lay enshrined. She placed Alix's hand in Bertie's, took both of them in her arms, and declared, *"He* gives you his blessing!" Alexandra already considered herself fortunate. The morning of the wedding she said to Vicky, "You may think that I like marrying Bertie for his position; but if he were a cowboy I would love him just the same and would marry no one else."

Ten months after her marriage, the Princess of Wales rose abruptly from watching her husband play ice hockey, rushed home, and delivered a son. Conforming to Queen Victoria's wish that all of her male descendants should be named Albert and all of her female descendants Victoria, the child was formally named Albert Victor Christian Edward (in the family, he was Eddy). The birth coincided with a dramatic and painful political event. On November 15, 1863, Princess Alexandra's father had succeeded to the Danish throne as King Christian IX. Ignoring an international treaty, he immediately annexed the partially independent duchies of Schleswig and Holstein into the Danish kingdom. The German Confederation objected and Prussia sent troops against the Danes, resulting in the first foreign victory of the Prussian minister-president, Otto von Bismarck. This war divided the British royal family. The Queen and her daughter Vicky, now Crown Princess of Prussia, were pro-German; Princess Alexandra, weeping bitterly for her own "poor Papa," along with Bertie, the government, and most of the press, strongly supported Denmark. Eventually, the Queen enforced domestic peace at Windsor by decreeing that the subject of Schleswig-Holstein not be discussed. Two years later, when Prussia itself annexed the duchies, Alexandra was permanently embittered. Years later, when Kaiser William II made her second son, Prince George, an honorary Colonel in a Prussian regiment, Alexandra spluttered: "So, my Georgie boy has become a real life, filthy, blue-coated, Picklehaube German soldier!!! Well, I never thought to have lived to see that!"

In 1867, twenty-two-year-old Alexandra came down with rheumatic fever. The attack began in February and it was July before she could be wheeled into the garden. Bertie, at first solicitous, soon grew bored. "The Princess had another bad night," wrote an indignant lady-in-waiting, "chiefly owing to the Prince promising to come in at 1 A.M., and keeping her in a perpetual fret, refusing to take her opiate for fear she should be asleep when he came! And he never came until 3 A.M.!" The illness left Alexandra with a permanently stiff knee and a limp. It also triggered a form of hereditary deafness, which worsened as the years passed.

For many years after Prince Albert's death, Queen Victoria withdrew, dividing her time between Windsor Castle and two houses which Albert had designed, Balmoral in the Scottish Highlands and Osborne House on the Isle of Wight. Her ministers, when they wished and needed to see her, traveled. She refused to accept the Prince Consort's absence. His rooms were left for forty years as if he were alive and might walk in. Every evening, his clothes were laid out with warm water and a fresh towel. His coats and trousers, hanging in his closets, were rigorously brushed and pressed. In their bedrooms, the Queen hung his portrait over the empty pillow. She fell asleep clutching his nightshirt and kept a cast of his hand on her night table so that she might reach out and hold it. As, in the Queen's mind, Albert still lived, she must be the messenger who could interpret his wishes and be certain that his commands were carried out. On this, Victoria was grimly determined. "I am anxious to repeat . . . that *my firm* resolve, my *irrevocable decision,* [is] that *his* wishes—*his* plans—about everything, *his* views about *everything* are to be *my law.* And *no human power* will make me swerve from what he decided and wished! I am *also determined* that *no one* person—may he be ever so good, ever so devoted . . . is to lead or guide or dictate *to me.* I know *how he* would disapprove it."

The principal object of this implacable injunction was the Prince of Wales. Later, Victoria admitted: "After '61, I could hardly bear the thought of anyone helping me, or standing where my dearest had always stood." Bertie, twenty when his father died, could not share in the great work of fulfilling Albert's will; indeed, Bertie now was one of her burdens. While Albert had lived, supervision of the Prince of Wales' training and conduct had been his father's concern. Now it was hers, and she pledged herself to exercise the same rigorous control over the errant son as Albert had. There would be no sharing of either the burden or the power of the crown with the Heir to the Throne. Bertie was immature, indiscreet. During the Schleswig-Holstein crisis, she informed the Foreign Office that the Prince of Wales was not to be told *"anything* of a very *confidential* nature." When Bertie asked to see diplomatic dispatches, the Queen sharply forbade any "independent communication" between the government and her son. "The Prince of Wales . . . has no right to meddle and never has done so before. . . . The Queen cannot allow any private and intimate communication . . . or all confidence will be *impossible!*"

Blocked from all but the most superficial, ceremonial participation in public affairs, the Prince of Wales still achieved at least a partial liberation from his mother. A married man and a father, he needed a separate establishment and his own domicile. In London, Marlborough House on the Mall, built by Christopher Wren for the first Duke of Marlborough, was remodeled for the Prince and Princess, who moved in in 1862. In Norfolk, Sandringham, an estate of seven thousand acres, abounding in pheasants and other game, was purchased.

If the Prince was excluded from politics, society was another matter. At a time when the Queen's seclusion rendered the royal court almost nonexistent, the young Prince and Princess of Wales became the center of society and the arbiters of fashion. Queen Victoria and Prince Albert, following Albert's inclinations, had come to regard society as frivolous and decadent, limiting their circle to royal relatives and a sprinkling of the oldest nobility. Society, which had laughed at Prince Albert and pitied Queen Victoria, now threw open its doors for the youthful Prince of Wales and his beautiful Princess. Bertie, especially, rushed to embrace all that was offered. Day after day, he hurried from one social engagement to the next, enjoying banquets, balls, operas, music halls, theater, garden parties, and private suppers. He could get by with little sleep. Sometimes, friends would be summoned to Marlborough House late at night for supper and whist until the early hours. At other times, he would sally forth with a party to explore London nightlife, using hired hansom cabs rather than royal carriages, often ending up at Evans Music Hall in Covent Garden, where he and his friends would sit in a reserved box protected by a screen from the audience's gaze.

The Prince's circle encompassed aristocrats, politicians, diplomats, financiers, merchants, physicians, explorers, actors, and actresses. This circle acquired a name, "the Marlborough House Set." Members, aware of Bertie's desire never to be alone, arranged to make themselves available at short notice. To institutionalize his friendships and provide a site for meetings, in 1869 the Prince formed the Marlborough Club at 52 Pall Mall, near Marlborough

House. Four hundred gentlemen, all acquaintances of the Prince of Wales, made up the original membership, and Bertie became the club's first president. Jewish members were welcomed and smoking was permitted in most rooms. On the lawn behind the club, there was a bowling alley where Bertie and his friends bowled in their shirtsleeves until the neighbors protested the rumbling of the balls. Until the Prince's death, all candidates for membership required his endorsement for election.

Bertie valued his companions and showed them intense loyalty, but a certain sensitivity was demanded in return. He liked wit, tolerance, and gaiety; he enjoyed a funny story, a good anecdote, or a tidbit of gossip properly presented. Snobs, prudes, prigs, and bores were made unwelcome. Bertie did not mind a measure of gentle chaffing, but there were limits; he expected respect and deference to his rank. The trick for those close to him was knowing where to draw the line between cordial good fun and excessive familiarity. Occasionally, men close to him trespassed, and the Prince reacted swiftly. Behind his back, his friends referred to his increasing girth, calling him "Tum Tum." One night at Sandringham, a visiting baronet was behaving wildly in the billiard room when the Prince put his hand on his friend's shoulder and remarked with a kindly smile, "Freddy, Freddy, you're very drunk." Sir Frederick immediately pointed to his host's waistline and said, "Tum Tum, you're very fat." The Prince turned on his heel and beckoned to an equerry. Before breakfast the next morning, Sir Frederick had left the house.

The Prince had a voracious appetite. At breakfast, before shooting, he had poached eggs, bacon, haddock, and chicken or woodcock. His dinner seldom consisted of fewer than twelve courses, the richer and more elaborate the better. He delighted in caviar at any hour, never tired of crayfish cooked in Chablis, and was especially fond of game birds—grouse, pheasant, partridge, snipe, or woodcock—boned, stuffed with truffles or foie gras, and bathed in a rich Madeira sauce. He insisted on roast beef and Yorkshire pudding at Sunday lunch after church and regarded grilled oysters as the ideal dish for an after-theater supper. His wife complained that he ate anything, refused to chew, and bolted his food. Bertie drank moderately, preferring champagne to wines and taking only a single glass of brandy after dinner. He loved to smoke, however. It was unpardonable in the Victorian Age for gentlemen to smoke in the presence of ladies, and considered vulgar even to smell of tobacco. Queen Victoria permitted no smoking in the royal palaces, even in guest bedrooms. Count Paul von Hatzfeldt, the German Ambassador, once was discovered at Windsor Castle, lying in his pajamas on the bedroom floor with his head in the fireplace, blowing smoke up the chimney. There was no smoking in the dining room after dinner, even after the ladies had withdrawn; gentlemen sat and drank port or brandy, avoiding tobacco lest the room be tainted by the smell. Only after the ladies had gone to bed might gentlemen switch into silk smoking jackets and puff away on cigars or cigarettes. The Prince of Wales was not able to change these rules while his mother was on the throne. In his own houses, however, and everywhere else, he smoked prodigiously. Beginning with a small cigar and two cigarettes before breakfast, he consumed an average of twelve large cigars and twenty cigarettes a day.

From afar, Queen Victoria disapproved of the behavior of what she called the "Marlborough House fast set." Describing Society as *"repulsive, vulgar, bad and frivolous in every way,"* she likened it to the nobility of France on the eve of the French Revolution. The Prince and Princess of Wales, particularly the Prince, seemed to her bent only on pleasure. "Bertie and Alix left . . . [Windsor] today, both looking as ill as possible," she wrote to Vicky. "We are all seriously alarmed about her. For although Bertie says he is anxious to take care of her, he goes on going out every night till she will become a Skeleton. Oh, how different poor, foolish Bertie is to adored Papa, whose gentle, loving, wise, motherly care of me, when he was not 21, exceeded everything."

In October 1871, soon after his thirtieth birthday, the Prince contracted typhoid fever while visiting a country house. Two others in the house party, an earl and a groom, also became feverish and ultimately died. Bertie was taken to Sandringham, where he steadily grew worse. By the beginning of December, his condition had worsened sufficiently to bring Queen Victoria hurrying to Sandringham, where she remained for eleven days. The rest of the royal family assembled in the overcrowded house, split into groups, sitting in parlors, waiting anxiously for news. Princess Alexandra sat by her husband's bedside, leaving only to pray in the village church. The Queen also sat in the sickroom watching her son, who was bathed in sweat, start up from a feverish sleep to hurl pillows at his nurse. No one forgot the approaching fatal anniversary—December 14—of the Prince Consort's death ten years before from the same disease. On December 11, Bertie raved incessantly, talking, singing, whistling. At seven P.M., the Queen was told that the end probably would come during the night. "In those heart-rending moments," Victoria wrote in her journal, "I scarcely knew how to pray aright, only asking God, if possible, to spare my beloved Child." In the morning, the Prince was slightly better, and by the fourteenth the fever had vanished entirely.

Bertie sought diversion in travel. In 1866, the Prince of Wales went to St. Petersburg to represent his mother at the marriage of Alexandra's Danish sister Minny to the Russian Tsarevich Alexander (known as Sasha). Alix, desperate to go, was pregnant and had to remain at home. In 1869, however, she accompanied the Prince on a six-month tour to Paris, Copenhagen, Berlin, Vienna, Cairo, Constantinople, Sebastopol, Yalta, and Athens. In Vienna, he found Hapsburg protocol onerous—it required him to call upon every member of the Emperor Franz Josef's extended family—"and as there are 27 archdukes now at Vienna, it is hard work." In Egypt, six blue and gold river steamers bore the royal party five hundred miles up the Nile, towing barges which carried three thousand bottles of champagne, four thousand bottles of claret, four French chefs, and a white donkey for the Princess to ride. Returning to Cairo, Bertie climbed the Great Pyramid, and Alix visited the Khedive's harem, where the women painted her face and eyes, wrapped her in a robe and veil, and sent her back to surprise her husband.

The Prince of Wales' favorite foreign country was France; his favorite Continental city, Paris. As a boy of fourteen, riding through the French capital in a carriage with the Emperor Napoleon III, he had announced, "I should like to be your son." In the last decade of the Second Empire (the 1860s), Bertie took every opportunity to visit Paris and bask in the brilliance of the imperial court. He became a familiar and popular figure in many Parisian circles: with the Bourbon princesses of the House of Orléans, the sons of the House of Rothschild, the dowagers of the Faubourg St.-Germain, and the ladies of the demimonde. After the fall of the Empire in 1870, Bertie remained a welcome figure, not only in the aristocratic French Jockey Club, of which he remained a member until his death, but among Republican politicians, who saw in England a counterweight to the massive power of the new German Empire. In France, the Prince usually traveled incognito and became "Baron Renfrew," or, when Alexandra was with him, "the Duke and Duchess of Lancaster," or even "Mr. and Mrs. Williams." No one was fooled, but the public understood that he wished to enjoy his privacy.

Every year at the end of the London season, the Prince went yachting at Cowes and then slipped away to a Continental spa to try to lose weight. When this took him to Austria, he called on the

Emperor. Protocol aside, he liked Franz Josef. "The weather is still excellent and the riding enjoyable on maneuvers," wrote the Hapsburg emperor in 1888, when he was fifty-eight and Bertie forty-seven. "I tried hard to shake off the Prince of Wales by continued hard trotting and by sustained gallop. But I didn't succeed. This chubby man kept right up with me. He showed incredible endurance and spirit, even after he grew a bit stiff. He wore through his red Hussar's trousers, which was pretty uncomfortable since he had nothing on underneath."

The Prince disliked Germany. Bernhard von Bülow, the German diplomat who later became Chancellor, knew the Prince well and said that Bertie "could never rid himself of the impression that the word 'German' was identical with the narrow-minded, moral preaching, drilling, and brute force. If he found a man to be dull, clumsy and uncouth, he would say of him: 'He is as tiresome and tedious as a German professor.' If a lady seemed to him to lack all grace and elegance, he compared her with a German *Frauchen.*" Bertie's view of Germany was reinforced by his wife, Princess Alexandra, who hated Germans for wrenching away Schleswig and Holstein from Denmark, and by his sister Vicky, the German Crown Princess and later Empress, who disliked almost everything in Berlin and Germany. Bertie was fond of his sister and her husband, Frederick, and if a visit to Germany involved a visit to them, he grumbled less about going. Later, when his nephew William became Kaiser, he avoided Germany whenever possible. The Prince made his feelings clear during the three short wars fought by Bismarck and Prussia to forge German unity: he described the war with Denmark which resulted in the annexation of Schleswig-Holstein as a "stain forever on German history"; he believed that right and justice were with Austria in the Austro-Prussian War of 1866; and his sympathy for France in the Franco-Prussian War of 1870–1871 was so pronounced that the Prime Minister, Mr. Gladstone, and eventually the Queen were obliged to insist on his silence.

To Queen Victoria, secluded at Windsor, Osborne, or Balmoral, it seemed that her son was always in motion. "The country, and all of *us* would like to see you a little more stationary," she wrote to him. He replied with as much patience as he could muster: "You remind me, my dearest Mama, that I am 45, a point I have not forgotten, although I am glad to say that I feel younger. You are, I think, rather hard upon me when you talk of the round of gaieties I indulge in at Cannes, London, [Bad] Homburg, and Cowes. . . . I like Cannes, especially for its climate and scenery, just the same as you do Aix [-en-Provence], which you tell me you are going to this year. . . . With regard to London, I think, dear Mama, you know well that the time we spend there is not *all* amusement, very much the reverse. To Homburg I go only for my health and to Cowes to get the sea breezes and yachting which, after the fatigue of the London Season, are an immense relaxation. Nobody knows better than I do that I am not perfect—still, I try to perform the many and ever-increasing duties which lie before me to the best of my ability, nor do I shirk many which I confess I would prefer not to have to fulfill. There is an old English saying that 'all work and no play makes Jack a dull boy'—and there is a great deal of truth in it. . . ."

Foreign travel did not calm the restless Prince. Beginning in his middle twenties and continuing for the rest of his life, Bertie was unfaithful to Alexandra. Once she was hampered by deafness, the Prince grew increasingly bored. She tried to keep up, but eventually abandoned the effort. He went out, stayed late, and was everywhere surrounded by appealing society women.

Gentlemen in Victorian England could amuse themselves as much as they liked with "actresses," the term society applied to women of the streets and special houses. Approaches to unmarried girls of good family were strictly forbidden. Once married, a young woman in society must not be approached until she had borne her husband several sons to carry on the family name and inherit the estates. The essential rule underlying the entire structure was discretion; everything might be known, nothing must be said. The ultimate disgrace was divorce, when charges and proceedings would get into the newspapers, informing the middle and lower classes that the standards upheld by Queen Victoria and the Church of England were habitually mocked by the nation's aristocracy.

The Prince of Wales rigorously observed these rules. His affair with Lillie Langtry, the professional beauty whom he subsequently helped to become a successful stage actress, was conducted with the public acquiescence of Edward Langtry, her husband. Nor was there any public unpleasantness from the husbands of Lady Brooke (later Countess of Warwick) or Mrs. George Keppel. Princess Alexandra also played her role to perfection in these royal bedroom dramas. It was the Princess's view that other women did not threaten—indeed had very little to do with—her own relationship with "my Bertie." As long as no public scandal was permitted, she remained gracious and forbearing, even tolerantly amused. An example of her attitude is presented by Georgina Battiscomb: "One day, she [Alexandra] chanced to look out of the window at Sandringham just as her husband and his mistress were returning from a drive in an open carriage. The Princess herself never lost her graceful slimness but Alice

Keppel, her junior by twenty-five years, had already grown very stout, whilst the Prince of Wales had long merited his disrespectful nickname of 'Tum-Tum.' The sight of these two plump persons sitting solemnly side by side was too much for her equanimity; calling her lady-in-waiting to come and view the joke with her, she dissolved into fits of laughter."

Queen Victoria complained that her son wasted his days with the Marlborough House "fast set," but whenever a prime minister attempted to break the pattern by finding real employment for the Prince, his mother balked. Gladstone, especially, tried. After visiting the Prince at Sandringham, the Prime Minister wrote to the Queen suggesting that the Prince be persuaded to adopt the habit of reading. The Queen replied, "She has only to say that the P. of W. has *never* been fond of reading, and that from his earliest years it was *impossible* to get him to do so. Newspapers and, *very rarely,* a novel, are all he ever reads."

Queen Victoria's reign stretched on and still the Prince had nothing serious to do. "The Prince of Wales writes to me that there is not much use his remaining at Cowes (though he is willing to do so) as he is not of the slightest use to the Queen," one of Bertie's aides wrote to another in 1892. "Everything he says or suggests is pooh-poohed." Bertie endured. He spent an extraordinarily long time—almost four decades from his coming-of-age and marriage— waiting for a human and political event he must simultaneously have wished for and dreaded.

Queen Victoria's family spread across Europe as first cousins routinely married each other and kings and emperors, privately known as Bertie and Georgie, Sasha and Nicky, Fritz and Willy, all referred to the little old woman in Windsor Castle as "Granny." All nine of her children and most of her grandchildren married, and there were thirty-seven living great-grandchildren at the time of her death. On family matters, there was no appeal from her dicta, and the smallest concerns of the youngest roused her passionate interest while she still treated the oldest almost as toddlers. On one occasion, aboard the royal yacht *Victoria and Albert,* four of her children, the Duke of Edinburgh, the Duke of Connaught, Prince Leopold, and Princess Beatrice, came up the gangplank to join their mother, who had come on board earlier and gone to her staterooms. The Duke of Edinburgh, a full admiral in the navy and Commander-in-Chief of the Mediterranean Fleet, informed the captain that the yacht could cast off. The captain apologized profusely and explained that he had no orders from the Queen. The children, all adults, looked at each other and said, "Did you not ask Mother?" "No, I did not. I thought you did." The Duke of Connaught was sent to ask permission for the yacht to leave. Victoria, who had anticipated the sequence and been waiting to see what would happen, nodded assent.

With the passage of time, the Queen's sense of humor, suppressed first by the rigid decorum imposed by Prince Albert, and then by the burden of grief imposed by Albert's death, resurfaced. Though Albert was never forgotten, and every day the Queen was at Windsor she visited the Frogmore mausoleum, she did begin to smile, then to laugh, then to roar with laughter, over pomposity undone, pretense revealed, or language ludicrously misused. At dinner one night at Osborne House, the Queen entertained a famous admiral whose hearing was impaired. Politely, Victoria had asked about his fleet and its activities; then, shifting the subject, she asked about the admiral's sister, an elderly dowager of awesome dignity. The admiral thought she was inquiring about his flagship, which was in need of overhaul. "Well, ma'am," he said, "as soon as I get back I'm going to have her hauled out, roll her on her side and have the barnacles scraped off her bottom." Victoria stared at him for a second and then, for minutes afterward, the dining room shook with her unstoppable peals of laughter. There was, of course, an opposite extreme. Rudeness, vulgarity, indecorum, anything hinting even slightly of lèse-majesté, called forth crushing disapprobation. The Queen's face would glaze, her eyes turn stony, and in a voice which often annihilated the social future of the transgressor, Her Majesty would say, "We are not amused."

Victoria in her later years as a queen and a woman required special handling. Benjamin Disraeli, Lord Beaconsfield, twice Conservative Prime Minister, explained at the end of his life to Matthew Arnold: "Everyone likes flattery and when it comes to royalty, you should lay it on with a trowel." Disraeli flattered profusely. He made Victoria Empress of India and then, on her birthday, produced this tribute: "Today, Lord Beaconsfield ought fitly, perhaps, to congratulate a powerful Sovereign on her imperial sway, the vastness of her Empire, and the success and strength of her fleets and armies. But he cannot; his mind is in another mood. He can only think of the strangeness of his destiny that it has come to pass that he should be the servant of one so great, and whose infinite kindness, the brightness of whose intelligence and the firmness of whose will, have enabled him to undertake labors to which he otherwise would be quite unequal, and supported him in all things by a condescending sympathy, which in the hour of difficulty, alike charms and inspires."

William E. Gladstone, four-time Liberal Prime Minister, lacked Disraeli's touch. Queen Victoria disapproved of some of Gladstone's policies—her tendencies were conservative rather than liberal—but during her long rule she had many Liberal ministers with whom she was congenial. When Gladstone replaced Disraeli as Prime Minister in 1880, the Queen informed her Private Secretary that she would "sooner abdicate" than send for Gladstone, "that *half-mad firebrand* who would soon ruin everything and be a Dictator." Twelve years later, Gladstone was back a fourth time as Prime Minister. The Queen bewailed "the danger to the country, to Europe, to her vast Empire, which is involved in having all these great interests entrusted to the shaking hand of an old, wild, and incomprehensible man of eighty-two and a half. . . . It is a terrible trial, but thank God the country is sound." Mr. Gladstone's problem was that he did not know how to please. It is impossible to imagine Gladstone, however polite, writing or speaking in Disraeli's language. Gladstone was respectful, even reverent, in his conversation and correspondence with the sovereign. But the Queen wanted to be treated as a woman, and "he speaks to me as if I were a public meeting," she said.

For the British people, Victoria was more than an individual, more even than the queen; she was—and had been as long as most of them could remember—a part of the fabric of their lives. She embodied history, tradition, government, and the structure and morality of their society. They trusted her to remain there, always to do her duty, always to give order to their lives. She did not disappoint them. In return, they gave her their allegiance, their devotion—and their esteem. One Victorian matron expressed it by turning to a friend as the curtain fell on Sarah Bernhardt's flamboyant performance as Cleopatra, and saying, "How different, how very different, from the home life of our own dear Queen."

CHAPTER 2

Vicky
and Willy

◆

O
h, Madam, it is a Princess," announced the physician who had presided over the delivery of Queen Victoria's first child.

"Never mind," crisply replied the twenty-one-year-old Queen, still energetic after twelve hours of labor. "The next will be a prince."

Bertie was born eleven months later. But her favorite child, and that of "Dearest Albert," was this first little girl, Victoria Adelaide Mary Louise, known as "Vicky," who grew up to become Empress of Germany and the mother of Kaiser William II.

Albert was enchanted with this bright little girl, who spoke German with her parents and English and French almost as well. Her mind was receptive, and the tutors who had such difficulty with the Prince of Wales sent glowing reports of his older sister. Vicky also was willful, obstinate, emotional; once as a child, she attempted to interrupt when her mother was talking to her ministers. When the gentlemen refused to be silent, the Princess stamped her foot and said, "Queen, queen, make them obey me!" Queen Victoria did what she could to control this behavior. Vicky, at thirteen, out driving with her mother, dropped her handkerchief out of the carriage so she could watch the equerries dashing to pick it up. Queen Victoria ordered the carriage stopped and its steps put down, and said, "Victoria, go and fetch it yourself." Nevertheless, the Queen compared her daughter's qualities favorably, not only to Bertie's, but to her own. "Bertie is my caricature," she wrote to Vicky when her daughter was an adult. ". . . You are quite your dear, beloved Papa's child. You are so learned and so fond of deep philosophical books that you are quite beyond me and certainly have not inherited that taste from me."

Prince Albert planned a special future for this special child. Albert dreamed of a Europe united in liberalism, progress, and peace. The constitutional monarchy of a liberal England would become one of the twin pillars of this noble edifice; a united Germany, gathered under the leadership of a newly liberalized Prussia, would be the other. The King of Prussia, Frederick William IV, and his brother, who would take the throne as King William I, both were rigidly conservative, but both were growing old. The future lay with William's son, young Prince Frederick. And Frederick, if not dazzlingly intelligent, was handsome, amiable, and dutiful; a man, Albert felt sure, who could be steered by a clear-headed, purposeful wife. Someone like Vicky.

Fritz, as Frederick was known, met Vicky at the Great Exhibition in 1851, when he was twenty and she was ten. Four years later, walking through the heather on a hillside near Balmoral, the tall, blond Prussian Prince proposed to the fourteen-year-old Princess Royal. The wedding, delayed until the bride reached seventeen, was the cause of competitive jostling between the British and Prussian dynasties. The Prussians announced that it was traditional for Hohenzollern princes to be married in Berlin. Queen Victoria commanded her Foreign Secretary to tell the Prussian Minister "not to entertain the possibility of such a question. . . . The Queen could never consent to it, both for public and for private reasons, and the assumption of its being too much for a Prince Royal of Prussia to come over and marry the Princess Royal of Great Britain in England is too absurd to say the least. . . . Whatever may be the usual practice of Prussian princes, it is not every day that one marries the eldest daughter of the Queen of England. The question must therefore be considered as settled and closed."

No more was said. On January 25, 1858, the wedding was celebrated in St. James's Chapel, and the bridal couple left the church to the strains of Mendelssohn's "Wedding March," the first time this music had been used for an actual wedding. Vicky tearfully departed for Germany. The Queen wept as she embraced her daughter. "Poor, dear child!" she wrote later. "I clasped her in my arms and blessed her and knew not what to say. I kissed good Fritz and pressed his hand again and again. He was unable to speak and tears were in his eyes." At Gravesend, the bride lamented, "I think it will kill me to take leave of dear Papa." Bertie sobbed as he stood beside his father on the Channel quay, waving at the boat which was carrying his sister to the Continent. Only Albert remained in control; but then he dashed back to Windsor to write to his daughter: "I am not of a demonstrative nature and therefore you can hardly know how dear you have always been to me. . . ."

Vicky's reception in Berlin was cool. Feeling at the Prussian court and in society ran so high against the "English" marriage that the British Minister, Lord Bloomfield, avoided even calling on his sovereign's daughter. Conservative Prussians, aware of Prince Albert's hopes for a liberal Germany, suspected his plan of using Vicky's marriage to advance his design. Otto von Bismarck, then Prussian representative to the Federal Diet in Frankfurt, wrote to a friend, "You ask me . . . what I think of the English marriage. . . . The 'English' in it does not please me; the 'marriage' may be quite good, for the Princess has the reputation of a lady of brain and heart. If the Princess can leave the English-woman at home and become a Prussian, then she may be a blessing to our country. If our future Queen on the Prussian throne remains the least bit English, then I see our court surrounded by English influence." The Prussian royal family seemed uninterested in making the seventeen-year-old bride feel welcome. Despite the long engagement, no home had been prepared for the newlyweds, who spent their first winter in a dark, cold apartment at the Berlin Castle. "Endless dark corridors connected huge, mysterious-looking rooms, hung with pictures of long-forgotten royal personages; the wind whistled down through the large chimneys . . . ," remembered a lady-in-waiting who suffered with them.

Vicky disliked the boots that Prussians always wore; she condemned the absence of bathrooms, the thinness of Prussian silver plate, and the formality, monotony, and length of Prussian court ceremonies. All these matters, she declared, were better done in England. In 1860, after three years in Berlin, she began to offer her husband political advice. "To govern a country is not a business that only a King and a few privileged men are entitled to do," she wrote to Fritz during a visit to England. "It is on the contrary the right and sacred duty of the individual as well as of the whole nation to participate in it. The usual education which a Prince in Prussia has hitherto received is not capable of satisfying present-day requirements, although yours, thanks to your Mama's loving care, was far better than that of the others. . . . You were not, however, sure of, nor versed in, the old liberal and constitutional conceptions and this was still the case when we married. What enormous strides you have made during these years!"

Vicky continued to speak of England as "home." In 1871, after thirteen years in Prussia, she wrote to a friend, "You cannot think how dull and melancholy and queer I feel away from you all and my beloved England! Each time I get there I feel my attachment to that precious bit of earth grow stronger and stronger." Kaiser William II wrote in his memoirs, "She delivered judgement on everything and found everything wrong with us and better in England which she habitually called 'home.' " William II explained his mother's behavior: "She came from a country which had had little to do with the Continent, which had for centuries led a life of its own . . . quite different from the traditions and growth of the country which she was to join. The Prussians were not Englishmen . . . they were Europeans. They had a different concept of monarchy and of class. . . . [Nevertheless,] my Mother set out with burning zeal to create in her new home everything which, according to her English education, convictions and outlook was necessary for the creation of national happiness."

On January 27, 1859, Princess Victoria, eighteen years old, gave birth to the son who was to become Kaiser William II. Vicky endured a long and painful breech delivery without anesthetics. The extraction with forceps was difficult and resulted in severe damage to the baby's left arm. This was not noticed for three days; then it was discovered that the arm was paralyzed and the muscles around it crushed. Examination showed that during delivery the arm had been wrenched almost out of its socket. Despite interminable exercises and constant treatment, neither the arm nor the hand recovered. Throughout William's life, both were miniaturized, feeble, and almost useless. The left sleeves of William's jackets and tunics were cut shorter than the right; the little left hand usually carried gloves or slipped into a carefully placed pocket or came out to rest on the hilt of a sword. William could not use an ordinary knife and fork; at dinners a footman or his dinner partner had to cut his meat for him.

When the child was very young, these distressing facts had yet to be learned. He was the first grandchild of the Queen of England (who was only thirty-nine) and, according to her wish, the baby was given the name of Albert. His full name was Frederick William Victor Albert, and he was known in the family as William or Willy. Queen Victoria was delighted. She saw him first at twenty months. "Our . . . darling grandchild . . . came walking . . . in a little white dress with black bows. . . . He is a fine fat child with a beautiful white, soft skin, very fine shoulders and limbs, and a very dear face, like Vicky and Fritz. . . . He has Fritz's eyes and Vicky's mouth and very fair, curly hair." When William was two and a half, Vicky brought him to Osborne; Grandfather Albert wrapped him in a large white damask table napkin and swung him back and forth while the little boy screamed with pleasure and his grandmother clucked her smiling disapproval.

At four, William was taken back to England to be present at the wedding of his Uncle Bertie to Princess Alexandra. William attended the ceremony in a Highland costume given to him by his grandmother; it came with a small toy dirk. During the ceremony, William was restless. His eighteen-year-old Uncle Alfred, Duke of Edinburgh, appointed to keep an eye on him, told him to be quiet, but William drew his dirk and threatened Alfred. When Alfred attempted to subdue the rebel by force, William bit him in the leg. The Queen missed seeing this fracas; to her William remained "a clever, dear, good little child, the great favorite of my beloved Angel [Vicky]."

Vicky was obsessed by William's damaged arm. She blamed herself for her child's handicap, for his appearance of being oddly off balance, for his so little resembling his tall, healthy father. Initially, she tried to conceal the handicap and her feelings; eventually, she spoke freely to her mother. "The poor arm is no better, and William begins to feel being behind much smaller boys in every exercise of the body—he cannot run fast because he has no balance, nor ride, nor climb, nor cut his food. . . . Nothing is neglected that can be done for it, but there is so little to be done," she wrote to Queen Victoria in May 1870. Seven months later she wrote again, "He . . . would be a very pretty boy were it not for that wretched unhappy arm which shows more and more, spoils his face . . . his carriage, walk and figure, makes him awkward in all his movements, and gives him a feeling of shyness, as he feels his complete dependence, not being able to do a single thing for himself. . . . To me it remains an inexpressible source of sorrow. . . ."

William repeatedly tried to correct or overcome the handicap. He did gymnastic exercises, learned to swim, sail, and fire a gun. "My greatest troubles," he said in his memoirs, "were with riding." His mother insisted that he perfect this skill. "The thought that I, as Heir to the Throne, should not be able to ride, was to her intolerable. But I felt I was not fit for it because of my disability. I was worried and afraid. When there was nobody near, I wept." Riding lessons, begun when the Prince was eight, became a matter of ruthlessness for the adults and endurance for William. Over and over, in the words of the tutor who supervised these lessons, "the weeping prince" was "set on his horse, without stirrups and compelled to go through the paces. He fell off continually; every time, despite his prayers and tears, he was lifted up and set upon its back again. After weeks of torture, the difficult task was accomplished: he had got his balance." Looking back on his boyhood, Kaiser William II decided that "the result justified . . . [the] method. But the lesson was a cruel one and my brother, Henry, often howled with pain when compelled to witness the martyrdom of my youth." William had no doubt as to who was ultimately responsible for this coldly rational treatment. "Hinzpeter [the tutor who supervised his lessons] was really a good fellow," he wrote. "Whether he was the right tutor for me, I dare not decide. The torments inflicted on me, especially in this pony riding, must be attributed to my mother."

Vicky also took responsibility for her son's general education. "His education will . . . be an important task," she wrote to Queen Victoria when her son was six. "I shall endeavour to make him feel that pride and devotion for his country and ambition to serve it. . . . And I may be able to instill our British feeling of independence into him, together with our brand [of] English common sense, so rare on this side of the water." William and his brother, Henry, three years younger, were turned over to George Hinzpeter, who prescribed Latin, mathematics, history, and geography; English and French under special tutors were added, and William read Shakespeare, Dickens, Sir Walter Scott, Byron, Macaulay, Tennyson, Defoe, and James Fenimore Cooper. Both boys spoke English regularly with their mother and used it as effortlessly as German; later William was said to be unaware which language he was speaking. When William was seven, lessons began at six A.M. and continued until six P.M. with two short breaks for meals and exercises. Hinzpeter's philosophy was based on "a stern sense of duty and the idea of service," William wrote later. "The character was to be fortified by perpetual renunciation . . . the ideal being the harsh discipline of the Spartans. . . . No praise: the categorical imperative of duty demanded its due; there was no room for the encouraging or approving word. . . . No word of commendation. . . . The impossible was expected of a pupil in order to force him to the nearest degree of perfection. Naturally, the impossible goal could never be achieved; logically, therefore, the praise which registers approval was also excluded."

Vicky occasionally wrote proudly about her son. When he was eight, she told her mother, "Willy is a dear, interesting, charming boy—clever, amusing, engaging—it is impossible not to spoil him a bit—he is growing so handsome and his large eyes have now and then a pensive, dreamy expression, and then again they sparkle with fun delight." When William was twelve, Vicky wrote to Queen Victoria, "I am sure you would be pleased with William if you were to see him—he has Bertie's pleasant, amiable ways—and can be very winning. He is not possessed of brilliant abilities, nor of any strength of character or talents, but he is a dear boy, and I hope and trust will grow up a useful man. . . . There is very little of his Papa or the family of Prussia about him." Mother and son shared pleasant moments. Vicky painted in oil and watercolors, doing landscapes, portraits, still lifes and flowers, and William remembered "happy hours spent in . . . [her] studio . . . my mother sitting at her easel, while I read aloud to her from some humorous English tale, and how she every now and then dropped her palette to enjoy a hearty laugh." The Prince of Wales, visiting his sister, approved of his nephews. "It is impossible to find two nicer boys than William and Henry," he wrote to Queen Victoria.

Vicky, eager for William's education to fit him for leading his country along the liberal path laid out by Prince Albert, did what she could to steer him away from the provincialism of the Prussian court. In 1874, William and Henry, fifteen and twelve, accompanied by Hinzpeter, were entered in a high school in Kassel where, for two and a half years, they mixed with other boys of good German families. In January 1877, William finished school and, on his eighteenth birthday, received as a present from his grandmother the Order of the Garter. (Queen Victoria originally had planned to send him the lesser Grand Companionship of the Bath. Vicky urged that the highest order be given. "Willy would be satisfied with the Bath, but the nation would not," she wrote to her mother.) After Kassel, William spent four terms at Bonn University, where he studied law and politics. He joined the exclusive Borussia student society, although he refused its traditional heavy drinking and was not permitted to duel. During his years in Bonn, William, then nineteen, spent many weekends with his aunt, Grand Duchess Alice of Hesse-Darmstadt (Queen Victoria's second daughter), and her children in Darmstadt, becoming almost a member of the family. His attention centered on his cousin Elizabeth, who was fourteen.* Ella, as she was called, found her Prussian cousin overbearing. He would ask to ride, then

---

* Elizabeth's younger sister Irene, twelve in 1878, would marry William's brother, Henry. Another sister, Alix, who was six in 1878, was to marry Tsar Nicholas II and become the Empress Alexandra of Russia.

demand to shoot, or row, or play tennis. When he was bored, he
would climb off his horse, or throw down his racket, and announce
that everyone should sit around while he read aloud from the Bible.
Whatever he was doing, he always wanted Ella next to him. His
infatuation received no encouragement and later, when he was German Emperor and she was the wife of Grand Duke Sergei of Russia,
he stubbornly refused to see her. As an old man, he admitted that he
had spent much of his time in Bonn writing love poetry to his cousin
Elizabeth.

When William finished his studies in Bonn, his mother wanted
him to travel widely to broaden his mind and experience. A trip to
Paris while still at the university had produced mixed results. William visited the Louvre, Notre Dame, and Sainte-Chapelle, and he
went up in a balloon launched from the Tuileries Gardens. But, he
said, "the feverish haste and restlessness of Parisian life repelled me.
I . . . never wanted to see the French capital again"—and although
he lived for sixty-three years after this visit, he never did. William,
on leaving Bonn, was "passionately interested . . . to go to Egypt."
But his grandfather, William I, King of Prussia and German Emperor, intervened. Prince William was second in line, after his father, to both those titles. It was time, according to his grandfather,
for his Prussian qualities to be emphasized. The years during which
Vicky had primary influence over the education and guidance of her
son ended.

When Vicky arrived in Berlin in 1858, King Frederick William IV of
Prussia was mentally ill; his brother William was Regent and Heir to
the Throne. In 1861, Frederick William died and William, sixty-
three, became King William I. William's son and daughter-in-law,
Fritz, thirty, and Vicky, twenty, became Crown Prince and Crown
Princess, expecting within a decade or so to mount the throne. Nine
months later, King William summoned the conservative politician
Otto von Bismarck to administer his government. Bismarck began a
twenty-eight-year tenure as Minister-President of Prussia and Chancellor of the German Empire. King William I lived past ninety. Bismarck, ruling in the King's name, united Germany and made his
elderly master an emperor, but it was not the liberal Germany desired by Prince Albert or by Fritz and Vicky.

Vicky was shocked and heartbroken by her father's death. As
with her mother, grief gave Prince Albert's precepts the force of
heavenly command and the young Englishwoman obediently set
herself to influence the course of Prussian affairs through her tall,

good-natured husband, who was devoted to his wife, admitted her intellectual superiority, and was willing to be guided by her vigorous opinions. Frederick, although trained as a soldier, was both a liberal and a nationalist. He longed for the re-creation of the medieval German Empire under a monarch like Charlemagne. His son Prince William remembered as a boy studying with his father a book titled *German Treasures of the Holy Roman Empire*. "It was so big that I had to spread it out on the floor, and I was never tired of looking at the pictures which my father would explain as he squatted beside me on the ground," said William. Thoroughly sympathetic with the hopes of his father-in-law, Prince Albert, Fritz was quickly estranged from his father's chief minister, Bismarck.

The breach between the King and Bismarck on the one hand, and Fritz and Vicky on the other, opened wide only nine months after Bismarck took office. Most Prussian newspapers in the 1860s were liberal and their editorial freedom was guaranteed by the constitution. They were critical of Bismarck's conservative policies. During the spring of 1863, the Crown Prince warned his father that Bismarck's encroachment on the constitution was opening a gap between the monarchy and the people. On June 1, at a Crown Council from which Frederick was absent on a military inspection tour, Bismarck retaliated by issuing a decree establishing censorship of press articles that might "jeopardize the public welfare." The Crown Prince, with Vicky's encouragement, protested publicly on June 5. "I knew nothing [about this order beforehand]," he told a political meeting in Danzig. "I was absent. I have had no part in the deliberations which have produced this result." King William, who in fact had signed the decree reluctantly, was enraged by his son's open opposition, characterizing it as military insubordination. He wrote to "Fritz a furious letter," Vicky wrote to her mother, "treating him quite like a little child, telling him instantly to retract in the newspapers the words he had spoken at Danzig." Frederick refused and offered to retire from the Army and politics and live in seclusion with his family. Bismarck, wishing to avoid creating a martyr in the Heir to the Throne, calmed King William and the threat of a court-martial was reduced to a military reprimand. Five months later, when the press decree was rescinded, Frederick wrote to Bismarck declaring his general opposition to the Minister-President's policies: "A loyal administration of the laws and of the constitution, respect and goodwill towards an easily led, intelligent, and capable people—these are the principles which, in my opinion, should guide every government. . . . I will tell you what results I anticipate from your policy. You will go on quibbling with the constitution until it loses all value in the eyes of the people. . . . I regard those who lead His Majesty the King, my most gracious father, into such courses as the most dangerous advisers for the Crown and the country." Vicky was pleased and apprehensive about what had happened. "Fritz . . . has for the first time in his life taken up a position decidedly in opposition to his father," she wrote her mother. But, she added, "we are dreadfully alone, having not a soul from whom to ask advice. . . . Thank God I was born in England where people are not slaves and [are] too good to allow themselves to be treated as such."

Bismarck did not forgive and the extended duel between the Bismarck party and what Bismarck deprecatingly referred to as the "Anglo-Coburg" party, was begun. The Crown Prince and Crown Princess, visiting Prussian towns, were received with ceremonies so minimal as to border on rudeness; Vicky assumed that instructions had come from Berlin. During the war with Denmark, Vicky loyally supported Prussia, and during the wars with Austria and France in which Fritz became a military hero she became enthusiastic. "I feel that I am now every bit as proud of being a Prussian as I am of being an Englishwoman and that is saying a very great deal as you know what a 'John Bull' I am," she told her mother. "I must say the Prussians are a superior race as regards intelligence and humanity, education, and kind-heartedness." But Vicky's enthusiasm never extended to Bismarck. "To us and to many quiet and reflecting Germans, it is very sad and appears very hard to be made an object of universal distrust and suspicion, which we naturally are as long as Prince Bismarck remains the sole and omnipotent ruler of our destinies. His will alone is law here," she wrote to Queen Victoria in 1875. "I wonder," she said in 1881, "why Bismarck does not say straight out, 'As long as I live, both the constitution and the crown are suspended' because that is the exact state of the matter."

The German Emperor, William I, watched from afar as his grandson Prince William, guided principally by Crown Princess Victoria, grew to manhood. Occasionally, when his parents were not in Berlin, Prince William was invited to dinner alone with his grandfather. The meal was served on a small, shaky, green card table in a drawing room of the royal palace on the Unter den Linden. "A bottle of champagne was put on the table," Prince William remembered, "which the Emperor himself uncorked and with his own hands always filled two glasses, for himself and for me. After the second glass he would hold the bottle up to the light and make a pencil mark on the label at the height of the contents for he was very economical. . . ." The Emperor decided that his grandson should begin the military phase of his preparation for the throne, and William, nearing twenty-one, was assigned as a lieutenant to the First Regiment of Foot Guards, stationed in Potsdam. William embraced regimental life. In the officers' mess, he was universally praised. In the Guards, William said, "I really found my family, my friends, my interests—everything of which I had up to that time had to do without. . . . Before I entered the regiment, I had lived through such fearful years of unappreciation of my nature, of ridicule of that which was to me highest and most holy: Prussia, the Army, and all of the fulfilling duties that I first encountered in this officer corps and that have provided me with joy and happiness and contentment on earth." The regimental atmosphere affected William's personality. As a boy and a student, his manner had been polite and agreeable; as an officer, he began to strut and speak brusquely in the tone he deemed appropriate for a Prussian officer. William's hardness distressed his parents; Crown Prince Frederick, a successful soldier, ruefully described William in the 1880s as "my son, the complete Guards officer." William made plain that he no longer much cared about his parents' opinions; he had the Guards and his grandfather. The Emperor, he said, was the only member of his family who appreciated his deep feelings for the army and for Prussia.

During his Potsdam years another formidable influence strengthened William's growing rejection of his mother. He married. William had met Princess Augusta Victoria of Schleswig-Holstein in 1868, when he was nine. Her father's principality, sandwiched between Prussia and Denmark at the base of the Jutland peninsula, had been annexed by Denmark, then conquered and annexed by Prussia in the war of 1864. Many Schleswigers and Holsteiners were aggrieved by their absorption by Prussia; Princess Augusta's father had decided to adjust to circumstances. William's suit for the Princess's hand (her family name was Dona) was his own decision; Dona's family was of minimal distinction, scarcely suitable for an heir to the throne of Prussia. Nevertheless, Vicky, Fritz, and King William I approved and on February 27, 1881, William and Dona were married in the Berlin Castle.

Dona, then twenty-three, a year older than her husband, was a tall, robust young woman with a rosy-pink complexion. Brought up amidst the rural nobility, she shared all its limitations and prejudices. She had been given a meager education and had developed few intellectual abilities or interests. She read neither newspapers nor books and had a simplistic understanding of politics. Her man-

ners were conventional, her morality puritanical. The Prince of
Wales once said that her only interests were "Kinder, Kirche,
Küche" (children, church, kitchen). An Englishwoman, living in
Germany, added "clothes," and described the future Empress as
"nice but silly." "For a woman in that position, I have never met
anyone so devoid of any individual quality of thought or agility of
brain and understanding," said another. "She is just like a good,
quiet, soft cow that has calves and eats grass slowly and ruminates. I
looked right into her eyes to see if I could see anything behind them,
even pleasure or sadness, but they might have been glass."

It was suggested that Dona's purpose was to breed some sturdy
stock into the Hohenzollern line. Dona produced seven children—
six sons and a daughter—within ten years (1882–1892), but her personality was more significant to William than her good health. William needed sympathy and warm emotional support; Dona supplied
him with unquestioning adoration. He was in revolt against his
mother, and the woman he chose was entirely unlike his mother. On
two subjects, however, Dona had strong views which delighted William: Dona was inflexibly opposed to liberalism in all areas and she
hated England. Liberalism, political, cultural, artistic, she equated
with license; Englishmen, whom she thought of as liberals, were
hypocrites, dangerously given to license. After her marriage, Dona
treated her mother-in-law with icy formality; Vicky scornfully referred to her daughter-in-law's rigidly Protestant ladies-in-waiting as
the "Hallelujah Aunts" or "a blessed set of donkeys." William supported his wife and referred to his parents and his three younger
sisters, who were close to his parents, as "the English Colony."

The division in the royal family was widely known in Berlin,
and Bismarck turned it to his purpose. The Chancellor, relying
solely for his power on the mandate given him by Kaiser William I,
needed a buttress against the liberal forces which looked for leadership to the Crown Prince. Prince William, at odds with his parents,
suited admirably. In 1884, Bismarck encouraged the Kaiser to delegate certain diplomatic missions, denied to the Crown Prince, to the
younger William. William was sent to St. Petersburg as the Kaiser's
representative at the coming-of-age ceremonies of the sixteen-year-
old Tsarevich Nicholas, the future Tsar Nicholas II. While there,
William became friendly with Bismarck's son, Herbert, who was
acting as Counselor of the German Embassy in the Russian capital.
William enjoyed the attention he received as his grandfather's envoy; on returning home, he wrote to his host, Tsar Alexander III,
that he would always take care to guard Russia's interests, especially
against the wiles of the Prince of Wales, who possessed "a false and

intriguing character." Tsar Alexander, who was Bertie's brother-in-law, considered William's letter rude and presumptuous. In August 1886, the Kaiser ignored his son and invited his grandson to accompany him to a meeting at Gastein with Emperor Franz Josef of Austria. He then sent William to Russia to report on the meeting to Tsar Alexander.

In the autumn of 1886, Bismarck appointed Herbert State Secretary for Foreign Affairs, the senior post in the German Foreign Ministry. Herbert suggested to his father that the connection with William be strengthened by bringing the Prince into the Foreign Ministry for training. The Kaiser, as pleased by the deferential attention of his grandson as he was dismayed by the disapproving manner of his son, agreed. William came twice a week to the Foreign Ministry building in the Wilhelmstrasse, where he was equipped with an office of his own and given lectures which explained the workings of the department, Germany's obligations under the Triple Alliance, and the nature of the Empire's overseas commercial and colonial policies. William also was informed, he said, of "our state of dependence on England which was principally due to the fact that we had no navy." Crown Prince Frederick objected to his son's indoctrination at the Wilhelmstrasse. "Considering the unripeness and inexperience of my eldest son, together with his leaning towards vanity and presumption, and his overweening estimate of himself, I must frankly express my opinion that it is dangerous as yet to bring him into touch with foreign affairs," he wrote to Bismarck. The protests did no good; the Chancellor had the support of the Kaiser; he ignored the Crown Prince. William, in his memoirs, suggests the flavor of his early relationship with the Chancellor: "My service in the Foreign Office brought me . . . into closer contact with the great statesman, so ardently revered, who moved through the days of my youth almost like some warrior figure out of heroic legend. . . . I was frequently invited to breakfast with the Prince [Bismarck] . . . the Princess, [and] Count Herbert Bismarck. . . . After the meal . . . [Bismarck] used to lie down on a couch and smoke his long pipe which I have often been allowed to light for him."

Against this coalition—the Kaiser, the Chancellor, and Prince William—Crown Prince Frederick could make no headway. Frederick, who had commanded armies in the wars against Austria and France, had wished to prove to Prussia, Germany, and Europe that a Hohenzollern prince who had played a major role in unifying Germany by victory in battle also could be a liberal and constitutional sovereign. In 1886, Crown Princess Victoria declared that many things would change when her husband succeeded his father. "Now Bismarck governs not only the German Reich but also the eighty-eight-year-old Kaiser," she said. "But how will it be when Bismarck is faced with a real Kaiser?"

The imminence of Frederick's reign drew increasing criticism of his character and abilities from those who would have most to lose from his succession. He was devoted to his wife and greatly respected her intellectual talents. "Have you asked the Crown Princess?" "We must see what the Crown Princess says about this," Frederick said frequently. His enemies underscored this deference and painted a picture of a weak, uncertain man, overshadowed by, dependent on, even dominated by his strong-willed, English wife. "Everyone agrees that the Crown Prince's character grows weaker year by year," Friederich von Holstein, a Foreign Ministry protégé of Bismarck, wrote in his diary in 1884. "His wife's influence is increasing every year." Even Frederick's private secretary scorned his master's apparent submissiveness to his wife. "You have only to look at what she's made of him," he declared. "But for her, he'd be the average man, very arrogant, good-tempered, of mediocre gifts and with a good deal of common sense. But now he's not a man at all; he has no ideas of his own, unless she allows him. He's a mere cipher." Vicky, the supposed cause of Fritz's emasculation, was unpopular. In a nation where wives remained in the background, her tactless and sometimes strident advocacy of political causes, as well as her indiscreet trumpeting of Britain's superior virtues, had alienated powerful sections of German society. No story denigrating the Crown Princess was too petty. Holstein, accusing her of prodigality, carped in his diary that her chef, "knowing her liking for stewed peaches, cooks a dozen peaches a day at three marks apiece throughout the summer and autumn on the chance she would ask for one."

William, secure in the bosom of his regiment, the esteem of his wife, and the approbation of the Bismarcks, was almost completely estranged from his parents. He opposed the liberal opinions of his father and believed that the strong English sympathies of his mother were anti-Prussian and unpatriotic. He was bitter and contemptuous of what he saw as his father's dependence. "My father . . . has a soft heart and is so unable to stand on his own two feet that one might say he is even helpless in domestic affairs," William said to Herbert von Bismarck in 1886. "Now I cannot talk to my father at any time in an open and relaxed manner because the Crown Princess [William at this time always referred to his mother as "the Crown Princess"] never leaves us alone for even five minutes for fear that my father—having at last recognized how honest my intentions towards him are—would come under my influence."

One formidable figure, beyond the reach of Kaiser William I and the Bismarcks, always supported the beleaguered Crown Prince and Crown Princess: Queen Victoria. The Queen could not intervene in German political affairs, but she knew how to make her opinions known and her weight felt on matters affecting the family. In 1885, when William's sister Victoria wanted to marry Prince Alexander of Battenberg—a match endorsed by the Crown Prince and Crown Princess—the Kaiser, the Bismarcks, William, and Dona opposed it on the ground that the Battenbergs were a family of little significance. Queen Victoria found William's opposition especially insufferable as he had himself taken a wife of minor royal distinction. "The extraordinary impertinence and insolence and, I must add, unkindness of Willy and the foolish Dona force me to say I shall not write to either," the Queen wrote to her daughter. "As for Dona, poor little insignificant princess, raised entirely by your kindness to the position she is in—I have no words. . . . As for Willy, that very foolish, undutiful and, I must add, unfeeling boy, I have no patience with him and I wish he could get a good 'skelping' as the Scotch say." The Queen added that William would not be welcome at Windsor, and an invitation to him was withdrawn. William's first reaction was vehement—he called his grandmother "the old hag"— then apologetic; he asked his mother to try to have the invitation reinstated. Vicky wrote to the Queen, attempting to explain her son's behavior: "William is always much surprised when he is thought unkind or rude . . . fancies that his opinions are quite infallible and that his conduct is always perfect—and cannot stand the smallest remark, though he criticizes and abuses his elders and his relations. . . . This only finds encouragement from Dona and all around him. I trust the faults which make him so difficult to get on with will wear off as he gets older and wiser and associates more with people who are superior to him and can laugh at many of his foolish ideas."

The relationship between mother and son did not improve. In 1886, Vicky wearily complained to her mother, "He did not condescend to remember that he had not seen me for two months, or that I had been to England . . . or that his sisters had the measles. He never asked after them or you, or any of my relations in England, so that I felt hurt and disappointed. . . . He is a curious creature. A little civility and kindness go a long way, but I never get them from him. . . ." A year later, in 1887, Vicky seemed resigned: "The dream of my life was to have a son who should be something of what our beloved Papa was, a real grandson of his in soul and intellect, a grandson of yours. . . . But one must guard against the fault of being annoyed with one's children for not being what one wished and hoped."

In January 1887, the Crown Prince became hoarse and had trouble clearing his throat. At first, this was blamed on his frequent colds, but at the beginning of March, when the symptoms persisted, Dr. Gerhardt, a professor of medicine at Berlin University, was summoned. Gerhardt found on the Prince's left vocal cord a small growth, which he attempted to remove, first with tweezers, then by burning with a hot wire. By May, the growth had reappeared and the wound caused by the treatment had not healed. Dr. Gerhardt called in another specialist, an eminent surgeon, Dr. Ernst von Bergmann. The two doctors considered the possibility of cancer; whether the growth was malignant or not, they proposed surgical removal of the diseased area. King William I and Bismarck were consulted, although Frederick himself had not been told. "The doctors," Bismarck wrote, "determined to make the Crown Prince unconscious and to carry out the removal of the larynx without having informed him of their intentions. I raised objections and required that they should not proceed without the consent of the Crown Prince." The Kaiser agreed and "forbade them to carry out the operation without the consent of his son." Three additional doctors who were summoned diagnosed cancer; they suggested removal, not of the entire larynx, but of the affected area of the vocal cords. If successful, the operation would leave the Crown Prince permanently hoarse but with a voice. Bergmann predicted good prospects: the disease had been caught early; the patient was in good health; the operation should be "not more dangerous than an ordinary tracheotomy." He promised, according to Prince William, the "recovery of my father's voice 'so that he would be able to command an army corps at a review.' " To this course, the Crown Prince and Crown Princess agreed, although Vicky trembled at "the idea of a knife touching his dear throat." The operation was scheduled for the morning of May 21.

Before proceeding, however, the German doctors unanimously recommended that one more laryngologist be consulted. The preeminent laryngologist in Europe, described as "the greatest living authority on diseases of the throat," was Dr. Morell Mackenzie, an Englishman. Dr. Mackenzie, urgently summoned to Berlin, arrived on the evening of May 20 and examined the patient. He insisted that unless it were proved that the growth was cancerous, the operation should be cancelled. In his opinion, the swelling was not cancerous; rather it was a "fibromatous swelling which could be removed without any operation in from six to eight weeks of treatment." The Crown Prince, "like any other mortal, must come to his clinic for treatment." The surgery scheduled for the following morning was cancelled. Dr. Mackenzie asked that a fragment of the larynx be removed and examined by Dr. Rudolf Virchow, the foremost pathologist in Germany, Director of the Pathological Institute of Berlin University and the creator of cellular pathology. Virchow examined the tissue and pronounced the growth benign. A second, larger fragment was taken a day later. Virchow again declared that he could find no evidence of malignancy. Dr. Gerhardt and Dr. Bergmann, protesting that pathology remained an unproved science, insisted that their original diagnosis was correct. They warned that the tumor was spreading to the other side of the throat and that if Dr. Mackenzie was wrong, valuable time was being lost. Mackenzie, relying in part on Virchow, remained emphatic. The final decision was left to the Crown Prince and Princess. The patient and his wife selected the hopeful English diagnosis over the gloomy German one.

Mackenzie examined Frederick in London early in June and recommended that his patient go to the Isle of Wight, whose mild climate, he said, would promote a cure of the throat infection. The German doctors, declaring that climate had no effect on swellings of the larynx, malignant or not, opposed this treatment but were overruled. The Crown Prince's presence in England permitted him to ride on June 21 in Queen Victoria's Golden Jubilee parade through London. None in the crowd cheering the tall, bearded figure in white uniform, silver breastplate, and eagle-crested helmet suspected that he could speak only in a tiny whisper. Fritz dutifully spent three months in Britain, dividing his time between the Isle of Wight and the Scottish Highlands. For a while, he seemed to be better. Queen Victoria acceded to her daughter's request and at Balmoral, in the present of Fritz and Vicky, knighted Morell Mackenzie for saving her son-in-law's life. In September the Crown Prince and his wife moved on to Venice and Lake Maggiore, where, at the end of October, his voice disappeared completely. Early in November, Vicky established him in a villa set in a grove of olive trees overlooking the Mediterranean at San Remo.

The growths steadily increased. The Crown Princess and Crown Prince still believed in Mackenzie's diagnosis but, in Berlin, Kaiser William I, Prince Bismarck, and the sick man's son, Prince William, did not. William asked his grandfather's permission to go to San Remo to verify his father's condition. The Kaiser agreed and assigned three new doctors, two Germans and an Austrian, to accompany him. William's sudden arrival at San Remo precipitated a clash. "My arrival gave little pleasure to my mother," Kaiser William II later recalled. "Standing at the foot of the stairs, I had to allow the flood of her reproaches to pass over me and to hear her decided refusal to allow me to see my father. . . . My father's condition, in my mother's opinion, gave no cause whatever for alarm, but the stony expression of her face . . . gave the lie to what her lips uttered. . . . Then I heard a rustling at the top of the stairs, looked up, and saw my father smiling a welcome to me. I rushed up the stairs and with infinite emotion we held each other embraced."

Vicky described the same scene to her mother: "You ask how Willy was when he was here. He was as rude, disagreeable and as impertinent to me as possible when he arrived, but I pitched into him with, I am afraid, considerable violence. . . . He began with saying . . . [that] he had to speak to the doctors. I said the doctors had to report to me and not to him, upon which he said that he had the 'Emperor's orders' . . . to report . . . about his Papa. I said it was not necessary, as we always reported to the Emperor ourselves. . . . I said I would go and tell his father how he behaved and ask that he should be forbidden the house. . . . Willy is of course much too young and inexperienced to understand this. He was merely put up to it at Berlin. He thought he was to save his Papa from my mismanagement. When he has not his head stuffed with rubbish from Berlin, he is quite nice and *traitable* and then we are pleased to have him; but I will not have him dictate to me—the head on my shoulders is every bit as good as his."

Vicky did agree to have Fritz examined again. Mackenzie, who was present, dramatically reversed his diagnosis: the Crown Prince was suffering from cancer, and would be dead within eighteen months. The other doctors agreed, adding that now even a complete removal of the larynx would do no good. "My father took his sentence of death—for such it was—like a hero, standing upright and looking the doctors firmly in the face," William said. Alone together after the doctors had left, Fritz and Vicky wept and clung to each other. "To think that I have such a horrid, disgusting illness!" shuddered Fritz. "That I shall be an object of disgust to everyone and a burden to you all!" To her mother, Vicky wrote, "My darling has got such a fate before him which I hardly dare to think of."

Through most of the winter the couple remained at San Remo while as many as fifty reporters, crowded into the Hotel Victoria, kept a macabre watch. There were demands from Berlin that the Crown Prince return; Kaiser William I, approaching ninety-one, was ill and could not survive much longer. Vicky refused. The only thing that mattered was her husband's health: Berlin was freezing and damp; if Fritz was to have any chance, it would be in the warm Mediterranean sun. Queen Victoria supported her daughter: "The more failing the Emperor becomes, the more Fritz must make sure of getting well."

The Crown Prince, sucking all day on ice cubes and with a bag of crushed ice tied around his throat day and night, began to suffo-cate. On February 9, 1888, a tracheotomy was performed and a permanent silver tube was inserted through his throat into his wind-pipe. On March 2, Prince William returned to San Remo. "[My father's] figure showed in its emaciation and the yellow color of the face unmistakeable signs of the rapid progress of the disease. He was perpetually tormented by a tearing cough, and no word passed his lips for his mouth was already forever dumb. Notes rapidly scrib-bled on bits of paper had to take the place of speech when gesture and mimicry failed."

A week later, Kaiser William I died in Berlin. In San Remo, the new Emperor, Frederick III, gathered his household in the drawing room. He invested his wife with the highest Prussian decoration, the Order of the Black Eagle, which only the sovereign could bestow. He wrote a note on a piece of paper and handed it to Sir Morell Mackenzie: "I thank you for having made me live long enough to reward the valiant courage of my wife." Finally, he sent a telegram to Queen Victoria: "At this moment of deep emotion and sorrow at the news of my father's death, my feelings of devoted affection to you prompt me, on succeeding to the throne, to repeat to you my sincere and earnest desire for a close and lasting friendship between our two nations. Frederick."

On March 11, the new German Emperor returned to his capi-tal. He was too weak to attend his father's funeral and stood weep-ing at a window as the funeral procession passed on its way to the Charlottenburg mausoleum. At his first Crown Council meeting, he asked questions and issued instructions by writing slips of paper. He made it clear that Bismarck would remain as Chancellor and that he would make no attempt to alter the Chancellor's policies. "In my entire ministerial career," Bismarck wrote in his memoirs, "the con-duct of business was never so pleasant or lacking in friction as it was during the ninety-nine days of the Emperor Frederick."

When the long reign of Kaiser William I had come to an end, the Queen had written a congratulatory note to Vicky: "My own dear Empress Victoria, it does seem an impossible dream, may God bless her! You know how little I care for rank or titles—but I cannot deny that after all that has been done and said, I am thankful and proud that dear Fritz and you should have come to the throne." At the end of April, Queen Victoria decided to visit her dying son-in-law. She went straight from her train to the Charlottenburg Palace and walked into the Crown Prince's bedroom. Wordlessly, he raised up both hands in a gesture of pleasure, then turned and handed her a nosegay. During the Queen's visit, Vicky brought Bismarck to see her. The Chancellor awaited his audience ill at ease; repeatedly, he asked the Queen's equerry where in the room the Queen would be and whether she would be standing or seated. To their mutual surprise, Victoria and Bismarck charmed each other. She asked him to stand by her daughter; "he assured me he would." "What a woman!" the Chancellor said afterwards. "One could do business with her." Later, he described her to his family as "a jolly little body." After the audience, the Queen said to the British Ambassador, "I don't understand why my daughter could not get on with Prince Bismarck. I think him a very amiable man and we had a most charming conversation." The grim purpose of the Queen's visit was never forgotten, however. During the three-day visit, Vicky often broke down. When it was time for the Queen to leave and she already had entered her railway carriage, Vicky followed and clung to her mother. "It was terrible," the Queen wrote in her journal, "to see her standing there in tears while the train moved slowly off."

On May 24, the dying Emperor appeared in the chapel of the Charlottenburg Palace at the wedding of his second son, Prince Henry, to Princess Irene of Hesse. He wore a uniform whose collar was cut high enough to cover the tube in his throat. Despite his feebleness and emaciation, he insisted on rising and standing during the exchange of rings. It was apparent to everyone that Frederick's reign would be short and that within a matter of weeks William would become Emperor. This tormented Vicky, not only because her husband was dying, but because, with Frederick's death, Prince Albert's dream of a liberalized Germany in partnership with England also would die. The Crown Princess tried to keep Frederick—and, it seemed to William, the Imperial crown—to herself for as long as possible. "I soon noticed that difficulties were being put in the way of my visits to my father," William wrote. ". . . Then I learned that spies were posted who gave timely notice of my arrival at the palace, whereupon I was either received by my mother or greeted at the house door with the information that the Emperor was asleep. . . . When at last I succeeded, with the help of the valet

. . . in slipping by the backstairs unnoticed into my father's bed-room, he showed himself greatly pleased to see me. . . . When he gave me to understand that I ought to visit him more often . . . and I answered that I had already called several times but had never been admitted, he was greatly astonished . . . he said that my pres-ence was welcome to him at any time." Colonel Swaine, the British Military Attaché in Berlin, wrote to the Prince of Wales: "We are living in sad times here in Berlin. . . . Not sad alone because we have an Emperor at death's door . . . but . . . because almost all officials . . . are behaving in a way as if the last spark of honor and faithful duty had gone—they are all trimming their sails. It seems as if a curse had come over this country, leaving but one bright spot and that is where stands a solitary woman doing her duty faithfully and tenderly by her sick husband against all odds."

Frederick's illness and approaching death summoned up poisons from the vast reservoir of Prussian antagonism to England. Already in September 1887, when the Crown Prince was leaving England to recuperate in Italy, Friederich von Holstein, First Counselor of the German Foreign Ministry, was spewing venom at the sick man's wife: "The Crown Princess's behavior is typical. Gay and carefree, with but one idea—never to return to Prussia. I persist in my view, which is now shared by others, namely that from the very beginning she accepted the idea that the worst would happen. Judging by all I have heard of her in recent months, I am tempted to call her a degenerate or corrupt character. Nature and pressure have com-bined to produce this effect. She came here thirty years ago, her father's spoiled darling, convinced she was a political prodigy. Far from acquiring influence here, she saw herself obliged to renounce any kind of open political activity and to conform to the restraint of the Prussian court which she hated. She has always despised her husband. She will greet his death as the moment of deliverance."

The new Crown Prince, William, torn between grief for his fa-ther and the prospect of becoming German Emperor, had little sym-pathy for "the English princess who is my mother," as he described her at the time. She had taken control of his father's medical treat-ment; now, as a result, his father was dying, and she was attempting to prevent father and son from meeting. At that time—and even more strongly as the years went by—William placed heavy blame on the English Dr. Mackenzie. "The decisive interference of the En-glishman Mackenzie . . . had the most disastrous consequences," William wrote. He questioned "whether the Englishman really pronounced his diagnosis in good faith. I am convinced that this was not the case. . . . He was out, not only after money, but also after the English aristocracy [referring to Mackenzie's knighthood]*. . . . When one considers that, if the English doctor had not intervened, my father would in all probability have been saved, one will understand how it was that I took every opportunity of opposing . . . this ostrich policy. That my mother could not free herself from the Englishman's authority, even when the facts had become clear to everyone else, had the worst possible effect upon my relations with her." William absolved his mother of the decision to summon an English doctor and of the specific choice of Mackenzie; he admitted that this was the "unanimous" decision of the Berlin doctors. But few in Germany knew this. Before long, it was a general belief in Germany that the English Crown Princess had insisted on summoning an English doctor, had insisted on following his incompetent advice against the recommendation of a phalanx of German physicians, and thus—even if she was not guilty of Holstein's vicious charge—was responsible for the needless death of a German emperor.

Early in June, Frederick, suffering from an abscess in the tracheotomy site and intermittent high fevers, was moved from the Charlottenburg Palace to the New Palace at Potsdam, where he had been born. In splendid weather he sat on a terrace and looked out at the gardens of Sans Souci, blazing with spring colors. On the morning of June 13, his friend King Oscar of Sweden visited him. The following day, Bismarck came to say farewell. Frederick reached for the Chancellor's hand and gave it to his wife. That evening, Frederick could not swallow even liquid food. Queen Victoria, receiving almost hourly telegrams at Balmoral, telegraphed William, "Am in

---

* William's charge was exaggerated, but Mackenzie, confronted by growing evidence that his diagnosis had been wrong, behaved evasively. In November 1887, after the Crown Prince had been told he had cancer, Mackenzie insisted to Queen Victoria's doctor that, the previous June when he had prevented an operation, there had been no malignancy. In January 1888, when Fritz was struggling to breathe and shortly before his tracheotomy, Mackenzie told the Queen at Osborne that "though he fully believed that there was nothing malignant, he could not say so positively for another six months." For the rest of his life, Mackenzie struggled to rebut the charge of misdiagnosis in this, his most famous case. His charge that the clumsiness of German physicians caused Fritz unnecessary suffering resulted in his expulsion from the Royal College of Surgeons for violating confidentiality and for unethical conduct. Mackenzie remained in private practice, but bitterness and controversy destroyed his health. In 1892, four years after his royal patient, Mackenzie died.

greatest distress at this terrible news and so troubled about poor dear Mama. Do all you can, as I asked you, to help her at this terrible time of dreadful trial and grief. God help us!" Frederick III died early in the morning of June 15.

"I am broken-hearted," Queen Victoria telegraphed her grand-son. "Help and do all you can for your poor dear mother. . . . Grandmama." To Vicky, she wrote: "Darling, darling, unhappy child, you are far more sorely tried than me. I had not the agony of seeing another fill the place of my Angel husband, which I always felt I never could have borne!" In her journal that night, the Queen wrote, "None of my own sons could be a greater loss. He was so good, so wise, and so fond of me!" The Prince of Wales wrote to his son, Prince George (later King George V): "Try, my dear Georgy, never to forget Uncle Fritz. He was one of the finest and noblest characters ever known. If he had a fault he was too good for this world."

Kaiser William II's first act was to throw a cordon of soldiers around the New Palace, where his father lay dead. No one could enter or leave the palace without permission; when Vicky, now Dowager Empress, went to the windows, she saw the red uniforms of the hussars patrolling the grounds. William was convinced that his mother would try to smuggle away to England his father's private papers. Officers went through the private rooms, opening drawers and searching in closets. Nothing was found. Two days later, Queen Victoria wrote in her journal: "Colonel Swaine arrived from Berlin. . . . He had brought some papers which Fritz had desired should be placed in my care."

The Prince of Wales hurried to Berlin for the funeral and found his sister bitterly angry. At William's command, despite her plead-ing, a postmortem was being performed on Frederick's body to ver-ify the cancer and embarrass the English doctor—and the English Princess. When Vicky had attempted to see Prince Bismarck to per-suade him to stop the postmortem, the Chancellor had sent word that he was too busy. William was making all the plans for his fa-ther's funeral, ignoring his mother's wishes; ultimately, she refused to attend the state funeral and held her own private service. The name Friedrichskron, which Frederick had given to the New Palace in his final days, was summarily changed back, on William's instruc-tions, to New Palace.

Queen Victoria felt the chill emanating from the new regime and repaid it in kind. On June 27, General Winterfeldt arrived from Berlin, bringing a formal letter to the Queen announcing William's accession. Soon, the new Kaiser was complaining about the cold manner in which his envoy had been received at Windsor Castle. The Queen wrote to her Private Secretary: "The Queen is extremely glad to hear that General Winterfeldt says he was received coldly . . . for such was her intention. He was a traitor to his beloved master, and never mentioned his name even, or a word of regret and spoke of the pleasure . . . at being chosen to announce his new master's accession. Could the Queen, devoted as she is to the dear memory of the beloved and noble Emperor Frederick, to whom, and [to] her daughter, General Winterfeldt has behaved so treacherously, receive him otherwise?" Five days later, the Queen tried a warmer approach with her grandson: "Let me ask you to bear with poor Mama if she is sometimes irritated and excited. She does not mean it so; think what months of agony and suspense and watching with broken and sleepless nights she has gone through, and don't mind it. I am so anxious that all should go smoothly, that I write thus openly in the interests of both." The Queen then turned to another troubling matter. "There are many rumors of your going and paying visits to Sovereigns. I hope that at least you will let some months pass before anything of this kind takes place, as it is not three weeks yet since dear beloved Papa was taken, and we are still in such deep mourning for him." William rebuffed his grandmother. He would soon be taking his fleet up the Baltic, "where I hope to meet the Emperor of Russia which will be of good effect for the peace of Europe. . . . I would have gone later if possible, but State interest goes before personal feelings and the fate which hangs over nations does not wait till the etiquette of Court mournings has been fulfilled. . . . I deem it necessary that monarchs should meet often and confer together to look out for dangers which threaten the monarchical principle from democratical and republican parties in all parts of the world. It is far better that we Emperors keep firm together." Queen Victoria was not amused. To Lord Salisbury, her Prime Minister, she telegraphed: "Trust that we shall be very cool, though civil, in our communications with my grandson and Prince Bismarck, who are bent on a return to the oldest times of government."

CHAPTER 3

"Blood
and Iron"

◆

After Waterloo and the dispatch of Napoleon Bonaparte to St. Helena, the Congress of Vienna redrew the map of Germany. The three hundred German kingdoms, electorates, principalities, grand duchies, bishoprics, and free cities which had made up the old Holy Roman Empire, bound by lip service to the Hapsburg Emperor in Vienna, were reconstituted into a loose confederation of thirty-nine states. Most remained small, a few were tiny, and there were five sovereign kingdoms: Prussia, Bavaria, Saxony, Hanover, and Württemberg. A Federal Diet to which all states sent representatives was established in the free city of Frankfurt on the Main. Its purpose was to settle disputes between the German states and, above all, to preserve the conservative status quo. In Germany and in the Diet, Austria—strictly speaking, not a German power at all—remained predominant. She possessed the prestige of an imperial ruler, the skillful diplomacy of the post-Napoleonic era's dominant statesman, Prince Clemens von Metternich, and the largest army in Central Europe.

Prussia, largest and strongest of the purely German states, was approaching Great Power status. Blücher's Prussians had relieved Wellington's exhausted army and turned the tide at Waterloo. The Congress of Vienna had added significant territories in the Rhine-

land and Westphalia to the Prussian Kingdom and the black and
white flag with the Prussian double eagle now flew from Aachen and
Coblenz to Königsberg near the Russian frontier. The new lands in
the west, among the most densely populated in Germany, were
heavily Roman Catholic, and rich in mineral wealth and industrial
potential. One of the King of Prussia's newly acquired subjects was
the ironmaster of Essen, Friedrich Krupp. The Prussian state, traditionally Protestant, overwhelmingly rural, with its Spartan military
tradition, nevertheless remained inferior to Austria in one essential
ingredient of national power: population. In 1815, there were 10
million Prussians, compared to 30 million Frenchmen and 30 million
subjects of the Austrian emperor.

Through the first half of the nineteenth century, the drive towards German unification gained momentum, speeded by the
growth of industry and railways. In 1834, a Prussian-organized customs union (*Zollverein*) lowered tariff barriers; in the 1850s, a doubling of trackage in the German railway network brought all
German states within hours of one another. Coal mined in the Saar
and in Silesia heated industrial furnaces in the Ruhr. The ports of
Bremen and Hamburg exported and imported goods for the whole
of Germany. Yet fifty years after the Congress of Vienna, Germany
remained a loose political confederation of thirty-nine states. Austria, continuing to dominate the Federal Diet in Frankfurt, opposed
any change; France, again risen to primacy in Europe under a new
Emperor, Napoleon III, reinforced Austria's policy. The statesman
who changed this—who expelled Austria from Germany, defeated
France and toppled Napoleon III, unified Germany, created the
German Empire, and transferred the capital of Continental Europe
from Paris or Vienna to Berlin—was Otto von Bismarck.

For twenty-eight years (1862–1890), the greatest German political figure since the Middle Ages loomed over Germany and Europe.
Bismarck's very appearance created an image of force and intimidation. Over six feet tall, with broad shoulders, a powerful chest, and
long legs, he gave up wearing civilian frock coats when he became
Imperial Chancellor and appeared only in military uniform: Prussian
blue tunic, spiked helmet, and long black cavalry boots which extended over the thigh. The top of his head was bald before he
reached fifty, but thick hair continued to sprout and tumble over his
ears, in bushy eyebrows, and in a heavy bushy mustache. The eyes,
wide apart and heavily pouched, glittered with intelligence and
flashed with authority. Despite the aura of power surrounding this
huge frame, there were contradictions: Bismarck's hands and feet
were small, even delicate; his waist, before it turned to paunch, was

abnormally narrow; his voice was not the deep bass or resonant baritone one might expect—it was a thin, high, reedy, almost piping tenor.

Bismarck's character was equally complex and contradictory. His greatest gift was intelligence; he possessed intellectual ascendancy over all the politicians of his time, German or European, and all—German and European—acknowledged this. He was self-confident, even daring, to the point of recklessness. He combined indomitable will and tenacity of purpose in reaching long-range goals with resourcefulness, suppleness, and virtuosity in improvising means. Bismarck was willing to work indefatigably, with exuberant energy, to create political and diplomatic situations from which he could profit; he was equally ready to seize an unexpected prize suddenly offered. His manner could be genial and charming; subordinates and enemies more often saw cunning, ruthlessness, unscrupulousness, brutality, and cruelty. Underneath, not surprisingly, lay restlessness, anger, myriad grievances, jealousy, and pettiness. Bismarck's politics and diplomacy were based on practical experience and he disdained theorists and sentimentalists. Near the end of his career, he was moody, suspicious, and misanthropic, bowed by the endlessly complicated business of governing. In Germany, he had no friends or colleagues, only subordinates. His assistant at the Foreign Ministry, Friedrich von Holstein, said that Bismarck treated people "not as friends, but as tools, like knives and forks, which are changed after each course."

Not all Germans approved of Bismarck. German liberals had fought for national unity, but they had wanted to achieve it in a democratic, parliamentary form, not have it thrust upon the nation by a powerful, conservative statesman wielding the power of a primitive, disciplined military state. Nevertheless, Bismarck had his way. He was the strongest personality and the most powerful political force Europe had known since Napoleon I. From the moment in 1862 when King William I of Prussia reluctantly made the Junker diplomat his Minister-President, Germany and Europe entered the Age of Bismarck.

Otto von Bismarck was born on April 1, 1815, two and a half months before the Battle of Waterloo, in Schönhausen in Prussia, near the Elbe River west of Berlin. His father, Ferdinand, a minor nobleman, possessed a typical Junker estate with cattle, sheep, wheatfields, and timber. The Junkers, whose nearest approximation was the rough English country squirearchy, lived close to the land, often milking their own cows, running their own sawmills, and selling their own wool at market. Although they worked their estates, they were proud of their ancient lineage. Bismarck sprang from a family older in Prussia than the Hohenzollerns, who had come from Stuttgart in 1415; Prussia's kings, Bismarck once said, derive from "a Swabian family no better than mine." Most Junkers were pious, rigid, and frugal, devoted to the land, to the Protestant church, and to their monarch, whose army they officered and government they administered. They cared nothing for the rest of the world and little for the rest of Germany; Bismarck himself never regarded South Germans or Catholic Germans as true Germans. Junkers were not interested in the great capitals of Europe: Paris, Vienna, and London. If they looked beyond their villages at all, it was to Berlin, the growing capital of their Spartan military state.

Ferdinand von Bismarck was a dull, easygoing Junker who managed his estate with only modest success. His wife, Wilhelmine, was a personality of striking contrast. The daughter of Ludwig Mencken, the trusted counselor of Frederick the Great, she had been brought up in Berlin, where she eagerly absorbed everything the capital had to offer. Her father died when she was nine and, in gratitude for his services, the royal family took Wilhelmine in hand and brought her up with the Hohenzollern children. Her marriage at sixteen to the ponderous, rustic nobleman over twice her age was considered a sound match—she was a commoner—but it was a mistake. Marooned on a farm, she compensated by ignoring her husband and concentrating on her children. She encouraged intelligence, ambition, restlessness, and energy, but gave little affection. At six, Otto was dispatched to school in Berlin, where he remained until he was sixteen. He grew up a strange mixture of his dissimilar parents: a tall, increasingly bulky boy, with a highly educated, tempestuous, romantic, passionate nature, bursting with strength and determination. In the words of a biographer, "he was the clever, sophisticated son of a clever, sophisticated mother masquerading all his life as his heavy, earthy father."

At seventeen, Bismarck enrolled at Göttingen University, the most famous liberal institution in Germany. There, he rejected contact with liberal, middle-class students, joined an aristocratic student society, drank exuberantly, neglected his studies, and, some say, fought twenty-five duels. He wore outrageous, varicolored clothes, challenged university discipline, and read Schiller, Goethe, Shakespeare, and Byron, preferring the English writers to the German. (His favorite author was Sir Walter Scott, whose novels stirred history into romance.) At Göttingen, Bismarck made a close friend of the American future historian John Motley, whose famous *Rise of the Dutch Republic* was to become a monument of nineteenth-century scholarship. Forty years later, as Imperial Chancellor, Bismarck often wrote to "Dear old John" and would happily abandon the duties of office to make Motley welcome.

Two years at Göttingen and a third at the University of Berlin equipped Bismarck for the entrance exams of the Prussian Civil Service. The tall young man's first assignment was to the city of Aachen in the western Rhineland. In 1836, when Bismarck arrived, the Catholic, free-thinking city was still disgruntled at having been handed over by the Congress of Vienna to Prussia. But the city's reputation as a spa still brought pleasure seekers from many nations, especially England. Bismarck, twenty-one, plunged into this urbane society, indulging happily in drink, gambling, and debt. He discovered the charms of well-born young Englishwomen and fell in love with Isabella Lorraine-Smith, the daughter of a fox-hunting parson from Leicester. When Isabella and her parents moved on to Wiesbaden, Bismarck took two weeks' leave to accompany them. In Wiesbaden, he spent extravagantly on midnight champagne suppers and, when she left for Switzerland, he followed. At the end of two months, when he wrote to his superior in Aachen that he would be absent for some additional time, he was suspended. The result did not trouble Bismarck. He "by no means intended to give the government an account of his personal relations," he said. A few weeks later, he was back at his family farm, his job terminated, his affair with Isabella over, but his knowledge of English greatly improved.

Bismarck returned to Berlin and endured one year of required military service in a regiment of Foot Guards. When he was twenty-four, his mother died and he resigned from the Civil Service to assist his father, who was ineffectually administering an estate in Pomerania. For eight long years while Otto and his brother Bernhard labored to restore the property to prosperity, the tempestuous youth with his romantic temper was chained to the barren life of a Pomeranian Junker. He found estate management, conversations with peasants, and the society of his Junker neighbors boring. Frustration turned to frenzy and the countryside rang with tales of the reckless, hard-drinking young landowner. He was said to ride hallooing through the night, to be ready to shoot, hunt, or swim anywhere in any weather, to be able to drink half a dozen young lieutenants from nearby garrisons under the table, to wake up his occasional guests by firing a pistol through their bedroom windows, to have seduced every peasant girl in all the villages, to have released a fox in a lady's drawing room. At the same time, he read hungrily, steeping himself in history and devouring English novels such as *Tom Jones* and *Tristram Shandy*. Mired in farm life, he thirsted for some noble or heroic purpose. Yet despite his boredom, there was a side of Bismarck's nature that loved the life of a Junker squire: the possession of land; riding or walking under his great trees. At twenty-seven, in the middle of these years, Bismarck made a three-month visit to Britain, passing through Edinburgh, York, Manchester, London, and Portsmouth. He liked England and, for a moment, toyed with the idea of joining the British Army in India. The impulse died when "I asked myself what harm the Indians had done me," he said later. In 1844, at twenty-nine, Bismarck's frustration drove him to reenter the Prussian Civil Service: he resigned two weeks later, explaining, "I have never been able to put up with superiors."

To steady himself, he married Johanna von Puttkamer, the daughter of another Pomeranian Junker. Simple, modest, patient, devoted, and ready to endure any behavior from the unstable, emotional volcano who was her husband, Johanna shared his opinion that wives belonged exclusively in the domestic sphere. "I like piety in a woman and abhor all feminine cleverness," he told his brother. Later, Johanna did not read his speeches even when the whole of Germany and all of Europe were discussing them. Her understanding of politics was personal: she was a friend of her husband's friends, she disliked or hated his opponents. When she married at twenty-three, Johanna von Puttkamer was not beautiful, but she possessed arresting dark eyes and a wealth of long, fine, black hair. She played the piano well and her playing of Beethoven's "Sonata Appassionata," Bismarck's favorite piece, could reduce her husband to tears. Bismarck wooed her mostly by talking about himself. Before their betrothal in February 1847, he wrote to her, "On a night like this I feel uncommonly moved myself to become a sharer of delight, a portion of the tempest and of night, and, mounted on a runaway horse, to hurl myself over the cliff into the foam and fury of the Rhine, or something similar." He had enough control, however, to add wryly, "A pleasure of that kind, unfortunately, one can enjoy but once in life."

Eighteen forty-eight was the Year of Revolution. France rose against the restored Bourbon monarchy and drove away King Louis Philippe; Metternich, the dominant figure at the Congress of Vienna, fled from Austria to England; Czechs, Magyars, and Italians rose in revolt. When revolutionary crowds filled the streets of Berlin, Prussian generals pleaded with King Frederick William IV to let them unleash the army. Frederick William refused and the army withdrew from the capital. The King agreed to a constitution and an elected parliament, and created a civilian militia responsible for law and order. Bismarck at Schönhausen became hysterical at the idea of the King of Prussia in the hands of the mob. He spoke of raising an army of peasants to march on Berlin and rescue the King. He entered the capital and went to the Castle, where he was denied entry. He suggested to Prince William of Prussia, Frederick William's brother, a lifelong army officer, that he succeed his brother and impose order; William refused. In the end, the army reoccupied Berlin without bloodshed. "We have been saved by the specifically Prussian virtues," Bismarck said. "The old Prussian concepts of honor, loyalty, obedience, and courage inspire the army. . . . Prussians we are and Prussians we remain." Nevertheless, the limited constitution and an elected assembly, the Landtag, remained.

In 1851, Prussia needed an ambassador to the new German Federal Diet at Frankfurt. No one much cared when it was given to Bismarck, considered by many to be a flamboyant reactionary from Prussia's backwoods. In Frankfurt, the nearest thing to an international capital Germany possessed, the predominant power was Austria. Bismarck's task was to make plain to the Austrians and to other German states that Prussia considered itself the equal in Germany of the Hapsburg Empire.

The Austrian representative, Count von Thun und Hohenstein, was an aristocrat who treated other members of the Diet as social inferiors. Bismarck bridled at Thun's behavior. When he called on Thun for the first time, the Austrian casually received him in shirtsleeves. Bismarck quickly stripped off his own jacket, saying, "Yes, it is a hot day." Traditionally, Thun was the only ambassador who smoked at meetings; Bismarck ended this when he pulled out his own cigar and asked Thun for a light.

Bismarck's eight years in Frankfurt added polish to his character. In the patrician town with its rich traditions, historic wealth, and cosmopolitan atmosphere, he became a serious diplomat. He lived well, smoked Havana cigars, and drank a concoction called Black Velvet, a mixture of stout and champagne. In the summer of 1855, his American friend, Motley, visited the Bismarck household in Frankfurt. "It is one of those houses," Motley wrote to his wife, "where everyone does as he likes. . . . Here are young and old, grandparents and children and dogs all at once, eating, drinking, smoking, piano playing and pistol shooting (in the garden), all going on at the same time. It is one of those establishments where every earthly thing that can be eaten and drunk is offered you—soda wa-

ter, small beer, champagne, burgundy, or claret, are out all the time
—and everybody is smoking the best Havanas every minute." Beneath this chaotic bonhomie, Bismarck was evolving a coolly cynical
approach to foreign policy. It had nothing to do with dynastic alliances or ethnic groupings. It concerned itself only with Prussia, its
security and prosperity; every other state was a potential ally or
enemy according to circumstance. "When I have been asked
whether I was pro-Russian or pro-Western," he wrote to a friend in
Berlin, "I have always answered: I am Prussian and my ideal in
foreign policy is total freedom from prejudice, independence of decision reached without pressure or aversion from or attraction to
foreign states and their rulers. I have had a certain sympathy for
England and its inhabitants, and even now I am not altogether free
of it; but they will not let us love them, and as far as I am concerned,
as soon as it was proved to me that it was in the interests of a
healthy and well-considered Prussian policy, I would see our troops
fire on French, Russians, English or Austrians with equal satisfaction."

In 1857 King Frederick William suffered a severe stroke and a
year later became hopelessly insane. His brother, Prince William,
was appointed regent. Bismarck, after eight years in Frankfurt, was
dispatched as Prussian Minister to St. Petersburg. Feeling isolated
from Berlin, Germany, and Europe, he grumbled that he had been
put "on ice." "Bismarck receives no news from Berlin," wrote an
assistant at the German Embassy. "That is to say the Wilhelmstrasse
[the Ministry of Foreign Affairs] simply does not write to him. They
don't like him there and they behave as though he does not exist. So
he conducts his own political intrigues, does no entertaining, complains incessantly about the cost of living, sees very few people, gets
up at 11 or 11:30 and sits about all day in a green dressing gown, not
stirring except to drink." Bismarck served four years in the city on
the Neva. Although he was popular with Tsar Alexander II, who
took him bear hunting, he avoided most social life.

When King Frederick William IV died childless in 1861, his
brother succeeded as King William I. The new King was sixty-three,
a tall, honest, decent soldier who cared only about the army. The
Prussian parliament insisted on reducing the period of required military service from three years to two. William and his War Minister,
General Albrecht von Roon, refused. The crisis extended over two
years. Roon, who knew and admired Bismarck, proposed to the
King that the Minister in Russia be brought home to fight the King's
battle in the assembly. William was reluctant and Bismarck, when
the idea was proposed to him, agreed only on condition that he also

be given charge of foreign policy. William refused. The double impasse—King versus parliament, King versus Bismarck—continued. Three times, in 1860, 1861, and 1862, Bismarck was offered the Minister-Presidency of Prussia without control of foreign affairs; three times, Bismarck declined. Nevertheless, William decided, just in case, to bring Bismarck closer and in May 1862 Bismarck was transferred from St. Petersburg to Paris. Bismarck, aware of the confused state of affairs in Berlin, behaved with deliberate casualness. In June, he went to London, then on to Trouville and Biarritz.

In Biarritz, Bismarck met Princess Katherine Orlov, the young wife of the elderly Russian Ambassador to Belgium. Detached from Johanna, who was in Pomerania with the children, Bismarck fell in love. Katherine Orlov was twenty-two, Bismarck forty-seven; they walked in the mountains together, picnicked, and bathed in the Atlantic surf; she played Beethoven, Mendelssohn, and Schubert while he listened, entranced. The intense relationship remained publicly acceptable: she called him "Uncle" and her husband did not appear to object. Bismarck wrote straightforwardly to Johanna. Describing a picnic, he said, "Hidden in a steep ravine cut back from the cliffs, I gaze out between two rocks on which the heather blooms at the sea, green and white in the sunshine and spray. At my side is the most charming woman, whom you will love very much when you get to know her . . . amusing, intelligent, kind, pretty, and young." Johanna's reaction, writing to a friend, was, "Were I at all inclined to jealousy and envy, I should be tyrannized to the depths now by these passions. But my soul has no room for them and I rejoice quite enormously that my beloved husband has found this charming woman. But for her he would never have found peace for so long in one place or become so well as he boasts of being in every letter." When the Orlovs left Biarritz, Bismarck accompanied them, as, twenty-five years before, he had followed Isabella Lorraine-Smith. The threesome went to Toulouse, then to Avignon. But the Orlovs were going to Geneva; Bismarck had been summoned to Berlin. On September 14, he said good-bye to Katherine. She gave him an onyx medallion, which he carried on his watch chain until he died.

In Berlin, the King and his parliament remained deadlocked. Twice, the assembly had been dissolved; twice, new elections had returned an even larger number of liberals determined to insist on a two-year term of service. William was adamant: he was Commander-in-Chief of the army; if he could not dictate the terms of military service, then being King was meaningless and he was prepared to abdicate.

Only the refusal of his son Frederick to succeed him had prevented him from doing so already. Roon, in extremis, waited no longer. He wired Bismarck in Paris: "PERICULUM IN MORA! DÉPÊCHEZ-VOUS!" ("Delay is dangerous! Hurry!")

On September 20, Bismarck, unbeknownst to the King, arrived in Berlin. When William that day admitted to Roon that only Bismarck could carry out the kind of unconstitutional action they were discussing, he added, reassuring himself, "But, of course, he is not here." Roon pounced: "He is here and is ready to serve Your Majesty." The climactic meeting between William I and Bismarck took place on September 22 in the summer palace of Babelsberg on the Havel River. The two men went for a walk in the park. William said that he could not reign with dignity if parliament overruled his royal prerogative on matters affecting the army. Bismarck replied that, given supreme power in domestic and foreign affairs, he would form a ministry and put through the King's demands regarding the army, with or without the consent of parliament. All he would need was the support of the monarch. Bismarck emerged from the audience as Acting Minister-President and Foreign Minister–Designate of the Prussian kingdom. Eight days later, he inaugurated twenty-eight years of rule with a famous speech which stated his philosophy and supplied a phrase which, more than any other, is identified with Bismarck. Explaining to the Budget Committee of the Landtag why, in the Prussian monarchy, the King must be allowed to make decisions about the army, he said, "Germany does not look to Prussia's liberalism but to her strength. . . . The great questions of the day will not be decided by speeches and the resolutions of majorities— that was the great mistake of 1848—but by iron and blood."*

The deputies voted 251 to 36 against the army plan and Bismarck sent them home. When they returned on January 27, 1863, he gave them a lecture on the relationship of the crown to a representative assembly in Prussia. If the assembly refused to vote necessary funds, the crown was entitled to carry on the government and collect taxes under previous laws. He, the King's Chief Minister, had not been appointed by and could not be dismissed by Parliament. "The Prussian monarchy has not yet completed its mission," he said. "It is not yet ready to become a mere ornamental decoration of your constitutional edifice." To Motley, he expressed his contempt for the deputies: "Here in the Landtag while I am writing to you, I have to listen . . . to uncommonly foolish speeches delivered by uncommonly childish and excited politicians. . . . These chatter-boxes

---

* Subsequently, the phrase was reversed to the more sonorous "blood and iron."

cannot really rule Prussia . . . they are fairly clever in a way, have a smattering of knowledge, are typical products of German university education; they know as little about politics as we knew in our student days."

It did not matter to Bismarck whether Prussian conscripts served two years or three in the army, but it mattered to the King and Bismarck needed the King. Bismarck cared about a free hand in foreign policy. His objective was to make Prussia, not Austria, predominant in Germany. Events soon played into his hands. The twin duchies of Schleswig and Holstein, northwest of Berlin at the base of the Jutland peninsula, had been ruled by the King of Denmark for four hundred years. The populations were mixed: Holstein, which reached to the outskirts of Hamburg, was mostly German; Schleswig, on the eastern side of the peninsula and containing the magnificent fjord and port of Kiel, was mostly Danish. In 1848, as the high tide of nationalism rolled across Europe, the German Holsteiners rose against the Danes. Prussia, with the approval of the Frankfurt Diet, sent troops to aid the Holsteiners. Conservative Europe, including Russia and Great Britain, rallied to Denmark and demanded that the Prussians withdraw. An international agreement, the 1852 Treaty of London, guaranteed the status quo: the two duchies would remain attached to the Danish Crown, but the King of Denmark would make no attempt to absorb them into his kingdom. In March 1863, six months after Bismarck became Minister-President of Prussia, the new King Christian IX of Denmark breached the Treaty of London by proclaiming the two duchies an integral part of Denmark. The Holsteiners refused to swear allegiance and again appealed to the Diet at Frankfurt.

Bismarck, for his own reasons, was pleased by the crisis. He had no interest in Holsteiner nationalism. "Whether the Germans in Holstein are happy is no concern of ours," he remarked. His interest was in the extension of Prussian power. While the majority of Germans in Schleswig, Holstein, and throughout Germany wanted only the restored independence of the duchies under a prince of their own choosing, Bismarck from the outset was bent on saving the duchies from Denmark in order to annex them to Prussia.

Austria was forced to support Prussia. Nominally, she was the first power in Germany and all Germany was demanding support for the duchies. To do nothing would mean abandoning leadership to Prussia. In January 1864, Prussia and Austria formed an alliance to enforce the Treaty of London. On January 16, Bismarck gave King

Christian an ultimatum to evacuate Schleswig within twenty-four hours. The Danes refused. Holstein was occupied without resistance. A combined Austro-Prussian army advanced into Schleswig, resisted by forty thousand Danes. Great Britain, tending toward sympathy with Denmark, was stymied by Denmark's incontrovertible breach of the Treaty of London; the British government restricted itself to insisting that the Austro-Prussian advance halt at the frontier of Denmark proper. On July 8, Denmark capitulated, formed a new cabinet, asked for peace, and surrendered the duchies.

At the end of August, Bismarck accompanied King William I to Vienna to discuss the future of the duchies with Emperor Franz Josef and his ministers. The Austrian response was vague, but Bismarck encountered immediate opposition from his own King. William I knew that he possessed no title, legal or historical, to the two duchies. He categorically refused to seize and annex them. No agreement was reached and both duchies remained under temporarily joint Austro-Prussian condominium. A year later, in August 1865, Holstein was assigned exclusively to Austria, Schleswig to Prussia. As evidence that Berlin considered Schleswig now permanently Prussian, the infant Prussian Navy began construction of its principal naval base at Kiel.

Victory over Denmark, for which William I promoted Bismarck to the rank of Count, was the Minister-President's first external triumph. He had "liberated" Schleswig and Holstein, entangled Austria in a corner of Germany far from home, and laid the basis for a confrontation he felt certain of winning. Over the winter and spring of 1866, Bismarck repeatedly provoked Austria. He demanded that the German Confederation be reformed by a new national German parliament, which would create a new German constitution from which Austria would be excluded. When Austria refused to abandon her primacy and give Prussia a free hand to organize a new federal system, Bismarck signed an alliance with Italy against Austria and let Vienna know that war was imminent. In May, he announced that Prussia had as much right to Holstein as to Schleswig. On June 6, he ordered Prussian troops to enter Holstein. On June 15, Prussia delivered ultimatums to neighboring Hanover and Saxony: Prussian troops would march through their territories to attack Austria; resistance would mean war with them also.

When war between Prussia and Austria began, Europe predicted overwhelming defeat for Prussia. The Hapsburg Empire had a population of 35 million; Prussia, 19 million. The German kingdoms of Hanover, Saxony, Bavaria, and Württemberg, and the grand duchies of Baden and Hesse—with combined populations of

14 million—sided with Austria. On June 23, General Helmuth von Moltke's three Prussian armies totalling 300,000 men marched swiftly into Bohemia. King William I was with the army, and Major Otto von Bismarck, costumed in a spiked helmet and cavalry boots, rode beside the King. At Königgrätz (or Sadowa, as it was called in France and England), the Austrians stood. Five hundred thousand men and fifteen hundred guns on both sides fought throughout the day, with heavy losses on both sides. At three-thirty in the afternoon, the Austrians appeared to be winning when Crown Prince Frederick with a fresh army of eighty thousand Prussians appeared on the Austrian flank. By evening the Austrian Army was in disorderly retreat toward Vienna. In a single day, Austria's position in Germany had been destroyed.

The question, in the days immediately following the battle, was what Prussia was to make of its victory. Moltke wished to pursue and destroy the retreating Austrian Army. King William, who had gone to war reluctantly and only after Bismarck had convinced him that Austria was about to attack, was now flushed with moral rectitude and military glory; wicked Austria must be punished by surrendering territory and submitting to a triumphal march of the victorious Prussian Army through Vienna. Bismarck was adamant: a total Austrian withdrawal from Germany was sufficient; in the years ahead, he would need Austrian support in his confrontation with France. Prussia would not be made stronger by annexing Austrian territory, he told the King. "Austria was no more wrong in opposing our claims than we were in making them," he said. To Johanna, he wrote that he had "the thankless task of pouring water into their [the King's and the generals'] sparkling champagne, and trying to make it plain that we are not alone in Europe but have to live with three other powers [Austria, France, and Russia] who hate and envy us."

For a while, it seemed that Bismarck and moderation would lose and that Moltke would march into Vienna and dismember the Hapsburg Empire. In a castle in Nikolsburg, where Austrian representatives were coming to sign an armistice, Bismarck decided that the King would favor Moltke. In despair, he withdrew from the King and climbed the stairs to his fourth-floor room; later, he said that he had considered throwing himself out the window onto the courtyard below. But as he sat, head in hands, he felt a hand on his shoulder. It was the Crown Prince. "You know that I was against this war," said Frederick. "You considered it necessary and the responsibility for it lies with you. If you now think that our end is attained and that it is time to make peace, I am ready to support you and defend your view against my father." He went down the stairs and later returned. "It has been a very difficult business but my father has consented," he said.

The Treaty of Prague, signed on August 23, redrew the map of Germany. Austria surrendered no territory but withdrew all claim of influence in Germany. The Diet at Frankfurt was dissolved. A new political entity, the North German Confederation, dominated by Prussia, was created north of the river Main. Schleswig and Holstein were annexed by Prussia. Those German states which had sided with Austria against Prussia suffered harshly. Hanover, most of Hesse, and the free city of Frankfurt were annexed, and the King of Hanover was dethroned. The King of Saxony kept his crown, but his kingdom was incorporated into the North German Confederation. The four states south of the Main—Bavaria, Württemberg, Baden, and Hesse-Darmstadt—retained their independence but were required to pay heavy war indemnities. Bismarck also insisted that they sign secret treaties of military alliance with Prussia, which included agreements to put their armies under Prussian command in wartime.

The reverberations of Prussia's victory rolled across the Continent. By showing itself the military superior of Austria, Prussia threatened France's position as the dominant power in Europe; French hegemony had been based in part on antagonism between Austria and Prussia. Adolphe Thiers, a French statesman, understood what had happened. "It is France which has been beaten at Sadowa," he said. Napoleon III, too late, decided to intervene and proposed calling a congress which would roll back some of Prussia's gains. Bismarck quickly showed his teeth. "If you want war, you can have it," he told the French Ambassador. "We shall raise all Germany against you. We shall make immediate peace with Austria, at any price, and then, together with Austria, we shall fall on you with 800,000 men. We are armed and you are not."

Bismarck's preoccupation for the four years that followed was France. The Empire of Napoleon III based its foreign policy on two assumptions: France was the greatest power in Europe, and its supremacy must not be challenged by a unified Germany. The North German Confederation, the result of Prussia's sudden, startling victory over Austria, was as far as France would permit Bismarck to go; any movement toward greater unification would lead to a Franco-Prussian war. Bismarck knew this and was determined to profit. To promote German unity, the Minister-President of Prussia, now also Federal Chancellor of the North German Confederation, required an enemy against whom all Germans could be rallied.

France—Bourbon or Bonapartist—which had been the strongest military power in Europe for more than two centuries, was the only plausible antagonist.

The pretext, when it came, did not originate with Bismarck. The government of Spain, having deposed a dissolute Bourbon, was seeking a new monarch. In September 1869, the Spanish crown was secretly offered to Prince Leopold of Hohenzollern, a distant cousin of King William I. The family relationship entitled William to approve or disapprove acceptance by a Hohenzollern of a foreign crown. William, interested only in Prussia, was not inclined to approve. Accordingly, Prince Leopold, a Roman Catholic then serving as an officer in the Prussian army, declined, citing the confused state of affairs in Spain. The Spaniards asked again. This time, Bismarck, who favored acceptance, badgered and bullied the King until William "with a heavy, very heavy, heart" agreed. No one—neither Spaniards nor Prussians—said anything to the French; it was understood that France, not wishing to be surrounded by Hohenzollerns in the event of war, would bitterly oppose Prince Leopold's candidacy.

When the French government and public first heard the news on July 3, 1870, there was an outburst of alarm and denunciation. "The honor and interests of France are now in peril," declared the Duc de Gramont, Napoleon III's Foreign Minister. "We will not tolerate a foreign power placing one of its princes on the [Spanish] throne and thus disturbing the balance of power." King William of Prussia, anxious to ameliorate the crisis, again encouraged Prince Leopold to renounce the Spanish crown, which Leopold was happy to do. Bismarck, his policy in apparent ruins, threatened to resign. And then, Gramont and France, having achieved a public diplomatic triumph, went too far. Gramont sent the French Ambassador to visit King William I, who was vacationing at the spa of Ems. France insisted, William was told, that the King of Prussia not only give his formal endorsement to the renunciation, but "an assurance that he will never authorize a renewal of the candidacy." William read this demand, coolly refused, and walked away from the Ambassador. Then he telegraphed Bismarck to tell him what had happened. Bismarck changed the wording of the telegram slightly, editing out moderating sentences and phrases, so as to make the King of Prussia's words seem more insulting to France. He gave the edited telegram to the press. The following day, Parisian newspapers demanded war and Parisian crowds shouted "À Berlin!" Germany rallied to Prussia, the armies were mobilized, and four days later, war was declared.

This time, Europe promised itself, Prussia was finished. The French Army possessed the reputation of the finest fighting machine in the world. Marshal Edmond Leboeuf had assured the Emperor Napoleon that his army was ready "to the last gaiter button." Moltke immediately began a carefully planned invasion of France by four hundred thousand troops—Bavarians, Württembergers, Hessians, Saxons, and Hanoverians, as well as Prussians. King William I, seventy-four, was in nominal command; at his side was Major General Otto von Bismarck, again in a blue Prussian uniform. This phase of the war lasted only a month. On September 1, Napoleon III personally surrendered at Sedan with an army of 104,000; on September 4, the Empress Eugénie fled Paris for a life of exile in England; on September 5, France proclaimed a republic. Bismarck recommended that the German Army halt and draw up a defensive line at its present positions in eastern France. This time Moltke and the King prevailed; the army marched on Paris, ringed the city with artillery, and, after a delay for early peace negotiations, began a bombardment which would last four months.

Once again, Bismarck confronted the generals. He wanted, as with Austria, a quick victory, followed by reconciliation. His objective was political, not military: establishment of a unified Germany by transforming the simple military alliances that bound South Germany to Prussia into a real political entity. Moltke's concerns were purely military: he wanted enough French territory to create a buffer for Germany from future attacks from the west; he asked for the city of Strasbourg, the fortress of Metz, and the provinces of Alsace and Lorraine. Bismarck was willing to compromise: Strasbourg and Alsace had been German two centuries before until wrenched away by Louis XIV. He was not eager to acquire Metz and Lorraine, both predominantly French in language and culture. "I don't like so many Frenchmen in our house who do not want to be there," he said. This time, the King ruled in favor of Moltke and both provinces were annexed to victorious Germany. This decision changed the international perception of the war; France had at first been seen to have begun it, but now the war seemed to be one of German aggression and conquest. "We are no longer looked upon as the innocent victims of wrong, but rather as arrogant victors," worried Crown Prince Frederick. Europe would see Germany, "this nation of thinkers and philosophers, poets and artists, idealists and enthusiasts . . . as a nation of conquerers and destroyers."

During the bombardment of Paris, German Army headquarters was established in Versailles. Because the King and Bismarck remained at headquarters, the governments of Prussia and the North

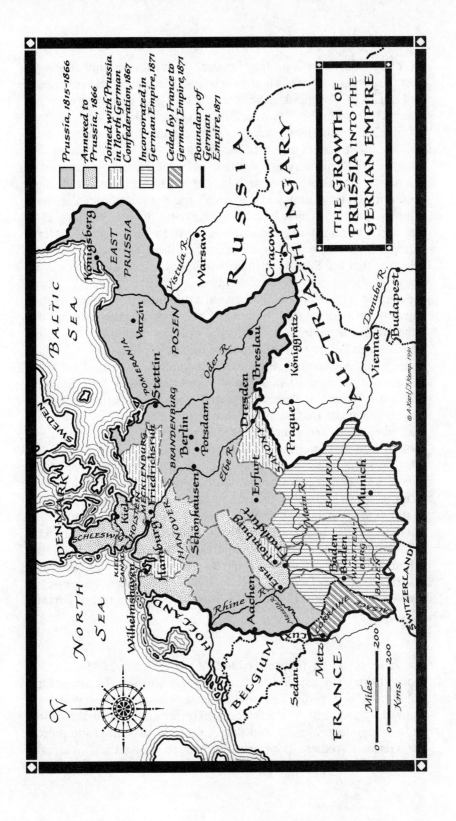

THE GROWTH OF PRUSSIA INTO THE GERMAN EMPIRE

Prussia, 1815–1866

Annexed to Prussia, 1866

Joined with Prussia in North German Confederation, 1867

Incorporated in German Empire, 1871

Ceded by France to German Empire 1871

Boundary of German Empire, 1871

BALTIC SEA

NORTH SEA

SWEDEN

DENMARK

Königsberg

EAST PRUSSIA

Vistula R.

Warsaw

RUSSIA

Varzin

POMERANIA

Stettin

POSEN

Cracow

HUNGARY

Oder R.

Breslau

Königgrätz

Dresden

SAXONY

Prague

Danube R.

Budapest

Vienna

AUSTRIA

Brandenburg

Berlin

Potsdam

Elbe R.

Erfurt

SCHLESWIG

HOLSTEIN

Kiel

KIEL CANAL

Wilhelmshaven

MECKLENBURG

Friedrichsruh

Hamburg

HANOVER

Schönhausen

Main R.

BAVARIA

Munich

HOLLAND

Rhine

Aachen

BELGIUM

Sedan

Metz

Moselle R.

FRANCE

Saar R.

ALSACE

LORRAINE

Ems R.

HOMBURG

Frankfurt

Baden-Baden

WÜRTTEMBERG

BADEN

SWITZERLAND

© A.Karl/J.Kemp, 1991

N

Miles   0   200

Kms.   0   200

German Confederation, the Prussian Court, and the courts of twenty German princes all crowded into the palace and town built by Louis XIV. Bismarck announced that his goal was the creation of a new German empire, built around Prussia, with the King of Prussia proclaimed the new emperor. The princes of the German states already in Versailles agreed. The obstacle was King William. The King regarded his hereditary title of King of Prussia as superior to the new imperial title Bismarck was about to give him; he disliked the South German states and worried about a dilution of the stern, military qualities which had brought Prussia to this summit. If he were to accept a new title, he wished it to be a significant one: "Emperor of Germany" or "Emperor of the Germans." Bismarck, knowing that the South Germans would not accept any such sweeping title, offered only "German Emperor," a glorified presidency of the empire. The dénouement came in a dramatic scene in the Hall of Mirrors on January 18, 1871, while the roar of guns bombarding Paris rattled the windows. William, hoping to foil Bismarck at the ceremony, asked the Grand Duke of Baden to raise a cheer for "the Emperor of Germany." Bismarck intercepted the Grand Duke on the stairway and persuaded him to compromise with "the Emperor William." When the cheer rang out, the newly proclaimed Emperor was so indignant that, stepping down from the dais to shake hands with his princes and generals, he walked past Bismarck, refusing to look at him and ignoring his outstretched hand.

On January 28, Paris capitulated, an armistice followed, and a treaty was signed. Strasbourg, Metz, Alsace, and Lorraine were stripped away and a war indemnity of 5 billion marks imposed. On March 6, Bismarck left Versailles, never to see France again; indeed, never thereafter to leave Germany. On March 21, the new Emperor William raised Count von Bismarck to the rank of Prince and granted him the estate of Friedrichsruh near Hamburg. Bismarck also received the Grand Cross of the Hohenzollern Order set in diamonds. "I'd sooner have had a horse or a good barrel of Rhenish wine," he said.

On June 16, 1871, under a cloudless sky, Bismarck, Moltke, and Roon, riding abreast, led a victory parade through Berlin. Alone, behind this trio, rode their new Imperial master, Kaiser William I, followed by a squadron of German princes, eighty-one captured French regimental eagles and flags, and forty-two thousand marching German soldiers. The crowds, massed along the boulevards, thronging around the triumphal arches, cheered and waved and cried. German unity, a dream since the Middle Ages, had been achieved in a glorious new empire which was now the most formidable military power in Europe. In the days that followed, there were notes of apprehension: victory had been achieved not, as the liberals wished, by the German people acting through representative assemblies, or even by the free will of the German princes, but by Prussian military might, which had conquered Germany as well as Denmark, Austria, and France. Some knew that it was not the wish of the King of Prussia that this unity be achieved and the Empire created. All Germans understood that the creation, structure, and future direction of the new Imperial state had been and were to be the work of one man: Otto von Bismarck.

For the moment, apprehensions were put aside; all was glory. Bismarck, at the pinnacle of his career, was the hero of Germany and the arbiter of Europe. His presence, his actions, his language, were said to be "haloed by the iron radiance of a million bayonets." "His words inspire respect, his silences apprehension," said Lord Ampthill, the British Ambassador.

The structure of the new empire represented Bismarck's solution to the problem of governing Germany. It was neither pure autocracy nor constitutional monarchy, although it had elements of both. The new Reich was a federal system like the United States; in creating the 1866 constitution of the North German Confederation, the precursor of the Imperial constitution, Bismarck had studied the American Constitution. As the American union had been created by sovereign states at the end of the eighteenth century, so the German Empire was nominally created by sovereign princely states. The differences, of course, were more significant than the similiarities. The American states had chosen voluntarily to unite and had worked out the structure of their new government in convention and prolonged debate; the German states were herded into union by the Prussian army and handed a constitution written by Bismarck. No single state in the new American union possessed the overwhelming dominance of Prussia. Prussia contributed two thirds of the land area, two thirds of the population, and practically all of the industry of the German Empire. Eighteen of Germany's twenty-one army corps were Prussian. Not only was it natural that Berlin should become the capital of the new empire and that the Minister-President of Prussia should be the new Imperial Chancellor; any other arrangement would have been unthinkable.

Bismarck's constitution created three separate branches of government: the Presidency (always to be held by the King of Prussia as German Emperor), the Federal Council (Bundesrat), and the parlia-

ment (Reichstag). The Bundesrat was Bismarck's gesture to federalism and the German princes. Nominally, the Empire still consisted
of twenty-five princely states, each ruled by its own government;
under the Empire, some of the German states still exchanged ambassadors with each other and even with foreign powers. Constitutionally, citizens of these states owed no allegiance to Emperor
William I. "The Emperor is not my monarch," said a politician from
Württemberg. "He is only the commanding officer of my federation.
My monarch is in Stuttgart." The princes were subordinate, not to
the Emperor, but to the Empire through the Bundesrat. Each German state sent a delegation to this body; each delegation was required to vote as a bloc. Of the Bundesrat's fifty-eight members,
seventeen were from Prussia, six from Bavaria, four each from Saxony and Württemberg. As no change could be made to the constitution if fourteen delegates were opposed, the seventeen Prussian
delegates, always voting en bloc, could make sure that the imperial
constitution remained unaltered.

The Reichstag, the democratic branch of the Imperial government, was elected by universal male suffrage and secret ballot, an
evolution of democracy which no other European state, not even
England, had yet attained. In Germany, the appearance was grossly
misleading; the German Social Democrat Wilhelm Liebknecht
scorned the Reichstag as "the fig leaf of absolutism." Although the
Reichstag voted on the federal budget and its consent was necessary
for all legislation, the restrictions placed on it were crippling: it
could not initiate legislation; it had no say in the appointment or
dismissal of the Chancellor or Imperial Ministers, and the Emperor
(or, in practice, the Chancellor) could with the agreement of the
Bundesrat dissolve the Reichstag at any time.

The position of the monarch who presided over this government was constitutionally peculiar. The German Emperor was not a
sovereign with ancient prerogatives; he had only the powers granted
him by the constitution. Article XI of the Imperial constitution
stated: "The presidency of the union belongs to the King of Prussia
who in this capacity shall be titled German Emperor." Nevertheless,
the Kaiser possessed several critically important powers: he had personal control of the armed forces and made all appointments and
promotions in the army and the navy. And he appointed (or could
dismiss) all imperial ministers including the Imperial Chancellor.

More unusual still was the office of Imperial Chancellor, which
Bismarck carefully crafted for himself. The Chancellor was appointed by the Emperor, entirely independent of the Bundesrat and
the Reichstag. His tenure of office depended wholly on the will—or

the whim—of the Emperor. Responsibility for foreign policy and war and peace were split; the Chancellor, not the Kaiser, had responsibility for German foreign policy, but the armed forces reported directly to the Kaiser and orders to the army and navy, including orders to begin a war, were exempt from requirement of the Chancellor's countersignature. The senior members of the imperial bureaucracy (the State Secretaries of Foreign Affairs, the Treasury, the Navy, Interior, and Education) were subordinates of the Chancellor, appointed and dismissed by him with the Kaiser's consent. They were not a Cabinet, either in the British or American sense; there was no collective responsibility as in England; there were no regular, joint meetings as in the United States. The overwhelming flaw in the constitution of the German Empire was that it was designed too closely to meet the needs and accommodate the talents of specific personalities. Fitted smoothly to the qualities of Bismarck and William I, it made the Chancellor the most powerful man in the empire. But, constitutionally, the Chancellor required the absolute support of the Kaiser. In other times, with other men— a restless, ambitious Kaiser, a weak, uncertain Chancellor—the Chancellor's position was certain to be fatally undermined.

Politically, it was Bismarck's extraordinary good fortune that William I remained on the throne as long as he did. Prince William of Hohenzollern was sixty-five in 1862 when he became King of Prussia, and seventy-four in 1871 when he assumed the imperial title; neither he nor Bismarck imagined that he would continue as Emperor for another seventeen years. During this span, Bismarck ruled the Empire and dominated Europe with no public sign of disapproval from the Emperor. In private, there were moments when the sovereign rebelled and threatened to step out from behind his role as figurehead; Bismarck usually dealt with these disturbances by threatening to resign. In fact, the Chancellor, venerating William in public, privately found the Kaiser dry and simplistic, and his insistence on faithfully executing his duty annoying. *Der Alte Herr* (the Old Gentleman), as Bismarck referred to him, demanded to be kept fully informed and then wished to discuss and approve all of the Chancellor's actions. William insisted on seeing all diplomatic dispatches, then writing his comments and questions, which, to Bismarck's chagrin, demanded answers. As much as possible, Bismarck withheld information from the monarch, not because he was not certain of overcoming William's hesitations, but simply because he did not wish to take the time to do so.

The two men irritated each other even in little ways. Bismarck, plagued by insomnia, would arrive at the Castle eager to describe his sleepless night. The Kaiser would open their conversation by innocently saying that he had slept badly. William disliked the confrontations to which Bismarck often exposed him; often, when the Chancellor asked for an audience, he would send word that he was too exhausted. One day, out for a walk, the Kaiser saw Bismarck approaching. "Can't we get into a side street?" William said to his companion. "Here's Bismarck coming and I'm afraid that he's so upset today that he will cut me." There were no side streets; Bismarck came up, and fifteen steps away took off his hat and said, "Has Your Majesty any commands for me today?" William dutifully replied, "No, my dear Bismarck, but it would be a very great pleasure if you would take me to your favorite bench by the river." The two, neither desiring to be with the other, went off to sit side by side. Bismarck expressed his sense of this burden by saying, "I took office with a great fund of royalist sentiments and veneration for the King; to my sorrow I find this fund more and more depleted." The Kaiser said simply, "It is not easy to be emperor under such a chancellor."

The years after 1871 seemed anticlimactic. The moments of daring calculation, of dramatic victories snatched from probable catastrophe, were over. "I am bored," Bismarck said in 1874. "The great things are done." He had no design in domestic politics beyond survival. In time, the national glow of triumph in unity wore off and each of the parties which made up the Reich grumbled that its interests were neglected. The wars had been won by the Prussian Army, the military embodiment of the Prussian Junker aristocracy, and the agrarian Junkers continued to demand predominance in the government of the empire. German liberals, the German middle class, and Germany's new industrialists often opposed the Junker elite, and the Reichstag became a field of open warfare. The rapid expansion of German industry also gave rise to a new industrial proletariat, whose ambitions and goals clashed with those of both the Junkers and the prosperous middle class. Bismarck had somehow to balance these factions to get legislation through the Reichstag.

Bismarck's decisions came after long periods of solitary brooding, not after lively discussions with others. Bismarck never exchanged ideas; he gave orders. Outside the Reichstag, he was rarely challenged. Yet neither mastery, success, nor fame calmed his loneliness or restlessness. Wherever he was, he felt out of place. "I have the unfortunate nature that everywhere I could be seems desirable to me," he said, "and then dreary and boring as soon as I am there." Bismarck acknowledged that his personality was complicated: "Faust complains of having two souls in his breast," the Chancellor

said. "I have a whole squabbling crowd. It goes on as in a republic."
Asked whether he really felt like the "Iron Chancellor," he replied:
"Far from it, I am all nerves." He admitted his unruly temper: "You
see," he said, "I am sometimes spoiling for a fight and if I have
nothing else at hand at that precise moment, I pick a quarrel with a
tree and have it cut down." He was lavish with insults; when a
subordinate, Baron Patow, had proved inept, another subordinate in
Bismarck's presence called Patow an ox. "That seems to me rudeness to animals," Bismarck said. "I am certain that when oxen wish
to insult each other, they call each other 'Patow.' " He made few
friends. "Oh, he never keeps his friends for long," Johanna sadly
told Holstein. "He soon gets tired of them." In his diary, Holstein
noted: "Part of the trouble was Prince Bismarck's habit of doing all
the talking himself. . . . He always monopolized the conversation.
He therefore preferred people who had not yet heard his stories."

In Berlin, Bismarck could be found either at the Reichstag, at
his office, or at home. He had no interest in society, never attended
dinners, balls, weddings, or funerals, and entertained the diplomatic
corps only once a year. Purporting to disdain the Reichstag, the
Chancellor actually spent many hours there when it was in session.
He entered through a private door, took his place on the dais, and
began turning through and signing government papers as if he were
in his office or his study at home. If personally attacked by a deputy,
he stopped writing and began stroking his mustache. When the
speaker finished, Bismarck immediately rose to reply, without asking permission from the Chair. He spoke in his high, thin voice,
meditating aloud, wrestling for words, shifting from one leg to the
other, pulling his mustache, studying his fingernails, spinning a pencil between his fingers, breaking off to drink a glass of brandy and
water, sometimes remaining silent for several minutes. The deputies,
losing interest, would begin to talk and laugh among themselves.
Then Bismarck would shake his fist and shout at them, "I am no
orator. I am a statesman."

Bismarck's office and home were on the Wilhelmstrasse, a fashionable and busy street extending north from Unter den Linden and
containing a number of old palaces and stately mansions which had
been converted into ministries. The Imperial Chancellory at No. 76
was an unimpressive two-story stucco building with a steep, red-tiled
roof. Its authority was inauspicious: the paint was peeling; the door
was guarded, not by a soldier or a policeman, but by an unliveried
porter with neither a staff nor a badge of office. Bismarck's office, a
corner room on the ground floor to the left of the entrance, possessed two windows, an enormous mahogany desk, a carved arm-

chair, and a massive leather couch on which the Chancellor liked to recline while reading official papers. The office displayed collections of meerschaum pipes, swords, buckskin gloves, and military caps, but no books. A bell sash hanging over the desk was used for summoning clerks, and a hole in the wall connected with an adjoining room which contained a telegraph to keep the Prince informed of what was happening in the Reichstag. Every ten minutes, while the Reichstag was in session, a length of tape was pushed through the aperture in the wall. Bismarck took it, read it, and threw it aside. While the Chancellor worked, his giant dog, Tiras, lay on the carpet, staring fixedly at his master. Tiras, known as the *Reichshund* (dog of the empire), terrorized the Chancellory staff, and people speaking to Bismarck were advised to make no unusual gestures which Tiras might interpret as threatening. Prince Alexander Gorchakov, the elderly Russian Foreign Minister, once raised an arm to make a point and found himself pinned to the floor, staring up at Tiras' bared teeth.

Until 1878, the Chancellory building at No. 76 Wilhelmstrasse had also been the Chancellor's home. In that year, as the Congress of Berlin was about to convene, the Imperial government, concerned about foreign opinion, purchased a separate residence for the Chancellor. The Radziwill Palace, next door to No. 76, was an elegant eighteenth-century building occupying three sides of a paved courtyard. Here, surrounded by his family, Bismarck was able to relax. Dinner was served at five; supper at nine. When the Chancellor was finished, the meal was over. He signalled this by rising from his chair and taking a seat at a small table in the parlor. Here, he filled his porcelain pipe and waited for coffee. He told stories, described what had happened in the Reichstag, joked with his grandchildren, and made the women laugh.

On the rare occasions when Bismarck entertained, guests were astonished by the lavish table spread by the Princess and the courtesy and warmth exhibited by the Prince. Visitors arriving at ten P.M. would find awaiting them Brunswick sausages, Westphalian ham, Elbe eels, sardines, anchovies, smoked herrings, caviar (usually a gift from St. Petersburg), salmon, hard-boiled eggs, cheeses, and bottles of dark Bavarian beer. Bismarck appeared at eleven. "I never saw Bismarck enter the room without the feeling that I saw a great man, a really great man, before me, the greatest man I ever saw or ever would see," said Bernhard von Bülow, the future Chancellor. Every male guest was greeted with a handshake; every woman with a slight bow and a kiss on the hand. In later years, when he was forced by gout to recline on a sofa, he asked forgiveness from the women for receiving them in this position. Bismarck always dominated the conversation, sometimes speaking so softly that his guests had to strain to catch his words. When he was silent, the company was silent, afraid of disturbing his thoughts or being caught speaking when he began to speak again.

When the Chancellor was not in Berlin, he was at one of his immense country estates, Varzin or Friedrichsruh. Varzin, in Pomerania, spread over fifteen thousand acres and containing seven villages, was purchased with a grant of money voted by the Prussian Landtag after Königgrätz. It was remote—five hours by train from Berlin, followed by forty miles on bad roads. Johanna thought the house "unbearably ugly"; Bismarck found it ideal. The forest was filled with giant oaks, beeches, and pines; there were deer, wild boar —and few neighbors. In 1871, after the proclamation of the empire, William I rewarded the new Prince Bismarck with Friedrichsruh, an even larger estate of seventeen thousand acres near Hamburg. It had the same stately forest, rich stocks of game, and sense of isolation. Bismarck could roam all day, carrying his gun, or, increasingly, only a pair of field glasses. The house at Friedrichsruh, originally a hotel for weekenders from Hamburg, was even less pleasing to Johanna. Bismarck installed his family without bothering to remove the numbers from the bedroom doors, refused to bring in electricity, and permitted illumination only with oil lamps. Soon, the cellar was filled with thousands of books which he had been given but would never read. Bülow, a visitor, struggled to describe the primitive state of the Chancellor's retreat: "Simplicity . . . complete lack of adornment . . . not a single fine picture . . . not a trace of a library . . . The whole house seemed to reiterate the warning: 'Wealth alone can destroy Sparta.' "

Bismarck complained constantly about his poor health but did nothing to improve it. He smoked fourteen cigars a day, drank beer in the afternoons, kept two large goblets—one for champagne, the other for port—at hand during meals, and tried to find sleep at night by drinking a bottle of champagne. Princess Bismarck believed that her husband's well-being depended on appetite. "They eat here always until the walls burst," reported a Chancellory assistant who visited Varzin. When the Prince complained of an upset stomach, Johanna calmed him with foie gras. When the pâté was brought to the table, the visitor reported, Bismarck first served himself a large portion, then followed the platter with his eyes around the table with such intensity that no one dared to take more than a small slice. When the platter came back to him, Bismarck helped himself to what remained. At night, he slept poorly or not at all. Often, he lay awake until seven A.M., then slept until two P.M. Lying in bed, he mulled over grievances. "I have spent the whole night hating," he said once. When no immediate object of hatred was available, he ransacked his memory to dredge up wrongs done him years before.

He suffered and complained continually. "This pressure on my brain makes everything that lies behind my eyes seem like a glutinous mass," he wrote to the Emperor in 1872. [I have] unbearable pressure on my stomach with unspeakable pains." Between 1873 and 1883, he suffered from migraine, gout, hemorrhoids, neuralgia, rheumatism, gallstones, varicose veins, and constipation. His teeth tormented him, but he refused to see a dentist; eventually his cheek began to twitch with pain. He endured the twitching for five years and grew a beard to hide it. In 1882, when the teeth were drawn, the twitching stopped, but the pain in the cheek remained.

Bismarck's appearance shocked those who saw him. His beard had come in white, his face and body were pink and bloated. His weight ballooned to 245 pounds. "The Chancellor has aged considerably over the last few months," Holstein recorded in 1884. "His capacity for work is less, his energy has diminished, even his anger, though easily kindled, fades more quickly than in his prime."

When the doctors announced to Johanna that her husband had cancer, she became sufficiently frightened to bring a new doctor, a young Berlin physician named Ernst Schweninger, to Friedrichsruh. Schweninger from the beginning confronted his patient head-on. At their first meeting, the Chancellor said roughly, "I don't like questions." "Then get a veterinarian," Schweninger replied. "He doesn't question his patients." Bismarck immediately gave in. Schweninger became a member of the Bismarck household and dictated to the Chancellor as if he were a schoolboy. He prescribed an exclusive diet of fish, mainly herring, forced Bismarck to drink milk before bedtime instead of beer or champagne, and curtailed his drinking of alcohol at other times. Within six months, the Chancellor's weight dropped to 197 pounds, his eyes became clear, his skin fresh, and he began to sleep peacefully at night. In 1884, he shaved off his beard. Schweninger left the household but returned often to monitor the Chancellor's diet. This was necessary, Holstein reported, because Bismarck's "inclination to transgress is reinforced by Princess Bismarck who is never happier than when watching her husband eating one thing on top of another."

Bismarck's affection for his three children, Marie, Herbert, and William (known all his life as Bill), was fierce, protective, and jealously possessive. At the height of the war with France, Bismarck, at army headquarters with the King, was told that Herbert had been killed and Bill wounded. He rode all night to find Herbert shot through the thigh but out of danger and Bill recovering from a concussion caused by a fall from a horse. Herbert, born in 1849, was his father's favorite; no man was closer to Bismarck. As a boy, Herbert was handsome, quick-witted, and spoiled. As he grew older, the power and deference that surrounded his father and his family had a destructive effect on the impressionable son. Attempting to copy his father, Herbert exaggerated. Where Otto was lofty, self-confident, and ironic, Herbert became arrogant, flamboyant, and sarcastic.

Once Herbert entered the Foreign Ministry, the Chancellor ensured choice assignments and quick promotions, while ruthlessly crushing Herbert's independence. Herbert had been in love for a long time with a married woman, Princess Elisabeth Carolath. In the spring of 1881, when Herbert was thirty-two, Elisabeth divorced her husband, expecting to marry Herbert. German newspapers speculated openly and uncritically about the marriage; unlike in Britain, where divorce was unthinkable, divorce was no handicap in Imperial Germany. But Herbert's decision stimulated violent antagonism in his father. Elisabeth Carolath was closely related to an old enemy of the Chancellor's. More important, Bismarck feared that the elegant and cosmopolitan Elisabeth would weaken Herbert's devotion to him. Using every available weapon, Bismarck threatened to discharge Herbert from the Foreign Ministry if he married Elisabeth; he persuaded the Emperor to decree that Varzin and Friedrichsruh could not pass to anyone who married a divorced woman; he sobbed that he would kill himself if the marriage took place. Herbert, subjected to this intimidation, torn between love and filial obligation, threatened with disgrace, disinheritance, and poverty, floundered helplessly. Eventually, Elisabeth, contemptuous, called off the marriage.

Shattered and surly, Herbert smothered his frustrations in drink. Bülow recalled staying up with him all night in Parisian cafés while Herbert drank bottles of heavy Romanée-Conti or dry champagne; then Herbert would appear at lunch the next day and finish off a bottle of port. First Counselor Holstein, who knew the Bismarck family intimately, observed: "Herbert's character is unevenly developed. He has outstanding qualities, first-rate intelligence and analytical ability. His defects are vanity, arrogance, and violence. . . . He is an efficient worker, but is too vehement. His communications with foreign governments are too apt to assume the form of an ultimatum. Bismarck is afraid of his son's vehemence. During our disputes with England over colonial affairs, Herbert once wrote [Georg Herbert von] Münster [German Ambassador to England] a dispatch which was, in tone, simply an ultimatum. The Chancellor laid the document aside, remarking that it was a bit too early to adopt that tone."

In 1885, Bismarck decided to catapult his son into one of the Reich's senior offices, the State Secretaryship for Foreign Affairs. Count Paul von Hatzfeldt, who preceded Herbert, was charming but weak; Herbert was already fulfilling many of the functions of the office. "Even now, the ambassadors seek out Herbert rather than Hatzfeldt because the latter is cautious and the former is talkative and informative and tells more than is good for us," Holstein wrote in his diary. "The way to loosen Herbert's tongue is to invite him to a morning meal or lunch and serve exquisite wines." On May 16, Holstein observed: "Both father and son are at present pursuing the aim of making the son State Secretary, not just yet, but as soon as possible." On June 28, he wrote of the Chancellor's "eagerness to get rid of Hatzfeldt. . . . My guess is that Hatzfeldt will have to go because Bismarck is firmly resolved that the post of State Secretary will fall vacant, come what may. . . . What is aimed at is a reshuffle of ambassadors in which something reasonable will be found for Hatzfeldt." In the autumn, the reshuffle took place. Hatzfeldt became ambassador to England. And Herbert, at thirty-six, replaced Hatzfeldt as State Secretary.

As State Secretary, Herbert's role was enhanced by his possession of his father's confidence; in time, he was regarded almost as the Chancellor's alter ego. Despite family closeness, official relations between father and son remained formal: Herbert addressed his father in official correspondence as "Your Highness." Nor did he presume that the Chancellor would forgive a lax performance. Planning to take one day away from his post in Berlin, he wrote to his brother-in-law at Varzin: "Please do not say anything about this. . . . Papa could find in it a dereliction of duty." In 1886, when Herbert became seriously ill and the Chancellor was told that his son's decline was due to the demands of office, Bismarck replied, "In every great state there must be people who overwork themselves."

Again, Herbert found solace in drink. In the evenings, the State Secretary was usually in a state of alcoholic befuddlement; in the mornings he suffered from debilitating hangovers. In restaurants, he was peevish, barking orders at waiters. Within a few weeks of becoming State Secretary, he lurched into the courtyard of the Foreign Ministry carrying a small rifle and began shooting at the windows of officials. Invited to Paris by the French Ambassador, he sneered, "I never go to Paris except in war time." When the Emperor Frederick was dying of throat cancer, Herbert told the Prince of Wales, the Emperor's brother-in-law, that "an emperor who could not talk was not fit to reign." The Prince said afterwards that if he had not valued good relations between Germany and England, he would have thrown Herbert out of the room.

Herbert's promotion to a key post in the Imperial Government seemed to mark him as the Chancellor's intended political heir. Herbert himself, having participated in many important decisions, felt his succession natural. At the same time, he knew the weakness of his position: whatever his talents, it would be said he had succeeded only because of his father. But it was the Kaiser who would appoint Bismarck's successor. There would, at least, be no further advancement under Kaiser William I, who had only reluctantly approved the appointment of the Chancellor's son as State Secretary. Subsequently, the old Kaiser regretted his decision: "These audiences with young Bismarck always take a lot out of me," he said. "He's so stormy—even worse than his father. He has not a grain of tact." Near the end of his life, William I said to a military aide, "Lately, it almost appears that the Prince would like to see Herbert take his place one day. That is quite impossible. As long as I live, I will never part from the Prince who will most probably, and as I hope, survive me. He is eighteen years younger than I am. Nor will my successors wish to make the Chancellor's office an hereditary one. That won't do." Bismarck, despite his hopes for Herbert's future, had no illusions about his son: "Herbert, who is not yet forty, is more unteachable and conceited than I, and I am over seventy. I have had a few successes." To an official who praised Herbert's industry as State Secretary, Bismarck said, "You need not praise him to me. I would have made him State Secretary even if he had not possessed all those qualities for which you praise him, since I want at my side a man in whom I can have complete confidence and whom it is easy for me to deal with. At my great age, when I have used up all my energies in the royal service, I think I have the right to ask that."

CHAPTER 4

Bismarck's Grand Design

◆

Despite his gruff, militaristic image, Bismarck had no intention of leading his new empire into another war. Beginning in 1871, the aggressive statesman, who in eight years had overturned European politics, defeating two emperors and creating a third, turned his energy to preserving the status quo. War offered more risks than opportunities; what had been won so brilliantly and swiftly might be lost with equal suddenness. "We are satiated," Bismarck said after the war with France. This opposition to war was not based on concern for human suffering. Rather, he considered war a clumsy way of settling international disputes. It took control away from him and placed it in the hands of the generals, whom he distrusted. "You know where a war begins but you never know where it ends," he said. The subsequent restless, expansionist policies which dominated the German Empire under William II played no part in Bismarck's design. Once he reached his goal of German unity, the maker of wars became a man of peace. And he succeeded: during Bismarck's nineteen years as Imperial Chancellor, there were no wars among the Great Powers of Europe.

Bismarck's tool was aggressive, ruthless diplomacy. He played a game of maneuver, constantly shifting tactics, smoothly alternating threats and blandishments, in pursuit of his twin goals of Continental peace and German hegemony. His technique of maintaining peace was not much different from the means he had employed in making wars: sowing suspicion and discord among other nations; provoking alarms, setting powers against one another as potential enemies, then offering one—or the other—or both—German support. His reputation made it easier: his achievement in creating the German Empire had been so extraordinary that other statesmen assumed that he possessed special powers, even special wisdom.

Bismarck had defeated each of his enemies—Denmark, Austria, and France—in isolation, but he realized that a powerful, united German Empire could not expect to fight another carefully insulated war. Between 1871 and 1890, there were five Great Powers in Europe—Germany, France, Austria, Russia, and Great Britain* —and the alignment of these five dictated the pattern of European diplomacy.

Great Britain, by choice, had isolated itself from peacetime Continental alliances; France, humiliated and embittered by defeat, also was isolated, although not by choice. That left three Great Powers: the empires of Germany, Austria-Hungary, and Russia. It was the purpose of Bismarck's diplomacy to influence and guide the policies of all three empires in the interest of Germany. "You forget the importance of being a party of three on the European chessboard," the Chancellor told the Russian Ambassador. "That is the object of all governments and above all of mine. Nobody wishes to be in a minority. All politics reduce themselves to this formula: try to be à trois in a world governed by five powers."

Germany had nothing to do with Britain's absence from the European chessboard; it bore a heavy responsibility for rendering France implacably hostile. King William I had had a chance of making with defeated France the same generous peace he had made with Austria; this time he rejected Bismarck's advice. The people of France had been accustomed to centuries of military glory. Tumbled from this summit, France could neither forget nor forgive. The choice of the Hall of Mirrors at Versailles as the site in which the new German Empire was proclaimed added a gratuitous insult. The heavy German war indemnity stimulated further resentment. In the years that followed, Bismarck and his successors periodically hoped that France might be reconciled to its losses and lured into the German diplomatic orbit. Always, the Germans were rebuffed. "We remember that they are waiting for us in Alsace-Lorraine," said

* Italy was approaching, but never quite reached, full Great Power status.

General Georges Boulanger, a French Minister of War and popular political figure in the 1880s.

The possibility of a France restored, powerful, and vengeful, in alliance with another power, haunted Bismarck. To keep France isolated, to seal her off from contact with other powers, to make her the pariah of Europe, became the cornerstone of the German Chancellor's foreign policy. In 1873, while German occupation armies still camped on French soil, Bismarck created his first anti-French coalition, the League of Three Emperors (*Dreikaiserbund*). It was a grouping *à trois* of Europe's three imperial dynasts, William I of Germany, Franz Josef of Austria-Hungary, and Alexander II of Russia. There was no formal alliance, merely an agreement to consult if circumstances warranted. The League was ideological rather than military, but in Bismarck's mind it was a pledge of conservative, monarchical solidarity against the volatile ambitions of unstable, republican France.

Bismarck kept a close watch on France itself. When French policies, external or internal, displeased him, France was hectored and bullied. "Remember, I forbid you to take Tunis," a German ambassador told a Foreign Minister of France. "Yes, I forbid you." Nevertheless, France recovered rapidly from her defeat. When Bismarck had saddled the new republic with a war indemnity of 5 billion marks, he had expected this burden to keep France supine for many years. Instead, France had paid off the debt in two years and, by the end of 1873, in accordance with the terms of peace, the last soldier in the German occupation army had gone home. The French also had set about restoring the strength of their army.

The possibility of French attack on Germany was nonexistent, but signs of French vitality irritated Prince Bismarck. Moltke, in Berlin, talked incessantly of the dire consequences of French rearmament and the advantages of preventive war. To the British Ambassador, he explained his theory of responsibility for war: peace was not broken, he argued, by the nation that marched first; the state that provoked the necessity for the other to march was the guilty party. Bismarck's policy trod a narrow line between peace and war. He never actually thought of unleashing Moltke, but he did attempt to intimidate France by showing that she was isolated and helpless in the face of German might.

In 1877, when Russia declared war on Turkey and marched on Constantinople, Austria and England combined to threaten Russia with war unless she drew back. When Count Julius Andrássy, the Austrian Foreign Minister, offered an international conference, Russia was wary. "If Vienna or London is chosen we shall not take part," announced Prince Alexander Gorchakov, adding, however, that Russia "had no objection to Berlin." Bismarck, eager to prevent a war between Austria and Russia which might entangle Germany, regarded the conference as a façade behind which the Russians could save face and offered his own services as an "Honest Broker." Tsar Alexander II, relying on his warm personal ties with Kaiser William I, expressed complete confidence in Bismarck's mediation. At the conclusion of the Congress of Berlin, when Russia was forced to give back many of the gains she had made at Turkey's expense, the Tsar and the pan-Slavs in St. Petersburg were bitter. They had been betrayed, they felt, by Bismarck.

Russian bitterness and recrimination were much on Bismarck's mind a year later when he arranged Imperial Germany's first military alliance. His choice of Austria as a partner seemed at first unlikely. Bismarck had once fiercely opposed an alliance with Austria; in 1854 he had protested "tying our neat, sea-worthy Prussian frigate to Austria's worm-eaten old galleon." Again in 1876, when Austria confronted Russia in the Balkans, Bismarck had stated that Germany had no interest in the Eastern Question "that was worth the bones of a single Pomeranian grenadier." His reason for change lay in the second axiom of the Chancellor's imperial foreign policy. The first was to ensure the diplomatic isolation of France; the second was to preserve peace between the Reich's two eastern neighbors, Austria and Russia. This had been the purpose of the League of Three Emperors, but in the crisis over the Russo-Turkish War, the League had disintegrated. As the Congress of Berlin concluded, Bismarck realized that antagonism between Austria and Russia in the Balkans was unlikely to disappear. His own effort to mediate had turned out badly; he had heard the grumbling and felt the growing estrangement from St. Petersburg. Better to begin with something solid: a defensive alliance with Austria. This could be used in two ways: it would ensure Germany's southern flank in case of war with Russia, and it could also frighten the Russians into seeking a closer relationship with Germany.

The choice of Austria was made easier because the peace imposed on Austria after the 1866 war had been generous. There were no "lost provinces" like Alsace and Lorraine to keep Vienna embittered. Austria was suitable on ethnic grounds: the Austrian population of the Hapsburg empire was ethnically compatible with and spoke the same language as the Germans; if necessary, the alliance could be tuned to the theme of Teuton versus Slav. Bismarck's larger purpose was to influence the relationship between Vienna and St. Petersburg as they moved towards a dangerous collision in the Balkans. To do this, he needed an ally he could dominate. Austria offered the better chance; Russia was too large, too remote, too far beyond his reach. "If I must choose," he said, "I will choose Austria, a constitutionally governed, pacific state, which lies under Germany's guns; whereas we cannot get at Russia." Russia, nevertheless, remained a part of Bismarck's equation. With Austria firmly in hand, he could reach out to Russia and offer her stability, managed and guaranteed by his iron hand in Berlin.

Bismarck's principal opponent in making the Austro-German Treaty of 1879 was the Emperor William I. William saw no reason for making an alliance with Austria, his former enemy, against Russia, Prussia's only permanent friend. Friendship between Hohenzollerns and Romanovs was a sacred bequest to William, handed down by his parents from the days of the Napoleonic wars. Tsar Alexander II was his uncle and his closest friend among European monarchs. Russia had stood by Prussia during Bismarck's three wars of unification; from Versailles, the new Emperor William I had telegraphed Tsar Alexander II: "Never will Prussia forget that it is due to you that the war did not spread." For Germany now to turn against Russia, the Kaiser said, would be a betrayal tantamount to treason. Bismarck, in order to influence William, said that Russian troops were moving towards the German frontier; he argued that a letter from the Tsar was offensively worded and portended an attack from the east. William, alarmed, hurried to meet Alexander at the frontier town of Alexandrovno. There, he assured the Tsar of his personal devotion and pledged German loyalty to a policy of friendship. Bismarck, meanwhile, proceeded to Vienna and, as if the Kaiser did not exist, drew up a treaty of alliance with Count Andrássy, the Austrian Foreign Minister.

When William returned to Berlin to find a telegram from Bismarck demanding his assent to a treaty with Austria, he was incredulous, then furious. "Prince Bismarck himself states . . . that I shall find it difficult to ratify this treaty," he said. "Not simply difficult but impossible: it would go against my conscience, my character, and my honor to conclude behind the back of my friend—my personal, my family, my political friend—a hostile alliance directed against him." William fought stubbornly. He cited the historic friendship between Hohenzollern and Romanov, the services Alexander had rendered Prussia, the danger in isolating Russia of driving her into the arms of France. He said that he would rather abdicate than sign an alliance against Russia. Bismarck countered by threatening to resign unless the Kaiser agreed to sign. William gave way. His threat to abdicate was meaningless: if he stepped down, the

Crown Prince, who favored the Austrian alliance, would become Kaiser and sign the treaty. "Bismarck is more necessary than I am," said William, but added, "My whole moral strength is broken." Signing the treaty, he wrote in the margin, "Those men who have compelled me to this step will be held responsible for it above."

The treaty, essentially a German guarantee of Austria against Russian attack, became the cornerstone of the foreign policy of Imperial Germany. It remained in force continuously for thirty-five years, until the outbreak of war in 1914 and then through the war until both Powers collapsed in 1918. Germany, by the act of signing, acquired a vital interest in the survival of the Austro-Hungarian Dual Monarchy. To maintain her only Great Power ally, she would be forced more than once to go to the brink. As long as Bismarck was in Berlin, he could control the Austrians and overawe the Russians. When Bismarck was gone, new patterns would form, new games would be played.

Austria, in Bismarck's mind, was a link, a secondary power, a useful supplement to German power. The keys to Bismarck's diplomacy were France and Russia. The Chancellor knew where he stood with France and could plan accordingly. Russia was an enigma. Bismarck never wished to fight the Russians. Despite periodic urging by Moltke that the time was ripe for crushing Russia, Bismarck did not believe that such a victory was either possible or wise. What would be Germany's objectives in such a war? he asked. Not territory; German expansion to the east could only be at the expense of Russian Poland, and Germany, he said, already had too many Poles. Besides, he told the German Ambassador to Vienna in 1888, one could not really defeat the Russians: "The most brilliant victories would not avail; the indestructible empire of the Russian nation, strong because of its climate, its desert, its frugality, strong also because of the advantage of having only one frontier to defend, would, after its defeat, remain our sworn enemy, desirous of revenge, just as today's France is in the West." Not wishing to fight the Russians alone, Bismarck assuredly did not wish to fight them if they were in alliance with the French. Nor did he wish the Austrians and the Russians to become embroiled so as to invoke the Austro-German Treaty. For all these reasons, once the Austrian treaty was signed, Bismarck moved quickly to bring the Russians into his European system. In mid-1881, he informed the Russian Foreign Office of the general nature of the Austro-German treaty, emphasizing that it was defensive. He invited the Russians to join in a broader defensive agreement; as a result the League of Three Emperors was resurrected. The three agreed that if one of them were attacked by a fourth power, the other two would preserve a benevolent neutrality. Thus, if Germany were attacked by France, Austria and Russia would remain neutral; similarly, if Russia were attacked by England, Germany and Austria would observe neutrality.

Bismarck still was not satisfied: the link with Russia was still too weak. Tension in the Balkans continued to mount, with Russia and Austria usually in opposition to each other. The League of Three Emperors, renewed in 1884, was allowed to expire in 1887. Bismarck then negotiated his final diplomatic masterpiece: a secret treaty with Russia against his ally Austria. Called the Reinsurance Treaty, it was defensive and promised only neutrality, not military assistance, if either party were attacked (German neutrality if Austria attacked Russia, Russian neutrality if France attacked Germany). Despite this limitation, it violated, as Bismarck well knew, the trust, if not the wording, of Germany's treaty with Austria. Bismarck obviously insisted on secrecy. The new Tsar Alexander III was no less anxious to hide the existence of the Reinsurance Treaty. Himself a pan-Slav, he could predict the reaction of other pan-Slavs. Alexander signed the treaty only because it gave him a promise of German neutrality in case Austria provoked a war with Russia. Russia did not wish to fight Germany; certainly the Russian Army was not prepared to fight Germany and Austria together.

The Bismarckian system was now in place, a network of inter-locking alliances, carefully balanced and kept in order by the master diplomat in Berlin. In Holstein's metaphor, Bismarck was the ultimate railway yardmaster: "Our policy with its criss-cross of commitments . . . resembles the tangle of tracks at a big railway station," he wrote in 1887. "[Bismarck] thinks he can click everything into its proper place and hopes particularly that the greater the confusion, the more indispensable he is."

Britain, the fifth of Europe's Great Powers, stood outside Bismarck's Continental system. This satisfied the Chancellor; he had no fear that England would engage itself in a Continental alliance which would upset his alignment of Germany à trois. Britain, he was convinced, never would enter into an alliance with Russia and the possibility of her siding with France seemed almost as unlikely. Nevertheless, before he signed the Austro-German Treaty of 1879, Bismarck considered offering England a German alliance. He proposed it to Benjamin Disraeli, Earl of Beaconsfield and British Prime Minister, one evening after dinner during the Congress of Berlin. Disraeli, surprised, said that he was favorably disposed, but needed time to prepare Parliament and British public opinion. After returning to London, Disraeli discussed the matter with Count Münster, the German Ambassador, who wrote to Bismarck, "I am convinced that he is sincere."

When, in March 1880, Disraeli's Conservative government was replaced by a Liberal cabinet headed by W. E. Gladstone, talk of an alliance evaporated. Bismarck detested Gladstone. The Chancellor was always suspicious of the manner in which the English conducted diplomacy; its dependence on public opinion seemed to him absurd. When Disraeli and Salisbury were in power, this nervousness was soothed; they were practical, conservative men who would find a way for realism to triumph. But Gladstone, a hero to German liberals, was a moralist who preached that conscience had a role in domestic politics and international affairs. The Chancellor referred to the Prime Minister as "Professor Gladstone" and "that big Utopian Babbler." Bismarck believed that Gladstonian morality, carried into diplomacy, led to murkiness, miscalculation, and bumbling, exemplified by England's confusion during the Gladstone years as to whether her enemy in the east was Russia or Turkey. To defend Turkey, England had stood against Russia in 1877 and at the Congress of Berlin. But in the 1880 election campaign which led to victory, Gladstone had passionately denounced the Turks for their atrocities against the Bulgarian Christians. Turks, Gladstone had thundered, were "that inhuman exception to the human race." Britain's swing back and forth on issues like this made it harder for Bismarck to maintain his delicately balanced European system.

In addition, the Chancellor considered Gladstone's government indecisive and ineffective in the overseas policy which most concerned Great Britain in the early 1880s: the occupation of Egypt. France, whose history in Egypt encompassed Napoleon's disastrous campaign on the Nile and Ferdinand de Lesseps' triumphant building of the Suez Canal, refused to give up its claims in Egypt despite the British occupation. The ensuing situation, in which England was embroiled in colonial conflict with France, was precisely the kind of confrontation on which Bismarck's European system was based. England and France opposed each other; neither possessed an ally; one or both would turn to Germany for support.

In September 1882, Herbert Bismarck arrived in London to establish contact with prominent Liberal politicians and attempt to discover Britain's ultimate purpose in Egypt. He was warmly received by British ministers and by London society; the Prince of Wales went out of his way to be cordial to the Chancellor's son and proposed him for honorary membership in the Marlborough Club.

Herbert was invited by Lord Granville, the Liberal Foreign Secretary, to Walmer Castle, Granville's country seat, where the visitor
spent several "very pleasant days discussing Egypt." Although Herbert said that annexation by Britain "would be compatible with
German interests," Granville replied that England did not wish to
possess Egypt and had not yet decided what to do. When the talk
turned to alliances, Granville told Herbert: "England does not need
an alliance with a European power and we do not pursue a policy of
alliances. Even quite different circumstances than the present ones
would never lead me to establish an alliance with a European
Power." Wherever he went, Herbert received thanks for German
support in Britain's Egyptian involvement. Sir William Harcourt,
the Liberal Home Secretary, told Herbert, "We are uncommonly
grateful to Prince Bismarck. Our being left a free hand in Egypt we
owe . . . to Germany's good will. We are all aware that at a particular moment Prince Bismarck could have upset the coach if he had
chosen to."

Encouraged by the talks with Herbert Bismarck, the Gladstone
Cabinet was astonished by the next twist in Anglo-German relations. The German Empire in 1883 had no colonies. Most of the
desirable regions of the globe had been seized before the Empire
was founded. Now, only marginal territories were left, in the barren
regions of South Africa and in the South Seas.

Believing that German security lay in a favorable balance of
power in Europe, Bismarck had previously rejected all arguments in
favor of colonies. Recognizing that a German drive for colonies
could upset his carefully calibrated equilibrium, Bismarck had encouraged French colonialism to distract France's attention from
Alsace-Lorraine. If Germany were to compete with France for colonies, French hostility towards the Reich would be violently restimu-
lated. Nor did Bismarck have any desire to compete with England in
the colonial sphere. The British and German empires were fundamentally different political organisms. One was a cluster of states in
Central Europe, welded into a powerful Continental empire. The
other was a global scattering of people and territories, knit together
by trade and sea power, with limited influence in peacetime on the
continent of Europe, but unchallengeable on the seas. German trade
flourished under the protection of the British Fleet; if colonial competition led to war with England, every German colony would be
gobbled up in the first few weeks.

In the summer of 1884, to the bewilderment of British statesmen, Bismarck suddenly changed direction. For a short period, less
than two years, colonies assumed importance and he wielded against

England all the intimidating power of German diplomacy. Colonies were the usual symbol of international prestige; Britain, France, and Russia—all weaker in Europe than Germany—had colonial empires. To some Germans, colonies were more than a matter of pride. German merchants, bankers, and entrepreneurs sought markets for their capital and products outside Europe; shipowners and trading firms in Hamburg and Bremen argued that colonies would provide markets for goods and sources of raw material. Yet wherever they looked, they found a French or British flag. In 1882, the German Colonial League (*Kolonialverein*) was formed to lobby, through the press and public opinion, for acquisition of German colonies. Newspaper editors, professors, industrialists, and middle-class Germans in general enthusiastically supported the movement. The clamor for colonies rose in the Reichstag, and the Imperial Chancellor yielded, not because of a shift in his private belief, but because he saw an opportunity to quiet the pan-Germans and the Colonial League by taking advantage of Britain's weakness in Egypt. And so, in the summer of 1884, the price was named: German support of Britain's involvement in Egypt was to be paid for by British acquiescence in German colonial expansion.

In the spring of 1883, a Bremen tobacco merchant, F.A.E. Lüderitz, established a small factory and trading post at Angra Pequena, a coastal bay 150 miles north of the Orange River, which marked the northern boundary of Britain's Cape Colony. Seeing no Europeans about, Lüderitz raised the German flag and, hoping for support, informed Berlin. The German government moved cautiously. In November, Count Münster, the German Ambassador in London, was instructed to ask whether Great Britain claimed to exercise sovereignty in that region. If the answer was yes, would Britain accept responsibility for protecting the lives and property of German subjects in the territory, thus exempting the Imperial Government from that obligation? The British government left the German inquiry unanswered for six months, first irritating, then infuriating Bismarck.

The cause of the delay in London lay in procedure and personalities. The German inquiry, an official communication from one European state to another, was properly addressed to the Foreign Office, where it came to the desk of the Foreign Secretary, Lord Granville. George Leveson-Gower, Second Earl Granville, was a gentleman who wished to give offense to no one. Although he was Leader of the Liberal Party in the House of Lords as well as Foreign

Secretary, he was, in 1884, well past his prime. Nearly seventy, he suffered from severe gout, complained frequently that he had too much to do, and gave the impression to those around him that his memory was slipping. Granville, thus, was not a man to reach a quick decision. Furthermore, Granville and the British government had no idea that Bismarck was seriously interested in colonial expansion and considered the note merely a request to protect German settlers. The German Chancellor's public pronouncements had opposed German colonies; he had communicated nothing in private to correct them. Once Granville focussed on the matter, he wished to accommodate Count Münster, but his path was obstructed by bureaucracy. Within the British Cabinet colonial matters were decided at the Colonial Office. Granville, therefore, had to consult Lord Derby, the Colonial Secretary. Derby was not at liberty to make a decision, for he in turn was required to consult the self-governing Cape Colony in South Africa. London might have no objection to a German foothold on the west coast of southern Africa, but Cape Town might have a different view. Indeed, a delegation of South Africans had already told Lord Salisbury, "My Lord, we are told that the Germans are good neighbors, but we prefer no neighbors at all." Granville explained these intricacies to Münster, adding his "sincere regrets." Bismarck impatiently sent Herbert to see the Foreign Secretary. Again, Granville turned up his palms, pleading goodwill and asking for time: "Neither my colleagues nor I have the slightest intention of obstructing German colonial aspirations and I beg you to say so plainly to Prince Bismarck. . . . If Germany pursues a colonial policy and opens barbarian lands to civilization and commerce we should rejoice at it. . . . The only representation which you can make against us is the slow progress of the negotiations; this happens owing to the independent position of our colonies which we cannot get over with the best will in the world." Candidly, Granville grumbled to Herbert about the extra burden the matter had imposed on him. "It is very hard for me as I have so much to do that I cannot well enter into these colonial questions." One solution, Granville suggested, would be for Herbert to discuss Angra Pequena "in my presence with Lord Derby since Derby is new at the Colonial Office. I will include his predecessor, Lord Kimberley." Herbert, appalled at this confused, casual way of handling business, wrote to his father, "I replied to the noble Lord that I cannot attend a ministerial conference."

Bismarck had already instructed Count Münster to demand of Lord Granville "why the right to colonize, which England uses to the fullest extent, should be denied us?" Now the excuses for delay seemed intolerable. London's claim that the Cape Colony was an independent government was incomprehensible to a mind accustomed to orders flowing from the top. Colonies were colonies, not independent governments. "So long as they remain under the Queen's sceptre and under the protection of the Mother Country . . . the game of hide and seek with the Colonial Office . . . is merely an evasion." The Chancellor ordered Münster and Herbert not to speak to Derby at all on the subject, but to confine all their discussions to Granville. He began to think in terms of threats. "Our friendship can be of great help to British policy," he reminded Münster, alluding to Egypt. "It is not a matter of indifference for England whether she has the good wishes and support of the German Empire or whether it stands coldly aloof." He became more fierce: "If we fail to push our rights with energy," he wrote to Münster, "we shall risk, by letting them sink into oblivion, falling into a position inferior to England's and strengthening the unbounded arrogance shown by England and her colonies in opposition to us. We may be driven to contemplate a complete rupture." Warned that he risked pushing Britain too far, he scoffed, "The English . . . have no reason at all for attacking us even if they are beginning to envy our industrial and commercial progress. The Englishman is like the dog in the fable who cannot bear that another dog should have a few bones, although the overfed brute is sitting before a bowl filled to the brim. An English attack would only be thinkable if we found ourselves at war with both Russia and France or did anything so utterly absurd as to fall upon Holland or Belgium or block the Baltic by closing the Sound."

In March 1885, on his father's instructions, Herbert pushed harder. The Liberal government was split and tottering, its prestige ruined by its failure to save Gordon at Khartoum. Accordingly, when Herbert went to see Granville, he felt empowered to be rude. It was his impression, he told Granville, that England deliberately stirred up trouble among her Continental neighbors and might even encourage war in order to "profit England by leaving her free to pursue her trading activities." These words, Herbert gleefully reported to his father, "produced violent gesticulations and exclamations of annoyance from Lord Granville." Herbert had gone too far. Sir Charles Dilke, a younger Liberal minister who was critical of Granville, was even more critical of the younger Bismarck: "Herbert Bismarck has come over again," he wrote. "He wanted us to dismiss Lord Granville and Lord Derby . . . [a] gross and unwarranted interference in our home politics, thoroughly Bismarckian in character."

Eventually, Britain acquiesced in Germany's colonial acquisitions, not because of Herbert's skill, but because Gladstone was determined not to quarrel. During a twenty-minute conversation with Herbert after dinner at Lord Rosebery's mansion, Gladstone said that he was willing to go any lengths to meet Germany's legitimate claims. He went further: "Even if you had no colonial aspirations, I should beseech you to go forward in this direction. I rejoice at your civilizing aspirations." Such innocence and idealism were almost too much for Herbert; his report to his father was filled with contempt: "There is no point in discussing the foreign policy of a great country with Mr. Gladstone as he has no comprehension of it whatever." Gladstone blandly assured the House of Commons that Britain welcomed with joy "the extension of Germany to these desert places." Nevertheless, the heavy-handed behavior of the Bismarcks, father and son, made an unfavorable impression on Gladstone and his colleagues. When Gladstone returned a year later for a brief third term as Prime Minister, his Foreign Secretary, Lord Rosebery, warned the German Ambassador that "they must take care in Berlin of their style of communication which is apt to savor distinctly of menace."

On June 8, 1885, the second Gladstone Cabinet resigned and Lord Salisbury formed a new Conservative government. Once more, British policy was in the hands of a man Bismarck trusted. The two statesmen quickly exchanged friendly messages. Salisbury wrote of his "lively . . . recollection of the kindness which your Highness showed me in Berlin in the years 1876 and 1878." Bismarck replied, describing his pleasure in seeing "by your own words that our former personal intercourse, which I am glad to renew, has left with both of us the same sympathetic recollection." Bismarck signalled his approval to everyone. "I value Lord Salisbury's friendship more than twenty swamp colonies in Africa," he said. The Chancellor's new rejection of colonialism was as swift and absolute as his pounce on the issue had been a year before. "Here is Russia and here is France, with Germany in the middle," he said to an African explorer. "This is my map of Africa." In one of his final speeches to the Reichstag, he declared, "I am not a colonialist."

Behind Bismarck's aberrant excursion into colonialism—along with the demands of German pride and desire for overseas markets —lay a domestic political motive: he wished to attack and neutralize the authority of the Crown Prince before Frederick became Emperor. The new reign could not be long postponed; in 1884, Emperor William I was eighty-six years old. Once on the throne, the liberal Fritz and his English wife were certain to choose their ministers from the liberal bloc in the Reichstag, giving Germany what the Chancellor contemptuously called "a German Gladstone ministry." The colonial policy was a defensive stratagem. It stimulated patriotism and produced votes; it created an enemy whom Germans could blame for the shabbiness of their overseas possessions. Best of all, inflaming anti-British feeling in Germany weakened the liberals in the Reichstag and undermined the position of the Crown Prince. Frederick, as Emperor, would scarcely be able to follow a pro-British policy if, because of the colonial confrontation, most of his people hated England. Privately, Bismarck admitted his scheme. In the autumn of 1884, when the colonial dispute was at its height, Bismarck confided to Tsar Alexander III that "the sole object of German colonial policy was to drive a wedge between the Crown Prince and England." And in 1890, after the Chancellor had fallen, Herbert Bismarck was asked how his father could have wandered so far from his anticolonialist views. Herbert replied, "When we entered upon our colonial policy we had to assume that the Crown Prince's reign would be a long one with English influence predominant. To prevent this we had to embark on a colonial policy because it was popular and also conveniently adapted to be able to provoke conflict with England at any given moment."

In sheer expanse of territory, Bismarck's brief colonial adventure produced spectacular results: in scarcely more than a year, the Chancellor acquired new land surface five times the size of the Reich itself. South-West Africa (now Namibia), German East Africa (now Tanzania), Togo and the Cameroons in West Africa, a third of New Guinea, most of the Solomon Islands (renamed the Bismarck Archipelago), the Marshall and Caroline Islands in the central Pacific, and a share of the islands of Samoa came under the German flag. But by every measure other than size, the new German colonial empire was a disappointment. South-West Africa and German East Africa were mostly deserts and dry riverbeds, containing few raw materials to tempt even the hardiest explorers or entrepreneurs. In the end, they proved an embarrassment. By 1914, fewer than twenty-five thousand German citizens, including soldiers and naval detachments, were to be found in all the German colonies combined. The cost to the homeland was many times the profits. In 1889, Bismarck even tried to persuade the British government to assume sovereignty over South-West Africa because of the expense to Berlin. A large volume of German trade continued to flow overseas, but not to and from German colonies. In the twenty-five years before the Great War, millions of Germans emigrated, but they went not to the deserts of German Africa, but to Milwaukee, Minneapolis, and other cities and towns in the American Middle West.

In his last two years of power, Bismarck again suggested an Anglo-German alliance. In November 1887, soon after concluding the secret Reinsurance Treaty with Russia, the Chancellor wrote privately to Lord Salisbury. He described Britain, Germany, and Austria as satiated states; the danger to peace, he said, came from Russia and France. If Britain were to join Germany and Austria in a defensive alliance, peace would be permanently secured. Holstein was surprised and impressed by Bismarck's move. "I know of no other case in which Bismarck addressed himself to a foreign premier in this direct form," he said. "And that he should have taken this most unusual step when at the height of his power shows what crucial importance he attached to Lord Salisbury's response." Salisbury politely declined. Again, in January 1889, Bismarck sent Herbert to London to propose a formal defensive alliance among Germany, Austria, and England. Salisbury, understanding that the alliance was aimed primarily at France and that Britain would be required to prop up Austria in the event of war with Russia, again declined. Future Parliaments would not be bound by the acts of present Parliaments, he told Herbert, and therefore England did not enter into peacetime treaties of alliance. "Meanwhile," he said politely of the offer, "we leave it on the table without saying yes or no. That is unfortunately all I can do at the present."

Although stymied, Bismarck displayed rare good humor. "The preservation of Anglo-German goodwill is, after all, the most important thing," he said on January 26, 1889. "I see in England an old and traditional ally. No differences exist between England and Germany. I am not using a diplomatic term if I speak of England as our ally. We have no alliance with England. However, I wish to remain in close contact with England."

On February 6, 1888, the Chancellor introduced a new Army Bill into the Reichstag. By raising the age limit for reservists from thirty-two to thirty-nine, the Bill would add 750,000 men to the wartime strength of the German Army. Bismarck, standing before the hall packed with deputies, foreign ambassadors, and visitors, delivered an emotional, patriotic speech. Germany, despite her alliances, must ultimately rely on herself: "We no longer ask for love, either from France or Russia. We run after nobody. We Germans fear God and nothing else on earth!'' The Reichstag erupted in cheering. Moltke burst into tears; Prince William of Hohenzollern, soon to be Kaiser, sitting in the gallery with his wife, applauded wildly. Four weeks later, on March 3, Bismarck appeared again at the Reichstag podium to announce the death of Kaiser William I. As he spoke of the sovereign whom he had made the most powerful monarch in Europe, the "Old Gentleman" whom he had served for twenty-five years, the Chancellor broke down. He attempted to continue, failed, and took his seat. To those watching, Bismarck's breakdown was a more impressive tribute than anything he might have said.

Despite the tears shed at the old Kaiser's death, Bismarck in 1888 was enjoying the rich fruits of a lifetime of achievement. His health was better than it had been for years. Herbert stood at his right hand, ably fulfilling a senior office. The Chancellor himself had finally managed to merge his own opposing desires: unchallenged power in the state and the life of a country gentleman. After Kaiser William II's accession, Bismarck left Berlin in July, not to return until January. At Varzin, he slept late, rose and swallowed two raw eggs, and set out for a walk. Wearing a long black coat and black, broad-brimmed hat, he resembled a venerable clergyman. After dinner—if he felt inclined—he would look over state documents forwarded from Berlin. Everything must await the Chancellor's approval—whenever he chose to give it. But why hurry? Everything —Germany, Europe, the young Emperor—all were fixed in a grand design, revolving with majestic precision in the balanced orbits he himself had long ago arranged. A lifetime of work and thought had gone into its creation. It should not be disturbed; certainly, not hurried.

Forty-four years' difference in age separated the old Chancellor and the new Kaiser: William II was twenty-nine in 1888, Bismarck seventy-three. To Bismarck, accustomed to rule behind a screen of deferential references to a passive sovereign, the possibility of trouble with a man almost young enough to be his grandson never occurred. William II, like William I, would become an honored figurehead. Bismarck had known the young Kaiser all his life. He was aware of William's impulsive self-confidence, his frenetic energy, his craving for flattery and applause. These could be managed. He also knew that William had an elevated view of his station in life and grandiose opinions as to his own qualities. These qualities in William, Bismarck had understood, could be not only tolerated but exploited. Through most of the reign of William I, the Chancellor had assumed that the threat to his power would come from Frederick. He had been prepared. A few years earlier, he had told the Crown Prince that he would remain in office under an Emperor Frederick on two conditions: the power of the Reichstag would remain limited and there would be no English influence on foreign policy. Frederick had agreed. To bolster his position, Bismarck had deliberately widened the breach between Prince William and his parents. William, born and bred in the authoritarian, militarist traditions of the Prussian Court, had been encouraged in his inclination towards autocracy. The Bismarcks, father and son, had drawn Prince William into their conservative fold, encouraged William's rebelliousness, and attempted to sharpen, not soften, the antagonism between the restless, ambitious son and his liberal parents. When Frederick unexpectedly died, the Bismarcks had on their hands a personality for which they themselves were partially responsible.

During the first year of the new reign, the young Kaiser and the elderly Chancellor remained on good terms. William was delightedly preoccupied with the ceremonial pleasures of his new rank. Bismarck's first complaints were minor and were not that his master was intruding on management of the state, but that, on the contrary, William was avoiding sustained and serious work. In February 1889, the Chancellor was heard to grumble that the Kaiser would rather attend a regimental dinner in Potsdam than a meeting with his ministers. General Count Alfred von Waldersee, Moltke's successor as Chief of the Army General Staff, noted in his diary that when William was required to sit and listen to oral reports by his generals or ministers, the Kaiser could not hide his boredom and sometimes yawned openly. William immediately began to travel: to all parts of Germany, to St. Petersburg, to Vienna, London, Constantinople, and Athens. Bismarck resented these journeys and worried that the impetuous young ruler would disturb his carefully balanced diplomatic arrangements. "The Kaiser is like a balloon," he said contemptuously. "If you don't hold fast to the string, you never know where he'll be off to."* William, for his part, let it be known that on these journeys he had listened to "too much talk of the Chancellor" and had heard the German Empire described as "the firm of Bismarck and Son."

---

* Bismarck also correctly judged these early journeys as lacking in benefit to William II's reputation. After the young Kaiser's visit to St. Petersburg in the summer of 1888, Tsar Alexander III told an aide that his guest was "a rascally young fop who throws his weight around, thinks too much of himself, and fancies that others worship him."

Gradually, the Chancellor realized that the new Emperor was no longer the fawning young Prince who had lit his pipe and complained about his parents. William was a versatile, ambitious, complicated man of considerable insecurity. This would require a relationship between Kaiser and Chancellor very different from that which had existed between William I and Bismarck. William II had grown up imbued with the lesson that Bismarck had taught: that although the German Empire was a constitutional state, he was also King of Prussia and had been granted this role—and that of German Emperor—by the Almighty. If God had put him in these places, no human, not even the founder of the Empire, should stand in his way. His education had stressed that ultimate political decisions—the decision for war or peace, the choosing of a Chancellor and Imperial and Prussian ministers—lay with the Emperor-King. William's belief had been buttressed by a growing Hohenzollern mystique, taught in thousands of schools, preached from hundreds of university lecterns throughout the Empire. Bismarck, too, had encouraged William to believe in his own special genius and divine mission.

William was not a fool; he had understood that he was being used in the Chancellor's game while his father was alive. He, in turn, had used Bismarck, extravagantly praising the Chancellor when he was at odds with his father and mother. But once he came to the throne, after his initial pleasure in dressing himself in glorious uniforms, hearing new forms of flattering address, inspecting troops, and riding in parades, he began to want more of the substance of power. He had no intention of playing only the passive role his grandfather had played. Soon enough, those opposed to the Chancellor found their way to the Emperor's ear. Bismarck's own subordinates, most prominently Holstein, leaked information in order to sabotage the Chancellor's policies or his standing with the Kaiser. Years of resentment found distillation in poisonous remarks. William would never be a real emperor, he was told, so long as he was only a tool in the hands of the Imperial Chancellor. Count Waldersee, no friend to Bismarck, said pointedly that "if Frederick the Great had had such a Chancellor, he would not have been Frederick the Great."

Sooner or later, a change was inevitable. Because Bismarck had no desire for change, it would be initiated by the Kaiser. The Prince would gladly have remained in office until his death; he loved power and genuinely believed that without him, Germany would be ruined. There was always Herbert, but Herbert still was young and unready. And Kaiser William, ten years younger than Herbert, had no experience at all. In fact, William felt his own inexperience and did not intend to dismiss Bismarck immediately. Rather, as the Chancellor aged, he meant gradually to take on more and more of Bismarck's powers.

William's relative lack of interest in politics during the first year of his reign lulled the Chancellor into underrating his former protégé. Instead of summoning his strength to solidify his control over the government and the Reichstag, Bismarck, sublimely overconfident, turned his back on Berlin, leaving Herbert to manage William. From Friedrichsruh or Varzin, the Chancellor conducted the government with little reference to the sovereign: if William asked a question or made a suggestion, Bismarck replied curtly, usually to observe how unwise or dangerous the Kaiser's suggestions were.

William, although offended by the Chancellor's prolonged absence and by his patronizing messages, did not challenge Bismarck on policy until May 1889. The first disagreement was over labor legislation. Bismarck, attempting to cope with the social repercussions of the rapid industrialization of Germany, already had given the German working class the most advanced social legislation in the world, including comprehensive social insurance and contributory old-age pensions. But he balked at restrictions on the age or sex of workers and on limiting the days and hours of work; forbidding a working man "to earn money on certain days and during certain hours" was "an encroachment upon personal freedom," Bismarck said. William had personal reasons for opposing the Chancellor's view. Although tutored in absolutism, the young Kaiser at the beginning of his reign craved the kind of popularity enjoyed by his father and grandfather. The means to achieve it, he decided, was to show that he was the Kaiser of all the German people. He would bind the workers to the crown with enlightened, cautiously liberal social and labor legislation; in this respect, laws protecting women and children from overwork and regulations on the hours and conditions of labor would be particularly popular and therefore useful.

The clash between these philosophies was precipitated by a strike of 170,000 Westphalian coal miners in May 1889. William, against the Chancellor's advice, received a deputation of the striking miners and appeared unexpectedly at a Cabinet meeting to announce (in Bismarck's words): "The employers and shareholders must give way; the workers were his subjects for whom it was his place to care; if the industrial millionaires would not do as he wished, he would withdraw his troops. If the villas of the wealthy mine owners and directors were then set on fire and their gardens trampled underfoot, they would soon sing small." Bismarck argued that the mine owners were also subjects who had a right to their sovereign's protection. The dispute festered and became a part of a larger crisis. In 1889, the seventy-four-year-old Chancellor was disinclined to make concessions to coal miners, factory workers, or Socialist deputies in the Reichstag. He believed that the time had come to deal forcefully with industrial turmoil and parliamentary upheaval. If the workers made trouble, the army would repress them; if the Reichstag misbehaved, he would simply dismiss it and turn the deputies into the street. To those who said that this coup d'état was unconstitutional, he would reply that he had created the constitution and could create another. Nor should anyone forget that he had begun his long service to the Prussian crown by ruling illegally for four years without the Prussian Landtag.

By January 1890, all parties in the Reichstag were in favor of legislation to restrict child labor, female labor, and work on Sundays. Bismarck refused to give way and William decided to act. On January 23, the Chancellor and all Prussian ministers were informed that the Kaiser had summoned a Crown Council (a session of the Prussian Ministry of State under the personal presidency of the King) for six P.M. on the following day. Herbert, charged by his father with learning the purpose of the Council, went to William and learned that the Kaiser intended to place his labor-reform plan before the ministers. Bismarck left Friedrichsruh, arrived in Berlin at two P.M., and summoned all Prussian ministers to meet in his office at three P.M. There, he told them what he knew of the Emperor's intentions and asked them to neither accept nor reject the plan but to ask for time to think it over. Without exception, the ministers agreed.

At six P.M. the Crown Council assembled. William, unaware of the earlier meeting, explained his proposals. Instead of repressing socialists, he wanted to win them over. He had nothing extravagant in mind; simply limitations on hours, restriction of labor by women and children, inspection of factories to check on working conditions. He complained that German employers were squeezing their workers like lemons and letting old people rot on a dunghill. Unless something was done, he said, he would become the king of the beggars. William pointed out that the day of the meeting, January 24, was the birthday of Frederick the Great; three days later, January 27, his own birthday followed. If the ministers agreed quickly, the Kaiser could issue a dramatic birthday proclamation which would bring glory to the crown. Bismarck listened and later condemned "the practical aimlessness of the scheme and its pretentious and exalted tone." In Council, he warned that "the increased expectations and the insatiable covetousness of the Socialist classes would destroy the kingdom. . . . His Majesty and the Reichstag were speaking of the protection of labor, but as a matter of fact it was a question of the compulsion of labor, the compulsion to work less." The ministers spoke one by one. All, as they had promised the Chancellor they would do, said that the Kaiser's proposals needed more time for consideration.

The Council turned to the repressive antisocialist bill before the Reichstag. William wished to moderate it by eliminating the state's power to eject troublesome socialists from their homes. Bismarck opposed the Kaiser. He said that the sooner the government took a firm stand, the less bloodshed there would be, but that ultimately, these social questions would have to be decided by force. If the Reichstag rejected the antisocialist bill, he wished to go back to his beginnings and use force. He would tear up the constitution and abolish the Reichstag and universal suffrage. He talked confidently of industrial disturbances, strikes, and civil war. "The waves will mount higher," he predicted; then "blood and iron" would rule again.

William pleaded that he did not wish to begin his reign by shooting his subjects. He appealed to the ministers, but they, not daring in Bismarck's presence to challenge him, meekly supported the Chancellor. What the young Emperor might do if they failed to support him, they did not know. What Bismarck would do if they opposed him, they knew exactly: he would destroy them. There was little William could do, and he left the Council dismayed and angry. "They are not my ministers," he said. "They are Bismarck's."

Bismarck had won a Pyrrhic victory. Between Kaiser and Chancellor, youth and age, the battle lines were drawn. The Kaiser had been humiliated; the old man had displayed his supremacy all too clearly. Bismarck sensed this; the following day a Chancellory official found him in tears lying on his office sofa. In the days that followed, he attempted to compromise. At the next meeting of the ministerial council, he agreed that the Kaiser should issue a proclamation declaring his interest in the welfare of the working class. William was also allowed to invite the European powers to an international conference in Berlin on labor and social problems.

William, only partially mollified, opened a campaign to win over the ministers one by one by receiving each individually every week to hear his report. This tactic alarmed Bismarck, who reacted by trying to control contacts between the Kaiser and the ministers more tightly than ever. He instructed Chancellory clerks to find an old decree, dating from 1852, which forbade Prussian ministers from speaking to the King except in the presence of the Minister-

President. On February 18, 1890, Bismarck reissued this regulation. Prussian ministers were ordered to "cease all direct correspondence with His Majesty, with the Bundesrat and the Reichstag. . . . Draft proposals must be sent to me for approval. Similarly, oral declarations to the Bundesrat or Reichstag are not to be made without my express approval." In his suspicion, the Chancellor was setting himself a Herculean task. At seventy-five, he would have to approve the Bundesrat agenda every day, chair all Bundesrat meetings, sign every order and bill in person, and approve every statement made by all government officials. Bismarck also refused to put his signature on the Kaiser's labor-protection proclamation when it was issued. Secretly, the Chancellor attempted to damage William's pet scheme, the international labor conference to be held in Berlin. He appeared uninvited at the French Embassy and proposed to the Ambassador that France should avoid the conference. "The Chancellor has unambiguously taken sides against his sovereign," the Ambassador hurriedly reported to Paris.

On February 20, Bismarck's coalition suffered heavy losses in elections for the Reichstag. Normally, Bismarck would have ignored this fact; as long as he possessed the confidence of the King-Emperor, he could continue to rule. Now, knowing that he was losing that confidence, Bismarck was in difficulty. He set about arranging new combinations in the Reichstag. At one point, he appeared before the Council and threatened to resign as Minister-President of Prussia and remain only as Imperial Chancellor. To his dismay, the ministers all agreed and one, Karl von Bötticher, the Interior Minister, made an eloquent farewell speech. Bismarck was enraged when, on March 9, the Kaiser summoned Bötticher and bestowed on him the Order of the Black Eagle, Prussia's highest decoration, usually reserved for royal persons. William, in turn, was infuriated to learn that Bismarck had attempted to draw Ludwig Windthorst, leader of the Catholic Center Party, into a new Bismarckian coalition, without consulting or even informing the Kaiser. Windthorst was an old enemy of the Chancellor; the interview on March 12 was a measure of Bismarck's desperation. Windthorst knew it; when he left the Chancellor's office after a conversation of an hour and a half, he said, "I am just leaving the political deathbed of a great man."

On March 14, William sent Bismarck a message that he proposed to call on him the following morning at the Foreign Minister's (Herbert's) residence. The Kaiser's message failed to reach the Chancellor before he went to bed. On Saturday the fifteenth, Bismarck was awakened at nine o'clock with the news that the Kaiser was waiting for him at Herbert's villa. Bismarck, accustomed to sleeping late, then having a cup of tea, a warm bath, and a massage in order to prepare himself for the day, hurriedly got out of bed, dressed, and walked in a cold rain through the garden of the Chancellor's palace to Herbert's villa. Both men were in a bad humor; William had waited twenty-five minutes for the Chancellor's appearance; Bismarck complained that he had known nothing of the interview until twenty-five minutes before, when he had been awakened. "So?" said the Kaiser. "I gave the order yesterday afternoon." The Chancellor told William what the Kaiser already knew: that Windthorst had called on him. "Well, of course you had him thrown out-of-doors," William flared. How dare the Chancellor attempt to make secret arrangements with an opposition leader without the Emperor's knowledge? Bismarck replied that, as Chancellor, he must be free to meet party leaders and said that he had received Windthorst as any gentleman had the right to receive friends in his home. "Not even when your sovereign commands it?" William demanded. "The power of my sovereign ends at the door to my wife's drawing room," Bismarck retorted so angrily that "it was all Bismarck could do to refrain from throwing an ink pot at my head," William said later. William demanded that the reissued order of 1852 forbidding ministerial access to himself in the Chancellor's absence be repealed. "How can I rule without discussing things with my ministers if you spend most of the year at Friedrichsruh?" he asked.

The conversation turned to Russia. William earlier had declared his intention of visiting Tsar Alexander III again soon; Bismarck now advised against it because, he said, he had received reports proving that the Tsar was unfriendly to the young Kaiser. Here, Bismarck played a trick. He picked up his dispatch case, fumbled with some papers, appeared to think better of it, and shoved them back into the case. William demanded to see the papers. Bismarck demurred, saying that it would be better if he did not. William insisted, reached out, and took the papers from the Chancellor's case. He found himself reading a confidential dispatch from St. Petersburg which included a report that the Tsar had described the German Emperor as *"un garçon mal élevé et de mauvais foi"* ("a badly-brought-up young man of bad faith"). Bismarck watched implacably, as William, humiliated, returned the paper and stalked back to his carriage.

It was the end and both men knew it. Three times the Kaiser sent emissaries to Bismarck requesting either cancellation of the 1852 order or the Chancellor's resignation. Bismarck refused and did not resign. On March 17, William sent a note, openly passed through departmental offices, complaining to Bismarck that he had not been informed of certain Russian troop movements: "I must greatly deplore the fact that I have received so few of the reports. You ought to have drawn my attention long ago to the terrible danger threatening." Bismarck now had the excuse he sought: the Kaiser was interfering in foreign policy and talking of war with Russia. On March 18, he sent in his resignation. Two days later, the official gazette published the Kaiser's letter of acceptance: "With deep emotion, I have perceived . . . that you are determined to retire from the offices which you have filled for many years with incomparable results. I had hoped that I should not be obliged to . . . part with you in our lifetime. . . . I confer upon you the dignity of Duke of Lauenburg. I will also have my life-size portrait sent to you. . . . I appoint you General Field Marshal [in the army]." Bismarck took these honors with cynical humor. The Kaiser had stated ill health to be a reason for the Chancellor's resignation: "I am in better health than I have been in for years past." William gave him a grant of money; Bismarck compared it to an envelope given to the postman at Christmas. As for the new dukedom: "I will use it when I am traveling incognito." Foreign ambassadors were informed that the resignation was due to ill health.* William telegraphed to Hinzpeter, "I am as miserable as if I had again lost my grandfather. But what God wills must be borne. . . . The position of officer of the watch on the ship of state has fallen to me. The course remains the same. Full steam ahead!"†

Bismarck left Berlin quickly. He filled three hundred packing cases with state papers and shipped thirteen thousand bottles of wine from the Chancellory cellar to Friedrichsruh. He paid a final call on his old enemy, the Empress Frederick. She asked whether there was anything she could do. "I ask only for sympathy," he replied. On March 28, he visited the Royal Museum at Charlottenburg to lay roses on the grave of William I. "I have bid farewell to my old master," he said. The roses were taken from the massive floral tributes which his own admirers had sent to him. On March 29, Bismarck departed the capital. Crowds lined the streets to the

---

* William telegraphed directly to his grandmother at Windsor Castle: "I deeply regret to inform you that Prince Bismarck has placed his resignation in my hands—his nerves and strength have given out."

† William's nautical language, published on March 22, was probably the inspiration for one of the most famous political cartoons ever drawn. Appearing in *Punch* on March 29 and captioned "DROPPING THE PILOT," it depicts Bismarck in mariner's cap, jacket, and boots descending a ship's ladder to a waiting rowboat while above on deck the Kaiser in crown and epaulettes leans languidly over the rail, watching.

station; he was seen off by a guard of honor, Imperial and Prussian ministers, generals, and ambassadors. Only the Kaiser was missing. As his train rolled out of the station, Bismarck leaned back in his seat and said wryly, "A state funeral with full honors."

Bismarck returned to Varzin, where he filled his diaries with the words "bored" and "tired." Ahead, on the day of his resignation, stretched eight more years of life. After forty years in state service and twenty-eight years of supreme power, it was difficult for him to believe that this was the end. The German Empire was his handi-work; he had created it and administered it throughout its existence. It was inconceivable to him that it could function without him. For a long time, he dreamed of being recalled, of making a triumphal return. He talked of those whom he would dismiss when he was restored to power. His return would not result from any winning-over of public opinion, but because of an appeal from the Kaiser; this was the only path allowed by the constitution he had written. But the Kaiser had no such intention and remained aloof. In June 1892, Prince Hohenlohe, Governor General of Alsace-Lorraine, told the Kaiser that people feared that Bismarck would return. William laughed. "They can make their minds easy," he said. "He will not return."

Out of power, Bismarck remained a factor in German politics. He spoke freely about William II's inexperience and volatility. For a while, Bismarck, on removing coins from his pocket, always turned the Kaiser's likeness to the table—"so that I will not have to see that false face." In 1891, he was elected by a Hanoverian constituency to the Reichstag. He never took his seat, explaining that he did not own a house in Berlin and was too old to live in a hotel. Eventually, he established an outlet for his views by contributing unsigned, but unmistakably authored, articles to Hamburg newspapers. These arti-cles, widely read and often highly indiscreet, hammered at the fool-ishness of the Kaiser and the blunders of his successors. He worked spasmodically on his autobiography, spinning and respinning tales until his assistant, dutifully transcribing Bismarck's words, had no idea where truth lay.

In May 1892, Herbert Bismarck became engaged to a Hun-garian noblewoman, Countess Hoyos. Kaiser William telegraphed his congratulations and Bismarck decided to attend the wedding, which was to be held in Vienna. He requested an audience with Emperor Franz Josef. The new German Chancellor, however, wor-ried about the possible ramifications of Bismarck's appearance in

Vienna and forbade the German Ambassador to attend the wedding. "We have not doubted for an instant that ovations will be prepared for the Prince in Vienna," Caprivi wrote. "We cannot prevent that but we must avoid the participation of the German Embassy in festivities that will be accompanied by demonstrations where one cannot tell whether they are meant as more pro-Bismarck or contra–Kaiser William." The Kaiser himself went further. In a private letter to Franz Josef he wrote: "He has planned an audience with you as the main event on his program. While most insolently ignoring my court and the Empress, he takes himself to Dresden and Vienna in order to parade himself there in the role of the grand old man. In the interest of myself and of my government, therefore, I should like to beg you as a true friend not to render the situation in the country more difficult for me by receiving this rebellious subject before he has approached me and said his *Peccavi*." William's letter made it impossible for Franz Josef to receive Bismarck and, during his stay in Vienna, the former Chancellor was ignored by Viennese society. No representatives of the Austrian court or the diplomatic corps attended Herbert's wedding. Bismarck was enraged. On his return from Vienna, he was cheered by crowds along his route. In Kissingen and Jena, he made speeches, declaring that, in writing the Reich constitution, he had given too much power to the crown.

In 1893, Bismarck, then seventy-eight, fell seriously ill with influenza and shingles. The Kaiser telegraphed sympathetically and sent Count Kuno von Moltke of his staff to Varzin bearing a personal letter along with a bottle of the finest Rhenish wine from the Imperial cellars. While there, Moltke also invited Bismarck to visit Berlin to help celebrate the Kaiser's birthday. News of Bismarck's acceptance raised fears in many government ministries that the former Chancellor might be returning to power. At noon on January 22, 1894, the fallen Titan made his triumphal return to the capital. Prince Henry of Prussia met him at the station and embraced and kissed him. A squadron of Cuirassier Guards escorted him through streets lined with cheering crowds, under balconies crowded with nervous government officials. At the palace, he mounted the steps, leaning on Herbert's arm. While the Kaiser received him, crowds outside repeatedly sang "Die Wacht am Rhein" and "Deutschland, Deutschland über Alles."

Bismarck had come to Berlin hoping that this was the beginning of his return to power, or, at the least, expecting to be consulted about political affairs. Nothing of the sort occurred. Bismarck did not see Caprivi, the Chancellor; Marschall, the State Secretary for Foreign Affairs; or Holstein, the First Counselor of the Foreign Office. At the formal dinner that evening, Bismarck sat next to the Kaiser with Herbert and Bill nearby, but William kept the talk firmly on trivialities. Bismarck, it was said, was treated like visiting royalty, not as a source of political wisdom. On February 19, the Kaiser returned the visit by coming to Friedrichsruh. Again, there was no talk of politics.

Near the end of 1894, Johanna died quietly at Varzin. Bismarck left the estate and moved permanently to Friedrichsruh. The Kaiser arrived to celebrate his eightieth birthday in April 1895, a visit which produced a memorable photograph of Bismarck, standing awkwardly and leaning on his cane because of pain in his joints, still towering over the youthful Kaiser. On this birthday, Bismarck received many congratulations but the German Reichstag refused to participate. This surliness and ingratitude moved the French Ambassador—representing a nation which had little reason to honor Bismarck—to say, "Whatever the Germans may say or do, they will never be a great people."

Bismarck's move to Friedrichsruh marked a final separation from his Junker origins. He had long before risen above purely Prussian concerns for preserving caste privileges, agrarian interests, and the supremacy of the army. Now, close to the cosmopolitan prosperity of the great commercial port of Hamburg, he glimpsed the future of the Germany he had created. Bernhard von Bülow described how Bismarck at eighty was taken to see the port of Hamburg: "He stopped when he set foot on a giant steamboat, looked at the ship for a long time, at the many steamers lying in the vicinity, at the docks and huge cranes, at the mighty picture presented by the harbor, and said at last, 'I am stirred and moved. Yes, this is a new age—a new world.' "

The quarrel between Bismarck and the Kaiser flared again in 1896 when the former Chancellor revealed in a Hamburg newspaper the previous existence of the secret Reinsurance Treaty with Russia and attacked William for refusing to renew it in 1890. William, infuriated, announced his intention to imprison Bismarck for treason in Berlin's Spandau Prison. Prince von Hohenlohe, then Chancellor, talked the Kaiser out of it, pointing out that the minimum sentence for treason was two years' hard labor, which would certainly kill the eighty-one-year-old Bismarck. Then would come the question of the funeral. The Kaiser certainly would wish to arrange and attend this event. "Would it be worthy of so great a monarch to have the funeral cortège of the first and most famous Imperial Chancellor proceed from a second-rate fortress such as Spandau?'' William ended his threats.

In December 1897, the Kaiser came to Friedrichsruh for the last time "to see how long the old man will last." William found his former Chancellor in a wheelchair. Bismarck, as host, tried repeatedly to begin a serious conversation. William evaded every political subject, listened absent-mindedly, replied with old barracks-room jokes from his regimental days in Potsdam. During the winter and spring of 1898, Bismarck declined rapidly, rarely left his wheelchair, and had difficulty breathing. He died on the night of July 30, 1898. William, cruising aboard the *Hohenzollern* on the North Sea, hurried back for the funeral. Bismarck had refused a state funeral in Berlin and was buried at Friedrichsruh. Herbert, who inherited the title of Prince on his father's death, met the Kaiser at the station. They kissed on the cheek, but at the funeral William and his staff stood on one side of the grave, the family on the other. On June 16, 1901, a monument to Bismarck was to be unveiled in Berlin. Bülow, now Chancellor, gave the Kaiser the news. William said he would not come. When Bülow insisted that this insult was too great, William reluctantly consented. "Very well, if you insist, I shall come," he said. "But only in a modest uniform."

CHAPTER 5

The New Course:
Kaiser William II,
Caprivi, and Hohenlohe

◈

Europeans who turned to look at the new German Emperor saw a short young man with restless, bright-blue eyes and curly light-brown hair. His most prominent feature was a brushy mustache with extended, upturned points, the creation of a skillful barber who appeared every morning at the palace with a can of wax. "[The Emperor] carries himself well. . . . [He] walks into the room with the stiff stride of a Prussian soldier," noted the English statesman John Morley. "If he laughs," wrote another English observer, "which he is sure to do a good many times, he will laugh with absolute abandonment, throwing back his head, opening his mouth to the fullest extent possible, shaking his whole body, and often stamping with one foot to show his excessive enjoyment of any joke. . . . He will continually shake the forefinger of his right hand into the face of anyone whom he wishes to convince or will rock slowly on his toes backwards and forwards." A drier, more disparaging view of the Kaiser was that of a third English eyewitness, a yachtsman who often sailed with William: "He was small and . . . handsome, with clear blue eyes . . . rather short in the neck and a little lopsided owing to his left arm being shorter than the other. . . . He spoke English very well, with no marked or unpleasant German accent, and took pride in picking up and making use of English slang expressions and colloquial phrases . . . which . . . in his anxiety to copy . . . he would often get wrong. His admiration of English gentlemen was extreme. . . . Sometimes, in moments when he was not on his guard, he found himself showing it too openly or plainly . . . and then he rather obviously tried to restrain it. . . . In particular his admiration turned towards the officers of our Royal Navy; his admiration of them and their appearance amounted to worship. I have often known his eyes [to] follow one of our young naval men who was, of course, quite unaware that he was the object of any special attention. He once told me: 'I like to look at your naval officers.' "

William II was the first German Kaiser who had the inclination and opportunity to glory in this role. William I had resisted the office, preferring what he considered the honest title of King of Prussia; Frederick III had no time to fulfill his dream of becoming a Charlemagne-like medieval emperor. William II, coming to the throne at twenty-nine, his head filled by Bismarck with notions of monarchical prerogative, was determined to invest the Imperial office with supreme power and brilliant prestige. He made plain from the beginning that his empire, the German Reich, was to be a military state; William II desired—even longed for—the approval and affection of his people, but ultimate power, he insisted, lay not in the people or their representatives in the Reichstag, but in the monarch loyally supported by the army. William's first proclamation, issued on the day of his father's death, was to the army: "So we are bound together—I and the army—so we are born for each other and will hold together indissolubly, whether it be the will of God to send us calm or storm." William repeatedly underscored this theme. In November 1891, he addressed a group of new soldiers being sworn in at Potsdam: "Recruits! You have sworn Me allegiance. That, children of My Guard, means that you are now My soldiers. You have given yourselves over to Me body and soul. There is only one enemy for you and that is My enemy. With the present Socialist agitation, it may be that I shall order you to shoot down your own families, your brothers, yes, your parents—which may God forbid—but then too you must follow my orders without a murmur." William's reign was filled with references to his own preeminence. "There is only one ruler in the Reich and I am he. I tolerate no other," he said in 1891. The sovereign, he told a military banquet in 1897, bears a "terrible responsibility to the Creator alone, from which no man, no minister, no parliament, no nation, can free him." The Reichstag, accordingly, was an object of contempt; Social Democrats were "enemies of the Empire and Fatherland . . . a gang of traitors." In 1903, he told

Bülow that he had no interest in the strength of different parties in the parliament, saying that it was all the same to him "whether red, black or yellow monkeys cavorted in the Reichstag cage." When shown the house of a native king at a colonial exhibition with the skulls of his enemies stuck up on poles outside it, William exclaimed, "If only I could see the Reichstag strung up like that!"

William's attitude towards England continued ambivalent. He oscillated between powerful attraction—"I adore England," he said in 1911 to Theodore Roosevelt—and petulant grievance which came close to hate. He wished to be understood and accepted as an English gentleman and, at the same time, feared as a Prussian warlord. He worked hard for British respect and his frequent failure caused him perplexity and irritation: "Not one of your ministers can tell me how many ships of the line you have in your Navy," he said to an English visitor. "I can tell him—he can't tell me." Part of the problem was the intensity of William's effort. Englishmen preferred understatement; the German Emperor seemed flashy, operatic, unreliable, or—the Englishman's ultimate word of censure—tiresome.

William's feeling about England centered on the British royal family, of which he felt himself a part—as much a member of the House of Windsor as of the House of Hohenzollern. When angry at his British relatives, he described them as "the damned family." His greatest respect was accorded his grandmother; his mother and his Uncle Bertie stirred mixed emotions. On assuming the throne, William could relegate his antagonism towards his mother to the past; Vicky's opinions no longer mattered. But his uncle, the Prince of Wales, could not so easily be set aside. He was the heir to a mighty throne; despite his flaws, the toast of Europe; and an uncle with eighteen years' seniority in age. William admired and was jealous of his uncle. Bertie managed, seemingly spontaneously, to please; if he did not, he did not care. William, caring desperately, tried too hard. Bertie looked down on William and William's country as pushy and parvenu, and William knew it. Each was cutting in private about the other: "William the Great needs to learn that he is living at the end of the nineteenth century and not in the Middle Ages," said Bertie on one occasion. "Willy is a bully and most bullies, when tackled, are cowards," he said on another. His nephew, he often announced, was "the most brilliant failure in history." William responded. His uncle, he said, is "an old peacock." "He is a Satan," he told his staff, "you can hardly believe what a Satan he is." Unsurprisingly, on both sides these words traveled far.

Early in his reign, William's decision to eschew a period of mourning for his father and to plunge immediately in the summer of

1888 into a round of visits to foreign capitals involved him in a flagrant snub of the Prince of Wales. The new Kaiser, after visiting St. Petersburg, next invited himself to Vienna. As it happened, the Prince already had been asked to Austria-Hungary during the same period. Bertie, on hearing of William's plans, wrote amicably to his nephew that he looked forward to seeing him in Vienna and would meet the Kaiser's train at the railway station wearing a Prussian uniform. William did not reply. The Prince, on arriving in Vienna, was told by an embarrassed Austrian Emperor that the Kaiser had insisted that no royal guest other than himself be present in Vienna during his stay; the Prince, accordingly, withdrew to Romania during the eight days of the Kaiser's visit. The day after his nephew left Austria, Bertie returned to Vienna to complete his visit.

Europe buzzed with accounts of the Prince's humiliation. Lord Salisbury summoned Count Hatzfeldt, the German Ambassador in London. The Ambassador offered the excuse that the Prince of Wales' presence at the time of the Kaiser's visit might have alarmed the Russians. Hatzfeldt also suggested that the Kaiser worried that the Prince would treat him "as an uncle treats a nephew, instead of recognizing that he was an emperor." Salisbury, attempting to put the incident in perspective, proposed that "discussions of this kind on personal questions, whatever we might feel about them, would not affect the general policy of the two nations." Hatzfeldt agreed.

Queen Victoria was enraged by her grandson's behavior. "As regarding the Prince's not treating his nephew as Emperor, this is really too vulgar and too absurd, as well as untrue, almost to be believed," she wrote to Lord Salisbury. "We have always been very intimate with our grandson and nephew, and to pretend that he is to be treated in private as well as in public as 'his Imperial Majesty' is perfect madness! He has been treated just as we should have treated his beloved father. . . . If he has such notions, he better never come here. The Queen will not swallow this affront. . . . William . . . also said . . . that, if his uncle wrote him a very kind letter, he might perhaps answer it!! All this shows a very unhealthy and un-natural state of mind; and he must be made to feel that his grand-mother and uncle will not stand such insolence. The Prince of Wales must not submit to such treatment. As regards the political relations of the two governments, the Queen quite agrees that that should not be affected (if possible) by these miserable personal quarrels; but the Queen much fears that with such a hot-headed, conceited, and wrong-headed young man, devoid of all feeling, this may at ANY moment become impossible."

William, in his new role as Kaiser, was anxious to visit England.

Salisbury warned Hatzfeldt that until the Vienna episode had been resolved, no invitation would be forthcoming. The Prince of Wales, to facilitate peace, asked his brother-in-law, Prince Christian of Denmark, to invite William to express his regrets in writing so that the English visit could be scheduled. "Most sincerely do I hope," Bertie wrote to Lord Salisbury, "that the young Emperor will accept the olive branch I offer him." The Kaiser refused. The Queen, now trying to achieve harmony, asked William "how this mistake could have arisen." "The whole affair is absolutely invented," William replied, "there not being an atom of cause to be found. The whole thing . . . originated either in Uncle Bertie's imagination or in somebody else's. Who put it into his head?" The Queen nevertheless decided to terminate the quarrel and wrote to William that he could come to England but must try not to offend his uncle again. William blandly replied, "I am happy to see that you regard the Vienna affair as concluded, in which I happily concur; I shall be happy to meet Uncle Bertie at Osborne."

Queen Victoria, in preparation for her grandson's first Imperial visit to England, and aware of his interest in the Royal Navy, decided to make him an honorary Admiral of the Fleet. William received the news with delight. "Fancy wearing the same uniform as St. Vincent and Nelson," he told the British Ambassador in Berlin. "It is enough to make one giddy." The commission, presented in August 1889 aboard the royal yacht *Victoria and Albert,* restored the Kaiser's admiration for England, and he returned to Germany glowing with warm feelings about his grandmother's country and his English relatives. "I now am able to feel and take interest in your fleet as if it were my own," he wrote to the Queen, "and with keenest sympathy shall I watch every phase of its further development knowing that the British ironclads, coupled with mine and my army, are the strongest guarantees of peace. . . . Should, however, the Will of Providence lay the heavy burden on us of fighting for our homes and destinies, then may the British fleet be seen forging ahead side by side with the German, and the 'Red Coat' marching to victory with the 'Pomeranian Grenadier'!!"

Vicky, a Dowager Empress at forty-seven, now had no influence on her son. Visiting Munich, the Kaiser wrote in the city's visitors' book: "Suprema lex regis voluntas est" ("The King's will is the highest law"). His mother, appalled, wrote to Queen Victoria, "A Tsar, an infallible Pope—the Bourbons—our poor Charles I—might have written such a sentence, but a constitutional monarch in the

19th century!!! So young a man—the son of his father—and your grandson—not to speak of a child of mine—should neither have nor express such a maxim!" She felt isolated and ignored. "William never comes and I am taken no notice of," she wrote in the summer of her husband's death. "Of course, it would be far better for me to go away from Berlin and not return, but I cannot be banished from the spot where my darling husband and two sweet children lie buried, nor leave the house for good and all where we spent so many years together, and where now recollections haunt every nook and cranny. . . . Besides, it would look as if I were afraid of them— William and Dona—if I gave up my rights."

In the autumn, Vicky turned over the New Palace to William and departed, first for England, where she spent three months with Queen Victoria, then for Kronberg near Frankfurt, where she purchased a small estate and built a private house in the style of an English country manor. She called it Friedrichshof and emblazoned on its front the inscription FREDERICI MEMORIAE. She continued, from afar, to disapprove of her son. "William is as blind and green, wrong-headed and violent on politics as can be," she wrote to England. "He is a big baby. . . . I wish I could put a padlock on his mouth for all occasions where speeches are made in public." William—now that he was Kaiser—adopted a more relaxed attitude towards his mother and her strictures. "My mother and I have the same characters," he said amiably to the British Ambassador. "I have inherited hers. That good, stubborn English blood which will not give way is in both our veins. The consequence is that, if we do not happen to agree, the situation becomes difficult."

Vicky outlived her husband by thirteen years. In November 1899, at fifty-nine, the Dowager Empress began to complain about "this awful lumbago . . . the constant pain." It was cancer of the spine. Her brother Alfred, Duke of Saxe-Coburg, former Duke of Edinburgh, died of cancer in July 1900; Vicky followed in August 1901. Near the end, her brother, now King Edward VII, came to visit, bringing with him English doctors who recommended more intensive doses of morphine to dull her pain. The German doctors resisted and again there was a medical confrontation across a sickbed. When his mother died, William repeated his performance at the death of his father: the house was sealed off and the rooms searched for the deceased's private papers. Again, Vicky outwitted him. All her letters and papers had been sent secretly back to England in the luggage of Sir Frederick Ponsonby, King Edward's private secretary. The morning after her death, the Kaiser, walking in the garden with Bülow, told the Chancellor that his mother had wished to be buried in England but that he could not permit this offense to German dignity. He did, however, endorse her other final wish, and her body, before being laid in the coffin, was wrapped unclothed in the English flag.

On March 18, 1890, the Kaiser summoned his senior generals and revealed the name of Bismarck's successor. The new Chancellor of the Empire and Minister-President of Prussia was to be General of Infantry Georg Leo von Caprivi, former State Secretary of the Imperial Navy, currently serving as commander of the Tenth Corps in Hanover. Caprivi, fifty-nine, was the model Prussian officer. He lived a Spartan life, had never married, did not smoke, and had few intimate friends and few enemies. He read history and spoke fluent English. His movements were quiet, his manner open and friendly, his language sensible. With a large round head, fringe of white hair, and sweeping mustache, he was, *The Times* told its readers, "a typical Teuton of the hugest and most impressive type. He might very well pass for a brother, or even a double of Prince Bismarck himself."

Caprivi, although of noble birth, possessed not an acre of land and prided himself on having managed for forty years on his army salary. He was born in 1831 into a family which mingled Italian, Slav, and Hungarian with Prussian blood and which had only recently acquired the noble "von." In 1849, at eighteen, he entered the army. He steadily climbed the ladder and established a reputation as a military administrator. In 1882, he was placed in charge of the German Navy, succeeding General Albrecht von Stosch. Caprivi had no interest in naval affairs and did not know the names of his officers or the emblems of rank on the uniforms they wore, but he accepted the assignment, which he performed for six years. Convinced that a war on two fronts against Russia and France was near (Bismarck had never troubled to reveal his secret Reinsurance Treaty with Russia to his Navy Minister), Caprivi chose the torpedo boat as the best and least expensive weapon to use against the Russian and French navies. Kaiser William II did not appreciate torpedo boats; he had no wish to appear at Cowes among his grandmother's huge battleships at the head of a squadron of small torpedo boats. Immediately after his accession, he began to interfere at the Admiralty. In July 1888, Caprivi resigned in protest and went back to the army.

Bismarck's dismissal signaled that the new Kaiser was unwilling to tolerate such a concentration of power outside the monarchy.

Why, then, did William, who wanted to be his own Chancellor, choose a general noted for his independence? And why did Caprivi, who already had left the navy because he didn't like the Emperor's interference, accept the assignment? William's reasons were pragmatic: he needed time to stabilize the state, and an honorable and unambitious Chancellor to administer the government. As the army was the strongest force in the Reich, the new Chancellor must be a general. Caprivi was the general with the most political experience; already, as State Secretary of the Navy, he had appeared before the Reichstag. If he was stubborn, he also was intensely loyal. No one expected the new Chancellor to remain in office long. Waldersee, the new Army Chief of Staff, who was ambitious to become Chancellor, did not envy Caprivi. "First, at least one successor to Bismarck must discredit himself," he confided to a friend. "Then perhaps one could be persuaded." Caprivi's reason for becoming Chancellor was simple: his monarch, the King of Prussia, had commanded him. He had no illusions about what it would mean to follow Bismarck. Once, walking past the Chancellor's Palace when Bismarck was still within, Caprivi had asked a friend, "What kind of a jackass would dare to be Bismarck's successor?" Caprivi left the army reluctantly. On his last evening with his officers in Hanover, he told them, "I know that I shall be covered with mud, that I shall fall ingloriously." His consolation, he said, was his belief that his army comrades would always remember him as a decent fellow.

When Caprivi first took office, he seemed to please everyone. Even Bismarck conditionally approved. "If anything can lighten for me the oppressiveness of this moment, it is the fact that you are to be my successor," he told Caprivi on the day he left the Wilhelmstrasse. "We are getting on well with Caprivi," William wrote to Queen Victoria on Christmas Day, 1890. "He is already adored by friends and revered by the opposition. I think he is one of the finest characters Germany ever produced." To the Emperor Franz Josef, William wrote that his new Chancellor was, "after Bismarck, the greatest German we possess, truly devoted to Me, and with a rock-ribbed character." Politically, the Kaiser positioned himself behind Caprivi. "If the Chancellor demands anyone's dismissal . . . [that person] must go, even if I myself like him."

Caprivi's purpose and style in administering the government were different from Bismarck's. His intention was "to lead the nation back to an everyday existence after the bygone epoch of great men and great events." In Bismarck's Reich, all the disparate, fractious elements of the state pivoted on the office and personality of the Iron Chancellor. Over the years, Bismarck had created a network of Prussian ministers, imperial state secretaries, and diplomats, subject to his autocratic whim, all instruments for carrying out his will. Now his sudden disappearance threw this balanced machinery into disarray. On his first visit to the capital after Bismarck's fall, Prince Hohenlohe, Governor General of Alsace, noted that "previously, independent statesmen were shriveled and dominated by the authority of Prince Bismarck. Now each personality is conscious of his own value. They have all swelled out like sponges placed in water."

Caprivi belonged to no political party. As Navy State Secretary, he had been on good terms with all parties in the Reichstag and his approach to that body, now that he was Chancellor, was moderate and conciliatory. He disdained Bismarck's policy of dividing the deputies into categories of "friends of the Reich" and "enemies of the Reich." Caprivi promised the deputies that he would "take the good wherever and from whomever it may come." The new Chancellor rescinded Bismarck's revival of the Cabinet Order of 1852, which forbade any direct contact, personal or written, between the monarch and individual ministers. As Chancellor, Caprivi no longer demanded the right to be present at every meeting between the Kaiser and other ministers. Further, Caprivi wished both the imperial state secretaries and the Prussian ministers to meet collectively and take decisions jointly in the manner of Western cabinets.

Caprivi's deliberate erosion of the Chancellor's office disturbed many government officials. They were accustomed to Bismarck's duplicity; Caprivi's attempt to introduce straightforwardness and simplicity seemed naïve. His innocence was widely remarked upon: on taking office, he had instructed the Foreign Office to trouble him after five P.M. only in case of real emergency; a few months later, when he announced that he would be working regularly until ten P.M., experienced officials smiled knowingly. Caprivi's unfamiliarity with the traditional workings of the Reich government extended to matters more serious than the hours of work. He knew little about Germany's relations with other powers and he did not speak the artful language of professional diplomacy. General of Infantry Caprivi, honest and blunt, wanted everything in plain view. Foreign Ministry officials disparaged him. "Caprivi has an absolutely stupid lack of knowledge in non-military matters," declared one German diplomat. "One might just as well make any good battalion commander Chancellor." Alfred von Kiderlen-Waechter, a counselor in the Political Section of the Foreign Ministry, observed more gently, "A horse which has done well out of doors is not one to be stabled."

■ ■ ■

Within a week of becoming Chancellor, Caprivi made the most significant foreign-policy decision of his term in office. The cornerstone
of Bismarck's Continental diplomacy had been the isolation of
France. To enforce this outcast status on France and to control conflicting Russian and Austrian ambitions in the Balkans, Bismarck
had followed the signing of his public treaty with Austria in 1887
with the conclusion of the secret Reinsurance Treaty with Russia.
On June 18, 1890, the three-year Reinsurance Treaty was due to
expire. Russia had warned that she could not allow herself to be
isolated as France had been. If Germany did not wish to continue
the alliance, warned Nicholas Giers, the Russian Foreign Minister,
the Tsar "would be forced, against his own convictions, to ally himself with the French Republic."

Negotiations for renewal had begun with Bismarck in February
1890. On March 17, the Russian ambassador to Germany, Count
Paul Shuvalov, returned to Berlin from St. Petersburg to confront
the final Bismarck crisis. On the night of March 20, Count Shuvalov
was pulled from his bed to be told that the Kaiser wished to see him
early in the morning. At this audience, William assured the ambassador that Bismarck's departure meant no change in German policies and that he, the Emperor, guaranteed renewal of the
Reinsurance Treaty. "I beg you to tell His Majesty [the Tsar] that
on my part I am entirely disposed to renew our agreement and that
my foreign policy will remain the same as it was in the time of my
grandfather," he said. Shuvalov, elated, cabled the news to St. Petersburg, where Alexander III noted on the margin of his Ambassador's report: "Nothing more satisfactory could be looked for. . . .
Entirely reassuring."

In the meantime, General Caprivi, knowing nothing of either
the Reinsurance Treaty or the Kaiser's assurances to Shuvalov, assumed the office of Chancellor. Caprivi had already admitted that
on questions of foreign policy he felt as if he had entered a dark
room. No successor to Bismarck would ever inspire the same blend
of fear and trust which Germany and Europe had given the Iron
Chancellor. His policy, therefore, would be one of openness and he
would be guided in practical details by his Foreign Ministry.

This office, however, also was in new hands. Three days after
Otto von Bismarck's resignation, Herbert von Bismarck had resigned as State Secretary for Foreign Affairs. The Kaiser and the
new Chancellor desperately needed a replacement. Holstein had
been proposed; he had brushed the offer aside, but used the oppor-

tunity to present his candidate, Baron Adolf Marschall von Bieberstein, the Ambassador of the Grand Duchy of Baden in Berlin.
Marschall, bulky and stooping, his face scarred by saber wounds
inflicted in student duels, a lawyer who had no diplomatic experience beyond representing his Grand Duke in the Imperial capital,
was appointed.

Because Marschall was new, it was Holstein who turned up at
Caprivi's door bringing a document which he urgently advised the
new Chancellor to read. It was the Reinsurance Treaty. The Russian
Ambassador, Holstein informed Caprivi, was waiting to begin negotiations. Caprivi asked Holstein's opinion. After having had Bismarck ignore his advice about Russia for five years, Holstein,
pleased to be consulted, strongly counselled letting the Treaty lapse.
Russia, whether in opposition to Germany or in alliance with her,
Holstein explained, posed a continuing threat. In order to oppose
this threat, Germany must have the support of Austria. And if Austria were to learn of the Reinsurance Treaty, the Austro-German
treaty would be undermined. On the other hand, in alliance with
Russia, there was a chance that Germany might be dragged into a
war between Russia and England. Marschall, under Holstein's influence, concurred. The German Ambassador to Russia, General von
Schweinitz, who also happened to be in Berlin, was consulted. He
supported Holstein, stressing the need to avoid misunderstanding
with Austria. If the existence of the Reinsurance Treaty leaked out,
Schweinitz said, the alliance with Vienna would not survive. "If Bismarck were still at the helm," Schweinitz said bluntly, "I would
advise that the Treaty be renewed. Under the changed circumstances, it would be dangerous to pursue such an ambiguous policy."
Caprivi was not offended by this statement; it was precisely his view.
"Bismarck was able to juggle with three balls. I can only juggle with
two," he said. The decision of the Chancellor and his advisors was
unanimous against renewal of the Reinsurance Treaty and in favor
of a "simple and transparent" foreign policy.

That afternoon, Caprivi and Schweinitz went to see the Kaiser.
Caprivi described the morning discussion and reported that he
would be unable to reconcile the Reinsurance Treaty with the treaty
with Austria. William asked the Ambassador's opinion. Schweinitz
supported the Chancellor and suggested that so noble a monarch as
William II would not wish exposure as being disloyal to his venerable colleague, the Emperor Franz Josef. William listened silently,
then stood up and declared, "Well, then, it can't be done whether I
like it or not." He said nothing about his personal guarantee to
Shuvalov that the treaty would be renewed.

The following day, Schweinitz called on Shuvalov, still euphoric over the Kaiser's promise, and told him that the decision had been reversed. Shuvalov, dumbfounded, then described his earlier meeting with William. Schweinitz, astonished in turn, quickly returned to Caprivi, who requested an immediate audience with the Emperor. William, confronting the distressed Chancellor, had created a crisis within a crisis. Rid of Bismarck little more than a week, free to rule as well as reign, he already had created an impossible situation. Either he must rebuff Shuvalov, Giers, and the Tsar and break the secret tie with Germany's eastern neighbor, or he had to dismiss his Chancellor of one week. William decided in favor of Caprivi and against Russia.

Schweinitz was dispatched to St. Petersburg to soothe the Russians. His task was difficult; Shuvalov could not forget William's promise: "One thing was said and another done," he complained. Stripped of Russia's only alliance, the Russian Foreign Ministry began to seek another. The events predicted by Bismarck and by Giers were not long in coming. On July 23, 1890, only four months after Germany's refusal to renew the Reinsurance Treaty, a French naval flotilla called at the Russian Baltic naval base of Kronstadt. Tsar Alexander III gave a dinner at Peterhof for the commander of the French squadron and stood bareheaded as a band played the "Marseillaise," the revolutionary anthem which had been prohibited within the borders of the Russian Empire. From Peterhof, Admiral Gervais, the French commander, went to Moscow, where he raised his glass and said, "I drink to Holy Moscow, the great Russian nation and its noble Tsar."

Caprivi knew from the beginning that the key to his Chancellorship would be his relationship with the young Emperor. People spoke "of the difficulties of my situation . . . at home and abroad," he told an acquaintance, "but the problem of which one speaks the least and the one which is the most fearful—not to say insurmountable—is that which comes from On High." At first, Caprivi managed to satisfy the Kaiser. As William had feared, an angry Bismarck had retaliated by giving interviews and writing articles, denying that he had resigned voluntarily and casting doubts on the Kaiser's competence. The new Chancellor considered it his duty to defend the monarch. Caprivi, believing that the Kaiser had been completely within his prerogative to dismiss Bismarck, regarded Bismarck's protests as improper and undignified.

It was as buffer as well as administrator that Caprivi made himself temporarily indispensable. Even when irritated by the unyielding old general, William restrained himself; he could not afford to dismiss a second Chancellor so soon after toppling Bismarck. Nevertheless, friction between the two was inevitable. In 1891, William, without consulting the Chancellor, drew up an Army Bill for submission to the Reichstag. Caprivi, offended by this lack of confidence, immediately wrote out his resignation. William withdrew the bill, but complained of his limited power. In private, William and his confidants, Philip von Eulenburg and Bernhard von Bülow, began to talk of the need for a coup which would strip the Reichstag of its power. (Kinderlen, who accompanied the Kaiser on his summer cruise to Norway in 1891, wondered how much of his master's bombast could be attributed to the new Imperial beard. "With a beard like this," Kiderlen heard William say on board the Hohenzollern, "you could thump on the table so hard that your ministers would fall down in fright and lie flat on their faces.")

Caprivi was not frightened. In March 1892, he resigned again, complaining that the Kaiser's interference made his work as Chancellor impossible. Caprivi's purpose was not to force William to modify his behavior; the Chancellor wished to leave office. Sensing this, William immediately backed down. "No, I would not dream of it," he scribbled on the Chancellor's request to resign. "It is not nice to drive the cart into the mud and leave the Kaiser sitting in it." Privately, William complained to his friends that Caprivi was becoming "a sensitive old fathead."

Caprivi's threats to resign increased the Kaiser's impatience. He complained to Philip von Eulenburg that he found it hard to deal with Caprivi's "indescribable obstinacy and . . . his unsuperable feeling that he is dealing with a very young man. He entirely overlooks the fact that I have acquired political judgement through my long association with Prince Bismarck and through my own experience." By the summer of 1893, William was covering Caprivi's memoranda with negative comments. "One can't get anywhere with these virtuous, hypocritical old bachelors," the Kaiser grumbled to a friend. Acknowledging that the Chancellor was completely honest and loyal, William decided the problem was a mismatch of personalities. "Caprivi, you get terribly on my nerves," the Kaiser told him one day. "Your Majesty, I have always been an uncomfortable subordinate," the Chancellor replied.

William persistently infringed on Caprivi's office. One day in 1893, an army captain, Natzmer, appeared in the Chancellor's office and announced that he was the newly appointed Governor of the German colony of Cameroon. Caprivi assumed that the man was deranged and attempted to calm him. But, as the officer described the events at a reception at the New Palace the previous night, culminating in the Kaiser's appointment of him to the vacant position, it became apparent that he was quite rational. Caprivi and Marschall drove together to Potsdam, where the Chancellor again raised the question of his constitutional responsibilities as head of the government. William capitulated and no more was heard of Captain Natzmer.

Episodes of this kind wearied Caprivi and he became increasingly anxious to escape. With every difference of opinion he tendered his resignation (during four and a half years as Chancellor, Caprivi offered or threatened to resign ten times). By early 1894, Eulenburg and Bülow were actively searching for another solution to the problem of the Kaiser's desire for personal rule. William talked about it openly. "For his successor, I shall take a younger man," he said. "Someone who will be closer to me personally and will not have any past experience to oppose me." Everyone in Berlin knew that Caprivi's days were numbered. Holstein remained loyal to the Chancellor to the end, but most politicians ignored Caprivi. At one dinner, the new Prussian Minister of War, General Walter Bronsart von Schellendorf, appointed to office without Caprivi's consent, publicly insulted, then turned his back on, the Imperial Chancellor. Caprivi understood. "My relations with the All Highest have become intolerable," he told a friend. "You just cannot imagine how relieved I will feel to get out of here." On October 26, 1894, he resigned. That night, he burned all his private papers in a Reichschancellory fireplace, and the following day he left for Montreux on Lake Geneva, where for many months he remained in seclusion. In the spring he returned to Germany and went to live with a nephew near Frankfurt on the Oder. There, in the midst of a deep pine forest, surrounded by grandnieces and grandnephews, he steadfastly refused all requests to speak or write about his career or his relationship with Bismarck or William II. "Nor would it do any good . . . rather harm," he said. "If unfavorable opinions of me grow out of . . . [this decision], I must bear it." Caprivi died in 1899.

"For his successor, I shall take a younger man," the Kaiser had announced as he prepared to replace sixty-three-year-old General Count Georg Leo von Caprivi. As it turned out, the third Chancellor of the German Empire, installed in October 1894, was Prince Chlodwig zu Hohenlohe who, on taking office, was seventy-five. Hohenlohe was not the Kaiser's first choice. William had had in mind someone like Bernhard von Bülow, the ambitious forty-five-year-old Ambassador to Romania who had been enthusiastically recommended by Philip von Eulenburg. Bülow was eager to be exactly what the Kaiser wanted—"some one closer to me . . . who will be mine alone"—but Eulenburg, William—and even Bülow—agreed that the time was not ripe. To present a façade of maturity and respectability, a man of more years would temporarily be necessary. Disappointed, the Kaiser had asked Eulenburg for suggestions. Eulenburg proposed Hohenlohe, a Bavarian Roman Catholic who had faithfully served Bismarck in the Diplomatic Service. The incumbent Governor General of the conquered provinces of Alsace-Lorraine was "a man neither conservative nor liberal, neither ritualist nor atheist, ultramontane nor progressive"—in short, a presentable stopgap who would not create conflict.

Hohenlohe stood at the summit of the German aristocracy. His brother Gustave, a cardinal, wielded great influence from his post in the Vatican. Hohenlohe's wife, a Russian, had possessed immense estates, which she had been forced to sell when she had married Hohenlohe, a foreigner. He was related to the House of Coburg and thus to the royal family of England, as well as to the House of Schleswig-Holstein, thereby to William II's wife, Dona. The Kaiser always referred to the new Chancellor as "Uncle," speaking to him with the familiar *du*.

Before the proclamation of the Empire, Hohenlohe had been Minister-President of Bavaria. In 1874, following the Franco-Prussian War, Bismarck appointed him Ambassador to Paris with instructions to do what he could to improve relations with the defeated nation. Hohenlohe managed adequately for eleven years, and his departure from Paris was a result not of any success or failure on his part, but of Herbert von Bismarck's ambition to become State Secretary. To make room at the top for Herbert, a number of ambassadorial appointments had to be reshuffled. "I've been trying to persuade my father for a year now to recall that hopeless idiot Hohenlohe from Paris," Herbert told Holstein in April 1885. "I'm vainly trying to persuade my father to dismiss this utterly incompetent Ambassador," he reported a few weeks later. Bismarck, persuaded by his son, suggested to Kaiser William I that Hohenlohe might move to Strasbourg to govern Alsace-Lorraine. The Kaiser approved, describing Hohenlohe as "a quiet man who never makes a mess of things." Holstein's opinion of Hohenlohe's abilities was not high. "The Chancellor will never send a man of outstanding intelligence to Strasbourg. . . . Hohenlohe [is] obviously elated.

. . . If only he knew that he was picked because they wanted a nonentity!''

Despite these unflattering assessments, Hohenlohe had served nine years in Strasbourg. When Kaiser William II asked him to become Chancellor, Hohenlohe was strongly disinclined and set down in writing the reasons he would be unsuitable:

1. Age, poor memory, illness
2. Poor public speaker
3. Unfamiliar with Prussian laws and politics
4. Not a soldier
5. Insufficient means. I could probably manage without the Governor General's salary, but not in Berlin. I shall be ruined.
6. My Russian connections
7. I have been in public life for thirty years, am seventy-five years old and do not wish to start something which I know will be too much for me.

These objections were overruled. Prince Hohenlohe was installed in office and served as Imperial Chancellor from 1894 to 1900.

Hohenlohe's appraisal of his talent as an orator was shared in the Reichstag. Deputies were shocked when they first saw "his shrunken figure with the head bent over to one side." The contrast with the first two chancellors, both tall, impressive men, was striking. His delivery of speeches was shy. When forced to parry an attack, he stammered out a few words read from a slip of paper handed to him by a subordinate. Hohenlohe himself was untroubled by these moments. "He felt such contempt for these parliamentary soap-boilers . . . [that] he came out of the Chamber in a pleasant, or at least a perfectly tranquil frame of mind," said a friend. His general conduct of the Chancellorship was equally weary. Under Caprivi, the power of the Imperial Chancellorship had declined; Hohenlohe made no attempt to restore it to its former state. He did not wish to quarrel with the Emperor, with ministers, secretaries, or departments, and he never threatened to resign. It was a point of pride with him that, although he was not a soldier like his predecessor, he—unlike Caprivi—did not threaten the Emperor with resignation over every minor difference.

This was why Hohenlohe lasted as long as he did. Having overthrown Bismarck and shed Caprivi, William, at thirty-five, felt ready to rule. Eulenburg, who had encouraged the Kaiser, wrote to Holstein in December 1894: "I am convinced that the Guiding Hand of Providence lies behind this elemental and natural drive of the Kaiser's to direct the affairs of the kingdom in person. Whether it will ruin us or save us I cannot say." Although William continued to treat the elderly Chancellor with respect in public and to call him "Uncle" in private, he began to intervene in domestic and foreign affairs to an extent unknown in Caprivi's time. Hohenlohe's indifference to, almost cynical acceptance of, this demeaned status increased the Kaiser's contempt and a cycle of humiliation began. In 1895, the Kaiser visited Bismarck at Friedrichsruh, an event of political significance; the Chancellor learned about it from the press. Hohenlohe, at Holstein's insistence, had retained Marschall as State Secretary for Foreign Affairs. The Kaiser despised Marschall and treated him with even greater disrespect than he displayed toward the Chancellor. In December 1895, the Kaiser told the British Military Attaché in Berlin, Colonel Swaine, that he suspected Britain and Russia of agreeing behind his back to an Anglo-Russian condominium over Constantinople and the Turkish Empire; he then telegraphed all German ambassadors to be on the lookout for evidence. Marschall and the Foreign Office learned of this conversation and message only by chance, from the coder who was sending it. Marschall was shaken by the episode. "Things are going badly with His Majesty," he wrote in his diary. "He interferes persistently in foreign policy. A monarch ought to have the last word, but His Majesty always wants to have the first, and this is a cardinal error."

Holstein understood the relationship between the Kaiser's absolutist beliefs and impulsive behavior in domestic policy, and his intervention in foreign policy. "Domestic politics make more noise," he wrote to Marschall, "but the other is much more dangerous. The fact that H.M. is now mixing into that, fresh from the smoking room, may have consequences which will astound both him and yourself." Hoping to block or at least to moderate the Kaiser's intrusions, Holstein sat in his office writing letters. He wrote to Hohenlohe asking the Chancellor to resist the monarch's more extravagant demands by employing the threat of resignation, at least occasionally. He wrote to Eulenburg and Bülow that he worried that the Kaiser's reach for absolute power, unchecked by the Reichstag, and unguided by cautionary advice from a respected Chancellor, would lead Germany to disaster. Initially, he believed that he could enlist Eulenburg. "Hohenlohe's back must be stiffened," Holstein wrote to Eulenburg. "In Hohenlohe's great compliance lies the overwhelming danger for the Kaiser, for it will actually strengthen his arbitrary tendencies. . . . When you deal with Hohenlohe, you must make a new man of him; you must advise him that . . . he must play the Chancellor of the Reich in dealing with the Kaiser. In reality, the old gentleman now behaves as though he were the second High Chamberlain of the Family." On Christmas Day, 1895, Holstein appealed to Eulenburg again. The Chancellor must "make one last, vigorous effort to bring about a change," by threatening to resign. "Remember that without this bitter medicine both the Kaiser and the Fatherland will meet with serious trouble. . . . 'The Kaiser as his own Chancellor' is a dangerous principle at the best of times. It is quite impossible with this impulsive and unhappily completely superficial ruler who has not the slightest idea of constitutional law, of political events, of diplomatic history and of how to deal with people." Receiving these letters, Eulenburg noted wryly of the writer: "The Holstein of 1888, with his old Prussian loyalty to the Monarch, has certainly not turned in 1896 into an anti-monarchist, but he has become a parliamentarian."

Holstein's letters had little effect; Hohenlohe grew steadily weaker. Occasionally, he tried to moderate the Kaiser's behavior: in March 1897, he wrote to William that the appointment of a committee on which the Kaiser had set his heart would be a diminution of the constitutional office of the Chancellor. "I know no constitution," William shouted. "I only know what I will." Hohenlohe, for once, argued back. "I felt it was my official responsibility, as Your Majesty's supreme adviser, to express my view frankly," he wrote to William. Preparing for his next audience with the Emperor, Hohenlohe decided to say: "If the word 'constitutional' gave offense, I regret that Your Majesty is not the Emperor of Russia. I am not the author of the constitution, but I am bound by it."

William began talking of a coup d'état against the parliament. Waldersee, the former Chief of the Army General Staff, was summoned and told to be ready to assume the Chancellorship from Hohenlohe. "I know that you will do the job well if shooting becomes necessary," William said to Waldersee. Hohenlohe understood his own position. "If the Kaiser wants to be his own Reich Chancellor, he will have to appoint a straw doll. I have no desire to be one," he wrote. "If I cannot get the Kaiser's consent to measures I regard as necessary, then I have no authority. . . . I cannot govern against public opinion as well as against the Kaiser. To govern against the Kaiser and the public is to hang in mid-air. That is impossible."

Nevertheless, Hohenlohe remained. For the next three years, 1897–1900, William enjoyed the personal rule he had always sought.

He dictated policy and supervised the preparation of legislation, sometimes even drafting bills himself. Hohenlohe, uninformed and uninvolved, was asked only to place his signature on state documents. Bülow, in 1898, described the Chancellor as "almost eighty years old, tired, ill, totally indolent, and completely passive."

CHAPTER 6

"The
Monster
of the Labyrinth"

◆

For sixteen years, from the fall of Bismarck in 1890 to his own forced retirement in 1906, Friedrich von Holstein played a principal role in making German foreign policy. Working beneath the surface at the Wilhelmstrasse, he was known as the "Éminence Grise," the "Empire Jesuit," and the "Monster of the Labyrinth." Holstein preferred this anonymity. Twice, he refused elevation to State Secretary; it would have meant wasting time before the Reichstag, seeing foreign ambassadors, and consorting with men who could not comprehend the intricacy and beauty of the diplomatic web he was constantly, obsessively spinning. In all his years as *Geheimrat* (First Counselor) of the Political Department of the Foreign Ministry, Friedrich von Holstein met his sovereign, Kaiser William II, only twice.

Holstein had a melancholy childhood. Born in 1837 in Pomerania, he was the son of a Prussian nobleman and retired officer, who, having married into a wealthy family and lost his wife, then married the elder sister of his dead spouse. It was this second wife who at the age of forty-six gave birth to Fritz, her only child. Fritz's mother became obsessive about his safety. During the revolutionary year of 1848, she took him out of Germany to protect him. He traveled with her and a tutor to France, Switzerland, and Italy, perfecting his mastery of French and Italian. At fifteen, he entered Berlin University to study law. After graduation, he applied for an army commission. He was rejected because of a "weak chest and general bodily weakness." Humiliated, Holstein enrolled in the Prussian Civil Service.

In 1859, citing his skill at languages, Holstein applied for a transfer from the Civil Service to the Prussian Diplomatic Service. Bismarck, who had known his father, stepped in and arranged that Holstein be appointed attaché to the Prussian Ministry in St. Petersburg where Bismarck himself was Minister. Setting off by train in December 1860, Holstein endured three days in a sleigh when his train was blocked by snow. In the ice-bound capital on the Neva, Bismarck, "tall, erect, and unsmiling . . . slightly bald with fair hair turning grey, sallow and not yet corpulent," held out his hand and said, "You are welcome."

Johanna von Bismarck immediately took the shy, awkward young man into her family, and Holstein was able to observe his patron at close range. Bismarck, although he lived simply, eschewing the court, society, and his fellow diplomats, behaved always as a man of importance. Returning to town one day from the Tsar's suburban palace at Peterhof, Bismarck and Holstein arrived at the station as the train was about to leave. Seeing them, the trainmen shouted, "Hurry up!" and Holstein instinctively broke into a run. Reaching the carriage door, he looked behind and saw Bismarck, still some distance away, approaching with a slow and dignified tread. The train waited. Climbing aboard, Bismarck said, "I'd rather be late ten times over than have to run once."

Holstein was miserable in St. Petersburg. Awkward, vain, and sensitive, he had never shared the camaraderie of regimental life common to most German, Russian, and other diplomats. He had little interest in women and light conversation, and did not blend into society. He came to dislike Russians, and his experience in the Tsar's capital produced a lifelong antipathy to Russia. Leaving St. Petersburg, Holstein was sent to posts he preferred: Rio de Janeiro (on leave, he explored the jungle of the Amazon), Washington (from which he went west and hunted buffalo on the Great Plains), Florence, and Copenhagen. In 1871, he was again on Bismarck's staff; this time in Versailles while German artillery hammered Paris and the Chancellor prepared to make peace with France and proclaim the German Empire. When peace came, Holstein—because of his familiarity with the treaty terms and his impeccable French—remained in Paris as Second Secretary of the German Embassy.

Here, he became caught in a scandal which affected his career. Bismarck was jealous of the ability and popularity of Count Harry von Arnim, the German Ambassador to Paris. Fearing that Arnim might one day be summoned home to replace him as Chancellor, Bismarck decided to remove this potential rival. Secretly, he assigned Holstein to find evidence of wrongdoing on Arnim's part. Holstein found his ambassador's signature on a payment of funds to a newspaper to run anti-Bismarck articles. He also discovered that Arnim had improperly removed a number of state documents from the Embassy. On a visit to Berlin, Arnim was arrested. At Arnim's trial, Holstein was required to testify against his former chief. Arnim fought vigorously, supported by many members of the Prussian nobility. Convicted and sentenced to a year in prison, Arnim escaped to Switzerland, from where he launched a virulent attack on Bismarck and Holstein. Berlin society, unable to make explicit its feelings against the Chancellor, heaped wrath on Holstein and boycotted him from fashionable life. Holstein withdrew, permanently and absolutely, into his work. In 1876, he returned from Paris and settled behind a desk at No. 76 Wilhelmstrasse.

Holstein's capacity for work was exceptional even by Prussian standards. From eight A.M. until late at night, he sat at his desk, tirelessly reading files and incoming memoranda, remembering everything, committing his thoughts to paper in the form of analysis, suggestions, corrections, and comprehensive, malicious gossip.

He remained Bismarck's man. Bismarck had given him his start in the Diplomatic Service, Bismarck had used him in the Arnim affair, Bismarck brought him back to Berlin in 1876, and now Bismarck made Holstein his private listening post and backstairs operator at the Foreign Office. Holstein performed this service eagerly. He was devoted to the Chancellor, whom in his journals he called "The Chief." He also served as Bismarck's private secretary during extended visits at the Chancellor's country estates, where he resumed his St. Petersburg role in the family as "Faithful Fritz." He was one of the few men who never bored the Chancellor. Holstein knew when to speak and when to keep quiet. When he spoke, it was in stimulating, pithy language. When he wished, he could draw on a spiteful and petty sense of humor which Bismarck enjoyed. On these visits, Holstein renewed his acquaintance with the Chancellor's sons, Herbert and Bill, whom he had known as adolescents in St. Petersburg and who now alternated with Holstein as their father's personal secretary. Holstein's friendship with Herbert became particularly close.

Holstein's position as Bismarck's favorite was an open secret at the Foreign Office, although the extent to which he enjoyed the Chancellor's confidence and the ways in which he earned further confidence revealed themselves only gradually. Beginning in the early 1880s, Bismarck authorized him to carry on an extensive private correspondence, dealing directly with ambassadors, ministers, and others in German embassies around the world, enabling him to provide the Chancellor (and himself) with political and personal information which did not find its way into official diplomatic communications. Year after year, his private letters and telegrams— clever, analytical, probing—went out to embassies in London, Paris, St. Petersburg, Vienna, and Constantinople. The responses kept Holstein well informed of the talents and personal shortcomings of every member of the Diplomatic Corps, from veteran ambassadors to youthful attachés. Holstein carefully directed incoming information to points where it would do him the most good.

Holstein's special position was unaffected by the superior office of State Secretary. In 1881, Holstein's friend Paul von Hatzfeldt, whom Holstein described as "incredibly able intellectually, but . . . a weak nature destined to be dominated," became State Secretary; Holstein was his principal advisor. In fact, in those years neither Hatzfeldt nor Holstein conceived German foreign policy; that was the prerogative of Bismarck whether he sat in the Chancellor's Palace in Berlin or wandered among his oaks at Varzin. As Bismarck's health declined after 1883 and his retreats to the country were prolonged, Holstein's power increased. Because Bismarck rarely set foot in No. 76 Wilhelmstrasse, the presence of Holstein, the trusted agent, his suspicious eye watching every movement, was all the more valuable. From the beginning, Bismarck brushed off criticism of Holstein. "He is very sensitive," the Chancellor told an earlier State Secretary, the elder Bernhard von Bülow. "I owe him many a useful warning, many a clever idea, and many a piece of good advice." Later, when an important German diplomat complained about having to deal with Holstein, Prince Bismarck had told him coldly, "I see. Then I cannot help you. I must have one man on whom I can depend entirely and that is Holstein." Herbert Bismarck shared his father's warm appraisal of "Faithful Fritz." Bill Bismarck, the Chancellor's younger son, was more skeptical. "You want to know what I think of Holstein?" he once replied to a question from the younger Bernhard von Bülow. "Well, that's a complicated matter. Father thinks him exceptionally useful and places implicit faith in him. Mother spoils him and gives him the best bits at the table. As for me, I don't deny his great talent, nor his brilliant French and English, or his quickness and cleverness. . . . But there are two things which do not please me about him. He suffers from an almost pathological delusion of persecution. As he is very sensitive and suspicious, this delusion is constantly finding new fuel. And so he is always stirring up my father who, in any case, is suspicious enough and always irritable with people. . . ."

When Herbert Bismarck became State Secretary in 1885, Holstein's special status and warm relationship with the Bismarcks, father and son, did not change. He continued to occupy an office adjoining that of the State Secretary, wading through a sea of reports from embassies and legations, writing his own memoranda, appearing unbidden, at his own discretion, through a private, unlocked door, at Herbert's desk. As time went on, Holstein's daily contact with Herbert made him increasingly critical of his old friend's arrogant, boorish behavior.

Holstein's defense against those with whom he felt uncomfortable was to withdraw. After Herbert's rifle-shooting incident in the garden of the Reichschancellory, Holstein wrote to a cousin: "I have described this scene . . . because it explains to you a good deal about myself. . . . With rough types like Herbert and his family, there is only one way of avoiding the alternative between degradation and conflict, namely to withdraw on one's own accord. That is what I have done, and at first it gave me rather a jolt. But when I see how others are treated I am glad I made a clean break. I hardly think that he would shoot through *my* window."

Gradually, the First Counselor began to oppose the Chancellor's conduct of foreign policy. Bismarck's policy had always been to keep in step with Russia; Herbert was encouraging this relationship to an extent which Holstein thought dangerous. Since his days in St. Petersburg, Holstein had not liked Russians. Now he felt that expansion of Russian power and increase in Russian prestige must be prevented. He urged maximum support of Austria. Through Hatzfeldt, who had been transferred to London, he tried to stir up British antagonism toward Russia. At first, Holstein refused to admit even to himself that he was attempting to thwart the Chancellor's policy. His explanation was that he was simply establishing a counterweight to Herbert's excessive pro-Russianism and that he, not Herbert, was conducting policy in accordance with the real intentions of the Chancellor. "I have sometimes gone beyond the intentions of the Big Chief, have occasionally even used *my* ways of reaching *his* goals," he told his journal. But by early 1886, with Herbert in the State Secretaryship, Holstein was alarmed. "For the first time in twenty-five years, I mistrust Bismarck's foreign policy," he wrote on January 13, 1886. "The old man is led by his son and the son is led by vanity and the Russian embassy." Holstein vigorously opposed the secret Reinsurance Treaty of 1887, concluded with Tsar

Alexander III behind the backs of the Austrian Emperor, the German Reichstag, and the Foreign Office bureaucracy. To Holstein, this network of interlocking alliances stemmed primarily from an old man's love of intrigue. Holstein's opposition was not hidden from either Bismarck, but father and son both believed that, whatever his opinions on policy, "Faithful Fritz" would continue personally loyal. When the younger Bülow once asked Herbert how he could tolerate Holstein's anti-Russian prejudice, Herbert smiled and said, "Holstein has once and for all a jester's privilege."

Holstein foresaw the coming clash between the restless young Kaiser William and the aging Chancellor. Increasingly, the calculating First Counselor began to correspond with Count Philip von Eulenburg, the Kaiser's friend. Through Eulenburg, he also was linked with young Bernhard von Bülow, son of the former State Secretary of the 1870s. By the time Bismarck fell, Holstein had made his own arrangements. He was offered the State Secretaryship and turned it down; he proposed Marschall instead. There were objections that with a new and inexperienced Chancellor and a new and inexperienced State Secretary, German foreign policy would founder. Holstein assured all worriers that the foreign policy of the Empire was in safe and experienced hands. He meant his own.

Neither Caprivi nor Marschall spoke French, the universal language of diplomacy, and they could not communicate easily with foreign ambassadors. Caprivi was honest and stubborn and Marschall gradually acquired confidence, but even two years later, in 1892, the Austrian Ambassador declared that without Holstein's approval, neither Chancellor nor Foreign Minister would make a move.

The decision not to renew the Reinsurance Treaty, the capstone of Bismarck's great arch of secret diplomacy, threw the retired Chancellor into a rage. The result, he predicted accurately, would be to force an isolated Russia into the arms of an isolated France. Within his circle, he rumbled threats to reveal that the secret treaty had existed, undermining Austrian confidence in German fidelity. (Bismarck made good on this threat in 1896; by that time it made little difference.) Holstein's switch in allegiance and his part in the nonrenewal of the treaty were never forgiven. Herbert, especially, regarded "Faithful Fritz" as a traitor. During the week after the resignation of both Bismarcks, when Holstein had gone to the files and brought the secret treaty to Caprivi, Herbert, still moving his belongings out of the building, flew into a rage. He sent for Holstein.

Queen Victoria, a Diamond Jubilee portrait, 1897

Alfred von Tirpitz

"You have been guilty of something which in past circumstances I should have obliged to punish most severely. All I can say is that you have been in too big a hurry to regard me as a back number." Soon after, when Herbert met Holstein on the stairs, he gave his former friend a deep bow and passed without a word. After Herbert's departure, tension between the two men grew, reaching an intense, mutual enmity. For many years after Prince Bismarck's dismissal, when Berlin was divided into the Court Party and the Bismarck Party, Holstein was a target of lively hatred by the latter without ever involving himself with the former. Until Prince Bismarck's death in 1897, Holstein's frantic concern was to prevent any reconciliation between the Kaiser and the Bismarcks. In any Bismarck restoration, Holstein knew, the first head to roll would be his own.

Otto and Herbert von Bismarck did not return. Year after year, Friedrich von Holstein sat at his desk in his little room on the ground floor at No. 76 Wilhelmstrasse. He unlocked the door himself in the morning, took his seat, and began a day which would last at least twelve hours. He worked slowly and deliberately, hampered as time passed by the growth of cataracts. He was disturbed only by messengers, who knocked softly, entered bowing, deposited or picked up documents, and departed noiselessly. Time passed and his routine never varied. Sitting at this desk, he watched Imperial chancellors come and go, state secretaries relieve each other, ministers and ambassadors march past. He alone remained. Never seen, he became a legend. Chancellors and state secretaries were dependent on him. He did everything for them, drafting their reports to the Emperor, writing their speeches, sending their dispatches, preparing memoranda, never relinquishing his own secret correspondence authorized years before by Bismarck, sharing it with no one. His memory astonished and terrified Foreign Office clerks; he knew what every document contained, what action had been taken, where every piece of paper was filed.

Holstein paused at midday for half an hour, when he ate a light lunch sent over from the Hôtel du Rome. At nine P.M., he turned off his desk lamp, which had a heavy red shade to protect his eyes, locked his door, and walked to a side entrance of the Restaurant Borchardt, No. 48 Französischstrasse. Here, a private room was held for him. Holstein was a gourmet and lover of fine wine. His instructions to the kitchen were as careful and precise as the orders he issued to diplomats; the chef and headwaiter appeared before him with as much apprehension as the clerks at the Wilhelmstrasse. Toward midnight, he ordered a cab. Other guests were delayed to permit him to pass down the hall and into the street alone.

Over the years, the social boycott of Holstein collapsed. Handsomely crested invitations began to arrive, but Holstein imposed his own boycott on society. Living in solitude in three small rooms in the Grossbeerenstrasse, he extended hospitality by inviting people to small supper parties at Borchardt, or, to show particular favor, to accompany him on one of his favorite long walks through the countryside around Berlin. The Kaiser and the Court were included in Holstein's boycott. On the Emperor's birthday, a huge reception massed all the dignitaries of the government and all the foreign ambassadors at the Berlin Palace. Naturally, First Counselor Baron von Holstein was always invited. The answer was always the same: "Geheimrat Holstein begs to be excused. He does not possess court dress." So reclusive was Holstein that in 1893, when William II had been on the throne for five years, he had not met Holstein. "I hear that I have an excellent official in the Foreign Office, Herr von Holstein," the Kaiser said one day to the Austrian Ambassador. "Unfortunately, I haven't yet succeeded in making his acquaintance." Holstein wished to maintain this distance. Once, hearing that the Kaiser was coming to the Foreign Office, Holstein hastily invited Baron Hermann von Eckardstein, a German diplomat assigned to London, temporarily in Berlin, to join him for lunch. Over the meal, Holstein talked for three hours, then strolled with his guest to Unter den Linden and asked a policeman whether the Kaiser had driven past. Learning that he had not, Holstein continued to walk with Eckardstein for another hour, then sent the younger man ahead to the Foreign Office to be sure the coast was clear. Ultimately, in November 1904, after William had been on the throne for sixteen years, he finally met Holstein socially. Bülow, then Chancellor, arranged a dinner. When they met, William talked about duck hunting.

In this fashion, the "Gray Eminence" and "Empire Jesuit" ruled his secret empire. Dedicated to work, worshipping power, he was furtive, crotchety, and suspicious. His mind was brilliant and complex—and also cantankerous. The more natural and obvious a thing was, the more Holstein suspected it. In his memoirs, Eckardstein recalled: "How often has it happened in important negotiations which he had himself initiated and in which he was personally interested, that I have been instructed to break off as soon as it appeared that the other party was ready to meet his wishes. I found that as a rule I could reckon on Holstein being willing only so long as the other side was unwilling." Holstein's web encompassed the whole of German diplomacy. He expanded his private espionage system, encouraging officials anxious to further their careers to keep him supplied with the sort of personal information on their superiors and colleagues which they knew Holstein liked and could use. He was master of malicious gossip and gleefully passed along poisonous innuendo. Holstein himself was easily offended; when excited in this way, he never looked anyone in the eye and made spasmodic clenching movements with the fingers of his right hand. He never forgave slights or insults. "The fellow didn't bow to me today," he would complain, refusing to accept the excuses that the offender had been across the street, was shortsighted, and had been looking in the opposite direction. Once offended, he was relentlessly vindictive. "As I perceive you are working . . . against me," he once said to Philip Eulenburg, "I shall be obliged to show my claws in some way." Even the Kaiser was not exempt from Holstein's demand for absolute loyalty: "If His Majesty does nothing against . . . [a Foreign Ministry official whom Holstein disliked], he ranges himself with my enemy." The extreme to which Holstein could go was illustrated by his treatment of Johann Maria von Radowitz, who served as German Ambassador to Turkey and Spain. When Radowitz accepted a Star to wear on his breast on the same honors list which produced for Holstein only a Cross to be worn around the neck, Holstein never forgave Radowitz and followed his career with pathological hatred. "His rage was all the more senseless," Bülow noted, "because since the Arnim case, Holstein has never been out in society, never put on a decoration, and does not even possess evening dress."

Holstein's influence on foreign policy remained powerful until his fall in 1906. Philip Eulenburg gave Holstein credit: "Neither Caprivi, nor Hohenlohe, nor Bülow ever promulgated an edict on even the most insignificant political matter without Holstein putting in an oar. Caprivi's and Hohenlohe's foreign policy was pure Holstein." The reason, Eulenburg explained, was that "Holstein's great talents [were considered] to be indispensable. No one could replace his understanding of complex questions of international importance. . . . In the Emperor's and the Government's interests, he had to be humored, as one humors a bad-tempered, erratic, positively dangerous sporting dog for the sake of his good nose."

Bülow, working closely with Holstein for nine years as State Secretary and Chancellor, treated the First Counselor warily. "The situation [at the Wilhelmstrasse] was made more difficult for me by the intrigues of Holstein," he sighed. "With all his unusual qualities, [he] was an incomparable intriguer . . . filled with pathological mistrust." Bülow also used a canine simile: "Holstein was like the watchdog which is very good at protecting the house against thieves and burglars, but of which one can never be sure whether he will bite his master's legs." In his *Memoirs*, Bülow chose a fiercer beast: "In his blind and petty hatred, old Geheimrat von Holstein, who for over thirty years had stood closer to the great Prince [Bismarck] than most others, seemed to me a cunning wolf who ought to be behind bars and not at liberty." Eulenburg's description was cruelest: "Bülow and I used to call him the 'weasel,' for that animal never stops until it has slaughtered the whole henhouse."

Holstein believed in a cautiously friendly German policy toward Britain. He shared the view of his old preceptor, Bismarck, that Germany, situated between France and Russia, must concern itself with the balance of power between the Triple Alliance of Germany, Austria, and Italy and the emerging anti-German Dual Alliance of France and Russia. Someday, Britain might be persuaded to join the Triple Alliance. In the interim, it was enough for Britain to maintain its Splendid Isolation. Holstein did not consider the possibility that Britain might join Germany's enemies; the antagonisms between Britain and France, and Britain and Russia were so deep that the First Counselor could not imagine that they could ever be bridged.

Accommodation with Britain assured German predominance in Europe, but also required moderation of German ambitions overseas. Germany must not alarm and provoke Great Britain by an aggressive colonial policy or by an extravagant increase in the size of the German Navy. In the 1870s and 1880s, Britain had assisted in the training of the small German fleet; in the 1880s Britain had endorsed Bismarck's brief excursion into colonialism. In overseas trade, German ships and traders enjoyed the protection of the Royal Navy and access to British colonial markets. Holstein saw no need to push for more.

It was on Holstein's advice that Caprivi, soon after becoming Chancellor, wrote a warm personal note to Lord Salisbury saying that he looked forward to friendly relations and close cooperation with the British Prime Minister. The German government, wary of a return to power of Gladstone and the Liberals, wished "to keep in mind the need to lighten Lord Salisbury's task to make possible his retention in office," Caprivi wrote at the same time to Hatzfeldt in

London. Hohenlohe's advent as Chancellor did not affect either German policy towards England or Holstein's influence at the Wilhelmstrasse. Before 1897, nothing occurred to change his belief that Britain would never join France and Russia; British antagonism towards those powers remained too strong.

CHAPTER 7

Bülow and Weltmacht

◆

Germany, in the first twenty years after the proclamation of the Empire, grew steadily in population and economic strength. Then, suddenly, beginning in the 1890s, the German population and industrial base exploded upwards. In 1871, the population of Great Britain (including Ireland) was 31 million; the new German Empire contained 41 million people. Twenty years later, in 1891, Britain's population had grown to 38 million, Germany's to 49 million. Then the growth rates changed. The number of Britons mounted to 41 million in 1901 and 45 million in 1911. But the German population soared to 56 million in 1900 and 65 million in 1910. The comparison with France is even more stark: between 1891 and 1910, while the Reich's population was swelling from 49 million to 65 million, the French population rose from 37 million to 39 million.

Coal- and steel-production figures were equally dramatic. In 1871, British coal dominated world markets with production of 112 million tons a year; Germany, the world's second-largest producer of coal, mined 34 million tons. By 1890, German coal production was half of Britain's; by 1913 it was equal. Steel production, an essential component of heavy industry and war, offered still more striking contrasts. In 1890, Britain produced 3.6 million tons of steel a year, Germany about two thirds of that. In 1896, German steel production first exceeded Great Britain's. In 1914, Germany (14 million tons) produced more than twice as much steel as Britain (6.5 million tons).

It was the same in almost every category and statistic by which economic strength is measured. The disappearance of customs barriers, the growth of railways, rapid urbanization, development of the chemical and electrical industries, the rise of the world's second-largest merchant fleet, booming overseas trade, extensive foreign investments—all added to a massive army of unique efficiency—created a state which dominated the European continent. With surging strength came a sense of national destiny. Young, self-confident, ambitious, the German Empire set out to follow the path taken by other powerful states.* Expansion became a matter of prestige and a measure of prosperity. By 1897, leading figures in the government, industry, the press, and the professions agreed that Germany's population explosion and industrial growth demanded colonies as sources of raw materials and markets for finished products. Unless the Reich acquired trading ports, naval bases, and coaling stations around the globe as Britain and, to a lesser extent, France, had done, her economy would atrophy and her greatness diminish. Thus the policy of *Weltmacht,* world power, was born. Bernhard von Bülow, with Admiral Alfred Tirpitz an architect of *Weltmacht,* expressed the issue in everyday terms. "The question is not whether we wish to colonize or not, but that we must colonize whether we want to or not. To say that Germany should cease its *Weltpolitik* is like a father telling his son, 'If only you would not grow, you troublesome youth, then I would not need to buy you longer trousers.'" Tirpitz was blunter: German overseas expansion, he said, was "as irresistible as a law of nature."

There were objections. The leaders of the German Social Democratic Party, Wilhelm Liebknecht and August Bebel, argued that Germany's future should rest on the solution of social problems at home rather than on expansion overseas. Their objections only added incentive to the imperialists: the forward policy was designed, at least in part, to divert the attention of the German public and German workers from social and political problems at home. Another argument, that the colonies already possessed by Germany

* The United States, whose population had increased from 50 million to 75 million in the twenty years between 1880 and 1900, was on this path. Americans had conquered a continent, created the world's largest industrial economy, and were looking to expand overseas. In 1898, the year after *Weltmacht* became the declared policy of the German Empire, the United States defeated Spain and swallowed the Philippines and Puerto Rico.

brought neither prestige nor profit to the Empire, was discounted. Even poor colonies, it was said, added territory to the German flag and might lead to something better. A further objection, that most of the areas of the world suitable for settlement already belonged to other European powers, failed to deter. Ernst Hasse, founder of the Pan-German League, whose program was the union of all members of the German race wherever they lived, declared: "One of the conventional lies of history is that the world is already divided. History, on the contrary, is merely the record of the partition and repartition of the world. . . . We want territory even if it belongs to foreigners, so that we may shape the future according to our needs." A corollary to this doctrine was that if direct exchanges of territory or revisions of colonial boundaries were made without German participation, then Germany had the right to demand territorial "compensation" from the powers involved.

A majority of Germans, convinced of the justice of their country's claims, believed that the world should and would accommodate German demands. If other powers—Britain, for example—were troublesome, Germany had the strength to deal with this. On January 6, 1897, Professor Schiemann, a member of the faculty of Berlin University, wrote in a newspaper: "England is still the state which has least adjusted to the fact that Germany is the strongest power on the continent and that she is prepared, if necessary, to compel this recognition."

Across Germany, professors proclaimed the glory of the Hohenzollern monarchy, the necessity for patriotic obedience, the historical inevitability of German expansion. No academic figure was more influential than Heinrich von Treitschke, Professor of History at the University of Berlin. In his *History of Germany in the Nineteenth Century,* published in five volumes, and in his university lectures through the 1880s and 1890s, Treitschke preached the ideology of power and the supremacy of the State. Born into the Saxon nobility, unable to follow a military career because of deafness, he considered war the instrument of the Divine Idea. "Only in war a nation will become truly a nation," he said. "Only common great deeds for the idea of a Fatherland will hold a nation together. . . . Social selfishness must yield. . . . The individual must forget himself and feel part of the whole; he must realize how insignificant his life is compared with the whole. . . ." The highest duty of the State, Treitschke said, was to develop and wield power. "The State," he not Holstein shouted in his lecture hall, "is not an Academy of Art. It is Power!" These words, delivered in a near-feverish howl, provoked roaring applause and chanting, foot-stamping adulation. Treitschke's rhetoric, intoxicating and mesmerizing, cloaked the new policy of the German Empire with philosophical purpose.

In 1896, Admiral Georg von Müller, Chief of the Kaiser's Naval Cabinet, translated Treitschke's philosophy into practical, contemporary terms. Writing to Prince Henry, the Kaiser's brother, Müller said: "General Caprivi believed that Germany had no chance at all of becoming a World Power and consequently his policy was designed only to maintain our position on the European continent. He was therefore acting quite logically in working at home for the strengthening of the Army, limiting the Navy to the role of defending the coastline . . . and seeking good relations with England as the natural ally against Russia, the country which threatened Germany's position in Europe." By 1896, Müller continued, Caprivi's policy was discredited and "widely ridiculed." "The German people . . . [are] coming to accept an entirely different opinion of their ability and indeed their duty to expand. . . . Our motto must be all or nothing. Either we harness the total strength of the nation quite ruthlessly, even if this means accepting the risk of a major war, or we confine ourselves to continental power alone." This choice, Müller said, would initially provide comfort and security but would eventually and inevitably lead to economic strangulation, decay, and backwardness. *Weltpolitik* realized that "world history is now dominated by the economic struggle, that Central Europe is getting too small and that the free expansion of the peoples who live here is restricted . . . by the world domination of England. . . . The war which could—and many say, must—result . . . would have the aim of breaking England's world domination so as to lay free the necessary colonial possessions for the Central European states who need to expand." Müller urged caution against any immediate challenge to England—the German Navy was insignificant—and he thought that Germany should first acquire some colonial possessions in alliance with England. Ultimately, however, Müller predicted that these "two Germanic world empires would . . . with absolute inevitability have to go to war to determine which of the two should dominate."

Above the philosophers and historians, the ministers and diplomats, the steel magnates, bankers, and shipping managers stood the leading advocate of *Weltmacht,* Kaiser William II. William saw his role in mystical as well as political terms: World Power became an extension of his Divine Right to rule. William I and his servant Bismarck had created a German Empire and a German Kaiser; now William II and *his* servants would transform the German Empire into a World Empire ruled by a World Kaiser. Germany, William II told the Austrian ambassador in 1898, "has great tasks to accomplish outside the narrow boundaries of old Europe." On January 18, 1896, at a celebration of the twenty-fifth anniversary of the establishment of the German Empire, William II had proclaimed: "The German Empire has become a world empire."

In December 1901, William wrote to his uncle, now King Edward VII, "I am the sole arbiter and master of German foreign policy and the Government and country *must* follow me. . . . May your Government never forget this. . . ." This was neither wholly accurate nor entirely hyperbole. The German constitution gave the Emperor sole responsibility for choosing a chancellor; the chancellor, assisted by the Foreign Ministry, was responsible for the administration of foreign policy. A Kaiser unhappy with a particular foreign policy could always dismiss one chancellor and select another. William's private opinion was that foreign policy was best handled directly between sovereigns. "I am at my very best," he said, "when I talk straight out to my colleagues," meaning the heads of the other ruling houses of Europe. Nevertheless, William accepted that on a day-to-day basis even the most gifted sovereigns required assistance from chancellors, prime ministers, foreign ministers, and diplomats. He wanted, as chancellor, a man who would transform his own ideas and inspirations into working policy—an able executor and faithful servant of his Imperial will. The obstinate Caprivi and the elderly Hohenlohe had disappointed him. Now, with the help of Philip Eulenburg, he had found the right man. "Bülow will be my Bismarck," William said. Bülow did everything to encourage this prophecy. If appointed, he wrote to Eulenburg in 1896, he would regard himself as no more than an executive instrument, an administrative assistant, to the monarch. "With me," he told Eulenburg, "personal rule—in the good sense—would really begin."

It was said of Bernhard von Bülow that he possessed every quality except greatness. Chancellor of the German Empire for nine years, State Secretary for Foreign Affairs for the three previous years, he was the most elegant, cosmopolitan political figure produced in Imperial Germany. Bülow was a consummate diplomat, urbane and polished, a man of wide culture who spoke several languages flawlessly and moved effortlessly in international society. As a politician, he dazzled even his political opponents with an endless outpouring of classical quotations, discreet jokes, and polished, charming repartee. He was a patriotic German who loved Paris and preferred Italy to most parts of Germany, especially Berlin. "Bülow," it has been written, "seemed more Latin than German, like some fabulous, many-colored bird in the Prussian aviary . . . always making new friends, nobody's enemy, captivating, graceful. . . ."

The façade was splendid. Behind lay the driving forces of Bülow's life: vanity and ambition. The characteristics of his work were laziness and cynicism. He grappled ruthlessly for power, but once it was in his possession, he ignored his duties, despised details, and left his subordinates to find their own way. A brilliant debater who won flashy triumphs in the Reichstag, he stepped down from the podium with his eyes glittering contemptuously as he spoke of those who had supported as well as opposed him. He practiced flattery as a high art, lathering and coating with layers of charm, but as soon as the back was turned, he let his malicious tongue dart forth to lacerate and ridicule the object just flattered. In the short term, Bülow had his way; as one observer noted, he was able to catch many mice by laying out for each its favorite kind of cheese. For twelve years, German foreign policy lay in the hands of a man who lacked purpose, scruples, courage, and a vision of his own. Power, which gravitates into the hands of men who know what they want, flowed out of Bülow's hands. It was wielded by Holstein, by the Kaiser, and by Alfred von Tirpitz.

People close to Bülow, watching his slippery passage through life, were fascinated and repelled by what they saw. Alfred von Kiderlen-Waechter, Political Counselor at the Foreign Office, called Bülow "an eel"; on hearing this, Tirpitz snorted that compared to Bülow "an eel is a leech." Holstein said that Bülow had read more Machiavelli than he could digest. Another contemporary declared that "underneath the shiny paint, there was nothing but plaster." Even Bülow's relatives admitted to Bernhard's flaws: "He would be quite a fellow if his character could only attain the height of his personality," said his younger brother Adolf. Bülow's aristocratic Italian mother-in-law ridiculed his absurdly exaggerated confidences. "Bernhard makes a secret of everything," she declared. "He takes you by the arm, leads you to the window and says, 'Don't tell anyone but there's a little dog down there who's pissing.' " The full range of Bülow's qualities, bright and dark, came out in his *Memoirs*. Four volumes, whose publication he deliberately postponed until after his death, attempted to enshrine his own reputation by ruining all others. Instead, these pages, brimming with vanity and malice as well as with brilliant scenes and sparkling dialogue, irreparably damaged Bülow's reputation. Kaiser William II, the object of much of Bülow's public flattery and target of much of his private venom, made one of his own few witty remarks when he declared that Bülow was the only case he knew of a man who first had died and then committed suicide.

From the first, this slender young man with his round, friendly face, his smiling blue eyes, and his carefully trimmed mustache had seemed destined for a golden life in Imperial Germany. He was born May 3, 1849, at Klein Flottbeck near Altona on the Elbe. His mother was a Hamburger, his father a Mecklenburg nobleman who had entered the Danish diplomatic service and represented the duchies of Holstein and Lauenburg at the Federal Diet in Frankfurt. Bismarck was in Frankfurt representing the King of Prussia. At the age of seven Bernhard von Bülow played with Bismarck's sons, and later described Herbert Bismarck as "the closest friend of my life." Bülow's introduction of Herbert is typical of his technique: in the same breath in which he describes Herbert as "the closest friend of my life," he tells an unpleasant little story: "My earliest memory of Herbert is of playing with him in the pretty garden of our house in the Neue Mainzerstrasse in Frankfurt with his brother Bill and a little girl named Christa. . . . There was a streak of German brutality in both brothers. Herbert and Bill both wanted to make Christa kiss a fat toad. . . ." As a child, Bernhard also visited Rumpenheim Castle near Frankfurt, where the Danish Prince Christian visited with his family. There he played with Princess Alexandra, who later married the Prince of Wales and became Queen of England. She was, Bülow remembered, "a beautiful girl, with a wonderful waist and a light, airy, swinging gait." When they met as adults, the Princess remembered his visits and that he had cuffed and scratched her in their games.

When Bernhard was thirteen, his father resigned his post in Frankfurt and left the service of Denmark to become Chief Minister of the Grand Duke of Mecklenburg. The family moved to Neustrelitz. Bernhard, fluent in French and English thanks to governesses, went to the local gymnasium and then to universities in Lausanne, Leipzig, and Berlin. During the Franco-Prussian War, he volunteered and put on the blue tunic, leather breeches, and yellow boots of a lance corporal in the King's Hussar Regiment. In December 1870, his squadron charged fifty French riflemen near Amiens. Bülow rode down a French soldier, slashed him on the head with his saber, and watched while his enemy "wavered and swayed, tottered, collapsed, gave a death rattle, and was dead." By the end of the war, Bülow was a lieutenant, but had turned down the plea of his colonel to make his career in the army. Greater opportunities beckoned.

In 1873, Bismarck installed his former Frankfurt colleague, Bernhard von Bülow the elder, as Imperial Secretary of State for

Foreign Affairs, a post Bülow held for six years until he died in office in 1879. Bulow *père* was stern, punctilious, and tireless. Bismarck valued him for his loyalty and his clear understanding that he and the Foreign Office were no more than instruments of the Chancellor's will.

In the year in which his father became State Secretary, young Bernhard von Bülow entered the German Diplomatic Corps. Naturally, all doors at court, in society, and in the foreign embassies in Berlin were open to the charming young man who had fought bravely in the war and whose father was Foreign Minister of the Reich. Bülow's first assignments were brief. He went to Rome—with which he fell in love—St. Petersburg, Vienna, and Athens. In 1876, he began six years in Paris as Second and then First Secretary of the German Embassy. In 1884, he hoped for assignment to London, but to his dismay, was sent instead to a second term in St. Petersburg. Before he left Germany, he was invited to spend two days at Varzin with the Bismarcks. He sat at the table, which he described as that of a German farmer, while Princess Bismarck plied him with delicacies and pressed him to drink more of the Prince's heavy Kulmbach beer. After dinner, the family sat around the table and gossiped unpleasantly about personalities in Berlin. The following morning, the Chancellor came to see Bülow about his assignment in St. Petersburg. "As I sat next morning in my room, eating a very large and excellent breakfast, the Prince entered. He sat down opposite with the words: 'Don't let me disturb you. Go on eating your eggs. I hope they have been boiled properly.' " Bismarck said that he understood Bülow's disappointment at being sent to the Russian capital rather than to London. "But the pivot of our position, and with that of our whole policy, the pivot on which things turn, is our relationship to Russia. . . . For us, therefore, St. Petersburg is now the most important diplomatic post. That is why I have transferred you there." Bülow listened carefully, but did not interrupt his breakfast of eggs, toast, and smoked herring. That afternoon, Bülow went for a walk with Bill Bismarck, who told him: "My father said some nice things about you. It pleased him especially that you went on calmly eating your eggs. 'He had good nerves. He pleases me altogether.' "

Along his smooth upward path, a second reputation began to form about Bernhard von Bülow. Ambition and careerism were seen behind the façade. Too often in private letters to influential people, Bülow took credit for the successes of his chiefs and detached himself from their failures. From St. Petersburg, where he was First Secretary and Counselor under General von Schweinitz,

Bülow delivered a litany of complaints to the Foreign Office. Ambassador Schweinitz was denounced as touchy, devious, egotistical, and unsophisticated in his analysis of Russian affairs. Unfortunately for Bülow, both Kaiser William I and Bismarck liked Schweinitz. Bülow's progress and tactics were observed from the beginning by one especially keen and suspicious eye in the Wilhelmstrasse: "Bernhard Bülow is clean-shaven and pasty, with a shifty look and almost perpetual smile," noted Friedrich von Holstein. "Intellectually plausible rather than penetrating. Has no ideas in reserve . . . but appropriates other people's ideas and skillfully retails them without acknowledging the source." Himself a master of intrigue, Holstein gave Bülow credit for his technique: "When Bülow wants to set one man against another, he says with an insinuating smile, 'He doesn't like you.' A simple and almost infallible method." Holstein noted another tactic: "A few days ago, Bulow sent me a letter to Herbert, unsealed, to be passed along to Herbert, sealed." In 1885, Bülow was intriguing for Prince Hohenlohe's removal from his post as Ambassador to France so that he could have the position himself. "The beauty of it," Holstein noted with cynical admiration, "is that all the while Bulow keeps up a continuous and friendly correspondence with Hohenlohe. . . ."

In 1886, while he was stationed in St. Petersburg, Bülow married. While his numerous love affairs, described in detail in his memoirs, had been matters of passionate dalliance, his marriage, undertaken at thirty-six, was a matter of career. His bride was born Princess Maria Camporeale, the daughter of Donna Laura Minghetti, the grande dame of Roman society. She had married, almost in girlhood, an older German diplomat, Count Karl Dönhoff, with whom she had three children. Bülow met her in 1875 in Florence, then again in Vienna. He admired "her wonderful eyes, black eyes," and her knowledge of German literature—"she had penetrated deeply into my pet philosopher, Schopenhauer." In 1885 she divorced her husband, and in 1886 she married Bülow. "For once in his life, Bülow has met a more skillful intriguer than himself," chortled Holstein. "This was the little Countess Dönhoff-Camporeale, who, after a marriage lasting sixteen years, divorced her husband to marry Bülow. . . . Bülow is certain that the little countess has never given a thought to anyone but him." Wickedly, Holstein then proceeded to list her previous lovers.

The new Maria von Bülow took a hand in her husband's career. In 1888, Herbert asked him whether he would prefer to go as minister to Bucharest or to Washington. Frau Bülow objected to the thought of a cold and stormy ocean between herself and her mother and children, so Bülow went to Bucharest for the next five years. There, he campaigned tirelessly for further advancement. His sights were set on Rome, where, through his wife, his connections were excellent. His stepfather-in-law ruled Roman society. King Humbert (Umberto) was persuaded to tell Kaiser William II that he would be pleased if the brilliant and charming Bernhard von Bülow became Ambassador in Rome.

On Monday morning, June 21, 1897, the beginning of a week during which newspapers in Rome were filled with descriptions of the celebrations in England of the old *regina inglesa*'s Diamond Jubilee, the German Ambassador, Bernhard von Bülow, found a telegram from Berlin lying on his desk at the Palazzo Caffarelli. The message commanded him to present himself as soon as possible to the Kaiser on board the *Hohenzollern* at Kiel. Bülow left Rome the next day. In Frankfurt, he changed trains, and while waiting the hour and a half for the train to Berlin, he had a conversation with Philip von Eulenburg, who had driven over from one of his Rhineland estates. The two men walked out of the station and sat beside a public fountain; Bülow remembered staring at a statue of Bacchus covered with vines. Eulenburg's message was simple and urgent: his friend must accept the Kaiser's commission and become State Secretary for Foreign Affairs. Assuming that Bülow would agree, Eulenburg added counsel on how to deal with the Emperor: "Only if you take the Kaiser in the right way can you be of use to your country. . . . William II takes everything personally. . . . He wants to teach others, but learns unwillingly himself. . . . He loves glory and is ambitious and jealous. In order to get him to accept an idea, you must act as though the idea was his. You must make everything easy for him. He readily encourages others to take bold steps but throws them overboard if they fail. Never forget that His Majesty needs praise. . . . He is as grateful for it as a good and clever child."

Stopping over in Berlin, Bülow went to the Kaiserhof Hotel for a haircut and shampoo and then began a round of calls. Holstein, whom Bülow saw first, would have preferred that Marschall remain Secretary of State because Marschall was easy to manage. But Holstein knew William II was determined to be rid of Marschall, and the wily First Counselor preferred Bülow to other possible successors. Holstein's fear was that the Kaiser might summon Herbert Bismarck. "Ever since his apostasy from the House of Bismarck," Bülow wrote, "Holstein on sleepless nights had terrifying visions of Herbert, with his father like a wrathful Titan standing behind him."

Accordingly, Holstein begged Bülow to accept the office. Next, Bülow visited Marschall, whom he found in bad humor. Marschall was angry not at Bülow, but at those whom he suspected of undermining his position with the Emperor. Like Holstein, he declared himself pleased that the Ambassador in Rome would be his successor. If possible, he said, he would like to be sent as Ambassador to Constantinople or Rome itself. Bülow promised to do what he could. Then Bülow went to see the Chancellor. He found Prince Hohenlohe, at seventy-eight, "older and weaker . . . with bowed head . . . his aged hand, with its very prominent bluish veins, caressing" a pale-brown dachshund. "Here I stand, a leafless trunk," the Chancellor greeted Bülow in a whispery voice. He declared his own wish to leave the Chancellorship as soon as possible, and mentioned that he assumed that Bülow eventually would be his successor. Bülow replied that if this were true, he would be grateful for every day the Prince remained in office while he prepared himself. In fact, Hohenlohe continued another three years.

On Saturday, June 26, the day of the Diamond Jubilee Naval Review in England, Bülow arrived in Kiel and went on board the *Hohenzollern*. He found the Kaiser alone, pacing the upper deck. "My dear Bernhard," William said, holding out his hand in welcome, "I'm sorry for you, but you must go to the front. The Badener [Marschall] has betrayed me." He accused Marschall of intriguing behind his back with opposition parties in the Reichstag and with attempting to diminish Imperial prerogatives. The job of the next State Secretary, he said, would be "to build a fleet for our defense and security without becoming involved in a war with England through the building of this fleet." "Not a very simple matter," Bülow noted to himself, and asked for five weeks to make up his mind. "Dear me," exclaimed the Kaiser, disappointed, "I thought we were going to be inseparable from now onwards." He granted Bülow's leave.

On August 3 Bülow reported again to the Kaiser at Kiel and accepted the office. William was in high spirits. "Now, what about my ships?" he asked, and the two men went ashore for a long walk among the sand hills to discuss the question. Bülow declared that he understood that the recent development of German industry, commerce, and shipping on the high seas must be protected. "Was that possible without coming to blows with England? It would certainly not be easy, as the policy of England towards economic competitors and especially seafaring competitors in the past had clearly shown. The best assurance of success would be a quiet, careful, and, if I might use the expression, elastic policy on our side." "Agreed, agreed," said the Kaiser, delighted. "Now that's your job."

Disingenuously protesting his sacrifice in leaving Rome, Bülow took up the job he had been seeking for years. He took to Berlin the French chef of the Palazzo Caffarelli and proclaimed the fellow's remarkable loyalty. "When one has shared bright days with his masters," Bülow quoted the chef as saying, "one does not quit them in their misery." Bülow's transition to Berlin was smooth. He was amiable, charming, always smiling, a splendid host, a talented raconteur. His wife was equally charming, elegant, and a close friend of the Dowager Empress Frederick. Bülow seemed to have no enemies. He had managed to remain close to the Bismarcks as well as to the Court. He had an excellent relationship with Hohenlohe. The Kaiser gushed in quick praise. "I adore him," William wrote to Eulenburg on August 20, only two weeks after Bülow had moved into the Wilhelmstrasse. "My God, what a difference from the South German traitor [Marschall]." Two days later, Bülow gave Eulenburg his first impressions of his new master: "As a man, His Majesty [is] charming, touching, enchanting to the point of adoration. As a ruler, [he] is threatened by temperament, lack of nuance . . . by a preponderance of will . . . over calm, clear reflection . . . unless he is surrounded by wise and especially by completely loyal and trustworthy servants." Six months later, Bülow waxed more eloquent to Eulenburg: "He is so *bedeutend* [distinguished]!! Of all the great kings and princes, he is by far the most significant Hohenzollern who has ever lived. He combines, in a manner such as I have never known before, geniality, the truest and most profound geniality, with the clearest good sense. He possesses a fantasy which raises me on eagle's wings above all pettiness and thereby gives me the clearest appreciation of the possible and the realizable. And, added to that, what energy! What memory! What swiftness and certainty of viewpoint! Today at the privy council I was simply overwhelmed!" William and Bülow each had found his man. The master had found the servant who would permit him his theatricality, overlook his casual attitude toward work, indulge his love of anecdote and gossip and keep him afloat on the tide of praise essential to his well-being. The servant had found a master whom he could manipulate without ever having to take an unpopular position or stand up and say no. "Bernhard the Obliging," he became known as to those around him. Bülow did not contest this; better to prevent by suppleness than lose by firmness, he believed. Often, he did what he liked even when the Kaiser had said no, knowing that William often changed his mind or frequently forgot what he had said in the first place.

Bülow's relationship with Hohenlohe never soured, partly because of Bülow's charm, but more because the Chancellor, old, sick, indolent, and passive, chose to overlook that he was being ignored. Now it was Bülow whom the Kaiser called on every morning and the Chancellor on whom he called only occasionally. Previously, State Secretaries for Foreign Affairs had been only functionaries; foreign policy had been made by the Chancellor and the monarch. Now, Bülow took control, making policy with Holstein and William, sending instructions to ambassadors, filling diplomatic posts, all without consulting Prince Hohenlohe. The Chancellor, reported the Austrian ambassador in 1899, was now "leading a contemplative existence."

Within the Foreign Office, Bülow was welcomed. He was the first professional diplomat to take the reins since Bismarck. He gave the Wilhelmstrasse a sense of professionalism and energy which it had lacked under Marschall. The key figure was Holstein. Bülow and Holstein had known each other for a quarter of a century, since twenty-three-year-old Bernhard had entered the diplomatic service. Holstein had kept an eye on the young man, realizing that the son of a State Secretary might be put to use. Bülow was always aware of Holstein's power and took care to propitiate it. Each understood that the other might be a powerful ally; neither wholly trusted the other. Bülow sensed that Holstein was keeping track of his own complicated efforts at self-promotion and he knew that the First Counselor disliked his continued relationship with the Bismarcks. In 1894, when Eulenburg first suggested to Bülow that he become State Secretary, Bülow emphatically declared that he would not accept the office as long as Holstein remained in the Wilhelmstrasse. When, in 1897, Bülow became State Secretary, Eulenburg, who was responsible for Bülow's promotion, encouraged him to deal firmly with Holstein from the beginning. "Build your nest as you need and want it," he urged. "Even the monster of the Labyrinth begins to moan, groveling before your feet." Bülow's position was strengthened by a coolness between the Kaiser and the reclusive First Counselor. In April 1897, William told Eulenburg that Holstein was "an old man full of specters and hallucinations for whom I broke many, many lances; a man who now and then had made the Wilhelmstrasse crazier than it already was." The Kaiser was pleased when Bülow took charge of the Foreign Office. "The sway of the counselors has almost stopped," he announced triumphantly to Eulenburg in 1899. "Who talks nowadays of Herr von Holstein? What is Herr von Holstein? . . . Since Bulow now has the reins in his hands, one no longer knows the names of his advisers."

Early in October 1900, the Kaiser summoned Bülow to Hubertsstock, his hunting retreat. Taking the State Secretary for a walk on the bank of Lake Werbellin, William brought the subject around to Prince Hohenlohe's health. The Chancellor's heart trouble was worsening; he had suffered two bad attacks within a month; Hohenlohe considered himself absolutely unable to continue in office and was begging for dismissal. Turning to Bülow, the Kaiser asked him point-blank: "Would you accept the succession?" The great moment in Bülow's life had come, but, knowing the prize was his, he turned coy. Had His Majesty considered other candidates? he asked. "Candidly, for me personally Phil Eulenburg would be much the most acceptable successor," William replied. "He is my best friend. I am his 'Highest.' But I do not know whether he is equal to it. I have the impression that he himself doubts it. . . . He has used up too much of his nervous energy in my service to be able to appear before the Reichstag." The State Secretary departed Hubertsstock having advised that William attempt to prolong Hohenlohe's tenure as long as possible. When he departed, the Kaiserin gave him her hand and said softly, "Do accept." There was not a chance that Bülow would not. Shortly afterward, on October 16, 1900, Bülow was called to the telephone in Berlin:

"Secretary of State Count Bülow speaking."

"Kaiser William speaking. Hohenlohe has told me that he cannot possibly carry on any longer. Come to Homburg."

Bülow went immediately, and the Kaiser did him the honor of meeting his train on the platform. After a brief talk, William gave him a hearty handshake and declared ebulliently, "My dear Chancellor, we shall meet at luncheon." Congratulations poured in. The Empress pressed his hand again and gave him fervent thanks. Herbert Bismarck wrote to express "satisfaction that Chlodwig, the old mummy, has finally been removed and that you have been appointed Chancellor." As Chancellor, Bülow moved immediately to confirm control over German foreign policy. "Under Prince Hohenlohe, I had administered our foreign policy," he wrote. Upon appointment as Chancellor he had no intention of allowing this critical role to fall into the hands of a new State Secretary at the Foreign Office. A replacement for himself as State Secretary was necessary; the position was first offered *pro forma* to Holstein, who, as Bülow confidently expected, declined. Holstein then made personnel suggestions which irritated Bülow: "Holstein . . . suggested several completely unqualified candidates as he hoped that the appointment of an ineffectual Secretary of State would give him a free hand in his swervings and intrigues." Bülow quashed this by persuading the Kaiser to elevate his own stolid Under Secretary, Baron von Richthofen, a "traditional Prussian" known for his "sobriety, objectivity, bee-like industry, conscientiousness and loyalty." Richthofen was exactly the kind of official the Kaiser could not bear listening to, but Bülow did not intend to permit the State Secretary to get anywhere near the Emperor. As in Bismarck's time, the Chancellor would once again be the maker of German foreign policy; the State Secretary would return to the role of instrument of the Chancellor.

To avert the possibility of a clash at the Foreign Office between Richthofen and Holstein, Bülow quickly made clear that he considered the State Secretary far less useful and important than the First Counselor. Bülow's support for Holstein contained a broad element of self-interest; Holstein could be far more destructive as an enemy outside the Foreign Office than while he remained at his desk in the Political Department. With Bülow's permission, Holstein continued to write private letters and transmit confidential documents to German ambassadors without troubling to show them to the State Secretary. Privately, the old Geheimrat trumpeted his victory. "Bülow gives me his full trust . . . ," he crowed in June 1905. "Richthofen is completely excluded, although he is useful to Bulow in parliamentary matters and as a intermediary with other ministries. From time to time, he inquires of me about the status of affairs."

As Chancellor, Bülow gave up tobacco, coffee, beer, and after-dinner liqueur, and limited his intake of alcohol to a half-bottle of red wine at dinner. Every morning, he threw himself into thirty-five minutes of rigorous exercise, including twenty-five knee bends. In good weather he took a daily ride through the Tiergarten, and every Sunday afternoon he tramped for several hours through the woods outside Berlin. Bülow, who took enormous pride in his horsemanship, reported that one of his proudest days came in 1905 when, at age fifty-six, he led his old regiment, the King William I Hussars, past the Kaiser on parade, first at a trot, then at a gallop.* At the close of this exercise, the Emperor handed him a brevet as Major General.

Bülow did not leave making a good impression entirely to charm. The Foreign Office press department was required to provide him with sketches of people he was to meet. In one such

---

* The impossibility of imagining Salisbury, Balfour, Campbell-Bannerman or Asquith donning a uniform, mounting a horse, and leading a cavalry charge past the sovereign suggests the differences between London and Berlin.

instance, the Chancellor was dining with an important newspaper owner whose father had played a role in the events of 1848. Bülow, prepared by the briefing, greeted the son by declaring his regret that "decades had to pass before I might make the acquaintance of the son of a man whom I revered from childhood as a great patriot." Following this meeting, the press lord and his newspaper lined up solidly behind the Chancellor. Bülow, meanwhile, laughingly confessed to his staff that he had never before heard of either the press lord or his father.

Bülow gave priority in his daily schedule to two concerns: his relationship with the Kaiser and his own comfort. Paperwork and staff discussions were limited to the hour between noon and one P.M. and visits from foreign ambassadors and other dignitaries to the hour between six P.M. and seven P.M. The morning was left free for the Kaiser, who when he was in Berlin paid the Chancellor a daily visit at nine A.M. to walk in the garden of the Chancellor's palace. Bülow encouraged William to seek him out and pass along all his thoughts. William found this invitation irresistible and on certain days the Kaiser walked with Bülow in the morning, met him again for lunch, and dined with him in the evening. Where William was not concerned, the Chancellor bestirred himself less vigorously. Nothing was allowed to interrupt his lunch hour, his evening program, his night's rest, or his vacations.

Bülow's sycophancy was remarkable even in the Kaiser's entourage. "The air is thick with incense," wrote William's household controller. "Whenever, by oversight, he [Bülow] expresses an opinion in disagreement with the Emperor, he remains silent for a few moments and then says the exact contrary, with the preface, 'As Your Majesty so wisely remarked just now, the matter stands thus and so . . .'" Count Robert von Zedlitz-Trützschler also was present on board the *Hohenzollern* on the day William complained to Bülow, "Your light trousers are enough to upset the best weather forecast." The Chancellor immediately retreated to his cabin and put on a darker pair. William trusted Bülow's judgment and, gradually, power transferred to him. "Since I have Bülow, I can sleep peacefully," William said to Eulenburg in 1901. "I leave things to him and I know that everything is all right."

CHAPTER 8

"Ships of My Own"

◆

I had a peculiar passion for the Navy," William II wrote in his memoirs, adding: "It sprang to no small extent from my English blood. . . ." William's feeling for ships and the sea began during his frequent boyhood visits to Osborne, Queen Victoria's seaside retreat on the Isle of Wight. "Osborne is the scene of my earliest recollections," William remembered. It was a happy place for children. Prince Albert had built for his own offspring a Swiss chalet with its own garden and kitchen so that they could grow their own vegetables, wash and iron their own clothes, and invite their parents to a tea they had prepared. For boys, there was a model fort. The next generation moved easily into these elaborate games. "I was allowed to play with the same toys and in the same places as did formerly my English uncles and aunts when they were my age," said William. He particularly liked the Osborne fort, where "I could play with the same old iron cannon on a model redoubt where my uncles played when they were boys."

The most appealing aspect of being at Osborne, for William, was its proximity to the sea. Down the hill on the Solent lay the little village of Cowes, home of the Royal Yacht Squadron, the premier sailing club of the United Kingdom. Across the Solent, five miles away, was the Royal Navy base at Portsmouth. "I often crossed over

. . . to Portsmouth and saw all classes of ships . . . and all the docks and shipyards," said William. "I climbed over the ship-of-the-line *Victory.* . . . On the three-decker *St. Vincent* . . . gunnery practice was just taking place as I boarded her. I was permitted to take part . . . and told off as gunner No. 1 to serve a gun. . . . I was not a little proud to have contributed my share to the deafening thunder of the broadside." William encountered his first German warship, the battleship *König Wilhelm,* when he was ten. "Heavy on the water lay the ironclad hull of this colossus, from whose gunports a row of 21 cm. guns looked menacingly forth," he wrote. "I gazed speechless on this mighty ship towering far above us. Suddenly, shrill whistles resounded from her and immediately hundreds of sailors swarmed up the sky-high rigging. . . . Three cheers greeted my father. . . . The tour of the ship . . . revealed to me an entirely new world . . . massive rigging, the long tier of guns with their heavy polished muzzles . . . tea and all sorts of rich cakes in . . . the admiral's cabin." When still a boy, William had other tastes of navy life: at thirteen, he learned to steer by a compass and to hoist signal flags, and he liked visiting the engine room and watching the heavy piston rods as they thrust back and forth. At fourteen, he witnessed the launching of the German Navy's first German-built ironclad, the turret ship *Preussen,* christened by his mother, the Crown Princess, at the Vulcan shipyard in Stettin. In 1880, at nineteen, he was back in Portsmouth, inspecting the new British battleship *Inflexible,* then the most powerful ship in the British Navy, about to go to sea under her first captain, John Arbuthnot Fisher. The following year, William represented Kaiser William I during the visit of an English squadron of eight armored ships to Kiel.

William never forgot or discounted the impact of England and the Royal Navy on his own perceptions. In June 1904, he managed to lure King Edward VII to Kiel, where every major ship of the German Navy was anchored. At a dinner aboard the *Hohenzollern,* the Kaiser attributed the building of this German fleet to his own feelings about the British Navy. "When, as a little boy, I was allowed to visit Portsmouth and Plymouth hand in hand with kind aunts and friendly admirals, I admired the proud English ships in those two superb harbors. Then there awoke in me the wish to build ships of my own like these someday, and when I was grown up to possess as fine a navy as the English."*

---

* The German people never read this Imperial reminiscence. Bülow listened to his master speak and quickly scribbled an alternative text for the press. When the Kaiser saw the new text, he complained to his Chancellor, "You have left out the best bits." "Believe

■ ■ ■

It was at Cowes and in the waters of the Solent in the 1890s that the rivalry between young Kaiser William II and his uncle the Prince of Wales gained momentum. The Prince of Wales had been slow to acquire a taste for competitive yachting. He was twenty-five when he bought his first sailing yacht, a thirty-seven-ton cutter which he named *Dagmar* after his Danish sister-in-law. Not until ten years later, in 1876, did he begin to race, winning the Queen's Cup at Cowes with the schooner *Hildegarde* and winning again with the racing cutter *Formosa*. Both boats were purchased from other yachtsmen; it was not until 1892 that the prince, at fifty-one, ordered a racing yacht built for himself. This was the 122-foot-long racing cutter *Britannia* (221 tons, designed by the preeminent British yacht designer, the Scot George Lennox Watson). *Britannia*'s mast towered 164 feet over the deck (a later mast soared 175 feet), and with all sails set she spread seventeen thousand square feet of canvas. *Britannia* was broad-beamed, allowing several comfortable cabins below for her owner and guests. She was sailed by a professional skipper and a crew of thirty-five, and she cost the Prince eight thousand pounds, sails and cabin fittings included.

The Prince was on board when *Britannia* raced for the first time at the Royal Thames Regatta on May 25, 1893. Thereafter, while his mother watched from her wheelchair, a telescope to her eye, from the balcony at Osborne House, he raced almost every day at Cowes regattas. He liked to race in the sunshine and took *Britannia* to the Mediterranean, racing on the Riviera and living on board. One day, he was sitting on deck in a canvas chair while *Britannia* was maneuvering for the start of the race. The yacht began heeling. At the last second, the Prince reached out and grabbed a rail just as his chair and newspapers went overboard. Calmly, the Prince asked if the papers might be fished out as he wanted to finish them. *Britannia* was jibed, a dinghy was lowered, the floating objects were retrieved and the newspapers were sent below to be dried out.

During her first season, May to September 1893, *Britannia* raced forty-three times and won twenty-four first prizes. In her five-year racing career, 1893–1897, she won 147 prizes in 219 races. When on July 3, 1895, *Britannia* defeated Lord Dunraven's *Valkyrie*

---

me, Your Majesty," Bülow explained, "if you describe our fleet, built with such heavy cost, sometimes with danger, so sentimentally, as the outcome of your own personal inclinations and juvenile memories, it will not be easy to obtain further millions for naval construction from the Reichstag."

III and Barclay Walker's *Ailsa,* the Prince wrote happily to his son Prince George, "Today's victory indeed makes *Britannia* the first racing yacht afloat."

If *Britannia,* at least for a while, was the first yacht afloat, her owner was, indisputably, the First Yachtsman Ashore. In 1863, the Prince had become Patron of the Royal Yacht Squadron, founded in 1815 and granted by King George IV the right to fly as its flag the White Ensign of the Royal Navy. In 1882, Bertie became Commodore, holding the office for nineteen years until he succeeded to the throne. The Squadron Club House was the Castle at West Cowes, a gray stone, turreted French-style château of modest size set directly on the sea at West Cowes. Nineteen brass saluting cannon were lined up on the esplanade before the Club House. The Squadron, a masculine retreat, boasted an excellent wine cellar, a celebrated chef, and a library stocked with French novels. No toilet facilities for women were installed until the 1920s.

There was racing in the Solent from May into autumn, but Cowes and the Royal Yacht Squadron blossomed into full glory during Regatta Week in August. Hundreds of great sailing yachts arrived from all parts of the British Isles, from the Continent, and even from America. Anchored in front of the Squadron esplanade, their varnished masts gleaming in the sunlight, they stretched into the shimmering haze of a summer morning. For the seven days of Regatta Week, England's fashionable world crowded into the little town on the Isle of Wight. Tiny bedrooms, even attics, were rented at exorbitant rates. Spectators flocked aboard steamers, passenger ferries, even tugboats to go out and watch the yachts race. The goal of every visitor—titled foreigners, young heiresses and their mothers, ambassadors, rich Americans—was the little stretch of lawn behind the Royal Yacht Squadron. Here, on this sloping bit of turf, members in short blue yachting jackets and white flannel trousers argued over the handicaps and tactics in that day's races. Duchesses sat in small wicker chairs, eating strawberries and nibbling ices. So many famous names were present that one wag described the Squadron lawn as "a marine Madame Tussaud's."

The central figure in this pageant, the royal patron who gave it luster, was the Prince of Wales. When the Prince was aboard his yacht, the Squadron lawn was listless; when he came ashore, it sprang to life. The latest beauties pushed forward hoping to be noticed, grizzled yachtsmen straightened their ties and broke into smiles. "I can recall the portly figure of . . . [the Prince] strolling across the green lawn of the Royal Yacht Squadron," wrote one of the privileged. "He wore a white yachting cap, smoked large cigars and always carried an ebony walking stick. His prominent eyes were china blue and kindly. . . . He was always followed by an entourage of intimate friends; . . . the beautiful Mrs. George Keppel, the notorious Mrs. Langtry, and sometimes his wife, Queen Alexandra, who seemed to me the most beautiful of the ladies."

Although the Prince reigned over the Squadron lawn on Regatta Week, he held no autocratic sway over clubhouse rules. Membership in this bastion of British aristocracy was exclusive; it was said to be far easier to enter the House of Lords than the Royal Yacht Squadron. One anonymous blackball was sufficient to exclude, and Sir Thomas Lipton, who built five great *Shamrock*s to challenge for the America's Cup and was proposed for the Squadron by the Prince himself, was not elected until the last year of his life. The Prince, as Commodore, tried to have the harshness of the single-blackball rule mollified, pointing out in 1900 that ninety-five names had been blackballed over the previous twelve years. The members, many already displeased to see the Squadron lawn cluttered with people who didn't know a cutter from a schooner, voted him down.

The Prince himself was responsible for introducing into the Squadron the member who did the most to spoil his own fun. In 1889, young Kaiser William II visited the Cowes Regatta and expressed an interest in yacht racing. Hospitably, the Prince proposed the Kaiser, who, with his brother, Prince Henry, was speedily elected. William bought an English America's Cup contender named *Thistle*, rechristened her *Meteor*, and, with an English captain and an all-English crew, began to race. It was his success with this first *Meteor* which prompted the Prince, in 1892, to order *Britannia*.

For four consecutive summers, 1892–1895, William appeared at the Regatta, mingling yacht racing with a family visit to his grandmother at Osborne House. Beginning in 1893, he lived on board his new white-and-gold steam yacht, *Hohenzollern*. Guests were often invited to breakfast, where they were served grilled salmon, filet of sole, deviled kidneys, ham and poached eggs (a favorite of the Kaiser's), and large quantities of fruit. Thus fortified, the party went out to race. Always, during Regatta Week, there was at least one formal dinner at Osborne House held in the Durbar Room. The Garter porcelain, with the insignia of the order emblazoned in deep blue and gold, was brought out and, in deference to the Kaiser's Anglophilia, the menu was as English as the Queen's chef could make it: ducklings, lamb with mint sauce, salmon with cucumber, and boiled potatoes. At first, William drank only sweet wines and champagnes until his English uncles, the dukes of Edinburgh and Connaught, taught him the delicate lure of dry vintages.

The burden of the Kaiser's annual visits fell on Bertie, who was detailed by his mother to look after her royal grandson. The toll on the Prince was heavy. With William yacht racing became more than a sport. He was obsessed by competition with his uncle and determined to win at all costs. He made endless trouble about handicaps and rulings, implying that the Committee was favoring the Prince of Wales and every other yachtsman. When engaged in a race, he refused to think of anything else. Once in 1893, when *Meteor* was racing *Britannia* around the Isle of Wight, the wind dropped in the late afternoon and both yachts were becalmed. The Prince, aboard *Britannia,* began to worry about the full-dress dinner which the Queen was giving that evening in William's honor. From his yacht he signalled *Meteor:* "Propose abandon race and return by train so as to reach Osborne in time for dinner." The Kaiser replied: "I object. Race must be fought out. It doesn't matter when we reach Cowes." Eventually, the breeze revived, but it was nine P.M. before the yachts made their moorings and ten before the royal yachtsmen reached Osborne House. The Queen had finished dinner. The Kaiser hurried up, kissed her hands, and apologized. The Queen gave him a thin smile. A few minutes later, the Prince of Wales arrived, taking cover briefly behind a pillar to wipe the perspiration from his brow. Then he came forward and bowed. The Queen gave him a stiff nod.

Eighteen ninety-five was the last year the Kaiser and the Prince of Wales raced against each other in person. As *Britannia* continued to triumph over *Meteor,* William loudly complained. Just before the beginning of the race for the Queen's Cup, the Kaiser announced that he was dissatisfied with the handicapping and withdrew *Meteor,* leaving *Britannia* to sail the course alone. The following winter, William sent his famous telegram to President Paul Kruger of the Transvaal Republic, an act which made the Kaiser persona non grata in England. He did not return to his grandmother's country for four years and never personally sailed at Cowes again.

The nephew's departure was happy news for the uncle. Cowes brought out the worst in William. The Kaiser never let the Prince of Wales—or those around him—forget that the older man was only heir to a throne, whereas he himself was a crowned sovereign. William insisted on the protocol of rank, effectively supplanting his uncle as the most prominent person attending the Regatta. Privately and publicly, the Kaiser let his feelings show. It was at Cowes, aboard the *Hohenzollern,* that William referred to the Prince of

Wales as "an old peacock." In public, he taunted the older man. One night, dining aboard the *Hohenzollern,* William heard that relations between England and Russia had reached a dangerous point. Laughing, he slapped his uncle on the back and said, "So, then, you'll soon be off to India to see what you are good for as a soldier." To Eckardstein, the Prince protested that "the Regatta used to be a pleasant recreation for me, but now, since the Kaiser takes command, it is a vexation." William, he declared, behaved not like a guest, but like "the Boss of Cowes."

The Kaiser himself was absent in the summer of 1896, but his yacht remained to vex the Prince of Wales. Having seen his *Meteor I* beaten for four years by *Britannia,* William decided to build a new boat. Before leaving the Solent at the end of the 1895 Regatta, he summoned G. L. Watson, who had designed *Britannia,* and ordered a new cutter, constructed along lines identical to his uncle's yacht, except that she was to be larger and faster—indeed, her sole assignment was to defeat *Britannia.* The result, *Meteor II,* appeared at the Cowes Regatta in 1896, sailing under the direction of the Kaiser's friend the Earl of Lonsdale and skippered by a great English captain, Bobby Gomes. *Meteor II* was a superb racing machine, carrying substantially more sail than *Britannia* but also, like *Britannia,* having comfortable cabins below for her owner and his guests. (Visitors were surprised to find not only an English captain and crew but an English chef and, on the shelves of the salon and staterooms, English novels, magazines, and newspapers.)

In the summer races of 1896, *Meteor II* proved that *Britannia* had been outbuilt. Chagrined and unwilling to bear either the gibes of his victorious nephew or the expense of building a new and more powerful boat himself, the Prince, in 1897, withdrew from racing and sold his beloved *Britannia.* He bought her back two years later. He sold her again in 1900 and again bought her back as King in 1902. To the end of his life, he continued to sail, either with his family on *Britannia* or, later, as a guest of his friend "Tommy" Lipton on board one of the tea magnate's giant *Shamrock*s (also designed by G. L. Watson). And, untroubled by further intrusions from his Imperial nephew, he attended the Cowes Regatta every year.

The Kaiser continued to race. In all, he owned four *Meteor*s, each larger and faster than its predecessor. In 1902, he replaced the yacht built in Britain with one built in America. Each year, the number of German seamen in the crew increased until, in 1909, *Meteor IV* was built to German design and sent to sea with a German captain and an all-German crew.

■ ■ ■

William, meanwhile, decided to establish at Kiel a Regatta Week in June to rival and eventually eclipse the Cowes Regatta Week in August. Kiel Week became a personal enterprise, on which the Kaiser lavished care and from which he drew enormous pride. He chose a magnificent setting. Kiel Fjord, wrested from Denmark after the 1866 war and now the eastern terminus of the Kiel Canal, was lined by granite cliffs and dark-green forests, with here and there a patch of sloping meadowland dotted with farmhouses. Here, aboard the gleaming white *Hohenzollern,* moored on the sparkling blue waters of the fjord, William felt completely at ease and in control. He often summoned his ministers to Kiel from Berlin and liked to discuss policy and world affairs, pacing the deck of the Imperial yacht.

The Kaiser's fervor drew others into the sport. As the social significance of Kiel Week grew, the hotel capacity of town and countryside was outstripped, and the Hamburg-America line annually dispatched one of its large transatlantic liners to serve as a floating hotel. Nevertheless, the enthusiasm of the German noblemen and industrialists who turned up on sailboats at Kiel Week was suspect. The Kaiser's brother, Prince Henry, himself a naval officer and an excellent yachtsman, stated bluntly: "There's no doubt about it, our people buy yachts and race them only to please my brother. . . . Half of them have never seen the sea. But if they go to the seaside and read about the Emperor's yacht . . . and if the wealthy merchants who know nothing of the sea become yachtsmen to please the Emperor, then it stirs up interest and we can get money for the Navy."

With all his ardor, William never fully achieved his goal. Germans might learn to jibe and come about (or hire English skippers who could do it for them), but Kiel never managed to radiate the social allure of Cowes. The German regatta was too formal, too heavy with court functions. There were too many glittering receptions and ceremonial dinners with heel-clicking generals and admirals, too many trumpets, brass bands, military marches, and goose-stepping soldiers. It was beyond the Kaiser's power to reproduce the casual garden-party atmosphere of Cowes, where the only music came from a string orchestra playing music-hall tunes and the nearest thing to a uniform were the blue blazers and white flannel trousers of the yachtsmen. Nor could William act the offhand seigneurial role created by his uncle. Gradually, the disappointed Kaiser realized that the beautiful Englishwomen who fluttered like butterflies around the genial figure of the Prince of Wales at Cowes would never travel across the North Sea to add luster to Kiel. He had better luck with rich Americans. William was always fascinated with enormous wealth, especially when it was self-made, and American millionaires such as J. P. Morgan, Cornelius Vanderbilt, and Andrew Carnegie, who had become yachtsmen, were flattered to be invited to Kiel Week.

Even at Kiel, the Kaiser never achieved the absolute ascendancy he desired for his *Meteor*s. His British skippers sought to win races, but on *Meteor III* at Kiel, William's captains' chances for victory declined dramatically when the Imperial owner seized the helm. The Kaiser cajoled and seduced them, slapping them on the shoulders in good fellowship, offering them cigarettes from his jeweled cigarette case. Using these tactics, he often succeeded and they ceded command. *Meteor III* usually paid the price. "If the Kaiser steered himself, we regularly hit the buoy," Bülow recorded.

In 1904, the fastest boat at Kiel Week was the new American schooner *Ingomar,* owned by millionaire Morton F. Plant and skippered by Charlie Barr, the finest American racing captain of the day. At the owner's request, Charles F. Robinson, Rear Commodore of the New York Yacht Club, took seagoing responsibility for the boat when she raced. In the 1904 regatta, *Ingomar* competed daily against *Meteor III,* but no race was more dramatic or significant than the first. Fifteen large yachts left their moorings in the harbor that morning in the fresh Baltic wind. Soon after the race began, *Ingomar* began to overtake the Imperial yacht with the Kaiser on board. The American boat was on a starboard tack, which gave her an indisputably legal right of way.

"Nevertheless," wrote Brooke Heckstall-Smith, a British yachting expert who was on board *Ingomar,* "as we approached *Meteor* . . . the Imperial yacht showed no signs of giving way! Not a word was spoken on our vessel; the silent crew lay flat on the weather deck. Morton F. Plant stood on the stairway in the companionway, his head just above the sliding hatch, his elbows resting on the coaming, a cigar in his mouth, a panama hat pulled over one eye. . . . Charlie Robinson, clad in his faultless flannel suit and showing his most elaborate silk socks, was reclining across the counter, chewing gum. . . . Captain Barr stood at the wheel. . . . I was crouching to leeward, my eyes riveted on *Meteor*. . . . Young Baron von Kotwitz, a German naval lieutenant who had been sent on board by the Kaiser as a pilot, was sitting on the deck with his mouth half open . . . wondering whether we had all gone stark raving mad . . . [and] were really going to send his All Highest Emperor to the bottom of the sea. . . . Closer and closer the yachts came together.

Our gigantic Oregon bowsprit was pointing straight at the *Meteor's* bow. . . . We should hit her fair slap amidships. . . . There was a fine breeze; we had every stitch of canvas on, including the jib topsail. . . . It was a silent, tense and terrible moment. Then Barr's voice rang out to me: 'Mr. Smith, Rule!' It was my duty to declare the Rule in a tight place; Barr knew it as well as I did, but it was a definite agreement between us that the responsibility was mine. '*Ingomar,* right!' I replied instantly. 'Mr. Robinson, what am I to do?' shouted Barr. 'Hold on!' came Charlie's instant decision. . . . I was prepared for a deuce of a crash. I heard old Morton F. Plant shout to his friend who was representing him: 'By God, Charlie, you're the boy. I'll give way to no man!'

"At that moment, the *Meteor's* helm was put down. Our bowsprit was within three feet of her rigging. Our helm was jammed down hard also, as quickly as the wheel would turn. Both vessels ranged alongside one another as they shot into the wind. . . .

"When we got back to Kiel, an admiral came alongside with a message from the Kaiser to say that His Majesty was to blame and regretted the incident. . . . But . . . we all felt that if we had allowed the Kaiser to bluff us that first day by giving way to him when we were in the right, he would only have taken advantage of us and bluffed us still more."

That summer at Kiel, *Ingomar* defeated *Meteor III* every time they raced.

CHAPTER 9

Tirpitz
and the German
Navy Laws

◆

The German Navy, like the German Empire, appeared late in the history of Europe. Fifteenth-century Germans had gone to sea in fighting ships; the Hanseatic League once sent out against Scandinavia a war fleet of 260 vessels. But the Thirty Years War, which killed half the population of Germany in the seventeenth century, eroded the power of the great Hansa ports, Hamburg, Bremen, Lübeck, and Rostock, and, for two hundred years, there were no German warships. In 1849, the German Confederation, the loose agglomeration of states formed by the Congress of Vienna, discovered a Leipziger who had learned seamanship in the America merchant marine and gave him command of twelve small fighting ships. Three of these vessels engaged a Danish ship off Heligoland until shots from the British-held island warned that the fracas was in British territorial waters. Great Britain did not recognize the Confederation's right to have a navy; Lord Palmerston, British Foreign Secretary, decreed that ships flying a German flag be treated as pirate vessels.

Prussia, strongest of the German kingdoms and principalities, traditionally had little interest in the sea, reserving its enthusiasm for soldiers and artillery. Then, in 1853, King Frederick William IV bowed to the appeals of his cousin, Prince Adalbert, and agreed to the establishment of a Prussian Admiralty. Adalbert, whose zeal stemmed from visits to British warships in England and the Mediterranean, was granted the title Admiral of the Prussian Coasts after the King had refused the rank of Fleet Admiral, "because we do not have a fleet." Adalbert began with no ships, no officers, no seamen, no naval bases, and—on the North Sea—no seacoast. This last deficiency was rectified in 1854, when Prussia persuaded the Grand Duke of Oldenburg to sell a five-square-mile plot on Jade Bay, where, over the next fifteen years, the naval base of Wilhelmshaven was constructed. In 1865, after defeating Denmark, Prussia annexed Kiel Fjord in the Duchy of Schleswig. Prince Adalbert's navy now possessed two designated "war ports": Wilhelmshaven on the North Sea and Kiel on the Baltic.

Adalbert began acquiring ships. He proposed a fleet of twenty armored vessels. A smaller program was authorized; the ships—as Prussia possessed no naval shipyards—would have to be purchased abroad. In 1864, Prussia's first ironclad, *Arminius,* was launched in England. Three years later, the ironclad *Friedrich Karl* was bought from France. In 1869, Prince Adalbert's navy acquired the 9,700-ton ironclad *König Wilhelm,* one of the largest warships in the world. This vessel, built on the Thames, remained Germany's most powerful ship for twenty-five years.

Adalbert needed officers. He began by using men trained in the navies of England, Holland, Denmark, Sweden, and the United States, or lured from the German merchant marine, or transferred, often against their will, from the Prussian Army. For the future, however, Adalbert wanted native Prussian naval officers, trained from boyhood. He established a training school aboard the corvette *Amazone,* but had difficulty attracting recruits. Most Junker families saw little use for a navy and withheld their sons. Prince Adalbert's task became more difficult when the *Amazone* went down in a storm, drowning most of the cadets on board; the year following, only three candidates applied.

By the summer of 1870, Prince Adalbert had assembled a squadron of four ironclads based at Wilhelmshaven. His troubles had not ended. The Franco-Prussian War, which resulted in overwhelming victory and military glory for the Prussian Army, brought disgrace to the Prussian Navy. When the war began, the Second French Empire was, after Great Britain, the strongest naval power in the world. French squadrons easily blockaded the German Baltic and North Sea coasts and seized forty German merchant ships. The Prussian ironclads remained at anchor, forbidden to fight against this overwhelming strength unless the French tried to force their way up the Elbe or Weser to attack Hamburg or Bremen. (The single naval action of the war took place three thousand miles away when the German gunboat *Meteor* fought a French dispatch boat off the coast of Cuba.) The greatest wartime danger to the passive squadron at Wilhelmshaven was that German mines, placed across the harbor entrance to protect German ships, would break loose and drift down among the anchored vessels.

The navy's behavior earned it contempt from the Prussian Army. German naval personnel were denied permission to count Franco-Prussian War duty as "war service" in their personal records. Admiralty officials found it difficult even to justify a navy. France, reputedly the greatest military and naval power on the Continent, had been swiftly defeated by the Prussian Army with no contribution from the Prussian Navy. If French naval superiority could do nothing to prevent France's humiliation, what was the point of Germany, now the supreme military power in Europe, having a navy? Bismarck had little interest in fleets; indeed, he once quoted approvingly the decision of the Prussian King Frederick William I, "who sold his last warship to create one more battalion."

It was a sign of the navy's low repute that, when Prince Adalbert retired in 1872, German Army generals commanded the German Navy for the next sixteen years. The first, General of Infantry Albrecht von Stosch, with a character "sharp as jagged iron," administered the navy like an army corps, applying the harsh parade-ground zeal of a Potsdam Guards regiment. Completing his inspection of one warship, he announced in a loud voice: "Sheer slop! From the commander to the lowest ship's boy." He insisted on full uniform at all times until an officer costumed in tunic and sash fainted on the bridge of a German warship in the tropics.

Stosch settled on coast defense as the navy's role. As France and Russia were the assumed enemies during his eleven-year term (1872–1883), he drilled his sailors to oppose a French or Russian landing on German beaches. In accord with this strategy, ironclads were distributed along the coast as floating forts. Designed to fight in coastal waters, these vessels were of shallow draft, which made them unsuitable for action in the open sea, where heavy swells would roll them back and forth. Stosch also persuaded Bismarck and the Reichstag to approve a ten-year building program of eight German-built, seagoing ironclads, to be used in sudden sorties against a blockading enemy fleet. (The money was obtained more easily because one quarter of it came from the war indemnity levied against defeated France.)

Stosch was replaced in 1883 by General Georg Leo von Caprivi, the future Chancellor. Caprivi, obsessed by the possibility of a two-front war with France and Russia, was determined to conserve "every man and every penny" for the great land battle. In Caprivi's mind, the ideal vessels for this purpose were small, inexpensive torpedo boats weighing only eighty or ninety tons, carrying three torpedo tubes; such boats could dash out among approaching enemy warships and troopships and torpedo them. Kaiser William II, assuming the throne in June 1888, was not interested in a navy of torpedo boats. William, indignant that during five years at the Admiralty Caprivi had built no big ships, embarrassed that Germany in 1888 spent less money on its navy than any great European power except Austria, accepted Caprivi's resignation three weeks after his accession and appointed a naval officer, Admiral Alexander von Monts. Within six months, Monts designed, and eventually the Reichstag approved, four ten-thousand-ton battleships—*Brandenburg, Kurfürst Friedrich Wilhelm, Worth,* and *Weissenburg,* the only modern battleships to enter the German Navy during William's first ten years as Kaiser.

William might proclaim—as he did in Stettin in 1891—that "our future is on the water," but few Germans agreed with him. This stemmed, in part, from the traditional Prussian belief that money spent on defense should be spent on the army. It also resulted from the Reichstag's reluctance to gratify any of the monarch's grandiose designs, especially those which seemed to enhance his personal rule and encroach on the parliament's own already limited constitutional privileges. But the primary reason for the inconspicuous success of the German Navy during William's first decade was the confusion in the Kaiser's mind and among senior naval officers as to how the navy should be administered and what its strategic purpose should be. In 1888, when William took the throne, the navy was administered by a single office, the Admiralty. In 1889, when Admiral Monts suddenly died, William abolished the Admiralty and split its functions between two offices: the High Command (*Oberkommando*), responsible for strategy and actual command of the fleet, and the Imperial Naval Office (*Reichsmarineamt*), charged with designing and building warships and wringing the funds for this purpose from the Reichstag. Admiral Eduard von Knorr, the Chief of the High Command in the 1890s, reported directly to the Kaiser, as Supreme War Lord; Admiral Friedrich von Hollmann, the State Secretary of the Navy Office during these years, was a Minister of the Imperial Government who reported to the Chancellor. The problems and frustrations were inherent: the Navy Secretary decided what ships to build without asking the High Command what ships it needed to implement its strategy. To complicate this administrative impasse, William at the same time created a third senior post: a personal naval aide on his private staff, titled Chief of the Naval Cabinet. This officer, Admiral Gustav von Senden-Bibran, inevitably became a private channel for dissident officers wishing to gain the Kaiser's ear. The result was constant bureaucratic warfare, which angered the Kaiser and confused the Reichstag.

The problem was conceptual as well as administrative: the Kaiser and the admirals could not agree on the purpose of a German Navy. William's ambitions were global. He wanted a fleet to inspire worldwide respect, to defend German colonies, and to protect German merchant ships on the high seas; for this purpose a large fleet of cruisers equipped for foreign service seemed more useful than squadrons of battleships riding at anchor in Kiel and Wilhelmshaven. Hollmann's strategy was based on coastal defense and commerce raiding: he wanted cruisers. Senden believed in battleships. He accepted Mahan's thesis that without a battle fleet as the hard core of national sea power, even swarms of cruisers would eventually be gobbled up by enemy battleships. Knorr waffled, frustrated that administratively it was Hollmann who decided what ships should be built. In fact, the real opposition to Hollmann and cruisers, the true intellectual proponent of battleships and a mighty German battle fleet, was a navy captain serving in the High Command. His name was Alfred Tirpitz.

Later, when the massive figure of Grand Admiral Alfred von Tirpitz with his bald, domed head, his famous forked beard, his reputation as the Father of the High Seas Fleet, was instantly recognizable in Germany and the world, no one remembered that during Tirpitz's first thirty years in the German Navy he had been a maverick. Tirpitz at the height of his power was—after Bismarck—the ablest, most durable, most influential and most effective minister in Imperial Germany. He was described as aggressive, ruthless, domineering, and obsessive. His favorite drink, it was said, was "North Sea foam." Having worked his way to the top, he had little use for young aristocrats who expected to rise on the strength of their names. Once, when a ballroom mariner asked the Admiral about his chances for promotion, Tirpitz replied, "You have very white hands for a man who hopes to command a cruiser." There were many complaints about Tirpitz. "You'll have to get along with him," the Kaiser always responded. "That's what I have to do."

Tirpitz had climbed the ladder rung by rung. He had served

aboard a sailing ship and an armored cruiser during the Franco-Prussian War, had commanded a torpedo-boat flotilla in the Baltic, a cruiser in the Mediterranean, and a cruiser squadron in the Far East. Ironically, never during fifty-one years of naval service did Tirpitz hear a naval gun fired in combat. His life was spent, nevertheless, in constant battle. He fought, not in North Sea gales, but at desks in Kiel and Berlin, in the chamber of the Reichstag, in the Kaiser's audience room at the Neues Palais or the imperial hunting lodge at Romintern. He was obsessive in his belief in German sea power and in his desire to create a fleet of mighty battleships. He thought only about the navy. He had no political or religious principles; he was willing to accept battleships from conservatives, Catholics, or socialists. In one argument with the Foreign Ministry, he said, "Politics are your affair. I build ships." When the wisdom or the direction of his shipbuilding was challenged by others, even an Imperial Chancellor, Tirpitz demanded and received the Kaiser's support and overrode the Chancellor.

The public image—and now the legend—of Tirpitz depicts a gruff curmudgeon, grimly resolved to have his way. But there was another side. He could be smiling, urbane, and conciliatory. In Berlin drawing rooms, with a glass of fine wine or a good cigar in his hand, Tirpitz played the polished, accomplished man of the world. Every year, he and his wife gave a party for all the officers and civilians in the Navy Ministry. During the evening, Tirpitz wandered from table to table, sitting and chatting amiably with each of his guests about whatever came into their heads. Hidden from the world, there was an even deeper layer. Tirpitz was highly emotional; his secretary reported that when he returned to his office from a difficult day at the Reichstag, he would sit at his desk and weep. He suffered from profound extremes of elation and depression. He was both a hypochondriac and an insomniac. His strength lay in his family, to which he was intensely devoted. To relax, he bought a house at St. Blasien in the Black Forest, far from Prussia, far from the sea. Here, sitting on his porch overlooking a pine-forested gorge, he could breathe the crisp mountain air and clear his mind of the tensions wrought in Berlin. At one point, even St. Blasien was too close and he bought a small house in Sardinia where, his daughter wrote, "one is so far from the world and civilization, in such primitive, 'bandit-like' conditions, that it is easy to imagine one is enchanted."

Alfred Tirpitz was born ten years before Kaiser William II, on March 19, 1849, into a professional, middle-class Prussian family.

His father was a lawyer who became a judge; his mother was the daughter of a physician. (The ennobling "von" would be added when Tirpitz was fifty-one as a mark of the Kaiser's favor.) Tirpitz' entry into the navy was not the result of boyhood enthusiasm. Rather, he admitted later, "I was very mediocre" in school. When a friend "expressed his intention of entering the Navy . . . it occurred to me that it might mean a certain relief for my parents if I too were to take up the idea." His father agreed, and in the spring of 1856, Tirpitz, at sixteen, became a cadet in Prince Adalbert's navy. Within a year, Prussia was at war with Austria and Tirpitz found himself aboard a sailing ship in the English Channel preparing for battle against an enemy steam corvette. Tirpitz' duty was to load cannonballs into the mouth of a gun and be ready with his nearby pike to repel boarders. Before shots were fired, the approaching "Austrian" vessel turned out to be Norwegian. Four years later, as a sublieutenant aboard the flagship *König Wilhelm,* Tirpitz shared in the Prussian Navy's humiliation as his ship spent the Franco-Prussian War lying at anchor.

Tirpitz, like William II, respected England and, also like William, admired the Royal Navy. During his cadet years, British naval officers treated the fledgling Prussian Navy as a diminutive offspring, deserving of nurture. "Between 1864 and 1870 our real supply base was Plymouth, where Nelson's three-deckers and the great wooden ships of the line of the Crimean War lay in long rows up the river," Tirpitz wrote. "Here we felt ourselves almost more at home than in the peaceful and idyllic Kiel, which only grumbled at Prussia. . . . In the Navy Hotel at Plymouth we were treated like British midshipmen. . . . Our tiny naval officers' corps looked up to the British Navy with admiration. . . . We grew up on the British Navy like a creeping plant. We preferred to get our supplies from England. If an engine ran smoothly . . . if a rope or a chain did not break, than it was certain not to be a home-made article, but a product of English workshops—a rope with the famous red strand of the British Navy. . . . in those days we could not imagine that German guns could be equal to English."

Tirpitz's esteem for the British Navy extended to esteem for English education and the English language. He spoke fluent English, read English newspapers and English novels, made a hobby of English philology, and enrolled his two daughters at Cheltenham Ladies' College. He bristled, however, at the patronizing attitude some Britons displayed towards Germany and the German Navy. As a young officer on the *Friedrich Karl,* he overheard an English-woman at Gibraltar say of his ship's crew, "Don't they look just like sailors?" When Lieutenant Tirpitz asked how they should look, she replied, "But you are not a sea-going nation." Tirpitz, in time, found himself sharing Bismarck's view: "I have had all through my life sympathy for England and its inhabitants. . . . But these people do not want to let themselves be liked by us."

Tirpitz's years as a gunnery officer aboard the *König Wilhelm* and *Friedrich Karl* were spent cruising the Mediterranean, the Caribbean, and the Pacific, showing the flag in ports which had never seen a German warship. In 1877, Tirpitz was assigned to visit the Whitehead Torpedo Centre at Fiume. When he returned to Germany, he was placed in charge of torpedo development for the German Navy. He started with the torpedoes themselves, working "like a mechanic with my own hands." In 1879, Emperor William I and Crown Prince Frederick visited the station, and Tirpitz arranged a demonstration of his torpedoes. "It was a tossup whether they would reach the target or ricochet wildly," he confessed afterwards.

From designing and testing weapons, Tirpitz proceeded to developing the boats that would launch the torpedoes and the tactics the boats would employ. This put him in contact with Navy State Secretary Caprivi, who happened to be a distant relation. "We do not know how we should fight," Tirpitz admitted to the State Secretary, and Caprivi instructed the young lieutenant to work out tactics. Although Caprivi envisaged the navy's role as defensive, Tirpitz persuaded him that when war began—France was assumed to be the navy's primary enemy—Tirpitz should lead his torpedo squadron in a dash into Cherbourg harbor, where his boats would torpedo every French warship in sight. Whatever armored ships Germany possessed would follow behind to bombard what remained of the French Northern Fleet. Tirpitz later referred to his duty with the "Black Host" of the torpedo flotilla as "the eleven best years of my life." In 1887, he met twenty-eight-year-old Prince William when his torpedo boats escorted the Prince across the North Sea to attend Queen Victoria's Golden Jubilee.

In 1888, when Monts succeeded Caprivi as Navy Minister, torpedo boats fell into disfavor and Tirpitz asked to be transferred. He was given command successively of the cruisers *Preussen* and *Württemberg*. In 1890, he was appointed Chief of Staff of the Baltic Squadron. He was sitting after dinner one evening in Kiel Castle with the Kaiser, General von Moltke, and a number of generals and admirals, when William asked for proposals on development of the navy. Tirpitz, a junior captain, remained silent while different theories were aired. Finally, the Kaiser said, "Here I have been listening to you arguing for hours that we must put an end to all this mess,

and yet not one of you has made a really positive suggestion."
Senden nudged Tirpitz, and Tirpitz declared that Germany must
have battleships. Nine months later, he was summoned to Berlin as
Chief of Staff to the High Command and commissioned personally
by the Kaiser to develop a strategy for a High Seas Fleet.

In Berlin, Tirpitz, surrounding himself with former "Black
Host" comrades, set to work. He changed the navy's annual training
cycle, terminating the army-based system of commissioning warships only for summer maneuvers, decommissioning them in autumn
and sending their crews ashore. In wartime, Tirpitz said, this system
would result in Germany possessing "a crowd of ships with men on
board, but no fleet." He drew up tactical exercises for operating a
battle fleet in the open sea. At that moment, ship design was ahead
of naval tactics; large armored ships were becoming available, but
no one knew how to use them in battle; some naval officers assumed
they would—as in Nelson's day—steer towards the enemy and attempt to ram and board. Tirpitz, unwilling to wait until Monts' new
battleships actually appeared, collected whatever ships he could find
—even training vessels and minesweepers—and used them to simulate larger ships. In this manner, he determined that a line of eight
ships was the most effective tactical unit; if more ships were available, a second line of eight could be formed, to work in unison with
or independently of the first eight.

Tirpitz' presentation to the Kaiser on December 1, 1892, of his
book of tactical exercises led to his first serious confrontation with
Navy State Secretary Hollmann. Admiral von Hollmann, Tirpitz
wrote in his *Memoirs,* was "a high-minded man who was never quite
clear as to the direction to be followed." His decisions were "absolutely devoid of principle and adapted only to the needs of the moment. . . . It was the tendency during this period to bring forward
demands in the Reichstag which were based not so much upon requirements as upon the probability of their being granted." This
produced "aimlessness," "chronic crisis," and "a confusion of opinions" which "displayed itself in a heterogeneous collection of vessels
from which one could not confidently expect any mutual cooperation in the event of war." Tirpitz's exercises assumed the eventual
availability of a fleet of relatively homogeneous ships which, possessing the same characteristics and fighting power, could operate
together. Hollmann, whose office was responsible for the design of
ships as well as obtaining money to build them from the Reichstag,
considered Tirpitz' theories a threat and demanded from the Kaiser
the right to overrule or amend the tactical exercise book. Tirpitz
fought back.

The battleground was the issue of battleships versus cruisers. William was caught in between. At one point, a number of Reichstag deputies were invited to a conference on naval matters at the New Palace. Tirpitz, seeing the Kaiser the day before, discovered that William intended to speak exclusively in favor of cruisers. Tirpitz objected, raising again the advantages of a battle fleet. William, disturbed, asked, "Why was Nelson then always calling for frigates?" "Because he *had* a battle fleet," Tirpitz replied. William subsequently blurred his address to the deputies the following day, calling for both cruisers and battleships, and sounding, to one observer, "like a gramophone record with two melodies playing at once."

Tirpitz, frustrated, asked in the autumn of 1895 to be relieved of duty with the High Command. William, not wanting to lose the services of this forceful, clear-thinking officer, parried by asking Tirpitz to comment on a recently received High Command recommendation on future naval construction. Tirpitz (who was largely responsible for writing the Oberkommando paper) obliged. On January 3, 1896, he handed the Kaiser a memorandum calling for two squadrons of eight battleships each, plus a fleet flagship. These seventeen battleships, he said, would constitute "a considerable force even against a fleet of the first rank." "Even the greatest sea state in Europe would be more conciliatory towards us if we were able to throw two or three highly trained squadrons into the political scales," he said. "We shall never achieve that using overseas cruisers."

Tirpitz's memorandum reached the Kaiser three days after news of the Jameson Raid into the Transvaal.* William passionately desired to intervene in this South African affair six thousand miles from Europe but was prevented by Germany's impotence at sea; caught up in his emotions, William thrust aside Tirpitz' memorandum. "My intentions . . . [are] altered by the Transvaal," he wrote to Hohenlohe. "We need . . . the purchase of armored cruisers and cruisers wherever we can find them as soon as possible. . . . At the same time, cruisers must be laid down in the homeland in numbers corresponding to the capacities of our dockyards." Tirpitz was dismayed by William's decision. "Tirpitz was here," Admiral Senden noted in his diary on January 12. "He was very dissatisfied that cruisers are now being demanded again and believes that, as a result, the whole program will break up." To Hohenlohe, all of the Kaiser's navy demands now seemed excessive. Consulting the lead-

* See Chapter 11.

ers of the Reichstag, he found "not a trace of enthusiasm for enlarging the Navy." Senden grimly confirmed this news to the Kaiser: "These are the facts: the . . . [Kaiser] has no majority in the Government . . . nor in the Reichstag. . . . I advise a change of personnel. . . . We must rule with one party only. . . . An energetic man with a broad view as State Secretary must bring about a change, perhaps Tirpitz." Near the end of January, Hollmann told Hohenlohe that "the Kaiser hopes to find a Chancellor who will introduce big naval demands, then dissolve the Reichstag and eventually carry out a *coup d'état.* That's all right with me . . . [but] I cannot see whom he will find to try out this experiment." Senden began pressing for Hollmann's replacement by Tirpitz. At the end of January 1896, when Tirpitz visited the Kaiser to discuss his battle-fleet memorandum of January 3, William impulsively announced that he intended to replace Hollmann and that Tirpitz would be the new State Secretary.

Hollmann, meanwhile, was pushing a shipbuilding program through the Reichstag. It included neither the numbers of battleships that Tirpitz had urged nor the swarm of cruisers for South Africa desired by the Kaiser, and it was obtained only by promising the deputies that, if the bill were approved, no additional request for funds would be made that year. In this budget, the Reichstag approved the building of one new battleship, *Kaiser Friedrich der Grosse,* and three large armored cruisers. William seemed pleased. He departed on a cruise, busying himself with sketches of a nine-thousand-ton battleship which, said Kiderlen, "was lovely only it could not float."

Hollmann's success eliminated Tirpitz' chance of succeeding the State Secretary that year. While the program was passing through the Reichstag, Senden wrote to Tirpitz: "Only the present State Secretary [Hollmann] has any hope of getting the Navy bill through peacefully. His Majesty shares the view . . . that a new State Secretary in the present parliamentary situation would arouse suspicion. . . . His Majesty has therefore decided to refrain from a change at present but wants you to be told that 'postponed' does not mean forever." Within a month of this decision, Tirpitz, promoted to Rear Admiral, departed Berlin to take command of the German cruiser squadron in the Far East.

The following year, William renewed his demand on Hollmann for more ships. Hollmann, unable to promise that he could persuade the Reichstag to grant this demand, found himself in growing disfavor. "He [William] seems to be toying with the idea of letting Hollmann go at the end of the year, because he is not the right man to carry the huge fleet plans through the Reichstag," the Chancellor wrote to Eulenburg. "I can tell you this here and now, that the monster fleet plan is a practical impossibility for the forseeable future. . . . I consider the whole idea still-born no matter which Navy Secretary or Reich Chancellor assumes the role of Godfather." In March, William told Hohenlohe that, if the Reichstag did not appropriate the money, he would build the fleet "and send the bill to the Reichstag later." When the Chancellor pointed out that, under the Empire's 1871 constitution, this was illegal, William grumbled, "The Kaiser has no rights."

On March 12, 1896, the Budget Committee of the Reichstag cut 12 million marks from Hollmann's 70-million-mark budget. Hollmann submitted his resignation; Hohenlohe, to the Kaiser's chagrin, refused to accept it. On March 30, William placed Hollmann on extended leave of absence. On April 3, Holstein wrote to Bülow, "Our doom embodied in Admiral Tirpitz is closing in upon us."

Tirpitz' primary assignment in the Far East had been "to seek out a place on the Chinese coast where Germany could construct a military and economic base." Upon arrival, he found the German cruiser squadron based at the British colony of Hong Kong, where drydock arrangements for German warships had to be made nine months in advance. Tirpitz and his ships cruised along the Chinese coast inspecting harbors, finally selecting Tsingtao* on the Yellow Sea. By the time the harbor was seized by German marines and "leased" from China in the autumn of 1897, Tirpitz had returned to Berlin.

In March, the Kaiser had summoned Tirpitz home to become Navy Minister. "I relinquished my command with a heavy heart," he said in his *Memoirs*. "Universal experience showed that to get . . . [shipbuilding legislation] through the Reichstag, a 'gift of gab' was needed which I did not possess." He went anyway, returning to Europe slowly, traveling across the Pacific, America, and the Atlantic. In Salt Lake City, he held a brief press conference; when asked about unfavorable comments in the German press concerning his appointment, he only smiled.

On June 6, 1897, Tirpitz arrived in Berlin. Great things were expected of him, but neither the Kaiser, the Chancellor, the Reichs-

* Tsingtao on Kiaochow Bay became the only overseas naval base ever possessed by the Imperial German Navy.

tag, nor the navy was prepared for the rapid succession of events that followed. On his desk, Tirpitz found a proposed Navy Bill drafted by Hollmann demanding more ships for the foreign-service cruiser fleet. He discarded it. On June 15, only nine days after taking office, Tirpitz visited the Kaiser in Potsdam and presented a 2,500-word "Very Secret" memorandum entitled "General Considerations on the Constitution of Our Fleet According to Ship Classes and Designs." Behind this technical language lay a document which would alter German and European history. Clearly, logically, relentlessly, like blows of a hammer, Tirpitz' sentences rolled out:

> "For Germany, the most dangerous naval enemy at the present time is England."
> "Our fleet must be constructed so that it can unfold its greatest military potential between Heligoland and the Thames."
> "The military situation against England demands battleships in as great a number as possible."
> "Only the main theatre of war will be decisive."
> "Commerce raiding [i.e., cruiser warfare] . . . against England is so hopeless because of the shortage of bases on our side and the great number on England's side, that we must ignore this type of war against England in our plans for the constitution of our fleet."
> "A German Fleet . . . built against England [requires]: 1 fleet flagship, 2 squadrons of eight battleships each, 2 reserve battleships for a total of 19 battleships."
> "This fleet can be largely completed by 1905. The expenditure . . . will amount to 408 million marks or 58 million marks per annum."

All previous German naval strategy was swept away. Cruiser warfare would be eliminated. The Reichstag's complaints about "limitless fleet plans" would be silenced. A battle fleet would be built for no larger annual sum than Admiral Hollmann's reduced 1896 budget of 58 million marks. The navy, hitherto an object of contempt, would become a powerful weapon in the hands of German admirals and an effective instrument in the hands of German diplomats. The international implications of Tirpitz' memorandum were even more far-reaching. To justify building battleships, a new enemy—England, at that time friendly to Germany—had been designated. To fight France and Russia, a powerful German battle fleet was unnecessary; the German Army would win or lose that war whatever might happen at sea. To fight England, however, Tirpitz had established that battleships would be necessary. Having established that premise, Tirpitz then brilliantly reversed the argument: in order to justify building battleships, the enemy must be England.

In a parliamentary sense, the memorandum's radical feature was that the Reichstag would be asked to commit itself to building a fixed number of warships over a number of years; this commitment would be binding and unalterable; for seven years neither these deputies nor future deputies would have the power to intervene and override. This was revolutionary: Admiral Hollmann had never objected to appearing annually, with that year's request, before the Reichstag. Indeed, Hollmann had considered this both a necessity and a virtue. "The Reichstag will never agree to be bound to a formal program for years in advance," he had argued. Besides, he continued, "the art of war is changeable on sea and no naval ministry can prophesy what we shall need ten years hence." Tirpitz, on arriving, had viewed the result of Hollmann's philosophy with contempt. "When I became State Secretary," he wrote, "the German Navy was a collection of experiments in shipbuilding surpassed in exoticism only by the Russian Navy of Nicholas II." Even the British Navy suffered from this syndrome, "but there, money is of no importance; if they built a class of ships wrongly, they just threw the whole lot into the corner and built another. We could not permit ourselves that. . . . I needed a Bill which would protect the continuity of construction of the fleet" and remove from the Reichstag "the temptation to interfere each year in technical details." The Reichstag, in other words, having voted a fixed number of ships, would have nothing further to say.

William approved Tirpitz' memorandum and the Navy Secretary moved quickly to draft a new bill. Delegating all routine administrative matters to a deputy at 13 Leipzigerplatz, he retreated first to Ems, then to St. Blasien, in order to think and work freely. He brought to the Black Forest a team of comrades and specialists from all parts of the navy, modeling it on Nelson's "Band of Brothers." Discussions were open and freewheeling; Tirpitz threw out ideas and then sat back, primus inter pares, to listen. No idea was sacred: "Every word of the draft Bill was altered probably a dozen times in our discussions at St. Blasien," he said. Ultimately, "we almost always came to a mutual decision."

The timetable was rigorous. Every document carried instructions: "At once," "Very urgent," "Finish today." On June 19, Tirpitz asked his colleagues to revise within six days all budget figures for the fiscal year 1898 in light of the new plan. By July 2, he was given a preliminary draft of the Navy Bill itself. Repeatedly, Tirpitz stressed to his coworkers that the key to their deliberations was that England was the enemy. An effective stimulus was provided by the June 26 Diamond Jubilee Naval Review, when the Royal Navy displayed 165 warships in five lines stretching over thirty miles.

By the end of July, reports of unusual activity in the Leipzigerplatz were spreading across Berlin. Tirpitz, to allay fears in the Navy High Command that its functions were being purloined, called on Admiral Knorr. The two agreed to establish a joint committee. Tirpitz saw to it that the committees received no information and had nothing to do. Six months later, when Knorr challenged Tirpitz directly, it was too late. The Navy Bill was before the Reichstag; Tirpitz went to the Kaiser and asked William to lay down, once and for all, the responsibility of the Navy Minister for ship types and shipbuilding. William obliged and Knorr was silenced. Tirpitz employed a similar tactic when the Treasury State Secretary expressed fears about the estimated costs of the new fleet. Tirpitz called on the State Secretary and deferentially promised formation of a joint committee. Meanwhile, he redoubled his efforts to win over the Kaiser and the Chancellor. In September, when the Treasury Secretary again raised objections, Tirpitz replied, "With all the good will in the world, I regret that I am unable to request the Reich Chancellor for any further decisions on a question which has already been decided on All-Highest level with the knowledge of the Reich Chancellor."

At the end of August, with the draft bill almost complete, Tirpitz embarked on a round of visits to leading German figures to obtain endorsements. On August 24 he called on Bismarck, who had been visited by no minister of the Imperial Government since his dismissal seven years before. To prepare the way, Tirpitz had persuaded the Kaiser to name the next large warship to be launched, a ten-thousand-ton armored cruiser, *Fürst Bismarck* (*Prince Bismarck*). William reluctantly had agreed and Tirpitz had written to Friedrichsruh requesting an audience. The letter had been returned with a message that the Prince did not open letters without the sender's name clearly written on the envelope. Tirpitz wrote a second letter, properly labeled, and was told to come.

He arrived at noon on August 24 to find the family already at lunch. Bismarck, at the head of the table, rose slightly when the visitor entered and gestured him to a chair. The former Chancellor, tormented by neuralgia, ate with difficulty, holding a hot-water bottle to his cheek, picking carefully over a plate of chopped meat, and refilling his glass until he had drunk a bottle and a half of champagne. When lunch was finished, Bill Bismarck's wife lit her father-in-law's long pipe and the women withdrew. The atmosphere was heavy. Bismarck, eighty-two, had no interest in *Weltmacht,* sea power, or battleships. Tirpitz, forty-eight, did not hope for serious endorsement, only a muting of opposition. Suddenly, Bismarck began to speak: His support for a fleet could not be purchased by flattery, even by the compliment of naming a warship *Fürst Bismarck.* Besides, he could not put on his uniform and come to Kiel to christen the new vessel; he did not wish to appear as a ruin in public. Tirpitz suggested that one of his daughters-in-law could perform the ceremony. That decision, said Bismarck, would be up to them. Tirpitz moved to his larger subjects: Germany, for political reasons, needed greater sea power, and modern sea power is embodied in battleships. The Prince replied that he preferred a swarm of small ships, attacking "like hornets." He wandered towards old grievances: Caprivi ("a wooden ramrod"), the failure to renew the Reinsurance Treaty with Russia ("a terrible disaster"). When Tirpitz argued that a fleet would make England more anxious for a German alliance, Bismarck responded that as individuals the English were worthy, but that the nation had "shopkeeper politics." England's military potential was contemptible; if they came to Germany, he said, "we should slay them with the butt ends of our rifles."

After two hours at the table, Bismarck invited Tirpitz to go for a drive in the forest. Two big bottles of beer were placed in the carriage, one on either side of the Chancellor. During the drive, he drank both. Speaking English in order to exclude the coachman, Bismarck reminisced over his career, lambasted William, talked of his dead wife, and said of the British Navy that "he liked the sailors but not the admirals." He had given up hunting, he said, because he could no longer bring himself "to put a hole in the shining coat of a beautiful animal." He ignored a rain shower, smoked his pipe, and apparently forgot about his neuralgia. At the end of the carriage ride, he invited Tirpitz to stay for supper. When Tirpitz left Friedrichsruh, he carried a letter in which Bismarck supported a modest increase in the navy. A few days later, the Bismarck press expressed a similar opinion.

Tirpitz repeated this success in visits to the King of Saxony, the Prince Regent of Bavaria, the Grand Dukes of Baden and Oldenburg, and the municipal councils of the Hanseatic towns. By September 15, the Navy Secretary was ready to meet the Chancellor and urge that the Bill be placed before the Reichstag as soon as possible. Hohenlohe consented and on October 19, the final draft of the Bill was forwarded to the Reich Printing Office with instructions to handle it as a state secret.

Preparing to convince the Reichstag, Tirpitz the naval strategist now transformed himself into Tirpitz the master politician. It was traditional in Imperial Germany for chancellors, ministers, and bureaucrats at all levels to scorn the members of the popularly elected body. Bismarck had shown an Olympian contempt for the parliament he had created; Hohenlohe's aloofness was shy and brittle; Bülow's attitude was to be supercilious, sardonic, and malicious. At times, the Reichstag's control of the national purse drove frustrated ministers to rage; Hollmann as Navy Minister was sometimes so irate at the repeated truncation of his budgets that he pounded the rostrum with his fists. Tirpitz approached the Reichstag differently. Possessed of the facts, Tirpitz seemed to imply, the deputies naturally would reach the correct conclusions. He devoted himself to influencing them. He was patient, courteous, and good-humored, always willing to repeat for a deputy who had not heard or understood. He flattered and entertained both leaders and rank and file. Groups of deputies were invited to meet the Navy Minister confidentially in his heavily curtained office in the Leipzigerplatz. Sitting around a big table, they found the Admiral beaming with goodwill, eager to answer questions and share opinions. Escorted tours of naval shipyards and visits to anchored warships were offered. But behind his smiling urbanity and deferential charm, Tirpitz never retreated an iota from his program. His tactics reminded one observer of the Rostand play in which a lady is asked how she managed to pass the grim sentries guarding a military fortress. "I smiled at them," she said.

On November 30, the Kaiser prepared the way for the Navy Bill by informing the Reichstag that "the development of our battle fleet has not kept up with the tasks which Germany is compelled" to assign to it, adding: "Our fleet is not strong enough to secure our home ports and waters in the event of hostilities." William denied any intent "to compete with sea powers of the first rank." Hohenlohe, speaking a week later at the first reading of the Navy Bill, seconded this promise: "We are not thinking of competing with the great sea powers . . . a policy of adventure is far from our minds. . . . [Nevertheless] in maritime questions Germany must be able to speak a modest, but above all, a wholly German word." Tirpitz' maiden speech also stressed the limits of the program: "Our fleet has the function of a protective fleet," he said. Its object would be to give Germany "a chance against a superior enemy," forcing "even a sea power of the first rank to think twice before attacking our coasts." The Navy Minister produced the letter from Bismarck, in which the Prince had written, "I find the totals demanded reasonable for our needs, although I should have preferred more attention to cruisers. This view would not restrain me, if I were a Reichstag deputy, from voting for the Bill." Tirpitz, reading the letter aloud, omitted the reference to cruisers. He stressed the administrative and political advantages of a fixed law which established for years in advance the strength of the navy and its annual building program. There would be no further alarm in the Reichstag over limitless fleet plans and an end would come to the disruptive parliamentary battles over types and number of ships to be built. Shipbuilding would be handled in a businesslike, Teutonic manner, shipyards would know what orders to expect, costs would be controlled. Above all, a fleet would be built; Tirpitz reminded his audience that after the 1873 Reichstag had authorized a navy of fourteen armored ships, it had required twenty-one years to obtain the funds from successive Reichstags to construct them.

The long-term, binding nature of the Bill and its proposed restriction of the Reichstag's right to control annual budgets worried the deputies. Most did not care whether the navy built battleships or cruisers; the sums proposed by Tirpitz seemed reasonable. But the prospect of making themselves irrelevant was alarming. The press stimulated their fears. "If the popular assembly allows itself to be bargained out of a part of its annual budget rights," warned the *Berliner Tageblatt*, "it will be sawing off the branch on which it sits." The *Frankfurter Allgemeine Zeitung* pointed out, "The present Reichstag is actually expected to rob its successors of a part of their rights."

The Center, heavily Catholic and South German, was inclined to support the Bill; opposition came from the conservative right, which preferred to spend money on the army, and from the Social Democratic left, which disliked spending money on armaments. Tirpitz reached out to all parties. A White Paper, "The Sea Interest of the German Empire," was distributed in the Reichstag. It contained statistics on population growth, emigration, trade, shipping, merchant-ship and harbor construction, development of colonies, and overseas investments, and a comparison of the battle fleets of Germany, England, France, Russia, Italy, Japan, and the United States. These figures proved that, in most measurements of national power, Germany had experienced spectacular growth since the formation of the Empire. But the record of the German Navy was woeful. Between 1883 and 1897, the Imperial Navy had declined from fourth in the world to fifth or sixth. In 1897, the White Paper declared, Britain possessed sixty-two armored ships of over five thousand tons, France had thirty-six, Russia eighteen, Germany twelve.

To supplement and broaden the effect of his personal lobbying, Tirpitz created a press bureau within the Navy Ministry. "I considered it my duty," he explained, "to bring home to the broader masses of the people the interests that were here at stake." The bureau, staffed by enthusiastic young naval officers, sought out journalists and plied them with information and suggestions; unfavorable comparisons with the size of foreign fleets were particularly stressed. Every article or letter hostile to the Navy Bill was answered and politely but firmly refuted. For small papers lacking naval correspondents, helpful articles already written were supplied. Special attention was devoted to newspapers in South Germany. Tirpitz' officers visited universities seeking professors, especially economists, who would speak in favor of the Navy Bill, stressing the value of a fleet as a protector of German industry and foreign trade. Professors and their students were invited to visit Kiel and Wilhelmshaven, where they were received by eager naval officers and ships' bands and escorted through the dockyards. In June 1898, the German Navy League (*Flottenverein*) was formed in order to propagate the theme of world power, sea power, and a larger navy. Fritz Krupp, whose giant factory at Essen made naval cannon and armor plate, was a major contributor; other industrialists anxious for titles, decorations or imperial favor contributed generously. The League's message was that colonies and fleets were essential to national greatness and prosperity; the corollary was that Great Britain, jealous of German sea power, was the enemy and would do everything possible to block Germany's "place in the sun." League membership rose rapidly, from 78,000 in 1898, to 600,000 in 1901, to 1.1 million in 1914. The league published a newspaper, *Die Flotte,* magazines, journals, and books glorifying naval history and spreading Anglophobia. A handsomely illustrated *Annual Naval Album* devoted to these themes appeared every Christmas; the Kaiser regularly bought six hundred copies, which he distributed as prizes in German schools.

When the Bill was referred by the full Reichstag to the Budget Committee, Tirpitz and his staff devoted special attention to Committee members. Interests and connections were analyzed to see where influence might be brought to bear. Fritz Krupp and Albert Ballin of the Hamburg-America Line spoke in favor of the Bill. The Association of German Industrialists and the presidents of seventy-eight chambers of commerce demanded a fleet. Unlikely statements came from surprising sources. "All peoples which have played a leading and creative role in the development of humanity have been mighty sea powers," an important banker was heard to say.

The German nation, and with it the Reichstag, began to respond. When the Bill reached its final debate on March 23, 1898, everyone knew it would pass. Eugen Richter of the liberal Radical Union, who opposed the Bill, prophesied: "If it is true that . . . Neptune's trident belongs in our fist, then for the great Reich with its great big fist, a little fleet is not enough. We shall have to have more and more battleships. . . ." August Bebel, patriarch of the Social Democrats, predicted the enemy against whom the fleet would be built: "There is, especially on the right side of this house, a large group of fanatical anglo-phobes made up of men who want to pick a fight with England. . . . But to believe that with our fleet, yes, even if it is finished to the very last ship demanded in this law, we could take up the cudgels against England, is to approach the realm of insanity. Those who demand it belong, not in the Reichstag, but in the madhouse." The Reichstag laughed.

On March 26, 1898 the Navy Bill passed, 212–139. Tirpitz and Bülow informed William, and Bülow added to his message the words "Long Live the Kaiser!" From Hong Kong, where he was serving with the German East Asian Squadron, Prince Henry, William's brother, telegraphed: "GERMAN EMPEROR, BERLIN. HURRAH! HENRY." Philip Eulenburg was rhapsodic: "On this day of honor for Your Majesty, I recall all the struggles and suffering out of which, like a phoenix, today's success has emerged. I thank God with overflowing heart for having granted us this Kaiser." William, in his joy at what Tirpitz had wrought, insisted that the Navy Minister be elevated to sit in the Prussian Ministry of State. The navy, he argued in a letter to Hohenlohe, "is like the Army a fully equal partner . . . in our national defense. . . . Moreover there is the Admiral himself. No sooner was he home from China, a man with a weakened constitution, than cheerfully and alone, he took up the awesome task of orientating an entire people, fifty million truculent, short-sighted, and foul-tempered Germans, and of bringing them around to an opposite view. He accomplished this seemingly impossible feat in eight months. Truly a powerful man! A man who so gloriously accomplishes such a gigantic work must be a full-fledged member of My administration!" Hohenlohe bowed and Rear Admiral Tirpitz took his seat in the innermost circle of the Imperial government. He would remain, the most influential of the Kaiser's ministers, for nineteen years.

■ ■ ■

The prominent feature of the First Navy Law—a fixed number of battleships not subject to alteration by annual vote of the Reichstag —had far-reaching implications, but the immediate military effect was not greatly significant. The seven battleships to be provided under the Law still would leave the German Navy weaker than the British or French fleet and still wholly unable to protect the extensive overseas trade which Tirpitz had cited as a reason for naval expansion. Neither in strength nor in organization would the German Fleet become a serious offensive weapon, although in a war with Russia, it could control the Baltic. Nevertheless, a year after his Reichstag victory, the Navy Secretary declared himself satisfied with the 1898 Navy Law. The Reichstag, he claimed, had provided a fleet which met the needs of the Empire. The Admiral may have hoped that, in 1904, when the First Navy Law had run its course, the Reichstag might again be persuaded to expand the fleet. Yet in February 1899, appearing before the Reichstag Budget Committee, he said, "I declare expressly that in no way has the intention to submit a new navy plan been manifested; that on the contrary in all quarters concerned the firmest intention exists to carry out the Navy Law and to observe the limits therein laid down."

One year after Tirpitz made this statement, the First Navy Law was superseded by a Second Navy Law, which doubled the size of the German battle fleet. The Boer War made this transformation possible. When the war began in October 1899, most Continental Europeans sympathized with the Boers. Germans, who considered themselves racially and culturally akin to the Dutch-related Boers, were especially aggrieved by what they perceived as British suppression of the "plucky little Boers." German indignation had no outlet, however, since the British Navy dominated the six thousand miles of ocean separating Europe from South Africa. German frustration surged to outrage in January 1900, when patrolling British cruisers stopped three German mail steamers off the African coast and searched them on suspicion of carrying contraband to the Boers. Britain quickly apologized, but the harm was done. Germany quivered with anger, and Tirpitz seized the opportunity immediately to draft a new Navy Bill. The Bill swept through the Reichstag on a tide of patriotism and became law on June 20, 1900.

The Second Navy Law increased the future German battle fleet from nineteen battleships to thirty-eight. There were to be two flagships and four battle squadrons of eight battleships each, with four battleships in reserve. The building program covered seventeen years, 1901 through 1917; the Fleet would reach full strength in 1920, when the last of the authorized ships was commissioned. This was no coast-defense fleet or sortie fleet; this was to be a formidable North Sea battle fleet which would catapult Germany into the rank of second naval power in the world. Equally significant, the Law publicly spelled out, for the first time, whom the fleet was intended to fight. Although the words "England" and "Great Britain" never appeared in its text, a preamble to the Second Navy Law was studded with references to "a great naval power," "a substantially superior sea power," "an enemy who is more powerful at sea," and, most tellingly, "the greatest naval power." The key sentences of this preamble offered the strategic rationale for the building of the German Fleet:

"To protect Germany's sea trade and colonies in the existing circumstances, there is only one means: Germany must have a battle fleet so strong that even for the adversary with the greatest seapower, a war against it would involve such dangers as to imperil his own position in the world.

"For this purpose it is not absolutely necessary that the German battle fleet should be as strong as that of the greatest naval Power because a great naval Power will not, as a rule, be in a position to concentrate all its striking forces against us. But even if it should succeed in meeting us with considerable superiority of strength, the defeat of a strong German fleet would so substantially weaken the enemy that, in spite of a victory he might have obtained, his own position in the world would no longer be secured by an adequate fleet."

This was Tirpitz' famous Risk Theory: As the larger British Navy must be scattered around the world, a smaller, concentrated German fleet would have a good chance of victory in the North Sea. But once the new German Fleet is built, Britain would be unlikely to risk war because, even if the Royal Navy were to defeat the German Navy in battle, the British Fleet would suffer such heavy losses that England would then be at the mercy of France or Russia. The element of risk, paradoxically, was not directed wholly at Britain. Along with the risk to Britain of offensive action and unacceptable losses at the hands of a powerful German fleet, there was the risk to Germany that Britain, fearing the growing threat of German sea power, might not wait until the mighty German Fleet was completed, but would first strike its own offensive blow. History offered precedent for such behavior: the Admiralty in 1801, fearing that France might acquire the neutral Danish Navy, sent Nelson sailing into Copenhagen harbor to destroy the Danish fleet at anchor. Germany, by building a powerful fleet so close to the British Home Islands, tempted Britain to destroy the fleet preemptively. Thus, as the risk to England rose, the risk to Germany also increased. Tirpitz understood and accepted this. He calculated the period of time through which Germany must pass before she was too strong for England to attack. He called this period of time the Danger Zone and, in 1900, he fixed its end as 1904 or 1905. But as England responded to the German challenge and laid down larger numbers of battleships itself, the Danger Zone kept expanding, and its terminal point receded into the future. By 1909, Tirpitz was forced to admit that Germany would not be out of the Danger Zone until 1915.

Passage of the Second Navy Law delighted the Kaiser who, as a reward, promoted his Navy Secretary into the hereditary Prussian nobility: Alfred Tirpitz became Alfred von Tirpitz.* Soon, the new nobleman was invited to Romintern. Tirpitz always used these visits for business. Every summer, the State Secretary retreated with his trusted aides to St. Blasien to work out details of forthcoming naval construction. Then, in September, Tirpitz carried his meticulously prepared brief to Romintern to discuss it with the Kaiser. Tirpitz liked Romintern, where "the fare was homely, the tables were decked with leaves" and "in the evenings, the company often read to each other." Nevertheless, the relationship between the Emperor and the Admiral remained formal. Both men understood that they needed each other: William had tried for nine years to build a fleet before Tirpitz took office and had failed; Tirpitz needed Imperial authority to overcome opposition in the government, in the Reichstag, and from within the navy. But Tirpitz never could be sure about William. "With his swift comprehension which was easily excited . . . and his self-consciousness, there was the danger that irresponsible influences would release impulses . . . impossible to carry out or . . . not in harmony with the whole course of action," the Admiral wrote of the Kaiser. Tirpitz preferred to consult William at Romintern, where "the air of the forest and complete quiet suited the Kaiser well. He was calmer and more collected and always ready to hear me and weigh reasons, with no sudden outbreaks of nervous excitement . . . announcing themselves by a certain restlessness in the eyes."

Throughout his reign, William bubbled with ideas and technical

---

* In 1903 Tirpitz was promoted from Rear Admiral to Admiral. In 1911, he became the Imperial Navy's first and only Grand Admiral.

suggestions about the navy. He drew sketches of ships and had them duplicated, distributed to the Reichstag, and forwarded to Tirpitz. For Tirpitz, these intrusions created difficulties. "I could never discover how to ward off the frequent interference of the Emperor, whose imagination, once it had fixed upon shipbuilding, was fed by all manner of impressions," he wrote. "Suggestions and proposals are cheap in the Navy and change like a kaleidoscope. If the Emperor had spoken with some senior lieutenant or had heard something aboard a ship, he was full of new demands, reproaching me with backwardness. . . . For example . . . the Emperor heard how difficult the improvement of modern shooting at sea and the great range of modern guns made it for torpedo boats to approach the enemy in battle. . . . The Emperor immediately became enthusiastic about an ideal ship which would be heavily armored and armed with many torpedo tubes. . . . Apart from the fact that speed and heavy armor plating compete against one another, the torpedo armament which was to be put below the waterline would have taken up the greater part of the engine and boiler space. We set to work, however, to comply with the command we had received and, in view of the impossibility of coming to any useful results, the department gave this project the name of Homunculus. . . . When I had an opportunity of presenting and explaining the draft plans [at Romintern], the Emperor abandoned his idea. . . . As a reward, I received permission to shoot a stag. I was able to telegraph to an aide in Berlin 'Stag and Homunculus dead.' "

The Second Navy Law of 1900 provided the basic framework for Imperial Navy legislation, but three Supplementary Navy Laws (Novelles) followed in 1906, 1908, and 1912. In each instance, Tirpitz manipulated a sense of crisis and frustration in Germany to ensure passage. Introduction of the Law of June 1906 followed the failure of the German demarche in Morocco and added six large cruisers to the German Fleet. The Supplementary Law of April 1908 originated in the perception that England and King Edward VII were weaving a web of encirclement around the Reich. This law reduced the age at which battleships and cruisers were to be replaced from twenty-five to twenty years; in effect, it increased the annual building tempo and made the fleet more modern and effective. The Supplementary Law of June 1912 was stimulated by Germany's retreat in the 1911 Agadir crisis; again, Tirpitz manipulated the public's sense of humiliation and outrage to push an increase through the Reichstag. Three additional battleships were added to previous programs. Total prescribed German battleship strength was raised to forty-one.

Great Britain reacted slowly to these expanding building programs. When Tirpitz in 1898 carried through the First Navy Law, Britain's potential enemies were France and Russia. In March 1898, the British Cabinet was so concerned about Russian pressure on North China that an ultimatum to St. Petersburg was drafted. Later that year, the arrival of a French expedition on the Upper Nile brought England close to war with France. Germany, in this period, appeared more as a potential ally for Great Britain than a potential enemy. The British Naval Defence Act of 1889 established a two-power standard for British naval strength: that is, the Royal Navy must always be superior to the fleets of the two next-strongest naval powers, then France and Russia. The prospect of a third Continental power increasing its naval strength was not seen as a threat in itself; Britain's concern was how it would affect the naval balance of power.

The number of new German ships to be built caused no alarm. Throughout the 1890s, British battleship building was substantial. Within sixteen months, December 1893 to March 1895, nine *Majestic*-class 15,000-ton battleships had been laid down. Between December 1896 and March 1901, an additional twenty battleships—improved *Majestics*—were begun. And, in response to the German Second Navy Law, the Admiralty ordered eight 16,300-ton *King Edward VII*s. It was this Second Navy Law and the rapid, efficient expansion of the German battleship fleet—five *Wittelsbach*s laid down in 1899 and 1900, five *Braunschweig*s in 1901 and 1902, five *Deutschland*s in 1903–1905—that seriously alarmed the British Admiralty. On November 15, 1901, Lord Selborne, First Lord of the Admiralty, informed Lord Salisbury, the Prime Minister, and the Cabinet: "The naval policy of Germany is definite and persistent. The Emperor seems determined that the power of Germany shall be used all over the world to push German commerce, possessions and interests. Of necessity it follows that German naval strength must be raised so as to compare more advantageously than at present with ours. The result of this policy will be to place Germany in a commanding position if ever we find ourselves at war with France and Russia. . . . Naval officers who have seen much of the German Navy lately are all agreed that it is as good as can be." Selborne's concern in this memorandum was the balance of naval strength. A year later, in October 1902, he focussed in a Cabinet paper directly on the German Navy's threat to England: "The more the composition of the new German fleet is examined, the clearer it becomes that it is designed for a possible conflict with the British fleet. It cannot be designed for the purpose of playing a leading part in a future war between Germany and France and Russia. The issue of such a war can only be decided by armies on land, and the great naval expenditure on which Germany has embarked involves deliberate diminution of the military strength which Germany might otherwise have attained in relation to France and Russia." A few weeks later, Selborne became more specific: "The Admiralty had proof," he told the Cabinet, "that the German Navy was being constructed with a view to being able to fight the British Navy: restricted cruising radius, cramped crew quarters, etc. meant that the German battleships were designed for the North Sea and practically nothing else."

Within a few years, the decision of the world's strongest military power to build a great battle fleet, making it the second naval power, forced fundamental changes in British naval strategy and diplomacy. As more German battleships slid down the building ways, more British battleships would be ordered. With a formidable German fleet concentrated only a few hours' steaming time from England's North Sea coast, the British Admiralty began to bring ships home from around the globe. And as the reality of Admiral Tirpitz' determination to build his "Navy Against England" penetrated English awareness, the British government prepared to alter the foreign policy which had served England since Trafalgar. The building of the German Fleet ended the century of Splendid Isolation.

PART II

THE
END OF
SPLENDID
ISOLATION

◆

CHAPTER 10

Lord
Salisbury

◆

Four eminent Victorian statesmen gathered at midday on Monday, June 24, 1895. The previous Friday, Lord Rosebery's Liberal government had been defeated in the House of Commons by a surprise vote on an insignificant issue. On Sunday Queen Victoria had summoned Lord Salisbury, the host of the gathering at 20 Arlington Street, and asked him to form a government. Salisbury had agreed and now, on Monday, he and his three guests were meeting to decide who should take which Cabinet office.

It was an odd quartet, socially and politically. The Marquess of Salisbury and the Duke of Devonshire were peers; Arthur Balfour and Joseph Chamberlain were commoners. Salisbury and Balfour were members of the same distinguished family, the Cecils, whose forebears had served at the elbow of Queen Elizabeth I. The modern Cecils, uncle and nephew, were the leaders of the Conservative Party, which would have the preeminent place in the new government. Devonshire and Chamberlain were Liberals who, on the tormenting issue of Home Rule for Ireland, had resigned from the leadership of the Liberal Party. Lord Salisbury wanted their support and the support of the substantial number of other disaffected Liberals in Parliament. He had received this support on a day-to-day basis while the Conservatives were in opposition; now, summoned to create a government, he wished to formalize it in an anti–Home Rule coalition. The new party and new government would have a new name: Unionist.

Lord Salisbury, naturally, would become Prime Minister. This was the Queen's decision and none of the men in Salisbury's drawing room questioned Her Majesty's choice. Lord Salisbury was the unchallenged leader of the Conservative Party and the last active great political figure of nineteenth-century England. He had first entered the Cabinet twenty-nine years before. Since then, he had served nine years as Foreign Secretary and seven as Prime Minister. Now sixty-five, he was six feet four inches tall, with heavy, rounded shoulders and expansive, unchecked girth. His head was huge, with a rounded bald dome, a thick beard of curly gray hair, and small, almost slitted eyes which peered at the world with what could be taken for suspicion; in fact, it was severe nearsightedness. With all his bulk, Lord Salisbury was not healthy. Now, accepting the premiership once again, he knew he would be obliged to spend long periods at his villa in the south of France, struggling to maintain his health.

The other peer in the Arlington Street drawing room, Spencer Compton Cavendish, eighth Duke of Devonshire, would have preferred to be somewhere else. Devonshire, at sixty-two, was a tall, thin-faced, bearded man with a jutting beak of a nose. Most of his life had been spent serving in government while he wished he were watching his horses run. As Lord Hartington, heir to the dukedom and scion of one of the great Whig families of England, he had served thirty-four years in the House of Commons. Under Lord Palmerston, Lord John Russell, and Gladstone, he had sat in Liberal Cabinets as War Secretary, Postmaster-General, and Secretary of State for India. Twice he had been offered and had declined the premiership. His departure from the Liberal Party leadership in 1886 had been a heavy blow to Mr. Gladstone; now, a duke sitting in the House of Lords, Devonshire had become almost a national institution. Queen Victoria treated him as such when she wrote to him in 1892, "The Queen cannot conclude this letter without expressing to the Duke . . . how much she relies on him to assist in maintaining the safety and honor of her vast empire. All must join in this necessary work." It was a commission that Devonshire, whatever his private desires, could not ignore.

Arthur Balfour, at forty-seven the youngest of Lord Salisbury's guests, was heir to his uncle's political estate. This succession had only a few years before seemed unlikely, even unthinkable. Nudged into politics by his uncle, Balfour had begun slowly. Tall and willowy, with large blue eyes, wavy brown hair, and a luxuriant mustache, the embodiment of landed wealth and languid charm, he appeared ill suited for the rough pummeling of House of Commons debate. Until his mid-thirties, Balfour appeared to take nothing seriously. His speeches were airy, frivolous, and seemingly unprepared. "His bitterest detractors could never say that Mr. Balfour's speeches smelt of the lamp," said an aristocratic admirer who approved of blue-blooded diffidence. But in 1886, when Balfour was thirty-nine, he was dispatched by his uncle to rule over Ireland, where he exceeded all expectations. This success led to leadership of the Conservative Party in the House of Commons (Salisbury, a peer, was restricted to the Lords). Balfour's manner in the House could be deceiving. Lolling on the Government Bench, he permitted himself to slide lower and lower, "as if," said an observer in the Gallery, "to discover how nearly he could sit on his shoulder blades." From this horizontal posture, he could rise up suddenly to intervene in debate. So great was Balfour's charm and so intricate the dialectic of his arguments that most members even across the aisle delighted in him. "Balfour," said one of them, "was one of the rare men who make public life tolerable and even respectable."

Balfour was in his uncle's house on this June day as ambassador. The foreign power to whom he would represent Lord Salisbury, the majority of the new Cabinet, and the Conservative Party was the fourth man present, Joseph Chamberlain. Lord Salisbury in 1895 may have been the most eminent statesman in England, but he was not the most popular. This description fitted Chamberlain. Had he not broken with Gladstone over Home Rule, Chamberlain would have succeeded to leadership of the Liberal Party and, eventually, to the premiership. This office was now gone forever. Still, as leader of the Liberal Unionists in the House of Commons and the country, he possessed the power to make or break the Unionist coalition. The alliance, at best, would be uncomfortable. Two political figures more unlike in background, character, and temperament than Lord Salisbury and Chamberlain could scarcely be found. For this reason, every bit of Balfour's canny, diplomatic charm was expected to be needed.

Joseph Chamberlain was fifty-nine in 1895. He had not attended Oxford or Cambridge or a public school. He had gone to work at sixteen and had made enough money to retire from business at thirty-four and go into politics as a Radical Liberal. Four years after entering Parliament, he sat in Gladstone's second Cabinet. In the House, he made a cool and elegant figure, with his black hair brushed carefully back over his small head. In Parliament and on podiums around the country, he was the voice of the shopkeeper, the middle class, and the Nonconformist. He sat with a marquess, a duke, and Arthur Balfour because his passion and eloquence had won him the allegiance of dozens of members of Parliament and hundreds of thousands of British voters. Salisbury had no choice but to invite Chamberlain into his Cabinet—the Liberal Unionists would be the margin of his majority over the Liberals and the Irish —but all four men were keenly aware of the differences that separated them. Chamberlain was the future; they were the past. He was energy and thrust; they stood for imperturbability, equanimity, sobriety, and caution. Chamberlain took risks, broke molds, was eager to build a new society and a new form of empire. By challenging Gladstone on Home Rule, he had splintered and broken one of England's two great political parties. Later, on the issue of free trade, he would bring down the other.

Salisbury opened the Arlington Street discussion by saying that, beyond the premiership and leadership of the House of Commons, all Cabinet offices were open. He offered Devonshire the Foreign Office. The Duke declined and became Lord President of the Council. Salisbury took the Foreign Office as well as the Premiership, a dual role he had performed in his first two Cabinets. He asked Chamberlain's wishes. Chamberlain said that he wanted the Colonial Office. Salisbury, surprised, suggested one of the more prestigious seats, the Chancellorship of the Exchequer or the Home Office. Chamberlain repeated that he would prefer to be Colonial Secretary. It was agreed. The other places were allotted. Another Liberal Unionist, the Marquess of Lansdowne, became War Secretary. The veteran George Goschen was offered the Exchequer but took the Admiralty. Sir Michael Hicks-Beach became Chancellor. In the end, Lord Salisbury formed one of the strongest Cabinets ever to hold office in the United Kingdom. Four members of the Cabinet besides the Prime Minister, declared the *Spectator,* were fitted to become Prime Minister: Devonshire, Chamberlain, Balfour, and Goschen. Overall, in the opinion of H. H. Asquith, who had been Home Secretary in the Liberal Rosebery Cabinet, Lord Salisbury's new administration displayed "an almost embarrassing wealth of talent and capacity."

Once installed, the new Prime Minister called a general election. The result was a sweeping Unionist victory: 340 Conservatives and 71 Liberal Unionists were elected along with 177 Liberals and 82 Irish members. Salisbury's Unionist majority was 152. This was the government which ruled Great Britain for ten and a half years. With the passage of time, there would be shifts in office and person-

nel. After seven years, Lord Salisbury, his health irreparable, resigned, to be succeeded by Arthur Balfour. The Duke of
Devonshire remained, as before, impressive even in lassitude.
Chamberlain's power expanded until he became almost coequal in
power to the Prime Minister when the premier was Salisbury, and
greater than the Prime Minister when the office was held by Balfour. Eventually, both Chamberlain and Devonshire resigned over
free trade, and Balfour, still deft, still charming, went on alone. In
the meantime, a decade of English history passed: the Jameson
Raid, the Kruger Telegram, Chamberlain's attempt to create an Anglo-German alliance, the Boer War, the Boxer Rebellion, the rise of
the German Navy, the Anglo-French Entente, the first Morocco
Crisis, and the laying of the keel of H.M.S. *Dreadnought.*

Robert Cecil, Third Marquess of Salisbury, four times Foreign Secretary and three times Prime Minister of Great Britain, grew up in
privileged but unhappy circumstances. His mother died before he
was ten and his father, a great Tory landowner and member of two
Conservative Cabinets, had little time for his numerous offspring.
Young Robert was miserable in every school he attended; he later
referred to those years as "an existence among devils." At Eton, he
was tormented. "I am bullied from morning to night," he wrote to
his father. "I am obliged to hide myself all evening in some corner.
. . . I am obnoxious to all of them because I can do verses, but will
not do them for the others." In London, during the holidays, he
lived in such dread of meeting his schoolmates that he avoided major streets. Eventually, Robert was withdrawn from Eton and
brought home.

The Second Marquess was annoyed with this second son. Having ten children somehow to raise, he had little taste for complaints
which, he thought, tended toward malingering and hypochondria.
The misunderstanding between the two was lifelong. "Never were
two men of the same blood more hopelessly antagonistic in all their
tastes and interests," Lord Salisbury's daughter was to write of her
father and grandfather.

Hatfield, the Cecil family estate in Hertfordshire, twenty miles
north of London, plays a role commensurate with the importance of
its owners, the Cecil family, in English history. When the estate
belonged to the Crown, the young King Edward VI lived for a while
at Hatfield; his half-sister Princess Elizabeth waited there in semi-
exile while the Catholic Queen Mary Tudor attempted to reimpose
her religion on the island. Portraits of English and European

monarchs, mingled with those of earlier Cecils, to whom the estate was given, hang on the walls of drawing rooms and corridors, and of the library into which Robert Cecil retreated. He became interested in botany and roamed the countryside collecting plants and flowers. Fluent in French, he eagerly obeyed his father's command that all family correspondence be conducted in that language. In 1847, he matriculated at Christ Church, where, because of the unusual brilliance of his essays, his fellow undergraduates predicted that he would one day be Prime Minister. Two years later, just after taking a degree, he suffered a nervous collapse. Throughout Lord Salisbury's life, accumulation of worry and physical exhaustion brought on severe migraines, which he called "nerve storms." The symptoms included black depression, digestive upheaval, crippling lassitude, and, at the peak of the crisis, an acute sensitivity to light, sound, or touch: the slightest increase in brightness or noise, or any physical contact, became excruciating. "It is the peculiarity of my complaint that it lays me up and makes me incapable, sometimes for days, without any warning," he explained to his father. "And I know by sad experience that unless I obey when it does attack me, the incapacity of a day may be turned into one of a week."

A worried doctor at Oxford convinced Lord Robert's father that only a long sea voyage would restore the young man's health, and he embarked for South Africa, Australia, and New Zealand. When he returned two years later at twenty-three, the Second Marquess, not knowing what else to do with his son, arranged for him to be elected to a safe Conservative seat in the House of Commons.

Lord Robert's early years in Parliament were undistinguished. His health and spirits were low and neither was improved by the late-night sittings common in the Lower House. His speeches were rebellious and cantankerous, as if all authority existed only to be insulted. A letter to his father from this period bordered on insolence: "Your prohibition gave me a stomach ache all morning. . . . I do not know whether I have sufficiently recovered my equanimity to write intelligibly but I will try."

Lord Robert defied his father in choosing a wife. He was, as a young man, tall, thin, stooped, awkward, shortsighted, shy, incapable of small talk, and atrociously dressed. Yet he was courteous, sensitive, and obviously brilliant, and when he proposed to Miss Georgina Alderson, she accepted. The Second Marquess thought that Miss Alderson's family connections made it an inferior match and declared that Lord Robert could expect no enhancement of his limited income. The result, the older man warned, would be "privations" and loss of social standing. Lord Robert replied that he was immune from worry on either count: "That which is my main expense—traveling—is almost always undertaken under pressure, either from you or others, which will cease on my marriage. [And] the persons who will cut me because I marry Miss Alderson are precisely the persons of whose society I am so anxious to be quit." The marriage went forward and the losses were minor, although one dowager did refuse to call at the young couple's first address, declaring that she "never left cards north of Oxford Street."

After his marriage, Lord Robert promptly got to work supplementing his small income by writing articles for the *Quarterly Review* and other journals. Here, in a clear, incisive style, he set forth his political philosophy. He believed in preserving traditional English views and institutions. He considered it the near-sacred duty of the Conservative Party to defend the hereditary rights and privileges of the propertied class. Democracy was a virus threatening to infect and strike down England. The votes of the working class were informed by a mingling of passion and greed which left no room for the patient, reasonable calculations required to guide the nation as a whole. Expecting government by numbers to produce government by the best was illogical, he said. "First rate men will not canvass mobs, and if they did, the mobs would not elect the first rate men." True to his principles, he vigorously opposed the reform-minded Tory democracy advanced by his own party leaders, Lord Derby and Benjamin Disraeli. In 1867, he resigned as Secretary of State for India rather than support the government-sponsored Second Reform Bill, which doubled the electorate by extending suffrage to town workingmen.

A year later, when his father followed his elder brother to the grave, Lord Robert Cecil left the House of Commons and entered the House of Lords as Third Marquess of Salisbury. In the Upper House, his star ascended rapidly. Soon, he was the dominant figure on the Conservative Front Bench. He spoke precisely and pungently, without notes, piling fact upon fact, adding epigram and irony, sometimes flinging little personal jibes—what one admiring opponent called "blazing indiscretions." His timing was theatrical. Often, he would pause before a critical passage, seeming to grope for the exact word required, sweeping up his audience in a compelling blend of suspense, recognition, and, ultimately, full-throated approval and applause. For all his success, Lord Salisbury disdained oratory as a lesser form of persuasion. Having given a speech, he never wanted to read it again. Being forced to do so for purposes of correction in *Hansard* was, he said, like "returning to the cold and greasy remains of yesterday's dinner."

For years, Salisbury's relations with Disraeli were crusty. Salisbury was scandalized that a Tory could also be a radical; he put it down to cunning and opportunism, declaring flat out, "I dislike and despise the man." For a while, he tried to deal with Disraeli by attacking him in Parliament and not speaking to him anywhere else. Disraeli, bold, imaginative, and incurably romantic, refused to accept the hostility of the intelligent, morose, standoffish younger man. Finding Salisbury at a garden party, Disraeli advanced rapidly, hand outstretched, and exclaimed, "Ah, Robert, Robert, how glad I am to see you!"

In 1874, as Disraeli was forming his second government, Salisbury was asked to resume the office of Secretary of State for India. He hesitated: "My impression is that D. [Disraeli] does not want to have me but is pressed by others. I am in precisely the same position." This was shadowboxing; Salisbury's entrance into the Cabinet was inevitable. No Conservative government could have been formed without including the most effective voice in the House of Lords. Before this government fell six years later, Lord Salisbury's situation had been transformed: he was Foreign Secretary of Great Britain and the Prime Minister's most effective and trusted lieutenant. In addition, he had become—with Prince Bismarck, Prince Gorchakov of Russia, and Austria's Count Andrássy—one of the handful of statesmen who determined the fate of Europe.

In 1876, Great Britain became embroiled in what was known in Europe as the Eastern Question, the array of diplomatic problems arising from the decay and impending disintegration of the Ottoman Empire. The powers principally concerned—other than the Turks themselves—were Russia, Austria, and Great Britain. In St. Petersburg, a strong pan-Slav party saw the Ottoman collapse as a glittering opportunity to realize a dream of four centuries: to restore the Cross to Hagia Sophia and seize control of the Straits. To Vienna, any retreat by the Sultan from his vast, ill-governed Balkan provinces was an automatic signal for Hapsburg aggrandizement. As for London, it was a long-established British policy to prop up the Sultan and resist any move to break up the Ottoman Empire. At stake was Britain's India lifeline, which ran through the Sultan's domains. Especially the capital, Constantinople, must not be allowed to come under the influence of another Great Power.

In April 1877, soon after Europe learned that twelve thousand Bulgarian Christians, including women and children, had been massacred by Turkish troops, Russia declared war. The Tsar's army advanced through the Balkans and by January 1878 stood in the suburbs of Constantinople. In England, apprehension gave way to hysteria. The Queen, passionately anti-Russian, raged at Gladstone for his condemnation of the Turks, referring to her former and future Prime Minister as "that half-madman." (The Duke of Sutherland went further and declared that Gladstone was "a Russian agent.") She was almost as displeased with her Conservative Foreign Secretary, the younger Lord Derby, a prudent, phlegmatic man, strongly opposed to war. "Oh!" Victoria wrote to Disraeli, "if the Queen were a man, she would like to go and give those horrid Russians, whose word one cannot believe, such a beating!" She threatened abdication. Disraeli did what he could to placate the Queen, hold back the Russians, and persuade Derby not to resign. The Cabinet was in chaos. Lord Derby, whose private meetings with the Russian ambassador in search of peace leaked out, began to despair, drink heavily, and neglect his work. Salisbury, from the India Office, began to perform many of the functions of Foreign Secretary.

Lord Salisbury did not entirely share the conviction that Constantinople was the key to India. Constantinople, after all, was eight hundred miles from Suez and Lord Salisbury had already observed that "much of the trouble came from British statesmen using maps on too small a scale." Nevertheless, he strongly believed that declared British interests should be firmly defended. Now, with Russian troops under the city's walls, Salisbury urged the Cabinet to send the Mediterranean Fleet through the Dardanelles to give visible strength to British warnings. Lord Derby resisted; the Cabinet wavered. Twice the fleet was ready; twice it was held back. Emboldened, the Russian Commander-in-Chief warned that if British warships appeared in the Bosphorus, his troops would occupy the city. Salisbury insisted that the fleet go forward. Eventually, on February 15, Admiral Hornby's ironclads splashed their anchors off the Golden Horn. The Grand Duke's army did not move. But for six months, British naval guns and Russian artillery lay within range of each other while the helpless capital of the Ottoman Empire stood between.

While the Cross was not yet on the Hagia Sophia and the Straits remained in Turkish hands, Russia had achieved much. The Tsar had forced the Sultan to sign the Treaty of San Stefano, in which most of the conquered Turkish Balkan territory reappeared as the new, Russian-sponsored state of Bulgaria. Great Britain, unwilling to accept these new arrangements, which so powerfully increased Russian influence in Constantinople, signed a defensive alliance with Turkey and began to mobilize reserves. Austria, also unhappy about the new "Big Bulgaria," followed suit. Suddenly, the prospect of renewed fighting seemed less appealing in St. Petersburg. Picking the bones of the dying Turk was one thing; fighting a war with Britain, Austria, and Turkey was quite another.

The prospect of war was also too much for Lord Derby, who resigned the Foreign Secretaryship. Indeed, Derby, a lifelong Tory, the son of a man who three times had been Conservative Prime Minister, was so upset that he deserted the party and joined Gladstone and the Liberals.* Salisbury succeeded Derby and the British Cabinet stood united for the first time during the crisis on a policy of strength. Salisbury took office on March 28. That day and the next, he concluded his business at the India Office. On the night of the twenty-ninth, he dined out, but excused himself after dinner to return to his house in Arlington Street. There, he locked himself in his study, and from eleven P.M. to three o'clock the next morning, without the help of assistants or memoranda, wrote a diplomatic note which affected the history of Europe. In polite but cogent language, he explained why the Treaty of San Stefano must not be allowed to stand. In effect, the note was an ultimatum to Russia: Britain would not submit to Russian dismemberment of the Ottoman Empire. Either the Treaty of San Stefano would be submitted to the judgment of a European conference or Britain and Russia must go to war. The Cabinet agreed to Salisbury's note without modification and forwarded it to the major powers.

At this point, Prince Bismarck stepped forward. The Chancellor cared very little about the fate of Turkey, but he cared very much that Germany not be compelled to take sides in a war between Austria and Russia. In a speech to the Reichstag, he suggested that Germany, placed as she was in the center of Europe and friendly to all the powers concerned, was admirably situated to play the role of "Honest Broker." He proposed an international conference in Berlin. All accepted.

The Congress of Berlin convened all the concerned powers in a dangerous and complicated dispute and resolved the matter so that peace was secured for a generation. Unlike the Congress of Vienna sixty-three years earlier, or the Peace Conference at Versailles forty-one years later, this was not a gathering of victorious powers to divide the spoils. No war had yet been fought. Russia, which came

---

* Of Derby, Disraeli, not inferior to Salisbury in flinging gibes, observed, "I do not know that there is anything that would excite enthusiasm in him except when he contemplates the surrender of some national possession."

to the conference a victor, was forced to give up some of her gains, but her defeat was not a humiliation. The Ottoman Empire, on the brink of death, gained another four decades of life.

At the Congress, Lord Salisbury remained in the shadow of his chief. Disraeli, now Earl of Beaconsfield, was admired by all; his progress across Germany had been slowed by curious and respectful crowds which packed the stations his train passed through. "Der alte Jude, das ist der Mann" was Bismarck's accolade. Beaconsfield delighted in royal audiences, elaborate banquets, and colorful ceremonies, and Berlin smothered him with invitations. The Crown Princess and the Chancellor competed for his evenings. His first weekend was spent with the Crown Prince and his wife at Potsdam and he wrote home rapturously about the visit. Salisbury was invited too, but his reaction was different. "Six hours of my day have been taken away by that tiresome Princess asking me to lunch at Potsdam," he complained to his wife. The Foreign Secretary also worried about his Premier. "He looks ill and sleeps badly," Salisbury reported. "[He] did not sleep this morning till six."

The Congress opened at two P.M. on June 13, 1878, with Bismarck in the President's chair, and lasted exactly one month. Bismarck ran the meetings like a drill sergeant. No one was permitted superfluous oratory; all items scheduled for a particular day had to be completed on that day. Bismarck had private reasons for this pace: he was due to leave in July for his annual cure ("Prince Bismarck with one hand full of cherries and the other of shrimps, eaten alternately, complains he cannot sleep and must go to Kissingen," Beaconsfield noted dryly). The Chancellor insisted that the language of the conference be French, although no Frenchmen were present and Beaconsfield did not speak French. Ignoring Bismarck, the Prime Minister spoke in English. As the Congress progressed, Beaconsfield's health deteriorated. He suffered from Bright's disease, asthma, bronchitis, and continuing insomnia. Before the end, he was near a state of collapse. Salisbury, working eighteen hours a day to make up for his countryman's incapacity, confided to his wife: "What with deafness, ignorance of French, and Bismarck's extraordinary mode of speech, Beaconsfield has the dimmest idea of what is going on—understands everything crossways—and imagines a perpetual conspiracy."

Nevertheless, the old man could still deal with a crisis. The Russians at one point dug in their heels about the location of a Turkish garrison south of the Danube. Britain sided with Turkey, reminding Russia that if the conference broke up, war would be declared. Beaconsfield ordered that a special train be held in readiness to take the British delegation to Calais. Gorchakov packed his trunks. Then Bismarck hurried to Beaconsfield's hotel and invited him to dine. During dinner, the Prime Minister later wrote in his diary, the Chancellor was "very agreeable indeed . . . made no allusion to politics, though he ate and drank a great deal and talked more." After dinner, the two retired to a private room. Bismarck had to discover whether the Prime Minister was bluffing. For an hour and a half, Beaconsfield insisted that he was not. "He smoked and I followed," Beaconsfield continued. "I believe I gave the last blow to my shattered constitution but I felt it absolutely necessary. . . . He was convinced that the ultimatum was not a sham and before I went to bed I had the satisfaction of knowing that St. Petersburg had surrendered."

On July 13, the conference concluded its work and Beaconsfield signed a treaty containing sixty-four articles. War had been averted. The Russian advance on the Straits had been rolled back as the new Bulgaria was drastically shrunk in size. Austria accepted payment for her support of Turkey in the form of a protectorate over the Turkish provinces of Bosnia and Herzegovina. Britain's fee was the cession of Cyprus. Together, Beaconsfield and Salisbury returned to London in triumph. The Queen conferred the Garter on the Prime Minister, who accepted only on condition that Salisbury, whom he called his "laboring oar" in Berlin, accept one too.*

Once the conference ended, Beaconsfield had fewer than two years remaining in office and only three to live. In that time, he visited often at Hatfield, and recognized the Foreign Secretary as his political heir. In Europe, the Foreign Secretary's circular dispatch and his performance at the Congress had made him a commanding reputation. In the company of the most powerful and celebrated statesmen and diplomats of Europe, the new British Foreign Secretary displayed a clarity and quickness of apprehension, a grasp of detail, a style of speaking and writing, and a dedication to his country's interests which were to give him a reputation for statesmanship second only to that of the Chancellor of the German Empire.

In the Conservative Party, once Beaconsfield was gone, Salisbury had no rival. In 1885, when the Tories returned to power, Lord

---

* At the end of the Congress, Lady Salisbury was presented by the Sultan with the "Order of Chastity Third Class." Only the wives of crowned monarchs received the Order First Class, Lord Salisbury was informed. Other royal ladies received the Order Second Class; the wives of diplomats were awarded Third Class.

Salisbury became both Prime Minister and Foreign Secretary.* The senior office was not one he cared about, although he held it three times for a total of thirteen and a half years. He disliked party and parliamentary politics and sponsored not a single measure of domestic legislation. He accepted the Premiership only because, by then, there was no one in the party to challenge his authority; a Cabinet including Lord Salisbury but with another at the top would have seemed ludicrously unbalanced. Lord Salisbury never flatly refused the Premiership, but several times tried to foist it off on others. Twice, he offered to relinquish it to his new Liberal Unionist ally, Lord Hartington, but ambition sat even more lightly on Hartington's shoulders than on Salisbury's and twice the future Duke of Devonshire refused.

As leader of the government, Salisbury differed in his conduct of the office from the two other great prime ministers of the age, Gladstone and Disraeli. Both of these were party men who kept their Cabinet colleagues on a short leash. Lord Salisbury, liking to run the Foreign Office without interruption, assumed that his colleagues would feel the same about their ministries, and he left them alone. The Prime Minister, he believed, was primus inter pares; ministers were members of a Cabinet, not henchmen of the Prime Minister. At the Foreign Office Salisbury's power was well-nigh absolute. Combining the positions of Foreign Secretary and Prime Minister, only vaguely responsible to his colleagues in the Cabinet, he was able for many years to conduct the foreign policy of England by himself. This policy, as he saw and conducted it, was simple and clearly defined. "France," he said in 1888, "is, and must always remain, England's greatest danger." The Germans he thought of as a race with whom "by sympathy, by interest, by descent," Britons ought always to be friends. He wished an alliance with neither power, telling the German Ambassador *"Nous sommes des poissons"* (We are fish) and that "the sea and her chalk cliffs were England's best allies." He understood both the advantages and weaknesses of sea power and once reminded Queen Victoria (who wanted him to do something about Turkish atrocities in Armenia): "England's strength lies in her ships, and ships can only operate on the seashore or the sea. England alone can do nothing to remedy an inland tyranny." He described his policy as "Splendid Isolation" and "the supremacy of the interests of England." With characteris-

---

* Because Salisbury sat in the House of Lords (the last British prime minister to do so), he was spared the burden of leading his party in the thrust and parry of Commons debate. This gave him time to act as both Prime Minister and Foreign Secretary.

tic diffidence, he made light of his task—"British foreign policy," he
once said, "is to drift lazily downstream, occasionally putting out a
boathook to avoid a collision"—but in fact he served with a dedication rarely seen at the Foreign Office.

Not that the Foreign Secretary was himself regularly seen at the
Foreign Office. Lord Salisbury refused to adjust his patterns of life
to the conventions of office. As Prime Minister, he refused to live at
10 Downing Street and made only occasional use of his rooms in the
Foreign Office across the street. He preferred to work in his own
London house in Arlington Street or, better yet, at Hatfield, where
he worked, for the most part, completely alone. His room was
equipped with double doors so thick and so far apart that when both
were shut, no amount of knocking or rattling at the outer portal
could disturb the solitary man within. He wrote many government
papers and much Foreign Office correspondence himself; he explained that if he had had more time, he might have delegated the
work, but as he was pressed, he had to do it himself. He did not
correct assistants' errors; the next time, he simply did the work himself. He answered all mail addressed to him from even the humblest
correspondent. Hour after hour, late into the night, he would produce long, handwritten pages on a bewildering variety of subjects.
"A great sleeper," his daughter called him, "finding eight hours
necessary and being happier if he could get nine."

In the morning, after a cold bath, Lord Salisbury continued his
paperwork. When he did go to the Foreign Office, he arrived after
luncheon, and devoted his afternoons to interviews with foreign ambassadors, many of whom came only to gather crumbs to include in
their weekly reports. "One subject only now occupies my thoughts,"
he wrote to a friend in 1887. "It is how shall I contrive to sit through
my interviews with ambassadors without falling asleep?" His solution was to conceal a sharp-edged wooden paper knife in his hand
beneath the table. When conversation grew arid and his eyelids
heavy, he prodded the knife point into his thigh.

At the Foreign Office, Lord Salisbury practiced the same detached administrative style employed with his fellows in the Cabinet. He chose ambassadors carefully and then treated them as
colleagues, not subordinates. Correspondence between the Foreign
Secretary and the Queen's ambassadors had the nature of crisp intellectual dialogue and mutual search for effective policy; there was
none of the tone of hectoring command which characterized Holstein's instructions sent out from the Wilhelmstrasse. Senior or junior, British diplomats were expected to cope. When a young
consular agent in Zanzibar, facing a palace revolution, mobs in the

street, and an endangered white colony, telegraphed home for instructions, Salisbury cabled back: "Do whatever you think best.
Whatever you do will be approved—but be careful not to undertake
anything which you cannot carry through." British subjects, roaming
the bush in search of profit, were permitted to fend for themselves.
One aggressive trader, having embroiled himself in a dispute with a
local potentate, demanded that the Foreign Office intervene and
punish the offending native. In the red ink reserved for the Foreign
Secretary's comment, Salisbury minuted dryly on this paper: "Buccaneers must expect to rough it."

When Lord Salisbury was in residence at Hatfield, his work and
interviews at the Foreign Office had necessarily to be concluded so
that he could catch a regular seven o'clock train from King's Cross
Station. His daily departure from the Foreign Office had the efficiency of a fireman sliding down a pole: one footman stood outside
his door holding his overcoat, another waited at the foot of the
stairs, ready to throw open the door of a one-horse brougham held
in readiness. From Downing Street to King's Cross—up Whitehall,
across Trafalgar Square, along Charing Cross, through Bloomsbury
—took exactly seventeen minutes, timed on his lordship's watch.
Boarding the train, he sank into a private compartment and invariably fell asleep for the whole of the journey.

Preferring privacy and shunning security, the Prime Minister
seemed to his friends excessively vulnerable. Once a genteel lunatic
did indeed enter his compartment. Lord Salisbury's vague concern
before nodding off was to try to recall the name of this agreeable
but unrecognized fellow traveler. When, at Hatfield station, his new
companion also got off, and then climbed into Lord Salisbury's
small carriage, the owner's worry increased: somehow he must not
only have forgotten the name, but also an invitation obviously issued. It was while jogging along that Lord Salisbury discovered the
truth: the man was both unbalanced and harmless. Arriving home
with no one about, the host excused himself and went off to work.
Some time later, when a footman found the Prime Minister bent
over his papers, Lord Salisbury glanced up and remarked that "he
had left a madman in the front hall."

No one was ever sure whether Lord Salisbury's famous inability
to identify friends and colleagues—even, one day, his own son walking in Hatfield Park—was due to towering absentmindedness or
flawed vision. Once, at a breakfast party, he leaned over and asked
in an undertone the name of the gentleman seated on the other side
of his host. The stranger, he learned, was W. H. Smith, who had
been Lord Salisbury's friend for many years and was, at that mo-

ment, his Chancellor of the Exchequer. Lord Salisbury's explanation for this curious blunder was that, in Cabinet meetings, Smith always sat across from him and that therefore he had never before observed Mr. Smith in profile. His forgetfulness made him useless as a gossip. To the despair of his wife and daughters, he would return from London to Hatfield and say, "I was told to be sure to tell you . . ." and then stop, having forgotten who was marrying, who was divorcing, and who was bankrupt.

Even on Sundays, Lord Salisbury buried himself in work, regarding a day free from interviews as an opportunity to catch up on his paperwork. He had no interest in any of the sports that preoccupied most of the country gentlemen of England; riding, shooting, yachting, and the racetrack. His Liberal Unionist ally, Lord Hartington, had opposite tastes and could not be found in London when important races were running at Newmarket. "Our political arrangements are necessarily hung up till some particular quadruped had run for something," Lord Salisbury huffed to his wife about Hartington. For a while, as a younger man, he attempted tennis, but his eyesight left him near defenseless. He read a great deal. He knew Jane Austen's six novels almost by heart. He disliked realism, rejected Balzac, and would put down any book which he found "left a nasty taste." He possessed small, portable volumes of Shakespeare, Virgil, Horace, and Euripides, and during railway journeys, long boat rides, or dry spells during a picnic, these little books would pop from his pocket and soon seal him off from his surroundings.

His real recreation lay in science. He remained an amateur botanist and, during his years of vacationing along the Channel coast of France, put aside his cares by collecting and analyzing seaweed. He was an early home photographer, packing heavy cameras, tripods, trays, bottles, red lamps, and black velvet cloths into his holiday luggage. In time, as the photographer metamorphosed into a chemist, the darkrooms installed in his houses were expanded into laboratories. One day, the new chemist staggered from his laboratory and collapsed, deathly pale, at the feet of his wife. Revived, he triumphantly proclaimed that he had succeeded in creating—and then unfortunately had inhaled—chlorine gas. Another time, the house was shaken by an explosion, and his horrified wife and family witnessed a figure, its face and hands dripping with blood, emerging from his laboratory door. An experiment with sodium, he said sadly, would need repeating.

Hatfield was one of the first private houses in England to be equipped with a telephone and electric lights, both installations being improvised by the owner. Soon after the first telephone appeared, Lord Salisbury spread wires over the floors at Hatfield, often tripping unwary guests. Voice reproduction was imperfect and only simple, recognizable phrases could be understood. The most common, booming out from various rooms in the master's unmistakable tones, was "Hey, diddle diddle, the cat and the fiddle, the cow jumped over the moon." Hatfield's electrification began with a primitive arc light glaring down from the middle of the dining-room ceiling. This was superseded by the new incandescent Edison light, which provided less glare but little increase in reliability. Power was drawn from a riverbank sawmill which still cut wood by day and now, brightly or dully—depending on the level of the river—illuminated the mansion by night. Electricity flowed on wires strung a mile and a half through the park and was subject to interruption when trees and branches bent with the wind. There were no fuses and the problem of surging had not yet been solved. "There were evenings," a member of the clan recalled, "when the household had to grope about in semi-darkness, illuminated only by a dim red glow such as comes from a half extinct fire; there were others when a perilous brilliancy culminated in miniature storms of lightning, ending in complete collapse. One group of lamps after another would blaze and expire in rapid succession, like stars in conflagration, till the rooms were left in pitchy blackness."

Lord Salisbury was the father of ten. He treated his children like small foreign powers: not often noticed, but when recognized, regarded with unfailing politeness. "My father always treats me as if I were an ambassador," reported one adolescent, "and I *do* like it." Classroom hours for small children were reduced by decree from five hours a day to four on the grounds that the shorter span would, paradoxically, produce more intellectual fruit. Lord Salisbury's basic educational philosophy was that higher authority could, at best, have only a marginal effect; real desire to learn had to come from within. "N. has been very hard put to it for something to do," he wrote of a son who had been left alone with him for a few days at Hatfield. "Having tried all the weapons in the gun-cupboard in succession—some in the riding room and some, he tells me, in his own room—and having failed to blow his fingers off, he has been driven to reading Sydney Smith's *Essays* and studying Hogarth's pictures." Lady Salisbury did not share her husband's detached approach. "He may be able to govern the country," she said, "but he is quite unfit to be left in charge of his children."

■ ■ ■

The one person in England to whom Lord Salisbury willingly deferred was the monarch. When Salisbury first became Foreign Secretary, Queen Victoria decided that this vigorous champion of Britain's greatness deserved her confidence. She gave it unstintingly for the rest of her life. He had been Prime Minister only the briefest time in 1885 when he was forced to step down in favor of Gladstone. "What a dreadful thing to lose such a man, for the country, the world, and *me!*" the Queen lamented. Nevertheless, she gratefully congratulated him on the "triumphant success of his conduct of foreign affairs by which he has in seven months raised Great Britain to the position she ought to hold in the world." On the spot, she offered him a dukedom. Salisbury declined, explaining that his "fortune would not be equal to such a dignity." But, he said, "the kind words in which your Majesty has expressed approval of his conduct are very far more precious to him than any sort of title." Ten years later, the queen's gratitude and confidence were undiminished. "Every day, I feel the blessing of a strong Government in such safe and strong hands as yours," she wrote. He had, she declared to a bishop, "if not the highest, an equal place with the highest among her ministers," including Lord Melbourne and Disraeli. As he aged and grew heavy, Salisbury's legs began to weaken. The Queen invited him to sit in her presence.

The sovereign, to Salisbury, was the embodiment of the nation and the focus of patriotism, the Crown indispensable to the functioning of Kingdom and Empire, its continued prestige the only guarantee of the nation's stability. Nevertheless, his feelings for the woman, Queen Victoria, went deeper. He was the first of her prime ministers to be younger than she, and he treated her with chivalry and personal devotion. He could not manage the courtly grace and flowery language which Disraeli had troweled onto his Faerie Queen, but he made up these lacks with an iron determination that she should be protected and obeyed. "I will *not* have the Queen worried," he would say to colleagues who wished to press this or that decision on the monarch. He most admired Queen Victoria's loyalty, her unflagging sense of duty, and her honesty. "Always speak the truth to the Queen" was his only advice to those approaching her for the first time. Her own candor was complete; the one offense which she could not pardon in others was any attempt to deceive or to conceal things from her. Salisbury's wife was under the impression that her husband told the Queen "everything."

Their correspondence was formal; each wrote in the third person. Lord Salisbury's letters always began with the phrase: "Lord Salisbury, with his humble duty to your Majesty, . . ." In cipher

telegrams, this was shortened to a terse "Humble duty." His deference was impeccable but underneath lay his steely will: "Lord Salisbury offers this suggestion with much diffidence and is quite
prepared to find that there are objections to it which are not evident
to him at the moment."

The Queen wrote back formally, although when she was upset,
she telegraphed excitedly, often bluntly, in the first person. "I am
too horrified for words at this monstrous, horrible sentence against
this poor martyr Dreyfus," she telegraphed in September 1899 from
Balmoral. "If only Europe would express its horror and indignation!
I trust there will be severe retribution!" Retribution was beyond
Salisbury's power, but he could and did agree: "Lord Salisbury entirely shares your Majesty's burning indignation at the gross and
monstrous injustice which has been perpetrated in France. It is perfectly horrible. . . ." Sometimes, when the Queen was truly
aroused, there was nothing that could be done. After the death of
the Emperor Frederick, the Queen wanted her widowed daughter to
come to England for a long visit. The Prince of Wales and Lord
Salisbury discussed the idea and decided that, for political reasons,
the Empress should not come. A telegram from Balmoral to Lord
Salisbury annihilated this recommendation:

> Letter received. Intention doubtless well meant, but it would be
> impossible heartless and cruel to stop my poor, broken-hearted
> daughter from coming to her mother for peace, protection, and
> comfort. She has nowhere to go; everyone expects her to come
> and wonders [why] she has not come before. It would be no use
> [to postpone the visit] and only encourage the Emperor [Wil-
> liam II] and the Bismarcks still more against us. You all seem
> frightened of them, which is not the way to make them better.
> Tell the Prince of Wales this, and that his persecuted and ca-
> lumniated sister has been for months looking forward to this
> time of quietness. Please let no one mention this again. It would
> be fatal and must not be.

Lord Salisbury knew when the battle was over and wrote
calmly to the Prince of Wales:

> Sir:
> In furtherance of the conversation I had with your Royal
> Highness on Monday, I wrote to the Queen that night, giving
> reasons why I thought it, and your Royal Highness thought it,

more prudent that the visit of the Empress Frederick should be deferred.

I have this afternoon received the enclosed answer from Her Majesty.

I have the honor to be your Royal Highness' obedient, humble servant,

SALISBURY

Salisbury's respect for the Queen's judgment was not based wholly on her rank. As he told the House of Lords after her death: "She had an extraordinary knowledge of what her people would think—extraordinary because it could not have come from personal intercourse. . . . I always felt that when I knew what the Queen thought, I knew pretty certainly what view her subjects would take, and especially the middle class of her subjects."

Lord Salisbury, averse to pretense and bombast, had little taste for the Queen's eldest grandchild. The Prime Minister's description of William II's qualities first appeared during the brief reign of Emperor Frederick. Queen Victoria was about to pay her son-in-law a final visit. Officials in Berlin worried that the grandmother might say something to irritate Prince William, her sensitive grandson, who soon would be Emperor. Count Hatzfeldt communicated these worries to Salisbury, who passed them along to the Queen:

"It appears that his [Prince William's] head is turned by his position and the hope evidently was that your Majesty might be induced to have a special consideration for his position. . . . Evidently, though Count Hatzfeldt's language was extremely guarded, they are afraid that, if any thorny subject came up in conversation, the Prince might say something that would not reflect credit on him; and that if he acted so as to draw any reproof from your Majesty, he might take it ill, and a feeling would rankle in his mind which would hinder the good relations between the two nations. . . . It is nevertheless true—most unhappily—that all Prince William's impulses, however blameable or unreasonable, will henceforth be political causes of enormous potency; and the two nations are so necessary to each other that everything that is said to him must be very carefully weighed."

Salisbury and Hatzfeldt were later involved in the family imbroglio which resulted from William's behavior towards his uncle in Vienna. The Prince of Wales was furious, and the queen had referred to her grandson as a "hot-headed, conceited, and wrong-headed young man, devoid of all feeling." In his conversations with Hatzfeldt, Salisbury found that the Ambassador had not reported any of these royal opinions to Berlin. "He was simply afraid to do so," the Prime Minister reported to the Queen. "From the hints he let drop, Lord Salisbury gathered that the young Emperor was difficult to manage, that Prince Bismarck was in great perplexity, and his temper had become consequently more than usually unbearable. . . . If nobody tells Prince Bismarck the truth, there is no knowing what he might do. Lord Salisbury's impression is that Count Hatzfeldt's position is very insecure."

When Bismarck fell in March 1890, Salisbury pronounced it "an enormous calamity of which the effects will be felt in every part of Europe." The manner of the Chancellor's dismissal, Salisbury noted to the Queen, had a certain poetic justice: "It is a curious Nemesis on Bismarck. The very qualities which he fostered in the Emperor [William II] in order to strengthen himself when the Emperor Frederick should come to the throne have been the qualities by which he has been overthrown." Nevertheless, the man who had created and controlled the carefully balanced interlocking alliance system was gone; Europe would be spared the bullying and secret treaties which doubled back on each other, but Bismarck's had been a policy of peace. The policies of the young Emperor and his new ministers were unknown.

The first signs were hopeful. The new German Chancellor, Caprivi, wrote a warm personal note to Lord Salisbury, appealing for friendly relations with England. Salisbury responded. The result in the summer of 1890 was an agreement between Germany and Britain in which the two empires exchanged colonial territories. Curiously, the agreement, which had Salisbury's support and which delighted the Kaiser, was opposed by most Germans and Englishmen, who each thought that their country had gotten the worse of the bargain.

The territories exchanged were Heligoland and Zanzibar, two small islands five thousand miles apart. Heligoland, a granite boulder less than a mile square, inhabited by fishermen, was set in the North Sea twenty miles north of the mouths of the Elbe and Weser rivers. Britain had seized and annexed the island from Denmark during the Napoleonic Wars. Although it commanded the sea approaches to Hamburg and Bremen, Germany's most important ports, Bismarck—uninterested in the sea, in colonies, and navies—ignored it. Britain scarcely noticed Heligoland—Lord Derby, as Foreign Secretary, called it "this perfectly useless piece of rock"—and never sought to fortify it; to do so would needlessly provoke a power which she had no intention of fighting. In 1887, Bismarck reluctantly authorized construction of the Kaiser William I (Kiel) Canal from the Baltic to the North Sea across the base of the Jutland Peninsula. German perception of Heligoland began to change. William II decided that "possession of Heligoland is of supreme importance to Germany." Once acquired, it would become the keystone of Germany's maritime defense, a shield for her North Sea coast, a launching point for future naval offensives against her potential enemies, France and Russia. Accordingly, the Wilhelmstrasse proposed that Great Britain cede Heligoland to Germany. In return, the German Empire would recognize an exclusive British protectorate over the island of Zanzibar, twenty miles off the eastern coast of southern Africa.

Salisbury saw no use for Heligoland, but could see value in acquiring Zanzibar, which commanded the north–south trade routes on Africa's eastern coast. Queen Victoria disagreed, Lord Salisbury pressed, and the Queen gave way: "The conditions you enumerate are sound and the alliance with Germany valuable; but that any of my possessions should be thus bartered away causes me great uneasiness, and I can only consent on receiving a positive assurance from you that the present arrangement constitutes no precedent." The Prime Minister telegraphed his reassurance:

"Lord Salisbury quite understands and so do his colleagues that this case is not and cannot be a precedent. It is absolutely peculiar. The island [Heligoland] is a very recent conquest. It became a British possession by Treaty in 1814. Why it was retained at the general settlement we do not certainly know. . . . No authority has ever recommended that it be fortified and no House of Commons would pay for its fortification. But if it is not fortified and we quarreled with Germany, it would be seized by Germany the day she declared war. . . . There is no danger of this case being made a precedent for there is no possible case like it."

From Balmoral, the Queen consented: "Your answer respecting Heligoland forming no possible precedent I consider satisfactory. . . . But I must repeat that I think you may find great difficulties in the future. Giving up what one has is always a bad thing."*

William II was delighted by the exchange. For the remainder of Salisbury's 1886–1892 term as Prime Minister, relations between the

---

* The cession of Heligoland also required approval by Parliament. In debate, Lord Rosebery asked whether the wishes of the island's inhabitants had been ascertained. The Prime Minister replied that they had been ascertained "confidentially."

Emperor and England were warm. William was proud of his rank in the Royal Navy and bombarded the Admiralty with advice. In 1891 he sent a detailed paper listing changes he recommended in the administration of the British Navy. Salisbury asked Lord George Hamilton, the First Lord, to prepare a polite reply: "It is wise to return a soft answer. Please send me a civil, argumentative reply, showing that in some directions we are adopting his recommendations . . . and that we will give our best consideration and attention to his valuable suggestions. It rather looks to me as if he was not 'all there.' " William, in these years, eagerly desired Lord Salisbury's good opinion. Making a state visit to England in July 1891, he asked to be invited to spend the night at Hatfield and, after his return to Berlin, he sent to Salisbury a full-length portrait of himself in the uniform of a British admiral as a memento of his visit.

Salisbury was uncomfortable with the Kaiser's attention and hoped that the advice from Berlin would cease. On April 14, 1892, he wrote to the Queen: "Lord Salisbury respectfully draws your Majesty's attention to the Emperor William's conversation as reported. He appears to be strangely excited; and it would be a very good thing if your Majesty would see him and calm him." A week later, Salisbury said again: "Lord Salisbury hopes that some opportunity may occur which will enable your Majesty to recommend to the Emperor calmness, both in his policy and in the speeches which he too often makes."

Soon after Salisbury returned to office in June 1895, the German Emperor became permanently embittered toward him. Always sensitive to English opinion or behavior, William believed that, during Regatta Week in August 1895, the Prime Minister had given him not one, but two, deliberate snubs.

The Kaiser was at Cowes, living on board the *Hohenzollern*. He had come in grand style, bringing along a naval flotilla which included the new German battleships *Worth* and *Weissenburg*. The presence of this squadron, which the Kaiser wished to show off to the Prince of Wales, already had frayed many nerves. "His Majesty gave the English a special treat by bringing along a fleet of four battleships and a dispatch boat," Alfred von Kiderlen-Waechter, the Foreign Ministry official assigned to the party, wrote ironically to Holstein. "They block the course of the racing vessels, every few moments they get an attack of *salutirium,* the sailors are flooding Cowes, the Queen has to invite the commanders, etc."

Simultaneously, Lord Salisbury was visiting Osborne House for an audience with the Queen. She suggested he call on her grandson to discuss the question of the future of the Ottoman Empire. Salisbury requested an audience. The interview was to be held on the *Hohenzollern*. The appointed hour came, but the Prime Minister did not arrive. William had been waiting impatiently for an hour when a steam cutter came alongside and Lord Salisbury hurried up the ladder, apologizing profusely for his tardiness. He explained that the launch bringing him from the landing in East Cowes had broken down and that he had had to wait for another to be brought. The Kaiser, rather than brushing the matter off, remained sullen throughout the interview, and Salisbury's proposal—that England and Germany combine in an approach to the problem of Turkey—was buried under his resentment. The unintended affront was compounded the following day. That afternoon, the Emperor asked to see Salisbury again, inviting him to come on board the *Hohenzollern* at four P.M. This time, William waited for two hours and Salisbury never appeared. The explanation was that when the Kaiser's invitation arrived, the Prime Minister was with the Queen. The telephone message was taken by a footman in the billiard room and delivered only at three forty-five P.M. Deciding that it was too late to call on the Emperor, whose request was doubtless only a courtesy since it had been delivered by telephone, Salisbury returned by boat to Portsmouth and took a train to London. The next day he received a message from the Queen: "William is a little sore at your not coming to see him, having waited some hours for you, thinking you would come after seeing me. . . . [I] think you should write a line to Count Hatzfeldt expressing regret at this." Salisbury apologized, but the Kaiser continued to speak of the Premier's "insulting behavior." Eventually, Lord Salisbury got tired of continued German references to his error and remarked to Eckardstein, "Your Kaiser seems to forget that I do not work for the King of Prussia, but for the Queen of England."

Returning to Berlin, William brooded over what he considered his rude treatment in England. Five months later, in early January 1896, events in southern Africa provided a flashpoint and William's anger exploded. Holstein blamed both the Emperor and Lord Salisbury. "Seeking an outlet for his resentment, he [the Kaiser] seized on the first available opportunity, which was the Jameson Raid," he wrote in his *Memoirs*. Earlier, he had written to Eckardstein: "By his boorish behavior in the autumn of 1895, Lord Salisbury succeeded in inducing in the Emperor, England's best friend in Germany, a temper which contributed to the sending of the Kruger Telegram."

CHAPTER 11

The
Jameson Raid
and the Kruger Telegram

◆

I would annex the planets if I could," Cecil Rhodes had cried one night, staring up at the heavens. In 1895, the most dynamic figure on the African continent was at the peak of his career. He was Prime Minister of the Cape Colony of South Africa, he had added territories as large as Western Europe to the British Empire, and he was one of the richest men in the world. At forty-two, he was called "the Colossus."

Rhodes was born in 1853, the sixth of nine children of a stern Hertfordshire vicar and his wife. Cecil was his mother's favorite among her seven sons; she called only him "my darling." At seventeen, he left England to join his older brother Herbert, who was growing cotton in Natal. When diamonds were discovered at Kimberley on the northern edge of the Cape Colony, Rhodes and his brother rushed to stake claims. In 1873, Cecil, twenty—already earning £10,000 a year—returned to England to pay his own way through Oriel College, Oxford. For the next eight years, Rhodes oscillated between two lives, doing a term or two at college, then returning, his Greek lexicon in his kit, to dig on the veldt. At Oxford, Rhodes, tall and slim with wavy, light-auburn hair and pale-blue eyes, played polo and joined clubs catering to dandies. He paid his bills by selling the uncut diamonds which he carried in a little box in his waistcoat pocket. "On one occasion," a fellow student recalled, "when he condescended to attend a lecture which proved uninteresting to him, he pulled out his box and showed the gems to his friends and then it was upset and the diamonds were scattered on the floor. The lecturer looked up, and asking what was the cause of the disturbance, received the reply, 'It's only Rhodes and his diamonds.' "

Rhodes' diamonds had made him rich. By 1891, his De Beers Diamond Company controlled South Africa's diamond production, which made up 90 percent of all the diamonds produced in the world. When gold had been discovered in 1886 in the Boer Republic of the Transvaal, Rhodes had become a leading investor in the Consolidated Gold Fields Company. Wealth had bought power. Rhodes had entered politics in 1878, and became an M.P. in the Cape Parliament ten months before he received his degree from Oxford. By 1890, at thirty-seven, he had become Prime Minister of the Cape Colony. It was not enough. Rhodes burned to extend the British Empire to the north, to bring southern Africa from Capetown to Lake Tanganyika into a single federated dominion of the British Crown. Britain's "younger and more fiery sons," he said, would thrust ahead and seize the land; the Crown would follow and annex. Bechuanaland, an area the size of Texas, was taken in this fashion; then the huge territory called Matabeleland, which Rhodes modestly named Rhodesia.* "What have you been doing since I saw you last, Mr. Rhodes?" Queen Victoria asked in 1894. "I have added two provinces to your Majesty's dominions," Rhodes replied. That year, Lord Rosebery, the Prime Minister, made Rhodes a Privy Councilor.

Rhodes' dreams extended beyond southern Africa. He wanted to build a railroad six thousand miles long up the eastern side of the African continent. He imagined the day when the Anglo-Saxons (to include Germans and Americans) would dominate a peaceful world in a permanent Pax Britannica. Rhodes once remarked, "If there be a God, I think that what He would like me to do is to paint as much of the map of Africa British as possible and to do what I can elsewhere to promote the unity and extend the influence of the English-speaking race." What troubled Rhodes was that right in the middle of this glorious dream, spoiling it all, stood a little cluster of Dutch farmers, led by a rigid, Bible-quoting old man, who, it seemed, had a vision of his own.

---

* Today, Northern and Southern Rhodesia have become, respectively, Zambia and Zimbabwe.

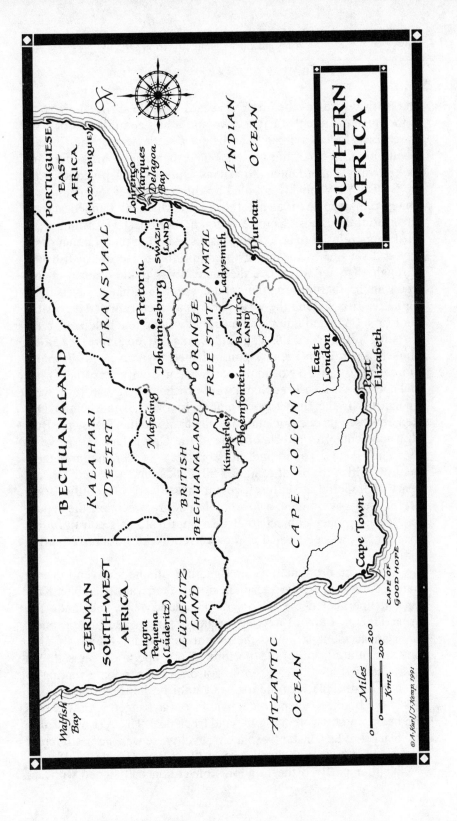

SOUTHERN AFRICA.

PORTUGUESE EAST AFRICA (MOZAMBIQUE)

INDIAN OCEAN

Lourenço Marques
Delagoa Bay

SWAZI-LAND

TRANSVAAL

Pretoria
Johannesburg

Durban

Ladysmith

NATAL

BECHUANALAND

KALAHARI DESERT

Mafeking

ORANGE FREE STATE

BASUTO-LAND

East London

BRITISH BECHUANALAND

Kimberley
Bloemfontein

Port Elizabeth

CAPE COLONY

GERMAN SOUTH-WEST AFRICA

LÜDERITZ LAND

Angra Pequena (Lüderitz)

Cape Town

CAPE OF GOOD HOPE

Walfish Bay

ATLANTIC OCEAN

Miles
0   200
Kms.
0   200

© A.Karl / J.Kemp 1991

■ ■ ■

The British were not the first Europeans to settle at the southern tip of the huge continent. In 1650, two and a half centuries before, the Dutch East India Company had begun a settlement at the Cape of Good Hope. In time, the settlers called themselves Afrikaners and spoke a variation of Dutch, Afrikaans. During the Napoleonic Wars, the British Navy quickly gobbled up the colony, but the majority of whites remained Afrikaners. In 1834, Parliament banned slavery throughout the British Empire. A fraction of the slave-owning Cape Afrikaners refused to accept this dispossession of their human property and set out to the north to escape the reach of English law. Through 1836 and 1837, five thousand Boers trekked north in covered wagons, taking along their cattle, sheep, and black slaves, fighting native tribes along the way. The Great Trek rumbled across the veldt for a thousand miles, and eventually came to a halt in a stretch of rolling hills beyond the Vaal and Orange Rivers. Here, the Boers climbed down from their wagons, hitched their oxen to the plow, and began to farm. Two small independent Boer states, the Transvaal and the Orange Free State, were proclaimed and, in 1854, were recognized by the British government. In 1877, Britain, under Disraeli, reversed its decision and formally annexed the Transvaal. British troops entered Pretoria and raised the Union Jack. Three years later, the Boers revolted and, in February 1881, defeated a detachment of British troops at Majuba Hill. Gladstone, now in office and weary of Imperial adventures, compromised and offered the Boers internal self-government, a form of autonomy which left the republics' foreign policy subject to British approval. This constitutional arrangement was embodied in the Convention of London, signed in 1881.

The most prominent Boer signature on the Convention was that of Paul Kruger, the President of the Transvaal Republic. Kruger's life paralleled the history of his country. He had made the Great Trek as a boy of ten. He became a farmer and hunter; once, when an accident required the amputation of his thumb, Kruger took his hunting knife and performed the operation himself. He always carried his Bible; when he got off a train, people waiting to see him on the platform had to wait until he finished reading and closed the book. Kruger's wide, pale face was fringed with whiskers and beard and he wore a top hat and frock coat. His eyes were small and black and he constantly spat. At seventy, he was the patriarch of the republic; his people knew him as Oom Paul (Uncle Paul).

Neither party to the London Convention had signed with enthusiasm. Kruger wrote his name on the document with great reluctance, making clear as time progressed that he would do his best to throw off the British yoke. Many Britons, especially officers of the army, considered the Boers and the Transvaal unfinished business. In their view, Gladstone had compromised too quickly, before the army had had a chance to vindicate its honor by reversing an early defeat.

Then, in 1886, huge reefs of gold ore, thirty miles long, 1,500 feet deep, were discovered in the Witwatersrand a few miles south of Johannesburg. Overnight, a city of tents sprang up, housing fifty thousand miners—Britons, Americans, Germans, and Scandinavians —the largest concentration of white men on the African continent. The city spread; tents became shacks, then barracks, then individual houses. Gigantic chimneys and mountains of slag arose beside the pit heads. The Rand was on its way to becoming the greatest source of gold in the world, exceeding the combined production of America, Russia, and Australia.

Gold produced social and political upheaval in the small republic of Bible-reading farmers. Foreign miners, called *Uitlanders* (outsiders) by the Boers, threatened to drown the state by sheer weight of money and numbers. Kruger and the members of the Executive Council—dressed like him in top hats, frock coats, brown boots—in their neat little capital of Pretoria with its careful streets lined with trees, shrubs, and flowers, were frightened by this rough mining-camp society. Uitlanders, Kruger believed, were godless, lawless, dirty, and violent; he characterized them publicly as "thieves and murderers." To maintain Boer political control, Kruger established a five-year residency requirement for citizenship and voting; then he extended it to fourteen years. Discriminatory taxes were levied against miners; their children, if any, were taught in Boer schools in Afrikaans. *The Times* in London stated the Uitlander case and warned of danger:

"When a community of some 60,000 adult males of European and mainly English birth find themselves subjected to the rule of the privileged class numbering only a quarter of that figure and are refused the enjoyment of the elementary liberties now conceded to the subjects of the pettiest German principality, we know there can only be one ending to the matter. It is most desireable, however, that this development of constitutional freedom should take place in accordance with the peaceful precedents of English history. . . . It would be, we feel, a calamity to civilization in South Africa if the controversy had to be decided by an appeal to force."

Talk of an armed uprising against the Boer government began

to spread among the miners. Often, this talk involved the name of Cecil Rhodes. Rhodes wanted Paul Kruger and the Transvaal government removed from his path. They were a major obstacle to Rhodes' imperial dreams: expansion of the Cape Colony to the north, a federation of South African states within the British Empire, a Cape-to-Cairo railway, the map of eastern Africa painted British red.

In the spring of 1895, Rhodes began to plot against the Transvaal government. Four thousand rifles, three machine guns, and over 200,000 rounds of ammunition were smuggled into Johannesburg under loads of coal or in oil tanks whose false bottoms had taps which would drip slightly if a customs official tried them. Four Uitlander leaders came to Cape Town, sat in wicker chairs on the Prime Minister's veranda, and looked out at Table Mountain while they conspired against President Kruger. The uprising would begin with an attack by armed Uitlanders on the Boer arsenal at Pretoria. The attackers would come with carts to carry away the weapons they found inside so that, as they disarmed the Boers, they armed themselves. Rhodes did not ask the Uitlanders to rise without outside help. British troops could not be used, but Rhodes had a private army of men recruited into the service of the chartered British South Africa Company, of which Rhodes was chairman. Already this semimilitary force had enforced Rhodes' will on Matabeleland. These men, Rhodes explained to the Uitlander leaders, would be stationed on the border of the Transvaal Republic; they would intervene if the uprising got into trouble. The commander of these troopers would be Rhodes' best friend and principal lieutenant, Dr. Leander Starr Jameson.

"Doctor Jim," as he was known in South Africa and later throughout the Empire, was an Elizabethan freebooter like Cecil Rhodes. A short, stocky, balding man, Jameson inspired comparison with loyal animals—which, from Englishmen, can be high recommendation. "The nostrils of a racehorse," declared George Wyndham. His wide-apart, brown eyes reminded Lord Rosebery of "the eyes of an affectionate dog . . . there can scarcely be higher praise." To one of his officers, Jameson's look of eager anticipation was that of "a Scotch terrier ready to pounce." A Scot, an eleventh and final child, trained as a surgeon, Jameson had come to Africa to practice in Kimberley, where his good nature and boyish grin quickly made him a favorite. He met Rhodes his first day in Kimberley and "we drew closely together," Jameson said. Rhodes moved into Jameson's one-story corrugated-iron bungalow, where the two lifelong bachelors shared two untidy bedrooms and a sitting room.

"We walked and rode together," Jameson continued, "shared our meals, exchanged our views on men and things, and discussed his big schemes." "All the ideas are Rhodes'," Jameson was to say and, at Rhodes' bidding, "Doctor Jim" abandoned his scalpel and rode off to build an empire. At the head of Rhodes' private army, Jameson had defeated King Lobengula of Matabeleland (and then had treated the captured King for gout).

In mid-October 1895, Jameson, on Rhodes' instruction, began assembling men on the Transvaal's western frontier about 170 miles from Johannesburg. He had 494 men, six machine guns, and three pieces of artillery. Three British army colonels, conveniently on extended leave from the Regular Army, were present to assist. His orders were to await word of the Uitlander rising, then, when summoned, to dash to Johannesburg across the veldt. Waiting, Jameson's men grew bored and restless. The days stretched into weeks and still the Uitlanders in Johannesburg kept asking questions: Would the rising succeed? If it did, what would be the relationship of their new multinational polity to the Cape Colony? To the Empire? Jameson observed this procrastination with impatience and anger. Time was passing; soon, Kruger would uncover the entire conspiracy. "Anyone could take the Transvaal with half a dozen revolvers," he declared. When the rising was fixed for December 28, and then postponed indefinitely, Jameson listened to the news and went outside his tent to pace. Twenty minutes later, he stepped back in and announced, "I'm going." The following evening, in the bright moonlight of a midsummer night in the Southern Hemisphere, the troopers rode into the Transvaal.

It was a fiasco. After four days, Jameson's men had ridden to within fourteen miles of the tall mine chimneys of Johannesburg. But they had been fighting all the way, they had not slept, and the deeper they penetrated into the Transvaal, the more Boers hurried out to bar the way. At eight o'clock on January 2, 1896, surrounded, outnumbered six to one, with seventeen dead, fifty-five wounded, and thirty-five missing, Jameson confronted the fact that his mission had failed. He raised a white flag. His men were disarmed and released immediately. Jameson himself and five officers, including the three British Regular officers, were handed over to the Cape government on the Natal border. From there, they were sent back to England for trial.

Five years later, when Great Britain attempted to subdue the Transvaal and the Orange Free State, it required three years and almost half a million soldiers.

■ ■ ■

In England, the public first heard about the Jameson Raid on the morning of New Year's Day when it picked up its newspapers and read—in the *Times* for example—"CRISIS IN THE TRANSVAAL: APPEAL FROM UITLANDERS. DR. JAMESON CROSSES THE FRONTIER WITH 700 MEN." Inside was the text of an appeal from five prominent Johannesburg Uitlanders asking Jameson to save them. "The position of thousands of Englishmen and others is rapidly becoming intolerable," declared the letter, dated December 28. "Unarmed men, women and children of our race will be at the mercy of well-armed Boers, while property of enormous value will be in the gravest peril." At the subsequent inquiry, it was revealed that the letter had been written in November and held by Jameson for release whenever an Uitlander rising signalled him to come. When there was no Uitlander rising and Jameson decided to go anyway, he released what came to be known as the "women and children" letter. England, not knowing this, waited excitedly to see how this melodrama would turn out. A new Poet Laureate of England, Alfred Austin, hastily cobbled up suitable doggerel:

> *There are girls in the gold-reef city,*
> *There are mothers and children too!*
> *And they cry, "Hurry up! for pity!"*
> *So what can a brave man do?*

The public cheered, but the British government promptly repudiated Jameson. The Colonial Secretary, Joseph Chamberlain, had been dressing for a ball at his house in Birmingham when a messenger brought him the news. Chamberlain immediately took a train for London, arriving before dawn on December 31. A stream of cables flowing from his office that day called the raid "an act of war," demanded that the raiders be summoned back, and offered his cooperation to President Kruger in making "a peaceful arrangement . . . which would be promoted by the concessions that I am assured you are ready to make." Chamberlain worried most about reaction to the raid in Germany. "If it [the raid] were supported by us," he said to Lord Salisbury, "it would justify the accusation by Germany and other powers that, having first attempted to set up a rebellion in a friendly state and having failed, we had then assented to an act of aggression."

■ ■ ■

Chamberlain's worries were well founded. The Transvaal Republic had always been a favorite of the German Empire: "a little nation which was Dutch—and hence Lower Saxon–German in origin—and to which we were sympathetic because of the racial relationship," the Kaiser explained in his memoirs. In 1884, Paul Kruger, fresh from London where he had signed the Convention specifically prohibiting his country from making treaties without British approval, had arrived in Berlin and called on Bismarck. "If the child is ill," Kruger observed, "it looks around for help. This child begs the Kaiser to help the Boers if they are ever ill." Bismarck, aware of the terms of the London Convention, was noncommittal.

German influence in the small republic grew quickly. Following the discovery of gold in 1886, fifteen thousand Germans swarmed into the Transvaal; German businessmen established branches in Pretoria and an energetic German Consul, Herr von Herff, missed no opportunity to stress German ties to the Transvaal. A railroad from Pretoria to the sea through the Portuguese colony of Mozambique was under construction, largely supported by German capital (making it, thus, entirely independent of British control). The Portuguese port of Lourenço Marques on Delagoa Bay where the new railway reached the Indian Ocean became a steamship terminus for the North German Lloyd and Hamburg-America lines.

From time to time, British diplomats, worried about encouragement given Boer aspirations, reminded their German colleagues of the 1884 Convention. This offended the Kaiser. "To threaten us when they need us so badly in Europe," he scoffed in October 1895. In 1895, German behavior stirred English suspicions. On January 27, the Kaiser's birthday, the German Club of Pretoria entertained President Kruger. Herr von Herff assured Kruger that Germany cared about the fate of the Boer state. Kruger again cast his state in the role of a child. "Our little republic only crawls about among the great powers," he said, "but we feel that if one of them wishes to trample on us, the other tries to prevent it." Germany, he proclaimed, "was a grown up power that would stop England from kicking the child republic." Sir Edward Malet, the British Ambassador in Berlin, protested this language to Marschall, the German Secretary of State. Marschall listened to Malet and retorted that the trouble in Africa was caused not by the Boers, but by the aggressive behavior of Cecil Rhodes. In July 1895, the Pretoria–to–Indian Ocean Railway was opened. William II telegraphed his congratulations and three German cruisers dropped anchor in Delagoa Bay.

In the autumn of 1895, rumors of an Uitlander rising spread to Europe. Malet, about to retire, used a final call on Marschall to warn of the danger of further encouragement of Boer aspirations. Marschall replied that, at the very least, the status quo must be maintained; any attempt to achieve Rhodes' dream of uniting the Transvaal, economically or politically, into British South Africa would be "contrary to German interest." The British and German press became belligerent. "The status [of the Transvaal to Great Britain] is one of vassal to suzerain," proclaimed *The Times.* "We will wash our own dirty linen at home without the help of German laundresses," growled the *Daily Telegraph.* Germany "needed no instruction as to the extent of her interests in South Africa," declared the *Vossische Zeitung.* "The Transvaal has a right to turn to Germany for support. The republic is in no sense an English vassal." When William II received Marschall's report of his talk with Malet, he flared with indignation. At a diplomatic reception, he snagged the British military attaché and complained that Malet "had gone so far as to mention the astounding word 'war.' . . . For a few square miles full of niggers and palm trees, England had threatened her one true friend, the German Emperor, grandson of Her Majesty, the Queen of Great Britain and Ireland, with war."

Then, on December 30, Herr von Herff telegraphed the Wilhelmstrasse that the raid had begun. He urged that a naval landing party from the ships in Delagoa Bay be brought by rail to Johannesburg to protect German citizens and property. On December 31, Hatzfeldt was instructed to ask officially whether the British government approved of the raid. If the answer were yes, he was to demand his passport and sever diplomatic relations. When Hatzfeldt called on Salisbury, he was assured that the government had nothing to do with the raid, was doing everything possible to suppress it, and recognized the dangers posed to the interests of other European powers in the Transvaal. Hatzfeldt returned to his embassy and cabled Berlin that the British government was not only not responsible for the raid, but was hugely embarrassed by it. In Berlin, Sir Frank Lascelles, the new British ambassador, delivered the same message, declaring that the raiders were "rebels" and that Jameson had been sternly commanded to withdraw.

In Berlin, however, the Kaiser was in a state of frenzied excitement. The Jameson Raid, following what he perceived as Lord Salisbury's rudeness the preceding summer, seemed evidence of a deliberate British policy of patronizing and ignoring German interests and the German Emperor. On January 1, General von Schweinitz described his Imperial master as "absolutely blazing and ready to fight England." The following day, the Prussian War Minister, General von Schellendorf, had an interview with the Kaiser during which William became so hysterical and violent that the War Minister told Prince Hohenlohe that "if it had been anyone else, he would have drawn his sword." That evening, still agitated, William wrote to the Russian Emperor, Nicholas II: "Now suddenly the Transvaal Republic has been attacked in a most foul way, as it seems without England's knowledge. I have used very severe language in London . . . I hope all will come right, but, come what may, I shall never allow the British to stamp out the Transvaal."

Later that night, after the Kaiser's message had been telegraphed to St. Petersburg, news of Jameson's surrender reached Berlin. William, pleased, was still determined to strike a blow at England. At ten o'clock on the morning of January 3, the Emperor arrived at the Chancellor's palace in the Wilhelmstrasse accompanied by Admirals Senden, Hollmann, and Knorr. Hohenlohe, the seventy-six-year-old Chancellor, and Marschall, the State Secretary, were there to receive them. Holstein and Kayser, Director of the Colonial Section, waited in a nearby room. "His Majesty," Marschall wrote later, "developed some weird and wonderful plans. Protectorate over the Transvaal. Mobilization of the Marines. The sending of troops to the Transvaal. And, on the objection of the Chancellor, 'That would mean war with England,' H.M. says, 'Yes, but only on land.'" The admirals doubted that Britain would be willing to fight Germany only on land in South Africa while observing peace in Europe and on the high seas. Discussion wandered. Someone suggested sending Colonel Schlee, Governor of German East Africa, disguised as a lion hunter, to Pretoria where he would offer himself as military Chief of Staff to President Kruger. Eventually Marschall, seeking to tone down the response, proposed that the Kaiser send a congratulatory telegram to President Kruger. William agreed and Marschall left the room to draft the message. Holstein, sensing danger, expressed misgivings, but Marschall silenced him quickly: "Oh, no, don't you interfere. You have no idea of the suggestions being made in there. Everything else is even worse." A telegram, actually drafted by Kayser, was sent back into the room, where it was approved. Couched as a personal message from the German Emperor to the Boer President, it read: "I express my sincere congratulations that, supported by your people without appealing for the help of friendly Powers, you have succeeded by your own energetic action against armed bands which invaded your country as disturbers of the peace and have thus been able to restore peace and safeguard the independence of the country against attacks from outside." William made one change to stiffen the language: congratulating the President on safeguarding "the prestige of the country" was changed to "the independence" of the country. "I express to Your Majesty my deepest gratitude for Your Majesty's congratulations. With God's help we hope to continue to do everything possible for the existence of the Republic," Kruger wrote back.

In Germany, the telegram was acclaimed. "Nothing that the government has done for years has given as complete satisfaction," declared the *Allgemeine Zeitung.* Marschall exalted over the "universal delight over the defeat of the English. . . . Our press is wonderful. All the parties are of one mind, and even Auntie Voss [the Radical *Vossische Zeitung*] wants to fight." The euphoria was short-lived. Bismarck called it "tempestuous." Bülow described it as "crude and vehement." Hatzfeldt "tore his hair over the incomprehensible insanity" that had overtaken the Wilhelmstrasse and was on the verge of resignation. Holstein, writing in 1907 after his retirement, regarded the telegram as the real beginning of Anglo-German antagonism: "England, that rich and placid nation, was goaded into her present defensive attitude towards Germany by continuous threats and insults on the part of the Germans. The Kruger telegram began it all."

The English immediately wanted to know whether the telegram was merely an impulsive message from the Kaiser or an official statement by the German government. On January 4, the day after the telegram was sent, the Empress Frederick asked this question of Hohenlohe at lunch. The Chancellor "answered that it certainly was in accordance with German public feeling at this moment. From which," the Empress wrote to her mother and brother in England, "I gather that the telegram was approved." Subsequently, Marschall took the *Times* correspondent in Berlin aside and told him that the telegram was *"eine Staats-Aktion"* (an official act of state).

In subsequent years, each of the participants in the January 3 meeting took pains to show that the action was forced upon him against his better judgment. Holstein supported Marschall, describing the telegram as "an expression of the Kaiser's annoyance, the result of disagreements of a personal nature which had arisen between the Kaiser and Lord Salisbury a few months previously during a visit to England. . . . Seeking an outlet for his resentment, he [William] seized on the first opportunity which was the Jameson Raid."

The Kaiser's story changed over time. When the telegram was published and all Germany was shouting its approval, William spoke and acted as if he were the sole author. Later, in his memoirs, William attempted to shift responsibility: "The Jameson Raid caused great and increasing excitement in Germany. . . . One day, when I

had gone to my uncle, the Imperial Chancellor, for a conference
. . . Baron Marschall suddenly appeared in high excitement with a
sheet of paper in his hand. He declared that the excitement among
the people—in the Reichstag even—had grown to such proportions
that it was absolutely necessary to give it outward expression and
that this could best be done by a telegram to Kruger, a rough draft
of which he had in his hand.

"I objected to this and was supported by Admiral Hollmann.
At first the Imperial Chancellor remained passive in the debate. In
view of the fact that I knew how ignorant Baron Marschall and the
Foreign Office were of English national psychology, I sought to
make clear to Baron Marschall the consequences which such a step
would have among the English; in this, likewise, Admiral Hollmann
seconded me. But Marschall was not to be dissuaded.

"Then, finally, the Imperial Chancellor [Prince Hohenlohe]
took a hand. He remarked that I, as a constitutional ruler, must not
stand out against the national consciousness and against my constitutional advisers; otherwise there was danger that the excited attitude of the German people, deeply outraged in its sense of justice
and also in its sympathy for the Dutch, might cause it to break down
the barriers and turn against me personally. Already, he said, statements were flying about among the people; it was being said that the
Emperor was, after all, half an Englishman, with secret English sympathies; that he was entirely under the influence of his grandmother,
Queen Victoria, that the dictation emanating from England must
cease once and for all. . . . In view of all this, he continued, it was
his duty as Imperial Chancellor, notwithstanding the fact that he
admitted the justification of my objections, to insist that I should
sign the telegram in the general political interest and, above all else,
in the interest of my relationship to my people. He and Herr von
Marschall, he went on, in their capacity of my constitutional advisers
would assume full responsibility for the telegram and its consequences. . . . Then I tried again to dissuade the ministers from
their project; but the Imperial Chancellor and Marschall insisted
that I should sign, reiterating that they would be responsible for the
consequences. It seemed to me that I ought not to refuse after their
presentation of the case. I signed.

"After the Kruger dispatch was made public the storm broke in
England as I had prophesied. I received from all circles of English
society, especially from aristocratic ladies unknown to me, a veritable flood of letters containing every possible kind of reproach; some
of the writers did not hesitate even at slandering me personally and
insulting me. . . ."

England's reaction to the Kruger Telegram was first amazement, then overwhelming hostility. The Kaiser implicitly had endorsed the Transvaal's "independence" and, by congratulating
Kruger on repelling the raid "without the help of friendly powers,"
had seemed to suggest that such help would have been—or in the
future might be—available. "The nation will never forget this telegram," proclaimed the *Morning Post.* "England will concede nothing to menaces and will not lie down under insult," said *The Times.*
Windows of German shops were smashed and German sailors were
attacked on the Thames docks. The 1st Royal Dragoons, of which
the Kaiser was the Honorary Colonel, took down the Imperial portrait and rehung it with its face to the wall. Satirical and ribald songs
about the German Emperor dominated the London music halls. A
Times editorial on January 7 restated Britain's position: "With respect to the intervention of Germany in the affairs of the Transvaal
. . . we adhere to the Convention of 1884 and we shall permit no
infraction of it by the Boers or anyone else. . . . Great Britain
must be the leading power in South Africa. She will not suffer any
policy calculated to lessen her predominance." The following day
the government announced the formation of a naval "Flying Squadron" of two battleships and four cruisers. The object, Parliament
heard, was "to have an additional squadron ready to go anywhere
either to reinforce a fleet already in commission or to constitute a
separate force to be sent in any direction where danger may exist."
In fact, the "Flying Squadron" got no farther than a cruise in the
Irish Sea. Later, Britain reinforced its point with three British cruisers, which arrived in Delagoa Bay to shadow the three German
warships already in the harbor.

The Royal Family disagreed as to how to react to "this most
gratuitous act of unfriendliness," as the Prince of Wales described
the telegram to his mother. "The Prince would like to know what
business the Emperor had to send any message at all. The South
African Republic is not an independent state . . . it is under the
Queen's suzerainty." The remedy the Prince urged on his mother
was to give the Emperor "a good snubbing." The Queen chose otherwise, deciding to deal with the Kaiser as an unruly grandson.
"Those sharp, cutting answers and remarks only irritate and do
harm, and in sovereigns and princes should be carefully guarded
against," she wrote to her son. "William's faults come from impetu-
ousness as well as conceit, and calmness and firmness are the most
powerful weapons in such cases." On January 5, from Osborne,
Queen Victoria wrote a grandmotherly letter:

"My dear William . . . I must now touch upon a subject which causes me much pain and astonishment. It is the telegram you sent to President Kruger which is considered very unfriendly towards this country, not that you intended it as such I am sure—but I grieve to say it has made a most unfortunate impression here. The action of Dr. Jameson was, of course, very wrong and totally unwarranted, but considering the very peculiar position in which the Transvaal stands towards Great Britain, I think it would have been far better to have said nothing." Lord Salisbury, receiving a copy of the Queen's letter, advised her that the letter "is entirely suited, in Lord Salisbury's judgement, to the occasion and hopes it will produce a valuable effect." At the same time, Queen Victoria asked the Prime Minister to "hint to our respectable papers not to write violent stories to excite the people. These newspaper wars often tend to provoke war, which would be too awful."

William's reply to the Queen on January 8 was a blend of deference and evasion:

Most beloved Grandmama:
Never was the Telegram intended as a step against England or your Government. . . . We knew that your Government had done everything in its power to stop the Freebooters, but that the latter had flatly refused to obey and, in a most unprecedented manner, went and surprised a neighboring country in deep peace. . . . The reasons for the Telegram were 3-fold. First, in the name of peace which had been suddenly violated, and which I always, following your glorious example, try to maintain everywhere. This course of action has till now so often carried your so valuable approval. Secondly, for our Germans in Transvaal and our Bondholders at home with our invested capital of 250–300 millions, which were in danger in case fighting broke out in the towns. Thirdly, as your Government and Ambassador had both made clear that the men were acting in open disobedience to your orders, they were rebels. I, of course, thought that they were a mixed mob of gold diggers quickly summoned together, who are generally known to be strongly mixed with the scum of all nations, never suspecting there were real English gentlemen or Officers among them.
Now, to me, Rebels against the will of the most gracious Majesty the Queen, are to me the most execrable beings in the world, and I was so incensed at the idea of your orders having been disobeyed, and thereby Peace and the security also of my Fellow Countrymen endangered that I thought it necessary to show that publicly. It has, I am sorry to say, been totally misun-

derstood by the British Press. I was standing up for law, order, and obedience to a Sovereign whom I revere and adore. . . . These were my motives and I challenge anybody who is a Gentleman to point out where there is anything hostile to England in this. . . .

I hope and trust this will soon pass away, as it is simply nonsense that two great nations, nearly related in kinsmanship and religion, should stand aside and view each other askance with the rest of Europe as lookers-on. What would the Duke of Wellington and old Blücher* say if they saw this?

Salisbury favored letting the incident drop and advised the Queen to accept William's explanations "without enquiring too narrowly into the truth of them." From the perspective of British politics, the Emperor had done the Salisbury Cabinet a favor. Jameson's caper had brought discredit on the government; many believed that the Colonial Secretary was personally involved. By bursting onstage in the middle of this drama, the German Emperor diverted attention to himself. Ironically, it was Rhodes who best explained this to the Kaiser. Visiting Berlin in 1899 in connection with the laying of a telegraph line through German East Africa, he was invited to lunch at the Castle. (The Empress had written to Bülow, "I should like to hear from you how I ought to treat Cecil Rhodes . . . whether rather coldly or whether one ought to be particularly friendly to him. My own choice would be for the former.") William, impressed by the great *conquistador,* listened tolerantly as Rhodes described how the Kruger Telegram had saved him. "You see, I was a naughty boy and you tried to whip me. Now my people were quite ready to whip me for being a naughty boy, but directly *you* did it, they said, 'No, if this is anybody's business, it is ours.' The result was that Your Majesty got yourself very much disliked by the English people and I never got whipped at all!"

Rhodes may have considered himself unwhipped, but both he and Jameson were punished for the raid. Jameson and his five chief officers were brought to London and tried at the Old Bailey for infringement of the Foreign Enlistment Act. In the months before the trial and even during the nine-day process in July 1896, the defendants remained free and Jameson was the toast of the capital. Arthur Balfour, the Government Leader in the House of Commons, declared that he "should probably have joined Jameson had he lived there." Margot Tennant Asquith, wife of the future Liberal Prime

* The commanders of the allied British and Prussian armies at Waterloo.

Minister, H. H. Asquith, sighed that "Dr. Jim had personal magnetism and could do what he liked with my sex." Although *The Times* urged that Jameson's sin was only "excess of zeal" and Lord Chief Justice Russell had to suppress pro-Jameson courtroom demonstrations during the trial, the verdict was guilty. Jameson was sentenced to fifteen months. (The officers, given shorter terms, were stripped of their commissions in the Regular Army.) Jameson went to a comfortable jail, but he moped, declined in health, and was sent home with a Queen's Pardon after only four months. Eight years later, in 1904, he became Prime Minister of the Cape Colony. In 1911, King George V made him a baronet, and the following year, Sir Leander Starr Jameson came back to England for good. He lived with his brother for five years and died at sixty-four, in 1917. From his sentencing to his death, he refused to speak about the raid.

Of greater political significance than the guilt of Jameson was the extent of the involvement of Cecil Rhodes and Joseph Chamberlain, the Colonial Secretary. These questions were the subject of a five-month inquiry by a Select Committee of the House of Commons in the spring of 1897. The raiders had been captured carrying copies of cipher telegrams which proved Rhodes' complicity in the proposed Uitlander uprising and the preparations for the raid. He had not authorized Jameson's decision to proceed; indeed, he had sent a cable halfheartedly telling him not to go. When Jameson went anyway, Rhodes acted as if he were horrified. "Old Jameson has upset my applecart," he said. "Twenty years we have been friends and now he goes and ruins me." Rhodes immediately resigned as Prime Minister of the Cape Colony and Managing Director of the Consolidated Gold Fields Company. In London, he appeared for six days before the Select Committee. He shouldered all the blame for the planning of the raid; when the Committee asked whether it was as Prime Minister or Managing Director that he had organized the incursion, Rhodes replied, "Neither." He had done it solely "in my capacity as myself."

The Committee found it impossible to establish that Chamberlain had prior knowledge of the raid. In the Colonial Secretary's favor was his immediate condemnation of the raid once he learned it was under way. While Rhodes was censured, Chamberlain and all other members of the Cape and British governments were exonerated. A few days after the inquiry ended, the House of Commons was shocked to find the Colonial Secretary rising to offer Cecil Rhodes a public testimonial. "As to one thing, I am perfectly convinced," Chamberlain said. "That while the fault of Mr. Rhodes is about as great a fault as a politician or a statesman can commit, there has been nothing proved—and in my opinion there exists nothing—which affects Mr. Rhodes's personal position as a man of honor." (Cynics suggested that Rhodes had wrung these words from Chamberlain by threatening to disclose hitherto unseen documents.)

Rhodes lived only six years after the raid. He suffered from cardiovascular disease, which he helped along by eating huge slabs of meat, drinking throughout the day, and smoking incessantly. His body near the end was bloated, his cheeks blotched and flabby, his eyes watery. His high-pitched voice became almost shrill; his handshake, offered with only two fingers of the hand extended, was weak; his letters, which had always ignored punctuation, left out words to the point of incoherence. He spent most of his time in his spacious Dutch farmhouse mansion, called Groote Schuur, at the foot of Table Mountain outside Cape Town. The rooms were beamed and paneled in dark teak and hung with African shields and spears. His vast bathroom of green and white marble boasted an eight-foot tub carved from solid granite. On his bookshelves he had placed the works of all the classical authors mentioned by Gibbon in *The Decline and Fall of the Roman Empire.* Rhodes had ordered these authors translated for himself at a cost of £8,000. On his bedroom wall, Rhodes had hung a portrait of Bismarck.

In 1896, when Groote Schuur was gutted by fire, Rhodes was told that there was bad news. He knew that Jameson was ill; now, his face white, he said, "Do not tell me that Jameson is dead." When he heard about the fire, he flushed in relief. "Thank goodness," he said. "If Dr. Jim had died, I should never have got over it." Jameson was at Rhodes' side in March 1902 when the Colossus, at forty-eight, met his own death. His last words were "So little done, so much to do."

Tension between the British and German governments ebbed quickly, although Lord Salisbury comprehended the potential danger that had been implicit in the situation. "The Jameson Raid was certainly a foolish business," he said to Eckardstein. "But an even sillier business . . . was the Kruger Telegram. . . . War would have been inevitable from the moment that the first German soldier set foot on Transvaal soil. No government in England could have withstood the pressure of public opinion; and if it had come to a war between us, then a general European war must have developed." As it was, the raid and the telegram altered the relationship between

Great Britain and Imperial Germany. In the popular view of Englishmen, the raid was a daring effort to protect legitimate British interests. The Kaiser's action had taken the British people entirely by surprise. Until publication of the telegram, Britons had traditionally looked upon France as the potential antagonist. The German Empire, ruled by the Queen's grandson, was assumed to be England's friend. The telegram indicated an unsuspected animosity. Feelings softened as time passed, but a residue of suspicion remained. The Princess of Wales declared to a friend that "in his telegram to Kruger, my nephew Willy has shown us that he is inwardly our enemy, even if he surpasses himself every time he meets us in flatteries, compliments, and assurances of his love and affection." In Rome, Sir Francis Clare Ford, the British Ambassador, warned his German colleague Bernhard von Bülow that "England will not forget this box on the ear your Kaiser has given her." When Bülow spoke of the many ties between the two countries, Ford explained that it was "just because of these many and intimate ties that the English people will not forgive your Kaiser this affront. The Englishman feels as a gentleman at a club might feel if another member—say his cousin with whom he played whist and drunk brandy and soda for many years—suddenly slapped his face."

The explosion of British anger, thoroughly reported in the German press, created its own backlash in Germany. One beneficiary was Tirpitz, who had opposed the sending of the telegram as unrealistic in view of Germany's impotence at sea. What could Germany have done, he asked, if Hatzfeldt had taken back his passport? What could fifty, or a hundred, or a thousand German marines or soldiers do in Africa as long as Britain controlled the sea? Mahan's thesis, that world power requires sea power, was glaringly displayed. "The incident may have its good side," Tirpitz wrote to General von Stosch, his former superior as Navy Minister, "and I think a much bigger row would actually have been useful to us . . . to arouse our nation to build a fleet." Years later, in his memoirs, the Grand Admiral concluded that "the outbreak of hatred, envy, and rage which the Kruger Telegram let loose in England against Germany contributed more than anything else to open the eyes of large sections of the German people to our economic position and the necessity for a fleet."

CHAPTER 12

"Joe"

◆

Lord Salisbury and Joseph Chamberlain worked together during the crisis of the Jameson Raid and Kruger Telegram, but the relationship between the two men had not always been amiable. As a young man, Chamberlain had flirted with republicanism. "The Republic must come and at the rate we are moving, it will come in our generation! I do not feel any great horror at the idea," he had said. As a junior minister in Gladstone's third government, Chamberlain had attacked the House of Lords. "The Divine Right of Kings—that was a dangerous delusion," Chamberlain had declared, "but the divine right of peers is a ridiculous figment. We will never be the only race in the civilized world subservient to the insolent pretensions of an hereditary caste." Chamberlain made his attack personal: "Lord Salisbury constitutes himself the spokesman . . . of the class to which he himself belongs, who toil not, neither do they spin, whose great fortunes, as in his case, have originated by grants made in times gone by for the services which courtiers rendered kings."

"Who toil not, neither do they spin"—the phrase rang through the nation. Lord Salisbury described the young Radical Liberal from Birmingham as "a Sicilian bandit." When Chamberlain threatened a march on London by tens of thousands of his Birmingham constituents to protest the power of the House of Lords, Lord Salisbury suggested that Mr. Chamberlain himself should march in the van. "My impression," Salisbury declared grimly, "is that those who will have to receive him will be able to give a very good account . . . and that Mr. Chamberlain will return from his adventure with a broken head if nothing worse." Chamberlain accepted the challenge and proposed that Lord Salisbury lead the Tory combatants. "In that case if my head is broken, it will be broken in very good company." He flung out another dare: "I would advise him [Lord Salisbury] to try another experiment. . . . He has had picnics at Hatfield . . . and picnics at half the noblemen's seats in the country. Now let him try to picnic in Hyde Park. I will promise him that he will have a larger meeting than he ever addressed and that it will be quite unnecessary for him to go to the expense of any fireworks."

This firebrand now sat with Salisbury at the Cabinet table. Joseph Chamberlain was born on July 8, 1836, into a middle-class family south of the Thames in London. In school, he took prizes in mathematics and French, but when he was sixteen his father insisted that he end his formal education and enter the family business, making fine Spanish leather boots and shoes. Two years later, Joseph, again at his father's request, went to live in Birmingham to help in a new metal-screw factory jointly owned by his father and uncle. For eighteen years, Chamberlain made screws; when he retired in 1872, his factory produced two thirds of all the metal screws manufactured in England. At thirty-six, a wealthy man, Joseph Chamberlain was able to concentrate on other things.

Wistful about his own truncated training, he had a lifelong interest in education. When John Morley took him to visit Oxford and they had gone "round the garden walks, antique gates and 'massy piles of old munificence,' " Chamberlain turned to Morley and said, " 'Ah, how I wish that I could have had a training in this place.' Yet [Morley said] he came to be more widely read . . . than most men in public life." Chamberlain's concern was for children's education. In 1870, 2 million of 4.3 million school-age children never attended school, and another million attended on a haphazard, intermittent basis. In Birmingham, children ran ragged, barefoot, and wild through the streets. Chamberlain became an advocate of compulsory, free education. While still making screws, he had been elected President of the Birmingham Board of Education. In 1870, as a private businessman, he had visited No. 10 Downing Street, where he had acted as spokesman for a delegation from the National Education League.

Within a year of retirement from manufacturing, Joseph Chamberlain was Mayor of Birmingham. Although he held office only three years, he developed an absolute political control over the city which he maintained for the rest of his life. This gave him an advantage over other national politicians; their followings were scattered throughout Britain while Chamberlain's was solidly concentrated in the middle class and urban proletariat of Birmingham and the Midlands. Here, his leadership was never challenged; where he led from one issue to another—even from one party to another—his followers marched behind.

Chamberlain commanded this allegiance even though he scarcely looked like a social reformer or a friend of the workingman. Of medium height, with a pale, clean-shaven face, Chamberlain was a self-creation sartorially as well as politically. He wore elegant cutaways and topcoats, a red cravat drawn through a gold ring, and a fresh orchid pinned daily in his buttonhole. A gold-rimmed monocle attached to a black ribbon popped in and out of his right eye. Once in Birmingham, he appeared at a municipal meeting wearing a tailored sealskin topcoat. His fellow citizens admiringly called him a "swell"; in the city and in wider circles too, he was known as "the King of Birmingham." In 1874, Mayor Chamberlain welcomed the Prince and Princess of Wales as visitors to Birmingham. Despite speculation in the Conservative press that the "Radical demagogue" who advocated a republic would show disrespect to the Heir to the Throne, Chamberlain ushered the royal couple through a parade, a reception, and a lunch at the Town Hall. Rising to toast the Prince, the Mayor declared, "Here in England the throne is recognized and respected as the symbol of all constituted authority and settled government." Not long after, Chamberlain was invited to dine at Marlborough House.

Chamberlain's life, blessed by early business and political success, was marred by personal tragedy. He had married at twenty-five and again at thirty. Both of his young wives—who were themselves first cousins—had died in childbirth while producing sons.* These shocks had left Chamberlain feeling that "it seems almost impossible to live." Soon after his second wife died, a report went around Birmingham that he had been killed in a carriage accident. "Unfortunately," he noted, "it wasn't true and the friends who came to look at my remains, found me presiding over a Gas committee."

In the summer of 1876, at forty, Chamberlain was elected unop-

---

* Austen, born in 1863, was Chancellor of the Exchequer, 1903–1905 and 1919–1921, and Foreign Secretary, 1924–1929. Neville, born in 1869, was Chancellor of the Exchequer, 1923–1924 and 1931–1937. From 1937 to May 1940, he was Prime Minister.

posed to Parliament. During the campaign, in a vituperative moment, he hurled abuse at the Conservative Prime Minister, Lord
Beaconsfield. Beaconsfield, Chamberlain said, was "a man who
never told the truth except by accident; a man who went down to
the House of Commons and flung at the British Parliament the first
lie that entered his head." Subsequently, Chamberlain apologized in
writing. Entering the Commons as a Radical member of the Liberal
Party, Chamberlain, unlike most M.P.'s, had had experience administering the affairs of a large city. He understood the problems of
housing, education, and sanitation as they affected the lives of the
urban poor, and he aired these problems in Parliament. His audience, expecting a fiery Radical demagogue, were surprised by his
incisive style. Chamberlain's beliefs were passionate, but his
speeches never passed the boundaries of logic. "His strength in debate," reported a journalist, "was that he always attacked and never
bothered to defend himself." Observers "watched him and wondered what answer he would give to this or that seemingly unan-
swerable point made by an opponent. In nine cases out of ten, he
made no answer, but by the time he sat down, he had changed the
entire issue and now the question was what answer the next man
was going to make to him." When he was challenged, Chamberlain's
figure stiffened and a cool smile fixed itself on his face. The im-
presssion was of "a man of obvious mystery with rather frightening
qualities held in leash . . . his voice was fascinating, but it had a
dangerous quality to it, and a sentence begun in a low tone, would
come to a trenchant conclusion with something like a hiss."

When the Liberals returned to power in 1880, Gladstone discovered that Chamberlain, an M.P. for only four years, expected to
be in the Cabinet. After negotiations which included a threat from
Chamberlain to lead a Radical splinter party if he was not included,
Gladstone made him President of the Board of Trade. The government was Liberal, but the member from Birmingham found himself
sitting at a Cabinet table with men quite different from himself. Half
his colleagues were peers; three fourths were hostile to his proposals
for social reform. Nevertheless, the arrangement succeeded. When
Chamberlain struck too harsh a note or advanced farther on a path
than his colleagues would follow, the Prime Minister wrote him a
fatherly note, stressing the need in politics for moderation and compromise.

In 1886, Gladstone decided to crown his long public career by
giving Home Rule to Ireland. A separate and independent parliament was to sit in Dublin with full powers of taxation and appointment of magistrates and other officials. The British Parliament in

London, stripped of Irish members, would retain control of defense and foreign affairs. Chamberlain, hearing Gladstone's proposal, was dismayed. In his view, "the Irish people are entitled to the largest measure of self-government consistent with the continued integrity of the Empire." But Gladstone, he thought, had gone too far. "It was mischievous or worse," Chamberlain said, "to talk of maintaining the unity of the Empire while granting Home Rule." He cited the precedent of the American Civil War: "To preserve the Union, the Northern States of America poured out their blood and treasure like water. . . . If Englishmen still possess the courage . . . we shall maintain unimpaired the effective Union of the three kingdoms that owe allegiance to the British Crown." As Gladstone plowed ahead, Chamberlain argued, again using the American example. Perhaps Britain, like America, should adopt a system of federalism: England, Scotland, and Ireland could each have its own parliament with certain powers, as the American state legislatures did. But it would not do for one nation, Ireland, to become almost independent, while the other two were not. Compromise became impossible. On March 26, 1886, Chamberlain resigned from the government and when the House voted, June 8, on Home Rule, Chamberlain led forty-six Liberal Imperialists into the lobby against the government. The bill failed, the government fell, and the Liberal party was split.

Chamberlain's action had dire consequences for himself as well as for his party. He was, after Gladstone, the most popular Liberal politician in Britain. Had he supported Gladstone on Home Rule, he would have succeeded to the leadership of the party and, one day, to the Premiership. As leader of a splinter faction, siding often with the Conservatives, he threw that chance away. Chamberlain never tried to reinstate himself. On the contrary, to the amazement and outrage of his former friends, he turned all his oratorical artillery against Gladstone and the Liberals. "It was unthinkable," wrote the journalist J. L. Garvin, describing the Liberal view of this apostasy. "Weapons made in their own arsenal, talents so obviously designed for the destruction of their opponents, a disposition so obviously Radical, a habit of speech so clearly intended for the chastening of dukes and Tories; that all this should be taken and placed at the disposition of the Tory Party was unheard of, impossible." He was accused of betraying the cause of the people for the society of duchesses. He was compared, unfavorably, to Judas: "Judas, after betraying his Master, did not attend public meetings; he did not revile his associates . . . he did not go swaggering about Judea saying he had now joined the gentlement of Jerusalem. No, Judas was contrite; he was ashamed; he went out and hanged himself." Irish members of the Commons stared at his infuriating monocle and orchid and screamed "Traitor!" and "Judas!" whenever he rose to speak. Once, when Chamberlain was firing directly at Gladstone, a mass of enraged Irishmen charged him from their benches. Fists flew, hats toppled, and Chamberlain was quite unmoved. To him, politics was a kind of warfare; beliefs must always be passionate; there must be "no fraternizing in the trenches and no wandering about in no-man's land."

Chamberlain was out of office for almost ten years, 1885–1895. As the Prime Ministership was beyond his grasp, he was resolved to make the best of second-best and use his leverage to compel the Conservative Party to take on his own Radical domestic program. He was technically still a Liberal; he and his followers remained on the Liberal benches, but gave their support on most issues to the Tories. In return, they demanded and received Tory backing for their proposals. In 1891, Lord Salisbury's government passed a law which had been one of Chamberlain's lifelong objectives: free education for all children in the United Kingdom. That same year, Chamberlain introduced for the first time in the British Parliament a bill establishing old-age pensions.

During his years of political loneliness, Chamberlain's private loneliness came to an end, a circumstance for which Lord Salisbury was indirectly responsible. In August 1887, the Prime Minister asked Chamberlain to lead a British delegation to Washington to attempt to settle a fishery dispute involving American fishing boats seized and confiscated in Canadian waters. Chamberlain, gloomy and restless, agreed on the day he was asked. He spent three months in the American capital, where he became a social favorite, dined frequently with President Cleveland, and concluded a treaty which pleased everyone. One night, at a reception in his honor at the British Embassy, the visiting Englishman was introduced to Mary Endicott, the daughter of Cleveland's Secretary of War. Once the presentations were over, he abandoned everyone else in the room and spent the evening talking to Miss Endicott. That night in his hotel, he sat for hours by an open window, smoking his cigar. Mary Endicott was twenty-three; he was fifty-one. He reached a conclusion. Miss Endicott accepted his proposal. When he sailed for England, Chamberlain wore a red rose instead of an orchid in his buttonhole.

The city of Birmingham greeted the young American bride: "Dear lady, welcome home." Queen Victoria, after their first meeting, entered in her journal: "Mrs. Chamberlain is very pretty and

young-looking and is very lady-like with a nice, frank, open manner." (A few years later, the Queen wrote: "Mrs. Chamberlain
looked lovely and was as charming as ever.") Lord Salisbury, according to his biographer, "was always ready to discuss politics"
with Mrs. Chamberlain. More important, the youthful stepmother
captured the affection of his children. "She unlocked his heart and
we were able to enter in as never before," one of his children said
later. "She brought my children nearer to me," Chamberlain acknowledged.

In 1892, Chamberlain's son Austen, twenty-nine, entered the
House of Commons. A year later, wearing a monocle like his father,
Austen gave his maiden speech. Gladstone, Prime Minister for the
last time, rose to congratulate the son of his former lieutenant and
current bitter enemy, observing that the speech and its accomplished delivery "must have been dear and refreshing to a father's
heart." Chamberlain bowed low to the old man and those nearby
said that they had never seen Joseph Chamberlain so moved.

Beyond politics, Chamberlain cared only for family and home.
He had no interest in sports, played neither golf nor tennis, never
hunted or went yachting. His days at Highbury, his house near Birmingham, were largely devoted to reading and raising orchids. He
extended his greenhouses again and again and loved to pace the
long glass corridors where his exotic plants stood in multicolored
ranks. He experimented, crossing hues and sizes, trying always for
something new and remarkable, which, when achieved, found its
place in his lapel.

The main business of Chamberlain's life was politics. By the
1890s he had linked all the major themes of his life: Democracy,
Radical Social Reform, and Empire. The package made a powerful
appeal to the British people. When the new anti–Home Rule coalition of Conservatives and Radical Liberals gave itself the party label
of "Unionist," Chamberlain declared that he was "proud to call
myself a Unionist . . . believing it is a wider and nobler title than
that either of Conservative or Liberal, since it includes both of them
—since it includes all men who are determined to maintain an undi-
vided Empire and who are ready to promote the welfare and union,
not of one class, but of all classes of the community." Chamberlain's
concept of Empire went beyond his refusal to see Ireland break the
integrity of the United Kingdom. He was thinking of a global bond,
linguistic, cultural, political, and commercial. This theme, addressed
to a Toronto audience during his North American visit in 1887, had
stirred his listeners to "frenzied enthusiasm." "I am an Englishman," he said. "I am proud of the old country from which I came.

. . . But I should think our patriotism was warped and stunted indeed if it did not embrace the Greater Britain beyond the seas—the young and vigorous nations carrying everywhere a knowledge of the English tongue and English love of liberty and law. With these feelings, I refuse to speak or think of the United States as a foreign nation. They are our flesh and blood. . . . Our past is theirs. Their future is ours. . . . Their forefathers sleep in our churchyards. . . . It may yet be that the federation of Canada may be the lamp lighting our path to the federation of the British Empire. If it is a dream—it may be only the imagination of an enthusiast—it is a grand idea. . . . Let us do all in our power to promote it and enlarge the relations and goodwill which ought to exist between the sons of England throughout the world and the old folks at home."

Chamberlain's interest in foreign affairs had evolved as his role in government broadened. In 1878, after only two years in the Commons, he warned his countrymen of the heavy burden of Splendid Isolation: "Already the weary Titan staggers under the too vast orb of her fate." In 1883, he asked Morley for help in defining a Radical position on such matters as National Defense, the Eastern Question, and Belgium. In 1884, Chamberlain, then President of the Board of Trade, had called on Herbert Bismarck in London to express his thanks for German support of the British role in Egypt. "Prince Bismarck," he had told Herbert, "has rendered us such great services that I only wish he could be convinced that towards no power are we so glad to be friendly as towards Germany. Without Germany's attitude, we would have fallen into great difficulties." Forwarding this message to his father, Herbert described Chamberlain as "this incarnate representative of the commercial class of Free Trade," who, at that moment, was "the most influential of English ministers." Chamberlain's gratitude had limits. When the Chancellor's tone turned rude, Chamberlain had bristled. "I don't like to be cheeked by Bismarck or anyone else," he had written to his friend Sir Charles Dilke, the Liberal Under Secretary at the Foreign Office. "I should let Bismarck know that if he is finally resolved to be unfriendly, we accept the position and will pay him out whenever the opportunity arises."

Chamberlain's decision to accept the Colonial Office when the Unionist government took power in July 1895 was a surprise; it seemed beneath his talents as well as his claim on the Prime Minister. Chamberlain felt differently. He had told Mary in 1887 that, although he might never hold office again, if the opportunity came

he would like the Colonial Office, where he "saw work to be done."
As Colonial Secretary, he became responsible for over 10 million
square miles—one fifth of the land surface of the globe—inhabited
by 50 million people. Chamberlain's intention was to bind all these
immense spaces and varied peoples closer to the crown. He thought
that a good start had been made—"I believe that the British race is
the greatest of the governing races that the world has ever seen"—
but that there was more to be done—"It is not enough to occupy
great spaces of the world's surface unless you can make the best of
them. It is the duty of a landlord to develop his estate."

In the first six months of his administration, the new Colonial
Secretary's Imperial dreams were brusquely overtaken by international events. When Leander Starr Jameson launched his quixotic
raid into the Transvaal and the Kaiser telegraphed his congratulations to the President of the Boer Republic, the Colonial Secretary
was indignant. He urged that Britain, beset on all sides, assert itself
forcibly. "My dear Salisbury," he wrote four days after Kruger's
receipt of the telegram, "I think that what is called an 'Act of Vigor'
is required to soothe the wounded vanity of the nation. It does not
much matter which of our numerous foes we defy, but we ought to
defy someone." Chamberlain suggested a "strongly worded dispatch
to Germany . . . declaring that we will not tolerate any interference in the Transvaal" and "an ostentatious order to commission
more ships of war."

When these crises had passed, Chamberlain drew a worried
conclusion: Britain, when challenged, had no friends. No help had
been expected from France or Russia. But the Transvaal affair had
brought confrontation with a power which Britain had reckoned
amiable: Germany. Speaking to the Canada Club in March 1896,
Chamberlain told his audience: "The shadow of war *did* darken the
horizon" in recent months. The cause, he said, was the "isolation of
the United Kingdom."

British colonial secretaries did not normally speak authoritatively
on foreign policy. Two factors made it possible in this instance: the
increasing overlap of responsibility between the Foreign Office and
the Colonial Office, and Lord Salisbury's willingness to cede power
in certain areas to his strong-minded and energetic colleague, Joseph Chamberlain. Historically, the Foreign Secretary's task was to
manage Britain's relations with foreign powers while the Colonial
Secretary's duty was to administer Britain's colonial empire. Now,
interlocking disputes involving British colonies and foreign powers

having arisen, both government departments were necessarily responsible. Questions about southern Africa, West Africa, Egypt, and the Far East arrived on the desks of both Cabinet ministers. Chamberlain, as Minister responsible for Hong Kong, was directly concerned with British policy in China. The Crown Colony handled more trade than the port of Liverpool. The impact of this trade on Britain's economy was suggested by a letter from the Duke of Devonshire to Eckardstein in March 1898: "If the panic that has seized the Lancashire cotton industry as to its Chinese markets goes on in this way, we shall soon have the greater part of the mills stopped and their hands out of work." Salisbury, despite this urgency, was little inclined to step forward in colonial disputes. His nature and experience equipped him to deal with the finely tuned Bismarckian system of quiet diplomacy and private understandings. To Salisbury, problems outside Europe were secondary; in most of these cases, he was content that Chamberlain, who had so much more vigor than he, take the lead.

As early as May 1897, Count Hatzfeldt was reporting to Chancellor Hohenlohe that "Chamberlain has rather risen above Lord Salisbury's head." The Kaiser subsequently referred to the "two-headed administration" in Britain and declared that "Chamberlain has Salisbury completely in his pocket." This was not true; final decisions were always the Prime Minister's. Chamberlain's letters to Salisbury were forceful, but always respectful. Salisbury's replies acknowledged the strength of Chamberlain's arguments, but wondered whether his good ideas could be achieved.

In the weeks following the Jameson Raid and the Kruger Telegram, Chamberlain, believing that the day was past when Britain could survive alone, forcefully stated his opposition to isolation. Salisbury, fearful of the risks of entanglement, declaring England had no history of peacetime military alliances, insisted on isolation. Queen Victoria, alarmed, wrote to the Prime Minister: "Affairs now are so different from what they used to be that the Queen cannot help feeling that our *isolation* is dangerous." Salisbury attempted to guide her back to his viewpoint. "Isolation is much less dangerous than the danger of being dragged into wars which do not concern us. . . . It is almost impossible for an English Government to enter into . . . an alliance . . . because when the crisis came, and the decision of peace or war had to be taken, the Parliament and people would not be guided . . . by the fact that the Government had some years before signed a secret agreement to go to war, but entirely by the cause for which it was proposed to go to war and their interests and feelings in respect to it. Their fury would be extreme when they discovered that their Ministry had tried to pledge them secretly beforehand."

Most Britons agreed with Lord Salisbury, and the glories of the Diamond Jubilee in 1897 seemed to confirm this viewpoint. With Dominion premiers and native princes gathering in London, with crowds flocking to Portsmouth to see the lines of anchored warships stretching into the Solent haze, the Empire seemed invulnerable. It was not until autumn of that year that events gave fresh strength to Chamberlain's argument that—in the queen's words—"isolation is dangerous."

These events occurred in China, where the Manchu Empire was in a state of decay. Since the middle of the nineteenth century, Britain had controlled Hong Kong and the trade of South China and the Yangtze Valley. France had acquired Indo-China; Portugal had taken Macao. Late in 1897, China lost additional territories. A German naval squadron seized Tsingtao and the Shantung peninsula. Three weeks later, a Russian squadron appeared at Port Arthur on the other side of the Yellow Sea. Two thousand Russian marines landed and raised the Russian imperial flag. Russian pressure on Peking intensified. In March 1898, the St. Petersburg government announced that it had obtained a twenty-five-year lease on Port Arthur and the right to build a railway across Manchuria to the Pacific.

Chamberlain watched these developments with alarm. The Russian advance into North China, threatening Britain's traditional interest in the center and the south, coming so soon after the triumph of the Diamond Jubilee, seemed a special humiliation. Talk in Europe attributed Britain's declining influence in China to a decay in national character. Chamberlain wrote to Salisbury that "public opinion . . . [will be] expecting some sensational action on our part." Salisbury replied, "I agree with you that 'the public' will require some territorial or cartographic consolation in China. It will not be useful and will be expensive, but as a matter of pure sentiment we shall have to do it." As Chamberlain had predicted and Salisbury agreed, the English public—most noisily the penny press —demanded action: the Russian menace to China must be confronted; why did the government not act?

In fact, the Cabinet, meeting at the end of March 1898, did not know what to do. Lord Salisbury was ill, recuperating at his villa on the Riviera. Arthur Balfour, substituting for his uncle at the Foreign Office, handled day-to-day problems, but was unprepared to initiate new policies. Chamberlain, determined to stop the Russians, stepped into the vacuum. "It is not the question of a single port in

China—that is a very small matter," he told a public meeting. "It is not the question of a single province. It is a question of the whole fate of the Chinese Empire and our interests in China are so great, our proportion of the trade so enormous . . . that I feel no more vital question has ever been presented for the decision of a Government. . . . If the policy of isolation, which has hitherto been the policy of this country, is to be maintained in the future, then the fate of the Chinese Empire may be, probably will be, hereafter decided without reference to our wishes and in defiance of our interests." British sea power alone, he argued, could not halt Russian expansion in Asia. A concert of powers was needed, or, if a concert was impossible, then a single, powerful ally. In Chamberlain's view, that ally was Germany, which could put pressure on the Russian frontier in Europe—indeed, this was the only power the Russians feared. That month, March, as the Cabinet wrestled with the problem of Russian encroachment on China, the Colonial Secretary resolved to try for an alliance with the German Empire.

Chamberlain's effort, essentially unsupported by his Cabinet colleagues, was fervently encouraged and abetted by an ally inside the German Embassy in London. During the 1890s, Baron Hermann von Eckardstein, six feet, five inches tall, was a striking figure. On ceremonial occasions, when he put on the white uniform and winged helmet of a Prussian cuirassier, he looked like a Norse god. Eckardstein had launched his career with a caper. As a lieutenant stationed at the German Ministry in Washington, D.C., he attracted the attention of Count Herbert von Bismarck. At dinner in a Washington restaurant with a group including the Chancellor's son, Eckardstein had bet his fellow diners that he could reach the street faster than they. They leaped from their chairs and ran down the stairs. Eckardstein calmly jumped out an open window. He sprained his ankle, but won the bet. It was the kind of flamboyant gesture to impress a Bismarck, and the young officer soon found himself posted in London. There, he met and married the daughter of Sir John Blundell Maple, a Conservative M.P. and the richest furniture manufacturer in England. A few years later, Sir John, who had no sons, made his German son-in-law heir to his fortune of two and a half million pounds. Bülow, impressed by Eckardstein's position in English society, promoted the Baron to First Secretary of the Embassy. Eckardstein was eager to promote friendship between his German homeland and the country in which his qualities had been recognized.

Eckardstein and Chamberlain had met in Newport, Rhode Island, in 1889, after Chamberlain's marriage to Mary Endicott. Over the years, Eckardstein had observed Chamberlain's rise, and in 1895 he had reported to Berlin that the Colonial Secretary was "unquestionably the most energetic and enterprising personality of the Salisbury Government." Then, in March 1898, Eckardstein arranged a meeting between Chamberlain and Count Hatzfeldt, the German Ambassador. Hatzfeldt was wary of the former screw manufacturer from Birmingham; he preferred to conduct diplomacy with an aristocrat like Lord Salisbury. Nevertheless, Salisbury had told him that Chamberlain would have the last word on colonial matters.

Ambassador Hatzfeldt faced a difficult task. In Berlin, Tirpitz' first Navy Bill was before the Reichstag. Passage of the Bill was Kaiser William's keenest political desire. Until this passage was achieved, relations with England must be managed so that Great Britain could continue to be presented as a threat. On the other hand, because the Royal Navy was so overwhelmingly superior, it did not seem politic to reject the British overture with excessive rudeness. "The English fleet," Bülow wrote to Hatzfeldt, "according to the unanimous estimate of all our naval authorities—I name above all, Admiral Tirpitz—is not merely equal to the combined fleets of any other two Great Powers, but superior." Tirpitz' proposal for building the German Fleet warned of years of risk in the face of this superior force. Better, therefore, to manage England prudently, to dangle German friendship in front of Chamberlain, and to pick up what one could in the colonial sphere. Hatzfeldt understood this strategy and assured Berlin that he would impress on Chamberlain that before an Anglo-German rapprochement could be contemplated, the Colonial Secretary "would have to show himself responsive on certain colonial questions."

Chamberlain and the German Ambassador met on March 29. Chamberlain emphasized, and Hatzfeldt agreed, that their conversation must be strictly unofficial. He would, of course, keep Mr. Balfour fully informed and ultimately no concrete step could be taken without the consent of Lord Salisbury. These things said, the Colonial Secretary then told Count Hatzfeldt that he favored a defensive alliance between Great Britain and Germany. On all great international issues, he argued, British and German interests were nearly identical. The Jameson Raid and the Kruger Telegram were aberrations. Britain, he confessed, needed friends: "I admitted that the policy of this country for many years had been isolation . . . [but this] may be changed." If Germany stood by England now in the Far East, said Chamberlain, she could count on Britain's help if she were attacked. Hatzfeldt listened carefully and confined his response to asking "if I thought that Parliament and the people . . . would accept the idea of an alliance."

Hatzfeldt had often heard from Lord Salisbury that Britain's security lay in isolation and that Parliament would never approve a peacetime alliance. Bülow, receiving Hatzfeldt's report of the first conversation, raised the same objection. Under the British parliamentary system, any new Cabinet could reverse the policies of its predecessor. It was impossible, therefore, for Great Britain to be a reliable ally. At his next interview with the German ambassador, Chamberlain endeavored to address this issue. It was true, he admitted, that a treaty would have to be approved by the House of Commons. But if Hatzfeldt would look back over English history, he would find no case in which a treaty made by one party in power had been repudiated by its successor. That kind of reversal, he suggested, was more likely in countries where the personality of the monarch was key; Imperial Russia, for example.

From Berlin, Bülow and Holstein, opposed to an English alliance but unwilling to affront Joseph Chamberlain, supplied Hatzfeldt with questions and objections which he could use to keep the powerful English Minister at bay. The Kaiser, reading Hatzfeldt's accounts, relished dangling a German alliance in front of England, but keeping it always just out of reach. It was satisfying to behold a senior minister of the British government admitting England's weakness and pleading, even unofficially, for German support. "The Jubilee swindle is over!" William wrote in the margin of one of Hatzfeldt's dispatches. On April 10, the Kaiser reminded the Wilhelmstrasse that he did not want an Anglo-German alliance. "At the same time," he continued, "it is of great importance to keep official sentiment in England favorable to us and hopeful. A friendly-minded England puts another card against Russia in our hands as well as giving us the prospect of winning from England colonial and commercial concessions. . . . To Count Hatzfeldt's skillful hands will fall the difficult task of putting off the conclusion of a formal alliance, not by a rejection wounding to English feeling, but so as to manifest a cordial wish for beneficent cooperation." Meanwhile, William used the well-meaning Eckardstein as a decoy. The baron, hearing from Chamberlain that the talks with Hatzfeldt were mired in German reluctance, rushed back to Germany. On April 9 he had an interview with the Kaiser. For an hour after dinner, Eckardstein and the Emperor walked up and down a terrace. William encouraged the airy dreams of his Anglophile diplomat, and Eckardstein hurried back to London to tell Chamberlain that the Kaiser had "said to me at Homburg that an alliance with England would be the best thing in the world. It would secure the peace for fifty years."

During his third and final interview with Hatzfeldt on April 25, Chamberlain heard nothing about this Imperial vision, only reiteration of the obstacles to an alliance. Perhaps someday, Hatzfeldt said, when feeling in Germany was warmer towards England, a closer relationship could be achieved. In the interim, the Ambassador suggested, nothing would be more helpful to advance that prospect than British colonial concessions. As the Birmingham screw manufacturer listened to the Rhineland aristocrat, his face grew hard. Chamberlain had been in business; he knew when he was being pushed too hard. There would be no buying of a future relationship with Germany by giving up bits of British territory. Instead, the Colonial Secretary swung the game around. Hatzfeldt's report to Berlin of this conversation contained surprising news: "Mr. Chamberlain . . . [said] that if his idea of a natural alliance with Germany must be renounced, it would be no impossibility for England to arrive at an understanding with Russia or France. . . . Mr. Chamberlain meant very deliberately to indicate that in case of a definite rejection on our side, England, so far as he has to do with it, will work for an understanding with Russia or France." In the margin of the dispatch, alongside Hatzfeldt's mention of an English understanding with Russia or France, the Kaiser wrote, "Impossible!"

This was the end of Joseph Chamberlain's first attempt to achieve an Anglo-German alliance. When Lord Salisbury returned from Beaulieu at the end of April, Chamberlain reported in detail what had taken place. The Prime Minister, neither surprised nor unduly distressed, consoled his energetic colleague: "I quite agree with you that under the circumstances a closer relation with Germany would be very desirable. But how can we get it?" Chamberlain was disappointed. His first effort had failed; other than Eckardstein, no one in Britain or Germany had supported him. Nevertheless, the unpleasant facts, as he saw them, did not go away. On May 13, 1898, he spoke in Birmingham Town Hall: "Since the Crimean War, nearly fifty years ago, the policy of this country has been a policy of strict isolation. We have had no allies. I am afraid we have had no friends. . . . We stand alone."

CHAPTER 13

Fashoda

Lord Salisbury refused to be agitated by the Far Eastern crisis which provoked Joseph Chamberlain's first attempt to achieve an Anglo-German alliance. The Prime Minister, like the Colonial Secretary, understood that Britain alone did not have the strength to keep Russia out of North China. But, as Chamberlain's reaction was to seek an ally, Salisbury's was to step back from confrontation. Before undertaking new commitments, Salisbury always measured Britain's resources; here he thought his country too weak. In April, a party of indignant fellow Cabinet ministers, come to urge strong action against Russia, learned something of his reasoning.

The delegation called on him in Arlington Street, where he lay ill with influenza. "His temperature was high and the doctor absolutely forbade an interview," recorded his daughter, who was present. "His colleagues therefore wrote a short draft of the message which they suggested sending to Russia, and I was asked to take it up to him for approval or rejection. He read it over, observed that its transmission would probably mean war, and then, after a short pause, said, 'Of course the Russians have behaved abominably and if it be any satisfaction to my colleagues I should have no objection to fighting them. But I don't think we carry enough guns to fight them and the French together.'

"I expressed somehow," Salisbury's daughter continued, "my incomprehension of what the French had to do with the matter. He turned to me with a look of surprise. . . . 'What had the French to do with it? Did I forget that Kitchener was actually on the march to Khartoum? In six months' time,' he went on, 'we shall be on the verge of war with France; I can't afford to quarrel with Russia now.'"

This message, brought downstairs to the waiting ministers, resulted in a milder dispatch to St. Petersburg. Six months later, as the Prime Minister had predicted, Britain was on the verge of war with France. In this confrontation, Salisbury made himself solely responsible for the foreign policy of England. He won his own last great diplomatic triumph, achieved in classic nineteenth-century British Imperial style: by skillful, independent diplomacy backed by the unchallengeable supremacy of the navy. War was averted and, with both Queen and Prime Minister sensitive to an adversary's pride, the French Republic was permitted to avoid humiliation. The crisis centered on a crumbling African mud fort called Fashoda.

Lord Salisbury did not care for Africa. His diplomacy, like Bismarck's, focussed on Europe, and the growing number of troubles emanating from Africa brought him only annoyance. "Africa was created to be the plague of foreign offices," he sighed. At first—he told the House of Lords in 1890—it had not seemed that there would be difficulties in Africa: "Up to ten years ago, we remained masters of Africa, or the greater part of it, without being put to the inconvenience of protectorates or anything of that sort, by the simple fact that we were masters of the sea and that we have had considerable experience in dealing with the native races. So much was that the case that we left enormous stretches of the coast to the native rulers in the full confidence that they would gradually acquire their own proper civilization without any interference on our part."

This hope was to fail. In 1869, the Suez Canal was opened and through the 1870s and 1880s an unseemly process known as the Scramble for Africa began. Great Britain, already positioned in South and West Africa, took more territory, and France, Germany, Italy, Belgium, Portugal, and Spain each acquired large areas. By 1890, England had swallowed Egypt, Kenya, and Uganda, and Britons at home, along with Cecil Rhodes in Cape Town, dreamed of a railway running the length of the continent. Essential to this dream was British control of the four-thousand-mile valley of the Nile. Cairo and Egypt had been in British hands since 1882, but the

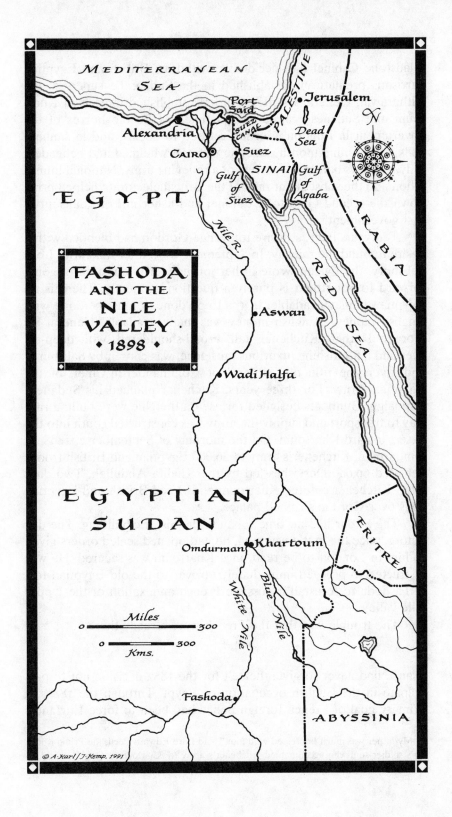

MEDITERRANEAN SEA

Port Said

•Jerusalem

PALESTINE

Dead Sea

Alexandria•

SUEZ CANAL

CAIRO◎

•Suez

SINAI

Gulf of Aqaba

EGYPT

Gulf of Suez

Nile R.

RED SEA

ARABIA

FASHODA
AND THE
NILE
VALLEY
◆ 1898 ◆

•Aswan

•Wadi Halfa

EGYPTIAN
SUDAN

Omdurman• •Khartoum

ERITREA

White Nile

Blue Nile

Miles
0 ——————— 300
0 ——————— 300
Kms.

Fashoda•

ABYSSINIA

© A. Karl / J. Kemp, 1991

Gladstone Cabinet had decided to withdraw British and Egyptian garrisons prematurely established in the Sudan. To supervise the withdrawal, General Charles Gordon established himself in Khartoum, the Sudanese capital. From this post, to the horror of the government in London, Gordon refused to depart, and in January 1885, after a nine-month siege, he was overwhelmed and beheaded, only two days before the arrival of a relieving army. National humiliation and the subsequent rage of the British electorate helped bring down the second Gladstone Cabinet and usher in Lord Salisbury's first government.

Ten years later, a desire to avenge Gordon had blended with a desire to build the railway. In September 1896, after talks with Lord Salisbury, the Queen wrote in her journal: "The question of going forward to Khartoum is purely a question of money. There is no Egyptian money available. If it is to be done, it must be done with English money." English money was made available. General Sir Horatio Herbert Kitchener, tall, broad-shouldered, with deep-set eyes and a flourishing luxurious mustache, was chosen by Salisbury* and given the title of "Sirdar," or Commander-in-Chief, of the Egyptian Army. For three years, Kitchener planned his Sudanese campaign. Gunboats designed for use on the Nile were built; a railway to transport and supply the army was constructed south into the desert toward Khartoum. On the morning of September 2, 1898, at Omdurman, Kitchener's army of 26,000 Egyptian and British troops defeated 60,000 Dervishes led by the Khalifa Abdullah. Two days later, Kitchener entered Khartoum and raised British and Egyptian flags over Gordon's ruined palace.

The Sirdar had no time to study the historic building. The day before, once the battle was won, he had opened sealed orders given to him in London to be read once Khartoum was secured. He was instructed to proceed immediately upriver to the old Egyptian fort at Fashoda to forestall a possible French annexation of the Upper Nile valley.

The trouble was that the French were already there.

France had never forgiven herself for the 1882 decision not to participate in the English occupation of Egypt. Through the 1880s, a primary goal of French foreign policy had been to force England's

---

* "My father was much impressed with him," said Lord Edward Cecil, the Prime Minister's soldier-son, who accompanied Kitchener's army to Khartoum. "That I clearly remember, for my father was not often impressed."

withdrawal from Egypt. A French diplomat once confided to an English colleague that "the French Embassy in London possesses little attraction for me, as the French ambassador is expected to get the English out of Egypt and the thing cannot be done." France, nevertheless, had wide possessions and great ambitions on the African continent. She held large territories in western North Africa, colonies at the mouth of the Congo and on the Niger, and settlements on the eastern coast at Djibouti in Somaliland. The French axis on the continent was east–west, the Indian Ocean to the Atlantic, as the British axis was north–south, Cape to Cairo. The two axes were competitive. Sooner or later, it was inevitable they would collide.

In 1894, French Foreign Minister Gabriel Hanotaux authorized a bold stroke of exploration and conquest. The Sudan and the Upper Nile had been unoccupied by a European power since Gordon's death. For a decade, the British in Egypt and the Lower Nile had made no move to retake the Sudan. From the French base at Brazzaville on the Congo, an expedition traveling across the breadth of Africa could seize the Upper Nile; once France had annexed the region, the east–west axis would be in place. A whisper of M. Hanataux's plan reached London. In March 1895, Sir Edward Grey, Parliamentary Under Secretary at the Foreign Office in Lord Rosebery's government, told the House of Commons: "The advance of a French expedition . . . into a territory over which our claims have been known for so long, would not merely be an inconsistent and unexpected act, but it must be perfectly clear to the French Government that it would be an unfriendly act, and would be so viewed by England." The enforcement of these British claims had provided an additional reason for sending Sir Herbert Kitchener into the Sudan. Equally, word of Kitchener's advance hastened French preparations in Brazzaville. The race for Fashoda had begun.

In the summer of 1896, Captain Jean-Baptiste Marchand of the French marines set out with eleven French officers and 150 Senegalese soldiers to cross the continent. They walked for twenty-four months, covering 3,500 miles. No army of Dervishes stood in their way; instead they fought swamps, hippopotami, crocodiles, scorpions, mosquitoes, fleas, and fever. Nevertheless, on July 10, 1898, the French expedition arrived at the old fort of Fashoda, built by the Egyptians in 1870 to combat the slave trade. Marchand raised the tricolor and claimed the Upper Nile as in the name of France. Britain refused to recognize any French claim. While Marchand's expedition was en route, Lord Salisbury warned the French government that Fashoda was indisputably part of the Sudan and therefore the property of the Khedive of Egypt.

Within a week of opening his sealed orders, Sir Herbert Kitchener (now Lord Kitchener by act of a grateful Queen) sailed upriver for Fashoda, accompanied by five gunboats pulling twelve barges in which were embarked one hundred Cameroon Highlanders, 2,500 Egyptian soldiers, and Maxim guns and field artillery. His officers included Lord Edward Cecil and—in command of one of the gunboats—Lieutenant David Beatty, who, eighteen years later, commanded the British Grand Fleet. The voyage up five hundred miles of river lasted a week. On September 19, Kitchener's flagship, flying only the Egyptian flag, encountered a rowboat which carried a large French tricolor at the stern. A French sergeant handed Lord Kitchener a message from Marchand: "I note your intention to visit Fashoda where I shall be happy to welcome you in the name of France." As it proceeded upstream, the British flotilla rounded a bend and beheld on the west bank a dilapidated fort surrounded by palm trees. In front of the fort, an honor guard of French African soldiers wearing red fezzes was drawn up on parade. In front of his men stood the small, bearded figure of Captain Marchand.

Herbert Kitchener was a Francophile who spoke French well. He admired Marchand's achievement in crossing the continent. Marchand's regard for Kitchener, who had defeated the Dervishes and in so doing eliminated a threat to his expedition, was equally great. They spoke in French.

"I have come to resume possession of the Khedive's dominions," Kitchener said.

"Mon Général, I, Marchand, am here by order of the French Government. I thank you for your offer of conveyance to Europe, but I must wait here for instructions."

"Captain, I will place my boats at your disposal to return to Europe by the Nile."

"Mon Général, I thank you, but I am awaiting orders from my Government."

"I must hoist the Egyptian flag here," Kitchener observed.

"Why, I myself will help you to hoist it—over the village."

"Over the fort."

"No, that I shall resist."

"Do you know, Captain, that this affair may set England and France at war?"

Marchand bowed without replying.

"You have achieved something remarkable, very remarkable, but you know the French Government will not back you up."

Marchand replied that, in any case, he would wait for his government's instructions. In the meantime, he declared, he would die before hauling down the flag of France.

Kitchener then turned slowly around and gazed at his own expedition of thousands of officers and men, flushed with victory. "We are the stronger," he observed. Marchand bowed again. They reached a compromise: the Egyptian flag was raised over an outlying section of the fort and the French flag remained where it was. Kitchener then detailed a strong force to garrison Fashoda and sailed away to Khartoum, Cairo, and eventually to Europe. Marchand remained behind, still awaiting orders. Colonel Reginald Wingate, who accompanied Kitchener to Fashoda, reported to a superior: "Here is Marchand in a perfectly untenable place, from which the state of the country makes retreat impossible, cut off from his nearest support by hundreds of miles of the most difficult country, short of ammunition and supplies and within easy striking distance of a huge Dervish army. . . . In short, our expedition has rescued the French expedition and . . . all of them thoroughly realize it. . . . I hope the instructions for Marchand's recall will not be long in coming . . . for the sake of the poor men who need feeding up and care after all their hardships."

At stake was not a mud fort, but two visions of Africa and the interest of two empires. Lord Salisbury instructed Sir Edmund Monson, the British Ambassador in Paris, to tell Théophile Delcassé, who had replaced M. Hanotaux as Foreign Minister, that "no title of occupation could be created by a secret expedition across unknown and unexplored wastes, at a distance from the French border, by Monsieur Marchand and a scanty escort." Indeed, Delcassé was to be told, all territories formerly subject to the Khedive and temporarily held by the Khalifa had passed by right of former possession and reconquest to the Egyptian government. This right, Salisbury declared, was not open to discussion. Indeed, "so long as the French flag flew at Fashoda, it was impossible for the British government to enter upon any territorial discussions." From this position, the Prime Minister and the British government did not waver. People, press, and opposition all ranked themselves firmly behind Lord Salisbury. Lord Rosebery, the most recent Liberal Prime Minister, declared at Epsom that "Great Britain has been treated rather too much as what the French call a *quantité négligeable* in recent periods. . . . If the nations of the world are under the impression that the ancient spirit of Great Britain is dead or that her resources are weakened, or her population less determined than ever it was to maintain the rights and honor of its flag, they make a mistake which can only end in a disastrous conflagration." The Admiralty mobilized a strong reserve squadron in the Channel. Some newspapers spoke of preventive war. "Fashoda is the last straw," announced the *Sheffield Daily Telegraph.* "A war with France would cut a good many Gordian knots in diplomacy . . . and when it was over, we should be able to start with a clean sheet." The Queen, however, worried about the consequences of war. "It seems a deadlock," she telegraphed Lord Salisbury on October 2. "The French Government do not telegraph Marchand to leave and he will be starved out and unable to remain for lack of water. Could we not delay till the French Government receive his report which can, I believe, come only through us." The Prime Minister, determined to see his policy through, did what he could to reassure the monarch: "I deeply sympathize with your Majesty's dissatisfaction at the present deadlock. We are, however, doing nothing, but only waiting and we cannot do anything else. No offer of territorial concession on our part would be endured by public opinion here." Queen Victoria resolved to trust Salisbury. "Received your cypher. Quite agree. We cannot give way. . . . If we wait, I think the force of circumstances will bring the French to their senses."

Across the Channel, Frenchmen saw things differently. According to the claims of possession and valor, France had a superior right to Fashoda and the Upper Nile. Marchand had survived an epic march; he had arrived first; he had planted the flag of the French Republic where no white men had ever been; he was a national hero. These arguments put Delcassé in an impossible position. He could not disavow Marchand without national shame and political disgrace. But the way to Fashoda lay through Egypt, and Egypt was in British hands. Marchand was isolated in the heart of Africa with a tiny band of brave men, dependent for supplies and security on the British Army. "We have only arguments down there and they have soldiers," Delcassé noted sadly. Britain was clearly ready to go to war over Fashoda; with public opinion split over the reopening of the Dreyfus case, France was not. The British Navy could destroy France's navy, cut all sea communications, and one by one pluck off France's colonies around the globe. Russia, abhorring the idea of war over a tiny colonial outpost in the middle of Africa, declared that the Franco-Russian Alliance applied only to Europe and refused any assistance. Delcassé thus faced the prospect of war with England, of losing the French colonial empire, of abandonment by Russia, all the while leaving a powerful, belligerent German Empire on France's European border.

When Delcassé struggled with this dilemma, the Queen of England insisted on peace. "Not a stone should be left unturned to prevent war," Queen Victoria instructed Lord Salisbury on October 25, "for I felt what an awful responsibility to God and man it would be were we to go to war and what a sacrifice of thousands of lives." Salisbury was anxious for a peaceful solution, providing France backed down. He understood that the most effective agent on the French side for reaching this solution was Delcassé. The French Foreign Minister made clear to his British adversaries that, unless he was permitted to retain a shred of self-respect, he would resign and turn his post over to someone less sensitive to the danger of war. Salisbury and Monson worked to convince Delcassé that "there would be no humiliation in withdrawing an expedition to which he had never explicitly given an official character and which had never been ordered to the Nile by the French Government. His [Delcassé's] position," Monson reported to his chief, "is that he must either accept a humiliation or go to war. His patriotism rejects the one solution; his conviction of the calamitous consequences to the two countries and the whole of Europe rejects the other." Lord Salisbury did what he could to help by describing Captain Marchand as merely "a French explorer who finds himself in a difficult position on the Upper Nile." The Queen continued to bring pressure: "I think a war for so miserable and small an object is what I could hardly bring myself to consent to," she telegraphed the Prime Minister from Balmoral on October 30. "We must try to save France from *humiliation*."

By then, the crisis was almost over. On October 28, Marchand arrived in Cairo, having come down the river on a British gunboat. Delcassé, furious at Marchand for having left Fashoda without instructions, ordered him back immediately. Meanwhile, on the twenty-seventh, Lord Kitchener landed at Dover. On November 3 he was sitting next to the Queen at dinner in Windsor Castle—"very agreeable, full of information," the Queen noted of her guest. The following night, November 4, the Sirdar was the guest of honor at a Guildhall banquet. Lord Salisbury was present, and when it came his turn to speak he rose and announced, "I have received from the French ambassador this afternoon the information that the French Government had come to the conclusion that the occupation of Fashoda was of no sort of value to the French Republic." On December 11, Marchand departed Fashoda for a second time, taking his men with him. A month later, Salisbury opened negotiations with Paul Cambon, a new French ambassador dispatched to London by Delcassé to work toward a rapprochement with England. On March 21, 1899, the Prime Minister telegraphed the Queen that he had reached an agreement with Cambon which "keeps the French entirely out of the Upper Nile valley." The watersheds of the two great African rivers, the Nile and the Congo, were to be the dividing line between the British and French spheres of influence; Britain would not move westward from the headwaters of the Nile; everything from there to the Atlantic would belong to France.

Settlement of the dispute disappointed the Kaiser, who had keenly looked forward to an Anglo-French war. From his yacht cruising in the Mediterranean, William had telegraphed the Tsar on October 28, 1898: "I have received news from London and Paris that both countries are mobilizing their fleets. . . . In case a collision between the two countries should occur, your position vis-à-vis them would be of the greatest value to me. How do you look at the situation?" Nicholas II replied that he "had no knowledge of an impending conflict between England and France" and added that "one might await events before taking any decision, the more so as it is always awkward to interfere without being asked with others' business." The Kaiser had a final comment on the Fashoda crisis: "Poor France: She acknowledges herself beaten without a shot having been fired. That is abdication on the sea. They have not read Mahan."

CHAPTER 14

Samoa
and William's
Visit to Windsor

◆

J oseph Chamberlain's second attempt to achieve an Anglo-
German alliance was delayed by a squabble over a cluster of
volcanic islands in the South Pacific and by a fuss over a birthday
party. The Samoan archipelago, lying between the Hawaiian Islands
and the northern tip of New Zealand, had been colonized in 1878 by
British, German, and American traders. Ten years later, a treaty
established a tripartite protectorate over the islands. In the spring of
1899, the King of Samoa died. The succession was contested, violence ensued, and British and American warships bombarded build-
ings, including, mistakenly, the German consulate. The German
government accepted an American apology for an errant American
shell, but promptly proposed to Great Britain that Britain join her
in asking America to withdraw from Samoa. Lord Salisbury declined. "You ask me to put my hand into a wasp's nest," he said.
Germany then suggested that Britain give up her stake in Samoa in
return for compensation elsewhere. Chamberlain, still aggrieved by
the rejection of his alliance proposal the year before, rejected the
German proposal. "Last year we offered you everything. Now it is
too late," he said to Eckardstein. Tempers flared. Suddenly, the
distant islands appeared on the front pages of newspapers in Lon-

don, Berlin, and Washington. "Instead of compliance, England has shown us harsh and open hostility," Bülow complained.

The Kaiser was indignant, not only because of thwarted German ambitions in Samoa, but because he had not been invited to Queen Victoria's eightieth birthday party on May 24. "I suspect that a great deal of His Majesty's ill-humor is due to the fact that he was not allowed to carry out his cherished scheme of presenting his younger children to the Queen on the occasion of her eightieth birthday," Sir Frank Lascelles, British Ambassador in Berlin, wrote to Lord Salisbury. Lascelles had mentioned this suspicion to Bülow, who—the Ambassador reported to Salisbury—"said that it was not for him to criticize the language of his sovereign, but I, who knew the Emperor so well, must know that his Majesty's impetuosity sometimes led to exaggeration of expression. . . . His Majesty was in fact more than half an Englishman and was extraordinarily sensitive to anything which he could regard as a slight either from the Royal Family or from Her Majesty's Government."

The Kaiser decided that both his troubles over Samoa and his exclusion from Windsor emanated from the same source: his old enemy, Lord Salisbury. On May 27, three days after the Queen's birthday, the German Emperor wrote:

> Dearest Grandmama:
> . . . I think it my duty to point out that public feeling [in Germany] has been very much agitated and stirred to the depths by the most unhappy way in which Lord Salisbury has treated Germany in the Samoan business . . . a way which was utterly at variance with the manners which regulate the relations between Great Powers according to European rules of civility. . . . This way of treating Germany's interests and feelings has come upon the people like an electric shock, and has evoked the impression that Lord Salisbury cares no more for us than for Portugal, Chile, or the Patagonians. . . . If this sort of high-handed treatment of German affairs by Lord Salisbury's Government is suffered to continue, I am afraid that there will be a permanent source of misunderstandings and recriminations between the two nations, which may in the end lead to bad blood.
>
> I, of course, have been silent as to what I have *personally* gone through these last six months, the shame and pain I have suffered, and how my heart has bled when to my despair I had to watch how the arduous work of years was destroyed, to make the two nations understand and respect their aspirations

and wishes, by one blow by the high-handed and disdainful treatment of [your] Ministers. . . . Now you will understand, dear Grandmama, why I so ardently hoped to be able to go over for your birthday. That visit would have been perfectly understood over here, as the duty of the grandson to his grandmother, putting 'Emperor,' etc., apart. . . . But a pleasure trip to Cowes, after all that has happened and with respect to the temperature of our public opinion here, is utterly impossible now. . . . I can assure you there is no man more deeply grieved and unhappy than me! and all that on account of a stupid island which is a hairpin to England compared to the thousands of square miles she is annexing right and left unopposed every year. . . . Good-bye most beloved Grandmama.

With much love and respect, believe me,
ever your most dutiful and devoted Grandson,
WILLIAM I.R.

Before replying, the Queen sent the Kaiser's letter to Lord Salisbury for comment. The Prime Minister carefully refuted the Kaiser's accusations of negligence and disrespect in dealing with Germany. He sent the memorandum to the Queen, noting dryly, "He [Lord Salisbury] entirely agrees with your Majesty in thinking that it is quite new for a Sovereign to attack in a private letter the Minister of another Sovereign; especially one to whom he is so closely related. It is not a desireable innovation and might produce some confusion."

The Queen's own reply was the angriest letter Queen Victoria ever wrote to her grandson. Her rebuff came from the heights, not of her throne, but of her position in the family. The German Emperor might have been a small boy in short pants standing before an outraged grandparent:

Dear William:

Your . . . letter, I must say, has greatly astonished me. The tone in which you write about Lord Salisbury I can only attribute to a temporary irritation on your part, as I do not think you would otherwise have written in such a manner, and I doubt whether any Sovereign ever wrote in such terms to another Sovereign, and that Sovereign his own Grandmother, about their Prime Minister. I never should do such a thing, and I never personally attacked or complained of Prince Bismarck, though I knew well what a bitter enemy he was to England and all the harm he did. . . . [As to] your visit to *Osborne, not to*

Cowes, . . . I can only repeat that, if you are able to come, I
shall be happy to receive you at the end of July or August. I can
have you and two of your sons as well as two gentlemen in the
house at Osborne, and you would leave the rest of your suite on
board your yacht.

Believe me, always your very affectionate grandmother,

V.R.I.

The Queen left it at that, but not Lord Salisbury. The Prime
Minister repaid his assailant with every delay available in his diplomatic drawer. For weeks, he kept the Wilhelmstrasse and the Kaiser
on tenterhooks about both Samoa and the Emperor's desired visit
to England. To Eckardstein, pressing for an answer, he declared that
he "wouldn't be dictated to by Berlin with a stop-watch." Holstein,
infuriated by the delay, instructed Hatzfeldt to let it be known that,
unless a Samoan settlement favorable to Germany was arrived at
quickly, the German Ambassador would ask for his passport. Lord
Salisbury reacted with sardonic lack of interest. "I am waiting daily
for Berlin's ultimatum about Samoa," he told the Duke of Devonshire. "Unfortunately it has not as yet arrived. For Germany, if it
doesn't send the ultimatum, will miss a splendid opportunity of getting rid respectably, not only of Samoa, but of all the colonies that
have cost so much. We English would then be in a position to come
to a permanent understanding with France by means of satisfactory
colonial concessions."

The more Salisbury toyed with them, the angrier the Germans
became. Chamberlain, still hoping eventually to improve the relationship between the two countries, had proposed that the dispute
be settled by Germany abandoning her claims in Samoa in return
for compensation in West Africa, adjacent to the German colony of
Togoland. Commercially, this offer was favorable to Germany. But
German eyes were fixed on Samoa; to the Kaiser it had become a
matter of personal honor; Tirpitz, thinking of overseas naval stations
for the future German fleet, insisted on Samoa in a letter which
Eckardstein described as "a document of frothy flummery, sauced
with bloody tears to suit the Kaiser's taste." German national pride
had become involved. Eckardstein noted ironically that most Germans knew not "whether Samoa was the name of a fish, fowl, or
foreign queen" but now that the issue had been raised, they insisted
"that this thing was German and for all time German it must remain." Bülow brought up his master's favorite project: "What has
happened in Samoa is a new proof that overseas policy cannot be
conducted without an adequate fleet," he told the Kaiser. "What I

have preached all through ten years to those blockheads . . . [in] the Reichstag," the Kaiser applauded in the margin. William said that he might never set foot in England again.

These German threats, disdained by Lord Salisbury during the summer, were not so pleasant for Joseph Chamberlain when autumn arrived. Over these weeks, the situation in South Africa had deteriorated. War with the Boers seemed imminent. Britain, in the Colonial Secretary's words, "stood alone." A margin of safety might be secured if German neutrality in South Africa could be established and publicly proclaimed. Nothing would give a clearer signal of this neutrality than a visit to England by the Emperor William, and Chamberlain did everything in his power to ensure that the visit would take place.

The Colonial Secretary prevailed, in part because Lord Salisbury and Count von Hatzfeldt, both skeptical as to the value of Imperial visiting, were ill. In July 1899, Lady Salisbury had suffered a stroke. Lord Salisbury, attending at her bedside, was tired of the Kaiser, tired even of Hatzfeldt. The German Ambassador, whose emphysema was worsening, could no longer stand up to the daily bombardment of demands and complaints from Berlin which had to be communicated to the Foreign Office. When the Samoan crisis was at its peak, weeks passed during which the Prime Minister and the German Ambassador never met. Negotiations were conducted between Eckardstein and Chamberlain. In Berlin, the split in the British government caused the Kaiser further vexation. "Your government in England appears to have two heads, Lord Salisbury and Mr. Chamberlain, and the one will not do what the other wants," he told Lascelles. "With Mr. Chamberlain the negotiations proceed smoothly . . . but what he agrees to Lord Salisbury refuses to sanction and so the affair is dragged out for months and months. I am not the King of Portugal and this treatment of the subject is evidence of very bad diplomatic manners. . . . I desire to remain friendly with England, but I have my duties as German Emperor to think of, and I cannot go on sitting on the safety valve forever."

On November 8 Great Britain and Germany came to terms on Samoa. The Kaiser acquired Western Samoa and a naval base at Apia. The United States kept the islands it possessed with its naval station at Pago Pago. Britain withdrew completely from Samoa and in return received Tonga and the German Solomon Islands (including Guadalcanal). German claims against British territories in West Africa were dropped. Everyone seemed pleased. Eckardstein wrote Chamberlain that the Samoan agreement "abolishes every colonial antagonism between the two countries." William cabled his grandmother that he was content with the settlement and she cabled back, "I AM EQUALLY PLEASED." To Bülow, the Kaiser telegraphed "BRAVO! YOU ARE A REAL MAGICIAN GRANTED TO ME QUITE UNDESERVEDLY BY HEAVEN IN ITS GOODNESS!"

The way was open for William to visit England.

It would be the Kaiser's first visit to his grandmother's country since August 1895, when Lord Salisbury had failed to appear for an audience aboard the *Hohenzollern*. For four years, although *Meteor* had continued to race at Cowes, the royal owner had not been present, nor had he been received by his grandmother at Osborne or Windsor. This upset William and, in the spring of 1899, he instructed Count Hatzfeldt to sound the British government about an invitation to the queen's eightieth birthday at the end of May. Socially, the greatest obstacle was the Prince of Wales. Hatzfeldt asked Eckardstein to assay the current state of the Prince's feelings towards the "Boss of Cowes." Eckardstein met the Prince at the Marlborough Club and steered the conversation towards yachting. "Yes, the last few years have been quite tolerable at Cowes," said the Prince. "No more of that perpetual firing of salutes, cheering, and other tiresome disturbances." When Eckardstein made his appeal, the Prince relented. "Let him come, so far as I am concerned. But don't let him make any bombastic speeches because the public over here won't have it." The visit was arranged for August. On July twentieth, the Empress Augusta broke her leg jumping her horse over a water obstacle. "I AM DÉSOLÉ," telegraphed the Kaiser, asking if they might come later in the year. He was reinvited for mid-November.

With the invitation in hand, William seemed to forget that it was he who wanted to visit. At Cowes in August, *Meteor* again won the Queen's Cup in the Kaiser's absence, and the Prince of Wales rose at the Royal Yacht Squadron banquet to congratulate his nephew. The following morning, a quarrelsome telegram from William was posted on the Squadron bulletin board. Addressed to the Race Committee, it complained about the conduct of the race: "YOUR HANDICAPS ARE PERFECTLY APPALLING." The Prince, staying aboard his yacht, sent for Eckardstein, who had a villa at Cowes. "It really is enough to make one despair," said the Prince. "Here I am taking the greatest trouble to put the Kaiser straight with the British public after all that has happened of late years. And here he is beginning to throw mud again at us. You know very well what the effect is on the British of such complaints . . . how sensitive we are about our national reputation for fair play in sport. Besides . . .

the best proof that our handicaps are fair is that his *Meteor* won the Queen's Cup yesterday." He shook his head and said sympathetically to the German diplomat, "I don't envy that Sisyphus job you have with the Kaiser."

Before the visit, a second disturbance agitated the Prince and his nephew. Running his eye down the list of German aides-de-camp accompanying the Emperor to England, the Prince found the name of Admiral von Senden, Chief of the Kaiser's Naval Cabinet. Senden had made occasional trips to England and once, in the company of the Prince of Wales and the Duke of York, he had heard indiscreet remarks about the Kaiser. Senden returned to Germany and reported what he had heard. William wrote immediately to his uncle to complain. The Prince replied diplomatically that nothing of the kind had been said. But Senden the tale-teller became non grata.

Seeing Senden's name, the Prince informed the Foreign Office that "the Kaiser could not possibly be accompanied on his visit by this person; he, the Prince of Wales, would absolutely refuse to receive such a *potin*." Eckardstein hurried to Berlin, where the Kaiser answered, "If I go to England at all this autumn, I shall take who I like with me." Eckardstein returned to England and pleaded with the Prince, who said, "I should be awfully glad to give way in this matter," but asked Eckardstein to make a final effort: "Do try to get the Kaiser to leave him at home." Eckardstein enlisted an ally, the German-born Duchess of Devonshire, who tackled the Prince of Wales at Newmarket. She arranged that the Prince withdraw his veto on condition that Senden apologize and agree not to accompany his master to Windsor or Sandringham. Eventually, Eckardstein was successful, although, he wrote, "It was not until shortly before the visit that I was able to forward to . . . Berlin the treaty concluded between the Prince and myself under which Admiral Senden was to be allowed to visit Windsor."

The forthcoming Imperial visit was unpopular in Germany. In the press and the Reichstag, there was talk of the scandal of visiting England at the moment when British "Mammonism" was "trying to strangle the brave little Boers." The Kaiserin, her leg now healed, urged Bülow to do something to prevent the trip: "I hoped . . . that the England visit was falling through. We really cannot go there. . . . I am afraid it will do the Kaiser any amount of harm in the country if we really go. Britain is only out to make use of us." Tirpitz, shepherding his Second Navy Bill through the Reichstag, worried about a display of Anglo-German amity just at the moment he needed to characterize the English as enemies to gather votes. Holstein, who ascribed the Kaiser's wish to make the visit to his unstable craving for the affection of his England relatives, worried what William might say once he was there. On the eve of the Kaiser's departure, Holstein presented him with an aide-mémoire which, cushioned by flattery, recommended that his royal master say nothing:

"Beyond any question your Majesty is more gifted than any of your relations, male or female. Your relations, however, do not extend to you a respect commensurate with the brilliance of your qualities—quite apart from the powerful position held by the German Kaiser. The reason is that your Majesty has always met your relatives openly and honorably, has initiated them into your plans and hopes, and has thus provided them with the opportunity of putting obstacles in your way. This English journey offers your Majesty the opportunity of righting this topsy-turvy situation and winning for your Majesty at a stroke the authority which is properly due to your Majesty's high qualities and great power. All that your Majesty need do to secure this is to avoid all political conversations.

"This applies above all to any talk with Lord Salisbury. . . . The impression made on him will be all the greater if your Majesty . . . at any meeting with him at Windsor or Osborne, merely disposes of him fairly quickly and with immaculate politeness, but with everyday small talk and no more, asking how his wife is and so on. . . . The same reserve, combined with the utmost graciousness, is desireable with Mr. Chamberlain. . . . Mr. Chamberlain will try to rush matters. . . . If your Majesty, finding Mr. Chamberlain irrepressible, will just listen politely to him and then give him the reply that his suggestion merits careful consideration and that your Majesty will give your full attention to it, I have no doubt that the offers which Mr. Chamberlain will be ready to make by way of payment for German's diplomatic cooperation and even for her firm neutrality, will grow in proportion as your Majesty exhibits quiet indifference."

At noon on November 20, 1899, the *Hohenzollern* edged alongside the Royal Quay at Portsmouth, where a special train waited to take the Kaiser to Windsor. On the platform at Windsor Station, the Prince of Wales, in a scarlet uniform, welcomed his nephew in the name of the Queen. The following night, Queen Victoria gave a formal banquet for 143 guests in St. George's Hall. "The entire service was gold," said Chamberlain, who was present. "All the candelabra and decorations [were] of gold, and three huge screens of velvet were covered with platters and every imaginable kind of piece in gold." The Colonial Secretary estimated the value of this treasure at £2 million and described it as one of the magnificent scenes of his life.

With her guests assembled in the hall, the Queen appeared, borne in a litter by four turbaned Hindus. William walked beside the litter, showing affection and deference to his grandmother. When the Queen was seated, William took his place across from her. Bülow, sitting nearby, found himself curiously touched by the "ruler of the world empire," who reminded him of "some good old soul of Hanover or Hamburg, as she carefully prodded the potatoes to find the softest, or cut the wing of her chicken." After dinner, the Queen gave each guest her hand to kiss and then retired. The party broke up for conversation. William, ignoring Holstein's advice, immediately walked up to Chamberlain. The two men talked for an hour. The Colonial Secretary reiterated his hope for an understanding between Britain and Germany. The Kaiser parried that Germany did not wish to disturb her excellent relations with Russia and reminded Chamberlain that Lord Salisbury's Great Britain had no tradition of formal peacetime alliances. Nevertheless, the Kaiser bubbled with good feelings: the recent agreement over Samoa had been helpful, and further British concessions would win over even greater segments of German public opinion. The average German, the Kaiser explained, was touchy, dogmatic, and sentimental. The best way to deal with him was to avoid trying his patience and show him much goodwill. At the end of their talk, before going off to bed, the Kaiser clapped Chamberlain jovially on the back.

The Kaiser's reception at Windsor was warm and, in his impulsive way, he responded. Enormously proud of his English family, he showed members of the German party around Windsor Castle, insisting that they admire the power of its massive battlements, the luxury of its appointments, the beauty of the paintings hung in its galleries, the charm of the gardens, the sweeping expanse of the Great Park. "From this Tower," he proclaimed to his retinue, pointing at the Great Tower, "the world is ruled." To Bülow, he confessed: "This is the finest reception and the most inspiring impression of my life. Here, where as a child I went along holding my mother's hand and marvelling modestly and timidly at the splendor, I am now staying as Emperor-King."

One afternoon, William visited the Queen. Alone together, the two—King-Emperor and Queen-Empress, grandson and grandmother—had their last conversation; fourteen months later Queen Victoria was dead. Afterwards, the Queen described their talk:

"William came to me after tea. . . . We spoke . . . of the shocking tone of the German press and the shameful misrepresentations and lies about the war, which he greatly deplores. But he says it is due to the 'poison' which Bismarck 'poured into the ears of the people' that the latter had hated England and wished for an alliance with Russia. If he had not sent him away, he does not know what would have happened, and he became even worse latterly in his abuse, which his son [Herbert] continued. William himself wishes for a better understanding with us."

There were notable absentees: throughout the Kaiser's visit, Lord Salisbury remained at Hatfield. Lady Salisbury had died a few hours after the Kaiser's arrival at Windsor. Count von Hatzfeldt was kept in Brighton by doctor's orders. For diplomatic counsel during his visit, William relied on Bülow. In mid-September, Salisbury had told the Queen that Hatzfeldt had asked three times whether the German State Secretary might be invited. "Lord Salisbury has heard nothing but good of Monsieur de Bülow," the Prime Minister told the sovereign, "and the German ambassador has pressed so earnestly that he should be invited that it is probably of some importance." Bülow came and his satisfaction at having been invited increased when, after tea on the fourth day of the visit, he was received by the Queen in her small private drawing room. Speaking in German, she asked him to sit beside her and told him that she had always strongly desired friendship between England and Germany. She asked Bülow to do something to tone down the attacks on England in the German press. The average Englishman was slow and indolent, she explained, "but if he was blamed too much and, as he believed, too unjustly . . . he might finish by losing patience." Bülow blamed it on "the immense harm that Bismarck had done by using all his influence to promote a bad feeling towards England."

The key political interview of the visit occurred when Chamberlain called on Bülow in his Windsor Castle bedroom. Bülow had learned that he would not be seeing Lord Salisbury and had received a letter from the Prime Minister asking him to talk to Chamberlain instead, emphasizing that the views expressed by the Colonial Secretary would be his own and not binding on the Prime Minister or the Cabinet. When Chamberlain walked into his room, Bülow was struck by his appearance: "Joseph Chamberlain was then sixty-three years old, but I should have taken him for no more than fifty." The Colonial Secretary impressed him as "an able, energetic, shrewd businessman, capable . . . of ruthlessness." Chamberlain went straight to the point: England, Germany, and America should collaborate; by so doing, they could check Russian expansionism, calm "turbulent" France, and guarantee world peace. Bülow repeated what Chamberlain had already heard from the Kaiser: by formally aligning herself with England, Germany would antagonize Russia, with whom she shared a long frontier. What good could the British Navy do if the Tsar marched on Königsberg and Berlin? In any case, if eventually there were to be an alliance, it would have to carry specific, detailed guarantees, endorsed by Parliament. Chamberlain, like the Queen, asked that the anti-British expressions of the German press be restrained. Bülow retorted that the Kaiser and government did not control German public opinion. Chamberlain deftly reminded Bülow that, when the Prince of Wales had thanked his nephew for coming to England in spite of anti-British sentiment in Germany, William had loftily proclaimed, "I am the sole master of German policy and my country must follow wherever I go."

In the aftermath, Chamberlain believed that he had achieved an important success; that he had been given a green light to campaign publicly for an Anglo-German alliance and that Bülow would support him in the Reichstag. Bülow afterwards maintained that although expressing a general appreciation of Chamberlain's idea, he had pointed out the difficulties a German government would have in following a pro-British policy, let alone making a formal alliance. He flatly denied giving Chamberlain assurances that he would promote an alliance in the Reichstag.

The German party departed Windsor for Sandringham, where the Prince of Wales waited to receive his nephew. Bülow, charmed by what he saw, praised England, as "the land par excellence of beautiful manors." Sandringham, "with its magnificent park . . . its fine oaks and beeches, its incomparably beautiful lawns, the rhododendron shrubs, the neat graveled paths and . . . hedges . . . fine stables . . . magnificent greenhouses . . . and kennels," was the examplar. Bülow was astonished at the complete freedom of movement enjoyed by guests, so different from the regimentation imposed on the Kaiser's guests. "One had only to appear at breakfast in the morning and there eat bacon, eggs, porridge and jam," and on Sunday to "attend Divine Service." Bülow's exuberance deserted him, however, as he observed the Prince of Wales in conversation with his own sovereign. The Prince, he said, reminded him of "a fat, malicious tom-cat, playing with a shrewmouse."*

While still in England, Bülow wrote his impressions of England and the English and sent them to Hohenlohe and Holstein: "British

---

* William's visit to Sandringham was a vexation to the Princess of Wales. She poked fun at the three valets and hairdresser brought along to maintain the Emperor and shook with laughter when told that there was an additional person, a hairdresser's assistant, whose sole function was to curl the Imperial mustache.

politicians know little of the Continent. Many of them do not know much more of Continental conditions than we do of the conditions in Peru or Siam. . . . The country exudes wealth, comfort, content, and confidence in its own power and future. . . . The people . . . simply cannot believe that things could ever go really wrong, either at home or aboard. With the exception of a few leading men, they work little and leave themselves time for everything." William, leaving England, was pleased by his reception. "The visit . . . has gone off excellently," he telegraphed to Berlin. "The consequences for the future will, in all human probability, be very satisfactory and favorable."

On November 30, the day after the Kaiser and Bülow had sailed, Joseph Chamberlain, suffering a heavy cold, rose at a Unionist luncheon in Leicester to present his British version of the Anglo-German campaign for better understanding. "Any far-seeing English statesman must have long ago desired that we not remain permanently isolated on the continent of Europe," he declared. Further, "It must appear evident to everybody that the natural alliance is between ourselves and the great German Empire." Enlarging his vision, the Colonial Secretary spoke of "a new Triple Alliance between the Teutonic race and the two great trans-Atlantic branches of the Anglo-Saxon race which would become a potent influence on the future of the world." Chamberlain's speech evoked congratulations from Eckardstein. The Kaiser, basking in the glow of Windsor and Sandringham, wired his compliments. Holstein attacked the speech as "an incomprehensible blunder." Bülow, surprised that Chamberlain had made his proposal public so quickly, described the speech as "a *gaucherie,* I believe unintentional, but still a *gaucherie.*" The Times icily rebuked the Colonial Secretary for using the word "alliance" and wondered why Mr. Chamberlain was trespassing into matters properly managed by Lord Salisbury. The Prime Minister said nothing.

Chamberlain waited confidently for the German State Secretary, in his speech to the Reichstag on December 11, to fulfill the bargain he believed had been struck at Windsor. Chamberlain's expectations were clear. The day after his Leicester speech, he wrote cheerfully to Eckardstein, "Count Bülow, whose acquaintance I was delighted to make . . . expressed a wish that I might be able at some time to say something as to the mutual interests which bind the United States to a triple understanding with Germany as well as to Great Britain. Hence my speech yesterday which I hope will not be unsatisfactory to him."

When Bülow rose in the Reichstag, it was to speak in support of

Tirpitz' Second Navy Bill. The future of the Reich, he declared, depended on linking strong naval power to overwhelming military force. "Without power, without a strong army and a strong navy, there can be no welfare for us." He went on to coin a ringing phrase: "In the coming century, the German nation will be either the hammer or the anvil." There was nothing in Bülow's speech about an alliance or even an understanding with Great Britain. Indeed, although the State Secretary spoke warmly of Russia, of the United States, and even of France, his references to England were cool. England was presented as a declining nation, jealous of the rising power of Imperial Germany, even vaguely hostile; a state which would oppose Germany's rightful destiny unless the Reichstag voted money for a fleet which would instill a proper respect.

Chamberlain read Bülow's speech with astonishment. "I will say no more about the way I have been treated by Bülow," he wrote to Eckardstein. "I consider it advisable to drop every kind of further negotiation as to the alliance question. I am really sorry that all your hard work should seem to have been in vain; but I am also sorry for myself. Everything was going so well and even Lord Salisbury had become quite favorable . . . to the future development of Anglo-German relations. But, alas, it was not to be."

Bülow did not completely dismiss his conversation with Chamberlain at Windsor. Through Hatzfeldt, he attempted to repair the damage he had done by having the ambassador stress to Chamberlain "the extreme difficulty of Count Bülow's position in the Reichstag. . . . The weapon of the Opposition is the repeated insinuation that the Government is carrying on secret political deals with England and sacrificing the true interests of Germany. The attack in the Reichstag has been so violent that Count Bülow has had to take it into account and compose his speech with reference to it. . . . We no longer live in the days when Prince Bismarck was all-powerful in foreign policy and had nothing to fear even when he took no account of public opinion. The present Chancellor [Hohenlohe] cannot do this and still less can Count Bülow."

It remained for Hatzfeldt to decipher and clarify for the Wilhelmstrasse the post-Windsor thinking of the British government and especially the murky relationship between the powerful Colonial Secretary and the ailing Prime Minister. "Chamberlain and Arthur Balfour are looked upon as the real supporters of a policy friendly to Germany," the Ambassador wrote, "while Lord Salisbury is credited, if not with a negative, at any rate with a passive part." Rejecting German speculation that Chamberlain's alliance proposal might have been an anti-Salisbury political maneuver designed to embarrass or even overthrow the Prime Minister, Hatzfeldt cautioned that Lord Salisbury "must not yet by any means be regarded as a spent political force." Perhaps, Hatzfeldt suggested, "when Mr. Chamberlain made his speech . . . he already had in his pocket Lord Salisbury's consent in principle, or else proceeded in the conviction that—as in the Samoan question—with the help of the majority of his colleagues, he would succeed in inducing the Prime Minister to accede to his wishes." Whatever Chamberlain's motivation, and despite his irritation at Bülow's behavior, the Ambassador concluded, the Colonial Secretary's interest in a German alliance was not dead. The correct German policy, therefore, was the one chosen by Holstein and Bülow: to encourage Britain to believe that a German alliance might come one day, but only if England continues "to show a spirit of accommodation towards us in . . . colonial questions."

CHAPTER 15

The
Boer War
and the Boxer Rebellion

While the Kaiser was still at Windsor and Sandringham, Britain's value as an alliance partner was being eroded by events in South Africa. As early as 1897, it had become evident that the Transvaal was preparing for war. President Kruger signed an offensive-defensive alliance with the sister Boer republic, the Orange Free State. Using the taxes collected from non-Boer Uitlanders, he bought cannon and Maxim guns from Germany. In negotiations with Joseph Chamberlain and the Colonial Secretary's representatives in South Africa, Kruger demanded indemnities for the Jameson Raid: £677,938 for material damages, £1 million for "moral and intellectual damages." He rejected outright the proposal that British and other Uitlanders be given full civic rights after five years' residence in the Transvaal; the time requirement was to be fourteen years. Kruger also claimed that the 1882 London Convention had lapsed and that Britain no longer held rights over the foreign and defense policies of the Boer republics.

Lord Salisbury, having entrusted the conduct of negotiations to Chamberlain, was wary of a confrontation in South Africa. "A war with the Transvaal will have a reaction on European politics which may be pernicious," he wrote to Chamberlain. Chamberlain disagreed and, arguing that "Kruger has never looked into the mouth of a cannon," persuaded the Cabinet to a show of force. At the end of August, Chamberlain switched metaphors and warned the Boer government that "the sands are running low in the glass." Kruger responded by rejecting all British suzerainty over the Transvaal. The British Cabinet dispatched a cavalry brigade, an infantry regiment, and two artillery batteries to reinforce the scanty British forces in the Cape Colony and Natal. Kruger demanded that British troops on the Transvaal frontiers be withdrawn and that all British reinforcements which had arrived in South Africa since June 1 be placed on ships and sent back home. This ultimatum, threatening war, was rejected. On October 11, Boer cavalry struck into the Cape Colony, Natal, and Bechuanaland. The towns of Kimberley, Mafeking, and Ladysmith were besieged. On December 15, a British army under General Sir Redvers Buller, marching to the relief of Ladysmith, was defeated at Colenso with the loss of eleven hundred men killed, wounded, or missing. That same week, other British forces were repulsed at Stormberg and Magersfontein. In England, these days were known as "Black Week." Queen Victoria did not share the national gloom. "I will tell you one thing," she said to Arthur Balfour, who had come to report to her at Windsor. "I will have no depression in my house. We are not interested in the possibilities of defeat." Lord Salisbury sorrowfully referred to "Joe's War" among his intimates, although in public he sturdily backed the Colonial Secretary.

Europe was pleased by Britain's defeats. "The vast majority of German military experts believe that the South African war will end with a complete defeat of the English," Bülow wrote to Hatzfeldt on December 26, 1899. Herbert Bismarck turned violently Anglophobe: "The South African question . . . will give the British Empire its death blow; for I believe that England is being smothered in its own fat and is no longer capable of severe exertion." From Paris, the British Ambassador wrote of "the infamous language and shameless mendacity of the French press." From St. Petersburg came news that the hostility of Russian society and newspapers was "phenomenal."

The Kaiser, in his Christmas greeting to his uncle, became lyrical in his lamentation: "What days of sad news and anxiety. . . . Many brave officers and men have fallen or are disabled after showing pluck, courage and determined bravery! How many homes will be sad this year and how many sufferers will feel agonizing pain morally and physically in these days of holy pleasure and peace! What an amount of bloodshed has been going on and is to be expected for the next months to come. . . . Your losses, as they are made known little by little, are quite appalling . . . especially the losses of the Highlanders . . . as they are much admired by my soldiers over here. . . . The sight of white men killing white is not good for the blacks to look on for too long; the simple suspicion that they might find it practical to fall on the whites in general is enough to make one's blood run cold."

A few weeks later, William urged his uncle to accept that defeat in South Africa meant no disgrace. "Last year," he pointed out, "in the great cricket match of England vs. Australia, the former took the latter's victory quietly, with chivalrous acknowledgement of her opponent." The Prince's reply was stiff: "I am afraid I am unable to share your opinions . . . in which you liken our conflict with the Boers to our cricket matches with the Australians, in which the latter were victorious and we accepted our defeat. The British Empire is now fighting for its very existence, as you know full well, and for our superiority in South Africa. We must therefore use every effort in our power to prove victorious in the end."

The Kaiser defended his metaphor in another letter to his uncle: "My last paragraph . . . seems to have given you some umbrage. But I think I can easily dispel your doubts about it. The allusion to Football and Cricket Matches was meant to show that I do not belong to those people who, when the British Army suffers reverses, or is unable at a given time to master the enemy, then immediately cry out that British prestige is in danger or lost. Forsooth! Great Britain has fought bravely for and lost the whole of North America against France and the Rebels, and yet has become the greatest Power in the world! Because her fleet remained unimpaired and by this the Command of the Sea! As long as you keep your fleet in good fighting trim, and as long as it is looked upon as the first and feared as invincible, I don't care a fiddlestick for a few lost fights in Africa. But the Fleet must be up-to-date in guns and officers and men and on the 'Qui vive' and should it ever be necessary to fall back upon it, may a second Trafalgar be awarded to it! I shall be the first to wish it luck and God-speed!"

In the middle of January 1900, three German steamers, *Bundesrat, Herzog,* and *General,* suspected of carrying rifles and cannon to the Boers, were stopped by British warships off the east coast of Africa. After a quick search at sea, two of the ships were released, but the *Bundesrat* was taken into Durban for a more thorough examination. No arms were found. When the news reached Berlin, howls of protest and demands for apology, compensation, and guarantees against recurrence filled the newspapers. Tirpitz seized the moment to declare that only a powerful fleet could prevent such national humiliation; the response must be a doubling of the 1898 Building Program. Lord Salisbury received German protests with detachment. Holstein telegraphed Eckardstein (again in charge of the German Embassy in the absence of Hatzfeldt) that "the Kaiser is considering whether someone should not be sent from here within forty-eight hours to get a definite answer by Thursday." The threat was a break in diplomatic relations. Eckardstein warned that it would do no good. "Lord Salisbury," he explained, "as on previous occasions when he considered himself insulted by the Kaiser's methods, went into the sulks and became almost unapproachable." The crisis was defused, according to Eckardstein, by his own prompt visit to the Prime Minister at the Foreign Office, where he turned the matter of eighteen large crates of Swiss cheese, seized on board a German ship near South Africa, into a joke. Lord Salisbury began to laugh and a peaceful settlement of the mail steamers' ultimatum swiftly followed.*

By spring 1900, the British military position in South Africa was much improved. Lord Roberts, the hero of India, and Lord Kitchener, hero of the Sudan, had relieved Sir Redvers Buller. The British Army in South Africa was swelling from the original garrison of 25,000 men to more than 250,000. The Boers had been thrown back, and relieving columns were approaching the besieged towns of Ladysmith and Mafeking. The Kaiser now proclaimed his pride in the success of his grandmother's army.† He informed the Prince of

---

* Shortly before calling on Lord Salisbury, Eckardstein spoke to the Swiss Minister, who told him about the cheese and asked him to do what he could to obtain its release. Eckardstein decided to put this triviality to use:

"On arriving at the Foreign Office, I was given to understand by the Private Secretary that his chief was in a great state of exasperation against the German Government and would not be easy to deal with. And, when I was received by Lord Salisbury, I found . . . [him] very stiff and distant in manner. 'Well, what news have you got?' he asked me very abruptly. 'No good news, I regret to say,' I replied. 'I am afraid we are faced by the most serious trouble.' 'Indeed, and what is that?' said he, more brusquely than ever. 'Yes,' I went on, '. . . if something isn't done at once, you will have to be prepared for an ultimatum from—the Swiss Government.' He looked up in astonishment and asked: 'From the Swiss Government? Whatever do you mean?' I replied, 'The Swiss Minister . . . told me . . . that if . . . [the crates of cheese] are not released, you may expect a forty-eight-hour ultimatum from Switzerland; and, if you then don't give way, you will have to take the consequences.' Thereupon, Lord Salisbury's face cleared, he began to laugh, and after a bit he said, 'Tell your friend, the Swiss Minister, that Her Britannic Majesty's Government would prefer to go into the matter in a friendly way.' "

† To the young Queen Wilhelmina of Holland, who appealed to the Kaiser to do something to save the crumbling Boers, William presented another face. He declined Wilhelmina's entreaties, declaring grandiloquently, "Yet whosoever believes in God the Lord as supreme judge of the world-order knows that He overlooks nothing and that He punishes injustice with relentless severity. . . . Therefore it is in the interest of world peace as well

Wales that, during the winter, he had spurned a Russian proposal that Germany and Russia offer mediation between the British Empire and the Boer Republic. "You have no idea, my dear William, how all of us in England appreciate the loyal friendship you manifest towards us on every occasion," the Prince replied. Johannesburg fell on May 31 and Pretoria on June 5. President Kruger took the railroad to Lourenço Marques, where he boarded a ship for Europe, leaving his invalid wife and South Africa forever. The war seemed over. In August the Queen proclaimed, "My armies have driven back the invaders beyond the frontier they had crossed and have occupied the two capitals of the enemy and much of his territory." In September, Great Britain annexed the Transvaal. Lord Roberts came home to become Commander-in-Chief of the British Army, leaving the tidying-up to Kitchener.

On June 6, 1900, news of the fall of Pretoria had been telegraphed to the Queen at Balmoral. Bells were rung, the guard of honor fired a salute, and the Union Jack was run up alongside the Royal Standard. That night, a procession of Highlanders accompanied by pipers had marched to the summit of Craig Gowan Height overlooking the Castle and lit a huge bonfire. The Queen, watching from the castle lawn, had drunk to the success of the British Army and continued to watch as the Highlanders marched down the mountain and danced reels on her lawn. The celebration had ended with everyone singing "God Save the Queen."

That same day, under a small headline which read "THE DISTURBANCES IN CHINA," *The Times* had reported that two British missionaries had been murdered by a Chinese group known as Boxers.

Over six decades, the Western Powers had been dismembering China, each scrambling for leases and concessions, tearing off pieces, dividing the vast country into spheres of influence. The Manchu government, nominally ruling the empire from the northern city of Peking, seemed powerless to halt this disintegration. Crippled by corruption, the Imperial Court lacked the will and power to galvanize and direct the political destiny of China's 350 million people. The army possessed neither modern weapons, nor central command, nor reason to fight. Not since the Manchus had come down from the north to overthrow the Ming Dynasty in the sixteenth century had the Celestial Kingdom been so helpless.

---

as of the Dutch-Frisian race on the Continent that a mighty [German] fleet shall be on the sea. . . . Till then Silence and Work."

And then, in the spring and summer of 1900, China's peasants in the northern part of the empire took matters into their own hands. A popular movement, whose purpose was to rid China of foreigners and their pernicious works, sprang up. The peasantry, usually noted for passive observance of the law, tied red ribbons around their waists, heads, wrists, and ankles, took up swords, spears, and old muskets, and left the fields which their ancestors had tilled for several millennia. They developed secret rites which, they believed, made them invulnerable to foreign bullets. Their battle cry was *"Sha! Sha!"* ("Kill! Kill!"). In Chinese, their name was "Fists of Righteous Harmony." To the rest of the world they were known as Boxers.

The Boxers objected to both the physical and spiritual pollution of the Celestial Kingdom. Foreign railroads stretched across the land, dispossessing peasants and violating sacred burial grounds. Trains carrying passengers and freight threw thousands of boatmen and carters out of work. Telegraph lines strung along the railways sang in the wind, affronting the spirits of the air. Worse still were the Christian missionaries with their fervent hymn-singing, their obsession with conversion, and their ridicule of traditional Chinese beliefs. And worse even than the foreign barbarians were the Chinese Christians, who had betrayed their countrymen by accepting these beliefs.

The immediate cause of the Boxer Rebellion was Germany's seizure of Kiaochow Bay and the city of Tsingtao in Shantung Province on the Yellow Sea. The Kaiser, itching to acquire a naval station and trading port on the China coast, had used the pretext of the murder of the two German missionaries in 1897 to wrench a ninety-nine-year lease on these territories. With Prussian thoroughness, German administrators began to transform the province into an island of Germany-in-Asia. Tsingtao became a city of German architecture, with clean, orderly streets and a German brewery which produced the best beer in Asia. Signs in German directed the peasants (most of whom could not even read Chinese) to obey German laws and regulations. The peasants of Shantung, among the most hardy and spirited in China, resisted these efficient foreigners almost at once. German punitive expeditions marching out to destroy villages maddened increasing numbers of peasants. Before the end of 1898, the first Boxers appeared. Their initial victims were native Christians. Then, on December 31, 1899, an English missionary in Shantung, the Reverend S. M. Brooks, was murdered. His assailants were captured and decapitated, but the central government carefully refused to suppress or even condemn the Boxer organizations.

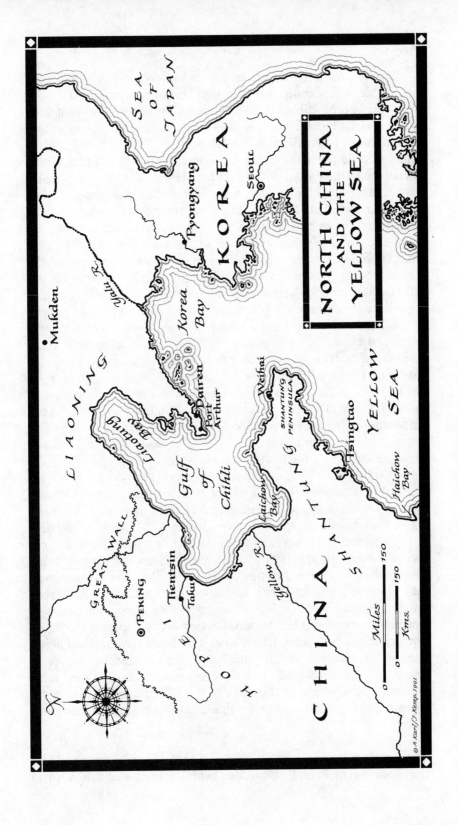

NORTH CHINA AND THE YELLOW SEA

SEA OF JAPAN

KOREA

Pyongyang

SEOUL

Mukden

Yalu R.

Korea Bay

LIAONING

Liaotung Bay

Dairen
Port Arthur

Weihai

Gulf of Chihli

SHANTUNG PENINSULA

Tsingtao

YELLOW SEA

GREAT WALL

Tientsin

Taku

PEKING

Laichow Bay

SHANTUNG

CHINA

Yellow R.

Haichow Bay

Miles   150
0

Kms.   150
0

© A. Karl / J. Kemp 1991

The central government in China in 1900 was, essentially, a tiny, ruthless, ambitious woman, the Dowager Empress Tz'u-hsi. From within the walls of the Forbidden City, served and protected by dozens of eunuchs, she ruled the Manchu Empire. Born in 1836, the daughter of an officer in the Household Guards, Tz'u-hsi blossomed into adolescent beauty and was accepted as a Third Grade Concubine in the harem of the Emperor Hsien-feng. She became his favorite and bore him a son, who on the death of the Emperor succeeded his father. Tz'u-hsi, Regent at twenty-six, moved pitilessly against her opponents. One, a powerful court official named Su Shun, soon became the subject of an Imperial decree: "As to Su Shun, he fully deserves the punishment of dismemberment and the slicing process. But we cannot make up our mind to impose this extreme penalty and therefore, in our clemency, we sentence him to immediate decapitation." When her son was old enough to govern, Tz'u-hsi thrust him into debauchery, cutting short his life. He was succeeded by another young man, Tz'u-hsi's nephew, for whom she also served as Regent. In 1898, not long after he came of age, the Dowager Empress overthrew this young Emperor with a coup d'état. He became a virtual prisoner while she resumed the task of ruling. In 1900, Tz'u-hsi was sixty-four, although sharp-eyed Western women who caught sight of her on ceremonial occasions said that she looked twenty years younger. Her voice was low and velvety and said to be filled with sexual insinuation.

Tz'u-hsi did not like what foreigners had done to China. Throughout the four decades of her rule, she had seen them steal ports from her empire, force unequal treaties upon her, dominate trade, and humiliate the Dragon Throne. The Regular Chinese Army seemed impotent to prevent these outrages. Now she observed the Boxers displaying all the courage and fervor which her own soldiers so embarrassingly lacked. Possibly, the Boxers, with their claim to 8 million "spirit soldiers," might actually defeat Western armies and navies. Carried away by this hope, the Dowager Empress first ordered her Imperial troops not to suppress the Boxer uprising in the provinces. Later, when the Boxers swept into Peking, Tz'u-hsi decided to ride the whirlwind and ordered her troops to join them. She wanted all foreigners and all Christian Chinese annihilated. At the height of the siege of the Legations, she said of the surrounded foreigners, "The foreigners are like fish in a stewpan."

The center of foreign influence in the Manchu Empire was the Legation Quarter in Peking. Near the heart of the great city with its endless grid of streets, tiny, gray, one-story houses, shops, and open-air markets, the Quarter occupied an enclave about three quarters of a mile square. Inside this small, unfortified zone lived the diplomatic representatives of nine European countries, the United States, and Japan. There were internal divisions—the British and Japanese distrusted the Russians, who seemed ready to annex all North China; no one much liked the Americans and their noisy preaching that they had no interest in acquiring Chinese territory—but to the Manchu Court, the foreigners presented a unified body. Collective documents addressed to the Chinese government were signed, simply, "Le Corps Diplomatique."

In the spring of 1900, the Diplomatic Corps received only bad news. Nature was stimulating anarchy in North China. Two harvests had failed and famine was widespread. That spring, the Yellow River flooded; then, when the waters receded, no rain fell. Hungry and desperate, the peasants listened to the Boxers. Reports coming into Peking from the countryside told of burning villages, massacred Chinese Christians, assassinated foreign missionaries. In May, frightened missionaries, engineers, and workers employed in mining concessions and railway projects began flocking into Peking and Tientsin from outlying stations.

On May 24, sixty guests were invited to dine at the British Legation in honor of Queen Victoria's eighty-first birthday. They sipped champagne and waltzed on the Legation tennis court by the light of paper lanterns hanging from branches. It was a last evening of frivolity. Four days later, the host, Sir Claude MacDonald, the British Minister, decided that the Legations were in danger. He asked that an Allied fleet of seventeen warships anchored at the mouth of the Pei-ho River, 110 miles away, provide security. On May 31, 337 foreign sailors and marines came ashore, boarded a train and, at eight that night, arrived in Peking. A few days later, they were joined by an additional eighty-nine German and Austrian marines.

The arrival of the foreign troops did not dispel the sense of imminent peril. On June 9, the grandstand of the Peking Race Course, a symbol of European exclusivism, was set on fire and burned to the ground, with a Chinese Christian roasted in the embers. Two days later, Chancellor Sugiyama of the Japanese Legation was returning from the railroad station in his tailcoat and bowler hat when his small carriage was stopped by a group of Boxers. Before the eyes of an appreciative crowd, he was dragged into the street and decapitated. The Boxers cut out his heart. Attacks on native Christians became more widespread. *The Times'* correspondent reported that he had seen "awful sights: women and children hacked to pieces, men trussed like fowls, with noses and ears cut off and eyes gouged out." On June 20, Baron Klemens von Ketteler, the German Minister to China, set out alone in a sedan chair to visit the Chinese Foreign Office. Along the way, a government soldier—not a Boxer—stepped from the sidewalk, aimed his rifle at the Baron's head, and fired, killing him instantly. That afternoon the fifty-five-day siege of the Legations began.

Some three thousand people were inside the foreign compound. Over two thousand were Chinese Catholics and Methodists who had been given sanctuary. There were four hundred foreign male civilians, 147 foreign women, and seventy-six foreign children. They were defended by 409 foreign soldiers, sailors, and marines who, among them, had three machine guns and four small cannon. There was plenty of water, five sweet-water wells within the British Legation grounds alone. Supplies of wheat, rice, and other staples were adequate, and 150 ponies, brought into the stables for Race Week, were available to provide meat. Sir Claude MacDonald assumed overall command of both the military garrison and the civilian population and each minister at least nominally commanded the troops of his own nationality. Messages between separate national compounds and barricades continued to be couched in diplomatic language: *"Veuillez agréer, M. le Ministre, l'assurance de ma très haute considération."*

The Chinese assault consisted of continual, ill-coordinated attacks on the walls and barricades which constituted the perimeter of the Legation defense, and constant bombardment by two modern Krupp cannon, sold to the Chinese by the German manufacturer. (After the siege, relieving troops discovered dozens of additional Krupp cannon in Chinese warehouses, still in their packing cases. Had they been used, the bombardment would have quickly demolished the Legation defenses.) As the siege continued, the red-sashed Boxers were replaced by regular Chinese troops. In the compound, ammunition dwindled, living conditions worsened, and the heat rose to 110 degrees. The stench of dead men and animals was thick and rich. A European professor, a man who knew and loved the Chinese, had crossed the lines in the first days of the siege. After being tortured, he was decapitated and his head mounted on a stick to give the Europeans on their barricades an excellent view. "The face," noted a witness, "has a most horrible expression."

They were cut off from the world. On June 10, after the murder of Chancellor Sugiyama, Vice Admiral Sir Edward Hobart Seymour, Commander-in-Chief of the Allied Fleet at Taku, had marched from Tientsin with a relief force of British naval infantry and other foreign troops.* Seymour's expedition of two thousand men, distributed in five trains, covered about half of the ninety miles between Tientsin and Peking before attacks on the trains and damage to the tracks forced him to halt. Waves of Boxers, disdaining death, hurled themselves against the rifles, machine guns, and field artillery of Seymour's troops. It became clear to Seymour that relief of the Legations was impossible; only with luck would he be able to save his own force. He began a fighting retreat to Tientsin, which by now was besieged by twenty thousand Chinese.

For almost eight weeks, the outside world remained ignorant of what was happening in Peking. All telegraph lines were destroyed. By the end of June, Seymour's column had battled its way back into Tientsin and other Allied troops had stormed the Taku forts and lifted the siege of that city. But nothing had been heard from the Legations since June 13. On June 29, a messenger got through with grim news: "Situation desperate. Make haste." In England, concern about China had pushed the Boer War out of the headlines, though there was little news to report. Rumors abounded. On July 16, under the headline "THE PEKING MASSACRE," the Shanghai correspondent of the *Daily Mail* reported the death of all foreigners in Peking. On the night of the sixth, the writer declared, a mass assault had overwhelmed the defenders, who had run out of ammunition. All survivors were "put to the sword in the most atrocious manner" except in cases where men had been able to shoot their own wives and children before the Chinese burst in. For two weeks, the story remained undisputed; Lord Salisbury wrote the Queen that it was "impossible to exaggerate the horror of the news from Peking." Then, suspicion set in and a mass service of mourning at St. Paul's was canceled until verification could be obtained.

In Peking, the defenders, alive but desperate, ate rice and pony meat. The Italian cannon had only fourteen shells. The Chinese had brought ten artillery pieces into action. From around the world, troopships were converging on the Yellow Sea. By the end of July, 25,000 foreign troops from eight nations were gathered at Tientsin and a Russian Commander-in-Chief, General Linevitch, had been appointed. On August 5, a new relief expedition started for Peking. It took nine days, but on the fourteenth, British and Japanese troops entered the city, reached the compound, and raised the siege. Sixty-

---

* Captain John Jellicoe and Commander David Beatty, later successive Commanders-in-Chief of the British Grand Fleet in the First World War, accompanied Seymour's expedition. Both were wounded, Jellicoe so severely that it was thought his wound was mortal.

six foreigners had been killed and 150 wounded. The Dowager Empress and her court fled to western China, the Boxers and Imperial Army melted away, and three fourths of the city's population vanished into the countryside. Within the empty city, looting became the principal activity of the remaining population, the relieving troops, and even the once-besieged civilians. "Lady MacDonald [wife of the British Minister] was out in Peking and devoted herself most earnestly to looting," a British officer in the relief force reported in a letter.

Kaiser William II burned with righteous indignation. "Peking must be stormed and leveled to the ground," he told Bülow. William basked in his new role as the avenging angel, the pillar of Christendom against the Yellow Peril. "Now it is a pleasure to be alive," he declared to Bülow, who later wrote, "I never saw him so excited as during the first phase of the Chinese affair." In a speech on July 2 at Wilhelmshaven, the Kaiser described the Boxer rising as "unprecedented in its impudence . . . [and] horrifying in its brutality" and demanded "exemplary punishment and vengeance." Without consulting the Chancellor or the Wilhelmstrasse, William ordered an expeditionary force of thirty thousand soldiers and marines to prepare to sail. From the beginning, he made clear that this military operation fell under his imperial prerogative. The China expedition would be "no business of the Foreign Office," but would be directed "from the saddle, as it were."

On July 27, he appeared at Bremerhaven to inspect the first contingent of German marines ready to leave for China. Standing before them, he gave what Bülow described as "the worst speech of this period and perhaps the most harmful that William II ever made." "You must know, my men, that you are about to meet a crafty, well-armed, cruel foe!" shouted the Kaiser. "Meet him and beat him! Give him no quarter! Take no prisoners! Kill him when he falls into your hands! Even as, a thousand years ago, the Huns under their King Attila made such a name for themselves as still resounds in legend and fable, so may the name of Germans resound through Chinese history a thousand years from now. . . ." Hohenlohe and Bülow were present at Bremerhaven and, as the Chancellor listened, his old face grew sad. He turned to Bülow and said, "I cannot possibly answer for this in the Reichstag. You must try to do something." Although Bülow did his best to suppress the speech, handing an expurgated copy to the press, one reporter obtained the real text and soon the Kaiser's words were circulating around the globe.

When he learned what Bülow had tried to do, William complained, "You struck out the best parts." Bülow pleaded with the Emperor to try to control himself. Speeches such as this, he explained, would be used by Germany's enemies to demonstrate that Germany was a land of barbarians. William accepted the criticism and reached for Bülow's hands. "I know you are concerned only for my best interest," he said, "but after all, I am just as I am and cannot change myself."

The Kaiser had set his heart on a particular prize: he wished a German officer to command the international expeditionary force. By early August, there were thousands of Allied troops in China or on the way, and it was obvious that some kind of supreme commander was necessary to coordinate their activities. Without the Kaiser's knowledge, Vice Admiral Sir Edward Seymour had commanded the first effort to relieve Peking and had failed; without William's consent, General Linevitch had been chosen on the scene to command the force which would eventually lift the siege. Still, William demanded priority. As the German Minister in China was the senior diplomat assassinated, the Kaiser reasoned that German precedence in extracting vengeance was justified. Hatzfeldt sounded out Lord Salisbury, who told him that it was a British characteristic, however unreasonable, "not to endure the command of a foreigner." Under pressure from William, the Wilhelmstrasse instructed Eckardstein to make a second attempt. This time Salisbury agreed; Britain was still involved in the Boer War and did not want the post for a British officer; the prospect of a Russian generalissimo in China had no appeal. Salisbury declared himself perplexed as to why the German Emperor wanted the post, but, as he did, he would have British support. William next telegraphed the Tsar. "The strongest corps only really worth speaking of will be the Russian, German, and Japanese. Is it your special wish that a Russian should be Commander-in-Chief? Or would you eventually wish one of my generals? In the latter case, I place Field Marshal Count Waldersee at your disposal." Nicholas II could see the thrust of William's offer. "I fully agree to the nomination of Count Waldersee," he replied. "I know him well; he is certainly one of your most able and experienced generals and his name stands high in the Russian army. With full confidence, I place my troops . . . under his command." On August 7, the Kaiser telegraphed General Count Alfred von Waldersee that he had been appointed.

Waldersee was a political general with a nose for power and a vehement American wife. Both Waldersees had attached themselves early to young Prince William. The Countess, outspokenly religious, preached vigorously against cigars, coarse language, and lascivious art. The Count, when he discovered that William's father, Crown Prince Frederick, was dying of cancer, remarked cold-bloodedly, "How wonderfully everything is turning out. All of us are looking with high hopes to . . . [William]." Three months after William became Emperor, Waldersee was appointed Chief of the General Staff, replacing Helmuth von Moltke, the hero of Bismarck's three wars, who, at seventy-seven, could no longer sit on a horse. Using his new position to cement his standing with the new Kaiser, Waldersee asked William to accept the rank of Field Marshal in the army. William consented and happily carried his beautiful gold-inlaid Marshal's baton at military parades and reviews.

Because William insisted on actual command of troops during army maneuvers, Waldersee got into trouble. The Kaiser, unlike his father, had no actual war experience. In maneuvers, he favored spectacular infantry attacks and mass cavalry charges, which in wartime would have been suicidal. "He is extraordinarily restless, rushes hither and thither, is much too far ahead of the fighting line, interferes in the leading of his generals, issues countless and often contradictory orders and pays little heed to his counselors," Waldersee noted of the thirty-one-year-old Emperor at the 1890 maneuvers in Silesia. "He is always determined to win and therefore takes in ill part any decisions given by the umpire against him." Caprivi, the former general just installed as Chancellor, remarked quietly that "the General Staff had offered many traps and the Kaiser had gaily fallen into every single one of them." Unfortunately for Waldersee, it was his duty as Chief of the General Staff to critique maneuvers, including the performance of his sovereign. Waldersee tried to be tactful, but he pointed out the Emperor's mistakes in front of a large audience. William looked astonished, then became grave. He "tried to make excuses and became very feeble in his explanations," Waldersee said. A few days later Waldersee was removed as Chief of the General Staff and sent to command the Northern District in Altona, near Hamburg. His successor was General Count Alfred von Schlieffen. For a while, Waldersee's banishment from Imperial favor was total; Bülow found the word "traitor" penned by William in a margin next to Waldersee's name. But by 1898, retired and living in Hanover, Waldersee had sufficiently regained the Kaiser's goodwill to be invited aboard the *Hohenzollern* for a summer cruise. And in 1900, needing a field marshal who could handle a role that was more diplomatic than military, William completely resurrected Waldersee. Once the Tsar and Lord Salisbury agreed to a German commander in Asia, the Kaiser appointed Waldersee without troubling to consult either Hohenlohe or Bülow. The German press gave Waldersee the title of "World Marshal." Beyond raising the siege of Peking, Waldersee was not sure what was expected of his mission. He spoke to Holstein, who was unable to give help. "It became obvious to me," the World Marshal wrote, "that apart from punishing the Chinese, our policy had no definite aims. The Kaiser had merely some vague ideas about the partition of China. The great thing for him was the necessity of playing a *role* in world politics."

On August 18, the Emperor received Waldersee and his staff to say good-bye. A few days later, news arrived in Germany that the Allied troops in China had relieved Peking and that the Boxers and Manchu Court had fled. "Naturally, this was a great disappointment for the Emperor," Waldersee wrote later. "He had got it firmly fixed in his head that . . . the Allied advance on Peking . . . would begin under my supreme command and mine would be the glory of capturing Peking." Privately, the Kaiser was furious, declaring that, by relieving the Legations too soon, Great Britain and Russia had deliberately "betrayed him." Nevertheless, William insisted that the German expedition proceed, impressing on Waldersee that "as big a war indemnity as possible should be imposed on the Chinese as he was needing money urgently for the Fleet."

Waldersee sailed on the North German Lloyd steamer *Sachsen,* proceeding via Naples, Suez, Colombo, Singapore, Hong Kong, and Shanghai. These ports were British, and the local authorities delighted the World Marshal by instructing all ships and forts to render a nineteen-gun salute whenever he passed. In Singapore harbor, he came on two French troop transports filled with soldiers bound for China. The commanders, he reported to the Kaiser, "were extraordinarily polite and . . . [said] that it would give them great honor and pleasure to fight under my command. . . . As I left the harbor and passed slowly by the two French ships at a distance of scarcely forty yards, the entire crews, numbering over 2,000, manned the rigging and played the *Präsentiermarsch* and then *Heil Dir im Siegerkranz,* the officers standing together on the bridge at the salute. I then had the *Marseillaise* played and they all broke out into loud cheers and the officers waved their tropical helmets."

Waldersee arrived in Peking in mid-October, making an entry which other foreigners present found "farcical" and "absurd." The troops were goose-stepping and wearing large straw hats; "This must be some Berlin tailor's idea of an appropriate headdress for a summer and autumn campaign in the East." Waldersee himself went everywhere wearing his cordon of the Order of the Black Eagle and carrying his Field Marshal's baton. He had brought along an experimental asbestos hut to use as field headquarters, but with no battles to be fought, he moved into the palace of the Dowager Empress; the palace burned down soon after, killing his German Chief of Staff. His relations with the French remained good. "Different staff officers with whom I have conversed, among them Lieutenant Colonel Marchand, famous in France in connection with the Fashoda affair, have openly proclaimed themselves friendly to Germany and admirers of our army organization," he wrote to the Kaiser. William was pleased. "I rejoice that the French and our men get on so nicely together," he replied to the Field Marshal. "Campaigns lived through together are a strong bond. They will get to know and appreciate each other, [and] the other nations, when they observe our men and our officers carry things through, will recognize the superiority of our system and be less inclined for a belligerent attitude towards us."

What most foreign soldiers and civilians observed, once the German troops arrived, was a resurgence of raping and looting, which had died down. A British officer was not surprised by this behavior. "They say that the Kaiser, in his farewell speech told the men to act this way. They are strictly obeying orders." Indeed, William's demand that "the name of Germans resound through Chinese history" for a thousand years was on Waldersee's mind. Determined to prove the mettle of German troops and to make the Chinese pay for the murder of Ketteler, the Field Marshal threw himself into the organization of punitive expeditions. There were no battles, but there was plenty of bloodshed. Waldersee, declared a member of his staff, wanted "to shoot all the headmen of every village for hundreds of miles around Peking." Before long, all North China trembled at the sight of German field-gray uniforms. Waldersee claimed that his men were "exerting a moral influence of far-reaching importance" and sent back to Berlin enthusiastic reports of the performance of his Krupp field artillery. The Kaiser was pleased. William was less pleased about the efficiency of German cannon when they were in the hands of the Chinese gunners. Hearing that a German gunboat sent from Shanghai to bombard Chinese forts on the Yangtze* had itself suffered seventeen hits by shells from the latest Krupp cannon, the Kaiser sent an angry telegram to Fritz Krupp: "This is no time, when I am sending my soldiers to battle against the yellow beasts, to try to make money."

---

* The German Admiralty explained the bombardment to the German Foreign Ministry by saying, "It was not a proper position for the Imperial German Navy to lie for whole weeks before Shanghai without doing anything."

While foreign soldiers burned villages and shot headmen, foreign diplomats argued with Chinese officials about the size of the indemnity to be paid for the Boxer outrages. The sum was finally fixed at £67,5000,000,* which China agreed to pay over a term of thirty-nine years. The Americans felt that the sum was too large; America, Waldersee crossly observed, "seems to desire that nobody shall get anything out of China." Once the agreement was signed, the Dowager Empress Tz'u-hsi returned to Peking and Allied soldiers began to think of returning home. The Russian Foreign Ministry circulated a note to all the powers in China suggesting a withdrawal timetable. The Kaiser did not want to withdraw. With much trumpeting, he had dispatched thirty thousand men to the Far East; they had arrived too late to win glory and there were no additional territories to acquire; now they were to return home with no more than a share of a thirty-nine-year indemnity. The Russians, he noted, would be withdrawing only to their Far Eastern provinces and Port Arthur, from which they could continue to exercise powerful influence over the Dragon Throne. The French would support their Russian allies. The Americans, entangled in a war in the Philippines, wished to leave China as quickly as possible. Only the British, wishing to check Russian influence in North China, had reasons to delay withdrawal. To avert further humiliation, it was important to Berlin that the other powers reject the Russian demand. The Germans had plunged in; now a rapid, wholesale withdrawal would make them a laughingstock. Yet if everyone else withdrew, they could not remain. Their position and prestige thus depended upon Britain. "At all costs, keep the British in Peking," Holstein telegraphed to Eckardstein.

In June 1901, Waldersee left Peking and sailed for home. He did so with regret. He had not been able to win the glory that the Kaiser so keenly desired. The World Marshal left behind in Peking a romantic partner, the wife of a former Chinese diplomat who had served in Berlin. He brought home with him from China an intestinal disease which eventually killed him in 1904 at the age of seventy-two.

---

* About $335,000,000 at the 1900 rate of exchange.

CHAPTER 16

The "Khaki Election"
and the Death of
Queen Victoria

◆

In September 1900, the government, riding the crest of South African victory, announced an election. Explaining his plans to the Queen, Lord Salisbury did not stress that the government intended to capitalize on the emotions generated by the war. Instead, he pointed out that "the Parliament is in its sixth year and precedents are in favor of a dissolution in the sixth year. . . . A critical period [has been] reached in the South African War and the Government will have more effect if they are fully acquainted with the views of the electors and are assured of their support." The Queen was happy to acquiesce in any measure likely to keep Lord Salisbury in office. Liberals complained about the unfairness of trying to translate pride in a military victory into votes for a party. The Unionist reply came from the Duke of Devonshire: "We all know very well that the captain of a cricketing eleven when he wins the toss, puts his own side in, or his adversaries, as he thinks most favorable to his prospects. And if there is not supposed to be anything unfair about that, then I think the English people would think it very odd indeed if the Prime Minister and leader of a great political party were not to put an electoral question to the country at a moment he thinks will be most favorable to his side."

The dissolution of Parliament was announced on September 18.

From the beginning, it was Chamberlain's campaign. (Salisbury's health was poor; he returned from four weeks of rest and mountain air in the Vosges at the outset of the campaign; he made no platform appearances.) Chamberlain roamed the land, hammering on a single issue: the conduct of the war. His purpose was to convince the electorate that a Liberal victory would mean the political defeat of British arms in South Africa. His theme became, "A vote for the Liberals is a vote for the Boers!" This charge was shouted from platforms, proclaimed by billboards and placards. Posters depicted prominent Liberals kneeling in tribute to President Kruger, helping him to haul down the Union Jack, even urging him to shoot British soldiers. One Liberal M.P. attacked in this fashion had lost two sons in the war and was actually visiting their graves in South Africa when the election was held.

The result of the "Khaki Election" was never in doubt. On October 6, the Queen wrote in her journal: "The elections are wonderfully good." The government was returned with a majority of 134 in the Commons. Salisbury and Chamberlain had a mandate to continue in power for another seven years. The vote did conceal weaknesses, since only one issue—the war—was put before the public. Unionist sloganeering had convinced the electorate that, with British troops still in the field, only an experienced government could be trusted to carry through its policy and win peace. But beneath concern about the war, other issues and resentments existed. The government's majority had been drifting downward. The number of Unionist votes in the Khaki Election was 2,400,000, but 2,100,000 voters had cast their votes for the Liberals. The truth was that the Unionist government was not generally popular and, as the journalist J. L. Garvin observed, many voters, "while marking their ballot papers in its favor, [vowed] never to vote for it again."

The election was followed immediately by a Cabinet shuffle. Mr. Goschen resigned as First Lord and was replaced by Lord Selborne, the Prime Minister's son-in-law. Other ministers packed up their papers in one office and walked across the street into another. Sir Henry Campbell-Bannerman, the Liberal leader, described the changes: "The stable remains the same, but every horse is in a new stall." The triumvirate at the top remained: Lord Salisbury was Prime Minister, Arthur Balfour was Leader of the House of Commons, and Joseph Chamberlain was Colonial Secretary.

There was one significant change: Lord Salisbury gave up the Foreign Office. Although only seventy, the Prime Minister, never physically strong, was aging. His eyesight grew worse, his girth became massive, and his bronchitis, stimulated by the smoke and fog of industrial London, drove him often to the milder climate and fresher air of the Riviera or the Vosges. His colleagues wondered how long he could last. Goschen, while still First Lord, had written to Chamberlain that Salisbury's reply to a letter sent from the Admiralty "makes one despair. . . . I do not know that more can be done. If some policy is forced on Salisbury which he disapproves of, it breaks down in execution."

Knowing that he had to curtail his responsibilities, Salisbury, a week after the election, raised the question of leaving the Foreign Office. Speaking to the Queen's private secretary, he confided that "his doctors had advocated his having less work . . . but that he was is ready to do whatever is most agreeable to the Queen." The Queen hated the thought of another man at the Foreign Office, but could not ask him to continue at the risk of his health. Her decision was ensured when she was shown a letter to the private secretary from Arthur Balfour: "I do very earnestly hope that the Queen will not insist upon Lord Salisbury keeping both offices. It requires no doctor to convince his family that the work, whenever it gets really serious, is too much for him. I have twice had to take the Foreign Office and three times, if I remember rightly, he has been called to go abroad at rather critical moments in our national affairs. He is over seventy and not an especially strong man." The Queen bowed. The new Foreign Secretary was to be Lord Lansdowne, who had been Secretary of War for five years. On October 23, the Queen sadly accepted Salisbury's resignation—but only conditionally. "Lord Salisbury thought the only person fit to take the Foreign Seals was Lord Lansdowne," she wrote that night in her journal. "But I said it must be on the strict understanding that it must be entirely under his personal supervision . . . and that no telegram or dispatch should be sent without first being submitted to him."

Salisbury's resignation as Foreign Secretary raised Joseph Chamberlain to an even higher level of importance. Winston Churchill, first elected to the House of Commons in the Khaki Election, later recalled his own contemporary view of the Colonial Secretary: "At the time when I looked out of my regimental cradle and was thrilled by politics, Mr. Chamberlain was incomparably the most live, sparkling, insurgent, compulsive figure in British affairs. Above him in the House of Lords reigned venerable, august Lord Salisbury, Prime Minister since God knew when. Beside him on the Government Bench, wise, cautious, polished, comprehending, airily fearless, Arthur Balfour led the House of Commons. But 'Joe' was the one who made the weather. He was the man the masses knew. He it was who had solutions for social problems; who was ready to advance, sword in hand if need be, upon the foes of Britain; and whose accents rang in the ears of all the young peoples of the Empire and lots of young people at its heart."

Lansdowne now was Foreign Secretary, but Chamberlain took charge of renewing the alliance proposal to Germany. Again, he made the initial proposal to Eckardstein. The German diplomat had a powerful ally in London society in Louise, Duchess of Devonshire. The Duchess was German, born Countess Alten of Hanover. Devonshire was, in fact, her second English duke; she had first come to England as the bride of the Duke of Manchester and, while still a young wife, had become the mistress of the future Duke of Devonshire, then titled Lord Hartington. The discreet liaison continued for twenty-four years, until Manchester died, leaving Louise free to marry Devonshire. London promptly dubbed her the "Double Duchess." Attached to both the country of her birth and the country of her marriages, she did all she could to assist Eckardstein in dealing with Chamberlain and the Cabinet. On January 9, 1901, Eckardstein and his wife received an invitation to a house party at Chatsworth. "Pray come without fail as the Duke has several urgent political questions to discuss with you," the Duchess wrote. "Joseph Chamberlain will also be here. As we shall have a large party of about fifty guests, you will easily get a chance for a quiet talk with the Duke and Jos., without attracting any notice. It is true, Asquith [the Liberal leader, Henry Herbert Asquith] and some other leading members of the Opposition will be with us too, but that will not matter for there are in the *Schloss* plenty of rooms where you will be able to talk without being noticed by anyone."

When Eckardstein arrived at Chatsworth, the holiday season was at its height. The Prince of Wales and Arthur Balfour had left, but Mrs. Keppel still was there, and amateur theatricals were presented every night. The conversation between Chamberlain, Eckardstein, and the Duke of Devonshire took place in the Duke's library after dinner on January 16. Eckardstein returned to London the next day and assisted Count Hatzfeldt in drawing up a telegram to Berlin: despite his earlier disappointment, Chamberlain's long-term aim remained the adherence of Britain to the Triple Alliance. "The Colonial Minister . . . and his friends had made up their minds that the day of . . . 'splendid isolation' was over for England," said the telegram. "England must look for allies for the future. The choice [is] either Russia or France or the Triple Alliance. . . . He [Chamberlain] was convinced that a combination

with Germany and an association with the Triple Alliance was preferable. . . . His advice was that matters should be taken up as soon
as Lord Salisbury left for the south and that the details should be
negotiated with Lord Lansdowne and himself. So long as he is convinced that a lasting partnership with Germany is possible, he will
resist to the utmost, the idea of an arrangement with Russia. Nevertheless, should it become evident that a permanent junction with
Germany is not practicable, then he too would advocate a settlement with Russia." Later that day, Hatzfeldt dispatched to Holstein
a private message making more explicit his and Eckardstein's impression that senior members of the British Cabinet were now
prepared to deliberately circumvent the Prime Minister: "It is particularly noteworthy that Chamberlain almost undisguisedly expresses the hope that he will soon be rid of Salisbury and thereby
become master of the situation. It seems certain that Salisbury is
leaving for the South for several months and that then Chamberlain
and his friends, of whom Lansdowne is very much one, will be in
control here."

Chamberlain's new overture was received in Berlin with a mixture of satisfaction and caution. "You and I are entirely in agreement that the idea of an alliance is premature," Hatzfeldt had begun
his message to Holstein, knowing how Chamberlain's ideas were
viewed in the Wilhelmstrasse. The German view continued to be
that Germany could afford to wait; as time passed and Britain's
difficulties increased, she would pay more for the security of a German alliance. "Better wait and leave the initiative to the English,"
Bülow telegraphed to Hatzfeldt on January 20. "There is no hurry. I
don't believe in an agreement between England and the Dual Alliance [France and Russia] until England has lost all hope . . . of
Germany's eventual support."

It was here that matters stood when, for a while, diplomacy
came to a halt. On the afternoon of January 18, after he had helped
Hatzfeldt draft the telegram to Berlin about Chamberlain's Chatsworth proposal, Eckardstein stopped off at his London club. There
he happened to meet a Court official who told him confidentially
that the Queen was dying at Osborne House.

Queen Victoria began the year 1900, the last full year of her life,
reading about British defeats in South Africa and poring over long
casualty lists, dreading to read familiar names. She sent letters and
telegrams to ministers and to officers in the field, exhorting them to
suppress gloom, to organize victory—and meanwhile to ensure that

everything was being done to provide for the safety and comfort of the cavalry horses making the long sea voyage to South Africa. In her wheelchair, she reviewed departing regiments and visited wounded soldiers in hospitals. "I was wheeled up to the bed of each man, speaking to them, and giving them flowers. They seemed so touched and many had tears in their eyes. There were a great number of Irish soldiers, chiefly from the Dublin Fusiliers, Inniskillens and Connaught Rangers. . . ."

A few days later the Queen made a dramatic change in plans for her usual spring holiday: instead of going to the Riviera, which she had visited annually for many years, she decided to visit Ireland, where she had not set foot for forty years. Her ministers were worried about the virulence of attacks in the Continental press against the Queen, the Prince of Wales, and England. Kiosks in Paris flaunted posters with vulgar, almost obscene caricatures of the Queen. Prominent Englishmen traveling in Europe attracted the cry of "Vive les Boers!" On April 4, as the Prince and Princess of Wales were aboard a train leaving the Gare du Nord in Brussels, a fifteen-year-old Belgian youth named Sipido jumped on the footboard outside their compartment and fired four shots at them from six feet away. Neither Prince nor Princess was hit. Captured, Sipido and four adult companions proved to be members of an anarchist group espousing anti-British, pro-Boer sentiments. Sipido declared that the Prince was his target because he was "an accomplice of Chamberlain in killing the Boers." No one in Britain wished to risk the Queen's life in such a climate.

Besides, Victoria herself had already decided to go to Ireland. "It was entirely my own idea as was also my giving up going abroad —and it will give great pleasure and do much good," she wrote to the Empress Frederick. She was grateful for the large number of Irish recruits who had signed up to go to South Africa and for their gallantry once in action. She decreed the wearing of the shamrock by Irish soldiers on St. Patrick's Day and authorized the creation of a new regiment, the Irish Guards, in the Brigade of Guards. Her visit to Dublin, which lasted almost the whole month of April, became a personal triumph. Overriding the views of her advisors, she drove through the streets without an armed escort, and the city which, sixteen years later, rose in the Easter Rebellion, cheered whenever she appeared.

During the spring of 1900, the tide turned in South Africa. On February 28, Ladysmith was relieved after a siege of 118 days. On May 19, five days before the Queen's birthday, the siege of Mafeking was lifted. On May 24, the Queen noted her birthday in her journal: "Again my old birthday returns, my 81st! God has been very merciful and supported me, but my trials and anxieties have been manifold and I feel tired and upset by all I have gone through this winter and spring."

The Queen's health was deteriorating. Rheumatic stiffness in her joints had required first a walking stick, then a wheelchair. In 1898, she developed cataracts. She had used reading glasses in private since 1877; now she was forced to wear them in public. She demanded larger and larger lettering and blacker and blacker ink in the confidential letters sent to her by Lord Salisbury. Everything else was read aloud to her by Princess Beatrice. In the summer of 1900, the strength and precision of her famous memory began to erode and she had trouble finding the words she wanted to use in conversation. By July, she was losing weight and complained of back pains and insomnia. The doctors recommended naps. "I now rest daily for a short while after luncheon which is thought good for me but loses time," she complained to her journal.

At the end of July, Queen Victoria suffered a personal blow. Cancer had already taken her son-in-law, the Emperor Frederick. Her daughter Vicky, the Dowager Empress of Germany, lay ill at Homburg, stricken by the same disease. Now came news that her second son, Alfred ("Affie" in the family), the former Duke of Edinburgh and a career naval officer who had been Commander-in-Chief of the Mediterranean Fleet before succeeding in 1893 to the hereditary Dukedom of Saxe-Coburg, was battling the relentless disease. Suffering from a painful tongue and throat, he had gone to Vienna for diagnosis. On July 25, the Queen recorded the terrible news: "The malady appears incurable, and, alas, one can only too well guess its nature. Affie himself is quite ignorant of the danger in which he is, and his doctors wish him on no account to be informed." Only six days later, the Duke's wife informed the Queen that he had died peacefully in his sleep, "having been with us in the garden in the afternoon." The Queen could not contain her private grief: "Oh God! My poor, darling Affie gone too! My third grown-up child,* besides three sons-in-law. It is hard at eighty-one. . . . I pray God to help me to be and have trust in Him who has never failed me."

The Queen's grief was kept mostly private, confided only to her

---

* With Alfred's death, the Queen had lost two of her five sons and one of her four daughters. Princess Alice, who married the Grand Duke of Hesse, died of diphtheria in 1878. Prince Leopold, Duke of Albany, was a hemophiliac and died of complications from that disease in 1884. Now came Prince Alfred in 1900. And her eldest daughter, the Empress Frederick, would follow in 1901, seven months after her mother.

family and her journal. A rare instance of semipublic complaint occurred during an exchange of letters with her old friend George
Goschen, a member of the Unionist Cabinet, who wrote that he
would not be standing for reelection in the autumn campaign. "He
has now been more than thirty-seven years in the House of Commons and being in his seventieth year, he felt that he may fairly
claim relief from its engrossing duties," Goschen wrote to the
Queen. "The last five years, during which he has been First Lord of
the Admiralty, have been a period of great and continuous strain,
and the overwhelming responsibilities of the post . . . have contributed to make him desire some rest." The Queen read the letter
with mixed feelings: certainly, Goschen had earned his retirement;
yet she always hated having to deal with new people; and if the
Admiralty was an "overwhelming responsibility," what about the
Crown? "The Queen feels that he is fully justified in wishing for a
rest," she finally wrote. "She wishes she could have the same, even
for the shortest period; for she does need it and feels the constant
want of it, at eighty-one—very trying and fatiguing." Goschen's
heart went out to the elderly monarch: "Your Majesty speaks pa-
thetically of the desire for rest often felt by your Majesty," he wrote
to her. "The nation knows the self-sacrifice and courage with which
your Majesty in your eighty-second year, discharges unremittingly
the most arduous duties, and endeavors to repay them with the
greatest devotion and affection ever paid to a sovereign."

In September, the Queen went to Balmoral. An attending gentleman, Lord James of Hereford, described her decline. "In May the
Queen was quite as of old—very cheerful and enjoying any anecdote or smart conversation. . . . When I returned in October I
found that the greatest change had taken place. The Queen had
shrunk so as to appear about one half the person she had been."
Queen Victoria described what was happening to her. Balmoral was
"gloomy and dark"; she felt "very poorly and wretched. . . . My
appetite is completely gone and I have difficulty eating anything."
By November 7, she was back at Windsor but felt no better:

> November 9: "Still have disgust for all food."
> November 11: "Shocking night and no draught could
> make me sleep as pain kept me awake. Very tired and un-
> well."
> November 28: "Bad, restless night, good deal of pain."
> December 2: "Could not leave room. My repulsion for
> food was great."
> December 3: "Very sleepy and slept before luncheon."

December 16: "Had a very bad night and only got up late. Slept most of the afternoon."

On the eighteenth, at eleven-forty A.M., she left Windsor for the last time. She slept for an hour on the train to Portsmouth, embarked on the *Alberta* at two P.M., and was at Osborne House by three-thirty. Even "magic Osborne" could not reverse what was happening:

December 22: "Slept until quarter to twelve at which I was very annoyed."
December 27: "Disturbed by the wind. Took some milk, fell asleep towards morning so did not get up till nearly one."

She continued faithful to duty. On January 2, 1901, Lord Roberts arrived, having sailed direct from Cape Town to Cowes to report to the sovereign on the progress of the war. The Queen received his report and gave him the Garter and an earldom. On January 10, Joseph Chamberlain, the last Cabinet Minister to see her alive, arrived with the latest news from South Africa. He stayed twenty minutes and later recalled: "She was thinner and there was a certain look of delicacy about her," but "she showed not the slightest sign of failing intelligence. . . . [She] spoke about the war, regretting its prolongation and the loss of life, but said earnestly, 'I am not anxious about the result.' " On January 13, she made a last entry in her journal: "Had a fair night, but was a little wakeful." Her last words were testimony to duty: "Rested again afterwards, then did some signing and dictated to Lenchen." The following day, January 14, there was no entry; it was the first time in nearly seventy years that Victoria had failed to write. On the seventeenth, her mind seemed clouded and she had difficulty speaking. Her children were summoned.

The Queen's eldest grandchild was not summoned, but appeared nonetheless. On January 18, the day after his return from Chatsworth, Eckardstein, hearing about the Queen's condition, rushed back to his embassy to telegraph Berlin. The Kaiser was in the middle of celebrating the bicentenary of the proclamation of the Kingdom of Prussia and had just declared his resolve to make the German Navy "as mighty an instrument" as the army. He broke off the celebration, cancelled all appointments, and announced that he was leaving immediately for England. Bülow, knowing that the visit would be bitterly unpopular in Germany, suggested that his master wait to see how the illness developed. Impatiently, William retorted that, where the life of his dear grandmother was concerned, no other considerations could be taken into account; in fact, he had already reserved cabins on the Flushing–Dover mail boat for that night. "I have duly informed the Prince of Wales, begging him at the same time that *no notice* whatever is to be taken of me in my capacity as Emperor and that I come as a grandson. . . . I suppose the petticoats [the Queen's three daughters, Princess Helena (Lenchen), Louise, and Beatrice] who are fencing off poor Grandmama from the world—and I often fear from me—will kick up a row when they hear of my coming. But I don't care, for what I do is my duty, the more so as it is this unparalleled Grandmama, as none ever existed before."

Although he came as a grandson, the German Emperor could not be ignored, and the Prince of Wales hurried back from Osborne to put on the uniform of the Prussian First Dragoon Guards and greet William at Victoria Station. On the morning of the twentieth, the nephew accompanied his uncle back to Osborne. The Queen barely recognized William, mistaking him for his father, the Emperor Frederick. William was extravagantly discreet. He waited tactfully in another room, declaring that while he wanted to see Grandmama as much as possible before she died, if that was impossible, he would quite understand. His attitude won the admiration of the family and he was invited to join the little party by the deathbed.

All through Sunday the twenty-second, while the Queen was dying, messages poured in. One came from President Kruger, wishing for her "prompt recovery." As the winter darkness fell about four P.M., the family group moved closer around the bed. The Prince of Wales kneeled beside his mother, while Prince Arthur, the Queen's other surviving son, and the German Emperor supported her in their arms with pillows. "The last moments were like a great three-decker ship sinking," reported the Bishop of Winchester, an old friend who was present. She rallied and gasped for breath, recognizing people, calling their names, then closing her eyes and slipping back into unconsciousness. Her last word was "Bertie." "Then came a great change of look and complete calmness," noted the Bishop. She died at half past six.

William's dignity and genuine sorrow had won his relatives' affection. Together, he and his uncle, the new King, lifted the body into the coffin. "She was so little—and so light," the Kaiser noted afterward. When the new King, who announced that he would call himself King Edward VII, departed for London for an Accession Council, he asked his nephew to take charge at Osborne. Moved by this new warmth, William decided to stay on in England through the funeral, almost a fortnight away. During the ten days the Queen lay in state at Osborne, William remained, living with the family despite the arrival of the *Hohenzollern*. King Edward invested William's son, the nineteen-year-old Crown Prince William, with the Order of the Garter and made the Kaiser a Field Marshal in the British Army. Impulsively, William responded by conferring the German Order of the Black Eagle on Lord Roberts, who was detested by pro-Boer Germans. The Kaiser's behavior was so new and remarkable that his uncle could find only good things to say. "William was kindness itself and touching in his devotion without a shade of brusquerie or selfishness," he wrote to his sister, who had been too ill to travel from Germany. A week later, he wrote to her again: "William's touching and simple demeanor, up to the last, will never be forgotten by me or anyone." The Kaiser also felt the closeness. In February 1906, when Britain and Germany sternly confronted each other at the Algeciras Conference, William wrote to his uncle, "Let us rather remember the silent hour when we watched and prayed at her bedside, then the spirit of that great Sovereign Lady passed away as she drew her last breath in my arms."

Queen Victoria had reigned for almost sixty-four years;* only subjects nearing seventy could remember another monarch. More than a sovereign, she was an institution, and most of her people thought of her as permanent, like the Houses of Parliament or the Bank of England. "She was the greatest of Englishwomen—I almost said of Englishmen—for she added the highest of manly qualities to the personal delicacy of a woman," said Joseph Chamberlain. The sense of loss was many-sided: loss of permanence, loss of authority, loss of security. On no one—not even on her Heir—did this loss have greater impact than on the Kaiser. In spite of all, the emotional link between them had never been broken. He was her eldest grandchild, she was his august, but also warmhearted Grandmama. The happiest days of his youth had been spent in the relatively informal atmosphere of Osborne and Windsor, an atmosphere dominated by the personality of the Queen. As the years went by, he never gave up his feeling of tenderness for his aging grandmother and respect for the Queen-Empress. She scolded him, but she also showed him

---

* Only two European monarchs have reigned longer than Queen Victoria: Louis XIV, who ruled for seventy-one years (1644–1715) and the Emperor Franz Joseph of Austria, who ruled for sixty-eight years (1848–1916).

affection and understanding. She criticized him to her ministers, but she also stood up for him, advising Lord Salisbury and others on how to deal with him. In many ways, she was like him: both were sentimental, subject to strong likes and dislikes, capable of gushiness and sharp anger in writing to subordinates. Because Victoria had had Albert and a series of independent prime ministers, she had learned to discipline her feelings and language as William never had. As long as she lived, she posed for William a model of how an Imperial sovereign should behave. When she died, that model vanished. His uncle, King Edward, could not replace her; for too long, Bertie, in William's eyes, had been the frivolous Prince of Wales. And so, at forty-two, the Kaiser was left alone to follow his own path, bereft of the presence, the counsel, and the affection of the one human he admired as well as loved.

On February 1, the Queen's body was carried to Portsmouth on board the *Alberta,* with King Edward following on the large *Victoria and Albert.* As the two yachts passed between the lines of saluting warships, the King noticed that the royal standard over his head was at half-mast. He asked the captain why. "The Queen is dead, Sir," was the reply. "The King of England lives!" declared the King, and the standard soared. A special train transported the coffin to London, past crowds of people kneeling in the stations, at crossroads, and in fields along the way. At times, the train seemed to be going recklessly fast; again, the new King was asserting himself. The train had left Portsmouth nine minutes late and the driver was told to "see what you can do to make it up as the King cannot stand people being late." In London, dense crowds lined the route between Victoria Station and Paddington as the gun carriage carrying the coffin rolled past, followed by three red-cloaked horsemen; the King; the Kaiser on the King's right; Prince Arthur, Duke of Connaught, on the King's left. At Windsor, the gun-carriage horses bucked in their harness and had to be unhitched and replaced by a party of navy bluejackets who pulled their royal mistress up the hill from the station. The funeral was in St. George's Chapel. Then Victoria was taken to the Frogmore Mausoleum, where after forty-two years she lay down at Albert's side.

William's private visit to England alarmed many in Germany. The Kaiserin had opposed the trip from the beginning and she wanted him to come home quickly. "I hope that you will be able to dissuade the Kaiser from staying for the funeral," she wrote to Bülow after the Queen's death. "And that you will persuade him to be satisfied with sending the Crown Prince or perhaps Prince Henry who is burning to go." William himself telegraphed his wife on January 23 his reasons for staying at Osborne: "My aunts here are quite alone [the new King had gone to London] and I must help them with many things. I must give then my advice whenever advice is necessary. They are so kind to me, they treat me like a brother and a friend instead of like a nephew. . . . It has been a terribly difficult and exciting time." When she got this message, the Empress worried even more: "The Kaiser is very tired and exhausted. But that occurs easily as you know . . . for he is so entirely absorbed by anything he does. But I think it is particularly dangerous the way everyone— especially the ladies—is trying to besiege his warm, friendly nature and turn his head (they all, of course, want to win him over for their own ends)." On the twenty-sixth, she had fresh news of English scheming: "To crown everything else, the new English King has made the German Emperor an English Field Marshal," she wrote to Bülow. "If this is not an irony in present circumstances [i.e., the Boer War], I do not know what is. It is supposed to be a gracious act, but I consider it tactless. The Kaiser, of course, has got to look pleased." For once, Eulenburg agreed with the Emperor's wife. "I am anxious when I think of the beloved Master in Osborne," he wrote to his colleague Bülow from Vienna. "He will be like a child amidst these people who are crude despite their mourning. Amongst them, he forgets all his shrewdness. A sort of trustful embarrassment takes possession of him and any one of them could easily get at the secrets of his soul (and our state secrets). And at the same time, he is really in the way. The family scold him behind his back and his own adjutants wring their hands and wish they could go home."

The Kaiser's visit and absorption into his English family also worried Bülow and Holstein. Chamberlain had just made his new alliance proposal at Chatsworth; now, they worried, the Kaiser was being exposed to the wiles of the English just at the moment when his emotional guard was down. To avert this danger, Eckardstein had been instructed to meet the Kaiser when he landed in England and ride with him to London in his private railway car. Along the way, the Baron informed William of his conversations with Chamberlain and Devonshire at Chatsworth. The Kaiser responded as he always did to Eckardstein, saying that he was delighted, that he completely favored an Anglo-German alliance which would protect mutual interests and serve world peace. Here, Eckardstein was forced to urge caution; before leaving London he had received urgent instructions from Holstein not to let the Kaiser discuss an alliance or any other political questions with British ministers during this private trip. "Accordingly, I told the Kaiser that I thought it would be best not to discuss the alliance and even to act as though he had no knowledge of what the Duke of Devonshire and Chamberlain had said," wrote Eckardstein. "He replied that he quite understood."

The shared death watch at Osborne had warmed the hearts of all participants. After investing the German Crown Prince with the Garter, the new King Edward had spoken of the close family ties between himself and the House of Hohenzollern and expressed the hope that the relationship might extend to the people of both countries. By hurrying to his grandmother's side, the King declared, the Emperor had aroused a profound feeling of gratitude, not only within the family but among the British people. William himself was moved by the outpouring of goodwill he felt from within the family and from the hushed British crowds who lined the streets. His inclination was to overrule Bülow and Holstein and to grasp the hand offered by Chamberlain. "Baron von Eckardstein tells me of Chamberlain's confidential intimation that it is all over with 'splendid isolation,' " he telegraphed to Bülow. "Britain must choose between the Triple Alliance and France-Russia. He [Chamberlain] is completely for the former. . . . Only if we are not willing, then the swing to the Dual Alliance. . . . So 'they come' it seems. This is what *we* have been waiting for."

The Kaiser's telegram dismayed the Wilhelmstrasse. Holstein urgently telegraphed Metternich, the senior diplomat in the Kaiser's party, and ordered him to pour cold water on the Emperor's enthusiasm. "Chamberlain's threatened understanding with France and Russia is a patent fraud," he asserted. ". . . We can wait. Time is on our side. As I see it, a rational agreement with England . . . will only come within reach when England feels the pinch more acutely than she does today." To Bülow, with his special talents for flattery, was assigned the task of communicating the Wilhelmstrasse's philosophy to the Kaiser:

"Your Majesty is quite right in the feeling that the English must come to us," wrote the new Chancellor on January 21. "South Africa has cost them dear; America shows herself uncertain; Japan unreliable; France full of hatred; Russia faithless; public opinion hostile in all countries. At the Diamond Jubilee English self-conceit reached its highest point. The English peacock spread its proudest display and preened itself in splendid isolation. . . . Now it begins to dawn gradually on the consciousness of the English that, by their own strength alone, they will not be able to maintain their world empire against so many antagonists. . . .

"Everything now depends on neither discouraging the English nor allowing ourselves to be prematurely tied to them. English troubles will increase in the next few months and with them the price that we can demand will rise. . . .

"Your Majesty will execute a very master coup if your All-Highness can succeed in leaving leading English personages with the hope of a future firm relationship with us, but without your All-Highness being at present prematurely bound or committed. The understanding threatened with the Dual Alliance is nothing but a scarecrow made up to intimidate us in the way the English have already practiced for years. . . . Your Majesty will of course know just how to rub their noses gently but firmly in this truth."

The Kaiser took the cue and did his best to suppress his feelings. When Lord Lansdowne, the new Foreign Secretary, called on him at Osborne for a general discussion of foreign affairs, there was no mention of an Anglo-German alliance. Instead, William lectured Lansdowne on the perfidy of the Russians, declaring that "the Russian Emperor [was] only fit to live in a country house and grow turnips" and that every "Russian Grand Duke likes Paris and a girl on each knee." Russia, he continued, "is really Asiatic," while Britain was European and should join in a general concert of Germany and France. When Lansdowne happened to mention the traditional balance of power in Europe, seeming to suggest that it still lay with Britain and the British Fleet, the Kaiser vehemently retorted, "It is not the British Fleet, but the twenty-two German Army Corps that are the Balance of Power in Europe."

William continued to be deeply troubled by his conflicting roles as the Queen's grandson and the German Emperor. He was respected by the family and was the hero of the British crowds; this was the acceptance and adulation in England he had always craved. The hand of permanent friendship was stretched across the old Queen's deathbed. William was anxious to take it, but the frantic messages from the Wilhelmstrasse restrained him. He expressed his dilemma when he turned to Metternich on the way to the Queen's funeral at Windsor and observed petulantly, "I cannot wobble forever between England and Russia. I would find myself forever trying to sit between two stools." Metternich replied as he had been briefed to: the choice of England was correct, but the time was not ripe; England could be made to pay a higher price. To illustrate the depths to which England was sinking, he reminded the Kaiser of what they had just witnessed during the funeral procession in London: "The military ranks stretched for miles. A muster of troops, morally degraded, idiots and undersized, pitiable human beings, the dregs of the population . . . the English have reached the end of their military capacity." (Metternich ignored the fact that over 250,000 British troops were in South Africa.)

Throughout his fortnight-long visit, William was torn by his divided impulses. As urged by his counselors, he made no move to see Chamberlain. Nevertheless, at a Marlborough House luncheon given in his honor by the King on the day of his departure, the Kaiser thanked everyone present for his "magnificent" reception in England and then gave them a glimpse of his own vision of the future:

"I believe there is a Providence which has decreed that two nations which have produced such men as Shakespeare, Schiller, Luther, and Goethe must have a great future before them; I believe that the two Teutonic nations will, bit by bit, learn to know each other better, and that they will stand together to help in keeping the peace of the world. We ought to form an Anglo-German alliance, you to keep the seas while we would be responsible for the land; with such an alliance, not a mouse could stir in Europe without our permission, and the nations would, in time, come to see the necessity of reducing their armaments."

Caught up in this glow, William returned to Germany. Bülow found him at his mother's bedside in Homburg "completely under the spell of his English impressions. As a rule, he could not change his military uniforms often enough, but now he wore civilian clothes as he had done in England, including a tie-pin with his grandmother's initials on it. The officers who were summoned from Frankfurt to dine with him were surprised to find their Supreme War Lord wearing civilian clothes . . . [and to hear] his constant enthusiastic allusions to England and everything English that, in his own words, 'ranked far above German habits and customs.' "

CHAPTER 17

The End of Anglo-German Alliance Negotiations

◆

Great Britain and Germany pursued alliance discussions through the spring of 1901. Salisbury played no part and was ignored, even scorned, by the Wilhelmstrasse. "Everything from London of late makes an impression of the most hopeless sloppiness as though Lord Salisbury's spirit breathed through it all," Holstein wrote to Eckardstein on March 9. Chamberlain had largely withdrawn. When Eckardstein called on him on March 18, the Colonial Secretary reaffirmed his view of the value of an Anglo-German alliance, expressed at Leicester sixteen months before, but had "no desire to burn his fingers again." It was, therefore, to Lansdowne that Eckardstein and—when he was well enough—Hatzfeldt brought a succession of messages from Berlin.

First came a proposal initiated by Bülow for an Anglo-German defensive alliance, good for five years, to be ratified by both the House of Commons and the Reichstag. Each power was to remain benevolently neutral if the other was attacked by one foreign state; if it was attacked by two, the ally would intervene. Thus, Britain could fight either France or Russia alone without drawing Germany in, while Germany also could fight either partner in the Dual Alliance without demanding British assistance. "The alliance is moving again," Eckardstein wrote to Holstein on May 23. "Lansdowne,

Devonshire and Chamberlain are fully determined. . . . Salisbury, who no longer has the same animus against us, still raises small objections now and then, as is his way; but is, as I learn from Devonshire and Lansdowne, quite satisfied that the policy of 'Splendid Isolation' is over and that something must be done. Anyway, these ministers hold so fast to their point of view that Salisbury cannot help himself. Lansdowne seems to manage him quite cleverly."

There was some disarray on the German side. Bülow decided that he wished to take the conduct of the negotiations "out of the hands of Eckardstein who was dominated by the English point of view and who was dependent upon English money." Accordingly, Holstein announced to Eckardstein that he was dispatching a more senior diplomat from Berlin to conduct the negotiations. Eckardstein promptly resigned. Although Holstein suspended the resignation, the British developed a sense of Eckardstein's eroding position: Lansdowne began to refer to him as "that person." The Kaiser intruded with an unfortunate turn of phrase. In a conversation with Sir Frank Lascelles, he referred to the ministers of the British government as "unmitigated noodles." He then repeated the phrase in a private letter to King Edward. The King summoned Eckardstein to his private study, read the Kaiser's letter aloud, and added, "There, what do you think of that?" Eckardstein thought for a moment and replied, "Wouldn't it be best if your Majesty treated that whole thing as a joke?" The King laughed and said, "Yes, you are quite right. I must treat the thing as a joke. But unluckily I have already had to put up with many of these jokes of the Kaiser."

When Hatzfeldt had sufficiently recovered his health, he resumed responsibility for the alliance negotiations. To Lansdowne's surprise, the ambassador brought another new German proposal to the table. The offer of a simple defensive alliance between the two countries vanished and in its place appeared a German invitation for Britain to join the Triple Alliance of Germany, Austria, and Italy. Berlin's logic, Hatzfeldt explained, was that if the British Empire, including India, Canada, and South Africa, was to be treated as a whole, then the Triple Alliance should be treated as a whole. If, for example, Germany was to be required to march against Russia because of a Russian attack on India, then Britain must fight Russia if the Russian army attacked Austria.

When news of this offer reached Lord Salisbury, the Prime Minister—thought by Holstein to guilty of "hopeless sloppiness," described by Eckardstein as "cleverly managed" by Lansdowne—wrote a memorandum so persuasively negative that it had the effect of vetoing any treaty on the spot. Salisbury restated that he was strongly averse to entangling his country in alliances with European countries. He pointed out that Great Britain was required to join the Triple Alliance as, in effect, a junior partner, subordinate to Germany; and guarantee the interests and frontiers of all three of the current members of the Alliance—Germany, Austria, and Italy —against threats from Russia and France. Salisbury was particularly opposed to any commitment of support to the shaky Hapsburg monarchy, "since the liability of having to defend the German and Austrian frontiers against Russia was heavier than that of having to defend the British Isles against France."

Further, he noted that an alliance with Germany would be certain to incur the bitter hostility of France, even if Britain could somehow avoid a German demand that Britain guarantee Germany's right to permanent possession of Alsace-Lorraine. Any peaceful resolution of the colonial disputes between Britain and France, especially the feud over Egypt, would be made impossible. Finally, the Cabinet would be unlikely to recommend such a treaty to the House; the Commons would be unlikely to approve the treaty if it did. No incumbent British government could commit a future government to declare war over an issue which was not supported by British public opinion at the moment of crisis. In such an instance, the treaty would be repudiated and the government would fall.

Salisbury's memorandum made any alliance agreement unlikely. In June, Alfred Rothschild, a friend of Chamberlain and Devonshire, wrote to Eckardstein: "Nobody here in England has any more use for the fine empty phrases of Bülow. Joe, who dined with me, is quite disheartened. He will have nothing more to do with the people in Berlin. If they are so short-sighted, says he, as not to be able to see that the whole new world system depends upon it, then there is nothing to be done for them." It was months, even years, before Bülow and Holstein understood that the alliance negotiations were over conclusively. "We ought not to show any uneasiness or anxious haste," Bülow commented to Holstein in October 1901. "We must just let hope shimmer on the horizon."

Originally, Joseph Chamberlain had sought an alliance with Imperial Germany because British markets in China were threatened by Russian expansionism in Asia. British sea power alone could not counter this threat; Chamberlain believed that only Germany, which could put military pressure on the Tsar's frontier in Europe, could moderate Russian penetration of China. Chamberlain's eagerness for an alliance became more urgent when the Boer War revealed the strength of hostility to Britain and the resulting weakness of Britain's diplomatic position in the world. From these specific needs, the Colonial Secretary molded an Anglo-German alliance, dominating the world, guaranteeing peace and prosperity, perhaps reaching out one day to include the United States.

With all its grandeur, Joseph Chamberlain's vision of the future was ill informed by history. Had Great Britain and Germany each overcome their hesitations and entered into alliance, then Russia and France inevitably would have been forced to come to terms with the Triple (now Quadruple) Alliance. Germany, the senior, dominant power, would have ruled over Europe. Britain, on all future issues, would have been forced to defer to Berlin. England would have had no choice: the Royal Navy would have been helpless against the aggregation of military and naval power arrayed against it.

In reaching out to Germany, Chamberlain ignored a centuries-old precept of English history: to survive and prosper, England must always ally herself with the weaker power or powers in Europe. Otherwise, allied to the strongest power, England finds herself in a subordinate role, her interests and independence subject to the dictates of the strongest power. Only by rallying the weaker states into a coalition to oppose the strongest power can England prevent Continental hegemony and preserve her own security. This was the lesson taught when England created alliances against Philip II of Spain, Louis XIV of France, and Napoleon Bonaparte. It was a lesson Joseph Chamberlain failed to apply.

Chamberlain's relationship with Bülow ended in personal bad blood. Their final quarrel had nothing to do with the alliance proposal, now moribund. In Edinburgh, on October 25, 1901, Chamberlain, the Cabinet minister chiefly responsible for prosecuting the war in South Africa, defended the tactics of the British Army fighting the Boer commandos on the veldt. These tactics—rounding up Boer women and children and placing them in concentration camps, burning Boer farms which sheltered the commandos—had set off a storm in England. Chamberlain acknowledged that the foreign press as well as English newspapers had criticized these tactics; he said that the methods might become even more harsh; in justification, he cited the practices of the armies of other countries in fighting irregular resistance. Condemnation of England was unacceptable, he said, from "nations who now criticize our 'barbarity' and 'cruelty' but

whose example in Poland, in the Caucasus, in Algeria, in the Ton-
kin, in Bosnia, and in the Franco-Prussian War, we have never even
approached." Implicit in this list were accusations against Russia,
France, Austria, and Germany, but it was from Germany alone that
a roar of indignation was heard. German newspapers vilified Chamberlain, "the bloodhound of the Transvaal," for presuming to compare the Prussian heroes of the Franco-Prussian War with
Kitchener's "butchers" in South Africa.

Bülow demanded an apology from Chamberlain. Paul Wolff-
Metternich, about to replace Hatzfeldt as German ambassador in
London, was instructed to make a formal protest at the Foreign
Office. Metternich did his best to dissuade Bülow, observing that
Chamberlain remained Germany's best friend in the British Cabinet. Bülow insisted. Metternich called on Lord Lansdowne. The
Foreign Secretary saw no prospect of an apology "for a speech
which in our opinion did not call for one." Metternich, pressured
from Berlin, called again to ask for a lesser expression of regret
which Bülow could wave before the Reichstag. Again Lansdowne
refused. Chamberlain told the Austrian Ambassador that "there
had been no warmer advocate than himself of England's adherence
to the Triple Alliance." Now, he said, he had been "subjected to
three weeks of measureless attack and abuse. . . . Since no insult
had been meant, no apology would be given."

Bülow refused to leave the matter alone. On January 8, 1902,
he rose in the Reichstag: "The German Army stands far too high
and its shield is far too bright to be touched by unjust attacks. This
business recalls Frederick the Great's remark when told that someone had been attacking him and the Prussian Army. 'Let the man
alone and don't be excited,' said the great King. 'He is biting granite.' " The Reichstag thundered applause, and Chamberlain was
alienated forever. Three days later, speaking in Birmingham, he
hurled defiantly: "What I have said, I have said. I withdraw nothing.
I qualify nothing. I defend nothing. I do not want to give lessons to a
foreign minister and I will not accept any at his hands. I am responsible only to my sovereign and my countrymen."

Chamberlain was cheered in the streets of London as well as of
Birmingham. "Mr. Chamberlain," said *The Times,* "is at this moment the most popular and trusted man in England." "You would
be interested to see the effect created in England by the German
treatment of us," a Foreign Office official wrote to a friend a few
weeks later. "The change is extraordinary. Everyone in the [For-
eign] Office talks as if we had but one enemy in the world, and that

is Germany. It is no good trying to assure us unofficially or officially that they are really our friends. No one believes it now."

Already, on December 19, 1901, before Bülow's speech, the British government had moved formally to terminate alliance negotiations. Lansdowne told Metternich that "the temper of the two countries was not in a particularly favorable state" and that "while we certainly did not regard the proposal with an unfriendly or critical eye, we did not think that for the moment we could take it up."

Chamberlain's dream of an Anglo-German alliance had ended, but his feeling that Britain could no longer afford to stand alone had not changed. On January 30, 1902, Metternich reported to Berlin, "I hear in the strictest confidence that negotiations have been going on for the last ten days between Chamberlain and the French ambassador for the settlement of all colonial differences between the two powers. . . ." More evidence followed quickly. On February 8, King Edward invited ministers of the Crown and all foreign ambassadors to Marlborough House, where he continued to live while Buckingham Palace was being refurbished. Eckardstein represented Germany. After dinner, while the company was having coffee and cigars, Eckardstein saw Chamberlain and Paul Cambon, the French Ambassador, go off together into the billiard room. Eckardstein lurked near the doorway. He strained to listen, but managed to pick up only two words: "Morocco" and "Egypt." As soon as Cambon departed, Eckardstein approached Chamberlain. The Colonial Secretary complained about the Chancellor's speech to the Reichstag and the German press. "It is not the first time that Count Bülow has thrown me over in the Reichstag. Now I have enough of such treatment and there can be no more question of an association between Great Britain and Germany." As Eckardstein was leaving Marlborough House, an equerry came up and said that King Edward would like to talk to him after the others had left. Eckardstein went to the King's private study. Fifteen minutes later, the King, having changed into less formal clothing, came in, shook hands, and offered Eckardstein an 1888 cigar and a whiskey and soda. He spoke frankly about British resentment of the abuse of Chamberlain and England in the German press. "For a long time at least," he said, "there can be no more any question of Great Britain and Germany working together in any conceivable matter. We are being urged more strongly than ever by France to come to an agreement with her in all colonial disputes and it will probably be best in the end to make such a settlement."

CHAPTER 18

Arthur Balfour

◆

In the spring of 1902 it seemed to Lord Salisbury that he might at last lay down the burden he had carried, as Foreign Secretary and Prime Minister, for the better part of twenty-four years. He was alone, weary, and aging rapidly. With increasing frequency, Cabinet ministers, hearing a slow, rhythmic breathing at the Cabinet table, would glance at their leader's chair and note that the Prime Minister had dropped off to sleep.

Salisbury would have departed sooner had the war been won more quickly. As the struggle on the veldt dragged on, the Prime Minister clung to office. At last, on May 31, 1902, a peace treaty was signed at Pretoria reincorporating the two Boer republics into the British Empire. The new King's coronation was only six weeks away, and Salisbury decided to stay until the formal transference had been achieved. When King Edward's sudden appendicitis forced an indefinite postponement of the ceremony, no further reason existed to delay. On July 11, 1902, without consulting or even notifying his colleagues, Lord Salisbury went to Buckingham Palace and resigned. His physician advised him to leave immediately for the Continent. He took the advice, but his health was ruined. When death came at Hatfield on August 22, 1903, he was prepared. "One might as well be afraid of going to sleep," he had noted earlier.

■ ■ ■

Four days before Lord Salisbury's resignation, Joseph Chamberlain had suffered a serious accident. On the morning of July 7, 1902, Chamberlain had stepped into the quadrangle of the Colonial Office and reviewed a battalion of West African troops brought to London for the coronation. After congratulating them on their loyalty, the Colonial Secretary suggested that some of them might be fortunate enough to glimpse "the King's face before you return to your homes." In the afternoon, Chamberlain had taken a hansom cab from the Colonial Office to his club. The day was hot and the glass front window of the cab, secured by a leather strap, had been folded up against the roof. To settle the dust, the pavements had been sprinkled and the footing was slippery. Near the Canadian Arch on Trafalgar Square, the horse shied, slipped, and fell, tipping the cab violently forward. Chamberlain was hurled out of his seat as the heavy glass pane snapped its restraining thong and crashed down on the Colonial Secretary's head. His scalp was penetrated to the bone in a three-and-a-half-inch gash running from the middle of his forehead across his right temple. Stunned, with blood pouring into his eyes, he was taken to Charing Cross Hospital. Despite the blow and loss of blood, Chamberlain seemed all right; his wife found her husband wreathed in a cloud of smoke from one of his cigars. He remained in the hospital several days and then went home to Prince's Gardens to rest. His injury was greater than had first appeared. "Joe Chamberlain was . . . very nearly killed," wrote Lord Esher. "The skull was bruised at a very thin place and he has not been able to read or think since."

Chamberlain was at home in bed when Lord Salisbury resigned. That afternoon, July 11, the King sent for Arthur Balfour and asked him to lead the government. Balfour received the King's messenger at the House of Commons and, before going to the Palace to accept, drove to Prince's Gardens to consult Chamberlain. The invalid was asleep and his doctor had left orders that he must not be disturbed. Mrs. Chamberlain, however, agreed to awaken her husband, and Chamberlain, lying in bed, promised Balfour his complete support. Then Balfour went to the King.

King Edward's choice was expected. Only two other candidates had been imaginable, Devonshire and Chamberlain, and both were disqualified because they came from the smaller Liberal wing of the Unionist coalition. Nevertheless, to many people, Chamberlain's position in the new government seemed awkward; some said bluntly that a Cabinet in which Mr. Chamberlain served under Mr. Balfour was upside down. Chamberlain had spoken for Britain on many of the issues of the day. He had led the party to victory in the Khaki Election. In the countryside, he was England's most popular politician and although the aristocratic Cecils, uncle and nephew, had ruled in Whitehall and Westminster, no one believed that either could rule without Joseph Chamberlain's support. Since the Khaki Election, Balfour and Chamberlain had in effect shared power, with Chamberlain managing the war and the Empire, while Balfour managed everything else. Chamberlain recognized that, when it came to confronting the constituencies and facing the rough and tumble of bringing out the vote, he was the one who kept the coalition in power.

Nevertheless, when Balfour was summoned, Chamberlain made no complaint. During Salisbury's decline, the succession had been decided. In February 1902, four months before Salisbury's actual retirement, Chamberlain had sought out Balfour's private secretary and emphasized—the private secretary reported—"that I was to understand that he was 'not a candidate for that office. I have my own work to do and it is not done yet and I am quite content to stay where I am. . . . I shall be quite willing to serve under Balfour.' "

The future of the Unionist government and the party depended on close cooperation between the new Prime Minister and his more famous subordinate. In temperament as well as ideology, the two men had little in common. Chamberlain was an innovator; Balfour, like his uncle, was a conserver. "The country is full of a vague desire for change, for great change," declared a fortnightly journal, "but Mr. Balfour is made Prime Minister precisely because it is desired by the ruling families that the minimum of change should be made." Chamberlain once described their differences: "Arthur hates difficulties. I love 'em." Balfour did not disagree. "The difference between Joe and me," he explained, "is the difference between youth and age. I am age." (In 1902, Balfour was fifty-four, Chamberlain sixty-five.) Nevertheless, at the beginning, each man, aware of the other's strengths and his own weaknesses, entered the partnership determined to make it work.

The new Prime Minister seemed to many of his contemporaries an embodiment of the Aristotelian philosopher-king. Blue blood, wealth, and charm, guided by what Austen Chamberlain called "the finest brain that has been applied to politics in our time," made up Arthur Balfour. Observers, struggling to describe Balfour's qualities, came up with words usually applied to aesthetic objects: "brilliant," "dazzling," "radiant," "resplendent." Indeed, John Maynard Keynes characterized Arthur Balfour as "the most extraordinary objet d'art our century has produced."

Arthur Balfour was born July 25, 1848, at Whittingehame House, a white Greek Revival mansion in the center of a ten-thousand-acre estate in the East Lothian region of the Scottish Lowlands. His paternal grandfather had gone to India in the eighteenth century, prospered with the East India Company, and returned to marry an earl's daughter. Balfour's father married the daughter of a marquess, Lady Blanche Cecil, one of Lord Salisbury's older sisters. At eighteen, Lady Blanche began producing children, giving birth to nine in eleven years before her husband died of tuberculosis at thirty-five. The eldest of her sons, named Arthur after his godfather, the Duke of Wellington, was seven when his father died.

Left to raise her children alone, Lady Blanche placed dust covers over the French furniture in Whittingehame House's yellow-damask drawing rooms and shifted her attention to the nurseries. She taught her children to read and write, heard their nightly prayers, and nursed them through diphtheria, typhoid, and whooping cough. Even before her husband's death, a friend described Lady Blanche's unusual character: "To know her slightly you would think she was a healthy-minded, happy wife, a mother of children, doing all the good she could. . . . You never could suspect the intense . . . feeling, dashing and flashing, and bursting and melting and tearing her at times to pieces. And she looks so quiet and pure and almost cold, aye cold." Nevertheless, her son Arthur always seemed to know how to handle her. As a little boy, he would climb into his mother's lap, put his arms around her neck, and ask, "Can you tell me why I love you so much?"

At eleven Arthur went off to school, where he was remembered by his masters as a fragile child with "a beautiful purity of mind." He had no stamina and, on doctor's orders, was required to lie down in the afternoons. He liked to rest in a room above the chapel where he could listen to the organ played in the hall below. At Eton, where he fagged for the future Marquess of Lansdowne,* he was solitary. Spectacles were not permitted at Eton, and Balfour, who was short-sighted, could not play cricket or other games with balls. Boys made fun of him, but, "if he was laughed at, he would join in the laugh, often shutting up his assailant by some witty repartee," recalled a schoolmaster.

At eighteen, Balfour entered Trinity College, Cambridge. He

* Who was to be Foreign Secretary in the Balfour Cabinet.

showed no interest in politics and avoided the Cambridge Union; instead, he attended concerts and recitals and developed a passion for Handel. He decorated his rooms with a collection of blue china, and here on Sunday evenings he served and presided over talk of books and philosophy. Some of his fellows considered him affected and nicknamed him "Pretty Fanny." Balfour did not mind; nor was he bothered that he took only a Second in Moral Science. He was being educated in another way outside Cambridge at Hatfield House in Hertfordshire, where Lord Salisbury was trying to assist his widowed sister to bring up her children. Balfour, only eighteen years younger than his uncle, was close enough in age to understand the ingredients of the older man's success without being overcome by awe. Salisbury fostered this understanding by always speaking to his nephew man-to-man rather than man-to-boy. A friendship, based on mutual respect as well as family affections, developed.

In 1872, Lady Blanche, debilitated by progressive heart disease, died at forty-seven. A few years earlier, Arthur had come of age and inherited his father's estate, estimated at four million pounds. In 1874, Salisbury proposed that Balfour enter Parliament and found him a safe seat in Hertfordshire. Balfour, still not much interested in politics, did not open his mouth during his first two and a half years in the House; when finally he did speak it was during the dinner hour, on the subject of Indian silver currency. "In these conditions," Balfour recalled, "I enjoyed to the fullest extent the advantages of speaking in a silent and friendly solitude." Two years later, he tried his hand at drafting legislation; his subject was a proposed reform of the Burial Law. "A very good bill," his uncle wrote to him, "but, if you bring it in, you will probably find yourself pretty well protected from the curse that attaches to those of whom all men speak well." In 1878, Salisbury, who had just become Foreign Secretary, took Balfour with him to the Congress of Berlin as his Parliamentary Private Secretary. The young man's principal memories were of banquets, balls, and parties, but he observed Bismarck, Disraeli, Salisbury, and Andrássy as they pressured Prince Gorchakov into giving up most of what Russia had won from Turkey. Bismarck, on learning Balfour's name, asked if he was related to a character named Balfour in one of Sir Walter Scott's novels. Balfour admitted that he was not and expressed surprise that the Chancellor knew Scott's novels. "Ah," said Bismarck, "when we were young, we all had to read Sir Walter."

A young man, handsome, charming, rich, and unmarried, had little difficulty making his way in London society. There was little he wanted that he could not have. Loving Handel, he paid for a performance of the full oratorio *Belshazzar* at the Albert Hall. Savoring philosophy, he wrote a book, *A Defence of Philosophic Doubt,* and published one thousand copies at his own expense. Balfour bloomed slowly in Parliament. In 1880, when he was thirty-two, an observer wrote: "The member for Hertford is one of the most interesting young men in the House . . . a pleasing specimen of the highest form of culture and good breeding which stands to the credit of Cambridge University. He is not without desire to say hard things of the adversary opposite, and sometimes yields to the temptation. But it is ever done with such sweet and gentle grace, and is smoothed over by such earnest protestations of innocent intention, that the adversary rather likes it than otherwise."

Balfour, a junior Conservative M.P., was a close friend of Mr. Gladstone, the Liberal leader. Balfour's London house, at No. 4 Carlton Gardens, was only a few doors from the house occupied by Mr. and Mrs. Gladstone when the Liberals were not in power. The new M.P. often met the older couple for dinner. Mrs. Gladstone referred to him as "that very pretty, quaint boy, tall and funny"; the Grand Old Man confessed to his wife, "I really delight in him, no more and no less." Balfour's inheritance, besides Whittingehame, included a Highland estate called Strathconan with a deer forest and a salmon stream. Balfour himself neither hunted nor fished, but in the autumn he kept the lodge filled with guests. Once, when Gladstone was Prime Minister, Mr. and Mrs. Gladstone came with their daughter Mary, who some thought was in love with Balfour. Gladstone enjoyed the visit and kept putting off his departure for a Cabinet meeting in London. Finally, with little time to spare, host and guest set off to walk the five miles of moor and heather between house and station. The station was some distance away when the train—"with ill-timed punctuality," Balfour wrote—appeared. Balfour charged ahead, splashing through pools, waving frantically to catch the eye of the engineer. He succeeded, and a few minutes later the Prime Minister arrived and clambered aboard. As the train left the station, Balfour reported, "I saw with intense thankfulness a pair of wet socks hanging out of the carriage window to dry. I had at least not inflicted on my distinguished guest the added horrors of a head cold."

Mary Gladstone's tenderness for young Arthur Balfour was typical of the interest women took in him throughout his life. His deepest attachment came at twenty-two when he fell in love, not with Gladstone's daughter but with Gladstone's twenty-year-old niece, May Lyttelton. Balfour's pursuit was slow and irresolute and, at one point, Miss Lyttelton gave up and agreed to marry someone else. Even after this suitor conveniently died, Balfour still hesitated. And then, after he finally had spoken to her, May Lyttelton died suddenly of typhoid. Stunned, dazed, Balfour wandered through the streets of London. Before the funeral, he sent an emerald ring which had been his mother's and which he had planned to give as an engagement ring, asking that it be placed in May's coffin. At the funeral service, Balfour broke down. His gloom persisted during a six-month trip around the world with her brother. "Comatose most of the time," reports Spencer Lyttelton's diary on the condition of his traveling companion.

May Lyttelton's death deprived Balfour of the woman he loved most, but there were other women. The most enduring of these discreet affairs was with Mary Wyndham, who became Lady Elcho and then, when her husband succeeded to an earldom, Countess of Wemyss. This relationship, which lasted over twelve years, occurred with the knowledge of Lord Elcho, nominally one of Balfour's friends. Balfour began the pursuit when Mary Wyndham was still unmarried, one of three beautiful Wyndham sisters who turned their father's country house at Clouds into a literary gathering place. Balfour never proposed to Mary Wyndham and Lord Elcho did, but the attraction reasserted itself. The affair was conducted in Victorian style: weekend house parties in labyrinthine mansions, golden afternoons on immaculate green lawns, tiny smiles during dinner, adjoining bedrooms. Balfour, never truly in love, did not flaunt his conquest, although at one point, Lord Elcho, fearing public exposure and ridicule, mentioned divorce.

The amused and approving attendants to this love affair were the "Souls," a close-knit group of friends who idolized Arthur Balfour and endeavored to share his tastes. Essentially young men and women who, in addition to noble blood, possessed wit and intellect, they had refused to restrict their talk to horses, clothing, and bridge. "Nearly all the young men in my circle were clever and became famous," was the way Margot Tennant, the most uninhibited of the Souls, described her male companions, most of whom were beginning their careers as junior ministers in Lord Salisbury's government. The women included Lady Elcho, Lady Desborough, Lady Horner, and the three spirited daughters of the Scottish millionaire landowner Sir Charles Tennant: Laura, who married Alfred Lyttelton; Charlotte, who became Lady Ribblesdale; and the irrepressible Margot. The Souls met regularly at No. 40 Grosvenor Square, Sir Charles' London house, and, on weekends, transplanted their activities to country mansions, where they took up tennis and bicycling and plunged into talk. Their conversation explored literature, art, music, science, and philosophy. Repartee was deft and rapier sharp. A newcomer who had wandered into the group one day announced, "The fact is, Mr. Balfour, all the faults of the age come from Christianity and journalism." Balfour replied with childlike innocence: "Christianity, of course . . . but why journalism?" Society was uncomfortable around the Souls and their serious talk—which is how the group got its name. "You all sit around and talk about each other's souls," grumbled Lord Charles Beresford, a famous hunter, naval officer, and close friend of the Prince of Wales. "I shall have to call you the 'Souls.' "

Balfour was the centerpiece around whom the Souls revolved. Slightly older than the others, he was admired by the men and adored by the women. "Oh dear," sighed Lady Battersea. "What a gulf between him and most men." Margot Tennant spoke of his "exquisite attention, intellectual tact, cool grace and lovely bend of the head [which] made him not only a flattering listener, but an irresistible companion." He was difficult "to know intimately because of his formidable detachment," she complained. "The most many of us could hope for was that he had a taste for us as one might have for clocks and furniture." One day, driven to exasperation by his cool self-containment, she burst out that he would not care if all his closest women friends—Lady Elcho, Lady Desborough, several others, and herself—were all to die. Balfour paused for a moment and then said softly, "I think I should mind if you *all* died on the same day."

Gradually, as marriage and other distractions came along, the Souls drifted apart, but Balfour remained the focus of the dinner parties he attended. Usually, his conversation was gentle and self-effacing, designed to bring out the best in everyone else. "After an evening in his company," wrote a friend, "one left with the feeling that one had been at the top of one's form and really had talked rather well." Occasionally Balfour snapped, as when he said of a colleague, "If he had a little more brains, he would be a half-wit." Once in a great while, he annihilated: after dinner in a country house, another guest told an off-color joke. The women had left the table, but two Eton boys remained with the gentlemen. Balfour's voice turned to ice. "Who did you say was the hero of this singularly disgusting tale?" he asked.

These flashes of anger, rarely revealed in society, stemmed from another side of Arthur Balfour, which the country and the House of Commons had only begun to observe when he was in his fortieth year. Under the charm lay hardness, even ruthlessness, which could be applied when the situation demanded. Friendliness could evaporate, friendship could be set aside, friends sacrificed in the name of what he considered a higher duty.

At the beginning of 1887, when Lord Salisbury's second government was settling in for what was to be a six-year term, the most pressing problem facing the Cabinet was Ireland. Gladstone's Home Rule Bill had been defeated and law and order on the island was breaking down. The source of the crisis was land tenure: when absentee land-lords attempted to collect rents from Irish tenants, many of whom had been on the land for generations, the impoverished tenants re-fused to pay or offered to pay only part of what they owed. All too frequently, the landlords called on the police to evict. When the police arrived, the countryside was often aroused against them and they became the targets of vitriol, stones, and pots of boiling water. Some landlords were implacable; Lord Clanricarde, an absentee millionaire who extracted every legal penny from his four thousand tenants in Galway, scoffed at threats. "If you think you can intimi-date me by shooting my agent, you are mistaken," he told his ten-ants.

When the Salisbury Cabinet was formed, Sir Michael Hicks-Beach, known as "Black Michael," had taken the Irish portfolio, but by March 1887, he was afflicted by painful eye trouble. He resigned and speculation about his replacement bubbled. The news that the Chief Secretaryship for Ireland, the most demanding, thankless, and personally dangerous post in the Cabinet, would go to the Prime Minister's nephew, Arthur Balfour, staggered the political world. In those days, although he was thirty-nine, Balfour still was known as a lightweight, delicate in health, a spineless charmer, "drifting with lazy grace in a metaphysical cloudland." An Irish newspaper de-scribed him as "a silk-skinned sybarite." Other papers called him Prince Charming, Pretty Fanny, and even Miss Balfour.

Balfour consulted his doctor to make sure his constitution could take the strain, then accepted. Before leaving for Dublin, he made out his will and sent it to a sister, observing that "accidents have occurred to a Chief Secretary for Ireland and (though I think it improbable) they may occur again." In Ireland, two detectives fol-lowed him everywhere. He consented to carry a loaded revolver, although he often forgot that it was in his pocket and dumped it out on the floor when he took off his coat. On arriving in Dublin he announced that Cromwell's Irish policy had "failed because he re-lied solely on repressive measures. This mistake I shall not imitate. I shall be as relentless as Cromwell in enforcing obedience to the law, but . . . as radical as any reformer in redressing grievances and especially in removing every cause of complaint in regard to the land." He proceeded ruthlessly to restore order. A police magistrate in Cork, hearing that a crowd of tenants meant to attack a small force of policemen, wired the threatened officers, "If necessary, do not hesitate to shoot them." Balfour publicly backed the order as being "best calculated in the long run to prevent injuries and loss of life." He elaborated on this view: "It is impossible to say, when the order to fire is once given, who will be the victims. That no doubt is a conclusive reason for deferring to the last dread necessity the act of firing. It has never been a reason, and if I have my way, will never be a reason for not firing when self-defence and the authority of the law actually require it." Those inciting tenants to refuse to pay rent were sent to jail, even though the inciters included Irish members of the House of Commons. When defaulting tenants began to fortify their houses, believing that the police lacked the equipment to force their way in, Balfour provided the constabulary with efficient battering rams which quickly ended the sieges, usually by destroying the houses. Accused of savagery in the House of Commons, he hurled back, "What I have done I have done, and if I had to do it again, I would do it again in the way I have done it." In Ireland, no one still called him Pretty Fanny; now he was known as Bloody Balfour.

As Chief Secretary, Balfour not only had to administer policy in Dublin, he had to defend it in Westminster. Every day during Question Period, he faced a ferocious, relentless attack from eighty Irishmen who screamed at him and shook their fists in his face. Balfour fought back alone, drawing on the versatile weaponry of his own personality. He met invective with serenity, rage with satire, passion with nonchalance. Sunk low on the Treasury Bench, his pince-nez drooping down his cheeks or dangling idly from his long fingers, he waited out the Celtic onslaught. When his moment came, his weapons flashed. "There are those," he said in one debate, "who talk as if Irishmen were justified in disobeying the law because the law comes to them in foreign garb. I see no reason why any local color should be given to the Ten Commandments." One day, an Irish M.P. let his voice rise to a shriek condemning Balfour, while the Chief Secretary sprawled languidly on the Treasury Bench, his face fixed in a mildly attentive smile. When the assailant, his face and clothing drenched with perspiration, finally finished, Balfour, affecting boredom, rose and disdainfully dismissed the whole performance by saying that his "jaded palate was no longer tickled by anything so lacking in flavor."

Balfour tried to redress grievances. Under his Chief Secretary-ship, the Unionist Party commenced an Irish land-reform program, based on voluntary sale and voluntary purchase, backed by a government fund of £33 million. The Chief Secretary proposed that a Roman Catholic college be built in Ireland and maintained with state funds. "My object is not to bribe the Irish people," Balfour said, replying to criticism. "My object is a simpler one—to afford Irish Roman Catholics some of that education which we in Scotland enjoy. . . . I desire to see them taught philology, philosophy, history, science, medicine. . . ." When he toured Ireland in 1891, at the end of his term, Balfour took no detectives and no revolver.

Balfour had gone to Ireland an expected failure and returned the strongest Conservative-Unionist Minister in the House of Commons. When the position of First Lord of the Treasury and Leader of the House fell vacant, Balfour succeeded by the unanimous choice of Unionist M.P.'s. He accepted, reported Lord Salisbury, "with rather a wry face." In his new post, Balfour modified his behavior. As Chief Secretary for Ireland, he had been a single gladiator, battling over issues personally felt. As Leader of the House, he was responsible for passage of the whole program of government legislation, including many items for which Balfour had little passion. All too often, the Leader displayed his apathy. Previous leaders had remained within the Houses of Parliament, if not actually on the Front Bench, throughout the hours the House was in session. Members were surprised, therefore, the first time Balfour returned to the Commons after dinner in evening dress; obviously he had left Westminster to dine in society. Leading the Opposition during Gladstone's last government, Balfour thrust and parried with the Grand Old Man, who was making his last fight for Irish Home Rule. Mr. Gladstone, now in alliance with the Irish Nationalists, was, said Balfour, "formerly as ready to blacken the Irish members' characters as he is now ready to blacken their boots." Yet Gladstone told Margot Tennant (who wrote to Balfour) that "he had never loved a young man so much as you and that your quickness had delighted him and your astonishing grip of difficult subjects." Balfour replied to Margot, "I am very glad you like the Old Man; for my part, I love him. . . ." Balfour's last visit to Gladstone's home at Hawarden came in 1896, two years after Gladstone had retired from politics and two years before his death. "I ran up from the station on my 'bike,' " Balfour wrote to Lady Elcho. "It shocked the Old Man. He thought it unbefitting a First Lord of the Treasury."

■ ■ ■

Balfour led the House of Commons for seven years, 1895–1902, in Lord Salisbury's third government. Because his uncle preferred to live in his own house in Arlington Street, Balfour as First Lord of the Treasury moved into No. 10 Downing Street. The relationship between uncle and nephew, built on family affection and mutual respect as well as an understanding of each other's views, was harmonious. Asked if there was a difference between his uncle and himself, Balfour replied, "There is a difference. My uncle is a Tory —and I am a liberal." Following the Prime Minister's lead, Balfour gave Joseph Chamberlain free rein in the Colonial Secretary's management of the growing crisis in South Africa. "My dear Uncle Robert," he wrote to Lord Salisbury in the spring of 1897. "You have, I suppose, by this time heard from Joe about his renewed proposal for an addition to our South African garrison. His favorite method of dealing with the South African sores is the free application of irritants. . . . [But] I cannot think it wise to allow him to goad on the Boers by speeches, and refuse him the means of repelling Boer attacks . . . it is a nice point whether the sending out of 3,000 men may prove to be a sedative or a stimulant." Balfour misjudged the outcome of Chamberlain's policy. "You ask me about South Africa," he wrote to Lady Elcho just before the fighting started. "I somehow think that war will be avoided." When war did come, Salisbury was already beginning to weaken physically. During the crescendo of military disasters that culminated in Black Week, Balfour attempted to buffer his aging uncle. "Every night I go down to the War Office between eleven and twelve at night, and walk up all the stairs . . . and there was never any news except defeats." It became apparent that Sir Redvers Buller would have to be replaced. Balfour went to see Lord Salisbury. Over the Prime Minister's initial objection, the decision was made to send out Lord Roberts.

In the new Cabinet formed after the Khaki Election, Lord Salisbury finally relinquished the post of Foreign Secretary in favor of Lord Lansdowne; but the number of the Prime Minister's relatives in the Cabinet still provoked the nickname "Hotel Cecil." In addition to Arthur Balfour, there was Arthur's brother, Gerald, who became President of the Board of Trade, and Lord Salisbury's son-in-law, Lord Selborne, who became First Lord of the Admiralty. Challenged on this point in the House of Commons, Balfour deftly replied that it was inconsistent to charge that "this unhappy and persecuted family" dominated the Cabinet and at the same time to say "that this Cabinet sits simply to register the decree of one too powerful Minister, and that too powerful Minister is not the Premier backed up by his family, but my Hon. friend the Secretary for the

Colonies. . . . These are two quite opposite views—not only oppo-site but inconsistent—both equally the creation of an uninformed imagination."

When Balfour became Prime Minister, he continued to be selective as to where he placed his energy and political support. On issues on which he could find no compelling advantage for one side over the other, Balfour took no strong stand. When it came to something which he regarded as essential to the defense or future of the realm —creation of a Committee of Imperial Defence, reequipping and redeploying of the Navy, furtherance of education, science, and technology—Balfour became tenacious. He would work day and night, applying the sharpest edges of his mind and tongue, worrying the issue, hounding colleagues, until he achieved his object. His po-litical philosophy was conservative. While not absolutely opposed to social reform—in 1902 he carried through the Education Act in the teeth of formidable opposition from both parties—he feared glib remedies. "It is better, perhaps, that our ship shall go nowhere than that it shall go wrong, that it should stand still than that it should run upon the rocks," he said. Like Lord Salisbury, Balfour had only a vague interest in party organization and campaigning. He could not simulate hearty backslapping or hand-shaking. Balfour's mien was politeness and distance; sometimes the politeness was so perfect and the distance so great that others were discomfited. King Edward VII complained that Mr. Balfour condescended to him.

Balfour's life was made up of opposites, each essential, each providing balance for the other: the serenity of philosophy and the thrust and parry of parliamentary debate, the clamor of Society and the quiet of solitude. "When I'm at work in politics, I long to be in literature and *vice versa*," he told John Morley. He made other men uneasy. His ability to see both sides of issues troubled political col-leagues and opponents, who sometimes charged him with cynicism. "Quite a good fellow," Balfour would say of an adversary. "Has a curious view. Not uninteresting." Once, as Chief Secretary for Ire-land, he was accused of planning to jail six Irish nationalist M.P.'s in the hope that they would die in prison. Balfour dismissed the charge as "ridiculous" and "grotesque" and continued, "I should like to say that I should profoundly regret the permanent absence of any of the distinguished men who lead the Parnellite Party. . . . If you sit op-posite a man every day, and you are engaged in fighting him, you cannot help getting a liking for him whether he deserves it or not." Temperamentally and philosophically, Balfour refused to see life in terms of absolutes. This was important, that was more important, neither was *really* important, he seemed to say. Margot Asquith decided that the secret of her friend's imperturbability was that he did not "really believe that the happiness of mankind depends on events going this way or that."

Behind this dispassionate approach to life lay a sober pessimism about human destiny. On the surface, Balfour was religious, a conventional Anglican who attended Sunday morning services and read Sunday evening prayers to his guests and servants sitting in chairs around his dining room. On another level, Balfour had learned from science that, set against the immensities of time, man was a puny, transitory creature. His view of man's ultimate fate was bleak: "Imperishable monuments and immortal deeds, death itself and love stronger than death, will be as though they had never been. The energies of our system will decay, the glory of the sun will be dimmed and the earth, tideless and inert, will no longer tolerate the race which has for a moment disturbed its solitude. Man will go down into the pit and all his thoughts will perish. The uneasy consciousness, which in this obscure corner has for a brief space broken the contented silence of the universe, will be at rest."

Arthur Balfour's retreat as Chief Secretary for Ireland, as leader of the House, and later as Prime Minister, was his childhood home at Whittingehame. The mistress of the house was his unmarried sister, Alice. Other residents, in the summer, included two brothers and their families with a total of three nephews and eight nieces. Balfour presided serenely over this establishment, playing hero to an eager bodyguard of giggling nieces. Each wanted to sit next to him at seashore picnics; all banded together to invade his sitting room, where "having cooked for him a sparrow rolled in clay according to a Red Indian recipe, [they] had presented it to him on a platter . . . in hopes of seeing him eat it."

Amid this activity, he preserved an attitude of calm. He breakfasted in bed and, until lunchtime, remained in his rooms dictating letters. Because he never read the newspapers, the family competed over lunch to tell him the news. In the afternoon, he sometimes played tennis on his own grass court (he played into his seventies) or rode his bicycle (the learning process took its toll, forcing the Leader to appear in the House at one point with an arm in a sling and a foot in a slipper). His obsession was golf. Every year, Balfour dedicated an entire month (usually August) to the then new sport. Tory aristocrats and country gentlemen snorted at their leader's middle-class recreations; men who killed birds and rode to the hounds had trouble understanding a man who wobbled about on bicycles and played "this damned Scottish croquet." But they recalled Balfour was a Cecil, and Lord Salisbury, the greatest Cecil of the day, shunned all sports and did not even go out of doors except to examine flora. Music surrounded Balfour. Two grand pianos filled his London parlor in Carlton Gardens, where the Handel Society often rehearsed. Even in Scotland, music followed dinner as a guest or an invited performer played Handel, Bach, or Beethoven on the concertina. Books were more important even than music. His library and sitting room overflowed from floor to ceiling with books. Between tea and dinner, and again for an hour or two before retiring, Balfour read. A new book on science might be propped on his bedroom mantelpiece so that he could read while dressing; his sister-in-law suspected him of "making a raft with his sponge" so that he could float a French novel on it when he bathed.

CHAPTER 19

Joseph Chamberlain
and Imperial Preference

◆

Joseph Chamberlain believed in imperialism. His design for the British Empire was of a worldwide family of nations, diverse, secure, prosperous—and closely tied to the United Kingdom. To promote this design he had taken the Colonial Office in 1895; to achieve it he had worked through the Boer War and the Khaki Election. By the summer of 1902, it still had not been accomplished. Britain's largest dominions, Canada and Australia, were secure and prosperous, but they were becoming independent. Their people still thought of themselves as subjects of the British Crown, but as Australian or Canadian subjects, not British subjects. "Colonies," wrote Robert Jacques Turgot, the eighteenth-century French economist and finance minister, "are like fruits which cling to the tree only until they ripen." Chamberlain concluded that the colonies needed incentives to remain attached to the Empire and that the incentives most likely to work were commercial. He therefore proposed building a tariff wall around the British Empire. All competing produce and goods from foreign states bound for any part of the Empire would be taxed once they crossed the tariff wall. This would benefit farmers and manufacturers throughout the Empire and bind them more closely to the mother country. The Colonial Secretary further anticipated that customs duties levied on foreign goods entering the United Kingdom would provide government revenues to pay for the social reforms he advocated. Chamberlain named his plan "Imperial Preference."

Chamberlain thought the country was ready for his proposal: under an imperialist banner, the nation had won the South African war; on an imperialist platform, the Unionist Party had won the Khaki Election. Imperial Preference, he believed, would ride the same tide of Imperial feeling. Other factors seemed favorable. Lord Salisbury, always dubious of Chamberlain and his schemes, had stepped down and been replaced by Arthur Balfour. In August 1902, the Fourth Colonial Conference had met in London and, although it rejected Chamberlain's suggestion that a Council of the Empire be formed, it passed a resolution favoring Imperial Preference. The British government was respectfully urged to grant preferential treatment to agricultural products and manufacturers of the colonies, "either by exemption from or reduction of duties now or hereafter imposed." In fact, Great Britain's historic adhesion to free trade had already been broken. In the 1902 budget, Conservative Chancellor Sir Michael Hicks-Beach had asked for and been given a small (one shilling per ton) duty on foreign corn* imported into the United Kingdom. Its purpose was to raise revenue to pay for the Boer War, but Chamberlain saw its acceptance by the Cabinet and the House of Commons as a starting point from which he could advance. If the shilling duty were kept on foreign corn, while corn grown in the Empire was exempted, it would be the beginning of Imperial Preference.

Chamberlain's idea found immediate favor with a faction of the Unionist Party: protection for British industry had long been a demand of the businessmen of the Conservative Party. But free trade remained an article of faith of many Tories and all Liberals. Indeed, Britain's attachment to free trade had been unchallenged by any major political figure since Peel's repeal of the Corn Laws in 1848. Hicks-Beach's small duty on corn was explained and accepted as a war tax only, to be lifted as soon as the end of the war made extra revenues unnecessary. To many in Parliament and the country, use of this temporary tariff as the first step in erecting a permanent tariff wall was a breach of promise and of Britain's tradition of free trade. In launching his crusade for Imperial Preference, therefore, Joseph Chamberlain was challenging history, as well as upsetting party alignments. Before the battle was over, he would split the Unionist

---

* "Corn," to Britons, is the grain Americans call wheat.

Party over free trade as dramatically as, twenty years earlier, he had split the Liberal Party over Home Rule.

Imperial Preference was not the only matter on Joseph Chamberlain's mind in the summer of 1902. "Joe's war" had finally ended in May, and the Colonial Secretary was planning a visit to South Africa to investigate personally the problems of reintegrating the Boer republics into the Empire. While there, he also hoped to persuade the wealthy Transvaal Uitlanders to contribute £30 million towards the cost of the war. He was to be away for four months, leaving England in November, staying through the South African summer, and returning home in March. Before leaving, he wanted the Cabinet to confront the issue of Imperial Preference, at least to the extent of deciding to retain the corn duty imposed by Hicks-Beach. The Cabinet met on October 21 and discussed the corn duty, but Chamberlain's proposal that it be the first step towards introducing the broader program of Imperial Preference was vigorously opposed by the new Chancellor of the Exchequer, David Ritchie. Balfour's report to the King of the Cabinet's deliberation was drafted in careful language. "It was suggested," the Prime Minister wrote, "that, while retaining the shilling duty on corn as regards foreign importation, our Colonies should be allowed to import it free. There is a very great deal to be said in favor of this proposal. But it raises very big questions indeed. . . . On the whole, Mr. Balfour leans towards it, but it behooves us to walk warily. . . ."

The Cabinet met again on November 19, a week before Chamberlain was to sail. Ritchie repeated his protest and handed his colleagues a confidential memorandum opposing Chamberlain's design: "Let us first be quite clear what preferential treatment involves. It involves the imposition of a charge on the taxpayers of the United Kingdom in order to benefit our kith and kin beyond the sea. Don't let us be under any delusion about that. . . ." Balfour, presiding, remained above the battle. The other ministers, turning their heads first to Chamberlain, then to Ritchie, kept silent. Chamberlain left the meeting convinced that he had the majority and that, in time, he might win over even Mr. Ritchie. In any case, it was agreed that, while he was away, the issue would be suspended and a final decision made only before the budget was presented to the Commons the following spring. The Colonial Secretary's impression of victory in principle is borne out by the Prime Minister's report that night to the King: "The Cabinet finally resolved that . . . they would maintain the corn tax but that a preferential remission of it would be made in favor of the British Empire."

During the four months the Colonial Secretary was away, Ritchie worked feverishly to reverse the Cabinet decision and do away with the shilling corn tax in the new budget. Armed with Treasury statistics, he pressed his Cabinet colleagues to reconsider their views. Early in March, before Chamberlain's return to England, the Chancellor asked Balfour to schedule a meeting and put the budget before the Cabinet. The Prime Minister, distressed to find his Chancellor and his Colonial Secretary still on a collision course, refused Ritchie's request and through Chamberlain's son, Austen, warned the Colonial Secretary, then aboard a ship approaching Madeira. Chamberlain considered his South African journey a success. He had toured the country, visiting Durban, Pretoria, Johannesburg, and Cape Town, making speeches and interviewing leaders of all parties; his only setback had been his failure to collect £30 million from the Uitlanders. Although disturbed by the message he received in Madeira, he arrived in Southampton on March 14, 1903, determined to press the Cabinet for maintenance of the corn tax as a first step to Imperial Preference.

At the Cabinet meeting three days later, on March 17, Ritchie demanded that the corn tax be abolished. Forewarned, Chamberlain was not surprised. What did surprise him was discovering that a majority of the Cabinet now seemed to favor the Chancellor. Balfour again did not take sides. He did not overrule Ritchie because he did not wish his new Chancellor to resign on the eve of his first budget presentation. Playing for time, the Prime Minister concentrated on mollifying Chamberlain, promising that if Ritchie were allowed to have his way with the budget in the Cabinet, the summer would be used to investigate and further analyze the matter. Chamberlain bowed and admitted that "there was no time to fight the question out in the Cabinet before the Budget had to be introduced." The budget Ritchie presented to the House on April 23 was a pure free-trade budget, and the Chancellor defended it with a full-blooded free-trade, free-food argument: "Corn is in a greater degree a necessity of life than any other article . . . it is the food of our people. . . ."

While Ritchie spoke, Chamberlain sat quietly. He maintained his silence for another three weeks. Then, on May 15 at Birmingham Town Hall, before his speech, he turned to the chief organizer and said grimly, "You can burn your leaflets. We are going to talk about something else." He began by apologizing that while doing the Empire's business in South Africa his "party weapons had become a little rusty." "In the calm which is induced by the solitude of the illimitable veldt," he had found himself looking beyond the petty issues of the day. He asked his audience to contemplate the glorious future of the British Empire: today, 40 million subjects in the United Kingdom; overseas, 10 million. One day, these 10 million would be 40 million. Did his audience wish these millions to continue in "close, intimate, affectionate" bond with the mother country or to break away and become independent nations? In preventing the disintegration of the Empire, "the question of trade and commerce is of the greatest importance." To achieve the promised glory of the Empire, Great Britain must favor its colonies by a policy of Imperial Preference. This question, he announced, must be an issue at the next General Election.

Balfour and Cabinet were stunned. On the very day that Chamberlain spoke in Birmingham, the Prime Minister was assuring a protectionist delegation in London that it was not the proper time to introduce Imperial Preference. Balfour recovered quickly enough to tell the press that Chamberlain's address was "a great speech by a great man." On May 28, Chamberlain repeated his challenge in the House of Commons. He was roundly cheered by many Unionist backbenchers and hooted by the Liberals while his colleagues on the Government Front Bench sat silent. Outside the Commons, other leaders of the Unionist Party, including the Duke of Devonshire, Lord President of the Council, who eighteen years before had joined Chamberlain in deserting the Liberal Party over Home Rule, now sided against the Colonial Secretary. The lines between free trade and protectionism were being drawn. "From that point on until the General Election of 1906," said H. H. Asquith, "it became the dominating issue of British politics."

The Prime Minister, who stood in the middle, pleaded for calm. "Chamberlain's views . . . commit no one but himself. They certainly do not commit me," he wrote to the Duke of Devonshire on June 4. He suggested to his Cabinet colleagues that "for the present it shall be agreed that the question is an open one and that no one stands committed by any statement but their own." His first speech to the Commons on the subject, delivered on June 10, followed this noncommittal path. He announced that he had not made up his own mind and therefore refused to take sides between free trade and Imperial Preference. To the House's astonishment, Balfour boldly ascribed his indecision—clearly an effort to keep both wings of his party in harness by criticizing neither—to moral rectitude and political wisdom: "I should consider that I was ill-performing my duty—I will not say to my Party but to the House and to the country—if I were to profess a settled conviction where no settled conviction exists." The Liberals hooted. Sir Henry Campbell-Bannerman, the Liberal leader, declared that it was intolerable that a British Prime Minister be without settled convictions on a fundamental issue of British politics. Sir Wilfred Lawson, a Liberal M.P., promptly scribbled a verse which circulated widely:

> *I'm not for Free Trade, and I'm not for Protection*
> *I approve of them both, and to both have objection*
> *In going through life I continually find*
> *It's a terrible business to make up one's mind*
> *So in spite of all comments, reproach and predictions*
> *I firmly adhere to unsettled convictions.*

For the Liberal Party, deeply divided by the Boer War, Chamberlain's proposal provided a simple, telling issue: the Unionists stood for a tax on food. Even better, from the Liberal standpoint, the electorate soon would be treated to the sight of free-trade Unionists and protectionist Unionists attacking each other. "This reckless, criminal escapade of Joe's is the great event of our time," Campbell-Bannerman chortled, adding that "to dispute Free Trade . . . is like disputing the Law of Gravitation. All the old war horses about me are snorting with excitement. We are in for a great time." Asquith instantly understood the implications: "On the morning of May 16, 1903, my husband came into my bedroom at 20 Cavendish Square with *The Times* in his hand," Margot Asquith recalled. " 'Wonderful news today,' he said, 'and it is only a question of time when we shall sweep the country.' Sitting upon my bed, he showed me . . . the report of a speech made at Birmingham the night before by Mr. Chamberlain." Many Unionists also glimpsed what was to come. Sir Michael Hicks-Beach, now a backbencher, warned, "Tariff Reform has united the Party opposite—divided for the last eight years—into a happy family. If persisted in, it will destroy the Unionist Party as an instrument for good."

Balfour's delaying tactic had been to persuade the Commons to suspend formal debate on Imperial Preference until the Board of Trade ascertained the economic facts, compiled statistics, and presented analyses and recommendations. Privately, he begged his colleagues not to speak on the subject until the report was in. The Prime Minister could control the House, but not Unionists outside the House. In the House of Lords, Lord Goschen, the former First Lord, denounced Imperial Preference and praised free trade. On July 1, fifty-four free-trade Unionist M.P.'s, calling themselves the

Unionist Free Food League, gathered to listen to fiery speeches by Lord Hugh Cecil—Lord Salisbury's son—and twenty-eight-year-old Winston Churchill, who had won his seat in the Khaki Election three years before. Initially, Balfour's delaying tactics succeeded. The Board of Trade assembled statistics in leisurely fashion and forwarded them to the Cabinet. Cabinet discussions drifted indecisively into August. On August 13, Parliament rose for the summer recess.

By the beginning of autumn, a reckoning could no longer be postponed. On September 9, Chamberlain sent a dramatic letter to the Prime Minister declaring that he wished to resign from the government and go out, a free man, to stump the country on behalf of Imperial Preference. Balfour, golfing at Whittingehame during the parliamentary recess, did not reply in writing. Instead, he summoned the Cabinet to meet on Monday, September 14. An hour before the Cabinet met, Balfour and Chamberlain met at a private flat. The Colonial Secretary firmly repeated his argument: the Cabinet as constituted, with Ritchie and other free-traders adamantly opposed, would not accept Imperial Preference. He agreed with the Prime Minister that public opinion was not yet ready for legislation involving a tax on food. Much convincing would first have to be done, and this he was prepared, even eager, to do. Balfour accepted Chamberlain's reasoning but still did not accept his resignation.

The Cabinet meeting lasted three hours. Confronting his Ministers, the languid and amiable Balfour displayed why, as Irish Secretary, he had been called "Bloody Balfour." He did not reveal his discussion with the Colonial Secretary. He said that he was determined to put an end to dissension, at least within his own Cabinet. He declared that some form of tariff was to be the government's policy and that any ministers opposed could not remain in the Cabinet. Ritchie and another free-trader promptly resigned. In fact, the astonished Duke of Devonshire wrote to a friend, "Ritchie and . . . [the other free-trader] did not really resign but were told they must go." To another friend, he added, "I never heard anything more summary and decisive than the dismissal of the two Ministers." The following day—the second of the Cabinet meeting—two more ministers, one of them the Duke himself, resigned. Only when they were gone, on September 16, did the Prime Minister accept Mr. Chamberlain's resignation as he had planned all along to do. The Duke, seeing that Chamberlain was leaving, withdrew his own resignation, responding as Balfour had calculated. That same day, September 16, the Prime Minister published a short pamphlet, entitled "Notes on Insular Free Trade," in which he analyzed England's dangerously isolated position as a free-trade island surrounded by a protectionist sea. Devonshire, feeling tricked, resigned a second time on October 6. With the departure of Chamberlain on one extreme and four free-traders on the other, Balfour had purged his Cabinet and hoped to govern amidst diminished rancor.

The only loss he regretted was that of the Duke. "The Duke, whose mental processes were not rapid," wrote a Liberal journalist, "had apparently been mystified by the dialectic of Mr. Balfour's pamphlet and dazed by the swiftness and subtlety of the transactions that followed. A fortnight later, he awoke with a crash." Balfour's own impression was similar: "The Duke never read it [Balfour's pamphlet], you know. I remember hearing he had confessed to somebody that he tried, but couldn't understand it. Dear Devonshire! Of course he hadn't. He told me once he had been content to leave his financial conscience in the hands of Mr. Gladstone. But it was all a muddle. He got himself into such a position that he had to behave badly to somebody—and there it was! But it never made the slightest difference to my love for him."

Balfour's "purging" of Chamberlain was less brutal than his dismissal of Ritchie and the free-traders, because Chamberlain had suggested his own resignation. The departure was even more friendly because, in parting, Balfour and Chamberlain had struck a bargain. The Prime Minister did not wish to break completely with the former Colonial Secretary, whose popularity he knew to be greater than his own. A bond would be maintained in the person of Chamberlain's eldest son, Austen, who was already in the Cabinet as Postmaster-General. Austen, then forty, would be offered Ritchie's post of Chancellor of the Exchequer, nominally the second most powerful office in the Cabinet and a traditional springboard to the Premiership. Balfour urged Chamberlain to persuade Austen to accept. Chamberlain did and Austen accepted.

There was more to the bargain. Chamberlain was not leaving the Cabinet simply to go home to his orchids or to hasten the advancement of his son. Despite differences, there was an area of agreement on fiscal reform between Balfour and Chamberlain and both men seized it. Balfour agreed that greater imperial unity was desirable and that Imperial Preference might be a way to achieve it. As party leader, however, he feared the domestic political cost if the public perceived the imposition of tariffs as a tax on food. Chamberlain agreed with Balfour that the sudden and sweeping nature of his proposal had alarmed the country and that before the enactment of legislation (and certainly before the public was asked to choose in the next election), a great deal more educating and persuading had to be done. This he was prepared to do himself. Balfour and Chamberlain, accordingly, agreed that the former Colonial Secretary, now a free man, would stump the country, propagandizing on behalf of Imperial Preference. When public opinion was swayed, the Prime Minister would lead the party onto this electorally safe new ground. Balfour would simultaneously follow with a minimum program which rejected free trade, but proposed only selective retaliatory tariffs, avoiding anything that smacked of a tax on food.

In early October, Chamberlain set out as a free-lance missionary of Imperial Preference, tariff reform, and protection. He was still the most popular politician in the country and he expected success preaching this new gospel. He began with a speech in Glasgow on October 6, 1903, in which he revealed his program: a two-shilling-per-ton duty on foreign wheat and flour, 5 percent tariffs on foreign meat and dairy products, and a 10 percent duty on foreign manufactured goods. Agricultural imports and manufactured goods from the British Empire would be exempted. He went from Newcastle to Cardiff, to Liverpool, Newport, and Leeds, concluding in the London Guildhall on January 18, 1904. Everywhere, he displayed an energy and zeal astonishing for a man of seventy. He had the support of most of the younger Unionist M.P.'s and of the entire Conservative press. As his progress continued, however, his message began to change. He had begun by demanding Imperial Preference solely for the sake of Imperial unity; with the passage of time his theme evolved increasingly into the protection of British agricultural products and British manufactured goods. His most vociferous backers were businessmen like himself who wanted protection for their own products against foreign competition. Chamberlain's speeches now rang with appeals to save this or that "dying British industry."

While Chamberlain preached, Balfour did his best to hold the Unionist free-traders on the leash. The Liberal Party was under no constraint. Asquith, the party's finest debater, set out in pursuit of Chamberlain and followed him around the country, speaking in the same town where Chamberlain had spoken, two or three evenings after the former Colonial Secretary had departed. Asquith's essential theme was that Chamberlain's tariffs would increase the price of food. Asquith also observed that the former screw manufacturer was a businessman who knew little of economics and whose arguments sometimes rested on flawed intellectual or even factual foundations. When he blundered, Asquith pounced and held up the error for public scrutiny and ridicule. After a few weeks of this relentless shadowing, Chamberlain angrily lashed back. At Cardiff, he dismissed Asquith as a mere lawyer with no business experience. Asquith tartly replied that he would "gladly defer to a businessman who understood and applied the rules of arithmetic." During the autumn, Chamberlain's campaign and Asquith's countercampaign, heavily reported in all the national newspapers, developed into a kind of rhetorical *mano a mano,* scrutinized, analyzed, and relished by the entire country.

Balfour—true to his bargain with Chamberlain—launched his own proposals for milder tariffs. Addressing a Unionist association at Sheffield on September 30, he sought a middle ground between free-trade absolutism and Chamberlain's Imperial Preference tariff on imported food. Abandoning the high-flown goal of Imperial unity, he asked only for weapons to combat the protectionist policies of other nations. He proposed that the government be empowered to apply selective tariffs against specific products from specific foreign countries. Such tariffs could be used as negotiating chips with foreign powers, or, if negotiating failed, to retaliate until the foreign powers removed their tariffs. Once this happened, Balfour explained, British tariffs could be removed and free trade would be reestablished. On its own, the Prime Minister's scheme might have been logical, but in the political atmosphere in which it was launched, it was received with contempt by free-traders and protectionists alike. Everyone on both sides understood that Balfour's real purpose was not a new system of selective tariffs, but a compromise —any compromise—that would hold his party together.

Rejection of Balfour's program did not mean rejection of Balfour. He was still Prime Minister and both Unionist free-traders and Unionist protectionists believed that this created an advantage for them. The Chamberlainites cited his selective tariffs as evidence that he was at heart a protectionist simply holding the government in line while Joe converted the country. The Unionist free-traders believed that Balfour was forced to indulge Chamberlain for the sake of party unity, but would in time declare himself, in party tradition, a pure free-trader. Both sides were willing for him to continue until— as seemed to each certain—he arrived in their camp. Balfour, clearly understanding that the moment he chose sides his government would collapse, found precarious safety by encouraging everyone to believe of him whatever suited them.

By the spring of 1904, Chamberlain sensed that something was wrong. His agreement with Balfour had been that he would lead and that once the path was cleared, Balfour, following behind, would catch up and embrace Imperial Preference. What Chamberlain had not realized was that, for Balfour, there was an escape clause: if

Chamberlain did *not* clear the path, there would be no catching up and no embrace. In fact, Arthur Balfour was not passionately interested in either Imperial Preference or free trade. He could watch Joseph Chamberlain proclaiming the glories of an imperial *Zollverein* and then observe his cousin, Lord Hugh Cecil, an ardent Tory, zealously defending the great legacy of free trade, and be moved by neither. Balfour did not much care which policy was adopted as long as the party survived. He waited to see how successfully Chamberlain was converting the country to protectionism. As the months dragged on, it became apparent that the former Colonial Secretary was in difficulty. At that point, Chamberlain, looking over his shoulder for Balfour's support, did not find the Prime Minister. Chamberlain's principal failure in his tariff-reform campaign lay not in his embarrassment by the gadfly stings of Asquith, or even in his inability to sweep the country with a slogan as he had in the Khaki Election, but in his failure to convince the Prime Minister that what he was doing was right and important. Balfour had the power to introduce—or to refuse to introduce—legislation. He had given Chamberlain a chance to convince the country; the country remained unconvinced. He had promised to follow and embrace once the path was cleared. The path had not been cleared. For Balfour, the important thing now was to save the party.

The task seemed hopeless. Mr. Balfour's own policy, the official policy of retaliation, had, by the beginning of 1904, become negligible. Except for the Prime Minister himself, no one propounded it or defended it or regarded it as anything other than a temporary shelter for a politician in distress. The Prime Minister, said an observer, was "a Free Trader who sympathized with Protection, a well-wisher of food taxes who was also their official opponent." By spring, Chamberlain's campaign and Balfour's equivocation had spread confusion and dismay through the party rank and file. In thirty-seven House of Commons by-elections held in 1904 and 1905, the Unionists lost twenty-eight seats and won only nine. Balfour's majority, which had been 134 when Lord Salisbury and Joseph Chamberlain won the Khaki Election in 1900, slid on some votes to only fifty. One celebrated party member was lost on May 31, 1904, when Winston Churchill, amid cries from the Unionist benches of "Blenheim Rat" and "Blackleg Blueblood," crossed the aisle and joined the Liberals. Churchill was an absolute free-trader as his father, Lord Randolph Churchill, had been, as Lord Salisbury had been, and as Churchill believed he had heard Arthur Balfour promise the Carlton Club he was when Balfour succeeded his uncle as Prime Minister. Now, as Churchill saw it, Chamberlain, a turncoat former

Liberal, was proposing protectionism and Balfour, guardian of Tory traditions, was, if not wholly supporting him, disgracefully waffling. Churchill fumed: "Some of us were born in the Tory Party and we are not going to let any aliens turn us out." His attacks on the Prime Minister in the House became violent: "To keep in office for a few weeks and months there is no principle which the Government is not prepared to abandon, and no quantity of dust and filth they are not prepared to eat," he said. "The dignity of a Prime Minister, like a lady's virtue, is not susceptible to partial diminution." Balfour, normally suavely immune to barbs hurled at him in the House of Commons, was stung by Churchill's malice. He rose to put the enfant terrible in his place: "It is not, on the whole, desirable to come down to this House with invective which is both prepared and violent. The House will tolerate, and very rightly tolerate, almost anything within the rule of order which evidently springs from genuine indignation aroused by the collision of debate. But to come down with these prepared phrases is not usually successful, and at all events, I do not think it was very successful on the present occasion. If there is preparation there should be more finish and if there is so much violence there should certainly be more veracity of feeling."

Somehow, Balfour survived. For sheer political nimbleness, few parliamentary achievements can match his performance in maintaining his government for over two years after Chamberlain's resignation. He endured the steady erosion of strength in by-elections, the constant bitter warfare in the House of Commons, and the rising chorus of press predictions that the government could not outlive each coming month. What struck everyone—delighting some, enraging others—was how much Balfour enjoyed it. There was no challenge in leading a government with a huge majority in which a prime minister's every whim glided submissively into law. Living on borrowed time, Balfour mobilized all his talents and maneuvered his government through session after session. Nevertheless, by artificially prolonging the Unionist government, Arthur Balfour ensured that when the fall came, it would be precipitous and catastrophic.*

---

* The campaign for Imperial Preference was Joseph Chamberlain's last political battle. On June 1, 1905, he suffered the first of a series of strokes which affected his ability to speak and largely confined him to a wheelchair. Balfour, visiting him in 1910, found him "very unintelligible." Chamberlain died on July 6, 1914, three weeks before the beginning of the Great War.

CHAPTER 20

Lord Lansdowne
and the
Anglo-French Entente

◆

When Lord Salisbury departed the Foreign Office in 1900, he was succeeded by a man whom an admiring fellow peer described as "possibly the greatest gentleman of his day." What set the Marquess of Lansdowne apart was not his ancient title, his enormous estates, or his great wealth, but his elegance, his air of serenity, and his unwillingness to cause other gentlemen distress. A small man with a narrow head and a bushy mustache, Lord Lansdowne was always immaculately tailored, whether wearing a gray frock coat and top hat in the House of Lords, or a tweed suit and panama hat when fishing for salmon. Membership in the aristocracy, Lansdowne believed, entailed unshirkable obligations. He himself served England, not from ambition or for pleasure, but as an obvious duty. Equally, the nation had an obligation to permit him to serve. "The longer I live," he wrote to his sister, "the more firmly do I believe in blood and breeding." Lord Lansdowne's most bitter battle, fought after he left the Foreign Office, was his attempt to prevent a Liberal government from nullifying the ancient privileges of the House of Lords.

On his father's side, Henry Charles Keith Petty-Fitzmaurice, Fifth Marquess of Lansdowne, was descended from the Normans. The First Marquess had been Prime Minister under George III; the

Third Marquess turned down the Premiership and a dukedom under George IV. In County Kerry, Ireland, the family owned 120,000 acres. Lansdowne House in Berkeley Square, London, was a majestic private palace in whose galleries hung two hundred paintings including Rembrandts, Reynoldses, Gainsboroughs, Hogarths, and Romneys. From his mother, Lansdowne acquired a more exotic strain: his mother's father was General Count de Flahaut de la Billarderie, an illegitimate son of Talleyrand and an aide to the Emperor Napoleon at the Battle of Borodino.

As a boy, Lansdowne, then Viscount Clanwilliam (the nickname "Clan" stuck all his life), served as Arthur Balfour's fag at Eton. At Balliol, he became an intimate friend of young Lord Rosebery. He was twenty-one in 1866 when his father died and he succeeded to both the title and the estate. The family was Liberal and, almost by hereditary right, the young Marquess entered Gladstone's government in 1872. In 1883, Lansdowne, thirty-eight, was sent as Governor General to Canada, where he spent five years. His tenure was marked by a record as a salmon fisherman: in four summers, he and his friends, casting with flies, managed to pull 1,245 fish from Canadian rivers. The average salmon weighed twenty-four pounds.

In 1885, while Lansdowne was in Canada, Lord Salisbury replaced Gladstone in office. Gladstone's position on Home Rule and Lansdowne's situation as a great Irish landowner had already brought the Marquess around to thinking of himself as a Conservative. Salisbury was willing to use whatever bait was required to reel in this catch; he offered the War Office, the Colonial Office, and the Viceroyalty of India. Lansdowne accepted India. Lansdowne's service in New Delhi was as unremarkable as had been his service in Ottawa. (In India, he made himself unpopular by raising the age of consent for girls from ten to twelve.) Nevertheless, when he returned from New Delhi, the Queen offered him the Garter and a dukedom. Lansdowne accepted the first and declined the second. The government offered the embassy in St. Petersburg; Lansdowne, having spent ten years on the Imperial frontiers, preferred to remain in England. He accepted the War Office, never imagining that he would be called upon to deal with a war. When the Boer War began, Lansdowne's work was impeded by his inability to put aside his gentlemanliness. Forced to remove Sir Redvers Buller from command in South Africa, he wrote to Buller, "[Lord] Roberts' appointment must, I fear, have been very distasteful to you. . . . It gave me pain to do what I knew would be very disagreeable to you." To the Queen, of his own performance as Secretary of State for War,

Lansdowne wrote "he must often have seemed to your Majesty to fall short of expectations."

Despite Lansdowne's perception of himself as a failure, Lord Salisbury thought highly of him and judged that a man with foreign blood and overseas experience would do well at the Foreign Office. Lansdowne was to justify Lord Salisbury's confidence although his diplomacy overturned the basic policy which Salisbury had practiced. Lansdowne's first significant achievement was to bring a formal end to Splendid Isolation.

A military alliance between England and Japan, two island nations separated by eight thousand miles, seemed an unusual diplomatic arrangement. But Britain needed an ally in the Far East to thwart Russian expansionism; when Bülow and Holstein turned Chamberlain down, Britain looked elsewhere. And Japan, alarmed by Russia's occupation of Manchuria and advance to the Yellow Sea, was unwilling to tolerate Russian penetration of the Korean peninsula, "a dagger" pointed at the Japanese home islands. In April 1901, Baron Tadasu Hayashi, the Japanese Ambassador in London, told Lord Lansdowne that his country "would certainly fight to prevent" Russian absorption of Korea. A basis for negotiations existed.

Talks between Lord Lansdowne and Baron Hayashi began in London in the spring of 1901 and continued through the summer and autumn. Salisbury, still Prime Minister, had little enthusiasm for any alliance; Chamberlain, gratified that Lansdowne recognized the need for an alliance and himself busy with South Africa, supported the Foreign Secretary but stayed out of his way. As the talks progressed, Lansdowne became aware that Japanese diplomacy was being conducted on two tracks. While he was negotiating an anti-Russian treaty in London with Baron Hayashi, Marquis Hirobumi Ito, a more senior Japanese diplomat, was in St. Petersburg negotiating an alternative treaty with the Russians. The Japanese explained that if nothing came of the talks with England, Japan would have to deal with Russia. One way or another, Russia must be kept out of Korea.

The London talks were successful. On January 30, 1902, Great Britain and Japan signed a military alliance for protection of their mutual interests in the Far East. The integrity of Korea was guaranteed. The treaty was to run for five years. If either power was attacked by only one power, the ally would maintain a benevolent neutrality. But if one of the allies was attacked by two countries, the other ally would go to war in support. On the surface, the treaty seemed to favor Japan: it isolated Russia in the Far East (France had no significant interests or military forces in northeast Asia; Germany would not side with Russia against England in an Asian war). Japanese military and naval officers began to plan the blow which fell on Port Arthur in 1904. But there were advantages for England. Should she find herself at war with France and Russia in Europe, Japan could be counted upon to distract the Tsar by attacking him from the rear. Most important, Britain now had powerful support in her effort to check Russian expansionism in Asia. The assistance which Chamberlain had sought from the Kaiser to protect British interests and markets in China had now been promised to Lansdowne by the Mikado.

German reaction to the new alliance was favorable. As the arrangement clearly was aimed at Russia, the Wilhelmstrasse understood that Russia now would encounter more resistance to her advance into the Far East; this, in turn, would relieve Russian pressure on Germany's eastern frontier. The Germans also were cheered by the anti-Russian character of the agreement, noting that it would widen the gulf between Great Britain and the Dual Alliance, making an understanding between Britain and France less likely. "I congratulate you on the conclusion of the new alliance, which we all look upon as a guarantee of peace in the East," the Kaiser wrote to King Edward on February 26, 1902. When he saw Sir Frank Lascelles at a garden party in Berlin, William said of the new treaty, "At last the noodles seem to have had a lucid interval."

French reaction to the Anglo-Japanese Treaty was mixed. Foreign Minister Théophile Delcassé understood that the alliance was aimed at France's Russian ally and therefore, indirectly, also at France. There was danger that if war broke out between the principals—Japan and Russia—the seconds—Britain and France—might have to fight each other. But there was an element in the new treaty which gave Delcassé hope. Joseph Chamberlain's policy had at last borne fruit; Great Britain was abandoning Splendid Isolation. Although Great Britain's liability was limited and the possibility of European implication seemed small, and although Lord Salisbury was still Prime Minister, the island nation had formally bound itself to a military alliance with a foreign power. In defending the new treaty in the House of Lords, Lord Lansdowne vigorously argued against the longstanding policy of his own Prime Minister:

"I do not think that anyone can have watched the recent course of events . . . without realizing that many of the arguments which a generation ago might have been adduced in support of a policy of isolation have ceased to be entitled to the same consideration now.

What do we see on all sides? We observe a tendency to ever-increasing naval and military armaments involving ever-increasing burdens upon the people. . . . There is this also—that in these days, war breaks out with a suddenness which was unknown in former days when nations were not, as they are now, armed to the teeth. When we consider these features of the international situation, we must surely feel that a country would indeed be endowed with an extraordinary amount of self-sufficiency . . . to say . . . that all foreign alliance were to be avoided. . . . Therefore, I would entreat you . . . to look at the matter strictly on its merits and not to allow your judgement to be swayed by musty formulae and old-fashioned superstitions as to the desireability of pursuing a policy of isolation for this country. . . . *Prima facie,* if there be no countervailing objections, the country which has the good fortune to possess allies is more to be envied than the country which is without them."

While an Anglo-German alliance was being discussed and an Anglo-Japanese alliance concluded, German diplomacy consistently failed to understand the basis and direction of British policy. Holstein and Bülow believed that Germany held the power of decision—that Germany had only to wait and, in time, England would come on German terms. In Holstein's view, the possibility of a diplomatic understanding between England and France was too remote to warrant serious concern at the Wilhelmstrasse. When Eckardstein warned that Chamberlain had threatened to look elsewhere if Germany refused an alliance with England, Holstein dismissed Eckardstein as "naive."

Holstein's opinion had firm historical backing. Antagonism between England and France went back to the Middle Ages; England's longest wars had been fought against the French. Through the century just ended, the Royal Navy had prepared to fight the fleet of a single enemy: France. In 1898, even as Chamberlain's plan for a German alliance was being launched, England and France had almost gone to war over Fashoda. Now, as the two nations competed for colonies, there were a dozen places around the globe where imperialist ambitions rubbed dangerously against each other.

The France of the Third Republic was querulous. Defeated by Germany, then—deftly encouraged by Bismarck—seeking to recover her lost pride by distant colonial adventures, France was restless, excitable, and unstable. No French government during these years enjoyed authority or longevity. Between 1873 and 1898 the British Foreign Office had negotiated with twenty-four French foreign ministers and twelve French ambassadors in London. During one five-year span, 1881–1886, ten French governments rose and fell. Although the years 1898–1905 saw six more French governments come and go, the Ministry of Foreign Affairs remained in the hands of a single man, Théophile Delcassé. Delcassé, a clever young provincial lawyer, had come to Paris, where he quickly had abandoned law for journalism and become a fixture in the lobby of the Chambre des Députés. At thirty-five, he had married a wealthy widow and, freed from financial worry, had run for office. He was elected to the Chambre in 1889 and, in 1894, became Minister of Colonies. Four years later, at forty-six, he was Foreign Minister. France needed allies to redress the balance with Germany and, one day, perhaps, regain the lost provinces of Alsace-Lorraine. He had strongly supported the French alliance with Russia, signed in 1894. When he entered the Quai d'Orsay four years later, he had a personal goal. "I do not wish to leave this desk," he told a friend, "without having established an entente with England."

At the moment Delcassé said this, Kitchener had just confronted Marchand at Fashoda and Delcassé's first weeks in office were spent negotiating France's humiliating withdrawal from the Upper Nile. The French public did not easily forget. For several years, French opinion was so violently anti-British that even the memory of Alsace-Lorraine seemed to have been obliterated. During the Boer War, not even German newspapers were as harsh in their criticism of England as the Parisian press. "The feeling of all classes in this country towards us is one of bitter and unmitigated dislike," reported the British Ambassador. Ignoring these feelings, Delcassé steered with consistent purpose. Removing the hostility in France's relationship with England by easing colonial frictions was the solution. Immediately after signing the Fashoda evacuation agreement, Delcassé launched his revolutionary policy. He dispatched to London as French Ambassador a prudent, far-sighted professional diplomat, Paul Cambon, who was instructed to do everything he could to effect a rapprochement. On December 9, 1898, before Marchand had even departed Fashoda, Cambon was seated at dinner next to Queen Victoria at Windsor Castle. The Queen, who throughout the crisis had bombarded Lord Salisbury with pleas that war be averted and France spared humiliation, found M. Cambon "very agreeable and well-informed. He told me a great deal about Constantinople [Cambon's previous post]." During the winter and spring of 1899, Cambon met often with Lord Salisbury to define the frontiers of the two empires in the center of Africa. Once agreement was reached, Cambon—following instructions from Delcassé—suggested that other matters might be solved in an equally friendly spirit. Lord Salisbury smiled and shook his head. "I have the greatest confidence in M. Delcassé and also in your present government," he said. "But in a few months they will probably be overturned and their successors will make a point of doing exactly the contrary to what they have done. No, we must wait a bit."

Delcassé and Cambon waited. In October 1899, on the eve of the Boer War, Cambon reported to Paris: "Everything is difficult for us here. The rage of imperialism turns all heads and I am not without disquiet about the future." In 1900, when Lord Salisbury retired from the Foreign Office, Delcassé hoped that because the new Foreign Secretary, Lord Lansdowne, had had a French mother, the chances for rapprochement had improved. But Joseph Chamberlain, not Lansdowne, was then the dominant figure in the British Cabinet, and Chamberlain still sought an alliance with Germany. Patiently, the French waited. In the spring of 1901, when the last Anglo-German alliance negotiations were ended by Salisbury's memorandum, Delcassé and Cambon saw an opportunity. The luster of Splendid Isolation was fading; Britain was already negotiating a military alliance with Japan, but still had no formal ally in Europe. Cambon quietly suggested to Lansdowne that the causes of friction in the colonial sphere should be examined and, if possible, eliminated. Lansdowne immediately passed this suggestion to Chamberlain, whose department would be affected by any talk involving colonies. The Colonial Secretary delayed, still hoping to reopen the door to Berlin. Then, in December 1901, Bülow made his famous "biting on granite" speech to the Reichstag, and Chamberlain was convinced that a German alliance was impossible. After the signing of the Anglo-Japanese alliance in January 1902, Delcassé and Cambon pursued more vigorously. In July 1902, Lord Salisbury stepped down as Prime Minister and was replaced by Arthur Balfour, but it was Chamberlain, Eckardstein wrote to Bülow, who still "exercises relentlessly the dominant influence in British policy." And now Chamberlain was interested in reconciliation with France. Passing through Egypt in November 1902, on his way to South Africa, the Colonial Secretary asked Lord Cromer to transmit, through the French Chargé d'Affaires in Cairo, his hope for an understanding with France. "Delcassé . . . seems to me to have done much to make possible an *Entente Cordiale* with France which is what I should now like. I wonder whether Lansdowne has ever considered the possibility of the King asking the President to England this year."

■ ■ ■

By the spring of 1903, the Boer War was over and the bitter French attacks on England had dwindled. King Edward VII planned a Mediterranean cruise with stops in Lisbon and Rome. On his own initiative, he decided also to visit Paris. Sir Edmund Monson, British Ambassador to France, was instructed to tell French President Emile Loubet that, on his return from his Mediterranean cruise, it would give the King great pleasure to visit the President of the Republic on French soil. President Loubet, who shared the hopes of Delcassé and Cambon, replied with enthusiasm that "a visit from the King would . . . do an amount of good which is probably not realized in England. . . . In this capital, His Majesty, while Prince of Wales, had acquired an exceptional personal popularity."

King Edward's zeal for the visit took his own government aback. Lansdowne worried that, with French antagonism still not completely abated, the King might be insulted or endangered. In addition, he and Balfour were affronted that the monarch had taken so much of the making of arrangements out of their hands; constitutionally, foreign policy was the government's, not the sovereign's, to make. Lansdowne therefore mentioned to Cambon that the visit should be "quite an informal affair." The King overruled him and told Monson and Cambon that he wished to be received "as officially as possible, and that the more honors were paid to him, the better." Cambon, taking his cue from the King rather than the Foreign Secretary, hurried to Paris to make arrangements.

On the first of May, King Edward, wearing the scarlet uniform and plumed hat of a British Field Marshal, descended from his private railway car at the Bois de Boulogne station and took his seat in a carriage next to President Loubet. As the carriage, surrounded by a screen of cuirassiers in silver breastplates, rolled up to the Arc de Triomphe and then down the Champs-Elysées, the crowd remained silent except for a few shouts of "Vivent les Boers!" "Vive Marchand!" and even "Vive Jeanne d'Arc!" The King behaved as if he were on the Mall, turning from side to side, gesturing with his Field Marshal's baton in reply to the salutes of French officers, smiling broadly whenever he heard a faint cheer. The rest of the English party, following in other carriages, was booed. "The French don't like us," a worried aide whispered to the King as the carriage came to a halt. "Why should they?" the King replied, and continued smiling and bowing from side to side.

King Edward's first speech was diplomatic: "A Divine Providence has arranged that France should be our near neighbor and, I hope, always a dear friend. . . ." The first evening, he went to the theater with President and Madame Loubet. The house was crowded, all eyes were on him, and the air was filled with tension. At intermission, the King left his box and plunged into the crowd. By chance, in the lobby he spied Mlle Jeanne Granier, a French actress whom he had seen on the stage in England. Extending his hand, he walked up and said, "Oh, Mademoiselle, I remember how I applauded you in London. You personified there all the grace and spirit of France." His words spread quickly. The next morning, on his way to a military review in Vincennes, the King continued to smile and scrupulously saluted every French flag and French officer in sight. Returning to the Hôtel de Ville, he told the Mayor of his pleasure at again being in Paris, "where I am treated exactly as if I were at home." His words rippled across the city. He went to the races at Longchamps, a ball at the Opéra, and a state dinner at the Elysée Palace. When he departed on May 4, enthusiastic crowds lined the streets and "Vivent les Boers!" had been replaced by "Vive le Roi!" and "Vive le bon Eduard!"

German reaction to the King's success was complacent. "The visit of King Edward to Paris has been a most odd affair, and, as I know for certain, was the result of his own initiative," Metternich reported to Bülow. "I am far from assuming that King Edward meant to aim a blow at Germany by his visit." Holstein characteristically dismissed any political significance, arguing that England's antagonism towards Russia was so strong that serious links would always be impossible with Russia's ally, France. Further, he did not believe in the role of personality: "So, although the Paris visit cannot be considered a very friendly action with regard to Germany, it is not likely to change the grouping of the Powers which is dictated by force of circumstances and not by the contribution of statesmen." The German press agreed. "A real Anglo-French Entente is in the long run impossible because in the colonial sphere differences will inevitably arise," the Berlin *Post* assured its readers. "Indeed, they will arise again very soon and these artificially spun threads will be severed with a jerk." Once again, on May 10, Eckardstein warned that a Triple Entente of Russia, France, and England was a possibility. Bülow asked for comment from leading German diplomats; all poured scorn on Eckardstein. "*Zukunftsmusik*" (music of the future), Holstein said.

The King was determined that his success be only a beginning, and in early July President Loubet, accompanied by M. Delcassé, paid a return state visit to Great Britain. King Edward's welcome was lavish, organized mainly by the monarch himself. After a visit to

Windsor Castle, the French President reviewed troops at Aldershot. There, on specific instructions from the King, the British Army band played the entire "Marseillaise" for the first time rather than stopping after the first four bars as had been customary. The ground broken by the heads of state, the diplomats set to work. On July 7, M. Delcassé called on Lord Lansdowne at the Foreign Office. When Delcassé returned to Paris, Cambon was assigned to pursue discussions with Lansdowne.

The talks continued for nine months. Their subjects were extra-European: Egypt, Morocco, fishing rights in Newfoundland, modification of the borders of Gambia and Nigeria, and problems having to do with Siam, Madagascar, and the New Hebrides. There was nothing of the sweeping, panoramic scope and language which Chamberlain had invoked in proposing an Anglo-German alliance. Some of the disputes were trivial, for example the Newfoundland fisheries disagreement. Under the Treaty of Utrecht, signed in 1713, French codfishermen had the right to land and dry their catch on the British shore. Recently, the French had begun catching lobsters, which had to be tinned as soon as they were caught. To house these operations, they had built primitive structures of timber and corrugated iron along the coastline. The Newfoundlanders protested that the right of drying codfish did not include that of building structures for lobster tinning. To which the French had replied that the Treaty of Utrecht said nothing of "codfish" but only of "fish" and that lobsters were "fish." The dispute had mounted the ladder at Whitehall until it reached the top, where it elicited a groan from the Prime Minister. "I am in despair over this grotesque lobster difficulty," complained Lord Salisbury.

Egypt and Morocco, on the other hand, were serious matters. France wanted a free hand to reorganize the affairs of the crumbling Moroccan sultanate, while England was equally anxious to end French opposition to her twenty-year occupation of Egypt. Agreement required concessions on both sides. France's desire to control Morocco was urgent, and Delcassé made this urgency plain in his first meeting with Lord Lansdowne on July 7: "Throughout our conversation," Lansdowne noted, "M. Delcassé spoke apparently with the utmost sincerity and he did not attempt to disguise from me the immense importance which the French government attached to obtaining from us a recognition of the predominance which they desired to obtain in Morocco." France had no wish to depose the Sultan or annex his country, Delcassé insisted, but the country was disintegrating and the Sultan was incapable of maintaining order. France would restore the Sultan's authority for the benefit of the

Moroccan people and of all foreign powers having commercial interests in the country. Delcassé said that France could not "admit that it was the business of any other Power but France to undertake the task of regenerating the country"; she hoped that Great Britain would support rather than obstruct her effort.

Lansdowne knew that French policy was inspired by the strategic dream of linking her North African with her West African territories; Morocco lay in the middle. He was aware that Britain's trade with Morocco was double that of France. On the other hand, he had before him the recommendation of one of Britain's most talented diplomats, Sir Arthur Nicolson, British minister in Morocco for nine years (1891–1900), that Moroccan affairs were so chaotic that, if France intervened and suppressed the country's disorder, it would save Britain the effort. Accordingly, Lansdowne told Delcassé that it was unlikely that Great Britain would oppose French intervention in Morocco, but that the situation in Egypt must also be discussed.

France's historical aspirations on the Nile stretched back to Napoleon and encompassed De Lesseps and the building of the Suez Canal; to renounce this heritage seemed a sure way to topple a shaky French government. Yet, if he could acquire Morocco, Delcassé reasoned, surrendering Egypt would be worthwhile, especially since what would be abandoned was a claim, not a presence. In these negotiations, Lansdowne's strongest supporter was Lord Cromer, the British Agent (in effect, Viceroy) in Egypt. Cromer's time in office and his experience gave him great influence with the British Cabinet. For Cromer, the Lansdowne-Cambon negotiations were a splendid opportunity to get the French off his back in Egypt, and he did not much care about the price. "The question comes down to have we any objection to Morocco becoming a French province? Personally, I see none," he wrote to Lansdowne on July 17. In general, Lansdowne accepted this approach, although his interests in the talks with France had a wider purpose than the establishment of an uncontested British claim to Egypt. From the beginning, the Foreign Secretary was as firm on Egypt as Delcassé and Cambon were on Morocco: "The Government of the French Republic should recognize that the British occupation of Egypt, which was originally intended to be temporary, has under the force of circumstances, acquired a character of permanency. It would therefore, as between Great Britain and France, be understood that the period of its duration should be left entirely to the discretion of His Majesty's Government."

On both sides, the bargaining required cessions of pride as well as of territories. Lansdowne had to consider Dominion concerns.

And Delcassé was never free of the pressure of French imperialists, who bristled at the suggestion of sacrificing France's traditional claims in Egypt. Cambon explained this consideration to Lansdowne. "You expect us to recognize your occupation [of Egypt]," he said. "I knew of nothing which France would find it more difficult to accept. I know that M. Delcassé sincerely desires to liquidate all our affairs, even Egypt, if it is possible. I believe him to be courageous enough to ignore it. But, if I may use a familiar expression, he would need a lot of *d'estomac* to assume responsibility for a settlement of the Egyptian question." "Do you think we do not need *d'estomac* to give you Morocco?" retorted Lansdowne.

On January 8, 1904, Lansdowne discovered that Delcassé had been acting entirely on his own authority and had not informed his Cabinet colleagues. Cambon was asked whether, in view of this, he and Delcassé were acting in good faith; if there was any doubt, the British government would immediately suspend the discussions. Mortified, Delcassé reacted quickly. As Lansdowne wrote to Cromer on March 14, 1904: "The French negotiations, after sticking in all sorts of ignoble ruts, suddenly began to travel with the speed of an express train. I attribute Delcassé's desire to get on quickly partly to doubts as to the stability of his own government and partly to similar suspicions as to the stability of ours." On April 7, 1904, the Anglo-French agreement was signed.

When the Anglo-French Convention was introduced in Parliament, it was presented as a purely colonial agreement, a sensible and modest elimination of sources of friction between neighbors. In England, both parties welcomed Lord Lansdowne's announcement. Most Liberals felt strongly that, if Splendid Isolation in Europe were abandoned, they preferred friendship with the French Republic to the alliance with Imperial Germany which Joseph Chamberlain had been advocating since 1899. The government made it clear that it was not proposing a military alliance. Lansdowne announced no revolutionary stroke of policy and claimed no great triumph of diplomacy. Throughout the debate, there was no reference to an alliance, to military or naval conventions; indeed, no third Power was even mentioned. Speakers in the Commons stressed that, by making this agreement, Britain did not exclude friendship with any nation. No one seems to have weighed the implications of the last article of the convention, which stated that the two governments "agreed to afford one another their diplomatic support to obtain execution of the clauses of the present declaration regarding Egypt and Morocco."

At the time the Convention was signed and presented to Parliament, no one in England considered asking German approval; it was assumed that no other power would object, or had the right to object, to two colonial powers securing peace between themselves by eliminating colonial frictions. The German government, although advised from the beginning that the negotiations were proceeding, had not complained. On March 24, 1904, two weeks before the signing, Delcassé had called in Prince Radolin, the German Ambassador in Paris, and given him the general terms of the agreement. Radolin responded that the arrangement seemed natural and justified. Two days later, the *Norddeutsche Allgemeine Zeitung,* a paper which generally reflected the views of the Wilhelmstrasse, declared that the agreement did nothing to prejudice German commercial interests in Morocco; on the contrary, the paper said, German as well as French traders would benefit from France imposing order and stability. Bülow quickly assured the British Ambassador that he was glad to see England and France liquidating their colonial differences. On April 12, the Chancellor informed the Reichstag that Germany had no objection to the agreement and felt no uneasiness about German interests in Morocco.

Holstein disagreed with Bülow. He believed that Morocco was one of the few countries where German commerce could compete equally with British and French and that the new agreement undermined these chances. In addition, he objected to the bilateral nature of the agreement. If France wished a special arrangement in Morocco, let her negotiate with all the Powers concerned, including Germany. "If we let ourselves be trampled in Morocco," he warned, "we invite similar treatment elsewhere. Not for material reasons alone, but even more for the sake of prestige must Germany protest against the intended appropriation of Morocco by France."

Parliament's enactment of the Anglo-French Convention was the crown of Lord Lansdowne's career. Splendid Isolation in Europe had come to an end and a vast upheaval in the Continental balance of power had begun. When Lansdowne was negotiating, first with Delcassé, then with Cambon, it never occurred to him that anything more than French and British colonies were involved. He did not see himself as preparing the ground for a military relationship with France and Russia, transforming the Dual Alliance into the Triple Entente. Delcassé saw further. Negotiation of the Convention and the appearance of the Anglo-French Entente were his creations. This was his patiently awaited reward for surrender at Fashoda six years before and for his firm refusal to permit France to take advantage of British difficulties during the Boer War. In dealing with England, Delcassé understood and accepted the nature of the British Constitution and the supremacy of the House of Commons. German insistence on a rigidly drafted treaty with clauses binding Britain to specific responses in every conceivable situation showed a lack of insight into how Great Britain was governed. The French were willing to begin with something small and unalarming, and proceed step by step.

Delcassé, the Foreign Minister of a nation isolated for a quarter of a century, had dreams of what the future might hold. Early in 1904, he had said: "If I conclude my agreements with England, Italy and Spain, you will see Morocco fall into our garden like ripe fruit." Later that spring, his vision expanded. Negotiations with England would wipe away all past quarrels. "This liquidation should lead us, and I desire that it shall lead us, to a political alliance with England. Ah, my dear friends, what beautiful horizons would open before us. Just think! If we could lean both on Russia and on England, how strong we should be in relation to Germany. A Franco-British alliance has always been my dream even during the Fashoda crisis. Now I can believe I am near my goal." The Foreign Minister paused at this point. After a moment, he went on: "It would be difficult to combine with the Russian alliance. But each day has its task."

CHAPTER 21

The Morocco Crisis of 1905

◆

On the evening of May 18, 1904, a wealthy retired American resident of Tangier named Ion Pedicaris sat in his dinner jacket drinking coffee in the wisteria-planted courtyard of his comfortable villa near the city. With him were his wife; his stepson, an Englishman named Varley; and his daughter-in-law, Mrs. Varley. Suddenly, shouts and then shots were heard from the back of the house. Varley and Pedicaris went to investigate. More shouts were heard. Fearfully, Mrs. Pedicaris and Mrs. Varley tiptoed to the servants' quarters. There, they beheld their husbands, bound and gagged, seated on the backs of mules. Men in brown cloaks gesticulated and pointed rifles. A moment later, the two husbands jounced off into the darkness.

The kidnapper, a local chief named El-Raisuli, who was in permanent rebellion against the Sultan of Morocco, soon forwarded his conditions for release of the prisoners. He demanded the dismissal of the Governor of Tangiers, the withdrawal of the Sultan's troops from the region, the cession to him of fifteen villages, the jailing of some of his enemies, the release from jail of some of his friends, and a ransom of ten thousand pounds. These conditions were granted and Mr. Pedicaris and Mr. Varley, after five weeks in a tent, returned to their wives. Mr. Pedicaris, having had enough of adventure, sold his villa and moved to Gloucestershire.

The seizure of two foreigners had terrified other Europeans in Morocco and affronted their governments. British and American warships had appeared in the harbor of Tangier. President Theodore Roosevelt had paced the White House and declared through clenched teeth that he wanted "Pedicaris alive or Raisuli dead." To Europeans and Americans, the episode demonstrated that the Kingdom of Morocco, the last independent African state in the northern half of the continent, could no longer maintain law and order. An imperialist power would have to pick up this burden and—as far as most foreigners in Morocco were concerned—the sooner this happened, the better.

Three European powers had shown interest in Moroccan affairs: France, ruler of Algeria, with which Morocco shared an eight-hundred-mile border; Britain, possessor of Gibraltar, the western gateway to the Mediterranean; and Spain, which owned four settlements on the Moroccan coast across the Mediterranean from southern Spain. To avoid the dangers of a quarrel over Morocco between these or other powers, the Sultan's kingdom had been specifically exempted from the "Scramble for Africa" by the Treaty of Madrid in 1880. The treaty, to which Germany and Italy were signatories along with France, Britain, and Spain, required that before one power overturned the agreement and seized political and economic power in Morocco, the other signatories had, at least, to be consulted. Imperial Germany had never expressed any ambitions in Morocco: indeed, when the Treaty of Madrid was signed, Bismarck had expressly declared that Germany had no significant interests in the kingdom. This German position had been restated in April 1904 when Bülow calmly reported the signing of the Anglo-French agreement to the Reichstag.

France, on the other hand, had desired for a long time to possess Morocco. In the nineteenth century French aspirations for a huge North African empire were partially fulfilled when Algeria (in the 1830s and 1840s) and Tunisia (in 1881) came under French control. Morocco managed to retain its independence because Great Britain opposed any European power obtaining a foothold on the Moroccan coast, which faced Gibraltar eight miles across the Straits. In 1880, the Sultan's tenuous sovereignty was affirmed by the Treaty of Madrid. Britain continued, through the end of the century, to be the power with the greatest political and economic influence in Morocco. From 1899 to 1905, Great Britain supplied 44 percent of Morocco's imports, France 22 percent, and Germany 11 percent. The commander of the Sultan's army was Kaid Maclean, a small, rotund Scotsman with a little white beard. Maclean had served in the post for twenty years and his cultural affinities had become mixed: he relaxed by dressing in a turban and white burnoose and walking in his garden blowing a bagpipe.

The Sultan, in 1894, was a puffy, overfed boy of fourteen, Abdul-Aziz. A new British Minister, Sir Arthur Nicolson, presented himself to this adolescent ruler and delivered a gift from Queen Victoria: a Maxim gun, which the Sultan took to a nearby square where he opened fire on a row of bottles. As he grew older, Abdul-Aziz showed a predilection for British friends, "grooms, gardeners, electricians, plumbers, cinema operators, commission agents, and the man who repairs his bicycles. These men," reported Nicolson, "show him photographs from the *Illustrated London News* of such things as lawn mowers, house boats, cigarette lighters, and gala coaches, and induce His Majesty to order such objects from London." Despite this influence at court, the British Foreign Office had little interest in expanding Britain's political role. In 1900, after five years at his post, Sir Arthur Nicolson was gloomy about Morocco's future. He described Morocco as "this loose agglomeration of turbulent tribes, corrupt governors, and general poverty and distress," and wrote to Lord Salisbury, "I do not believe that it is possible to reform this country from within. It is sad to admit it, but I fear that the country is doomed." With the Boer War absorbing British resources, England shunned the labor of reorganizing Morocco as she had reorganized Egypt. Since France was willing to undertake the task, the British saw a solution. And if France was willing to pay for this privilege by terminating its twenty-year harassment of the British in Egypt, so much the better. One point on which Great Britain insisted—and it was written into the Anglo-French agreement in 1904—was that "in order to secure the free passage of the Strait of Gibraltar," the stretch of African coast opposite the Rock was to remain unfortified.

France, by 1904, was eager to incorporate Morocco into its North African empire as soon as possible. In the months following the signing of the Anglo-French Convention, as the Sultan's kingdom slid further into chaos, France offered the Sultan assistance in reorganizing his army. The Sultan declined. Over the winter, the Paris press and public began to demand French pacification of the Sultan's kingdom. On February 21, 1905, the French Ambassador, M. René Taillandier, arrived in the royal city of Fez and demanded that the Sultan turn over his police and army to French officers and his customs houses to French inspectors. The Sultan, fearing for his throne and knowing that his English friends would no longer help him, called in the German Ambassador to inquire whether France spoke for Europe. The reply from Berlin, in sharp contrast to the position taken only ten months earlier by Chancellor Bülow, was a stinging slap at France and Foreign Minister Théophile Delcassé: the German government continued to recognize the independence of the Sultan's government as guaranteed by the Treaty of Madrid.

Behind this reply to the Sultan lay a major, carefully planned German diplomatic offensive. At the time of the signing of the Anglo-French agreement assigning Morocco to France, Bülow had accepted it as a means of restoring "tranquillity and order" in the Sultan's kingdom. First Counselor Holstein had disagreed, arguing that German commercial interests and German prestige both would be trampled by establishment of a French protectorate, but Bülow as Chancellor had prevailed. In the months that followed, Bülow had come around to Holstein's view, Delcassé had acted hastily and arrogantly. Required by the Madrid treaty to consult all signatories before acting in Morocco, he had consulted all except Germany. Warned that he was trespassing on German rights and that Germany would not accept being pushed aside, the French Foreign Minister had blandly asserted that France had absolutely "nothing to fear from this [German] quarter."

These slights were not the only, or the most serious, German concern. When Bülow had welcomed the Anglo-French agreement, he had not recognized its larger significance. With the passage of time, the implications of Delcassé's achievement dawned: the French Foreign Minister was not simply attempting to remove points of colonial friction; he was trying to change the balance of power in Europe. His long-range objective was to create an Anglo-French-Russian Entente to confront the Triple Alliance of Germany, Austria, and Italy. Secretly, the Wilhelmstrasse believed, a policy of encirclement against Germany had been worked out; the authors were King Edward VII and Théophile Delcassé. Holstein was ready to admit that his belief that England would never join France had been mistaken. Now, in 1905, "when this danger was clear before my eyes, I became convinced that, before the ring of the Great Powers enclosed us, we ought to try with all our might to break through the ring, and we must not shrink from the most extreme measures."

Circumstances favored a German diplomatic offensive. Imperial Russia, the ally on which France counted for military support against Germany, had suffered serious defeats in the Far East. Emboldened by Russia's weakness and by the already overwhelming superiority of the German Army, Holstein and Bülow decided that the moment had come to humiliate France and demonstrate to Paris and the world that the Third Republic, despite its ties to Russia and Britain, remained essentially as it had been in Bismarck's time: alone. British support would be shown to be, in Holstein's word, "platonic," and the Anglo-French Entente, unable to withstand the pressure from Berlin, would collapse.

Bülow's first move was to push Germany forward as the champion of treaty rights, of the independence of small states, and of the principle of the Open Door. This principle—the equal right of all colonial powers to exploit what they perceived as backward, disintegrating kingdoms and empires—had already been established in China and enthusiastically supported by a new imperialist power, the United States. When Bülow demanded that the Open Door now be applied to Morocco, the German Ambassador in Washington passed along the comment of President Roosevelt: "That is just exactly what we also want." Bülow triumphantly reported the President's words to the Kaiser.

William supported Bülow's position. France's forward policy in Morocco seemed to treat the German Empire and the German Emperor alike as *quantités négligeables* in world affairs. Unveiling a statue of his father in Bremen on March 22, 1905, William announced that God had destined Germany for a great future and predicted "a world-wide dominion of the Hohenzollerns." General Alfred von Schlieffen, Chief of the German General Staff, assured the government that France was unprepared for war in Europe; that Russia, overwhelmed by defeat in the Far East, was in no position to give support to her European ally; and that any aid Britain could give on land would be too small to make a difference. Schlieffen offered his opinion that "if the necessity of war with France should arise for us, the present moment would doubtless be favorable." He urged "the earliest possible thorough cleaning up with France at arms. No waiting ten or twenty years for a world war, but so thorough a settlement that thereafter there should be no fear of a world war. France should be provoked until she had no course but to take up arms."

Bülow did not seek war or intend to unleash Schlieffen. But the threat of war was a useful weapon; properly wielded, it could help him win almost as sweeping a triumph as could be achieved by war. Thus, when addressed by the Sultan of Morocco, Bülow's answer was very different from the mellow acquiescence of ten months earlier. "In the face of this chain of aggressions," Bülow said later, "it seemed to me necessary to remind Paris again of the German Empire. It was not only the extent of our economic and political interests in and about Morocco which decided me to advise the Kaiser to set his face against France, but also the conviction that in the interests of peace, we must no longer permit such provocations. I did not desire war with France either then or later. But I did not hesitate to confront France with the possibility of war because I had confidence in my own skill and caution. I felt that I could prevent matters coming to a head, cause Delcassé's fall, break the continuity of aggressive French policy, knock the continental dagger out of the hands of Edward VII . . . and simultaneously preserve peace, preserve German honor, and improve German prestige."

In preparing this challenge, Bülow decided that it must be dramatized in the most flamboyant possible way. The instrument he chose was Kaiser William.

Morocco had never interested William. He once told Eckardstein that "when, as Prince of Prussia, he had been attached to the Foreign Office for instruction, he had heard a lot of talk about Morocco, but he had never understood why so much importance was attached to it." In March 1904, the Kaiser told King Alfonso of Spain that Germany had no special interest in Morocco and would concentrate solely on Europe. At the Kiel Regatta in June, William repeated to King Edward that Morocco had never interested him. After the signing of the Anglo-French Entente, the Emperor had told Bülow that "it was in Germany's interest for France to engage and commit herself in Morocco. This would turn the eyes of Frenchmen away from the Vosges and they might, in time, forget Alsace-Lorraine." To another diplomat he said that it would be "a good thing that France should have to pacify Morocco and work there to establish law and order. This pioneer work would cost [France] heavily in blood and treasure."

William wanted to visit Tangier; "I have been to Asia [Jerusalem] and I would much like to set my foot on African soil [Tangier]." Bülow and Holstein decided to exploit this wish and use the Imperial traveler to assure the Sultan of German support for Moroccan independence. "Your Majesty's visit will embarrass Delcassé, upset his plans, and foster our economic interests in Morocco," Bülow wrote to the Kaiser. "Tant mieux!" ("So much the better") noted the Kaiser in the margin, setting aside, in his eagerness to leap into the international limelight, his lack of interest in Morocco.

On March 28, 1905, the Kaiser embarked at Cuxhaven aboard the Hamburg-America steamer *Hamburg*. While he sailed down the Channel and around the coast of Spain, Europe heard rumors that he would land at Tangier. The Paris press rumbled that such a visit would be unfriendly to France. As he approached the Pillars of Hercules, William began to have doubts. He reflected that Bülow's Moroccan policy was risky. He had been looking forward to visiting Gibraltar, where Queen Alexandra would be aboard her yacht and where there would be ceremonial occasions for him to wear his British admiral's uniform. And there was the matter of his personal safety. Tangier had become a haven for many exiled European anarchists; an emperor—any emperor—made a tempting target. Perhaps, William wired to Bülow, a visit to Tangier would be undignified, even unsafe. Bülow quickly announced the impending landing to the German press and then telegraphed the Kaiser that it was too late; to back out now would give France a public victory and proclaim the German Emperor a coward.

Nevertheless, as the *Hamburg* lay off the port of Tangier on the morning of March 31, the Kaiser's reluctance intensified. The ship was too big to dock in the harbor and a storm had churned up a heavy sea. Baron von Richard Kühlmann, the German Chargé d'Affaires in Tangier, coming out in a small boat to greet his sovereign, had to leap from the boat onto a rope ladder snaking along the *Hamburg*'s hull. From there, Kühlmann, costumed in the full-dress uniform of the Bavarian Lancers complete with *tchapka,* high boots, and spurs, had to come up hand over hand, drenched by spray, and present himself on deck standing in a pool of water. William, who had no stomach for such athletics, announced that he would not go. Then, quite suddenly, the wind and sea died down and the Kaiser decided to proceed with the visit.

He arrived at the dock to find not the Sultan to welcome him, but an aged uncle sent as a substitute. William gave the speech Bülow had written for him: Germany continued to recognize the Sultan as an independent monarch. Presented to the diplomatic corps, he told the French Minister that Germany stood for equal rights and an Open Door for trade by all nations as guaranteed in the Madrid Treaty. "When the Minister tried to argue with me, I said 'Good morning' and left him standing." A white Barbary stallion was led forward. The horse, strange to its rider, unprepared for the fireworks and gun salutes which welcomed the Emperor, bucked, and William nearly fell off. Clinging to the saddle, he wondered which faces in the crowd belonged to anarchists; he was not reassured to know that the Sultan had ordered that "all were to be exterminated if the Kaiser came to any harm." Later, William listed his complaints for Bülow: "I landed because you wanted me to in the interests of the Fatherland, mounted a strange horse in spite of the impediment my crippled left arm causes to my riding, and the horse was within an inch of costing me my life. I had to ride between Spanish anarchists because you wished it and your policy was to profit by it."

The Kaiser remained in Tangier only a few hours. He returned to the *Hamburg* and sailed immediately for Gibraltar, only to find that Queen Alexandra had left, leaving him no message. One of his escort vessels in the process of mooring managed to ram a British cruiser. "The British generals and admirals stood stiffly and coldly to receive me without a single word more than was necessary," he grumbled. He sailed into the Mediterranean. In the Sicilian castle of the Holy Roman Emperor Frederick II, he observed, "It is wonderful to think what this great Emperor achieved. If I were able to have people beheaded as easily as he could, I could do more." Back in Berlin, he found Bülow "trembling with emotion and showing in every word and gesture his devotion and affection." Bülow assured the Kaiser how much he had worried. "When the news reached me that Your Majesty had come away alive out of Tangier, I broke down and sat weeping at my desk while I uttered a thanksgiving to Heaven."

"But why did you send me there?" the Kaiser asked.

"It was necessary for my policy," the Chancellor replied. "Through Your Majesty I threw down the gauntlet to the French. I wanted to see whether they would mobilize."

The German press quickly blossomed with Morocco stories describing the trampling of foreign rights by a grasping France, while noble, disinterested Germany stood up alone to defend the rights of all other nations. Europe was not fooled. It was unclear, however, what profit the Wilhelmstrasse wished to make from its challenge. Bülow gave substance to the German challenge by sending the Sultan a message offering German diplomatic support in his refusal to accept French officers. The Chancellor also suggested that the Sultan invite all governments signatory to the Madrid Treaty to a new international conference to reconfirm Moroccan independence. "I emphasized again that Germany was not seeking her own advantage in Morocco but only desired the maintenance of a treaty which had been violated," Bülow declared. German ambassadors in London, St. Petersburg, and Vienna were instructed to inform their host governments that Germany had acted as she did because she "could not recognize the right of France, England and Spain to settle the Moroccan affairs independently." German rights were not to be disposed of by anyone without German participation and consent. If foreigners probed deeper "about the purpose of the [Kaiser's] visit," Bülow's instructions continued, "do not answer them but keep a serious and impassive face. Emulate the sphinx who, surrounded by tourists, reveals nothing."

Germany's silence as to its ultimate goals in Morocco and the refusal of German diplomats to provide any explanation for the Emperor's dramatic landing at Tangier left European foreign offices confused and alarmed. Why, if the Wilhelmstrasse had been unhappy with the Anglo-French Moroccan understanding, had no complaint been made in 1904? Why, if it was believed that German rights were about to be trampled, had the matter not been addressed to the French government through diplomatic channels? Gradually, the larger purpose began to reveal itself: the Kaiser's landing, the future of Morocco, were only factors in a German attempt to humiliate France. The collapse of Russia had provided the opportunity; France's moves in Morocco provided the pretext.

In Paris, from the day the Kaiser landed at Tangier, Delcassé told the Chambre des Députés that the Imperial visit would not affect France's policy in Morocco. When the German-encouraged invitation to an international conference arrived in Paris, Delcassé declined on behalf of France. The rest of the French Cabinet, especially the new Premier, a financier named Maurice Rouvier, was uneasy. Behind the German demand for a conference lay the threat of war. While the Russian Army was unavailable, France was not ready for war with Germany. The Sultan of Morocco, assured of German support, refused to turn his army and customs over to French officials. Delcassé found he was attacked on all sides. In the Chambre des Députés, Delcassé was condemned by the right for having given away Egypt without acquiring Morocco, and by the left for pushing the Republic to the brink of war. President Loubet continued to support Delcassé, but Rouvier and the Cabinet clearly wished the Foreign Minister to resign. Isolated and shaken, Delcassé belatedly attempted to mollify the Germans. After a dinner at the German Embassy on April 13, he told his host, Prince Radolin, that he desired to eliminate the misunderstanding. Coldly, Radolin told him that he had no instructions from Berlin but that it was too late for bilateral negotiations. Soon after, Delcassé told Loubet that he would resign. Loubet requested him not to act in haste.

At this point, the beleaguered Delcassé found an unexpected champion. King Edward VII's view of the crisis had focussed first on what he considered the deplorable, operatic behavior of his nephew at Tangier, a performance the King described as "the most mischievous and uncalled-for event which the German Emperor has been engaged in since he came to the throne. He is no more nor less than a political *enfant terrible*. . . . Can there be anything more perfidious and stupid than the present policy of the Kaiser?" As the scope of the German demarche and the difficulties of M. Delcassé became more pronounced, the King rallied to the French Foreign Minister. On April 23, as he cruised on his yacht in the Mediterranean, he took the unprecedented step of personally telegraphing the French Foreign Minister and urging him not to resign. Before returning to England, the King spent a week in Paris. He saw Delcassé twice. Although the British government insisted that the King's visit was private, Bülow and Holstein could not help regarding it as a conspiratorial gathering of the two leading proponents of encirclement.

The King's support of France and her Foreign Minister reflected the view of the British people, press, and government. Lord Lansdowne, who had not anticipated that his colonial agreement with France would lead within a year to a European crisis, was wholly sympathetic to Delcassé. He understood that the German challenge was not simply a defense of legitimate German economic and treaty interests, but an attempt to smash the Entente. With Cabinet support, he refused to back away from Britain's commitment to France. There was another factor in British policy. By the spring of 1905, many Britons were worried about the growth of the German Navy. The new First Sea Lord, Sir John Arbuthnot Fisher, had proclaimed that Great Britain had only one enemy at sea: the German Empire. Fisher's reaction to the Morocco crisis was typically impetuous. "This seems a golden opportunity for fighting the Germans in alliance with the French, so I earnestly hope you may be able to bring this about," the First Sea Lord wrote to Lansdowne on May 22. "Of course I don't pretend to be a diplomat, but it strikes me that the German Emperor will greatly injure the splendid and growing Anglo-French Entente if he is allowed to score now in *any way*—even if it is only getting rid of M. Delcassé. . . . All I hope is that you will send a telegram to Paris that the English and French fleets are one. We could have the German Fleet, the Kiel Canal, and Schleswig-Holstein within a fortnight."

Fisher's belligerence was not government policy. When President Theodore Roosevelt offered to mediate the dispute between Britain and Germany, Lansdowne coldly telegraphed to Washington: "We have not, and never had, any intention of attacking Germany; nor do we anticipate that she will be so foolish as to attack us." But Lansdowne fully agreed with Fisher on one point: Germany must not, as a result of the crisis, be allowed to obtain a naval base, or even a coaling station, on Morocco's Atlantic coast, from which she could threaten the sealanes to South Africa and around the Cape. On April 25, Lansdowne sent a message to Delcassé that, if the Germans asked for a port, the British government would join France in opposition. Lansdowne never diluted his offer; indeed, on May 25, he suggested that the two countries discuss in confidence all contingencies. Delcassé believed he was on the verge of an Anglo-French military alliance.

Meanwhile, German pressure on France was mounting. The Cipher Department of the Quai d'Orsay routinely intercepted and deciphered communications between the Wilhelmstrasse and the German Embassy in Paris. As the crisis intensified, the decoded messages on the desks of French foreign ministers were increasingly belligerent. In Berlin, Bülow called in the French ambassador and informed his guest "in a friendly manner" that "if he was convinced that England would come to France's aid, I did not wish to question this surmise. . . . I also acknowledged that England could deal our industry a heavy blow and could also destroy the fleet that was in the course of construction. But, as things stood in the war which I desired to avoid as much as . . . [the French Ambassador] himself, France would be the unfortunate who would suffer most. It is you who will pay *les pots cassés,* not because of our *méchanceté* but by the force of circumstances." Under this pressure, Rouvier crumbled.

At dinner with Prince Radolin on April 26, the French Premier pleaded that France would do her best to be a good neighbor and that war over Morocco would be a crime. Delcassé had exceeded his authority, the Premier claimed. On May 7, Radolin passed along to Rouvier a declaration from the Wilhelmstrasse: good relations were possible only with a French foreign minister whom the German government could trust.

Convinced that the Germans were bluffing—as he had been convinced that the English were *not* bluffing at Fashoda—Delcassé struggled to stay in office. Paul Cambon was brought from London to tell President Loubet and Premier Rouvier that Great Britain might consider extending the Entente into an actual alliance. Rouvier listened and then demanded that all such negotiations be stopped immediately. "If the Germans find out about them, they will declare war," he said. On June 3, the Sultan, pushed by the Germans, formally rejected France's proposal for internal reform. Instead, as suggested by Bülow, he invited eleven European powers and the United States to attend a conference on his country's future. France immediately refused; Great Britain, Italy, and Spain declared that their acceptance would be conditional on that of France. By the first of June, German patience was at an end. Prince Radolin passed a further message from Berlin to M. Rouvier: "The Chancellor of the German Empire does not wish to have any further dealings with Monsieur Delcassé." On June 5, Delcassé was summoned to the Elysée Palace to meet the President and the Premier. Delcassé suggested sending French cruisers to Tangier to enforce France's demands to the Sultan. "That would mean war with Germany," said Rouvier. "Do not believe it, it is all bluff," Delcassé responded. "Tomorrow, I will ask the Cabinet to choose between his policy and mine," Rouvier told the President. "Tomorrow one of us will resign."

At ten A.M. on June 6, the French Cabinet met, but not until eleven did the President enter the room, followed by the Premier and the Foreign Minister, both pale. Delcassé stressed the possibilities of an English alliance and declared that, if war came, a British army of a hundred thousand men could be landed in Schleswig-Holstein to divert the Germans from France's eastern frontier. Rouvier noted that "the British Navy does not run on wheels" and that he doubted that British battleships "would be much help in keeping the German Army from reaching Paris." His voice filled with emotion: "Are we in a condition to sustain a war with Germany? No! No! Even with the aid of the British Fleet we should be in for a worse catastrophe than in 1870. We should be criminals to indulge in such an adventure. France would not recover." Delcassé hoped that Loubet would speak on his behalf, but the President remained silent. Rouvier called for a vote and every minister voted against Delcassé. The Foreign Minister immediately resigned and returned in tears to the Quai d'Orsay. Sixty-six days had passed since the Kaiser had landed at Tangier.

That night in Berlin, Bülow was sitting on a terrace outside his study, cooling himself from the heat which had settled on the city. The telephone rang at midnight. It was the Kaiser "telling me that he had just received news of Delcassé's fall." The following morning —the wedding day of the Emperor's eldest son, Crown Prince William, to Grand Duchess Cecile of Mecklenburg—the Kaiser arrived at Bülow's office. "You can't escape me this time," William chuck-

led. On the spot, he promoted his Chancellor to the rank of Prince
of the German Empire.

Delcassé's resignation was a German diplomatic victory, but Bülow
and Holstein wanted more. There were still the fruits of Delcassé's
work to be destroyed: Morocco must be internationalized and the
Entente must be demolished. Rouvier, ironically, was the first to
realize what lay ahead. Having assumed the role of Foreign Minister
in addition to that of Premier, he received the German Ambassador
four days after the climactic meeting of the French Cabinet. All
smiles, Rouvier said that he assumed that with Delcassé removed,
Berlin would drop its demand for an international conference on
Morocco. Prince Radolin gave him a nasty shock. Germany "absolutely insisted" on the conference, the Prince announced. Further,
Radolin continued, "it is my duty to declare to you that if France
were to attempt to change in any way whatever the status of Morocco, Germany would stand behind the Sultan with all its forces."
Rouvier was stunned and outraged, but given the state of the French
Army, he could not protest. France would attend the conference.
    The British government was dismayed by Delcassé's resigna-
tion. Lansdowne had believed that the Entente was a colonial agreement which contained nothing harmful to other powers, including
Germany. When the German offensive was launched, he was surprised; when the Foreign Minister with whom he had negotiated the
agreement was forced to leave the French government, he was appalled. "The fall of Delcassé is disgusting and has sent the Entente
down any number of points in the market," the Foreign Secretary
said. On June 8, two days after the event, Balfour drew gloomy
conclusions in a letter to the King: "Delcassé's dismissal or resignation under pressure from the German Government displayed a
weakness on the part of France which indicated that she could not at
present be counted on as an effective force in international politics.
She could no longer be trusted not to yield to threats at the critical
moment of a negotiation. If, therefore, Germany is really desirous of
obtaining a port on the coast of Morocco, and if such a proceeding
be a menace to our interests, it must be to other means than French
assurance that we must look for our protection." "Other means"
meant, of course, the Royal Navy and, during the summer, measures
were taken to display the navy's strength and demonstrate Britain's
support of its Entente partner. In July, the British Atlantic Fleet was
warmly welcomed when it visited Brest. The visit was returned in
August when the French Northern Squadron called at Portsmouth.

King Edward did everything possible to make the visit a success. He inspected the French flagship, reviewed the French squadron, invited the French admiral and his captains to dine aboard *Victoria and Albert,* gave a dinner at Windsor Castle, and saw to it that the French officers were given luncheons, first at the Guildhall and then by the Houses of Parliament.

On September 28, France and Germany agreed to the agenda of a conference which would open in mid-January 1906 in the Spanish town of Algeciras, across the bay from Gibraltar. The Germans could not hide their satisfaction. The Kaiser, unveiling a statue of Helmuth von Moltke, proclaimed, "You have seen in what position we found ourselves a few months ago before the world. Therefore, hurrah for dry powder and well-sharpened swords!" Bülow spoke of the superiority of the Teutonic character over the Gallic: "Peaceful, good-humored, rather naive, with little political insight in spite of otherwise great and splendid qualities, the German judges the Frenchman too much according to his own lights and underestimates the French ambition, the boundless French vanity, the French hardness and cruelty."

As January approached, Bülow instructed Radolin to make sure that France understood that Germany expected French concessions at the conference. Bülow called in the French Ambassador in Berlin and advised France "not to linger on a road bordered by precipices and even abysses." These constant threats hardened Rouvier. "I have had enough of German intrigues and recriminations," he said. "If the Berlin people imagine they can intimidate me, they are mistaken. I will yield nothing more, come what may."

The Algeciras Conference, the most important European diplomatic gathering since the Congress of Berlin twenty-eight years before, formally opened at Algeciras Town Hall on January 16, 1906. New red carpets had been laid in the corridors and on the stairways, and the long table at which the Municipal Council usually met was covered with fresh green baize. The diplomats representing the thirteen powers attending were senior ambassadors; at the suggestion of the German delegation, the Duke of Almodóvar, representing the host nation of Spain, was elected chairman. The Wilhelmstrasse had sent two senior diplomats, Herr von Radowitz, the German Ambassador in Madrid, and Count von Tattenbach, the former Minister to Morocco. Radowitz, appointed by Bülow, a man who—the Chancellor himself declared—"had a great future behind him," was assigned to make certain that Germany remained at the head of the majority, and was not maneuvered by the French and British into a position of isolation. Tattenbach, appointed by Holstein, had a reputation as "the most violent of German diplomatists," "a sergeant-major in face and voice, cracking rude jokes, waves of German national anger flushing the scalp under his upright, stubble hair." His mission was to concentrate on the future of Morocco and to strip away France's claim to exclusivity in the kingdom. M. Révoil, the French delegate, a small man with a waxed mustache, smiled at everyone except the Germans, whom he was determined to foil. The British delegate, Sir Arthur Nicolson, bent with arthritis, seemed even smaller than M. Révoil, until he began to speak. Then this shy, frail man, who had spent seven years as Minister to Morocco and was now British Ambassador to Spain, spoke with impressive authority.

Nicolson's instructions were furnished by the new Liberal Foreign Secretary, Sir Edward Grey, who had replaced Lord Lansdowne in December when Balfour's Unionist government resigned. Lansdowne's policy had been reconfirmed by the Liberal Cabinet: Nicolson was to support France as agreed in Article IX of the Anglo-French Convention. The Liberals, like the Unionists, meant to interpret this article generously. "Tell us what you wish, on each point, and we will support you without restriction or reserve," King Edward VII had said to Paul Cambon in London. Grey also told the German Ambassador, Count Metternich, that England would honor its commitment to France.

When the conference opened, Count Tattenbach went on the offensive. He declared that France could be permitted some authority to restore order in those parts of Morocco near the Algerian frontier, but that France's wish for a mandate to establish order throughout the country was inadmissible. He described German policy as an attempt "to secure full guarantees for the open door," and tried to persuade Nicolson that Britain should be supportive. If Britain arranged for France and M. Révoil to make concessions, Tattenbach continued, the threat to peace would quickly disappear and the conference promptly and successfully end. Nicolson replied that his country had special treaty obligations to France and that "it was not for me to urge concessions on my French colleague." After this meeting, Nicolson wrote to his wife, "I felt really insulted and really furious . . . so that I could eat nothing afterwards. . . . He [Tattenbach] is a horrid fellow, blustering, rude, and mendacious. The worst type of German I have ever met."

The central dispute was control of the Moroccan police: "He who has the police has Morocco," Metternich told Grey. Germany insisted that the police force be internationalized. M. Révoil replied that France would prefer a continuation of the status quo to an internationalized force. The status quo, of course, meant continued kidnappings and chaos. The Germans would not yield; neither would the French. Premier Rouvier had sacrificed Delcassé and agreed to attending the conference; he was in no mood to concede anything else. "We are close to a rupture," Nicolson wrote to his wife. "The Germans have behaved in a most disgraceful way. Their mendacity has been beyond words. I would not have thought Radowitz capable of such unblushing lying and double dealing." Nicolson was not always comfortable with his French colleague, whom he found "changeable—sometimes firm and positive, at other times, weak and vacillating."

During the conference, Gibraltar was visible from Algeciras, the gray granite mass looming above the mimosas and orange trees. On March 1, the combined British Atlantic and Mediterranean fleets appeared in the harbor: twenty battleships, dozens of cruisers and destroyers, an immense display of naval power. At Nicolson's suggestion, Admiral Lord Charles Beresford, the British Commander-in-Chief, invited all of the delegates to dinner on board his flagship, *King Edward VII.* To avoid difficulties of protocol, no national anthems were performed and the single toast of the evening was to "All Sovereignties and Republics." The massed bands of the fleet played and, as the diplomats were being ferried back to Algeciras, one hundred and forty fleet searchlights beamed into the night sky. Thereafter, when the delegates looked towards Gibraltar and saw the ships lying beneath the towering rock, Count Tattenbach's bad temper seemed less threatening.

German diplomacy fared poorly at the conference. On March 3, Nicolson outmaneuvered Radowitz on a procedural vote and the Germans were defeated 10–3. Holstein, furious, wanted to threaten war against France, but Bülow drew back. Worried that, because the conference was going badly, Holstein in frustration might push Germany and France over a precipice, the German Chancellor forbade Holstein from having anything further to do with Morocco and the Algeciras Conference. A few days later, the Germans had one more chance. On March 7, Rouvier was defeated on a domestic issue in the Chambre des Députés and the French government resigned. "Tattenbach is again talking of war," Nicolson wrote, but this talk faded quickly. Nicolson had become exasperated by Révoil: "This is the third time that I have raised his banner and on each occasion he has hid behind a bush and only come out when the fighting was over. He is so dreadfully weak and irresolute that he puts me in a false position and gives ground for the charge that the Germans are

always bringing against me that I am more French than the French."
By the beginning of April, Bülow wanted only to end the Conference as quickly as possible. It was agreed that France should have
special responsibilities for preserving order along the Moroccan-Al-
gerian frontier, and should share with Spain the supervision of the
police with a Swiss inspector general in command. The document
was signed on April 7 and the Conference ended.

At first, because outright French predominance in Morocco had
been postponed, some considered the conference a German victory.
President Roosevelt congratulated the German Ambassador in
Washington on the Kaiser's "epoch-making success," and said that
"His Majesty's policy has been masterly from beginning to end."
The Ambassador, Hermann Speck von Sternburg, passed the President's compliment along to Berlin, although he added cautiously
that the view from the White House "did not appear to agree with
the facts." In time, it became obvious that the Algeciras Conference
was a significant defeat for German diplomacy. While France had
not won the clear predominance she had sought in Morocco, she
had gained something more precious, something of which M. Delcassé had dreamed: the active diplomatic support of Great Britain.

At Algeciras, Germany achieved the opposite of what she intended. She meant to break the Entente before it took on meaning
and strength. Instead, German bullying succeeded in driving France
and England closer together. Metternich saw clearly what was happening and, in the middle of the conference, reported from London:
"The Moroccan Question is regarded by everyone here as a trial of
strength with the Anglo-French Entente and our Moroccan policy as
an attempt to smash it. Hence the determined opposition." When
the Conference was over, Metternich forwarded unwelcome news to
Berlin: "The Entente Cordiale has stood its diplomatic baptism of
fire and emerged strengthened." Bülow and Holstein were responsible for this defeat. Had they been content with the fall of Delcassé
and willing to negotiate their grievances in Morocco with Rouvier,
the Algeciras Conference would not have been summoned and Article IX of the Convention never called into play. In the end, Delcassé
had the final triumph: as a result of his policy, France acquired a
second ally.

This was as clear in Germany as it was in the rest of Europe.
Pan-Germans in the press and the Reichstag raised a storm over the
meager results of Algeciras. Stung by this criticism, Bülow defended
his policy in the Reichstag on April 5. "The treaty may not have
given us all we wished," he declared, "[but] it did represent the
essentials of what we had striven to attain. It reaffirmed the sover-

eignty of the Sultan. . . . France did not obtain the Protectorate at which she had aimed. . . . We had stood unshakeably by the great principle of the Open Door. . . . The attempt to exclude us from a great international decision had been successfully thwarted." A number of other speakers followed Bülow to the rostrum and, during a violent attack on the Chancellor by the Socialist leader August Bebel, Bülow fainted. He was carried to his office, where he awoke to find his feet being rubbed and his fellow ministers discussing the question of his successor. The Kaiser hurried to the Reichstag, but was forbidden by Bülow's doctor to see the Chancellor. Eventually, when it was determined that the cause was exhaustion and not a stroke, Bülow was sent home for three weeks to read French novels. "I got through a whole series of them," he noted cheerfully. "Some of these seemed very well-written."

The Chancellor's collapse, later attributed to overwork, and sojourn at home proved the occasion for the political demise of First Counselor Friedrich von Holstein. Someone had to be blamed for the failure of the Bülow-Holstein Moroccan policy, and Bernhard von Bülow, having been made a Prince when success seemed to glitter, needed another to accept censure. Holstein was brought down by tactics he might have admired. The First Counselor throughout his career had gotten his way by threatening to resign. In January 1906, as the Algeciras Conference was convening, Secretary of State Oswald von Richthofen, Holstein's nominal superior, died in office, and was replaced by Heinrich von Tschirschky. Holstein had approved Tschirschky's appointment, but the two soon were at odds. At first, Holstein had continued to use the back door between his office and the State Secretary's room. Then one day, he found that door locked. Tschirschky, Bülow explained, "was too emotional to be able to support with ease a continual threat of the sinister presence of Holstein discovered unexpectedly at his back. When, irritated by this exclusion, Holstein entered the room of the Secretary of State by the corridor, with a great bundle of documents under his arm, Tschirschky, in a cold discouraging voice, requested him to put them on the table and go outside and wait until he was called. With Holstein's nature this could only lead to a breach. He at once handed in his resignation but was convinced I would prevent its being accepted. . . . Fritz von Holstein, though in the main his calculations were right, had forgotten one eventuality! that I might be taken ill and, by doctors' orders, shut off from all enquiries and documents at the moment when his resignation was in the hands of Secretary of State Tschirschky who was now his enemy." Tschirschky "in the most cold-blooded manner persuaded the Kai-

ser to accept the Privy Councilor's resignation." Bülow at a stroke
had toppled a rival and provided a scapegoat. Enraged, Holstein left
the Wilhelmstrasse, where he had worked for thirty years, and retreated to his rooms at the Grossbehrenstrasse to plot his revenge.

PART III

THE
NAVY

CHAPTER 22

From
Sail to Steam

◆

The Victorian Age, the Pax Britannica, Splendid Isolation, the Empire on Which the Sun Never Sets, existed because Britannia Ruled the Waves. Essentially, she ruled unchallenged. Her former antagonists, the Spanish and the Dutch, had no navies to speak of; Russia and the United States were deeply engaged in consolidating control over their own continental landmasses; the German Empire did not exist. Despite its shattering defeat by Nelson, the French Navy remained throughout the century the world's second-largest. But France, after Bonaparte, faced decades of political instability and institutional change: empire, monarchy, republic, empire again, then, following crushing military defeat, another republic. Only briefly, at the height of the Second Empire, did France build ships which caused alarm in England. Even then, Great Britain's naval supremacy remained unshaken.

At the end of the Napoleonic Wars, the British Navy shrank. The number of ships fell drastically. In 1815, when the Emperor was dispatched to St. Helena, the British Fleet possessed 214 ships-of-the-line and 792 other vessels of all types. By 1817, there were 80 ships-of-the-line active and in reserve; in 1828 there were 68; in 1835, 50. The reduction in manpower was even more drastic. Of 145,000 sailors and marines in the wartime fleet, only 19,000 remained in 1820. Moments still came when the Fleet was summoned. In 1827, against the Turks at Navarino, a Royal Navy squadron fought its last battle in Nelsonian style: oak-hulled sailing ships forming a line of battle and British broadsides rolling out from gunports lining three-tiered decks. In 1855, the Queen went to war against the Tsar, but the Russian Navy remained in harbor, so the British Fleet was needed only to bombard fortresses and convoy troopships.

Unable to fight other major warships, British captains and seamen took on new duties. The Royal Navy became the policeman of the oceans. Pirates were attacked and exterminated along the Barbary Coast of North Africa, in the Aegean, the Red Sea, the Caribbean, the East Indies, and the coastal waters of China. British warships attempted to suppress the slave trade by patrolling the coast of West Africa, intercepting slave ships, and freeing their suffering cargo. To fulfill these duties, the distribution of the British Fleet dramatically changed. Once consisting primarily of ships-of-the-line concentrated in home waters and the Mediterranean, the Fleet had broken up into squadrons of smaller ships scattered around the globe. In 1848, twenty-five ships were assigned to the East India and China Station, twenty-seven served against the slavers off West Africa, fourteen patrolled the east coast of South America, ten were in the West Indies, and only thirty-five remained in home waters.

Manning these far-flung ships were dozens of captains, hundreds of officers, thousands of seamen, many of whom spent an entire career at sea without ever being in a battle. Individual ships saw action, and individual officers and seamen won medals—but often for heroism on land, as participants in one of the naval brigades landed on unfriendly coasts throughout the century. Most of the admirals who were to lead the Royal Navy into the twentieth century and the First World War were baptized by fire in colonial wars. Several were wounded or decorated: Lord Charles Beresford, speared in the hand in the Sudan; Arthur Wilson, fighting with his sword hilt and then with his fists, also in the Sudan, winning the Victoria Cross; John Jellicoe, shot in the chest and feared lost in the failure of the naval-brigade relief column during the siege of the Peking Legations. These men stepped out of the Victorian Royal Navy, when sea power exercised a wider influence on history than ever before or since. Going from ship to ship as they progressed in age and rank, they experienced the sea and learned to command. The ultimate lesson was constant: in the British Navy it was not ships but men who won.

■ ■ ■

A ship of war is an entity, a city, a kingdom. In the nineteenth-century Royal Navy, ruling despotically over each of these far-flung floating kingdoms, wielding power benevolently or otherwise as was his nature, stood a Royal Navy captain. No longer could he hang a man for mutiny, but he could do almost anything else. As Her Majesty's ships went about their duties in the distant reaches of the globe—patrolling Oriental rivers, anchored in sleepy South Pacific harbors, steaming off sunbaked African coastlines—peculiarities appeared and eccentricities blossomed in the behavior of some of Her Majesty's captains. Many were entirely harmless. Captain Houston Stewart of the three-decker *Marlborough,* flagship of the Mediterranean Fleet in the early 1860s, enjoyed fishing from the window of his stern cabin when the ship was at anchor. Required occasionally to leave his line, he tied it to a rail but returned eagerly every few minutes to see whether he had a catch. Admiral Kingcome, Commander-in-Chief of the Pacific Station during the same decade, delighted in beating the drum for night quarters himself. He strapped on the drum and away he went down the lower decks, bending double beneath the hammocks of the sleeping seamen.

On board ship, especially when far from the spyglass and signal flag of his admiral, the captain of a British warship had virtually unlimited authority. One captain, commanding a ship in West African waters, always took off his uniform to read his Bible and removed his cap and jacket when conducting divine service on deck for his crew. A British captain, he believed, could recognize no higher authority than himself. Another captain advanced Christmas Day to December 18 because the pork brought on board for Christmas dinner was "feeling the tropical heat." The same captain once appointed one of his officers a bishop so that the new prelate could consecrate a patch of ground in which the captain wanted to bury a seaman. After performing this service, the new bishop was returned to the laity. Still another British captain, invited by the governor of the nearest British colony to dine on the Queen's birthday fourteen days hence, declined on the ground that he would have a headache. Reported by the angry governor to his admiral, the captain blandly explained that "he had had a headache every day for six months and he did not see why he should be spared one on Her Majesty's birthday."

Captains assumed wide latitude in matters of dress. If the captain liked gold braid, he wore gold braid and all his officers wore gold braid. If the officers next went to a ship whose captain thought gold braid pretentious, all the embroidery came off. There was great variety in hats. One admiral wore a tall white top hat, another a white billycock hat. Eventually, these eccentric sartorial proclivities confronted a powerful opposing force. The Prince of Wales cared deeply about uniforms and he liked them properly worn. In 1880, even on home stations, naval officers were wearing practically whatever they liked. Under the prodding of the Prince, a committee was formed to meet three days a week in London until standards were set. The Prince, declaring that he could understand pictures better than words, demanded drawings. Drawings were made, choices discussed, and decisions reached. Thereafter, on and near the shores of England at least, officers wore uniforms which were, by the Prince's pleasure, uniform.

Another perquisite of rank was the right to bring animals on board ship, either for nourishment or for companionship. One admiral who liked fresh milk brought two cows to sea. Officers frequently brought sheep and chickens. Some captains kept parrots, dogs, or cats in their cabins and some harbored larger and more exotic pets. Captain Marryat of the corvette *Larne,* in Burmese waters, owned a pet baboon named Jacko, who bit the crew and tore off buttons.

One of the most tolerant officers in Her Majesty's Navy was Her Majesty's second son, H.R.H. Prince Alfred, Duke of Edinburgh, a career officer. In 1870, when Prince Alfred commanded the wooden frigate *Galatea,* he permitted one of his officers, twenty-four-year-old Lieutenant Lord Charles Beresford, to bring an elephant on board the ship in India. The elephant lived in a house built on the afterdeck and fed on branches of trees, bran, biscuits, and anything else that came his way. Lord Charles trained him to clew the mainsail by picking up a line and walking along the deck. The elephant avoided seasickness by balancing himself carefully, rolling to and fro with the motion of the ship. When the *Galatea* returned to England, the elephant was sent to the London Zoological Gardens, but not without difficulty; only Lord Charles could persuade the happy pachyderm to abandon his seagoing home.

Nine years later, when Prince Alfred had advanced in rank to admiral and was Commander-in-Chief of the Mediterranean Fleet, he agreed to a brown bear named Bruin as a pet for the midshipmen aboard his flagship. At sea, Bruin liked wrestling on the quarterdeck with the boys after supper, and when the ship moored in the Grand Harbor at Malta, Bruin swam ashore and walked down the main street, the Strada Reale. Bruin's favorite trick, however, was to slip into the water when the fleet lay at anchor and swim up to the boats of another warship. Approaching stealthily, Bruin would reach out and lay one paw on the gunwale and another on the shoulder of the unsuspecting boatman. Bruin and his young masters, watching with binoculars and telescopes, enjoyed the reaction.

Bruin's fate was a watery one. His berth was in one of the ship's boats, hung above the edge of the deck out over the water. One evening, Bruin, disoriented, climbed out the wrong side of the boat and fell into the sea. The cry of "Bear overboard" was raised and the midshipmen were frantic. But neither Prince Alfred nor the captain could bring themselves to stop one of Her Majesty's battleships to pick up a mere bear, and Bruin was left behind.

When peculiar behavior in a naval officer fermented into madness, the most common cause was isolation. After years on a foreign station, crowded into a tiny wardroom, officers often ate without speaking to each other. Drink, permitted on British warships to break down tensions and mitigate the effects of isolation, sometimes made things worse. A visitor once came aboard a ship in Bermuda and found every officer drunk in the wardroom. Two were suffering from delirium tremens; one was picking the bodies of imaginary rats from the floor with a stick. Aboard another ship, an engineer officer was confined in his cabin because he believed himself to be the ship's boiler. All day long, he lay on his back, puffing vigorously, shouting that if he stopped he would burst. Still another case involved a gentle, retiring officer who went berserk. The ship's chart house was padded and he was locked inside, but somehow the ship's cat strayed within his reach and was torn limb from limb.

Captains, of course, were the most isolated of all. After years of being part of an Officers' Mess, a man on becoming a captain was suddenly condemned to live and dine alone. He could modify his predicament by inviting his officers to dine with him or by speaking to them on deck, but it was expected on both sides that distance would be maintained.

One captain of a ship lost in the immensity of the South Pacific appeared one morning on the poop of his ship with his salmon rod in hand. To the horror of the crew, he began casting long and accurately at the first lieutenant standing below him on the quarterdeck. Another captain suddenly turned and shouted at the ship's quartermaster to bring him a bucket because the commander, his second in command, made him sick. Officers afflicted by disagreeable captains had means of retaliation providing they proceeded with caution. If invited to dinner, they were free to decline. One captain, faced with refusals from his entire company of officers, countered by giving each a written order to come to dinner. The officers could not disobey this command and they came to his table, but refused to look at the captain, or to speak, or to eat the food which was placed before them.

Not all British captains were demented or foolish, of course. Most were respected, many were admired, and some learned to rule their floating kingdoms with near-Solomonic wisdom. There was, for example, the captain of a troopship engaged in ferrying soldiers, officers, and sometimes officers' wives between England and India. On one voyage a dispute broke out among the ladies as to who should have the privilege of bathing first. The ship's captain pondered and then solemnly declared that the oldest lady should have precedence. Thereafter, it is said, the younger ladies splashed happily while the more elderly female passengers gave up bathing for the remainder of the voyage.

Officers gave their orders to boatswain's mates, whereupon these grizzled noncommissioned officers, themselves promoted up from the ranks, used a blend of shouts, curses, coaxings, and explanations to pass the orders to the men. Their usual tone was exasperation. "You're a bloomin' Portuguese army, you are," one boatswain's mate complained to his men. "I say to one of you beggars, go, and he comes, and to another, do this, and he sees me damned first." Sir Percy Scott once overheard a boatswain's mate explaining to a group of seamen how they were to behave when Queen Victoria presented them with medals at Windsor Castle. "Now do you 'ear there," said the boatswain's mate, "when you come opposite 'er Majesty you don't go down on your knee. You stand up, take your 'at off, hold your 'and out, and 'er Majesty puts the medal in the palm. When you get it, don't go examining it to see if it 'as got the proper name on it; walk on; if it's not the right one, it will be put square afterwards."

Years at sea taught most boatswain's mates exactly how far they could go in dealing with the ship's officers. One captain who took to sea a coop filled with chickens excoriated his boatswain's mate in public because the birds and their pen were dirty. Whereupon the mate cleaned the pen, whitewashed the chickens, and blacked their legs and beaks. The chickens died and the captain fumed, but he was helpless.

For ordinary seamen, it was a harsh life in a Darwinian world; those who were not fit did not survive. Everything was done at the run to the insistent clamor of hoarse shouts. There was no privacy and little rest. Men stood four-hour watches, four on and four off. Seamen off duty slept, as in Nelson's day, in hammocks slung over the guns. At night, flickering candles, hung in lanterns, threw shadows across the sleeping, swaying men and the polished, gleaming guns. In peacetime, there was far too little to do to occupy the time of the huge crews which had to be maintained on board in case of war. Idleness was dangerous and thus, over the centuries, evolved the practice of daily holystoning of the decks, the entire crew in rows on their knees rubbing the deck with a kind of sandstone until it shone like the floor of a London ballroom—until flying salt spray covered it again with gumminess which would be removed by holystoning again the following day.

The food, too, was cheerless; this had changed little since Trafalgar. Lime juice, a preventive against the dreaded scurvy, was served once a week, not to please the men but to keep them healthy. Water was drawn from casks where it had stood for months; what came out was often a foul-smelling, syrupy brew. The ration of rum, served on British ships since the days of Francis Drake, was halved in 1825 and then halved again in 1853. Salt beef and salt pork, preserved in brine, were drawn out in stiff slabs which had to be soaked for hours in fresh water before they could be cooked and eaten. As the century progressed, beef was preserved in tins; the sailors called it "bully beef" or "Fanny Adams" after an English girl who had mysteriously disappeared near a tinning factory. Biscuits, hard as stones and the abode of weevils, were a staple. On sailing ships, British seamen ate with their fingers; later, when knives and forks were issued, old admirals grumbled that the Navy was pandering to luxury which would undermine discipline.

Discipline in the Royal Navy had always been stern. The great eighteenth-century admiral John Jervis, Earl St. Vincent, had decreed that shipboard discipline must rest on fear. In the Napoleonic era, harsh discipline was essential to harness and coerce seamen dragged aboard ships, cursing and kicking. The operation of the press gang, less conscription than kidnapping authorized by Parliament, was simple and violent: when a ship needed men, the captain sent a press gang ashore. They overpowered and captured as many civilians as were needed and carried them, subdued by violence or drink, back to the ship. Once aboard, there would be no escape for many years. They were kept in subjugation by the cat-o'-nine-tails, wielded by boatswain's mates, a collection of "brutes who rejoiced in their muscular arms and were charmed with the sound of the heavy, dense blows which they dealt in sheer wantonness."

The ultimate reaction to this ill-treatment, desertion, was perilous: a seaman caught in an attempt to desert was condemned to the dreaded penalty of "flogging around the fleet." This meant that he would be tied to a capstan in a small boat which would proceed in stages between the anchored vessels of the fleet. Alongside each ship, the victim would receive twenty-five lashes of the cat-o'-nine-tails on his bare back, the time between ships being used to revive him by pouring wine down his throat. This ended before mid-century, and by the 1870s a captain's right to order flogging was severely restricted by law, although floggings continued on more distant stations. It was not until 1879 that flogging was finally abolished in the Royal Navy and the last cat-o'-nine-tails permanently put away in a boatswain's mate's locker.

The cat was silenced, but leave was rare or granted grudgingly, and the impulse to desert remained strong. In 1865, when H.M.S. *Sutlej,* flagship of the British Pacific Squadron, put into San Francisco, a third of the crew deserted, taking the ship's boats with them. Safely immune from British authority, these former sailors enjoyed insulting their former officers when they came on shore. Seamen given liberty who did return to their ships usually came back drunk and penniless. Conditions improved with the passage of time but even in 1890, the men of the cruiser *Hawke* were allowed on shore only once a month, and men with bad records only once in three months. There was a solution, found by captains willing to defy St. Vincent's decree. One captain, following this course, had to deal with an excellent seaman who habitually returned late from leave. Summoning the man, the captain told him how valuable he was and instructed him to come to him personally and ask for forty-eight hours' leave whenever he wanted it. The seaman was never late again.

A sailing ship's most valuable men were those who went aloft. Three huge pine masts thrust up from the deck and were crossed at different levels by wooden yards from which as many as twenty canvas sails were hung and stretched. By changing the alignment of the yards and thus the angle of the sails to the wind, the ship could be made to sail in almost any direction. For the men who worked there, this interlocking web of wood, canvas, and rope made an extraordinary gymnasium in the sky. Men scampered through the rigging, sometimes running along the yards without holding on even though the ship was rolling wildly. Sometimes they fell, usually catching the yard or a line to save themselves. When a ship changed course, falling off before the wind, the heavy rolling caused the great yards to strain and shudder; the sails went slack and the huge sheets of canvas rolled and crackled like thunder. If a line parted, the violent backlash could kill anyone in the way. Topmen developed arms and hands as strong as a gorilla's. Everyone who went aloft went barefoot, not only because the grip of the toes was essential, but so that shoes would not hurt the hands or heads of men below or alongside. Feet thus exposed became horny and callused, and most topmen could not wear boots without discomfort; indeed, they went ashore barefoot, with their boots slung around their necks for the sake of propriety. When winter came and Her Majesty's ships remained at sea, men worked aloft in icy wind, sleet, and snow, dressed only in flannel vests and trousers with their heads, arms, ankles, and feet bare. When their work was done, they would swing down the lines, land on deck with catlike spring, and go below—to find a freezing gundeck awash in water, the galley fire out, and nothing but cold water and hard biscuits.

And yet despite flogging, poor food, no leave, and constant danger, the average seaman had immense pride in himself and the navy. One had only to see a competitive sail drill among the ships of the Mediterranean Fleet moored in Malta's Grand Harbor to understand the spirit of the fleet. General sail drill was carried out every Monday morning. Crowds gathered along the yellow stone ramparts to watch the ships compete in making sail, shifting topsails, striking topgallant masts and upper yards, all against the clock.

The men who worked aloft had been picked for their quickness, agility, and courage and they had a fierce pride in their ability and their ship's standing. The elite were the upper yard men, who attracted the eyes of the entire fleet; to be known as the smartest Royal Yard Man in the fleet was to reach a pinnacle of fame.

At one moment, the fleet would be silent and immobile, the men frozen on each deck. At the flagship's signal, the fleet erupted into life. Men swarmed aloft, darting along the yards, shifting lines and moving sails with astonishing speed. Time was at stake, not life, and with the ship's reputation to make, men took extraordinary risks so that for a while it was necessary after each drill to make the signal "Report number of killed and injured." At fault were not the officers but the men themselves, who cared passionately about winning at these perilous but thrilling games. It was this same spirit which maintained the tradition that when a ship sailed for home from the Grand Harbor in Malta, a man would be standing erect on the top of each mast—main, mizzen, and fore. "Many a time have I seen these men, balanced more than 200 feet in the air, strip off their shirts and wave them," recalled Lord Charles Beresford. In 1909, one of these old topmen wrote to Lord Charles about the sailing-ship navy of fifty and sixty years before: "I am doubtful if there are many men in the Navy today who would stand bolt upright upon the royal truck of a line-of-battle ship. I was one of those who

did so. Perhaps a foolish practice. But in those days fear never came
our way."

Along with her officers, boatswain's mates, and ordinary seamen, a
great Royal Navy man-of-war in the nineteenth century was home
to a small group of adolescent boys, the midshipmen. Until the great
reforms of Jacky Fisher, these future officers were almost exclusively the sons of gentlemen. Not necessarily aristocrats—the dashing young earls and viscounts tended to go into the Brigade of
Guards or the elite cavalry regiments of the army. The navy, with its
long stretches of sea duty and service on foreign stations, seemed
too far away from the attractions of living in England. When a boy
bearing a title did go into the navy, he was likely to be a younger
son. Queen Victoria's second son, Prince Alfred, Duke of Edinburgh, became a career officer, eventually rising to the rank of admiral and command of the Mediterranean Fleet. King Edward VII's
second son, Prince George, was a career navy man until his elder
brother died and he stepped forward as Prince of Wales and eventually became King George V. Most midshipmen, however, were of
neither royal nor noble blood, but the offspring of the solid, conservative gentry of rural England. It was essential that a boy's parents possess sufficient connections to have their son nominated by
the First Lord of the Admiralty and sufficient money to pay the
expenses of his schooling and training until he received an officer's
commission.

A prospective cadet had to be nominated by the First Lord
before his thirteenth birthday. This achieved, he traveled to Portsmouth for a written and physical examination. Neither exam was
onerous, particularly if the boy had some education. A little English,
some French or Latin, a "satisfactory knowledge of the leading facts
of Holy Scripture and English history, a certain amount of geography, and an elementary knowledge of arithmatic, algebra and geometry" were what was required. Lord Charles Beresford, second son
of the Marquess of Waterford, signed his application and was asked
if he always signed his middle name, "William," with a single "l."

Beresford paused only a second. "Only sometimes, sir," he
said. He passed.

Prince Louis of Battenberg, entering the Royal Navy at twelve,
survived his physical by a different application of wit. Bothered by
shortsightedness and knowing that his vision would be tested by
being asked to read the time on the Naval Dockyard Tower clock,
Battenberg carefully set his watch by the clock before going in to be

examined. Just before the question was asked, he managed a furtive peek at his watch.

Not all candidates survived the hurdles. In a typical mid- to late-nineteenth-century year, of one hundred boys presenting themselves for examination at Portsmouth, sixty-four would pass and become Royal Naval Cadets. They were dispatched to H.M.S. *Britannia,* an old three-deck ship-of-the-line brought into the river Dart and permanently moored in 1863 just above the town of Dartmouth. The following year, the two-decker *Hindustan* was moored upstream of *Britannia.* Most of the masts and rigging were removed from both ships, a walkway connected them, and together they became a floating school for future officers of the Royal Navy.

New cadets joined the *Britannia* twice each year and settled in for two years of courses which included seamanship, navigation, mathamatics, and French (France remained the likely foe). It was a Spartan life of exercise and discipline. *Britannia*'s upper deck had been enclosed and converted into classrooms and officers' quarters. Belowdecks, all the guns had been removed and the gundecks transformed into dormitories and messrooms for the cadets. The boys slept like ordinary seamen in hammocks slung close beneath the low-beamed ceilings. Each kept all his belongings in his sea chest, fitted with a mirror on the inside of the lid and a small washbasin which nestled among his clothing. The day began with a cold saltwater bath on deck and progressed through dressing, prayers, inspection, meals, classes, and exercise.

A single mast had been left in place on *Britannia.* Towering 120 feet above the deck, with safety nets stretched beneath, it was used to train cadets in sail drill; the boys could also climb it for fun whenever they liked. Before the end of his second term, each cadet was required to touch the truck, the round piece of wood at the top of the mast. This could only be done by shinnying up the last fifteen feet of bare pole. Every term, a few boys, dizzied by the height, fell into the nets; some were so badly injured that they had to be sent home for good.

Officially, discipline rested with the officers and consisted of confinement on bread and water or caning with trousers lowered. In fact, the older boys kept the younger in line. As late as 1893, Cadet (later Vice Admiral) K.G.B. Dewar considered himself "comparatively lucky in receiving only two really severe beatings whereas some of my contemporaries were kept in a state of constant terror by frequent thrashings." This kind of bullying and beating of thirteen-year-old boys by fifteen-year-olds tended, Admiral Dewar noted dryly, to "suppress independence and initiative in our future naval officers."

After two years, cadets who survived their courses, *Britannia*'s foremast, and the older boys left the school and went to sea as midshipmen. Here their home was the Gunroom, a tiny cabin on the lower gundeck next to the ordinary seamens' quarters. They slung their hammocks just as they had done on the *Britannia*. Each boy got a pint of water every morning for washing. He opened his sea chest and put the water in his basin inside. In a heavy sea, water slopped over onto his clothing, but this was infinitely preferable to having it spill onto the spotless deck, an infraction which brought swift punishment. The midshipmen ate simply and sparingly, salt pork one day, salt beef the next, and many of them carried memories of pangs of hunger through the rest of their lives.

Discipline remained strict. Midshipmen could not be flogged; it was thought too degrading for one of Her Majesty's future officers to bear the stripes of the cat. They could be ordered to the top of the mast as punishment ("Masthead for the midshipmen, the cat for the men" was a navy saying). Cadet John Jellicoe, future Commander-in-Chief of the Grand Fleet, did not mind; he enjoyed the view, and once that grew boring he pulled out a book. Harsher discipline lay in the hands of the older midshipmen. Younger midshipmen who misbehaved or somehow displeased their seniors were subject to Gunroom trials. If found guilty, they could be bent over the Gunroom table and beaten with a dirk scabbard. On occasion, midshipmen, bullied or beaten beyond endurance, rose in revolt. In 1905, on board the cruiser *Kent,* a desperate young midshipman fired a revolver at the senior midshipman. The tormentor must have opened his mouth very wide in surprise at this behavior, because the bullet passed through both of his cheeks without touching his teeth.

The midshipmen's purpose at sea was learning to sail and fight a ship. Boys soon discovered that climbing the mast of a ship at sea was quite different from climbing the mast of the stationary *Britannia.* High in the rigging, a midshipman looked down between his feet at the deck pitching and rolling, the sea hissing and seething. There were no safety nets. Sir Percy Scott, who survived to become an admiral, vividly recalled this part of a midshipman's training: "On a dark night, with the ship rolling, [a midshipman] was awakened from his slumbers by a scream, 'Topmen of the watch in royals!' In a pouring rain squall, he had to feel his way aloft to a yard 130 feet above the deck. . . . There the sail was aback, wet and stiff as a board, the clewlines fouled. But the sail had to be furled. . . . Fine training for a boy," said Scott, placidly adding: "although it cost a good many lives."

Down from the yards, during the long nights at sea, midshipmen made up their own games. Cockroaches were trapped, a spot of melted candle wax was dripped on their backs, and a piece of spun yarn planted in the wax. The yarn was lighted and the insects released; if they could be made to go in the same direction, it became a race. (On one ship, the cockroach escaped, its yarn still burning, and set the ship on fire.) Maggots, coaxed from bad meat, were saved for maggot derbies. The course was the Gunroom table, lined with books to define the track. Each maggot owner was allowed to touch his entry on the tail with a pencil to spur it on or to prevent it from climbing the books or reversing course. Sometimes, when two maggots collided, one climbed on the back of the other and rode piggyback, confusing the outcome.

It was a mixture of danger, excitement, fear, and boredom, and in later life most midshipmen looked back with fond memories on their early years aboard sailing ships. Part of the reason was the ship and the sea, and part was the friendship they felt for each other and the companionship they found among the older men. On a sailing ship, the young midshipmen lived close to the ordinary seamen, working side by side aloft in the rigging, barefooted as the men had taught them. When they were hungry, they chewed tobacco because the men advised that this would dull the pangs. This juxtaposition of ordinary seamen and future officers bred respect on both sides: the men were quicker to obey an officer who knew what it was to reef a sail in the teeth of the wind; the officers were more effective in command because they understood and admired the stuff of which British seamen were made.

Sir Percy Scott, the gunnery Jeremiah of the Royal Navy, looked back warmly on "those old sailing days in fine weather" and on the soft nights on the warm trade winds when "in the evening the men always sang and it was fine to hear a chorus of eight hundred men and boys. We midshipmen knew all the men's songs . . ."

Before 1851, the British ship-of-the-line was built as she had been for centuries: a three-deck, wooden sailing vessel propelled by the wind, armed with tiers of smoothbore cannon firing solid round cannonballs. In that year, the first major change in this traditional construction occurred. A British three-decker was equipped with a steam engine deep inside her oaken hull. A funnel was raised above her decks, a propeller shaft protruded through her stern, and H.M.S.

Sans Pareil could go where she wished, with or without the wind. By 1858, the British Navy had built or converted thirty-two steam-fitted ships-of-the-line. The French Navy, spurred by the ambitious Emperor Napoleon III, followed the same course and by the end of that year also possessed thirty-two propeller ships-of-the-line. It was not this temporary equality, however, that brought momentary jeopardy to Britain's otherwise serene domination of the oceans.

On March 4, 1858, in Toulon, the French Navy laid the keel of the frigate *La Gloire,* the world's first oceangoing ironclad. *La Gloire* was not truly an iron ship; rather, she was a wooden-hulled frigate with iron plates bolted to her timber sides above the waterline. The plates were a response to new rifled guns which, tests had proved, could hurl a solid shot through the oaken sides of wooden ships. Convinced that his ironclad, protected by her heavy metal shielding, would be able to overwhelm any number of conventional ships, Dupuy de Lôme, her designer, proclaimed that *La Gloire* amidst a fleet of wooden vessels would be like a lion amidst a flock of sheep.

Britain refused to believe that her wooden walls were crumbling. With splendid British disdain, the Lords of the Admiralty reacted to this French impertinence by ordering another, bigger three-decker of 131 guns. H.M.S. *Victoria,* launched in 1859, was a larger edition of Nelson's *Victory,* built exactly a century before. Like *Victory, Victoria* had a solid hull of oak, and dumpy, muzzle-loading cannon, poking out through gunports as British warships had been designed since the time of Sir Francis Drake.

Two years after learning the details of *La Gloire,* the Lords of the Admiralty thought better. Tradition was important, but the new French warship must not be allowed to threaten British naval supremacy. They concluded that British counterparts were necessary and in December 1860, H.M.S. *Warrior,* Britain's first seagoing ironclad, was launched. She was a hybrid vessel. Forty of her guns were old-fashioned muzzle-loaders, fourteen were new breech-loaders. Her hull was made of oak, but iron plates four and a half inches thick were bolted to her sides. She was a full-rigged sailing ship, but the enormous extra weight of her iron plates made her slow and cumbersome under sail, so she was equipped with a powerful steam engine which could drive her at fourteen knots.

Within a year of *Warrior's* launching, confirmation of De Lôme's metaphor of the lion among the sheep came from across the Atlantic. Since the outbreak of the American Civil War, the superior Union Navy had blockaded Confederate ports. Squadrons of wooden sailing ships cruised in Chesapeake Bay and off Charleston, Savannah, Mobile, and New Orleans, blocking all trade. Southern cotton could not reach Europe, and crucial war materials, paid for by the cotton, could not return. Desperate to break the blockade and failing to persuade Britain or France to sell an ironclad, the Confederate Navy decided to make one for itself. When the Norfolk Navy Yard fell to the South upon Virginia's secession from the Union, the 4,636-ton frigate *Merrimack* had been captured. Her masts and upper decks were stripped down to the lowest deck on the waterline. Here a casement of heavy armor was installed to protect a battery of ten guns, four nine-inchers on each side and a pivoting seven-inch gun on the bow and the stern. Jutting from her bow was a twenty-four-foot ram. The vessel was rechristened C.S.S. *Virginia;* her mission was to attack the Union frigates blockading Norfolk.

This unusual vessel had only a single day of glory. On the morning of March 8, 1862, the *Merrimack/Virginia* steamed out of Norfolk into Hampton Roads, her single smokestack belching black smoke. With Union shells bouncing off her armor, she made straight for the Union sloop *Cumberland,* her own bow gun mowing down the men on the *Cumberland*'s deck. *Merrimack* rammed *Cumberland* in her starboard bow, wrenching off her own ram but opening a giant hole in the Union ship. *Cumberland* listed and, as she began to fill, the angle permitted her to fire three broadsides at point-blank range at her oddly shaped assailant. *Merrimack* was unharmed. As the *Cumberland* sank, *Merrimack* turned and made for the steam frigate *Congress.* Her guns set the Union ship ablaze. Two other Union frigates, maneuvering to engage the Confederate vessel, went aground. At the end of the day, the *Merrimack* withdrew, preparing to return and complete the slaughter the following day.

That evening, another, equally strange vessel appeared in Hampton Roads. The U.S.S. *Monitor* had been built in response to the *Merrimack;* over the winter, the North, aware of the work on the *Merrimack,* had created a smaller ironclad to engage her. *Monitor* was 987 tons and had only two guns, but they were eleven-inch cannon set in a revolving turret on the middle of her deck. Laid down in New York City in October 1861, she was launched at the end of January and towed to Chesapeake Bay. Few had much faith in her. When she was launched, her officers refused to stand on her deck, believing that she might go straight to the bottom. Only her designer, John Ericsson, remained on board, waving his hat triumphantly as she floated on the New York tide.

On the morning of March 9, when *Merrimack* reappeared,

Monitor was waiting. The ships fought for two hours, *Monitor* enjoying the advantage of her revolving turret, not needing to maneuver to bring her guns to bear. Neither ship seriously damaged the
other, but after two hours *Monitor* ran out of ammunition and withdrew to replenish. *Merrimack* then turned her attention to the
wooden Union frigate *Minnesota.* In desperation, the *Minnesota*
loosed a broadside from two ten-inch guns, fourteen nine-inch, and
seven eight-inch. The shells hit *Merrimack* and bounced off. *Merrimack* then set *Minnesota* on fire. At this point, the *Monitor* returned. The *Merrimack* aimed at her opponent's armored pilot
house, hit the small shelter with a shell, and wounded *Monitor*'s
captain by driving iron splinters into his eyes. Both ships retreated
and the engagement was not renewed. The battle was a draw: *Merrimack* had routed the Union squadron off Norfolk but she could not
steam up the bay to the Potomac to bombard Washington as long as
Monitor was there. Neither was she sufficiently seaworthy to go out
and attack other blockading Union flotillas in the open ocean.

In fact, both ships were of limited use. Neither had the ability to
go to sea or remain there for weeks. In the rough waters of the open
sea, *Monitor* would have become a floating coffin. She had come
close to sinking twice under tow from New York to Hampton
Roads; she did eventually sink under tow off Cape Hatteras. But the
battle between these two awkward ships did have one far-reaching
result: it proved beyond doubt the advantage of an iron hull over a
wooden one.

The Royal Navy's response was measured. More ironclads were
ordered, but until 1866 wooden hulls were laid down as well. In 1861
and 1862, the flagship of the Mediterranean Fleet was the old three-
decker wooden line-of-battle ship *Marlborough,* carrying 121 guns.
A decade later, Midshipman John Jellicoe joined *Newcastle,* a full-
rigged, four-thousand-ton wooden-hulled frigate. As part of the
Royal Navy's Flying Squadron, available for rapid deployment to
troubled areas, she sailed in company with four similar wooden frigates and one frigate whose wooden hull was covered with iron
plates. A number of older wooden ships underwent conversions:
they were brought into the yard to have armor plates bolted to their
sides. The older ships often took less than kindly to this tampering;
the hull of the converted wooden battleship *Orion* was so abused
that her seams often cracked open and squirted jets of water in
heavy weather.

The trend was to iron, and with it from sail to steam. As
wooden hulls were sheathed in iron plates, vessels became heavier
and the ratio of sail area to the weight of the ship declined. At first,

in an effort to push these ponderous hulls through the water, designers added more and taller masts; the ten-thousand-ton ironclads
Agincourt, Minotaur, and *Northumberland,* laid down in 1861, each
had five towering masts. This design had limits; one was tragically
exceeded in September 1870 when H.M.S. *Captain,* a full-rigged armored ship with colossal masts and clouds of sail, heeled over in a
Channel storm. Unable to right herself because of her top-heavy
construction, she capsized and went down, taking with her all but
eighteen of her five-hundred-man crew.

The lesson of the *Captain*—that iron ships required steam propulsion—was one that most British captains were reluctant to grasp.
Sailing ships had been fitted with steam engines since well before
the Crimean War. The majestic *Marlborough* and the more modern
Victoria both had steam engines tucked away on a lower gundeck;
when the engines were put in use, slender funnels were raised between the masts. To their captains, however, the use of an engine for
entering and leaving harbor or even in an emergency seemed disgraceful. *Marlborough* was famous throughout the fleet for her elegance and efficiency; this meant the smartness and precision with
which her seamen could manage her sails. In 1859, when the ironclad *Warrior* was being constructed, Captain Alston's *Manual of
Seamanship,* published for midshipmen, assigned steam propulsion
its proper subordinate place: "Although we are living in what may
be termed the steam era and our Navy is a steam navy, I have in this
work wholly excluded the consideration of steam power, as, owing
to the great cost of coal and the impossibility of providing stowage
for it except to a limited extent, the application of steam power for
ordinary purposes must be strictly auxiliary and subordinate and its
employment on general service the exception rather than the rule."

It was not, of course, the price of coal that kept the engines
silent. In those days a man-of-war under sail looked like a gigantic
yacht, scrupulously clean, with no sounds other than the creak of
timbers, the sighing of the wind in the rigging, and the shouts of the
boatswain's mates. The eye caught the curve of the sails against the
blue sky.

In 1865 young Lord Charles Beresford went aboard the frigate
Tribune, commanded by Captain Lord Gillford. Lord Gillford
prided himself on the speed of his ship under sail, and nothing could
persuade him to employ his steam engine. Indeed, Lord Gillford
refused to shorten sail in heavy weather and ordered that no sail
should ever be taken in without his personal permission. One night
in a storm, Beresford went down to the captain's cabin to ask permission to take in one topsail. The ship was heeling over at an

alarming angle. The captain stuck one bare foot out of his bed and put it against the side of the ship. "I don't feel any water here yet," he declared and sent Beresford back on deck. The next minute the sail blew away.

Lord Gillford's passion was shared by most of his colleagues. As late as 1874, the Royal Navy Flying Squadron proceeded everywhere under sail. *Newcastle,* Jellicoe's ship, was fitted with an engine, but the whole emphasis of training on the ship was placed on sail drill. Occasionally, an elderly captain simply forgot about his ship's engine. One such veteran, entering a harbor under sail and steam, ordered the sails struck and the anchor dropped. To his amazement, the ship continued forward, snapping the anchor cable. Moments before the ship ran aground, the captain was reminded that he had forgotten to order the engines stopped. "Bless me, I forgot we *had* engines," he replied.

Well into the 1880s, British warships continued to be rigged with masts and sails. *Inflexible,* Captain John Fisher's first command, had many features of a modern warship. She was made of solid iron and she carried massive eighty-ton guns in twin turrets. But she also boasted tall masts, yards, and sails. Officially, the reason was that steam engines might break down and that ships of war must always have an alternative means of locomotion. But the real reason was that officers and men alike hated engines and loved sails. "I did not like the *Defence.* I thought her a dreadful ship. After the immaculate decks, the glittering perfection, the spirit and fire and pride of the *Marlborough,* I was condemned to a slovenly, unhandy tin kettle." Thus did Lord Charles Beresford react to his transfer from the proud three-decker to a new steam-driven ironclad. Everyone hated the black smoke pouring out of the funnels, dirtying the masts and yards and sooting the white, holystoned decks. Even worse was the process of coaling. As sacks of coal were brought on board and stowed below, a fine black dust spread everywhere, covering sails and decks, officers and men.

Nevertheless, by the end of the eighties, sails were mostly gone. In 1887, Captain Penrose Fitzgerald, himself a splendid sailing-ship captain, called on his colleagues to face facts: "The retention of masts and sails in men of war diverts so much attention and energy and resources of both officers and men from the real work of their profession and from the study of modern naval warfare. . . . Evolutions aloft are so attractive and so showy and there is so much swagger about them . . . that we seem to have lost sight of the fact that . . . [they] have nothing to do with the fighting efficiency of a ship in the present day." In 1886, *Colossus,* the first battleship built of steel instead of iron, was commissioned at Portsmouth. *Colossus* was also the first British battleship to have electric lights throughout. Soon the hybrid battleships with their eccentric distributions of modern guns, their low freeboard, side-by-side funnels, and bulky, pagodalike structure were gone. When the Naval Defence Act of 1889 passed Parliament, the navy was authorized to build eight modern steel battleships, weighing over fourteen thousand tons and capable of more than sixteen knots. With these ships of the *Royal Sovereign* class came the announcement of the Two Power Standard. The "cardinal . . . policy of this country is that our Fleet should be equal to the combination of the next two strongest navies in Europe," declared the First Lord in March 1889. The transformation was extraordinarily rapid. Every captain commanding a great steel battleship at the beginning of the twentieth century had trained in the Old Navy of masts and sails. None would dispute the retired sailor who looked back on those days and said, "No doubt the present fleet far excels the old wooden walls, but those old wooden walls made sailors."

In spite of its traditions of gallantry and seamanship, the nineteenth-century Royal Navy was unready for war. Responsibility for this lay at the top. Weapons and tactics in naval warfare were changing rapidly, but many senior officers preferred not to notice. They were assigned to ships, they served in them, eventually they commanded them, without ever giving a serious thought to the design of their vessels, their fighting efficiency, or their tactical employment in battle. Anything new was suspicious and potentially dangerous. By getting out of step, one might make a mistake; by remaining in step, one eventually reached the top. Midshipmen became lieutenants, lieutenants became commanders, then captains, then admirals, all in stately procession, no one making a fuss, each waiting placidly in line for his seniors to retire so that he could succeed.

One problem was the Nelsonian tradition. Nelson had achieved absolute victory, Nelson was a naval legend. Therefore, Nelson's way was the only way. Nelson had ordered his captains to lay alongside the enemy; therefore, even though modern guns could reach out to far greater distances, British captains still dreamed of closing to point-blank range. No matter that Nelson throughout his career had been a practitioner of boldness and innovation. His words had been graven in stone, his tactics hardened into glorious tradition. To make matters worse, officers who had fought under Nelson were still around. Any junior innovator thinking of proposing change had to deal not simply with hoary tradition, but with the bleak eye of the old admiral pacing the quarterdeck.

Another problem was the human material. The brightest boys in England did not instinctively become navy midshipmen. Nepotism was the rule as fathers steered their sons, and uncles their nephews, into the navy; the result was a "self-perpetuating . . . semi-aristocratic yacht club." This tradition ensured good breeding and solid courage, but not necessarily vision. As noted, even among the aristocracy and the gentry, the Royal Navy did not often attract the most intellectually gifted; there were many ways to spend one's life more appealing than months on a rolling deck. As the peacetime years stretched on, there was little incentive to weed out dullards and incompetents, most of whom had friends at the Admiralty, or in Parliament, or even at Court.

When bright young men did come into the navy, they had few opportunities to learn and nowhere to take their ideas. There was neither a naval college to instruct and stimulate nor a naval staff to filter and promote new suggestions and theories. The only school was the sea. Once in a while, a cry of protest was heard from the ranks. In 1878, *Macmillan's* magazine published an accusing article by a serving junior officer: "I call the whole system of our naval education utterly faulty. . . . I say that we, the Navy's youth, are in some professional matters most deplorably ignorant, and the day will come when we, and England, will wake up to the fact with a start. It sounds impossible, inconceivable, that it is only a privileged few who are allowed to make a study of gunnery . . . only a privileged few who are initiated into the mysteries of torpedos; only a privileged few who are taught . . . surveying and navigation; not even a privileged few who are taught the science of steam; and yet all this is so!"

The article was signed "A Naval Nobody." Had it not been published under a cloak of anonymity, it might have ruined the career of its author, Lieutenant John Jellicoe, future Commander-in-Chief of the Grand Fleet in the First World War.

The Admiralty and most senior officers looked upon any expression of ideas from junior officers as impertinence. On one occasion when a good idea had been forwarded to the Admiralty, a Sea Lord scribbled across the paper: "On what authority does this lieutenant put forward such a proposal?" This, as many young officers saw it, was the crux: the old sea dogs saw any questioning of the old ways as a challenge to authority. It flew in the face of the oldest law of the sea: absolute obedience to orders. From a boy's first day on the *Britannia* the first principle had been obedience. This was true not only in the 1860s but in the 1890s. "As a midshipman, I was often told that it was not my duty to think but only to obey," wrote Vice Admiral K.G.B. Dewar of his years as a cadet and midshipman in the middle nineties. No matter that Nelson himself had repeatedly disobeyed orders, that one of the most glorious moments in British naval history had been when Nelson put his telescope to his blind eye at Copenhagen and claimed that he did not see the signal to withdraw. Rigid obedience stifled initiative and even obliterated common sense. When in the spring of 1893, junior officers were compelled blindly to obey a superior even though it was clear that disaster would follow, H.M.S. *Camperdown* rammed H.M.S. *Victoria.*

Vice Admiral Sir George Tyron, Commander-in-Chief of the Mediterranean Fleet, was regarded as a man who one day would be First Sea Lord. A brilliant officer and an outstanding seaman, Tyron also possessed a mathematical mind which he applied in devising ever more intricate and daring maneuvers for his ships to perform. He delighted in changing formations from column in line to column abreast and back again, setting his ships on seemingly irretrievable courses, then saving them from collision with a signal from his flagship at the last possible minute. If these novel and spectacular maneuvers, intricate as a quadrille, astonished and frightened his captains, so much the better. It was Tyron's worry that Royal Navy captains would lose their edge in peacetime; his complicated naval ballets were designed to keep them on their mettle. Nor did Tyron's officers dare to question his orders. The Admiral was an overbearing man and an iron disciplinarian; besides, he had always been right. No matter how baffled his captains were by Tyron's mysterious orders, everything always seemed to come out splendidly. Even Tyron's second in command, Rear Admiral A. H. Markham, admitted that he rarely comprehended Tyron's ingenious evolutions.

In June 1893, Tyron took the fleet, consisting of eight battleships and five cruisers, to the eastern Mediterranean. Tyron flew his flag in H.M.S. *Victoria* and Markham flew his in H.M.S. *Camperdown.* On June 23 the fleet, which was anchored off Beirut, weighed anchor and went to sea for exercises. It was a bright sunny day, with clear visibility and a calm sea. By mid-afternoon, the ships were steaming in two columns, 1,200 yards apart. At two-twenty P.M. Tyron hoisted a signal for the next maneuver: the vessels were to change formation, passing through each other's columns by turning inward towards each other. Immediately, there were questions throughout the fleet. With the ships steaming at nine knots only 1,200 yards apart and the turning radius of some of the ships at that speed as much as 1,600 yards, the margin of safety seemed nonexistent. Captain Gerard Noel of the battleship *Nile,* immediately astern of Tyron, said: "I thought we had taken it [the signal] wrong." He asked for a repeat, which was given. "I still thought there was something wrong," he said later.

At three thirty-seven P.M., Tyron signaled that his command was to be executed: "Second division alter course in succession 16 points to starboard" and "First division alter course in succession 16 points to port." Captain Arthur Moore of the battleship *Dreadnought,* immediately behind *Victoria* and *Nile,* told his officers: "Now we shall see something interesting." He meant that although the situation seemed perilous and he couldn't understand it, he assumed that the audacious Tyron had some trick up his sleeve. On board the flagship *Victoria* her captain, Maurice Bourke, standing next to the Admiral, was uneasy. He knew that the maneuver would take his ship very close to *Camperdown.* To indicate his fears, he had already loudly asked a midshipman on the bridge to sing out the distance to the *Camperdown.* But when his own second in command, *Victoria*'s commander, urged him to speak to the Admiral, Bourke angrily told him to be silent. To question Tyron, one needed a braver man than Bourke.

On *Camperdown,* Admiral Markham could have issued orders which would have saved the situation. Markham was a competent officer and later behaved heroically on an expedition to the Arctic. But he was outweighed not only in rank, but in experience of seamanship. His first reaction when Tyron's original signal was reported to him was "It's impossible. It's an impossible maneuver." He asked the admiral to confirm the order. Instead, *Victoria* signaled impatiently, "What are you waiting for?" This was a public rebuke, witnessed by the entire fleet, which Markham could not ignore. Along with *Victoria, Camperdown* put her helm over and the two ships headed for each other, their heavy rams gliding beneath the water like giant knife blades.

It became obvious what was going to happen. "We shall be very close to that ship, sir," Bourke forced himself to say. Tyron stood frozen in silence, his eyes on the approaching *Camperdown.* "May I go astern with the port engine?" asked Bourke. Tyron remained silent and turned to look at the ships behind him. "May I go astern full speed with the port screw?" appealed Bourke. Tyron turned to look again at the *Camperdown,* now only 450 yards away. "Yes," he finally said. Bourke then cried, "Full astern both engines!" and followed immediately with "Close all water-tight doors!" Both orders had already been given on the *Camperdown.*

Tyron was as convinced of his own infallibility as his officers were; perhaps he simply thought that *his* ships could not collide. As *Camperdown*'s ram struck *Victoria* on her starboard bow, the Admiral was heard to murmur, "It's all my fault." Both ships were still making five or six knots, and the impact of the blow forced *Victoria* seventy feet sideways in the water. She was mortally wounded: *Camperdown*'s ram, twelve feet beneath the water, had penetrated nine feet into *Victoria*'s innards. With both ships still moving, *Camperdown*'s ram, like a giant can opener, tore a wider gap as it wrenched free. When the ships came apart, the flagship had a hole nearly thirty feet across below the waterline through which water rushed into the ship. Most of the watertight doors were open on that hot Mediterranean afternoon and the command to close them had come too late. *Victoria* began to sink by the bow and heel over to starboard. Soon, the foredeck was awash and the fore turret rose like a steel island from the sea. Twelve minutes after the collision, the battleship rolled over and went down, bow first. Of a crew of almost seven hundred officers and men, 358 went down with the ship. Tyron went with them. One survivor was the *Victoria*'s second in command, Commander John Jellicoe, who had spent the day in bed with a fever of 103 degrees. On feeling the impact, Jellicoe had gone to the bridge and from there, down the side into the water.

Twenty-two of the ship's fifty-one officers were drowned along with the admiral. The other twenty-nine were court-martialed, along with Rear Admiral Markham. All were acquitted, although Markham's career ceased to prosper. The grounds of his acquittal were that "it would be fatal to the best interests of the service to say that he was to blame for carrying out the orders of the Commander-in-Chief present in person."

In the years before the turn of the century, the Mediterranean Fleet, the cream of the navy, reached a peak of Victorian splendor. From its base in the Grand Harbor at Valletta, Malta, the fleet made seasonal cruises to the different shores of the inland sea. On the coast of Spain and the Riveria, in the ports of Italy and Greece and the exotic harbors of the Near East and North Africa, the great ships would silently appear from over the horizon to manifest the majesty and power of England. Anchored in rows, hulls black, superstructures a dazzling white, funnels buff yellow, flags flying stiffly in harbor breezes, boats plying back and forth, they made a colorful sight. Gold-encrusted admirals came ashore to call on local potentates and dignitaries, officers to attend balls, play polo, or hunt snipe and woodcock. Fierce competition in sail drill gave way to equally passionate competition between ships in boat races at fleet regattas or timed coaling contests. In 1880, the Commander-in-Chief of the Mediterranean Fleet, Admiral Sir Frederick Beauchamp Seymour, led his officers through such a hectic round of balls, teas, receptions, polo, and other sports that he was known as "The Swell of the Ocean."

The fiercest competition of all was in polishing the ships. Every metal surface in the Mediterranean Fleet blazed like the sun. Battleship and cruiser crews devoted enormous energy to burnishing the great guns. Massive armored watertight doors were taken off their hinges and filed and rubbed until they gleamed—and, incidentally, were no longer watertight. On some ships, even the little ring bolts on deck were polished and fitted with little flannel nightcaps to protect them from salt air between inspections.

This cult of brightwork originated in the need to keep the men busy. When sails gave way to steam, the time given to tending the rigging, furling and mending sails, straightening and coiling ropes was given instead to polishing. Like holystoning, which continued on the wooden decks of steel ships, it was absurd; the process made men's hands and clothes filthy with metal polish and as soon as salt spray hit the gleaming metal, copper turned green again and brass blue. In the early nineties, as the last sailing ironclads were replaced by modern battleships without masts, the paint-and-brightwork cult reached a peak. A sparkling ship reflected well on the captain and his second in command, the commander, and commanders spent large sums out of their private pockets, often far more than they could afford. "It was customary," wrote Sir Percy Scott, "for a Commander to spend half his pay in buying paint to adorn Her Majesty's ships as it was the only road to promotion."

Appearances were often deceiving. "When I went to sea in 1895," wrote Vice Admiral K.G.B. Dewar, "snowy, white decks, enamel paint, shining brasswork, and an air of spic and span smartness became the criteria by which ships were judged. In my first ship [the cruiser] *Hawke,* scrubbing, painting, and polishing absorbed an enormous amount of time and energy. . . . The basins on the Gunroom bathroom had to be polished till they shone like mirrors, the doors being locked to prevent them being used. . . . Thus, on a sunny Mediterranean day, the *Hawke* glistened and sparkled on the waters of that ancient sea, but she was infested with rats which contaminated the food . . . ran over the hammocks and swarmed into the Gunroom at night. No attempt was made to get rid of them, beyond the dirks of the midshipmen accurately employed."

One aspect of shipboard life which no one worried much about was gunnery; the few officers who did worry were ridiculed as fanatics. As one former officer explained: "Had anyone suggested that fighting efficiency lay in knowing how to shoot the guns and not polishing them, he would have been looked at as a lunatic and treated accordingly." The most persuasive reason was that firing the guns, like using the steam engine on sailing ships, spread dirt and grime. "It was no wonder the guns were not fired if it could be avoided," wrote Sir Percy Scott, acidly, "for the powder then used had a most deleterious effect on the paintwork and one Commander who had his whole ship enameled told me that it cost him £100 to repaint her after target practice."

Gunnery could not be wholly avoided as Admiralty orders decreed that target practice be held at least once every three months. "No one except the Gunnery Lieutenant took much interest in the results," recalled Admiral Sir Reginald Tyrwhitt. "Polo and pony racing were much more important than gun drill." Nevertheless, the ammunition had to be disposed of. On the designated day, the flagship hoisted the signal: "Spread for target practice, expend a quarter's ammunition and rejoin the fleet." Ships then steamed off in all directions and did what they liked. Many simply loaded the guns and pumped three months' allowance of ammunition at the horizon. A few ships quietly dumped the shells overboard. There was little risk; admirals understood the nasty way that gun smoke dirtied a ship. Indeed, when flagships engaged in target practice, their admirals often remained ashore to escape the din.

The fleet's attitude towards gunnery and the range at which ships fired both were legacies of Nelson's day. On board H.M.S. *Marlborough,* the Mediterranean Fleet flagship of the 1860s, "it was considered that anyone could fire a gun and that the whole credit of successful gunnery depended upon the seamanship of the sailors who brought the ship into the requisite position," reported Lord Charles Beresford, who had been a *Marlborough* midshipman. The optimum position was close range; if possible, alongside. "We used to practice firing at a cliff in Malta Harbor at a range of a hundred yards," Beresford recalled. After practice, he would be sent ashore to collect the used cannonballs and bring them back to the ship.

A decade later, Midshipman John Jellicoe, on board the frigate *Newcastle,* found that practice ranges still had not risen to much over a thousand yards. "Gunners looked along the barrels of their guns and fired at what they saw in a way which had not changed since Nelson's day," he said. Technically, the gunners did not have a choice, as no system of controlling long-range firing had been developed. In fact, it seemed, no such system was really desired in the British Navy. Ships were expected to fight at close range; close action was more decisive and better suited to British pluck. Once British captains had brought their ships within close range, their gun crews would pour shell into their enemies with such élan that they would either surrender or be destroyed. Long-range firing would ignore these traditional and successful tactics.

There were, of course, objections to this revered naval dogma, some based on historical fact. In the War of 1812, only eight years after the death of the great Nelson, British pluck had not been enough to win in the face of superior gunnery emanating from a supposedly negligible foe, the Americans. Within a few months of the outbreak of war, three veteran British frigates were humiliatingly defeated by hard-hitting American ships in single-ship actions. The defeats were not hard to explain: the American ships were newer, bigger, and better manned than the weather-beaten, foulbottomed Royal Navy ships. More important, the American crews served their guns more efficiently. These actions, which in America created a new public interest and pride in the young United States Navy, horrified the British Admiralty and public. Powerful British flotillas sailed across the Atlantic and stifled the upstart Americans by weight of numbers.

Beyond facts, there was logic: suppose an enemy admiral irritatingly refused to oblige the British naval tradition of close action. Suppose he perversely trained his own gunners to shoot accurately at six thousand or seven thousand yards. Then the British fleet might all be sunk and British sailors could exercise their pluck only by swimming about in the sea. This was the nightmare of one British naval officer who crusaded all of his life for accurate long-range gunnery. Percy Scott was a short, round-faced boy who entered the navy in 1866 and two years later arrived as a midshipman on board the fifty-gun frigate *Forte*. The *Forte*'s commander was a jolly soul, kind to his midshipmen and deeply concerned about appearances. "He gave us midshipmen plenty of boat sailing, took us on shore to play cricket, and encouraged sport of every kind," Scott recalled. "He made us dress properly and in appearance set us a fine example. He took a long time over his toilet, but when he did emerge from his cabin it was a beautiful sight, though he might have worn a few less rings on his fingers." The commander's ship was to be as beautiful as his person. The *Forte* was "absolutely transformed. All the blacking was scraped off the masts and spars and canary yellow was substituted. The quarter deck was adorned with carving and gilt, the coamings of the hatchways were all faced with satin wood, the gun carriages were French-polished, and the shot were painted blue with a gold band around them and white top. Of course, we could not have got these shot into the guns had we wanted to fight, but that was nothing. . . ."

In 1881, the British Navy was called upon to fight. Scott was present at the bombardment of Alexandria and he was appalled by what happened: "[The Egyptians] had forty-two modern heavy guns varying from 10 inch to 7 inch." They were bombarded by "eight battleships carrying eighty guns from 16 inch to 7 inch," not counting lighter calibers. "The fleet fired in all 3,000 rounds at the forts and . . . made ten hits. One would have thought that this deplorable shooting would have brought home to the Admiralty the necessity of some alteration in our training for shooting, but it did not. They were quite satisfied in that it was better than the Egyptian gunners' shooting."

In 1886, Scott was promoted to commander and sent as second in command to *Edinburgh,* the most modern turret ship of the day. He seized the opportunity to institute regular gunnery practice. "But the innovation was not liked," he said; "we were twenty years ahead of the times, and in the end we had to do as others were doing. So we gave up instruction in gunnery, spent money on enamel paint, burnished up every bit of steel on board and soon got the reputation of being a very smart ship. She was certainly very nice in appearance. The nuts of all the aft bolts on the aft deck were gilded, the magazine keys were electroplated and statues of Mercury surmounted the revolver racks."

Ten years later Scott was given command of his own ship, the 3,400-ton cruiser *Scylla* of the Mediterranean Fleet. He came on board, hoping that fleet gunnery had progressed during the time he had been away. Instead, he found that nothing had changed; paintwork was still what counted. And with paintwork, cleanliness. Admirals, writing reports after the all-important annual inspections which could promote—or fail to promote—ships' captains and commanders, stressed cleanliness: "Ship's company of good physique, remarkably clean and well-dressed; state of bedding exceptionally satisfactory. The stoker division formed a fine body of clean and well-dressed men. . . . The ship looks well inside and out and is very clean throughout. . . ." This report on H.M.S. *Astraea,* Scott noted bitterly, "contained no reference to the fact that *Astraea* was one of the best shooting ships in the Navy, nor did her captain and gunnery lieutenant get one word of praise for all the trouble they had taken to make the ship efficient as a fighting unit of the fleet."

Percy Scott was a practical sailor, not a visionary. What he wanted was a navy trained to use the more powerful guns with which technology was providing it. He wanted British gunners trained to hit the target, and to hit it often, at ever greater ranges, in all kinds of weather and sea conditions. To him, it was ludicrous and dangerous that in 1896 the crew of the modern steel battleship *Resolution* was still being mustered on deck for cutlass drill, training to parry and thrust, for the moment their ship would grind alongside an enemy and they would swarm over the side in boarding parties.

Alone, Percy Scott would have made no difference. He would have been shunted aside as a fanatic who disturbed the tranquillity of the peacetime navy. But Scott was not alone, and he was promoted to stations where his obsession could benefit the Fleet. He became commanding officer of H.M.S. *Excellent,* the navy gunnery school at Portsmouth; later he was assigned to a role in which he could exercise his talents: Inspector of Target Practice for the Fleet. The man who promoted Scott was a naval visionary, a man obsessed not just with gunnery, but also with naval strategy, tactics, ship design, and organization of personnel. Throughout his fifty years of service, from cadet to Admiral of the Fleet, he pressed for change. As First Sea Lord before the First World War, he revolutionized the British Navy.

CHAPTER 23

Jacky Fisher

◆

John Arbuthnot Fisher, England's greatest admiral since Nelson, was not cast from the Nelsonian mold. Whereas the hero of Trafalgar was a calm, quiet man whose private arrangements were a national scandal, Fisher, the tempestuous builder of the modern Royal Navy, rushed through life from one seething, volcanic controversy to the next, all the while serving at home as the exemplary head of a model family. A more important distinction, of course, is that Nelson was a fighting admiral, while Fisher, although he commanded fleets at sea (most notably the Mediterranean Fleet, from 1899 to 1902), never did so during wartime. His role and his great service to the navy and his country were as an administrator and reformer. In this sense, Fisher can better be compared to St. Vincent than to Nelson, for it was the magisterial and autocratic John Jervis, Earl St. Vincent, England's First Sea Lord during the Napoleonic Wars, who appointed Nelson to command and provided him with the ships and men to vanquish the French. Similarly, Fisher appointed Admiral Sir John Jellicoe to command the Grand Fleet during the Great War and provided Jellicoe with the vast agglomeration of ships—battleships, battle cruisers, cruisers, destroyers, and submarines—with which Great Britain guarded the exits from the

North Sea, shielded her coasts, and foiled the purposes of the German High Seas Fleet.

Fisher (who behind his back was known universally as Jacky) was First Sea Lord from 1904 to 1910 and again from 1914 to 1915. During these years, he dominated the Admiralty, ruled the Royal Navy, and dictated British naval policy. It was a time of tension and growing danger. As the German navy laws ground inexorably forward and new German battleships slid one after the other into the water, Fisher was convinced that only he could prevent a naval defeat of England with consequent starvation or invasion of the homeland and ruination of the Empire. His priorities were clear: he did not want war, but if—through international misbehavior or political blundering—war was to come, Fisher wanted the British Fleet poised to "hit first, hit hard, and keep on hitting."

It was, in almost every sense, *his* fleet. For fifty years, from naval cadet to Admiral of the Fleet, Jacky Fisher had stood for change, reform, efficiency, readiness. Over the years, as the navy converted from sail to steam, from wooden hulls to iron and steel, Fisher was first to demand reforms in technology, in personnel handling, in tactics and strategy at sea. He was a leading proponent of improved naval gunnery: firing at longer ranges, with greater accuracy and faster rates of fire. Yet he believed that the torpedo would eventually supersede the great gun as the primary naval weapon. He believed in large, fast surface ships with heavy guns, and he supervised the design and construction of the *Dreadnought,* the first all-big-gun battleship. Yet he was convinced that the submarine was the warship of the future and he urged the Royal Navy to invest in these sneaky undersea craft and develop tactics for them to sink battleships. He introduced destroyers and gave them their name. He began substitution of turbines for reciprocating engines and he urged the use of oil fuel rather than coal. Even on what seemed the smallest matters, Fisher demanded change. Remembering the hard, weevily biscuits which he had eaten as a cadet and midshipman aboard sailing ships, he converted the fleet to fresh bread baked daily in ovens aboard the ships.

In appearance, this naval titan was short and stocky; an average Englishman, perhaps, until one looked at his face. It was round, smooth, and curiously boyish. His mouth was full-lipped and sensual and could be merry, but as he aged it tightened and the corners turned down with bitterness and fatigue. The extraordinary feature was the eyes. Set far apart, almost at the edges of his face, they were very large, and light gray. Heavy eyelids, which tended to droop, gave them an almond shape. When he looked at a person, Fisher's gaze was fixed and compelling and gave no clue to the patterns of thought or emotion behind the façade. When he was happy, all this stone could melt and his eyes would glow with warmth. When wrath entered his soul, the lips thinned, the jaw clenched, and the eyes narrowed and glittered.

There was another curious quality about Jacky Fisher's face. It had a strange yellowish tint, which, together with the quasi-Oriental shape of his eyes, gave birth to the rumor, given wings by his enemies, that he was partly Malayan, "the son of a Cingalese Princess," it was said. In fact, he had suffered severely from dysentery and malaria while in his forties and almost died from this combination of diseases, which took a number of years to cure. It was this that had given him his yellowish hue, but this fact did not stop his opponents, who used it to explain what they called his "Oriental cunning and duplicity." In 1904, Captain Wilhem Widenmann, the German Naval Attaché in London, passed the rumors along to Berlin, referring to the new First Sea Lord as "an unscrupulous half-Asiatic."

Fisher was not a Malay or a Cingalese, but he was barely a gentleman by birth and not truly one in behavior. He owed nothing to family, wealth, or social position and everything to merit, force of character, and sheer persistence. "I entered the Navy penniless, friendless and forlorn," he told everyone who would listen, including the king. "I have had to fight like hell and fighting like hell has made me what I am." He brought to the fight an exceptional inventory of qualities: Herculean energy, burning ambition, towering ego and self-confidence, and fervent patriotism. He was bold, quick-witted, and original, and in everything he did he was passionately involved: for or against, yea or nay. This was true from the beginning. "I remember the intense enthusiasm which he displayed in everything . . . he was easily the most interesting midshipman I ever met," recalled an early shipmate.

Fisher's correspondence and conversation mirrored his exuberant nature. His letters, written in large, bold letters and filled with exclamation points and double and triple underlining, frequently ended with "Yours till we part at the pearly gates," "Yours till Hell freezes," or "Yours till charcoal sprouts." His phraseology ranged from the Bible to the street and he threw in quotes and historical facts with less regard for accuracy than for making whatever point he had in mind. He never reread or edited his letters before putting them in the mail. As an eighteen-year-old midshipman, he explained this practice, which he followed for the rest of his life: "I can't bear to read them [letters] over twice. I like putting things down as I think of them, and if I was to read them over twice, I should get disgusted . . . and tear the letter up and consequently never write a letter at all." His conversation was similar. Rarely worrying about the impression his listener might be forming, Fisher cared only about making his point as he riveted a man with his eyes and pounded his fist on the palm of his hand. Sometimes, he quite forgot to whom he was speaking. "Would you kindly leave off shaking your fist in my face?" King Edward once said to the Admiral.

Fisher knew the Bible intimately and he reinforced his knowledge with constant reading and visits to church. When at the Admiralty, he went every morning to early service at Westminster Abbey or St. Paul's and sometimes would listen to three sermons on a single Sunday. When the Dean of Westminster heard that the First Sea Lord had been seen listening to four sermons on one day, he wrote to Fisher, warning him of "spiritual indigestion." Fisher did not ride horses and played no sport. He liked to walk—or, better, pace—so that he could think. His single relaxation and exercise was dancing. He began as a young man on ship or shore, dancing with women, or fellow officers if women were not available, and singing or whistling the tune himself if he could not find a band. "I believe, dear Admiral, that I would walk to England to have another waltz with you," wrote one of his partners, Grand Duchess Olga, a younger sister of Tsar Nicholas II of Russia.

Fortunately for Fisher's career, his blunt words and sometimes tactless behavior were buffered by an extraordinary ability to charm. He could charm Russian grand duchesses and Royal Navy boatswain's mates, a Sultan of Turkey and a roomful of American millionaires. He charmed two monarchs of England: the tiny reclusive widow who lived at Windsor and her bon vivant son who traveled the world in pursuit of pleasure. Both Queen Victoria and King Edward VII put up with impertinence from Fisher because he delivered it with an impish smile and contagious high spirits which cut through the pomp and boredom surrounding Royal Persons. Once at a dreary formal luncheon, Fisher blurted out to the King: "Pretty dull, Sir, this. . . . Hadn't I better give them a song?" The King was delighted and the First Sea Lord then rendered a music-hall ditty about two drunken tramps in Trafalgar Square. Fisher was on shakier ground one evening at dinner when the King was teasing him about sailors having a wife in every port. Smiling, but with narrowed eyes, Fisher shot back, "Wouldn't you, Sir, have loved to be a sailor?" For a moment, the King's face clouded and the table fell ominously silent. Then the King roared and everyone else guffawed and chuckled.

Within the navy, Fisher's credo, "The efficiency of the Fleet and its instant readiness for war," won him a band of devoted followers, many of them exceptional younger officers who, like Jellicoe, would go on to higher command and fame. But not everyone in the navy liked or admired Fisher. His thrusting ambition, his certainty that he was always right, his blunt language, and his ruthless treatment of officers he thought were unfit made him enemies, especially among older, more conventional officers already shocked by the nature of his reforms. It was argued that he showed favoritism; he admitted it, declaring that "favoritism is the secret of efficiency," by which he meant selection on the basis of merit, not seniority. Besides, he pointed out, "if I haul a man up over the shoulders of his seniors, that man is going to take care to show I haven't made a mistake." As he grew older, he became more autocratic, showing contempt and hatred of anyone who stood in his way. His opponents were "pre-historic admirals," "mandarins," or "fossils." "Anyone who opposes me, I crush," he once hissed at an opponent in an Admiralty corridor. Not surprisingly, an anti-Fisher faction grew up in the navy. Fisher was described as reckless, duplicitous, abusive, and vengeful. Behind his back, he was "The Malay," "The Yellow Peril," and "that hobgoblin whose name is Fisher."

People outside the navy constantly groped for sticks with which to beat the First Sea Lord. The Admiral remained elusive. "A silly ass at the War Office wrote a paper to prove me inconsistent," he wrote to Arthur Balfour, who as Prime Minister brought Fisher to the summit of the Admiralty. "Inconsistency is the bugbear of fools! I wouldn't give a damn for a fellow who couldn't change his mind with a change of conditions. Ain't I to wear a waterproof because I didn't when the sun was shining?" Fisher's general opinion of politicians was not high. He never lost his respect for Balfour, admiring his keenness of mind and grateful for Balfour's constant support as Prime Minister and then as Leader of the Opposition. He served under four First Lords during the prewar period: Lord Selborne from 1904 to early 1905, Lord Cawdor for eight months until the fall of the Unionist government at the end of 1905, Lord Tweedmouth, the Liberal First Lord from 1906 to 1908, and Reginald McKenna from 1908 until Fisher's retirement in 1910. All worked well with Fisher, except Lord Tweedmouth, whose indecision in Fisher's long battle with Lord Charles Beresford helped to undermine the Admiralty and precipitate Fisher's ultimate fall. Cabinet ministers in general Fisher likened to "frightened rabbits," and he once declared that the existence of politicians had "deepened his faith in Providence. How else could one explain Britain's continued existence as a nation?"

There were some who charged that Fisher was a warlord who thirsted for blood. The image was supported by the story that he once suggested to the King that the navy be sent to "Copenhagen" the growing German fleet as Fisher's hero Nelson had destroyed the Danish Fleet by a surprise peacetime blow. "My God, Fisher, you must be mad!" King Edward cried. Fisher's real view of war was more complicated. He had been in battle and witnessed carnage. He knew that war was something other than a path to glory. "Personally, I hope that war will not come," he told an American friend in 1898, when press and public opinion in the United States were clamoring for war with Spain. He pointed to "the fearful miseries it always entails amongst those poor widows and orphans and dependant relatives whose sufferings pay for the fortunes of war contractors and the power of politicians who run no risks."

Nevertheless, Fisher understood what wars were about and what nations meant when they said they wanted peace: "All nations want peace, but they want a peace that suits them." A decision for war, he felt, came from a weighing of factors; if a nation felt that it risked losing more in war than it could possibly gain, there would be no war. Thus, for Fisher, the key to peace as well as security lay in the strength of the British Navy. "The French, no doubt, sincerely desire peace with England," he wrote in 1894, "provided they can replace England in Egypt and the Nile Basin and elsewhere. To obtain peace on these terms they would not shrink from trying a fall with England, if they thought there was a fair chance of success. The deadlock that ends in war can only be avoided by one of two means. Either the French may abandon their claims, or the English may strengthen their seapower to such an extent that the probable chances of an international struggle would leave France worse off than she is today." It all came back to the Fleet. "On the British fleet rests the British Empire," he said, and "Only a congenital idiot with criminal tendencies would permit any tampering with the maintainance of our sea supremacy." If war did come, it might come suddenly and, in the case of a great sea battle, all could be decided within a few hours. Throughout his career Fisher hammered on the theme of "the suddenness . . . and finality of a modern sea fight . . . once beaten the war is finished. Beaten on land, you can improvise fresh armies in a few weeks. You can't improvise a fresh Navy; it takes four years." The suddenness and decisiveness of a sea battle put a premium on intelligent, courageous leadership. "The generals may be asses, but the men, being lions, may pull the battle through on shore," he said. "But in a sea fight, if the admiral is an ass, millions of lions are useless!"

For most of Fisher's naval career, England's presumed enemy was France. Nevertheless, by 1901 he was writing from the Mediterranean, where he had trained a vast fleet to fight the French: "We must reconsider our standard of naval strength in view of the immense development of the German Navy." He admired the Kaiser ("a wonderful man," "a wonderful fellow") for his interest in the sea and for the efficient way he was building up a fleet. The Kaiser returned the sentiment. "I admire Fisher, I say nothing against him," he told a foreign visitor. "If I were in his place I should do all that he has done and I should do all that I know he has in mind to do." Despite this exchange of compliments, Fisher was convinced throughout his term as First Sea Lord of the inevitability of war with Germany. When war did come, he thought, it would come suddenly. "The German Empire," he told the King in 1906, "is the one Power in political organization and in fighting strength and in fighting efficiency, where one man (the Kaiser) can press the button and be confident of hurling the whole force of the Empire instantly, irresistably, and without warning on its enemy." Specifically, Fisher thought that the Germans would choose a weekend, probably a weekend with a bank holiday. He had no difficulty pinpointing the date, the name of the British admiral, and the name of the battle in which Britain's future would be decided. "Jellicoe to be Admiralissimo on October 21, 1914 when the Battle of Armageddon comes along," he wrote in 1911. Fisher's premise and most of the details of his prediction were correct. He picked the date because it corresponded with the probable completion of the deepening of the Kiel Canal, which would permit the passage of German dreadnoughts from the Baltic to the North Sea. War did come on a bank holiday weekend, although it was in August, not October, 1914. (The Kiel Canal had been completed in July.) At the Battle of Armageddon, which was the Battle of Jutland, when the whole strength of the German High Seas Fleet was hurled against the Royal Navy, the Commander-in-Chief of the Grand Fleet—the Admiralissimo—was Sir John Jellicoe. Jellicoe was in command because, over the years, Fisher had guided his career and insisted that no one else would do.

On January 25, 1841, in Rambodde, Ceylon (now Sri Lanka), a twenty-year-old Englishwoman, Sophie Fisher, wife of Captain William Fisher, aide-de-camp of the Governor of Ceylon, gave birth to the first of her eleven children, a son whom the parents named John Arbuthnot. As Fisher himself described his parents: "[My mother was] a most magnificent and handsome, extremely young woman who married for love exactly nine months before I was born! My father was 6 feet 2 inches, a Captain of the 78th Highlanders, also very young, also especially handsome. . . . Why I am ugly is one of those puzzles of physiology which are beyond finding out."

In the same year as his first child's birth, Captain Fisher unwisely resigned his army commission and began to plant coffee. Within a few years, his crop was obliterated by disease and he took work as Inspector General of Police, a low-paying job which left little to bring up the eleven children whom his bountiful wife provided. To lessen the burden, "little Jack," as he was known, was sent back to England at the age of six. He never saw his father again; Captain Fisher was thrown from a horse and killed when the boy was fifteen. Two years before his death, when the son he hadn't seen for seven years entered the navy, Captain Fisher wrote a letter which, in its pathetic apologies and awkward attempt at warmth, suggests how distant from his family and thoroughly alone young Jack must have felt:

> My dear Jack:
>
> You must recollect I am very poor and that you have a great many brothers and sisters, and that I cannot give you much pocket money. But I will give you what I can afford, and mind you, never get into debt. . . . From all that I have heard . . . you are a very good boy and very clever, and I expect you to get on well. Perhaps you may see some fighting. . . . God help you, my dear Jack.

Fisher's destination in England was the house of his London grandfather, Sophie's father, a wine merchant who had lost all his money ("A simple-minded man," Fisher described his grandfather, "fleeced of a fortune by foreign scoundrels") and existed by taking in lodgers. The boy lived mainly on boiled rice and brown sugar, sometimes gratefully receiving from a charitable lodger a piece of bread thickly spread with butter. He had almost no contact with his mother, now living in penury in Ceylon, struggling to bring up her many children on the negligible income of her husband's negligible estate.*

---

* Four of Fisher's siblings died in infancy. Two of his younger brothers followed him to England and entered the navy. One, Philip, became a lieutenant and drowned at twenty-seven when his ship foundered and went down in a storm at sea. A second brother, Frederick William, became a full admiral and was knighted. But he was nine years younger than Jack, who left home before he was born. They scarcely knew each other, and William appears in Fisher's correspondence even more rarely than his mother.

Fisher's sense of abandonment created a gap between him and his mother which he could never overcome. When he was twenty-nine and stationed aboard a ship in Hong Kong, he wrote to his wife, Kitty, "I heard from my mother. . . . She contemplates coming to see me. . . . I am in a horrid fright of my mother turning up some day unexpectedly; I am sure we couldn't live together. I hate the very thought of it and, really, I don't want to see her. I don't see why I should as I haven't the slightest recollection of her."

Although he helped his mother as much as possible from his skimpy navy pay and sent her an allowance until her death in 1891, Fisher resented her constant requests for more money. Thus, two months after complaining to his wife about his mother's drawing money from his agent in England, Fisher was proposing to his wife that they give away eighteen pounds, five shillings a year "to charity." He understood the sadness of the situation, but saw no remedy. "[I have] none of the feelings of a son for his mother," Fisher admitted to his wife. "I do so much pity her when I think how I love Beatrix and Cecil [his own two oldest children] and what a grief it would be to me were they to grow up without loving me."

Later in life, Fisher told everyone who would listen (including King Edward VII) that he had entered the navy "penniless, friendless and forlorn," but it wasn't quite true. He had very little money, but he had important friends. His godmother, the widow of the Governor of Ceylon whom Fisher's father had served as aide-de-camp, now lived in a sumptuous country house in Derbyshire, where young Jack was often invited. "I had happy days there," he remembered. "The Trent flowed past the house and I loved being on the river and catching perch." One of Lady Horton's neighbors was Sir William Parker, the last of Nelson's captains, now a senior admiral and Commander-in-Chief of the naval base at Plymouth. Lady Horton requested Sir William to nominate her godson Jack Fisher for the navy. At the same time, "strange to say," said Fisher, "another dear old lady took a fancy to me, and she was Lord Nelson's own niece, and she [also] asked Sir William for me." Sir William obliged and on July 13, 1854, thirteen-year-old Jack Fisher went on board Nelson's flagship, H.M.S. *Victory,* at Portsmouth to be examined for the navy. The test was simple: "I wrote out the Lord's Prayer and the doctor made me jump over a chair naked and I was given a glass of sherry." He was certified "free from defect of speech, vision, rupture, or any other physical disability," and was accepted.

H.M.S. *Britannia* had not yet been established as a school for cadets, and in 1854 boys accepted by the navy went directly to sea on a warship to learn by doing. Fisher's assignment was to *Calcutta,* then in port at Plymouth. Fisher traveled to Plymouth, where he called on the port admiral, his sponsor, Sir William Parker, whom he had never met. Parker invited the boy to dinner, "but I told him I thought I had better get on board my ship. . . . [Sir William] was amused and told me to dine and sleep at his house. He told me all about Lord Nelson whom he had served under a great many years. Only his wife was at dinner—he wore tiny little epaulettes at dinner and the next morning he sent me off to my ship . . . as I stepped on board I had a bucket of salt water over my feet. They were holystoning decks and the white-haired First Lieutenant, with his trousers turned up above his knees and no shoes or stockings, roared at me like a Bull of Bashan and afterwards gave me an orange. . . . The oldsters among my messmates all had white hair. . . . They had been all their lives in a Midshipman's berth—they were failures. Our ship had the failures as the Captain had been tried by Court Martial in his last ship for cruelty—he had flogged all his crew."

Fisher had entered on a stern life. "The day I joined as a little boy, I saw eight men flogged—and I fainted at the sight," he was to write. He found that he suffered from seasickness, which continued to plague him all his life. The food was still Old Navy: maggoty biscuits, foul water. "Whenever you took a bit of biscuit to eat," he remembered, "you always tapped it edgeways on the table to let the 'grown-ups' get away. . . . A favorite amusement was to put a bit of this biscuit on the table and see how soon all of it would walk away. . . . The water was nearly as bad as the biscuit. It was turgid, it was smelly, it was animally."

Calcutta was an old, second-rate ship-of-the-line with two gundecks and eighty-four smoothbore muzzle-loading cannon mounted in broadside array. She had been in reserve and was being recommissioned for service in the war with Russia when Fisher boarded. In June 1855, she sailed for the Baltic, where an Anglo-French fleet was blockading Russian ports on the Gulf of Finland. Without an engine, however, she was useless and on arrival she had to be towed into the anchorage by a paddle-wheel steam gunboat. After two months, the Admiral rid himself of her by sending her home. The following March, Fisher joined his second ship, *Agamemnon,* at Constantinople, where she was anchored after serving with the Allied fleet off the Crimea. Once again, Fisher arrived too late for action, and when peace was declared his ship was used as a troop carrier to return soldiers to England.

Up to this point, Fisher's short naval career had provided him with little excitement. Then, on July 12, 1856, he was promoted from cadet to midshipman and embarked in the twenty-one-gun steam corvette *Highflyer*. At fifteen, he was about to enter five colorful years on the China Station.

Highflyer's captain was Charles F. A. Shadwell, whom Fisher later described as "about the greatest saint on earth. The sailors called him, somewhat profanely, 'Our Heavenly Father.' He was once heard to say 'Damn' and the whole ship was upset. . . . He always had the Midshipmen to breakfast with him, and when we were seasick he gave us champagne and gingerbread nuts. . . . His sole desire for fame was to do good, and he requested that when he died he should be buried under an apple tree so that people might say, 'God bless old Shadwell!' He never flogged a man in his life."

Saintly Captain Shadwell was especially fond of young Jack Fisher. Shadwell was fascinated by astronomy, had published works on the subject, and, in consequence, had been elected a Fellow of the Royal Society. Alone with this unusual interest among naval officers on the China Station, he seized the opportunity to pass it along to this lively midshipman. "He was always teaching me in his own cabin," Fisher remembered. "He taught me all I know [on the subject]. I could predict eclipses and occultations and play with the differential calculus through him."

Shadwell also gave Fisher a lesson on style in command. In June 1857, *Highflyer* joined in an attack on hundreds of pirate junks on the Canton River. When the Chinese abandoned their junks to flee across the rice paddies, a British landing party swarmed in pursuit. Under heavy fire, Fisher recalled, "our captain [Shadwell] stood on the river bank (everyone else took shelter). I shall never forget it. He was dressed in a pair of white trousers, yellow waistcoat, a blue tail coat with brass buttons, and a tall white hat with a gold stripe on the side . . . and he was waving a white umbrella to encourage us . . . to go for the enemy."

The following spring, attacking a network of Chinese forts at the mouth of the Pei-ho River in North China, Captain Shadwell and the British China Squadron suffered a bloody defeat. The river mouth was barred by heavy chains strung between iron stakes, this apparatus being covered by the guns of the forts. Bombardment of the forts had little effect, while the British gunboats were badly hit. In *Plover,* the flagship, twenty-six of thirty-six men on board were killed or wounded, including the Admiral, who had part of his thigh shot away. A landing party, Fisher among them, was sent ashore to try to seize and silence the guns by assault. Crossing a wide flat of soft mud, the British sailors and marines were caught by heavy, accurate fire. "You sank up to your knees at least every step," said

Fisher. "They had horrid fire-balls firing at us. . . . I saw one poor fellow with his eye and part of his face burnt right out. If a piece struck you, it stuck to you and burnt you away till it was all gone." In the slaughter on the mud flat and aboard the ships, 89 men were killed and 345 wounded. "I never smelt such a horrid smell in my life as . . . bringing the wounded out [to the ships]. Abaft the mainmast it was nothing but blood and men rolling about with arms and legs off." When the sun came up another horror met British eyes. During the night, the Chinese had come down from the forts to the mud flat "and hauled what fellows they could find out of the mud, cut off their heads, and stuck them on the walls."

Captain Shadwell was wounded in the action by a musket ball which lodged in his foot. A series of operations was performed, the last emergency surgery for a burst artery. "They had not time to give him chloroform," Fisher reported, "so you can fancy the agony the poor old gentleman endured, and the old fellow said quite innocently afterwards, 'Well, Fisher! I am afraid I made a great deal of noise this morning.' " Eventually, it was decided to invalid Captain Shadwell back to England. "We are all *very, very* sorry," said Fisher. "He doesn't like leaving the ship at all. He says perhaps someone will succeed him that doesn't understand the boys and won't know how to bring us up." Before leaving, Shadwell gave Fisher a pair of his own studs carrying his family motto, "Loyal au mort," which Fisher wore until he died sixty years later. And when the Admiral came to see Shadwell off and asked what he could do to be helpful, Shadwell pointed to Fisher and said, "Take care of that boy!"

In March 1860, Fisher was promoted to acting lieutenant and in June he went aboard *Furious,* a sixteen-gun wooden paddle-wheel sloop. Within two weeks, Fisher was writing: "She [*Furious*] is such a horrid old tub . . . and Oliver Jones, the Captain . . . is an awful scoundrel. There has been one mutiny on board her already." Years later, looking back, Fisher broadened his first impression: "[He was] Satanic . . . for like Satan, he could disguise himself as an angel. . . . He told me that he had committed every crime except murder . . . [but he was] fascinating . . . he had such charm, he was a splendid rider, a wonderful linguist, an expert navigator, and a thorough seaman. . . . This man led me a dog's life . . . he used to send me up to the maintop in my tailcoat and epaulettes after I had been dining with him . . . he being 'three sheets in the wind' as the sailors say. He was a rich man and had unparalleled champagne and a French chef. He might tyrannize us but he fed us."

Captain Jones hated higher authority, but he insisted on absolute obedience to himself. Ordered to leave the Gulf of Pechili (now

Po Hai) in North China before winter set in, he deliberately remained behind until his ship was seized and held fast in drifting ice.
Then, with the temperature below zero, Jones decreed battle drill at
four A.M. with shot passed up to the guns and all the yards and
topmasts struck. Grumbling ensued among the officers as well as the
men; indeed, said Fisher, "I believe I was the only officer he did not
put under arrest." Nevertheless, on this captain so very different
from the saintly Shadwell, Jacky Fisher managed to make his mark.
When the twenty-year-old acting lieutenant left his ship, Captain
Jones wrote of him: "As a sailor, an officer, a Navigator, and a
gentleman, I cannot praise him too highly."

By the time *Furious* reached England in August 1861, Fisher had
spent five years in China, served in five ships, risen from naval cadet
to acting lieutenant, and marked himself among his superiors as an
exceptional young officer. Once home, he scored brilliantly in the
examinations required to confirm his permanent lieutenant's commission and then was reassigned to the Navy's Gunnery School
aboard H.M.S. *Excellent. Excellent,* an old, mastless three-decker
moored in Portsmouth Harbor, focussed primarily on gunnery, but
it was also a research center where innovative officers attempted to
adapt developing technology to use in naval warfare. Fisher managed, over the next twenty-five years of his career, to spend four
tours of duty totalling fifteen years in this elite establishment, leaving it finally as commanding officer. On board *Excellent* and her
sister H.M.S. *Vernon,* moored nearby, which Fisher developed into
an independent torpedo school, he worked out systems and tactics
with modern breech-loading guns and different types of torpedos.
Here was the core of the navy, not aboard the far-flung ships where
tradition, seniority, and brightwork ruled with a lifeless hand.

Fisher never laid ambition aside. During his first tour in Portsmouth, he spent his free afternoons walking the downs behind the
base, shouting into the wind to develop a voice of command. Nor
was he shy. "The Lords of the Admiralty were paying their annual
visit to the . . . [*Excellent*]," an old seaman remembered, "and one
of the Admirals was heard to remark, 'Is this Lieutenant Fisher as
good a seaman as he is a gunnery man?' Lieutenant Fisher at once
stepped forward and said . . . , 'My Lords, I am Lieutenant Fisher,
just as good a seaman as a gunnery man.' "

In April 1863, after fourteen months on *Excellent,* Fisher became gunnery officer on H.M.S. *Warrior,* Britain's first ironclad,
then assigned to the Channel Fleet. *Warrior,* like *Inflexible* in 1882

and *Dreadnought* in 1906, was not only the most modern and powerful ship in the Fleet, but the forerunner of new ship designs for years
to come; Fisher, by a blend of ability and luck, managed to connect
himself with each of these pioneer vessels. Aboard the huge, black-
hulled hybrid with her three towering masts and two funnels, Fisher
commanded the battery of forty guns. Her captain was the able and
respected Sir George Tyron, subsequently to become one of the
most famous officers of the nineteenth-century Royal Navy. "She
had a picked crew of officers and men, so I was wonderfully fortunate to be the Gunnery Lieutenant and at so young an age." Fisher,
still only twenty-two, was blissfully happy: "I got on very well except
for skylarking in the wardroom," which brought admonitory frowns
to the face of Sir George Tyron. Fisher was exceedingly popular
with his fellow officers, for good reason: "I never went ashore so all
the other lieutenants liked me because I took the duty for them.
One of them was like Nelson's signal—he expected every man to do
his duty."

When he left *Warrior,* Fisher returned to *Excellent,* where he
remained five years as a gunnery instructor, switching just before his
tour was up to torpedoes. He was fascinated by these new weapons.
First introduced in stationary form (we would call them mines) during the American Civil War, they took advantage of the hydrostatic
principle that an explosion under water against the side of a ship has
more effect than a shell with the same explosive charge bursting on
deck because the force of the explosion is compounded by water
pressure and thus can punch a hole in the side of the ship. The first
moving torpedoes were developed by a Briton, Robert Whitehead,
working independently of all governments at Fiume on the Adriatic
in the 1860s. Although Whitehead's first primitive weapon traveled
at only seven knots for a distance of only a few hundred yards and
exploded only a few pounds of powder, Fisher was intrigued. His
advocacy of the possibilities was not always enthusiastically supported. "A First Sea Lord told me that there were no torpedoes
when he came to sea and he didn't see why the devil there should be
any of the beastly things now," Fisher wrote later. He advised his
lordship that a Whitehead torpedo, "costing only £500, would make
a hole as big as His Lordship's carriage (then standing at the door)
in the bottom of the strongest and biggest ship in the world and she
would go to the bottom in about five minutes."

Fisher's recognition as a torpedo expert procured for him, in
June 1869, a trip to Germany where, along with taking note of German developments in this field of weaponry, the twenty-eight-year-
old lieutenant had lunch with King William I of Prussia (soon to

become Emperor William I of Germany), the Prussian Chancellor Otto von Bismarck, and Helmuth von Moltke, Chief of the Prussian General Staff. The occasion was a ceremony inaugurating a small fishing village on the river Jade as a naval port for the new North German Confederation. The port, named Wilhelmshaven after the King-soon-to-be-Emperor, would later become the main base of the High Seas Fleet. Sitting at the table, Fisher spoke to the King and to Bismarck in English. Later, half jestingly, he said, "I never can make out why I didn't get a German decoration. I think perhaps they thought me too young. However, I had the honor of an empty sentry box placed outside the little inn where I was staying; and if I had been of higher rank there would have been a sentry in it."

It was during his second tour in H.M.S. *Excellent* that Fisher married. The marriage was unusual in that he married young. Most Royal Navy lieutenants could not afford a wife; they married late or not at all. Nor did young women looking for husbands search with diligence among a group of men famous for their long absences at sea. Fisher's passion and vitality simply overrode such objections, although when he married in 1866, he and his wife were both twenty-five.

Frances Katherine Broughton, whom Fisher always called Kitty, was a Victorian maiden with a long neck and an oval face. She was of modest family: her father was a village rector and her two brothers were junior officers in the navy. Her goals in marriage were the same as her husband's. During their engagement, she wrote to a cousin that "Jack would certainly rise to the top" and that she had promised herself and him never to stand in his way. Through fifty years of marriage, she was faithful to her promise, remaining in the background, bringing up his children, a son and three daughters, during his years at sea. (Kitty cannot have complained too much; all three of her daughters married naval officers.) Fisher himself was deeply in love when he married and remained a devoted husband all his life. Although Kitty could not match him in either intellect or energy, his brimming high spirits never spilled over into infidelity— despite his rash boast to King Edward that he had ravished every virgin in London. ("Splendid," the King replied. "If true.")

Fisher's next assignment was as commander (second-in-command) of the battleship *Ocean,* flagship of the China Station. He did not want to go; he was much happier living at home with Kitty and working at the torpedo school. In addition, China was far distant from the navy's center stage. "The mere fact of . . . [visiting] the

Admiralty gives one a great lift, as one gets to know the bigwigs intimately," he wrote to Kitty. "I feel quite sure that it is a most horrid mistake being so far away from England—one . . . gets forgotten."

The prolonged two-and-a-half-year absence from Kitty was painful for Fisher, and during these thirty months in the Far East, love and aching loneliness poured from his pen: "My own most darling Kitty . . . I really do not think there is any man and wife who have more perfect love for each other and trust in each other than we have." "I think it must be true . . . that God in some mysterious manner does make man and wife one body in those cases in which their love for each other is pure." "In 17 days it will be two years since we said 'goodbye.' . . . I never can again feel so miserable as I did then." He also missed his children and admonished her about their health: "Dorothy requires cod-liver oil. She dislikes fat and occasionally has little rough places on her face . . . signs showing that the child is wanting in fat. Cod liver oil is the way to put it into her." Much of their correspondence was about religion, and Fisher lectured and urged her in her faith: "Mind, my own darling, that you do your very utmost to have Him always in your mind." "I so often hope, my darling, that we may be able to make our children love our Savior with all their little hearts." Kitty responded by sending him little prayers which she had written and which he was to repeat daily to ward off temptation. To Kitty, Jack confessed that he was not completely the serenely confident young man the world took him to be. He admitted that he delighted in his ability to stir the men or rouse the midshipmen, "but, my darling, this is just the point in which I am such an arrant imposter and take so many people in by my manner: really and truly, I'm a humbug." He doubted his ability ever to learn a foreign language, a lack which would bar him from one avenue of advancement, the post of Naval Attaché at a foreign court: "I feel my want of French and German the more I think of it, and I almost despair of ever learning them." As the long tour neared an end, he began to dream of being home: "Now, my darling, I must say good night as it's past 10 p.m. and I have to be up at 4 a.m. What shall you say to my getting up at 4 a.m. every morning when I'm at home . . . but I daresay a week or two will soon get me back into those dear old habits of waking about 7:30 as on a Saturday morning and being down to breakfast at sharp 10!!! Eggs & bacon, hurrah . . ."

■ ■ ■

Fisher found H.M.S. *Ocean* in Hong Kong in December 1870. His new home was an elderly wooden line-of-battle sailing ship with armor bolted on her sides, an auxiliary steam engine, and a broadside armament of muzzle-loaded guns. Fisher immediately got to work, and, applying lessons learned on *Excellent,* installed a system of electrical firing so that all the guns on each broadside could be fired simultaneously by the push of a button. Venerable *Ocean* thus became the first vessel in the Royal Navy with this advanced technology. Nor did Fisher neglect the traditional duties of a ship's commander. Using his own brisk methods, he saw to it that the ship's white superstructure and black hull always glistened with fresh paint. "Every man was provided with painting pots improvised out of bully tins," recalled a member of the crew. "When the ship went into harbor . . . immediately after the anchor was dropped, the whole of both watches would . . . scramble over the ship's side, and in half an hour the ship would be painted from stem to stern."

Even so, *Ocean*'s old timbers, straining under the weight of additional armor, leaked at the seams, and "when we got into heavy weather, the timbers of the ship would open when she heeled and squirted water inboard," Fisher wrote. "Always we had many fountains playing in the bottom of the ship." Returning at last to England around the Cape of Good Hope, she ran into enormous gales. Mountainous seas washed away two boats, smashed in the side of the quarterdeck, and buried the men on deck in water up to their waists. (In the teeth of this gale, with the ship rolling 41 degrees, thirty-one-year-old Commander Fisher climbed the foremast to help his seamen furl a foretopsail.) Nevertheless, by the time the ship reached Plymouth all damage was repaired and the admiral of the naval dockyard reported to the Admiralty that "his ship is a perfect yacht. The crew . . . have shown the most perfect discipline . . . [They are] contented, active and cheerful . . . *Ocean* fulfills all the conditions entitling her to be called a British man-of-war in its most comprehensive meaning."

Fisher's shore assignment was back to H.M.S. *Excellent* as head of torpedo instruction. Eventually, during his four-year tour, he managed to separate torpedo training from the gunnery program and have it established as a separate school. H.M.S. *Vernon,* another dismasted three-decker, was brought into Portsmouth Harbor, moored next to *Excellent,* and became the Royal Navy Torpedo School. Thirty-three-year-old Jacky Fisher, newly promoted to captain, was its first commanding officer.

Fisher's devotion to torpedos did not mean that he had forgotten gunnery. It was simply that he applied himself to whatever task he was given. He explained his attitude to his own student officers on board *Vernon:* "If you are a gunnery man, you must believe and teach that the world is saved by gunnery, and will only be saved by gunnery. If you are a torpedo man, you must lecture and teach the same thing about torpedoes. But be in earnest, terribly in earnest. The man who doubts, or who is half-hearted, never does anything for himself or hs country. You are missionaries; show the earnestness—if need be, the fanaticism—of missionaries."

In December 1876, Fisher went back to sea for six years, holding command of five ships during this period. The first was the old corvette-ram *Pallas,* a vessel so decayed that "in order to keep her [iron] plates from falling off, a chain cable was passed under her hull to hold them in place." *Pallas* was with the Mediterranean Fleet and, in company with the major vessels, Fisher took his ship through the Dardanelles and anchored off Constantinople. He and a party of British naval officers dined with the sultan, Abdul-Hamid II, "a little man with a hook nose, a very black beard and whiskers cut close, and looking very delicate and careworn, but with a most sweet smile when he spoke."

Fisher moved up to a cruiser and two battleships, the most interesting being the old battleship *Bellerophan*, which was in the middle of a fourteen-year tour as flagship of the West Indies Station. Known affectionately in the navy as "Old Billy," *Bellerophan* was suffering, when Fisher came aboard, from a sense that the Admiralty was indifferent and that her chances of ever engaging an enemy were practically nil. Captain Fisher had a different vision: he wanted any ship he commanded to sparkle with discipline, pride, and fighting efficiency as if she were the flagship in the Mediterranean and an enemy squadron were on the horizon, clearing for action. Upon arrival, Fisher assembled his crew, promising them three months of hell. At the end of this span, if the ship was not ready, there would be another three months of hell. The second term was unnecessary, and although discipline was rigorous, one of his officers remembered that the men "were very proud of their captain." The same officer had other recollections of Fisher: "[When in port] he attended morning and evening sermons [at a church ashore]. . . . His spirits were inexhaustible . . . he developed a most extraordinary passion for dancing . . . he would come to the schoolroom or the verandah or the lawn, it did not matter where, and we would dance for any length of time to his own whistling . . . And on shipboard eventually."

Success on these ships prepared Fisher for the prize appointment in the Royal Navy: command of the newest, most powerful vessel in the fleet, the battleship *Inflexible*. Fisher was only forty and still a relatively junior captain in January 1881 when the assignment came, but his reputation was shining and every officer he served under added to its luster. Old Shadwell, his China captain, was now an admiral and went around introducing Fisher to his fellow admirals as "my boy"—adding, in a stage whisper: "the best boy I ever had." Fisher himself told a tongue-in-cheek story about how he was selected: "As each name was discussed by the Board of Admiralty it got 'butted,' that is to say, it would be remarked: 'Yes, he's a splendid officer and quite fit for it, but—' and then some reason was adduced why he should not be selected (he had murdered his father, or had kissed the wrong girl!). Lord Northbrook, who was First Lord, got sick of these interminable discussions as to who should be captain of the *Inflexible,* so he unexpectedly said one morning: 'Do any of you know a young captain called Fisher?' And they all— having no notion of what was in Lord Northbrook's mind, and I being well known to each of them—had no 'buts'! So he got up and said: 'Well, that settles it. I'll appoint him captain of the *Inflexible.*' "

Inflexible was not only the prize appointment in the navy, she was also a prize anomaly, the last queen of the hybrids. Fisher described her as "a wonder . . . with the thickest armor, the biggest guns, the largest of everything, beyond any ship in the world," but she was also the last battleship in the Royal Navy built to carry canvas. *Inflexible* was an 11,880-ton armored vessel carrying two masts, two smokestacks, two propellers, and twelve steam boilers. Her guns, four sixteen-inch muzzle-loaders each weighing eighty tons and mounted in two turrets amidships, were the largest ever installed in a British warship at that point ("A man could crawl up inside the bore of one of her guns," noted Fisher). Their rate of fire was supposed to be one shell every two minutes, but they "took so long to load that they could be fired only once in five minutes, and for a long time after they had been fired the whole ship would be enveloped in a yellow fog while the projectile could be seen soaring away in the distance like a huge bird." If, in battle, one of these shells were actually to hit another ship, that ship would surely sink, although most navy men reckoned the likelihood of hits from the occasional discharge of *Inflexible*'s guns as remote.

Inflexible was seven and a half years under construction and, Fisher noted with mixed amusement and exasperation, she contained "endless inventions, accumulated by cranks in the long years she took building. There were whistles in my cabin that yelled when the boiler was going to burst or the ship was not properly steered and so on." When he came aboard, her complicated internal structure, a maze of compartments and tortuous passages, had thoroughly confused the crew, who sometimes "knew not what deck they were on or what compartment they were in, or whether they were walking forward or aft." Fisher's solution was to paint compartments and passages different colors, each with specific directional or locational meaning. Because there were no portholes, all drills and daily life inside this iron labyrinth would have been by the flickering light of candles—except that *Inflexible* was the first ship in the fleet to be equipped with electric lights (she was also the first British warship in which a sailor was fatally electrocuted).

The best measure of *Inflexible*'s hybrid uniqueness was that she possessed both sails and torpedo tubes; the latter, a pair submerged in her bow. Fisher lacked complete faith in the efficacy of these two tubes, so he carried on board two large steam launches, each also carrying a torpedo tube. When action impended, these launches were to be lowered over the side to bedevil the enemy. As for the sails, they were little used for motive power and Fisher held them in high contempt. Nevertheless, when he found his ship was ranked low in the Mediterranean Fleet because his crew could not shift topsails as quickly as others, he sent his men aloft to drill. Soon, his men could shift topsails faster than any ship in the Fleet, and the Admiral wrote home—Fisher reported wryly—that *Inflexible* was regarded as "the best ship in the Fleet."

In the spring, Fisher took his new ship to the Mediterranean, where *Inflexible*'s first assignment was to act as guard ship during Queen Victoria's visit to Menton on the Riviera. The Lords of the Admiralty, proud of their new ship, seized the occasion to anchor *Inflexible* in the harbor at Villefranche and thus display the world's most powerful warship both to their sovereign and to the French. Captain Fisher was invited ashore to dine with the Queen and her visiting grandson, Prince Henry of Prussia, the future Admiral of the Imperial German Navy. Fisher's infectious enthusiasm charmed the reclusive widow and, when she left for England, she sent him a print of herself and a photograph of her daughter Princess Beatrice.

That summer of 1882 the British Navy fired its guns for the first time in a major action since the Crimean War a generation earlier. It was the first time Fisher had heard serious gunfire since China. Egypt, nominally a vassal state of the crumbling Ottoman Empire, was ruled by a local khedive. An Egyptian general, Ahmed Arabi (also known as Arabi Pasha), rebelled against the Khedive and his European advisors. To protect their citizens and commercial inter-

ests, Britain and France both dispatched warships. Thirteen vessels
of the British Mediterranean Fleet, commanded by Sir Beauchamp
Seymour ("The Swell of the Ocean") steamed into Alexandria's
harbor and anchored. When a mob poured through the streets, killing, burning, and looting, and besieging the Khedive in his palace,
hundreds of European refugees were brought out to the warships;
seven hundred civilians crowded the deck of H.M.S. *Monarch* alone.
Arabi's soldiers began strengthening the harbor forts, whose guns
were aimed at the fleet. Although reluctant to provoke more trouble, the Gladstone government eventually authorized Seymour to
demand that this work be stopped. Shortly before this ultimatum
expired on July 11, the French squadron weighed anchor and disappeared. All refugees aboard British warships were transferred to
commercial vessels, which left the harbor. On July 12, work on the
forts having continued, the Mediterranean Fleet went into action.

Seymour's fleet of eight battleships accompanied by five gunboats was a hodgepodge collection, typical of the navy in that era.
The battleships had each come from a different drawing board; each
had its own design, machinery, and armament. Among them, they
mounted ninety heavy guns—sixteen-inch, twelve-inch, nine-inch,
eight-inch, seven-inch, and six-inch. All they had in common was
masts and sails.

In the bright sunlight and gentle offshore breeze of early morning, the bombardment began, soon enshrouding masts and spars in
smoke. Each captain was permitted to anchor or steam slowly back
and forth while firing at the fort selected as his target. Aboard some
vessels trained to fire from a rolling deck in the open sea, the calm
waters were a problem; one captain assembled on deck all members
of his crew not serving the guns and had them run back and forth
from one side to the other to create a roll which would assist his
gunners. *Inflexible* anchored outside the breakwater and began spasmodically belching sixteen-inch shells. A cloud hundreds of feet
high formed over her masts. By five-thirty P.M., when the bombardment ceased, she had fired eighty-eight sixteen-inch projectiles. The
fleet as a whole had fired three thousand shells—with a lack of
success which disgusted Scott and other gunnery experts. Ten of
forty-four modern Egyptian guns had been hit and silenced; several
dozen of the older smoothbore Egyptian cannon no longer fired.
Fifty percent of all British shells fired malfunctioned, either exploding prematurely or failing to explode at all. Damage to the British
fleet was slight; Fisher's *Inflexible,* hit by a ten-inch shell, was the
most seriously hurt. Five British sailors died and forty-four were

wounded; the Egyptian figures were 150 killed and four hundred wounded.

The bombardment achieved its purpose: Arabi's soldiers withdrew from the forts and the city. A naval landing brigade of 150 sailors and 450 marines came ashore to protect the Khedive's palace and form a defense perimeter around the town. Its commander: Captain Fisher of *Inflexible,* who two weeks earlier had written to Kitty, "You need not have the least worry about me as there is not the slightest prospect of my landing with the men." Fisher's arrival was the beginning of Britain's involvement in Egyptian affairs, which lasted until after the Second World War.

Fisher established his headquarters in the harem chamber of the Khedive's palace and defended the city until regular British troops arrived from Malta to relieve his landing force. During this period, Fisher, lacking cavalry for reconnaissance, came up with the idea of attaching iron plates to the sides of a locomotive and eight railway cars. On the cars, he mounted three Gatling guns and a naval cannon—thus creating the world's first armored train. Manned by two hundred sailors, it sortied daily into the city's outskirts, usually with Fisher in command. The sailors were excited by their new weapon and adapted quickly: when one, stationed as a lookout on a roof, was hit by a bullet, he reported faithfully in naval terms, "They've found the range, sir." Correspondents and illustrators covering the fleet heard about Fisher's train and hurried to observe. Their reports and sketches of the armored train and its inventor brought Captain John Fisher his first reputation with the general British public.

Fisher's duty ashore left him with an unpleasant aftereffect: a severe case of dysentery. Despite eight pills of ipecacuanha and a dose of opium every four hours, "the sickness was simply indescribable," he wrote to Kitty. He remained in his cabin aboard ship, anchored first at Alexandria, then at Port Said at the mouth of the Suez Canal. The disease worsened and then was complicated by malaria. *Inflexible* sailed for Malta, where although Fisher was offered home leave, he refused. He feared that if he left the ship, he would lose this prize command. Further, he could not afford to go on sick leave at half pay; he had only £50 in the bank and travelling home on a private steamer would have swallowed it all. Finally, Lord Northbrook intervened, declaring that "the Admiralty could build another *Inflexible* but not another Fisher," and ordered Fisher invalided home. As he was being carried aboard at Malta, he overheard a doctor say, "He'll never reach Gibraltar." "Then and there," Fisher said later, "I determined I would live." In England, at home in Chelsea with his family, Fisher was unable to leave the house for months.

Fisher's illness was the subject of much solicitous concern. One letter he treasured and promised to frame came from the entire ship's company of H.M.S. *Inflexible:* "Sir . . . it is our whole wish that you may speedily recover and be amongst us again, who are so proud of serving under you. . . . Sir, trusting that you will overlook the liberty we have taken in sending this to you, We beg to remain, Your faithful and sympathizing ship's company, INFLEXIBLES." There were other letters from more exalted pens. The Prince and Princess of Wales wrote, through an equerry, to Mrs. Fisher, asking for information as to the progress of her husband's illness. The Queen asked repeatedly for news of the irrepressible young captain who had come to dinner and charmed her on the Riviera, inviting him to come to visit her at Osborne House as soon as he felt better.

In January 1883, Jacky Fisher, who had entered the navy "penniless, friendless, and forlorn," traveled to the Isle of Wight and for two weeks, joined the household of his sovereign. "I am all right," he wrote to his wife, who had stayed home. "Two cups of tea and bread and butter, and a very comfortable sofa and a delightful sitting room . . . [next to] my bedroom, deliciously quiet, have all combined to rehabilitate me." In March, Fisher's former Commander-in-Chief, Sir Beauchamp Seymour, now elevated to the peerage as Lord Alcester, was invited to Osborne House and wrote to ask Fisher about dress and protocol. Briefing the Admiral, Fisher sketched a picture of his own visit. The prescribed dress for dinner, he said, was knee breeches and pumps, "but I was let off with trousers on account of being an invalid. . . . She [the Queen] talks to one a good deal more than I expected. . . . She is sometimes silent for awhile, preparing her next subject of conversation, and I believe the [best] plan is to remain silent also. They say 'Your Majesty' to her much more frequently than I was led to suppose. The Princess [Beatrice] sits next to her, and the most pleasant place is next to the Princess, as she is so very pleasant and helps on the conversation. The other folks at the table talked in a very low tone. . . . I would suggest your asking Ponsonby if you are to kiss the Queen's hand on first seeing her. I ought to have done so, but they did not warn me about it, so when she put her hand out I was all adrift. . . . You are very much left to yourself during the day. . . . You had better take some matches with you in case you want a light in the night, as they don't have them. A little oil lamp burns all day in all the rooms and passages. . . . Dinner is not till 9 o'clock . . . breakfast at 9:30

and lunch at 2 p.m. . . . . The Queen is uncommon particular about medals, etc. being put on the right way."

One night at dinner during this stay, when Fisher was seated far down the table from the Queen, an uncharacteristic burst of laughter from this quarter reached the ears of the august lady. She inquired as to its cause. Fisher spoke right up: he had been telling Lady Ely, he said, that there was enough flannel wrapped around his tummy to go around the room. The Queen laughed too. Thereafter, every year until her death, she invited Fisher to come to Osborne if he was stationed in England.

In April 1883, Fisher's health was sufficiently improved for him to return to duty. Lord Northbrook, the solicitous First Lord,* sent him back to *Excellent,* this time—twenty-one years after his first arrival—as commanding officer. From this point, Fisher was not to go to sea again for fifteen years. He remained on *Excellent* only two years, but in this time he developed a devoted coterie of younger officers who shared his sense of alarm and urgency about improving the offensive power of the fleet. Two of these lieutenants, both to be heard from in the future, were especially concerned about the accuracy of naval gunnery; they were Percy Scott and John Jellicoe.

In the summer of 1885, when Fisher left *Excellent,* he began a span of fifteen months when the navy could find no job for him. Not surprisingly for a man of his energy, these doldrums were cause for despair. Besides, he found that he still suffered from his old Egyptian malady, dysentery. It was in the summer of 1886 that, in order to treat this lingering disease, he first went to the famous Bohemian spa of Marienbad. Set amidst pine forests two thousand feet above sea level, Marienbad offered the curative balm of the sparkling spring waters of the Kreuzbrunnen. Those who came were not all invalids, nor were their diets always rigidly simple. Trout, grouse, and peaches from local streams, farmlands, and orchards appeared regularly before the visitors, who might have spent the day playing golf, fishing, or shooting and who could look forward to an evening

* During this winter, while Fisher was recovering, Lord Northbrook gave a party to which he was invited. Mr. Gladstone was present. The First Lord took Fisher up to the Prime Minister and said, "I want to introduce Captain Fisher who commanded the *Inflexible,* our biggest battleship with 24 inches of armor and four 80-ton guns." Gladstone looked at Fisher for a moment and then said slowly, "Portentous weapons! I really wonder the human mind can bear such a responsibility." "Oh, sir," Fisher quickly replied, "the common vulgar mind doesn't feel that sort of thing." A witness observed the old statesman take another look at Captain Fisher and then permit himself a slight smile.

of music, cards, or conversation. The Prince of Wales discovered Marienbad in 1899, and thereafter beautiful women and distinguished and fashionable gentlemen crowded into the spa's splendid little hotels. Every morning, some of the most famous faces in Europe could be seen strolling along the Promenade, discreetly watched by detectives keeping an eye out for anarchists or jewel thieves. Among the detectives, other men with notepads, busily sketching, turned out to be tailors, fixing their gaze on the figure of Prince of Wales, moving slowly along the Promenade in a blue jacket, white flannel trousers, and a soft felt hat. Within a season, fashionable gentleman across Europe would wear what the tailors had seen and copied.

Fashion added glitter to Marienbad's attractions, but most people still came to improve their health. Fisher's account of his experience is typical: "When all the doctors failed to cure me, I accidentally came across a lovely partner I used to waltz with, who begged me to go to Marienbad in Bohemia. I did so and in three weeks I was in robust health . . . it really was a miracle and I never again had a recurrence of my illness." Thereafter, whenever he could, he spent several weeks in the summer at his "beloved Marienbad." Usually he went alone, although at least once he was accompanied by his daughter Dorothy. He traveled eight hundred miles from London, crossing the Channel at Calais, going by train through Cologne, Mainz, and Nuremberg to the Austro-Hungarian frontier and on to Marienbad. Once there, he stayed in a modest hotel, the Zum Grünen Kreuz, next door to the famous Hotel Weimar where the Prince and his retinue put up. He had little money and he spent it carefully: "I got breakfast for tenpence, lunch for a shilling, and dinner for eighteen pence . . . and a bed for three and a sixpence. . . . Once . . . I did a three weeks' cure there, including railway fare and every expense, for twenty-five pounds."

Fisher thrived in the cross section of men and women he met at Marienbad. "Every day is happy in this delightful place, even when it is raining cats and dogs as it is at present," he wrote. He met many distinguished English countrymen: judges, generals, ambassadors, and businessmen. "If you are restricted to a Promenade only a few hundred yards long for two hours morning and evening, while you are drinking your water, you can't help knowing each other quite well. . . . I almost think I knew Campbell-Bannerman the best. He was delightful to talk to. I have no politics. But in after years I did so admire his giving Freedom to the Boers. Had he lived, he would have done the same to Ireland without any doubt whatever."

In 1895, Fisher went on from Marienbad to Switzerland. He

climbed to the top of the Gorner Grat above Zermatt, reaching nearly 10,300 feet "fresh as a daisy"; but he had to come down after only an hour, "the sun so burning hot . . . our faces and necks so fearfully burnt." He watched with amusement the behavior of two tall young ladies who, one of his companions observed, "were husbandeering and not mountaineering." By the time he reached Geneva, Fisher's sunburn was painful and his temper was foul. He called Geneva "over-rated . . . a very second-class place" and Mont Blanc "a fraud." He unleashed his feelings against other tourists, particularly "the flood of Americans . . . so overwhelmingly nauseous and disagreeable . . . [that] I will never come abroad again. . . . Foreigners cannot distinguish them from English, and so I am not surprised we are so unpopular abroad." There were too many Americans in Paris, too: "The Americans swarm so everywhere that the whole place abroad is quite nauseous to me. Such vulgar brutes they all are, both men and women."*

In November 1886, fully recovered, Fisher became Director of Naval Ordnance, a post he held for five years. His field was the design and construction of all guns, torpedoes, and ammunition aboard British warships. His greatest triumph was the development of quick-firing, breech-loaded guns which could get off a shell every seven seconds and thus help to deal with the growing threat of fast French torpedo boats swarming out from their bases at Brest on the Atlantic or Bizerte on the Mediterranean to attack the British battle fleet. Fisher himself laconically claimed a different achievement: it

---

* Fisher's antagonism towards Americans continued for another decade. In 1901, as Commander-in-Chief of the Mediterranean Fleet, he approvingly quoted the Kaiser's pronouncement that "what the world had to fear were the Slavs and the Yankees." "The Yankees are dead set against us," Fisher quoted another source. "Only 1/4 of the population of the United States are what you may call natives; the rest are Germans, Irish, Italians and the scum of the earth! all of them hating the English like poison."

Like many of Fisher's opinions, especially outside the naval field, these views were subject to sudden, violent change. In 1906, Fisher's only son married a Philadelphia heiress. Fisher went to America for the wedding and fell in love with everything he saw. His son's father-in-law, he wrote to a friend in England, worked in a forty-story building filled only with clerks employed by his business. He went to a luncheon with "about 70 multimillionaires and . . . told them it was a damned fine old hen that hatched the American Eagle! They all stood up and cheered like mad!" His conclusions were not that different from Joseph Chamberlain's: "Their language [is] English, their literature English, their traditions English, and, quite unconsciously to themselves, their aspirations are English. What damned fools we shall be if we don't exploit this into a huge Federation of English-speaking peoples!"

was during his term at Naval Ordnance, he said, "that wooden boarding pikes were done away with" in the Royal Navy.

Fisher's task was complicated by the fact that in 1886 control of naval gun manufacture and supplies of ammunition, which had been lifted from the Admiralty during the Crimean War, still remained in the hands of the War Office. The army, with little knowledge or interest in naval requirements, was responsible for delays in arming new ships and for keeping the Admiralty generally in the dark as to the quantity of naval ammunition it had on hand. Fisher, frustrated by this irrational arrangement, fought it vigorously, with the full support of an admiring First Lord, Lord George Hamilton. But the soldiers were well entrenched and it was not until another two decades had passed and Jacky Fisher was First Sea Lord that the navy finally gained full control over the design of guns for its ships. Even then, naval ammunition continued to be stored ashore in army depots.

In 1890, Fisher was promoted to Rear Admiral, and from May 1891 to February 1892 he served a brief stint as Admiral Superintendant of the Portsmouth Dockyard. He was impatient with all delay and relentless in his demand for efficiency. The most important construction in the yard during his tenure was *Royal Sovereign,* the first of a new class of seven 14,500-ton battleships designed by Sir George White and armed with four 13.5-inch and ten six-inch guns. Fisher was generally irritated by the fact that it took at least three and a half years to build a battleship and some took up to seven. He was specifically angry because *Royal Sovereign,* which had been laid down twenty months before his arrival at the yard, was still less than half completed. Fisher's solution was to pull workmen off other ships and concentrate them on the most important ship "like a hive of bees." He was constantly at the building slip, learning workmen's first names, praising, joshing, bullying. As a result, *Royal Sovereign* was finished and commissioned twelve months after Fisher's arrival; her total building time of thirty-two months from laying of the keel to commissioning into the fleet was a record for that day. Fisher's approach to ships which came into his dockyard for repairs was similar. One battleship came in needing replacement of a single heavy gun barrel, normally a two-day job. Fisher had a chair put on the gun platform the first morning, declaring that he would sit there until the job was done. At midday, a table was brought and his lunch was served. The new gun was installed in four hours.

In May 1892, Fisher went back to the Admiralty to commence five and a half years as Third Sea Lord, charged with designing, building, fitting out, and repairing all the ships of the fleet. Once again, imagination and innovation held sway. Under Fisher's leadership, the water-tube boiler was introduced into British warships. Traditionally, heat from the furnaces passed in tubes through large tanks of water to raise the temperature and make steam. Fisher reversed the process, passing water in tubes directly through the furnaces, raising steam much more rapidly and with less expenditure of coal. He introduced a new class of small, fast ships into the fleet to screen the big ships and deal with the growing mass of French torpedo boats. Fisher himself supplied the name "destroyers" for these craft; they were meant to "destroy" the French torpedo boats.

During these years, Fisher was knighted (1894) and promoted to Vice Admiral (1896). In August 1897, he went back to sea for the first time in fifteen years, as Commander-in-Chief of the North Atlantic and West Indies Station. He had only one battleship (his flagship, the light, fast *Renown)* and five cruisers, but he whipped things into shape as if war were imminent. Suddenly, everything on this peaceful, almost sleepy station was bustle and speed. "There were no half-measures with Jacky," a junior officer remembered. "It was first in everything or Look Out! We were beaten once getting out torpedo nets. Result: no leave for the next few days until we reduced time to what was afterwards . . . never beaten again. . . . Jacky was never satisfied with anything but 'Full Speed.' We shoved off from the accommodation ladder at full speed, then reversed engines at full speed. He loved dash and making a fine effect."

On board ship, he inspired fear and awe. "He had a terrific face and jaw, rather like a tiger, and he prowled around with the steady, rhythmical tread of a panther. The quarterdeck shook and all hands shook with it. The word was quickly passed from mouth to mouth when he came on deck, 'Look out, here comes Jack.' Everyone then stood terribly to attention while the great one passed on and away." Officers who did not measure up were sent home in ignominy. "On the other hand, if any of us were in trouble or any of the youngsters were sick, he and Lady Fisher were the first to enquire about it." While at Halifax and Bermuda, he regularly asked a group of midshipmen ashore to join himself and his wife for the weekend. There, off duty, he encouraged junior officers and midshipmen to talk freely and give him their ideas. He did not mind when they stood up to him, providing their arguments were sound. "Williamson and Paine pulled his leg and chaffed him in the most astounding way," reported an awed lieutenant. "Repartee was bandied about and Jacky used to go into convulsions of merriment."

When in 1898, the Fashoda crisis threatened to actually produce a war with France, Fisher's war plans were dramatic. He would send *Renown* to the Mediterranean to bolster the fleet in the main theater of action, and he and his cruisers would attack and mop up the French West Indies. The high point would be an assault on Devil's Island designed to kidnap the celebrated Captain Alfred Dreyfus, whose arrest and trial in 1894 had convulsed the French Army and French society. It was Fisher's intention to carry Dreyfus across the Atlantic and set him ashore on the French coast where, Fisher believed, the captain's appearance would confuse and disrupt the officer corps of the French Army. When the French stepped back from Fashoda and the crisis ended, Fisher was sad. "One ought not to wish for war, I suppose," he said, "but it was a pity it could not have come off just now when I think we should have made rather a good job of it."

Fisher was happy in the North American and West Indies command and not at all pleased to learn that his tour was being terminated eighteen months early so that he might serve as British naval delegate to the forthcoming First Hague Peace Conference. Fisher's selection had been made personally by Lord Salisbury, who remembered how effective Fisher had been in fighting the War Office on the issue of naval gun manufacture. (Lord Salisbury remembered even more clearly because Fisher's principal military antagonist had been Colonel Alderson, Salisbury's brother-in-law.) Salisbury declared that he expected Fisher to fight with the same vigor at the peace conference. "So I did," said Fisher, "though it was not for peace." Fisher's disappointment at his premature removal from his term of sea duty was appeased by the promise that, when the peace conference was over, he would be given the Mediterranean Fleet, "the tip-top appointment of the Service," he told his daughter.

The first Hague conference originated in a proposal issued by Count Mikhail Nikolaevich Muraviëv, the Russian foreign minister, in the name of the young Tsar Nicholas II. Mankind would benefit, the Russian proposal suggested, if the nations could agree on limitation of armaments, on rules to mitigate the horrors of war, and on establishment of permanent machinery to arbitrate international disputes. Many disdained the proposal. "It is the greatest nonsense and rubbish I ever heard of," King Edward said to Lady Warwick. "France could never consent to it—nor *We*." For once the King and his nephew were in agreement. The Kaiser wrote disapprovingly to his cousin Nicky: "Imagine a monarch holding personal command of his army, dissolving his regiments sacred with a hundred years of history . . . and handing his towns over to Anarchists and Democracy." The Admiralty's view was offered by the First Lord, Edward Goschen, when he presented the Naval Estimates (the Admiralty's annual budget request) to the House of Commons: "If you think that war is simply an absurd possibility, if you think you can have peace without power, if you believe in the sweet reasonableness of Europe in arms, then I admit that these Estimates are a crime."

Despite all doubts, no nation could afford to offend the Tsar by outright refusal to come, and twenty-two states sent delegates to the conference, which lasted from mid-May to the end of July 1899. The chairman of the British delegation, Sir Julian Pauncefote, British Ambassador to the United States, had strict instructions from the Cabinet: Great Britain must retain her supremacy at sea; no limitation of naval armaments could be permitted to threaten her maintenance of the Two Power Standard. The Sea Lords, the army, and the Cabinet also opposed any restrictions on new weapons or explosives. Fisher's presence in the delegation was intended to make sure that no mischief come from the conference. With forty-five years of naval service behind him and command of Britain's primary fleet ahead of him, the colorful Admiral was a highly visible symbol and reminder of Britain's naval might. Fisher himself made no bones of what he thought of limiting armaments. No foreigner, he declared bluntly to anyone who listened, should have the power to limit the size, strength, or freedom of action of the British Navy. Signing his name in a journalist's autograph book before the conference began, he wrote, "The supremacy of the British Navy is the best security of the peace of the world."

Personally, Fisher was "instantly acclaimed as the heartiest, jolliest, smartest delegate at The Hague." At a party at the British Legation on the first evening of the conference, Fisher, then fifty-nine, "danced down everyone else in the ballroom." Socially, "by the charm of his manner, the frank heartiness of his conversation and the genuine, unmistakeable earnestness with which he applied himself," he swept all before him. He stayed in Scheveningen in a seaside hotel which was swamped by the conference. "Such a rush always going on," he wrote to his wife. "Band plays at breakfast, and at lunch and at dinner!!! Huge boxes arrive continuously and the *portier* rushes about like a wild animal." On a day off, he visited Amsterdam, which he thought "detestable and smelly," dined in "a beastly, stuffy little hole over a stinking canal," and went to see Rembrandt's "The Night Watch," the only Dutch painting he decided he liked. Ruefully, he stared at the English naval flags captured by the famous Admiral Michiel de Ruyter in the Anglo-Dutch naval wars of the seventeenth century.

At public meetings, Fisher said little, but he made his weight felt walking the corridors, talking informally. Here, the dancing charmer became the grim little warrior admiral. Although dressed in white top hat, frock coat, and gray gloves, he created an impression not unlike that produced aboard *Renown:* that of a dangerous jungle cat on the prowl. In forceful, often luridly exaggerated language, he hammered home his belief that war could only be deterred, not by a limitation of armaments, but by making war too horrible to contemplate. "The humanizing of war? You might as well talk about humanizing Hell!" Fisher said bluntly. "The essence of war is violence! Moderation in war is imbecility! . . . I am not for war, I am for peace. That is why I am for a supreme Navy. . . . If you rub it in both at home and abroad that you are ready for instant war . . . and intend to be first in and hit your enemy in the belly and kick him when he is down and boil your prisoners in oil (if you take any) . . . and torture his women and children, then people will keep clear of you." He derided the idea of granting immunity to neutral ships bound for enemy ports. "Look," he said to an English journalist walking away from church one morning, "when I leave The Hague I go to take command of the Mediterranean Fleet. Suppose that war breaks out and I am expecting to fight a new Trafalgar on the morrow. Some neutral . . . [freighters loaded with coal] try to steam past us into the enemy's waters. If the enemy gets their coal into his bunkers, it may make all the difference in the coming fight. You tell me I must not seize these colliers. I tell you that nothing that you, or any power on earth, can say will stop me from seizing them or from sending them to the bottom, if I can in no other way keep their coal out of the enemy's hands; for tomorrow I am to fight the battle which will save or wreck the Empire. If I win it, I shall be far too big a man to be affected about protests about the neutral colliers; if I lose it, I shall go down with my ship into the deep and then protests will affect me still less."

Fisher's vehemence particularly impressed the German military and naval delegates, Colonel von Schwarzkopf and Captain Siegel. Reporting to Berlin, Siegel gave a concise summary of the principles of British sea power, stripped of pretense and façade:

I. England holds . . . the fixed conviction that her position in the world, her power and her prosperity, depend on the fleet. . . .

II. Currently, the fleet has attained a strength that is equal

to all demands. It suffices on its own to crush a combination
of all states. . . .

　　III. England is firmly resolved to employ with all cunning
and ruthlessness, the instrument of war which she possesses
in her Fleet, according to the principle 'Might is Right.'

　　When the debate on extending the rules of the Geneva Convention to naval warfare was over, Sir Julian Pauncefote was able to
report to London, "Thanks to the energetic attitude and persistent
efforts of Sir John Fisher, all provisions . . . which were likely in
any way to fetter or embarrass the free action of the Belligerents
have been carefully eliminated."

　　In the end, the conference rejected the Tsar's appeal and refused any general limitation of armaments, although it did ban three
methods of warfare which it considered especially pernicious: the
use of expanding "dumdum" bullets, the use of poison gas, and the
dropping of explosives from balloons. Despite furious opposition
from the Kaiser, the conference agreed to a permanent panel of
arbitration; this became the International Court of Justice, sited,
appropriately, at The Hague. Fisher left to take command of the
Mediterranean Fleet, and three months after the peace conference
ended, Great Britain went to war with the Boers in South Africa.

CHAPTER 24

Ut
Veniant Omnes

◆

H.M.S. *Renown* was not and never had been a first-line battleship of the Royal Navy. Laid down in 1893 and commissioned in 1897, she was one of three "light battleships" specifically built for colonial wars and foreign stations. Her ten-inch guns were insufficient to match European battleships, but would presumably suffice to sink European cruisers or heathen ships in distant waters. It was on such a remote station, North America, that Fisher had found *Renown* and fallen in love with her. She was his flagship there and he liked her silhouette, her broad teak decks, her high speed (eighteen knots) and sea-keeping characteristics, her captain, her officers, and her crew. And so, when Vice Admiral Sir John Fisher was appointed Commander-in-Chief of Britain's principal battle fleet, he took with him to the Mediterranean as his flagship not one of Britain's principal battleships, but H.M.S. *Renown*.

It was highly irregular and tongues wagged. Captain Prince Louis of Battenberg, Assistant Director of Naval Intelligence, observed to a friend, "*Renown* . . . should not be the flagship; in fact, she ought to be in China. We want the biggest and best in the Mediterranean; J.F. of course, won't part with his 'yacht' but it is quite wrong." George, Prince of Wales, an old navy man, shared Fisher's sense of the personality of vessels and supported the Admiral: "I must say your old ship is one of the most beautiful ships I have ever been on board," he wrote. "She is absolutely steady and no vibration whatever at 13 knots."

Steady underfoot and handsome to the eye, *Renown* steamed through the Strait of Gibraltar and, on a westerly course, began to plow the blue waters of the Mediterranean. It was early September 1899. For the next three years, the ship would be the post from which a great fleet, the primary instrument of British influence in that ancient sea, would be commanded. Influence in the Mediterranean had been important to Britain since the early eighteenth century; Fisher himself subscribed to Mahan's theory that command of the sea in any European war meant safety of the Home Islands and control of the Mediterranean. Since the opening of the Suez Canal in 1869, over a quarter of Britain's imports and 30 percent of her exports had come from or gone to the Mediterranean Basin or passed through the canal. The highway to India and China, the lifeline of the Empire, passed through the Mediterranean. Two great naval bases, at Gibraltar and Malta, sustained the fleet which guarded the lifeline.

The view from Paris was different. The axis of British interests in the Mediterranean was west–east: Gibraltar-Malta-Suez. France's concerns lay on a north–south axis: between Marseilles and Toulon, in France, and Algiers and Tunis, the gateway ports to her vast North African empire. Beginning in 1888, the French Admiralty had moved its most powerful battleships from Brest and Cherbourg to Toulon. The British Admiralty, taking note, began to follow suit. British admirals in the Mediterranean had also to worry about the Russians. British policy for most of the century had been to support the Ottoman Empire against Russian pressure on the Straits. The instrument of this support was the British Mediterranean Fleet. Since 1894 and the signing of the Franco-Russian Alliance, there was always a chance that the French and Russian fleets would somehow merge to sweep the British Navy out of the inland sea.

During the years of Fisher's command, 1899–1902, the danger to Britain became immediate. The difficult and humiliating war against the small Boer republics had taken most of the British Army out of England and stretched the navy thin escorting troops and supplies and maintaining sea communications over seven thousand miles. Britain, militarily extended, was also diplomatically isolated. In some circles in Europe, there was talk that the time had come to settle accounts with the proud, insufferable British. Given these factors, during Fisher's tour the safety of the Empire depended heavily on the readiness for war of the Mediterranean Fleet. Fisher's purpose was to make war with England and confrontation with the British Mediterranean Fleet an uninviting prospect. He was aware of the great difference in the importance of sea power to Great Britain and to its principal potential adversary, France. "If . . . the whole of the French Fleet were sent to the bottom," he said, "France would still remain a first class power. Her position . . . depends on her Army and . . . France is independent of the sea for her supplies. . . . On the other hand, any disaster to the English Fleet would be fatal to the power of England." "Preliminary failure in Naval War means the ruin of the British Empire," he put it another time. "You can replace cavalrymen and artillerymen within a few months, but you can't simply go around to the green grocers, and buy new battleships, cruisers and destroyers."

With so much dependent on the force he commanded, Fisher was determined not to be taken by surprise. His tactics emphasized getting in the first blow. "Success in war depends upon the concentration of an overpowering force upon a given spot in the shortest possible time," he told his officers. "Our frontiers are the coasts of the enemy and we ought to be there five minutes after war is declared." (Subsequently, he amended this to "five minutes before war is declared.")

Unfortunately, the stately British Mediterranean Fleet which Fisher inherited was anything but prepared for the role of naval lightning bolt. Fisher arrived determined to jolt the fleet out of its sleepy routine. He began with an inspection of every ship in his command. Within minutes of the Admiral's barge coming alongside and the Admiral's feet touching the deck, the ship involved would be a maelstrom of shouted orders, running men, and clanking machinery. "General Quarters" would sound, then "Out torpedo nets," then "In nets," "Lower all boats," and "Abandon ship." Sometimes these exercises lapped on top of one another so that wild-eyed officers had to decide which to begin with and which to let go. "When Fisher left the ship," wrote Sir Reginald Bacon, commander of the battleship *Empress of India*, "she would resemble a wreck, with her upper deck a mass of ropes and debris." The Admiral's eyes, however, had followed everything and everyone. Aboard one destroyer, he saw the sign "UT VENIANT OMNES" in gold letters mounted on the bridge. "What does that mean?" he asked. "Let 'em all come," replied the youthful lieutenant in command. Fisher beamed with pleasure and the story found its way into his talks and letters for months. But the blow could come as quickly as the smile: "As the Commander of one ship did not show the ability to cope with this volcanic inspection, he was discharged from his ship and sent home the same evening, most of his belongings having to follow in a subsequent steamer," Bacon recalled. "At another inspection, a lieutenant in command of a destroyer exhibited gross ignorance of the details of his ship; he left the next day for China." When Fisher discovered incompetence or inefficiency, he was merciless; it did not matter to him that he was ruining a man's career "I am sorry for your wife and children," he said to one departing officer. "But in war I should have had you shot."

Fisher began a series of lectures at Malta's Admiralty House on naval strategy, fleet tactics, individual ship handling in preparation for battle, gunnery, and the use of torpedoes; all fleet officers, not merely ship captains, were invited. His listeners never forgot these hours, sitting in chairs before him, their bodies bathed in the dampness of ninety-degree heat. He was an electrifying speaker whose fiery language, sparkling wit, and sly digs at naval bureaucracy and tradition kept his audience laughing and applauding even as their starched white uniforms wilted into sogginess. "I went to a lecture by Jacky Fisher on Naval Gunnery and Strategy," said one of his lieutenants. "He used hardly a single note and talked for two hours. Simply magnificent . . . His smile is irresistible."

In his lectures, Fisher did not assume superior knowledge and expound from a lofty pulpit of rank. He admitted that he needed information on many points and welcomed ideas and suggestions, however unconventional, from any officer. He was particularly anxious, he said, for any ideas regarding defense of the fleet against attack by torpedo boats. At The Hague, he explained, the German naval delegates had told him that Britain's battleship squadrons were useless as, in war, they would inevitably be sunk by German torpedo boats. More immediately, he reminded his officers, they all had to be concerned with the twenty-two French torpedo boats based at Bizerte, only nine hours away.

Fisher's energy seemed limitless. He kept paper and pencil by his bed at night and rose every morning at four or five to put into effect the notes he had scribbled to himself during the night. Fisher never played any sort of game, but when the fleet was in port he exercised daily, pacing the ramparts fronting Admiralty House and overlooking his ships moored below in the Grand Harbor. (He preferred to pace back and forth rather than take walks, he once explained, and chose the flattest place he could find so that he would not always have to be thinking about where to put his next footstep; thus he could concentrate his mind on whatever he was wrestling with.) All had free access to him while he was taking his daily exercise and it was not uncommon to see the Commander-in-Chief walking the ramparts, deep in debate on some point of tactics or technology with a junior commander or lieutenant.

Besides making himself available, Fisher encouraged original thought by offering cups for prize essays on cruising and battle formations. A special table was placed in a large room on the ground floor of Admiralty House and on it were different-sized blocks of wood, representing all the ships of the fleet. Officers were invited to come at any hour to work out tactics and play war games. When one young lieutenant brought him a carefully worked-out plan for defending the fleet against torpedo attack, Fisher immediately ordered his captains to practice these tactics at sea the following week.

Flinging open the door to new ideas and hobnobbing with lieutenants instead of senior captains sent startling messages through the fleet. Fisher's behavior was unprecedented; some found it disgraceful. Heretofore, admirals had consulted no one—or at the very most had looked to a flag captain for a confirming nod of the head. Fisher's behavior, ignoring seniority and showing little interest in the views—or feelings—of senior officers who preferred traditional ways, was alarming to these older men. "It was brought home to them," said Bacon, "that the brains which were to be useful to the Commander-in-Chief were not of necessity to be found in the heads of the most senior of officers." When the older officers began to complain, the seeds were sown for a violent antagonism which would divide the Royal Navy. It was not just what Fisher did; it was how he did it. Looking back, Lord Chatfield, who was in the Mediterranean Fleet in Fisher's era and later became an Admiral of the Fleet and First Sea Lord, tried to see both sides: "Fisher had a practice of consulting young officers which was proper enough in itself," he wrote. "But, regrettably, he spoke to them in a derogatory way about their superiors. It was his ruthless character and his scorn of tact that led to violent criticism and enmities that shook the Service. . . . Fisher's greatness was not then realized. There were many who hated him and he hated them. His was not the method of leading smoothly, but of driving relentlessly and remorselessly. He prided himself on this policy, and boasted of it and of his scorn of opposition."

It was exactly this driving, ruthless search for efficiency, this remorseless hounding of the inefficient, which inspired and awed Fisher's young admirers and acolytes. As Bacon remembered: "It is impossible to exaggerate the new ardor and the feeling of relief among younger officers. They felt that the day had dawned when mere peace ideas and maneuvers were about to give way to real preparations for meeting a war when it came." Fisher's credo—"the efficiency of the Navy and its instant readiness for war"—became the watchword of this band of reformers which, within the navy, came to be called the Fishpond. Their argument at the time hinged on dramatic improvements made in the Mediterranean Fleet during Fisher's years of command. Later, they believed—and in time the navy and the nation came to agree—that it was because of their idol that the British Navy was ready for the Great War.

The crux of the debate—past versus present, tradition versus reform, young versus old—was Jacky Fisher. How an officer felt about the navy, which ladder of success he chose to climb, focussed on this one, small, restless figure. Junior officers had to make a choice—and the choosing began during Fisher's galvanic years with the Mediterranean Fleet. His impact, and the change it made in one young officer of the fleet, can be traced through the letters of Captain Maurice Hankey of the Royal Marines, stationed on board *Ramillies*. Hankey's first mention of the new Commander-in-Chief is made up of general rumor and innuendo: "The new Admiral—Fisher—has just joined the fleet; he is said to be a complete scoundrel. . . . He has got Siamese blood in him." Then Hankey, who himself despaired at the complacency and lethargy he found in the fleet, began to hear interesting things about Fisher: "I fancy the new admiral, of whom the executive branch can say nothing too bad, is going to shake them out of their fool's paradise a bit . . . [He] is very keen on dancing and in spite of the great heat and the scarcity of ladies is giving a dance next Saturday." Soon afterwards, Hankey got his first look at Fisher: "I had not seen Admiral Fisher before; he is a queer looking cuss, but very affable and he capered about all the evening like a junior . . . [officer]." And then, before long, Hankey was fiercely defending his new hero: "The present admiral . . . doesn't care a fig for the Admiralty and tradition and dares to look facts in the face as they are. He has already done incalculable good out here and may do more if he can keep afloat with the awful millstone of naval prejudice trying to sink him."

Forty years later, as Lord Hankey, the former marine, looked back on what he had witnessed: "It is difficult for anyone who had not lived under the previous regime to realize what a change Fisher brought about in the Mediterranean Fleet, and, by example and reaction, throughout the Navy. . . . Before his arrival, the topics and arguments of the officers' messes . . . were mainly confined to such matters as the cleaning of paint and brasswork, the getting out of torpedo nets and anchors and similar trivialities. After a year of

Fisher's regime, these were forgotten and replaced by incessant con-
troversies on tactics, strategy, gunnery, torpedo warfare, blockade,
etc. It was a veritable renaissance and affected every officer in the
Navy."

Inspiring lectures and prizes for essays were only the beginning;
the real revolution in the Mediterranean Fleet became evident when
Fisher took the ships to sea. Exercises were realistic: ". . . a night
attack on Malta . . . landing 5,000 men from the Fleet . . . exer-
cising the boom defense at Malta, putting it in place in two hours
instead of two days, . . . [essential] with Bizerte only 9 hours off
with 22 torpedo boats. . . . It was pitch-dark night when we had
the most exciting time . . . there was fighting going on all over the
horizon with destroyers chasing cruisers and other destroyers . . .
the destroyers all dashing about like mad in the middle of it all and
torpedoing everything. . . . [it was] the best thing I have ever seen
and the most realistic. . . . We finished part of the maneuvers yesterday. They were quite splendid and everyone is delighted with
themselves. Beresford came on board to tell me he had made up his
mind now not to re-enter Parliament, but to remain out with the
Fleet his whole time! as he had learnt more in the last week than in
the last 40 years. . . . I never had any sleep for 48 hours, nor did
anyone else . . . we had a final battle between the two parts of the
Fleet, one against the other, all hands firing like mad, and it was a
splendid sight."

Fisher's exercises stressed real wartime tactical situations:
blockade of the French naval base of Toulon; moving the fleet along
the Algerian coast from Malta to Gibraltar while protecting his battleships against French torpedo boats stationed along that coast.
Underlying the exercises were two basic changes: he forced the fleet
to move at higher speeds, and he persuaded and cajoled it to practice more accurate, long-range gunnery. When Fisher took the Mediterranean Fleet to sea, it automatically steamed at high speed.
"Woe to the captain and fleet engineer of the ship who could not
maintain its speed. All the 'chiefs' were shaking their heads at the
probable effects on engines and boilers, which they said were being
rattled to pieces." Bacon quotes the captain of the small Third-Class
cruiser *Barham* to illustrate what happened to a ship which might
slow down the fleet. *Barham* had arrived at Malta from England
with defective boilers. When the captain went to see the Admiral
Superintendant of the Malta dockyard to arrange repairs, he found
Fisher "sitting in the Superintendant's chair with the Dockyard Officers in a row before him, and they were directed to work day and
night on my vessel's defects until completed. The Commander-in-

Chief then visited *Barham* and while in the engine room, he asked me what I considered her sea speed to be. I replied 'Sixteen knots,' on which he said, 'If you don't do seventeen knots I'll hunt you down until you do.' His secretary, who was behind me, murmured sotto voce, 'He'll do it too' and always afterwards, the *Barham* was hustled along at seventeen knots."

Fisher was able to lead his fleet at constant high speeds from one end of the Mediterranean to the other. He was particularly proud of one voyage of 740 miles at fourteen knots from Malta to Trieste, and having the entire fleet of forty-three vessels arrive at the exact moment his schedule had called for. "I have burnt 10,000 more tons of coal than my predecessor," he trumpeted. "I am sure it's the right thing to move the fleet at high speed always and to practise at the speed to be employed in action."

The same passion was applied to gunnery. Where previously ships had fired individually at ranges of two thousand yards, Fisher had them steaming in company, firing at targets three thousand or four thousand yards away. The battleship *Caesar* began carrying out practice at six thousand yards. Fisher bought a fifty-guinea gold cup and offered it to the ship winning a competition in heavy-gun shooting. Ships began installing telescopic sights. Still Fisher was unsatisfied with the technology of his fleet's gunnery. "The other day I couldn't see a blessed thing on account of the smoke of the barbette guns, and so cursed the delay of smokeless powder."

Exercises at sea taught Fisher something about the increased pressure placed on an admiral in a new age of warfare, when events were accelerated and the time for decision compressed by the advent of steam propulsion. "I had a tremendously long day yesterday," he wrote to Kitty in August 1900. "I was at it from 4 a.m. till 8 p.m. and hardly time to eat, but . . . it was very exciting and interesting with such a large number of vessels, nearly 40 in all, maneuvering about . . . it requires an Admiral to be like the four beasts in Revelations, full of eyes behind and before." "Suddenness is the characteristic feature of naval operations [today]," he wrote to Lord Selborne. "In former days," he instructed Joseph Chamberlain, "the wind affected both sides alike and 'a stern chase was a long chase' if one side did not wish to fight. But now within 20 minutes of seeing— not the enemy himself (he is out of sight)—but his smoke on the horizon, you are alongside each other and passing each other at a greater combined speed than the express trains on the South Eastern Railway!"

At Trafalgar, Fisher continued, once Nelson had given his orders, he had nothing to do but walk "up and down the quarterdeck of the *Victory,* having a yarn with his Captain! He had got his ships alongside those of the enemy and had nothing more to do, and then it became a sailors' battle. But now it's the Admiral's battle. All is worked from the conning tower. You press a button and off go the torpedoes. Another electrical signal fires the guns, a third works the engines, and so on."

Hard as he worked the fleet during maneuvers, Fisher was equally passionate about his duties as a host and a diplomatic representative of Britain. He gave banquets and balls on board his flagship, inviting Austrian officers and Hungarian aristocrats in Trieste and Fiume, and sent "the bill to the Admiralty afterwards without having first received their permission." He took the fleet to Constantinople, had three interviews with the Sultan, and received an order set in brilliants. Lady Fisher and two of their daughters who accompanied him received lesser decorations. To the ships of the fleet, the Sultan sent 640,000 Turkish cigarettes. In Morocco, Fisher entertained the Governor and twenty Moorish chiefs, "all such splendid men, all of them Othellos. . . . I gave [the governor] a couple of revolvers, a case of *eau de cologne,* which he loves, and a quarter of a ton of ice. . . . It is a fine sight, this immense fleet, and he told me that now he knew why England was so great and so feared by all nations. . . ."

Despite a dramatic improvement in the fleet's efficiency and readiness, Fisher was not content. He complained to anyone who would listen that the force at his disposal was grossly inadequate to carry out its mission. He bombarded the Admiralty with demands for more ships and predictions of doom if he didn't get them. He bemoaned his own prospective fate, if as he predicted, his fleet was beaten. "The admiral commanding the British Mediterranean Fleet . . . being the man who will probably preside at the Battle of Armageddon which will probably be fought off Port Mahon in Minorca . . . has to bear in mind that Admiral Byng was shot . . . for not getting a victory near that spot,"* he wrote to Joseph Chamberlain. "Who is going to be hung if we don't lick the French fleet?" he cried to a journalist. "I have the rope round my neck," he declared to Lord Selborne, the new First Sea Lord. Specifically, he wanted more cruisers and destroyers. "In this famous Mediterranean Fleet," he wrote to Chamberlain, "we only recently had three cruisers. The Admiralty total for war is 36 cruisers on this station! Were I a

---

* In 1756, Admiral John Byng, sent with a squadron to relieve a French siege of Minorca, hesitated too long, forcing the British garrison to surrender. Byng was court-martialed and shot "*pour encourager les autres*" (to encourage the others), observed Voltaire.

Frenchman I should watch with malignant glee the denuding of the English Mediterranean Fleet of its practised vessels to send them to China and the Cape. . . . Please do not think me a pessimist but . . . 'God is on the side of the big battalions' and Nelson said truly, 'Only numbers can annihilate.' "

Fisher's letters to Lord Selborne, the new First Lord, hammered at this theme: "I maintain it to be a cardinal principle that the Mediterranean Fleet should be kept constituted for instant war . . . [but] the fleet as now constituted is not prepared for war and cannot be exercised for war because we have an insufficiency of cruisers and destroyers." Selborne and the Admiralty attempted to quiet him by promising that, if war threatened, additional ships would be sent from England. Fisher was skeptical, doubting that the Foreign Office would permit this when relations became strained. To Lord Rosebery, he wrote: "Lord Selborne says 'Trust us to send you the ships when the time comes.' I don't trust them! They will be afraid to precipitate matters." Besides, even if the ships did come, Fisher feared that they would be useless or in the way. "Unless I have the use of these vessels to cruise with the fleet during peace exercises, I cannot find out their deficiencies or the best way of applying them in war. They will come upon us, crude, unorganized and unpractised in their duties. . . . What a burden to throw on the Admiral, suddenly to pitchfork onto him a mass of crude material at the moment when all his time and energies are required elsewhere. . . . I would sooner have 14 battleships always with me than the 18 or 20 they would pitchfork out when war was declared."

If the reinforcing ships could not actually be sent in peacetime, then, Fisher told Lord Rosebery, he had a compromise proposal: "[The Admiralty] admit an immense number of vessels of every class must be added to the Mediterranean Fleet in the event of war. I ask that these vessels should be named, their captains named, that they shall be collected at one port at home—say Portsmouth—that the Admiral who is going to bring them out shall be appointed to take charge of them at once, that this Admiral should be put under my orders; he would see everything ready, he would know quite well that I would shoot him like a dog when he came out if there was the slightest deficiency in any one fighting requisite, however trivial. I give you my solemn word of honor I would shoot him and he would know that for certain! See the result of this: I apportion all these vessels beforehand, knowing their qualities and the capabilities of their captains, instead of being harassed and overwhelmed with such a mass of work on the outbreak of war or when imminent." Fisher's prediction on this point was illustrated and underlined when the battleship *Hood,* newly arrived in the fleet, rammed a French steamer going out of Grand Harbor. "It was splendid for me that it happened," Fisher told Lord Rosebery, "as I had told them over and over again it was against all human reason to expect a newly joined ship to be worked with the precision and nerve of the rest of the Fleet."

Fisher was insistent that he needed more destroyers immediately. The number of destroyers in the Mediterranean Fleet in 1900 was sixteen; Fisher demanded an additional thirty-two. "If more destroyers are not obtained," he warned, "we shall have the Boer War played over again at sea." "To steam a fleet at night without a fringe of destroyers is like marching an army without an advance guard, flanking parties or scouts."

Fisher's demands were received at the Admiralty with irritation. Lord Walter Kerr, the First Sea Lord, whose duty was to decide where to station the vessels of the Royal Navy, began to bridle at Fisher's incessant claims and dire predictions. Kerr expressed "serious disappointment at having received such a wholly unscientific document from the Commander-in-Chief. . . . The Commander-in-Chief has a habit, noticeable in some of his communications, of indulging in strong phrases to emphasize his arguments such as 'disastrous consequences,' 'imperative necessity.' . . . These must be regarded as the outcome of impulse rather than of calm and deliberate judgement and must not be taken too seriously. . . . No one knows better than Sir John Fisher that the proposal . . . is an impossibility under existing conditions, yet he calmly proposes it. . . . Their Lordships have a right to expect something better than a demand for impossibilities from an officer holding the position of Commander-in-Chief, Mediterranean."

Fisher did not reduce his demands; he augmented them. Fifty-four destroyers, not forty-eight, was now the minimum. At the end of the year, he raised his demand to sixty-two. The Admiralty gave way only slightly; they sent him an additional eight, to raise his total to twenty-four. That was all, Fisher was told, that he would get in peacetime. Meanwhile, Lord Walter Kerr was bristling. Officially, he wrote: "I must call attention to a tendency the Commander-in-Chief has of endeavoring to impose his policy on the Government. He forgets that the Government is responsible for policy and for the forces placed at his disposal—it is his business to make the best use of them." Privately, Kerr declared of Fisher: "His reiterated demands become tedious."

Fisher aimed his belligerence, which could be venomous, at Kerr. "The First Sea Lord is a nonentity because he tries to do everything and succeeds in doing nothing," he wrote to J. R. Thursfield, naval correspondent of the *Times*. Kerr was less interested in preparing for war than in the regulations for the cuffs of flag officers' full dress coats, he charged. Fisher also attacked Kerr's Roman Catholicism: "Walter Kerr . . . is a slave to the Roman Catholic hierarchy and he won't be allowed to leave the Admiralty however much he may wish it. . . . I believe the Roman Catholic influence far transcends anything people have any notion of. . . . In the Navy their one mainstay is Walter Kerr and they will make him die at his post." (The appointment of Kerr, who was practically the same age as Fisher, to the post of First Sea Lord seemed to preclude any chance of Fisher being given the top role in the navy.)

During the Mediterranean years, Fisher made regular excursions behind the backs of his civilian and naval superiors to communicate his views to the press. A number of journalists interested in naval affairs, most notably Thursfield of *The Times* and Arnold White of the *Daily Mail,* received regular letters from Fisher, who fed them information on which to base articles pushing his views, most prominently the urgent need to reinforce the Mediterranean Fleet. Bacon, one of the ablest young officers in the Fishpond and later Fisher's first major biographer, put the best face he could on this practice, claiming that Fisher was "careful never to give away any secret information" and did what he did because he was "a firm believer in the need for the press to be fed with the truth and not with lies." Fisher's letters to Thursfield and White are filled with numbers and deployments of ships, proposed war plans, estimates of French tactics, and fiery denunciations of all who oppose his own point of view. Fisher's language was so colorful that many of his words and phrases were lifted and put into print despite his fervent injunctions to "Keep all this STRICTLY private!" and "BURN THIS!" Writing to Kitty, he defended his practice of leaks to the press by saying, "I . . . can't help it for it is all quite true and I should be a traitor if I did disguise my views, considering that the safety of the Empire is at stake." Nevertheless, his method was more than brash or outrageous; it was sly and unscrupulous. He would write to the Admiralty, deploring the "mischievous" article which Thursfield had written in *The Times,* especially the "unpleasant prominence" given himself, and then, a few days later, send off another letter to Thursfield packed with information, violent rhetoric, and chuckling asides about his chiefs. Eventually, some in London began to smell a rat. Lord Walter Kerr noted that one "warmed-over," "mischievous" article was written "in many instances in identical terms . . .

[to] the views expounded . . . by the Commander-in-Chief [that is, Fisher]."

Sometimes, despairing of getting his way, Fisher thought of resignation. He would leave the navy and enter the House of Commons to press his charges against the Admiralty and attack the government for national unpreparedness. Or he would accept a post with one of the great armaments manufacturers. In 1900, he heard that he might be offered the chairmanship of Elswick, a giant shipbuilding firm, a post which paid a salary of £10,000 a year. "It's a place I should revel in," Fisher confided to Arnold White. "I should immediately set to work to revolutionize naval fighting by building on speculation a battleship, cruiser and destroyer on revolutionary principles—oil fuel, turbine propulsion, equal gunfire all around, greater speed than any existing vessels of their class, no masts, no funnels, etc. And I should build them all in 18 months and sell them for double their cost . . . and put up Elswick's shares 50 percent."

Intriguing though this vista is—privately built superwarships presumably available to the highest bidder—Fisher's real goals lay within the navy: first, reinforcement of the Mediterranean Fleet; eventually, appointment to the post of First Sea Lord. Although his method of achieving the first—constant badgering of the First Lord and the Admiralty—seemed unlikely to lead to the second, Fisher persisted. And, by the spring of 1901, his shouts and groans produced a result: Lord Selborne announced that he was coming to Malta and bringing with him the First Sea Lord, Walter Kerr, and the Director of Naval Intelligence, Rear Admiral Reginald Custance. They would sit down with the Commander-in-Chief on his own home ground in Malta and sort things out.

When the visitors arrived on board *Renown,* the four men went to Fisher's cabin. The Commander-in-Chief stated his complaints: he needed more ships; "when the time comes" would be too late.

"You seem to place no trust whatever in the Admiralty, Sir John," Lord Selborne chided him.

"No, I do not," Fisher answered. "I know your intentions are good, but Hell is paved with good intentions."

From these discussions came compromises. The eight promised additional destroyers were dispatched (although not the thirty-two or forty-six Fisher had demanded). More important, Admiral Sir Arthur Wilson's Channel Fleet was officially assigned to Fisher's wartime command and annual joint maneuvers between the Mediterranean and Channel Fleets were authorized. Fisher was publicly mollified and privately pleased. A visit of this kind by Admiralty brass was "unprecedented," he trumpeted. He had not gotten everything he wanted (about this he would continue to complain publicly and privately), but during the remaining eighteen months of his command, the power of the fleet was to grow enormously. Elderly battleships were replaced by modern ships. Armor-piercing shells, telescopic sights, and gyroscopes were issued or installed. Supplies of coal increased.

In September 1901, there were joint exercises between the Mediterranean and Channel fleets, which would act together in war but had never actually practiced with each other. At the conclusion of the maneuvers off Gibraltar under Fisher's overall command, a jubilant Fisher wrote to the First Lord: "All has gone exceedingly well and Wilson, who is not given to compliments, made the following signal when I ordered the Channel Fleet into Gibraltar for coal: 'The officers of the Channel Squadron have profited much from their association with the Mediterranean Fleet whilst under your command.' Both Wilson and Beresford handled their squadrons most admirably when working independently against each other. . . . [Thereafter, with] the whole fleet working together as one, it was rather a gigantic business with eighteen battleships all in a row and others of the 50 [other ships] all close around."

After the maneuvers, while Wilson was still at Gibraltar, Fisher and his colleague locked themselves into a cabin to talk privately about war plans. "I believe in the various talks I had with Wilson that we have arranged for every eventuality in case of war and are in complete accord on every point," Fisher wrote to Lord Selborne. "He has one copy, copied by himself from the one copy I made out in my own writing so no one will or ought to know our plans, except that they are in accord with the general principles laid down by the Admiralty." (This policy, useful for preventing unauthorized leaks —other than those committed by Fisher himself in sharing his thoughts with the London press—would not have been helpful were either or both admirals to be rendered insensible early in war.)

In the spring of 1902, Fisher's three-year command of the Mediterranean Fleet was coming to an end. It had been a great success— "Nearly everything I have asked for has been given eventually," he wrote to his daughter—and Fisher was looking beyond. The Anglo-French colonial agreement had been signed, Entente was in the air, and, instead of worrying about the French fleet at Toulon and the French torpedo boats at Bizerte, Fisher was writing to England about the alarming growth of the German Navy. "Personally, I have always been an enthusiastic advocate for friendship and alliance with France. . . . The Germans are our natural enemies everywhere. We ought to be united with France and Russia." He did not think his own future particularly bright. He was sixty-one in 1902 and although he had been promoted to the rank of full admiral while in the Mediterranean, he doubted that there was much prospect of higher office. "I am 'tabooed' by the Admiralty . . . and in consequence the Mediterranean will probably be my last appointment," he wrote to Arnold White. To Thursfield, he added: "I hear a syndicate of Admirals (mostly fossils) has been formed to prevent my future employment." His best hope, he thought, was to be made Commander-in-Chief of one of the great naval bases like Devonport as a dignified stepping-stone to retirement. Already, he had written his son, Cecil, asking him to keep an eye out for "a few acres of land and nice cottage" near Bury St. Edmunds.

Lord Selborne, however, had other ideas. On February 9, 1902, he wrote to Fisher:

> My dear Admiral:
> . . . You have several times pressed me to relieve you in the Mediterranean . . . [to] allow you to see if you cannot grow better cabbages than anyone else in a secluded English village. I am now going to take you at your word, only instead of growing cabbages I want you to come . . . and take Admiral Douglas' place as Second Naval Lord.
> . . . [In making this offer] I want to make an observation or two to obviate any possibility of misunderstanding in the future. . . . I make no promise as to your succeeding the present First Naval Lord when his time is up. I reserve complete freedom of choice of his successor for myself or my successor when the time comes.
> My second point is that if we ever differ, as in the natural course of events we probably occasionally shall, no one off the Board must ever know of our differences. Each member of the Board has his eventual remedy in resignation, a remedy which a wise man reserves for some special occasion only. But so long as we do not resign, our solidarity to the service and world outside must be absolute.

Fisher was overjoyed and quite prepared to accept the discreet admonition from a man eighteen years his junior about his bad habit of running to the newspapers. "I think it shows an extraordinary Christian spirit on the part of Lord Selborne and the Admiralty to ask me to come and sit amongst them, after the way I have harassed them, blackguarded them and persecuted them for the last three years," he wrote to his daughter. Writing his last letters from Malta,

Fisher glowed with pride in his own accomplishments: "I feel very sad at leaving such a fine fleet, and so much increased since I joined it when practically we had only 8 battleships of an old type, and now we have practically 15 brand new ones. Then we had only 8 destroyers. Now we shall have practically 32, etc. etc. etc. . . . We had 53 vessels in all with us last time and it was a very goodly show."

From a different quarter, that of the Foreign Office, came another favorable view of Fisher's tenure as Commander-in-Chief. Writing to bid the Admiral farewell, the British Ambassador to the Ottoman Empire wrote from Constantinople: "My object was to keep things as quiet as possible during the South African troubles and that I could follow this policy without any fear that it would be put down to timidity was in great measure due to the state of efficiency to which you had brought the Fleet in the Mediterranean and to the fact that foreign powers knew and fully understood this."

Fisher's accomplishment was best known and appreciated within the fleet. The week of his final departure from Malta was filled with testimonials. A dinner was given in his honor by the officers of the fleet; eight hundred asked to come and only 170 could be admitted because of the size of the hall. The governor gave a dinner, other admirals gave dinners, there was a dance on board *Ramillies,* and a dinner and smoking party aboard *Renown* for all fleet officers. ". . . They began singing 'Auld Lang Syne' and 'Goodbye Dolly Grey' and then danced the 'Lancers,' Father with the old Chief Engineer of the Dockyard," Fisher's daughter wrote to her brother.

Fisher's actual departure was done in bravura style. At noon, when a gun was fired, *Renown* slipped her mooring and steamed out of the Grand Harbor at sixteen knots "like a torpedo boat with the largest Admiral's flag that has ever been flown." As she passed beneath the ramparts, her own guns thundering out a salute to the Governor, Fisher caught sight of companies of soldiers running to line the ramparts in his honor. "As usual, they were all half an hour late," he noted, "and we saw them all doubling up just as we were leaving the harbor. One does not wonder at South Africa when one sees every day the utter ineptitude of Military Officers." Fisher's daughter Beatrix watched her father go: "As we passed the ships they cheered over and over again, drowning the bands and [gun] salutes, 'Auld Lang Syne,' etc.—the soldiers on shore cheering too. You never saw anything so lovely as the *Renown* as she fired the parting salute to the Governor with the sun shining on the smoke. . . . They say over a thousand copies of Father's photo were bought by bluejackets last week. . . ."

■ ■ ■

In June 1902, Fisher returned to the Admiralty as Second Sea Lord.* His province was personnel, and he focussed his attention on the selection and training of officers. Cadets were to be enrolled at twelve and thirteen as they had been in Fisher's own youth half a century before, and not at fifteen as the practice had evolved in the later years of the nineteenth century. This change especially pleased the Prince of Wales,† an old navy man. "You can't get them too young," he wrote approvingly to Fisher.

More controversial were Fisher's attempts to break down the traditional barriers of social class that afflicted the navy. Jacky Fisher's own origins had been as far down the social scale as the navy was likely to reach. Fisher wanted to deepen the pool. "Surely we are drawing our Nelsons from too narrow a class," he said. "Let every fit boy have his chance, irrespective of the depth of his parents' purse." The new Second Lord also wanted to drop the bar between deck officers and engineer officers. Traditionally, the deck officers, who would advance to become captains and admirals, came from the upper levels of British society, while the engineer officers, who spent their lives in the bowels of the ships, came from the lesser classes. The two trained in separate schools and wore different uniforms. Only recently had engineer officers been permitted to enter and dine in the wardroom; still, they could never expect to command a ship.

Fisher's plan was that all cadets, no matter what their social origins or eventual assignments, should receive the same education in seamanship and engineering. At twenty-two, on reaching the rank of lieutenant, an officer would specialize in engineering or deck. But an engineering officer would still be competent to stand watch on the bridge and a deck officer to take his turn watching gauges in the engine room. On reaching the rank of commander, all officers would drop their specialties and have equal opportunity to proceed to higher command.

Fisher's scheme stirred great resistance. Members rose in Parliament to protest the disgraceful proposal to send "our officers

---

* Four Sea Lords, all naval officers, administered the Admiralty. The Fourth Sea Lord was responsible for supplying the Fleet, the Third Sea Lord for the design and construction of ships, the Second Sea Lord for manning them with officers and men, and the First Sea Lord for directing naval operations in peace and war. The First Lord, a politician and member of the Cabinet, was responsible to the Prime Minister and to Parliament for the navy as a branch of government.

† The future King George V.

. . . down in the coal hole." From the fleet came the story of the uppish deck officer who said to a chief engineer, "Look here, Brown, it doesn't matter what rank the Admiralty like to give you, and I don't care whether you walk in to dinner before me or after me. All I know, Brown, is that my Ma will never ask your Ma to tea." The old admirals, whom Fisher dubbed "the Mandarins" and "the fossils," fought hard. "They look on me," he wrote to his son, "as a sort of combined Robespierre and Gambetta." "My dear Walker," he wrote to a friend, "I had no idea that admirals could be so rude to each other."

But Fisher also had powerful support: from the King, the Prince of Wales, Prime Minister Arthur Balfour, and the First Sea Lord. More important to him personally, he had the fervent backing of the abler young senior officers of the navy. "I have in my drawer letters from 24 Captains and Commanders, the very pick of the service, in favor of the scheme," he wrote to Thursfield. "I prefer these 24 opinions of the coming admirals who are going to command our fleets and administer the Admiralty, to any 24 admirals now existing but who are passing away."

As always, Fisher's energy and appetite for work were phenomenal. When he could find nothing to do in his office, he walked the corridors with a placard hung around his neck proclaiming, "I HAVE NO WORK TO DO" or another commanding, "BRING ME SOMETHING TO SIGN." He gave one of his rare public speeches at the banquet of the Royal Academy on May 2, 1903, managing in ten minutes to provide the audience with laughter and cheers, chaff the army, spill wine on the Secretary of State for War, and provide the nation with a pithy, oft-quoted phrase of reassurance about the navy. "On the British Navy rests the British Empire," he declared. "Nothing else is of any use without it, not even the army. . . . No soldier of ours can go anywhere unless a sailor carries him there on his back." Fisher emphasized this statement by a sweep of his arm which propelled a glass of port onto the immaculate white waistcoat of St. John Broderick, the Army Secretary, who was sitting next to him. Fisher rushed on in high spirits: "I am not disparaging the Army. . . . The Secretary for War particularly asked me to allude to the Army or else I would not have done it. . . ." In conclusion, Fisher told his listeners to have confidence in the navy and the Admiralty, assuring them that "you may sleep quietly in your beds." Afterwards, Fisher was elated by the reception he received. "The Lord Chief Justice [who sat on Fisher's other side] told me that my speech was the best that had been delivered inside the walls of the Royal Academy. . . . The Prince of Wales was very delighted and cheered me like anything. . . . The Archbishop of Canterbury, Mr. John Morley, Sir Ernest Cassel. . . . in fact, shoals of them came up to me afterwards and congratulated me."

Command of the great naval base at Portsmouth, the senior command in the Royal Navy other than that of First Sea Lord, often served to prepare an officer for that ultimate post. On August 31, 1903, Fisher hoisted his flag in H.M.S. *Victory* as Commander-in-Chief, Portsmouth. Here, his role was to preside over all the activities of the largest naval base, naval dockyard, and cluster of naval training schools in Great Britain. His duties included supervision of the training of naval cadets, of the naval gunnery and torpedo schools, and of the building and repair of ships in the dockyard. Fisher stepped beyond these official boundaries. It was during his brief (fifteen-month) tour at Portsmouth that he turned serious attention to submarines.

Fisher was already convinced that the torpedo was the naval weapon of the future. The problem was delivering the torpedo to the target. In 1903, the effective range of torpedoes was one thousand yards; any ship firing torpedoes had to close to that range. Fisher, as Director of Naval Ordnance in the 1880s, had worked to make that as difficult as possible for French torpedo boats attacking British warships. He installed quick-firing guns on the decks of Her Majesty's ships which would blanket the Frenchmen in a barrage of fire. Later, he developed fast, anti-torpedo-boat vessels which could screen the heavy ships and keep torpedo boats out of range (he called these vessels destroyers). Between them, quick-firing guns and destroyers made surface torpedo attack almost impossible in daylight. And thus the importance of the submarine. Fisher, switching his perspective from defense to attack, realized that the underwater craft was a means of bringing torpedo launching tubes within range of major enemy warships in daylight.

When Fisher first looked into them, submarines were far from the deadly weapons they became in the two world wars. Lack of speed, limited radius of action and time underwater, restricted vision in daylight, and total blindness at night made them seem harmless, even risible. Admiral Lord Charles Beresford dismissed them as "Fisher's toys." As the potential of the undersea craft became more apparent, scorn was mingled with fear. The British Navy did not wish submarines to become effective. Britain had invested the safety of her islands and empire in surface sea power. Submarines could put battleships, and the huge sums invested in them, at risk.

Submarines, grumbled the British admirals, were unmanly, unethical, and "un-English," the weapon of cowards who refused to fight it out on the surface and should be banned from civilized warfare. Admiral Sir Arthur Wilson, Commander-in-Chief of the Channel Fleet, so despised "this underhand method of attack" that he bade the Admiralty to announce publicly that all submarine crews captured in wartime would be treated as pirates and hanged.

Fisher saw things differently. It was true that the submarine was the weapon of the weaker power; it was true that he had worked to protect British surface sea power from all craft which could launch torpedoes; and it was true that he was working on plans for a giant new surface warship, a super battleship. But, as he saw it, Britain should disdain no new weapons. Submarines might be un-English, but if they could sink English battleships, they could also sink foreign battleships. Fisher's objective was to send enemy ships to the bottom of the sea. He did not care whether the weapons that sent them there were cowardly, underhanded, or un-English; he only cared that they worked. If submarines could fire torpedoes into enemy warships, Britain should have submarines, and the more the better.

When Fisher arrived in Portsmouth, Captain Reginald Bacon had just been assigned to the newly created post of Inspecting Captain of Submarine Boats. Under the supervising guidance of the Commander-in-Chief, Bacon had been given the navy's entire submarine force—six small boats—and instructed to experiment and develop tactics. Fisher and Bacon suited each other perfectly; the Admiral described the captain as "the cleverest officer in the Navy," and Bacon later said of his patron, "The submarine was Lord Fisher's child and his dynamic energy overrode all naval and departmental obstruction."

Bacon's officers and crews considered themselves an elite corps and, in fleet maneuvers in March 1904, they made a distinct impression. Their "enemy" was the Home Fleet, and they kept hitting Sir Arthur Wilson's proud battleships and cruisers with so many unarmed torpedoes that umpires had to rule two of the surface ships "sunk"—which did not at all please "Tug" Wilson. (Unfortunately, one of Bacon's submarines was rammed and sunk with all hands by a passing merchant ship, which had not been warned that an undersea craft might be lying beneath its bow.) The real lesson of the maneuvers, Bacon reported, was that the presence of submarines "exercised an extraordinary restraining influence on the operations" of a battle fleet: battleships always had to be accompanied by a large screen of destroyers. Fisher enthusiastically pronounced the submarines a huge success: "I don't think it is even faintly realized the immense impending revolution which submarines will effect as offensive weapons of war."

Fisher was looking far ahead. Essentially, until the outbreak of war in 1914, the submarine was still considered a defensive weapon, useful in defending harbors and coastlines in conjunction with mine fields, which they might one day replace. Submarines could establish a mobile defense and make the approach of enemy surface ships extremely hazardous. Strung across a narrow waterway, such as the Straits of Dover or the Strait of Gibraltar, a group of submarines could make passage by enemy ships almost impossible. Bacon was emphatic on the point: "The risks of allowing a large ship to approach such a port [defended by submarines] are so great that I unhesitatingly affirm that in wartime it should never be allowed." This was the beginning of the end of the classic British naval strategy of close blockade of enemy ports. Faced with the likely presence of enemy submarines, British ships could not lie close off enemy harbors waiting to intercept enemy ships or squadrons which ventured out. Instead, the blockading fleet would have to withdraw over the horizon, maintaining only the thinnest screen of surveillance and then, when the alarm had sounded, come thundering up, surrounded, as Bacon had said, by clouds of destroyers to protect the big ships from the lurking submarines.

For four months in the autumn of 1903, Fisher sat on a panel whose assignment was to reorganize the British Army. The Boer War had revealed much bumbling in the army and, once the war was over, the Balfour government appointed a Royal Commission to find out what was wrong. Lord Esher was the chairman and Sir George Clarke and Sir John Fisher the other members. Fisher's selection came as a not unpleasant surprise to him and rather a shock to the Admiralty, which had not been consulted. "Lord Selborne and all the rest seem very jealous at my being selected by the King and Prime Minister, and apparently His Majesty and the P.M. made up their minds without consulting anyone, but that's not my fault," he wrote to his son. "I am the target for envy, hatred, malice and all uncharitableness." Then, good news: "The King will never forgive anyone who stands in the way of my being on the committee," he reported cheerfully. The Admiralty, whose opposition had been based on its belief that being Commander-in-Chief, Portsmouth, was a full-time job, grudgingly gave way. "The Board will expect me to fulfill all my duties at Portsmouth," Fisher wrote, and he agreed to do so. To facilitate the arrangement, meetings of the Royal Commission were held in Fisher's office on the base.

If the navy was upset, the army was outraged. Not only was the only professional military officer on the commission an admiral, not a general, but Jacky Fisher was an admiral whose contempt for the army was delivered with the roar of a broadside. Fisher's feelings went back a long way. Thirty-eight years before, as a twenty-four-year-old lieutenant, Fisher had attended a course on musketry at an army school. "I was asked the question, 'What do you pour the water into the barrel of the rifle with when you are cleaning it?' Both my answers were wrong. I said, 'With a tin pannikin or the palm of the hand.' The right answer was 'With care.' " Later, as Director of Naval Ordnance, struggling to regain control of the design of naval guns and the storing of naval ammunition, he said that the War Office "makes my blood boil. Which reminds me of the Colonel of Cavalry who was appointed Controller of Stores to the Indian Navy and some ship expended her main yard as 'carried away.' So he sent down an order that whoever took it away was to bring it back immediately."

Fisher's view of the army's proper role infuriated the generals, "The Regular Army should be regarded as a projectile to be fired by the Navy," he declared, recommending that battalions of soldiers be stationed aboard warships as they had been in Nelson's time so that they could be trained in amphibious warfare and supplemental naval duties. This would decrease the need or opportunity for army officers to make major decisions; his opinion of their talents and mental abilities was manifested in his little joke: "A prayer for the War Office: 'Give peace in our time, O Lord!' "

What Fisher learned when he gleefully jumped into the work of the Royal Commission did nothing to change his views. "The military system is rotten to the very core," he wrote. "The best of the generals are even worse than the subalterns because they are more hardened sinners." He wanted the men at the top—"the Old Gang" —swept away en masse and young officers promoted.

At the end of its review, the Royal Commission advised abolishing the traditional office of Commander-in-Chief of the British Army, a post which had been held for years by Queen Victoria's cousin, the Duke of Cambridge, and replacing it with an Army Council similar to the Lords of the Admiralty. The commission also recommended decentralizing the home army into seven territorial commands. When the report was submitted and presented to the Prime Minister, Fisher insisted that all three commissioners threaten to resign unless the report was adapted in its entirety.

A personal result of this Royal Commission was Fisher's permanent friendship thereafter with Reginald Brett, Lord Esher, whom he admired immediately and extravagantly. An alliance was formed which, because of Esher's intimacy with the King, was to sustain Fisher through many battles at the Admiralty. Their correspondence crackled with ideas and, on Fisher's side, colorful invective. He blazed away at his enemies, knowing that Esher would chuckle and agree.

The Commander-in-Chief, Portsmouth, was given a large salary of £4,000 a year with which to extend the Royal Navy's hospitality. London was only an hour and a half away by train, and Fisher seized the opportunity. "We have 550 people coming to a ball here tonight who have been asked," he wrote to Esher, "and have just been told that another 150 will come who have not been asked." Invitations flowed from Admiralty House to politicians, to journalists, even to royalty; to anyone who could be bent to the navy's—or Jacky Fisher's—purpose. When Fisher was advocating submarines, the Prince and Princess of Wales were invited to Portsmouth. The Prince went to sea in a submarine which submerged. The Princess, watching from an observation ship, was heard to say under her breath, "I shall be very disappointed if George doesn't come up again."

The premier visitor was, of course, the King, and it was during his command at Portsmouth that Fisher became close to Edward VII. Queen Victoria had been susceptible to the daring captain's impish charms, but she had had little liking for the Admiralty or the navy ever since their refusal to make the Prince Consort an Admiral of the Fleet. Edward, on the other hand, during his long years as Prince of Wales, had made many friends in the navy, was well informed on naval matters, and shared most of the opinions and prejudices of his admirals and senior captains. Fisher, the most colorful and outspoken of the lot, knew a powerful potential ally when he saw one. The King, an expert judge of character, had no difficulty identifying the outstanding officer in his navy.

Fisher had just taken over the Portsmouth command when he was summoned to spend a week at Balmoral. The King and the Prime Minister had decided to appoint the Admiral to the Royal Commission to reorganize the army and the King wanted a look at Fisher at close quarters. Fisher was as excited and delighted as a child. "My rooms are next the King's," he wrote from the Highlands to his wife, "and his piper plays opposite our windows every morning about eight. . . . I sat next the King at dinner last night and talked to him the whole time and so as usual didn't get much dinner, but I made up with sandwiches in the evening. They have a most excellent plan of having orangeade and lemonade besides whiskey and soda all put on a side table and the most delicious sandwiches always under a silver cover . . . always a lot of ham sandwiches. . . . I was out alone with him most of yesterday forenoon, walking about the grounds and he seemed greatly interested in all I told him. . . . You can't think how very friendly the King is." The King gave a ball for Fisher on Friday night and presented him with a pair of white gloves to wear on the occasion. He had a hat especially rushed from London, "so I'm all right for church."

In that first week of talks, Fisher captured the King's confidence and Edward thereafter backed the controversial Admiral and his policies. Lord Selborne, the First Lord, arrived at Balmoral to find Fisher firmly ensconced in the monarch's affection and about to be appointed to the Royal Commission. "Lord Selborne arrived last night," Fisher told Kitty, "and I am much amused at his asking me to help him by speaking to the King about something he is greatly interested in, as if I was the Grand Vizier or the Sultan's Barber." Even when Fisher's original invitation had expired, the King was reluctant to see him go. "You must stay till Monday," the sovereign urged. "I want more talks with you. Besides, the air does you good."

A few months later, in February 1904, the King visited Fisher at Admiralty House in Portsmouth. The Admiral pretended to grumble: "I wasn't master in my own house. . . . The King arranged who should come to dinner and . . . how everyone should sit at the table." But Fisher's cook, a young woman named Mrs. Baker, prepared the meal; the King liked it so much he gave her a brooch. Some time later, Fisher noticed that his soup wasn't up to Mrs. Baker's standards. He asked his butler, who admitted that Mrs. Baker was not in the kitchen. "Sir John, she has been invited by His Majesty to stay at Buckingham Palace." Mrs. Baker's subsequent explanation was that the King had said to her while visiting Portsmouth that he thought she would enjoy seeing how a great state dinner was managed and told her that he would invite her to Buckingham Palace or Windsor Castle to see one.

As Fisher became closer to the King, Esher explained how King Edward's thinking processes worked: "H.M. has two receptive plates in his mind. One retains lasting impressions . . . The other, only most fleeting ones. On the former are stamped his impression of *people* and their relative value. On the latter, of *things,* and these are apt to fade or be removed by later ones. But, and this is the essential point, if you can stamp your image on number one—which you have long since done—you can rely on always carrying your point. . . . The King will not go into details, for his life is too full for that, but he will always say to himself, 'Jack Fisher's view is so and so, and he is sure to be right.' I don't think you need trouble about H.M. for he will always back you."

Having befriended the King, Fisher also befriended the Queen. At Queen Alexandra's sixtieth birthday party at Sandringham, Fisher discovered that all the other guests had brought prepared remarks to honor their hostess. Fisher had none and so he improvised. "Have you seen that halfpenny newspaper about Your Majesty?" he asked. The Queen said she hadn't and asked what it was. " 'The Queen is sixty today! May she live till she looks it!' " Fisher declared. Delighted, the Queen asked for a copy. Three weeks later, she reminded him. Staggered for a moment, Fisher recovered and said, "Sold out, Ma'am; couldn't get a copy." Chuckling, he added privately (in his *Memoirs*): "I think my second lie was better than my first."

Once in Marienbad, Fisher was deliberately excluded from a luncheon party where the King had expected to find him. Fisher happily described what happened: "The King came in and said 'How d'ye do?' all round, and then said to the host, 'Where's the Admiral?' My absence was apologized for—lunch was ready and announced. The King said 'Excuse me a moment, I must write him a letter to say how sorry I am for the oversight'; so he left them stewing in their own juice. . . . He came back and gave the letter to my friend and said, 'See he gets it directly . . . tonight.' "

It helped their friendship that King Edward and Jacky Fisher were born in the same year. The King once told Fisher that his outspokenness would ruin him and Fisher promptly replied, "Anyhow, I am stopping with you at Balmoral and I never expected that when I entered the Navy penniless, friendless and forlorn." What sealed their mutual affection was the honesty, originality, and human warmth each found in the other. Occasionally, Fisher irritated the King. Once, riding in the King's open carriage in London, the Admiral spotted a handsome woman he knew and stood up in the carriage and waved his umbrella. The King was furious at this breach of propriety and gave Fisher a tongue-lashing; later, His Majesty asked the woman to dinner. Fisher also sometimes ran afoul of King Edward's obsessive concern about uniforms and decorations. One night, needing help, Fisher "got the King's nurse to dress me up; she put the ribbon of something over the wrong shoulder, and the King harangued me as if I'd robbed a church."

Despite these thundershowers, the King was deeply fond of Fisher. "I had four and a half hours alone with him and he was most kind and cordial, and took me to the station finally and saw me off, and told me at parting how much he had enjoyed my company,"

Fisher wrote to Esher from Carlsbad in September 1904, a few
weeks before he became First Sea Lord. That autumn, a scene at
Sandringham made the royal affection even plainer. Fisher was invited for the weekend: "As I was zero in this grand party, I slunk off
to my room to write an important letter, then took off my coat, got
out my keys, unlocked my portmanteau, and began unpacking. I had
a boot in each hand; I heard somebody fumbling with the door
handle and, thinking it was the footman . . . I said, 'Come in; don't
go humbugging with that door handle!' and in walked King Edward
with a cigar about a yard long in his mouth. He said (I with a boot in
each hand), 'What on earth are you doing?' 'Unpacking, Sir.'
'Where's your servant?' 'Haven't got one, Sir.' 'Where is he?'
'Never had one, Sir; couldn't afford it.' [The King said,] 'Put those
boots down and sit in that armchair.' And he went and sat in the
other on the other side of the fire. I thought to myself, 'This is a rum
state of affairs. Here's the King of England sitting in my bedroom
on one side of the fire, and I'm in my shirt-sleeves sitting in an
armchair on the other side!'

   " 'Well,' said His Majesty, 'why didn't you come and say "How
do you do?" when you arrived?' I said, 'I had a letter to write and
with so many great people you were receiving, I thought I had better
come to my room.' Then he went on with a long conversation until it
was only about a quarter of an hour from dinner time and I hadn't
unpacked. So I said to the King, 'Sir, you'll be angry if I'm late for
dinner, and no doubt Your Majesty has two or three gentlemen to
dress you, but I have no one.' And he gave me a sweet smile and
went off."

CHAPTER 25

First
Sea Lord

◆

The Second Earl of Selborne had been First Lord of the Admiralty since 1900 when, in the wake of the Khaki Election, Lord Salisbury had reshuffled his Cabinet and promoted Selborne—who was only forty-one but happened to be the Prime Minister's son-in-law—from Undersecretary for the Colonies to responsibility for the navy. Fisher's relationship with Selborne had been contentious but respectful; as Commander-in-Chief of the Mediterranean Fleet, the Admiral had demanded more ships; not getting them, he complained, but always within limits. Selborne recognized Fisher's exceptional qualities. In 1902, he brought the Admiral home as Second Sea Lord; in 1903, he made him Commander-in-Chief, Portsmouth; both assignments were established stepping-stones to the office of First Sea Lord. In May 1904, Selborne went down to Portsmouth to make a formal offer. Fisher relished the moment: "4 days ago Selborne told a friend of mine that he was afraid of me . . . [but that] my going to the Admiralty was 'simply unavoidable,' " Fisher wrote to Esher. Fisher seized the offer: "The die is cast!" he told Esher. "I accepted yesterday on the understanding I commenced work on October 21st (Trafalgar Day!). Nothing like a good omen!"

Through the summer, Fisher worked hard on the drastic reforms he meant to impose on the navy. On July 30, he spent three and a half hours explaining them to Balfour in the Prime Minister's room in the House of Commons. The following week he was twice with the King on board *Victoria and Albert* and then the yacht *Britannia*. On August 17, Selborne came back to Portsmouth to be briefed on Fisher's plans. "Selborne was so cordial and responsive that I made the plunge and with *immense success*," Fisher wrote to Esher. "He has swallowed it all whole. . . . I sat him in an arm chair in my office and shook my fist in his face for 2 1/4 hours without a check. Then he read 120 pages of foolscap and afterwards collapsed!" On August 21, an exultant Fisher wrote to Arnold White, "I am ready for the fray. It will be a case of *Athanasius contra Mundum*. Very sorry for Mundum as Athanasius is going to win!"

Within twenty-four hours of Fisher's arrival at the Admiralty on October 21, Britain was close to war with Russia. On the night of the twenty-second, the Russian Baltic Fleet, steaming off the North Sea's Dogger Bank on the first leg of its doomed voyage to the Far East, suddenly found itself surrounded by an unidentified cluster of small boats. Somehow mistaking the craft caught in their searchlights for Japanese torpedo boats, the Russian sailors opened fire. One Hull fishing trawler was sunk and others damaged; two English fishermen were decapitated and several were wounded. The London press screamed for war. "This fleet of lunatics" was the description of one Service journal; the Russians are "no more to be trusted with a battleship than a six year old infant with a new penknife," roared another. As it happened, Fisher had reported to the Admiralty on the twenty-first with severe influenza and a high fever. When the news from Hull arrived, he was home in bed. Hearing that the Cabinet was meeting and that war was in the air, he got up, took a cab to the place of meeting, and demanded to be admitted. Before the Cabinet, he argued against war with Russia, which was France's ally. The enemy, he reminded the ministers, was Germany. The crisis continued for another week. On November 1, Fisher wrote to Kitty, "I've been with the Prime Minister all day, morning and afternoon. It has very nearly been war again. Very near indeed, but the Russians have climbed down again. . . . Balfour a splendid man to work with. Only he, I, Lansdowne and Selborne did the whole thing. . . ."

Coughing badly for several weeks, Fisher plunged into his work with a series of sixteen-hour days. He began at five A.M. and worked three hours before breakfast, was erratic about eating lunch, and left the Admiralty at nine P.M. Sundays were no different except that Fisher slipped over to Westminster Abbey for morning and evening services. After this burst of energy had extended for eleven weeks, Lady Fisher grew worried about her sixty-four-year-old husband. Sitting next to the King one night at dinner, she told him her fears. The King promptly reached for a menu and wrote on the back: "Admiral Sir John Fisher is to do *no* work on Sundays, nor go near the Admiralty, nor is he to allow any of his subordinates to work on Sundays. By command, Edward R." Fisher ignored the royal decree, but not without reminding the King *why* he was working so hard. After an hour with King Edward, he wrote to Kitty: "We never ceased talking (or rather I did not!) for a whole hour and he seemed intensely to enjoy it and kept on saying Bravo! Bravo! That's right! Of course you're right! etc., etc." Fisher husbanded his own energy by ignoring petty details, locking into a drawer argumentative papers which failed to interest him, and sending other irritants up in smoke. When a Highland regiment landed by the navy on a beach found its spats wet and discolored, the War Office demanded that the navy pay the cost of replacements. The Admiralty refused. When the correspondence was brought to Fisher, he tossed it into the fire. If anyone asked for it, he said, they should be told that Admiral Fisher had taken the papers home with him.

Fisher was revolutionizing the navy. All of his ideas, many of them hatched in the Mediterranean, elaborated and polished at Portsmouth, suddenly became the marching orders of the Fleet. Fisher's first reform, having to do with personnel and the selection and training of young officers, already had been announced in December 1902 when he was Second Sea Lord and put into effect under the Admiral's own eyes during his year at Portsmouth. The next three were announced simultaneously in an Admiralty Memorandum issued on December 6, 1904, when Fisher had been First Sea Lord for only six weeks. They were sweeping and interlocking; one could not be done without the others; there was not enough money and there were not enough men. Fisher hammered on this theme of interdependency: this is "the house that Jack built," he declared, and "so we must have no tinkering! No pandering to sentiment! No regard for susceptibilities! No pity for anyone! We must be ruthless, relentless, and remorseless! And we must therefore have The Scheme! The Whole Scheme! And nothing but The Scheme!!!" The fifth of Fisher's great reforms, the one which had the most dramatic effect on the naval balance of power and the prewar diplomatic history of Europe—the one by which the era came to be known—was the decision to build a fast, all-big-gun battleship, H.M.S. *Dreadnought*.

All of Fisher's reforms were controversial. The one which attracted the least opposition, because the argument in its favor was so unchallengeably logical, was the redistribution of the Fleet. For decades, British fleets and squadrons had been scattered around the globe. In 1904, there still were nine, including squadrons in China, the South Atlantic, and North America and the West Indies. Some of these outlying fleets were formidable: the China Squadron possessed five battleships. But all were much weaker than the fleets of the local powers which occupied those regions. The British China Squadron, although far superior to the naval forces of any other European power in the western Pacific, was woefully inferior to the navy of Japan—but in 1902, the Anglo-Japanese Alliance had been signed primarily so that Japan would look after British naval interests in the Far East. The North American Squadron, unassisted, could not have begun to deal with the growing strength of Theodore Roosevelt's United States Navy—but war between the two Anglo-Saxon powers seemed remote, if not unthinkable. The South Atlantic Squadron was weaker than either the navy of Brazil or the navy of Argentina—but neither Brazil nor Argentina seemed likely to attack Great Britain; both, in fact, were soon to place orders for battleships in British shipyards.

Closer to home, British fleets seemed oddly distributed. The Mediterranean Fleet, with the twelve most powerful battleships, was the navy's premier striking force, available for war against France. But the Foreign Office had been negotiating for a year, and was soon to conclude, a colonial entente with France, greatly diminishing the prospects of such a conflict. Meanwhile, alarm was spreading about the rise of the German Navy. To meet the growing threat of the High Seas Fleet, the Royal Navy deployed the Channel Fleet, whose responsibilities and cruising grounds included everything north of Gibraltar. This fleet had eight somewhat older battleships. To cover the Home Islands when the Channel Fleet was at Gibraltar, three days away, the navy had the Home Fleet, made up of eight even older battleships.

Fisher, who since the autumn of 1902 had looked upon Germany as Great Britain's most probable naval opponent, moved quickly to redistribute the Fleet so that the latest and most powerful ships would be concentrated against the most dangerous potential enemy. Four new battleships were withdrawn from the Mediterranean Fleet and attached to the Home Fleet, which was renamed the Channel Fleet and told to remain close to the Channel. When, in 1905, the five battleships were withdrawn from China, they too were attached to the Channel Fleet, whose strength then rose to seventeen battleships. The former Channel Fleet, now redesignated the

Atlantic Fleet, was based at Gibraltar and assigned eight battleships, which could steam either north towards home waters or eastward into the Mediterranean, depending on where they were needed. The Mediterranean Fleet, its strength now reduced by one third, was instructed to think in terms of fighting a war alongside France, not against her. The China, North American, and South Atlantic squadrons were disbanded and their useful ships, mostly cruisers, reassigned. Naturally, the admirals commanding these flotillas were not pleased. The Commander-in-Chief of the Mediterranean Fleet protested violently against the reduction of his force. The Admiral of the China Squadron argued against sending home his five battleships; ordered to comply, he begged to be allowed to keep at least one battleship as his flagship for reasons of prestige. The Admiralty insisted that all five come home and instructed him to come home with them.

The criticism applied to Fisher's redistribution of the Fleet was mild compared to the censure he took for his next reform: the scrapping of scores of useless and obsolete ships. Throughout the nineteenth century, the Pax Britannica had been policed around the world by British warships. Scattered around the globe were dozens of small, elderly gunboats and tired Second- and Third-Class cruisers, usually at anchor in a sleepy harbor, occasionally putting out to sea to parade the White Ensign along the coast and remind the natives that behind this little ship lay the mighty battleships and armored cruisers of the greatest navy on earth. To Fisher, this policy of soaking up crews and money in ships which, he said contemptuously, were "too weak to fight and too slow to run away" was absurd. The smallest gunboat cost the Admiralty £12,000 a year to maintain. Each had a captain, officers, and seamen, whose skills were going to waste and whose training was lagging every month they were kept away from the fighting fleet.

Not all the ships disdained by Fisher were small or on foreign stations. There were battleships, too slow and lightly armored to be allowed to wander within the range of enemy guns, each costing £100,000 a year to keep in service. The five battleships of the *Admiral* class, "magnificent on paper, splendid when weight of broadside is taken as a criterion, but in reality . . . absolutely useless for fighting," were prime examples. All had to go. "The first duty of the Navy is to be instantly ready to strike the enemy and this can only be accomplished by concentrating our strength into ships of undoubted fighting value, ruthlessly discarding those that have become obsolete," declared the new First Sea Lord.

The blow fell ruthlessly. One hundred and fifty-four ships were struck off the active list "with one courageous stroke of the pen," as an admiring Prime Minister Balfour described it. Ninety of these ships, classified by Fisher as "sheep," were condemned as totally useless and put up for sale as scrap. Thirty-seven were classified as "llamas" and transferred to future peripheral wartime duties such as laying mines. Twenty-seven, including four old battleships, became "goats," allowed to retain their guns but to be the object of no further expense for repair or maintenance. Both the "llamas" and the "goats" were to be laid up without crews in British home ports. A few gunboats—*Woodcock*s, *Woodlark*s, *Sandpiper*s and *Snipe*s— were retained for service on Chinese rivers and along the west coast of Africa.

The scrapping policy brought reproof. The Foreign Office disliked having the the navy unavailable to its diplomats. Fisher's reply: "It appears necessary to repeat, as the Foreign Office pays no attention to this point, that visits of powerful ships and squadrons have largely taken the place of desultory cruising by small, isolated vessels and that, so far from injuring, this has greatly enhanced the prestige of British naval power." More serious was the criticism of many admirals, some on active duty, others—described by a pro-Fisher journalist as the "Bath Chair Flotilla"—retired admirals who complained that the navy was being deprived of ships which would be essential in wartime. No matter how weak or slow, they argued, old Second- and Third-Class cruisers could be used to escort British merchant ships and to mop up enemy merchantmen. Fisher's rebuttal was that the most likely commerce raiders of a future war were armored cruisers which could annihilate British Second- and Third-Class cruisers with minimum effort. The admirals could not know it, but Fisher had a remedy for German armored cruisers firmly fixed in his mind: it was to be the battle cruiser, larger, faster, and more powerful than any armored cruiser in the world. These revolutionary ships, which were to become the Royal Navy's *Invincible*-class battle cruisers, were part of Fisher's interlocking plan—"The Scheme! The Whole Scheme! And nothing but the Scheme!"

The next part of Fisher's Scheme evolved coherently from the scrapping policy. Bringing home 154 ships provided the navy with a large surplus of officers and seamen. Fisher used them to establish a fleet of reserve ships ready for war, each carrying a nucleus crew. Under the previous system, ships which were not fully manned and in commission were assigned to the Reserve Fleet, where they were laid up in harbors without crews, with only maintenance parties poking about. Upon mobilization, entirely new crews from the Naval Reserve were to be brought on board. These officers and men, wholly unfamiliar with the ships, would have to learn the idiosyncrasies of the guns, the peculiarities of the engines—even each others' names—as they were putting out to sea to face the enemy. On the rare occasion when Reserve ships were sent to sea to drill, the results were appalling: frequent engine breakdowns, and gunnery results the Admiralty preferred not to release.

Fisher's purpose was to bring the Reserve Fleet to war readiness. He did so by manning the most useful ships in that fleet with nucleus crews: that is, two fifths of the vessel's normal wartime complement of officers and men. These men, including the specialists in fire control, gunnery, and engineering necessary to fight the ship effectively, lived aboard the ships and became thoroughly acquainted with their turrets and boiler rooms. When the alarm was sounded for either war or drill, the remainder of the crew was drawn from the large numbers of Regular Navy personnel in naval schools or shore barracks nearby. This fleshing out was necessary to fight the ship, but the hundreds of men engaged in passing coal to the furnaces or projectiles and powder to the guns did not need the training or familiarity with the ship required of the nucleus-crew specialists. Four times a year, exercises were held in which nucleus-crew ships took aboard hundreds of men within a few hours and put to sea for two weeks of maneuver with the active squadrons of the fleet. Even in harbor, care was taken to preserve the psychological impression among nucleus crews that they were part of a war fleet, instantly ready to sail. They were not tied up to quays and jetties with gangplanks permanently down, as Reserve Fleet ships had been in the past. Instead, nucleus-crew ships were moored far out, to break the link with land and let the men feel the tug of the sea. One officer, visiting a group of nucleus-crew ships lying between Sheerness and Chatham, looked out and could see nothing but water and mud flats. He asked an old petty officer whether he did not mind being moored so far from shore. "No, bless you, sir," replied the old sea dog. "What the eye can't see, the 'eart don't long for." Fisher was delighted by the results of his nucleus-crew system and described it as "the keystone of our preparedness for war." The whole fleet, he said, was now "instantly ready . . . Suddenness is now the characteristic feature of sea fighting! . . . Readiness for sudden action has to be the keynote of all we do!" Balfour was enormously impressed by the Admiral's new creation, which, he declared, "has augmented the fighting power of the British Fleet not once or twice, but threefold."

Within five months of becoming First Sea Lord, Fisher acted to correct the deplorable state of fleet gunnery. The navy had been stung when, in testimony before a Royal Commission investigating the errors of the Boer War, a British general had described the marksmanship of the naval gunners sent to help in the defense of Ladysmith as something "which would have disgraced a girls' school." Fisher was furious, the more so because he knew it was true. From Portsmouth, he had recalled Percy Scott, who had served under him in the Mediterranean and who had demonstrated rapid, accurate fire, and had given him command of the gunnery school H.M.S. *Excellent.* In March 1905, as First Sea Lord, Fisher created the new post of Inspector of Target Practice, appointed Scott, and told him to do for the fleet what he had done for the ships under his own command. That same autumn, Scott introduced competitive firing into the fleet. By 1908, ships were hitting the target more often at six thousand and seven thousand yards than they previously had at two thousand yards. Conventional officers disliked Scott, who was small, cocky, and obsessed with gunnery. Fisher backed him nonetheless. "I don't care if he drinks, gambles, and womanizes," the First Lord said. "He hits the target."

Fisher's reforms brought not only more efficiency to the Fleet, but greater economy in naval expenditure. When Fisher took over the Admiralty, the Navy Estimates were continually rising. From £27.5 million in 1900, they had increased to £36.8 million in 1904, the year before Fisher arrived. Even those who favored a powerful navy were uneasy with this relentless growth. "Unless retrenchment comes from within, there will come upon us an irresistible wave of reaction which will do infinite mischief," *The Times'* naval correspondent, Thursfield, wrote to Fisher, adding, "It haunts me like a nightmare." Fisher entirely agreed. He rejected the principle that "fighting efficiency is inalienably associated with big Estimates! The exact opposite is the real truth! Lavish naval expenditure, like human high living, leads to the development of parasitical bacilli which prey on and diminish the vitality. . . . Parasites in the shape of non-fighting ships, non-combatant personnel, and unproductive shore expenditure must be extirpated like cancer—cut clean out." Fisher went after the bacilli, great and small. Scrapping obsolete ships saved £845,000 a year in repair costs alone and permitted the discharge of six thousand redundant dockyard workers. He discovered that the navy kept ten thousand extra chairs in stock. "There is only so much money available for the Navy," he roared. "If you put it into chairs that can't fight, you take it away from ships and men who can." He was told that an "amazing array of tumblers" was kept on hand. "The surgeon had his own particular pattern of tumbler, and the purser his, and they had to be stored in enormous quantities so that neither the pursar nor the surgeon should run the horrid risk of being short of his own particular tumbler." To their dismay, the First Sea Lord insisted that both professionals drink from similar goblets. Fisher's eagle eye brought dramatic results: in the 1905 Naval Estimates, £3.5 million was lopped off the previous year's expenses; in 1906, the Estimates dropped another £1.5 million; in 1907, still another £450,000. By 1907, the navy was costing the government and the taxpayer £31.4 million a year, which was £5.4 million less than it had cost when Fisher took office. The budget was reduced, not only as the fighting power of the British Fleet was augmented "not once or twice, but threefold"; it was done while Fisher was building a new ship and a new class of ship that would revolutionize naval warfare. This ship, which gave its name to all subsequent battleships from every nation, was H.M.S. *Dreadnought.*

CHAPTER 26

The Building of the Dreadnought

◆

A battleship is a floating platform for naval guns designed to destroy enemy ships. Assuming equal marksmanship on both sides, the ship with the larger number of guns, firing heavier shells at longer range, will prevail. Speed is also a factor, giving a captain the power to choose the moment of action—whether to pursue or withdraw. In battle in mid-ocean, where an enemy ship cannot flee to a friendly harbor and where there is no hiding place other than in rain clouds, fog, or darkness, destruction of the slower, weaker vessel is almost inevitable. Range is important because a ship which can fire and score hits out of range of the guns of her enemy is fighting a helpless foe. Range, size of the guns, and destructive power go hand in hand; the larger the shell, the greater the range, and the heavier its penetrating and blast effect.

When she was designed and built, the *Dreadnought* was the supreme embodiment of these concepts. Her main armament consisted of ten 12-inch guns, each capable of hurling an 850-pound projectile. If all eight guns of the *Dreadnought*'s broadside fired simultaneously, 6,800 pounds of steel and high explosive would plummet down on an enemy. Until she appeared, standard battleship armament in all major navies had consisted of four 12-inch guns, supported by a mixed battery of guns of smaller calibers. The summit of this earlier design had been reached in *Dreadnought*'s immediate predecessors, *Lord Nelson* and *Agamemnon,* designed to carry four 12-inch and ten 9.2-inch guns. At three thousand or four thousand yards, ranges which the smaller guns could manage, these ships were formidable. But Fisher, since his days with the Mediterranean Fleet, had dreamed of six thousand, eight thousand, even ten thousand yards. At these distances, all previous British battleships and all foreign battleships could fire only four guns.

The genesis of the *Dreadnought* traditionally is traced to an Italian, Vittorio Cuniberti, the chief constructor of the Italian Navy. Cuniberti had already designed four light battleships, the *Vittorio Emanuele* class, each carrying two 12-inch and twelve 8-inch guns, for his own navy. When his design for a larger, more heavily armed ship for the Italian Fleet was rejected, he received permission to write an article for *Jane's Fighting Ships,* calling for a 17,000-ton ship carrying twelve 12-inch guns. The article appeared in the 1903 annual edition of the publication and although it galvanized naval thinking on the matter of the all-big-gun ship, it may not have had quite the pioneer effect claimed for it at the time. Several powers, including the United States and Japan, were moving in the direction of larger, faster, heavier-gunned ships. In the spring of 1904, the U.S. Navy presented to Congress an appropriation request for two 16,000-ton ships each carrying eight 12-inch guns. The Americans moved slowly; the *South Carolina* and *Michigan* were not authorized until the spring of 1905 and not laid down until the autumn of 1906. Japan laid down two large 20,000-ton, 20-knot "semi-dreadnoughts" (they carried four 12-inch and twelve 10-inch guns) in the spring of 1905.

Cuniberti's article and reports of American and Japanese designs may have reinforced Fisher's belief that the fast, all-big-gun ship was the warship of the future, but, in his *Memoirs,* the British admiral gives no credit to Cuniberti or any other foreigner. He states that he personally first conceived the fast, big-gun battleship (which he half-facetiously dubbed H.M.S. *Untakeable)* at Malta in 1900, where he discussed his ideas with W. H. Gard, then chief constructor of the Malta dockyard. When he returned to England, he talked with Sir Philip Watts, the navy's chief designer, whom he had known since serving as captain of the *Inflexible,* for which Watts had designed a set of then unique antiroll tanks. Their friendship had continued, and in 1902 Watts, who also believed in fast, powerful ships, had succeeded Sir William White as civilian Director of Naval Construction. In October 1904, on becoming First Sea Lord,

Fisher immediately reinforced his staff by bringing Gard to London as Watts's Assistant Director of Naval Construction.

On December 22, 1904, Fisher created the Committee on Designs to work out details and produce drawings for his new battleship. The committee had a membership of nine civilians and seven naval officers, most of them Fisher's protégés. The officers included Rear Admiral Prince Louis of Battenberg, then Director of Naval Intelligence and future First Sea Lord; Captain John Jellicoe, Director of Naval Ordnance and future Commander-in-Chief of the Grand Fleet; and Captain Reginald Bacon, who was naval assistant to the First Sea Lord and would become the first captain of the *Dreadnought.* Fisher was not a member of the actual committee and did not sit in on their deliberations, but he supervised. As he explained the arrangement in a letter to Esher: "Selborne has agreed to my being President of a committee to devise new types of fighting ships. I explained to him that I had got the designs out of what had to be, but it was a politic thing to have a committee of good names, . . . [so that critics] will fire away at them and leave me alone."

Fisher knew what he wanted when he formed the committee and, although their instructions were to advise, a better description of their task would be that they were to "confirm," "refine," and "implement" the First Sea Lord's ideas. The basic decision had already been made by Fisher with Gard's help: they were to consider a battleship with uniform armament of 12-inch guns and 21 knots of speed. But the committee were not puppets, although it was later charged that the *Dreadnought* was entirely a product of Fisher's megalomania and that he imposed his views on a helpless committee. Fisher did not know quite how to get what he wanted, and he kept an open mind as different ideas were proposed and explored. He respected the men on the committee, the more so because they were youthful and exceptionally able—and also because they had shown themselves eager to embrace new ideas.

The committee sat for seven weeks, from January 3 to February 22, 1905. At the first meeting, Fisher stood up and read a statement of purpose: "Two governing conditions [of naval warfare] are guns and speed. Theory and actual experience of war dictate a uniform arrangement of the largest guns, combined with a speed exceeding that of the enemy so as to be able to force an action." About the same time he laid a memorandum before Balfour and the Cabinet explaining his priorities, first guns, then speed: "In designing this ship, the most powerfully arranged armament has been made the first consideration. Absolutely nothing has been allowed to stand in the way of the most nearly perfect power and scope of the guns.

. . . Being a battleship, she will have to fight other battleships. Having speed, she can choose the range at which she will fight."

Some of the reasons for uniform big-gun armament were obvious. The purpose of battleships was to throw the maximum weight of shells at the enemy battle line; thus, why not make all the guns the biggest possible? Uniform big-gun armament meant that a ship would have to stock only a single caliber of ammunition, and parts for all her guns would be interchangeable. There was a more important reason, developed and hotly urged by dedicated gunnery officers like Percy Scott and Jellicoe: accurate fire control. An enemy ship moving fast ten thousand yards away is a difficult target to hit. Percy Scott discovered that the problem was a little easier if one used salvo firing—that is, firing a number of similar-caliber shells simultaneously at the target. If the splashes of the shells striking the water are behind the target, the guns should be lowered slightly; if in front, they should be raised; if before the target, they should be trained back a bit; if behind, they should be trained forward. This salvo firing continues until finally the huge columns of water straddle the target. Then the gunners know they have the correct range and sooner or later they will obtain hits. It was impossible to use guns of different caliber for this purpose; different-sized shells would have to be fired at different angles of gun-barrel elevation, at different velocities, and on different trajectories, and once they hit the water, no one could tell which splash was a product of which gun.

The argument that larger, uniform armament was more effective was supported by the experience of Admiral Count Heihachiro Togo's victory over the Russian Baltic Fleet at Tsushima on May 27, 1904. There, firing at seven thousand yards, both sides demonstrated the hitting power and accuracy of large naval guns at long range, and, further, the advantage of a maximum number of big guns. Captain William Pakenham, a Royal Navy observer aboard Admiral Togo's flagship, noted that "when 12 inch guns are fired, shots from 10 inch guns pass unnoticed, while, for all the respect they instill, 8 inch or 6 inch might just as well be pea shooters."

The new ship's speed and the range of her heavy guns also entered the equation. Speed would enable her to choose the range at which she would fight and, with her uniform armament of great guns, she could stay out of range of any lesser guns mounted by the enemy. Six-inch guns would be useless, as she would fight beyond the range of these guns; further, she would not need 6-inchers as a defense against torpedo-carrying destroyers, for she would fight well out of range of torpedo attack. Thus, all available weight devoted to guns should be invested in the heaviest guns possible. Fisher summed up these arguments: "The fast ship with the heavier guns and deliberate fire should absolutely knock out a vessel of equal speed with many lighter guns, the very number of which, militates against accurate spotting and deliberate hitting. . . . Suppose [once the range was obtained] a 12 inch gun to fire one aimed round each minute. Six guns would allow a deliberately aimed shell with a huge bursting charge every ten seconds. Fifty percent of these should be hits at 6,000 yards. Three 12 inch shells bursting on board every minute would be HELL!"

Along with deciding the number of heavy guns, the committee wrestled with the problem of siting the turrets. A sailing ship fired broadsides from rows of guns running down both sides of the hull and thus had to turn on a course roughly parallel to that of an enemy in order to fire her guns. At that, she could only fire half of her armament at the enemy (unless a second enemy ship conveniently appeared on her opposite side). Modern battleship guns, usually mounted two to a turret, revolved in the turret so that the guns could fire in almost any direction. Turrets placed on the bow or stern could fire to either side as well as forward or aft. Fisher wanted as many guns as possible able to fire forward; the proper position of a British battleship should be in pursuit of an enemy. "I am an apostle of 'End-on Fire,' for to my mind broadside fire is peculiarly stupid. To be obliged to delay your pursuit by turning even one atom from your straight course on to a flying enemy is to me being the acme of an ass!"

Various arrangements were tried, including superimposing of turrets on the bow and stern so that a higher turret was mounted above and slightly behind a lower turret. This novel arrangement was rejected, it being wrongly supposed that when the upper-turret guns were fired, the blast effect on the turret beneath would make the lower turret unlivable. This view was disproved when the first two U.S. dreadnoughts, *Michigan* and *South Carolina,* were built with superimposed turrets which worked perfectly well. Not until 1909, when the American dreadnoughts were completed and Great Britain had already built ten dreadnought battleships and four battle cruisers, did the British Navy switch, in the *Orion*-class battleships and the battle cruiser *Lion,* to superimposed turrets.

In the end, three of the *Dreadnought*'s five turrets were placed in a position to fire ahead. This was done by placing one turret in front of the bridge on the bow and a wing turret on either side just aft of the bridge (see diagram). The wing turrets could also fire broadside or astern, so that the ship was ready to fire six 12-inch

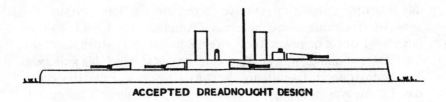

ACCEPTED DREADNOUGHT DESIGN

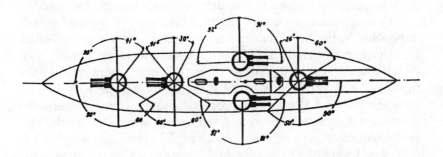

guns forward, six astern, or eight on either broadside. As theretofore no previous battleship, British or foreign, had carried more than four 12-inch guns, two firing ahead, two astern, or four broadside, the *Dreadnought* was the equivalent of two or even three earlier ships. Or, from the point of view of an admiral, a line of ten dreadnoughts would be equal to thirty pre-dreadnoughts firing ahead or astern, and twenty pre-dreadnoughts firing broadside.

A related problem was to raise the turrets as much as possible above the main deck without unbalancing the ship and making her top-heavy. In earlier ships with low bows and gun turrets placed on the main deck, the sea often poured over the bows and into the turrets, swamping guns and gunners. Fisher demanded that "no guns be carried on the main deck. In this position they are practically useless. Half the time they cannot see the objective for want of a view and may hit a friend as readily as an enemy, and the other half they are flooded out by the sea." On January 12, the committee partially obliged and placed at least the forward turret on a raised fo'c'sle so that it could be fought even when the ship was taking waves over the bow.

The committee then turned to the problem of attaining the high speed on which Fisher was adamant. "It is clearly necessary to have superiority in speed," Fisher had written to Selborne, "in order to compel your opponent to accept battle or to enable you to avoid

battle and lead him away from his goal 'till it suits you to fight him."
(This was as close as Fisher would come to admitting that occasionally a British warship might have to run away.) Here, too, the lessons of Tsushima were relevant. Admiral Togo had had an
advantage of six or seven knots over Admiral Z. P. Rozhestvensky.
This enabled him to stay at the greater range at which his gun crews
had been trained. Eventually, he was able to execute the classic
naval maneuver, crossing the Russian "T," bringing all his guns to
bear on the ships at the head of the Russian line. Fisher argued that
Togo's success at Tsushima was due primarily to superior speed.

Fisher wanted 21 knots for the *Dreadnought,* a speed clearly
impossible with the standard reciprocating steam engines which
then powered the British Fleet. Although most British pre-
dreadnoughts were designed for 18 or 19 knots, they rarely attained
this speed and certainly could not sustain it for long periods. Experience showed that British squadrons steaming at even 14 knots for
more than eight hours began to suffer breakdowns. The problem lay
in the nature of the engines themselves. Reciprocating engines had
cylinders, inside of which were heavy pistons which steam pressure
pushed once up and once down during each revolution of the propeller shaft. The engines revolved at 120 revolutions a minute, so
the huge momentum of the heavy pistons and other moving parts
had to be created and destroyed four times every second. As a result, the brass bearings were subjected to heavy stress and wear.
After a few hours' steaming at high speed, a number of bearings had
to be adjusted and if the engines were not stopped, a breakdown
would occur. After a battleship had run a four-hour full-speed steam
trial, she often had to spend ten days in port to adjust her main
bearings. It was this characteristic which caused Cuniberti to refer
disparagingly to the eight new British battleships of the *King Edward* class, then under construction and scheduled to join the fleet in
1905 and 1906, as "monsters with short legs."

A solution was available in the form of turbine engines: discs
mounted on a single shaft which spun continuously in the same
direction as steam pressed against their blades; thus, no motion or
energy was lost and little stress or wear ensued. But in January 1905
turbines were still on the frontier of technology. Many naval officers
remembered the performance of Charles Parsons' launch *Turbina* at
the 1897 Diamond Jubilee Review, but most considered this a taste-
less spectacle rather than a vision of the future. Two destroyers,
Viper and *Cobra,* completed in 1905, had been equipped with turbines and, at 36 knots, were to leave all other destroyers far astern.
The small cruiser *Amethyst* was given experimental turbine engines,

but when she went to sea for trials in 1904, she cracked a large casting and had to be brought home for repairs. Cunard, to which speed meant profit, had decided to install turbines in its two great liners *Lusitania,* to be launched in 1906, and *Mauretania,* scheduled for completion in 1907. Weighing what they knew and what they didn't, Fisher's committee hesitated. To go ahead and order an essentially untried system for a ship of the size and significance of the *Dreadnought* was an enormous risk. As the moment of decision approached, Philip Watts, who had expressed no opinion, was asked what he thought. Watts replied succinctly. "If you fit reciprocating engines," he said, "these ships will be out of date within five years." That decided it; the *Dreadnought* would have turbines.

The engine room of the *Dreadnought* was transformed to a place unrecognizable to British naval officers. As Bacon, the ship's first captain, and previously captain of the battleship *Irresistible,* described the difference: "[The turbines] were noiseless. In fact, I have frequently visited the engine room of the *Dreadnought* when at sea steaming 17 knots and have been unable to tell whether the engines were revolving or not. During a full speed run, the difference between the engine room of the *Dreadnought* and that of the *Irresistible* was extraordinary. In the *Dreadnought,* there was no noise, no steam was visible, no water or oil splashing about, the officers and men were clean; in fact, the ship to all appearances might have been in harbor and the turbines stopped. In the *Irresistible,* the noise was deafening. It was impossible to make a remark plainly audible and telephones were useless. The deck plates were greasy with oil and water so that it was difficult to walk without slipping. Some gland [valve] was certain to be blowing a little which made the atmosphere murky with steam. One or more hoses would be playing on a bearing which threatened trouble. Men constantly working around the engine would be feeling the bearings to see if they were running cool or showed signs of heating; and the officers would be seen with their coats buttoned up to their throats and perhaps in oilskins, black in the face, and with their clothes wet with oil and water." These old engine rooms, Bacon said elsewhere, resembled "a glorified snipe marsh."

Armor, the defensive shield, was next. Heavy armor was of less importance to Fisher than gunpower or speed and he begrudged the weight alloted to inert steel plates. "Speed is armor," he declared, and "Hitting is the thing, not armor." The *Dreadnought*'s skin, however, was to be thick. She carried five thousand tons of armor, almost eight hundred tons more than either of the two *Lord Nelson*s. This was redistributed, and more was added to the belt and below the waterline so that the ship could absorb at least two torpedo hits and still survive. Turret armor was reduced on Jellicoe's recommendation that the concussive effect of a direct hit on a 12-inch gun turret, even if the projectile did not penetrate the turret before exploding, would almost certainly put the turret out of action at least temporarily.

Although "speed is armor," no ship could outrun all shells or avoid all torpedoes and Fisher wanted the *Dreadnought* to be unsinkable. Most warships of the day had extensive watertight compartmentation below the waterline, each compartment being sealed off from those adjacent by watertight doors that remained open most times for easy access within the hull, and then were bolted shut when action impended. But there were occasions—as in the ramming of H.M.S. *Victoria*—when danger struck unexpectedly; the doors remained open and the sea, once admitted, spread rapidly, taking the ship to the bottom. Fisher's solution was radical: all watertight doors were to be eliminated; "no holes in the bulkheads whatsoever," he decreed. Instead, each compartment in the hull was to become a self-contained unit with no horizontal access at all. Men were to enter these spaces on ladders or electric elevators, from a hatch on the main deck. Once inside, enclosed in steel, they could communicate by telephone with other parts of the ship (tiny holes were permitted to pierce the bulkheads for electric wires and steam and hydraulic pipes), but otherwise they lived in a little, metallic world of their own. If the sea came in, they would drown, but the rest of the ship would live.

There were other changes. The heavy, sharp-edged ram bow, until then a fixture on British battleships, disappeared. Fisher saw no need for it, as his heavy guns would ensure that the battle would be fought at long ranges and steel battleships would no longer be closing on each other to ram. In addition, he pointed out, "the extra length [of a ram] will make it more difficult to dock a ship, and more of a peril to friends in peacetime than of any probable use in war."* Still another change moved the living quarters of the captain and officers' to the forward part of the ship. Throughout the long sailing-ship era, when vessels were commanded and steered from the quarterdeck aft, officers' quarters had been in the stern section of the ship. Captains and admirals lived in glorious cabins with carved windows and gallerys looking out over the rudder. In the early steel battleships, this tradition of officers' quarters aft was continued,

---

* Ironically, the one enemy ship sunk by H.M.S. *Dreadnought* was the German submarine *U-29*, which she rammed and sank in the English Channel on March 18, 1915.

even though ships were now steered and fought from a bridge or conning tower looking out over the bow. The *Dreadnought* committee took the logical step: captains and officers were moved to sleep and work at points closer to their battle stations. (Ordinary tars, hearing that the officers were moving forward and they were going aft, suspected that the reason lay in the presumed vibration of the new ships' engines, which would shake men sleeping nearby out of their bunks. In fact, the *Dreadnought*'s turbines produced so little vibration that the seamen soon rejoiced in the change, especially as they now had the relatively dry afterdeck for exercise and taking the air.)

Fisher demanded two final and key specifications—containment of the *Dreadnought*'s overall size and cost—that stemmed as much from political as from purely naval considerations. Although more powerful than any of her predecessors, the new ship was not to be much larger or more expensive than the twins, *Lord Nelson* and *Agamemnon*, which had just been laid down in October and November 1904. *Dreadnought* was only eighty-five feet longer, two and a half feet wider, and 1,400 tons heavier than these pre-dreadnought battleships and she was to cost only an additional £181,000. Because of her revolutionary design, Fisher reasoned, the ship would be subjected to many criticisms. He did not mean to abet this criticism with excessive size and cost and see his brainchild sink in Parliament.

On February 22, 1905, after only seven weeks of deliberation, the design committee submitted its recommendations. Fisher immediately went to work. The Admiralty's policy, he declared, would be to lay down the ship as soon as possible, and by giving the project the highest priority, to complete the vessel within a year of launching.

No new British battleships would be designed until the *Dreadnought* had gone to sea and the results of her trials evaluated. The two big pre-dreadnought battleships *Lord Nelson* and *Agamemnon* were too far along to be redesigned and would be completed as originally planned, but work on them would slow as priority was given to the *Dreadnought*. *Lord Nelson*'s and *Agamemnon*'s first sacrifice would be the eight twelve-inch guns scheduled to be divided between them; these were commandeered for the *Dreadnought*.

Fisher intended from the beginning to electrify the world with a record building time for the *Dreadnought*, and he carefully selected the dockyard to achieve his purpose. The Royal Naval Dockyard at Portsmouth could build more rapidly than any other private or naval yard. Portsmouth's record building time for a battleship was thirty-one months; Fisher wanted the *Dreadnought* built in twelve. Seven hull models were built and tested in the Admiralty tank at Haslar. Eventually, a shape was found which would require only 23,000 horsepower, not 28,000 as expected, to drive 17,000 tons through the water at twenty-one knots. This saving in engine weight was transferred to armor. Wherever possible, novelty was introduced as simplicity. Much of the saving in time was achieved by standardization. Instead of having each of the ship's great steel plates cut individually, he ordered them in advance by the dozen in standard sizes and had them piled up in readiness in the yard.

In London, Fisher also was moving at full speed. Parliament was informed of the general plan and the basic dimensions of the ship in the First Lord's Statement on Naval Estimates in March 1905. By then, of course, the Admiralty already had issued orders for construction materials; Fisher had Balfour's promise that the Estimates would be accepted by the Commons. On June 24, 1905, the main propulsion machinery—turbines, pipes, boilers—was ordered. In July, the first 2,200 tons of steel plates and other structural material arrived in Portsmouth and were stacked for future use. In August, the ship's armor was ordered and by September 1, 1,100 men were engaged in sorting, preparing, and assembling materials. The *Dreadnought*'s keel was laid on Monday, October 2, 1905. Thereafter, work accelerated. On Wednesday, October 4, the first middle deck beams and inner bottom plates were fitted to the keel. By Saturday the seventh, most of the middle deck beams were in position. A week later, on Saturday the fourteenth, the middle deck plating was installed. The main deck beams went in on November 25 and on December 28, the center lines of her propeller shafts were sited in. By the last day of the year, the hull was almost complete. This rate of building was unprecedented and, in recognition, on January 1, 1906, Thomas Mitchell, the Chief Constructor of the Portsmouth dockyard, was knighted.

By early February, four months after the keel was laid, the hull was ready. The Admiralty chose for the ship the ancient and illustrious name *Dreadnought,* previously borne by eight Royal Navy vessels.* The King was invited to launch the ship. King Edward came down to Portsmouth on Friday afternoon, February 9, bringing a

---

* The first *Dreadnought,* a vessel of 400 tons carrying 200 men, was launched in 1573 and sailed against the Spanish Armada. Queen Elizabeth I chose its name "to infuse her own dauntless spirit into the hearts of her subjects and to show . . . Europe . . . how little she dreaded, and how little such a people could dread, the mightiest armaments of their enemies." The fifth *Dreadnought,* a three-decker of 98 guns, fought with Nelson at Trafalgar.

triumphant Jacky Fisher as his guest on the royal train. The Queen did not come because her father, King Christian IX of Denmark, had died a few days before. When the train arrived at the dockside jetty at six P.M., the monarch led his guests on board the *Victoria and Albert* for dinner and the night. The weather that day had been cold and bright, and the sunset light on Portsmouth harbor that evening reminded one observer of a Turner. All night, however, the barometer fell and by early Saturday morning a southwesterly gale was bringing rain in sheets. At nine A.M. the King's guests breakfasted on the yacht and apprehensively looked out through rain-blurred windows. By mid-morning, the rain had stopped and the sun shone through fitfully between scudding banks of clouds.

All morning, special trains from London had been disgorging crowds of spectators at Portsmouth station. By ten A.M. people were streaming through the main gate of the navy yard and wending their way along the network of dockyard roads and lanes, past huge workshops of brick and corrugated iron, to the north corner of the yard, where the *Dreadnought* was waiting. There, they saw the huge hull resting in its cradle, the lower half painted a reddish brown, the upper half, which would rise above the waterline, a bluish gray. The hull was supported by only a few of the large wooden blocks which had held it during construction. Most had already been removed and the last few were being knocked away by gangs of men who were singing "Rule, Britannia!", "Suwanee River," and "Lead, Kindly Light" as they worked. Towering over the crowd rose the great hull itself and before the bow, an enormous wooden platform on which the King and a thousand dignitaries and guests were to stand during the ceremonies.

King Edward, wearing his uniform of Admiral of the Fleet with its cocked hat and his broad blue ribbon of the Order of the Garter, left the yacht at eleven-fifteen A.M. and boarded his train for the short trip through the yard. The death of his father-in-law had curtailed some of the planned display, but the King's train nevertheless passed between solid lines of sailors and marines along a route which included four triumphal arches draped with naval flags and scarlet bunting. At eleven-thirty the train arrived beneath the wooden platform and the King climbed stairs lined with red and white satin to find himself in an enclosure surrounded by admirals, government officials, a naval choir, members of the press, and all the foreign naval attachés, senior among them Rear Admiral Carl Coeper of the Imperial German Navy. Over their heads loomed the bow of the *Dreadnought,* garlanded with red and white geraniums.

Fisher was irrepressible. Standing next to the King, he was seen continually gesturing and describing features of the ship. The Bishop of Winchester began the service with the 107th Psalm: "They that go down to the sea in ships, that do business in great waters; these see the works of the Lord, and his wonders in the deep," and ended it by raising his hand to bless the ship and all who would sail in her. When the last blocks had been knocked away and the *Dreadnought* was held only by a single, symbolic cable, the King plucked a bottle of Australian wine from a nest of flowers before him and swung it against the bow. The bottle bounced back. Again His Majesty swung and this time the bottle shattered and wine splashed down the steel plates. "I christen you *Dreadnought!*" cried the King. Then, taking a chisel and a wooden mallet made from the timbers of Nelson's *Victory,* he went to work on the symbolic rope holding the ship in place. This time, one stroke did the job. The great ship stirred. Slowly at first, then with increasing momentum, she glided backwards down the greased building way. A few minutes later, the giant hull floated serenely on the water, corraled by a flotilla of paddle tugs. The band played "God Save the King," the crowd gave three cheers, and His Majesty descended the steps, reboarded his train, and returned to the *Victoria and Albert,* which cast off immediately for Cowes in a fresh storm of rain and wind.

The launching of the great ship made news around the world. From Washington, the London *Times'* correspondent reported: "The building and launching of the *Dreadnought* have aroused interest here which is both professional and political. Nobody is more interested than the President [Theodore Roosevelt] to whom all things naval are of deep concern. That such a ship could have been built so quickly and so secretly astonishes naval experts." *The New York Times* worried about the close connection between Great Britain and a nation which worried Americans: Japan. "The *Dreadnought* is a symbol of the effectiveness, the sincerity, and the power of the alliance between Great Britain and Japan, for she is a direct outcome of the naval lessons of the Russo-Japanese War. It is now known, though it was quite unknown while the war lasted, that Great Britain was permitted by Japan to station naval attachés in the vessels of Admiral Togo's fleet . . . it is hinted that they included at least one naval constructor. The results of what they learned are all to be incorporated in the giant *Dreadnought.*"

In the months that followed, the empty hull was converted into a ship. The hull is the easiest part of a warship to build; the engines take longer; turrets, gun mountings, and guns take longest. On February 15, 1906, only five days after the launching, Fisher again speeded up her schedule. Now the ship was to be completed by

January 1, 1907, rather than by mid-February of that year. The acceleration meant another increase in effort for the Portsmouth navy yard. Normal working hours were eight and a half hours a day, beginning at seven A.M., five and a half days a week. The *Dreadnought*'s builders began at six A.M. and worked eleven and a half hours a day, six days a week. Of the eight thousand men employed by the yard, three thousand were at work on this single ship.

By March 2, 1906, all the ship's boilers were on board and two thousand tons of armor plate had been bolted into position. A month later, the total weight of the ship was 10,000 tons. In May, the first turbines arrived from Parsons and the weight of the ship reached 11,500 tons. By May 23 she received her sixth coat of paint. In June, all of her turbines were installed and six of the 12-inch guns had been hoisted into position. The ship's weight reached 13,100 tons. In July, the other four 12-inch guns were mounted and the ship weighed 14,000 tons. By August 3, 15,380 tons had been worked into the ship and her foremast was raised above the superstructure. On September 1, the *Dreadnought* was placed in reserve commission and the first members of a nucleus crew came aboard to sling their hammocks in her spaces.

The *Dreadnought* tested her engines alongside a dock. "It was an exciting moment when steam was first put into the turbines," recalled Bacon, the ship's first captain. "How would they work? The clearance between the thousands of blades on the rotating and static drums was a matter of a few thousandths of an inch only. One defective blade might become loose, come out, and strip the turbines completely." There were stories of shattered turbines whose blades had been removed by the bucketful. Happily, the *Dreadnought*'s turbines worked splendidly. The boilers were fired up, steam was let gently into the turbines, the rotors turned, blades revolved precisely as designed, and then the engines were cut off.

On October 1, 1906, a year and a day from the laying of her keel, H.M.S. *Dreadnought* went to sea. Bacon was on the bridge. Leaving her fitting-out basin, the battleship had an embarrassing moment: she got stuck in the basin entrance. There was plenty of water under her keel, but the basin had been built when ships did not bulge as much under water as the *Dreadnought* did. Fortunately, the tide still had another hour to rise; at full tide, the *Dreadnought* barely slipped out. Bacon did not enjoy imagining the glee of the ship's critics had she had to wait while her turrets were lifted off to reduce her draft and permit an escape.

The *Dreadnought*'s first excursion into the English Channel was

for contractor's trials, prescribed tests of her seaworthiness and capabilities before formal acceptance into the Royal Navy. It was
quickly apparent that she took the sea well. Because of her size and
the height of her bows, she steamed at 19 knots through fifteen-foot
waves, remaining steady and keeping her fore turret dry. On October 3 and 4, she steamed for thirty hours at moderate speed with all
gauges holding firm. On the fourth and fifth she conducted a series
of high-speed, three-hour runs. The new turbine system, Bacon signaled the Admiralty, was "markedly successful." On October 6, he
was handed a telegram from Balmoral: "The King is greatly pleased
at the satisfactory report of *Dreadnought*'s trials." On October 8,
the battleship steamed for eight hours at full speed without incident
and the following day returned to port, her officers jubilant.

The battleship sailed again on October 17, this time to fire her
guns. The *Dreadnought*'s full broadside was a matter of concern to
her designers, the Admiralty, and above all, to the officers and men
on board. No one knew whether or how badly the recoil effect of
eight huge guns fired simultaneously would damage the ship. For the
occasion, an anxious Sir Philip Watts, the ship's designer, had come
on board to see what happened. Seeking the best spot from which to
observe the effect of the broadside on the ship's structure, Watts left
the bridge and placed himself on the mess deck. "He looked very
grave and serious," said Bacon of Watts. "I am quite sure that he
fully expected the decks to come down wholesale. Presently, there
was a muffled roar and a bit of a kick on the ship. The eight guns
had been fired and scores of men between the decks had no idea
what happened."

Trials continued through October and November, and on December 3, the *Dreadnought* returned to the Portsmouth yard. On
December 11, 1906, three weeks short of Fisher's accelerated schedule, H.M.S. *Dreadnought* was accepted into the Royal Navy. These
records—a year and a day from laying the keel to going to sea; ten
months from launching to full commissioning into the navy—had
never been equalled in the history of capital ships. Previous to that,
the average building time for British battleships had been thirty-
three months. No battleship had been built in less than thirty-one
months.

Early in the new year, 1907, Bacon took the *Dreadnought* on
her first voyage. She steamed down the Atlantic coast of Spain to
Gibraltar and then into the Mediterranean, where the Home Fleet,
commanded by Sir Arthur Wilson, was cruising off the north coast
of Sardinia. During this voyage, a major steering problem came to

light. When the *Dreadnought* was moving faster than 15 knots and the helm was put over more than 10 degrees, the vessel had so much momentum that the rudder engine could not bring the rudder back to zero; thus the ship continued turning in a circle. In the Strait of Bonifacio off Corsica, this defect caused a near collision. Bacon did not report the problem immediately to the Admiralty. The difficulty could be fixed with a stronger rudder engine once they returned to England; meanwhile he could stay out of trouble by limiting turns at higher speeds. If he had made a report, he probably would not have been allowed to proceed on the next phase of his ship's shakedown cruise, a 10,000-mile round-trip voyage across the Atlantic to the West Indies. Keeping mum, Bacon returned to Gibraltar, coaled his ship, and sailed westward, maintaining a constant speed of seventeen knots for 3,400 miles. His destination was Trinidad, selected by Fisher for its remoteness from the eyes of British critics and foreign naval attachés. There, for six weeks, the new battleship carried out extensive tests on her guns and machinery. One night, intending to check her searchlights, Bacon took the big ship into the mouth of a small creek and dropped anchor. The plunging anchor stirred up the largest shark Bacon had ever seen, "a great, white-bellied brute who rose to the surface to see what had happened to disturb its habitual quiet." When the crew saw the fish, their enthusiasm for tropical swimming dwindled.

The *Dreadnought*'s return to England was marred by new troubles. Bacon came down with malarial fever of 103 degrees, a recurrence of an illness contracted as a young officer in a naval landing-party expedition against African headhunters in 1897. One of the ship's boiler tubes burst, injuring three men. And the ship almost ran out of coal. Steaming nonstop for ten days across the Atlantic, the *Dreadnought* arrived at Spithead down to her last eighteen tons, enough for about four hours of steaming.

Upon her return to England, the *Dreadnought* became the flagship of the Commander-in-Chief, Home Fleet. In the spring of 1907, she made a series of visits to ports around the British Isles, and in June she traveled across the North Sea to Bergen, Norway. From July 30 to August 7 she was at Spithead for the annual naval review and there, on August 5, 1907, King Edward paid her another visit, this time bringing the Queen and the Prince of Wales. With Fisher standing at his elbow on the bridge, the King watched the hoisting of both the Royal Standard and his personal flag as an Admiral of the Fleet. At ten A.M. the ship weighed anchor and steamed down the lines of anchored battleships and cruisers whose cheering crews lined the rails. Reaching the sea, the *Dreadnought* increased speed to twenty knots. A party of journalists invited on board were surprised by the absence of vibration. The naval correspondent of *The Times* went below to the starboard engine room and subsequently told his readers: "It was far cooler than any other engine room I have visited; there were no moving parts visible except the governors of the two turbines and there was very little noise. As to the engineers in charge, they seemed to have very little or nothing to do except to stand by for orders from the bridge."

The main purpose of the excursion was to demonstrate to the royal party the firing of the battleship's 12-inch guns. Once south of the Isle of Wight, the *Dreadnought*'s two after turrets trained around to slightly ahead of amidships and then, with the monarchs watching from the bridge, opened fire. The Queen, peering aft at the muzzles of the guns, was startled by the flame and blast as the projectiles belched forth. In less than three minutes, twelve rounds had been fired, six by each turret, and the exercise was over. The targets, two floating canvas structures fourteen feet by fourteen feet, were only a mile and a half away, the range being drastically cut so that the King and Queen could observe the shells either striking the targets or falling into the sea. In spite of the close range, the marksmanship was impressive: of twelve rounds fired, eleven hit the target and nine were bull's-eyes. This shooting was even more impressive to *The Times'* correspondent when he discovered that the firing had been done, not by specially picked gunnery marksmen, but by the regular gun crews which manned the two turrets.

After firing, the ship steamed close to the targets so that the royal couple could see the results for themselves. The King was so pleased that he climbed inside both turrets to congratulate the gunners. Fisher, Scott, Jellicoe, and Bacon, all of whom were aboard, all with much at stake in the *Dreadnought,* were exultant. The Queen was excited and asked that the targets be hoisted aboard and displayed like trophies on the fantail so that she could take snapshots. (Later, when the *Dreadnought* returned to Portsmouth, steaming past other battleships with her targets displayed, there were grumbles that Bacon was "a cheap swaggerer.")

From the beginning, the Germans had been curious about the development of the *Dreadnought.* Their curiosity was heightened by the unusual secrecy surrounding all details connected with the ship. The *Times* noted "the air of mystery in which she had been officially enveloped and which is still to be maintained." The key details did leak out. The 1905 edition of *Jane's Fighting Ships* reported that the new ship would be laid down before the end of that year, that she would be an all-big-gun ship with 12-inch guns, and that she would be powered by turbines which would give her a speed of 21 knots. *Jane's* was impressed: "It is hardly too much to say that, given her speed, gun power, range and the smashing effect of the concentrated force of heavy projectiles, the *Dreadnought* should easily be equal in battleworthiness to any two, probably to three, of most of the ships now afloat."

This, of course, included German ships, and Admiral Tirpitz and the German Admiralty paid careful attention. In December 1904, even as Fisher was announcing the formation of the Committee on Design, Admiral Carl Coeper, the German Naval Attaché in London, was reporting to Berlin that Vickers Limited, a British shipbuilding firm, was drawing plans for a new battleship armed with ten or twelve 12-inch guns. The Kaiser noted Coeper's news approvingly, scribbling on the dispatch: "In my opinion, this is the armament of the future."

Despite the Kaiser's opinion, his navy was bound on a different course. As the *Dreadnought* was emerging from the drawing board, Tirpitz was launching the *Deutschland,* the first of five new German battleships which, with their 13,400 tons, four 11-inch and fourteen 6.7-inch guns, and 18-knot speed, were inferior even to the British pre-dreadnoughts *Lord Nelson* and *Agamemnon*. To follow the *Deutschland* class, Tirpitz was thinking of two larger ships of sixteen thousand tons with eight 11-inch guns and twelve 7.6-inch guns, but beyond this limit in size and tonnage he could not go. The obstacle was the depth of the Kiel Canal, the path by which the fleet shuttled between the North Sea and the Baltic. It was a cruel choice: either the ships remained the same size or the canal would have to be enlarged. And redigging the canal would require years of effort and millions of marks. As a result, when confirmation of the size, speed, and armament of the *Dreadnought* reached Berlin, something close to panic ensued. Admiral Müller, subsequently Chief of the Naval Cabinet, wrote to Tirpitz on the subject on February 8, 1905. Müller was a waffler and, typically, he explored both sides of the argument and then hopped back up on the fence: "If there were no natural obstacles, we should be bound to choose the very large ship of the line as the type for the future. . . . But we are faced with a natural obstacle: the Kiel Canal. One might indeed say that the concentration of power in a 17,000 ton or 18,000 ton ship is so very important that we must do without the canal rather than the big ships. But I do not value the big ships as highly as this."

Tirpitz knew better, and his decision, not made easily, was to build bigger ships and to enlarge the canal to accommodate them.*

When speculation about the new British ship first appeared in the winter of 1904–1905, Tirpitz was engaged in building the *Deutschland* class. The *Deutschland* herself had been laid down in 1903 and was launched in November 1904, before Fisher's Committee on Design held its first meeting. Two more ships, *Hannover* and *Pommern,* had been laid down in 1904 and were launched in September and December 1905 respectively, as *Dreadnought*'s own keel was being laid and construction begun. The fourth and fifth ships of this now hopelessly obsolete class, *Schlesien* and *Schleswig-Holstein,* were laid down in 1905 and launched in May and December 1906. Although by the latter date H.M.S. *Dreadnought* had been commissioned, Tirpitz doggedly went ahead and finished all five ships. The *Deutschland*s were thus brought into service over a two-year period, 1906 to 1908, when the *Dreadnought* was already proving herself at sea and nine additional dreadnought ships were under construction for the British Navy.

An even better measure of the disarray in Berlin can be seen in the timing of Tirpitz's own dreadnought program. In July 1906, when the British *Dreadnought* was already in the water fitting out for sea trials, Tirpitz laid the keel of Germany's first all-big-gun battleship, S.M.S. *Nassau,* of 18,900 tons and twelve 11-inch guns. Then, suddenly, Tirpitz reversed himself. On orders from Berlin, all work on the new ship at Wilhelmshaven was halted; the workmen were commanded to lay down their tools and walk away. This hiatus, while German designers struggled to obtain and analyze details of the *Dreadnought,* lasted an entire year. Not until July 1907 was work resumed on the *Nassau.* At that point, Tirpitz plunged forward. In the same month, besides resuming work on the *Nassau,* he laid the keels of two more dreadnoughts, *Westfalen* and *Posen,* and a month later, in August, the keel of a fourth sister, S.M.S. *Rheinland,* was laid down in Stettin. Nevertheless, in terms of time lost, the damage was done. For twelve long months, the Imperial German Navy had not driven a single rivet into this new class of supership.

---

* Later it was said that forcing the Germans to spend time and money widening and deepening the Kiel Canal was part of the brilliance of Fisher's scheme. Fisher himself subsequently saw the advantages and exulted that Germany had been "paralyzed by the *Dreadnought* which had halted all German construction for a year and converted the Kiel Canal into a useless ditch," but this was after the fact. There is no evidence that Fisher or his design committee were thinking about the problems Tirpitz would face with the Kiel Canal; if they were thinking of Germany when they designed the *Dreadnought,* it was of sinking German battleships on the high seas.

■ ■ ■

Despite her triumphs, the *Dreadnought* and Fisher were assailed from many sides. The brilliant achievement was declared to be, not a stroke of genius, but a horrendous blunder. By enormous effort and at vast expense over many years, Britain had built an over-whelming supremacy in pre-dreadnought battleships. Now, charged Fisher's critics, at the whim of a foolish First Sea Lord, she had thrown it all away. By introducing a new class of ship so powerful that all previous battleships were instantly obsolete, she had doomed the long lines of *King Edward*s, *Canopus*es, and *Majestic*s— forty battleships in all. Germany was to be given a chance to begin a new race with Britain for naval supremacy on equal terms.

Protests poured into the Admiralty, rang in the House of Com-mons, inundated the press. "The whole British Fleet was . . . mor-ally scrapped and labeled obsolete at the moment when it was at the zenith of its efficiency and equal not to two but practically to all the other navies of the world combined," roared Admiral of the Fleet Sir Frederick Richards, a former First Sea Lord. David Lloyd George, a member of the Radical wing of the Liberal Party, de-nounced the *Dreadnought* as "a piece of wanton and profligate os-tentation" and thunderously demanded to know why Fisher had not left well enough alone. "We said, 'Let there be dreadnoughts,' " declared the fiery Welshman. "What for? We did not require them. Nobody was building them and if anyone had started building them, we, with our greater shipbuilding resources, could have built them faster than any country in the world."

There were conceptual arguments from naval personages such as Sir William White, who had designed most of Britain's pre-dread-nought battleships, and Lord Charles Beresford, a popular admiral and Member of Parliament. White complained that building dread-noughts was "putting all one's naval eggs into one or two vast, costly, majestic but vulnerable baskets." Better to have a greater number of smaller ships, he argued, because the loss of one in battle meant a smaller fractional reduction in fighting strength. There were practical complaints from serving officers about design mistakes. Lieutenant K.G.B. Dewar, a gunnery officer, could not imagine the thinking of the designer who had placed the forward tripod mast, which carried the fire-control station, behind and not in front of the forward funnel. This unfortunate juxtaposition ensured that when Lieutenant Dewar was sitting aloft on the mast trying to use his binoculars or telescope to spot the fall of shells, he would receive the full blast of black smoke pouring out of the forward funnel directly into his eyes and lungs.

As well as he could, Fisher ignored the politicians, but at White, Beresford, and his naval antagonists he roared defiance. "I wish to God I could bite them," he wrote of his enemies on May 12, 1905. "I will if I get a chance." He rebutted the "too many eggs in too few baskets" argument, saying that bigger, stronger ships were not only more dangerous to the enemy but more survivable. Larger ships could carry greater guns and more armor; large hulls could be designed to better resist torpedo attack and enclose more powerful engines, thus giving higher potential speed. Besides, Fisher declared, all these advantages were being obtained without actually increasing either the size or the cost of the *Dreadnought* markedly over the *Lord Nelson*s. For an increase of only 1,500 tons and 10 percent more money, he was equipping the navy with a ship two or three times as powerful.

Against one of Beresford's arguments—that *Dreadnought*s should not be built because they would not fit into Britain's existing drydocks—Fisher turned withering scorn: "It should clearly be borne in mind that the docks and harbors exist for our ships, not the ships for the docks. If the necessity for larger ships be shown, the other expenditure which they entail must be faced, for otherwise, if we continue to build ships only because they will go into the existing docks, we shall not require any docks at all—in the day of action our ships will all go to the bottom."

One objection, Dewar's complaint about smoke in the eyes of the fire controllers, was acted upon and in the seven new battleships which followed *Dreadnought*, the forward mast was placed in front of the funnel. Then, inexplicably, in *Colossus, Hercules, Orion, Thunderer, Monarch, Conqueror,* and the battle cruiser *Lion,* the original error was repeated. *Dreadnought,* obviously, was not always steaming directly into the wind and smoke was not always pouring directly into the face of her fire-control spotters. In 1907 target practice, the ship scored twenty-five hits in forty rounds fired at eight thousand yards, which ranked her third in the fleet. But in weight of shell thrown at the target—a crucial factor in battle—the *Dreadnought* stood unchallengeably supreme. In eight minutes, she hurled 21,250 pounds of shells from her guns, 75 percent more than any other British battleship.

These statistics still failed to convince Sir William White. In 1908, he wrote an article, "The Cult of the Monster Warship," which reiterated his opposition. But he was fighting a losing battle;

more dreadnoughts, British and foreign, were sliding down the ways. Noting his views, the *Observer* commented dryly: "When Sir William White suggests that both the United States and Germany are foolish and deluded powers, slavishly copying the errors of a blind [Admiralty] Board in Whitehall, he surely takes up the position of the dissenting juryman who had never met eleven such obstinate fellows in his life."

In the end, Fisher and the Admiralty built the *Dreadnought* not only because they believed they were right, but because they believed it was their duty. As Bacon put it: "Knowing as we did that the *Dreadnought* was the best type to build, should we knowingly have built the second-best type ship? What would have been the verdict of the country if Germany had . . . built a *Dreadnought* while we were building *Lord Nelson*s, and then had forced a war on us and beaten our fleet? What would have been the verdict of the country if a subsequent inquiry had elicited the fact that those responsible at the Admiralty for the safety of the nation had deliberately recommended the building of second class ships?" Bacon's own suggestion was that the guilty parties be hanged from lampposts in Trafalgar Square.*

* In February 1910 the *Dreadnought,* lying with the Home Fleet in Weymouth Bay, received word that the Emperor of Abyssinia with a small suite was on his way to visit the ship. The telegram was signed "Hardinge" (Sir Charles Hardinge was Permanent Under Secretary of the Foreign Office). The Emperor's party—four Abyssinians, a young man from the Foreign Office, and a European translator—were met by a red carpet and a saluting naval officer at Weymouth Station. Escorted to *Dreadnought,* they found the battleship dressed with flags, lines of marines drawn up on deck, a band playing, and the admiral and his staff in gold-laced uniforms waiting to greet them. The visitors inspected the ship and saw the sick bay, the wireless room, the officers' wardroom, and one of the gun turrets, which was rotated and its guns elevated and depressed. The admiral wanted his explanations translated, but the translator had difficulty. Told the difference between the marines in red uniforms and the marines in blue, he said, "I am afraid it will be rather hard to put that into Abyssinian, sir. However, I'll try." He turned to the Emperor: "Entaqui, mahai, kustufani." The Emperor nodded. "Tahli bussor ahbat tahl aesque miss," the translator continued. "Erraema . . ." The Emperor repeated a few of the words, nodding that he understood. The British officers were excellent hosts; one young lieutenant was particularly delighted at the astonishment of the native visitors when he switched on an electric light. At the end of the tour, the admiral invited his guests to remain for a meal, but the translator replied that "the religious beliefs of Abyssinia made it impossible for the Royal family to touch food unless it was prepared in special ways." With salutes, bows, and smiles all around, the Imperial party left the ship and returned to London.

A few weeks later, the *Daily Mirror* got wind of the story and the truth emerged. The "Emperor" was a young man named Anthony Buxton, disguised with greasepaint, a false beard, a turban, and robes. His suite, similarly costumed, was made up of friends, including the painter Duncan Grant. The language employed, after the first three words of impromptu Swahili, were the translator's adaptation, suitably mispronounced, of the

■ ■ ■

Although Fisher's design committee sat for only seven weeks, it
produced plans not only for the *Dreadnought,* but for a second new
type of revolutionary and controversial warship. This was the very
large, very fast, heavily gunned, but lightly armored ship originally
called a large armored cruiser and eventually known as the battle
cruiser. Between 1906 and 1914, ten battle cruisers were constructed
in Great Britain; across the North Sea, six were built for the High
Seas Fleet. From the beginning, the battle cruisers captured the public imagination. They weighed as much as battleships (*Dreadnought*
at 17,900 tons and *Invincible* at 17,250 tons were the two largest
warships Britain had ever built up to that time), carried 12-inch
battleship guns, and were extraordinarily fast. When they put to sea,
with black smoke pouring from their funnels and waves curling back
from their bows, with their turrets and long gun barrels training
around towards a target, they were intimidating symbols of naval
power. People began to think of them in simile. Their speed and
huge guns called forth the image of great jungle cats, swift and
deadly, with large shining claws. Others likened them to cavalry, a
highly mobile force, hanging on the flanks of battle, ready to charge
in for the kill. The most famous of the battle-cruiser admirals, the
brave, impetuous Beatty, handled his ships like cavalry. In the navy
and in society, he and his officers radiated the glamour of hussars,
appearing more dashing than the captains of the plodding dreadnought battleships, the infantry of the sea, the backbone of the fleet.
But despite their speed, their power, and their glamour, their beauty
was flawed, and doom rolled over them at Jutland. On a single
afternoon, four of these sixteen giants, three British and one German, went to the bottom of the sea.

Originally, these big, fast, powerful ships were intended as super-
cruisers with the duties that cruisers had always had: scouting for the
battle fleet, commerce raiding or hunting down enemy commerce
raiders, patrol, and blockade. In sailing-ship days, the antecedent of
the cruiser was the frigate. Nelson's majestic three-deck ships-of-

---

Fourth Book of the *Aeneid,* which he had memorized in school. The navy reddened with
embarrassment; questions were asked in Parliament; the hospitable admiral was followed
through the streets by boys shouting "Bunga-Bunga!" When the hoaxers called on the
First Lord and offered to apologize, Mr. McKenna frowned and bundled them out of his
office. It was particularly mortifying that one of the costumed Abyssinians had been a
woman. This was Virginia Stephen, who was to become Virginia Woolf.

the-line, carrying eighty to one hundred guns, were too big, too slow, and too valuable to be risked for this kind of work, and frigates—smaller, faster, more versatile—were assigned these duties.

The frigate's first and crucial mission was to be the eyes of her admiral, observing and reporting the size and movements of the enemy fleet. Speed was essential and, by carrying three masts and spreading almost as much canvas as a ship-of-the-line, a frigate was able to thrust her lighter hull through the water much faster than a larger, heavier ship. This enabled her to approach a hostile squadron while staying just out of range, to establish its numbers, course, and speed, and to return to her own admiral to tell him what she had learned. Once battle impended, the frigate withdrew. With her lighter timbers she was too thin-skinned to lie in the line of battle and her smaller guns could not contribute much to a heavy cannonade.

Ships evolved from wood to steel and propulsion changed from wind to steam, but admirals still needed the same information. The job of scouting was assigned to fast, lightly armored cruisers. By the 1890s, British cruisers had been given a second assignment, the protection of merchant shipping. France—still the potential enemy—had provoked Admiralty concern by suddenly launching a series of big cruisers capable of 21 knots. These ships were the brainchilds of a school of French admirals who, despairing that France would ever be able to match Britain battleship for battleship, concluded that the best way to bring down the maritime colossus was to unleash a pack of swift, deadly cruisers and torpedo boats that could attack and cripple Britain's vulnerable overseas merchant trade.

British admirals grasped the threat. Their reaction was to produce the anticruiser cruiser, a ship even faster, stronger, and more heavily gunned, to hunt down and sink anything the French sent out. These ships, designed to fight, not simply to shadow and report, were given more armor and called armored cruisers. Class after class was designed, launched, and sent to sea: six ships of the *Cressy* class, 12,000 tons, laid down in 1898 and 1899; four ships of the *Drake* class, 14,100 tons, laid down in 1899; nine ships of the *County* class, 9,800 tons, laid down in 1900 and 1901; six ships of the *Devonshire* class, 10,850 tons, laid down in 1902; two ships of the *Duke of Edinburgh* class, 13,500 tons, laid down in 1903; four ships of the *Warrior* class, 13,550 tons, laid down in 1904; and finally three ships of the *Minotaur* class, 14,600 tons, whose design had been completed and funded by Parliament before Fisher took office and which were laid down in January and February 1905, even as his own design committee was sitting. In all, there were thirty-five of these British armored cruisers, some of them as big as or bigger than the *Royal Sovereign* and *Majestic*-class battleships. Yet no matter how big they got or how impressive they looked, they were never expected to fight battleships. Indeed, their own survival, like that of the frigates that preceded them, lay in keeping out of range of battleship guns.

This was Fisher's understanding and purpose too, at least in the beginning. His first battle cruisers were intended to be the ultimate in armored cruisers, so fast and heavily gunned that they could overtake and destroy any other cruiser in the world. As early as March 1902, when he was Commander-in-Chief of the Mediterranean Fleet, Fisher wrote to Lord Selborne that he was working with Gard, the Chief Constructor of the Malta dockyard, on a design for an armored cruiser which would make all existing armored cruisers obsolete. Fisher called the hypothetical ship H.M.S. *Perfection*, and at the top of the list of her design characteristics he put "Full Power Speed of 25 knots." In his letter, he wrote gleefully: "there would be no escape from her 25 knots." Once *Perfection* put to sea, all other armored cruisers might as well head for the scrap heap: "A single fast armoured cruiser would lap them up like an armadillo let loose in an ant hill. . . . The decisive factor upon which the fate of the ants will thenceforth hang will not be the efficacy of their bite, but the speed of their legs." In fact, Fisher advised Lord Selborne, he had already tested his theory in exercises at sea during his tour as Commander, North American Station, in the fast battleship *Renown:* "I on one occasion 'mopped up' all the cruisers one after another with my flagship the battleship *Renown.* The heavy swell and big seas had no corresponding effect on the big *Renown* as it had on the smaller . . . cruisers."

The Sea Lords' response was not everything Fisher had hoped. They authorized the *Warrior* and *Minotaur* classes, big ships with 9.2-inch guns and a speed of 23 knots, two knots beneath that which Fisher had demanded for *"Perfection."* Meanwhile, other admiralties were experimenting. Towards the end of 1904, word reached London that Japan was laying down two large, 21-knot armored cruisers, each carrying four 12-inch guns and twelve 6-inch. In Italy, four Cuniberti-designed ships carrying two 12-inch and twelve 8-inch guns and capable of 21 knots were on the ways. Foreigners were creeping up on *Perfection.*

In February 1905, once Fisher's design committee had completed the plans for the *Dreadnought, Perfection* appeared. No longer did Fisher have to urge his projects on the Admiralty; now he *was* the Admiralty. And in the Fisher era, he immediately made clear, British commerce was to be protected not by scattering armored cruisers around the world, but by building a few, immensely fast, powerful ships which could hunt down and destroy enemy cruisers wherever they fled—if necessary, "to the world's end."

By then, of course, the potential threat had changed nationality; it was not French cruisers that worried the Admiralty, but German ocean liners, the huge, swift, blue-water greyhounds, of the North German Lloyd and Hamburg-America lines, being constructed with a capacity to carry 6-inch guns. Designed to whisk passengers across the North Atlantic in five or six days, they could easily outrun any existing British cruiser.

Speed, then, was the preeminent requirement; speed to overtake the enemy and speed also for the new ship's own defense: she must be able to keep out of range of battleship guns. Fisher fixed the minimum absolute margin at four knots and, since he was building the *Dreadnought* to steam at 21 knots, H.M.S. *Perfection* must be able to steam at 25 knots.

Fisher also wanted maximum firepower. The biggest guns available were 12-inch, already being installed on new armored cruisers and fast battleships by the Italians and Japanese. Having successfully argued the case for the all-big-gun battleship, Fisher now demanded an all-big-gun armored cruiser. Once again, the faithful and imaginative Gard gave the Admiral what he wanted. *Perfection,* which was to become the *Invincible*-class battle cruiser, came off the drawing board with eight 12-inch guns in four twin turrets. Fisher was overjoyed. With 25-knot speed and eight 12-inch guns, here was a warship capable of destroying any vessel fast enough to catch it, and fast enough to escape any vessel capable of destroying it. She could "mop up" a whole squadron of enemy cruisers with the greatest of ease, using her speed to establish the range and her long-range guns to sink the enemy without exposing herself to return fire.

She had only a single flaw: her armor was too light. Like Sleeping Beauty, for whom life was serene as long as she stayed away from spindles, the *Invincible* and her sisters could lead happy lives as long as they stayed away from battleships. Her speed was a precious, expensive commodity and had been purchased at a heavy price. The three vital characteristics of a warship—guns, speed, and armor—are interrelated. A designer could not have everything: if heavy guns and heavy armor were required, then speed had to be curtailed; this was the compromise built into most battleships. If a higher speed was demanded and heavy guns retained, armor had to be sacrificed. This was the case with the *Invincible* and her sisters. To gain four precious knots of speed, the *Invincible* gave up one turret and two twelve-inch guns of *Dreadnought*'s armament. This saved two thousand tons, which could be invested in propulsion machinery. A more dangerous sacrifice was made in armor. The *Dreadnought,* intended to steam through a cataclysm of shell bursts, was fitted along her belt amidships with armor plate eleven inches thick, enough to stop a plunging heavy shell. Over the *Invincible*'s vital midships spaces, the belt armor was only seven inches thick. If the battle cruiser's mission was to scout or to engage enemy cruisers, seven inches of armor would keep her safe. But if she were to be deliberately taken within range of enemy battleships, seven inches was not enough.

What was responsible for the catastrophe that lay ahead for Britain's battle cruisers? The design flaw was their thinness of skin, but it was compounded by confusion of purpose and even confusion in nomenclature. The purpose of the battleship was always clear: to sink enemy battleships and dominate the ocean surface. But the purpose of the battle cruiser was never so clear, even from the beginning. She had the original mission of the frigate: to scout for the battle fleet. Fisher had enthusiastically endorsed the second mission acquired in the 1890s: to hunt down and destroy enemy commerce raiders. Once the ships had been given 12-inch guns—the basic armament of battleships—a third possibility began to creep into Admiralty thinking: they should be prepared to participate in a general fleet engagement. Instead of remaining as inactive as frigates, battle cruisers could form a fast auxiliary squadron operating in the van or to the rear of the main battle fleet. Possessing the same heavy long-range guns as battleships, they could reinforce the dreadnoughts by adding to the weight of metal raining down on enemy decks. Fisher described this as a fullfillment "of the great Nelsonic idea of having a squadron of very fast ships to bring on an action or to overtake and lame a retreating foe."

A shift in nomenclature added to the confusion. Originally, the *Invincible* class had been announced as "large armored cruisers," a more accurate designation than the subsequent "battle cruiser." In fact, the ships were very large, very heavily gunned, very fast, armored cruisers. But because of their size and armament, naval authorities began almost immediately to count them as capital ships along with dreadnoughts, and by 1912, when the term "battle cruiser" was coined, the impression of equality was firmly fixed. If they had remained "large armored cruisers," perhaps the Admiralty and many admirals and the naval press would not have permitted thinking to drift towards the belief that battle cruisers were intended to stand up against battleships.

Some naval experts saw the potential danger. *Brassey's Naval*

Annual said: "[The problem with] vessels of this enormous size and cost [is that] an admiral having *Invincible*s in his fleet will be certain to put them in the line of battle where their comparatively light protection will be a disadvantage and their high speed of no value." In short, because she looked like a battleship and carried a battleship's guns, sooner or later *Invincible* would be expected to fight like a battleship.

In time, Germany began to construct similar ships. Fisher's certainty that his battle cruisers could hunt down and destroy enemy armored cruisers was valid only as long as the enemy did not also build and send out battle cruisers. Once German construction was under way, the value of the *Invincible* and her sisters deteriorated and the threat to them increased. Given the nature of war, admirals on both sides could be expected to employ their battle cruisers on similar missions. Thus the great ships were likely to find their way to each other. Under those circumstances, two large vessels, each one firing heavy shells capable of penetrating the light armor of its opponent, would be locked in a deadly embrace. Neither, given the high speed of both, would be able to escape. The decision would likely be quick; accurate gunnery and luck guiding a 12-inch shell into an opponent's propulsion spaces or powder magazines would end the battle suddenly.

Lord Cawdor, Selborne's successor as First Lord, announced the first three British battle cruisers in the House of Commons in March 1905. In addition to the new *Dreadnought,* Lord Cawdor declared, construction would begin on "three large armoured cruisers . . . to be delivered in thirty months." In the spring of 1906, six months after the *Dreadnought,* the three keels were laid, *Invincible* at Newcastle-upon-Tyne and *Inflexible* and *Indomitable* along the Clyde near Glasgow. Fisher hovered over all three and, not surprisingly under this surveillance, they were completed on schedule and joined the fleet in 1908. Visually, they were impressive, and their speed exceeded Fisher's most extravagant dreams. In sea trials, *Invincible* reached 26.2 knots and later surged to 28 knots.

The appearance of these ships provoked more frustration in Berlin. The First Sea Lord had announced the three *Invincible*s to the Commons without details as to their armament, saying only that they would be large, fast, armored cruisers. The *Blücher,* the Kaiser's first battle cruiser, was intended as the German response. She was big—at 15,500 tons, much bigger than the *Deutschland*-class battleships. With a speed of 25 to 26 knots, she was fast enough. But to the London circle of naval attachés, naval correspondents, and other interested parties, Fisher had leaked the false information that the *Invicible*s would mount the same 9.2-inch guns which the *Warrior* and *Minotaur* classes had carried. Accordingly, Tirpitz armed his *Blücher* with twelve 8.2-inch guns, a match, it was felt, for the British 9.2-inch. While this unfortunate ship was still up on blocks, the three British *Invincible*s went to sea and their massive armament of eight 12-inch guns was revealed. Tirpitz once again had been outfoxed. *Blücher* was obsolete two years before she reached the water.

When intelligence of the *Invincible*s' true capability arrived in Berlin, Tirpitz set grimly to work. The German battle cruiser *Von der Tann,* 19,400 tons (2,000 heavier than the *Invincible*s) with eight 11-inch guns and 25 knots' speed, was laid down in October 1908. Britain replied in February 1909 with the *Indefatigable,* a bigger *Invincible* with the same armament and speed, but additional tons of armor spread over her sides and decks. Tirpitz came back in April and July 1909 with the *Moltke* and the *Goeben,* each 23,000 tons, with ten 11-inch guns and 27 knots' speed. *Seydlitz*—25,000 tons, with ten 11-inch guns and 26.5 knots' speed—and *Derfflinger* and *Lützow*—each 28,000 tons, with eight 12-inch guns and 27 knots' speed—followed. Britain's reply to *Moltke* and her sisters was the four "Cats," *Lion, Princess Royal, Queen Mary,* and *Tiger,* 27,000 tons, with eight 13.5-inch guns and 28 knots' speed. (The *Lion* exceeded 31 knots in her trials.) All of these ships, although laid down only three to five years after the *Invincible*s, were a hundred feet longer and 10,000 tons heavier than the earlier vessels. Most of this weight went into more propulsion machinery and bigger guns; armor was increased only marginally.

The first thunderous use of battle cruisers was exactly as Fisher had envisaged. At the Battle of the Falkland Islands, December 8, 1914, two British battle cruisers, *Invincible* and *Inflexible,* engaged a squadron of smaller German cruisers under Admiral Count von Spee. Using his greater speed and the greater range of his larger guns, the British Admiral stayed mostly out of reach of the lighter German guns, while, in a textbook application of Fisher's "hunt down and mop up" theory, his ships methodically blew the German ships to pieces. At Jutland, the opposite tactics were applied and opposite results achieved. Rather than using his speed to stay out of range of enemy heavy guns, Beatty led the five ships of his Battle Cruiser Squadron in a cavalry charge straight at the German battle cruisers and, behind them, the seventeen dreadnoughts of the High Seas Fleet. Two of Beatty's ships, the *Indefatigable* and the *Queen Mary,* penetrated by heavy shells, blew up with the loss of almost everyone on board. Two and a half hours later, in another phase of the battle, the *Invincible* herself blew up. One thousand twenty-six men of her company were drowned; five were saved. A naval expert eulogized the battle cruisers at Jutland: "Their speed . . . should have kept the ships out of range of battleships and heavy guns . . . but when occasion arose for gallant leadership in the face of the enemy, dictates of design were brushed aside and the *Invincible* steamed at full speed into annihilation."

CHAPTER 27

Lord
Charles Beresford

◆

As First Sea Lord, Jacky Fisher had roughly two years (from the autumn of 1904 to the autumn of 1906) before his critics mustered sufficient strength to challenge the reforms he was bringing to (they would have said "inflicting on") the navy. There had been murmurs and grumbles, although they were directed at different issues. "One complains of the new scheme of naval education, but approves the distribution of the fleet and the present types of the ships," McKenna explained to Asquith. "Another likes Osborne [which became the new cadet-training school] but hates dreadnoughts. A third likes both Osborne and dreadnoughts but wants a fleet double the size and reviles the policy of scrapping old vessels." What most critics, particularly those within the navy, had in common was a dislike of Fisher's methodology: "Ruthless, Relentless, and Remorseless! . . . Never explain! Never apologize!" Nevertheless, for twenty-four months, at least as far as the world could see, the First Sea Lord had his way.

Even during the first two years, however, Fisher had had to fight, threaten, and compromise to get what he wanted. In March 1905, when Lord Selborne left the Admiralty to become High Commissioner to South Africa (Fisher wrote reproachfully to Selborne, "I wish South Africa was at the bottom of the sea!"), the Prime

Minister seemed about to appoint Walter Long, a Conservative politician whom Fisher detested, to be First Lord. Fisher informed both
Balfour and the King that, coincidentally, he had just had a visit
from Sir Andrew Noble, chairman of Armstrong, Whitworth, &
Company, who was about to form "an immense combination of the
greatest shipbuilding, armor plate, and gun-making firms in the
country. . . . [They] are willing to unite under my presidency (and
practical dictatorship!), and I fancy I should have about £20,000 a
year. . . ." Fisher, whose navy pay was about one fifth that amount,
dangled the idea long enough to alarm the King and the Prime
Minister, and the Earl of Cawdor, not Walter Long, became First
Lord. In November 1905, Lord Cawdor issued the Cawdor Memorandum, declaring it to be British government policy that four
dreadnoughts be laid down every year.

On December 5, the short-term Earl of Cawdor, along with the
rest of the Balfour Cabinet, stepped down from office. The incoming
Liberal government of Sir Henry Campbell-Bannerman had sterner
views on defense spending: in the election campaign, severe cuts had
been promised. Although on first taking office, the new government
endorsed the Naval Estimates prepared by the Earl of Cawdor, including construction of four new dreadnoughts, this decision rapidly
was overturned. By May 1906, the new Chancellor of the Exchequer, H. H. Asquith, was demanding that at least one of the proposed four ships be dropped. "Nothing that Sir John Fisher could
say would affect" his thinking, Asquith proclaimed. Lord Tweedmouth, the new First Lord, preferred to compromise, and Fisher
conceded. One ship was dropped from the 1906 Estimates, one from
the 1907 Estimates, and two from the 1908 Estimates. Over the
three years, eight new dreadnoughts were authorized for the navy
rather than the twelve envisaged by the Cawdor Memorandum. In
1909, the country would suddenly decide that a mistake had been
made and in the ensuing panic, eight additional dreadnoughts were
authorized in a single year.

Deleting unbuilt ships saved money, but not enough. In July
1906, under further pressure from the government, the Sea Lords
decided to lower the strength of the active fleet by seven battleships
and four armored cruisers. Three battleships were to be drawn from
the Channel Fleet, whose strength would sink from seventeen to
fourteen. Two battleships were to be taken from the Atlantic Fleet
and two from the Mediterranean Fleet; each would have six battleships instead of eight. The seven withdrawn battleships were not to
be deactivated, however; they would join the nucleus-crew fleet although their crews would remain at three fifths normal strength.

Like all nucleus-crew ships, they would go to sea frequently and remain, in Fisher's language, "instantly ready for war." The move would allow a reduction in personnel of two thousand men, saving a quarter of a million pounds a year.

The decision, made secretly in July, began to leak to the press in September. To dampen the outcry from navalists in the Unionist Party and the press, Fisher found a positive way to announce the change. In October a new Admiralty Memorandum announced with a flourish the creation of a new Home Fleet as the logical development of the policy of concentration in home waters which had begun when Fisher came to the Admiralty in 1904. The core of the new fleet would be the seven battleships withdrawn from the Channel, Atlantic, and Mediterranean fleets; the balance would be formed by the nucleus-crew battleships already at hand.

In arguing his case, Fisher never complained about the economic limitations placed upon him by the government. Instead, he concentrated on the strategic soundness of establishing the new Home Fleet. "Our only probable enemy is Germany," he told the Prince of Wales, who was dubious about the new disposition. "Germany keeps her whole fleet always concentrated within a few hours of England. We must therefore keep a Fleet twice as powerful concentrated within a few hours of Germany. If we kept the Channel and Atlantic Fleets *always* in the English Channel . . . this would meet the case, but this is neither feasible nor expedient, and if, when relations with foreign powers are strained, the Admiralty attempt to take the proper fighting precautions and move our Channel and Atlantic Fleets to their proper fighting position, then *at once* the Foreign Office and Government veto it, and say such a step will precipitate war. . . . The Board of Admiralty don't intend ever again to subject themselves to this risk and they have decided to form a new Home Fleet always at home, with its Headquarters at the Nore and its cruising ground the North Sea. ('Your battleground should be your drill ground,' said Nelson.)"

The Prince's skepticism reflected the stronger feelings of many senior and retired naval officers, much of the Conservative press, and numerous Conservative politicians. For the first time, these hostile entities converged to oppose Fisher. Their complaints centered on two points: First, the active fleet in home waters, the Channel Fleet, was to be reduced; second, the new Home Fleet was to have its own Commander-in-Chief, separate in peacetime from the Commander-in-Chief of the Channel Fleet. But who knew how suddenly war might come? If the Germans struck from the blue, they would find Britain's naval defenses divided. The plan was everything

Fisher had lectured against at Malta, where he had told his audiences that concentration of force and command was the key to victory. Even some of his admirers were appalled. "As you know," Admiral Prince Louis of Battenberg wrote to Thursfield of the *Times*, "I am a firm believer in the genius of John Fisher . . . [but] this 'Home Fleet' . . . is simply topsy-turveydom . . . the feeling amongst all thinking naval men is one of consternation. . . . I shall not rest until this whole monstrous scheme is knocked on the head."

If Prince Louis was alarmed, other officers were enraged. Gradually, there formed what Fisher called the "Syndicate of Discontent," made up, he said, of "pre-historic fossils," whose opinions he scorned and whose opposition drove him to rage. "An attack should always be met by a counterattack! We pander to traitors in our own camp . . . and we fawn on our foes and give them barley sugar instead of a black eye! I am getting very sick of this *'taking it lying down'* apologetic line of policy. *The Admiralty policy has not failed in any one single point and will not fail. Success is absolutely assured!*"

In January 1907, when this letter was written, the elements opposed to him in the navy, in the press, and in society had rallied around a leader. From then until he left the Admiralty three years later, the First Sea Lord was bedeviled. "Lest I should be exalted above all measure," Fisher declared, citing II Corinthians 12:7, "there was given me a thorn in the flesh."

In the century's first decade, the most famous officer in the Royal Navy was not Sir John Fisher. It was instead an enthusiastic, courageous, impetuous and charming Irishman, Charles William de la Poer, Lord Beresford. Other adjectives applied to Lord Charles— bluff, hearty, breezy, sporting, irrepressible—and all were used in abundance. He was always in the newspapers: the wealthy aristocrat who became a popular hero; the captain and admiral idolized by common seamen; the persistent parliamentary champion of a bigger navy. To most Britons, he was John Bull the Sailor. Photographs of Lord Charles, standing legs apart on a warship deck, his sleeves striped in gold braid, a small naval cap sitting atop his broad, round face, and his pet bulldog squatting worshipfully at his feet, gave a sense of security: England was safe as long as Lord Charles and the navy were on guard.

For almost forty years, Beresford served England, not only in the navy but in the House of Commons. Coming ashore between seagoing assignments, he would run for a seat and never fail to be elected. Changing his blue uniform and gold stripes for a top hat, frock coat, and gloves, he would go to the House and exhort the members to spend more money on the navy.

In the fleet, Beresford was a man of action, rather than a man of vision. In war, his tactic was to attack; in peacetime, he burned his restless energy in riding, hunting, and fishing. At forty-six, Lord Charles, the captain of a cruiser, rowed stroke in his ship's boat in fleet regattas. His reputation for attention and kindliness to the men under his command went around the navy. When he realized that space aboard ship permitted only one bathtub for every twenty stokers, he devised a nest of galvanized-iron tubs which could be spread out and used by the men to wash the coal grime from their bodies and then restacked in less space than a single regulation tub. He had a gift for noticing individuals, for commending as well as condemning. In most commands, admirals followed the old navy tradition of never praising anything done well; to do well was considered no more than a sailor's duty. Beresford operated differently: "Any smart action performed by an officer or man should be appreciated publicly by signal," he said. "This is complimentary to the officer or man and to the ship in which he is serving. . . . Everyone is grateful for appreciation."

Beresford had faults: colossal vanity; exceptional, almost dangerous, resistance to authority; love of publicity. Nevertheless, from 1902 to 1909, in succession, he commanded Britain's most important fleets. His last command, of the Channel Fleet, made him admiralissimo of all Royal Navy ships in home waters. Had war come, the public and many in the navy believed, gallant, popular "Charlie B." would become the Nelson of his day.

Lord Charles Beresford stepped forth from one of the wealthiest, most patrician families of Ireland. His ancestors were Englishmen who had come to Ireland in the time of James I and stayed to rule. One of his forebears governed the whole island under Pitt; his own great-uncle was Archbishop of Armagh and Primate of All Ireland. Lord Charles himself was the second of five sons of the Fourth Marquess of Waterford. He spent his boyhood on the family estate, Curraghmore, a domain of 100,000 acres near Waterford in southeastern Ireland. His home was a country mansion set against rolling hills covered with oaks, but Beresford family life revolved around the stables. Beresfords hunted six days a week, and the perils of the chase played a significant role in the lives and deaths of the clan. The Third Marquess, Lord Charles's uncle, had killed two foxes in one day and was in pursuit of a third when his horse stumbled, pitching the rider onto his neck, which snapped. He was succeeded by his brother, Lord Charles' father, who happened to be a cleric in holy orders. The Reverend Lord John set the church aside to become Marquess, and his wife, transforming herself from the wife of a well-bred clergyman into a countess, took up hunting and rode enthusiastically every day. She was spared serious accidents, but the carnage continued elsewhere. Lord Charles' elder brother, who eventually became the Fifth Marquess, was hopelessly crippled by falls from his horse. Lord Charles did not escape. By the time he had reached middle age, he had broken his chest bone, his pelvis, his right leg, his right hand, a foot, one collarbone three times, the other once, and his nose in three places.

Beresfords tended to serve their country in the army (Lord Charles' younger brother, Lord William, won a Victoria Cross in the Zulu War of 1879), but Lord Charles lost his heart to the navy at the age of twelve when he visited the Channel Fleet (the admiral was a friend of his father's). In 1859, at the age of thirteen, he enrolled as a cadet aboard *Britannia.* Unlike Midshipman Jacky Fisher, who began his career "friendless and forlorn," Beresford's early assignments were always splendid. His first ship was the pride of the navy, *Marlborough,* flagship of the Mediterranean Fleet. Climbing the side of the giant three-decker as she lay at anchor in Malta's Grand Harbor, Beresford looked up into the faces of two grizzled boatswain's mates and heard one say, "That white-faced little beggar ain't long for this world." Nevertheless, Beresford survived and prospered. He voyaged around the world on *Galatea,* commanded by Queen Victoria's second son, the Duke of Edinburgh. In Japan he met the Mikado, witnessed two decapitations, and had himself tattooed. Later, he was tattooed again in England, reporting cheerfully in his memoirs that "both methods are beautifully illustrated on my person."

In 1874 when Beresford was twenty-eight, he became a member of Parliament. His brother, now the Fifth Marquess, asked Lord Charles to stand for the local seat for Waterford, and for the next forty years Beresford was in and out of the House of Commons. He managed this without having to resign his commission in the navy, a particularly awkward situation for the Lords of the Admiralty. As an M.P., this junior officer could rise in the House and lambaste the government and Admiralty on matters which, coming from any other lieutenant, would seem outrageous indiscipline. Eventually, when Beresford was almost commuting to the House of Commons from his billet aboard the battleship *Thunderer* of the Channel

Fleet, the Admiralty became so incensed that the intervention of the Prime Minister, Disraeli, was required to save Lord Charles his seat. (Beresford cleverly pointed out to the Prime Minister that if he were forced to resign, a new election in Waterford would probably turn the seat over to a Liberal Home-Ruler.)

In 1874, the Prince of Wales chose Beresford as one of the thirty-two aides who would accompany him on his eleven-month trip to India. The Queen, disliking what she had heard of Lord Charles' boisterous enthusiasm, objected to his inclusion, but in this small matter the Prince had his way. The trip was a lively progression of receptions, balls, investitures, and hunts for elephants and tigers. The Prince shot an elephant, and Beresford had climbed up on the rump to dance a jig when suddenly the beast arose, shedding Beresford, and rumbled off into the jungle. There was trouble with the Duke of Sutherland's passionate addiction to driving the engines of the Prince's trains. Sent to retrieve him, Beresford would find him sitting by the throttle, "his red shirt flung open, his sun helmet on the back of [his] head . . . refusing to budge. 'Can nothing be done?' the Prince asked sadly." At night, Beresford took his turn with other members of the suite, sitting with a pair of loaded pistols outside the door of the sleeping Prince. Beresford was also present when the Prince, insisting that his gentlemen dress for dinner even when they were living in tents, lopped the tails off their formal evening wear and thus invented the dinner jacket or tuxedo.

In 1878, Beresford was appointed to command the smaller of the royal yachts, *Osborne,* used in the summer by the Prince of Wales. Even on this small side-wheeler, Beresford managed to enjoy himself and push for change. He took the Prince to Denmark and went hunting with three kings and five crown princes—"I was the only person present who was not a king actual or a king prospective," he observed cheerfully. Finding that one of his officers had served on the *Osborne* for fourteen years, Beresford recommended to the Prince that, for the benefit of their careers, all officers be transferred every two years. The Prince agreed, but the Queen refused to have the reform extended to the *Victoria and Albert.* "I am an old woman now," she explained to Beresford, "and I like to see faces I know about me and not have to begin again with new faces."

The summer of 1882 marked a turning point in Beresford's life as it had in Fisher's. As a result of the bombardment and occupation of Alexandria, both men became national heroes; in fact, Beresford's figure in the popular press loomed larger than Fisher's. Fisher, of course, was celebrated as captain of the navy's newest and most powerful ship, *Inflexible,* and then as commander of the naval landing brigade and deviser of the armored train. Beresford commanded only the 780-ton sloop gunboat *Condor,* but he was also a member of Parliament, the son of a marquess, and an intimate friend of the Prince of Wales. When the Mediterranean Fleet sailed to Alexandria to deal with Arabi Pasha's revolt, Beresford waited expectantly for action. Believing that the Gladstone Cabinet was treading too softly, Lord Charles wrote to the Prince of Wales that, as he saw it, unless Arabi was quashed, England's position in Egypt and her new grip on the Suez Canal were doomed. The Prince discreetly informed the Liberal Foreign Secretary, Lord Granville, of the contents of Beresford's letter, only to learn that his impetuous friend had forwarded a similar letter to the ultra-Conservative *Morning Post,* which planned to use it to attack the government. The Foreign Secretary, infuriated that a serving officer should communicate with the press, demanded that Beresford be arrested and court-martialed. The Prince hastened to intervene and save his friend. "He is an Irishman," the Heir wrote to the Foreign Secretary, "and in consequence hasty and impulsive, but I feel sure that the Queen does not possess a more zealous and loyal officer than he."

By fending off the blow, the Prince saved Beresford's career; less than a week later, Lord Charles proved the Prince a prophet. With the British and French fleets lying in the roadstead, the Egyptians began bolstering the defenses of the harbor forts. On July 9, the British Commander-in-Chief, Admiral Sir Beauchamp Seymour, issued an ultimatum that unless work was suspended forthwith, he would open fire. At this point, the French squadron, on orders from Paris, hoisted its anchors and disappeared over the horizon. Work on the forts continued and on July 10, Seymour signalled the fifteen ships of the British fleet to prepare for action. The four most powerful ships, *Inflexible* included, were to engage the forts in the northern harbor, the other large ships the forts to the west. The gunboats, *Condor* among them, were positioned between the two divisions of large armorclads to act as signal-relay points for passing the admiral's orders. To Beresford's dismay, the gunboats were instructed to stay out of the fighting. Lord Charles chafed at this command and, the night before the bombardment, called his crew on deck and told them that if they would leave it to him to find an opportunity for action, he would leave it to them to make the most of any opportunity he brought their way.

At dawn on the eleventh, the muzzles of the naval guns belched flame and shell at the Egyptian forts. The Egyptians replied briskly, and for most of the day the bombardment continued. The second largest entrenchment, Fort Marabout, being some distance from the position of the eight large ironclads, had not been targeted by British fire. When, in the afternoon, Fort Marabout suddenly opened fire and began sprinkling shells close to the British battleships, Beresford saw his chance. "Seeing the difficulty," he wrote, ". . . I steamed down at full speed and engaged Fort Marabout. . . . I knew of the heavy guns and I knew that one shot, fairly placed, must sink us. But I hoped to be able to dodge the shoals, get in close when I was quite sure they would fire over us." "Good God!" cried Admiral Seymour, "she'll be sunk!" But then he heard his men beginning to cheer. Steaming so close that the heavy guns of the fort could not bear down on him, Beresford fired his own three small guns so rapidly and accurately that the Egyptian heavy guns were silenced, one by one. *Condor* did not go unharmed: one seaman had a foot shot off; he picked it up in his hand and hopped below to see what the ship's doctor could do about it. On the flagship, Seymour, about to signal "Recall *Condor*," changed his signal to "Well done, *Condor*." That evening, when the guns were secured, he summoned Lord Charles on board the flagship and shook him warmly by the hand.

The bombardment of Alexandria was the first major British fleet engagement since the Crimean War, and the British press revelled in the action. With typical foresight, Beresford had as his guests on board *Condor* that day a correspondent from *The Times* and an artist from *The Illustrated London News*. Together, the two journalists made England ring with the exploits of "the gallant Charlie B." The navy and even the Queen joined the chorus of praise. Beresford was promoted to captain and he received the personal congratulations of the sovereign. "I am very glad to give you this, Lord Charles," she said later as she pinned a C.B. to his coat, adding in a low voice, "I am *very* pleased with you."

Meanwhile in Alexandria, Arabi's troops had withdrawn from the forts and an eight-hundred-man naval brigade under Fisher's command had landed to face the Egyptian troops still menacing the city's outskirts. Inside the city, the streets were in the hands of a mob. Fisher recommended that Beresford be appointed provost marshal and chief of police, and Lord Charles set out with a tiny force of sixty bluejackets and marines to restore order. "Arabs were murdering each other for loot under my nose," Beresford said, "and wretches were running about with fire balls and torches." Within five days, the city was calm. "I only had to shoot five men by drumhead courtmartial besides flogging a certain number," One episode suggests Beresford's style of command:

"I was at work . . . [when] a sudden tumult arose in the street. I went out to perceive a huge Irish Marine Artilleryman engaged in furious conflict with five or six men of the patrol. They had got handcuffs on him and he was fighting with manacled hands. I asked the sergeant what was the matter.

" 'He's drunk, sir. We are going to lock him up.'

" 'Let him go,' I said.

"The men fell back and the Irishman . . . turned upon me like a wild beast at bay. The man was in a frenzy. Standing directly in front of him, I spoke to him quietly.

" 'Now, my lad, listen to me. . . . You're an Irishman and you've had a little too much to drink, like many of us at times. But you are all right. Think a moment. Irishmen don't behave like this in the presence of the enemy. Nor will you. Why, we may be in a tight place tomorrow and who's going to back me then? You are. You're worth fifty of the enemy. You're the man I want!'

"As I talked to him, the expression on his face changed from desperation to a look of bewilderment, and from bewilderment to understanding; and then he suddenly broke down. He turned his head aside and cried. I told the sergeant to take him away and give him some tea."

Two years later, the Prince of Wales interceded again and Beresford returned to Egypt, high adventure, and personal glory. At the Prince's request, Lord Wolseley agreed to take Lord Charles as his naval aide-de-camp with the army attempting to relieve Khartoum, where the Mahdi was besieging General Gordon. The Sudan, as big as India, possessed no roads, so the British troops toiled up the river Nile, 1,650 miles from Cairo to Khartoum. Nearing the end and fearing that Gordon could not last, Wolseley sent a desert column ahead, cutting across one of the giant loops in the ancient river. Sixteen hundred men, Beresford among them, set off across 176 miles of baking sand. Water gave out and camels died. Then came the Arabs. "With a roar like the roar of the sea, an immense surging wave of white-sashed black forms, brandishing bright spears and flashing swords," rolled down on the British column. The soldiers formed a hollow square; Beresford's place was firing a naval Gardner gun straight into the onrushing tide of green and white banners and shining metal. When the wave rolled into the British line, all the men at Beresford's guns were killed except Lord Charles. He killed a man simply by holding "my sword rigid at arm's length. He ran right up the blade to the hilt." Another Arab thrust at Beresford with his spear. Beresford deflected the point with his hand, which was ripped to the bone. The wave rolled back and the British marched on to the river below Khartoum. A boat sent up to the city found the Mahdi's flag floating on the ramparts: the city had fallen two days before. But Beresford's adventures were not over. Now in command of a makeshift river gunboat, he had to run a gauntlet of enemy forts to rescue the crew of another English boat. His own boiler was holed and he spent a desperate night making repairs while lying within range of the Mahdi's artillery. Once the boiler was patched and fresh steam raised, Beresford ran back down the river, all guns blazing. It was the stuff of legend.

On Beresford's return to London, the Prince of Wales helped him to obtain the post of Fourth Sea Lord, the junior Lord of the Admiralty. Inside the navy's citadel, Beresford continued to attack his superiors. He wrote a secret memorandum showing that the British Fleet was unprepared for war; the document leaked out into the columns of the *Pall Mall Gazette.* The other Sea Lords had had enough of him and, to get him out of the Admiralty, out of the House of Commons, out of London, out of England, he was posted to command of the cruiser *Undaunted* in the Mediterranean. By the time he left, it was not only the admirals who had seen enough of Lord Charles Beresford.

During these years in London, Lord Charles—then in his early forties—almost capsized socially by becoming involved in a luridly reckless attack on his old friend and patron, the Prince of Wales. Ferocious, insulting letters flowed from Beresford's busy pen and at one point, blind with rage, he raised his fist to strike the Heir to the Throne. It happened, of course, because of a woman. Or rather, two women, Lady Brooke and Lady Charles Beresford.

The youthful Lord Charles had been one of the Prince's closest companions. It was Lord Charles who introduced the Prince to one of the passions of Bertie's life, the racetrack; the Prince's first racehorse was an animal named Stonehenge, bought for him by Beresford. The Prince enjoyed Lord Charles' high spirits and rollicking good humor. He stood up for his excitable friend against ministers of the Crown and even against his mother. The Prince was familiar with Beresford's famous Irish temper but, until the affair of Lady Brooke, had never felt it directed against himself.

Returning to London from the Sudan, Beresford became involved with Frances (known as Daisy), Lady Brooke,* then in her late twenties, the most dazzling of the beauties in the Marlborough

---

* Later, Countess of Warwick.

House set. The affair ran its course and Beresford returned to his wife. But Lady Brooke, to her way of thinking abandoned prematurely, wrote a passionate letter of appeal to Lord Charles. This document fell into the hands of Lady Charles, who turned it over to her lawyer as insurance on her husband's future good behavior. Lady Brooke, unable to abide the thought of her unexploded bomb resting in enemy hands, decided to seek a white knight.

The distressed beauty went to see the Prince of Wales, beseeching him to help her save her reputation by retrieving the incendiary letter. The Prince, always susceptible to beauty, called on the lawyer, read the letter, and decided that it should best be burned. Twice he called on Lady Charles to ask her permission that this be done. Bluntly, she advised her future sovereign to mind his own business. Lord Charles, now firmly reinstalled in his role as faithful husband, vigorously supported his wife.

In the meantime, Lady Brooke and the Prince of Wales discovered other interests in common, and she was seen constantly at his side. Bertie, no doubt frequently reminded of Lady Charles' rude intransigence in rebuffing his good offices, instructed that she be dropped from the invitation list to Marlborough House. Beresford, believing his wife condemned to social oblivion, called on the Prince on the eve of leaving to take command of the *Undaunted*. Forgetting himself, he called the Prince "a coward" and "a blackguard" and clenched his fist to strike. Bertie begged his old friend to desist, reminding him that the blow would cost him his commission in the navy and condemn him to eternal social darkness. Lord Charles, only slightly cooled off, went to sea, and Lady Charles, still excluded from the golden circle, threatened to abandon England and live abroad.

Beresford, steaming up and down the Mediterranean, paced his cabin and composed a sulphurous letter to the Prince, threatening public exposure of many aspects of the Prince's private behavior. "The days of duelling are past," he wrote to the Prince, "but there is a more just way of getting right done than can duelling, and that is— publicity." Instead of sending it directly to the Prince, however, he mailed the letter to his wife, instructing her to show it to the Prime Minister. Lord Salisbury's style of business was to avoid all avoidable storms, but a hot-tempered Irishman threatening to drag the Heir to the Throne into the mud could not be ignored. Salisbury called on Lady Charles and wrote to her husband to calm their mutual rage, now bordering on hysteria. The Princess of Wales, who normally overlooked her husband's indiscretions, was sufficiently upset to remain in Russia with her sister, the Empress Marie, and

did not return to England for the celebration of her husband's fifti-
eth birthday. She did hurry home, however, when typhoid struck her
son Prince George, and once back, joined the fray, committing herself loyally and absolutely to her husband and pouring her fury on
both Beresfords. From Malta, Beresford, undaunted, delivered another salvo, declaring: "I now demand an apology from Your Royal
Highness, failing which . . . I shall no longer intervene to prevent
these matters becoming public." Unless the Prince made amends for
ostracizing his wife, Beresford thundered, he would resign his commission and take his wife to live in France.

Eventually, Lord Salisbury resolved the matter by drafting a
letter to Lord Charles and persuading a reluctant Prince to sign it.
"Dear Lord Charles Beresford," the letter read, "I regret to find
from your letter of the 23rd instant that circumstances have occurred which have led Lady Charles Beresford to believe that it was
my intention to publicly wound her feelings. I have never had any
such intention and I regret that she should have been led to conceive such an erroneous impression upon the point. I remain, Yours
truly . . ."

Lord Salisbury's plan then called for the return of the letter to
the author, which occurred, whereupon the visible storm clouds
lifted. Inwardly, however, the Prince of Wales continued to seethe.
Writing to Lord Charles' brother, the Marquess of Waterford, the
Prince declared, "I have no desire to advert to what occurred at the
end of last year; but I can never forget and shall never forgive the
conduct of your brother and his wife towards me. His base ingratitude, after a friendship of about 20 years, has hurt me more than
words can say. You, who have so chivalrous a nature and are such a
thorough gentleman, will be able to form some opinion of what my
feelings on the subject are. . . ." Twenty years later, when Lord
Charles was locked in battle with a mighty adversary, First Sea Lord
and Admiral of the Fleet Sir John Fisher, his erstwhile comrade the
Prince of Wales—now become King Edward VII—was his patron
no longer. Throughout the trials which shook the Admiralty from
1907 to 1909, the King's friendship was the rock on which Fisher
stood.

CHAPTER 28

Fisher
Versus Beresford

◆

Beresford's career continued to advance. After four years as
captain of the *Undaunted* in the Mediterranean, he spent
three years ashore at the Chatham Naval Dockyard. Then, like most
naval officers, he languished on half pay, awaiting his next command. It was during these periods, when he was away from the navy,
that Beresford's life was unlike that of other navy captains. On a
visit to Berlin, for example, Lord Charles was invited to lunch by
Bismarck, then newly ejected from the Chancellorship. The old man
told Lord Charles that he liked the English and that he believed that
"the British fleet was the greatest factor for peace in Europe." "We
drank much beer," Beresford reported of their two hours together,
"and all the time his gigantic boar-hound, lying beside him, stared
fixedly at me with a red and lurid eye." Beresford was constantly
seen on speakers' platforms throughout England; seeking to benefit
from his popularity, forty parliamentary constituencies approached
him about becoming their candidate. In 1897, he ran for a seat for
York and was elected. That same year, a book, *Life of Nelson and
His Times,* was published under the names of Lord Charles and a
collaborator. In 1898, Lord Charles traveled to China at the behest

of the British Chamber of Commerce to investigate commercial, social, and military conditions. He returned across the Pacific, stopping to call on the Emperor of Japan and, after crossing America by train, on President McKinley. In New York, trading was halted for two minutes on the New York Stock Exchange so that the famous British visitor could address the members from the floor. His short speech, he was told, cost the exchange $100,000 a second in lost time.

At the end of 1899, Beresford, now promoted to Rear Admiral, was appointed second in command of the Mediterranean Fleet to fly his flag in the battleship *Ramillies*. The Commander-in-Chief, his immediate superior, was Vice Admiral Sir John Arbuthnot Fisher. Beresford's path had not crossed Fisher's since the bombardment of Alexandria seventeen years before, but each was aware of the other's career. Fisher, along with many of his colleagues, was offended by Lord Charles' constant criticism of the Admiralty from places where he was relatively immune, such as the House of Commons, on lecture platforms, and in the press. "He really is very stupid," Fisher wrote of Beresford to the First Lord in 1894, "but he can't resist self-advertisement." For his part, Beresford recognized and admired Fisher's dedication to improvement in gunnery and fighting efficiency. What he may have felt about Fisher the man (and social inferior) he kept to himself, at least for the moment.

Both men were well known in the country, but at that time Beresford's popularity and celebrity were greater than Fisher's. Lord Charles always made good copy and when the press learned that the new admiral and his bulldog were going to the Mediterranean, stories appeared announcing that Lord Charles would soon whip the fleet into fighting shape. The implied slur—that the actual fleet commander was not competent—was perhaps unintended, but it did not at all please Sir John Fisher. Unfortunately, and probably unintentionally, Beresford had scarcely arrived when he seemed to infringe upon the prerogative of his sensitive superior. One day a party of *Ramillies* signalmen landed on the parade ground at Malta, accompanied by Lord Charles and a number of other officers. Each signalman—Beresford announced to his guests—represented a battleship, and Beresford's handling of this human battle squadron on the parade ground would demonstrate the tactics which he would later employ with the battle fleet at sea. News of this unusual drill quickly reached Fisher and a series of flags immediately soared up the halyards of Fisher's flagship: "*Ramillies* signalmen to return to their ship immediately. Report in writing why station orders not obeyed." (Malta station orders were that seamen were not to be

landed for drill without permission of the chief of staff and, therefore, of the Commander-in-Chief.) Beresford brought his explanation to Fisher's cabin, whereupon Fisher told him that it was he,
Fisher, who commanded the fleet and would supervise its training
and maneuvers. Beresford accepted the rebuke and apologized.

Soon another incident occurred. The Grand Harbor at Valletta,
Malta, is small and crowded. All around are hills, covered with
houses, palaces, ramparts, and fortified towers, rising steeply from
the water's edge. The entrance to the harbor is narrow, the channel
tortuous. Despite this, it was Fisher's habit to lead the fleet in at
high speed, moor quickly, go ashore, and mount the ramparts to
watch the rest of the fleet enter the harbor. On this occasion, *Ramillies,* Beresford's flagship, came in, tried to pick up her buoy, failed,
and swung around, blocking the harbor and delaying the ships behind her. Disgusted, Fisher signalled to Beresford (who was not
responsible for the ship-handling of his flagship): "Your flagship is
to proceed to sea and come in again in a seamanlike manner."
Within minutes, this signal, a public rebuke from the Commander-
in-Chief to his second in command, was being discussed in every
ship of the fleet. Beresford did not complain.

Fisher, who spoke in strong language and clearly expected
those around him not to take offense, had no grudge against Beresford and was as quick to praise as he was to criticize. "Beresford did
uncommonly well," he wrote after fleet maneuvers in 1900, "and is
much pleased at my praising him, which he thoroughly deserved."
"He is a first rate officer afloat, no better exists in my opinion,"
Fisher said in 1902. "In the two years he has been under my command he has never failed once to do everything he has been ordered, cheerfully and zealously and has always done it well. In the
Atlantic last year, the tactical handling of the two fleets under Wilson and Beresford, pitted against each other off Cape St. Vincent
for two days was . . . simply admirable on both sides. If anything,
Beresford had the advantage and Wilson admitted it."

Fisher recognized Beresford's popularity with the British public
—"He could do so much good for the Navy . . . there is no doubt
the 'oi polloi' believe in him and listen to him like no one else"—but
he deplored his subordinate's freewheeling ways. "I am very sorry
about Beresford's extravagances," he wrote to Lord Selborne. "He
promised me faithfully (for we have been great friends) he would be
circumspect and judicious. He has been neither. . . ." And again to
Selborne: "There is a good deal in what Beresford urges but he
exaggerates so much that his good ideas become deformities and are

impractical, and his want of taste and his uncontrolled desire for notoriety alienates his brother officers."

Beresford's acknowledgment of Fisher's achievement with the Mediterranean Fleet was generous. "Under the command of Sir John Fisher," Beresford wrote, "its efficiency was admirable. . . . From a 12 knot fleet with breakdowns, he made a 15 knot fleet without breakdowns." Fleet training and exercises were based "not on tradition, but on the probabilities of war."

Fisher's presence did not change Lord Charles' habits of a lifetime. While his ship was at Gibraltar, he arranged and won a motor-car race from the bottom of the Rock to the top; not long after, he cracked his pelvis when his hunter failed to clear a hedge and came down on top of its rider. Returning to England in 1902, he was elected to the House for Woolwich and promptly moved a reduction in the First Lord's salary as penalty for defects in Admiralty administration. In New York City, he told a Pilgrims' Society meeting at the Waldorf-Astoria that "battleships are cheaper than battles," a phrase which the navalist President Theodore Roosevelt picked up and repeated.

In February 1903, Lord Charles, now a vice admiral, took command of the old Channel Fleet. (This force was later renamed the Atlantic Fleet.) It was the first of three major fleet commands assigned to him within the next five years. He began with six first-class battleships and soon was given two more. He worked his ships and seamen as hard as Fisher did: "The Navy, unlike the Army, is always on active service. . . . In the Navy, the only difference between peace and war is that in war the target fires back." Beresford ordered his ships "never to go to sea or steam from port to port without practising some exercise or tactical problem. For every pound's worth of coal burnt, a pound's worth of training."

For all his fleet's efficiency, Lord Charles could still put on a show. When the Kaiser, an honorary admiral in the Royal Navy, visited Gibraltar in March 1904, Beresford stood up at dinner to propose a toast. As the words "German Emperor" fell from his lips, a rocket soared from the deck of his flagship and every ship in the fleet fired twenty-one guns. "As the Emperor was leaving that night, the German flag and the Union Jack were hoisted on the Rock, half the searchlights of the Fleet being turned on one flag, and half on the other." Later, as the Kaiser's ship sailed out of the breakwater, two thousand rockets placed on either side of the embankment blazed upward to form a triumphal arch of fire.

The responsibilities of the Channel Fleet, which Fisher redesignated the Atlantic Fleet in December 1904, ran from the western end of the English Channel down to the Strait of Gibraltar. During Beresford's tour of command, the Channel Fleet almost became involved in hostilities with the Russian Baltic Fleet. This ill-fated flotilla, bound on its voyage of doom for the Strait of Tsushima, had fired on the British trawler fleet off Dogger Bank, then proceeded to the port of Vigo in Spain. The Channel Fleet was at Gibraltar. While London's popular press demanded war and Sir John Fisher, then fulfilling his first day as First Sea Lord, met with the Cabinet, Beresford's fleet prepared to deal with the Russians. Lord Charles did not have much stomach for the assignment: "The Russian ships were so loaded with coal and stores that their upper-deck guns could not have been worked and a fight would have been murder," he explained, ever the sportsman. Beresford's tactic, had he been ordered to engage, would have been to use only four of his eight battleships: "It appeared to me that this would be only chivalrous, under the circumstances. If the Russian ships had commenced to knock my ships about, I would have engaged them with the whole eight Channel Fleet battleships." This statement did not sit well in London. "If . . . [Beresford's] statement became public property," noted the Director of Naval Intelligence, "the taxpayers would probably enquire why they were paying for the other half of the fleet." Fisher, who did not want war to be a sporting event, was furious: "Lord Nelson's *dictum* was 'the greater your superiority over the enemy, the better' and he was a chivalrous man!" Unconvinced, Beresford repeated his original claim that if he had opened fire with all his guns, it would have been "a massacre." The battle never took place, because Nicholas II quickly apologized.

It was Beresford's curse that wherever he went, Jacky Fisher had been there before him; wherever he wanted to go, Jacky Fisher seemed to be blocking his path. In June 1905, Lord Charles went to the Mediterranean Fleet as acting Admiral and Commander-in-Chief and in 1906 he was promoted to full Admiral. His tour in command of what had been, in Fisher's day, Britain's primary fleet, coincided with Fisher's naval revolution at the Admiralty. One of Fisher's reforms was redistribution of the Fleet, bringing ships back from foreign stations in order to concentrate British naval strength in home waters. Accordingly, even as Beresford was assuming command, his fleet was being reduced in numbers and its ships transferred to the new primary force, the Channel Fleet, commanded by Sir Arthur Wilson. It was natural that Lord Charles should have been displeased; it was characteristic when he turned his exasperation into a public grudge.

The real blow which Fisher delivered to Beresford fell on December 4, 1905. On this day, the last of the Balfour government, Admiral Sir John Fisher was promoted to Admiral of the Fleet, a rise in rank which permitted him to remain on active duty another five years, until he reached the age of seventy in January 1911. Until that moment, Beresford had expected that Fisher would be forced to step down as First Sea Lord and retire in 1906 at sixty-five, whereupon he, Lord Charles Beresford, would have had an excellent change of succeeding Fisher at the Admiralty. Immediately upon his promotion, Fisher annihilated Beresford's hopes by announcing that he would indeed remain as First Sea Lord for another five years. Lord Charles, realizing that he now had no chance of achieving the ultimate ambition of every naval officer, reacted as if Fisher's decision were a breach of naval etiquette directed specifically at himself. He ignored the fact that the two First Sea Lords immediately preceding Fisher had done the same thing: that is, hold on to office after being promoted to Admiral of the Fleet. Lord Charles' frustrated rage was matched, if not exceeded, by that of his wife, who wanted her husband's promotion to consolidate the social position which had been jeopardized by her husband's quarrel with the King.

Beresford revealed his vexation in a number of ways. To the First Lord he complained in March 1906, "The Service is very sore and irritated throughout, not so much upon what is done, as upon the way in which things are done." The "little gentlemanly etiquettes" which have "made the Service run smoothly" now were "entirely abandoned," he charged. He made no attempt to hide his feelings from the officers in his fleet. At dinner with a number of officers and visitors, he complained about the short-service sailors used aboard ship for unskilled tasks—passing coal and ammunition. On the morrow, he proposed, he would put some of these men on shore and march them around to demonstrate to his guests what "rotters" the Admiralty expected him to work with. Beresford's remarks drew hearty laughter and great applause. Captain Reginald Bacon, a former Fisher aide devoted to the First Sea Lord, now commanding the battleship *Irresistible* in Beresford's fleet, reported privately to Fisher that Lord Charles and Admiral Lambton, commanding Beresford's cruiser division, were publicly "wailing and bemoaning" Fisher's reforms. When the Mediterranean Fleet joined the royal yacht off Corfu, both the King and the Prince of Wales summoned Bacon to express doubts. "What is upsetting the King and the Prince of Wales so much is what they call 'a feeling of unrest' in the Service," Bacon wrote to Fisher. Fisher immediately called Bacon's letter to the attention of Lord Tweedmouth: "It is with extreme reluctance that I feel compelled . . . to bring before the Board the unprecedented conduct of the Commander-in-Chief Mediterranean in publicly reflecting on the conduct of the Admiralty and inciting those under his command to ridicule the decisions of the Board." Fisher cited the "extraordinary conduct of a Commander-in-Chief canvassing his captains as to whether or not they approved the policy of the Board of Admiralty."

Curiously, considering Fisher's knowledge of Beresford's habits and dislike of Beresford's behavior, the next assignment offered to Lord Charles was the premier appointment afloat, command of the new Channel Fleet. Lord Tweedmouth's wish to conciliate those opposed to Fisher's reforms was a factor. "I thought Lord Tweedmouth a most pleasant man," said a visitor to the Admiralty, "but he gave me the idea of being much torn between the Fisherites and anti-Fisherites, and no wonder, considering that he can't possibly know enough of the subject himself to be able to form any sort of opinion." Fisher could have objected but, at least in his correspondence, he did not. Beresford's appointment was announced in July 1906, to take effect the following spring. For over six months, Beresford's name does not appear in Fisher's letters at all.

It was during this period that the Admiralty began to create the new Home Fleet. Certain battleships were to be withdrawn from the Channel Fleet, manned only by nucleus crews and stationed at the Nore, essentially in reserve. As the new dreadnoughts joined the fleet, they too would go to the Home Fleet, not the Channel Fleet. In wartime, the Home Fleet as well as the Atlantic Fleet would come under the command of the Commander-in-Chief, Channel Fleet; in peacetime, each would be commanded by an independent admiral. The reasons given were economy (the new Liberal government insisted that more money be saved) and increased security (the Home Fleet would remain in home waters to protect the country when the Channel Fleet and Atlantic Fleet were away on maneuvers). Lord Charles Beresford did not see it this way. In his view, just as he was about to join a new command, its importance and its numerical strength were to be diminished. Once again, the devilish Jacky Fisher had stepped across his path.

Nearing the end of his Mediterranean tour, Beresford took two months' leave in Mexico to deal with the estate of his younger brother, who had been killed in an accident. When he returned to London, Fisher summoned him to the Admiralty in order to clarify the nature of Lord Charles' new Channel Fleet command and make sure that the incoming Commander-in-Chief understood and accepted the limitations on his control over the various fleets in home waters. The meeting appeared successful and an agreement was drawn up: battleships, cruisers, and destroyers of the Home and Atlantic fleets would be detached from those organizations and placed under Lord Charles' command for exercises and maneuvers, but administratively they would remain beyond his reach. And the decisions as to the timing and length of these temporary assignments would be made by the Admiralty, not by Lord Charles. Beresford declared that he understood and accepted the arrangement, and he initialed the document on which it was set forth.

Despite the appearance of harmony, Fisher's dislike and distrust of Beresford did not change. To a friend, he described the Admiralty interview with caustic humor:

"I had three hours with Beresford yesterday and all is settled and the Admiralty don't give in one inch to his demands; but I had as a preliminary to agree to three things:

"I. Lord Charles Beresford is a greater man than Nelson.

"II. No one knows anything about naval war except Lord Charles Beresford.

"III. The Admiralty haven't done a single d———d thing right."

Writing another friend, Fisher dropped any semblance of humor: "Lord Charles Beresford now dictates terms before he will accept the command of the Channel Fleet. He required that Fleet to be increased by cruisers and destroyers and that the Home Fleet shall come under his command. . . . If acceded to, it means that the Board of Admiralty will abdicate its functions and take its instructions from an irresponsible subordinate who is totally unacquainted with the world requirements of the British Navy and is only thinking of magnifying his own particular command." To Lord Knollys, the King's private secretary, Fisher revealed the depth of his animus against the Beresford appointment: "I followed your advice and wrote a most cordial letter to Beresford. . . . It will not be my fault if he resigns as Tweedmouth says he will. My conviction is he wants to get into parliament and hates the Channel." Fisher was even more bitter in a letter to his newspaper friend Arnold White: "My conviction is that Beresford funks the Channel and wants to clear out! Fogs and short days and difficult navigation very different to Mediterranean white trousers!!! Wilson also very hard to follow." A month after the Admiralty interview and still a month before Beresford actually took command of the Channel Fleet, Fisher grimly warned Lord Tweedmouth that accepting Beresford meant a "blow to discipline and the lowering of Admiralty authority. *It is only putting off the evil day!* But having adopted the policy of endeavouring to keep him, and in view of the action that has been taken, there seems no other course but to go on as now arranged."

Beresford hoisted his flag on *King Edward VII* on April 16, 1907, and for a few days he and Fisher endeavored to be polite to each other. "All I wish to assure you is that so far as I am concerned I am most anxious that we should avoid friction and undesirable correspondence—and so I think [it] in all ways desirable that we should discuss things personally," the First Sea Lord wrote to the Commander-in-Chief. Beresford's reply came back coated with honey. "There is not the slightest chance of any friction between me and you, or between me and anyone else," he assured the First Sea Lord. "When the friction begins, I am off. If a senior and a junior have a row, the junior is wrong under any conceivable condition, or discipline could not go on. As long as I am here, I will do my best to make the Admiralty policy a success."

As senior flag officer afloat, Beresford now stood at the pinnacle of the seagoing British Navy. He commanded the most powerful fleet then in existence, consisting of fourteen battleships including the eight new ships of the pre-dreadnought *King Edward VII* class. His Channel Fleet, as Fisher described it, "is of itself a match for the German Fleet, and reinforced by the Atlantic Fleet, it has an overwhelming superiority." If war came, Beresford as admiralissimo would command 244 warships, the mightiest fleet in history. In some respects, Lord Charles was well equipped for this role; in others, less so. His seamanship was outstanding; his personal bravery, displayed at Alexandria and in the Sudan, was undisputed. How successful he would have been as a wartime admiral, we shall never know. He was not much interested in strategy and tactics. His character was impulsive, even reckless; in wartime, blessed with luck, these qualities could lead to brilliant success. If luck was elsewhere, Lord Charles might not have been able to look defeat in the eye, coolly cut his losses, and save what was left of his fleet for the next day's battle. As a peacetime admiral, he was enormously popular both with officers and men. Lamed by gout, he would be carried by four Royal Marines, "looking very like a Roman Emperor," and enthroned on the bridge of his flagship. From there, he ruled his fleet with benevolent despotism. Everything centered on his own person. "My principal recollection," recalled a former Channel Fleet officer, "is of endless piping, callings to attention, and buglings." A stickler for the old navy rule that the senior officer present make every decision, including what uniforms all officers and men were to wear, what awnings the ships were to spread, when the men were to wash their clothes, when the washed clothes were to be hung up, and when they were to be taken down, Lord Charles watched his fleet with an eagle eye. Whatever his flagship did, the rest of the fleet had to do; if the flagship forgot to do something, the other ships must forget it too. Sir Percy Scott, the fanatical gunnery expert who commanded the First Cruiser Division of Beresford's Channel Fleet, found this rule nonsensical. "I remember coming up on deck once and finding that, although it was pouring with rain, the guns were not covered. I pitched into the Officer of the Watch, but got the worst of it; he informed me that he could not cover the guns as the flagship had not covered hers." For the most part, the fleet was kept extremely smart and clean. Lord Charles liked to invite his society friends and their elegant ladies aboard and have his wife, to whom he referred as "my little painted frigate," serve as hostess beneath the yawning muzzles of the enormous guns. Beresford's men did not mind these moments of social frippery; they were a welcome change from the austere regime of Sir Arthur Wilson, Lord Charles' bachelor predecessor.

Despite his undeniable talents and his enjoyment of the pleasures of rank, Lord Charles remained unhappy. From the moment he took command of the Channel Fleet, he took out his dissatisfaction by challenging the Admiralty. Every man in his fleet knew that he called Fisher "our dangerous lunatic" and that he had opposed most of Fisher's reforms: the building of the *Dreadnought* ("We start at scratch with that type of ship"), the scrapping of dozens of older ships, and, most vehemently, the creation of the Home Fleet. Although at his January meeting with Fisher he had accepted, in writing, the new arrangement of fleets in home waters, Beresford informed the First Lord on May 13 that the Home Fleet was "a fraud upon the public and a danger to the Empire." A few days later, he repeated and broadened this charge in a letter to Knollys (and therefore the King): "I am most distressed and alarmed at the complete absence of organization and preparation for war in the Fleet. . . . The Home Fleet is the greatest fraud ever perpetrated on the public. . . . I am doing the best I can to help Authority get things right." Meanwhile, he warned, "if Germany attacked us suddenly, she would inflict terrible disasters on us and she might win."

Fisher, made aware of Beresford's behavior and language, was beside himself. "The truth is that such language on the part of Lord Charles Beresford . . . besides being insubordinate is perfectly preposterous," he informed Lord Tweedmouth. "Our superiority over Germany is so overwhelming and the superiority of our personnel and of our gunnery practice is so great, that the Germans know it would be madness for them to provoke a war." He asked the First Lord to write to Beresford "with the object of disabusing him of the idea that now possesses him that his is the sole responsibility for the conduct of a naval war. . . . It is also imperative that Lord C. Beresford should be distinctly informed that the British Admiralty has no . . . intention of abdicating its functions." Tweedmouth declined to satisfy the aroused First Sea Lord by censuring Beresford. Instead, he asked Fisher to be more tolerant of the Commander-in-Chief. "I know him to be ambitious, self-advertising and gassy in his talk," Lord Tweedmouth wrote of Beresford, "but we all knew those bad qualities of his and no one better than you when you very wisely recommended his . . . appointment. . . . There must always be a good deal of difference of opinion as to the manner of administrating so great a business as the British Navy and I feel very much . . . the responsibility . . . of consulting and conciliating the opinion of all whose experience qualifies them to form opinions on the subject whether they are in exact accord with the Admiralty Board views or not. . . . I am the last person in the world to abrogate one iota of the supremacy of the Board of Admiralty but I do think we sometimes are inclined to consider our own views to be infallible and are not ready enough to give consideration to the views of others who may disagree with us. . . ." et cetera, et cetera.

Tweedmouth's schoolmasterish lectures astonished and dismayed Fisher, but there was nothing he could do except to accept them or resign. Soon Beresford was back with another complaint: the Admiralty had sent him no war plans. For over a century, British Admiralty procedure had been to issue each Commander-in-Chief a set of "War Orders," dealing with broad political and military objectives. Within this framework, a fleet commander was expected to draft his own detailed, operational "War Plan," assigning tasks to the ships and squadrons under his command. Once drafted, these "War Plans" were to be sent to the Admiralty for examination, amendment, and approval. In Beresford's case, he was handed the same Admiralty War Orders which had been given to his predecessor Sir Arthur Wilson two years before. In addition, purely for illustrative purposes to help him draw up his own War Plan, he was sent a 188-page document entitled "War Plans," which had been drawn up at the Admiralty. Beresford quickly drew up his own War Plan for war against Germany which involved using more battleships and cruisers than the Royal Navy possessed. The Admiralty rejected his plan, issued new War Orders, and directed Lord Charles to submit a revised War Plan. Beresford responded by asking to see Sir Arthur Wilson's War Plan. Wilson replied that his War Plan had been inside his head except for specific orders that had been drafted during the Morocco Crisis and were now no longer valid. Matters were at an impasse. Meanwhile, Beresford buttressed his case that the Admiralty was thwarting his efforts by complaining that no one had told him what ships would be sent to him as reinforcements when war broke out. "It is manifestly impossible," he wrote on June 27, "for me to submit detailed plans for the carrying out of operations . . . unless I know what ships are available to carry these plans out." The Admiralty replied that this was impossible as it could not know, on any specific day, which ships would be in drydock or under other repair, or detached for training or other use.

By the end of June, only two months after Beresford arrived at the Channel Fleet, his relations with the Admiralty were strained to the point of breaking. Tweedmouth suggested a personal talk to avoid further "improper" and "provocative" letters. On July 5, Lord Charles sat down at the Admiralty with the First Lord and the First Sea Lord. Unfortunately for Beresford, a transcript was kept. It shows the Commander-in-Chief uncertain as to what he wanted, unable to explain his views and—in Fisher's presence—cowed and anxious to please. Fisher began by talking about numbers of ships:

SIR JOHN FISHER: "We simply want to know what you are driving at, because we seem to give you everything you require, and then, as I hardly like to use the word 'compromise,' or anything like that, because it is not a word that the Admiralty should use to anyone, we say, 'Shall you be satisfied if we do with you as we did with Sir Arthur Wilson?' which is the point you seem to be going on making. There cannot be any doubt about the battleships of the Channel Fleet being far superior to the German Fleet. Shall you be satisfied if we make your armoured cruisers up to six, the same as Sir Arthur Wilson had, and give you the whole of the two divisions of destroyers at Portland under Admiral Montgomerie, all to come under you? We think the present arrangement better. You say you would like these vessels permanently, so as to bring your squadron up to what you say were Admiral Wilson's component parts. We do not agree, but we say, 'This is our chief executive officer afloat; we do not agree, but we will give him the armoured cruisers, the destroyer flotillas, and the attendant vessels, as he presses for them.' "

LORD CHARLES BERESFORD: "I cannot see the thing straight off. I will write to you."

SIR JOHN FISHER: "You must have thought about it. You have been writing about it for months."

LORD CHARLES BERESFORD: "I am not sure that I have not asked for more cruisers than that in my plan."

FIRST LORD: "I do not think the Board will agree to more than I have told you."

LORD CHARLES BERESFORD: "I see. It's a fair offer on the part of the Admiralty to meet me, and it shows you see the danger I see."

SIR JOHN FISHER: "We think it is very undesirable for the Admiralty to remain in a state of tension with you, and the First Lord said (I think with great propriety), 'Let us have a talk with Lord Charles and see if we can arrange matters in this way and finish off the business without further irritating correspondence.' Do not let us have any more letters about it. It was hoped you would say, 'After meeting round this table this morning I can quite see that the Board of Admiralty are anxious to meet me in every way they can, as it is also my duty to meet the Board of Admiralty in every way I can; we have fixed up the matter and here is an end of it.' "

LORD CHARLES BERESFORD: "I never come to a conclusion myself with anything without I think. On principle, being a public man, I never say a thing straight off. Have those ships you are going to give me nucleus crews?"

SIR JOHN FISHER: "No, they are fully manned. They are complete, the destroyers are at Portland, and they will remain at Portland under you. Simply as regards the cruisers, what we shall do is to knock two cruisers off the 5th Cruiser Squadron, and turn them over to you."

LORD CHARLES BERESFORD: "That gives me the force I am halloing for. You may depend on it, the cordiality between us exists. There is no want of cordiality on my part."

Tweedmouth then picked up this point, asking Beresford: "Why do you not try to cultivate good and cordial relations with the Admiralty?" and why he persisted in saying that "the Home Fleet is a fraud and danger to the Empire."

BERESFORD: "You will allow me to smile for at least ten minutes over [the question about cordial relations]. Although my views are very drastic, there is not any question of want of cordial relations with the Admiralty. Not privately or publicly have I ever said anything against the Admiralty . . ."

TWEEDMOUTH: "If you say, in a letter to me, as First Lord, that our Home Fleet 'is a fraud and a danger to the Empire,' that is not very pleasant to the Admiralty, and you have repeated that again and again. . . . I must tell you that to tell the First Lord of the Admiralty that what is a very important part of his Board's policy is absolutely useless and is a fraud and a danger to the Empire, I do not think that is very friendly to the Admiralty."

BERESFORD: "It is a private letter. We have all written much stronger things than that on important questions of that sort. . . . It was only a 'term.' If we went to war suddenly you would find it is true. If I had said officially that the Admiralty had created that, or if I had pitched into the Admiralty about it, it would be different. . . . That I had any notion of insubordination I absolutely deny. That letter of mine to the First Lord has no right to go before the Board, a private letter like that . . ."

TWEEDMOUTH: "It is not marked private. Other letters have been marked private."

BERESFORD: ". . . I ought to have put 'private' and 'confidential' on it."

TWEEDMOUTH: "I cannot look on that as simply a private communication to me. I think that is a very important letter."

FISHER: "I am quite sure you understand we are all equally interested, as you are, in having friendly and cordial relations, but it is absolutely impossible if the Chief Executive Officer of the Admiralty afloat is going to be 'crabbing' the Admiralty in everything the Admiralty is doing, and writing such letters to the First Lord. . . ."

TWEEDMOUTH: "I think so serious a charge against the Home Fleet ought to be substantiated; you ought to say how it is a fraud, and how it is a danger to the State."

BERESFORD: "It is a 'term.' I can write it all out to you in detail. The public think it is ready for instant action. What is your own term?—Without an hour's delay: well, it is not."

Before the interview was over, Lord Charles made another placatory statement, seeming to defer to the First Lord and the First Sea Lord: "I do not dictate to the Board of Admiralty. The Board has the right—it is the constituted authority, and so long as it is the constituted authority, it is responsible and no one else. It may do wrong things, but it is the responsible authority."

Beresford got part of what he wanted—two additional armored cruisers and twenty-four destroyers were added to the Channel Fleet—and he declared himself satisfied: "I can now make out a plan of campaign on definite lines," he wrote on July 18. In fact, a

War Plan from the Channel Fleet arrived at the Admiralty only eleven months later.

Long before that, matters had grown worse. In November 1907, Beresford complained to the Admiralty about the forthcoming transfer of three officers under his command. "It has come to my notice that a feeling has arisen in the Service that it is prejudicial to an officer's career to be personally connected with me on Service matters," he wrote. "This may not be a fact, but the impression I know exists. It is certainly borne out by the late procedure. . . . The removal of three such important officers from my command at or about the same time will add enormously to my already exceptionally hard work. . . . It may not have been intended, but it most certainly has the appearance of a wish to handicap and hamper me in carrying out the responsibilities with by far the most important appointment within the Empire." Patiently, the Admiralty rebutted these charges. Captain Frederick Sturdee, Beresford's chief of staff, was being transferred to command a battleship, a necessity for promotion; Beresford himself had been urging this promotion. Explaining this and the other cases to Lord Charles, the Admiralty noted that "you continue to employ language which had no parallel within their experience as coming from a subordinate addressed to the Board of Admiralty."

As relations continued to deteriorate, incidents involving Beresford began to multiply. Most famous was the ludicrous "Paint Work Affair," also in November 1907, which coupled Lord Charles with Rear Admiral Sir Percy Scott.

Scott, the foremost gunnery expert in the Royal Navy, was a self-made man of no private means whose lifelong obsession was hitting the target with naval gunfire. "Like most specialists who propound innovations," declared a contemporary newspaper biography, "he has aroused bitter hostility alike to his schemes and himself personally." He was entirely Fisher's kind of naval officer and Fisher had always supported him. Initially, although their professional paths had never crossed, Beresford also endorsed Scott's crusade, and in 1903 had declared that "I would rather go into action with 6 ships trained on Captain Scott's principle than with 12 trained on any other." Scott's defect, from Beresford's point of view, was that he was Fisher's man. And when Scott was posted by the Admiralty to command the First Cruiser Division of the Channel Fleet, Lord Charles saw the assignment as another of Fisher's attempts to place a spy in his nest.

In the presence of the Commander-in-Chief, the movements of all ships of the Channel Fleet were dictated by Beresford. But when the First Cruiser Division was operating independently, Scott was in command. On November 2, Scott's cruisers had concluded maneuvers with the fleet in Scottish waters and been detached to return independently at high speed to Portland; Beresford and the battleships would follow later. By Monday, the fourth, Scott's flagship, *Good Hope*, already was anchored inside the breakwater at Portland but one of his ships, *Roxburgh*, remained outside, practicing the independent gunnery exercises which Scott had enthusiastically encouraged. At some point during the morning, a message arrived from Beresford directing that all ships of his fleet terminate exercises at sea and come into harbor in time to clean and paint ship by the eighth, on which day they would be inspected and reviewed by the German Emperor. Scott was eating lunch on board *Good Hope* when he was handed a signal from *Roxburgh*'s captain, asking permission to remain outside the harbor a little longer to finish a round of gunnery exercises. Scott was sympathetic, but, bowing to Beresford's command, ordered the cruiser to come in immediately. His signal, intended to be read solely by *Roxburgh*, had an irritated, sarcastic tone: "Paintwork appears to be more in demand than gunnery so you had better come in in time to make yourself look pretty by the 8th." A few hours later, Beresford's big ships appeared and entered the harbor, and *Roxburgh* followed them in.

For four days, nothing happened.* Then an officer on Beresford's staff visiting *Good Hope* heard about Scott's signal and reported it to Lord Charles. Beresford erupted in rage. He summoned Scott aboard *King Edward VII*, where, in the presence of two other admirals and members of his staff, he bathed the diminutive Scott in a torrent of abuse. Scott opened his mouth to reply, but was silenced by another deluge of wrath. Finally, leaving Scott in no doubt that he was to be court-martialed and replaced, the Commander-in-Chief turned on his heel and walked away. White-faced and silent, Scott returned to *Good Hope*. A few minutes later, Beresford hoisted a general signal to all ships in his fleet. Repeating Scott's offending signal to *Roxburgh*, Beresford declared that "this signal, made by the Rear Admiral commanding the First Cruiser Squadron, is contemptuous in tone and insubordinate in character." Publicly, the Commander-in-Chief ordered Scott's signal expunged from the signal logs of *Good Hope* and *Roxburgh*. Not satisfied with this public humiliation of his subordinate, Lord Charles then sat down and wrote to the Admiralty demanding Scott's head. Scott's signal, he

* As it turned out, the entire brouhaha was unnecessary: the Kaiser arrived too late and the inspection and review were cancelled.

complained, was "totally opposed to loyalty and discipline . . . pitiably vulgar, contemptuous in tone, insubordinate in character, and wanting in dignity. . . . It is impossible that the matter rest where it is. . . . I submit that Rear Admiral Sir Percy Scott be superceded from command of the First Cruiser Squadron."

The Admiralty did not approve. Their Lordships replied that they did not approve of Scott's signal, concurred in the Commander-in-Chief's reprimand, to which they would add their own "grave disapprobation," but did not wish either to remove the Rear Admiral or make any public announcement. Unmollified, Beresford complained that as Scott's "act of insubordination to my command was of a public character," his censure by the Admiralty should be public. The Admiralty declined. When Scott returned to *King Edward VII*, he began to say, "I should like to take the opportunity of apologizing to you for the incident—" He got no further. Red-faced, Beresford roared that he would accept no private apology for the public insult he had received. He ordered Scott off his flagship and commanded him not to speak to him in the future; all communications between them were to be in writing or by signal between ships. Scott thereafter was ostracized from all of Beresford's social functions and, as much as possible, the First Cruiser Squadron was banished to regions distant from the Channel Fleet.

The press had a field day with the story. Conservative papers unanimously favored Beresford and demanded that Scott be stripped of his command. The Liberal press and many of the popular papers thought it odd that an admiral famous for trying to overthrow his superiors at the Admiralty should be protesting so loudly that one of his own subordinates was guilty of disloyalty. The Service journals, which recognized Scott's value to the navy, deplored both Scott's signal and Beresford's overreaction.

Not surprisingly, Lord Charles detected Fisher's hand in most of what had happened: Scott's impudence in sending the original signal was the kind of insubordination to himself which Fisher encouraged; the Admiralty's subsequent refusal to honor his request and rid him of Scott stemmed solely from Scott's presence in the Fishpond. To his friend and fellow Irishman, Sir Edward Carson, Beresford wrote grimly: "There is no doubt" that the "determined, audacious, treacherous, and cowardly attacks on me" had been "inspired by the gentleman from Ceylon."

By the beginning of 1908, the Fisher-Beresford vendetta had escalated into open civil war. Mere mention of Beresford's name could drive Fisher into a rage; every officer in the Commander-in-Chief's camp had become "a traitor." Captain Edmund Slade, the

Director of Naval Intelligence, kept a worried eye on the First Sea Lord. "Sir J[ohn] is in a most nervous state as regards Lord C[harles] and what he may do," Slade wrote in his diary on January 7. "He is so bitter against Lord C. that anything he does or says is wrong," Slade added on April 11. "Sir J. is not well and looks very old and worn today," was the entry on April 24. Beresford also was not well and spent part of this period in bed at Claridge's Hotel in London. Here Slade called on him, hoping somehow to mend relations between the two admirals. In the sitting room, he encountered Beresford's wife, Lady Charles, whom Fisher already had dubbed "a poisonous woman." Slade soon realized, more from talking to Lady Charles than to Beresford himself, that no closing of the breach was possible. "As long as they are in their respective positions, they will fight each other," he noted gloomily. One reason was Lady Charles: "She is a terrible looking woman," Slade wrote, "very stout, very much got up, rouged apparently, with fair hair and a sort of turban which she apparently always wears." Having suffered substantial social disfavor in her life, she was determined that her husband would rise to the top of his profession and that no middle-class officer born in Ceylon would bar his path. According to Slade, whenever Lord Charles began to drift towards a resolution of his differences with Fisher, "the influence of Lady C." would be employed to steer him back to hostility.

For a while, it seemed that Beresford might win. Sir Edward Grey, the Liberal Foreign Secretary, who believed in Fisher, sadly told the First Sea Lord that it had been represented to him "that Beresford had the whole Navy." Lord Charles' friends in the navy, in society, and in Parliament pressed hard for the inquiry into Admiralty policy for which they had been asking since 1906. Fisher adamantly refused and told the Cabinet in an Admiralty memorandum on January 25 that "the Admiralty fear no inquiry; but it would be simply impossible for the Members of the Board to retain office if such a blow to the authority of the Admiralty as the investigation of its fighting policy by its subordinates were to be sanctioned." Campbell-Bannerman did not want the Sea Lords to resign en masse, and one of his last acts as Prime Minister was to promise Fisher in writing that no form of inquiry would be held. Asquith, succeeding to the Premiership on April 7, confirmed this pledge.

The change in Downing Street greatly benefitted Fisher by precipitating a much-needed retirement at the Admiralty. A strong First Lord would not have tolerated the schism which had divided the navy and threatened the nation's security; he would have conducted his own investigation, made a decision, and ordered either

Beresford or Fisher to resign. Lord Tweedmouth was not up to it. A journeyman politician who had served Mr. Gladstone as chief Liberal whip, then gone to the Lords as Lord Privy Seal, he had not adjusted easily to the impatient and sometimes irritable Fisher. And when called upon to decide between the competing arguments of the First Sea Lord and the popular and charismatic Lord Charles Beresford, Tweedmouth's mind began to sag.

Early in 1908, Tweedmouth's troubles multiplied rapidly. On February 6, Lord Esher wrote a letter to *The Times* defending Fisher against a demand by the Imperial Maritime League that the First Sea Lord be removed. At the end of his letter, Esher delivered a powerful blow: "There is not a man in Germany from the Emperor downwards who would not welcome the fall of Sir John Fisher." When the Kaiser read the letter in his copy of *The Times,* his temperature began to rise. Furious at Esher, he sent a nine-page handwritten letter of complaint to Tweedmouth. "I am at a loss to know whether the supervision of the foundations and drains of the Royal palaces [from 1895 to 1902 Esher had served as Permanent Secretary to the Office of Works] is apt to qualify somebody for the judgement of naval affairs in general," the Emperor wrote with heavy sarcasm. "As far as regards German affairs naval, the phrase is an unmitigated piece of balderdash and has created intense merriment in the circles of those who know here. But such things ought not to be written by people who are highly placed as they are liable to hurt public feelings over here." The Kaiser's act in writing directly to a British Cabinet minister created its own disturbance in London. The King, much annoyed, wrote to his nephew:

> My dear William:
> Your writing to my First Lord of the Admiralty is "a new departure" and I do not see how he can prevent our press from calling attention to the great increase in building of German ships of war which necessitates our increasing our Navy also.
>> Believe me,
>> your affectionate uncle,
>> EDWARD R.

Tweedmouth, however, infinitely surpassed William in indiscretion. He replied to the Kaiser's letter by privately sending His Majesty the forthcoming British Naval Estimates without informing the Cabinet and before they were presented in Parliament. Then, addled by flattery, he gossiped about the Emperor's letter, carried it with him, and showed it around London, even reading parts of it

aloud to astonished fellow guests in private drawing rooms. Naturally, the press soon was on his trail and the opposition demanded
that, because a foreign monarch was attempting to influence Britain's Naval Estimates, the Imperial letter be laid before the House
of Commons. A few weeks later, Tweedmouth was shunted into the
harmless job of Lord President of the Council. There, he deteriorated rapidly. In May, he wrote to Lord Knollys to announce that he
had "about 15 young unmarried nieces who would be delighted" if
the King would join them in staging a little variety entertainment,
"very bright but very proper," with "a stand up supper" to follow.
Shocked, Knollys concluded that Tweedmouth's mind was "seriously unhinged." Reading these documents, the King noted in the
margin, "This is very sad but explains his extraordinary behavior on
so many occasions."

Tweedmouth's replacement was Reginald McKenna, moved to
the Admiralty from the presidency of the Board of Education. Having won a First in Mathematics at Cambridge and rowed bow in the
Cambridge boat, McKenna seemed, at forty-five, a thin, lithe,
"youngish man with a bald head covered with down as if he was
using a hair restorer." He made a favorable impression on Fisherites
at the Admiralty. Slade thought him "pleasant in manner, sharp and
quick." Initially, Fisher worried that McKenna was one of the Liberal naval "economists" who saw the navy only as a place where
budgets might be cut to obtain money for social programs. If this
were so, Fisher would not agree and become expendable. The King
reassured him. "When I agreed to McKenna's appointment," he
wrote to Fisher, "it was on condition that you kept your present
post. The Prime Minister never made the *slightest* objection—on the
contrary, he was most desirous that you should remain."

For all his quickness, it was bound to take McKenna time to
immerse himself in Admiralty affairs. Beresford used this period to
carry his feud with Fisher openly into society. Society, it seemed,
was entirely on his side, the more so because the jovial and gallant
Lord Charles had inherited a considerable fortune on the death of
his brother and was able to entertain on a lavish scale in his large
house on Grosvenor Street. "Beresford . . . can do more with his
chef than by talking," Fisher noted wryly, and Lord Charles' drawing room was always filled with society women, ancient admirals,
Conservative M.P.'s, and newspaper editors—anti-Fisherites all.
Fisher lumped them together as "the Dukes and Duchesses" and
told the Prince of Wales that his skin "was like a rhinoceros and all
the envenomed darts don't pierce it." Nevertheless, they hurt. When

he retired, he told a friend, he would write his reminiscences and title them *"Hell. By One Who Has Been There."*

Throughout his ordeal, Fisher was sustained by a few loyal, highly placed friends. One was Esher, who counseled Fisher to remain calm: "In a country like ours, governed by discussion, a great man is never hanged. He hangs himself." The First Sea Lord's greatest supporters were the royal couple. Queen Alexandra regularly sent for the Admiral to tell him what was being said in the drawing rooms. The King consistently threw his full weight on Fisher's side, telling him, "Keep your hair on," and urging him to curb the extravagance of his language and stop insulting his enemies in places where it would get back to them. At one point the King summoned Fisher and lectured him "that I was Jekyll and Hyde!" Fisher wrote to Esher. "Jekyll in being successful at my work at the Admiralty—but Hyde as a failure in society! That I talked too freely and was reported to say (which of course is a lie) that the King would see me through anything!" Bravado of this kind, the King declared, "was bad for me and bad for him as being a constitutional monarch." Fisher denied indignantly that he ever said such things and suggested that they were lies concocted by his enemies. Whereupon, "having unburdened his mind . . . [the King] smoked a cigar as big as a capstan for really a good hour afterwards, talking of everything from China to Peru." Fisher was grateful for the King's support and expressed his feelings in extravagant terms: "When Your Majesty backed up the First Sea Lord against unanimous Naval feeling against the *Dreadnought* when she was first designed, and when Your Majesty launched her, went to sea in her, witnessed her battle practice (which surpassed all records), it just simply shut up the mouths of the revilers as effectively as those lions were kept from eating Daniel! *And they would have eaten me but for Your Majesty!*" On another occasion when the King warned Fisher, "Do you know I am the only friend you have?" the Admiral replied with that trace of pixieish impertinence which King Edward found so captivating, "Your Majesty may be right, but, Sir, you have backed the winner!"

While the new Prime Minister and new First Lord still were getting the feel of their offices, Beresford escalated his vendetta against Fisher. At the Academy Dinner on May 1, he attempted to hide from Fisher, but the First Sea Lord discovered him, came up, and insisted on shaking hands. At the Royal Levee at St. James's Palace on May 11, Lord Charles displayed a shocking public rudeness to his superior. Fisher was standing against a wall, talking to Lloyd George and Winston Churchill. Beresford arrived, bowed to the King, and passed close by the three men. He shook hands and spoke to Lloyd George and Churchill. Fisher put out his hand but Beresford refused to take it and, in full view of everyone present, turned his back on the First Sea Lord. Within a few days, all London and the entire fleet were humming with the story. The King, who along with everyone else had witnessed the affront, denounced the Cabinet as "a pack of cowards" for not removing Beresford immediately.

Fisher meanwhile was busy making sure of the new First Lord. "What really amounts to incipient mutiny is being arranged in the fleet," he told McKenna on May 16. "Beresford evidently thinks you will . . . funk." He urged McKenna to tell the Commander-in-Chief that he could not continue his campaign of criticism in uniform; rather, he should resign, run for Parliament, and—in a political instead of a military forum—attack the Admiralty.

Fisher (who liked calling Beresford a "gasbag") put it succinctly: "Either the quarterdeck and silence or Westminster and gas." McKenna quickly agreed with Fisher and tried to get Cabinet approval to relieve Beresford "in the interests of the Naval Service and for the safety of the Empire." The Prime Minister and other ministers gave "strong objection" and nothing was done. "They are all 'blue funkers' about Beresford and overrate his power of mischief and his influence," Fisher lamented.

In June, Lord Charles was involved in another incident with Percy Scott which again burst out in the press and stimulated new demands that something be done about the chaotic situation in the navy. The Channel Fleet, accompanied by Scott's cruiser division, made a summer cruise to Norway. Maneuvering in those waters, Beresford signalled Scott's division to take a new position astern of the column of battleships led by the flagship *King Edward VII.* H.M.S. *Good Hope,* Scott's flagship, had begun to turn when Beresford hoisted another signal, taking control of the cruisers out of Scott's hands. The cruiser division now was ordered to turn inward on itself, a maneuver which, had Scott complied, would have rammed *Good Hope* into H.M.S. *Argyle,* a repetition of the *Victoria-Camperdown* tragedy. Scott instantly countermanded Beresford's order and the Commander-in-Chief, once he had grasped the situation, approved the action: "If . . . the Rear Admiral [Scott] thought *Good Hope* was too close to *Argyle* the Rear Admiral was right in turning to starboard."

Under the heading "A STRANGE OCCURRENCE IN THE CHANNEL FLEET," *The Times* told the story to the world, and new demands in the press and Parliament rose up against an admiral who, in addition to troublemaking and insubordination, now was endangering the safety of his ships at sea. Beresford's feud was described as "a gross scandal," "sapping the foundations of dicipline," "a serious menace to our national security," and a "sickening tale of effeminate sensitiveness and huff." On July 6, Arthur Lee, a former Unionist Civil Lord of the Admiralty, wrote to *The Times* that "It can no longer be denied that the Commander-in-Chief of the Channel Fleet (who presumably is the Admiralissimo in the event of war) is not on speaking terms with the admiral commanding his cruiser squadron, or with the First Sea Lord of the Admiralty." *The Times,* editorializing on Lee's letter, declared, "We say frankly that . . . Lord Charles Beresford is . . . in the wrong. . . . The Commander-in-Chief of the Channel Fleet must be confronted with the historic alternative, submit or resign."

Still, nothing was done. To the numerous questions submitted and shouted before the House of Commons, Asquith blandly remarked that the government had no knowledge of the "alleged dissensions" other than "unverified rumours." Beresford used the King's visit to the Channel Fleet in August as an opportunity to attempt to win the sovereign over by reminding him of their past friendship. "Personally," he wrote, "I shall never forget the day, as Your Majesty's kindness and charm reminded me so clearly of those happy days gone by which can never be erased from my memory." The King's reply was distinctly cool: "My dear Lord Charles Beresford," King Edward began, and went on to express his hope that "nothing may occur to prevent your continuing to hold the high and important position which you now occupy." The letter was signed "Very sincerely yours." With the Cabinet refusing to act and the King now worried that, out of office, Beresford would "make a disturbance and give trouble and annoyance," Fisher was becoming frantic. "Knollys [the King's private secretary] dead on for my leaving Beresford alone," he wrote to Esher. "*It's impossible!* You can't let authority be flouted as he continually flouts the Admiralty. Daily he is doing something traitorous and mutinous." The poisonous struggle continued until December 1908 when, between them, the First Lord and the First Sea Lord found a way to rid themselves of the Commander-in-Chief. Fisher's Home Fleet had now grown so much by the incorporation of powerful new ships that it was time to arrange the merger of the Channel and Home fleets. Accordingly, it was decided in December (but not announced until February) that command of the Channel Fleet had been reduced from a three-year to a two-year appointment and, in consequence, Lord Charles

Beresford would be giving up his command in March 1909 rather than in March 1910.

Although at sixty-three he still had two years to go before reaching compulsory retirement age, Beresford hauled down his flag on March 24, 1909. Coming ashore from *King Edward VII,* boarding a train in Portsmouth, and, later that day, arriving in London, he received the adulation of a great naval hero, home from a victory. The platforms both at Portsmouth station and at Waterloo were massed with admirers who cheered, threw their hats in the air, waved handkerchiefs, and sang "For He's a Jolly Good Fellow." Excited and encouraged by this show of support, Lord Charles went immediately on the offensive. On March 26, he called on Balfour. The leader of the opposition had permitted a wary friendship which, by then, had progressed to writing each other as "My dear Arthur" and "My dear Charlie," but he had no intention of being dragged into a condemnation of Fisher, whom he had installed as First Sea Lord and whom he continued to respect. Balfour's differences with the Admiralty were political—he had just used the Naval Scare* to hammer the government for more dreadnoughts—and it was blindingly clear to him that much of Beresford's antagonism was personal. On this occasion, Lord Charles' purpose was to sound Balfour on the likelihood of an election and the possibility of a new Unionist government. Should this come to pass, he wondered whether he might expect to be appointed First Sea Lord in Sir John Fisher's place? Balfour easily evaded the question by saying that he did not expect a new election for at least two years. When Beresford then declared that he meant to take his case to the country in public speeches, Balfour advised him first to talk with the Prime Minister.

On March 30, Beresford saw Asquith and on April 2 he wrote a long letter outlining his case. "During the whole of my tenure of the command of the Channel Fleet," he declared, "that force . . . has never, even for a day, been equal to the force which it might have to encounter in home waters. During that period, the fleets in home waters have not been organized in readiness for war and they are not organized in readiness for war today." Unless the government took action, he threatened, he would stump the country, raising alarm. This prospect was disagreeable to Asquith. His Cabinet had just undergone three harrowing months of internal strife related to the German Navy Scare, and the government was about to plunge into the unknown with the Chancellor of the Exchequer's revolutionary "People's Budget"; the last thing the Prime Minister wished

* See Chapter 33.

was a popular admiral stumping the country declaring that the Admiralty was incompetent and the navy impotent. He knew nothing about the navy himself, and McKenna had been First Lord only a year. Accordingly, Asquith appointed a committee. This was a subcommittee of the Committee of Imperial Defence and, as all members were Cabinet ministers, also a subcommittee of the Cabinet. Asquith himself took the chair, and Grey, Haldane, and Morley sat with him. Originally, the Prime Minister also wished to include on the committee Admiral of the Fleet Sir Arthur Wilson, Beresford's predecessor as Commander-in-Chief of the Channel Fleet and the most experienced and respected blue-water officer in the navy. King Edward agreed, but Beresford objected that Wilson was prejudiced in favor of Fisher, and Asquith yielded.

Fisher was infuriated by the establishment of the subcommittee. He looked on an inquiry as an insult to the navy, the Admiralty, and himself. Even calling the First Lord and the First Sea Lord to account on the basis of the charges of a subordinate had no precedent in the history of the navy; for the government to participate in these charges even to the extent of calling an inquiry smacked of deeper humiliation. Fisher spoke of resigning. McKenna argued that this would imply to the public that he feared Beresford's attack. King Edward remained a bulwark and commanded Fisher not to resign "even under pressure." Fisher, never intending to leave, acquiesced. "I shall of course obey His Majesty," he wrote to Sir Frederick Ponsonby, the King's assistant private secretary, "but it is almost past belief how Beresford has been pandered to. . . . The Prime Minister without consulting the Admiralty decides on Sir A. Wilson being a Member of the Committee of Enquiry—a very good decision—but Beresford objects and he is taken off the Committee. Esher is especially invited to serve on the Committee at a personal interview by the Prime Minister and is appointed—Beresford objects and Esher's appointment is cancelled. Beresford summons as witnesses my own personal staff at the Admiralty to cross-examine them as to the way I conduct business and this is to be allowed. . . . The object is to discredit me."

Even as the committee inquiry was beginning, a powerful private effort to discredit Fisher was under way. Early in May when Admiral Sir Francis Bridgeman arrived in London to join the Admiralty as Second Sea Lord, he went to Grosvenor Street to pay a courtesy call on Lord Charles, who had been his Commander-in-Chief in the Mediterranean. The butler, not knowing that this admiral was different, took his hat and ushered him into a room where seven other admirals, including Lord Charles, were seated around a table, conspiring against Fisher. Astonished, the plotters looked up —then one dropped his pen and crawled under the table to look for it, another turned his back and poked the fire, a third bent over to retie his shoelaces. Lord Charles leaped to his feet and hurried Bridgeman into another room.

More damaging to Fisher was the hostility of Sir George Armstrong, a former officer and bitter enemy of the First Lord's, who in speeches and in a letter to *The Times* revealed that Fisher had received and had had privately printed letters critical of Beresford, from a captain then serving in Beresford's Mediterranean Fleet. The accusation of espionage—that Fisher placed men in key spots throughout the navy to spy on their superiors—was revived and sensationalized. The basic charge was untrue: only with great reluctance had Fisher permitted his naval assistant, Captain Reginald Bacon, to leave his staff and join Beresford's command as captain of the battleship *Irresistible*. It was Bacon, who needed a seagoing command to qualify for promotion, who insisted on the transfer. Once in the Mediterranean Fleet, Bacon—by his own admission— was enthusiastic about many of the qualities of his new chief: "I always look upon Lord Charles Beresford as the most charming Commander-in-Chief under whom I ever served," he wrote. "All his subordinates loved him, for he was an ideal leader of men, and, had he been given a good staff, he would have been a great admiral in wartime; but he was essentially an admiral who was dependent on his staff. His mercurial temperment militated against deep study or concentrated thought, but a natural quickness and alertness of intellect enabled him to seize on important points."

Occasionally, Bacon wrote from the Mediterranean to Fisher on an intimate and—he assumed—confidential basis, reporting sometimes on reactions, positive and negative, of officers in the fleet to the drastic reforms Fisher was making in the navy. In March 1906, Bacon was summoned to a private interview with King Edward aboard the royal yacht at Corfu, on which occasion "the King pointed out that it was his [Bacon's] duty as late confidential Naval Assistant to keep Fisher *au courant* with the general opinion of the Fleet." In one of his letters to the First Sea Lord, Bacon described criticism of the reforms being expressed in the fleet and to the King by Beresford and Admiral Lambton, his second in command. The letter began with the unfortunate phrase "Lord Charles and Admiral Lambton have been getting at the King." Bacon years later said that he wished he had written, "The King has spoken to me of the objections to the schemes that have been placed before him by Lord Charles and Admiral Lambton." But Bacon thought he was writing only to his old chief with whom, in the course of years of intimate contact, a certain informality of expression had developed. What Bacon could not know, and where Fisher transgressed, was that the First Sea Lord, without Bacon's permission, would have the captain's letters privately printed and circulated among his friends. These were the letters which had fallen into the hands of Sir George Armstrong.*

For a number of weeks, the press and Parliament were filled with sharp words directed at the First Sea Lord's indiscretion. Revelation of the Bacon letters brought the Prince of Wales, theretofore neutral despite a general predisposition toward the conservative side of the navy, into Lord Charles' camp. The Prince, Beresford cheerfully told a friend, had become "quite violent" against Fisher: "He said . . . that he must go or the Navy would be ruined." Eventually, McKenna had to rise to defend the First Sea Lord in the House of Commons: "Is the House seriously going to be asked to condemn a great man because, at a time of great labor, he has ordered to be printed a number of letters it would have been better, I would say, not to have printed at all? This sort of attack is doing a cruel injustice to the First Sea Lord who has had the unreserved confidence of successive First Lords of the Admiralty. . . . I appeal to the House not to be misled by any such trumpery matters as these into censuring in the slightest degree a man who has given the very best service to the country that any man could give."

No censure of Fisher by the House was contemplated or even possible; Balfour probably would have prevented the Unionists from supporting such an effort and, in any case, the Liberal Party so thoroughly dominated the Commons that any Unionist motion of censure would easily have been defeated.

As for the Liberal government, the Prime Minister's method of dealing with all questions about the navy—Beresford versus Fisher included—was the subcommittee inquiry. Fifteen meetings of the subcommittee were held between April 27 and July 13. Over 2,600 questions were asked of Beresford, Fisher, McKenna, Sir Arthur

* Fisher's indiscretion in having the letters printed, and their revelation to the navy and the public by Armstrong, ruined Bacon's career. An exceptionally imaginative and talented officer whom Fisher had called "the cleverest officer in the Navy," Bacon was responsible for the early development of the Royal Navy's submarine force and was the first captain of the *Dreadnought*. In the aftermath of the letters scandal, he left the navy.

Remarkably, Bacon bore Fisher no ill will for what had happened. "Fisher, of course, had no right to circulate copies of the letter privately to his friends without the writer's permission but that was Fisher all over," Bacon wrote. In 1929, still loyal to his dead chief, Bacon published a two-volume biography of Fisher.

Wilson (who was called as a witness), and others. McKenna conducted and argued the case for the Admiralty. Fisher sat silent unless specifically asked a question by a member; McKenna had extracted a promise of muteness lest the First Sea Lord's fury at some of Beresford's statements "lead to the harmony of the meeting being rudely interrupted." Even so, the glowering look on Fisher's face kept the room in a state of tension. "It was dramatic—," Haldane wrote to his mother after the first meeting, "Beresford and Fisher in a deadly fight before us."

The inquiry began with Beresford presenting his case: despite Great Britain's overwhelming superiority in warships, her naval defense was inadequate and the Fleet unprepared for war. He attacked the organization of the Fleet in home waters, most notably the fact that in peacetime the Home Fleet had not come under the command of its wartime admiral; that is, himself as Commander-in-Chief of the Channel Fleet. He complained that during his tenure, the Channel Fleet itself was never up to full strength due to the constant withdrawal of ships for repairs. He accused the Admiralty of permitting a dangerous deficiency in cruisers and destroyers, both as compared to the numbers of German ships in both those categories, and relative to the needs of guarding Imperial lifelines. Finally, he charged that the Admiralty lacked any sort of serious war plan.

McKenna countered that Beresford knew when he accepted the Channel Fleet, that he was taking command during a transitional period. Even as constituted under Beresford (and even deducting ships under repair) the Channel Fleet was always more powerful than the High Seas Fleet. Now, McKenna pointed out, what Lord Charles was advocating—and what the Admiralty had always planned—was being carried out: the Channel Fleet was merging with the Home Fleet. As to the shortages of cruisers and destroyers, the Admiralty produced figures which proved Beresford wrong. The question as to whether the Sea Lords should provide an admiral afloat with a detailed war plan received careful consideration. Fisher was against it, but more important for the purposes of this inquiry, so was Sir Arthur Wilson. Wilson "did not consider it either practicable or desirable to draw up definite plans in peace which would govern the action of the fleet on the outbreak of war. . . . If such plans were forwarded to the Admiralty by a Commander-in-Chief they would pass through so many hands that secrecy could not be guaranteed . . . a plan, such as Lord Charles Beresford had required, in which every ship is told off by name for its duties, as practically impossible."

In presenting his case, Lord Charles proved to be his own worst enemy; when he spoke, he rambled; applying logic, he contradicted; offering illustration, he was irrelevant. Fisher, more or less gagged by McKenna, observed his enemy's ineffectiveness, but also noted with dismay that Asquith and the committee seemed easy on him. "We have . . . roped him [Beresford] in on every single point so far, but the disquieting aspect is the obvious desire of the Committee to get him out of his mess," Fisher wrote to Ponsonby—and thus to the King. "He refuses to answer questions when we get him into a tight place and makes long, irrelevant, wild speeches instead—or else he says the question is too absurd to answer—and the Committee let him have his way and don't insist on his answering. He makes the most malignant misstatements, and when we bring him to book, he appeals to Asquith whether his word ought to be doubted, etc., etc., and Asquith glosses over the matter and asks a question to get round the ugly corner." Beresford's case also was damaged by the discovery that he was being supplied with facts and figures from inside the Admiralty by two of his supporters—information which they had no right to pass along and he no right to receive.

In its findings, issued as a parliamentary paper on August 12, the subcommittee noted that all naval forces in home waters had been merged, which "satisfies in substance all of Lord Charles Beresford's requirements." As to the claimed deficiency in destroyers, the subcommittee declared itself "satisfied . . . there is no such deficiency"; as to the shortage of cruisers, "there is no sufficient foundation for Lord Charles Beresford's apprehensions." When it came to Beresford's complaint about war plans, "the Committee are satisfied that he had no substantial grounds for complaint in this matter." Nevertheless, there was uneasiness at the fact that all navy war plans seemed to be locked up in the heads of two or three admirals, especially when those admirals were scarcely on speaking terms. The "General Conclusion" to the committee findings contained a passage equally critical of Beresford and Fisher: "[The committee] feel bound to add that the arrangements [for war] were in practice seriously hampered through the absence of cordial relations between the Board of Admiralty and the Commander-in-Chief of the Channel Fleet. The Board of Admiralty do not appear to have taken Lord Charles Beresford sufficiently into their confidence as to the reasons for dispositions to which he took exception; and Lord Charles Beresford, on the other hand, appears to have failed to appreciate and carry out the instructions of the Board and to recognize their paramount authority."

Although Fisher's partisans, beginning with the King, hailed the report as a clear verdict in the First Sea Lord's favor, Fisher himself was bitterly disappointed. In his view the Admiralty did not need to take a subordinate into its confidence or offer him reasons for the orders they gave; the fact that the board (he knew the words were directed at himself personally) was chastised on this point he considered unjust and humiliating. Beresford considered himself the victor and went about London trumpeting that opinion. From the South Tyrol, where he had gone to escape all the tumult, Fisher boiled with frustration. "The Committee, by not squashing Beresford when they had the chance and so utterly discrediting him thereby in the face of all men, have given Beresford a fresh leash of insubordinate agitation," he wrote to a friendly admiral. "Had they smashed him, as they could have by the evidence, as a blatant liar, he would have been so utterly discredited that no newspaper would have noticed him ever again," he wrote to a friendly journalist. The villains, Fisher believed, were the four committee members: Asquith, Grey, Haldane, and Morley. "I thought they were great men," he wrote to McKenna. "They are great cowards." He closed that letter by wishing all five in hell—"on earth . . . instead of waiting."

Fisher's view was shared by many, including Knollys, who wrote from Balmoral that he was "disgusted" by the report, that "Asquith 'watered it down' to such an extent that it amounts to a verdict in Beresford's favor" and that "the fact is that the Committee . . . were afraid of Beresford, and this has been proved by their treatment of him. . . ." The King himself wrote privately that he hoped the Admiralty "will consider most seriously C.B.'s outrageous conduct, which if tolerated undermines all discipline in the R[oyal] N[avy]." Despite these endorsements, it became increasingly clear that Fisher's days at the Admiralty were numbered. Beresford was still on the loose, charging that "a system of espionage, favoritism, and intimidation exists at the Admiralty." In letters, he referred to Fisher as "the mulatto." He let it be known that he meant to run for Parliament in the next election and hinted that he had a commitment from Balfour to make him First Sea Lord if the Unionists won. Balfour said nothing. Both political parties, the navy, and the public were weary of the vendetta and anxious about the harm it had caused to the service. Beresford was gone; now to balance the scales Fisher also had to leave.

On the King's birthday, November 9, Fisher was raised to the peerage as Baron Fisher of Kilverstone, taking as a motto for his coat of arms "Fear God and Dread Nought."* He did not object to

---

* Fisher struggled in choosing a motto and wrote to his daughter and others about his dilemma. First he considered simply "Dreadnought" but decided that this was "too

retiring. He was leaving only one year early and his departure would make it possible for Sir Arthur Wilson, who had only two years of active service left, to succeed him as First Sea Lord. On January 25, 1910, his sixty-ninth birthday, after fifty-five years of service, Fisher left the navy. That evening, a group of his enemies held a dinner to celebrate his retirement. Unable to be present, Beresford sent a telegram:

SO REALLY SORRY THAT I CANNOT COME TO CELEBRATE THE GREAT DAY AT YOUR DINNER. MUST GO TO DEPTFORD TO SPEAK. YOUR TOAST SHOULD BE—'TO THE DEATH OF FRAUD, ESPIONAGE, INTIMI-DATION, CORRUPTION, TYRANNY, SELF-INTEREST, WHICH HAVE BEEN A NIGHTMARE OVER THE FINEST SERVICE IN THE WORLD FOR FOUR YEARS.'

In the General Election of January 1910, Beresford overcame the overall Liberal victory to win a seat for Portsmouth in the House of Commons. There, he continued to harangue the government and the Admiralty on naval matters, although to less and less effect. Still nominally on the navy list until his sixty-fifth birthday in 1911, he did not cease aspiring for promotion to supreme command. In December 1910, only seven months after the Prince of Wales had become King George V, the new monarch urged Asquith to make his friend Beresford an Admiral of the Fleet like Fisher and Fisher's successor as First Sea Lord, Sir Arthur Wilson. Saying that he "had no personal objections," Asquith referred the request to McKenna, who firmly scotched it. He did so by comparing Beresford to Wilson, the most recent Admiral of the Fleet: "Sir Arthur Wilson stands out by universal acknowledgement as the greatest sailor we have had for many years, whose incomparable merits could only be rewarded by exceptional distinction. . . . Judged by these standards, what claim has Lord C. Beresford to an extraordinary promotion? His services are no longer required. He has commanded at sea with much, but not unusual, success. . . . He has not been responsible for, or associated with, any development of naval science, strategy, or training. . . . To single him out for exceptional honor would lower the value

egotistical," "too arrogant and boastful." Then he pondered, "Perhaps in two words, 'Dread Nought.' " This still did not please him, and he wondered to a friend, "It wouldn't do to take 'Dreadnought' as a motto, but how would 'Fear God and nothing else' do? . . . which is a paraphrase of 'Dreadnought' and Psalm 34, verse 9." Eventually, he made a final choice: "Dread Nought is over 80 times in the Bible ('Fear Not'). So I took as my motto 'Fear God and Dread Nought.' "

of our naval rewards. . . . The Service would not think it right to
rank Lord Charles Beresford with Sir Arthur Wilson."

Asquith passed this letter along to the palace and no more was
heard on the subject. In 1912, Beresford published a vitriolic book,
The Betrayal, rehashing all of his arguments presented in the inquiry. Times had moved on, and the new First Lord, Winston Churchill, ignored the book and demolished Beresford in the House
whenever the member for Portsmouth rose to speak. In 1916, the
King raised Lord Charles to the peerage as First Baron Beresford of
Curraghmore. He died in 1919.

In another time, Lord Charles Beresford might have gone to
the pinnacle of the navy. His qualities, those of a brave, patriotic
officer and good commander, were those of innumerable other
Royal Navy officers who had advanced steadily through the ranks to
admiral, commanded major fleets, served a few years as First Sea
Lord, and then retired into happy oblivion. Beresford's misfortune
was to come along in the time of a naval genius. Jacky Fisher possessed gifts which Beresford lacked. Beresford stood for things as
they were, for orthodoxy and tradition. Fisher looked beyond, imagined new men, new rules, new ships, new worlds that broke tradition
so violently that they constituted revolution. Both men had colossal
egos, but over a lifetime of service, Beresford's ego tended to focus
on himself, while Fisher's was devoted to the advancement of the
Service. Despite his bonhomie, Beresford was a social snob. Fisher's
seniority appeared to him a subversion of the natural order and it
galled him that "the Malay" or "the Mulatto" should always give
the orders. Disappointment became humiliation, bitterness led to
insubordination and a crusade against the First Sea Lord.

Fisher was more sensitive to Beresford's opposition than to that
of any other officer. Once he discovered that Beresford was to be his
principal antagonist within the Service, he automatically opposed
any suggestion Lord Charles had to make. As Commander-in-Chief
in the Mediterranean, Fisher advocated concentration of force, unified command, and the dispatch of more ships to his fleet. When he
didn't get the ships, he criticized the Admiralty and the First Sea
Lord, often behind their backs. When Beresford, as Commander-in-
Chief of the Channel Fleet, demanded the same concentration, unified command, and increase in strength, Fisher denounced him as
insubordinate. To Beresford, it did not seem fair.

Esher, writing to Balfour's private secretary, declared of Fisher,
"I do not say he has not made mistakes. Who has not? But he is a
great public servant, and at the end of a long life devoted to his
profession and to the state, he is the victim of Asquith's want of

moral courage." As it turned out, the epitaph was premature. None of those who followed him at the Admiralty approached him in imagination or drive. Soon after the outbreak of war, responding to Churchill's plea, Admiral of the Fleet Lord Fisher of Kilverstone, then seventy-three, returned to the Admiralty as First Sea Lord.

PART IV

BRITAIN
AND GERMANY:
POLITICS AND
GROWING TENSION,
1906–1910

◆

CHAPTER 29

Campbell-Bannerman:
The Liberals
Return to Power

◆

Henry Campbell (for thus he was born in 1836) grew up in an orderly, businesslike atmosphere of politics, religion, and commercial prosperity. His father, Sir James Campbell, was simultaneously a successful importer of foreign goods and Lord Provost of Glasgow. Campbell's sons, destined for the business, were exposed early to foreign places and tongues. Henry and his elder brother, James, often accompanied their father on visits to France; when Henry was fourteen, he toured Europe with James for ten months. Still fourteen, thoroughly grounded in French language and literature, he entered Glasgow University, remained four years, then moved along to Trinity College, Cambridge, where he took an undistinguished Third in classics. In 1858, he returned to Glasgow to work for his father. In 1860, at his brother's wedding, he met and fell in love with Charlotte Bruce, daughter of the major general commanding the Edinburgh garrison. Their marriage, when he was twenty-five and she twenty-eight, was, he said, the happiest day of his life. They had no children and shared every thought and possible moment. They laughed at the same jokes, often spoke French to each other, and made up private names for political figures. Charlotte had a strong will and judged men shrewdly. Her duty, as she conceived it, was to protect her husband from those who were anx-

ious to take advantage of what she considered his excessively trusting nature. His duty, as he saw it, was to nurture her by constant
presence and sustained affection through repeated and prolonged
periods of illness. He trusted her absolutely and, particularly when it
came to judging character, would make no move without her counsel. "We will refer it to The Authority," he once told a friend, "and
she will decide. Her judgment is infallible."

In 1868, after ten years in business, Henry Campbell was
elected to the House of Commons as Member for Stirling. Three
years later, he changed his name. A rich uncle, Henry Bannerman,
died leaving a large inheritance to his nephew on condition that he
add "Bannerman" to his name. Campbell agreed although he came
to regret it. "I see you are already tired, as I long have been, of
writing my horrid long name," he wrote to a friend. "I am always
best pleased to be called Campbell and most of my friends do so.
. . . An alternative is C.B." His wife, even less pleased by the
change, for years went on signing herself simply "Charlotte Campbell."

C.B. rose slowly in Liberal Party politics. He spent seventeen
years in the House of Commons before ascending to Cabinet rank in
1885 as Secretary of War. To his dismay, he found himself at his first
Cabinet meeting seated next to the seventy-six-year-old Prime Minister, Mr. Gladstone. "I sat down timidly," recalled Campbell-
Bannerman, "on the edge of the chair, like a *fausse marquise,*
abashed to be under the wings of the great man." C.B. remained at
the War Office through the balance of Gladstone's third government, returned when the Grand Old Man came back to form a
fourth government, and stayed on through the brief term of Gladstone's mercurial heir, the Earl of Rosebery.

Inadvertently, Campbell-Bannerman was the cause of the fall
of Rosebery's government. The Liberal majority in the Commons
had been declining; Rosebery had replaced Gladstone without an
election and the voters did not like a Gladstone ministry without
Gladstone. For weeks, the government had been stumbling with
majorities of seven or eight. On June 21, 1895, the subject, Army
Estimates, was one which usually emptied the House, leaving only a
handful on the opposing benches. The government's case was in the
hands of C.B. as War Minister. Suddenly, in a move carefully plot-
ted by Unionist leaders, the opposition moved a one-hundred-
pound reduction of Campbell-Bannerman's salary on the grounds
that he had not provided the army with a sufficient reserve of cordite. C.B. replied that, in the opinion of his expert advisors, the reserve was ample. He refused to give the figures in public but offered

to show them in private to opposition leaders. They were not interested. Balfour and Chamberlain appeared on the scene to join in the attack. Liberal whips rushed to locate and rally members but when the vote was taken, the government was short by seven votes. Rather than continue its hand-to-mouth existence, the Rosebery government resigned. The Queen sent for Lord Salisbury. C.B. was defiant about the alleged shortage of cordite: "As to the censure, I am very proud of it. It was a blackguard business. We have too much ammunition rather than too little."

The early years of Lord Salisbury's long rule were difficult for the Liberal Party. Leadership was uncertain: Gladstone, well up in his eighties, lived in restless retirement; Lord Rosebery, Gladstone's successor as Prime Minister, remained leader of the opposition, but his grip on the party was weak. He was an earl, young, handsome, stylish, an eloquent orator, and the darling of the press. His marriage to a Rothschild brought him £100,000, with which he kept a racing stable and a yacht. During the sixteen months he was Prime Minister, two of his horses won the Derby in successive years. Rosebery was immensely proud, almost more so than of any political achievement. The turf world loved him, but rank-and-file Liberals, stern Nonconformist followers of Mr. Gladstone, looked askance at the spectacle of a Whig aristocrat distracted from the Premiership by cheering a horse. But Rosebery had greater political handicaps than his passion for the track. To many, he seemed in the wrong party; on South Africa, on Home Rule, on land and tax policies, his views were more Tory than Liberal. Gladstone, who appointed him Foreign Secretary, summed up his opinion by saying that "Rosebery was one of the ablest as well as one of the most honorable men he had ever known, but that he doubted whether he really possessed common sense."

Out of office, still party leader, Rosebery sulked. Gladstone, in his eighty-seventh year, continued to speak in public, attracting huge crowds. Rosebery complained that this undermined his position; eventually, finding himself "in apparent difference with a considerable mass of the Liberal Party . . . and in some conflict of opinion with Mr. Gladstone," he resigned the party leadership. Sir William Harcourt, Liberal leader in the Commons, succeeded for one year and then, he too withdrew. The party whips offered the leadership to Herbert Henry Asquith, the most accomplished orator in the party, but Asquith, forty-six, needed to earn a living at the bar to support his family; he urged that the post go to Campbell-Bannerman, sixteen years his senior.

C.B. accepted reluctantly. He was a solid, reassuring figure, a conciliator, faithful, humorous, shrewd, kind, good-natured. He had been faithful, but not especially active on the front bench. Beatrice Webb described him as "well-suited to a position of sleeping partner in an inherited business." He had no ambition to succeed to the leadership. His health was uncertain; his wife's health was poor. That he would harness himself to the heavy and constant burdens of the leadership seemed improbable. C.B. did so because, there being no one else, he saw it as his duty. In the beginning, this situation conferred certain advantages: he did not want the job and could not be accused of snatching it from anyone else. He had no enemies; all were grateful. In 1898, Gladstone died, removing the great figure which had shadowed every other Liberal statesman for forty years. Some Liberals missed the brilliance and charm of Lord Rosebery, others were glad that the haze of doubt surrounding the party leader's intentions had finally lifted. There was nothing enigmatic about C.B. He stood stoutly for Liberal ideas in their simplest form and worked avowedly to bring the Liberal Party back to power. It was said that "Campbell-Bannerman's great advantage was that he always seemed to be in the battle while Lord Rosebery always seemed to be above it." During the seven years of C.B.'s leadership before the Liberals returned to power in 1905, he modestly said that the question of who should be Prime Minister in the next Liberal government should be decided only when the moment came. For part of this time, C.B. told friends that Rosebery could have the leadership back any time he wanted it. "The door has always been open for Lord Rosebery's return," he said.

The issue that made Rosebery's return impossible and so deeply divided the Liberal Party that it could not transform itself into a government was the Boer War. From the beginning, Campbell-Bannerman realized that the war would wreak havoc on party unity. The majority in the party, following the tradition of Gladstone, was against the war. This included C.B., Morley, and Lloyd George, among the leadership. They opposed imperialism, as Gladstone had, and viewed the Empire as much as an instrument of intimidation and exploitation as a civilizing influence. In this instance, they found the cause of the war in the iniquity of certain government ministers, primarily Chamberlain. The Colonial Minister, in alliance with Rhodes, had engineered a squalid intrigue in the interests of a gang of profiteers who wished to use the power of a large nation to squelch the liberty and steal the treasures of a small and helpless one. The Boers, from this perspective, were "a small people, struggling to be free," and Kruger's ultimatum was a desperate challenge into which the Boer President had been trapped by an astute course of provocation.

Rosebery rejected this position and, on the issue of the war, supported the government. The former Prime Minister had drifted so far away from the mass of the party, however, that his views had little impact. More significant was the position taken by three active younger Liberal leaders, H. H. Asquith, Sir Edward Grey, and Richard B. Haldane, who, while remaining firmly pledged to the party, supported the government on South Africa. Fifty Liberal back-benchers stood with this triumvirate; together the group was called the Liberal Imperialists. For Asquith, a former Home Secretary and the most prominent of this faction, the key point was, Who started the war? For him, the decisive acts were the Boer ultimatum and invasion of adjacent British territories. "We [the Liberal Imperialists] held that the war was neither intended nor desired by the Government and the people of Great Britain but that it was forced upon us without adequate reason and entirely against our will," he explained. Grey wholeheartedly agreed: "We are in the right in this war. It is a just war. It is a war which has been forced upon this country," he said. Campbell-Bannerman did not dispute that, in the narrow sense, the Boer ultimatum had made war inevitable. "The Boers have committed an aggression which it is the plain duty of all of us to resist," he declared. His complaint was that the situation had been inflamed by British government policy. As C.B. put it, he was "anti-Joe, but never pro-Kruger." In the middle, standing between the Liberal Imperialists and the Liberal pacifists, was Campbell-Bannerman, who respected Asquith, if not Asquith's position. For the other Liberal Imperialist leaders, he had contempt. Applying the term "Master" to people he disliked, C.B. referred to "Master Haldane" and "Master Grey," but never to "Master Asquith."

The political reckoning of the Boer War came in September 1900 after the British Army, having recovered from its early defeats, had occupied Pretoria and Johannesburg. Chamberlain persuaded Salisbury to call a general election to take advantage of the euphoria of victory and exploit the split among the Liberals. C.B.'s divided party had no chance. Chamberlain, a master political propagandist, pounced on the theme that Liberal candidates were friends of the nation's enemies and would undermine British policy and stab British soldiers in the back. The election was a test of patriotism, Unionist orators relentlessly proclaimed; the issue was patriotism versus treason. "A vote for the Liberals is a vote for the Boers," screamed placards and speakers around the country. This attack aggravated the deep split in the Liberal Party. Liberal candidates found them-

selves condemning each other, not the Unionists, while Chamberlain rode triumphantly over both, declaring that even the slightest
Liberal success would weaken the hand of the government in ending
the war and dealing with the rebellious Boers. Campbell-Bannerman's situation was hopeless. He was aware that many voters resented the tone of Unionist oratory and knew that calling an
election at that point was a political trick. He also understood that
many of these same voters believed that defeat of the government
would be considered by the Boers and by foreign powers as a rejection of the South African policy into which the nation had poured a
torrent of blood and wealth.

Chamberlain, exulting in his anticipated victory, sought not just
to defeat but to destroy his former party. He asked for a landslide
which would sweep away the Liberals. The vote, when it came—
2,428,492 to 2,105,518—was not the hoped-for annihilation; indeed,
by Chamberlain's definition, over 2 million British voters had proclaimed themselves "traitors." The Khaki Election, fought on a single issue, ensured the Unionist Party another six years of rule. From
Campbell-Bannerman's practical point of view, this was not entirely
bad; the Liberal Party, still in the throes of internal division, was
unready to govern.

Politics was only one part of Campbell-Bannerman's life. He gave
seven months a year to London, the Liberal Party, the House of
Commons, and government office. During these months, he gave
himself completely, weekends included. He was not invited to dinner parties and late-night suppers and did not go to the great house
parties which lured Balfour and Asquith. In compensation, C.B. demanded five months away for his wife and himself. Three of these
months were spent at his home in Perthshire: Belmont, a rambling
Victorian mansion furnished with soft carpets, deep leather armchairs, and big, open fireplaces. Outside, a broad expanse of lawn
stretched to a circle of giant ash, beech, spruce, and pine trees. On
arrival at Belmont, C.B.'s first concern was to visit his trees, sometimes bowing to them and bidding them "Good morning." To one
magnificent specimen, he always raised his hat and, in a courtly
manner, inquired after "Madame's health." Nothing unfamiliar was
permitted at Belmont. There were no motorcars, only old horses,
old carriages, old dogs—many dogs, his and hers—and old servants.
C.B. was loyal; what had served him well would not be put by. He
had a large collection of walking canes. Each day, as he chose the
one to be given an outing, he would murmur affectionately to the

others, consoling them for being left behind. A drawer in his desk contained a mass of pencil stubs—old friends, he explained, "who deserved to be decently cared for when their day was done."

Every year, Campbell-Bannerman and his wife spent two months on the Continent, travelling through France, Switzerland, Italy, or Spain, always arriving punctually in Marienbad, where Charlotte could rest and take a cure, at the beginning of August. C.B. loved France and would often be seen sitting in a restaurant or poking through shops in Paris. Sometimes, he would escape from London to Dover to sit on the pier and watch the Channel steamers come and go. Occasionally, he improved on this pastime by taking the morning boat to Calais, enjoying an excellent lunch at the Gare Maritime, and returning to England in the afternoon. Among his papers, he always carried a novel by Balzac, Flaubert, Anatole France, or Zola, but his primary pleasure was to sit and look at people. Few looked at him, and to the end he scorned the idea that he was a person of importance.

The Unionist government's claim of victory in South Africa was hollow. Although the Union Jack waved in Johannesburg and Pretoria and triumphant beacons illuminated the hills above Balmoral, Boer fighting men were still in the field. They were no longer organized into regiments; instead, they assembled secretly as guerrilla commandos, small bodies of horsemen who struck suddenly at slow-moving British infantry detachments and supply columns, then vanished into the veldt. Orthodox military tactics were useless; by the time a force of British or Imperial cavalry came up to pursue, the guerrillas had transformed themselves into peaceful Boer farmers, plowing the land in the same baggy work clothes in which they had fought a few days before. Their weapons were hidden in their houses, and the swift work ponies that made the raids possible were grazing in their fields.

Kitchener, who succeeded Lord Roberts as Commander-in-Chief in December 1900, addressed this problem with brutal logic: if he could not pin down twenty thousand Boer horsemen with 250,000 British troops* in a war of movement, he would reduce and then eliminate the commandos' ability to maneuver. Eight thousand cor-

---

* Over 447,000 British, Imperial, and colonial troops fought in South Africa. Twenty-two thousand were killed in action or died of wounds. On the Boer side, eighty-seven thousand men took up arms, of whom seven thousand died. Another eighteen thousand to twenty-eight thousand men, women, and children died in Kitchener's concentration camps.

rugated iron and stone blockhouses were stretched first along the railway lines, then across the countryside. Eventually, the veldt was laced with a network of small blockhouse forts, linked by barbed wire, within rifle shot of one another. Once the countryside was compartmentalized, Kitchener swept through in the manner of a pheasant shoot in Norfolk. The language of Kitchener and his intelligence officers was that of the hunt: so many "drives" and "bags" and "kills." Sweeping everything before them, the army "sanitized" the ground behind. All crops, potential food for the commandos, were burned. Every farm which could be used as a shelter or rendez-vous point was burned. Every rural inhabitant caught in the net, mostly women and children, was uprooted, hustled into a wagon, and driven off to one of twenty-four concentration camps built and administered by the army. The camps, hastily constructed tent cities, were exposed to sun and rain in summer and icy winds in winter, and had inadequate latrines and insufficient fresh water. Because the inmates were reckoned to be the families of Boer guerrillas still in the field, they were given reduced-scale army rations. There was no meat, no vegetables, no milk for children, no soap; the water was contaminated. Typhoid appeared. Over fourteen months, during which the population of the camps bulged to 117,000, 18,000 to 28,000 inmates, most of them women and children, died.

Britain learned about these horrors from the testimony of an impassioned middle-aged woman, Emily Hobhouse, who toured the camps and returned to England. She went to see St. John Broderick, the Unionist Secretary of State for War, who listened politely but refused to commit himself. Then she went to see Campbell-Banner-man. The Liberal Party leader sat quietly as she poured out her story: "wholesale burning of farms . . . deportations . . . a burnt-out population brought in by the hundreds of convoys . . . de-prived of clothes . . . semi-starvation in the camps . . . fever stricken children lying . . . upon the bare earth . . . appalling mortality." C.B. decided to speak. A week later, on June 14, at a Liberal dinner at Holborn Restaurant, he talked about the nature of war. "A phrase often used [by the government] was that 'war is war,' but when one came to ask about it one was told that no war was going on, that it was not war. When was a war not a war? When it was carried on by methods of barbarism in South Africa."

A storm of anger burst over his head. He was denounced in the popular press, excoriated in private clubs, excluded from polite soci-ety. The leader of the Liberal Party, a former War Secretary, had appallingly defamed the British Army. Pro-Boerism had reached the point of treason. Obviously, this man could never become Prime

Minister. Campbell-Bannerman did not flinch. Three days later he repeated his words in the House of Commons. He absolved the soldiers who carried out the orders: "I never said a word which would imply cruelty or even indifference on the part of officers or men of the British Army. It is the whole system I consider, to use a word I have already applied to it, barbarous." The repetition inflamed both Unionists and Liberal Imperialists. Haldane rose to regret that the word "barbarous" had been used and to disassociate himself and his colleagues from their party leader. In the division that followed, fifty Liberals, including Asquith, Grey, and Haldane, abstained from voting. Three days later, Asquith gave his reply in a speech at Liverpool Station Hotel. "We have not changed our view," he said. "We do not repent of it . . . and we shall not recant it." Public dinners and counterdinners followed; one observer described this contest as "war to the knife—and fork." A dinner for Asquith was planned; C.B. appealed to Asquith to postpone it and substitute a unity dinner over which he himself would preside. Asquith declined. Rosebery spoke at a luncheon, attacking C.B.'s "methods of barbarism" phraseology but not aligning himself with Asquith. "I must plough my furrow alone," he told his audience. "That is my fate, agreeable or the reverse. But before I get to the end of that furrow it is possible that I may find myself not alone." By the spring of 1902, Asquith and Rosebery still were apart, but both had repudiated Campbell-Bannerman's leadership of the party.

It was at this moment, when the Liberal future looked blackest, that Joseph Chamberlain shattered the Unionist government by proposing a duty on imported wheat. For three years, the battle over Imperial Preference dragged on, pitting Prime Minister against Colonial Secretary, spurring resignations and defections, accompanied all the while by Unionist losses in by-elections. By the autumn of 1905, there was little doubt that when a General Election was called, the Liberal Party would win. Arthur Balfour, politically weary and suffering from bronchitis and phlebitis, seemed anxious to go.

The King let it be known that if Balfour resigned, Campbell-Bannerman was his choice. King Edward had not always felt this way about C.B. After the "methods of barbarism" speech, the monarch had asked Lord Salisbury whether the Liberal leader could be silenced. The Prime Minister replied that any attempt to do so would be unwise; it would be seen as Court interference in party politics. The King had to be satisfied with extending only the minimal necessary politeness when he and C.B. were forced to meet. With the passage of time, these feelings mellowed. The two men had similar tastes: both loved France and Paris; both went annually for a cure at Marienbad. It was in Bohemia that the King and the Liberal leader talked informally and the King discovered C.B. to be "so straight, so good-tempered, so clever, and so full of humor that it was impossible not to like him." Campbell-Bannerman's solid, unpretentious qualities were quite different from Balfour's airy graces. In conversation, the King found Sir Henry to be "quite sound on foreign politics." Above all, King Edward was a realist. For seven years, C.B. had been leader of the Liberal Party. It was plain that the Liberals were coming to power. The King would be dealing with Sir Henry as sovereign to minister; why not try to make him a friend? "I lunched with the King," C.B. wrote to a friend from Marienbad in August 1905. "He said he was glad to exchange views with me as I must soon be in office and very high office." The intimacy flourished: "about half my meals have been taken in H.M.'s company," Campbell-Bannerman continued. "I think my countrymen [in Marienbad] were astounded to find with what confidence, consideration, and intimacy he treated me."

As the election approached, the only issues were the margin of victory and whether the Liberals, so long out of power, were ready to govern. Campbell-Bannerman believed they were and, while ready to accept the Premiership himself, was equally ready to step aside if another Liberal seemed able to provide greater harmony. For a while, in the spring and summer of 1905, it seemed that Lord Spencer, Liberal leader in the House of Lords, might be chosen. Dubbed "the Red Earl"—because of the color of his beard rather than the hue of his politics—he had had long service during the Gladstone years and his placid, undemanding ways seemed likely to offend the fewest in the party. Rosebery remained a remote possibility but his maverick political behavior had alienated him from both the leaders and the rank and file. In the autumn the breach between Campbell-Bannerman and Rosebery was further widened by their differing positions on Home Rule. Campbell-Bannerman advocated genuine Home Rule ("the effective management of Irish affairs in the hands of a representative Irish Authority"), albeit step by step. Rosebery rejected ultimate Home Rule in any form and declared in ringing tones: "Emphatically and explicitly, once for all, I cannot serve under that banner."

In the autumn of 1905, Lord Spencer suffered a cerebral seizure which ended his political career. Rosebery had removed himself from consideration. Campbell-Bannerman, the overwhelming preference of the Liberal rank and file, the clear preference of the King, was now the overwhelming favorite. Suddenly, new obstacles rose in his path. If C.B.'s ascent to the summit could not be denied, three men in his party meant at least to limit his power. Early in September, the three leading Liberal Imperialists, Asquith, Grey, and Haldane, gathered at Grey's fishing lodge at Relugas in northeastern Scotland to discuss the prospects of a Liberal government and their roles should one be formed. Their doubts about C.B.'s leadership went beyond their differences with him over South Africa. In Haldane's words, "Campbell-Bannerman . . . was genial and popular and respected for the courage with which he had resisted the policy of the Government in South Africa. But he was not identified in the public mind with any fresh ideas, for indeed he had none. What was wanted was not the recrudesence of the old Liberal Party, but a body of men with life and energy and a new outlook on the problems of the state. At these problems some of us had been working diligently. . . ."

There was also concern about Campbell-Bannerman's health and its effect on his capacity for leadership. On the podium, C.B. had always been dull; now, old and weary, he—and therefore the party—were certain to be minced in debate by the brilliant parliamentary skills of Arthur Balfour. Accordingly, the trio's decision, which came to be known as the Relugas Compact, was to support C.B.'s installation as Prime Minister, but to make their support conditional on his leaving the House of Commons for the House of Lords. The party in the Commons would be led by Asquith, an acknowledged master of debate. This arrangement had precedent: Salisbury had sat in the Lords while Balfour managed the Commons; Lord Spencer, had he become Prime Minister, would have governed from the Upper House. The bludgeon to enforce the trio's demand was powerful: if C.B. did not agree, Asquith, Grey, and Haldane would refuse to accept office. Assuming that Campbell-Bannerman would give way, the three picked out the offices they wished: Asquith would become Chancellor of the Exchequer as well as Leader of the House of Commons; Grey would go to the Foreign Office; Haldane would become Lord Chancellor and preside over the House of Lords. Control of these three offices would allow the trio to dominate the government; the weakened Prime Minister would occupy a largely figurehead role. Before leaving the fishing lodge, Asquith, Grey, and Haldane pledged themselves to one another: unless C.B. went to the Lords, all would stay out; unless all came in together, none would accept office.

The trio's first move was to inform the King. Haldane visited the sovereign at Balmoral, insisting that his colleagues' decision was based on concern for Campbell-Bannerman's health. The King, aware that C.B. was not robust, accepted the wisdom of the new Prime Minister's going to the Lords and agreed to suggest it to him. But King Edward objected to the trio's threat to remain outside the Cabinet. The government, he pointed out, would be crippled from the beginning and he, as monarch, would be in an awkward position. On November 13, Asquith confronted Campbell-Bannerman with the Relugas Compact. C.B. listened carefully. He was anxious, he said, to have Asquith as Chancellor and agreeable to Grey as Foreign Secretary, but at Haldane, he bucked violently. He blamed the suggestion that he go to the House of Lords on "that ingenious person, Richard Burdon Haldane." He would go to the Lords, "a place for which I have neither liking, training nor ambition," he said, only "at the point of a bayonet."

On Monday afternoon, December 4, Balfour went to Buckingham Palace and resigned. That evening, knowing the King would summon Campbell-Bannerman the following day, Grey called on C.B. and told him bluntly that he would not take office in the new government unless the Prime Minister went to the Lords, and Asquith—who, Grey said to C.B. was "the more robust and stronger leader in policy and debate"—was permitted to lead the Commons. Campbell-Bannerman was surprised, hurt, and indignant. Grey, he said later, had come to him "all buttoned-up and never undoing one button." Grey explained his harshness as honesty: "I wanted him to know just where I stood and to feel that I was not suppressing in his presence things that I had said about him elsewhere."

The next morning, Tuesday, December 5, the King asked Campbell-Bannerman to form a government. During their interview, the monarch urged his friend to accept the proposal of the Liberal trio and take a peerage. C.B. was noncommittal. He told King Edward that he must talk to his wife, who was still in Scotland. On Wednesday evening, Lord Morley and Lord Tweedmouth, both about to enter the Cabinet, appeared in Campbell-Bannerman's house in Belgrave Square. The new Prime Minister still was undecided. Lady Campbell-Bannerman was soon to arrive and Morley and Tweedmouth were asked to return after dinner. When they returned, they found C.B. exultant. "No surrender!" he cried. Lady Campbell-Bannerman, despite worries over her husband's health and her jealousy of his time spent away from her, so loathed the

Relugas trio that she had put her fears aside and urged her husband to remain in the Commons.*

Asquith, informed of C.B.'s decision, immediately deserted his friends. "The conditions are in one respect fundamentally different from those which we, or at any rate I, contemplated when we talked in the autumn," he wrote to Haldane. "The election is before us and not behind us. . . . I stand in a peculiar position which is not shared by either of you. . . ." Asquith felt that if the trio refused to come in, "a weak Government would be formed . . . and the whole responsibility would be mine." Having decided to enter the government, Asquith wanted his friends to join him and began doing his best to negotiate on their behalf. Grey and Haldane, weakened by Asquith's defection, repledged to each other that neither would take office without the other. Grey was staying at Haldane's flat in Whitehall Court, and when Haldane came home at six P.M. on December 7 he found Grey reclining on a sofa in his library "with the air of one who had taken a decision and was done with political troubles." Neither had eaten and Haldane proposed that they go to the Café Royale, where they could take a private room, dine, and talk. Over a fish dinner, it became apparent to Haldane that Grey keenly wanted to find a way to back down and join the government. He could do so easily on his own—it was clear that C.B. wanted him —but he was refusing to ask for a place unless Haldane was taken, too. Haldane understood that the next move was up to him. Leaving his dinner on the table, he took a hansom cab to Belgrave Square. The Prime Minister was dining with his wife; Haldane was shown into the study. C.B. entered and Haldane said that he had come to ask whether Campbell-Bannerman still wanted Grey at the Foreign Office. The Prime Minister said that he did, very much. Haldane said that he thought that Grey would be willing. C.B. sensed the unspoken half of Haldane's message and asked whether Haldane would consider the Home Office or the Attorney Generalship.

"What about the War Office?" Haldane asked.

"Nobody will touch it with a pole," Campbell-Bannerman replied.

"Then give it to me," Haldane said. "I will come in as War

---

* The decision was a reversal of an earlier private agreement between Campbell-Bannerman, his wife, and Dr. Ott, the Viennese specialist whom they consulted at Marienbad. That agreement was exactly the arrangement proposed by the Relugas trio: that if C.B. became Prime Minister, he go to the House of Lords. On December 9, a shocked Dr. Ott learned of the decision and wrote to the new Prime Minister: "I am sure that those who are persuading you to remain in the House of Commons are not your true friends . . . and that they do not think of your precious health as the most important matter."

Secretary if Grey takes the Foreign Office. I will ask him to call on you early tomorrow to tell you his decision which I think may be favorable."

The arrangement was made. Haldane returned to tell Grey. Grey agreed. The following morning he went to see C.B. and accepted the Foreign Office, which he was to hold for eleven years. During the two years of C.B.'s Premiership, Grey and Campbell-Bannerman worked closely together; the Prime Minister relied almost completely on the Foreign Secretary to manage the nation's relations with other states. Before Campbell-Bannerman stepped down, Grey offered an apology for his earlier behavior: "My thoughts have often gone back to the days when this Government was being formed and I have felt from the early days of this Parliament that all my forecast before the elections was wrong, and that your presence in the House of Commons has been not only desirable but essential to manage this party and keep it together; and so it continues to be."

Haldane was the single member of the Relugas trio who did not achieve the office to which he aspired. (Eventually, in 1911, Asquith as Prime Minister appointed his friend Lord Chancellor.) In the early days of the new Cabinet, Haldane and Campbell-Bannerman avoided each other. C.B. spoke of his War Minister with disparagement. "Haldane is always climbing up and down the backstairs but he makes such a clatter that everyone hears him," the Prime Minister said. "We shall see how 'Schopenhauer' gets on," Campbell-Bannerman grumbled another time, applying his penchant for nicknames to Haldane, who was steeped in German philosophy. "Myself he did not like at first," was Haldane's way of putting it. "For some months he said nothing to me and encouraged me but little in Cabinet." With the passage of time and mounting evidence of Haldane's loyalty, hard work, and efficiency in the reform of the British Army, C.B. mellowed.

The Liberal government which presented itself at the Palace on December 11 was studded with talent. Besides the Relugas trio, it included Morley at the India Office; Lloyd George as President of the Board of Trade; Herbert Gladstone, son of the Grand Old Man, as Home Secretary; Tweedmouth at the Admiralty; and Winston Churchill, just below Cabinet rank, as Under Secretary for the Colonies. John Burns, the first workingman in English history to reach Cabinet rank, became President of the Local Government Board. "I congratulate you, Sir Henry," chortled the delighted appointee when told that the post was his. "It will be the most popular appointment that you have made."

While the new ministers were at the Palace receiving their seals of office, a thick fog crept over London. When the ceremony was over, Grey and Haldane set off in a carriage down the Mall for their respective offices. Along the way, the fog was so dense that the driver was forced to halt. Haldane got out to see where they were and could not find his way back to the carriage. After a while, Grey stepped down and after prolonged wandering around eventually reached the Foreign Office. Haldane by "feeling among the horses' heads" at last stumbled into the War Office, where he handed his seals to the Permanent Under Secretary and asked the tall ex-Guardsman on duty as a footman for a glass of water. "Certainly, sir," replied the old soldier. "Irish or Scotch?"

The following morning, the generals of the Army Council trooped in to discover what they could of the new War Minister. Haldane said that "as a young and blushing virgin just united to a bronzed warrior . . . it was not expected by the public that any result of the union should appear at least until nine months had passed." Delighted, the generals passed this phrasing along to the King, who roared with laughter.

Within a month of taking office, the new government faced a General Election. The campaign began after Christmas and polling took place over the last three weeks of January. The result was a Liberal landslide. Traditionally safe Unionist seats were swept away. Over two hundred Unionist M.P.'s, including Arthur Balfour, were defeated. The Liberal Party stormed into the House of Commons with 379 members, a clear majority of 88 over all other parties in the House. With the backing of 83 Irish Nationalists and 51 Labourites, Campbell-Bannerman and his fellow ministers could look down on a woeful Unionist remnant from a summit of 513 votes to 157 .

When the new Parliament met on February 13, Campbell-Bannerman seemed transformed. He spoke with an authority and dignity which surprised the opposition and delighted the hundreds of Liberal members crowded into the seats or jostling for standing room behind the Government Front Bench. A month later, when Balfour returned to the Commons, having found a seat in a by-election, the Unionist leader made the mistake of attempting to trifle with the sturdy Scot. Offering his views on a resolution favoring free trade, Balfour launched into one of his rhetorical performances, articulate, ambiguous, evasive, and, to both the hostile majority and its leader, patronizing. Grimly, Campbell-Bannerman replied.

"The Right Honorable gentleman is like the old Bourbons—he has learned nothing," the Prime Minister threw back at his predecessor. "He comes back to this new House of Commons with the same airy graces, the same subtle dialectics, the same light and frivolous way of dealing with a great question, but he little knows the temper of the new House of Commons if he thinks those methods will prevail here. . . . They are utterly futile, nonsensical and misleading. They were invented by the Rt. Hon. gentleman for the purpose of occupying time on this debate. I say, enough of this foolery! . . . Move your amendments and let us get to business."

The schism between traditional Gladstonian idealism and a harsher view of the realities of wielding Imperial power that had split the party during the Boer War was not fully closed. Campbell-Bannerman, Morley, Lloyd George, and the majority of Liberals in the House of Commons and the country yearned to remain aloof from European power politics and to put moderation and reconciliation ahead of expansionism in Imperial affairs. Asquith, Grey, and Haldane, the Liberal Imperialists of the Relugas Compact, saw Britain's role differently: as an Imperial power whose territories bordered on those of other nations around the globe, and whose Home Islands neighbored a continent seething with tensions. The differences were apparent early in the new government. In his first speech as Prime Minister, on December 21, 1905, Campbell-Bannerman told a packed house in the Albert Hall that he meant to conduct a milder foreign policy than the Unionists had. He was a Francophile and he welcomed the Entente with France "so wisely concluded by Lord Lansdowne." "In the case of Germany," he continued, "I see no cause whatever for estrangement in any of the interests of either people." He favored disarmament and pledged his government to work for it at the coming second Hague convention. "The growth of armaments is a great danger to the world," he said. "[It] keeps alive and stimulates and feeds the belief that force is the best if not the only solution of international differences. It is a policy that tends to inflame old sores and to create new ones."

In March 1907, shortly before the opening of the Second Hague Peace Conference, the Prime Minister published an article in a Liberal weekly, the *Nation*, urging that disarmament be given a chance. Britain, he asserted, was attempting to reduce expenditure and armaments and would go further if other nations would follow suit. In this area, the Liberals faced a domestic political dilemma: how—after years of demanding decreases in defense spending, after pledging to the voters that once in power they would reduce the army and navy Estimates—were they to pay for certain army and navy policies adopted by Balfour's government? Fisher had been called in to remake the navy; ships had been scrapped and fleets redistributed. The *Dreadnought* had been designed, laid down, and launched and would be commissioned by the King even before the meeting of the first Liberal Parliament; this work could not simply be halted. The decision was to trim here and there and insist on efficiency. One dreadnought was dropped from the 1906 Naval Estimates; Fisher declared that three rather than four was acceptable. Haldane attacked the army with the same zeal for reform and efficiency. His promise, when he became Secretary of War, was to cut £3 million from the Army Estimates while simultaneously creating a more effective weapon. To the amazement of Campbell-Bannerman, who fully expected "Master Haldane" to fall on his face at the War Office, Haldane carried out his pledge. He reorganized the army into two forces, a professional Regular Army Expeditionary Force of six divisions and 160,000 men, and a second-line Territorial Army to be raised in the counties, organized into fourteen divisions, and held as reserve to back up the Expeditionary Force. C.B. was delighted by the manner in which Haldane defended his policies in the Commons against Unionists—Balfour, most skillfully—who attempted to point out flaws and inconsistencies in the planned army reforms.

The greatest triumph of Campbell-Bannerman's brief occupancy of 10 Downing Street was his political reconciliation in South Africa. Since the beginning of the Boer War, through years of abuse, he had preached the same message. To him, the war seemed a wound which could be healed only by understanding and generosity on the part of the British government. As Prime Minister, he was ready to effect his belief. He proposed granting self-government to the Boer republics and then bringing them into a federation of self-governing states as a Union of South Africa. C.B.'s suggestion that Britain hand back to the defeated Boers the powers of government it had stripped from them in a war which had cost thirty thousand lives and £250 million raised desperate Unionist opposition. Backed by his huge majority, however, the Prime Minister granted self-government to the Transvaal and the Orange Free State. He did so by letters patent, which needed the approval only of the House of Commons and not of the Lords. In 1909, eighteen months after C.B.'s death, the South Africa Act, establishing the Union, passed both houses of Parliament. Louis Botha, the Boer general who became the first Prime Minister of the Union of South Africa, expressed his gratitude to Asquith, Campbell-Bannerman's successor, adding, "My greatest regret is that one noble figure is missing—Sir

Henry Campbell-Bannerman. For what he has done in South Africa alone, the British Empire should always keep him in grateful memory." To a journalist, Botha explained: " 'Three words made peace and union in South Africa: "methods of barbarism." ' . . . [Botha] went on to speak of the tremendous impression . . . made upon men fighting a losing battle . . . by the fact that the leader of one of the great English parties had had the courage to say this thing, and to brave the obloquy which it brought upon him. So far from encouraging them to a hopeless resistance, it touched their hearts and made them think seriously of the possibility of reconciliation."

In the spring of 1906, C.B. seemed at the summit of his career. In fact, his private life was filled with anguish and exhaustion. His wife, his comrade and advisor of forty-six years, was dying. Charlotte Campbell had always had mixed feelings about her husband's political career. She was ambitious for him and fiercely defensive when he was attacked. "Henry is a good man," she declared, "how good no one knows but myself." But ambition mingled with resentment of the amount of time his career took him away from her. She disliked the minutiae of politics and rarely was seen in the House Gallery even when her husband was speaking. Her possessiveness grew stronger as she succumbed to a painful nervous disease. Increasingly, Campbell-Bannerman was forced to choose between his public duties and care for his wife. Away from her, he was troubled by the knowledge that she was at home, lying on a bed or a chaise longue, her eyes fixed on the clock, counting the minutes until he returned. More and more, as leader of the opposition, then Prime Minister, he would fail to return to the House after dinner, sending a note that his wife's health required him to be with her.

In 1902, Lady Campbell-Bannerman, whose weight was over 250 pounds, suffered a stroke which left her partially paralyzed. The move into 10 Downing Street in January 1906 was a trial, but she managed to give a large party for her husband on the eve of the opening of Parliament. Unable to stand, she sat propped up for two hours, making herself agreeable to a crowd of guests. Through the spring and summer, her health deteriorated. She disliked professional nurses and would take food and medicine only from her husband's hands. Whenever she called, he rose and sat with her, through the night if necessary. One night that summer, his own worsening health compelled him to spend an entire night apart. "How strange to have spent a whole night in bed," he wrote. "It has not happened to me for six months." In the mornings, he fell asleep over his government papers.

In August 1906, they decided to risk the journey to Marienbad. They traveled slowly, in easy stages, arriving on the thirteenth. Lady Campbell-Bannerman was exhausted but happy. The King came on August 16, accompanied by the beau monde and a swarm of journalists. For two weeks, the Prime Minister was obliged to attend upon the sovereign at lunches, dinners, and teas, always hurrying back to bring news and gossip to his invalid. When she worsened, the Prime Minister began taking meals in a sitting room next to her bedroom. The door was ajar and, in the course of a meal, she called two or three times. Each time, he sprang up and hurried to her side. August 30 was a blazing summer afternoon, silent in the heat except for the clicking of horses' hooves in the street below and the sound of labored breathing from the dying woman. At five o'clock she died.

The King, sitting on the balcony of his own hotel suite, took a pen and wrote: "I know how great your mutual devotion was and what a blank the departed one will leave in your home. Still, I feel sure that you can now only wish that your beloved wife may be at peace and rest, and free from all further suffering and pain."

Campbell-Bannerman carried on for less than two years. In public, he tried to be cheerful, but a friend, seeing him talking and laughing with his guests, would go upstairs later to find the Prime Minister with his head in his hands, sobbing. His own body was spent. On November 13, Campbell-Bannerman collapsed in Bristol. His doctors commanded six weeks of complete rest and the Prime Minister decided to go to Biarritz. On the way, he suffered another heart attack in Paris and was forced to pause while his doctor came from London. Moving to Biarritz, he remained until mid-January, when he returned to London. There, a friend reported that he "seemed to have recovered all his old buoyancy and energy." On February 12, 1908, Campbell-Bannerman made his last speech in the House of Commons. That night, he was stricken again and taken to his bedroom at Number 10. He did not leave this room until his death ten weeks later. The King, the Queen, and the Prince of Wales visited him as he sat by the window in Downing Street. Leaving for a royal gathering in Copenhagen, the King asked to be kept constantly informed of the Prime Minister's condition. "Don't telegraph to 'The King,' " the monarch instructed. "There will be so many kings about. Telegraph to 'King Edward.' "

For two months, the Cabinet marked time, postponing important decisions and looking increasingly to Asquith, the designated heir. On March 27, the Prime Minister sent for the Chancellor to tell him that he meant to resign. "You are a wonderful colleague," he said to Asquith, "so loyal, so disinterested, so able. You are the greatest gentleman I have ever met." His parting words were optimistic: "This is not the last of me. We will meet again, Asquith." On April 1, the Prime Minister sent his resignation to the King in Biarritz. On April 3, the King accepted. Campbell-Bannerman died on the morning of April 22, 1908.

CHAPTER 30

The
Asquiths,
Henry and Margot

◆

Herbert Henry Asquith's beginnings were more modest than those of any prime minister before him. He was born in 1852, the son of a wool merchant in a Yorkshire village. When Herbert* was eight, his father twisted an intestine in a village cricket game and, a few hours later, died. From the age of twelve, Asquith lived as a paying boarder with families in London so that he could attend a better school. As a student, he excelled. "[The school] simply . . . put the ladder before him and up he went," said his headmaster. At seventeen, Asquith won a Classical Scholarship to Balliol. His arrival coincided with Benjamin Jowett's first term as master of the college and Jowett, who had a keen eye for potential, kept Asquith under close scrutiny. Asquith devoted himself to the Oxford Union. He spoke in almost every political debate, became president, and changed the society's rules so that smoking was permitted and afternoon tea served. In spite of this distraction, Asquith

---

* Until he was forty, Asquith was known to his family and friends as Herbert. His second wife, Margot Tennant, called him Henry. Throughout his life, Asquith always referred to himself as H. H. Asquith, even signing letters to his mother in this fashion when he was nine.

in 1874 was the only Balliol man to take First Class Honors in Classics.

Asquith could have remained at Oxford as a don, but this was not his ambition. He moved to London and began to prepare for the bar. Without money and with no social connections, Asquith plunged into marriage at twenty-five and quickly became a father. To supplement his meager earnings from the law, he regularly wrote for the Liberal weeklies, *The Spectator* and *The Economist.* He wrote lead articles, mostly on politics, but could move into other arenas—economics, literature, social customs—without losing facility.

One night in 1881, at a dinner at Lincoln's Inn, Asquith sat next to another young barrister, also a moderate Liberal with political ambition. Richard Burdon Haldane, a Scot four years younger than Asquith, who became Asquith's closest friend and strongest political ally, had studied in Germany, where he had acquired fluency in the language and a strong taste for German philosophy. Haldane had the private money that Asquith lacked. The two dined together at a restaurant two or three times a week; afterwards Asquith returned to his family. Haldane often came home with Asquith and was a favorite with his wife and children. Haldane admired his friend's strengths and noted his weaknesses. Asquith, said Haldane, had "the best intellectual apparatus, understanding and judgement that I ever saw in any man," but he was better at explaining than creating. "Asquith did not originate much," Haldane continued. "He was not a man of imagination, but when we had worked anything out we always chose him to state it for us—a thing he did to perfection." On one point, Asquith was consistently clear: "We were both rising at the Bar, but to Asquith eminence in the law at no time presented any attraction," Haldane recalled. "From the beginning, he meant to be Prime Minister."

It was Haldane who first persuaded Asquith to run for Parliament. Haldane himself had been elected to the House of Commons in 1885 and the following year urged his friend to seek election from the Scottish constituency of East Fife. Asquith was elected by a narrow margin and continued to represent these electors for thirty-two years. When he gave his maiden speech in March 1887, members on both sides were struck by his self-confidence, authority, and eloquence. "His diction was even then faultless," said an admiring Haldane. Mr. Gladstone was less impressed; when asked whether he thought young Asquith's oratory would carry him to political greatness, the Liberal leader shook his head. "Too forensic," he said. Nevertheless, five years later, when Gladstone embarked on his fourth and last Cabinet, he named Asquith, at forty, to be Home Secretary. On August 18, 1892, the new ministers went to Osborne House to receive the seals of office from the Queen. Crossing the Solent from Portsmouth, the incoming Liberal ministers passed another boat carrying the outgoing Unionist ministers back to Portsmouth; both groups raised their hats in silent salute. On that occasion, Queen Victoria did not speak to the new Home Secretary, but recorded in her diary that he seemed "an intelligent, rather good-looking man." Soon after, Asquith was summoned back to Osborne for dinner and overnight, and this time the Queen noted that she had "had a conversation with Mr. Asquith whom I thought pleasant, straight-forward and sensible."

Asquith's ascent to the Cabinet had been accompanied by years of domestic tranquillity. At eighteen, he fell in love at the seashore with a fifteen-year-old girl, Helen Melland, the daughter of a successful Manchester physician. They wrote to each other regularly, and, four years later, while he was still at Balliol, secretly became engaged. In 1877, when he was twenty-five and she twenty-two, they married. Asquith's earnings as a barrister and her small income from her father permitted the purchase of a white-walled house, set in a garden in Hampstead, which remained their home for fourteen years. Helen Melland was a tall, brown-haired, attractive woman. "A beautiful and simple spirit," remembered Haldane. "No one would have called her clever or 'intellectual,' " said her husband. "What gave her her rare quality was her character." She was "selfless and unworldly . . . warm . . . and generous." At one point, still struggling at the bar, he expressed his love by spending £300 to buy her a diamond necklace.

Helen Asquith was happy with life in Hampstead. Five children arrived over nine years and while her husband worked over his legal briefs and went to the House of Commons—sometimes dining with friends and returning home late—she supervised his home and family. As the years passed, he changed; she did not. Asquith's career brought him onto the fringes of society. Invitations arrived; he was pleased, Helen dismayed. At first, Asquith was not socially adept; it was noticed that, on going in to dinner, he offered his arm to his own wife. He corrected these flaws, developing an appreciation for fine wines and a talent for small talk with titled ladies. His wife had no such appreciation or talent. Society, curious about the new couple, commented on his ambition and her reluctance. In a word, Helen was seen as holding her husband back.

One observer of the Asquith marriage was the tempestuous, extravagantly social Margot Tennant, a member of the Souls and a passionate admirer of Arthur Balfour's. "When I discovered that he [Asquith] was married," Margot later wrote, "I asked him to bring his wife to dinner, which he did, and directly I saw her I said: 'I do hope, Mrs. Asquith, you have not minded your husband dining here without you, but I rather gathered Hampstead was too far away for him to get back to you from the House of Commons. You must always let me know and come with him whenever it suits you.'

". . . She was so different from me that I had a longing for her approval. She was gentle, pretty and unambitious, and spoke to me of her home and children with a love and interest that seemed to exclude her from a life of political aggrandizement which was what from early days had captured my imagination. . . .

"I was anxious that she should . . . know my friends, but after a week-end spent at Taplow with Lord and Lady Desborough [Margot Tennant's sister and brother-in-law] where everyone liked her, she told me that though she had enjoyed her visit she did not think that she would ever care for the sort of society that I loved, and was happier in the circle of her home and family. When I said that she had married a man who was certain to attain the highest political distinction, she replied that that was not what she coveted for him. Driving back from Hampstead where we had been alone together, I wondered if my ambition for the success of her husband . . . was wrong."

Margot Tennant's friendship with Helen Asquith was brief. In September 1891, while on vacation in Scotland, Helen Asquith contracted typhoid fever. She died within three weeks. Asquith returned to Hampstead with five motherless children. The eldest, Raymond, was twelve; the youngest was eighteen months old.

Before his first wife died, Asquith felt an attraction for Margot Tennant. In her memoirs, she described the scene of their first encounter: "The dinner where I was introduced to my husband was in the House of Commons and I sat next to him. I was deeply impressed by his conversation and his clear Cromwellian face. He was different from the others and, although abominably dressed, had so much personality that I made up my mind at once that here was a man who could help me and would understand everything. It never crossed my brain that he was married, nor would that have mattered. . . .

"After dinner we all walked on the Terrace and I was flattered to find my new friend by my side. . . . [We] retired to the darkest part of the Terrace, where, leaning over the parapet, we gazed into the river and talked far into the night.

"Our host and his party—thinking that I had gone home and

that Mr. Asquith had returned to the House when the division bell rang—had disappeared; and when we finished our conversation the Terrace was deserted and the sky light.

"We met a few days later dining with Sir Algernon West . . . and after this we saw each other constantly."

Margot already had made up her mind. After the first night on the Terrace she told her sister Lady Ribblesdale: "Asquith is the only kind of man that I could ever have married—all the others are so much waste paper." Only a month after Helen's death, Asquith and Margot began to write long and intimate letters. "You tell me not to stop loving you as if you thought I had done or would or could do so," Asquith wrote.

Margot Tennant was the daughter of Sir Charles Tennant, a wealthy Lowland Scottish baronet, whose three daughters had stormed London society. Margot, the most articulate and provocative, also had a reputation as a horsewoman. She was not beautiful; her own word portrait of herself serves best: "Small, rapid, nervous, restless, her eyes close together, a hawky nose, short upper lip, large, bony, prominent chin . . . conversation graphic and exaggerated . . . highest vitality, great self-confidence . . . warm-hearted, fond of people, animals, books, sport, music, exercise . . . intellectually self-made, ambitious, independent and self-willed . . . fond of admiration from both men and women and able to give it . . . Loves old people because she never feels they are old. . . ."

Many of Margot's happiest moments were on horseback. "I ride better than most people," she announced, "and have spent or wasted more time on it than any woman of intellect ought to." Across the rural counties of England, she cleared fences and hedges, helping to kill as many as three foxes a day. The pleasure was not without cost: "I have broken both collar-bones, all my ribs and my kneecap, gashed my nose and had five concussions of the brain," she declared. Once, astride a horse while waiting for her father in front of his house on Grosvenor Square, an impatient Margot rode up the front steps into the front hall, where the animal's legs gave way on the marble floor. Horse and rider collapsed—both, this time, unhurt.

In society, Margot Tennant was equally impulsive. Sitting next to Randolph Churchill at dinner, she told the former Chancellor, "I am afraid you resigned more out of temper than conviction, Lord Randolph." "Confound your cheek!" said the astonished Churchill. "What do you know about me and my convictions?" Nevertheless, provoked, he went on: "I hate Salisbury. He jumped at my resignation like a dog at a bone." By the end of the evening, Margot had conquered Lord Randolph. He invited her to a supper for the Prince of Wales. Determined to shock, she arrived in a white muslin dress with a transparent chemise. "Do look at Miss Tennant!" tittered the other women. "She is in her nightgown!" Margot overheard and, when the Prince arrived, immediately told him what was being said. The Prince asked her to sit next to him at supper.

Margot Tennant's intelligence was quick, perfect for word games and brittle repartee. At eighty, Gladstone wrote her a poem and left her father in the drawing room to come to her bedroom for a talk. Tennyson read his poems to her. Skilled at verbal jousting, she was ruthless with fashionable women who challenged her. Lady Londonderry once thought to unseat Margot by saying to her before an audience, "I am afraid you have not read the book." "I am afraid, Lady Londonderry, you have not read the preface," replied Margot. "The book is dedicated to me."

It was not easy for Margot to decide whom to marry. When she met Asquith she was twenty-seven; ten London seasons had passed and she still was not ready to choose. She idolized Arthur Balfour and at one point there were rumors that Balfour and Margot were engaged. Balfour disposed of them quickly. "I hear you are going to marry Margot Tennant," a friend said to him. "No, that is not so," Balfour replied. "I rather think of having a career of my own." Margot's most serious suitor appealed to the outdoor side of her nature. Peter Flower, a younger brother of Lord Battersea, was handsome and charming, a famous amateur boxer, and one of the best horsemen in England. They met when he rushed to her side after she fell from a horse. Margot wrote to Peter every day for nine years and finally agreed to an engagement. "I will marry you, Peter, if you get some serious occupation," she said. "But I won't marry an idle man." Peter Flower could not reform. He continued to gamble and waste money until, eventually, to avoid his creditors, he sold his horses and moved to India.

Asquith was different. And yet she kept him waiting for two years while she made up her mind. He continued his pursuit. He kneeled with her and prayed at the grave of her sister Laura, who had died in childbirth. To a note she sent him in the House of Commons, he replied, "This afternoon as I sat on the Treasury Bench answering questions, I got your telegram and read it furtively, and crammed it hastily into my trousers pocket, until I could get out of the House and read it over and over again in my little room."

When it came, the news that the brilliant Liberal Home Secretary was going to marry the vivid Margot Tennant amused and alarmed London society. His friends worried that marrying so frivolous a person as Margot would ruin his career; her friends were concerned that taking on a man who disliked hunting and outdoor games, and who had five children, would extinguish Margot's spirit. Margot herself had turned the idea over and over: "I was filled with profound misgivings when I realized that the man whose friendship was what I valued most on earth wanted to marry me. Groping as I had been for years to find a character and intellect superior to my own, I did not feel equal to facing it when I found it. . . . I realised the natural prejudice that all children since the beginning of the world must have against stepmothers. . . ." Jowett, Margot's friend as well as Asquith's, had warned her that she would have to change. He saw her, he had written to her, as a young woman who "wastes her time and her gifts scampering from one country house to another . . . she has made a great position, though slippery and dangerous." Specifically, he warned, "It is not possible to be a leader of fashion and to do your duty to the five children."

Margot decided that Jowett was wrong and her own misgivings unfounded. She married Asquith on May 10, 1894, at St. George's Church in Hanover Square. The first meeting of the Rosebery Cabinet was postponed in order not to clash with the ceremony. Haldane served as best man, and four prime ministers, past, present, and future, were on hand: Gladstone, Rosebery, Balfour, and Asquith himself. The family moved into a comfortable house at 20 Cavendish Square, which, except for the eight years in Downing Street, they occupied for a quarter of a century. As Margot had calculated, it was Asquith's life, not hers, that changed. Fourteen servants at Cavendish Street were kept busy with luncheon and dinner parties. The Asquiths were guests at dinners, summer balls, and weekend house parties. Asquith fitted in smoothly and seemed to enjoy himself. He balked only at riding and hunting. Soon after his marriage to Margot, he went deer hunting for the first and only time. "I fired two shots and killed two stags," he wrote. "Content with this proof of my prowess, I put by my rifle and have never used it since. I believe I still hold the record among deer stalkers of never having fired a shot without killing my quarry."

When the Rosebery Cabinet left office, beginning the long decade of Salisbury-Balfour Unionist rule, Asquith went back to the bar, mixing law with service in the House of Commons. Cavendish Square and the social pace which Margot set required money, and Asquith brought in between £5,000 and £10,000 a year.

As a former Cabinet Minister and Privy Councillor, he outranked most of the judges before whom he appeared and he could afford a touch of irreverence. "Supposing I were to give you an area marked by meridians of longitude. Would that constitute a place, Mr. Asquith?" asked Mr. Justice Wright. "That, my Lord," Asquith shot back, "would be merely a matter of degree."

Asquith disapproved of the Jameson Raid. "An adventure more childishly conceived or more clumsily executed it is impossible to imagine," he said. When the captured raiders were brought to London for trial, he condemned their reception: "Having done by their blundering folly as great a disservice as it is possible to render . . . to the best interests of the Empire, [they] were, on their arrival in England, acclaimed and fêted by a section of London society as the worthy successors of Drake and Raleigh." Curiously, two members of that section of London society were Mr. and Mrs. Asquith. "Dr. Jim had personal magnetism and could do what he liked with my sex," Margot confessed. "My husband and I met the Doctor first —a week or ten days before his trial and sentence—at Georgina Lady Dudley's house; and the night before he went to prison he dined with us alone at Cavendish Square." In these early years, Margot proved Jowett wrong by establishing a good relationship with Asquith's five children, particularly Raymond. She lost her own first baby in May 1895 and, eventually, two others. Two children, Elizabeth, born in 1897, and Anthony, born in 1902, survived.

During ten years in opposition, Asquith's political reputation continued to grow. In 1898, when Lord Rosebery resigned the party leadership and Sir William Harcourt declined to accept it, there remained only Campbell-Bannerman and Asquith. Asquith had youth and energy, and was far more effective as a speaker, but ruled himself out because he was poor. Margot did not give up so easily. She wrote to Arthur Balfour, asking him to persuade her wealthy father to make Asquith independent of the bar. Balfour, although he was leader of the Unionist Party in the Commons, agreed and wrote to Sir Charles Tennant that the greatest position in the Liberal Party was within his son-in-law's reach, but that Asquith could not compete without jeopardizing Margot's comfort. "No man can lead either the Opposition or the House of Commons if he is tied by a profession. A party may not give much but it claims everything," Balfour urged. Sir Charles refused. He was a dedicated Liberal and believed in seniority and precedence. Campbell-Bannerman was sixteen years older than Asquith, had served longer in the Cabinet, and was entitled to the leadership. He, Tennant, would do nothing to obstruct this natural succession. Asquith accepted C.B.'s leadership until they were separated by the Boer War. Even then, he maintained politeness and respect. During the "war to the knife—and fork" over C.B.'s "methods of barbarism" speech, Asquith said publicly, "There is nothing in the world so uncongenial to me as to enter on any kind of public disputation with an old friend and colleague by whose side I have often fought in the past and by whose side I hope to fight again in the future." Even Asquith's part in the Relugas Compact was excused (the more easily, no doubt, because C.B. triumphed).

As Chancellor of the Exchequer in Campbell-Bannerman's Cabinet, Asquith introduced two budgets and powerfully supported his chief in parliamentary warfare. (Asquith once described one of his own speeches as one "to which I can fairly say no answer was possible.") C.B.'s command, on occasions when Balfour was shredding a Liberal argument in debate, was "Go and bring the sledgehammer." Thus summoned, Asquith appeared in the House to reply.

In March 1908, when the King was leaving for Biarritz, the Prime Minister, Sir Henry Campbell-Bannerman, was dying at 10 Downing Street. Before he left, King Edward told Asquith that if anything happened to C.B., he meant to send for the Chancellor. On April 1, the Prime Minister sent a letter of resignation to the King; on April 4 the sovereign wrote to Asquith, asking him to form a government and to come to Biarritz to kiss hands. The following day, this news was across London and sixty reporters waited outside the house on Cavendish Square. Asquith remained secluded until the night of the sixth, when, after dinner, he left his house in secret, drove to Charing Cross Station, and took the nine o'clock boat train to Paris. Traveling alone, wearing a thick overcoat and a cap pulled down over his eyes, he eluded pursuit. In Biarritz, he put on a frock coat and called on the King who, in deference to his doctors, had taken a ground-floor suite at the Hôtel du Palais to avoid the strain of climbing stairs. In King Edward's reception room, Asquith accepted the commission as Prime Minister, kissed the monarch's hand,* and went to lunch in the next room. King Edward spoke genially to Asquith between bouts of bronchial coughing. That night, the new Prime Minister returned through driving rain to dine with the King and his vacation companions, Sir Ernest Cassel and Alice Keppel.

In Biarritz, Asquith gave the King the names of his new Cabinet. Most of Campbell-Bannerman's Cabinet would remain, but he

* It was an odd arrangement: The King of England, incognito as Duke of Lancaster, appointing a prime minister in a foreign hotel. *The Times* characterized it as "an inconvenient and dangerous departure from precedent."

would promote Lloyd George to Chancellor of the Exchequer. The resulting vacancy at the Board of Trade would be filled by thirty-four-year-old Winston Churchill. Lord Tweedmouth, increasingly erratic at the Admiralty, would be replaced by the efficient Reginald McKenna, the son of a London civil servant. The most significant of these changes was the promotion of Lloyd George to the number two position in the Liberal government. Originally, Asquith, having prepared but not yet introduced his third budget, had planned to continue as Chancellor in addition to serving as Premier, as Gladstone had done. He changed his mind in order to give the Cabinet political balance. With Asquith as Prime Minister, Grey as Foreign Secretary, and Haldane at the War Office, the Cabinet had lost the balance between Liberal Imperialists and Radical pacifists which C.B.'s position as Prime Minister had provided. The Radicals now feared that the imperialist wing of the party could act as it liked. To calm these fears, Asquith established Lloyd George, the ablest of the Radicals, at his side.

Asquith, during his eight years of Premiership, was determined to maintain a balance, to go down the center, not to stray to right or left. He always warmly supported Grey and Haldane, who remained his closest friends in the Cabinet, permitting Grey almost absolute authority over British foreign policy. But in Cabinet meetings, in the Commons, and on the stump, he was Everyman's leader. It was said of Asquith that he had no party within his own government. It was not that Asquith did not know his own mind. "Asquith was a man who knew where he stood on every question of life and affairs . . . scholarship, politics, law, philosophy and religion," wrote Churchill. "When the need required it, his mind opened and shut smoothly and exactly, like the breech of a gun . . . once he had heard the whole matter thrashed out, the conclusion came with a snap; and each conclusion, so far as lay with him, was final." Nor did Asquith shy from the ruthlessness required of those in power. "The first essential for a Prime Minister is to be a good butcher," Asquith said to Churchill when he offered Cabinet office to the younger man in 1908. "There are several who must be pole-axed now," he added. Time was a favorite instrument of Asquith's government. "The Right Honorable Gentleman must wait and see," was his frequent retort in Parliament. In Cabinet, where the gravity of an issue could lead to the resignation of important ministers or even the breakup of the government, Asquith ruled by postponement. "What we have heard today leaves much food for thought," he would say at the end of a meeting. "Let us all reflect before we meet again how we can bring ourselves together." He conducted Cabinet meetings as a chairman of the board, seeking consensus and effectiveness. "In Cabinet, he was markedly silent," Churchill said. "Indeed, he never spoke a word . . . if he could get his way without it. He sat, like the great Judge he was, hearing with trained patience the case deployed on every side, now and then interjecting a question or brief comment . . . which gave matters a turn towards the goal he wished to reach."

As a young man in the 1870s and 1880s, Asquith's recreation had lain in political discussion. Haldane, who had known the Asquith of Helen Melland and Hampstead, mildly disapproved of the change effected after his friend married Margot. "In his earlier days, Asquith was a very serious person," Haldane noted. "By degrees, particularly after his second marriage, he went more and more into society and was somewhat diverted from the sterner mode of life with which he and I were familiar." By the time he was Prime Minister, Asquith made absolute distinction between work and play. "He disliked 'talking shop' out of business hours," Churchill said. "With Asquith, either the Court was open or it was shut. If it was shut, there was no use knocking on the door. . . . When work was done, he played . . . he delighted in feminine society; he was always interested to meet a new and charming personality. Women of every age were eager to be taken in to dinner by him. They were fascinated by his gaiety and wit, and by his evident interest in all their doings."

In 1908, when he became Prime Minister, Asquith was fifty-six, Margot forty-four. Over the years, a distance had appeared between them. Childbirth was difficult and dangerous for her and she spent months recovering. "For many years after my first confinement, I was a delicate woman," she wrote. She suffered severe insomnia. "No one who has not experienced . . . real sleeplessness can imagine what this means," she said. "Insomnia is akin to insanity." Her last surviving child, Anthony, was born in 1902, but she lost another at birth in 1907. In 1908, "when my husband became Prime Minister, I went to St. Paul's Cathdral and prayed that I might die rather than hamper his life as an invalid." The vivacious and indefatigable Margot, the brilliant conversationalist of the Souls who had kept the young Home Secretary up until dawn on the terrace of the House of Commons, did not enjoy the subordinate role of a politician's—even a prime minister's—wife. When, in her presence, he repeated old stories for new audiences, she was visibly bored. "I am horribly impatient and it is only by strong self-control that I ever listen at all," she admitted in 1905. She offered advice to everyone, requested or not. "Margot I find rather trying as a visitor," said

Pamela McKenna. "She criticizes everything incessantly . . . and always in the unkindest way." She departed from gatherings "leaving a wake of injured and weeping people." Ironically, as Asquith turned away from political discussion as recreation, Margot found it increasingly fascinating. He came home from his desk or the House of Commons to a political gadfly. "I have sometimes walked up and down that room till I felt as though I was going mad," he told his daughter Violet, describing his home life. "When one needed rest, to have a thing like the *Morning Post* leader flung at one—all the obvious reasons for and against more controversially put even than by one's colleagues." Violet's sympathetic reaction to her father's complaints strained her own relationship with Margot. In 1909, Asquith wrote to Margot, "It is a grief to me that the two women I care for most should be on terms of chronic misunderstanding."

Asquith admitted "a slight weakness for the companionship of clever and attractive women" and found relief in their society. At dinner parties, on weekends at country houses, the Prime Minister would often be found flirting, holding hands, and playing bridge late at night with young women charmed to be noticed by the most influential political figure in the land. Margot refrained from objection and even declared that Henry needed his "little harem" to take his mind from his work.

In 1912, at sixty, Asquith fell in love, perhaps more completely than he ever had been with Helen Melland or Margot Tennant, with Venetia Stanley, twenty-six. Venetia, the youngest daughter of Lord Sheffield, a Liberal nobleman, and a first cousin of Clementine Churchill, was a contemporary and close friend of Asquith's daughter Violet; she was a frequent guest at 10 Downing Street. Venetia was tall, with dark eyes and a strong nose and face; a young male friend described her as "a splendid, virginal, comradely creature" with "a masculine intellect." She was widely read and vaguely eccentric; she kept as pets a bear cub, a penguin, and a fox. In 1910 and 1911, Asquith wrote occasionally to Venetia, unburdening himself of some of the cares of daily life. In February 1912, she accompanied him and Violet on a Sicilian holiday. Later that spring, on a Sunday morning, he and Venetia were sitting in the dining room of a country house "talking and laughing just in our old accustomed terms . . . Suddenly," he wrote in notes for a never-published autobiography, "in a single instant without premonition on my part or any challenge on hers, the scales dropped from my eyes; the familiar features and smile and gestures and words assumed an absolutely new perspective; what had been completely hidden from me was in a flash half-revealed, and I dimly felt, hardly knowing, not at all understanding it, that I had come to a turning point in my life."

Over the next three years, the Prime Minister wrote 560 letters —over 300,000 words—to Venetia Stanley.* Most of the letters were on paper emblazoned "10 Downing Street," although they were written from many different places. By 1914, the letters began "My darling," "My own darling," or "My own most beloved." He declared his love and need, and begged for a sign that she returned his passion: "You have given me, and continue to give me, the supreme happiness of my life." "Without you, I must often have failed, and more than once gone down. You have sustained and enriched every day of my life." He also wrote about literature and politics, gossiped about society, and described in intimate detail meetings of the Cabinet and War Council.

By July 1914, Asquith's love for Venetia dominated his thoughts; he signed one letter: "Your lover—for all time." During the deadlock over Ulster and the crisis preceding the war, he wrote to her two or three times a day, sometimes during Cabinet meetings, sometimes while sitting on the front bench of the House of Commons. On Fridays, he took her for drives in his chauffeured car. Occasionally, in the early evening, he would call on her at her parents' London house. There seems to have been no physical intimacy; Asquith described in 1915 what Venetia meant to him:

"Darling—shall I tell you what you have been and are to me? First, outwardly and physically unapproachable and unique. Then, in temperament and character, often baffling and elusive, but always more interesting and attractive and compelling than any woman I have ever seen or known. In solid intellect, and real insight into all situations, great or small, incomparably first. And above all, and beyond all, in the intimacy of perfect confidence and understanding, for two years past, the pole star and lode-star of my life."

Asquith's obsession did not escape notice. Lady Sheffield, Venetia's mother, worried about her daughter's involvement with the married Prime Minister and had planned in August 1914 to send Venetia on a lengthy Mediterranean tour; war intervened. Margot knew about Venetia. Although, years later, she wrote, "No woman should expect to be the only woman in her husband's life," at the time she was deeply wounded. Venetia, she said, was "a woman without refinement or any imagination whatever." As for her hus-

* Asquith's letters to Venetia were discovered by her daughter after her death in 1948. Venetia's letters to Asquith have never been found.

band: "I'm far too fond of H. to show him how ill and miserable it makes me." "Oh," she cried, "if only Venetia would marry."

In the middle of May 1915, the relationship ended abruptly when Venetia told Asquith that she had accepted the proposal of Edwin Montagu, one of the Prime Minister's former private secretaries. Montagu had proposed to Venetia in 1912 and been turned down. Early in 1915, she changed her mind. Even so, she continued to write to Asquith for three months until, at Montagu's insistence, she admitted the truth. Venetia renounced Asquith reluctantly. "Why can't I marry you and yet go on making him happy?" she pleaded with Montagu. "But neither of you think that fun and I suppose my suggesting it or thinking it possible shows to you how peculiar I am emotionally." Once her decision was made, she looked back on the three years that had ended and said, "I know quite well that if it hadn't been me it would have been someone else or a series of others."

CHAPTER 31

Sir Edward Grey
and Liberal
Foreign Policy

◆

Sir Edward Grey was a country man. He regarded the Foreign Office, where he spent eleven years as Foreign Secretary, as a dungeon from which he escaped on weekends to the sunlit glades of the New Forest or to the waters of a Hampshire trout stream. At his desk, he worked with devotion but without joy; he preferred talking about the majesty of Handel or the beauty of Wordsworth to talking about the balance of power or the Triple Alliance. He left Britain only once during his term of office, and spoke only a few phrases of primitive French, but he was the greatest British Foreign Secretary of the century.

Grey was the junior conspirator of the Relugas Compact trio. He was born in 1862, ten years after Asquith, six years after Haldane. His roots were at Fallodon, the family estate in Northumberland near the Scottish border, within sight of the North Sea. His grandfather, Sir George Grey, was a country baronet who spent forty years in the House of Commons and served as Home Secretary in the Liberal Cabinets of Lord John Russell and Viscount Palmerston. Grey's father was a retired colonel who fought in the Crimean War and the Indian Mutiny and then continued for fifteen years as one of the Prince of Wales' rotating equerries. During one period of attendance on the Prince, Colonel Grey suddenly died of pneumonia at Sandringham. He left his wife with seven children; Edward, twelve, was the eldest. Sir George Grey promptly retired from Parliament and assumed a paternal role with his fatherless grandchildren.

At fourteen, Edward Grey went to Winchester. He was marked by his skill at Greek and Latin and by his desire to be alone. He was an exceptional tennis player and cricketer, but preferred to wander off to the river Itchen, which flowed past the school playing fields. There, the distant schoolboy shouts were erased by the babble of the water and Grey lost himself casting his fly between the reeds. From Winchester, Grey went to Balliol, where he led a life "of pure pleasure . . . it led to nothing but left no scars, nothing to be regretted or effaced." When he was twenty, his grandfather died, leaving him the baronetcy, the Fallodon estate of two thousand acres, and responsibility for his mother and younger brothers and sisters. He still did no work and in 1884 was sent down by Jowett. "Sir Edward Grey," wrote the Master of Balliol, "having been repeatedly admonished for idleness, and having shown himself entirely ignorant of the work set him during the vacation, was sent down." Grey returned to Fallodon, where, left to himself, he began to read the books he had ignored at Oxford. At the end of the term, he returned to Balliol, took his examinations, and won an undistinguished degree.*

Eighteen months after leaving the university, Grey married a Northumberland squire's daughter, Dorothy Widdrington, whom he had met at a shooting party. She, like Grey, was a proud, interior person, uneasy in society. Her mind was subtle and worked rapidly; she judged questions on their merits "in the clear, cold light of reason." She was as disdainful of cant as she was of trivia. "Her downright question 'Why?' often startled and almost terrified a careless talker." Grey, whose stern exterior belied an inner gentleness, depended on Dorothy. A few weeks before their marriage, he wrote to her: "I believe, however busy, however active, however flustered a man may be with the battle of life, he is always looking for some place where he may lay his inner heart, his soft and tender nature, in safety; else there is danger that he may lose it altogether or find it injured in the rough struggle. Such a place he finds in a woman, and when he really loves, he confides it all to her freely without reserve." They had no children and were content; each wrote to the other every day they were apart.

* Forty-four years later, in 1928, Sir Edward Grey was elected chancellor of Oxford University.

In November 1886, a month after his marriage, Grey, twenty-three, won a seat in the House of Commons, defeating a Percy from the clan which had been lords of Northumberland since the Middle Ages. Soon after Grey's arrival in Parliament, Gladstone split the Liberal Party over Home Rule. During the next six years of opposition, Grey met Asquith and Haldane and formed lasting friendships and a lifelong political alliance.

In 1892, Gladstone returned to Downing Street for the fourth and last time. Grey was selected by the Foreign Secretary, Lord Rosebery, as Parliamentary Under Secretary for Foreign Affairs. He had no previous experience, training, or special interest in foreign affairs, but, in the parliamentary system, expertise is supplied, not by the politicians who move in and out of senior government offices, but by the permanent civil servants who function at a level just below. Grey had no say in the making of policy; his assignment —Rosebery was in the House of Lords—was to explain and defend the government's policy in the Commons. The House soon noticed that when Grey spoke it was with precision and authority. The most important of his statements was made on March 28, 1895. Rumors had reached London that France was preparing an expedition across Africa to the headwaters of the Nile. Great Britain claimed predominance over this region for Egypt and herself. "I cannot think it possible these rumors deserve credence," Grey told the House, "because the advance of a French expedition under secret instructions right from the other side of Africa into a territory over which our claims have been known for so long, would not be merely an inconsistent and unexpected act, but it must be perfectly well-known to the French Government that it would be an unfriendly act, and would be so viewed by England." Joseph Chamberlain immediately rose from the Opposition Bench to declare that what Grey had said was "the fullest and clearest statement of the policy of the Government with regard to this subject that we have yet had from a responsible Minister." In fact, Grey's statement—which came to be known in diplomatic history as the "Grey Declaration"—had not been approved by the Cabinet. The morning after, it was the subject of a lively debate at 10 Downing Street. Lord Rosebery, then Prime Minister, eventually won endorsement of Grey's position against the opposition of ministers who felt that Britain had no business on the Upper Nile, or, indeed, in Egypt.

In 1895, Lord Rosebery's government fell over the question of the supply of cordite and the Liberal Party stepped aside for another ten years of Unionist rule. Grey was not unhappy to leave office. "There was no pleasure for me in the House of Commons work," he wrote. "I could express clearly to others what I had previously made clear to my own mind, but beyond that there was no natural gift for speaking." Grey remained in Parliament between 1895 and 1906, but, out of office, he was able to devote more time to private life.

The appeal of a peaceful life, primarily a life spent amidst nature, was at war with political ambition in both Edward and Dorothy Grey. In 1893, when Grey was Under Secretary at the Foreign Office, Dorothy explored the subject for three hours with Haldane. At the end, Haldane went away saying, "I understand at last. You must not stay in politics. It is hurting your lives. It is bad." Dorothy immediately wrote to Edward at the House of Commons: "I . . . said that if we went on crushing our natural sympathies we should probably end by destroying our married life, because the basis and atmosphere of its beauty would be taken away and it would die. . . . He [Haldane] said he had felt in himself how much your unhappiness in office made it difficult to talk to you or be intimate, and that he had been feeling there was no spring or heart in either of us. . . . We talked for a long time, he arguing in favor of giving up politics and I against it, and I believe he had the best of it. I was quite touched by him; we must be nice to our Haldane. He thinks now that it would be quite reasonable if you resigned at once, though I told him we had no idea of that." Haldane stuck to his view only a few months. Before long, he was writing to Dorothy: "The one blow that I should feel a heavy and even a crushing one would be that Edward should leave politics. For me it would rob the outlook of much of its hope and meaning. I think his presence is of the . . . [greatest] importance to the Liberal Party. And how much I believe in that Liberal Party and in the work we have to do, you know." The issue was to perplex Grey all his life: on the one hand, he believed that the best life possible lay in contemplation of God's world of nature; on the other, his stern sense, stemming from a Whig ancestry, of duty to party and country, forbade him the naturalist's life he craved.

They found a solution in compromise. From the moment they arrived in London, Edward and Dorothy Grey agreed that town life was "intensely distasteful." Needing a refuge, and finding Northumberland and Fallodon too distant for weekends, Grey recalled the rippling, trout-filled waters of the river Itchin flowing past the playing fields of Winchester. He and Dorothy acquired half an acre of meadow sloping down to the stream and built a small weekend cottage of brick and wood. Buried in roses, it became a haven and sanctuary. Nothing was allowed to intrude; politics were banished and weekend invitations refused. "The cottage became dearer to us than Fallodon itself," Grey wrote. "It was something special and sacred, outside the normal stream of life." There were no servants; a village woman came across the fields on weekends to clean and cook. This style of life met Grey's definition of luxury: "that of having everything that we did want and nothing that we did not want."

In London during the spring and summer, Grey and his wife waited eagerly for Saturday mornings. On Saturdays, they rose by alarm clock, left their house on Grosvenor Road at five-thirty A.M., walked across Lambeth Bridge, and took a six o'clock train from Waterloo Station. By eight A.M. they were having breakfast in their cottage. On midsummer Saturdays, Grey fished from ten until two, and then again from seven until nine in the evening, when the river faded into dusk. He described these days as "an earthly paradise."

"The angler is by the river not later than ten o'clock: the stream is lively but quiet, and here and there the surface is broken by the recurring swirl of a swaying reed; but no life disturbs it. . . . Not a bird skims the surface of the water, not a fly is to be seen, not a sign of a living creature under it. But the fresh light air is like a caress, the warm sun shines interrupted only by the occasional passage of small, white clouds, the water meadows are bright with buttercups, and the woods and hedges that are on their borders are white with hawthorne blossoms or lit by the candelabra of horse-chestnut flower. Birds of many sorts, most notably blackbirds, are singing, and the angler in his hour of waiting has such entertainment as seems more than imperfect man can deserve or comprehend. Presently—it may be soon or not till after an hour or more—flies begin to appear on the surface of the water, the rise of a trout is seen; in a short time all is life and agitation. Trout are rising everywhere, some audibly, some without a sound; flies are hatching out all over the river, sitting or skipping in little flights on the water or rising into the air; a moving network of birds, swifts, swallows, and martins is on the river; a rush of bird life and the swish of the wings of the swifts is heard as they pass and repass up and down the stream; and the angler, no longer inert, is on his knees in the midst of it all, at convenient distance from a rising trout, one arm in constant action and the rod and line making a busy sound in the air as he dries and casts his fly. Now for two hours or more his life is energy, expectation, anxiety, resource and effort. . . ."

Sundays, Grey read, took walks, bicycled, or simply sat with Dorothy watching the birds. He was a serious reader and quoted with approval the story of a man happy in his country home when unexpected visitors were announced. The man greeted his visitors, declared that he was delighted to see them, and then said, "And now what would you like to do? We are reading." Both Greys were fascinated by birds: their diversity of plumage, their multifarious songs, their ability to fly. "If you will lie on your back on a fine day, you may see gulls sailing high in the air, without apparent effort or movement of wing, as though it was not necessary for them to descend at all," he marvelled. Dorothy Grey shared in everything. Sometimes, she fished beside her husband; more often she brought a book and alternated between reading and watching him fish. She was the keener and more expert bird-watcher. When Edward could not come to the cottage, she went alone, spending the entire weekend in solitude.

In March, Grey went to Scotland to fish for salmon. "The greatest of all sport in fly-fishing is that for spring salmon in a big river," he said. Beginning in October, he would lie awake in bed fishing in his imagination the deep pools where the salmon were resting on their passage up the river. A strong and undeniable pull from a salmon weighing fifteen, twenty, even thirty pounds was "one of the great moments of joy in life." The most memorable of these Highland fishing expeditions came in the late summer of 1905, when Grey leased Relugas House, which looked down on the wild gorge of the Findhorn River. Here, Dorothy wrote to Haldane, "in his few intervals indoors, he sits by a window which overlooks a good pool and murmurs, 'What a nice word *river* is!' "

It was the last blissful summer of Edward Grey's life. Three months after leaving Scotland, he was Foreign Secretary, embarked on an eleven-year journey. On February 1, 1906, five months after leaving the Highlands, two months after her husband had taken office, Dorothy Grey was at Fallodon waiting for her husband. She went for a drive alone, the horse shied, and she was thrown out of the small cart onto her head. She never regained consciousness. Grey was attending a meeting of the Committee of Imperial Defence when the telegram came. He took the night train from King's Cross and sat with her for forty hours before she died.

He was alone, but not deserted. His biographer writes: "The memories he amassed in those twenty years with Dorothy among the woods and the birds, or alone with his rod by the waters, were the capital on which he lived during the long years of his widowerhood, his grim struggle to guide the brute forces of Europe onto the paths of peace, and the blindness that mocked his final escape from office." Even as Edward Grey lost his sight, those memories did not dim. In his mind, he could still see "the luxuriance of water meadows, animated by insect and bird and trout life, tender

with the green and gay with the blossoms of early spring; the noble-
ness and volume of the great salmon rivers, the exhilaration of looking at any salmon pool, great or small; the rich brownness of
Highland water. . . . [An angler who has known these things] will
look back upon days radiant with happiness, peaks of enjoyment
that are not less bright because they are lit in memory by the light of
a setting sun."

Grey had no particular liking for foreign countries. Unlike Lord
Salisbury, Arthur Balfour, Joseph Chamberlain, or Sir Henry Campbell-Bannerman, all of whom relaxed by reading French novels, or
Richard B. Haldane, whose recreation lay in German philosophy
and literature, Grey preferred Wordsworth and George Eliot. Grey
never visited Marienbad, Biarritz, or the Riveria; he spoke no German and only a schoolboy French. In London, he avoided the society of foreign diplomats as he avoided society in general. At one
point, exhausted by a prolonged period of crisis, he retreated to
Fallodon. "I am alone here for a few days," he wrote to a friend. "I
like to be alone at first after a strenuous time. . . . My squirrels
come on to my writing table and take nuts from my hand as if I had
never been away. There is something restful in the unconsciousness
of animals—unconscious, that is, of all the things that matter so
much to us and do not matter at all to them."

For ten years, this reclusive man guided the foreign policy of
England. From Campbell-Bannerman, Grey was detached, politically and personally. He had opposed the Liberal leader during the
Boer War and he had joined in the awkward and unsuccessful effort
to force C.B. from the Commons to the Lords. In the twenty-seven
months of Campbell-Bannerman's Premiership, the two rarely saw
each other outside of Cabinet meetings. Nevertheless, C.B. and
Grey were in accord on the general lines of British foreign policy:
maintaining the Entente with France, endeavoring to reach a similar
agreement with Russia, and restraining German ambitions through
British naval supremacy while seeking a mutual lowering of levels of
naval armaments. As Prime Minister, Campbell-Bannerman left
these matters mostly in Grey's hands. When Asquith succeeded
C.B. in 1908, Premier and Foreign Secretary were personal friends
and trusted political allies. More even than C.B., Asquith left foreign policy to Grey. In the Cabinet and the Commons, Grey was the
government spokesman; Asquith intervened only to confirm and reinforce. Grey rarely consulted the Cabinet and even more rarely
spoke in the House; he spared the Prime Minister most details.

Grey based policy exclusively on what he perceived to be the interests of England. In 1895, when he was Parliamentary Under Secretary and the threat to those interests had come from France, Grey had firmly warned that Captain Marchand's expedition to the Nile headwaters would be viewed in England as an "unfriendly act." Nine years later, Grey—out of office—read the agreement Lord Lansdowne had negotiated with France with "a feeling of simple pleasure and relief . . . the menace of war with France had disappeared." Grey's attitude towards Germany was guided solely by how German policies affected England. He had learned early that dealing with the Wilhelmstrasse could be difficult. Soon after he became Under Secretary, British and German firms were competing for railway concessions in Anatolian Turkey. "Suddenly," said Grey, "there came a sort of ultimatum from Berlin requiring us to cease competition . . . and stating that unless we did so, the German consul in Cairo would withdraw support from the British Administration in Egypt. . . . [This was followed by] a despairing telegram from Lord Cromer [British agent in Egypt] pointing out that it would be impossible to carry out his work in Egypt without German support in the face of French and Russian opposition." In diplomacy, Grey admitted, one expects quid pro quos. But "it was the abrupt and rough peremptoriness of the German action that gave me an unpleasant surprise. . . . The method adopted by Germany in this instance was not one of a friend. There was no choice for us but to give way . . . but it left a sense of discomfort and bad taste behind." Thereafter, Grey regarded Britain's involvement on the Nile "like a noose round our neck . . . In this case, the noose had been roughly jerked by Germany."

Grey had been surprised and distressed by Holstein's and Bülow's bludgeoning attempt to shatter the new Anglo-French Entente when the Kaiser landed at Tangiers. During the months that followed in the summer and autumn of 1905, he sympathized with Lansdowne and the Unionist Cabinet. "The French were being humiliated because of an agreement we had made with them," he wrote later. "The agreement bound us only to diplomatic support, but . . . if Germany used force and France was in serious trouble, what was our position to be?" Before the question was answered, the Balfour government resigned, the Liberals came in, and members of the new Cabinet, including the Prime Minister, Campbell-Bannerman, left London to campaign for the January general election. The only member of the government who continued to work three days a week in London was the new Foreign Secretary, Sir Edward Grey.

Grey was quickly made aware that France was seeking a British military commitment in the event of war with Germany. Major Victor Huguet, the French Military Attaché in London, had seen Major General J. M. Grierson, Director of Military Operations in the War Office, and had talked for five hours with Colonel Charles Repington, the influential military correspondent of *The Times*. On December 29, Repington wrote to Grey that Huguet did not question the British government's sympathy for France, but that he had asked "what the British Government were prepared to *do*." On January 9, Grey wrote to Campbell-Bannerman in Scotland: "Indications keep trickling in that Germany is preparing for war in the spring. France is very apprehensive. I do not think there will be war. . . . But the War Office ought, it seems to me, to be ready to answer the question of what they could do, if we had to take part against Germany." The following day, Paul Cambon, the French Ambassador, came to see Grey.* "He put the question to me directly and formally," the Foreign Secretary wrote to the Prime Minister, ". . . whether in the event of an attack by Germany arising out of Morocco, France could rely upon the armed support of England. I said that I could not answer this question. I could not even consult the Prime Minister or the Cabinet during the Election. . . . M. Cambon said he would again ask after the Election was over."

Haldane urged that Huguet and Cambon deserved a quicker response. Accordingly, on January 16, without the approval of either the Prime Minister or the Cabinet, secret talks between British and French staff officers began. They focussed on plans to send 100,000 British soldiers to the Continent within two weeks of an

* Although Paul Cambon served as French ambassador in London for twenty-three years, he never learned to speak English. Cambon experienced no embarrassment with Lord Salisbury or Lord Lansdowne, the two previous foreign secretaries with whom he had dealt; both were fluent in French, the international language of diplomacy. Grey, however, spoke French poorly and, taking office at a moment of crisis, worried that communication with Cambon would be difficult. He explained in his memoirs how the difficulty was overcome:

"I could read French easily, but had no practice, and therefore no power of expressing myself in it," Grey said. "Cambon's position respecting English was exactly the same. He understood, but could not speak it. He spoke his own language so distinctly and with such clear pronunciation that every word could be visualized when listening to him. To listen to him was like reading French. Each of us, therefore, spoke his own language, and each understood perfectly. To make sure that we did understand we each exchanged the record that we had made separately . . . of one of these early conversations. The comparison of our records left no doubt that each of us had followed every word spoken. From that time we trusted each other completely. . . . All the other ambassadors of the Great Powers spoke English and spoke it well; so that the drawback of my deficiency in French was less than I had feared it would be."

outbreak of hostilities. On January 26, when Campbell-Bannerman returned to London and was informed, he approved. On the thirty-first, Grey responded officially to Cambon: the military conversations would continue with the proviso that they not bind England in advance to war. "In the event of an attack upon France by Germany arising out of our Morocco agreement," Grey said, he did not doubt that "public feeling in England would be so strong that no British government could remain neutral." But Parliament would not be committed before the event and it would be impossible for any Cabinet to sign a defensive alliance with any foreign power without the knowledge and consent of Parliament.

On the same day, January 31, 1906, before seeing Cambon in the afternoon, Grey had attended a morning meeting of the new Cabinet, where he had informed the ministers that he had promised France unreserved diplomatic support in the Morocco crisis. Neither he, Campbell-Bannerman, nor Haldane had mentioned the military conversations. On the following day, February 1, Dorothy Grey was thrown from a cart in Northumberland. After her death on the fourth, Grey, in shock, offered to resign or take a lesser role. C.B., Asquith, Haldane, and the Cabinet begged him to persevere. Gradually, he regained his grip. The Algeciras Conference, begun in January, went forward through February and March, and ended in April, when Germany gave way. The threat of war receded and ministers in London turned to other problems. But the military staff conversations continued. And for six years, the Cabinet was not told.

Before and after the war, Grey was criticized for keeping most ministers of the British government in ignorance of detailed military talks with a foreign power. Grey's tactic was to play down the importance of the conversations: Grierson and Huguet had been required to state in writing that their talks, although officially sanctioned, did not commit either of the governments to go to war; on this ground, Grey steadfastly insisted that neither Cabinet nor Parliament ever lost its freedom of action. Harold Nicolson's explanation of Grey's view was that "[Grey] did not attribute any but a purely technical and conditional importance to such conversations as soldiers or sailors might hold. These conversations, to his mind, were mere matters of routine which could be reversed with the stroke of a pen. They possessed to his mind, no more importance than discussions between the London Fire Brigade and the Westminster Water Works."

The final responsibility for not informing the Cabinet rested with Campbell-Bannerman. It was *his* Cabinet, not Grey's, and whatever the Foreign Secretary recommended, the Prime Minister had the power to overrule. The ingredients of a discussion between the two men can be imagined: within months, a successful colonial settlement with France had evolved into a threat of war with Germany. A new government, faced with an imminent General Election, risked distraction and a potential split if there was debate over entering a Continental military alliance. The new Cabinet, unaccustomed to working together, still lacked cohesion, and revelations in Cabinet might easily find their way to Parliament and the press. Better, then, to continue the conversations in secret, reminding all concerned—the officers involved, the French Ambassador, and his government in Paris—that nothing was guaranteed, that ultimately the House of Commons must decide.

The extent to which the military conversations committed Britain to France remained unclear to Asquith when he succeeded C.B. in 1908. Grey wrote to Asquith in 1911:

"Early in 1906 the French said to us, 'Will you help us if there is war with Germany?'

"We said, 'We can't promise, our hands must be free.'

"The French then urged that the military authorities should be allowed to exchange views, ours to say what they could do, the French to say how they would like it done, if we did side with France. Otherwise, as the French urged, even if we decided to support France, on the outbreak of war we should not be able to do it effectively. We agreed to this. Up to this point, C.B., . . . [Haldane] and I were cognizant of what took place—the rest of you were scattered in the Election.

"The military experts then conversed. What they settled, I never knew—the position being that the Government was quite free, but that the military people knew what to do if the word was given."

Asquith, still nervous a few months later, wrote to Grey: "Conversations such as that between Gen. Joffre and Colonel Fairholme seem to me rather dangerous; especially the part which refers to British assistance. The French ought not to be encouraged, in present circumstances, to make their plans on any assumptions of this kind." Grey's reply was testy; he was performing a delicate balancing act between his obligations to Parliament and his personal commitment to France.

"My dear Asquith," Grey wrote. "It would create consternation if we forbade our military experts to converse with the French.

No doubt these conversations and our speeches have given an expectation of support. I do not see how that can be helped."

During his first weeks in office, Grey set his course for the next eight and a half years. The restrictions imposed by parliamentary government sometimes made him appear evasive, even devious. He always insisted that, until the ultimate moment of decision, Parliament's freedom of action had been preserved. On the other hand, it was equally clear to Grey personally—and he made his belief known to everyone else—that Britain's national interest dictated support of France if war came between France and Germany. While Grey acknowledged this contradiction, he overcame it by saying that, although England was not legally bound to France, his own conviction decreed that he could not remain in a government which refused to stand by its Entente partner. Grey knew that Asquith would resign if he did; this meant that the Liberal government would fall. A Unionist government, returning Balfour and Lansdowne to office, would stand by France.

Underlying Grey's policy was the imperative of British naval supremacy. He was a Liberal and advocated government spending for social reform, but once the German challenge was raised, he accepted that no matter how many ships Germany built, Britain must build more. As long as the only adversary was Germany, it could be done. There was, however, a grimmer possibility: if Germany achieved hegemony on the Continent, England would find herself at bay against the combined sea power of a united Europe. "What really determines the foreign policy of this country is the question of sea power," Grey told an audience of Dominion delegates in 1911. "There is no . . . appreciable danger of our being involved in any considerable trouble in Europe unless there is some power or group of powers . . . which has the ambition of achieving what I call the Napoleonic policy.* That would be a policy on the

---

* Grey's apprehension about Germany and her ambitions regarding Continental and world hegemony received continual, powerful stimulus from the senior Foreign Office clerk supervising the Western (European) Department. Eyre Crowe, the son of an English father and a German mother, lived in Germany until he was seventeen. His wife and many of his friends, including Admiral Henning von Holtzendorff, Commander of the High Seas Fleet from 1909 to 1913, were German. Crowe's intimate knowledge of Germany led him to deep suspicions of German militarism. On January 1, 1907 he submitted a lengthy memorandum on Anglo-German relations which was to exercise a strong influence on Foreign Office thinking in the years before the war. Germany, he argued, had achieved massive national power through a policy of "blood and iron." It was natural that she now would wish to find her "place in the sun" as a world power. Finding Great

part of the strongest power in Europe . . . of . . . separating the other powers . . . from each other, taking them in detail, crushing them if need be, and forcing each into the orbit of the policy of the strongest power. The result would be one great combination in Europe, outside which we would be left without a friend. If that was the result, then . . . if we meant to keep command of the sea, we should have to estimate a probable combination against us of fleets in Europe, not of two powers, but five powers."

For a century, British naval supremacy had made allies superfluous. Now, in Grey's view, allies had become essential to the maintenance of British naval supremacy.

Britain and the British Navy across her path, it was also natural that German policy toward England would be dominated by hostility. Britain should react to this challenge, Crowe advised, with "the most unbending determination to uphold British rights and interest in every part of the globe. There will be no surer or quicker way to win the respect of the German government and of the German nation." Grey, impressed, forwarded Crowe's analysis to Campbell-Bannerman, Asquith, Haldane, and Morley.

CHAPTER 32

The Anglo-Russian Entente and the Bosnian Crisis

For a generation the Triple Alliance had dominated Europe. German military power had smashed Denmark, Austria, and France, and then, with the passage of time, increased. The addition of Austria and Italy to this potentially formidable war machine simply tipped the balance further in Germany's favor. When France and Russia formed the Dual Alliance, the Wilhelmstrasse did not feel seriously threatened. Britain's first attempt to abandon isolation and enter the Continental alliance system on Germany's side would, if successful, have given the Reich absolute supremacy in Europe. But Chamberlain's overtures were spurned and Britain reached out to France. The Anglo-French Entente surmounted the German challenge in Morocco. At Algeciras, observers noted that the primary agent of Germany's defeat was a British diplomat, Sir Arthur Nicolson. Those seeking the source of Sir Arthur's authority had only to lift their eyes from the negotiating table at Algeciras and look across the bay to Gibraltar where, under the frowning mass of the great Rock, lay the ships of the British Fleet. A Russian representative, Count Cassini, who had been present at Algeciras, reported the firmness and skill with which the Englishman wielded British diplomacy and power on behalf of France. It registered in St. Petersburg that for Russia, which needed years of peace to recuperate from the war with Japan and the 1905 revolution, Great Britain could be a useful ally.

The chance of an agreement between Britain and Russia seemed remote. Antagonism ran deep; German statesmen assumed it was permanent. In private, Queen Victoria described Tsar Alexander III as "barbaric, Asiatic, and tyrannical." Conservatives feared Russia thrusting towards the Dardanelles, into the Far East, against the frontiers of India, through Persia towards the Gulf. Liberals rejected the Russian autocracy as antidemocratic. Britain's first step away from Splendid Isolation had been the alliance with Japan, a treaty specifically aimed at containing Imperial Russia.

In Russia, distaste for Britain was equally deep-rooted. The aristocracy and government bureaucracy despised British constitutionalism and were suspicious of British diplomacy. Japan, they felt, would never have dared challenge Russia had she not been supported by her English ally. Liberals welcomed closer ties with England's parliamentary democracy, while conservatives feared opening further doors to political contamination. Already they disliked the principles of their ally, France, governed by Republicans, Catholics, and atheists. The country conservative Russians admired was Germany. In Berlin, at least, there was strength, order, religion, and efficiency. "My own opinion," Sir Arthur Nicolson was to write from St. Petersburg, "is that if the Emperor and the Russian Government were free from any other political ties, they would gladly form an intimate alliance with Germany. German influence today is predominant both in court and Government circles." The reason, Nicolson noted, was that in addition to a common conservative tradition, German handling of Russia was surprisingly civilized and sophisticated. "The alternate hectoring and cajolery which are a distinctive feature of German diplomacy in other countries are not employed here," Nicolson wrote to Grey. "A suave, conciliatory attitude and a gentle solicitude are characteristics of German diplomacy in this capital."

Despite this array of obstacles, the appeal of an Anglo-Russian rapprochement continued to grow. King Edward, visiting his father-in-law, King Christian, in Copenhagen, met Alexander Isvolsky, the Russian Minister to the Danish court. Isvolsky had trained under Prince Gorchakov, and served as Minister to the Vatican, where he became friendly with Bülow, then German Minister to Italy. From Rome, Isvolsky went to Tokyo, then Copenhagen. When he met the King in the spring of 1904, he was fifty, plumpish, and costumed in Savile Row suits with a white waistcoat, white spats, and a pearl tiepin. Strutting through diplomatic gatherings "on little lacquered feet," he peered at the world through a lorgnette and then passed by, trailing the scent of violet eau de cologne. Isvolsky was a commoner and had seen the need to make a good marriage. He courted the young widow of a distinguished general; she rejected him. Later, when Isvolsky became Minister of Foreign Affairs, she was asked whether she did not regret having lost such a good match. "Every day," she replied, "I regret it, but every night I congratulate myself." In the end, Isvolsky married the sister of Peter Stolypin, who became Premier of Imperial Russia.

Isvolsky spoke fluent English and was familiar with English literature and history. His words, carefully chosen, always deferential, pleased King Edward. The King told Isvolsky that he hoped that England and Russia might smooth out their differences as England and France had done; the Minister replied that this was his own dearest wish. After this conversation, the King wrote to the Tsar, declaring his "great pleasure" in talking with M. Isvolsky. "In him," the King continued, "you have a man of remarkable intelligence who is, I am sure, one of your ablest and most devoted public servants." This endorsement did no harm to Isvolsky's career and in May 1906, when the Russian Foreign Minister, Count Vladimir Lamsdorff, exhausted by the war and revolution, begged to retire, Nicholas selected Isvolsky to replace him.*

In the meantime, events in the Far East and their European repercussions had damaged the prospects of Anglo-Russian rapprochement. The surprise attack on the Russian Fleet in the harbor of Port Arthur by Japan, England's ally, angered Russians. Admiral Rozhdestvensky's sinking of British fishing trawlers on the Dogger Bank outraged Britons. Nicholas II, with one disastrous war on his hands and no desire to begin a second, quickly wrote a letter of regret to King Edward. The Russian Ambassador in London, Count Alexander Benckendorff, as anxious as Isvolsky to better relations with Britain, proposed that the matter go before the International Commission of Inquiry at The Hague. Great Britain agreed, and the Russian government paid £65,000 in damages.

Russia's problems multiplied. Admiral Rozhdestvensky's fleet was destroyed in the Strait of Tsushima on May 27, 1905, and a peace treaty with Japan was made at Portsmouth, New Hampshire, under the eye of President Theodore Roosevelt. Protests against the

---

* Learning that a reshuffling of diplomatic posts was in the offing, Isvolsky sent an aide to St. Petersburg to discover which embassy he might get. The results of this secret inquiry were to be wired back to Copenhagen in code: if the posting was to be Italy, the agent was to write "Macaroni"; if Berlin, "Sauerkraut." Once in St. Petersburg, the aide learned that his master was to become Foreign Minister. The telegram to Isvolsky read: "CAVIAR."

mismanagement of the war swept across the country. Troops fired on a crowd marching to the Winter Palace with a petition for the Tsar; by mid-October, the nation was paralyzed by a general strike. On October 30, Nicholas II issued an Imperial Manifesto, transforming Russia from an absolute autocracy into a semiconstitutional monarchy. The principal embodiment of change was to be an elected parliament, the Duma.

These events occurred in Russia in the final weeks of the Balfour Unionist government. Although Benckendorff already had spoken to Lord Lansdowne about the possibility of an Anglo-Russian understanding, by December 5 Lansdowne was out of office. On December 13, two days after becoming Foreign Secretary, Sir Edward Grey received Count Benckendorff to promise that the foreign policy of the Liberal government would follow the lines drawn by its Unionist predecessor; as Lord Lansdowne had achieved a settlement with France, so the new government hoped for a resolution of difficulties with Russia. A few days later, in his first speech as Prime Minister, Sir Henry Campbell-Bannerman told a capacity audience in the Albert Hall that the new government had "nothing but good feelings for the people of Russia."

Once the Algeciras Conference concluded on April 2, 1906, the two countries moved quickly. The new British ambassador to Russia —appointed before his triumph at Algeciras—was Sir Arthur Nicolson. Reporting to London to receive instructions, he went to dinner at Grey's house in Queen Anne's Gate with Asquith, Haldane, and Morley, the Secretary for India. They talked for four hours about Anglo-Russian relations. Two objectives were set. The longer-range was to establish a better overall relationship with Russia, a temporarily weakened but potentially formidable state. The second, more immediate purpose was to secure the Indian frontier from the threat of Russian invasion. For more than thirty years, British statesmen had feared that Russia might march into Afghanistan and seize the Khyber Pass, the gateway to India. The method would be to strengthen the buffer states of Tibet and Afghanistan and to seal off Russia penetration to the Persian Gulf by propping up the crumbling political structure of the Persian monarchy.

On May 12, 1906, Isvolsky succeeded Lamsdorff as Russian Foreign Minister. On June 6, he sat down to begin negotiating with Nicolson. As a backdrop to their conversations, the First Imperial Duma had been received by the Tsar in the Winter Palace on May 9, and then gone off to meet in the Tauride Palace and begin the first parliamentary session in Russian history. The Duma's first act was to formulate a sweepingly aggressive "Address to the Throne" demanding universal suffrage, universal primary education, absolute freedom of speech and assembly, expropriation and redistribution of large landed estates, release of all political prisoners, and dismissal of all ministers appointed by the Tsar, to be replaced by ministers acceptable to the Duma. The Imperial government refused. Ministers attempting to address the Duma were howled into silence. Nicholas II, appalled by the Duma's behavior, appointed as Prime Minister Peter Stolypin, who, on July 22, locked the doors of the Tauride Palace and posted an Imperial decree suspending the Duma.

London's reaction to these events made the diplomats' task more difficult. The Duma had sent a delegation to participate in an interparliamentary meeting scheduled to gather in London in July. The Prime Minister was to open the proceedings and welcome the delegates. On the morning Campbell-Bannerman was scheduled to speak, news reached London that the Tsar had suspended the Duma. Attempting to reassure the shocked and crestfallen Russian delegation, the Prime Minister said, "New institutions often have a disturbed if not a stormy youth. The Duma will revive in one form or another. We can say with all sincerity, 'La Duma est morte. Vive la Duma!' " This phrase, reported to St. Petersburg, hindered the British Ambassador. The more abusive the British press became, the more "Isvolsky's former eagerness has been replaced by silence and indifference," Nicolson noted in his diary. "When I mentioned . . . that I should like to have some outline of his views on Persia, he looked blankly at me and said that he had no views at all."

Isvolsky's slow pace stemmed also from his anxiety about German reaction to these negotiations. Much as he wished an agreement with Britain, he wished also to avoid offending Prince von Bülow. As Nicolson explained to Grey: "He fears, I think, that we are weaving webs and foreign rings around Germany and he will not allow himself to be drawn into any combinations, or place his signature to any document which might in his opinion be aimed, however indirectly, at Germany. . . . He has always as a warning before him the fate of M. Delcassé." In October, Isvolsky went to Berlin to explain his intentions to Bülow and to ask for German approval. The German Chancellor replied that Berlin would welcome an Anglo-Russian agreement as long as it did not adversely affect German interests. Isvolsky also faced opposition within the Russian Council of Ministers and from the Russian General Staff, which was reluctant to give up its ability to menace Britain's huge Indian empire.

Patience was required, and Grey did not push. "I do not wish the negotiations to go to sleep," he wrote to Nicolson. "But on the other hand, we must avoid raising in M. Isvolsky's mind the suspicion that we wish to force the pace in order to take advantage of Russia's present situation." In November, with Grey's permission, Nicolson hinted that once agreement was reached, Britain might be willing to discuss proposals for improving Russia's position on the Dardanelles. This suggestion set Isvolsky to "beaming with pleasure" and restored momentum to the talks. Nicolson's technique, as described by his son and biographer, Harold Nicolson, was to adopt "the methods of a humane and highly skilled dentist dealing with three painful teeth. He would work a bit on Afghanistan, proceeding delicately and firmly; at the first wince of pain, he would close the cavity with anodynes, cotton wools and gutta-percha, and proceed, at the next sitting, with Tibet. He was enabled by these methods to win the entire confidence of M. Isvolsky and gradually bring his three tasks to a simultaneous state of readiness without at any moment jabbing the nerve." Early in February 1907, the Russian Council of Ministers approved. In March, a Russian naval squadron visited Portsmouth and the officers and men were cheered in the streets of London. On August 31, 1907, Nicolson and Isvolsky signed the convention at the Russian Foreign Ministry.

The Anglo-Russian Entente of 1907 was similar to the Anglo-French Entente of 1904. It was not a treaty of alliance; there were no military clauses; the words "war," "aggression," and "defense" did not appear. Its professed purpose was to eliminate friction between two empires at three points in the Middle East and Central Asia where their territories rubbed abrasively. Tibet and Afghanistan were left as buffer states, their territorial integrity guaranteed. China's nominal sovereignty over Tibet was recognized. Russia agreed that Afghanistan was "outside the Russian sphere of influence" and that Russian officials and agents could "only enter into political relations with that country through the intermediary of His Majesty's Government." Britain agreed to share the Afghan trade with Russian companies and entrepreneurs. The agreement over Persia was more complicated. The Shah's kingdom was divided into three zones or spheres of interest, the Russian in the north, the British in the south, and a neutral zone in the center. In the northern zone, Russia was to have exclusive political and commercial concessions. Britons would have similar exclusivity in the south; both empires could scramble for whatever they could get in the center. This de facto partition was masked by a declaration that the two governments were "mutually agreed to respect the integrity and independence of Persia." In fact, the St. Petersburg negotiations had been conducted without the knowledge of the Persian government. When the Shah complained that his country's future had been settled without its knowledge or consent, the Foreign Office replied stiffly that the convention was specifically intended "to preserve the integrity and independence of Persia."

Grey, presenting the convention to the House of Commons, argued that it banished the old nightmare of a Russian invasion of India and relieved the government of the burden of spending large sums for defense of the subcontinent. The larger benefit, he declared, was the transformation of an antagonist into, if not an ally, at least a friend. Most Conservatives (including Balfour) welcomed the agreement. Labour and Radical members denounced the signing of any agreement with a morally abhorrent autocracy and declared that Persia had been sacrificed to "that foul idol, the Balance of Power."

German official reaction was muted. Bülow, consulted throughout by Isvolsky, reacted as he had originally to the Anglo-French convention: he accepted the agreement as a settlement of specific colonial differences which did not affect German interests. "We watch the end of the negotiations without anxiety," he declared at the end of April 1907. "I may be told that I take the Anglo-Russian rapprochement too calmly. I take it for what it is—an attempt to remove difficulties . . . the antagonism of the whale and the elephant was not unalterable. That we are surrounded by difficulties and dangers no one is aware better than myself. They are the result of our exposed position. We need not be alarmed by ententes in regard to matters which do not directly concern us. We cannot live on the enmities of other nations. Let us grant to others the freedom of movement which we claim for ourselves."

The German Chancellor and the Wilhelmstrasse had failed to realize the convention's deeper significance. A cardinal point of German diplomacy had been that England and Russia must always remain hostile. First Bismarck, then Holstein, had poured scorn on the idea that England and Russia could ever find common ground. The Anglo-Russian Entente of 1907 removed from the armory of German diplomacy the weapon of exploiting Anglo-Russian differences that had been used effectively for almost half a century. Not every German was deceived. The German ambassador in St. Petersburg reported: "No one will reproach England for such a policy; one can only admire the skill with which she has carried out her plans. These plans need not necessarily be ascribed to any anti-German tendency, yet Germany is the country most affected by this agreement." The Kaiser agreed. "Yes, when taken all round, it is aimed at us," he wrote in the margin of this dispatch.

Nicolson attempted to defend the convention. "There was no question of 'encircling' Germany," he said later. "In dealing with both France and Russia we had honestly no other object than to place our relations on a safer and more secure basis in the general interests of peace." But in his next sentence, Nicolson admitted: ". . . yet the subconscious feeling did exist that thereby we were securing some defensive guarantees against the overbearing domination of one Power. . . ." Great Britain had decided not to tolerate German hegemony on the Continent. From this vague but powerful instinct flowed the entente with France, the rebuilding of the Royal Navy, and the entente with Russia. The result was a restoration of the balance of power in Europe. Theobald von Bethmann-Hollweg, the future German Chancellor, understood: "You may call it 'encirclement,' 'Balance of Power' or what you will, but the object aimed at and eventually obtained was no other than the welding of a serried and supreme combination of states for obstructing Germany, by diplomatic means at least, in the full development of her growing power," he said.

The King, who had played a part in bringing the Anglo-Russian Entente to fruition, put his seal on the bargain by traveling to Reval (now Tallin) in June 1908 to meet Tsar Nicholas II. Announcement of the visit upset radical Labour M.P.'s. "An Insult to Our Country" was the title of an article published by James Ramsay MacDonald, who described Nicholas II as "a common murderer" and demanded that the King not go "hobnobbing with a blood-stained creature like the Tsar." The King went anyway, taking with him on the *Victoria and Albert* the Queen, Sir Arthur Nicolson, and Sir John Fisher. The voyage across the North Sea was rough, with everyone seasick. "The Queen lay on deck like a corpse," Fisher wrote to his wife.* In the calm waters of the Kiel Canal, the King sent for Fisher to talk while he had his breakfast and watched the escort of German cavalry trotting along the banks. At Kiel, Prince Henry of Prussia greeted the visitors and assigned four German destroyers to escort the British yacht up the Baltic.

On a spring morning, *Victoria and Albert* anchored off Reval

---

* To Lady Fisher, Fisher insisted that he himself "wasn't actually sick" but remained in his cabin because of a "horrible sick headache." Nevertheless, he admitted, "I look with horror to the trip back across the North Sea and would like to come back by train. . . ."

near the two Russian Imperial yachts, *Standart* (used by the Tsar) and *Polar Star* (used by the Dowager Empress Marie, Queen Alexandra's sister). During the visit, which lasted two days, no member of the English party set foot on shore; luncheons, teas, banquets, and balls took place in the salons, in the dining rooms, and on the decks of the yachts. This arrangement was prompted by what were tactfully referred to as "unstable conditions" inside the Russian Empire. Nicholas II was accompanied by his wife, his mother, his sister, Grand Duchess Olga, his Prime Minister, Peter Stolypin, and Isvolsky. One evening when the Tsar and the two Empresses were on board *Victoria and Albert,* a Russian steamer bearing a choral society approached and anchored close enough so that the singers could perform for the royal guests. Some in King Edward's suite were nervous about the proximity of the steamer; a strong arm could have thrown a bomb across the water. The chief of the Russian police assured them that all of the singers, women as well as men, had been stripped and searched.

Good weather and family feeling put the King and Fisher in high spirits. On his own initiative, the King suddenly declared that he was making Nicholas II an Admiral of the Fleet in the British Navy. The Tsar, he explained, needed a British naval uniform to supplement his uniform as colonel of the Scots Greys, since "he was more likely to meet British warships in future than he was to encounter British troops." The Tsar, reported Fisher, "is simply like a child in his delight" and quickly made the King an admiral in the Russian Navy. Back in England, the Cabinet and First Lord Reginald McKenna grumbled that constitutionally they should have been consulted. Fisher pooh-poohed these technicalities: "It's a jolly good thing to have a King who knows how to act, as Cabinet Ministers seem to me to be always like a lot of frightened rabbits." Following the state banquet on the British royal yacht, Fisher waltzed the "Merry Widow" with Grand Duchess Olga, in the center of a circle formed by the company. Then Fisher went up on deck and, at the request of the King, danced a solo hornpipe. "What a very nice time we spent at Reval," Grand Duchess Olga wrote her dance partner. "I hadn't laughed so much for ages!"

Entente with England was only the first of the diplomatic triumphs with which Isvolsky intended to adorn his career as Russian Foreign Minister. During the negotiations in St. Petersburg, Grey and Nicolson had dangled the lure of British support for a paramount Russian objective: opening the Dardanelles to the passage of Russian warships. Since the major powers had signed the Treaty of London in 1871, the strait had been closed to all foreign warships. For Russia, this had the advantage of protecting the Empire's Black Sea coast from European warships. But Russian warships were prevented from exiting through the Dardanelles into the Mediterranean. The Russian Black Sea Fleet had therefore played no part in the war with Japan. Russian nationalists viewed closure of the strait as humiliating to a Great Power's prestige. Nicolson's suggestion that England might help Russia break this barrier had pleased Isvolsky, but, curiously, once Isvolsky decided to attempt this objective, he did not work through England. Instead, he went through Austria.

His partner was Count Alois Lexa von Aehrenthal, the Austrian Foreign Minister. Isvolsky knew Aehrenthal well: the Austrian, a tall, broad-shouldered man with drooping eyelids and a weary, indolent air—"amiable and chatty, but not brilliant" was Nicolson's description—had been Hapsburg ambassador in St. Petersburg. Aehrenthal was well aware of Isvolsky's ambitions on the Dardanelles. When a change in the government of Turkey confronted Austria with an opportunity, Aehrenthal realized that he and Isvolsky might work together to achieve their national objectives and to defy the rest of Europe.

The treaty negotiated at the Congress of Berlin by Bismarck, Disraeli, and Gorchakov was the cornerstone of European diplomacy in the Balkans. Any admission that the Ottoman Empire was disintegrating would unleash a race for spoils which could plunge Europe into war. Accordingly, shams were employed: for thirty years the Christian provinces of Bosnia and Herzegovina had been occupied and administered by Austria; Bulgaria had ruled itself for the same period as a "self-governing principality." In both cases the façade of Turkish sovereignty remained in place. In the summer of 1908, the Ottoman Sultan Abdul Hamid II was overthrown by a group of revolutionaries calling themselves Young Turks. Aehrenthal feared that the new Turkish government might attempt to reassert full control over Bosnia and Herzegovina; in order to forestall this, he decided that Austria-Hungary should formally annex the two provinces. Normally, Imperial Russia would strenuously, perhaps forcibly, have resisted. The one million people of Bosnia and Herzegovina were Slavs who, through the long years of Austrian occupation, had dreamed of the day they would unite in a purely Slav nation around the independent kingdom of Serbia. To these aspirations—shared and encouraged by Serbia—Russia had given its blessing. Now, in pursuit of his goal of opening the Dardanelles, Isvolsky was about to sacrifice these promises.

On September 19, 1908, interrupting his cure at Karlsbad, the Russian Foreign Minister secretly visited Buchlau, the Bohemian castle of Count Leopold von Berchtold, Aehrenthal's successor as Austrian ambassador in St. Petersburg. Aehrenthal was waiting there. Together, the two foreign ministers worked out their scheme: Austria would support a Russian demand that Turkey open the Dardanelles to passage by individual Russian warships; in return, Isvolsky would turn his back while Austria annexed Bosnia and Herzegovina. Since both halves of the plot were in violation of European treaties signed by all the Great Powers, the two foreign ministers agreed to synchronize their moves: announcement of the annexation and presentation of the demand on the Dardanelles were to be simultaneous. No date was set for the twin faits accomplis; Isvolsky explained later that it was understood that no step would be taken until he had had a chance to prepare the ground with his Entente partners; Aehrenthal admitted that he had agreed to wait until he had received from Isvolsky a written summary of their conversation and, in any event, not to act without giving his partner fair warning.

Isvolsky had placed himself in a precarious position. He was preparing to betray the Balkan Slavs, to whom Russia had deep historical and psychological commitments. He was preparing to defy the Great Powers, possibly including his Entente allies. And, desiring exclusive credit for his coup, he had informed neither the Tsar nor Prime Minister Stolypin. Unfortunately for Isvolsky, before he was ready to betray the Balkan Slavs, Aehrenthal betrayed him. Thinking he had plenty of time, Isvolsky left Bohemia, crossed the Alps, stopped in Rome, and arrived in Paris on October 3. Here he was handed a letter from Aehrenthal informing him that circumstances compelled him to proceed at once. Two days later, Bulgaria proclaimed its independence. On October 6, Emperor Franz Josef formally proclaimed the annexation of Bosnia and Herzegovina. Nicholas II was furious. "Brazen impudence," he wrote to his mother. "The main culprit is Aehrenthal. He is simply a scoundrel. He made Isvolsky his dupe."

Isvolsky had sacrificed Russian honor without having been paid his price. He was left to rush about Europe, endeavoring to find support for a Russian move which had depended for its success on a simultaneous move by Austria. In France, Russia's ally, he found little. Stéphen Pichon, the French Foreign Minister, was evasive: Go to London and see what support you can get, he advised his Russian colleague.

Isvolsky arrived in London on October 9. He found Sir Edward

Grey outraged by Austria's action. "The Whig statesman, the monitor of public law in Europe, the English gentleman, the public school boy: all these elements in [Grey's] character were equally affronted," wrote Winston Churchill. To Grey, "it mattered not to us that Austria should annex instead of merely occupying Bosnia and Herzegovina. But . . . we felt that the arbitrary alteration of a European treaty by one Power without the consent of the other Powers who were parties to it struck at the root of all good international order." On October 5, Grey had sent telegrams to all major capitals insisting that "it is an essential principle of the law of nations that no Power can free itself from the engagements of a Treaty nor modify its stipulations except by consent of the Contracting Parties." Britain, Grey declared, would refuse to recognize the annexations at least until the views of other Powers were known. When Sir Charles Dilke complained in the House of Commons that the Foreign Secretary was making too much fuss, Grey retorted that the sacredness of international agreements was at stake.

Grey was icy when Isvolsky appealed for Britain's support in opening the Dardanelles. Having condemned the breaking of one treaty, Grey would not condone the breaking of another. Consideration of the strait at that moment, he said, was "inopportune." His reputation and career collapsing, Isvolsky mingled pleas with threats. "Isvolsky went on to say that the present was a most critical moment," Grey reported to Nicolson. "It might either consolidate and strengthen the good relations between England and Russia, or it might upset them altogether. His own position was at stake, for he was entirely bound up with the policy of good understanding with England which he had advocated against all opposition."

Neither pleas nor threats made any impression on Grey; Britain would not support Russia in any demand on the new Turkish government. When Isvolsky, desperate to salvage something, proposed holding a conference to discuss the annexation and the Dardanelles, Grey agreed. If other Powers were willing to sanction what Aerenthal had done and Isvolsky proposed to do, Britain, Grey said, might also be willing.

On October 22, Aehrenthal declared that he would attend a conference only if it was agreed in advance that the annexation of Bosnia and Herzegovina was accepted and that the subject would not be discussed. Isvolsky, now assailed by a betrayed and outraged Serbia, refused, whereupon Aehrenthal rejected the invitation. The role of Germany became critical. Neither the Kaiser nor Chancellor Bülow had been informed of the planned annexation. William's first reaction was that Aehrenthal's act was "a piece of brigandage" which "confronted us with the dilemma of being unable to protect our friends the Turks" because "our ally has injured them." "Thus my Turkish policy, so carefully built up over twenty years, is thrown away. A great triumph over us for Edward VII." Bülow insisted that he learned of the annexation "only at the same time as the news was communicated to London and St. Petersburg." Nevertheless, Germany had no choice except to support Austria. Two years earlier, in 1906, Bülow had written: "Our relations with Austria are now more important than ever because Austria is our one sure ally. We must reveal as little as possible of our relative political isolation to the Austrians. It is only human nature that if I tell a man I need his horse, he puts a very high value on the horse." Aehrenthal already had comprehended this, and before the annexation remarked that Germany must support Austria's move as the Reich had no other serious ally. Bülow found related reasons: "Austria-Hungary behaved totally loyally to us at Algeciras . . . like should be paid with like." Accordingly, Berlin supported Austria's rejection of Isvolsky's invitation. "The conference won't come off," said Bülow. "We shall have nothing to do with it."

Isvolsky was trapped. For weeks, he complained to anyone who would listen that Aehrenthal was "duplicitous" and "no gentleman." Aehrenthal silenced him by threatening to publish the correspondence between them before the meeting at Buchlau, implying that the Russian Foreign Minister had made statements which might further compromise his position.

War seemed imminent. Serbia mobilized; Russian and Austrian troops took up positions on the frontier. On November 6, Balfour, leader of the opposition, wrote to Lord Lansdowne, who led the Unionist Party in the House of Lords:

> Asquith asked me to speak to him last night after the House rose. He was evidently extremely perturbed about the European situation, which, in his view, was the gravest of which we have had any experience since 1870.
>
> He said that, incredible as it might seem, the Government could form no theory of German policy which fitted all the known facts, except that they wanted war. . . . [I]t would certainly involve Russia, Austria, and the Near East—to say nothing of ourselves. I observed . . . that it was difficult to see what Germany expected to gain by a war . . . Asquith's only answer . . . was that the internal condition of Germany was so unsatisfactory that they might be driven to the wildest adventures in order to divert national sentiment into a new channel.

Aehrenthal understood the strength of his position. He did not fear war; in fact, he already had promised General Count Franz Conrad von Hötzendorf, chief of the Austrian General Staff, that unless Serbia gave way and recognized the annexation of the two Slav provinces, he would approve an Austrian assault on Serbia. He disdained talk of the sanctity of treaties. "Your Sir Edward Grey wants peace," he said disparagingly to a group of English visitors in Vienna. Besides, he scoffed, "What can England do to us?"

In March, Bülow brought the crisis to a head. On the twenty-first, he instructed Count Friedrich von Pourtalès, German Ambassador in St. Petersburg, to tell Isvolsky that "unless Russia agreed to recognize the annexation of Bosnia-Herzegovina, Germany would leave Austria-Hungary a free hand." The message was clear: Austria would overwhelm Serbia; if Russia attempted to aid her Serbian client, the German Empire would stand beside Austria. "We expect a precise answer, Yes or No," Bülow instructed Pourtalès. "Any vague, complicated or ambiguous reply will be treated as a refusal." Nakedly confronted by the threat of war, Russia backed down. The Russian Council of Ministers sat for three hours on March 22 and advised the Tsar to consent. Nicholas telegraphed William that he accepted the annexation, adding, "with God's help war would thus be avoided." In the Reichstag, Bülow paid the Tsar an ironic tribute: "Russia's recent conduct has won the gratitude of all friends of peace." Most of the credit Bülow kept for himself. "I solved the Bosnian crisis," he announced in his memoirs, and cited the words of Emperor Franz Josef to support his claim. Bülow "managed the affair excellently," the Chancellor quoted the Emperor. "On the one hand, he carried our claims on Bosnia and Herzegovina through to a successful conclusion. . . . On the other hand, he did not let things go as far as war. I must give him all the praise for an old man like me does not want to have a war again." Along with praise, Franz Josef sent Bülow a signed photograph in a gold frame, a full-length portrait of himself, and the Order of St. Stephen—highest in the Hapsburg Empire—set in diamonds. A year later, on a visit to Vienna, the Kaiser—who originally had described the annexation as "a piece of brigandage"—also claimed credit, for having "taken his stand in shining armor at a most grave moment by the side of "[Austria's] Most Gracious Sovereign [Franz Josef]."

The abruptness of the Russian capitulation surprised Europe. "Russia was stiff for a time and then suddenly threw up the sponge and collapsed," Grey observed. "The strain on Isvolsky's temperament had been very great and he seemed to have had a sudden reaction at the end to despair and disgust." In Russia, the spectacular collapse was humiliating. "I have been assured by those who have witnessed many phases in the recent history of Russia that there has never previously been a moment when the country had undergone such humiliation," Nicolson wrote to Grey. "Although Russia has had her troubles and trials, both external and internal, and has suffered defeats in the field, she has never had, for apparently no valid excuse, to submit to the dictation of a foreign power." Tsar Nicholas explained the crisis to his mother: "Germany told us we would help solve the difficulty by agreeing to the annexation, while if we refused, the consequences might be very serious and hard to foretell. Once the matter had been put as definitely and unequivocally as that, there was nothing for it but to swallow one's pride and agree. But," added the Tsar, "German action towards us has been simply brutal and we won't forget it."

The triumph in which Aerenthal, Bülow, and the Kaiser exulted came at high cost. Russia resolved that she would never submit again. If a second challenge came, Russia would accept. From 1909 onward, the commander of the Kiev Military District in the Ukraine had standing orders to be ready within forty-eight hours to repel an invasion from the west. The Bosnian Crisis left Isvolsky bitter and unforgiving. Although he remained Foreign Minister for three more years, his effectiveness was diminished. In 1911, he resigned and was appointed Russian Ambassador to France. In Paris, he worked vengefully day and night to strengthen the Franco-Russian alliance. When war came, Alexander Isvolsky boasted, "This is *my* war! My war!"

CHAPTER 33

The
Navy Scare
of 1909

◆

On December 8, 1908, at the Monday-morning meeting of
the British Cabinet, Reginald McKenna, who had replaced Lord Tweedmouth as First Lord of the Admiralty, gave his
fellow ministers a nasty shock. The navy, McKenna declared, would
ask for six new dreadnoughts in the Estimates he would present to
Parliament in March; the ministers had expected him to ask for four.
Further, in addition to these six, another six would be needed in
1910 and a third six in 1911. He based this request on alarming
information he had received about the accelerated building program
of the German Fleet. Two prominent ministers, David Lloyd
George, Chancellor of the Exchequer, and Winston Churchill, President of the Board of Trade, adamantly opposed anything more than
four dreadnoughts. McKenna and the Sea Lords, led by Fisher, insisted that, unless six ships were authorized, they would not remain
in office. The Navy Scare, which gripped Parliament, press, and
country in the winter and spring of 1909, was under way.

At the center of this battle lay the Liberal Party's election
pledge to spend less money on armaments and more on social reform. Liberal M.P.'s saw dreadnoughts as a horrid form of profli-
gacy; battleships represented staggering sums of money wasted on
floating mountains of steel. In 1907, 136 M.P.'s had petitioned

Campbell-Bannerman to reduce spending on armaments; in 1908 a similar petition was signed by 144 M.P.'s. The government and Admiralty had obliged by sacrificing ships. Before leaving office in December 1905, Lord Cawdor, the Unionist First Lord, had issued a memorandum to guide British dreadnought building: "Strategic requirements necessitate the building of four armored ships a year. . . . The period of building is two years, therefore eight ships will be building at any given time." Within weeks of taking power, the Liberals swung the axe: one dreadnought of the *Bellerophon* class was cut from the 1906 Estimates. In 1907, the cut was repeated and one dreadnought was lopped from the *Collingwood* class. In 1908, the four-ship program was cut to two. By July 1908, Great Britain had twelve dreadnoughts, instead of sixteen, built, building, or authorized by Parliament.*

Asquith, who replaced Campbell-Bannerman in April 1908, was content with this slowing tempo in dreadnought building. Indeed, he wondered if it had slowed enough. "As you know," he wrote to McKenna in July, "I have for a long time been growing skeptical . . . as to the whole dreadnought policy. I don't want to press you, but as you have now surveyed the whole situation from the inside, I should be very glad to know if you have come to any conclusion of your own as to the lines upon which construction ought to proceed for the next few years. There is much money in it —and more than money." The Prime Minister was dismayed five months later when his First Lord proposed that the navy be given, not two new dreadnoughts as in the 1908 budget, not four as recommended in the Cawdor Memorandum, but six.

McKenna's argument was based on the German building pro-

* 1905 Estimates	Dreadnought
	Invincible
	Inflexible
	Indomitable
1906 Estimates	Bellerophon
	Superb
	Temeraire
	(one ship cut)
1907 Estimates	Collingwood
	St. Vincent
	Vanguard
	(one ship cut)
1908 Estimates	Neptune
	Indefatigable
	(two ships cut)

gram. The keel of the first German dreadnought, *Nassau,* had been laid in July 1906. In the summer of 1907, within a few weeks of one another, three additional German dreadnoughts, *Westfalen, Posen,* and *Rheinland,* each similar in most characteristics to the first eight British dreadnought battleships, had been laid down. The German 1907 program also included the first German dreadnought battle cruiser, *Von der Tann,* with its eight eleven-inch guns and twenty-five-knot speed a match for the British *Invincible.* In 1908, the Reichstag authorized four more German dreadnoughts, the battleships *Thüringen, Helgoland,* and *Ostfriesland,* and the battle cruiser *Moltke.* In 1909, the German Navy Law called for three more battleships and another battle cruiser to be laid down.

Within two years, beginning in the summer of 1907, Germany had laid down or ordered nine dreadnoughts. Beginning in 1905, Great Britain had ordered twelve dreadnoughts over four years. If the British and German programs for 1909 each included four new ships, then in 1912, when all these ships were completed, Germany would possess thirteen dreadnoughts and Britain sixteen. This did not seem to McKenna and the Sea Lords a sufficient margin on which to rest British naval supremacy. It rendered illogical Asquith's statement that the Two Power Standard, to which he said Britain remained committed, required "a preponderance of ten percent over the combined strengths in capital ships of the next two strongest powers."

More ominous from McKenna's viewpoint were Admiralty suspicions that the Germans were accelerating secretly: gathering essential shipbuilding materials, acquiring guns, turrets, and armor well in advance of actually building the hulls. Reports reached London that dreadnought keels were being laid down months before the dates scheduled by the German Navy Law—in advance even of the appropriating votes in the Reichstag. For several years, it had been evident that Germany's shipbuilding capacity was significantly expanding. By 1908, seven shipyards in the Reich were capable of constructing dreadnoughts.* From keel-laying to launching required an average span of one year. Immediately after the hull was launched and towed to a fitting-out dock for installation of turrets, guns, and propulsion machinery, a new keel could be laid on the building way. Theoretically, the German Navy could begin seven new dreadnoughts every year. In fact, there was a brake on this

---

* Wilhemshaven Dockyard in Wilhelmshaven; Weser Works in Bremen; Vulcan Works in Stettin; Blohm and Voss in Hamburg; Schichau Works in Danzig; and Germania Works and Howaldt's Works in Kiel.

tempo. The governing factor in rate of dreadnought construction was not the time required to build a hull, but the time needed to manufacture the guns, gun mountings, and armor that transformed a floating hill into a fighting ship. The date of laying down could therefore be delayed without affecting the date of completing a vessel, provided work was proceeding on these more intricate components.

The making and accumulation of these components was much easier to hide than the laying of a keel and the building of a hull. Naval guns, mountings, and armor for the German Navy were made in the workshops of Krupp of Essen. Krupp, already the largest business enterprise in Europe, was expanding rapidly, from 45,000 workers in 1902 to 100,000 in 1909. There were rumors that Krupp was secretly buying quantities of nickel, a metal essential to the process of hardening steel and therefore integral to the manufacture of guns and armor. It was said that rows of huge naval gun barrels lined the sheds at Essen, awaiting shipment to the naval shipyards.

Contracts for three German dreadnoughts in the 1909 program were supposed to have actually been placed with shipyards ahead of the dates scheduled by the Navy Law and before the Reichstag had authorized the money to pay for them. If these reports were true, the British Admiralty was being stripped of a guideline for predicting the future size of the German Fleet. The Admiralty had assumed an average building period for German dreadnoughts of three years. Now, it seemed, ships were being laid down ahead of time and constructed more quickly because guns, gun mountings, and armor had been manufactured in advance. The three years might be shrinking to two and a half, or even two, which was the average time Britain allowed for construction of a dreadnought. (England, as the world's most advanced industrial power, had always been able to build ships faster than any other nation. Even when another power began a ship of advanced design, Britain had always been able to adapt and overtake.) Using the published Navy Law schedules, the dreadnought ratio in 1912 would be 16:13. But if the Germans had laid down early and were accelerating construction, the Admiralty declared, as "a practical certainty" Germany would have seventeen dreadnoughts in 1912. And, if the maximum capacity of German shipyards were utilized, the High Seas Fleet could have twenty-one dreadnoughts in 1912 to pit against Britain's sixteen.

McKenna presented these fears to Grey on December 30, 1908:

My dear Grey:
    . . . The argument . . . may be summarized as follows: German shipbuilding is in excess of the monetary provision for

it made under the Fleet Law and the Estimates. . . . Hence
the terms of the Law are no guide to the dates when the ships
will be completed. We are bound therefore to look at the German capacity to build, and we can best judge what they can do
by what they are doing. . . . If by any spurt Germany can once
catch us up, we have no longer any such superior building capacity as would ensure our supremacy. . . .

Four days later, on January 3, 1909, the First Lord wrote to
Asquith:

My dear Prime Minister:
 . . . It seemed to me that an examination of the German
Naval Estimates might prove helpful in showing how far Ger-
many is acting secretly and in apparent breach of her Law. . . .
I am anxious to avoid alarmist language, but I cannot resist the
following conclusions which it is my duty to submit to you:

1) Germany is anticipating the shipbuilding program laid
   down by the law of 1907.
2) She is doing so secretly.
3) She will certainly have 13 big ships in commission in the
   spring of 1911.
4) She will probably have 21 big ships in commission in the
   spring of 1912.
5) German capacity to build dreadnoughts is at this moment equal to ours.

The last conclusion is the most alarming, and if justified
would give the public a rude awakening should it become
known.

This closing shot in McKenna's letter was shrewdly placed. The
First Lord knew that a consummate political animal like Asquith
would be influenced by a sense of political risk. Already the country
was uneasy, knowing that Germany had laid down four ships in 1908
to Britain's two. Once McKenna's worries reached the Unionist
M.P.'s and the Unionist press, a howl of alarm would rise up. The
First Lord's recommendations therefore could not—as Asquith
might dearly have wished—be ignored.
On the Liberal side of the House and in the Liberal press, any
increase over the planned four dreadnoughts would be strongly opposed. "I will not dwell upon the emphatic pledges given by all of us
before and at the last General Election to reduce the gigantic expen-

diture on armaments built up by the recklessness of our predecessors," Lloyd George wrote to Asquith. "Scores of your most loyal supporters in the House of Commons take these pledges seriously and even a three million pound increase will chill their zeal for the Government . . . an increase of five to six million will stagger them." Churchill also did not accept McKenna's case: "I found the Admiralty's figures exaggerated," he wrote. "I did not believe the Germans were building dreadnoughts secretly in excess of their published laws." Germany had a constitution; dreadnoughts could not be built without a vote of money by the Reichstag. If the German Navy was building in secret from England, it was also building in secret from the Reichstag; Churchill thought this unlikely. Thus, he concluded, "I believed four ships sufficient."

In January 1909 the Admiralty, instead of paring down from six to four, suddenly asked for two additional dreadnoughts, raising the total requested to eight. On January 3, Lloyd George warned Churchill: "The Admiralty mean to get their six dreadnoughts . . . the Admiralty have had very serious news from their Naval Attaché in Germany since our last Cabinet meeting and . . . McKenna is now convinced we may have to lay down eight dreadnoughts next year." He had feared "all along this would happen," the Chancellor said. The struggle continued through January and most of February. Lloyd George and Churchill, supported by Morley, Burns, and others, wanted four. Grey and Haldane wanted six. McKenna wanted at least six, possibly eight. The Liberal press warned against "Panicmongers"; Conservative papers attacked "Pacifists," "Little Englanders," and "Economaniacs." Personalities became involved. "What are Winston's reasons for acting as he does in this matter?" asked Knollys, the King's private secretary. "Of course it cannot be from conviction or principle. The very idea of his having either is enough to make anyone laugh." Resignations were in the air. "The economists are in a state of wild alarm, and Winston and Lloyd George by their combined machinations have got the bulk of the Liberal press into the same camp," Asquith wrote to Margot on February 20. "They . . . go about darkly hinting at resignation (which is bluff) . . . but there are moments when I am disposed summarily to cashier them both."

The Cabinet was deadlocked and the Prime Minister faced loss either of his Foreign Secretary and First Lord, or of his Chancellor and Board of Trade President. On February 24, a special meeting was called in Grey's room at the Foreign Office. The Sea Lords were present. Lloyd George rose from his chair and began to pace the room. When the discussion turned to Krupp's increased capacity for making gun turrets, the Chancellor burst out, "I think it shows extraordinary neglect on the part of the Admiralty that all this should not have been found out before. I don't think much of any of you admirals." McKenna, who now violently disliked Lloyd George, held his temper and replied calmly, "You know perfectly well that these facts were communicated to the Cabinet at the time we knew of them, and your remark [then] was, 'It's all contractor's gossip.'"

There seemed no way out of the impasse, when Asquith suddenly made a proposal which satisfied everyone: the government would ask for four dreadnoughts in the 1909 Estimates, two to be laid down in July and two in November. In addition, it would seek authority to build four additional dreadnoughts to be laid down no later than April 1, 1910, *if* careful monitoring of the German construction program proved them necessary. The contingent four, as well as the first four, would be completed in 1912, the British "danger year" as seen by the Admiralty. And, if the contingent four were built, this would have no effect on the regular 1910 program, under which it was assumed that still another four dreadnoughts would be ordered.

Although all in the Cabinet agreed to the four-now, perhaps-four-later compromise, it displeased extremists on either side. Lloyd George and Churchill, realizing that they were outmaneuvered, suddenly expressed willingness to vote for six. It was too late. Meanwhile, McKenna, Fisher, and the Sea Lords worried that *they* had been tricked and that the six they had demanded and the eight they had hoped for all would vanish in Parliament. "We are placing our whole and sole trust in you that these two jugglers [Lloyd George and Churchill] don't outwit us," Fisher wrote to McKenna. "There was a certain sweet certainty about 'six' . . . which is lacking in a bill with possibly evading phrases capable of being twisted against us, but I've no doubt of your seeing to it." McKenna took the Admiral's case to Asquith, saying that if the four-plus-four bill "is rejected either in the Commons or the Lords, I understood from you yesterday that you would instantly resign." Asquith replied, "I do not see how it is possible for me to say more than that I regard my personal and public honor pledged. . . . My one predominant desire is to attain the end which we both have in view. I have never before made—as I make to you now—so clear and direct an appeal for trust and confidence."

Fisher, fighting for eight, sent to McKenna (who forwarded it to the Prime Minister) a report from an Argentinian naval mission which had just visited the Krupp works and a number of German shipyards. Hoping to attract orders, the Germans had shown their visitors everything. According to Fisher, the visitors were overwhelmed by the size and capacity of the German plant and shipyards. They reported twelve capital ships on the building ways and, at the Krupp plant in Essen, they counted one hundred eleven-inch and twelve-inch barrels nearing completion. The lesson, the First Sea Lord said, was that "nothing less than eight ships would do."

Asquith adhered to the four-plus-four compromise. McKenna put it before the House of Commons on March 16. When the First Lord rose, members listened intently and for the most part silently. Tea hour came and nobody left. The Prince of Wales sat in the Peers' Gallery, his head thrust forward to catch every word. Fisher was present, sitting behind the Speaker's Chair. McKenna's speech was blunt: "No matter what the cost, the safety of the country must be assured. We do not know, as we thought we did, the rate at which German construction is taking place." He spelled out the possibilities from the grimmest to the least grim. The House listened, mostly in silence. Balfour followed, then Asquith. Both supported McKenna. When Asquith sat down, the Speaker looked at the House and the House looked at the Speaker and for several minutes no one got up. Nothing further was heard of a motion to reduce the Estimates, made by the 140-member Little Navy group.

The country, which, like the House, had heard only rumors about the battle going on inside the Cabinet, was stunned by McKenna's speech. The Liberal press, despairing at the damage increased dreadnought building would do to social programs, took the position that if the four contingent ships were to be laid down, they must be credited against the 1910 naval budget; it was intolerable that Britain might pay for eight dreadnoughts in a single year. But Asquith could manage the Liberals. The real attack on the Estimates came from the Unionists. Before March 16, Conservatives had agreed that six new ships would be enough. Now, facing the threat of possible German acceleration as revealed by the First Lord, Conservatives in the Commons, the Lords, the press, and the country demanded that all eight ships be laid down at once. "We want eight and we won't wait!", a slogan coined by M.P. George Wyndham, became the battle cry of the Unionist Party. Accusations of incompetence and of abdicating supremacy at sea were flung at the government, at the Admiralty, and at Fisher himself. "Citoyens, la patrie est en danger!" declared the *Daily Telegraph*. "We are not yet prepared to turn the face of every portrait of Nelson to the wall." *The National Review* described Fisher as the "reincarnation of Marshal Leboeuf," the French Minister of War who boasted on the eve of the Franco-Prussian War that the French Army was ready to the last gaiter button! When Asquith refused to pledge himself to the immediate building of the four contingent ships, the *Daily Telegraph* prounced that "since Nero fiddled there has never been a spectacle more strange, more lamentable, than the imperilling of the whole priceless heritage of centuries to balance a party budget." On March 19, Balfour gave notice of a motion of censure: "In the opinion of this House, the declared policy of His Majesty's Government respecting the immediate provision of battleships of the newest type does not sufficiently secure the safety of the Empire."

On March 29, another packed house heard the debate on Balfour's censure motion. Grey, rather than McKenna or Asquith, was the principal government speaker. His speech ranged widely, from the crushing burden of armaments on all countries, to the essential role of the navy in Britain's security, the state of Anglo-German relations in general, and the Admiralty's fears that Germany's expanding capacity, rather than her moderate intentions, might govern German naval construction: "The great countries of Europe are raising enormous revenues and something like half of them are being spent on naval and military preparations . . . [which are], after all, preparations to kill each other. Surely . . . this expenditure . . . becomes a satire . . . on civilization. . . . If it goes on . . . sooner or later I believe it will submerge civilization."

Britain, Grey argued, could not unilaterally drop out of the arms race: "If we, alone among the great powers, gave up the competition and sank into a position of inferiority, what good should we do? None whatever. . . . We should cease to count for anything amongst the nations of Europe, and we should be fortunate if our liberty was left, and we did not become the conscript appendage of some stronger power."

In this area, the strength of the navy played a critical role in British policy: "There is no comparison between the importance of the German Navy to Germany, and the importance of our Navy to us. Our Navy is to us what their Army is to them. To have a strong Navy would increase their prestige, their diplomatic influence, their power of protecting their commerce, but . . . it is not a matter of life and death to them . . . [as] it is to us. No superiority of the British Navy over the German Navy could ever put us in a position to affect the independence or integrity of Germany because our Army is not maintained on a scale which, unaided, could do anything on German territory. But if the German Navy were superior to ours, they, maintaining the Army which they do . . . our independence, our very existence would be at stake."

Anglo-German relations, Grey believed, were friendly and would remain so as long as both Powers respected each other's vital interests: "I see a wide space in which both of us may walk in peace and amity. . . . In my opinion two extreme things would produce conflict. One is an attempt by us to isolate Germany. No nation of her standing and her position would stand a policy of isolation assumed by neighboring powers. . . . Another thing which would certainly produce a conflict would be the isolation of England attempted by a great Continental Power so as to dominate and dictate the policy of the Continent. That has always been so in history."

Where did Grey find the road to peace?

"If I was asked to name the one thing which would mostly reassure . . . Europe . . . I think it would be that the naval expenditure in Germany would be diminished, and that ours was following suit. . . . On what basis would any arrangement have to be proposed? Not the basis of equality. It must be the basis of a superiority of the British Navy. No German, so far as I know, disputes that that is a natural point of view for us."

Grey turned finally to the specific problem of apparent German acceleration and the British response. He spoke of German capacity ("Your intention to accelerate is one thing while your power to accelerate is another"). The only way to *know* what was going on in another country's shipyards was for naval attachés to have free access.

On strict party lines, Balfour's censure motion was defeated, 353 to 135. Four ships were to be built; four more were authorized and waited in the wings. Churchill himself later ruefully described what had happened: "In the end a curious and characteristic solution was reached. The Admiralty had demanded six ships; the economists offered four; and we finally compromised on eight."

From the beginning of the Navy Scare, the British government attempted to learn the facts, not only from its Naval Attaché in Berlin and from shadowy unofficial sources, but from the German government. In the autumn of 1908, McKenna, hearing reports of materials collected in German shipyards and of contracts awarded to shipyards before funds were voted in the Reichstag, put these matters before Captain Widemann, the German Naval Attaché in London. Widemann denied everything. Indeed, he said, he was shocked that the First Lord would attribute such obviously unconstitutional behavior to State Secretary Tirpitz. McKenna, believing his own information, not Widemann, did not consult the Naval Attaché again.

Grey became involved in January 1909 after reading McKenna's persuasive memorandum on German shipbuilding. Grey understood the importance of British naval supremacy; at Scarborough on November 20, 1908, he had said, "There is no half-way house in naval affairs . . . between complete safety and absolute ruin." But, as Foreign Secretary, he felt an additional concern: if the German government were deliberately lying to conceal an acceleration of its building program, then the whole of German policy, not just the number and delivery dates of ships under construction, was thrown into question. From the beginning of January until the publication of the British Naval Estimates on March 12, Grey struggled to extract from Paul Wolff-Metternich, the German Ambassador in London, a straightforward statement about German naval building. In dealing with Metternich, the Foreign Secretary faced two problems: first, the German Ambassador was kept in the dark by Admiral Tirpitz; second, even when Metternich was accurately informed, he was often instructed not to pass the information along to the British. The Grey-Metternich conversations, therefore, were an exercise in frustration for both men.

Grey's first meeting with Metternich took place on January 4, 1909, immediately after the Foreign Secretary had read the First Lord's memorandum. Grey referred to the rumors and reports which the British Admiralty had heard and received; Metternich said they were untrue. Grey pointed out that Britons were worried because of the large theoretical capacity Germany had for building dreadnoughts; Metternich replied that the entire German program was laid down in the Navy Laws and that any sudden shift of German shipyards to dreadnought construction was forbidden by those laws. Grey suggested that the best way of ascertaining facts was to let the naval attachés visit shipyards in both countries and see what ships had been laid down and how far along they were. Metternich said that the Kaiser would never permit this.

By the time the second conversation took place, on February 4, Metternich knew that the evidence in British hands of accumulation of advance materials in German shipyards was incontrovertible; therefore, he admitted it. The reason, he explained, was simply foresightedness on the part of the contractors, who were proceeding at their own risk. He insisted that no acceleration was intended and that the rate of shipbuilding was fixed by law. It was true, he conceded, that the rate of building *could* be accelerated, but only by a public vote in the Reichstag. Grey was in a difficult position. He respected Metternich, but he suspected that the Ambassador was withholding information. Metternich had admitted only belatedly the advance accumulation of materials; he still had not acknowledged that contracts for two of the four 1909 ships had been let in October 1908. Grey could not accuse the Ambassador of passing false information, yet he could not believe the information Metternich gave him. Once again, Grey suggested an exchange of attaché visits to the shipyards. Metternich replied that the Emperor had refused absolutely. There was little more that Grey could do beyond warning that Britain would have to consider German capacity as well as the German Navy Laws in formulating its own building plans. On March 10, just before publication of the British Naval Estimates, Metternich officially informed Grey that German building would not be accelerated and that the High Seas Fleet would not possess thirteen dreadnoughts until the end of 1912. That night, Metternich warned Berlin that the British Admiralty would ask for more ships.

On March 12, the day of the publication of the British Naval Estimates and four days before they were to be presented to the House of Commons, Asquith summoned Metternich to reinforce Grey's warning. As reported to Berlin by Metternich, this is how the Prime Minister explained the British program: "According to information received by the British Admiralty, three of the four [German] dreadnoughts of the . . . 1909–1910 year have been under construction for several months. Not only has the material been collected, but the keel of one dreadnought of the 1909–1910 program has been laid in the Schichau yard. If preparations are made for building, and ships are actually begun some months before they are voted [by the Reichstag], it is clear that the completion of these ships can be antedated by a corresponding number of months. Mr. Asquith had no wish to complain [Metternich was paraphrasing and summarizing the Prime Minister's words] and had no justification for any complaint about this procedure. Germany alone had the right to determine the rate of her shipbuilding, and no responsible persons in England would have the right to object; but the British Government . . . (in estimating their own program) could not avoid taking account of the development of the German program."

The Prime Minister promised that Britain would withhold the laying down of the four contingent dreadnoughts until the pace of German construction made it imperative.

Metternich sent this report to Berlin; the answer was silence. Four days later, just two days before the opening of the naval debate in the Commons, Metternich urgently telegraphed Berlin, asking for permission to explain the German program in greater detail. Tirpitz was opposed and the Kaiser agreed with Tirpitz. "I think it would be better for Metternich to hold his tongue. He is incorrigible," William wrote in the margin of the Ambassador's telegram.

The stark nature of McKenna's Naval Estimates speech and the passion of the Commons debate forced German reactions. On March 17, the day after the debate, Metternich complained to Grey that the British government had ignored his March 10 assurance that the German naval program was not being accelerated. Grey's response was to say for the third time that the best way to clarify such misunderstandings and get accurate facts was for the naval attachés of each country to visit the other's shipyards.

The same day in Berlin, Tirpitz publicly supported the position the beleaguered Metternich had been required to take. Opening the Reichstag debate on the German Naval Estimates, the State Secretary officially declared that British fears were groundless: Germany, he announced, would possess thirteen, not seventeen, dreadnoughts in 1912. Privately, however, Tirpitz decided to admit to Metternich a fact which Metternich had not known and which, on instructions, he had been denying vigorously: that the contracts for two of the four 1909–1910 German dreadnoughts had indeed been placed with private shipyards in the autumn of 1908, six months before the Reichstag could authorize funds. Now, since the British Admiralty and government already knew, Tirpitz decided that Metternich should confirm this information in London, and explain that the contracts had been given early not to steal a march on England, but solely to get lower, competitive prices from the builders while, at the same time, preventing the yards from having to dismiss any workers.*

Humiliated by his own government, Metternich had no choice but to obey instructions. On March 18, he admitted that the contracts for two of the four ships had been placed in October 1908. His miserable situation got no sympathy from Fisher, who by now believed that both Tirpitz and Metternich were dissembling. "We have got to have a margin against lying," he declared. Meeting Metter-

---

* An additional fact Tirpitz did not pass on either to the Kaiser or to Metternich: actual construction of one of the ships had begun on March 1, 1909. When William found out five months later he was furious: "His Majesty the Kaiser sees in this a justification, though only a formal one, for the English claim that building is being accelerated," Admiral Müller, the Kaiser's Naval Secretary, wrote to Tirpitz. "His Majesty has always emphasized that no acceleration of building has taken place." Tirpitz denied any acceleration, claiming that "start of building . . . is solely a private business matter for the firms. In my opinion, therefore, there was no reason to notify His Majesty. Schichau [the shipyard] began the ship in March at its own risk and with its own money to avoid dismissing workers."

nich by accident on March 24, he glared at the German and burst out, "How all this scare would vanish, Ambassador, if you would let our Naval Attaché go and count them [the ships under construction]." "Impossible," Metternich replied. "Other governments would also want to. Besides, something would be seen which we wish to keep secret." Fisher assumed that the German ships, or the guns they carried, were even bigger than the published figures suggested.

Metternich continued to try to make his government understand the British viewpoint until he left London. He wrote early in April, admirably summarizing the cause of the Navy Scare in London:

"Until November last (1908) the British Government believed that in our Naval Law it possessed a standard of reasonable accuracy with which to regulate its own annual shipbuilding requirements. . . . Until last November it was assumed here that the execution of our program depended on the annual financial vote of the Reichstag. This security has now disappeared. The present Government has indeed our assurance that we do not wish to accelerate our 'tempo' and that we shall have no more than thirteen dreadnoughts in the year 1912. But the Government maintains that, although these may be our intentions at present, we have every right to change them at any moment we may wish to do so. The Government feels that in this important question it is groping in the dark in respect to our ship-building, and that it must not be dependent upon the good intentions of a foreign government—intentions which may change."

When Metternich's dispatch reached the Kaiser's desk, William covered it with marginalia: "Nonsense!" "This is absolutely not so!" "No!" . . .

After Grey's speech and the defeat of Balfour's censure motion, parliamentary debate was over, but the furor in the Cabinet and country continued. Lloyd George and Churchill persisted in trying to stave off the four contingent dreadnoughts and to ensure that, if they were to be built, they would be part of the 1910 program. (Fisher wrote chaffingly to Churchill that if Churchill would permit the four additional ships to be built, he would see that they were named *Winston, Churchill, Lloyd,* and *George.* How they would fight!!") McKenna was "very sore with his colleagues about the way he had been treated" and reiterated his threat to resign unless the four contingent ships were ordered. Grey supported McKenna. The

Conservative press hammered the government. "If the Government is not composed of stony-hearted pedants, the shipbuilding . . . [orders] should be given out now," declared the *Daily Mail*. "Eighty percent of the cost of a battleship goes in wages to the British worker." "Our Navy and our unemployed may both be starved together and soon will be if you don't turn this Government out."

Ironically, the decision to build the contingent four, when it came, was prompted not by Germany, but by Austria and Italy. In July 1909, London learned that Austria was planning to build three and possibly four dreadnoughts. The Italians reacted swiftly; although Austria and Italy were nominal allies in the Triple Alliance, each regarded the other as a potential enemy. Italy immediately announced that it would build four dreadnoughts. Therefore, looking ahead to 1912, Britain would face a minimum of thirteen German dreadnoughts in the North Sea, plus Austrian and Italian dreadnoughts in the Mediterranean. The Admiralty case became irresistible. On July 26, McKenna announced that the four contingent ships would be laid down "without prejudice" to the 1910 program. Asquith, fulfilling his promise—and also keenly aware of the results of a recent by-election in Croydon in which the Liberal candidate had been overwhelmingly defeated—backed the First Lord. Liberals grumbled that there was still no sign of German acceleration and that the Austrian and Italian dreadnoughts cancelled each other out; Conservatives cheered; the Navy Scare was over.

The resolution was painful for a Liberal government which had taken office pledging to reducing the armaments burden. For three years, the government had met this pledge. Now, within twelve months, it had ordered eight costly ships.* Indeed, it was to acquire more. Two of the dominions, New Zealand and Australia, aware of their reliance on the Royal Navy, were alarmed by McKenna's portrayal of the narrowing margin of British naval supremacy. On March 22, only six days after the First Lord's presentation of the Naval Estimates to the House of Commons, the government of New Zealand cabled an offer to pay the cost of building one dreadnought. In June, the Australian government followed with a similar proposal. Both offers were accepted and in 1910 two additional battle cruisers, *New Zealand* and *Australia*, were laid down. Directly and indirectly, the Navy Scare of 1909 resulted in a single year's harvest of ten new dreadnoughts for the Royal Navy.

In retrospect, the grounds for the scare turned out to be false.

---

* Six battleships, *Colossus, Hercules, Orion, Conqueror, Monarch,* and *Thunderer,* and two battle cruisers, *Lion* and *Princess Royal.*

The Germans were acquiring materials and gun mountings in advance, and shipyards had begun construction early, but there was no acceleration in the delivery dates of German dreadnoughts. The four ships of the 1908 program and the four ships of the 1909 program were delivered on time and the four ships of the 1910 program were actually delayed eight months to permit a design change made necessary by the increase in gun caliber from 12-inch to 13.5-inch in six of the ten British ships.* At the end of 1912, there were—as promised by Tirpitz and Metternich—thirteen German dreadnoughts in commission. They were faced by twenty-two British dreadnoughts. Later, Churchill assessed the results and the significance of the Navy Scare:

"In the light of what actually happened, there can be no doubt whatever that, so far as facts and figures were concerned, we [Lloyd George and himself] were strictly right. The gloomy Admiralty anticipations were in no respect fulfilled in the year 1912. There were no secret German dreadnoughts, nor had Admiral Tirpitz made any untrue statement. . . . But although the Chancellor of the Exchequer and I were right in the narrow sense, we were absolutely wrong in relation to the deep tides of destiny. The greatest credit is due to the First Lord of the Admiralty, Mr. McKenna, for the resolute and courageous manner in which he fought his case and withstood his Party on this occasion. Little did I think, as this dispute proceeded, that when the next Cabinet crisis about the Navy arose, our roles would be reversed; and little did he think that the ships for which he contended so stoutly would eventually, when they arrived, be welcomed with open arms by me."†

The 1909 Naval Scare in Britain had other effects. There were those—Sir Edward Goschen, the British Ambassador in Berlin, was one—who were convinced that the building of the four additional dreadnoughts had a favorable impact on Anglo-German relations. In Berlin—this argument went—the decline in British dreadnought building during the early Liberal years bore out German theorizing that Britons were becoming soft and effete and would—in the natural Darwinian order—soon be replaced as rulers of the world by the virile Teutons. The British government's decision to double its annual shipbuilding program, Goschen argued, replaced this growing

---

* The three German battleships of the class, *Kaiserin, König Albert,* and *Prinzregent Luitpold,* had two fewer twelve-inch guns than their predecessors. The weight saved was given to thicker armor to deal with the greater penetrating power of the heavier British shells.

† In October 1911, McKenna and Churchill swapped jobs, with McKenna becoming Home Secretary and Churchill First Lord of the Admiralty.

contempt with respect and greater desire for friendship. A second effect was clearly apparent. The Two Power Standard, the historic guideline by which Great Britain had reckoned the sufficiency of its naval strength, was defunct. As recently as November 1908, at the outset of the Naval Scare, Asquith had restated that Britain required "a preponderance of ten percent over the combined strengths in capital ships of the next two strongest powers, whatever those powers might be." In fact, the world's third-largest navy, ranking not far behind the German Navy, belonged to the United States; no British politician or admiral envisaged war with the Americans. The 1909 Naval Scare marked the beginning of a one power standard for the British Navy; Britain was building only against Germany. Churchill, as First Lord, stated the fact officially on March 28, 1912, when he told the House of Commons that Britain's standard was one of 60 percent superiority over Germany.

There were two further effects of the 1909 Naval Scare and the decision to build eight dreadnoughts in a single year. Alarm in Parliament and hysteria in the press as to the condition of Britain's naval defenses prompted criticism of the aging First Sea Lord who directed the Admiralty and advised the government. Why, if Britain suddenly needed eight ships in a single year, had she built only two the year before? Justified or not, mounting complaints and criticism eroded Jacky Fisher's credibility. No sooner had the 1909 Naval Estimates been voted than a government inquiry began to look into these matters. The Naval Scare also deeply affected the Chancellor of the Exchequer, David Lloyd George. The decision to build eight dreadnoughts in a single year upset his budget calculations. To raise millions of additional pounds, the Chancellor set himself to find new sources of revenue and the taxes he proposed became even more politically controversial than the decision to build additional ships. They led, in 1910 and 1911, to a tumultuous and historic confrontation between the House of Commons and the House of Lords.

CHAPTER 34

Invading
England

◆

The role of the navy in Britain's wars was defensive; the offensive weapon was the army. And so the metaphor: the navy, the shield; the army, the spear; or, as Fisher modernized it: "the Army is a projectile to be fired by the Navy." The navy's primary mission was to defend the British Isles and the trade routes of the Empire. Yet, no matter how great its power, it could reach no farther than an enemy's coast. Alone, it could not defeat a great Continental enemy; decades of war against the Sun King and against Napoleon had proven that. Naval officers admitted that Britain needed an army; their preference was for a small, highly professional expeditionary force which, given the mobility provided by dominant sea power, could strike suddenly at any point on a hostile coastline with an impact out of all proportion to its numbers. In conceiving the role of the British Army, however, British admirals and captains never imagined that it should be responsible for the defense of the Home Islands. Since the Armada, it had been the duty of the Royal Navy to sink the warships, troopships, and barges of any invading power before a single enemy soldier set foot on an English beach.

...

As the nineteenth century approached an end, some in Britain began to doubt the navy's ability to perform even its defensive role. Much of this doubt was deliberately stirred by army officers. Was it wise, they asked, for Britain to put all her eggs in a single basket? "I know of nothing that is more liable to disaster than anything that floats on the water," Lord Wolseley, Commander-in-Chief of the British Army, declared in 1896. "We often find in peace and in the calmest weather our best ironclads running into one another. We find great storms dispersing and almost destroying some of the finest fleets that ever sailed. Therefore, it is essentially necessary for this country that it should always have a powerful army, at least sufficiently strong to defend our own shores." Even if British battleships managed not to run into one another or were not swamped by storms, there was always the chance that they might be decoyed away from the Channel long enough for an invading army to slip across. For these reasons, the army suggested, the army ought to be larger.

The army's initial defeat in the Boer War strengthened this argument. Heavy reinforcements of troops had to be sent from England, denuding the homeland of soldiers. The Continental press, vociferously pro-Boer, fumed against Britain's "free-booting enterprise in South Africa" and urged a European coalition to take advantage of Britain's vulnerability at home. That vulnerability was more psychological than real—the British Fleet remained on station in European waters—but it was keenly felt. "The Empire, stripped of its armor, with its hands tied behind its back and its bare throat exposed to the keen knife of its bitterest enemies," was the graphic description of the celebrated journalist W. T. Stead. As there were almost no troops in England, the French might lure the Fleet away long enough to ferry across fifty thousand or a hundred thousand men and march into London unopposed. Even Lord Salisbury, who customarily ignored talk of any threat to Britain, took note. In May 1900, when his countrymen felt most exposed, he proposed the formation of private rifle clubs throughout the country; invaders were to be deterred by the prospect of amateur riflemen popping up from behind the hedgerows.

Despite the Prime Minister's suggestion, the government maintained faith in the navy's ability to prevent invasion. During the Boer War, the Fleet had, in fact, played its traditional role. Absolute command of the sea had made possible the uninterrupted transport of 250,000 soldiers and their munitions and supplies over a route of six thousand miles. Meanwhile, talk in the Paris and Berlin press notwithstanding, no Continental soldiers had set foot in England.

The First Sea Lord of the period, Sir Walter Kerr, explained with professional calm: "Unless our Navy was quite wiped out in home waters, the risk to an invading force would be enormous and I suspect this is fully realized across the Channel." As it happened, no European government had any intention of challenging Great Britain, no matter how far away her soldiers might be. And no European fleet had the capacity to challenge the Royal Navy. The French Fleet, the only force which might conceivably have posed a threat, was throughout the span of the Boer War wholly unprepared for action. By December 1900, the sense of vulnerability in England had passed. The *Naval and Military Record* had regained a properly British sense of aloofness regarding threats from abroad: "The only difficulty we see in the way of an invasion of England—and it may arise through our insular prejudice—is that the French troops would have to be conveyed across the water."

After South Africa, the British Army naturally wished to correct the organizational and material flaws which had led to its embarrassment at the hands of the Boer commandos. Many officers also wanted a general expansion to give Britain the army of a Great Power. In 1901, St. John Broderick, Unionist Secretary of War in Salisbury's last Cabinet, introduced a plan for an army of 600,000 men structured in six army corps. One hundred and twenty thousand of these soldiers would be given the traditional role of an expeditionary force; 480,000 were to be assigned the new role of home defense. The reason, Broderick explained, was that something might happen to the navy. "Invasion may be an off-chance," he declared, "but you cannot run an Empire of this size on off-chances." The War Secretary's scheme met with general disapproval. "A great defensive army will never have anything to do in this country that is worth doing," announced the *Times*. "Not thirty army corps could redress the balance if the fleet were swept from the seas," Lord Rosebery declared in the House of Lords. Winston Churchill expressed the argument succinctly: "As to a stronger Regular Army, either we had command of the sea or we had not. If we had it, we required fewer soldiers; if we had it not, we wanted more ships."

The army persisted. Field Marshal Lord Roberts, the famous "Bobs," Britain's greatest living military hero, winner of the Victoria Cross, veteran of India, victor in South Africa, and, from 1901 to 1904, Commander-in-Chief of the British Army, became its advocate. Roberts' fear was that if the shield of the navy were to be broken or misplaced, the British Army would pose no obstacle to an invading force from any Continental power. His proposal was to create a large British Army based on compulsory conscription.

When the Unionist government of Arthur Balfour turned him down, he resigned from the army to devote himself to this cause. In 1905 , he became president of the National Service League, a militant group favoring conscription. Freed from the restraints of office, Lord Roberts, over seventy, became a familiar figure speaking on behalf of conscription in the House of Lords and at public meetings. When, in the last months of his Premiership, Balfour assured the House of Commons that invasion was "not an eventuality which we need seriously to consider," Roberts replied in the Lords: "I have no hesitation in stating that our armed forces, as a body, are as absolutely unfitted and unprepared for war as they were in 1899–1900."

Roberts' hostility towards Balfour was mild compared to his feelings about the new Liberal government which took power in December 1905. Looking to find money for social programs, Campbell-Bannerman and Asquith cut both the Army and the Navy Estimates. Soon, Lord Roberts was writing regularly to Mr. Balfour, who was the acknowledged authority in the Commons on defense as well as leader of the opposition. Roberts calculated that if, for one reason or another, the British Navy did not intervene, it would require only ninety-four hours for a Continental enemy to hurry seventy thousand soldiers across the Channel or the North Sea. Once in England, these invaders would be augmented by eighty thousand foreigners, all trained soldiers, already living in Great Britain. Many of the latter, he charged, worked in large hotels at the country's chief railway stations, where they could step out on the tracks to tie up Britain's transportation system.

Balfour was sufficiently impressed by Roberts' warnings to suggest that the Committee of Imperial Defense reconsider England's vulnerability to invasion. Before and during his Premiership, the potential invaders had been French; now they had become German. A subcommittee met and began to hear evidence. In April 1908, when Asquith became Prime Minister, the matter was taken more seriously. Because of his expertise, Balfour was asked to appear and to analyze the information gathered. In the presence of Asquith, Grey, Haldane, Lloyd George, and Lord Roberts, Balfour spoke for an hour. It was, said a witness, a "luminous" exposition, "quite perfect in form and language" which so "dumfounded" the committee that none of them, not even Roberts, could think of a single question to ask. "The general opinion was that no finer exposition of this question has ever been made." Balfour's opinion and the subcommittee's conclusion was that the navy should be the first line of defense and that as long as its supremacy remained assured, England could not successfully be invaded.

Fisher, who had little respect for the army, had always been contemptuous of suggestions that the navy could not fend off an invasion. "The Navy," he said on becoming First Sea Lord in 1904, "is the 1st, 2nd, 3rd, 4th, 5th . . . ad infinitum Line of Defence! If the Navy is not Supreme, no army however large is of the slightest use. It's not invasion we have to fear if our Navy is beaten, IT'S STARVATION!" As to enemy soldiers suddenly rushing across the North Sea and landing on an English beach, Fisher snorted: "I am too busy to waste my time over this cock and bull story." It would take months of preparation to assemble transports and embark soldiers; this could not go unnoticed. As to seventy thousand men, Fisher pointed out that during the month of October 1899, at the beginning of the Boer War, the greatest maritime power in the world, possessing the world's largest merchant fleet and using five great seaports, managed to send to sea only thirty thousand troops with less than four thousand horses. Fisher bristled that the Committee of Imperial Defence had bothered to meet to listen to Lord Roberts. At a Guildhall banquet in 1907, in one of the two public speeches Fisher ever made, the First Sea Lord ridiculed the idea of a German army arriving in England like a bolt from the blue. "You might as well talk of embarking St. Paul's Cathedral in a penny steamer," he declared. "No, gentlemen, you may go home and sleep quiet in your beds."

Although the subcommittee's conclusion and the government's endorsement were decisive as far as policy was concerned, both remained secret and had no effect on the raging public debate over invasion. Despite the First Sea Lord's assurances, despite the new dreadnoughts joining the Fleet, despite Haldane's efficient reorganization of the army, English men and women still worried. Henry James, almost an Englishman, living at Rye on the Channel coast, worried that he might one day look out to sea and spot the light-gray ships of the German Fleet, training their guns on his house. "When the German Emperor carries the next war into this country," he said, "my chimney pots, visible for a certain distance out to sea, may be his very first objective." The *Daily Mail* gave advice to diners: "Refuse to be served by an Austrian or German waiter. If your waiter says he is Swiss, ask to see his passport."

These worries were aggravated by a growing torrent of special literature—books, pamphlets, plays, and newspaper stories—based on the imminence of foreign invasion. With the growth of literacy and the rise of mass-circulation newspapers, a boom in sensational writing was on. Invasion literature erupted in the form of spy stories, imaginary-war novels, and invasion novels. For twenty years, from the beginning of the 1880s until 1903, when a colonial agreement with France was near completion, the fictional invaders had always been French. Britain's diplomatic quarrel with France over Egypt was a factor, heightened in 1898 by the war scare over Fashoda, but the roots of the antagonism went back centuries. In the late Victorian Age, the English explained it as purely a matter of France's envy: "envy of England's great Empire, envy of her freedom, envy of the stability of her Government, or her settled monarchy, or her beloved Queen."

In 1882, a flurry of invasion fears titillated England. A scheme, proposed that year in Parliament, envisaged digging a twenty-mile railway tunnel from Dover to Calais. In the subsequent outcry, rational discussion of the commercial advantage of opening this avenue for trade was forsaken. On the surface, the sole issue became whether the Channel tunnel might function as a breach of Britain's guardian moat. Underneath lurked other fears. A tunnel would mean the end of Splendid Isolation. It would force Britons to cast aside images of themselves as inhabitants of "this sceptred isle . . . set in a silver sea," as defenders of "this fortress built by Nature for herself." No stranger to England could understand. A generation earlier, Prince Albert, always enthusiastic about technology, had proposed a tunnel to Lord Palmerston; the Prime Minister, who never strayed far from the views of the average Englishman, replied "without losing the perfectly courteous tone which was habitual to him, 'You would think very differently, Sir, if you had been born on this island.' " Most Englishmen still shared this view. In 1882, impassioned citizens descended upon the London offices of the Channel Tunnel Company and broke the windows. A mass antitunnel petition signed by Browning, Tennyson, Huxley, Cardinal Newman, the Archbishop of Canterbury, five dukes, ten earls, fifty-nine generals, seventeen admirals, and twenty-six members of Parliament solemnly declared that the digging of a tunnel "would involve this country in military dangers and liabilities from which, as an island, it has hitherto been happily free." The uproar fired the imagination of writers. A torrent of pamphlets, tracts, and penny novels poured off the presses, with titles such as *The Channel Tunnel, or England in Danger; The Seizure of the Channel Tunnel; Battle of the Channel Tunnel; Surprise of the Channel Tunnel;* and *How John Bull Lost London*. A stock character appeared in this school of fiction: the

French waiter, working in England, with a rifle hidden in his luggage. Trained as soldiers, he and his compatriots would seize their arms, sneak from their lodgings, and, in the dark of night, capture the English terminal of the Channel tunnel. The following morning, a conquering French Army would arrive in England by train. The tunnel itself would make the influx of a number of foreigners seem unsuspicious: "The great increase in prosperity that the Tunnel brought to Dover," one novelist explained, "caused a large number of French restaurateurs, waiters, bootmakers, milliners, and pastry-cooks to settle in that town."

Great Britain's two most senior military officers added to the uneasiness. Field Marshal His Royal Highness the Duke of Cambridge, Commander-in-Chief of the British Army (and cousin to the Queen) wrote that if the English terminal to a tunnel were seized by surprise, Britain could not hope to oppose any great Continental power. "We might, despite all our precautions, very possibly some day find an enemy in actual possession of both its ends and able at pleasure to pour an army through it unopposed." Lord Wolseley, Adjutant General, thought that it might be possible for an enemy to invade without waiters and pastrycooks. "A couple of thousand armed men might easily come through a tunnel in a train at night, avoiding all suspicion by being dressed as ordinary passengers, or passing at express speed through the tunnel with the blinds down, in their uniforms and fully armed." As the years went by—with no tunnel present or in the offing—Channel tunnel invasion stories dwindled. One of the last, written in 1901, focussed on a tunnel being secretly bored from Calais. The clandestine terminus was to be established on a farm in Kent belonging to a French spy who had taken the name and manners of an Englishman. The plot was frustrated, but English readers were warned that "the tube of steel still lies beneath the sea. . . ."

As relations with France grew warmer and relations with Germany chilled, the source of fictional invasions shifted: it was from across the North Sea and not the Channel that England's despoilers were to come. In the best of the invasion genre, Erskine Childers' *The Riddle of the Sands,* published in 1903, the invaders were Teutons. Childers' tale is one of adventure at sea: two young Englishmen on holiday aboard a small yacht are sailing and duck shooting amidst the elaborate web of sand banks, estuaries, and tidal pools that stretch along the German North Sea coast from the Dutch frontier to the mouth of the Elbe. Here, in this shifting maze of sand and water, they stumble upon a mysterious enterprise, avoid attempted murder, dine with a gentlemanly English traitor, overhear shocking plans, and, one dark night, hidden aboard a German tugboat, one of the two young sailors catches a glimpse of His Imperial Majesty, the German Emperor. The Kaiser is present to verify the feasibility of the enterprise; the stowaway realizes what it is when he realizes where the tugboat is going:

"The course . . . was about west, with Norderney light a couple of points off the port bow. The course for Memmert? Possibly; but I cared not, for my mind was far from Memmert tonight. *It was the course for England too.* Yes, I understood at last. I was assisting at an experimental rehearsal of a great scene, to be enacted, perhaps in the near future—a scene when multitudes of sea-going lighters, carrying full loads of soldiers, not half-loads of coal, should issue simultaneously, in seven ordered fleets, from seven shallow outlets, and, under escort of the Imperial Navy, traverse the North Sea and throw themselves bodily upon English shores."

The Riddle of the Sands is more than a spy story; it is also a sailor's book. Childers himself was a yachtsman; he writes of "the wind humming into the mainsail," "the persuasive song the foam sings under the lee bow," and "the noble expanse of wind-whipped blue, half surrounded by distant hills." His own preference among his two young heroes is Davies, the owner of the yacht, a resourceful sailor whose daring and skill at the helm pilot the craft to the point where the secrets of the sands can be discovered. Davies has been to Oxford, been turned down by the navy, and now lives on his old thirty-foot sloop, its rigging and decks turned gray, its brass tarnished green. Davies' shipmate is Carruthers, an Oxford friend in the Foreign Office, whose world consists of writing reports and dining and dancing at country-house weekends. When Carruthers arrives, dressed in flannels and blazer, one look from Davies is enough; Carruthers changes into old clothes. Davies, not Carruthers the Foreign Office professional, understands what is going on. Sitting one day belowdecks, while the yacht lies in a harbor wrapped in clammy, silent fog, Davies puffs on his pipe and rolls out his charts on the cabin table. He is filled with respect, even admiration, for Germany:

" 'Here's this huge empire, stretching half over Central Europe —an empire growing like wildfire, I believe, in people, wealth, and everything. They've licked the French and the Austrians and are the greatest military power in Europe. . . . What I'm concerned with is their seapower. It's a new thing with them but it's going strong and that Emperor of theirs is running it for all it's worth. He's a splendid chap, and anyone can see he's right. They've got no colonies to speak of, and must have them, like us. They can't get them and keep them, and they can't protect their huge commerce without naval strength. The commerce of the sea is the thing nowadays, isn't it. I say, don't think these are my ideas. . . . It's all out of Mahan and those fellows. Well, the Germans have got a small fleet at present, but it's a thundering good one and they're building hard.' "

England, on the other hand, ignores the source of her greatness and spurns the zealous "sun-burnt, brine-burnt" sailors who understand these things and know how to save her:

" 'We're a maritime nation,' " Davies tells Carruthers. " 'We've grown by the sea and live by it; if we lose command of it, we starve. We're unique in that way; just as our huge Empire, only linked by the sea, is unique. And yet, my God! . . . see what mountains of apathy and conceit have had to be tackled. It's not the people's fault. We've been so safe so long, and grown so rich, that we've forgotten what we owe it. But there's no excuse for those blockheads of statesmen as they call themselves, who are paid to see things as they are. . . . By Jove, we want a man like this Kaiser, who doesn't wait to be kicked, but works like a nigger for his country and sees ahead. . . . We aren't ready for her [Germany]; we don't look her way. We have no naval base in the North Sea and no North Sea fleet. . . . And, to crown all, we were asses enough to give her Heligoland which commands her North Sea coast . . . . We can't talk about conquest and grabbing. We've collared a fine share of the world and they've every right to be jealous. Let them hate us and say so; it'll teach us to buck up; and that's what really matters.' *

* *The Riddle of the Sands* was the only novel written by this passionate, quixotic man. A well-bred Englishman who went to Cambridge, Erskine Childers worked as a clerk in the House of Commons, where the lengthy recesses and vacations provided him leisure to enjoy what he loved best: yachting in the North Sea and the Baltic. He was an English patriot who served his country with the horse artillery in the Boer War and as an aerial observer and intelligence officer in the First World War. Before the Great War came, however, a new passion had entered Childers' life. In 1908, he visited Ireland. He became a fervent Home Ruler and quit his job in the House of Commons to devote himself to the Irish cause. In July 1914, as the Protestants of Ulster were arming to resist Home Rule, Childers and his American wife rendezvoused their fifty-foot yacht with a German tugboat off the coast of Belgium and took aboard hundreds of Mauser rifles and thousands of rounds of ammunition to supply the Irish nationalists. This secret act preceded his service to England in the Great War. After demobilization, Childers gave himself again to Ireland. Entangled between factions of Irish nationalists, he chose the most extreme, which was temporarily to lose. Arrested by soldiers of the Irish Free State, he was found to be carrying a small pistol and, on this pretext, he was condemned and executed by a firing squad on November 24, 1922. "I die full of intense love for Ireland," he wrote to his wife

Growing public concern over the danger of German invasion can be measured by comparing Childers' innocent, windswept tale with a lurid, melodramatic book which appeared three years later. In March 1906, when Campbell-Bannerman's Liberal government had been in power only three months, the London *Daily Mail* began to serialize *The Invasion of 1910* by William Le Queux. Behind the book lay Lord Roberts' warnings that, despite the navy, Britain lay open to foreign invasion. Le Queux also believed in conscription and building a larger army; the purpose of his book was to shock the nation into believing the same.

In *The Invasion of 1910,* the invading army assembles in exactly the spot reconnoitered by Erskine Childers' two yachtsmen: amidst the tidal sands of the Frisian coast. Charging suddenly across the North Sea, it falls upon an unprepared England. Although untrained —because Lord Roberts' call for conscription has gone unheeded— England's soldiers and civilians fight with desperate bravery, but are no match for the efficient, professional enemy. On both sides, the war is fought with ferocity. The Germans are monsters who bayonet women and children, force terrified citizens to dig their own graves, and, in retaliation for the ambush of a German supply party, slaughter the entire population of an English town. The Kaiser is not a "splendid chap," but a bloodthirsty barbarian who craves the bombardment and sacking of London. "The pride of these English must be broken," commands the All-Highest. The English are almost as brutal: any German who falls into their hands is shot, stabbed, hanged, or garrotted. .

In Le Queux's plot, London is subjected to bombardment with heavy loss of life, then to fighting in the streets. Covered with gore, the Germans capture the city but cannot hold it. An enraged England rises up, forces the surrender of the invading army, and wreaks vengeance. German prisoners are lynched, torn limb from limb, or die in ways "too horrible to here describe in detail." The war ends in uneasy compromise. Germany, having annexed Holland and Denmark, ponders its chances in another invasion. England's economy, finances, and trade are demolished. Those wealthy enough to get away have fled; those left behind are starving.

The moral of this tale is hammered home by Le Queux when a character says, "Had we adopted his [Roberts'] scheme for universal

---

the night before he died. In reply to Winston Churchill's charge that he hated England, he told his wife, "It is not true. I die loving England and passionately praying that she may change completely and finally towards Ireland." In 1973, Erskine Childers' son, Erskine Hamilton Childers, became President of the Republic of Ireland.

service, such dire catastrophe could never have occurred." The point also was made in a foreword written by Roberts, in which he declared that "the catastrophe that may happen if we still remain in our present state of unpreparedness is vividly and forcibly illustrated in Mr. Le Queux's new book which I recommend to the perusal of everyone who has the welfare of the British Empire at heart."

The idea for the novel was born in the restless mind of Alfred Harmsworth, Lord Northcliffe, who ceaselessly strove to boost the circulation of his London *Daily Mail*. Roberts' constant warnings that a weak and complacent England was open to invasion suggested a story, and Le Queux was hired to write it. For four months, financed by the *Daily Mail,* the novelist roamed the east coast of England, scouting invasion beaches and sites for his fictional battles. He took his research to Lord Roberts and, together, hack writer and former Commander-in-Chief sat down to plot the course of the German campaign. Their work went to Lord Northcliffe, who initially vetoed it on the grounds that, although militarily sound, it overlooked the fundamental truths of newspaper circulation. For Northcliffe's purposes, the German Army had to battle its way through big cities and large towns, "not keep to remote, one-eyed villages where there was no possibility of large *Daily Mail* sales."

Lord Northcliffe launched *The Invasion of 1910* with sandwich men in spiked helmets and Prussian blue uniforms parading down Oxford Street, their boards proclaiming imminent invasion. Each day thereafter, advertisements advised which towns would be invaded the following morning in the *Daily Mail.* Success was overwhelming: newspapers sold out, again and again; published in book form, the novel was translated into twenty-seven languages, including Japanese, Chinese, and Arabic, and sold over a million copies around the world. The German edition chagrined Le Queux. Its cover depicted a triumphant German Army marching into the smoking ruins of a shattered London, and the translator's editing left the invading army in possession of the British capital. The Kaiser, who read both editions, ordered that the General Staff of the Army and the staff of the German Admiralty analyze the book for useful information.

Again, foreigners living in Britain became suspect. "Most of these men," Le Queux told his readers, "were Germans who, having served in the army, had come over to England and obtained employment as waiters, clerks, bakers, hairdressers, and private servants, and being bound by their oath to their Fatherland, had served their country as spies. Each man, when obeying the Imperial command to join the German arms, had placed in the lapel of his coat a button of a peculiar shape with which he had long ago been provided and by which he was instantly recognized as a loyal subject of the Kaiser." Across England, worried citizens looked up from the *Daily Mail* or Le Queux's book, casting about for potential "enemy agents." The War Office was flooded with reports of German plots to seize dockyards and naval bases, thereby putting the Fleet out of action as a prelude to invasion. Mysterious airships were rumored floating over British towns at night. The number of potential enemy warriors already in England escalated from Le Queux's relatively innocuous "6,500 spies" to Lord Roberts' "80,000 trained soldiers" to the revelation by a Colonel Driscoll that "350,000 trained German soldiers" resided in Britain. A Conservative M.P., Sir John Barlow, asked Haldane, the War Secretary, to tell the House of Commons what he knew about the 66,000 German Army reservists living near London. While he was at it, Barlow suggested, the War Secretary might also investigate the secret cache of thousands of German rifles stored in the cellars of a bank in Charing Cross. Another Tory M.P., Colonel Lockwood, asked that something be done about the "military men from a foreign nation" who had been busy for two years in the neighborhood of Epping "sketching and photographing the whole district."

The government attempted to deal with these fears. The "mysterious airships" turned out to be small balloons put up to advertise new automobiles. The German rifles in Charing Cross were traced to a purchase of old pieces by the Society of Miniature Rifle Clubs, temporarily stored by the society's bankers. Haldane, disgusted by Le Queux, Roberts, and the entire spy-invasion mania, sarcastically suggested that the enemy agents near Epping had been wasting their time as the information they required was already available in public ordnance survey maps. "Lord Roberts' repeated statements that we are in danger of invasion and are not prepared to meet it . . . are doing a good deal of mischief," he told the House. "Worse still is the effect on the public mind that Germany is the enemy which renders any attempt to improve relations increasingly difficult. The King is a good deal worried about this and I have told him that I would myself back up Lord Roberts' proposal for Compulsory Service in order to restore confidence and banish the German bogey if I were not convinced that it was both impracticable and dangerous."

In part, the Liberal government's annoyance at *The Invasion of 1910* and similar works stemmed from the Tory prejudice of most of the authors of these books. Le Queux made his views explicit, ascribing the initial success of his German invasion to the fact that "a strong, aristocratic Government had been replaced by a weak administration, swayed by every breath of popular impulse. The peasantry, who were the backbone of the nation, had vanished and been replaced by the weak, excitable population of the towns." Irritated by such slurs, Liberal M.P.'s rose in Parliament to ask what could be done to limit the damage done by vulgar, inaccurate books which aroused passions and inflamed hatreds. Campbell-Bannerman, the Prime Minister, advised leaving the book "to be judged by the good sense and good taste of the British people." The government, of course, could decide on the policy matter of compulsory conscription. It decided against Lord Roberts: peacetime conscription of men into the British Army never occurred.

Roberts, nevertheless, continued to speak, and accounts of fictional invasions continued to appear. In January 1909, at the height of the Naval Scare, when the Cabinet was locked in fierce debate over whether to authorize four or six dreadnoughts, a new play, *An Englishman's Home,* opened at London's Wyndham's Theatre. The playwright was Guy du Maurier, a Regular Army officer who had never written a play or anything else and who at that moment was in South Africa serving as second in command, Third Battalion, the Royal Fusiliers. Before leaving England, Major du Maurier, affected by Roberts' warnings, had written the play and given it to his brother, Gerald du Maurier, the actor and theatrical manager.* Gerald du Maurier read his brother's work and, without troubling to inform the far-off major, put it on the stage.

In the play, England is invaded by a foreign army. The Lord Chamberlain's office, which approved and licensed theatrical works, worried that a specific foreign power might be offended; thus, the nationality of the invaders was unspecified. Accordingly, the enemy soldiers swear allegiance to "the Emperor of the North" and their country is known as "Nearland." The action takes place in the parlor of Mr. and Mrs. Brown, a middle-class English family whose house is suddenly surrounded and entered by a troop of Nearland soldiers. The names of the invaders—Prince Yoland, Thol, Garth, and Hobart—vaguely disguise their national identity, but their spiked helmets provide an unmistakable clue. Initially, Mr. Brown is apathetic, declaring that wars should be fought between professional soldiers. The enemy commander, Prince Yoland, treats the Englishman and his family with rigid civility and arrogant contempt. When household articles are destroyed or confiscated, the damage or loss is paid for. As the play develops, Brown becomes increasingly indignant at the presence of intruders in his domestic castle and verbally

---

* Father of novelist Daphne du Maurier.

lashes out. Ultimately, he seizes a rifle and points it at his enemies. Prince Yoland coolly reminds him of his own previous statement that civilians have no role in fighting wars. Brown replies, "Bah! What does that matter? I am an Englishman!" Nightly, at this line, the theater rang with sustained applause. In the end, brave Mr. Brown kills two Nearland soldiers and then is himself executed, a hero but also a victim of England's unpreparedness. At the final curtain, patriotism is avenged when British regulars arrive to expel the invaders.

The play played to packed houses for eighteen months. The sight, even on stage, of foreign soldiers in spiked helmets trampling across an English lawn and bursting through French windows into the parlor of an English house was too much for many a fervent theatergoer. The army set up a special recruiting station in the lobby of the theater so that fiery young men, erupting out of the stalls once the curtain had fallen, could volunteer on the spot for Haldane's new Territorial Army.

CHAPTER 35

The Budget
and the
House of Lords

◆

In January 1906, after the Liberal Party had spent a decade in the political wilderness, Sir Henry Campbell-Bannerman led it back into power. The General Election that month had produced a landslide Liberal victory. Sir Henry and his Cabinet had no doubt as to what their followers expected: they had been elected on a classic Liberal platform of Peace, Retrenchment (i.e., cutting military spending and, therefore, taxes), and Reform. The new Entente with France and a similar arrangement with the Russians would help maintain peace, while the Germans were kept in check by Sir John Fisher and his dreadnoughts. Retrenchment was achieved when Haldane at the War Department and Fisher at the Admiralty produced greater fighting efficiency for less money. The area of greatest expectation, however, was Reform. The party had promised significant changes in the patterns of British life. Elimination of religious instruction in state-supported schools, extension of the temperance laws, establishment of old-age pensions, limitations on hours of work, better housing, and land reform all were parts of the Liberal program. Many new M.P.'s, along with the voters who supported them, believed that it would not take long to transform the promise into legislative reality. The experienced politicians who sat on the Government Bench knew better; before a single item of the new government's reform program could become law, it had to be passed by the House of Lords. And, in 1908, the Lords, with five hundred Unionist peers and only eighty-eight Liberals, were adamantly, viscerally opposed to reform.

The dukes, marquesses, earls, viscounts, and barons who made up the Lords Temporal of the House of Lords (the Lords Spiritual were the archbishops of Canterbury and York and twenty-four other bishops) were accustomed to ruling England. They were the old landed nobility; they owned the most property, and, having the largest stake in the country, thought it normal that they be expected to look after it. The rest of the population—workers, townspeople, tradesmen, and middle classes—would, of course, be fairly treated according to station. In determining the most effective blend of firmness, kindness, and condescension to be meted out, the aristocracy had the benefit of generations of experience with grooms, gamekeepers, gardeners, and indoor staff. The rise of the House of Commons in Tudor times, the temporary victory of the Parliamentarians and Oliver Cromwell, made no essential difference in this pattern of oligarchic rule. Even the wide expansion of the electorate through the great Reform Acts of the nineteenth century brought little change in the character and breeding of the men at the top. The public voted in larger numbers, but it still voted to choose *which* of the great noblemen, Whig or Tory, would serve as ministers of the Crown and custodians of the national destiny.

The institutional embodiment and ultimate political bastion of the landed aristocracy was the House of Lords. Here, whether they chose ever to enter the chamber or not, all hereditary peers were entitled to sit. The hall, eighty feet long, forty-five feet wide, was illuminated by high windows in which portraits of England's monarchs were set in stained glass. Peers sat on four rows of red leather benches, ascending on either side of the center aisle. Two golden royal thrones, almost never occupied, and the Woolsack, a large red cushion stuffed with wool,* from which the Lord Chancellor presided and, when necessary, called for order, dominated the chamber.

Admonition from the Woolsack was rarely heard. Their lordships were too well behaved to bark and hiss at an opponent, and the political issues which embattled the House of Commons only a few yards away seemed to lose their virulence when brought into the House of Lords. Usually, even in session, the chamber was empty.

---

* Placed in the House in the fourteenth century to proclaim the nation's wealth in the wool trade.

"The cure for the House of Lords is to go and look at it," said the journalist Walter Bagehot. "In the ordinary transaction of business there are perhaps ten peers in the House, possibly only six; three is the quorum for transacting business. A few more may dawdle in or not dawdle in." Numerous peers never entered the House of Lords at all, preferring to live "an obscure and doubtless a useful existence on their country estates scattered through the length and breadth of England [where they] were locally familiar as landlords, magistrates and Lords Lieutenant." They came up to London only to bring out a daughter or occupy a seat at a coronation. If they went to the House of Lords, it was usually to look up a friend whom, unaccountably, they had not encountered at their club. David Lloyd George, the Radical Welshman who was Chancellor of the Exchequer in Asquith's Cabinet, dubbed these rustic noblemen Backwoodsmen.

In 1906, the House of Lords retained a significant constitutional function: when a piece of hasty, ill-conceived legislation was passed by the Commons and forwarded to the Lords, their lordships had the power to veto it. In theory, this was supposed to exercise a wise restraint on the lower House. Rebuff in the Lords might lead to cooler reconsideration in the Commons. Or, by provoking the resignation of the government, it could bring on a new General Election in which the public would have an opportunity to express its view at the polls. To this power of rejection, there was one long-established exception: it was accepted that the House of Lords could not amend or reject any bill having to do with money. For 281 years, this understanding—unwritten like the rest of the British Constitution—had gone unchallenged. In fact, the huge party imbalance in the upper house made a farce of the Lords' supposed role as an impartial revisionary body. The permanent Unionist majority swept away any trace of impartiality. When the government was Conservative, bills arrived from the Commons and passed effortlessly through the Lords without amendment, and sometimes even without discussion. But when a Liberal government came to power, the House of Lords suddenly awakened to its duty to scrutinize, amend, and reject. This was the fate of Gladstone's Home Rule bills in 1884 and 1893. In the decade of rule by Lord Salisbury and Arthur Balfour, 1895-1905, the Lords had retreated into somnolence, their watchdog powers unrequired and unexercised. Then came the election results of January 1906. "We were all out hunting in Warwickshire when the final results of the election arrived," wrote one nobleman. Peers, greatly alarmed, turned up at the House of Lords to ask what they should do to help turn back the socialist tide. They were counseled not to worry; nation and empire were safe. The Liberal majority, it was explained, although formidable in the House of Commons, could do nothing in the face of the veto power of the House of Lords. Soon— the explanation continued—in a few more years at most—the country would return to its senses and, in the next General Election, return control of the Commons to the Unionist Party. In the meantime, Mr. Balfour and Lord Lansdowne, respectively the leaders of the party in the Commons and the Lords, would wield the powers of the upper house to keep the country safe.

It was this formidable pair, the former Prime Minister and his lieutenant, the former Foreign Secretary and maker of the Anglo-French Entente, who blocked the Liberal path to social reform. The two Conservative leaders did not act in secret. They did not need to. What they planned and did was constitutional and legal; in their view it was also patriotic and right. The new Liberal majority contained men who were professionals, from the middle class, possessing small means; some of the Labour M.P.'s had actually worked with their hands. To Lansdowne, who believed that "the man in the street is the most mischievous product of the age," a House of Commons composed of poor men and workingmen could not effectively govern the nation. Balfour agreed, and in Nottingham on January 15, 1906, the night of his own electoral defeat, he urged that it was the duty of everyone to see that "the great Unionist Party should still, whether in power or in opposition, control the destinies of this great Empire." From the beginning of the new Parliament, Balfour and Lansdowne worked together. In an exchange of letters in April 1906, they both used a military metaphor: "It is essential that the two wings of the army should work together . . . ," Lansdowne wrote Balfour. Balfour agreed: "The Party in the two Houses shall not work as two separate armies but shall cooperate on a common plan of campaign." The campaign was to be ruthless, the power of the House of Lords to be applied nakedly and unashamedly. Liberal bills which challenged the status or wealth of the landed nobility, or their supporters or constituents, were to be slaughtered without mercy.

The first victim was a Liberal Education Bill designed to remedy the grievances of the Nonconformists, who had provided massive electoral support to the Liberal cause. The Bill, which would have abolished teaching Anglicanism and Roman Catholicism in state-supported schools, stirred the wrath of High Church Tories in both the Commons and the Lords. Introduced early in April 1906, it emerged from the Commons in autumn and went up to the Lords. Lord Lansdowne, with Balfour's advice in his ear, knew how to deal with it. The Bill was allowed to pass its early readings, then was sent to committee, where it was so mutilated by amendments that it came out legislating the opposite of its original purpose. This mutant was returned to the Commons, where the government, horrified, refused even to consider the Lords' amendment and simply let it die. A quicker, less complicated fate met a Plural-Voting Bill, intended to repeal an ancient law which gave certain landowners holding property in different constituencies the right to vote in each. (One great nobleman thus empowered had the right to vote twelve times.) The Lords began to debate the bill, soon ran out of things to say, and killed it in an hour and a half. The only major piece of legislation allowed to pass the 1906 Parliament was a Trades Disputes Act, which exempted trade unions from legal actions for damages. The growing trade-union movement was expanding its political and economic power; sensing danger in direct repression, the Lords warily stood aside.

Liberals were enraged by the massacre of their bills. The House of Lords had become, in Lloyd George's phrase, "not the watchdog of the Constitution, but Mr. Balfour's poodle." Campbell-Bannerman, expressing frustration at the end of the session, announced grimly, "The resources of the House of Commons are not exhausted and I say with conviction that a way must be found, and a way will be found, by which the will of the people, expressed through their elected representatives, will be made to prevail." In June 1907, the Commons resolved, 432 to 147, to curb the veto power of the House of Lords. Nevertheless, in the 1907 parliamentary session, the Lords destroyed or sterilized almost every Liberal bill. The only important legislation allowed to pass was Haldane's Army Reform Bill which, by making the Regular Army more efficient and creating the Territorial Army and a General Staff, all the while cutting £2 million from annual military expenditure, was difficult to oppose.

In January 1908, as the Liberal government entered its third year, the party in the Commons and the country was losing patience. Virtually none of the legislation promised in the election had been enacted; everyone realized that none would be until something was done about the House of Lords. But what could be done? Any legislation designed to restrict the powers of the Lords would have to pass *through* the House of Lords. Meanwhile, the Prime Minister was ill (Campbell-Bannerman was to resign on April 3 and die on April 22), the government seemed ineffective, and the public was disgusted. The electorate—as Balfour had predicted—was beginning to swing back to the right. A series of Liberal by-election losses (seven seats over the year) were not enough to threaten the government's huge majority in the Commons, but they were a warning of what might happen in the next General Election.

To reverse this trend, in 1908 the Cabinet proposed two significant pieces of legislation: an Old-Age Pensions Bill and a Licensing Bill. The concept of pensions for the elderly had overwhelming support from the British working class, and enactment had been pledged by Liberal M.P.'s. The proposed plan was modest: any person seventy or older who did not have an income of more than ten shillings a week would receive a weekly pension of five shillings (seven shillings and sixpence for married couples). Recipients had to pass a character test; any person who "has habitually failed to work according to his ability, opportunity, and need, for the maintenance of himself and those legally dependent on him" was declared ineligible. To preempt interference by the Lords, the government invoked the argument that it was a finance bill to which amendments by the upper house were inadmissible. Their lordships grumbled but let it pass.

In its treatment of the Licensing Bill, the House of Lords showed no such caution. Carefully framed, supported by a far wider section of the public than simply Liberal Nonconformists who believed passionately in temperance, the bill was intended to cut down the number of public drinking houses in neighborhoods which had too many. A fixed number of pubs, proportionate to local population, was established and a lengthy grace period of fourteen years granted in which to adjust to the appropriate number. Conservatives fell upon this bill with fury. It was described as a vindictive government intrusion on a traditional and honorable form of private enterprise. One peer, arguing that the number of public houses had no relationship to drunkenness, declared that he did not feel sleepier in his country house, where there were fifty bedrooms, than he did in his seaside villa, where there were only a dozen. Brewers threatened to withdraw their generous support of the Unionist Party if the bill became law. The King, endeavoring to protect the Lords from themselves, summoned Lord Lansdowne and urged that the upper house not be seen lining up on the side of intemperance. Lansdowne carried the plea to his fellow Unionist peers meeting informally in the drawing room of Lansdowne House on Berkeley Square. (There was no chamber in the Houses of Parliament large enough to accommodate this number except the House of Lords itself, which could not be used except for official—and recorded—debate.) Of two hundred peers present, all but twelve favored rejecting the bill. When it was formally brought before the House of Lords on November 24, the vote to reject was 272 to 96. The House, said Lord

Edmond Fitzmaurice, Lord Lansdowne's brother, gave it "a first class funeral. A great many noble lords have arrived who have not often honoured us with their presence." In announcing the results, the Liberal Lord Chancellor, Lord Loreburn, declared that the Licensing Bill had not died that night in the House but already had been "slain by the stiletto in Berkeley Square."

At the end of 1908, the Liberal Party seethed with frustration over the government's impotence and its apparent unwillingness to challenge the provocations of the upper house. News from by-elections continued to depress and it was generally felt that if an election were held, the Unionists would win by a majority of a hundred seats. The problem, as everyone realized, was that the Lords were exploiting the letter of the constitution while ignoring its spirit. Balfour, with only 147 Unionist members in the Commons, supported by five hundred Unionist peers, was restricting the exercise of government to a single party.

One solution—provoking an immediate General Election—seemed to the government too full of risks. None of the bills rejected by the Lords was in itself persuasive enough to convince the country to make a basic constitutional change regarding the upper house. Another path suggested itself: the Lords could not amend a Finance Bill; during the passage of the Old-Age Pensions Bill, the majority of peers had made no attempt to conceal their hostility to the legislation, but when the Commons firmly announced that any upper house amendment to this money bill was constitutionally unacceptable, the Lords had backed down. Finance bills—a Budget Bill, specifically—seemed to offer a means of social advance for the Liberal government. Should the Lords attempt to block legislation, the Liberals saw a basic constitutional issue they could take to the country. The issue of Who Rules England? The Peers or the People? was something the public could understand.

It was during the weeks early in 1909 when the Cabinet was deadlocked on the issue of four dreadnoughts or six in the Naval Estimates that David Lloyd George, the Chancellor of the Exchequer, devised his 1909 budget. He approached his task with zest. With £8.7 million needed to fund the old-age pensions and £3.7 million required in the first year to pay for new dreadnoughts,* Lloyd George faced an immediate prospective deficit of £16 million. To raise the money, the Chancellor would be forced to increase revenue through new taxes. This prospect cheered him enormously.

* Dreadnoughts cost roughly £1.5 million apiece; the eight authorized in 1909 eventually cost British taxpayers at least £12 million.

"I shall have to rob somebody's hen roost," he said, "and I must consider where I can get most eggs and where I can get them easiest and where I shall be least punished." By April, the Chancellor had located a number of suitable hen roosts. Paying for the extra dreadnoughts—whose authorization he had strenuously opposed—offered considerable retributional pleasure; the Unionists who had shouted loudest for the additional battleships would now be taxed to pay for them. The other items on his tax list also could be counted on to agitate the country's Establishment. Better, he had calculated a way to overcome their opposition: all these measures, which included a healthy ingredient of social reform, could be wrapped into a finance bill, the annual budget, with which the Lords would tamper at their peril.

Lloyd George introduced his historic budget before the House of Commons on April 29, 1909, one month after the conclusion of the censure debate on the Naval Estimates. He called it the "People's Budget" and said it was intended "to raise money to wage implacable warfare against poverty and squalor." The bill slashed at wealth and property in a variety of ways. The only new taxes which hit all classes were increased duties on alcohol and tobacco. Taxes on motor cars and gasoline fell on the upper classes and the affluent. Lloyd George hit back at the brewers who had helped kill the Licensing Bill by increasing the cost of liquor licenses for public houses. He graduated income taxes from ninepence per pound to one shilling and twopence per pound (from slightly under 4 percent to a little less than 6 percent). He imposed a "Super Tax" on all incomes over £3,000 per year and substantially increased death duties. What most enraged Conservatives was that the Chancellor inserted into the Finance Bill a Land Valuation Bill intended to prepare the way for new taxes on land. For the first time, all private land in England was to be appraised. This was perceived—as was intended—as an attack on the great landowners. It created a storm. The image of strangers tramping over ancient lands to assess their value in order to levy taxes threw English noblemen into a frenzy; if the Bill could not be defeated in the House of Commons, then it must and would be vetoed in the House of Lords.

The long battle over the House of Lords evolved in two phases: the initial battle over the 1909 budget; then, overtaking and overshadowing the budget, the fundamental constitutional question as to whether the House of Lords should retain its power to overrule the House of Commons. As long as the issue was primarily financial,

Lloyd George fought the government's case. Once the battle shifted onto constitutional grounds, the Prime Minister, Asquith, stepped forward to lead his party.

The Chancellor was an eager, active, sometimes inflammatory spokesman. In Parliament and the country, he delivered speeches, "something between incomparable drama and a high class vaudeville act," which left his audiences "howling with alternate rage and laughter." The most famous was delivered on a summer evening at Limehouse in London's East End where, before an audience of four thousand Cockneys, he described the government's fight to pass the Old-Age Pensions Bill and the resistance of the nation's landlords and property owners. The highlight was his description of his visit to a coal mine:

"We sank into a pit half a mile deep. We then walked underneath the mountain. . . . The earth seemed to be straining, around us and above us, to crush us in. You could see the pit props bent and twisted and sundered until you saw their fibers split in resisting the pressure. Sometimes they give way and there is mutilation and death. Often a spark ignites, the whole pit is deluged in fire, and the breath of life is scorched out of hundered of breasts by the consuming flame. In the very next colliery to the one I descended, just a few years ago three hundred people lost their lives that way. And yet when the Prime Minister and I knock at the door of these great landlords and say to them—'Here, you know these poor fellows who have been digging up royalties at the risk of their lives, some of them are very old . . . they are broken, they can earn no more. Won't you give them something towards keeping them out of the workhouse?'—they scowl at us and we say—'Only a ha'penny, just a copper.' They say, 'You thieves!' And they turn their dogs on to us."

Lloyd George embraced all peers, magnates, and landowners great and small in an inclusive, generic, derogatory term, "the dukes." Describing these landed noblemen to his audiences, for the most part workers and townspeople, he painted scenes of rustic barbarians who sat around rough tables before vast fireplaces in their castles, wearing coronets like the peers in *Iolanthe,* occasionally ordering their horses saddled so they could ride up to London and gleefully vote against Liberal bills. At Newcastle on October 9, the Chancellor was in good form. He had good news to work with: Conservatives had predicted that the introduction of his budget would depress the economy; in fact, it was healthy and rising. "Only one stock has gone down badly," he reported. "There has been a great slump in dukes." And no wonder: "A fully equipped duke costs as much to keep up as two dreadnoughts and dukes are just as great a terror and they last longer." He turned to the issue of the Lords' veto: "The question will be asked 'Should 500 men, ordinary men, chosen accidentally from among the unemployed, override the judgement—the deliberate judgement—of millions of people who are engaged in the industry which makes the wealth of the country?'"

The Chancellor's provocative speeches did their work; as Lloyd George sharpened his stick and prodded mercilessly, cries broke out all over England. From country shires and mountain fastnesses, noblemen emerged. The Duke of Portland earnestly explained how the budget would spread unemployment through the country as great estates were forced to dismiss gardeners and gamekeepers. The Duke of Somerset announced that he would be compelled to reduce his contributions to charity. The Duke of Beaufort grimly wished that he could see Mr. Lloyd George caught in the middle of his pack of hounds. Experienced politicians were goaded by the Chancellor's speeches. Lord Lansdowne likened Lloyd George to "a swooping robber gull, particularly voracious and unscrupulous, which steals fish from other gulls." Lord Rosebery, who since formation of the Liberal government in 1906 had remained detached, describing his own speeches as "the croakings of a retired raven on a withered branch," suddenly burst into partisan flame with a speech in Glasgow. Attacking the budget, he said bitterly, "I think my friends are moving on the path that leads to Socialism. How far they are advanced on that path I will not say. But on that path, I, at any rate, cannot follow them an inch. Socialism is the end of all, the negation of Faith, of Family, of Property, of Monarchy, of Empire." Rosebery's words brought joy to the country houses of England. If this great Liberal orator and former Prime Minister was, after all, "on the side of the angels," all was not lost.

Asquith left most of the argument at this stage to his fiery Welsh colleague, providing the Chancellor with support which Lloyd George characterized as "firm as a rock." The Prime Minister's single major speech of the autumn, an address to thirteen thousand people in Birmingham on September 17, treated passage of the budget as certain: "Amendment by the House of Lords is out of the question," he declared. "Rejection by the House of Lords is equally out of the question. . . . That way revolution lies." Nevertheless, the unthinkable happened. On November 4, the House of Commons passed Lloyd George's budget. Debate moved to the Lords. Lord Lansdowne reminded the House that Oliver Cromwell, the greatest English republican, had said that a House of Lords was necessary to protect the people against "an omnipotent House of Commons—

the horridest arbitrariness that ever existed in the world." Lord Curzon declared that never in human history had poverty been cured by taxation and that the taxes now proposed would grow from sporadic confiscation to complete and uniform confiscation. On November 30, the Lords rejected the budget by a vote of 350 to 75, the first time in 250 years that the Upper House had repudiated a finance bill. Asquith promptly moved a resolution in the Commons describing the Lords' action as "a breach of the Constitution and a usurpation of the rights of the Commons." Privately, Liberals who wished a showdown with the Lords were delighted. "If you gentlemen throw out the Budget, we shall have the time of our lives," one Cabinet minister told a Conservative friend. "We have got them at last," Lloyd George exulted.

The way lay open for a General Election. On December 10, 1909, in the Albert Hall, Asquith announced that the Liberal Cabinet would not again submit to the rebuffs and humiliations dealt by the Lords over the preceding four years. "We shall not assume office and we shall not hold office, unless we can secure the safeguards . . . necessary for the legislative utility and honor of the party," he said. Surprisingly, the election held in January 1910 was dull. Both parties campaigned on the merits of the budget, but the real issue was the veto power of the House of Lords. The country voted in moderate numbers and the result was a loss for both sides. The Liberals won a majority with 275 seats, but suffered a huge shrinkage from the 377 seats they had gained four years earlier. The Unionists gained 105 seats and came back to Westminster with a total of 273, but remained a minority. Eighty-two Irish Nationalists and forty Labour members were certain to vote with the government. The Unionist defeat ensured that the budget would pass; Lord Lansdowne had promised that if the Liberals won the election the House of Lords would let it through. In order to pass the bill through the Commons, however, with a government majority of only two, the Cabinet needed the Irish—and the Irish were only available for a price. They wanted Home Rule, and the only way to pass Home Rule through the British Parliament was to annul the veto power of the House of Lords. The price of passing the "People's Budget" through the House of Commons, therefore, was Asquith's promise to make a powerful assault on the Lords. For the next year and a half the Prime Minister attempted to carry out this promise.

When the new Parliament assembled in February 1910, Asquith immediately announced that the government intended to eliminate the veto power of the House of Lords. On April 14, he introduced a

Parliament bill into the House of Commons, declaring that "if the Lords fail to accept our policy, or decline to consider it . . . we shall feel it our duty immediately to tender advice to the Crown as to the steps which will have to be taken. . . ." The rumor, awful to Unionist peers, was that the Prime Minister had obtained the King's promise to create enough new peers—as many as five hundred—to carry the bill through the House of Lords. Distracted by this prospect, Unionists scarcely noticed as the Chancellor's budget, land valuation and all, passed through the Commons on April 27 and the Lords the following day. That evening, exhausted by their labors, needing a respite before they continued, members of both houses adjourned for the Easter recess.

Ultimately, the King would have to decide. Lansdowne had averted an immediate crisis by carrying out his pledge that, if the Liberals won the General Election, the Lords would pass Lloyd George's budget. This was no longer enough. The government now was committed to Irish members and thus to stripping the power of veto from the House of Lords. King Edward agreed that some reform of the upper house was necessary; in October 1909, Lord Knollys, his private secretary (who shared and reflected the monarch's view), wrote to a friend, "I myself do not see how the House of Lords can go on as presently constituted." Yet while the cosmopolitan King did not share the tastes of all peers, particularly some of the Backwoodsmen, the exclusiveness of the aristocracy and the privilege of the House of Lords were part of the England into which he had been born. Although Asquith told Parliament in February 1910 that he had neither requested of nor received from the King any pledge to create five hundred peers to subvert the House of Lords, even the hint that such a request might someday arrive worried the monarch.

King Edward was in poor health. For four years, his bronchitis and gout had worsened. Despite nights of coughing and a constant increase in weight, he refused to obey his doctors. "Really, it is too bad," he would complain. "There is the attack again, although I have taken the greatest care of myself"—and then sit down to a dinner of turtle soup, salmon steak, grilled chicken, saddle of mutton, snipe stuffed with foie gras, asparagus, fruit, dishes of flavored ices, and a savory, after which he would light up an enormous cigar. In addition to his physical ills, there were the obligations of constitutional monarchy: he must, in public, always be cheerful, patient, and wise.

One burden the King found heavy was the need to be civil to

his nephew the Emperor William. This made even more difficult a duty on which the British Foreign Office now insisted. King Edward had been on the throne for eight years. He had made state visits to all the major—and a number of minor—European capitals, but he had never formally visited Berlin. (His many trips to Germany to see his dying sister or to call on his nephew had all been private and informal.) The Kaiser felt this keenly, German diplomats mentioned it frequently, and the Foreign Office pressed hard. The King, ill and melancholy, agreed reluctantly and in February 1909 he went.

The visit was plagued by mishaps. The first occurred as the King's train reached Rathenow, on the Brandenburg frontier, where a military band and a regiment of hussars were drawn up. When the royal train pulled into the station, the King was unready; the train had crossed into a different time zone and his valet, having failed to adjust his watch, had not laid out His Majesty's uniform. When the King's suite in full uniform descended from the train, the band, expecting the monarch to follow, struck up "God Save the King." For ten minutes, while King Edward struggled into the uniform of a German field marshal, the band played "God Save the King" over and over, "till we all nearly screamed," said a member of the British suite. Eventually, King Edward appeared and, walking so briskly that he lost his breath, inspected the hussars.

In Berlin, the Kaiser awaited his uncle at the place on the station platform where the King's railway car was to stop; the King, however, was in the Queen's carriage a hundred yards away. The Kaiser, the Kaiserin, and the rest of the welcoming party had to run down the platform and line up again to greet their guest. A long cavalcade of carriages waited to carry them to the Palace, but there was trouble with the horses. Some of the carriages were bunched together, and the footmen following one had to keep turning around to make sure they would not be bitten by the horses immediately behind them. Nearing the Palace, the horses pulling the carriage in which the Empress was riding with Queen Alexandra suddenly stopped and refused to move, and the two women had to descend and climb into another, hastily emptied carriage. Two horses in the cavalry escort became frightened, threw their riders, and galloped disruptively along the procession. The result of these misadventures was that the Kaiser and the King arrived at the Palace, looked behind them, and saw no one. William, humiliated, turned his anger on Baron von Reischach, Master of the Horse, declaring that of all the people in the world, this should not have happened in front of the English who were, to a man and woman, all experienced riders.

The state visit, which lasted three days, included a heavy schedule of family luncheons and dinners, civic receptions, visits to regimental headquarters, a drive to Potsdam, a performance of the Berlin Opera, and a Court ball. Throughout, King Edward persevered, but he was weary, kept his remarks to a minimum, and was anxious to abbreviate each event. The question of which English decorations to bestow on German officials, normally a matter which would have occupied him for hours, interested him scarcely at all. He tolerated the Kaiser, who tried to please, but whose forced jokes and continual grunts of approval frayed King Edward's nerves.

The King's night at the opera gave him a scare. The performance was of *Sardanapalus,* one of the Kaiser's favorites. The last scene was a realistic portrayal of the funeral pyre of Sardanapalus. King Edward, weary from a tiring day and nodding off during the opera, suddenly awoke. Alarmed, believing that the fire was real, he demanded to know why the fireman stationed in the wings had not taken action. The Empress, sitting beside him, convinced him that there was no danger.

There was a moment of real danger. The King had a bronchial cough, but refused to moderate his use of cigars. After a luncheon at the British Embassy, he went into a parlor with Princess Daisy of Pless, a young Englishwoman married to one of the premier noblemen of Germany. She curtsied before him and, in Bülow's words, "the head of the British Empire inspected her with all the satisfaction of an old connoisseur of female beauty." They sat together for almost an hour while the King smoked his immense cigar and tugged at the collar of his tight-fitting Prussian uniform. Suddenly, King Edward broke into a spasm of coughing, and then fell back against the sofa. The cigar fell from his fingers, and his eyes stared. "My God, he is dying!" thought Princess Daisy. She tried to undo the collar of his uniform and failed. Queen Alexandra rushed in and the two women tried together. They failed. The King revived and opened it himself. Sir James Reid, the King's doctor, hurried in and asked everyone to leave the room. Within fifteen minutes they were invited to return. The King, insisting that nothing serious had happened, would not let Princess Daisy leave his side.

Upon his return to England, King Edward's health continued poor. He began falling asleep over luncheon and dinner, and sleeping soundly through performances at the theater and the opera. He wheezed painfully when required to climb stairs. He went to Biarritz and then on to the Mediterranean, but he could shake neither his pallor nor his cough. That winter at Sandringham he seemed in better spirits, playing bridge until midnight and up every morning to shoot. The January 1910 General Election made certain that the budget would pass, but it also ensured that the Prime Minister would call upon the sovereign to use (or at least to threaten to use) his prerogative of creating additional peers. King Edward, sympathetic to the peers' desire to maintain their dignity, saw their die-hard position as suicidal. As a constitutional monarch, he could not refuse the advice of a prime minister backed by a majority of the House of Commons. What he could do and did do was to tell Mr. Asquith that before he would agree to create the swarm of Liberal peers necessary to subvert the House of Lords, the issue must be submitted again to the country in a second General Election.

King Edward's doctors were eager to get him away from the fogs and damp of London into the sun of Biarritz. He left on March 8, 1910, stopping in Paris, where he suffered an attack of acute indigestion with shortness of breath and pain near the heart. On the Basque coast, he struggled for six weeks with severe bronchitis. Mrs. Keppel helped to distract him, and on April 26 he returned to England, apparently refreshed. That evening he felt well enough to go to the opera at Covent Garden. The following morning, he resumed his appointments, seeing Asquith and Kitchener; the next day he received Haldane, Morley, and the Russian Ambassador, Count Benckendorff. Friday night he was back at the opera for five hours of *Siegfried.* On Saturday he left for Sandringham and seemed in good form, telling stories at dinner and afterwards enjoying bridge. Sunday, May 1, a cold wind and showers of rain swept over Norfolk, but the King insisted on taking his regular Sunday afternoon walk to inspect his farm and pedigree animals. He caught a chill. Monday, he turned to London in a pouring rain and, by the time he was back in Buckingham Palace, he had a severe bronchial attack and was breathing with difficulty. Queen Alexandra, discreetly vacationing in Corfu while her husband was with Mrs. Keppel in Biarritz, was notified. Assuming the King's illness to be another of his recurrent attacks, she started home slowly; upon reaching Venice, she thought of spending twenty-four hours in the city.

On Tuesday, May 3, the King saw the American Ambassador, Whitelaw Reid, to discuss the forthcoming visit to London of former President Theodore Roosevelt, whom King Edward had never met. "Our talk," said Reid, "was interrupted by spasms of coughing." That night, the King skipped dinner but smoked a huge cigar and played bridge with Mrs. Keppel. He could not sleep. Through Thursday, the King continued to receive visitors, saying of his illness, "I must fight this." When visitors begged him to rest, he replied, "No, I shall not give in. I shall go on. I shall work to the end." Ponsonby, bringing him papers to sign, found him sitting at his writing table with a rug around his legs. "His color was grey and he appeared to be unable to sit upright and was sunken. At first he had difficulty with his breathing . . . but this gradually got better." The King signed some papers and then looked at Ponsonby and said helplessly, "I feel wretchedly ill. I can't sleep. I can't eat. They really must do something for me." That afternoon, Queen Alexandra reached Calais and, a few hours later, London. It was the first time during their marriage that her husband, while present in the city, had not welcomed her at the station. When she reached the Palace, the sight of the King fighting for breath, his face chalky and gray, told her the truth.

The next day, Friday, May 6, was King Edward's last. In the morning, he insisted that his valet dress him formally in a frock coat. He received his friend Sir Ernest Cassel and said, "I am very seedy but I wanted to see you." Then he collapsed. Through the afternoon, he sat hunched in his armchair as a series of heart attacks hammered at his stricken body. Five doctors declared there was no hope. Morphine was administered to dull the pain. He had moments of consciousness, during which friends appeared. One of these was Mrs. Keppel, whom the Queen, in a display of generosity, had sent for so that she might say good-bye. At five P.M., the Prince of Wales informed his father that one of the King's horses, a two-year-old named Witch of the Air, had won a race at Kempton Park. "I am very glad," said the King. Early in the evening, he sank into a coma. At eleven-thirty, he was carried to his bed and at eleven forty-five, with the Archbishop of Canterbury pronouncing a blessing, he died.

Queen Alexandra, looking at her husband's body, said to Ponsonby how peaceful he looked and that it was not the cold wind at Sandringham but "that horrid Biarritz" that had killed him. She said she felt as if she had been turned to stone, unable to cry, unable to grasp the meaning of her husband's death, unable to do anything. She mentioned that she would like to go and hide in the country, but there was the state funeral, and all the arrangements that had to be made. King Edward's son, now the new King George V, wrote that night in his diary, "I have lost my best friend and the best of fathers. I never had a word with him in my life. I am heartbroken and overwhelmed with grief." Jacky Fisher, newly retired, sat for half an hour with Queen Alexandra and, at the lying in state, felt that, if he could touch the body, the King would awake. "The world [is] not the same world," he wrote. "I've lost the greatest friend I ever had. . . . I feel so curious a sense of isolation—which I can't get over— and no longer seem to care a damn for anything. . . ."

Bernhard von Bülow recorded that "the death of Edward VII

. . . was of the greatest assistance to our foreign policy. I do not think he had really wanted to fight us. . . . But inspired by hostility to his nephew, by his fear of our economic rivalry, and the accelerated rhythm of our naval tempo, Edward VII created difficulties and, whenever he could would put a spoke in our wheel."

The Kaiser privately hailed "the death of the 'Encircler' " and rushed immediately to London to participate in the public pageantry of a state funeral.

H. H. Asquith was using the Easter recess to escape politics on board the Admiralty yacht *Enchantress,* accompanying the First Lord, Reginald McKenna, on an inspection trip to Gibraltar. Informed by radio that the King's condition was worsening, Asquith decided to turn the yacht around immediately. At three A.M. on the morning of May 7, he was handed a wireless message from the new King: "I am deeply grieved to inform you that my beloved father the King passed away peacefully at quarter to twelve tonight (the 6th). George." Asquith went up on deck and found himself surrounded by a predawn twilight dominated by the blaze of Halley's comet: "I felt bewildered and indeed stunned. At a most anxious moment in the fortunes of the State, we had lost without warning or preparation, the Sovereign whose ripe experience, trained sagacity, equitable judgement and unvarying consideration counted for so much. . . . His successor, with all his fine and engaging qualities, was without political experience. We were nearing the verge of a crisis almost without example in our constitutional history. What was the right thing to do?"

The Kaiser enjoyed his uncle's funeral. He relished the prominent place accorded him among his relatives. He preened himself that "the entire royal family received me at the railway station as a token of their gratitude for the deference to family ties shown by my coming." In Westminster Hall, he admired the "gorgeously decorated coffin" and the "marvelous play" of colors created when rays of sunlight filtering through the narrow windows touched the jewels in the Crown of England surmounting the coffin. He delighted in prancing through London on horseback beside his cousin, the new King George V, past "the vast multitude . . . clad in black," at the head of a "splendid array" of "gorgeously" dressed English guardsmen: "Grenadiers, Scots Guards, Coldstreams, Irish Guards—in their perfectly-fitting coats, white leather facings, and heavy bearskin headgear; all picked troops of superb appearance and admirable martial bearing, a joy to any man with the heart of a soldier." In another way, it also gladdened the Emperor to telegraph his new Chancellor, Theobald von Bethmann-Hollweg, that the Liberal government of England was in trouble. His impressions, based on "many talks with . . . relatives, with gentlemen of the Court, with certain old acquaintances, and many distinguished persons," were "somewhat as follows: People's minds are wholly occupied with the internal situation. . . . The outlook all around is black. The Government is thoroughly hated. . . . It is reported with satisfaction that on the days after the King's death and during the lying-in-state, the Prime Minister and other of his colleagues were publicly hissed in the streets, and that expressions like 'you have killed the King' were heard. A demonstration against the Government is looked for . . . and a strong reaction in a Conservative sense is thought not improbable." The Kaiser's skills as a political reporter can be judged by the fact that the "regicide" government had five months earlier won a seven-year term in a General Election and eight months later was to reconfirm its authority in a second General Election.

Nevertheless, it was true that King Edward's death had put the government in an awkward position. Asquith could not now avoid attacking the veto power of the House of Lords even if he wished to; it was part of his commitment to the Irish members who gave him his majority. Yet the only power that could humble the Lords was the royal prerogative. Everything rested on the King; first King Edward, now King George. Only the monarch could create the mass of new peers necessary to vote the Upper House into political impotence. And the new King was, as the Prime Minister had described him, "without political experience." To pressure him immediately after his accession was, at the least, distasteful. At worst, it might be damaging to the government. The alternative, proposed on June 6, was an armistice and a conference in which four leaders from each party, including Asquith and Lloyd George, Balfour and Lansdowne, would meet quietly and seek to resolve their differences. Although a fervent minority in both parties—extreme Radicals on one side, extreme Tories on the other—objected to their principles being compromised behind closed doors, and strict constitutionalists worried at the nation's basic political structure being altered in secret, the first meeting was held, at 10 Downing Street, on June 17. Twenty-one meetings were held during the summer and autumn of 1910—without success. Along the way, Lloyd George grew impatient, proposed a coalition government, and admitted that his desire to create hundreds of new Liberal peers was no greater than Balfour's. "Looking into the future," he told the Unionist leader, "I know that our glorified grocers will be more hostile to social reform than your Backwoodsmen." Balfour did not want a coalition; neither did Asquith; and on November 10, 1910, it was officially announced that the Constitutional Conference had failed.

Asquith moved immediately. On the afternoon of November 10 the Cabinet agreed that Parliament should be dissolved and the issue of the veto power of the Lords put to the country. The following day, the Prime Minister called on King George at Sandringham to ask that, if the General Election produced another Liberal victory, the King pledge himself to create enough new peers to pass a Parliament bill through the House of Lords. On November 16, Asquith went to Buckingham Palace for the King's answer. In great distress, King George asked if the Prime Minister would have made the same request of his father. "Yes, Sir," said Asquith, "and your father would have consented." Reluctantly, the King agreed. With this promise—kept secret for the moment—Asquith led his party into a December election, the second within a year. Despite the excitement at Westminster, the country appeared to be even more bored than it had been in January. Five hundred thousand fewer voters went to the polls, and the results were almost identical: the Liberals lost two seats and returned to the House of Commons with 272. The Conservatives gained two seats and returned to Westminster with 272. As before, the Irish Nationalists (84 seats) and Labour (42 seats) held the balance and would vote with the government.

Nothing now could save the Lords. Asquith had a specific mandate from the country, a majority in the House of Commons, and the King's secret promise to create new peers. In February 1911, the Parliament bill was introduced in the Commons. By May, the bill had passed and come to the Lords. Still not knowing that the King was pledged, if necessary, to overwhelm them in their own chamber, the peers treated the bill with traditional disdain, referring it to committee, where it was sufficiently disfigured by amendment to render it harmless. On July 18, Lloyd George called on Balfour and revealed the promise extracted from the King the previous December. Balfour and Lansdowne immediately saw that they were defeated; the best that could be managed now was a graceful surrender. In order to convince his followers, Lansdowne asked the Prime Minister to state his intentions in writing. On July 20, Mr. Asquith obliged with identical letters to the Unionist leaders in both houses:

Dear Lord Lansdowne (Mr. Balfour):
I think it courteous and right, before any public decisions are announced, to let you know . . . [that] should the necessity

arise, the Government will advise the King to exercise his prerogative to secure the passing of the Bill in substantially the
same form in which it left the House of Commons; and His
Majesty has been pleased to signify that he will consider it his
duty to accept, and act on, that advice.

Yours sincerely,

H. H. ASQUITH

The following morning, July 21, Lord Lansdowne brought the
Prime Minister's letter to a meeting of two hundred Unionist peers
at Grosvenor House, the London mansion of the Duke of Westminster. Lansdowne read Asquith's letter and said that he believed the
government was not bluffing.* He advised that, to avoid dilution of
the peerage, the Lords pass the bill as sent from the Commons.
Either way, he pointed out, the House of Lords would lose its veto
power.

Lord Lansdowne's argument failed to persuade a number of his
titled listeners, who declared themselves implacably opposed to
passing the bill no matter what the consequences. Lord Curzon, a
former Viceroy of India, himself a fledgling peer and therefore anxious to prevent devaluation of a recent honor, defied the government, the monarch, and Lord Lansdowne by crying, "Let them
make their peers. We will die in the last ditch before we give in!"
thus giving the name "Ditchers" to the bill's diehard opponents.
"Ditcher" resistance rallied around the stumpy, red-faced figure of
Lord Halsbury, a former Lord Chancellor, then eighty-eight (he
lived to be ninety-eight), who as a lawyer and judge had worked his
way up to the Woolsack and an earldom, and who, said one of his
followers, "invariably objected on principle to all change." Lord
Halsbury already had announced that he would vote against the bill
as a "solemn duty to God and country." At Grosvenor House, he
cried that he would cast that vote "even if I am alone, rather than

---

* Asquith was not bluffing. Although, at one point, he declared that he would ask the
King to create only enough new peers to carry the Parliament bill through the House of
Lords by a majority of one, he already was drawing up lists of Liberal gentlemen whom
the King might be asked to ennoble. One list of 249 names survives. It contains men of
varied distinction: forty-four were baronets and fifty-eight were knights; there were four
generals and one admiral (one of the generals was Baden-Powell, defender of Mafeking
and founder of the Boy Scouts); history was represented by G. M. Trevelyan and G. P.
Gooch; the law by Sir Frederick Pollock; commerce by the South African millionaire Abe
Bailey; classics by George Gilbert Murray; philosophy and mathematics by Bertrand
Russell; the theater by J. M. Barrie; and fiction by Thomas Hardy and Anthony Hope
(author of *The Prisoner of Zenda*).

surrender." At least sixty Ditchers stood with this bantam gladiator, and the number was thought to be growing.

Those who supported Lord Lansdowne were known as "Hedgers."* And no one hedged more carefully than Arthur Balfour. Perhaps because he sensed that nothing he could say would deter Lord Halsbury; perhaps because, after thirty years of party leadership, he was weary and wanted only to lose gracefully and move on to other issues; perhaps because for Arthur Balfour politics was never more than a game; perhaps for all these reasons, Balfour was reluctant to become involved. Unwilling to appear before the angry peers, he would only agree to writing a letter to the *Times:* "I agree with Lord Lansdowne and his friends," he announced. "With Lord Lansdowne, I stand. With Lord Lansdowne, I am ready, if need be, to fall." It was the statement of a man who knew and accepted that he was about to be beaten. In ultra-Tory clubs in London and at weekend parties in the country houses of England, the cry "B.M.G.— Balfour Must Go" grew louder.

Balfour's abdication of leadership became manifest at a scene in which Asquith suffered the most conspicuous public humiliation of an English Prime Minister in the history of Parliament. On July 24, Asquith arose in the House of Commons to announce the King's promise and to explain how this would affect passage of the Parliament bill. The opposition, believing the government had forced the pledge from the King and was bent on the destruction of not only the House of Lords but the class system, private property, the Anglican Church—everything that for centuries had made England "a green and pleasant land"—refused to let him speak. From the seats behind Balfour, Unionists shouted "Traitor!" It was the beginning of a cannonade of vilification. Whenever the rage ebbed slightly, Asquith began a sentence; immediately he was drowned by hoots and jeers: "Traitor!" "Dictator!" "Who killed the King?" Lord Hugh Cecil, a son of Lord Salisbury, stood repeatedly and screamed, "You have disgraced your office!" A Labour M.P., staring in disgust at Lord Hugh, finally rose and shouted back, "Many a man has been certified for less than half of what the noble lord has

---

* *The Times,* the stalwart, schoolmasterish voice of Conservative England, stood with Lansdowne. It reproached Lord Halsbury and his "Ditchers" for their use of "picturesque phrases, such as 'nailing the colors to the mast,' 'going down with the flag flying,' and 'dying in the last ditch' . . . [phrases which, in real life] stir the heart and fire the blood. What makes . . . [these phrases] so splendid is the majesty of death. But the heroic peers will not go down or die in the last ditch; they will only be out-voted. That is not the majesty of death but the bathos of the stage; and to assume airs about it is not tragedy but melodrama."

done this afternoon!" For forty-five minutes, Asquith stood at the dispatch box waiting to speak. In the Gallery, Margot Asquith, blazing with fury, scribbled a note and sent it down to Sir Edward Grey, who sat behind Asquith on the Government Bench: "For God's sake, defend him from the cats and cads." Grey could do nothing and sadly tore up the note. Eventually, the Prime Minister gave up. "I am not going to degrade myself," he said and sat down. The din continued; fists were brandished on both sides, until the Speaker halted the proceedings.

Through the afternoon, Arthur Balfour lounged on the Opposition Front Bench, taking no part in the brawl, but doing nothing to halt it either. Some observers thought they saw concern on his face, others thought he seemed revolted. Nevertheless, out of a sense of weariness, or understanding that there were pleasures—in philosophy, perhaps—superior to involvement in such a scene, or perhaps from sheer indifference, Balfour did not act.

In the end, to save the House of Lords from ridicule, Lansdowne persuaded the majority of Unionist peers to abstain from voting on the bill. The vote was narrowed to the Liberals versus the Ditchers. Even then, as Lord Halsbury increased the numbers of his adherents, it seemed that the bill must die. On the day of the vote, August 10, with the temperature at one hundred degrees, the greatest heat recorded in England in seventy years, many Ditchers still believed that the government's threat to create new peers was "pure bluff." The Liberal Lord Morley, who had moved the bill, attempted to disabuse them: "I have to say that every vote given tonight against my motion is a vote in favor of a large and prompt creation of peers." In the end, it was Lord Curzon, hating what he had to do, who saved the House of Lords from an invasion of Liberal "grocers." When the final division took place, Curzon grimly led thirty-seven Unionist peers into the lobby *in favor* of the government bill. They were joined by eighty-one Liberals and thirteen bishops and opposed by 114 Ditchers; the final vote was 131 to 114. The Parliament bill became law and the House of Lords lost its power to veto. The Ditchers were "boiling with rage." Lady Halsbury hissed from the Gallery when the result was announced and subsequently refused to shake Lord Lansdowne's hand. That night at the Carlton Club, peers who had voted with Lord Curzon and the government were denounced to their faces as "Traitor!" and "Judas!"

The scene in the House of Commons on July 23 was too much for Arthur Balfour. On August 9, the day *before* the climactic vote in the House of Lords, the leader of the opposition departed England for a vacation in the Austrian Alps. There, amid "the cataracts, the pines, and the precipices" of Badgastein, he reflected upon his life, then in its sixty-fourth year. Politics seemed "quite unusually odious"; it was time to devote himself to philosophy; he already had a short article in mind. That autumn on returning to England, the elegant prince of the House of Commons resigned the leadership of the Unionist Party. His successor was a Glasgow steel manufacturer, born in Canada, named Andrew Bonar Law.

CHAPTER 36

The Eulenburg
Scandal

◆

When Asquith drew Balfour aside in November 1908 to say that he could give no explanation for Germany's behavior except that "the internal condition of Germany was so unsatisfactory that they might be driven to the wildest adventures," he was referring to the upheavals caused by the Eulenburg Affair and the Kaiser's *Daily Telegraph* interview. "PRUSSIAN COURT SCANDALS" headlined the London *Times,* as reporters from around the globe sat in a Berlin courtroom writing stories which bathed the leadership of the German Empire in a lurid glow. Before the conclusion of these events, shock waves had rolled through German society, the Kaiser had suffered two nervous collapses, and the Chancellor had announced in the Reichstag, "It is false and foolish to suppose that because some members of society have failings, the nobility as a whole is corrupt or the army destroyed."

The diplomatic policy of Bülow and Holstein—threatening war with France over Morocco; attempting to smash the Anglo-French Entente before it took root—had spectacularly failed. The Kaiser, who in his delight at the fall of Delcassé had made Bülow a prince, was frustrated and angry. Someone would have to pay. Bülow, who had adopted, administered, and taken credit for Holstein's strategy as long as it was successful, was determined not to be the scapegoat.

In the spring of 1906, during the humiliation at Algeciras, Holstein's personal position in Berlin worsened. State Secretary von Richthofen, whom Holstein was accustomed to ignoring, died in January and was replaced by Heinrich von Tschirschky, a friend of the Kaiser's whom Holstein disliked. Tschirschky reciprocated the feelings. After Algeciras, it occurred simultaneously to Bülow and Tschirschky that the moment had come to rid themselves completely of Holstein. The First Counselor, aware of the tremors beneath him, resorted to his customary tactic: on April 2, he handed his resignation to Bülow. On April 4, Bülow told Holstein that he would do nothing until he had discussed the matter with the Kaiser. On April 5, before he had seen William, Bülow fainted on the floor of the Reichstag and was carried home to bed. From his bed, the Chancellor instructed Tschirschky to forward Holstein's resignation to the Emperor with the recommendation that it be accepted. When William received the document, he signed it immediately.

Holstein, stunned at his sudden downfall, quickly turned his formidable powers to ferreting out the enemy who had brought it about. He discounted Bülow: the Chancellor had been his protégé and ally for thirty years; Bülow always had been elaborately respectful of the First Counselor's special role at the Wilhelmstrasse; besides, Bülow had been home in bed. Tschirschky, he knew, lacked the authority to persuade the Kaiser to such a deed. Then Holstein learned that, on April 17, the day William had countersigned the resignation, Prince Philip von Eulenburg had been at the Palace for lunch. Holstein looked no further. This friend of the Kaiser, who had helped overthrow chancellors and state secretaries during the nineties, had once again wielded personal power over the Emperor. His enemy, Holstein was convinced, was Prince Philip von Eulenburg.

The greatest influence on Philip von Eulenburg's life, he always said, was his mother. Alexandrine von Rothkirch-Eulenburg was a woman of artistic temperament who delighted in music and showed considerable skill as an amateur painter. From his mother, Philip inherited his enthusiasm for nature, art, music, and poetry, and a desire for intimate friendships. Countess von Eulenburg lived until her son was fifty-five and spent as much time at his side as possible; when apart, they wrote to each other daily.

Eulenburg's father, an old-fashioned, hardbitten Prussian who had been a soldier, found little good in the artistic interests of his wife and children. Philip was as closed with his father as he was open with his mother. "I could never put into words," he wrote later, "what the world of the imagination meant to me in childhood. . . . The narrow world in which my parents lived at that time, my father's perpetual injunctions to reduce expenses, filled me with bitterness."

Heir to a Junker, a young Count von Eulenburg would become a soldier, and Philip was entered as a cadet in the Garde du Corps (the Royal Bodyguard Regiment) at Potsdam. He was inept and hated the "torment of unfair, narrow-minded, and coarse-natured superiors." When the Franco-Prussian War broke out and the regiment went to the front, his commanding officer left him behind. Eventually, he was transferred to a staff position in which he so charmed his new commander that, although Philip had never been in combat, the officer procured for him an Iron Cross for bravery. When the war ended, his mother won his father's permission for Philip to leave the army. He went to Leipzig and Strasbourg universities, earned a doctorate in law, and began to work, without enthusiasm, in the courts. At twenty-eight, he married a Swedish countess, who over eleven years produced eight children. Marriage was an ordeal for Eulenburg. His wife, said a friend, was "terribly boring." "Her conversation was negligible," said another friend. "She was entirely eclipsed by the brilliant Phili whom she looked up to in idolizing love and wonderment." "I enjoy family life little," said Eulenburg. "I gladly go my way."

Eulenburg embarked on a diplomatic career believing that this profession would give him more time to develop as an artist. "My official career as a diplomat was to me a torment," he said later. "An artist every inch of me, and certain of success, I fought like a desperate creature against my father, who in his Old Prussian way recognized nothing but an official career, and looked upon all artistic activity as a pastime, a toy, for a Count Eulenburg." He entered the Foreign Office at thirty through his friendship with Herbert Bismarck. (Eulenburg's sister, Adda, was an intimate of the Chancellor's daughter, Marie.) During Herbert's unhappy love affair with Princess Elisabeth Carolath, Eulenburg had played a dual role: to the lovesick son he was the intimate friend to whom all could be confessed; to the worried parents he was the sensible young man who could guide their son back to the path of reason. Subsequently, a grateful Herbert had suggested that "dear Phili" join him in the diplomatic service.

Eulenburg's career proceeded slowly. He was thirty-four before he received his first foreign assignment, in 1881, as Third Secretary of the German Embassy in Paris. His six-month tour was marked by the beginnings of a friendship with the Embassy's Second Secretary, Bernhard von Bülow. Eulenburg's second post was Munich, where he served as First Secretary of the Prussian Legation. His official duties were light and he was able to plunge into the cultural and artistic life of the Bavarian capital. Eulenburg had considerable amateur talent, and in each field he was self-taught. He wrote children's stories which extracted enthusiastic praise from as unlikely a source as Friedrich von Holstein. Eulenburg's plays were professionally produced in Berlin and Munich. Without formal architectural training, he designed Italianate halls and pavilions for the family estate at Liebenberg. He was proudest of his music. His "Rosenlieder" (Rose Songs) had three hundred printings over twenty-five years and sold 500,000 copies; he created ballads, "Skaldengesänge," based on Norse sagas; these songs and ballads he frequently sang himself in a pleasant voice. He hoped to write an opera. Once in Paris, he sang one of his compositions for a famous professional singer, who urged him to study counterpoint. Offended, Eulenburg told Bülow as they were leaving, "I shall take care never to study counterpoint. It would only lame the wings of my genius."

These talents, along with his brilliance as a conversationalist and raconteur, appealed to Prince William of Hohenzollern when Eulenburg, at thirty-nine, met the twenty-seven-year-old future Kaiser at a hunting party in May 1886. Eulenburg, tall, with a broad forehead, neatly trimmed beard, and large, expressive eyes, immediately captivated the younger man. While Philip sat at the piano, playing and singing his songs, William turned the pages. Beginning that summer William and Augusta invited him frequently to Reichenhall, where, William wrote later, Eulenburg "used to enliven our evenings with his piano playing and ballad singing. One of his finest compositions, the 'Submerging of Atlantis,' was my favorite piece of music. He was, like me, a great lover of nature and my wife and I had long, stimulating talks with him on art, music, and literature on our walks. He was great on the Italian Renaissance especially, and had many friends and acquaintances among notable artists in Munich." William noted his new friend's storytelling ability: "He was one of those fortunate people to whom, particularly when traveling, something comical always happens. Phili could tell these stories to universal hilarity." Soon, William was introducing Eulenburg to his former tutor, Hinzpeter, as "my bosom friend, the only one I have." "Whenever he came into our Potsdam home," William recalled later, "it was like a flood of sunshine on the routine of life."

Eulenburg responded enthusiastically to William's friendship. His letters to the Prince were flowery: The Prince's friendship, he said, "has become a radiance in my life; a letter from Prince William "I will lay among my most treasured gifts"; a visit to Eulenburg's home drew from Eulenburg's children the relayed expression "that Prince William looked 'so very handsome' in uniform." When William was downcast, Eulenburg lavished sympathy; when William was excited, Eulenburg heaped on praise. William received an unpleasant telegram: "He was very pale," Eulenburg wrote to his friend Bülow, "and looked at me, half afraid, half miserable, questioning me with his beautiful blue eyes." As Kaiser, William had given a speech: afterward, Bülow recorded, "Phil was so excited that he ran up . . . and kissed both His Majesty's hands with the words, 'I am overcome. I am overwhelmed!' "

The Bismarcks approved of the friendship. "It was very useful, your going to see Prince William," Herbert wrote to Eulenburg in August 1886. "He thinks a great deal of you and has sung your praises to me in every kind of way. You must make use of this and . . . talk to him and get an influence over him. For the heaven-storming strain in most of his opinions must be more and more toned down, so that the Potsdam lieutenant's outlook may gradually give way to statesmanlike reflections. Except for that, the Prince is really a pearl." At the end of the summer, the two friends, William and Philip, set out together for Bayreuth to listen to *Tristan und Isolde* and *Parsifal* and to meet Wagner's family, whom Eulenburg already knew. Again, Herbert Bismarck wrote approvingly: "So you are going to be in Bayreuth with Prince William. . . . I hope you will distract his mind so that the Wagnerian trombones may not damage his bad ear with their discords. Six hours of the Music of the Future would inflame even my drums. I am always afraid that the Prince will do too much, so energetic as he is in everything; and he must be prevented from that, for his health is of quite inestimable importance to the German nation."

At this time, with Prince William's father, Crown Prince Frederick, in apparent good health, it seemed unlikely that Prince William's health would matter much to the German nation for a number of years. In fact, twenty-four months later, the young man was to become German Emperor. Even then, the Bismarcks continued to approve of the friendship. When William as Kaiser was forming a party for his first Norwegian cruise, Herbert suggested that Eulenburg go. "Your influence on His Majesty is an excellent one," he said. Eulenburg's unique relationship as bosom friend of the Emperor and trusted confidant of the Bismarcks ended in March 1890 with the Chancellor's dismissal. In the great schism which divided society and the bureaucracy in the 1890s, Eulenburg chose William. When he attended Otto von Bismarck's funeral in 1897, he walked up to Herbert to offer sympathy. Herbert coolly and ostentatiously turned his back.

When William ascended the throne, Eulenburg worried that the friendship would end, but the new monarch reassured him. "I would never have dreamed that my Kaiser would be the one who *alone* understands . . . [my] sensibility," Eulenburg wrote to William. His intimacy with the young, assertive Emperor quickly gave Eulenburg a key role in the Imperial Government. Once Caprivi had replaced Bismarck and Marschall became State Secretary, Holstein assumed a dominant role at the Foreign Office. William and the reclusive First Counselor did not meet and the task of mediating between them fell to Eulenburg, whose unofficial title became "Ambassador of the German Government to the Kaiser." In 1890, Marschall, nominally Eulenburg's superior—Eulenburg was serving as Prussian Minister to the German state of Oldenburg—recognized Eulenburg's influence: "If I feel a certain degree of confidence in setting to work, I owe that feeling not least to the kind, cordial words which you have been so good as to say to me. The confidence and friendly feeling that you offer me, I respond to with the heart-felt request that you will help me further by word and deed, in case of necessity, as also by unhesitating criticism."

Holstein wrote to Eulenburg almost daily, requesting help in steering the Kaiser: "Perhaps His Majesty could say . . ."; "A useful subject for conversation would be . . ."; "You might suggest to His Majesty that he . . ."; "You must utter a warning against . . ." Holstein motivated Eulenburg with a blend of gratitude and warning about the Kaiser's position: "Your letter of today . . . gives me hope that with your help we may still restrain the Emperor—without it, we shall not . . ."; "The reason I feel it my duty to inform you in good time is that this directly concerns the personal prestige of your Imperial friend. That prestige is not in any case increasing—on the contrary. The nation does not take him seriously."

Eulenburg carried out his "Embassy to the Emperor" primarily by letter; when the matter was urgent, he traveled to Berlin. Eulenburg also saw the Kaiser regularly at the annual *Kaiserjagd* (Royal Hunt) at Romintern; at shooting parties at his own Liebenberg estate near Berlin; sailing aboard the *Meteor* at Kiel Week (the only picture on William's desk in his small cabin was Eulenburg's), and on the annual all-male Norwegian cruises every July. During these Wilhelmine vacations, Eulenburg enjoyed special privileges. His cabin aboard the *Hohenzollern* was always next to the Kaiser's. When William summoned his elderly generals on deck for morning exercises, making them squat so that he could come up behind to give them a push and send them sprawling, Eulenburg was absent. "The Emperor has never touched me," he said. "He knows I would not suffer it." At shooting parties, where all were forced to wear green court shooting-dress with choking high collars and high brown boots with silver spurs, Eulenburg alone dared to reach up and un-fasten his collar so that he could breathe.

Eulenburg's great influence on the Kaiser in the middle 1890s led to speculation that he might be appointed State Secretary, or even Chancellor. Eulenburg rejected this talk, explaining that an official relationship with the Emperor "would impair my influence." In 1894, when Caprivi was weakening and Eulenburg's name was mentioned as a replacement, he begged the Kaiser never to ask him to accept the office. William laughed. "I agree with you that in one way you are entirely unfit to be Imperial Chancellor—you are too good-natured."

Eulenburg felt comfortable rejecting the demanding role of State Secretary because he had found an intimate friend—an alter ego—who could do it for him. Bernhard von Bülow, Eulenburg's Paris colleague, was ambitious and had the taste for power that Philip lacked. From the beginning, Bülow had seen in Eulenburg a useful friend. "I soon fell under the spell of 'Phili' Eulenburg," Bülow wrote of their early years. Subsequently, Bülow said, Eulenburg became "the friend who has been nearest to my heart." Eulenburg quickly put his talents to Bülow's use. When Bülow was maneuvering to marry the divorced Countess Maria Donhoff, Eulenburg worked to smooth Bülow's path at the Wilhelmstrasse. In 1888 Bü-low was posted to Bucharest, where he was marooned for five years —and counted on Eulenburg to rescue him. Bülow understood Eu-lenburg's effusive nature and wrote to him in the same language: "I have a great longing to see you again, dearest Philip"; "Nothing will ever be able to part us from each other"; "in the depths of our souls we think and feel alike . . . ever since I have known you I have . . . loved you from my heart." In 1893, when there was talk that Eulenburg would replace Marschall as State Secretary, Philip shared his reservations with Bernhard: "A poor barndoor fowl like me, cockered up into an eagle. I can hear myself cackling instead of clawing, and see myself laying an egg instead of sitting with flaming eyes on the gable of 76 Wilhelmstrasse. The thing is out of the question." Bülow indignantly rejected this self-description: "I—not as a friend but quite dispassionately speaking—consider you the ideal Secretary of State. You would not run about in the yard like a barnyard fowl, but as a faithful, wise and noble watchdog would guard the Emperor's door. You have . . . intuitive genius . . . His Majesty's complete confidence . . . a great name, social charm—in short, you have everything."

Bülow also understood the need to mirror Eulenburg's fervent admiration of William II. "We cannot be sufficiently thankful that we have a monarch who always reminds me of the heroic . . . emperors of our medieval period," he wrote to Eulenburg in August 1890. "The Emperor's personality grows indubitably more arresting every day." Eulenburg, naturally, was delighted to help the career of a man who seemed so warm and wise. Bülow's promotion from Bucharest to Rome in 1893 was largely Eulenburg's doing. In 1895, when Bülow had been at the Palazzo Caffarelli for only two years, Eulenburg, who had still larger ambitions for his friend, wrote to the Kaiser, "Bernhard is the most valuable official Your Majesty possesses—the predestined Imperial Chancellor of the future." William liked the idea. "Bülow will be my Bismarck," he told Eulenburg.

The two friends—Eulenburg was Ambassador to Austria, Bülow Ambassador to Italy—met secretly in the Tyrol in 1896. The meeting, Eulenburg wrote afterwards to Bülow, was based "on our boundless love for our King [of Prussia; i.e., William]. How, in this complicated world, could . . . [anyone] have understood this personal, human love for the best of all Kings, or our natural, heartfelt friendship for one another?" Eulenburg, meanwhile, was working steadily to have Marschall removed as State Secretary. "Your Majesty will allow me to remind you that I made full arrangements for Marschall's dismissal last year," Eulenburg wrote to William. "Your Majesty decided to keep him in office for opportunistic reasons." At last, in June 1897, Eulenburg was successful: Marschall was dismissed; Bülow was summoned from Rome and made State Secretary. Bülow paid for his promotion with a letter he knew Eulenburg would like: "As a personality, His Majesty is charming, touching, irresistible, adorable. . . . I hang my heart more and more every day on the Emperor. He is so remarkable! . . . far and away the greatest Hohenzollern that has ever existed. He combines in a manner that I have never seen before the soundest and most original intelligence with the shrewdest good sense. He possesses an imagination that can soar on eagle wings . . . and what energy into the bargain! What a memory! What swiftness and sureness of apprehension!"

Eulenburg, overjoyed, replied: "You are our dear good sovereign's last card. No other can—and still less will—do all for him that you are doing. . . . Another might have genius or erudition but love and loyalty will always be lacking, the love of a faithful servant which with you has taken the form of a father's love for a difficult child. How terribly *alone* the poor Emperor stands." When Bülow was appointed Imperial Chancellor, Eulenburg congratulated him again: "One of the best things God has given me to do was my intervention in your career—an intervention which I always felt to be my mission. I am possessed by the sense that after terrible storms I have at last steered the ship we may call 'The Emperor's Reign' into at least a tolerably safe anchorage."

With Bülow at the helm, Eulenburg's direct political influence diminished, which, he said, was his wish. He maintained his personal friendship with the Kaiser through the annual cruises to Norway and the hunting parties at Romintern and Liebenberg. His friendship with William became, if anything, more possessive. At Romintern, Eulenburg told Bülow, he had been appalled by the Empress's "wrinkled, prematurely aged face and grey hair" and by the fact that "all night long, the Empress made scenes with her weeping and screaming." Eulenburg was deeply upset. He "told me with feverish agitation," said Bülow, "that the Empress was in such a nervous state that it would be very advisable if she were separated from the Kaiser soon." Dona remained and Eulenburg's revulsion continued. Three years later, he complained that the Empress's "love for His Majesty is like the passion of a cook for her sweetheart who shows signs of cooling off. This method of forcing herself upon him is certainly not the way to keep the beloved's affections."

Meanwhile, Eulenburg had begun to weary of official life. "Ten years of uphill work for our dear Master have completely exhausted me," he wrote to Bülow in 1898. The following year, he broke with Holstein. Although in 1900, William elevated his old friend to the rank of prince, Eulenburg's fortunes were declining. His "sweet, affected piety . . . repulsed" a diplomatic colleague. Eulenburg himself explained, "At a certain age, men go through a period of bodily change, just as women do." This was particularly true, he said, of "men who in their sensitivity have . . . a kind of feminine sensibility." In 1902, Eulenburg's mother died. Plagued by worries, heart disease, and gout, he departed Vienna after eight years as ambassador, and secluded himself at Liebenberg. Eulenburg continued to be invited to autumn hunts and on Norwegian cruises, but declined on the grounds of health. On Eulenburg's birthday, the Kaiser always visited Liebenberg. "As Phili will never come to me now," said William, "I have to come to him." In an exception to his normal seclusion, Eulenburg made the Norwegian cruise of 1903.

He was ill throughout the voyage and found that his distaste for the holiday had grown; he described the *Hohenzollern* as "this floating theatre," where "things were much as in the most frivolous lieutenant's mess." By 1905, Eulenburg seemed better. That autumn, the Russian Count Sergei Witte, returning home from negotiating the Russo-Japanese peace treaty at Portsmouth, New Hampshire, visited the Kaiser at Romintern. He found Eulenburg seated grandly like a monarch in a huge armchair, while William sat on the arm of the same chair, excitedly talking and gesticulating like a lieutenant. It seemed that Philip Eulenburg, the Kaiser's dearest friend, was resuming his role as a maker and breaker of men in Imperial Germany.

Once Holstein had decided that it was Eulenburg who had brought him down, he burned for revenge. For years, through his spidery network of sources, he had made himself privy to police files on leading government figures. He was aware that in the eighties Philip Eulenburg's name had been included on the secret list of persons suspected of homosexual behavior. On May 1, 1906, Eulenburg received a letter from Holstein. It began with accusation: "My dear Phili—you needn't take this beginning as a compliment since nowadays to call a man 'Phili' means—well, nothing very flattering. You have now attained the object for which you have been intriguing for years—my retirement. And the general press attacks on me are also all that you can wish." In the letter, Holstein hurled an insult: "I am now free to handle you as one handles such a contemptible person with your peculiarities."

Eulenburg understood that Holstein meant to ruin him. Considering it "a matter of life and death," Eulenburg decided that only a duel could clear his name. He challenged Holstein to "exchange pistol shots until disablement or death." When he informed Tschirschky, the State Secretary—imagining the scandal of two prominent, elderly men, formerly occupying the highest positions in the German Empire, attempting to maim or kill each other—"literally collapsed into his chair." Withdraw the challenge "for God's sake and the Emperor's," Tschirschky begged Eulenburg. Eulenburg agreed to do so if Holstein would apologize. On May 3, Holstein wrote: "Prince Eulenburg having assured me on his word of honor that he had neither hand, act, nor any part in my dismissal, and has in no way been concerned in any of the attacks on me in the press, I hereby withdraw the offensive remarks made upon him in my letter." Despite this retraction, Eulenburg—who once had lik-

Lord Salisbury

H.M.S. Dreadnought assuming the role of flagship of the Home Fleet in 1907.

ened Holstein to a bloodthirsty weasel—did not feel safe. "I cannot say that I consider Holstein's attacks really disposed of," he wrote. "He will revenge himself in his accustomed fashion."

Holstein was already at work. He enlisted the aid of a man he had for years despised, Germany's most famous journalist, Maximilian Harden, founder and editor of the Berlin socialist weekly *Die Zukunft* ("The Future"). That summer and autumn, when a series of critical articles began to appear in *Die Zukunft*, Eulenburg understood that a new alliance had been formed. The articles blamed Germany's defeat at Algeciras on the sinister, pacifist influence of what Harden described as the "Liebenberg Round Table," the group of friends who gathered every autumn with the Emperor at Prince von Eulenburg's Liebenberg estate. The group, Harden wrote sardonically, consisted of "nothing but good people. Musical, poetic, spiritualistic; so pious that they expect better cures from prayer than from the wisest doctor. . . . In their intercourse, oral and written, [they are] of touching friendliness. This would all be their private affair if they did not belong to the Kaiser's closest round table and . . . from visible and invisible positions, spin the threads which suffocate the German Empire." Harden described Eulenburg, the leader of the circle, as an "unhealthy, late romantic and clairvoyant" who "with unflagging zeal has whispered and whispers still to William the Second that he is chosen to rule alone." "For years," Harden charged, "no important post was filled without . . . [Eulenburg's] help" and during this time, "he took care of all his friends."

Harden had three reasons for attacking Eulenburg. He opposed the Kaiser's inclination toward personal rule, which, he—rightly— believed was encouraged by Eulenburg. He had agreed with Holstein's policy of humiliating France and sundering the new Anglo-French Entente. When that policy was frustrated at Algeciras, Harden blamed Eulenburg for persuading the Kaiser to be conciliatory. Further, because of Eulenburg's close friendship with Raymond LeCompte, First Secretary of the French Embassy in Berlin, Harden suggested that Eulenburg was passing to LeCompte assurances that Germany was not prepared to back her diplomacy with threats of war. Harden's third reason was more personal and more poisonous. LeCompte, one of the German experts in the French Foreign Office, had known Eulenburg years before in Munich; once assigned to Berlin, LeCompte was included in the annual *Kaiserjagd* at Liebenberg. Harden had evidence that LeCompte was homosexual. Adding this to rumors he had heard about Eulenburg—rumors now reinforced by information from Holstein's files—Harden created, first by innuendo, then by increasingly direct accusation, the image of a circle around Eulenburg which was at least homoerotic if not openly homosexual.

Harden was treading on dangerous ground. Homosexuality was officially repressed in Germany, as elsewhere in Europe. In the Reich, it was a criminal offense, punishable by prison, although the law was rarely invoked or enforced. Still, the very accusation could stir moral outrage and bring social ruin. This was especially true at the highest levels of Society. In Austria, the Archduke Ludwig Victor (known as "Luzi-Wuzi"), brother of Emperor Franz Josef, had an affair with a masseur and was sent into exile. In Germany, Fritz Krupp, head of the giant armaments firm and friend of the Kaiser, was accused of pedophilia on Capri and, amidst the scandal, killed himself. A shadow had fallen close to Eulenburg in 1898 when his only brother, Friedrich von Eulenburg, a cavalry officer, was convicted of homosexuality and forced to resign from the army. The Kaiser, outraged, had demanded that Philip Eulenburg never see or speak to his brother again. A bitter Eulenburg told Bülow that he would not obey. Harden, by accusing Eulenburg and his Liebenberg circle, drew close to accusing the Kaiser himself. Philip Eulenburg had been William's closest friend for over twenty years. If the charge were true and the Emperor had not known, what did that suggest? Worse, what if the Emperor had known?

Eulenburg asked Bülow how he should respond to Harden's attacks. The Chancellor, aware that Holstein's vendetta against Eulenburg sprang from the former First Counselor's belief that Eulenburg was responsible for the Kaiser's acceptance of his resignation, advised his friend to leave Germany for a while, until things calmed down. Since his other friend, the Kaiser, who did not read Die Zukunft, treated him as warmly as before, Eulenburg did not heed the advice. In October, the Emperor joined his friends as usual at Liebenberg; in January 1907 he summoned Eulenburg to Berlin, where he invested his "dear Phili" with the highest Prussian decoration, the Order of the Black Eagle.

Harden waited until April 1907 before renewing his attack. In that month he published an article specifically naming three of the Kaiser's military aides-de-camp, all members of the Liebenberg group, as homosexuals. The story astounded Berlin; still, the Kaiser was oblivious. Eventually, when they were alone in the Palace garden, Crown Prince William showed the Kaiser the Zukunft article and other press clippings. "Never shall I forget the pained and horrified face of my father who stared at me in dismay," reported the

Crown Prince. "The moral purity of the Kaiser was such that he could hardly conceive the possibility of such aberrations."

William reacted quickly. He demanded the immediate resignation of the three aides-de-camp and of Count Kuno von Moltke,* military commander of Berlin, whom Harden had also implicated. If Moltke was innocent, the Kaiser insisted that he immediately sue Harden for libel. As for Eulenburg, also included in Harden's attack, the Emperor wrote to Bülow: "I insist that Philip Eulenburg shall at once ask to be retired [from the Diplomatic Service]. If this accusation against him of unnatural vice be unfounded, let him give me a plain declaration to that effect and take immediate steps against Harden. If not, then I expect him to return the Order of the Black Eagle and avoid scandal by forthwith leaving the country and going to reside abroad."

Eulenburg resigned immediately and sent back his Black Eagle. To Bülow, whom Eulenburg still considered a friend, he wrote: "The loss of an old imperial friendship was not the cruel deception which perhaps you expected it to be since I know, only too well, the character of this pilot who shouts 'abandon ship' in every case long before it is necessary." As to Harden's accusation, he said, "I know myself to be entirely innocent." Bülow, in his *Memoirs,* claimed that at this stage he believed Eulenburg: "I was convinced that the accusations of unnatural practices brought against him were unfounded. His affectionate relations with wife and children, the deep and passionate love with which his charming and distinguished wife still clung to him, made such vile assertions appear monstrous."

Obeying the Imperial command, Moltke and Eulenburg moved to sue Harden for libel. As both had been government officials, they asked the Prussian Crown Prosecutor to take the case; he refused, claiming that the matter was personal. Eulenburg then withdrew, but Moltke persevered. Harden's trial began in Berlin Municipal Court on October 23, 1907. The editor was represented by Max Bernstein, Crown Prosecutor of Bavaria, acting in a private capacity. Bernstein immediately seized the offensive, attempting to implicate both Moltke and Eulenburg in the unquestioned activities of the three aides-de-camp. "Disgusting orgies" involving soldiers of the elite Garde du Corps Regiment at the home of one of the incriminated aides were described. One witness "thought he recognized Count Moltke as one of those present." Another witness

---

* Moltke had been the Kaiser's senior aide-de-camp for eight years, 1894–1902. When William sent two bottles of old wine to Bismarck at Friedrichsruh in 1894 as a conciliatory gesture, Moltke was the messenger.

testified that he had been debauched ten years before by a man who might have been Count Eulenburg. Moltke's former wife declared that Eulenburg had gone down on his knees before her, begging that she give up her husband. Harden, who had been an actor before he became an editor, played his role with flair. At one point, the judge begged him "in the interests of our whole country" to compromise. Harden melodramatically leveled his finger at Moltke across the courtroom and shouted, "Between that man and me, there is no possibility of compromise on this earth." Bernstein scored his most damaging point when he emphasized that the Emperor had demanded Moltke's and Eulenburg's resignations and that both had immediately complied. Harden was acquitted and walked out of the courtroom into a street filled with cheering people.

During the trial, Bülow privately continued to pose as the sympathetic friend and confidant of the embattled Eulenburg. In fact, the Chancellor and the government remained deliberately aloof. "In these painful circumstances," Bülow wrote the Kaiser, "we must see that the Crown is kept . . . completely removed from all connection with the affair." Eulenburg always assumed that the friend whom he had enthusiastically supported remained a friend. During the Harden-Moltke trial, Eulenburg repeatedly wrote to the Chancellor, "begging me," said Bülow, "to see that his name did not appear; to use all my influence to keep him out of the case. 'I ask for your protection and friendship,' " Bülow quoted Eulenburg. " 'I do not beg for myself, but for my wife and children. . . . Stand by me, if only for their sakes. . . . I know myself entirely innocent.' " Bülow received these appeals coldly, writing in his *Memoirs*, "As the highest official in the Empire, I could not interfere with the action of an independent judiciary."*

Harden's triumph was brief. On December 19, the government overturned the Municipal Court verdict on a technicality and ordered a new trial. This time, Eulenburg was summoned and, under oath, testified that he had never violated Paragraph 175 (prohibiting anal intercourse) of the Criminal Code. Pressed by Bernstein as to whether he had engaged in other homosexual acts, Eulenburg declared, "I have never done anything dirty"; "I have never practiced

---

* Immediately after the Moltke-Harden trial, Bülow himself was accused of homosexuality by Adolf Brand, a journalistic crusader for homosexual rights. The Crown Prosecutor, who had refused to undertake libel cases on behalf of Moltke and Eulenburg, quickly took up the case on behalf of the Imperial Chancellor. Eulenburg, cited as a witness, appeared on Bülow's behalf. Bülow's name was rapidly cleared and Brand was sentenced to eighteen months in prison. During the trial, Bülow testified that he "considered the practices in question loathsome in the highest degree and quite incomprehensible."

any abominations." Moltke's former wife was proven a liar and the testimony of other witnesses in the first trial was discredited. The second trial ended on January 3, 1908, and Harden, found guilty of libel, was sentenced to prison. Moltke, presumably vindicated but socially ruined, retired to his country estate.

Harden, free on appeal and foiled by Moltke, redoubled his attack on Eulenburg. Eulenburg had testified under oath that he was not homosexual; if Harden could prove that he was, Eulenburg would be guilty of perjury. In April 1908, Harden opened a new case in Munich, promising evidence of Eulenburg's flagrant homosexual behavior when he was in the Bavarian capital twenty-five years before. On May 8, Bülow intervened. He ordered his old friend arrested and charged with perjury. The case was transferred to Berlin. Eulenburg, who suffered from heart trouble and severe rheumatoid arthritis, was ill and his doctors pleaded that he not be held in prison; a compromise was reached and the Prince was incarcerated for five months in Berlin's Charity Hospital. When the trial began on June 29, the defendant was carried into court every day on a stretcher.

In preparation for the trial, Harden and Bernstein assembled 145 witnesses against Prince Eulenburg. One by one—thieves, blackmailers, mentally ill persons, and homosexuals—each was brought into Eulenburg's hospital room to stare at the prince for identification. Before the trial began, most had been dismissed; twelve remained. During the first week of court proceedings, the twelve were reduced to two. One of these had thirty-two previous convictions, running from bribery to indecent exposure. He was disqualified when it was learned that, even after the trial had begun, he had tried to blackmail Prince Eulenburg. This left only Jacob Ernst.

Ernst's connection with Eulenburg went back twenty-five years, to the early 1880s. While serving in Munich, Eulenburg had taken a villa on Lake Starnberg, between the city and the Alps. He liked to compose music and poetry while fishing on the lake. His regular boatman on these excursions was a seventeen-year-old boy, Jacob Ernst. Eulenburg employed Ernst, who seemed to him simple and innocent, as a house servant, and took him along on trips. When Ernst married, he was put in charge of the Starnberg villa. Twenty-five years later, at the time of the trial, Ernst had fathered eight children, was partially deaf, and was addicted to alcohol. Before any legal proceedings had begun, when rumors of homosexuality were at first whispered, Ernst—unaware of his future involvement—had written to Eulenburg:

"Could you ever have believed, my lord Prince, that any people in this world could behave like that to such a good man as you are? I couldn't. . . . I have known you for a long time, my lord Prince. You have never shown me or my family anything but kindness, and never been the slightest trouble to any of us. Don't be afraid—it will be all right. I made someone explain the paragraph to me—it is simply shocking to say such things about you. Such a normal healthy man as you are. I will close now, hoping you will get the better of the scandal."

In the Munich trial, Ernst had sworn that he had never had indecent relations with Eulenburg. In Berlin, when Bernstein cross-examined him, threatened him with confrontation by a witness, with conviction of perjury, and with speedy removal to prison, Ernst changed his story. On one occasion in 1883, he said, Eulenburg had made advances to him in a boat and he had accepted. Bernstein also produced a letter from Eulenburg to Ernst, written after Ernst had first appeared before the court in Munich. "Besides," Eulenburg had written, "if anything of the kind ever had taken place, it was such an old story that there could no longer be any question of punishment." Bernstein described this as an admission of guilt; Eulenburg explained it as an attempt to calm and reassure a terrified former servant.

Bernstein's case hinged entirely on Ernst. "Harden sent 145 printed accusations into court against me," Eulenburg wrote to Bülow. "Of these—all of which were exposed for the lies they were—one was enough to ruin me." The trial was never completed. Before Princess von Eulenburg could present her testimony—"in the long period of 34 years comprising our married life, I have never perceived the smallest sign of anything but a perfectly normal emotional life or manner of life"—Philip Eulenburg fainted in court. His leg was badly swollen; doctors diagnosed thrombosis and refused to allow him to return to court. The court moved to Charity Hospital. Eulenburg's health worsened and the trial was adjourned. In September, he was no better and the case was suspended. The following summer, 1909, the trial resumed, Eulenburg collapsed again, and the case was postponed indefinitely.

Bülow, by August 1909, was no longer in power. In writing to him, Eulenburg, still unaware of the former Chancellor's role in Holstein's downfall, allowed himself only a mild reproach for Bülow's behavior: "Only one thing seemed difficult to explain: the fact that neither the official nor even the semi-official press cared to take up the cudgels on behalf of one of the highest German functionaries and fight scandal and scandal-mongering newspapers." From Rome, where he lived in retirement, Bülow oozed condolence: "My dear

Phili: For many years we lived on the closest terms of friendship. How could I, therefore, ever be indifferent to your misfortune? All I could do within the limits of my duty as Chancellor, I did, to prevent these deeply tragic events which, as a man, cut me also to the heart. I did whatever was in my power to make your position somewhat easier." In writing his *Memoirs,* Bülow appeared to make up his mind about Eulenburg. His friend, he said, was a man of "abnormal instincts," "perilous inclination," and lack of "erotic integrity." The fate of "poor Phili," he said, suggested "an obvious comparison with both the fate and the abnormal inclination . . . of Oscar Wilde."

Eulenburg lived at Liebenberg in seclusion until his death in 1921. From time to time, during these twelve years, court-appointed doctors burst in on him unexpectedly to see whether he was strong enough to return to court. Always their verdict was "Prince Eulenburg is not fit to stand trial."

The scandal horrified the Kaiser—but William missed his friends. In October 1907, as the first Moltke-Harden trial was beginning, William suffered a nervous collapse and went to bed for two days. At Christmas that year, he wrote to Houston Stewart Chamberlain: "It has been a very difficult year which has caused me an infinite amount of worry. A trusted group of friends was suddenly broken up through . . . insolence, slander and lying. To have to see the names of one's friends dragged through all the gutters of Europe without being able or entitled to help is terrible." William never saw Philip Eulenburg again, although from time to time he was heard to sigh, "Poor Phili." In 1927, nine years after his abdication and flight to Holland, ex-Kaiser William II wrote to Eulenburg's son that he believed Philip Eulenburg had been "absolutely innocent."

CHAPTER 37

The
Daily Telegraph
Interview

◆

At the end of October 1907, as the first Moltke-Harden trial was beginning in Berlin, the Kaiser—ordinarily eager to travel, especially to England—faced an English trip he dreaded. William had been shocked and infuriated by the alleged actions of his intimate friends, and was mortified that these charges had been published in newspapers throughout the world. What were the English thinking? What must his English relatives be saying about him behind his back? The questions were urgent because he and the Empress Augusta were about to set out on a state visit to Great Britain. The trip, scheduled to begin November 11, had been planned months in advance. In June, William had written to his uncle King Edward VII that he looked forward to seeing Windsor Castle and to "good sport in the dear old park I know so well." Then, on October 31, William telephoned Chancellor von Bülow to say that he had had an accident. An attack of giddiness had forced him to stretch out on a sofa; there he had fainted and rolled onto the floor. "My head hit the ground so hard that my wife was alarmed by the noise and came rushing to me, terrified," he told Bülow. Because of this, he continued, he could not possibly think of undertaking the exhausting trip to England; already he had wired this news to King Edward. In fact, the telegram to the King described the illness differently: "bronchitis and acute cough . . . a virulent attack of influenza. . . . I feel quite unable to meet the strain of the program so kindly prepared for me." The King was furious: "I cannot say how upset I am," he told Knollys. Sir Edward Grey immediately telegraphed Sir Frank Lascelles, the British Ambassador in Berlin, that "there is little doubt that this decision would be attributed to the recent scandals in Berlin and nothing that we could say or do would alter the impression." Lascelles delivered this message to the Chancellor and added, "The worst of it is that about an hour ago I was in the Tiergarten and met the Emperor, who is alleged to be so seriously ill, galloping along . . . with a group of his aides, in very good spirits."

In his *Memoirs,* Bülow said bluntly that William was too embarrassed to go to England. After seeing Lascelles, the Chancellor sent a sharp note to the Kaiser. William immediately changed his mind. He invited the Chancellor to join him that evening at the theater, where he informed Bülow that his indisposition had disappeared, he had taken a refreshing gallop, eaten a hearty meal, and now was ready to go wherever the Chancellor wished. Bülow informed Lascelles that the Kaiser would be coming to England as planned.

On November 11, an unusually thick fog hung over the Channel and southern England. As the *Hohenzollern* approached Portsmouth, reported *The Times,* "the German squadron and the Admiralty were practically engaged in a game of hide and seek." Later that day, when the German party reached Windsor Castle, the fog was so thick that from a window in St. George's Hall, it was impossible to see across the Quadrangle as the state carriages arrived through the Royal Entrance. William, wearing his British admiral's uniform, nevertheless was ebullient. "It seems like coming home again to Windsor," he told the Mayor. "I'm always glad to be here." At a state banquet for 180 guests the following night, King Edward inserted a mischievous dig into his formal welcome: "For a long time we had hoped to receive this visit, but recently we feared that, owing to indisposition, it would not take place. Fortunately, Their Majesties are now both looking in such good health that I can only hope their stay in England will much benefit them."

The visit's public climax was a reception in London. "Sunshine and breeze and cloud-flecked blue sky, more reminiscent of April than November" greeted the Kaiser as he drove through cheering crowds and waving banners from Paddington Station to the Guildhall. One large banner, "BLUT IST DICKER ALS WASSER" ("Blood is thicker than water"), touched him especially and he added the expression to his speech later that morning. His address to the Lord Mayor referred to his first visit as Emperor in 1891, when he had been given the Freedom of the City: "Sixteen years ago, I said that my aim was above all the maintenance of peace. History, I venture to hope, will do me the justice that I have pursued this aim unswervingly ever since. The main support and base for the peace of the world is the maintenance of good relations between our two countries and I shall further strengthen them as far as lies within my power. Blood is thicker than water. The German nation's wishes coincide with mine."

Haldane, whose German was fluent, was called upon for extra duty, as some of the German guests did not speak English. One day, he escorted General Karl von Einem, the Prussian War Minister, and other members of the Kaiser's party to London, where he showed them the War Office and invited them to lunch at his house in Queen Anne's Gate. (Afterwards, he noted, they wished to visit, not the Tower of London or Westminster Abbey, but Harrods.) Einem had special reason to be grateful to Haldane. After the Windsor Castle banquet, when the gentlemen were sitting in the smoking room with the King and the Kaiser, Haldane, "next to General von Einem . . . noticed that he was in pain. . . . [I] tracked the source of his discomfort to his feet; his pumps were too tight across the instep. As soon as the two sovereigns left, I turned to the War Minister and said it was the custom of Windsor Castle as soon as royalty left to kick off our shoes, and I set the example. He looked at me gratefully."

It was understood before the visit that political issues would not be discussed at Windsor. The Kaiser, however, was incapable of compartmentalizing his conversation and, while talking to Haldane, brought up the matter of the Berlin-to-Baghdad Railway. Germany had obtained a concession from the Sultan to build the Turkish section of the new line; the project was delayed by British concern that the railroad would open a potentially hostile approach to India through the Persian Gulf. What did England want? William asked. "I said I knew we wanted a 'gate' to protect India from troops coming down the new railway."* "I will give you the 'gate,' " William replied. That night, during the theatrical performance which followed dinner, Haldane sat behind the Kaiser. Leaning forward, he asked William whether he was serious about "giving us a 'gate.' . . . Next morning, a helmeted Prussian guardsman, one of those

---

* The "gate" was control of the final section which would reach the Gulf.

the Emperor had brought with him, knocked loudly on my door and handed me a message from the Emperor that he had meant what he said." That evening, the Kaiser invited Haldane to his apartment after the theatricals. Haldane went at one in the morning and discovered William talking and smoking with Baron Wilhelm von Schoen (the State Secretary for Foreign Affairs), Einem, and Metternich. Haldane bowed and began to withdraw, saying, "I feel myself an intruder because it is like being at a meeting of Your Majesty's Cabinet," he said. "Be a member of my Cabinet. I appoint you," William responded. At three A.M. Haldane left the Kaiser's apartments and groped his way down dark passageways back to his own room in a different part of the castle.

Politicians in both countries were pleased by the visit. "I wish to express my satisfaction at the welcome of the Imperial couple by the King and people," Bülow told the Reichstag. "I believe that when the history of the last decade is written . . . it will appear that the tension between England and Germany which has long oppressed the world was due in the last resort to a great mutual misunderstanding. Each attributed to the other purposes that it did not entertain. . . . I am certain that I speak for this House and the German people when I say that such peaceful and friendly feelings are shared by us." Sir Edward Grey agreed: "It is bound to have a good effect." Morley hoped that "the visit of the German Emperor . . . will much improve the chances of a little decent calm in Europe." Esher, writing in his journal, introduced a discordant note: "Our King makes a better show than William II. He has more graciousness and dignity. William is ungrateful, nervous, and plain. . . . Grey had two long talks with him. At the first, he declaimed violently against Jews. 'There are far too many of them in my country. They want stamping out. If I did not restrain my people, there would be Jew-baiting.' "

The state visit lasted a week. At the end, the Empress Augusta returned to Germany. William, delighted by his enthusiastic reception, so different from the murky atmosphere of Berlin, decided to prolong his stay on a private basis. He rented Highcliffe Castle near Bournemouth in Hampshire and invited the owner, Colonel Edward Montague Stuart-Wortley, a Regular Army officer, to stay on as his guest. William delighted in these surroundings: "The great British people . . . received me with warmth and open arms. During my stay, I sampled, as I had long wanted to do, all the delights of English home and country life. Comfortable affluence, excellent people in all walks of life, with all classes giving clear evidence of culture in their elegance and cleanliness. Pleasant intercourse between gentlemen on an equal footing without all the ceremonial of royalty. I found it immensely refreshing and soothing."

During this happy sojourn on the British coast, William talked freely to Colonel Stuart-Wortley about his desire for England's friendship and his frustration that England constantly misunderstood and rejected his good intentions. Stuart-Wortley took careful notes.

During the week in October 1908 in which Austria precipitated an international crisis by annexing Bosnia and Herzegovina, Bernhard von Bülow was at his seaside villa on Norderney, a Frisian island on the North Sea coast. "Overwhelmed with work, absorbed from morning to night in these difficult problems," Bülow "received from the Kaiser, who was at Romintern, a bulky, almost illegible manuscript, written on bad typing paper, with a covering letter asking if I saw any objection to its publication." The manuscript, written in English, was the draft of an extended interview with Kaiser William II on the subject of Anglo-German relations. Using remarks William had made during his three weeks at Highcliffe the previous autumn, Colonel Stuart-Wortley was asking permission to publish the interview in the London *Daily Telegraph.* In Stuart-Wortley's view, if the English public knew the extent of the Kaiser's Anglophilia, relations between the two countries would greatly improve. The Kaiser, too, wished for publication, but, in accordance with the German constitution, was asking the Chancellor's advice and approval. William demanded only that Bülow "on no account forward it to the Foreign Office in Berlin."

Bülow ignored the Kaiser: "Without the slightest suspicion in my mind of the ominous contents of the manuscript, which I could not find the time to read, I sent it off to the Wilhelmstrasse with a note: 'Please read the enclosed article carefully, transcribe it in clear, official script . . . duplicate it, and enter in the margin such corrections, additions or deletions as may seem suitable.' "

State Secretary Schoen was absent from No. 76 Wilhelmstrasse when the manuscript arrived; accordingly, it went to Under State Secretary Stemrich, who read the draft and forwarded it untouched to Reinhold Klehmet, for the previous twelve years a Counselor in the Political Division. Klehmet interpreted Bülow's instructions literally: he was to correct any errors of fact and not to express an opinion as to the advisability of publication. He made two minor corrections and returned the manuscript—now written neatly on good paper—to the Chancellor. Bülow stated he again did not read the interview. He sent it back to the Kaiser, saying that he saw no reason not to publish. William sent it to Stuart-Wortley, who gave it to the *Daily Telegraph.*

On the morning of October 29, Bülow found on his desk a long message from the Wolf Telegraph Agency office in London, summarizing an interview with the German Emperor published the previous day in the *Daily Telegraph.* In the interview, given to an anonymous person "of unimpeachable authority," the Kaiser protested that he had always been a friend of England but that his friendship was unappreciated. "You English are mad, mad as March hares," he said. "What on earth has come over you that you should harbor such suspicions against us, suspicions so unworthy of a great nation." He took "as a personal insult," William continued, the "distortions and misinterpretations" of the British press in describing his "repeated offers of friendship" with England. This hostility made his own effort to promote friendship all the more difficult as the majority of Germans disliked the English. Then came what Bülow, in his *Memoirs,* was to call "the three enormities": when the Boer War was at its height, Russia and France had urged him to save the Boer republics by joining a Continental coalition which would "humiliate England to the dust." He had refused, the Kaiser declared, and had informed the Russians and the French that "Germany would use her armed might to prevent such concerted action." He had sent this letter to his grandmother, Queen Victoria, and it had been placed "in the archives of Windsor Castle."

"Nor was that all," the Kaiser continued. "Just at the time of your Black Week [early in the Boer War], when disasters followed one another in rapid succession . . . I worked out what I considered to be the best plan of campaign . . . submitted it to my General Staff . . . then . . . despatched it to England. That paper is likewise among the State Papers at Windsor Castle awaiting the severely impartial verdict of history. And as a matter of curious coincidence, let me add that the plan which I formulated ran very much on the same lines as that which was actually adopted by Lord Roberts. . . .

"But, you will say, what of the German Navy? . . . Against whom but England is it being steadily built up?" Its purpose, William explained, was to protect Germany's growing worldwide trade. "Germany looks ahead. Her horizons stretch far away. She must be prepared for any eventualities in the Far East. . . . Look at the accomplished rise of Japan. . . . It may even be that England herself will be glad that Germany has a fleet. . . ."

Bülow's reaction was utter dismay. The interview revealed,

"more than any previous manifestation of the kind, the Emperor's intellectual extravagance, his incoherent regard of facts, his complete lack of political moderation and balance, combined with an excessive urge towards . . . display." "As I read these sad effusions, which could scarcely have been surpassed in tactless stupidity, I sent for Klehmet and asked him how he could ever have let pass such incredible expressions of opinion. He replied that he had received the definite impression that His Majesty personally was very anxious to have the whole article published." Bülow exploded: "And haven't you learned yet that His Majesty's personal wishes are often sheer nonsense?"

Bülow had chosen his own defense: busy with a crisis, the Chancellor had trusted the Foreign Office; the Foreign Office—which, Bülow knew, the Kaiser intensely disliked—had betrayed the trust and, therefore, the Kaiser and himself. The Foreign Office, then in the hands of the weak Baron von Schoen, was ill equipped to refute this charge. It had obeyed specific orders to make "such corrections, additions or deletions as may seem suitable." Beyond this, it had in the Bismarckian tradition left the ultimate decision as to the advisability of publication up to the Chancellor.

The vital point, on which no one except Bülow could supply the truth, was whether Bülow had actually read the interview before approving publication. He claimed that he had not; he clung to this through the parliamentary storm that followed and maintained it even in his *Memoirs*. Yet no one had greater experience with the Kaiser's inflammatory exaggerations and rhetorical bluster than Bülow. As Chancellor, he lived in constant apprehension of William's indiscretions; he was constantly editing, suppressing, rewriting the Kaiser's speeches. Further, a German Emperor did not publish a lengthy interview in an English newspaper every day. If not as a duty, then out of sheer curiosity, would not the Chancellor have wished to know what William was saying? Schoen, Stemrich, and others at the Wilhelmstrasse were convinced that Bülow was lying. Some have suggested that he read the interview, anticipated the result, and permitted publication in the hope of using the subsequent constitutional crisis as a means of improving his own position in relation to the Crown.

The interview startled the world. Japan wondered what "eventualities" might involve the German Fleet with its own navy. France and Russia denied that they had proposed a coalition against England during the Boer War; indeed, Tsar Nicholas II told Sir Arthur Nicolson, it was the Kaiser who had suggested Continental intervention. The English reaction ranged from amusement to contempt.

Lord Roberts threatened to return his Order of the Black Eagle. The *Times* observed that if Germany were planning a naval war in the Pacific, the accumulation of a powerful, short-range battle fleet in the North Sea seemed odd. Grey wrote to a friend: "The German Emperor is aging me; he is like a battleship with steam up and screws going, but with no rudder, and he will run into something some day and cause a catastrophe." In the House of Commons, Haldane was asked whether the plan of campaign which had won the Boer War could be made public. The War Minister replied that the War Office had been unable to locate the document in its archives. Consequently, he said, "I am not in a position to fulfill the wish of those who want the document published."

In a Germany just emerging from the first Eulenburg trial, the interview ignited a new firestorm of shock, embarrassment, and indignation. The ruler who seemed to have chosen his friends so indiscreetly had now proclaimed to Germany and Europe that the Empire was ruled by a man who was constitutionally irresponsible and possibly mentally unbalanced. Sir Edward Goschen, the new British Ambassador, was amazed. "To a newcomer like myself, imbued with the idea that His Majesty was more or less outside public criticism, this onslaught upon him comes as a most striking surprise," he reported to Sir Edward Grey. The Austrian ambassador sent a similar report to Vienna: "Never before in Prussian history have *all* circles been captured by such deep resentment against their sovereign." Germans, most of whom had passionately supported the Boers, were furious that the Kaiser claimed to have drawn up the plan of campaign by which the British had conquered the South African republics. Why alienate the Japanese? Why antagonize the French and Russians? Why provoke the British by saying that most Germans hated them?

Underlying specific criticism of the Kaiser's unguarded remarks was the general complaint that William was attempting again to exercise personal rule—a right he had not been granted by the Imperial constitution. The left reacted by demanding greater limits on the monarchy and tighter restriction of the Emperor's right to interfere in domestic and foreign policy. The Conservatives wanted the monarchy left unfettered, but desired restraints placed on the eccentric, damaging behavior of *this* monarch. When a majority in the Reichstag, including many Conservatives, demanded a censure debate, Bülow sent Theobald von Bethmann-Hollweg, the Imperial Secretary of the Interior, to assess the mood of the assembly. Bethmann-Hollweg reported to the Chancellor that "it will be impossible to limit the present uproar to the *Daily Telegraph* or to formal mistakes committed in the treatment of the document" by the Foreign Office. "What is erupting now with primeval force is resentment against the personal regime, dissatisfaction over the Emperor's attitude of the last twenty years, of which the conversations in the *Daily Telegraph* are only one among many symptoms."

Before he could deal with the Reichstag, Bülow had to make sure of the Kaiser. Under the German constitution, the Chancellor was chosen by the Emperor and could remain in office as long as the Emperor wished, no matter what the views of the members of the Reichstag. William II, who had agreed to publication of the interview to contribute, he thought, to friendly relations with England, was stunned by the personal criticism directed at him from all sides. He had behaved in strict accordance with the constitution by forwarding a draft of the interview to the Imperial Chancellor for approval. The Chancellor had approved, the interview had been published—and now he, the German Emperor, was everywhere regarded as a menace or a fool.

Bülow's most effective weapon had always been the threat of resignation; he used it now. He wrote to the Kaiser, who was still at Romintern, declaring that though he had not read the interview, he had submitted it to the Foreign Office. "If Your Majesty is displeased with my having failed under pressure of business to go through the English manuscript in person, and blames me for the carelessness shown by the Foreign Office, I humbly beg to be relieved of my Chancellorship. If, however, I have not lost Your Majesty's confidence, I feel I cannot remain at my post unless I am given the freest scope to defend Your Majesty openly and vigorously, against the unjust attacks on my Imperial Master." As soon as Bülow saw the Kaiser, on William's return from Romintern, the Chancellor realized that he had no need to worry. "He was," said Bülow, "as he always was at moments of crisis, very pale, very pitiable." William did not reproach the Chancellor; this time Bülow did not even need to blame the Foreign Office. He informed the Kaiser that the Reichstag debate would begin on November 10. "Go ahead," said William. "Say what you like. But, however you do it, bring us through." "His trustful, childlike attitude touched me more than I can say," Bülow observed.

With the Kaiser submissive, Bülow had no difficulty getting permission to publish a statement in the official government gazette, the *Norddeutsche Allgemeine Zeitung.* The statement ignored the content of the interview and dealt solely with responsibility for publication. The guilty party was the Foreign Office; the Chancellor had taken the blame; the Emperor had refused the Chancellor's resignation.

In the Reichstag, which debated both the content of the interview and the responsibility for publishing it, the targets of attack were the Foreign Office and the Kaiser. Speakers on all sides condemned the carelessness and incompetence of the Foreign Office; members on the left demanded constitutional changes which would restrict the authority of the Emperor; Conservatives expressed "the wish that in future the Emperor will maintain greater reserve in his conversation." Bülow successfully avoided the storm, managing to incriminate the Kaiser, exonerate himself, and present the image of a brave and chivalrous Chancellor, willing to absorb all blows, just and unjust, and persevere for the sake of Crown and nation. The interview, he said when he rose to speak, contained incorrect facts: No plan of campaign had been worked out or sent to Windsor, rather the Boers had been warned that they would have to fight alone; there had never been a proposal of a Continental alliance against England; the majority of Germans were not hostile to England; Germany had no ambition to threaten Japan in the Far East. "For the mistake which was made in dealing with the manuscript, I take the entire responsibility," Bülow continued. "It is repugnant to my personal feelings to brand as scapegoats officials who have done a life-long duty."* Bülow characterized the Kaiser as a willful, clumsy child, anxious to be useful and important, who stumbled badly when left untutored. "Gentlemen, the knowledge that the publication of his conversations had not produced the effect which the Emperor intended in England, and has aroused deep excitement and painful regret in our country will—and this is the firm conviction which I have gained during these days of stress—will induce His Majesty in future to observe that reserve which is as essential in the interests of a coherent policy as in those of the authority of the Crown. If this were not so, neither I nor my successors could accept the responsibility."

Bülow emerged triumphant. "When, amid a roar of cheering, I sat down, I felt that the battle had been won," he said. Holstein, watching from retirement, supported the Chancellor's tactics: "In view of the Kaiser's indiscretions, no defense was possible," he wrote in his journal. The *Berliner Tageblatt* openly attacked Kaiser William: "We have a population of more than sixty million, a highly

---

* Two weeks later, Bülow transferred Klehmet from Berlin to the post of Consul in Bucharest.

intelligent nation, and yet the fate of the Chancellor as well as the choice of his successor rests with one man! Such a situation is intolerable to a self-respecting nation. The events of the last few days have made it clear that the German people will not continue to allow their vital interests to depend on the mood of a single individual whose impulsiveness they have once again had the opportunity of witnessing."

The Kaiser was not in Berlin during the Reichstag debate. His schedule, established well in advance, had called for a visit to the Archduke Franz Ferdinand, the Austrian Heir, and then attendance at a hunting party at Donaueschingen, the Black Forest estate of his friend, the multimillionaire German-Austrian Prince Max von Fürstenberg. William's decision to go ahead with his journey at a time when the nation was convulsed by talk of the monarch's indiscretion had drawn bitter comment in the Reichstag. In fact, before his departure, the Kaiser had asked Bülow whether he ought to remain in Berlin during the debate. Bülow had told him to go: "He was longing for Donaueschingen where fox-hunting, cabaret entertainments and every kind of amusement were in prospect," the Chancellor explained. "I yielded to his wish." Once the Kaiser had gone—and despite the fact that William was being roundly condemned in the Reichstag for his absence—Bülow did nothing to bring him back. When Holstein questioned Bülow, "Did you, as people are saying, dissuade the Kaiser from returning to Berlin?" Bülow replied, "No, I said nothing either way." In fact, during William's stay at Donaueschingen, he received a lengthy, coded telegram from the Chancellor, stating that it was unnecessary for him to return to Berlin during the debate.

When the Kaiser arrived at Donaueschingen, his host was struck by William's look. "If you met Kaiser William, you would not know him," Prince Max said. At first, the visit distracted the Kaiser. "The two days here have gone off very harmoniously and gaily," he wrote to Bülow. "The shoot went splendidly. I brought down sixty-five stags. I remember you in all my prayers, morning and evening. . . . There is a silver lining in every cloud. God be with you! Your old friend, William I.R." Then, one evening after dinner, William suffered a personal blow. The ladies "in full evening dress with all their jewels, the gentlemen in green or black swallowtails . . . were assembled in the Great Hall of the Castle, with a band playing on the staircase. Suddenly, Count Hülsen-Haeseler appeared in pink ballet skirts with a rose wreath and began to dance to the music." General Count Hülsen-Haeseler, a friend of the Kaiser's since boyhood, and Chief of the Military Cabinet, had performed in this manner before. "It is an unusual experience to see a Chief of the Military Cabinet capering about in the costume of a lady of the ballet," said a new member of the Kaiser's suite. Exhausted by his pirouettes, the Count stopped, bowed—and then sagged to the floor. The Castle was in pandemonium: a doctor worked over the stricken dancer; Princess von Fürstenberg sat in a chair and wept; the Kaiser paced frantically up and down. After an hour and a half, the Count was pronounced dead of heart failure. Rigor mortis had set in and only with great difficulty was the General's body stripped of its tutu and dressed in proper military uniform.

William, already agitated by the *Daily Telegraph* affair, was further unnerved. Meanwhile, Bülow's success before the Reichstag was evaporating. To secure his position as Chancellor, he needed a public endorsement by William of the stand he had taken in the debate. On November 17, Bülow went to see the Kaiser, who had returned to Potsdam. William and Augusta awaited him on the terrace in front of the New Palace. As he approached, the Empress hurried forward and whispered in his ear, "Be really kind and gentle with the Emperor. He is quite broken up." William led Bülow into his study. The Kaiser, pale and dejected, was "in such a depressed and pessimistic mood that I had to comfort him more than criticize his past conduct," said Bülow. With the monarch deep in melancholy, the Chancellor had no difficulty. He drew from his pocket a prepared statement:

"Uninfluenced by the exaggerations of public criticism, which seem to him unjustified, His Majesty the Emperor regards it as his chief Imperial task to assure the continuity of Imperial policy, while, at the same time, maintaining his constitutional responsibilities. His Royal and Imperial Majesty has accordingly approved all declarations by the Imperial Chancellor in the Reichstag, at the same time assuring Prince von Bülow of the continuation of his confidence."

William eagerly endorsed the document and, said Bülow, "grasped my hand convulsively. 'Help me! Save me!' He embraced me and gave me a hearty kiss on both cheeks." As Bülow bowed and was leaving, the Kaiser said again, "Thank you! Thank you with all my heart!" Returning home, Bülow told his wife, "I've managed, once more, to get the Crown and the Emperor out of a scrape."

When Bülow left, William began to weep and went to bed. The following day, Bülow was informed by telephone that the Kaiser intended to abdicate. The Chancellor hurried back to Potsdam. The Empress, her eyes red with tears, received him on the ground floor. "Must the Emperor abdicate?" she asked. "Do you wish him to abdicate?" Bülow attempted to calm her, assuring her that, thanks to his speech in the Reichstag, "the storm had begun to abate."

Bülow left without seeing the Kaiser. The Crown Prince arrived. "I rushed upstairs," he recorded in his *Memoirs.* "My father seemed aged by years; he had lost hope and felt himself to be deserted by everybody. He was broken down . . . his self-confidence and his trust were shattered. He talked vehemently . . . bitterness aroused by the injustice . . . kept reasserting itself. I stayed with him for an hour sitting on his bed, a thing which, so long as I can remember, had never happened before."

William never mentioned abdication again, but his depression was evident. "The Emperor made no attempt to conceal the deep dejection of his soul," said Princess Victoria Louise's English governess. "[He] moved about—this man usually so loquacious, so pleased with himself and the world—in a mournful silence, speaking seldom and then in an undertone. . . . Everyone else, too, seemed to talk in whispers." In his rare public appearances, William veered to the opposite extreme, affecting a forced cheerfulness, cracking jokes and laughing louder than anyone else. The Kaiser avoided Bülow. The morning visits to the Wilhelmstrasse and strolls in the Chancellory garden ceased; Kaiser and Chancellor saw each other only when business required it. At the end of six weeks, William began to recover. On New Year's Day, as he drove through the streets and the crowd broke into cheers, William's self-confidence and self-esteem began to creep back. Public sympathy for the Emperor increased; his silence and withdrawal were ascribed, not to collapse, but to a becoming royal dignity. Blame was directed at the Chancellor: the Emperor, after all, had done his constitutional duty by showing the draft of the interview to Prince von Bülow. The Chancellor had betrayed his master twice: first, by failing to read the document before publication; second, by not sufficiently defending the monarch in the Reichstag. In private, then gradually, in a wider circle, William accepted and repeated this view. He had been "left in the lurch," he said; "I became the scapegoat and my Chancellor washed his hands in innocence." To Archduke Franz Ferdinand, the Austrian Heir, he wrote: "You will understand what agony it is for me to behave as though everything were normal, and to go on working with people whose cowardice and lack of responsibility has [sic] deprived me of the protection which anyone else would have accorded to the Head of State as a matter of course. The German people is beginning to look into its soul and to realize the deed which has been done to it." Bülow, sensing that public opinion was shifting to the Emperor, became alarmed. He wrote to William on

February 13 that everything he had said and done in November had been motivated "solely and exclusively by loyalty to Your Majesty's house and country and inner love for Your Majesty's . . . Person." In the margin of this letter, William wrote "Pharisee!"

On March 11, 1909, with the Bosnian Crisis at a critical stage, William received Bülow in the picture gallery of the Berlin Castle. "I walked up and down with him," the Kaiser said, "between the portraits of my ancestors and the paintings of the battles of the Seven Years War . . . and was amazed when the Chancellor harked back to the events of the autumn of 1908 and undertook to explain his attitude." Bülow employed the technique which had worked in the past, telling William that "I could not continue to shoulder the heavy burden of office unless I felt that I had the entire confidence of my sovereign." The Kaiser countered bluntly that, in the autumn, the Chancellor had not "shown sufficient energy in contradicting attacks" against the Crown. "Froben," he said, "would not have spoken as you did in the Reichstag debate on November 10." As he spoke, William stood before a portrait of Froben, a royal equerry, who, at the Battle of Fehrbellin in 1675, had mounted the piebald horse of the Great Elector in order to attract enemy musketballs away from his master. As Chancellor, said William, Froben would have declared that he had advised the Emperor to say what he did in the *Daily Telegraph*. Bülow replied that he could not have said this since, knowing his beliefs, the public would not have believed him. "Which simply means," retorted William, "that you consider me a donkey, capable of blunders you yourself never could have committed." Bülow apologized, extolled the Kaiser's remarkable qualities—and William swung around. "This frank conversation released the tension between us," the Kaiser said. "Haven't I always told you that we complete one another famously?" he asked Bülow. "We should stick together and we will." He pumped the Chancellor's hand and took him in to lunch. "I've just been having it out with the Imperial Chancellor and everything has been put right between us," the Kaiser announced to the waiting entourage. "If anyone says anything against Prince Bülow, I shall punch his nose for him." That night, William wired his brother, Henry, "Have just forgiven Bülow who begged my pardon in a flood of tears." The following night, at Bülow's request, the Imperial couple dined with him. William walked in the door and greeted Princess von Bülow: "How happy I am to be here again! What a terrible winter this has been! But now it's all going to be perfect."

Despite this jaunty talk, the Kaiser's renewed affection for his Chancellor had a hollow quality. To a friend he confided that the whole reconciliation has been "a comedy" and that as soon as the political situation permitted, he intended to remove Bülow from office. The opportunity arrived in June; the occasion was the Chancellor's defeat on a key vote in the Reichstag. By the spring of 1909, the building of the fleet had created a fiscal crisis in Germany. Five hundred million additional marks were required. In deference to the power of the conservatives in the Reichstag, four fifths of the new revenues—400 million marks—was to be raised from sales taxes, which hit the lower and middle classes hardest. Some concession, however, had to be made to the liberals; Bülow proposed that one fifth of the required sum—one million marks—be raised from property owners by means of an inheritance tax. Conservatives stiffly opposed death duties, which had never before been imposed in Germany. The Kaiser supported the Chancellor, but he made it clear that if Bülow failed to deliver the vote for the inheritance tax, he must resign. One June 24, the inheritance tax was defeated by eight votes, 195 to 187.

On June 26, 1909, twelve years to the day after he had accepted the State Secretaryship from the Kaiser on board the *Hohenzollern* at Kiel, Bülow returned to the same site to offer his resignation as Chancellor. William was waiting on deck, impatient and nervous. "As a matter of fact, I'm in rather a hurry," the Emperor said. "In an hour I have to have lunch with the Prince of Monaco." He told Bülow that his successor would be Bethmann-Hollweg, the Imperial Secretary of the Interior. "I'm sure you'll agree with me," the Kaiser said. "He'll soon put the Reichstag down a peg or two. Besides, I shot my first roebuck at his estate in Hohenfinow." Bülow's response was tentative: "As far as domestic policy is concerned, Bethmann-Hollweg is perhaps the best man . . . [but] he understands nothing about foreign policy." "You leave foreign policy to me," William said. "You've managed to teach me something, you know." When Bülow recommended that the Kaiser do everything possible to reach a naval agreement with England, William frowned. "I cannot and will not allow John Bull to give me orders on how many ships I can build." Cheerily, the Kaiser returned to Bethmann-Hollweg: "Just wait till that great tall fellow stands up in the Reichstag and glares at all the 'honorable' members. Why, he'll scare them to death. They'll run off and hide in their mouse holes." When it was time to leave, the Kaiser took Bülow with him to lunch on the Prince of Monaco's yacht. At the table, where most of the other guests were French, William was in high spirits and laughed loudly. "I had the peculiar sensation I had eaten the condemned man's last meal in the presence of foreigners," Bülow remembered.

For three weeks, the Chancellor lived in limbo, hoping that William might change his mind. On July 14, the announcement came: Prince von Bülow, who was resigning as Imperial Chancellor, would receive for his services the Order of the Black Eagle set in diamonds. That night, the Kaiser invited himself to dinner at Bülow's table. William presented to Princess von Bülow a bouquet of roses which he said he had picked himself; he also offered her an enameled portrait of himself set in diamonds. His remarks over dinner were less generous. When the Princess said she was sad at what had happened, the Kaiser replied, "I feel even worse than you do. I've fought against it tooth and nail, but Bernhard was determined to go." Princess von Bülow mentioned the Reichstag tax vote as the reason for her husband's resignation. William disagreed. "You mustn't think that the . . . Death Duties are what made Bernhard retire," he said. "The real reason was the events of last November. You see, those fellows let me know privately that they didn't really mind the death duties. They overthrew him because they didn't think he showed enough zeal defending his Imperial Master." What, asked the Princess, did the Emperor think her husband should have done in November? "He ought to have declared in the Reichstag: 'I won't have any more of this insolent speech about the Emperor. How dare you speak like this? Quick march! Get out!' "

William evolved different versions of his role in Bülow's departure. In his *Memoirs,* he recorded, "I decided to acquiesce in the wish of Prince Bülow to grant his request for retirement." Soon after the resignation, he explained to his entourage that the Chancellor was becoming senile and could not remember one day what he had said the day before. To the King of Württemberg, standing under the same tree in the garden of Sans Souci where the Kaiser had held his last interview with the fallen Chancellor, William boasted: "This is where I gave that sweep the boot!"

CHAPTER 38

Naval Talks
and Bethmann-Hollweg

◆

As Kaiser William was enjoying "dear old sport" in Windsor Park, basking in the cheers of London crowds, proclaiming friendship at the Guildhall, and being "soothed and refreshed" by Colonel Stuart-Wortley and his friends at Highcliffe Castle, the German Admiralty was preparing a new Supplementary Navy Law. The useful life of battleships, set by the Navy Law of 1898 at twenty-five years, was to be reduced to twenty years, after which a new, replacement ship would be laid down. To effect the new law, the 1906 program of two dreadnoughts a year, increased to three in 1907, would increase to four dreadnoughts annually. For four years—1908, 1909, 1910, and 1911—three battleships and one battle cruiser were to be authorized. In 1912, when these sixteen capital ships were built or building, the program would drop back to two a year. In March 1908, the Reichstag passed this Supplementary Navy Law.

The new German Navy Law alarmed the British government. The Liberals, in power for two years in 1908, had attempted to diminish armaments costs to devote more money to social programs. There had been no effort to reach an understanding with Germany on shipbuilding; instead, Campbell-Bannerman had tried to lead by example. In 1906 and 1907, the four dreadnoughts a year of the

Unionist program had been cut to three a year. In 1908, British dreadnought building had been cut even further, to two a year. The Germans were moving in the opposite direction. It was disheartening; surely the Germans understood that no British government, Unionist or Liberal, could permit a potential enemy to equal or surpass British naval strength. German shipbuilding could only provoke increased British building and a consequent waste of money by both countries. Surely, rational discussion could persuade the government in Berlin to put a reasonable limit on its naval ambitions.

One British Cabinet Minister acutely affected by the new German Navy Law was David Lloyd George, the Chancellor of the Exchequer, who would have to find the money to pay for any increase in the size of the British fleet. Sir Edward Grey decided to put the Chancellor in touch with Count Metternich, the German Ambassador to England; Lloyd George could then express his views in person to a representative of the German government. On July 14, 1908, Grey invited Lloyd George and Metternich to lunch at the Foreign Office.

Count Paul Wolff-Metternich was an Anglophile. A Rhineland aristocrat and a Roman Catholic, he had first arrived in London in 1900 to assist the Ambassador, Count Hatzfeldt, who was gradually succumbing to emphysema. In November 1901, when Hatzfeldt died, Metternich—as envisaged—slipped smoothly into the post which he was to hold for ten years. The Kaiser, introducing his new representative to his uncle, then Prince of Wales, in 1900, called Metternich "no ordinary man. He is by conviction a staunch friend of England and was chosen by me on that account. But he is at the same time a trusted and true friend of mine, enjoying my fullest confidence." Metternich, a bachelor, was little seen in London society and, although a niece lived with him to act as his hostess, during his term the immense German Embassy at 9, Carlton House Terrace, was closed to music, dancing, and laughter. Nevertheless, the Ambassador held the respect of both the British and German governments. He had, said Bülow, "an open mind for the . . . enormous latent power of the British Empire. The underestimation of this power was an error particularly deep-rooted . . . in Prussian military and aristocratic circles." Sir Edward Grey respected Metternich's professionalism: "I always felt, with Metternich," wrote Grey, "that whatever I said would be faithfully reported by him; that no chance and unintentional slip of mine . . . would be distorted or misrepresented."

In conversation at the Foreign Office lunch, Grey and Lloyd George emphasized that Anglo-German relations hinged on the naval competition. Ruinous expenditure for battleships would not improve Germany's relative position, they argued, because "every Englishman would spend his last penny to preserve" British supremacy at sea. But the shipbuilding race and the waste of millions of pounds and marks would embitter relations. German fears of a British attack and arguments that a fleet was needed to deter such an attack were groundless; Lloyd George jokingly reminded Metternich of Bismarck's quip that, if an English army landed on German soil, he would "leave it to the police to arrest" it. Lloyd George suggested that a slowing of the tempo of German battleship construction would be the most effective way of reassuring English public opinion. Britain, he said, would be "most ready to meet Germany half way in establishing a joint basis for curtailment of the fleet building on both sides."

The Kaiser, who regarded the Fleet as his private preserve, treated any advice that it be limited as a personal insult, an attack on his prerogative. Across the margins of Metternich's dispatch he scribbled: "Such insolent talk has never been heard from England"; "First-class cheek!"; "We shall never be dictated to as to how our armament should be constituted"; "We should look upon that as a declaration of war"; "No! There will be no talk about that at all!" At the end of the letter, William let his feelings flow at length:

> Bravo! Metternich! Has done his business very well, except in one point, which is the most important. The Ambassador has overlooked entirely that he was not permitted, even if entirely non-committally and only as a private opinion, to [agree] to the insolent demands of the English Ministers to make their peacefulness dependent on the diminution of our sea force. Through that he has put himself on a very dangerous slope. I am sorry for him because of that. It must be pointed out to him that I do *not* wish a good understanding with England at the expense of the extension of the German fleet. If England only intends graciously to hold out her hand to us with the indication that we should curtail our fleet, then this is an excessive impudence, which contains a great insult for the German people and its Kaiser, and which should be refused *a limine* by the Ambassador! By the same rights France and Russia could then demand a curtailment of our land force. As soon as one allows any foreign Power under any pretext whatsoever to have something to say about our own armaments, then one may retire, like Portugal and Spain! The German fleet is not built *against* anybody and not *against* England either! But according to *our* needs! This

has been said quite clearly in the Navy Law and has remained unchanged for eleven years! This law is being carried out to the very last tittle: whether the British like it or not does not worry us. If they want a war, *they* must *start* it, we are not afraid of it!

(Signed) WILHELM R.I.

Two weeks later, Metternich invited Grey and Lloyd George to the German Embassy. The two English ministers returned to their original theme: "The naval question [was] the central point of German-English relations." "Mr. Lloyd George," Metternich reported to Berlin, "then returned to his pet idea, the slackening down in the speed of naval construction and exhorted me to make use of the time during which the peace-loving Liberal Government was at the helm." The Kaiser's colorful marginalia continued violent: "This is talk which until now has been only used against creatures like China or Italy! It is unheard of!"; "If England want to have war, just let her start it, we'll give her what for!" In his long footnote to this second report, William vented his anger on Metternich:

"This sort of conversation as it has been carried on between Lloyd George and Metternich is utterly unworthy and provoking for Germany! I must beg him in future to have nothing to do with that sort of expectoration. Here he has accepted very patiently as a listener the opinions and orders of English statesmen, and has only ventured protests which had no effect at all. He should give these gentlemen . . . an answer like 'Go to Hell,' etc. That would bring these fellows to their senses again. That Lloyd George even dared to come out with an order for defining the speed of OUR building is beyond the limit, but is a result of Metternich putting himself during the first discussions on the dangerous path of *'a possibility not being out of the question.'* The clever British are trying to hook him, and sooner or later they will pull the string and drag him out; despite this 'private talk,' 'non-committal character of expression of opinion,' etc.! He should *ab ovo* refuse everything with such remarks as, 'No country allows itself to be dictated to or admonished by another country about the size and kind of its armaments.' 'I refuse to discuss such a matter.' . . .

"Metternich should give that sort of fanatic a kick in the ass; he is too soft!"

Despite the Kaiser's anger, Metternich remained at his post. He continued to report his observations and opinions, attempting to explain the British perspective to Berlin: "The English are afraid of our fleet because we are their nearest neighbors and we appear to them more efficient than other people. . . ." The Kaiser growled:

the English "will just have to get used to our fleet. And from time to time, we must assure them that it is not directed against them."

The Kaiser did not wish to fight the Royal Navy and he never dreamed of invading the British Isles. He was building a fleet to proclaim Germany's Imperial grandeur, to make the world listen respectfully to the German Emperor, and, above all, to earn England's approval and reduce German independence on England's favor on the oceans of the world. Because the British Navy was so much stronger, he regarded British complaints about the size of his fleet as impertinent and offensive. In August 1908, William forcefully expressed these feelings to Sir Charles Hardinge, Under Secretary of the Foreign Office, who was traveling with King Edward VII in Germany. After lunch at Kronberg, Hardinge's conversation with the Kaiser turned to naval limitation. Because, up to that point, the Kaiser had been so amiable, Hardinge forgot himself and said, "But you must build slower." Instantly, William drew himself up, and announced that no one could use the word "must" to a German Emperor. If England insisted on German limitation, he said, "then we shall fight. It is a question of national honor and dignity." Later, William reported the scene to Bülow: "I looked him straight in the eye. Sir Charles became scarlet, made me a bow, begged pardon for his words and urged me expressly to forgive and forget and treat them as remarks made inadvertently in a private conversation." After dinner, the Kaiser continued, "when I gave him the Order of the Red Eagle, First Class, he was ready to eat out of my hand. . . . My frank words, when I had showed him my teeth had not failed in their effect. You must always treat Englishmen thus."

Bülow, as Chancellor, had the constitutional right to have final say about the foreign policy of the Empire. He had supported the building of the fleet; he owed his appointment as State Secretary and Chancellor to his acceptance of William's conviction that Germany's future lay on the water. He had embraced the Risk Theory, the Danger Zone, and the argument that once the Danger Zone was passed, the German Fleet would be a means of putting diplomatic pressure on Great Britain. Bülow also was aware of the political invulnerability of Tirpitz' relationship with the Kaiser. Any challenge to the Navy Minister would be hazardous; Bülow sensed that the one figure in the Reich government the Emperor would choose over him was Tirpitz. Accordingly, in the summer of 1908, when William was complaining bitterly about Metternich, Bülow repledged his faith in the fleet: "I beg Your Majesty not to doubt that I support Your Majesty's naval plans with heart as well as head," he wrote. "I know that the creation of the fleet is the task which history assigns Your Majesty."

Nevertheless, Bülow was impressed by Metternich's views. He respected the Ambassador's warnings that the acceleration in German dreadnought building was frightening the Liberal government and alienating English public opinion. He worried that the British Cabinet, goaded by Sir John Fisher, might authorize a preemptive attack on the young German Fleet. In November 1908, emboldened by his triumphant *Daily Telegraph* speech in the Reichstag, the Chancellor questioned Tirpitz. The English government and people were apprehensive about the German Fleet, he said, and the idea of preventive war was widely mentioned in the English press. Thus, "I must ask Your Excellency whether Germany and the German people can look forward to an English attack with quiet confidence."

Tirpitz waited three weeks to reply, before admitting that in view of the overwhelming superiority of the British Fleet, Germany would lose a naval war. But this, in Tirpitz' opinion, was an argument for increasing, not diminishing, the size of the German Fleet: "Our duty is to arm with all our might. . . . Every new ship added to our battlefleet means an increase in the risk for England if she attacks us." Besides, Tirpitz continued, Metternich misunderstood the root of British anxiety and antagonism: it was not the building of the fleet, but German economic competition. Naval concessions would not remove this rivalry and lessen resentment. Tirpitz scorned talk of British attack: "The possibility of a preventive war is a scarecrow and a fiction of our diplomats [i.e., Metternich] to make people who resist them pliable." From London, Metternich contradicted Tirpitz: "The cardinal point of our relations with England lies in the growth of our fleet. It may not be pleasant for us to hear this, but I see nothing to be gained by concealing the truth."

This internal debate at the highest level of the German government continued through the winter and early spring of 1909. In Britain, the new German Navy Law with its four dreadnoughts a year, the fear that Germany was secretly accelerating, led to the celebrated Navy Scare. The result: Asquith's ingenious compromise of four ships now, four later if necessary. In Berlin, the Kaiser gradually recovered from his nervous collapse after publication of the *Daily Telegraph* interview. Bülow's reputation, at a peak after his Reichstag appearance on November 10, was in the descendant. "Feeling that [he] might soon cease to be Chancellor," he summoned a conference in the Chancellor's Palace on June 3, 1909. The subject was the naval question and the possibility of reaching an understanding with England. Metternich was summoned from London; Moltke, Chief of the General Staff; Bethmann-Hollweg, Vice Chancellor and future Chancellor; and Schoen, State Secretary for Foreign Affairs, were present along with Tirpitz. Bülow began with a defense of Metternich: the first duty of a representative abroad, he announced, is to report the truth. The Ambassador and the Navy Minister then traded familiar arguments, with Metternich asserting that the building of the German Fleet was the only cause of British annoyance and Tirpitz protesting that the cause was commercial rivalry. Bülow asked whether any shipbuilding ratio between Germany and England would be acceptable to Tirpitz. Tirpitz suggested three German dreadnoughts for four British. Metternich interjected that this would quickly lead to war. Bülow asked Tirpitz what Germany's chances would be in case of war. The Admiral replied that "our Navy [is] not at present in a position to come out of a fight with England as victors." Moltke declared that, in that case, it seemed wise to try for an understanding based on slowing construction. Bethmann-Hollweg agreed. Bülow attempted to mollify Tirpitz by narrowing the scope of any potential agreement. He was not thinking of a permanent agreement with England, he said, only one long enough to get Germany through the Danger Zone without a preventive war. Asked how long the Danger Zone would last, Tirpitz replied, "Five to six years . . . say, in 1915, after the widening of the Kiel Canal, and the completion of the fortifications of Heligoland."

When Bülow reported the conference to the Kaiser, William "pooh-poohed my fears," said the Chancellor. "The English will never attack us alone," the Kaiser elaborated, "and at the moment they will not find allies." Nevertheless, on June 23, Bülow sent instructions to Metternich in London to begin to work towards "an entente on the Naval Question . . . provided it is combined with a general orientation of English policy in a sense more favorable to Germany." The following day, the Reichstag defeated Bülow's death-duties bill. Two days later, on board the *Hohenzollern,* the Chancellor offered his resignation, and on July 14 it was accepted.

The new Imperial Chancellor, Theobald von Bethmann-Hollweg, was a tall, gaunt, broad-shouldered man of fifty-two with a high forehead, a Vandyke beard, and a pensive, professorial air. To relax he read Plato and played Beethoven sonatas on the piano. His life had been spent in the Civil Service of Prussia and the Empire, where he was known for thoroughness, fairness, pragmatism, and perseverance. His rise through the bureaucracy had made him few enemies. He benefitted from a close family connection with Kaiser William II, nourished by his own respect for the Crown and Prussian traditions and his enthusiasm for German unity. Unlike his clever, ambitious predecessor, Bethmann was regarded as a man unconcerned with advancement; his moves up the ladder were attributed to obedience to duty.

Bethmann lacked Bülow's cleverness, adroitness, and facility as a speaker. He had no experience in foreign affairs. Because of his tendency to brood and procrastinate, his decisions were often delayed. Bülow, in recommending him to the Kaiser for an earlier promotion, had said that Bethmann was neither a thoroughbred nor a jumper, but a good plowhorse who would proceed steadily and slowly. Albert Ballin, the shipowner who was the Kaiser's friend, said that Bethmann had "all the qualities which honor a man and ruin a statesman." For this reason, Ballin also sometimes referred to the new Chancellor, whose appointment had been endorsed by his predecessor, as "Bülow's revenge."

Bethmann-Hollweg's father, Felix, was a maverick. Descended from a wealthy Frankfurt banking family ennobled in 1840, as a young man he abandoned his urban Rhineland origins and became a gentleman farmer in Prussia. With his inheritance he purchased Hohenfinow, a run-down 7,500-acre estate of forests, meadows, and ponds thirty miles from Berlin. For thirty-five years, he poured his energy into restoring the estate to prosperity. He planted wheat fields, imported cattle, installed a sawmill and a trout hatchery. He tried but abandoned operating his own small steel mill. A three-story seventeenth-century brick manor house at the end of an avenue of majestic linden trees was refurbished with tapestries and hand-carved furniture. Gruff and headstrong, Felix Bethmann-Hollweg ruled the countryside as District Magistrate. His opinions were Conservative, pro-Bismarck, and antidemocratic. In 1865, he deplored the fall of Richmond and the defeat of the Confederacy in the American Civil War. "I do not know whether I am more repelled by the depravity of slavery or that of the Northern democracy," he said. He married a French-speaking Swiss, Isabella de Rougemont, an elegant and sophisticated woman who secretly longed for the life of her sister in Paris. Together, they had two sons and three daughters. Theobald, the second son, was born in 1856.

Felix's sons were awakened at five A.M. and plunged into cold baths. They were educated by tutors and rigorously trained to ride. Theobald, intense and idealistic, absorbed his father's passionate belief in the splendor and destiny of the Prussian monarchy. In Berlin, at ten, he witnessed the spectacular torchlight homecoming parade of the victorious Prussian Army after its defeat of Austria. "I

cannot believe that our beloved German people is incapable of being one people and one state," he wrote in adolescence. A few years
later, he stood "late at night, at the open window, looking from the
castle to the river flowing majestically in the moonlight" and decided that "my whole being and life are more and more determined
and uplifted by my Germanness and by my desire to be a true and
brave son of Germany."

In 1877, eighteen-year-old Prince William of Hohenzollern, a
lieutenant in a Guards regiment quartered near Hohenfinow, was
invited to shoot deer in the Bethmann-Hollweg park. William arrived in uniform and was forced to borrow a shooting jacket from
Theobald, who was three years older and six inches taller. "[The
jacket] looked like a summer overcoat," William recalled. William,
because his left arm was useless, had never shot a deer. "Are the
bucks close enough for me to shoot?" he asked anxiously. Though
semi-tame deer had been provided, William missed his first three
shots. Finally, as dusk approached, William rested his rifle on Felix's
shoulder, fired, and brought down a buck. "This little episode provided the impetus for a lasting friendship," the elder Bethmann-
Hollweg recorded. Felix marked the spot where the buck had fallen
with a boulder and a newly planted tree. William frequently returned. "I spent many happy hours in their congenial, happy circle,"
he said. And this contact led to his "esteem for the diligence, ability
and noble character of Bethmann. . . . These qualities clung to
him throughout his career."

The elder brother, Max, was a disappointment. Handsome and
affable, he plunged so deeply into the pleasures of riding and drinking that he did poorly on his first law exam. Rather than face a
second, he fled to America. Provided with 150,000 marks by his
father, Max failed on Wall Street and moved to Texas, where he
speculated in land which he hoped to sell to German immigrants.
Too few immigrants arrived. In 1897, in his mid-forties, the future
Chancellor's brother died of stomach cancer.

Theobald's rise, although unspectacular, was steady. He did
brief service in an elite cavalry regiment, studied at Bonn University
and took a doctorate in law from Leipzig, then returned to Hohenfinow and succeeded his father as district magistrate. In 1889, at
thirty-three, he married a tall, cheerful young woman from the Prussian aristocracy. Four years later, in recognition of Theobald's services as magistrate, the Kaiser presented him with the Order of the
Red Eagle, Fourth Class. "One day I'll make a minister out of your
son," William told Felix. Two years later, Theobald became a Provincial Counselor and in 1899 he was installed as Oberpräsident

(Governor) of the Mark Brandenburg. Bülow promoted him in 1905 to Prussian Minister of the Interior. He had begun to be mentioned as a possible successor to Bülow despite his wife's protests: "It disconcerts me whenever I hear it, since at the bottom of his heart, Theobald does not aim for it at all." Bethmann-Hollweg continued to be promoted. When in 1907 he was named Imperial Secretary of the Interior and Vice Chancellor, the usually critical *Die Zukunft* called him "a man of strong gifts." In the spring of 1909, rumors of Bethmann's succession were everywhere. At first, the Kaiser resisted. "I know him well," he said of Bethmann. "He is always lecturing me and pretends to know everything." Besides, Bethmann's loyal support of Bülow during the November Reichstag debate appeared to have soured the Kaiser. "I cannot work with him," William announced. Nevertheless, when Bülow failed in the death-duties vote and offered his resignation, the Kaiser seized the opportunity. On July 8, 1909, Bethmann was told that he would be appointed. With "grave doubts" he accepted. "Dear Theo, you cannot do that," his wife exclaimed. Bethmann-Hollweg explained to a friend: "Only a genius or a man driven by ambition and lust for power can covet this post and I am neither. An ordinary man can only assume it when compelled by his sense of duty."

During the *Daily Telegraph* crisis, as the Reichstag had demanded that the Kaiser abide by the constitution and leave foreign policy to the Chancellor, Bethmann-Hollweg had urged Bülow to defend the authority of his office. "Your Excellency is not only the Kaiser's Chancellor," he had told Bülow, "but also the Chancellor of the empire." Now Chancellor himself, Bethmann hoped to implement this view. He faced an uphill battle. The office had been weakened since Bismarck, enjoying the silent, unquestioning support of Emperor William I, had wielded unchallenged power. Bülow, spinning out nine years of sycophancy, had dissipated the Chancellor's powers in favor of the Crown. The Reichstag had gained in relative strength. Although constitutionally a Chancellor was responsible only to the Emperor, to be successful he needed money from the Reichstag. When Bülow lost the Kaiser's confidence, he quickly lost control of the Reichstag. The Kaiser in 1909 was a diminished figure, but he retained, independent of the Reichstag, the power to appoint and dismiss chancellors and ministers. Bethmann therefore had to be wary of William's volatile tendency to barge into delicate political and diplomatic arrangements. The *Daily Telegraph* affair had somewhat curtailed these tendencies, but the Kaiser still required constant vigilance.

At first, Bethmann and the Kaiser behaved politely towards each other. William resumed his daily visits to the Chancellor's Palace, walking in the garden, discussing political events and issues as he had with Bülow. He dined frequently with the Chancellor. "It was a pleasure for me to visit Bethmann's house since Bethmann's spouse was the very model of a genuine German wife," he said. William sometimes complained about the Chancellor's pedagogical manner—"He laid down the law as dogmatically as a school-teacher"—but Bethmann always gave William the deference due a German Emperor and King of Prussia. Behind the Kaiser's back, the Chancellor complained: "The idea that he will ally himself with the [other German] princes in order to chastise the Reichstag and eventually to abolish it, or that he will send one of his Adjutant Generals [with soldiers] into the Reichstag if I am not tough enough constantly crops up in conversations with me. I do not take these things too seriously, although they increasingly prevent mutual trust and agreement on the policies to be followed. They personally demand much strength or nerve."

Bethmann was handicapped in dealing with other ministers within the government. He was a civilian who had worked his way up through the domestic civil service. His lack of experience in foreign affairs meant that he did not personally know either Germany's ambassadors in other countries or foreign ambassadors in Berlin. He was unable thoroughly to control the Foreign Office; it was not Bethmann-Hollweg who provoked the 1911 crisis at Agadir. The other ministry partially beyond Bethmann's reach was the Navy Ministry. Under the constitution, the armed forces were the Kaiser's to command. Tirpitz, as Navy Minister, had only to please this single constituent. As long as William stood behind him, Tirpitz was more or less independent of both Chancellor and Reichstag. Bethmann's communications with Tirpitz took the form not of instructions, but of irritated appeals: "If you cannot avoid conversations with foreign diplomats, I would appreciate your making sure that your statements do not go beyond the outlines of the foreign policy of the empire, directed by me."

But in one area of foreign policy, relations with England, Bethmann moved immediately to take control. In his memoirs, the new Chancellor described the circumstances in the summer of 1909: "England had firmly taken its stand on the side of France and Russia in pursuit of its traditional policy of opposing whatever continental power for the time being was the strongest; . . . Germany held

fast to its naval program. . . . If Germany saw a formidable aggra-
vation of all the aggressive tendencies of Franco-Russian policy in
England's pronounced friendship with this Dual Alliance, England
on its side had grown to see a menace in the strengthening of the
German Fleet. . . . Words had already passed on both sides. The
atmosphere was chilly with distrust." On July 26, less than two
weeks after Bethmann-Hollweg became Chancellor, the British government announced that the second four dreadnoughts of the 1909
Estimates would be laid down. The Danger Zone which Tirpitz had
said would last until 1915 was now extended. Bethmann concluded
that with three Great Powers united against Germany, and the main
irritant to Britain the German Fleet, his duty was to negotiate with
England and, if he could obtain firm commitments, attempt to limit
the Fleet.

Bethmann acted authoritatively. He had been in office only
three weeks when, on August 3, he heard Albert Ballin propose a
meeting on naval matters between admirals Tirpitz and Fisher. "I
respectfully protest," Bethmann said to the Emperor, who had just
returned from his annual cruise to Norway. "I consider as my particular province and the principal object of all my efforts, the establishment of confidential and really friendly relations with England. In
Your Majesty's absence, I have been studying the matter in depth
with all the documents. It is my special field and I cannot allow it to
be encroached upon." The Chancellor was so vehement that, after
he left, William turned to Ballin and said, "Your proposal won't
work. You see how vexed he was. I cannot afford a Chancellor crisis
just a few weeks after appointing him." On August 17, Bethmann
circulated a directive to all department heads, including Tirpitz, that
naval discussions with England would be supervised by him.

On August 21, Bethmann informed Sir Edward Goschen, the
British Ambassador, that he was prepared to open naval talks with
Britain. On October 15, the Chancellor gave Goschen his plan. The
basic German Navy Law would have to be carried out, he said; the
Kaiser, Admiral Tirpitz, the Reichstag, and the German people
would not permit a reduction in the ultimate number of ships. But
for two or three years, to gratify England, the government was prepared to build fewer ships annually. The new supplementary program of four dreadnoughts a year might, he suggested, be reduced
to three. But this concession by Germany would require something
from Britain. Pressed by Goschen, the Chancellor specified that, in
return for a naval agreement, Germany wanted assurance of British
neutrality if Germany became involved in war.

Alfred von Kiderlen-Waechter, whom Bethmann had chosen as

his new Secretary of State for Foreign Affairs, supported the Chancellor's proposal: If British sea power were neutralized, Germany would not need as large a navy. "It would be almost incomprehensible to serious opinion in Germany that we should lose the advantage of a friendly rapprochement with England for the sake of a few ships more or less, as long as the defense of our coasts is assured," Kiderlen said. On October 20, Metternich was instructed to emphasize to Sir Edward Grey that a general assurance of friendship would be insufficient; there must be an explicit pledge of British neutrality. Germany further insisted, Metternich was told, that Britain give this pledge *before* Germany would agree to slow the building of her fleet.

Grey was skeptical. From the beginning, he had been wary of Bethmann-Hollweg's "political agreement." "I want a good understanding with Germany," Grey said, "but it must be one which will not imperil those we have with France and Russia." Foreign Office professionals worried that Britain might be asked to accept the status quo in Europe, including recognition of Germany's annexation of Alsace-Lorraine. Although the 1904 Entente agreement had said nothing about Alsace-Lorraine, these diplomats realized that a formal guarantee to Germany on this politically charged issue would have powerful repercussions in France and could mean the end of the Entente. Grey had a deeper concern. In his view, a British guarantee of absolute neutrality would ultimately lead to German hegemony in Europe. France and Russia, estranged from Britain, would face Germany alone. Either they would come to terms with her and swing into her orbit or, if war were declared, they would be defeated. In either case, an isolated England would face a German-dominated Continent. Faced with a choice between even a crushingly expensive naval race or a pledge of neutrality that would lead to German hegemony, Grey, Asquith, and their Liberal colleagues chose the first course. Metternich understood this. "The English friendship with France would be almost worthless," he told Berlin, "if England were to say plainly that under no circumstances would she help France against us." Grey also refused to negotiate any political agreement, even a vague one, unless naval limitation had first been accepted. How could he defend a political agreement before the House of Commons, he asked Metternich, when British taxpayers still were being asked to pay enormous sums for dreadnoughts?

The issue was never resolved. For the remainder of 1909, all of 1910, and part of 1911, the two powers sparred with each other. In Bethmann-Hollweg's mind, naval concessions depended upon a binding political agreement. British statesmen, eager though they were to limit the German Fleet and reduce their own shipbuilding costs, refused any agreement that made it impossible to assist a beleaguered France and prevent German dominance. The armaments race continued. In the spring of 1910, the First Division of the High Seas Fleet, made up of the four latest German dreadnoughts, shifted home port from Kiel on the Baltic to Wilhelmshaven on the North Sea. Simultaneously, the Reichstag voted funds for four additional dreadnoughts, bringing the total ordered to seventeen. The German Navy League warned against the "siren song" of a naval agreement with England which "represents a policy of diminishing our forces at sea . . . in the vain hope of composing an antagonism which lies in the conditions of existence of the two peoples." In Britain, First Lord Reginald McKenna asked Parliament for five new dreadnoughts, raising the Naval Estimates by £5.5 million pounds to over £40 million. Within little over a year, the Admiralty had been given fifteen dreadnoughts: eight from the four-plus-four; two colonial ships; and now five more. The Liberal press was dismayed. "The appetite of this monster of armaments grows by what it feeds on," warned the *Daily News*. "Give it four dreadnoughts and it asks for eight, eight and it asks for sixteen, sixteen and it would still be undiminished. It is an appetite without relation to needs or facts. It is the creation of irrational hates and craven fears." Within the Cabinet and in the House of Commons the point was made by Lloyd George. In July, Asquith replied to his colleagues:

"I see quite as clearly as my Right Hon. friend the Chancellor of the Exchequer that every new dreadnought that you build postpones the achievement of some urgent work of social reform; but national security, national insurance, after all, is the first condition of social reform. You may say 'Is it not possible to come to some kind of arrangement between the nations of the world, particularly between ourselves and the great friendly Empire of Germany, by which this kind of thing might be brought to a close?' I wish it were. The German Government told us—I cannot complain, I have no answer to make—their procedure in this matter is governed by an act of the Reichstag under which the program automatically proceeds year by year. . . . If it were possible even now to reduce the rate of construction, no one would be more delighted than His Majesty's Government. We have approached the German Government on the subject. They have found themselves unable to do anything. They cannot do it without an Act of Parliament repealing their Navy Law. They tell us, and, no doubt, with great truth, they would not have the support of public opinion in Germany to a modified program. These are the governing and unalterable facts of the situation for the moment."

On August 14, 1910, the British government made a partial shift in its position. Previously, Grey and Goschen had shown no interest in the German offer to slow the tempo. Britain had wanted an outright reduction in the number of ships; the Germans had refused. Now, Goschen reported to Bethmann, England was willing to negotiate the original German offer: a reduction in the tempo without alteration of the basic Navy Law.

Grey made an additional suggestion. It would lessen anxiety, he contended, if the two navies could make periodic exchanges of technical information: the dimensions of ships being built, their armament, armor, speed, and completion dates. To verify this information, he suggested that the naval attachés of the two powers be permitted periodic visits to the shipbuilding yards to examine the building. Two months later, on October 14, Bethmann formally accepted this proposal, but reiterated that a political agreement was "an indispensable preliminary condition for any naval agreement."

The British General Election in January 1911 delayed negotiations, but in February, Goschen was instructed to open discussions on an exchange of information. The German government was coolly receptive. The Kaiser disliked the idea and, on March 3, announced publicly that an exchange of naval information would have no value; a political understanding was crucial: "England and Germany together would ensure the peace of the world." Bethmann-Hollweg refused to abandon his own objective. "He reminded me," Goschen told Grey, "that he had always said that the atmosphere must be thoroughly cleared and a good understanding secured before any reduction in naval armaments could be made." On March 30, Bethmann gave a pessimistic speech in the Reichstag: "I consider any control of armaments as absolutely impracticable. . . . Who would be content to weaken his means of defense without the absolute certainty that his neighbor was not secretly exceeding the proportion allowed to him? . . . No, gentlemen, any one who seriously considers the question . . . must inevitably come to the conclusion that it is insoluble so long as men are men and states are states."

Despite the Chancellor's pessimism, talks continued on the subject of an exchange of naval information. On July 1, 1911, the British Embassy in Berlin telegraphed London that the German government had agreed to exchange information on the number of ships to be laid down in the coming year and to provide additional technical data on each ship when its keel was laid.

That same day, another message reached the Foreign Office in

London. The German gunboat *Panther* had appeared and dropped anchor in the harbor of the Moroccan port of Agadir. France protested the *Panther*'s presence and, by the terms of Britain's 1904 agreement with France, the British government was bound to support France's position in Morocco. Before the month was over, British and German statesmen were talking of war.

PART V

THE
ROAD TO
ARMAGEDDON

CHAPTER 39

Agadir

◆

Alfred von Kiderlen-Waechter, Germany's most significant Imperial State Secretary for Foreign Affairs after Bernhard von Bülow, was born in Stuttgart in 1852. His father, a banker, became a senior official at the Württemberg Court and was about to be ennobled when he died unexpectedly; the honor was given posthumously and Kiderlen, his mother, and his siblings acquired the "von." At eighteen, Alfred volunteered for service in the Franco-Prussian War. After the war, he finished University and law school and entered the Foreign Service. His first foreign assignment was to St. Petersburg, where he arrived in 1881. A large, florid, fair-haired young man whose face was slashed with student duelling scars, he became known as a heavy drinker and troublemaker. Young bachelors from the embassies of several European nations gathered nightly at a regular table in a French restaurant to gossip, laugh, and carouse. Much ribbing passed back and forth, but none of it in Kiderlen's direction. Any teasing pointed at him was likely to provoke growls and perhaps a threat of swords or pistols.

Kiderlen spent four years in St. Petersburg, two in Paris, and two in Constantinople. He attracted Holstein's attention. Holstein's first impression was that Kiderlen was "a typical Württemberger with a gauche exterior and a crafty mind," but in time the suspicious older man came to trust and value the younger. Bülow, who always disliked other men of talent in the diplomatic service, declared that Kiderlen was "a tool of Holstein," but he admitted that Kiderlen had useful qualities. "Kiderlen was to Holstein what Sancho Panza was to Don Quixote," Bülow announced. "He was incapable of enthusiasm and of any idealistic conceptions. His feet were always firmly on the ground but he had a very strong feeling for the prestige and advantages of the firm and he watched the competitors with great vigilance." During the Caprivi Chancellorship, when the inexperience of both the Chancellor and State Secretary Marschall left Holstein supreme at the Wilhelmstrasse, Kiderlen flourished as head of the Near Eastern Section. By 1894, his prominence and his close ties to Holstein had been noted by *Kladderadatsch,* a satirical journal favorable to Bismarck and hostile to his enemies. When the paper attacked Holstein, Eulenburg, and Kiderlen, bestowing on each an unfavorable nickname (Holstein was the "Oyster-fiend," Eulenburg the "Troubadour," and Kiderlen "Spätzle"—Dumpling —after the South German dish of which the Württemberger was fond), Kiderlen challenged the editor to a duel, pinked him in the right shoulder, and was sentenced to four months in the fortress of Ehrenbreitstein. He was released after two weeks, his career undamaged. In 1895, as Ambassador to Denmark, he artfully deflected a riot from the German Embassy. Slipping out into the crowd, he pointed to a harmless storehouse, shouted at the top of his lungs, and began hurling stones at the storehouse windows.

In 1888, Bismarck selected Kiderlen to accompany the Kaiser as the Foreign Ministry representative on board the *Hohenzollern* cruises to Norway. William liked the rough, intelligent Württemberger, who told good jokes and seemed to enjoy the exuberant pranks and crude horseplay that characterized those nautical holidays; the invitation to Kiderlen was renewed every year for a decade. Then, in 1898, his participation in the Imperial cruises—and very nearly his career—terminated. In fact, Kiderlen had been appalled by the false heartiness and schoolboy intrigue practiced on board the yacht and he wrote of his feelings, privately, to State Secretary Marschall. When Marschall departed Berlin for Constantinople in 1897, he failed to clean out his office and the new State Secretary, Bülow, discovered the letters in the files. They found their way to the Emperor, who read Kiderlen's biting descriptions of behavior on board the yacht, of rudeness to the Prince of Wales, of boorishness at the Royal Yacht Squadron at Cowes. Kiderlen was banned from the yacht and the Kaiser's presence and, as soon as a place could be found for him, exiled from Berlin. For the next ten years—from the age of forty-eight to the age of fifty-eight—he labored at the Embassy in Bucharest. One after the other, less able men—first Tschirschky, then Schoen—went to the top of the Foreign Ministry while one of the most vigorous and experienced men in the diplomatic service, trained by Bismarck and Holstein, was stuck in a Balkan cul de sac.

In Romania, Kiderlen had no difficulty expressing his contempt for the post he held. Every year on New Year's Eve, King Carol held a reception for diplomats, followed by a court ball, the most important diplomatic event of the year in his country. Every year, Kiderlen departed on Christmas leave before the ball, declaring to any Romanians who would listen that the King was unwise to make plans which so seriously conflicted with his own holiday arrangements.

In Kiderlen's time, the principal social gatherings at the German Legation in Bucharest were rowdy "beer evenings" during which male members of the German colony gathered to carouse and sing in a manner reminiscent of student days. Ladies of the German Colony and the diplomatic corps never visited the German Legation because of the private life of the German Minister. Kiderlen had a mistress, Frau Hedwig Krypke, a widow two years younger than himself with whom he lived the last eighteen years of his life. She was handsome and discreet; she lived with him in Copenhagen and Bucharest and when he was State Secretary, but he never showed any intention of making her his wife. As a result, she—and to some extent, he—was ostracized in Berlin and in the foreign capitals in which he served; the Kaiserin was particularly incensed that this unrepentant sinner should rise so high in the Imperial government. Nevertheless, Kiderlen robustly defied convention and managed to maintain both his career and his liaison with Frau Krypke.

The Wilhelmstrasse was not so rich in talented diplomats that it could afford permanently to ignore Kiderlen's qualities. Twice during his long exile in Bucharest Kiderlen was temporarily transferred to the larger post at Constantinople to substitute for Marschall when Marschall was on leave. In 1908, when Baron Schoen, the State Secretary, fell ill, Kiderlen was summoned to Berlin to fill in. "I am to pull the cart out of the mud and then I can go," grumbled the Württemberger. Kiderlen remained unforgiven by his sovereign; when he went to the Palace to pay his respects, the Kaiser shook hands without a word. Kiderlen's brief tenure as a substitute was crowded with significant events. He arrived at the peak of the Bosnian Crisis and helped to force a Russian retreat without war. With Jules Cambon (Paul Cambon's brother), the French Ambassador in

Berlin, he negotiated a new Franco-German agreement on Morocco, reinforcing guarantees to German commerce and investments in that country. He stumbled when Bülow, heavily criticized in the Reichstag for his handling of the *Daily Telegraph* affair, put the Acting State Secretary in front of the deputies to distract attention from himself. Kiderlen's speech was not a success and his attempt to explain the working of the Foreign Ministry, along with his proposal to increase efficiency by increasing staff, provoked "a general outburst of hilarity." Bülow later mocked his lieutenant's distress, comparing the Reichstag's contemptuous mirth to that of a band of students or young regimental officers baiting an awkward new colleague. "Kiderlen's debacle," Bülow noted, was helped along by "his pronounced Swabian accent and . . . the extraordinary yellow waistcoat he wore." Kiderlen himself was serene throughout; he did not care what either the Chancellor or the Reichstag thought of him. In his view, Bülow was finished as Chancellor and parliament had neither the competence nor the right to participate in the making of foreign policy.

Bülow's departure cleared the way for Kiderlen's permanent return to Berlin. By 1909, the Chancellor, far more than the exiled Minister in Bucharest, was the object of the Kaiser's displeasure. When Bethmann-Hollweg, who knew nothing of foreign affairs, was chosen to succeed Bülow, the outgoing Chancellor advised the Kaiser that the Foreign Ministry would have to be given to someone of greater ability than the amiable Schoen. William did not think so. "Just leave foreign policy to me," he said to Bülow. "I've learned something from you. It will work out fine." Bethmann was aware of his own limitations, however, and as soon as he took office, an urgent summons went to Kiderlen in Bucharest: "The new Chief is extremely anxious to meet you." Schoen did not mind being replaced. "Bethmann is a soft nature," he observed, "and I am also rather flabby. With us two a strong policy is impossible." Nevertheless, it required almost a year and a rising chorus of voices, including that of the Crown Prince, to overcome the Kaiser's opposition. In June 1910, when Kiderlen at last was appointed State Secretary, William warned Bethmann, "You are putting a louse in the pelt."

In office, Kiderlen took charge in a manner which brooked no opposition. Subordinates were soon referring to him as Bismarck II. He ignored his own ambassadors in foreign capitals, including two former State Secretaries, Marschall in Constantinople and Schoen, who had been sent to Paris; he himself handled all negotiations with the foreign ambassadors posted in Berlin. When he discovered that the Kaiser was communicating privately with Metternich in London, he stormed and threatened to resign. William's habit of calling at the Wilhelmstrasse every day to see what was going on vexed Kiderlen, and he parcelled out information to the sovereign only in the briefest form. He had left neither his gruff manner nor his tactlessness behind in Bucharest. Once, he announced that he had never set foot beyond the European continent. "Really?" said the American Ambassador. "No, thank God, never!" replied the State Secretary. Kiderlen's relationship with Bethmann began with mutual respect, then eroded as the State Secretary decided that the Chancellor's grasp of foreign affairs would never be more than amateurish. Bethmann referred to Kiderlen as "*Dickkopf*" ("Thick Head") and Kiderlen to the Chancellor as "*Regenwurm*" ("Earthworm"). At times, Kiderlen treated Bethmann like a subordinate, saying that he could not give details of foreign-policy issues to the Chancellor because Bethmann simply would not understand them. When Bethmann fussed, Kiderlen offered to resign. When foreign ambassadors complained that Kiderlen told them nothing, the Chancellor replied, "So. Do you think he tells me more?" Nor could Bethmann find sympathy for his troubles with Kiderlen by turning to the Kaiser; William was quick to remind that he had warned against putting *eine Laus in den Pelz.*

Morocco, which had brought Europe close to the precipice in 1905, was a source of permanent turmoil in international affairs. On paper, the Act of Algeciras had endorsed the independence of the Sultan's realm and guaranteed an open door for the commerce of all nations. In fact, France had assumed a primary political role, although not the full protectorate which she desired, while Germany had been guaranteed commercial rights and access. Great Britain, whose trade in Morocco was larger than that of either France or Germany, was content to remain generally mute while giving support to her Entente partner. Despite this agreement, friction between France and Germany continued. In 1908, German consular officials helped German deserters to escape from the French Foreign Legion through Casablanca; the French found out and dealt roughly with the offending diplomats. Berlin was enraged and there was talk of war. In January 1909, Kiderlen, then substituting in Berlin for Schoen, negotiated a new bilateral treaty with Jules Cambon, the French Ambassador. In a declaration signed February 8, 1909, the German government recognized "the special political interests of France in Morocco" and declared itself "resolved not to thwart those interests." In return, the French government promised "to safeguard the principle of economic equality and consequently not to obstruct German commercial and industrial interests in the country." Both parties were momentarily happy. Kiderlen was rewarded with a Sèvres dinner service to take back to Bucharest.

The détente in Morocco was short-lived. As France moved confidently ahead in the political sphere, assuming that the phrase "special political interests" gave her a free hand to deal with the Sultan, Germans complained that their businesses were not receiving the increased commercial concessions they felt were due. Southern Morocco, for example, was believed in Germany to be "exceedingly fertile" and "highly suitable for European settlement." Treasures of iron and other ores were said to lie beneath the surface, and these supposed riches had attracted the attention of major German firms. In 1909, the Düsseldorf metallurgical company of Mannesmann Brothers established a subsidiary, Marokko-Mannesmann, to explore and exploit the ores of southern Morocco. About the same time, Max Warburg created Hamburg-Marokko Gesellschaft to investigate the same opportunities. Although the region was closed by the Act of Algeciras to all international commerce, the German firms assumed that, with French cooperation, these limitations could be overcome. The French refused to cooperate. In December 1910, Bethmann rose in the Reichstag to warn, "Do not doubt that we will energetically defend the rights and interests of German merchants." It did no good. Two months later a German diplomat reported that "in Casablanca, one can no longer escape the feeling of living in a purely French colony."

Meanwhile, Sultan Abdul-Aziz, who had progressed from Gatling guns and bicycles to photography and collecting expensive watches, was overthrown in 1908 by his brother Mulai Hafid in a civil war which bankrupted the state treasury. In 1909, the new Sultan confronted claims, primarily French and Spanish, for damages during the fighting. The claims totalled sixteen times the Sultan's annual revenue. To pay the debts, Mulai Hafid imposed new taxes; these stirred fresh discontent. In January 1911, a French officer was murdered. In April, the tribes near Fez, the capital, revolted and still another brother of Abdul-Aziz proclaimed himself Sultan. The French Consul in Fez reported that the situation was perilous and that the Europeans in the city were threatened with massacre. Under the Act of Algeciras, each of the Great Powers was permitted to intervene if the lives or property of its citizens were in danger. Accordingly, France informed the other powers that a French military column would be dispatched from Casablanca to Fez.

Always sensitive to any pretext the French might employ to

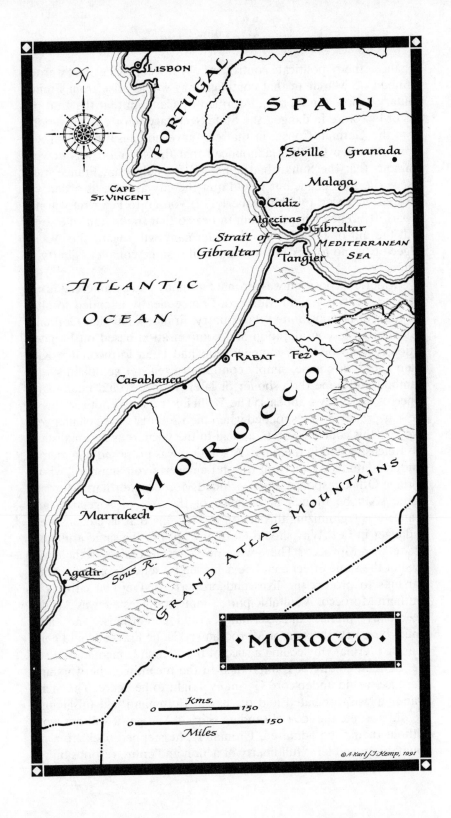

N

LISBON

PORTUGAL

SPAIN

Seville   Granada

Malaga

CAPE
ST. VINCENT

Cadiz

Algeciras

Gibraltar

Strait of
Gibraltar

MEDITERRANEAN
SEA

Tangier

ATLANTIC

OCEAN

Rabat   Fez

Casablanca

MOROCCO

Marrakech

GRAND ATLAS MOUNTAINS

Agadir   Sous R.

• MOROCCO •

Kms.
0 —————— 150

0 —————— 150
Miles

© A. Karl / J. Kemp, 1991

enhance their political control of Morocco, Kiderlen warned Cambon on March 13 that complications would arise from French military action. On April 4, informed by Cambon that the Europeans of Fez were in danger, the State Secretary retorted that reports from the German Consul in that city gave no cause for alarm. On April 28, when Cambon announced that the situation was now so ominous that the Sultan had appealed for help, that France must rescue the Europeans but would quit the city as soon as order was ensured, Kiderlen told him soberly, "If you go to Fez, you will not depart. If French troops remain in Fez so that the Sultan rules only with the aid of French bayonets, Germany will regard the Act of Algeciras as no longer in force and will resume complete liberty of action."

Kiderlen's position was strong: Germany had commercial interests and treaty rights in Morocco; France clearly intended to alter the basis of her position in the country; France knew that Germany was entitled to consideration and compensation based on France's action; yet no offer of compensation had been forthcoming. Kiderlen could, of course, simply continue to register complaints with Cambon and hope that, sooner or later, France would take cognizance of Germany's appeals. The Wilhelmstrasse did not see this as the way great states responded when their interests were challenged. Nor was this course likely to appeal to the vociferous nationalists in the Reichstag and in the press. A solution was proposed in a memorandum, dated May 30, from Baron Langwerth von Simmern, whose Foreign Office responsibilities included Morocco: northern Morocco would soon be French in defiance of the Act of Algeciras, and France was legitimizing this action by claiming that its citizens were in danger in Fez. Why should Germany not use the same argument in southern Morocco? There were no German soldiers in the country, but the same effect could be achieved by sending one or several warships to protect the lives and property of German citizens in southern Morocco. A suitable port, Simmern suggested, was Agadir. Eventually, France and Germany would compromise and there would be a new division of Moroccan spoils, or France would compensate Germany by ceding a slice of the French Congo adjacent to the German colony of Cameroons. In the meantime, the warship's presence would underscore Germany's right to be heard. The memorandum was circulated and discussed. Bethmann had misgivings. He did not like the idea of sending ships. "And yet it will not work without them," he admitted. Ultimately, he stepped back from accountability and left "full liberty of action and entire responsibility" to Kiderlen.

The German move was political, but it had to seem to be a protection of commercial interests. Accordingly, on June 19, Dr. Wilhelm Regendanz, the new managing director of Max Warburg's Hamburg-Marokko Gesellschaft, was summoned to the Wilhelmstrasse and told to draw up a petition from German firms active in southern Morocco, appealing to the government for help from marauding natives. Regendanz was to collect signatures from as many firms as possible. His task was particularly delicate and arduous because he was not permitted to show the signers the document they were signing; the Foreign Ministry considered this a necessary precaution against leaks. In spite of this hindrance, Dr. Regendanz successfully collected the backing of eleven firms.

There was a snag in working out the scheme: at that moment there were no German citizens or commercial interests in southern Morocco. Despite the grandiose talk by the Mannesmann Brothers and the Hamburg-Marokko Gesellschaft, no German explorers had yet traveled to see the "exceedingly fertile" valley of the Sus or to test-bore the imagined ore deposits of the southern Atlas Mountains. Dr. Regendanz considered this only a temporary embarrassment. When the warship arrived at Agadir, he promised, endangered Germans would be there to welcome it.

Meanwhile, negotiations were proceeding with France. On June 11, Kiderlen having retreated to Kissingen for his annual cure, Cambon called on the Chancellor in Berlin. The Ambassador found Bethmann unusually agitated and talking of "extremely grave difficulties." Cambon said jauntily that "no one can prevent Morocco falling under our influence one day," but for the first time he spoke of compensation, something "which would allow German opinion to watch developments without anxieties." Bethmann, nervously aware of the developing plan to send ships to Agadir, advised Cambon to "Go and see Kiderlen at Kissingen." Cambon went, and at the spa on June 21 he told the State Secretary that he hoped the German Empire would not insist on a partition of Morocco because "French opinion would not stand for it. But," he added significantly, "one could look elsewhere." Kiderlen declared himself ready to listen to "offers." Cambon replied that he was on his way to Paris and would discuss it with his government. On parting, Kiderlen said to the Ambassador, "Bring something back with you."

The Cabinet to which M. Cambon was on his way to report was in exceptional confusion. There had been a frightful accident. At dawn on May 20, M. Ernest Monis, the Prime Minister, had been standing at the edge of a small airfield at Issy-les-Moulineaux, watching the start of a Paris-to-Madrid air race. One of the planes developed engine trouble on takeoff, barely rose from the ground, swerved, and plunged into the crowd of spectators. The Premier was struck in the face and chest by the propeller and rendered unconscious; the War Minister, standing next to him, was killed. For several days, M. Monis's life was in danger, then, partially recovered but maimed, he attempted to direct the nation's affairs from his bed. On June 27, he resigned and M. Joseph Caillaux, the Minister of Finance, stepped up to the Premiership. Caillaux, considered able but unscrupulous, was one of a group of international French financiers with close ties to Berlin, and it was expected that his foreign policy would be Franco-German rapprochement. As Foreign Minister, Caillaux chose M. de Selves, a local government official with no experience of foreign or even national affairs. Observers took this to mean that the Prime Minister meant to conduct foreign affairs himself.

Aware that the French government was in turmoil, State Secretary Kiderlen made up his mind. On June 24, after Cambon had departed for Paris, Kiderlen traveled to Kiel to report to the Kaiser and persuade William to dispatch the warship.

William sensed more acutely than Kiderlen or Bethmann that a new adventure in Morocco was likely once again to embroil Germany with England. The Kaiser had no wish to do this; now that his sinister uncle, "Edward the Encircler," was gone, William felt cozily comfortable with his cousin "Georgie," whom he could hector and intimidate as he did the Tsar. He accepted eagerly King George's invitation to witness the unveiling of a statue of their mutual grandmother, Queen Victoria, in front of Buckingham Palace. On May 16, the Kaiser arrived with the Kaiserin and their nineteen-year-old daughter, Princess Victoria Louise. As always, William was exhilarated by British military pageantry: "The big space in front of Buckingham Palace was surrounded by grandstands . . . filled to overflowing. In front of them were files of soldiers of all arms and all regiments of the British Army . . . the Guards . . . the Highlanders. . . . The march past was carried out on the circular space, with all the troops constantly wheeling; the outer wing had to step out, the inner to hold back, a most difficult task for the troops. The evolution was carried out brilliantly; not one man made a mistake." The public caught the good mood between the cousins. One night, the King took his guests to a play at the Drury Lane Theatre. Between acts a curtain was lowered which depicted a life-size King and Kaiser mounted on horseback, riding toward each other, saluting.

The audience rose and cheered. Haldane, who had suggested giving a lunch for the German generals in the Kaiser's party, was told that the Emperor himself would like to come. Haldane arranged an eclectic guest list including Lord Kitchener; the First Sea Lord, Sir Arthur Wilson; Lord Morley; Lord Curzon; Ramsay MacDonald, leader of the Labour Party; and the painter John Singer Sargent. William enjoyed himself, although he could scarcely believe that a British Minister of War could live in a house so small that the Emperor dubbed it the "Dolls' House."

The Kaiser had been asked by Bethmann to bring up Morocco with his British cousin. Obediently, William asked whether King George did not agree that France's policies seemed incompatible with the Algeciras Convention. The King's reply was candid. "To tell the truth," he said, "the Algeciras Convention is no longer in force and the best thing everyone can do is to forget it. Besides, the French are doing nothing in Morocco that we haven't already done in Egypt. Therefore we will place no obstacles in France's path. The best thing Germany can do is to recognize the *fait accompli* of French occupation of Morocco and make arrangements with France for protection of Germany's commercial interests." William listened and promised the King that, at least, "We will never make war over Morocco." Returning home, he reported this conversation to the Chancellor, concluding that England would not oppose French occupation of Morocco and that if Germany meant to do so, she would have to do it on her own.

A month later, on June 21, when plans to send a ship had long been hatched, and Dr. Regendanz was gathering signatures from German firms appealing for help for their endangered interests, the Kaiser still was not aware of his Foreign Minister's plans. William continued to say that he had no objection to greater French involvement in Morocco because "France would bleed to death there." Constitutionally, the command to send a ship had to come from the Kaiser, the supreme warlord. Somehow, he would have to be told and persuaded. On June 26, William was on board the *Hohenzollern* attending the Lower Elbe Regatta, with Bethmann also on board and Kiderlen expected. When Kiderlen arrived, the two men tackled the Emperor. William balked; he was willing to accept expansion of the German Empire but had little stomach for a direct military challenge to France. He protested that sending a ship was too big a risk, that no one could predict the consequences, and that a step of such far-reaching importance should not be taken without consulting the nation. The Chancellor and the State Secretary persisted. "We will have to take a firm stand in order to reach a favorable result,"

Kiderlen insisted. "We cannot leave Morocco to the French. . . . [Otherwise] our credit in the world will suffer unbearably, not only for the present, but for all future diplomatic actions." In the end, the monarch who boasted to his relatives and in his marginalia that he, not his ministers, was the sole master of German foreign policy, reluctantly consented. In his memoirs, he disavows responsibility: "During the Kiel Regatta Week, the Foreign Office informed me of its intention to send the *Panther* to Agadir. I gave expression to strong misgivings as to this step, but had to drop them in view of the urgent representations of the Foreign Office." From the *Hohenzollern*'s radio room, Kiderlen crisply telegraphed Berlin: "Ships approved."

A signal flashed from the German Admiralty to the gunboat *Panther,* then proceeding north off the West African coast, bound for home after a voyage around the Cape. Built for colonial service a decade before, the light-gray, two-stack *Panther* was not the ship the Kaiser would have chosen to advertise his powerful fleet. She was short, fat, and lightly armed*; her crew of 130 included a brass band; and her primary mission was impressing natives or bombarding mud villages rather than fighting other ships at sea. Suitable or not, *Panther* had been tapped and she entered the historical limelight on July 1, 1911, when she steamed slowly into the Bay of Agadir and dropped her anchor a few hundred yards from the beach.

The view from the ship was magnificent. A broad bay of sparkling blue water was framed by steep brown cliffs rising seven hundred feet from the sea. At the top stood the walls and towers of Agadir Castle, an imposing Portuguese bastion built centuries earlier, when Portugal reached out across the globe. Below, at sea level, in the small fishing village of Funti, people lived and worked in an ageless fashion. No Europeans and no sign of European life were present; the port had been closed to international shipping for many years.

One European was on the way. Doing his best, as instructed, to arrive before the warship sent to protect him, Herr Wilburg, subsequently nicknamed the "Endangered German," was a representative of the Hamburg business consortium in Morocco. On June 28, he was in Mogador, seventy-five miles north of Agadir. Because all telegrams to Morocco had to be sent in French and French officials were free to read them, a code had to be worked out in which Wilburg's instructions and destination were hidden in a seemingly innocuous text. Three telegrams were necessary, and it was not until

---

* 211 feet long, 32 feet in beam, one 4-inch gun forward, one aft.

the evening of July 1 that Wilburg was able to start. His journey was arduous and miserable. The heat which afflicted Europe that summer was even more intense in Africa. Wilburg found all the grass and shrubs burned up by the sun; he even found that goats had climbed into trees to escape the scorching rays. The road was no more than a track, sometimes only a few feet wide, winding through hills strewn with rocks and stones. On corniches along the sea, on one side he touched a cliff and on the other, he looked down on a precipitous drop. Caravans of mules and camels came toward him, forcing him to press his horse against the rock.

When Wilburg arrived at Agadir on the afternoon of July 4, the *Panther* had been at anchor for three days. Wilburg saw the warship, but was too exhausted to make contact. The next morning when he awoke, he saw that a second, larger German ship had entered the bay and anchored during the night. This was the 3,200-ton light cruiser *Berlin,* with ten four-inch guns and a crew of three hundred. Immediately, Wilburg tried to let his countrymen know that he was present. At first, he had no luck; the men on the *Berlin* took the man on the beach running up and down, waving his arms and shouting faint cries, for an excited native, perhaps with something to sell. The Admiralty had given strict orders that men were not to be landed without further instructions. Wilburg, seeing the men on the ships staring at him without apparent interest, became dispirited and stood motionless, looking back at the two gray ships lying silent in the bright sunlight. His posture identified him: suddenly an officer on the *Panther* was struck by the lonely figure on the beach standing with his hands on his hips. Africans did not employ this stance. A boat was launched and soon Wilburg, the "Endangered German," was taken under the protection of the Imperial Navy. It was the evening of July 5.

News of the *Panthersprung* (panther's leap) created a sensation in Europe. At noon on July 1, German ambassadors in all capitals delivered the following note to their host governments:

"Some German firms established in the south of Morocco, notably at Agadir and in the vicinity, have been alarmed by a certain ferment which has shown itself among the local tribes. . . . These firms have applied to the Imperial Government for protection for the lives of their employees and their property. At their request, the Imperial Government has decided to send a warship to the port of Agadir, to lend help and assistance, in case of need, to its subjects and employees, as well as to protect the important German interests in the territory in question. As soon as the state of affairs in Morocco has resumed its former quiet aspect, the ship charged with this protective mission will leave the port of Agadir."

Within the Reich itself, Kiderlen's move had overwhelming support. "Hurrah! A deed!" shouted the headlines of the *Rheinisch Westfälische Zeitung*. "Action at last, a liberating deed . . . Again it is seen that the foreign policy of a great nation, a powerful state, cannot exhaust itself in patient inaction." Pan-Germans assumed that the partition of Morocco was at hand, that Germany would annex a piece of the seaboard. On June 12, the Crown Prince, a fervent nationalist, expressed this view to Cambon. Inviting the Ambassador to the Imperial box at the Grunewald Races, he spoke of Morocco as "un joli morceau," adding, "Give us our share and all will be well." On the day of the *Panther*'s leap, Arthur Zimmerman of the Foreign Office assured the Pan-German League, "We are seizing this region once and for all. An outlet for our population is necessary." Kiderlen kept silent, refusing to reveal whether his goal was a piece of Morocco or a larger slice of territory somewhere else. Either way, the *Panther*'s spring would serve: "Little by little we will make ourselves at home in the ports and the hinterland and then at the right moment, attempt to come to an understanding with France on the basis of the division of Morocco or of compensation by a part of the French Congo."

Jules Cambon, the French Ambassador in Berlin, was immediately affected by the sudden coup. A week before, he had left Kiderlen at Kissingen, having been asked to "bring back something" from Paris. In his own capital, he had found the government in disarray, the Foreign Ministry in chaos. Before anything could be decided, the *Panther* was at anchor in the Bay of Agadir. Cambon did not know what it would take to persuade the ship to sail away. He knew that negotiations must continue and that "serious colonial compensation" would have to be considered. But now it seemed that Kiderlen thought seriously of annexing part of southern Morocco. Kiderlen himself was unhelpful in determining the goal of German policy; the State Secretary now employed the same sphinx-like behavior as Bülow had in 1905. "The more silent we are, the more uncomfortable the French will become," Kiderlen noted cheerfully.

Negotiations began on July 9 when the French Ambassador, icy and austere, called on Kiderlen. "*Eh bien?*" he said, inviting the State Secretary to explain reasons for the *Panther*'s leap. "*Vous avez du neuf?*" ("Do you have anything new?") replied Kiderlen, tossing the ball back to his guest. Gradually, the shape of the negotiations began to emerge. The French government could not agree to acquisition of Moroccan territory by Germany because of French public opinion, but was ready to offer compensation elsewhere, perhaps in the French Congo. Kiderlen, certain of his negotiating advantage, observed that the hopes of the German public for a piece of Morocco had now been raised and could be satisfied only if the compensation elsewhere was substantial. He declared to a friend, "The German Government is in a splendid position. M. Cambon is wriggling before me like a worm."

Although Kiderlen expected to deal directly—and only—with France, the *Panther*'s arrival in Agadir concerned other powers. Kiderlen, in calculating his move, had not given the reaction of other nations much thought. Russia, he sensed, would give only half-hearted support to her ally; St. Petersburg had never been anxious to fight a war over a French colony in Africa. England's role in the matter Kiderlen had scarcely considered. Thus, when Sir Edward Grey called in Count Metternich on July 4 to discover Germany's intentions, the Ambassador could not be helpful. He did not know himself; Kiderlen had not informed him. When Grey asked whether German troops would be landed, Metternich pleaded ignorance. Grey made the point that while Germany had taken an overt step by sending a ship, Britain "had not taken any overt step, though our commercial interests in Morocco were greater than those of Germany." He left the Ambassador with the statement that Britain's attitude toward what happened in Morocco "could not be a disinterested one" and reminded his guest of "our treaty obligations to France."

Great Britain's apprehension over the *Panther*'s appearance at Agadir arose from several sources. There was dislike for the suddenness and roughness of the German move; it smacked of the same shock tactics Bülow and Holstein had employed in the Kaiser's sudden descent on Tangier. There was concern that Germany intended to acquire a naval station on Morocco's Atlantic coast; this could threaten the Imperial sealanes to South Africa and around the Cape. (Careful analysts at the Admiralty and in the press discounted this danger, pointing out that a base at Agadir, 1,500 miles from the North Sea, would be highly vulnerable and ultimately a source of weakness rather than strength for the Imperial Navy. The First Sea Lord, Sir Arthur Wilson, assured Grey that neither Agadir or any other Moroccan site could quickly or easily be transformed into a fortified and formidable naval base.) Finally, Grey was concerned about France and the Entente. Once again, as at Tangier and Algeciras, Germany seemed intent on humiliating France, either by forcing a partition of Morocco or by stripping France of an embarrassingly large slice of French territory elsewhere. Such a loss of French prestige, while England stood by, would gravely damage the Entente. Grey was resolved that England should not merely stand by.

In the face of London's concerns and Grey's questions, Berlin remained silent. Asquith, speaking in Parliament on July 6, suggested that the government would welcome a statement of German intentions. Crowe, writing on July 17, asked himself: "What is Germany driving at? Herr von Kiderlen's behavior seems almost inexplicable." From Paris came reports that the French government was being squeezed to give up the entire French Congo; from Morocco, that German troops had landed at Agadir and that German officers were negotiating with tribal chiefs. Days passed and still Germany offered no explanation other than that endangered Germans were being protected. This passage of time added conspicuous insult to possible injury. Grey had stated in his July 4 conversation with Metternich that Great Britain had a vital interest in the future of France's role in Morocco, yet for over two weeks, the Imperial government had ignored that concern. Officials at the Foreign Office, many considerably more Germanophobic than Grey, were alarmed and angry. "This is a test of strength, if anything," Crowe argued. "Concession [by France] means not loss of interests or loss of prestige. It means defeat. The defeat of France is a matter vital to this country." Sir Arthur Nicolson, who in 1910 had returned from St. Petersburg to become Permanent Under Secretary of the Foreign Office, agreed. Without a strong show of England's support, he advised the Foreign Secretary, German pressure would soon compel France either to fight or to yield. If France yielded, he continued, German hegemony on the Continent would become permanent.

By July 19, Grey was convinced that he must have information as to German intentions. He asked Asquith to allow him to "make some communication to Germany to impress upon her that, if the negotiations between her and France come to nothing, we must become a party to a discussion of the situation." Otherwise, he feared that the "long ignorance and silence combined must lead the Germans to imagine that we don't very much care." The Prime Minister agreed and Grey summoned Metternich to an interview on the afternoon of July 21.

From the British perspective, the twenty-first was the critical day of the Agadir Crisis. The Cabinet met in the morning, the Foreign Secretary saw the German Ambassador in the afternoon, and a historic speech was given in the evening. During the day, several conversations between leading members of the British government gave clear definition to British policy. The previous morning *The Times* had published an accurate but unauthorized story from Paris, describing Germany's sweeping demands on France. British public opinion, previously dubious about France's Morocco policy, had turned against the Germans. When the Cabinet met in the morning, Grey summarized the state of the Franco-German negotiations as reported to him by the French government. He pointed out that seventeen days had elapsed without any notice being taken by Germany of the British query about German intentions. He announced that he was seeing Metternich in the afternoon and would ask for clarification. Meeting the German Ambassador at four P.M., Grey explained that Britain had waited in hopes that France and Germany would reach agreement, but that he had heard that German demands were too excessive for France to accept. Meanwhile, the German presence continued at Agadir: no one knew "whether German troops are landed there, whether treaties were concluded there which injure the economic share of others," whether, perhaps, the German flag had been raised. Metternich, as much in the dark on these matters as Grey, was, the Foreign Secretary minuted, "not in a position to give any information."

Meanwhile during the day, another drama was unfolding in Whitehall. For weeks, David Lloyd George, the volatile, Germanophile Chancellor of the Exchequer, had been wrestling with the implications of the *Panther*'s leap. He wished to give Germany time to explain, yet the long silence from Berlin was ominous. That morning, before the Cabinet meeting, Winston Churchill visited him in his office. "I found a different man," Churchill was to write. "His mind was made up. He saw quite clearly the course to take. He knew what to do and how and when to do it. . . . He told me that he was to address the Bankers at their Annual Dinner that evening and that he intended to make it clear that if Germany meant war, she would find Britain against her. He showed me what he had prepared and told me that he would show it to the Prime Minister and Sir Edward Grey after the Cabinet." Lloyd George was irritated and concerned: "When the rude indifference of the German Government to our communication had lasted for seventeen days . . . I felt that matters were growing tensely critical and that we were drifting clumsily towards war," the Chancellor wrote. "It was not merely that by failing even to send a formal acknowledgement of the Foreign Secretary's letter, the Germans were treating us with intolerable insolence, but that their silence might well mean that they were blindly ignorant of the sense in which we treated our obligations under the Treaty [of 1904], and might not realise until too late that we felt bound to stand by France."

Lloyd George did not speak up at the meeting of the Cabinet and thus, when Grey met Metternich, the Foreign Secretary was unaware of the new resolution found by his colleague. The Foreign Secretary learned about it only in the late afternoon when, he wrote, "I was suddenly told that Lloyd George had come over to the Foreign Office and wanted to see me. He came into my room and asked if the German Government had given any answer to the communication I had made on behalf of the Cabinet on July 4. I said that none had reached me. . . . Lloyd George then asked whether it was not unusual for our communication to be left without any notice and I replied that it was. He told me that he had to make a speech in the City of London that evening and thought he ought to say something about it; he then took a paper from his pocket and read out what he had put down as suitable. I thought what he proposed to say was quite justified and would be salutary, and I cordially agreed. . . . The speech was entirely Lloyd George's own idea. I did nothing to instigate it, but I welcomed it." On Grey's recommendation, Asquith approved.

On the evening of July 21, Lloyd George arose before the assembled bankers of the City of London at the banquet given them at the Mansion House by the Lord Mayor. The bulk of his speech dealt with politics, the budget, inequities of property and wealth, and the prospects for world prosperity. Peace, he declared, was the "first condition of prosperity." Then, halting the flow of extemporaneous words, he picked up a piece of paper and read slowly the carefully considered words he had showed to Grey and Asquith:

"I would make great sacrifices to preserve peace. I conceive that nothing would justify a disturbance of international good will except questions of the gravest national moment. But if a situation were to be forced upon us in which peace could only be preserved by the surrender of the great and beneficent position Britain has won by centuries of heroism and achievement, by allowing Britain to be treated, where her interests were vitally concerned, as if she were of no account in the Cabinet of nations, then I say emphatically that peace at that price would be a humiliation intolerable for a great country like ours to endure. . . ."

The message was not remarkable: Britain, in matters affecting her interest, did not intend to be ignored. Sir Edward Grey had been passing this message to the diplomatic chancelleries of Europe for six and a half years. What gave the Mansion House speech significance were the lips from which this message sprang. Lloyd George was a radical, a pacifist. His views on foreign affairs, insofar as they were known, were considered to be pro-German; certainly he had always strongly favored an Anglo-German understanding. The fact that he had stood up in public and warned that Britain would fight to maintain her prestige came as a shock to many in both England and Germany. During the furor that followed, Grey reckoned that the speech had a positive effect. "Lloyd George was closely associated with what was supposed to be a pro-German element in the Liberal Government and the House of Commons," the Foreign Secretary wrote. "Therefore, when he spoke out, the Germans knew that the whole of the Government and House of Commons had to be reckoned with. It was my opinion then, and it is so still, that the speech had much to do with preserving peace in 1911. It created a great explosion of words in Germany, but it made the Chauvinists doubt whether it would be wise to fire the guns."

Lloyd George's speech had made no reference to any specific nation, but Germans recognized that the Chancellor's warning was addressed to them. The German press quickly turned violent against England, protesting that here was yet another episode in the age-old story of Britain interfering in a question which did not concern her. Her real aim, declared *Germania,* was to make certain that she shared in any partition of Morocco: "Whenever a country occupies one village, England immediately demands three and preferably four." Indignant cries mingled with blustering anger. "The German people refuse to be dictated to by foreign powers," said the *Kölnische Zeitung.* "Strong in the justice of her cause, Germany admonishes the stupid disturbers of the peace, 'Hands off!'" shouted the *Lokal Anzeiger.*

In the Wilhelmstrasse, Kiderlen was angry because the British Chancellor's speech, by encouraging the French, could only make his negotiations with Paris more difficult. And the State Secretary was furious at what he considered a breach of diplomatic manners. The British Foreign Secretary had asked the German Ambassador for a clarification of the German position in Morocco. The Ambassador had promised to contact his government in an effort to provide what was asked. Yet that very same evening, before the Ambassador's message could even be decoded in Berlin, a senior minister of the British government had issued a public warning to the Imperial government. Kiderlen assumed that the entire British Cabinet had drafted or at least approved Lloyd George's speech and then chosen the leading pacifist and Germanophile among them as a mouthpiece to increase the harshness of the insult. Kiderlen seethed: "If the English Government had intended to complicate the political situation and to bring about a violent explosion, it could certainly have chosen no better means than the speech of the Chancellor of the Exchequer."

Kiderlen had to do something. If he ignored the speech completely, France might decide that it had England's backing and break off negotiations. And if he ignored Grey's request to Metternich, the unpredictable English might encourage France to defy the German Empire. Britain had to be mollified in a way that did not seem a response to the Mansion House speech or to any other form of British pressure; nationalist opinion in Germany would never forgive that. Kiderlen decided to approach Grey confidentially and explain German objectives in Morocco.

On Monday, July 24, Metternich asked to see Grey, saying that he brought news from Berlin. The Ambassador began by announcing that the *Panther* had been sent "to protect German interests . . . the special cause was the attack of natives on a German farm." Grey took him up on this point: "I observed that I had not, I thought, heard of this attack before. I had understood that the dispatch of the ship had been due to apprehension as to what might happen, not to what had actually happened." Count Metternich admitted that he had not heard of the actual attack before, either. "I observed that there were no Germans in this region," Grey continued. "Count Metternich said he had no information on this point." The Ambassador assured the Foreign Secretary, however, that "not a man had been landed" and that no troops would be landed. Further, Metternich continued, "Germany had never thought of creating a naval base on the Moroccan coast and never would think of it." Germany had no intention of taking any Moroccan territory. All she asked was compensation for France's breach of the Act of Algeciras. Grey was satisfied and asked whether he could communicate what Metternich had told him to the House of Commons. Metternich said that he would ask permission from Berlin.

Grey's request, relayed by Metternich, made Kiderlen even angrier. The next day, Tuesday, July 25, the German Ambassador returned to see Grey with the answer from Berlin: Kiderlen would not permit the Foreign Secretary to announce in Parliament what he had been told in confidence. The reason was Lloyd George's speech. "That speech had been interpreted without contradiction as having a tone of provocation for Germany and the German Government could not let the belief arise that, in consequence of the speech, they had made a declaration of intentions about Morocco"—this was how Grey reported his interview with Metternich. As to German negotiations with France: "If, after the many provocations from the side of France and her free-and-easy manner in Morocco, as if neither Germany nor a treaty existed, France should repel the hand that was offered to her by Germany, German dignity as a Great Power would make it necessary to secure by all means, and if necessary also, alone, full respect by France of German treaty rights." Grey, angered by the barely concealed charge that he had conspired with his Cabinet colleagues to impugn German national honor, drew himself up to defend the dignity of the British government. Since the Germans "had said that it was not consistent with their dignity, after the speech of the Chancellor of the Exchequer, to give explanations as to what was taking place at Agadir," Grey declared that it was "not consistent with our dignity to give explanations as to the speech of the Chancellor of the Exchequer." The gunboat at Agadir, German intentions in Morocco, the Franco-German negotiations—all had now been subordinated to an affair of national prestige. The air was filled with tension; many—Lloyd George among them—thought that war was near.

That same afternoon, about five-thirty P.M., Lloyd George and Churchill "were walking by the fountains of Buckingham Palace," as Churchill recalled. Running after them came a messenger, asking that the Chancellor go immediately to see Sir Edward Grey. Churchill went too and together they found the Foreign Secretary in his rooms at the House of Commons. Grey, who had just walked over from the Foreign Office after his interview with Metternich, was pale. "I have just received a communication from the German ambassador so stiff that the Fleet might be attacked at any moment. I have sent for McKenna to warn him," the Foreign Secretary told his colleagues. While they were speaking, the First Lord came in, listened for a few minutes, and then hurried away to send orders to the Fleet.

Grey was alarmed; already that day he had sent a note to McKenna emphasizing that "we are dealing with a people who recognize no law except that of force between nations and whose fleet is mobilized at the present moment." Four days before, on the twenty-first, *The Times* had announced that the German High Seas Fleet of sixteen battleships and four armored cruisers had put to sea and "vanished into the desolate wastes of the North Sea."* Grey's

---

* In fact, the Admiralty had been aware of the plans and the destination of the German Fleet. Indeed, the British Atlantic Fleet under Sir John Jellicoe was at Rosyth, on the Firth of Forth, preparing to sail for joint exercises with the German High Seas Fleet in Norwegian waters. Sailors on both sides had been looking forward to the maneuvers as a chance both to renew old acquaintances and to scout the tactics and equipment of a

warning to McKenna resulted in a general alert to the British Fleet. There were rumors, following the *Times* story, that the Germans might attempt "a bolt from the blue" against the Royal Navy. "Supposing the High Seas Fleet, instead of going to Norway as announced, had gone straight for Portland, preceded by a division of destroyers, and, after a surprise night torpedo attack, had brought the main [German] fleet into action at dawn against our ships without steam, without coal, without crews . . ."

The First Sea Lord, Sir Arthur Wilson, evidently thought little of this alarm and left on July 21 for a weekend of shooting in Scotland. Winston Churchill found this shocking. "Practically everybody of importance and authority is away on holiday," he complained to Lloyd George. As Home Secretary, Churchill had no responsibilities in the Agadir Crisis except a general one as a member of the Cabinet. Nevertheless, his blood was up. When, at the peak of the crisis, he learned that the navy's reserves of gunpowder were unprotected, he plunged into action:

"On the afternoon of July 27, I attended a party at 10 Downing Street. There I met the Chief Commissioner of Police. . . . He remarked that by an odd arrangement, the Home Office [which was Churchill's responsibility] was responsible, through the Metropolitan Police, for guarding the magazines . . . in which all the reserves of naval cordite were stored. For many years these magazines had been protected without misadventure by a few constables. I asked what would happen if twenty determined Germans in two or three motor cars arrived well armed upon the scene one night. He said they would be able to do what they liked. I quitted the garden party.

"A few minutes later I was telephoning from my room in Home Office to the Admiralty. Who was in charge? . . . An Admiral (he shall be nameless) was in control. I demanded Marines at once to guard these magazines, vital to the Royal Navy. . . . The admiral replied over the telephone that the Admiralty had no responsibility and no intention of assuming any; and it was clear from his manner

---

potential foe. But neither Whitehall or the Wilhelmstrasse wished the fleets to meet in a time of tension such as this. "At the end of three days," Kiderlen had said to Goschen on June 14, "they might either fraternize too much . . . or they might on the contrary be shaking their fists in each other's faces." The Kaiser also was cruising in Norwegian waters, on board the *Hohenzollern,* and the prospect of him becoming involved worried Kiderlen almost as much. "You know the Emperor pretty well," he said to Goschen, "and you can imagine how excited he will be at the sight of the two Squadrons. He will certainly want to make the most of the opportunity and there is every chance that, as an Admiral of both Navies, he will amuse himself by putting himself at the head of the combined squadron and going through a series of naval maneuvers—ending with a great banquet, toasts, and God knows what!"

that he resented the intrusion of an alarmist civilian Minister. 'You refuse, then, to send the Marines?' After some hesitation he replied, 'I refuse.' I replaced the receiver and rang up the War Office. Mr. Haldane was there. I told him that I was reinforcing and arming the police that night and asked for a company of infantry for each magazine in addition. In a few minutes the orders were given; in a few hours the troops had moved. By the next day, the cordite reserves of the Navy were safe."

Kiderlen was unaware of the movements of the British Fleet, but he knew from Lloyd George's speech and from Metternich's reports of his interviews with Grey that England was in earnest about France and Morocco. These manifestations of English "meddling" in German affairs may have been much resented in Germany, but they helped to focus the Wilhelmstrasse on the reality of the situation: if France was pushed into war by German pressure, England would fight beside its Entente partner. German objectives in Morocco or elsewhere in Africa were not worth a war with France, England, and probably Russia as well. Once Kiderlen grasped this, he began to moderate his demands, look for compromise, and speak in conciliatory terms.

On July 26, Metternich received new instructions from Berlin, and on Thursday, the twenty-seventh, he again called on Grey at the Foreign Office. This time, Grey said, the atmosphere was "exceedingly friendly." The German government had reversed its earlier position. Now, Metternich asked that Parliament be told that, while the Franco-German negotiations would remain exclusively Franco-German, they would not touch on British interests. Any territories exchanged would be exclusively French or German, although Metternich requested that Grey not give M.P.'s any details. Further, the Ambassador said, if the British government could make a public statement saying that it would be pleased by a successful conclusion of the negotiations, this would have a beneficial influence. He meant, on France.

This information was passed along in the House of Commons that afternoon, not by the Foreign Secretary, but by the Prime Minister. Asquith said: "Conversations are proceeding between France and Germany; we are not a party to those conversations; the subject matter of them may not affect British interests. On that point, until we know the ultimate result, we cannot express a final opinion. But it is our desire that those conversations should issue in a settlement honorable and satisfactory to both parties and of which His Majesty's Government can cordially say that it in no way prejudices British interests. We believe that to be possible. We earnestly and sincerely desire to see it accomplished. The Question of Morocco itself bristles with difficulties, but outside Morocco, in other parts of West Africa, we should not think of attempting to interfere with territorial arrangements considered reasonable by those who are more directly interested. Any statements that we have interfered to prejudice negotiations between France and Germany are mischievous inventions without the faintest foundation in fact. But we have thought it right from the beginning to make it quite clear that, failing such a settlement as I have indicated, we must become an active party in discussion of the situation. That would be our right as a signatory of the treaty of Algeciras, it might be our obligation under the terms of our agreement of 1904 with France; it might be our duty in defence of British interests directly affected by further developments."

The Anglo-German phase of the crisis was over. The moderate German press was vastly relieved. "Peace or war hung upon Herr Asquith's words," wrote the *Vossische Zeitung* the following day. "His was perhaps the gravest responsibility of any statesman in recent years. It was a peaceful speech." The Franco-German dispute was not resolved. But the speeches of Lloyd George and Asquith and the conversations between Grey and Metternich clearly established in the minds of both French and German negotiators that Britain hoped for a successful outcome to the talks and that Britain advised reasonable concessions by France to square its increased role in Morocco. But it was also established that where France dug in against what she considered excessive German demands, Britain stood by her side.

From that point until the Agadir Crisis was finally resolved in mid-October, negotiations were exclusively Franco-German, conducted in Berlin between Kiderlen and the French Ambassador, Jules Cambon. Britain's warning on Morocco had hedged German ambitions, but Kiderlen's policy had to produce some fruit. The talks turned to compensation and Kiderlen demanded the entire French Congo. The French refused to surrender an entire colony; the government would not survive. France, feeling the presence of Britain behind her, became defiant. Pierre Messimy, the War Minister, announced that "we are not going to stand any more nonsense from Berlin . . . and we have the nation behind us." There was talk of sending a French cruiser to Agadir. Both governments, in fact, found themselves tormented by the fierceness of their own public opinion. Grey observed from London: "The Germans at first made such huge demands on the French Congo as it was obvious that no French Government could concede," he wrote later. "The fact was that both Governments had got into a very difficult position; each was afraid of its own public opinion. The German Government dared not accept little. Their own Colonial Party had got their feelings excited and their mouth very wide open. If the mouth was not filled—and it would need a big slice to fill it—there would be great shouting. The French Colonial Party would revolt if their Government gave up too much. Probably after a time the German Government was as anxious as the French Government to get out of the business by a settlement, but neither dared settle."

Kiderlen was trapped between France's refusal to grant the sweeping compensation which would mask his failure in Morocco, and the vehement cries of German nationalists. Most German nationalists had little interest in the steamy equatorial forests of the Congo, "where the fever bacillus and the sand flea say good night to each other" and where the "only prospect of of profitable traffic [lay] in sand for our breeders of canaries." They still wanted a piece of Morocco, and as they sensed this possibility ebbing away they trumpeted their impatience and frustration. "Has the spirit of Prussia perished?" demanded the *Post*. "Have we become a generation of old women? What has become of the Hohenzollerns?" France's seizure of Morocco was said to be a military threat to the Reich; the French would use native soldiers to fill out the gaps in the French Army caused by a declining birthrate. (A German cartoon displayed a ragged file of apes and monkeys dressed in French uniforms parading past a French officer. The caption read: "The last class of reserves.") General Moltke, the Chief of the General Staff, was indignant. "If we slink out of this affair with our tails between our legs, and if we do not make a demand which we are prepared to enforce with the sword, I despair of the Empire's future," he growled.

The Kaiser was skittish. As the crisis with England mounted, William—fearing war with Great Britain—nervously telephoned Kiderlen and Bethmann to report to him at Swinemünde. William complained that Kiderlen was going beyond the limits agreed on board the *Hohenzollern*. Kiderlen replied by drafting a letter of resignation. France, he insisted, would make a major offer only if she was convinced that Germany was serious. "I do not believe that they would take up the challenge but they must feel that we are ready for everything." If that policy was unacceptable to his sovereign, he would resign. Bethmann had gone this far with Kiderlen and decided that he had to continue. If the State Secretary was allowed to resign, he said, he would submit his own resignation. William gave in. "The Kaiser was very humble in Swinemunde. Kiderlen returned very pleased," said Kurt Riezler, the Chancellor's personal assistant. But Bethmann, finding himself with almost no voice, was thoroughly unhappy. "Kiderlen informs nobody, not even the Chancellor," reported Riezler. "Bethmann said yesterday he wanted to give Kiderlen a lot to drink in the evening in order to find out what he ultimately wants." Meanwhile, William, stung by the contempt of the nationalist press, reverted to bombast. "I am not going to dance attendance on the French any longer," he declared on August 7. "They must make an acceptable offer at once or we will take more, and that immediately." On August 13, he spoke of using his sword. "We will insist upon our demands, for it is an affair of honor for Germany." Unless the French gave Kiderlen whatever the State Secretary asked, William announced, he would "not be satisfied until the last Frenchman was driven out of Morocco—by the sword if necessary."

By August 16, Kiderlen and Cambon together announced that the situation was "grave." Six French offers of territorial concession in the Congo had been rejected by Germany, and seven German proposals had been rejected by France. On the eighteenth, the talks in Berlin were suspended. Cambon went to Paris for further instructions. Kiderlen, inexplicably, departed on vacation for Chamonix in the French Alps. Frau Krypke accompanied him; they were met by the local French prefect, who had instructions from M. Caillaux to make the German couple as comfortable as possible. Apparently, Kiderlen had suspended the negotiations in the hope that the rising tension would compel the French to give in. In fact, the passage of time worked against the State Secretary. Cambon returned from Paris at the end of August, instructed to secure definite German acquiescence to a French protectorate in Morocco *before* he agreed to *any* further discussions of compensation to be paid in the Congo. With the French standing firm, Kiderlen's confidence began to falter. Commercial barons such as Ballin, who had cheered the *Panther*'s spring in the beginning, did not approve Kiderlen's demand for the entire French Congo with the consequent rumors of war. Nine weeks of fruitless bargaining had filled the air with suspense and exhausted the public patience. The Kaiser was impatient and fidgety. "What the devil will happen now?" he asked. "It is pure farce. They negotiate and negotiate and nothing happens."

The resumption of talks between the French Ambassador and the German Foreign Minister was scheduled for Friday, September 1. It was postponed with no reason given. Cambon was slightly ill, but Kiderlen failed to pass this news to the press. The result was a panic on the Berlin stock market on the morning of September 2. Although the talks began on Monday, September 4, there were runs on banks as nervous depositors withdrew their capital. Waves of selling orders came in from the provinces, and the day was known as Black Monday. During the week, the market rallied, then plunged again on Saturday the ninth. This was too much for Ballin, who told his friends that, thanks to Kiderlen, Germany was cornered: she would either have to go to war over an African swamp or back down and appear ridiculous. Under pressure from all sides, the State Secretary began to retreat. He agreed to recognize a de facto French protectorate in Morocco provided the word "protectorate" itself did not appear on paper. On October 11, a draft of the Morocco Convention was initialed by Kiderlen and Cambon. In return for her political protectorate (the term was not used), France pledged to safeguard for thirty years the principle of the Open Door in Morocco. By the twenty-second, the sacrifices France was to make in compensation had been agreed: 100,000 square miles of territory in the French Congo were ceded and added to the German colony of Cameroons. On November 4, the final Franco-German agreement was signed in Berlin. In over a hundred meetings, Kiderlen and Cambon had developed affection for each other. They exchanged photographs inscribed "A mon terrible ami" and "A mon amiable ennemi."

The result was a triumph for France and a defeat for Germany. Sir Edward Grey called it "almost a fiasco for Germany; out of this mountain of a German-made crisis came a mouse of colonial territory in Africa." Kiderlen had taken great risks, had made a massive display of diplomatic force, and had achieved nothing in Morocco: no slice of territory, no naval base on the Atlantic, no retreat of the French from Fez. Even in the Congo, he had finally accepted less than half the territory he had earlier fixed as an irreducible minimum. For this he had provoked a prolonged international crisis, called the world's attention to Britain's support of France, and raised the French Republic to a level of prestige the country had not enjoyed since the Second Empire.

There was no way to mask these facts, and the air in Berlin filled with anger and recrimination. The nationalist press roared that the settlement was "the last nail in the coffin of German prestige." Harden complained, "Without acquiring anything of moment, we are more unpopular than ever." Friedrich von Lindequist, the German Colonial Secretary, resigned, declaring that he could not defend the agreement before the Reichstag. Bülow called the episode "deplorable . . . a fiasco . . . like a damp squid, it startled, then amused, and ended by making us look ridiculous." According to Bülow, Kiderlen himself blamed the disaster solely on William II, who "throughout this whole diplomatic campaign veered from absurd threats and demands to utter discouragement and pessimism leading to unnecessary concessions."

Responsibility for the *Panther*'s spring had been Kiderlen's, but it was Bethmann who rose to defend the Franco-German agreement in the Reichstag. He pointed out that the government had achieved "a considerable increase of Germany's colonial domain" without giving up anything in Morocco that Germany had ever had and that "an important dispute with France had been settled peacefully." "We drew up a program and we carried it out," he declared—and the chamber burst into laughter and derisive shouts. When the Chancellor concluded, "We expect no praise but we fear no reproach," the atmosphere changed, but not for the better. "The silence," reported the *Berliner Tageblatt*, "was like that of the grave. Not a hand moved, no applause rang out." The reply to the Chancellor, primarily from the nationalists, but in which all parties participated, was savage. Ernst Basserman, the National Liberal leader, wanted to know why military pressure had not been exerted on France in the Vosges, where the German Army was powerful, rather than at Agadir by a mere gunboat. Ernst von Heyderbrand, the Conservative leader, complained loudly of the decline of German prestige and pointed the finger of blame at England:

"Like a flash in the night, all this has shown the German people where the enemy is. We know now, when we wish to expand in the world, when we wish to have our place in the sun, who it is that lays claim to world-wide domination. . . . Gentlemen, we Germans are not in the habit of permitting this sort of thing and the German people will know how to reply. . . . We shall secure peace, not by concessions, but with the German sword."

Heyerbrand's speech was punctuated by hearty, ostentatious applause from the royal box, where the Crown Prince was sitting with one of his younger brothers. Bethmann was infuriated by this expression of partisan, antigovernment sentiment and demanded of the Kaiser that he discipline his Heir. William obliged. Summoning both his son and his Chancellor, he allowed Bethmann to remonstrate with the Crown Prince and explain in detail the position of the Imperial government. Afterward, Bethmann was content with his own role. "My conscience lets me sleep," he said. "War for the Sultan of Morocco, for a piece of the Congo or for the Brothers Mannesmann would have been a crime." . . . "If I had driven toward war, we would now stand somewhere in France, our fleet would largely lie at the bottom of the North Sea, Hamburg and Bremen would be blockaded or bombarded, and the entire nation would ask me, Why this? . . . And it would rightly string me up on the nearest tree." About this time, when his friend Sir Edward Goschen, the British Ambassador, asked whether he still had time to play his usual Beethoven sonata before going to bed, Bethmann replied, "My dear friend, you and I like classical music with its plain and straightforward harmonies. How can I play my beloved old melodies with the air full of modern discord?"

For Kiderlen, the debacle was personal. In January 1912, less than two months after signing the convention with Cambon, Kiderlen appeared in Rome, where Bülow was living. "I thought he looked ill," Bülow observed. "His face had a worn and puffy look and certainly he drank far too heavily." Bülow cautioned him to slow down, but Kiderlen replied that he would not last long in any case. His influence in the government had eroded almost to nothing; when Haldane, the British Minister of War, came to Berlin to discuss Anglo-German relations, the German Foreign Minister was excluded from most of the negotiations. On December 30, 1912, one year after his humiliation, Kiderlen, home for Christmas in his native Stuttgart, drank six glasses of cognac after dinner, collapsed, and died of a heart attack.

CHAPTER 40

"I Do Believe That I Am a Glowworm"

◆

One consequence of the Agadir Crisis was a change within the British Cabinet: Reginald McKenna was replaced as First Lord of the Admiralty by Winston Churchill. The cause was a sudden worry about the direction of the navy. In the middle of August, before Kiderlen left Berlin for his Alpine holiday and Cambon returned to Paris for instructions, a serious war scare gripped the British government. Sir Edward Grey had urged that the navy be kept in readiness and, accordingly, the Atlantic Fleet was concentrated at Portland and not allowed to sail on its summer cruise to Norway. Special night guards were posted at the Admiralty, large orders for naval ammunition were placed, and the tunnels and bridges of the South Eastern Railway were patrolled day and night. Meanwhile, staff officers of the British and French armies bent over maps to prepare the landing of four to six British divisions on the Continent.

On August 23, after Parliament had risen, Asquith called a secret, all-day meeting of the Committee of Imperial Defence and asked for a presentation of the war plans of the British Army and Navy. Grey and Lloyd George were present, along with Churchill, who, as Home Secretary, would not normally have been involved. The services were represented by the two Cabinet ministers,

Haldane and McKenna; Sir William Nicholson, Chief of the Imperial General Staff; Sir Henry Wilson, Director of Military Operations; and Sir Arthur Wilson, the First Sea Lord. The meeting began at eleven-thirty A.M. and continued until six P.M.; the army was given the morning, the Navy the afternoon.

General Sir Henry Wilson presented the army's war plan in a detailed exposition. Standing before a large map of northwestern Europe, he described the threat perceived by the French and British General Staffs. German mobilization would produce 110 army divisions, French mobilization only eighty-five divisions. The moment war began, Moltke would turn three quarters of his strength against France, leaving only twenty-two divisions to screen the east against Russia. The right wing of the German offensive against France would wheel through Belgium in order to bypass the fortress system on the Franco-German frontier. Even if the Belgian Army were to fight—which was by no means certain—the dispatch of a British Expeditionary Force at the earliest possible moment would support the French left flank. Six regular British infantry divisions and one cavalry division, 160,000 men, had been assigned this role, and plans had been carefully worked out with the French to hurry them across the Channel and into the line. Railway timetables had been worked out in such detail that there were even ten-minute breaks to allow the troops to have tea. The War Office had printed thousands of terrain maps of Belgium and northern France and Haldane had already designated Sir John French to command the Expeditionary Force. The British force, Wilson declared, would help to dam the German flood; in addition, their presence would be important psychologically. French soldiers would know that they were not fighting alone. Before he sat down, Wilson asked Sir Arthur Wilson for Admiralty assurance that the transport of the Expeditionary Force across the Channel would be guaranteed by the navy. The meeting adjourned for lunch at two.

When it reconvened at three, Admiral of the Fleet Sir Arthur Wilson stood up to present the navy's plans. Wilson resented being forced to do what he was doing. There was no Naval War Staff because both Wilson and Fisher had resisted any dilution of the prerogatives of the First Sea Lord. Both admirals preferred to maintain absolute control over administration, training, and deployment of the fleet. They believed that war plans should be prepared and held in great secrecy by the First Sea Lord and the Commanders-in-Chief and, for fear of leakage, not divulged to the army or to politicians. Nevertheless, at that moment, under the direct order of the Prime Minister, Sir Arthur Wilson had no choice.

Admiral Wilson's presentation was rambling and opaque. The navy's strategy in a war against Germany, he announced, would be to clamp a close blockade on the German coast, provoke a great sea battle, and annihilate the German Fleet. Light forces—destroyers and light cruisers—would prowl close to shore while, over the horizon, battleships and battle cruisers would prowl in wait for the High Seas Fleet. Every vessel in the navy would be devoted to these tasks and Wilson regretted that he could not give assurances regarding escorting troopships to the Continent. Perhaps, once the German Fleet had been defeated and the seas swept clean, troops could be transported. But not, he thought, to France, where a tiny British Expeditionary Force would be overwhelmed and devoured by the huge Continental armies.* Wilson subscribed to Fisher's thesis: the British Army should be used as a projectile to be fired by the navy. The navy's choice for military operations would be the seizure of Heligoland and then, eventually, a landing inside the Baltic on the coast of Pomerania, from where the British Army could threaten Berlin.

Wilson's listeners, particularly Haldane and the generals, were aghast. So much effort had been put into building an efficient Regular Army which could be used as an Expeditionary Force; so much planning had gone into coordinating initial operations with the French; now the navy was refusing even to transport the troops to the battlefield. At the First Sea Lord's proposal that the British Army be "projected" onto the German coast, Haldane snorted with disgust. Any force landed in Pomerania would necessarily be so small that, as Bismarck had said, it could be "rounded up by a few Prussian policemen." Sir William Nicholson asked why the British Navy thought itself better qualified than the British Army to plan a land campaign against the German Army. Did the Admiralty possess maps of the German railway system? Disdainfully, Admiral Wilson replied that it was not the Admiralty's business to have such maps. "I beg your pardon," said Nicholson. "If you meddle with military problems, you are bound not only to have these maps but to have studied them." McKenna backed up his Sea Lord, arguing that sending the British Expeditionary Force to France would doom it and that Britain's efforts ought to be concentrated on the war at sea. Sir Henry Wilson hit back by reminding the committee where the principal danger lay: in the massive power of the German Army. French generals, facing this juggernaut, did not place much value on

---

* Sir Arthur Wilson also argued that the British Army could not fight in France because British soldiers did not speak French.

sea power. A naval correspondent for *The Times* had written that British sea power was worth 500,000 bayonets to France. "Our Navy is not worth 500 bayonets to them," Henry [General] Wilson declared. Indeed, "[General] Joffre did not value it as one bayonet."

By the time the meeting broke up, the navy had done itself great harm. No decision had been made between the fundamentally divergent war strategies of the two fighting services, but it was clear that the army's careful analysis and detailed planning had made a far better impression than Admiral Wilson's vague and imperious monologue. Haldane, who had spent five years at the War Office fashioning the British Army into a modern weapon, was particularly appalled. He went directly to Asquith and threatened to resign unless something was done. "The fact is that the admirals live in a world of their own," he wrote to the Prime Minister. "The Fisher method, which Wilson appears to follow, that war plans should be locked in the brain of the First Sea Lord, is out of date and impracticable. Our problems of defense are far too numerous and complex to be treated in that way. . . . Unless this problem is tackled resolutely, I cannot remain in office." Asquith replied that the Admiralty plan was "puerile and I have dismissed it at once as wholly impracticable," and he informed the Admiralty that the Cabinet sided with the War Office; the Expeditionary Force must be transported to France. When McKenna and the admirals continued to resist, it became obvious that a change would have to be made.

It was easiest to replace McKenna. Haldane believed that the solution lay in stripping the office of First Sea Lord of autocratic power by forming a Naval War Staff similar to the Army General Staff, and he believed that he was the best man to do that job. His task at the War Office was finished. "In 1911 I had begun to feel that the back of the necessary work had been broken and to fear that I was becoming stale," he wrote later. He told Asquith that he had no great desire to become First Lord but that, practically speaking, no one else could create a Naval War Staff. Asquith, characteristically, shrank from decision. With feelings between the two services running high, it would insult the navy to send an army broom to clean up the Admiralty. Besides, Haldane had just been made a Viscount and had moved from the Commons to the Lords. Asquith wanted his First Lord to sit in the Commons, where he could lead the debate on Naval Estimates and deal with the querulous old admirals and amateur naval experts who habitually made trouble and needed silencing.

In addition, there was another candidate. Winston Churchill attended the August 23 meeting because, throughout the summer of

Agadir, he had thrust himself into issues of foreign and defense policy. On August 13, he had sent Asquith a powerful memorandum analyzing the first stages of a Continental war in which the German Army swept into France through Belgium. "By the twentieth day," Churchill forecast, "the French armies will have been driven from the line of the Meuse and will be falling back on Paris." To blunt this threat, Churchill had recommended that four Regular Army divisions, 107,000 men, be dispatched immediately to France, with two more divisions, another 53,000 men, to follow as soon as the naval blockade of the German coast was in place. Meanwhile, he said, 100,000 soldiers of the British Indian Army should be brought to France via the Mediterranean and the port of Marseilles. Churchill's grasp of the subject and eloquence on paper impressed the Prime Minister. While favoring the army war plan, Churchill also cast doubt upon the navy. After the August 23 meeting, he wrote a series of letters to Asquith, probing for soft spots in the Admiralty's planning. "Are you sure that the ships we have at Cromarty are strong enough to defeat the whole High Seas Fleet?" he wrote to Asquith on September 13. "If not, they should be reinforced without delay."

Asquith took five weeks to make up his mind. By mid-September, Kiderlen and Cambon had returned to Berlin to negotiate and the danger of war was quickly receding. Asquith began going to a rented country house on the coast of East Lothian in Scotland, traveling from London in a sleeper compartment on Friday nights and returning on Sunday nights. It was a restful place, with an avenue of lime trees, an exceptional library, and a private golf course stretching down to the sea. Even here Churchill followed him, ostensibly to play golf in the autumn sunshine. On September 27, he was there when Haldane drove over from his family home at Cloan to see the Prime Minister. "As I entered the drive . . . I saw Winston Churchill standing at the door," Haldane wrote. "I divined that he had heard of possible changes and had come at once to see the Prime Minister." Unhappy at having to make a choice, Asquith at one point put the fifty-five-year-old Haldane and the thirty-six-year-old Churchill in the same room and told them to decide what was best. Haldane, aware of the drawbacks of his own candidacy, offered to take the Admiralty for one year and then relinquish it to Churchill. Sensing victory, the Home Secretary declined. Finally, Asquith made up his mind. "He and my father played golf together in the afternoon," remembered Violet Asquith, the Prime Minister's daughter. "I was just finishing tea when they came in. Looking up, I saw in Winston's face a radiance like the sun." She asked whether he would like tea. He looked at her "with grave but shining eyes. 'No, I don't want tea, I don't want anything, anything in the world. Your father has just offered me the Admiralty.'"

Churchill recalled that day in language of power and portent: "Mr. Asquith . . . asked me quite abruptly whether I would like to go to the Admiralty. . . . I said, 'Indeed I would.'. . . The fading light of evening disclosed in the far distance the silhouettes of two battleships steaming slowly out of the Firth of Forth. They seemed invested with a new significance to me.

"That night when I went to bed . . . my mind was dominated by the news I had received of the complete change in my station and of the task entrusted to me. I thought of the peril of Britain, peace-loving, unthinking, little prepared, of her power and virtue, and of her mission of good sense and fair play. I thought of mighty Germany, towering up in the splendour of her Imperial State and delving down in her profound, cold, patient, ruthless calculations. I thought of the army corps I had watched tramp past, wave after wave of valiant manhood, at the Breslau maneuvres in 1907; of the thousands of strong horses dragging cannon and great howitzers up the ridges and along the roads of Würzburg in 1910. I thought of German education and thoroughness and all that their triumphs in science and philosophy implied. I thought of the sudden and successful wars by which her power had been set up."

Filled with excitement and disquiet, Churchill opened the Bible lying on the table beside his bed. At random, he read from the ninth chapter of Deuteronomy: *"Hear, O Israel: Thou art to pass over Jordan this day, to go in to possess nations greater and mightier than thyself. . . . Understand therefore this day, that the Lord thy God is he which goeth over before thee; as a consuming fire he shall destroy them. . . ."*

For Winston Churchill, who in a lifetime never questioned Britain's virtues or the wickedness of her enemies, "it seemed a message full of reassurance."

From the beginning, Winston Churchill knew he was unique. Youth and early manhood only strengthened this impression. One evening in 1906 after the Liberals had been swept into power and Churchill was holding office as Under Secretary for the Colonies, he was seated at a dinner party next to Violet Asquith, daughter of the new Chancellor of the Exchequer. For a long time, Churchill did not speak. "Then he appeared to become suddenly aware of my existence," Violet wrote. "He turned on me a lowering gaze and asked me abruptly how old I was. I replied that I was nineteen. 'And I,' he said almost despairingly, 'am thirty-two already. Younger than anyone else who *counts,* though,' he added, as if to comfort himself." Churchill then launched into a savage attack on the shortness of life as opposed to "the immensity of possible human achievement:" . . . "Curse ruthless time! Curse our mortality! How cruelly short is the alloted span for all we must cram into it." By the end, Violet was dazed, but not so much that she did not remember the words with which he concluded his outburst: "We are all worms. But I do believe that I am a glowworm."

Winston's grandfather was the seventh Duke of Marlborough, and Winston was born in one of the 320 rooms of Blenheim Palace, which had been built by parliamentary grant to reward the military exploits of the first Duke. His father, Lord Randolph Churchill, was a second son who had done brilliantly at Eton and Oxford and then, at twenty-five, met a nineteen-year-old American heiress, Jennie Jerome, and proposed to her on their third evening together. Jennie's father worked on Wall Street, which the Duke vaguely disdained. Randolph persisted and the Prince of Wales, always a romantic, lent a hand. The couple were married in April 1873 in the chapel of the British Embassy in Paris. Jennie became pregnant immediately.

Seven and a half months later, she came to Blenheim to hunt, suffered a slight fall, and began to have contractions. Because she could not make it upstairs to her bedroom, Winston was born in a small ground-floor room, just off the great library. Jennie was only twenty and her own life seemed to have just begun, so, in the manner of the upper classes, the tiny baby with pinkish curls and upturned nose was immediately turned over to a nanny, Mrs. Everest. "Woom," as Winston always called her, was the maternal influence in his life. Jennie was always out—"We seemed to live in a whirl of gaiety and excitement," she remembered later. "Many were the delightful balls I went to which . . . lasted till five in the morning." In her absence, "Woom" cradled Winston, fed him, toilet-trained him, dried his tears, and made him feel that he was loved. "Mrs. Everest it was who looked after me and tended all my wants," Churchill recorded. "It was to her I poured out my many troubles."

Troubles appeared early in his parents' marriage. Somehow, Randolph had contracted syphilis, some say from an aged prostitute while he was at Oxford, others believe from a parlormaid at Blenheim with whom he slept soon after Winston's birth. Although the symptoms were not disabling, once the disease was clearly diagnosed he no longer could sleep with his wife. Jennie had an extraordinary beauty. One who saw her described her as "a dark, lithe figure . . . appearing to be of another texture to those around her —radiant, translucent, intense. A diamond star in her hair, her favorite ornament—its lustre dimmed by the flashing glory of her eyes. More of the panther than of the woman in her look." Margot Asquith, who met Jennie Churchill at Newmarket, also used the feline simile: "She had a forehead like a panther's and great wild eyes that looked through you." Jennie took lovers; one estimate was that she had two hundred. Society did not doubt that one conquest was Albert Edward, Prince of Wales. Jennie did not flaunt her lovers and Randolph—who had no choice—accepted them, although on one occasion he ordered the Prince of Wales out of his house and on another, he attacked one of her companions with his fists. The couple took long, separate vacations to Switzerland, Paris, the south of France, sometimes not seeing each other for weeks. When Winston was seven, his mother spent time on the Irish estate of Colonel John Strange Jocelyn, a famous horseman. Jennie became pregnant, and when the child was born named it John Strange Churchill . . . Winston's only brother, Jack.

Unfortunately for Winston, these private circumstances reinforced the natural disinclination of upper-class Victorian parents to have much to do with their children. Winston saw his parents rarely. His earliest memory of his mother is "in Ireland . . . in a riding habit, fitting like a skin and often beautifully spattered with mud . . . My mother always seemed to me a fairy princess: a radiant being possessed of limitless riches and power. . . . She shone for me like the Evening Star. I loved her dearly—but at a distance." Winston's own son Randolph, the grandson of Lord Randolph and Jennie Jerome, declared of his father's childhood: "The neglect and lack of interest in him shown by his parents were remarkable, even judged by the standards of late Victorian and Edwardian days." William Manchester offers a perceptive view of the effect of this deprivation of parental love: "Most infants are loved for themselves; they accept that love as they accept food and warmth. . . . [But in Winston's case] that anyone should love him became a source of wonder. . . . Affection from others had to be earned; eventually he would win it by doing great things. At the same time—and this would cripple his schooling—the deprivation of parental attachment bred resentment of authority. One might expect that his mother and father, the guilty parties, would be the targets of his hostility. Not so. The deprived child cherishes the little attention his parents do give him; he cannot risk losing it. Moreover, he blames himself for his plight. Needing outlets for his own welling adoration, he enshrines his parents instead, creating images of them as he wishes they were, and the less he sees of them, the easier that transformation becomes. By this devious process, Lord Randolph became Winston's hero, and his mother . . . 'a fairy princess.' . . . His own resentment had to be directed elsewhere. Therefore he became, in his own words, 'a troublesome boy.' "

At seven, Winston was plucked from Mrs. Everest's care and on a dark November afternoon deposited at St. George's School in Ascot, a fashionable preparatory school. "I hated this school . . . [and the] life of anxiety I lived there for more than two years," Churchill recalled. "I made very little progress in my studies and none at all in games. . . . My teachers saw me at once backwards and precocious, reading books beyond my years and yet at the bottom of my Form. They were offended. They had large sources of compulsion at their disposal but I was stubborn. Where my reason, imagination or interest were not engaged, I would not or I could not learn." Pugnacious, resistant to discipline, Winston's behavior provoked those "sources of compulsion" which were later described by another boy at the school. Boys who did poorly in class were summoned to the Headmaster's study: "In the middle of the room was a large box draped in black cloth and in austere tones the culprit was told to take down his trousers and kneel before the block over which I and the other Head Boy held him. The swishing was given with the master's full strength. It took only two or three strokes for drops of blood to form everywhere and it continued for fifteen or twenty strokes when the wretched boy's bottom was a mass of blood. Generally, of course, the boys endured it with fortitude but sometimes there were scenes of screaming, howling, and struggling which made me almost sick with disgust."*

The liverish welts on Winston's buttocks, exposed at home, first to Woom, then to Jennie, were sufficient evidence. Winston was removed from St. George's and entered in a school in Brighton where "I was allowed to learn things that interested me: French, History, lots of Poetry by heart, and above all Riding and Swimming." His dearest wish, however, was not fulfilled. "Will you come and see me . . . I shall be miserable if you don't . . . Please do come, I have been disappointed so many times"—the letters flowed to Jennie, week after week, year after year, in a hundred variations.

---

* The beating of small boys in English public schools was unremarkable. Earlier in the nineteenth century the headmaster of Eton was a Dr. Keate, "who on heroic occasions was known to have flogged over eighty boys on a single summer day; and whose one mellow regret in the evening of his life was that he had not flogged far more."

She never found the time. Once, his father came to Brighton for a political meeting and did not cross the street to visit his son. Winston waited in vain and then wrote sadly, "I was very disappointed but I suppose you were too busy."

At twelve, Winston was put up for Harrow. First, there was an entrance examination. "I should have liked to be asked to say what I knew," he wrote. "They always tried to ask me what I did not know. When I would have willingly displayed my knowledge, they sought to expose my ignorance. This sort of treatment had only one result: I did not do well on examinations." The Harrow examination contained no grammar, no French, neither history nor geography, and only a few questions on arithmetic. Most of it involved translation from Latin and Greek. "I found I was unable to answer a single question on the Latin paper," Churchill recalled. "I wrote my name at the top of the page. I wrote down the number of the question '1.' After much reflection, I put a bracket round it thus '(1).' But thereafter I could not think of anything connected with it that was either relevant or true." Harrow took him anyway—his grandfather was the Duke of Marlborough, his father Lord Randolph Churchill—and for five years he remained at the bottom of his class. "We were considered such dunces," Churchill wrote, "that we could only learn English." Day after day, he went through the drill of diagramming sentences. "I learned it thoroughly. Thus I got into my bones the essential structure of the ordinary British sentence—which is a noble thing. And when in after years my school fellows who had won prizes and distinction for writing such beautiful Latin poetry and pithy Greek epigrams had to come down again to common English, to earn their living or make their way, I did not feel myself at any disadvantage."

From Harrow, Winston continued to plead for a visit. "Do try to get Papa to come. He has never been here," he wrote to his mother. Jennie replied, "I would go down to you but I have so many things to arrange about the Ascot party next week that I can't manage it." When he was seventeen, a crisis arose. Winston was refused permission to come home for Christmas, but was to be sent to stay with an unknown French family in Versailles to improve his French. He begged for a reversal. Jennie was adamant: "I have only read one page of your letter and I send it back to you—as its style does not please me." Winston wrote back: "My darling Mummy: Never would I have believed that you would have been so unkind. I am utterly miserable. That you should refuse to read my letter is most painful to me. There was nothing in it to give you grounds for rejecting it. . . . I can't tell you how wretched you have made me feel. . . . Oh my Mummy." No reply. Winston wrote every day, building a crescendo: "Darling Mummy: . . . I am so wretched. Even now I weep. Please my darling Mummy be kind to your loving son. Don't let my silly letters make you angry. Let me at least think that you love me—Darling Mummy, I despair. I am so wretched. I don't know what to do. Don't be angry I am so miserable. . . . Please write something kind to me. I am very sorry if I have 'riled' you before. I did only want to explain things from my point of view. Good Bye my darling Mummy. With best love I remain, Ever your loving son, Winston." Jennie complained to Randolph, "He makes as much fuss as though he were going to Australia for two years." Winston remained at the bottom of his class; his only distinction at Harrow was winning the school fencing championship. During these years, he developed a stammer to complement his lisp.

In the Harrow years, Winston's persistent dullness in his studies convinced Lord Randolph that his son could not qualify for Oxford or Cambridge and that an attempt to enter the Royal Military College at Sandhurst was the proper goal for this obtuse boy. When Winston was fourteen, his father asked whether he would like to enter the army. Winston said yes at once. "For years I thought my father with his experience and flair had discerned in me the qualities of military genius. But I was told later that he had only come to the conclusion that I was not clever enough to go to the Bar." Winston's first two efforts to pass the Sandhurst entrance exam seemed to justify his father's gloom. He failed, and in the interim before the third attempt, he almost accidentally killed himself. At his aunt's estate near Bournemouth, he was being chased in a game with a cousin and his brother, Jack. He found himself on a bridge over a deep ravine with one of his pursuers standing at each end of the bridge: "Capture seemed certain. But in a flash there came across me a great project. The ravine which the bridge spanned was full of young fir trees. Their slender tops reached to the level of the footway. 'Would it not,' I asked myself, 'be possible to leap onto one of them and slip down . . . ? I looked at it. I computed it. I meditated. Meanwhile I climbed over the balustrade. My young pursuers stood wonderstruck at either end of the bridge. . . . In a second I had plunged, throwing out my arms to embrace the summit of the fir tree. The argument was correct; the data were absolutely wrong. It was three days before I regained consciousness and more than three months before I crawled from my bed. The measured fall was 29 feet onto hard ground." Winston's plunge, which ruptured a kidney, at last brought his parents rushing to his side. And during his recovery period a celebrated "crammer" for the Sandhurst exams was enlisted on Winston's behalf. On his third attempt, he passed with a score not high enough to admit him to the infantry, but sufficient to allow him to enter the cavalry. His own delight at his achievement was destroyed by a letter from his father:

My dear Winston:
I am rather surprised at your tone of exultation over your inclusion on the Sandhurst list. . . . The first extremely discreditable feature of your performance was your missing the infantry, for in that failure is demonstrated beyond refutation your slovenly, happy-go-lucky, harum-scarum style of work for which you have always been distinguished at your different schools. Never have I received a really good report of your conduct in your work from any master or tutor. . . . Always behind-hand, never advancing in class, incessant complaints of total want of application . . . thus you have failed to get into the '60th Rifles' one of the finest regiments in the Army. . . . By . . . getting into the cavalry you have imposed on me an extra charge of some £200 a year.
. . . Now is a good time to put this business plainly before you. Do not think I am going to take the trouble of writing to you long letters after every folly and failure you commit and undergo. I shall not write again on these matters and you need not trouble to write . . . because I no longer attach the slightest weight to anything you may say about your own acquirements and exploits. . . . If your conduct and action at Sandhurst is similar to what it has been in the other establishments . . . then my responsibility for you is over.
I shall leave you to depend on yourself, giving you merely such assistance as may be necessary to permit of a respectable life. . . . If you cannot prevent yourself from leading the idle, useless, unprofitable life you have had during your schooldays and later months, you will become a mere social wastrel, one of the hundreds of the public school failures, and you will degenerate into a shabby, unhappy and futile existence. . . . Your mother sends her love. . . .

The letter wounded; Winston's replies were frantically apologetic. A few months later, in his second term at Sandhurst, an accident again stirred Lord Randolph's wrath. He had given Winston an expensive gold watch and Winston had allowed it to slip out of his pocket into a stream. His father happened to see it under repair at the watchmaker's and asked Winston what had happened. "While walking along Wish Stream I stooped down to pick up a stick and it fell out of my pocket into the only deep place for miles," Winston explained.

> The stream was only about five inches deep—but the watch fell into a pool nearly six feet deep.
>
> I at once took off my clothes and I dived for it but the bottom was so uneven and the water so cold that I could not stay longer than 10 minutes and had to give it up.
>
> The next day I had the pool dredged—but without result. . . . I then borrowed 23 men from the Infantry Regiment—dug a new course for the stream—obtained the fire engine and pumped the pool dry and so recovered the watch. I tell you all this to show you that I fully appreciated the value of the watch. and that I did not treat the accident in a casual way. The labor of the men cost me over £3.
>
> I am very, very sorry that it should have happened. But it is not the case with all my things. Everything else you have ever given me is in as good repair as when you gave it first.
>
> Please don't judge me entirely on the strength of the watch. I am very very sorry about it.
>
> I am sorry to have written you such a long and stupid letter. . . .

Winston was a success at Sandhurst; he entered near the bottom of his class of 102 and graduated near the top. "At Sandhurst I had a new start," he explained. "We had now to learn fresh things and we all started equal." True, when he first arrived, his amazed officers found that he wanted to argue about the commands on parade-ground drill. But he persevered, became again a champion fencer and a passionate horseman. At Aldershot, where he joined a cavalry regiment after receiving his commission, he was in the saddle, either at drill or at polo, eight or nine hours every day.

He learned to stand up to his mother on behalf of one he dearly loved, Mrs. Everest. Once Winston and Jack were away at school, Woom had passed into the employ of the boys' grandmother, the Duchess of Marlborough. Facing a shortage of funds, the Duchess proposed to fire the erstwhile nanny, who had worked for the family for nineteen years. Winston rebelled and, once again, Jennie refused to read his letter. This time Winston stormed back: "It is quite easy, dear Mamma, for you to say that it is not my business or for you to refuse to read what I have got to say, but nevertheless I feel I ought in common decency to write to you at length on the subject. . . .

She is in my mind associated—more than anything else—with *home*. . . . She is an old woman who has been your devoted servant for nearly 20 years—she is more fond of Jack and I than of any other people in the world and to be packed off in the way the Duchess suggests would possibly if not probably break her down altogether. . . . At her age she is invited to find a new place and practically begin over again. . . . I think such proceedings cruel and rather mean. . . . It is in your power to explain to the Duchess that she *cannot* be sent away until she has got a good place. . . . If you can't, I will write and explain things to Papa. . . ." There was no reply, and Mrs. Everest was let go. From Sandhurst, Winston regularly dug into his own skimpy funds to send money to his beloved Woom.

Winston's painful experience with parental neglect paralleled and was in part caused by one of the most dramatic stories in British political history. Winston's father, Lord Randolph Churchill, soared briefly and brightly like a meteor over the political landscape. In 1886, at the age of thirty-seven, he was both Chancellor of the Exchequer and Leader of the House of Commons in Lord Salisbury's second government. A Tory democrat, restless under Lord Salisbury's careful, conservative hand, Randolph let his own ambition ride too freely. Challenging the War Minister, the Prime Minister, and the whole Cabinet, he demanded that the Army Estimates be cut. To get his way, he talked of resignation. When that did not work, he did resign, confident that the party would turn to him. It did not. Lord Salisbury refused to reappoint him, explaining, "When you have had a boil on your neck and it has been removed, you do not wish it back." Randolph slid into owning racehorses, party-going, and foreign travel. Gradually, his disease began to tighten its grip. His speeches, both in the House of Commons and on the stump, became embarrassing; he became confused and forgot the line of his argument; his friends discreetly stole away or sat in grieving silence. "There was no curtain, no retirement," Lord Rosebery wrote of his friend. "He died by inches in public."

By the summer of 1894, when Winston was in his second year at Sandhurst, Lord Randolph's condition could be hidden from no one. He was thin and pale, with deep lines in his face. His hair was mostly gone. His hands shook and his speech was slurred and stuttering. At dinner, a guest saw "gleams of hate, anger and fear in his eyes." At one point, unable to speak, Randolph pointed to a dish and squealed "E-e-e-e-e!" The host asked what he would like. Randolph pointed and squealed again: "E-e-e-e-e! I want that!" The guest was convinced that Randolph had entered "what I called 'the malignant monkey' stage of insanity."

Jennie took him on a world cruise, hoping he might improve and, if not, to take him out of the limelight.* By the time the party reached Madras, it was clear that Randolph was dying; the cruise was broken off and he returned to London. Winston, who had seen so little of his father that he was shocked to learn that he was ill, was in his last month at Sandhurst. The chance he had hoped for, to earn his father's respect, to form a friendship, to stand at his side, now would never come. He had to cling to a single meeting when, after his father had raged at him for some offense, Randolph quieted down and said sadly to Winston, "Do remember that things do not always go right with me. My every action is misjudged and every word distorted. . . . So make some allowances." In spite of his harsh and lonely childhood, Winston was stricken when on January 24, 1895, his father died. "All my dreams of comradeship with him, of entering Parliament at his side and in his support, were ended," he wrote much later. "There remained only for me to pursue his aims and vindicate his memory."

Within six months of Lord Randolph's death, Woom also was dead. Winston's devotion to her had never wavered. When she came in her old poke bonnet to visit him at Harrow and Sandhurst, he escorted her on his arm around the grounds and then, in sight of everyone, kissed her good-bye. In the summer of 1895, she was stricken with peritonitis. Winston rushed up from Aldershot, stopping in London to collect a doctor. He came to her bedside out of the rain and immediately Woom was worried. "My jacket was wet," Churchill recalled. "When she felt it with her hands she was greatly alarmed for fear I should catch cold. The jacket had to be taken off and thoroughly dried before she was calm again."

Mrs. Everest died in Winston's arms and he left immediately for Harrow in order to break the news in person to his brother, Jack. Winston organized the funeral and even provided a wreath in the name of his mother, who was in Paris, too busy to attend. These two deaths, Lord Randolph's and Mrs. Everest's, marked the end of youth for Winston Churchill. He commemorated his father with a two-volume biography; Woom's picture remained in his room until his own death seventy years later.

Randolph's death gave Winston freedom. "I was now in the

---

* During his illness and after his death, Jennie sternly refused to permit anyone to name the disease which killed her husband. Winston never did and even in 1966 Winston's son Randolph referred to his grandfather as suffering from a "severe mental disease."

main the master of my fate," he wrote. Lieutenant Winston Churchill was graduated from Sandhurst the winter his father died. "Raise the glorious flag again," he later wrote, recalling his feelings at the time. "Don't take No for an answer. Never submit to failure. . . . You will make all kinds of mistakes; but as long as you are generous and true, and also fierce, you cannot hurt the world or even seriously distress her. She was made to be wooed and won by youth. She has lived and thrived only by repeated subjugations."

A description of the next five years of Churchill's life reads more like the plot of a "tuppenny" Victorian novel than a true account of the adventures of a young British officer. Somehow, in this short span of time at the high-water mark of European colonialism, this young man managed to place himself under fire in four different wars in four widely separate corners of the earth. In the autumn of 1895, he campaigned with the Spanish Army against guerrillas in Cuba; in 1897 he fought in a campaign against Pathan tribesmen on the Northwest Frontier of India; in 1898 he served under Kitchener in the Sudan and participated with the 21st Lancers in the famous "last cavalry charge of the British Army"; a year later the British armored train in which he was riding in Natal province was ambushed by Boers, and Churchill was captured. He escaped, returned home a hero, wrote the third of three books about his adventures, and—now the most famous young man in England—was elected to the House of Commons in the Khaki Election of 1900.

None of this could have happened without Winston's relentless, thrusting ambition and Jennie's formidable help. Almost from the moment of Randolph's death, his relationship to her changed. Churchill himself summarized their new connection: "I was now in my twenty-first year and she never sought to exercise parental control. Indeed, she soon became an ardent ally, furthering my plans and guarding my interests with all her influence and boundless energy. She was still, at forty, young, beautiful and fascinating. We worked together on even terms, more like brother and sister than mother and son." Winston knew about her lovers: at sixteen he wrote to his brother that he had arrived home unexpectedly from Harrow and "found Mamma and Count Kinsky breakfasting." He seems not to have minded, and eventually he employed his mother's lovers on his own behalf with the same insistence he used on her.

In arranging his first war, the campaign in Cuba, Winston required no more of his mother than her consent. His new regiment, the 4th Hussars, was scheduled to sail for nine years' service in India and all the officers were granted ten weeks' leave. Most went off to fox hunting, steeplechasing, or racing yachts, but Winston decided to visit a war.

There was a tradition in the army of officers, bored by peacetime routine, traveling at their own expense to war zones, where they waited and pleaded to be taken into combat in almost any capacity. Winston's approach was through an old friend of his father's who was the British Ambassador in Madrid. Once permission to observe the war in Cuba was arranged with the Spanish authorities, he persuaded his mother that, at £37 for a round-trip ticket to New York and Havana, the excursion would cost less than two months of fox hunting. On November 30, 1895, he celebrated his twenty-first birthday by listening to bullets whistle over his head and thunk into the trunks of palm trees. He found he liked it: "There is nothing more exhilarating than to be shot at without result," he wrote. His accounts, published as *Letters from the Front,* brought him five guineas apiece from the *Daily Graphic.*

Winston was thrilled to be under fire, but back in London he reflected gloomily on the prospect of an army career. Nine years in India, barracks life without action, without advancement, without celebrity, palled even before it began. Through his mother's connections, he met and dined with Chamberlain, Balfour, Asquith, and other leading politicians. He planned to succeed his father, to be elected to Parliament. But how could he escape the army; where would he find the money to enter politics? He turned to Jennie: "I cannot believe that with all the influential friends you possess and all those who would do something for me for my father's sake," she could not arrange something. He asked to go to South Africa or Egypt. This time, she could not help him. He went to India. He was stationed at Bangalore in the southern Indian hills, three thousand feet above sea level, where mornings and evenings were fresh and cool. Winston lived in a "palatial bungalow, all pink and white" with a tile roof, and a columned veranda set in a garden of purple bougainvillea. Officers drilled for an hour and a half every morning; afterward Winston played polo and read. Doggedly, the young man who had never attended a university worked his way through twelve volumes of Macaulay and four thousand pages of Gibbon. He practiced elocution; all his life Churchill suffered from a speech impediment, part stammer, part lisp. He had difficulty pronouncing the letter "S" and used to pace his room repeating, "The Spanish ships I cannot see for they are not in sight." Bored, he bombarded his mother with appeals to find him a war. In April 1897, when fighting broke out between Greece and Turkey, he thought he saw his chance. He would take leave and cover the war as a special correspondent. He didn't care which side he was on, he wrote to Jennie. "If you can get me good letters to the Turks—to the Turks I will go. If to the Greeks—to the Greeks." The war ended before he could get to either.

In August 1897, Winston was in England on leave when the Pathan tribesmen on the Indian-Afghan frontier revolted. A British-Indian force of three brigades, the Malakand Field Force, was to be sent to put down the insurrection. Churchill had met the commander of the force, Major General Sir Bindon Blood, and extracted a promise that if he ever took troops into action on the frontier, he would permit Churchill to join him. Seizing on Blood's commitment, Winston cut short his leave and took the first steamship for Bombay. Behind, he left instructions for his mother to find a paper for which he could act as correspondent. Jennie found the *Daily Telegraph,* and Blood, having no room for Churchill as an officer, agreed to take him along as a journalist. The Pathans could not tell an officer from a journalist and, when the force was ambushed near the Khyber Pass, Winston fought them off with his revolver. When the campaign was over, he returned to Bangalore and began working on a book, *The Story of the Malakand Field Force.* His descriptions brought the terrain vividly before the reader's eye: "The Himalayas are not a line, but a great country of mountains. Standing on some lofty pass or commanding point . . . range after range is seen as the long surges of an Atlantic swell, and in the distance some glittering snow peak suggests a white-crested roller yet higher than the rest." . . . "Bright sunlight shining on the swirling muddy waters; the black forbidding rocks; the white tents of the brigade a mile up the valley; the long streak of vivid green rice crops by the river; and in the foreground the brown-clad armed men." He wrote it in two months and sent it to his mother to find a publisher; Jennie asked Arthur Balfour's advice and a publisher was found. Speed was paramount—another book on the expedition was being written—and when Winston saw the proofs, he writhed in embarrassment and shame. It was filled with "about 200 misprints, blunders, and mistakes" which "destroys all the pleasure I had hoped to get from the book and leaves only shame that such an impertinence should be presented to the public—a type of the careless, slapdash spirit of the age and an example of what my father would have called my slovenly, shiftless habits." Churchill was too sensitive. The book had an enthusiastic reception. Reviewers and readers alike skipped over the errors to hail the author's "wisdom," "comprehension," and "style." Churchill was surprised and moved. "I had never been praised before," he wrote. "The only comments which had ever been made upon my work at school had been 'Indifferent,' 'Slovenly,' 'Bad,' 'Very bad,' etc. Now here was the great world with its leading literary newspapers and vigilant erudite critics writing whole columns of praise." The Prince of Wales read the book and sent a copy to his sister, the Empress Victoria. "My dear Winston," he wrote to the author, "I cannot resist writing a few lines to congratulate you on the success of your book! I have read it with the greatest possible interest and I think the descriptions and the language generally excellent. Everybody is reading it and I only hear it spoken of with praise."

Winston wanted to be where the fighting was fiercest, but as a correspondent, not as an officer. Already, before his book was published, he had raged at Jennie for permitting his *Daily Telegraph* dispatches to be published anonymously. "I had written them with the design . . . of bringing my personality before the electorate," he told his mother. "If I am to do anything in the world, you will have to make up your mind to publicity. . . . Of course a certain number of people will be offended." Because of the anonymous byline, he said, "I regard an excellent opportunity of bringing my name before the country in a correct and attractive light—by means of graphic and forcible letters—as lost."

The next famous campaign was to be Kitchener's march up the Nile to reconquer the Sudan and avenge the death of General Gordon. In April 1898, even as *The Story of the Malakand Field Force* was being devoured in London drawing rooms, Churchill was imploring his mother to pull every string she could reach. "You must work for Egypt for me. . . . You have so many lines of attack. . . . I beg you—have no scruples but worry right and left and take no refusal." Two months later, still in India, he was growing desperate: "Oh, how I wish I could work you up over Egypt. I know you could do it with all your influence—and all the people you know. It is a pushing age and we must shove with the best." Jennie took up the challenge and—Winston wrote later—"left no wire unpulled, no stone unturned, no cutlet uncooked." The Prince wired Kitchener on Winston's behalf; the Sirdar, who did not like junior officers writing campaign accounts in which senior officers were criticized, refused. "Do not want Churchill as no room," he declared. Jennie went to Cairo to fire at close quarters. No effect. In June, Winston took more leave and came home from India to plead his case in person. He found two hundred other officers at the War Office urging themselves for the campaign. Then, fate intervened. Lord Salisbury had read *The Story of the Malakand Field Force* and invited Lord Randolph's son to come and tell him more. The Prime

Minister received the Lieutenant in his large Foreign Office room overlooking the Horse Guards Parade, and with Old World courtesy led him to a small sofa. He told Winston that he had found the book fascinating "not only for its matter but for its style," and said that he had been able "to form a truer picture of the kind of fighting that has been going on in these frontier valleys from your writings" than from any official documents he had been given to read. At the end of the interview, leading his visitor to the door, Lord Salisbury added, "If there is anything at any time I can do which would be of assistance to you, pray do not fail to let me know." Winston marshalled his courage and three days later wrote, "Dear Lord Salisbury: I am very anxious to go to Egypt and to proceed to Khartoum with the Expedition." His purpose, he explained, was to write another book. "I am loath to afflict you with this matter," he concluded. "Yet the choice lies between doing so and abandoning a project which I have set my heart on for a long time. . . . I venture to think that no hurt will result but rather benefit. The affair is after all of extreme insignificance to any but me." A few days later, Lieutenant Churchill was assigned as a supernumerary officer to the 21st Lancers for the Sudan campaign. Winston made an arrangement with the *Morning Post* to write a series of articles at £15 apiece, and then bolted for Egypt. He took a train to Marseilles and a "filthy tramp" steamer to Alexandria, and joined the 21st Lancers in Cairo just as they were embarking by riverboat and railroad fourteen hundred miles up the Nile to join the Sirdar's army.

"Nothing like the Battle of Omdurman will ever be seen again," Churchill wrote. "Everything was visible to the naked eye. The armies marched and maneuvered on the crisp surface of the desert plain through which the Nile wandered in broad reaches, now steel, now brass." The British-Egyptian Army, 26,000 men, lay behind temporary fortifications in a great crescent with its back to the Nile, where eight British gunboats were anchored, their guns trained out over the desert. At sunrise on September 2, 1898, the Dervish Army, sixty thousand strong, began to move across the sandy plain. Churchill, with a patrol of lancers, looked down on the enemy: "Their front was nearly five miles long . . . relieved and diversified with an odd-looking shimmer of light from the spear points. . . . I suddenly realized that all the masses were in motion and advancing swiftly. Their Emirs galloped about and before their ranks. . . . Then they began to cheer. . . . To us, watching on the hill, a tremendous roar came up in waves of intense sound, like the tumult of the rising wind and sea before a storm. In spite of the confidence which I felt in the weapons of civilization . . . the formidable aspect of this great host of implacable savages, hurrying eagerly to the attack . . . provoked a feeling of loneliness."

Despite the Khalifa's superiority in numbers, it was an unequal fight. The "weapons of civilization"—Kitchener's four batteries of howitzers, the guns on the boats on the Nile, the modern rifles held by British and Egyptian troops—cut "wide gaps and shapeless heaps" in the onrushing Dervish Army. Before even reaching the British lines, the Dervishes faltered. Twenty thousand men lay dead and wounded. For no more legitimate purpose than that which sent the Light Brigade up the Valley of Death, the 21st Lancers were then ordered to charge. Churchill rode at the head of his squadron, holding his Mauser pistol: "The collision was now very near. I saw before me, not ten yards away, the two blue men who lay in my path. I rode at the interval between them. They both fired. I passed through the smoke conscious that I was unhurt. The trooper immediately behind me was killed."

A Dervish charged with his sword: "I had room and time enough to turn my pony out of his reach and leaning over on the off side I fired two shots into him at about three yards. As I straightened myself in the saddle, I saw before me another figure with uplifted sword. I raised my pistol and fired. So close were we that the pistol itself actually struck him." Another Dervish "staggered toward me raising his spear. I shot him at less than a yard. He fell on the sand and lay there dead." The brief battle was over. "But now from the direction of the enemy there came a succession of grisly apparitions: horses spouting blood, struggling on three legs, men staggering on foot, men bleeding from terrible wounds, fish-hook spears stuck right through them, arms and faces cut to pieces, bowels protruding, men gasping, crying, collapsing, expiring." The 21st Lancers had lost a quarter of its men and a third of its horses, killed and wounded, in two minutes of battle.

As soon as the campaign was over, Churchill returned to England. "Come and see me and tell me about your future plans," wrote the Prince of Wales, who invited Winston to dine at Marlborough House, where he urged the young man to write another book. Churchill resigned from the army, began working on *The River War,* about the Sudan Campaign, and ran for Parliament. He lost, but not badly. When Britain's argument with the Boers concluded in a Boer ultimatum, Churchill sensed war and further opportunity for glory. On October 14, 1899, he sailed for South Africa to cover the story for the *Morning Post.* Within two weeks of arriving in Capetown, Churchill had been in action and was behind barbed wire in Pretoria, a prisoner of the Boers.

The escapade was a spirited piece of Churchillian melodrama. While waiting for the main campaign to start, he was invited to accompany a British armored train proceeding through Natal toward the besieged town of Ladysmith. The train, carrying two companies of British troops, was "cloaked from end to end with thick plates," but any damage to the tracks would render it immobile. General Louis Botha, commander of the Boer forces besieging Ladysmith, was out with five hundred mounted men when he spotted the train huffing north. All he had to do was to litter the rails with large rocks once the train had passed, frighten it into retreat by firing a few shells ahead of it, then wait while it piled into the rocks at full speed reverse. Three cars were derailed; the stunned British soldiers found themselves under heavy, accurate fire from the Boer riflemen. Although technically Churchill was only an observer, he assumed responsibility for trying to save the men. For seventy minutes, fully exposed to enemy fire, he labored to clear the track of derailed cars in order to free the engine. He succeeded partially and sent the locomotive off to safety, packed with wounded men. Coming back on foot to try to lead the other soldiers out, he found himself standing in front of a man on horseback, looking down the barrel of a Boer rifle. The rifleman was none other than Louis Botha, one of the best marksmen in South Africa, later the first Prime Minister of the Transvaal and a lifelong Churchill friend. Winston remembered a quote from Napoleon. "When one is alone and unarmed, a surrender may be pardoned." He raised his hands in the air. "We're not going to let you go, old chappie, although you are a correspondent," one of his captors told him cheerfully. "We don't catch the son of a lord every day," they said.

Churchill remained in captivity for less than a month. One night he leaped onto the wall behind the camp latrine, dropped to the other side, and was free. He walked boldly through the streets of Pretoria, jumped aboard a moving coal train, and left the city. Still, he was three hundred miles from friendly or neutral territory, did not know the language, and had only a little chocolate and a few biscuits. The first house he tried belonged to an English mine operator, who hid him at the bottom of a coal mine for three days while the Boers posted notices all over the Transvaal describing the fugitive: "Englishman 25 years old, about 5 ft. 8 in. tall, average build, walks with a slight stoop, pale appearance, red brown hair . . . cannot pronounce the letter 'S' . . ." Churchill lay with rats running across his face until his benefactor could smuggle him away, hidden behind bales of wool, on a train bound for Lourenço Marques in Portuguese East Africa. When Churchill arrived in the first town across the border and went to the British Consulate, a minor official took one look at his ragged clothes and told him to go away. Churchill stepped back into the street, looked up at the upper story where the Consul's office was located, and roared: "I am Winston Bloody Churchill. Come down here at once."

Back in South Africa, Churchill was a hero. He reapplied for an army commission, joined a South African cavalry regiment, and fought in some of the bloodiest battles of the war. He was recommended for the Victoria Cross, which Kitchener vetoed, and rode in the first columns to liberate Ladysmith and capture Pretoria and Johannesburg. He returned to England to find his mother about to marry George Cornwallis-West, "the handsomest man in England," who was only sixteen days older than Winston and twenty years younger than the bride. Her friends were appalled, but Jennie didn't care. "I suppose you think I'm very foolish," she said to a friend, "but I'm having such fun." Winston loyally stood by her. He wrote a new book, *London to Ladysmith, via Pretoria,* made a lecture tour of the United States, and collected £15,000 in book royalties, journalist's pay, and lecture fees. Then, the most famous young man in England, now properly financed, ran again for Parliament. In September 1900, he was elected to the House of Commons, where he was to remain for sixty-five years.

At first, the appearance of this pink-faced young man with bright blue eyes and reddish hair provoked memories of his father. *The Daily Mail* correspondent noted "the square forehead and the full bold eye . . . the hurried stride through the lobby." The observer from *Punch* reported that "When the young member for Oldham addresses the House, with hands on hips, head bent forward, right foot stretched forth, memories of days that are no more flood the brain." It was not long, however, before Winston was known for himself: "restless, egotistical, bumptious, shallow-minded and reactionary, but with a certain personal magnetism, great pluck and some originality," thought Beatrice Webb. When Churchill spoke, the Press Gallery stirred. How many horses and mules had been sent to South Africa, Winston asked the War Secretary, whom he disliked. When the answer was given, Churchill had another question: "Can my Right Honorable Friend say how many asses have been sent to South Africa?" By 1904, Churchill could no longer tolerate the Balfour-Chamberlain split on free trade and crossed the aisle to join the Liberal Party. Campbell-Bannerman gave the new recruit an important sub-Cabinet position as Under Secretary for the Colonies in the Liberal Cabinet of 1905; Asquith promoted him into the Cabinet, first as President of the Board of Trade, then as Home Secretary.

By 1911, Churchill was the only man in England instantly identifiable by his first name. "If it had not been for me, that young man would not have been in existence," Edward VII told Lord Esher. "How is that, sir?" asked the startled Esher. "The Duke and Duchess both objected to Randolph's marriage," the King explained. "It was owing to Us that they gave way." At thirty-six, Winston had almost everything he wanted: celebrity, a podium, a place at the table of the mighty. On a Scottish golf course one autumn afternoon, Asquith gave him a responsibility and an opportunity suited to his talents: he handed Winston the Royal Navy.

CHAPTER 41

Churchill
at the Admiralty

◆

O n Monday, October 25, 1911, Churchill and McKenna exchanged offices. In the morning McKenna came to the Home Office and Churchill introduced him to the leading officials; after lunch Churchill went to the Admiralty, where McKenna presented the Sea Lords and heads of department. McKenna's attitude throughout was gloomy but correct. He was not happy to be shunted out of the Admiralty, and his friends and supporters in the navy and around the country shared his view. Telegrams and letters poured in, expressing gratitude for his struggle against the economizers during his three and half years as First Lord. The blow was heightened by the fact that McKenna's replacement was one of the two arch-economizers in the Cabinet, Winston Churchill.

Some in Parliament and elsewhere did not understand McKenna's chagrin at switching from the Admiralty to the Home Office. In the informal ranking of Cabinet posts, the Home Secretary was Number Three, just behind the Prime Minister and the Chancellor; the First Lord stood further back. Indeed, this had been Churchill's own opinion in 1902, when he had scorned Austen Chamberlain's desire to become First Lord as "a poor ambition."

Apprehension about the new figure moving into the Admiralty was widespread. Observers saw a brilliant, self-confident young man of great physical courage and inexhaustible energies, with eloquent powers of expression. His rise had been meteoric. A Cabinet Minister at thirty-three, two years at the Board of Trade, twenty months at the Home Office; now, at thirty-six, he was still half a generation younger than his colleagues (Lloyd George was forty-eight, Grey forty-nine, Haldane forty-five, and Asquith fifty-nine). Yet despite his talent, he bore a heavy weight of disapproval. The stigma of having changed parties never left him. "Turncoat," "opportunist," "wind bag," "self-advertising mountebank" were some of the names flung at him. The Conservative *Spectator* greeted his appointment by saying, "We cannot detect in his career any principles or even any constant outlook upon public affairs; his ear is always to the ground; he is the true demagogue. . . ."

Churchill did not care what anyone said about him. Once past the two carved stone dolphins which guarded the entrance to the Admiralty building, ensconced in the furniture, carved with dolphins, that dated from Nelson's day, Churchill was in rapture. "That is because I can now lay eggs instead of scratching around in the dust and clucking," he explained. "It is a far more satisfactory occupation. I am at present in the process of laying a great number of eggs—good eggs." He moved swiftly. His first act was to hang on the wall behind his desk a large chart of the North Sea. Every day the duty officer marked with small flags the position of the principal ships of the German Navy. Each morning, on entering the room, Churchill stood before the chart and studied the whereabouts of the High Seas Fleet. His purpose, he said, "was to inculcate in myself and those working with me a sense of ever-present danger." He made quick decisions on a number of matters. Orders had not been placed for twenty new destroyers authorized in the 1911 Estimates; the new First Lord placed the orders immediately. The unguarded naval magazines which had kept him awake as Home Secretary the previous summer were transferred to the Admiralty and put under permanent guard by Royal Marines. Before his arrival, only a clerk stood guard at the Admiralty nights, weekends, and holidays to respond to reports and alarms arriving from around the globe. Churchill initiated a watch system of naval officers to stand duty around the clock. He ordered the Sea Lords to stand watch; one of the four was always to be near the Admiralty building.

He made a controversial appointment to the key role of Private Naval Secretary to the First Lord. Rear Admiral David Beatty, at forty the youngest flag officer in the navy, was not a conventional officer. His career had been splendid and celebrated: he had commanded a Nile gunboat at the Battle of Omdurman; he had been

with the Naval Landing Party during the Boxer Rebellion; he had
been promoted rapidly, some thought too rapidly. Handsome and
dashing, he had married a daughter of Marshall Field, the Chicago
Department-store mogul, and his wife had brought him a dowry of
£8 million; this sat poorly with admirals and captains struggling to
make ends meet on regular navy pay. Others complained that he
was too fond of life ashore; Beatty and his beautiful wife were often
seen in society; he rode superbly and followed the hounds with relish—good stuff for a cavalry officer, but odd for an admiral. Worst,
he was arrogant: offered the post of second in command of the
Atlantic Fleet, a billet for which many officers would have been
grateful, he had turned it down as not sufficiently interesting. Not
surprisingly, the Admiralty turned its back. Beatty had been left to
languish ashore on half pay for eighteen months. The prospect was
that before long he would be retired.

When Churchill became First Lord, Beatty asked for an appointment. Everything that Churchill had heard was favorable:
youth, enterprise, courage. Beatty's father had been in the 4th Hussars, Churchill's regiment. Beatty's gunboat on the Nile had used its
guns to support the charge of the 21st Lancers at Omdurman. Churchill was not influenced by Admiralty complaints that his visitor
"had got on too fast" and "had too many interests ashore." When
Beatty walked in, Churchill looked him over and said, "You seem
very young to be an admiral." Unfazed, Beatty replied, "And you
seem very young to be First Lord." Churchill took him on immediately. Beatty set to work in a room adjoining the First Lord's, accompanied him on all his inspection tours, and provided a sounding
board across every field of strategy and technology. In April 1913,
when one of the most sought-after commands in the navy, the Battle
Cruiser Squadron, fell vacant, Churchill appointed Beatty. Beatty
led the battle cruisers into the most violent actions of the North Sea
war. After Jutland, as Admiral, he took command of that huge agglomeration of dreadnoughts on which Britain's security rested: the
Grand Fleet.

Seeking guidance, Churchill turned to Jacky Fisher, now retired. They knew each other well, having spent two weeks together
in Biarritz in 1907 at the house of a mutual friend. Fisher, then First
Sea Lord, had talked through the days and nights while Churchill
listened. Fisher "fell desperately in love with Winston Churchill. I
think he's quite the nicest fellow I ever met and such a quick brain
that it's a delight to talk to him." The King, also in Biarritz, noticed
the new relationship and told Lady Londonderry that he found
them "most amusing together. I call them 'the chatterers.' " Chur-

chill's opposition to the 1909 Naval Estimates cast a shadow over the relationship, although the younger man wrote to assure the Admiral of his "unaltered feelings."

After leaving the Admiralty, Fisher left England to live in retirement in Lucerne. He had been fond of McKenna and his wife (writing to them as "My Beloved First Lord" and "My Beloved Pamela"), but as soon as he learned that Churchill was to become First Lord, he began sending recommendations: Battenberg to succeed Wilson as First Sea Lord, Jellicoe to go as Second in Command of the Home Fleet, and so on. Churchill anticipated Fisher's letters. On the morning of October 25, before leaving the Home Office to go over to the Admiralty, he wrote:

> My dear Lord Fisher,
>   I want to see you very much. When am I to have that pleasure? You have but to indicate your convenience and I will await you at the Admiralty.
>
> Yours vy sincerely,
WINSTON S. CHURCHILL

Fisher came like a shot. Three days later, Churchill and both McKennas met the boat train at Charing Cross. Fisher spent three hours with the McKennas, both of them "fearfully cut up at leaving the Admiralty," then motored with Churchill to Reigate, a small town south of London, where Asquith and Lloyd George were waiting for them. The dialogue was primarily between the First Lord and the Admiral. "I had certain main ideas of what I was going to do and what, indeed, I was sent to the Admiralty to do," Churchill said. "I intended to prepare for an attack by Germany as if it might come the next day. I intended to raise the Fleet to the highest possible strength. . . . I was pledged to create a War staff. I was resolved . . . to provide for the transportation of a British Army to France should war come. . . . I had the Prime Minister and the Chancellor of the Exchequer at my back." In Fisher, Churchill found "a veritable volcano of knowledge and inspiration; and as soon as he learned what my main purpose was, he passed into a state of vehement eruption. . . . Once he began, he could hardly stop. I plied him with questions and he poured out ideas." When the Reigate conversations began, Churchill had no thought of recalling Fisher to the Admiralty. "But by the Sunday night the power of the man was deeply borne in upon me and I had almost made up my mind to do what I did three years later and place him again at the head of the Naval Service. . . . All the way up to London the next morning I was on the brink of saying 'Come and help me' and had he by a word seemed to wish to return, I would surely have spoken. But he maintained a proper dignity, and in an hour we were in London." Fisher returned to Lucerne.

Three weeks later, he was back for a secret weekend meeting on board the *Enchantress* at Plymouth, three days of "continuous talking and practically no sleep." A professional bond was established and the Admiral began to bombard the new First Lord with densely written ten-page letters, beginning "My beloved Winston," studded with underlinings and exclamation points, containing "every sort of news and counsel, from blistering reproach to supreme inspiration," and ending with "Yours to a cinder" or "Yours till Hell freezes" or "Till charcoal sprouts." Fisher's urgent advice was that Churchill promote Jellicoe to Second in Command of the Home Fleet to give him the experience and seniority necessary to take command of Britain's main fleet on the outbreak of war. Churchill acceded; Jellicoe, although twenty-first in seniority among vice admirals, was appointed. Ecstatically, Fisher reported the news to his daughter-in-law:

> The greatest triumph of all is getting Jellicoe Second-in-Command of the Home Fleet. He is the future Nelson SURE!" To Pamela McKenna, he elaborated: "In two years he [Jellicoe] will be Commander-in-Chief of the Home Fleet. . . . The Battle of Armageddon comes along in September 1914. That date suits the Germans, if ever they are going to fight. Both their Army and Fleet then mobilized and the Kiel Canal finished and their new [naval] building complete.

Basking in his new role, Fisher wrote in glowing terms about Churchill: "So far every step he contemplates is good, *and he is brave which is everything. Napoleonic in audacity, Cromwellian in thoroughness.*" This praise halted abruptly in April 1912 when Churchill promoted three admirals who were close to the King and who had sided with Beresford during the schism in the navy. "I regret that in regard to . . . what you have done in the appointments of Sir Hedworth Meux, Sir Berkeley Milne, and Sir Reginald Custance, I fear this must be my last communication with you in any matter at all," Fisher wrote to Churchill. "I am sorry for it but I considered you have betrayed the Navy in these three appointments, and what the pressure could have been to induce you to betray your trust is beyond my comprehension." To Esher, Fisher made the nasty supposition that the appointments were the fault of

Churchill's young wife, Clementine: "Winston, alas! (as I have had to tell him) feared for his wife the social ostracism of the Court and succumbed to the appointments of the two Court favorites recently made—a wicked wrong in both cases! Winston has sacrificed the Country to the Court and gone back on his brave deeds . . . so I've done with him!"

Fisher continued to grouse and harrumph, at one point describing the First Lord as "a Royal Pimp," but Churchill ignored both complaints and insults. Soon Fisher was boasting to his son: ". . . as regards Winston Churchill . . . no doubt, I sent him an awful letter and he really has replied very nicely that no matter what I like to say to him, he is going to stick to me and support all my schemes and always maintain that I am a genius and the greatest naval administrator, etc., etc., etc. . . . However, there is no getting over the fact that he truckled to Court influence . . . and I have rubbed this into WC and he don't like it. . . . Still, for the good of the Navy I am reluctantly feeling compelled to continue my advice to him as to new Dreadnoughts and other fighting business."

Churchill was coming to the Mediterranean and, as Fisher would be in Naples, the First Lord decided to woo the old lion in his lair: "My dear Fisher," he wrote on May 15, "The Prime Minister and I are coming to Naples on the 24th. . . . I shall look forward to having a good talk with you and I therefore defer replying to your last letter which I was so glad to get. If the consequences of the recent appointments were to be what you apprehend, I should feel your censures were not undeserved. But they will not be. The highest positions in the Admiralty and in the Fleet will not be governed by seniority; and the future of the Navy rests in the hands of men in whom your confidence is as strong as mine. . . . For the rest let us wait till we can talk freely. Writing is so wearisome and unsatisfactory."

Churchill was going to Malta and Gibraltar to meet the Mediterranean admirals and discuss—along with Kitchener, who was coming from Egypt—the defense of the Imperial lifeline through the inland sea.* For this reason, he was accompanied by the Second Sea Lord, Prince Louis of Battenberg, and by Beatty, his Naval Secretary. But he was also going to relax under blue skies and, to share this pleasure, he invited Clementine, her sister, his sister-in-law, and Asquith, who brought along his twenty-five-year-old daughter, Vio-

---

* The visit was to result in the decision to transfer Britain's Mediterranean battleships to the North Sea and to leave guardianship of British interests in the Mediterranean in the hands of the French Navy.

let. The party embarked in the *Enchantress* in Genoa and two days later found themselves entering the Bay of Naples. In her diary, Violet Asquith described what happened: "Some of us went ashore . . . straight to the museum . . . back to the yacht for luncheon and *there was Lord Fisher*! His eyes, as always, were like smouldering charcoals. . . . He was very friendly to Father and Prince Louis but glowered a bit, I thought, at Winston. . . . As the day wore on I noticed signs of mellowing in Lord F. which I feel will turn to melting before long. I whispered at tea to Winston: 'He's melting.' His mind was far away. He gazed at me blankly and said in a hard, loud voice: '*What's* melting?' Distracted, I replied: 'The butter.' which brought an old-fashioned look from our hostess [Clementine] who eyed the bread and butter anxiously. When we got back to the *Enchantress* Lord F. and W. were locked together in naval conclave. . . . I'm sure they can't resist each other long at close range." Fisher remained on board overnight, and the next morning Violet reported: "Danced on deck with Lord Fisher for a very long time before breakfast. . . . I reel giddily in his arms and lurch against his heart of oak." Between Violet's dancing and Winston's wooing, Fisher was conquered. "I was nearly kidnapped and carried off in the Admiralty yacht!" Fisher wrote to a friend. "They were very sweet about it! My old cabin as First Sea Lord all arranged for me! I had a good time and came out on top! The Prime Minister is 'dead on' for my coming back, and he has put things so forcibly to me that, with great reluctance to re-enter the battlefield, I probably shall do so. . . ." To Lady Fisher, the Admiral listed Churchill's compliments: "WC said the King was always talking about me to him, and had acknowledged how much I had done, but that I was absolutely wedded to certain ideas he couldn't approve of. WC turned round to him [the King] and said that everything now that was said at home and abroad of the 'present overwhelming supremacy and efficiency of the British Navy' was solely and only and entirely due to me! and that 'there would shortly be 16 ships with 13½ inch gun, when not a single German ship had anything but a 12 inch gun, which compared to the British 13½ inch gun, was only a pea-shooter and he said the King shut up then. I also heard indirectly from Esher that Winston Churchill always sticks up for me to all the Court people besides the King. . . ."

The new First Lord's relationship with the navy was not all paperwork and strategic talk. For Churchill, bursting with excitement and energy, it was Fun. One of the perquisites of office was that he selected the women who christened new dreadnoughts. Within seven weeks of his appointment, Winston stood by while Clementine christened the battleship *Centurion.* Two years later, Jennie christened the battleship *Benbow.* There were sweeter delights: the First Lord was the only man in the kingdom other than the monarch to have a yacht paid for out of the public purse. The Admiralty yacht *Enchantress,* a handsome 3,500-tonner, came with comfortable staterooms, an excellent wine cellar, and a crew of one hundred to take the First Lord wherever he wished to go. Winston made it "largely my office, almost my home" and, during his first eighteen months in office, spent 182 days on board, visiting every British naval station and dockyard in the United Kingdom and the Mediterranean. As lord of the *Enchantress,* he could play host to whomever he liked, including the Prime Minister, who did not have a yacht, and who keenly enjoyed cruising under the warm sun of the Mediterranean.

Churchill used the yacht to visit the Fleet; he wanted to know the ships and the men—*his* ships and *his* men, as he thought of them. "These were great days," he wrote in *The World Crisis.* "From dawn to midnight, day after day, one's whole mind was absorbed. . . . Saturdays, Sundays, and any other spare day, I spent always with the Fleet at Portsmouth or at Portland or Devonport or with the Flotillas at Harwich. Officers of every rank came on board to lunch or dine. . . . I got to know what everything looked like and where everything was and how one thing fitted into another. In the end, I could put my hand on whatever was wanted."

The navy never knew where he would turn up. Suddenly, he would appear, ebullient and inexhaustible, bounding up the gangways of the dreadnoughts, disappearing down the hatches of the submarines, eager to see everything and have everything explained. He communicated his enthusiasm to everyone. He took Arthur Balfour and Lord Morley into one of the turrets of the dreadnought *Orion,* where "in cramped and oily quarters, with a mass of machinery penning them on every side," he lectured on how the guns were worked. Asquith was amused by Winston's exuberance. The Prime Minister went to witness target practice and soon the First Lord was "dancing about the guns, elevating, depressing, and sighting." "My young friend yonder," Asquith observed, "thinks himself Othello and blacks himself all over to play the part." When Violet Asquith accompanied her father to the Mediterranean she observed "W[inston] in glorious form though slightly over-concentrated on instruments of destruction. Blasting and shattering are now his *idées fixes.* As we leaned side by side against the rail, past the lovely,

smiling coastline of the Adriatic bathed in sun, and I remarked
'How perfect!', he startled me by his reply: 'Yes—range perfect—
visibility perfect'—and details followed showing how effectively we
could lay waste the landscape and blow the nestling towns sky-
high." Beatty, also on the cruise, wrote to his wife that "Winston
talks about nothing but the Navy and all the wonderful things he is
going to do." Back in London, Lloyd George chided his former ally
in naval economy: "You have become a water creature. You think
we all live in the sea and all your thoughts are devoted to sea life,
fishes and other aquatic creatures. You forget that most of us live on
land."

May 1912 saw Churchill's first great naval review as First Lord:
"The flags of a dozen admirals, the broad pennants of as many
commodores and the pennants of a hundred and fifty ships were
flying together. The King came in the Royal Yacht. . . . One day
there is a long cruise out into the mist, dense, utterly baffling—the
whole Fleet steaming together all invisible, keeping station with
weird siren screamings and hootings. It seemed incredible that no
harm would befall. And then suddenly the fog lifted and the distant
targets could be distinguished and the whole long line of battleships,
coming one after another into view, burst into tremendous flares of
flame and hurled their shells with deafening detonations while the
water rose in tall fountains. The Fleet returns—three battle squadrons abreast, cruisers and [destroyer]flotillas disposed ahead and
astern. The speed is raised to twenty knots. Streaks of white foam
appear at the bows of every vessel. The land draws near. The broad
bay already embraces this swiftly moving gigantic armada. The ships
in their formation already fill the bay. The foreign officers I have
with me on the *Enchantress* bridge stare anxiously. We still steam
fast. Five minutes more and the van of the Fleet will be aground.
Four minutes, three minutes. There! At last. The signal! A string of
bright flags falls from the *Neptune*'s halyards. Every anchor falls
together; their cables roar through the hawser holes; every propeller
whirls astern. In a hundred and fifty yards every ship is stationary.
Look along the lines, miles this way and miles that, they might have
been drawn with a ruler. The foreign observers gasped."

Prompted by Fisher, Churchill took an interest in the lot of the
common seamen and petty officers. Navy pay, which had not
changed in sixty years, was raised; annoyances in the form of petty
discipline, inadequate leave, and slow promotions were eliminated.
"No First Lord in the history of the Navy has shown himself more

practically sympathetic with the conditions of the Lower Deck than Winston Churchill," wrote an unofficial navy magazine. A reporter for the *Daily Express* accompanied him on a visit to a submarine in 1912: "He had a yarn with nearly all the lower deck men of the ship's company, asking why, wherefore, and how everything was done. All the sailors 'go the bundle' on him because he makes no fuss and takes them by surprise. He is here, there, everywhere." Sympathy with enlisted men and encouragement that they and their petty officers voice their grievances did not increase Churchill's popularity with officers. On one occasion, poking about a cruiser, he had the officer guiding him show him the brig. When the officer returned to the wardroom, his fellow officers shouted, "Why didn't you lock him up?" What Churchill saw as a proper interest in the condition of the men, officers scorned as an attempt to curry favor with the lower ranks. Once, visiting a battleship, the First Lord ordered the ship's company assembled on deck for his inspection. Then he put the officer in charge to a test:

"Do you know your men by name?" the First Lord asked.

"I think I do, Sir; we have had many changes recently, but I think I know them all," the officer replied.

"What is the name of this man?"

"Jones, Sir."

"What is your name?" asked Churchill, addressing the seaman.

"Jones, Sir."

"Is your name really Jones or do you say so only to back your officer?"

"My name is Jones, Sir."

When Churchill departed, the officer and his fellow officers on the ship were in a "choking wrath."

To senior captains and admirals—some almost old enough to be his father—Churchill seemed especially disrespectful. A bumptious young man of thirty-six with a ballyhooed experience of war as a junior cavalry officer was overriding professional naval opinion, interfering in technical matters, jumping to harebrained conclusions. They dealt with him their own way. Churchill watched the old battleship *Cornwallis* firing at a target and, as soon as the guns were silent, wanted to know how many hits had been scored.

"None," replied the admiral.

"Not one? *All* misses? How do you explain it?"

"Well, you see, First Lord, the shells seem to have fallen either just short of the target or else gone just a little beyond it."

The Sea Lords confronted the problem every day. The First Lord treated them as his subordinates, issuing orders rather than asking for their advice. From his dicta and personality there was no appeal; Prime Minister and Cabinet were firmly behind him. On one memorable occasion when one of the Sea Lords accused Winston of ignoring the time-honored traditions of the Royal Navy, the First Lord replied savagely, "And what are they? I shall tell you in three words. Rum, sodomy, and the lash. Good morning, gentlemen."

Eventually, in the Bridgeman Affair, Churchill's bruising treatment of the Sea Lords reached the attention of the House of Commons. Admiral Sir Francis Bridgeman was a competent, colorless officer who had been happily serving as Commander-in-Chief of the Home Fleet when Churchill brought him ashore to replace Sir Arthur Wilson. Bridgeman came, reluctantly but dutifully, "to help things along if I can." By October 1912, the mild-mannered Bridgeman already had locked horns on a variety of issues with the tempestuous First Lord. Eventually, he stated that Churchill's constant interference in technical decisions and repeated overriding of naval traditions were denigrating the authority of senior officers and would harm the efficiency of the service. The First Lord did not take this criticism well, and Bridgeman threatened to take his case to the Prime Minister and the King.

From that moment on, Bridgeman's doom was certain. On November 14, Churchill mentioned to Prince Louis that he would soon be moving up to First Sea Lord. Bridgeman was recuperating from appendicitis and two attacks of bronchitis. In letters to Battenberg and Beatty, he had mentioned the possibility of resigning and spoken wistfully of going to a warmer climate where he could sit in the sun and recover. Reports of these letters reached Churchill, who seized on Bridgeman's health and wrote to the Admiral that he was aware of the great sacrifice the First Sea Lord was making by remaining at his post. "If, by any misadventure, we were to be involved in war," the First Lord continued, "I feel that the burden might be more than you could sustain." Bridgeman misinterpreted what in fact was a buffered call for his resignation as simply a well-wisher's concern about his health, and replied that he was already better and fit to carry on. This letter was highly unwelcome to Churchill, who, foolishly headlong, already had submitted Bridgeman's resignation to the Prime Minister and the King. On December 2, Churchill dropped his pretence of solicitude and bluntly informed Bridgeman that his resignation had been accepted.

A change of this magnitude attracted comment in the press, particularly as Churchill had already forced the resignations of four Sea Lords within the year. On December 11, Lord Charles Beresford rose to ask about the matter in the House of Commons. Beresford saw Churchill not only as a youthful interloper at the Admiralty, but also as the agent of his own archenemy, Fisher.

"Might I ask the First Lord if it is a fact that ill-health and no other cause was the reason for the First Sea Lord's resignation?" Beresford asked.

"So far as I am aware, no other cause whatever," Churchill replied.

"Might I ask on which side the proposal for resignation emanated—from the Admiralty or from the First Sea Lord?" Beresford continued.

"Very well," Churchill declared. "Since the Noble Lord presses it: the proposal emanated from me."

Churchill worried that the affair was getting out of hand. The press trumpeted that a distinguished sailor with a long and honorable career was being summarily cast aside by a tyrannical Minister who knew nothing about the navy, but who dismissed everyone who did not bow to his demands. Even people who did not know the details, or who thought well of Winston, felt that Bridgeman had been mistreated. Attempting to improve his position, Churchill bullied Bridgeman even further, commanding him to state that health alone, rather than policy disagreements, had brought his resignation. Bridgeman replied to this browbeating by replying honestly that he could not do it; he reminded Churchill of specific disagreements and of the fact that, on one occasion, he had suggested his own resignation as a remedy.

Frustrated and furious, Churchill turned all his rage on Beresford in the House of Commons. When the former Admiral rose again at Question Time, Churchill attacked him with rhetorical violence.

"What I ask the Noble Lord to do is to state specifically what he had in his mind—if he has anything in his mind."

"It is his habit in matters of this kind to make a number of insinuations—" Churchill began.

"That is not true," Beresford interrupted.

"Insinuations of a very gross character," persisted Churchill, "some of which transgress the limits of Parliamentary decorum; to cover the Order Paper with leading and fishing questions, designed to give substance and form to any gossip or tittle-tattle he may have been able to scrape together, and then to come down to the House, not to attempt to make good in fact or in detail . . . but to skulk in the background, waiting for an opportunity. . . . I have not ever since I became First Lord of the Admiralty made any reply to the Noble Lord's scurrilous and continuous personal attacks, none. I sought no quarrel with him. . . . but within a fortnight he made a speech in which he said I had betrayed the Navy . . . and ever since he has been going about the country pouring out charges of espionage, favoritism, blackmail, fraud, and inefficiency."

"I deny that entirely," Beresford interrupted again. "I never used the word 'blackmail.' Give the date and the place."

"Certainly," Churchill replied evenly. "In the constituency of the honorable member for Eversham—my memory is very good on these points—he used the great bulk of those offensive expressions, needless to say, unsupported by any facts or arguments. . . . I have never taken these things too seriously. I am not one of those who take the Noble Lord too seriously. I know him too well. He does not mean to be as offensive as he often is when he is speaking on public platforms. He is one of those orators of whom it was well said, 'Before they get up, they do not know what they are going to say; when they are speaking, they do not know what they are saying; and when they have sat down, they do not know what they have said.' . . . Under a genial manner . . . the Noble Lord nourishes many bitter animosities on naval matters."

Ultimately, the House, which was familiar with Beresford's obsession with Fisher, sustained the First Lord. Significantly, even Bridgeman sided with Churchill, writing after the exchange in the Commons: "I do hope the whole business is now at an end, but I hear rumours of a deep-laid agitation against Churchill; I am using every bit of influence I possess to arrest it. . . . I am afraid Beresford is difficult to hold and I unfortunately can do nothing with him."

Churchill's relations with King George V were correct but cool. Having spent fifteen years in the navy and risen by merit to the rank of Captain before his brother's death made him Prince of Wales, George V shared most of the views and prejudices of the navy's senior officers. In the Fisher-Beresford contest, the King became a Beresford man, and accordingly was not pleased when Churchill made the former First Sea Lord his principal advisor. For his part, Churchill respected the monarch without placing much weight on his opinions. After a royal visit to the *Enchantress,* Winston reported to his wife that the King had talked more stupidly about the navy than anyone he had ever heard. Three times in three years, the two became entangled over the names to be given to new dreadnoughts. Traditionally, a First Lord proposed names and the King amended, counterproposed, and then agreed. In November 1911, immediately after becoming First Lord, Churchill proposed *Africa, Assiduous, Liberty,* and *Oliver Cromwell* for the four battleships in that year's Estimates. The King rejected naming a dreadnought *Cromwell* after the man who had chopped off the head of King Charles I. He accepted *Africa* and proposed *Delhi, Wellington,* and *Marlborough.* The four ships eventually went to sea with the names *Iron Duke* (which Churchill liked better than *Wellington), Marlborough, Emperor of India,* and *Benbow.* The following year, the First Lord proposed four names from England's warrior history for the four great fifteen-inch-gun, oil-burning superdreadnoughts of the 1912 class. On his desk, the King read: *King Richard the First, King Henry the Fifth, Queen Elizabeth,* and—again—*Oliver Cromwell.* Lord Stamfordham, the King's Private Secretary, immediately wrote to Churchill that "there must be some mistake . . . that name was proposed for one of the ships of last year's program; His Majesty was unable to agree to it and . . . personally explained to you the reasons for his objection." This time, Churchill persevered. "Oliver Cromwell was one of the founders of the Navy and scarcely any man did so much for it," he wrote to Stamfordham. "It seems right that we should give to a battleship a name that never failed to make the enemies of England tremble." King George refused to budge and the First Lord declared, "I bow." The new ship was named *Valiant,* and of Churchill's original choices, only *Queen Elizabeth* went to sea. The other two dreadnoughts were named *Warspite* and *Barham,* and a fifth sister of the class, *Malaya,* was named after the colony that paid to build her.

Churchill's final brush with the King on the subject of names occurred over two ships of the 1913 class. The First Lord proposed *Ark Royal* and *Pitt.* The King had various arguments against *Ark Royal,* but he rejected *Pitt* on an intuition derived from his own many years at sea. Sailors, he knew, tended to find obscene or scatological nicknames for the ships they served on; *Pitt* was much too easy and would have an inevitable result. Churchill, presented with the argument, grumbled that this suggestion was "unworthy of the royal mind." The 1913 dreadnoughts, the last of the prewar building program, were given names to please a monarch: *Royal Sovereign, Royal Oak, Ramillies, Resolution,* and *Revenge.*

As peacetime First Lord, Winston Churchill's most significant achievement was the design and building of the *Queen Elizabeth* class of superdreadnoughts. This division of five large, fast, heavily armored ships, powered by oil and carrying heavier guns than those on any previous dreadnought, played a decisive role at the Battle of Jutland, the long-awaited Armageddon of Jacky Fisher's dreams. Immeasurably superior to any earlier battleship, they continued to form the backbone of British naval strength well into the Second World War, when Winston Churchill, once again First Lord and then Prime Minister, had reason to be grateful for their presence.

The dominant naval weapon of the era, despite the advent of the torpedo, was the great gun: the long-barreled naval cannon which fired a heavy shell down a rifled tube, lofting the spiralling projectile thousands of yards to plunge onto an enemy ship, piercing and penetrating heavy armor to burst inside turrets or hull, spreading fire, devastation, chaos, and death. The size and weight of one of these shells grew immensely as the diameter of the barrel and the projectile increased. *Dreadnought,* Fisher's first all-big-gun ship, was armed with ten heavy guns, each firing a shell 12 inches in diameter and weighing 850 pounds. In the building programs that followed, 1906 through early 1909, a total of sixteen dreadnoughts—ten battleships and six battle cruisers—were equipped with 12-inch guns. In the 1909 program, at Fisher's urgent demand, the diameter of barrel and shell was dramatically increased to 13.5 inches.* This addition of only an inch and a half in the diameter of the shell increased the projectile's weight from 850 pounds to 1,250 pounds.

By the time Churchill arrived at the Admiralty, eighteen dreadnoughts with 13.5-inch guns had been launched, laid down, or authorized, although none had gone to sea. Nevertheless, as soon as he became First Lord, he immediately sought to go one size better. Within a few months, he would have to stand before the House of Commons and, in the 1912 Naval Estimates, ask for money to build five more giant ships. He decided to propose an even bigger gun, which would hurl a mammoth 15-inch, 1,920-pound projectile 35,000 yards. He took his plan to Fisher. "No one who has not experienced it has any idea of the passion and eloquence of this old lion when thoroughly roused on a technical subject," Churchill wrote. "To shrink from the endeavour was treason to the Empire," Fisher roared at Churchill. "What was it that enabled Jack Johnson to knock out his opponents? It was the big punch."

Emboldened, Churchill ordered the new gun designed and produced. Redesigning dreadnoughts to carry the new weapons was complicated and risky. If the guns were enlarged, everything must

---

* The first two ships of the 1909 "We Want Eight!" program, *Colossus* and *Hercules,* were equipped with 12-inch guns. The next six, *Orion, Conqueror, Monarch, Thunderer, Lion,* and *Princess Royal,* were given the new 13.5-inch guns.

be enlarged: turrets, armor, the ships themselves. This meant a significant increase in cost. And all this had to be done before it was known whether the new gun would work. "If only we could make a trial gun and test it thoroughly before giving the orders for the whole of the guns of all the five ships, there would be no risk," Churchill wrote about his dilemma. "But then we should lose an entire year and five great vessels would go into the line of battle carrying an inferior weapon to that which we had it in our power to give them." Worried, the young First Lord went back to Fisher: "He was steadfast and even violent. So I hardened my heart and took the plunge." Forty of the huge rifles were ordered. One gun was rushed along four months ahead of the others to test it for stress, range, and accuracy in actual firing. Even so, Churchill and the navy were irrevocably committed. The first of the new ships, *Queen Elizabeth,* did not go to sea for three years. During all this time, Churchill waited in suspense: "Fancy if they failed. What a disaster. What an exposure. No excuse would be accepted. It would all be brought home to me—'rash, inexperienced,' 'before he had been there a month,' 'altering all the plans of his predecessors' and producing 'this ghastly fiasco,' 'the mutilation of all the ships of the year.' What could I have said?" The gun was a brilliant success, and British dreadnoughts which carried it were able to fire a shell 40 percent heavier than any that could be fired back at them. Even during his long, anxious wait, Churchill was entranced with what he was creating. In May 1912, he told the annual banquet of the Royal Academy that "everything in the naval world is directed to the manifestation at a particular place during the compass of a few minutes of a shattering, blasting, overbearing force." A few days later, describing the impact of a heavy shell upon a warship, he gave the House of Commons a graphic metaphor. In order to imagine "a battle between two great modern iron-clad ships, you must not think of . . . two men in armor striking at each other with heavy swords. It is more like a battle between two egg shells striking each other with hammers. . . . The importance of hitting first, hitting hardest, and keeping on hitting . . . really needs no clearer proof."

The new ships could deliver a knockout punch; it remained to provide them with armor and speed. In the *Queen Elizabeth*s there was no skimping on armor; key areas such as the waterline and turrets were covered by thirteen and a half inches of solid steel. Churchill's ships could deliver and take a punch. Still, he was not satisfied. He wanted speed. The standard twenty-one knots of British dreadnoughts was not enough to overtake a fleeing enemy and bring it to battle. He needed battle-cruiser speed, twenty-five or twenty-six knots.

Here, as in almost everything, he followed Fisher's constant cry: "Speed! Speed! Do you remember the recipe for jugged hare in 'Mrs. Glasse's Cookery'? First, catch your hare. . . ." "The first of all necessities is speed so as to be able to fight When you like, Where you like, and How you like. . . ."

The battle cruisers had achieved their speed by sacrificing armor. This Churchill would not do. "I do not believe in the wisdom of the battle cruiser type," he wrote. "To put the value of a first class battleship into a vessel which cannot stand the pounding of a heavy action is false policy." The First Lord and his designers tried other avenues. They could give up a turret. All previous dreadnoughts had carried ten 12-inch or ten 13.5-inch guns paired in five turrets. A full broadside from the ten rifles of a 13.5-inch-gun ship, an *Orion,* a *King George V,* or an *Iron Duke,* weighed fourteen thousand pounds. But the great weight of the fifteen-inch shells in the new class gave a broadside of even greater weight, sixteen thousand pounds, fired from only eight guns. Two guns, an entire turret, were sacrificed and this two thousand tons devoted to propulsion machinery. More boilers were installed. Still it was not enough.

The solution was oil fuel. Oil burned more fiercely than coal and gave off more heat. Steam created under higher pressure drove the shafts and turned the propellers faster. The ships moved more quickly through the water. Oil had other advantages. Oil could be transferred at sea from tankers to warships, dispensing with the constant need to go into port to take on coal.

"The ordeal of coaling ship exhausted the whole ship's company," Churchill wrote. ". . . With oil a few pipes were connected with the shore or with a tanker and the ship sucked in its fuel with hardly a man having to lift a finger. . . . Oil could be stowed in spare places in a ship from which it could be impossible to bring coal. As a coal ship used up her coal, increasingly large numbers of men had to be taken, if necessary from the guns, to shovel the coal from remote and inconvenient bunkers to bunkers nearer to the furnaces or to the furnaces themselves, thus weakening the fighting efficiency of the ship. . . . For instance, nearly a hundred men were continually occupied in the *Lion* shoveling coal from one steel chamber to another without ever seeing the light of day or of the furnace fires."

Oil fuel was already in use in many smaller ships. Submarines could not run on coal, and when Churchill arrived at the Admiralty, seventy-four submarines and fifty-six destroyers dependent exclusively on oil were built or building. Two American battleships, *Oklahoma* and *Nevada,* ordered in 1911, were to be oil powered. But America produced its own oil; the British Isles did not. Here lay the risk and gamble for Churchill. Converting dreadnoughts to oil meant giving them greater speed; it also meant basing British naval supremacy on a fuel obtainable only from overseas. Oil would have to be found, acquired, transported, and stored in enormous reserve tanks in quantities sufficient for many months of fighting.

Even the vigorous Churchill could not accomplish all this by simple decree. He needed advice. He needed facts. He needed enthusiasm. He turned to Fisher and asked the Admiral to return to England and preside over a Royal Commission on Oil Supply. His letter was warm, blunt, stern, and supplicatory: "This liquid fuel problem has got to be solved. . . . [It requires] the drive and enthusiasm of a big man. I want you for this, viz. to crack the nut. No one else can do it so well. Perhaps no one else can do it at all. I will put you in a position where you can crack the nut, if indeed it is crackable.

"I recognize it is little enough I can offer you. But your gifts, your force, your hopes, belong to the Navy . . . and as your most ardent admirer and as the head of the Naval Service, I claim them now, knowing you will not grudge them. You need a plough to draw. Your propellers are racing in air."

Fisher could not resist; he returned immediately and plunged into the work of the Royal Commission. Within six months, the Commission made its recommendation: the advantages of oil for the fleet were so overwhelming that a four-year reserve should be obtained and stored. Parliament authorized the spending of £10 million for storage tanks. Churchill simultaneously sent experts to the Persian Gulf to examine the potential of oil fields in that region. In July 1914, another £2.2 million was authorized to acquire a controlling interest in the Anglo-Persian Oil Company. From the *Queen Elizabeth*s forward, the new ships of the Royal Navy burned oil. The "lamentable exception," as Churchill termed it, was the 1913 *Revenge* class of fifteen-inch-gun battleships, which because of fears that wartime oil supplies would be inadequate were designed for coal. When Fisher returned as First Sea Lord at the outbreak of war, one of the first orders he gave was that *Revenge, Royal Oak, Royal Sovereign, Resolution,* and *Ramillies*—their hulls still on the building ways—be redesigned for oil.

■ ■ ■

The navy benefitted from another important technical change during the Churchill years, although in this instance the First Lord served as referee rather than as instigator. Sir Percy Scott had never been satisfied with the state of Royal Navy gunnery. The greater range of the new guns created more problems in hitting the target. Artillerymen on land train their cannon around in the direction of the target, elevate the muzzle to achieve the proper range, and fire until the target is destroyed or they are told to stop. At sea, it has never been this easy. Besides the ceaseless roll of the deck, which requires constant changes in elevation, both firing ship and target ship are moving across the water, creating endlessly changing angles. Traditionally, solving these angles, estimating distances, feeling the roll of the deck were the task of the gunlayer, one to each great gun, inside the turrets of the battleships. In peacetime the system worked. Firing practice usually involved stationary targets, positioned at ranges no greater than two thousand yards. Under these conditions, the gunlayers, peering down their barrels, could see where their shells were falling, make corrections, and—to the delight of senior officers and astounded spectators—pulverize the target. Sir Percy Scott considered this a dangerous exercise in fantasy. In wartime, he argued, individual gunlayers in the turrets would face not only the concussive blast of the guns, billowing heavy smoke, and spray resulting from high speed, but the fact that the target would be shooting back. At ranges four and five times greater than in peacetime, the individual gunlayer at turret level could not even see where his shells were landing. The result would be catastrophic: gunlayers who could not see, guns which could not be aimed, shells which could not strike—a fleet blind and helpless. Scott's solution was what he called Director Firing.

A single master gunlayer, posted high in the conning tower or on the foremast, would aim and fire simultaneously all the heavy guns on the ship. From this eyrie, above the blast and smoke of his own guns and the spray from the splash of enemy shells, with an excellent line of vision to the target, he and his assistant could observe the geysers as their own shells struck the sea near the enemy. They could calculate what adjustments were required, electrically transmit their orders to the guns, and then, when all was ready, press a key to fire all guns at once in a mighty broadside salvo. Broadside firing was an integral part of Scott's concept: not only was the master gunlayer more likely to select the right target than blinded individual gunlayers, but once the target had been selected and range accurately measured, the simultaneous arrival of a blizzard of heavy shells would be far more devastating than even the accurate delivery of a single burst.

Scott's dream remained locked in his head when in 1910 he retired and went to work for Vickers. But he remained in constant contact with Jellicoe, who as Director of Naval Ordnance had recommended that all capital ships be equipped with Director Firing. Jellicoe carried his enthusiasm to the Home Fleet when, in December 1911, Churchill appointed him second in command. But the innovation continued to be rejected; Admiral Sir Francis Bridgeman, Commander-in-Chief of the Home Fleet and Jellicoe's superior, was one of many admirals who were determined to keep the old and—as they saw it—tried and true system of independent gunlaying. Director firing, they argued, was putting all one's eggs in a tiny, exposed basket. What would happen if the electrical lines from the director's perch to the guns were severed by shell fire—not to mention if the entire unarmored director's platform were shot away?

Scott knew he was right, and once he was out of the navy he could not be muzzled. He carried his case to Churchill and, with Churchillian persistence, insisted that the First Lord listen. Churchill warned that the Sea Lords were opposed, but in the end, Scott's demand that his system be exposed to a competitive trial appealed to him. By command of the First Lord, the new 13.5-inch-gun dreadnought *Thunderer* was equipped with Scott's director system. Her officers were dismayed—"We were by no means pleased at having this unpopular new system thrust upon us," discreetly complained the ship's gunnery officer—but worked diligently to master the techniques.

On November 12, 1912, off Berehaven, the trial toward which Scott had worked finally took place. Two new dreadnoughts, identical except that one had director firing and one did not, were to fire under the same conditions of range, light, and state of the ocean. *Thunderer*'s challenger was her sister *Orion,* which, using the old system of individual aiming and firing, had the best gunnery record in the Fleet. The sea was up, giving each ship a roll to the side of five degrees. They raised speed to twelve knots and then, steaming in line, each trained its guns on its own separate towed target nine thousand yards away. When the order to fire was given, each dreadnought had three minutes to bombard its own target. Time after time *Thunderer*'s salvos, sometimes of five guns, sometimes of the full ten, rolled out and smothered the target. She fired thirty-nine heavy shells in three minutes, scoring thirteen direct hits, two ricochets onto the target, and ten "possible hits" in the water (close enough to have hit a real ship bigger than the towed target). *Orion*'s

individual gunlayers could hardly find the target at all. The battleship fired twenty-seven times, scoring two hits, one ricochet, and one
"possible." The press, invited to observe, trumpeted the dimensions
of Scott's triumph: three times as many hits for *Thunderer,* said the
Daily Telegraph; five times as many, said *The Times;* the correct
figure was six times as many. Even after this test, "a very large
number of officers remained sceptical," wrote Jellicoe. "There was
considerable opposition and the great majority of ships were not
fitted with it." In fact, progress was slow, but steady. At Jutland,
only two of the thirty-six British dreadnoughts of Jellicoe's Grand
Fleet opened fire without benefit of Percy Scott's ingenious system.

As First Lord, Churchill focussed his prodigious energy and powers
of concentration on the navy. He was fascinated by the development
of technical innovations, which, incorporated into ships, could provide the fleet with a margin of superiority on the day of battle. But
there was more. Churchill was a romantic with a historical vision on
the grandest scale. He saw the great ships with which he had been
entrusted as figures in a gigantic drama of human destiny. On them,
on their sailors and officers, on the Admiralty, and on himself rode
the enormous weight of Britain's future. In a memorable passage in
The World Crisis, he described these feelings:

"I recall vividly my first voyage from Portsmouth to Portland
where the Fleet lay. A grey afternoon was drawing to a close. As I
saw the Fleet for the first time drawing out of the haze, a friend
reminded me of 'that far-off line of storm-beaten ships on which the
eyes of the Grand Army never looked' but which had in their day
'stood between Napoleon and the dominion of the world.' In Portland harbour the yacht lay surrounded by the great ships; the whole
harbour was alive with the goings and comings of launches and small
craft of every kind, and as night fell ten thousand lights from sea and
shore sprang into being and every masthead twinkled as the ships
and squadrons conversed with one another. Who could fail to work
for such a service? Who could fail when the very darkness seemed
loaded with the menace of approaching war?

"For consider these ships, so vast in themselves, yet so small, so
easily lost to sight on the surface of the waters. Sufficient at the
moment, we trusted, for their task, but yet only a score or so. They
were all we had. On them, as we conceived, floated the might, majesty, dominion and power of the British Empire. All our long history built up century after century, all our great affairs in every part
of the globe, all the means of livelihood and safety of our faithful,

industrious, active population depended upon them. Open the sea-cocks and let them sink beneath the surface, as another Fleet was one day to do in another British harbour far to the North, and in a few minutes—half an hour at the most—the whole outlook of the world would be changed. The British Empire would dissolve like a dream; each isolated community struggling forward by itself; the central power of union broken; mighty provinces, whole empires in themselves, drifting hopelessly out of control, and falling a prey to strangers; and Europe after one sudden convulsion passing into the iron grip and rule of the Teuton and of all that the Teutonic system meant. There would only be left far off across the Atlantic unarmed, unready, and as yet uninstructed America to maintain, single-handed, law and freedom among men. . . ."

CHAPTER 42

The
Haldane Mission

◆

The Agadir Crisis presented Admiral von Tirpitz with an opportunity. In the same week that Kiderlen was sitting down to bargain with Jules Cambon, and as the Berlin bourse sagged, rose, and finally crashed, Tirpitz went to the Palace and asked the Kaiser to endorse a new Supplementary Navy Law. Press, public, and the Reichstag were aroused against England. Some Germans wanted a showdown: "We all know that blood is assuredly about to be shed and the longer we wait, the more there will be," declared the *Post*. The showdown, Tirpitz urged, should come in the form of new ships. William embraced the idea and the *Novelle* was drafted. The "Risk Fleet" theory which had justified German shipbuilding since Tirpitz proposed the First Navy Law in 1898 "had fulfilled its purpose," William declared. The new objective would be a 2 : 3 ratio of dreadnoughts with the British Navy. A third battle squadron of eight dreadnought battleships would be added to the two battle squadrons now building. To achieve this, a faster building rate ("tempo") would be imposed. Instead of building two dreadnoughts a year beginning in 1912 and continuing for five years, the Imperial Navy would build three new ships every other year. The tempo over six years thus would rise from 2-2-2-2-2-2 to 3-2-3-2-3-2.

By 1918, the High Seas Fleet would possess fifteen new dreadnoughts rather than twelve.

Bethmann-Hollweg was aware that announcing a 2 : 3 ratio would alarm the British. They would react to the increased numbers of new ships and the admission that Germany was now building specifically against England; the German Fleet had always been described as being constructed "for our needs alone," without reference to any foreign power. During the autumn of 1911, the Kaiser and the Admiral did their best to persuade the Chancellor of the wisdom of the 2 : 3 ratio. "It readily grants the English an important supremacy and cuts short the talk of 'competitive building,'" William wrote to Bethmann-Hollweg. "It is at the same time a commitment to them, such as they have wished for, and surprises on our part are excluded, since the ratio is determined once and for all. . . . Whether they accept the ratio or not is immaterial."

Tirpitz argued a larger theme: "The purpose of our naval policy is political independence from England—the greatest possibility of security against an English attack. . . . To accomplish this . . . we must diminish the military distance between England and ourselves, not increase it. If we do not succeed, then our naval policy of the last fourteen years has been in vain."

Reports of a new Navy Bill and further expansion of the German Fleet reached England. Churchill, making his first speech as First Lord on November 9, 1911, offered conciliation and compromise. If no change was made in the long-established German building program, he said, Britain might be able to make large reductions in her Naval Estimates. Lloyd George agreed with the First Lord. "He [Lloyd George] felt that any effort should be made to heal friction with Germany and to arrive at a common understanding on naval strength," Churchill wrote. "We knew that a formidable new Navy Law was in preparation. If Germany had definitely made up her mind to challenge Great Britain, we must take it up; but it might be possible by friendly, sincere, and intimate conversation to avert this perilous development. We were no enemies to German colonial development. . . ." If the effort failed, the next step would be less difficult; "I felt I should be all the stronger in asking the Cabinet and Commons for money [for the Navy] if I could go hand in hand with the Chancellor of the Exchequer and testify that we had tried our best to secure a mitigation of the naval rivalry and failed."

In both countries there was support for resumption of the talks; in both countries there was opposition. Because of the opposition, the talks could not begin on an official level. Better that private, unofficial conversations take place between discreet nongovernmental figures. If these exploratory talks succeeded, official doors might open.

Two men, private citizens and friends, one in London and one in Hamburg and Berlin, were eager to serve as a link between their governments. Both were businessmen: one a financier, the other a shipping magnate. Each was close to his own monarch. Although one was now a British subject, both had been born in Germany. And although one was now a Roman Catholic, both had been born Jewish.

The King of England's most intimate friend was born into a German Jewish family in Cologne in 1852. Ernest Cassel was ambitious, self-confident, and tenacious of purpose; throughout his life he displayed judgment, drive, and unimpeachable integrity. Cassel's father, a bank official, took it as natural when his youngest son left school at fourteen to become a clerk and again when at seventeen Ernest emigrated to England with nothing but a valise and his violin. By twenty-two, Cassel had become London manager of the international financial house of Bischoffsheim and Goldschmidt at a salary of £5,000 a year. At twenty-six, he married Annette Maxwell, a Roman Catholic Englishwoman, celebrating the event by becoming, on the same day, a naturalized British subject. Three years later, in 1881, when Cassel was twenty-nine, Annette Cassel died of tuberculosis, leaving her husband with one daughter, Maud. He never remarried.

Cassel invested money in risky overseas projects with high profit potential. His specialty was railroads. He made a fortune developing Swedish railways that transported Swedish iron ore to ports for export. He acquired interests in Egypt, in Mexico, in South America, and in the United States, where railway building was heavily dependent on European capital.

A frequent visitor to New York, he formed a lifelong friendship with Jacob Schiff, the American railroad financier of the house of Kuhn, Loeb. Cassel had many American friends, who admired not only his great success and financial wisdom but his blunt speaking and his willingness to share contacts and information.

Penetrating the world of the landed aristocracy in England was more difficult. Wealth acquired in business closed as many doors as it opened. Cassel doggedly pursued entry into the patrician world. He rented, then purchased estates and country houses, showering invitations on the gentry and the peerage. He presented himself at the places they felt comfortable; he was seen at shooting parties, at the racetrack, at card tables. He learned to ride and hunt, although his seat was not firm and gates and hedges demanded courage. While he preferred the talented self-made men and women on the periphery of the social elite—Randolph Churchill and his son Winston, the Asquiths—he persevered with witless bores if their blood was sufficiently blue. He achieved success in 1901 when Maud married the Hon. Wilfred Ashley, a great-grandson of Lady Palmerston and heir to the stately Broadlands House in Hampshire.

It was Cassel's business reputation, not his social climbing, that brought him into contact with the Prince of Wales. The Prince liked self-made men; their conversation was generally more interesting. He liked men who were willing to spend their money on the diversions of life. Some—the Rothschilds, Baron Moritz Hirsch, Cassel— were Jews; others—Sir Thomas Lipton, the tea manufacturer and yachtsman, and Sir Blundell Maple, the furniture manufacturer— were not; the Prince did not care where or whether a man worshipped. Hirsch, who was born in Germany and had huge estates in Austria, was close to the Prince despite repeated snubs by both Continental and English aristocracy. Cassel met the prince through Hirsch; on Hirsch's death in 1896, Cassel became his executor. He also took over Hirsch's role as chief financial advisor to the prince. He assumed control of all of the Prince's investments and made it possible for the Heir to ascend to the throne in 1901 free of debt. In gratitude, the new King made Cassel a Privy Councilor in 1901. At the ceremony effecting this promotion, everyone except the King was astonished when Cassel asked to be sworn in on a Roman Catholic Bible; at that moment Sir Ernest revealed that his wife on her deathbed had begged him to be received into the Catholic church and that he had been converted soon after she died.

Cassel's friendship with the King was based on harmony of opinions and tastes. During the later years of his reign, the King visited Cassel's house in Park Lane almost every day for bridge. King Edward's death in 1910 was a blow; a heavier one fell a year later, when Cassel's daughter died, like his wife, of tuberculosis. Cassel was left with two granddaughters, on whom he lavished affection. By then he lived in Brook House, an enormous mansion in Park Lane filled with Old Masters, Renaissance bronzes, Chinese jade, Dresden porcelain, old English silver, and French and English inlaid furniture. It boasted an oak-panelled dining room capable of seating one hundred, six marble-lined kitchens, and an entrance hall paneled alternately with lapis lazuli and green-veined cream-colored marble. He also possessed three English country houses, a stud farm at Newmarket, an apartment in Paris, and villas in Switzerland and the south of France.*

Alfred Ballin, who built the Hamburg-America Line into the largest steamship company in the world, was a Hamburger. He was born one hundred feet from the harbor of the great port on the river Elbe sixty miles inland from the North Sea. His career was bound up with ships, free trade, and peaceful, international competition, the elements which had brought the city prosperity for over five hundred years. Hamburg's traditions as a free Hanseatic city and its role as gateway to the cluster of German states to the south and east went back to the Middle Ages. Prussia, geographically close, with its harsh military structure and agricultural economy, seemed remote in customs and feeling from democratic, mercantile Hamburg. For much of its history Hamburg's principal trading partner had been England. Well into the nineteenth century, there were more British ships in the harbor than vessels of any other nation, including Germany. Cargos of wool and coal came in from England; the ships refilled with grain and other foodstuffs for the voyage back. Then, after the middle of the century, a new cargo began passing across the Hamburg docks: people. As the population of the Empire increased, German peasants began leaving the land. In the 1860s, 1870s, and 1880s, waves of emigration passed through Hamburg and its sister port, Bremen on the river Weser. In 1881, 123,000 passengers sailed down the Elbe from Hamburg on a one-way trip to New York.

The North Atlantic passenger trade was Albert Ballin's proving ground. By 1886, at twenty-nine, Ballin was chief of the Passenger Division of the Hamburg-America Line (HAPAG). The competitive North German Lloyd Shipping Company, based in Bremen, predominated on the North Atlantic. NGL had forty-seven transatlantic steamships; Hamburg-America had only twenty-four. Ballin began to launch ships, among them a class of fast new luxury liners designed to make the voyage a pleasant rather than a disagreeable experience for those who could travel First Class. Ballin himself traveled frequently aboard his ships, always keeping an eye out for

---

* During the war, like many other naturalized British subjects born in Germany, Cassel was attacked for his birth. He died in 1921 at sixty-nine, while sitting at his desk in Brook House. Although he had given away over £2 million, primarily to schools and hospitals, his estate was worth over £7 million. A substantial sum went to his granddaughter Edwina Ashley, who soon after married Lord Louis Mountbatten. From her father, Edwina inherited Broadlands, which thus entered the Mountbatten family.

flaws. On board, moving from passenger to passenger, asking their impressions and recommendations while the nervous crew hovered nearby, he jotted entries in a notebook. One voyage to New York produced these items: "Notices on board to be restricted as much as possible; those which are necessary to be tastefully framed—no room for portmanteaux and trunks—towels too small—soiled linen cupboard too small—butter dishes too small—toast to be served in serviette *hot*." By 1899, when Ballin was forty-two, his innovations and relentless attention to detail had brought him rewards: his company was the largest in the world, possessing more tonnage than the combined merchant marine of any nation other than Great Britain or Germany. Albert Ballin was appointed managing director, a post he held for the rest of his life.

Ballin had a large round head framed by tight black curls, a large nose, and puffy lips. Nevertheless, he turned himself into the image of dapper charm. He grew a mustache, employed a pince-nez, and always appeared in elegant clothes, whether he wore a top hat at the Hamburg stock exchange or was dressed in yachting costume aboard one of his ocean liners. He was warm and graceful, possessed faultless manners, and had numerous friends in his own city, in England, and in America. His wife, whom he married when he was twenty-six, was a middle-class Protestant woman, several years older and a few inches taller than her husband. She was warm and immensely proud of him, but preferred to remain in the background. When, after eleven years, no children were born, they adopted a daughter.

As managing director, Ballin was in a position to open Hamburg-America's lead over the competition. Other companies and other nations did not give up. In 1902, the British government, distressed to see the mercantile trident passing into German hands, awarded Cunard an annual subsidy of £150,000. In the years that followed, Cunard began to build two 32,000-ton transatlantic express liners, *Mauretania* and *Lusitania*. The British White Star Line countered by launching the *Olympia*, the *Titanic*, and the *Gigantic*. Ballin refused to be outbuilt. Three new Hamburg-America liners were ordered from the Vulcan Works in Stettin and Blohm and Voss in Hamburg. *Imperator* came down the ways in 1912; *Vaterland* followed in 1913 and *Bismarck* in 1914. The most famous of these ships was *Vaterland*, a mammoth 54,000 tons, not only the largest vessel in the world, but—as the steamship company proudly pointed out—the largest moving object ever created by man. She was designed to carry over five thousand people (a crew of 1,234 and 4,050 passengers) at twenty-four knots across the Atlantic in less than a week. The first-class passengers would travel in unparalleled luxury. Ladies could bathe in the indoor Pompeii-style "swimming bath," which extended through three decks and offered water eight feet deep. Gentlemen, after dining in the Ritz-Carlton restaurant, where tables were set with flowers produced in the ship's own greenhouse, could retire to sit in high-backed chairs before the glowing hearth of an enormous fireplace in a high-beamed, oak-paneled smoking room which smacked more of a Bavarian castle than an ocean liner. For those who could afford it, the ship supplied extravagant space; the largest suites aboard the *Vaterland* each contained twelve rooms.

Ballin's first meeting with the Kaiser was in 1891, when the young Emperor brought his wife to inspect the new *Auguste Victoria,* which Ballin had named after her. William first took Ballin's measure, however, at a conference at the Berlin Castle in 1895, called by the sovereign to discuss the celebrations which were to surround the opening of the Kiel Canal. It was arranged, the Kaiser announced, that the *Hohenzollern* would steam down the Elbe to the mouth of the canal followed first by a North German Lloyd steamship, then by a vessel of the Hamburg-America Line. Ballin asked to speak: as the ceremonial voyage was to commence in Hamburg he said, perhaps it would be more appropriate for a Hamburg-America steamer to have the place of honor behind the Imperial yacht. Frostily, the Kaiser replied that he had already promised the place to the Bremen company. Ballin declared that, then of course, the matter was settled "and that he would withdraw his suggestion, although he considered himself justified in making it."

The development of a great merchant marine was closely connected in William's mind with the rise of the Imperial Navy, and he was proud of the success of HAPAG. He took a proprietary air toward the steamship line, frequently sending Ballin suggestions and even drawings concerned with equipment and design. On every occasion when the company made news—when launching a new ship or adding a new route—a congratulatory Imperial telegram arrived on Ballin's desk. William liked Ballin personally; they shared a fascination for ships and the sea, an itch to travel, and a desire for German greatness. The Kaiser sent Ballin Christmas cards and dropped him postcards from his travels. When Ballin suffered neuralgic pains, William recommended doctors and even proposed sending a court official to Ballin's office to help diminish the workload on his overburdened friend.

Beginning with an invitation from Ballin in 1899, the Kaiser and his entourage began attending the annual HAPAG dinner every

June before the Lower Elbe Regatta and Kiel Week. Ballin understood his sovereign's weakness for pageantry and elegance, and he
had the means to play upon it. His ships, floating palaces, were
always at the Emperor's disposal. Every year, Ballin dispatched one
of his finest ships to serve as a floating hotel for guests of the Kaiser,
the Court, or the government. Rising up behind the lines of gray
warships and the flocks of steam and sailing yachts anchored in the
fjord, the great black-hulled HAPAG liner with its white superstructure and blue trim added a touch of splendor. On several occasions,
the Kaiser himself chose to cruise aboard HAPAG liners rather
than on board the *Hohenzollern.* (One such cruise occured in 1905
when William descended over the side of the Hamburg-America's
Hamburg to make his famous landing at Tangier.) For many years,
all HAPAG liners kept several cabins ready to be used by any persons designated by the Emperor. In 1905, during his visits to Hamburg, William began to dine at Ballin's house. In time, these visits
became so frequent that Ballin's house was called Klein Potsdam
(Little Potsdam). But when he accepted Ballin's hospitality, the Kaiser did not bring his wife. The Kaiserin Augusta Victoria did not
approve of her husband's friendship with the steamship owner. Ballin was a Jew.

Heinrich von Treitschke at the University of Berlin helped give respectability to German anti-Semitism. In his writings and lectures,
he warned against the growing power of the Jews and their subversion of German ideals. Jews who wished to enjoy the full privileges
of German citizenship should give up their religion and embrace
Christianity, Treitschke argued. Otherwise, Jews should be barred
from service in the institutions of the state. In practice, this was
largely the case. There were no practicing Jews in the Imperial Diplomatic Service and very few in the officer corps of the army; those
who did get in were assigned to inferior posts and never promoted.
Jews unwilling to give up their faith and be baptized were barred
from the Imperial Navy; the official excuse was "dietary difficulties."

The German Jew who rose highest in German society during
the Imperial years was Gerson Bleichroder, Bismarck's banker. His
rise dramatized the power of money. He was the richest man in
Berlin, possibly the richest in Germany. He managed the Chancellor's fortune and made the Chancellor rich. He was the first German
Jew to be ennobled without converting to Christianity. Bleichroder
hungered for acceptance into Prussian society. In his huge Berlin

mansion, he gave lavish balls, inviting the cream of society, persuading even Princess von Bismarck to attend. But many stayed away, including the young officers whose presence graced every other ball. Bleichroder's daughter was left in her chair at balls in her own house because no young man would ask her to dance. No Jews, not even relatives, were invited to these parties lest the other guests be offended.

Bismarck's anti-Semitism was bland, but ingrained. He gave Bleichroder a *von* but never allowed the banker to forget his origins. Referring to Harden, the editor of the *Zunkunft*, the Chancellor said that he was "a quiet unpretentious man of great tact, not at all like a Jew." Commenting on the qualities of two Prussian officials whose German fathers had married Jewish women, Bismarck observed that "the pairing of a German stallion with a Semitic mare occasionally did not produce bad results." Other Prussian aristocrats expressed themselves bluntly. "I am no friend of Jews," Eulenburg announced. Holstein wrote in his journal, "I heard a few days ago that Bleichroder wants to get his son into the diplomatic service. He will not succeed."

William II's attitude toward Jews was that of many of his countrymen. Bülow considered the Kaiser "in no way prejudiced against Jews" but William's conversation and correspondence belied this absolution. With wealthy Jews, successful in business and finance, William's relations were good, even cordial; to Jewish press lords and socialists he was vindictively, sneeringly hostile. Once, in the middle of a diatribe, William was reminded that his friends Ballin and the banker Franz von Mendelssohn were Jews. The Kaiser paused, then declared that he did not consider them to be Jews at all. Being received by the monarch did not mean, however, that these Jewish financiers and industrialists were admitted into Prussian society. They saw the Emperor during the day at luncheons at the Schloss or Potsdam or even in hunting parties at Romintern. Very rarely did a Jew receive an invitation to one of the formal Court evenings which were the pinnacle of Berlin society. Nor was the Prussian aristocracy enthusiastic about the Kaiser's friendship with certain Jews. The old accusations bubbled up: the ancient supremacy of the land was being undermined by money; the Jews were acquiring too much influence and social respectability; too many Jews were marrying off their daughters to poor aristocrats and government officials. Princess Daisy of Pless spoke of "the Jewish peril." The Kaiser's title "Seine Majestät" (His Majesty) was sneeringly twisted into "Siegfried Meyer."

Ballin did his best to ignore anti-Semitism. He was not a religious man. He rarely attended synagogue, preferring to work on weekends through the Jewish and Christian sabbaths alike. He considered himself a Hamburger; he ate, drank, smoked, and spoke as a Hamburger. He was aware that there was anti-Semitism in Hamburg, but the lines were clearly defined and, in the cosmopolitan atmosphere of the old port city, there was no animosity. His business colleagues and his employees were mostly Christian, yet when he took coffee at a table in the Alster Pavillion, his companions usually were Jews. His greatest friend was Max Warburg of the dynasty which had presided over one of Europe's great international banking houses since the eighteenth century. Most of Ballin's vacations were taken on board his own ships; when he went to a sanatorium at Kissingen to relax by reading detective thrillers, the other guests at the sanatorium were exclusively Jewish. Ballin's view was that this was the world and he accepted it. He disdained the efforts of some wealthy Jews to break into the upper reaches of German society; these efforts, he believed, increased anti-Semitism.

Although Ballin had little in common with the Prussian aristocracy, he shared its fervent belief in maintaining order and upholding the rights of property. He was a dedicated monarchist— "The essential thing is the throne," he wrote to Harden in 1909, "the republicans . . . are loathsome"—and vociferously supported the government's policy of promoting Germany's economic role in the world. He despised Social Democrats and worried about the growing power of socialists in the Reichstag. The German Foreign Office he considered "very largely a special preserve for aristocratic incompetents" and the bureaucracy in general petty and obtuse. But on a day-to-day basis it was predictable and efficient, and this was good for business. Ballin believed that the role of government was to clear the path for the real pioneers of Germany's future, the great financiers and industrialists. In this sense, his building of the Hamburg-America Line with the Kaiser's enthusiastic support was an example of how things should work.

When Tirpitz proposed the First Navy Law in 1898, Ballin was among his firmest supporters. Hamburg-America was a shipping line whose operations and viability depended on keeping the sealanes open and world markets available to its ships. The huge fleet of passenger liners and freighters which Ballin had built up could not be left unprotected by warships. In 1898, HAPAG informed the Emperor that the "strengthening of the war fleet necessary for Germany's welfare" gave the company "great pleasure." By 1900, Ballin's support had become grandiloquent: "The fleet is . . . the embodiment of the national purpose of a 'greater Germany' and of imperial power. . . . In the brutal struggle of nations for light and air, strength alone counts. . . . Germany has an incomparable land army, but beyond the seas only its warships can create respect for it. Without the support of a strong fleet, whose iron core can only be made up of battleships, Germany has no real power against the tiniest exotic state." Ballin assisted Tirpitz in practical ways, sending the Admiral a constant stream of information on matters of naval interest, gleaned from his own reading and the reports of his ship captains and engineers. He served on the governing board of the Hamburg chapter of the Navy League, and when the League convened in Hamburg he invited hundreds of members to cruise on the Elbe aboard HAPAG steamships.

As the High Seas Fleet continued to grow, it was obvious that it was not being built to deal with "tiny exotic states." Ballin had known that it was being built against England and he had publicly expressed his agreement with Tirpitz's Risk Theory. Eventually, however, his German national pride and his common sense as a shipowner came into conflict. Ballin knew England as well as any foreigner. He visited frequently in London, had many English friends, and was a regular reader of the London papers. As a businessman, he saw the British as competitors, not enemies. Over the years, despite overwhelming naval supremacy, Great Britain had done nothing to prevent Germany from acquiring colonies or creating the largest merchant steamship company in the world. In Singapore, Hong Kong, and dozens of other British colonial ports, German merchant ships had been welcomed and serviced as quickly and efficiently as British competitors. Where there was a threat from pirates or exotic potentates to the ships or citizens of any European nation, the Royal Navy had stepped in as an international police force. It would be better, of course, if this overwhelming world sea power were German, but since Britain would do whatever was necessary to maintain her naval supremacy, Germany was unlikely to overtake her. Once the German Fleet had reached respectable size, why not stop at a point which the British found unthreatening?

It was this kind of reasoning, and his growing awareness that German fleet-building was stirring British fears and forcing England into anti-German diplomatic alignments, that led Ballin in 1908 to turn against Admiral von Tirpitz. After the war began, Ballin wrote to Harden about the Admiral's obsession with ships. By implication, he was admitting his own failure to recognize this obsession earlier, when he might have done something to combat it:

"Tirpitz . . . did not wish to negotiate. He wanted no settlement, he wanted only to build ships. He put obstacles in the way of every understanding with England, even though at the time [Ballin was speaking of 1908–1909] every intelligent man had to admit that limitless construction on the part of both sides was a race which England was always destined to win because of much greater resources."

In June 1908, Max Warburg introduced his Hamburg friend Albert Ballin to his London friend Ernest Cassel. The two men spoke of the deterioration in Anglo-German relations. Cassel said frankly that his friend King Edward was worried about the menace posed to Britain by the rapid increase in the strength of the German Fleet. Ballin retorted that the British Navy with its overwhelming numbers had nothing to fear from Germany. He reported the conversation to the Kaiser, to Bülow (still Chancellor), and to Schoen, the State Secretary. A year later, in June 1909, Ballin met Cassel again. By then, the atmosphere had been disturbed by William's letter to Lord Tweedmouth and by his *Daily Telegraph* interview. Cassel had written to Ballin earlier in the spring that German shipbuilding was the "Alpha and Omega of English mistrust." At Kiel Week, just before he left for London, Ballin had proposed to the Kaiser that he sound out Cassel about the prospect of direct Anglo-German talks on naval arms limitation. Ballin's idea was that Tirpitz meet Fisher. Cassel confided in Ballin that the Liberal government felt burdened by the arms race and wanted to shift its focus to social programs. Britain would insist on maintaining naval supremacy, but was not averse to seeking some mutually acceptable ratio of naval strength. The government, he had ascertained, would be ready to hold discussions. "Such a meeting," Ballin reported to the Kaiser, "would have to be kept absolutely secret and both parties should agree that there should be no victor and no vanquished if and when an agreement was concluded." William congratulated Ballin on the skill with which he had conducted his mission.

This private effort by the two businessmen was sidetracked by a political event four days after Ballin's report to the Kaiser: on June 14, 1909, Bülow resigned. Bethmann, new to his office and untried in diplomacy, was disturbed by the concept of private citizens holding diplomatic discussions, even with the approval of their governments. The Imperial Chancellor and the Foreign Office were the proper institutions for conducting foreign policy, Bethmann believed, and he meant to take Anglo-German relations firmly into his own hands. Relations with England were "*his* department" and "*his* specialty," the Chancellor declared. It was the end of the first mutual effort of Ballin and Cassel to stop the armament race.

Bethmann's efforts were unsuccessful, and by the beginning of

1912 the Agadir Crisis and the proposal for a new German Supplementary Navy Law had made the prospects for arms limitation even more bleak. Neither Ballin or Cassel had given up hope, however, and the appointment of Winston Churchill as First Lord seemed to open a new path to negotiations. Early in January, Ballin wrote to Cassel suggesting that on his next visit to Germany he bring Churchill along. If this could be arranged, Ballin would endeavor to produce Admiral von Tirpitz so that the two navy ministers could sit down face to face in the manner of businessmen and iron out their differences. Cassel spoke to Churchill, who demurred from travelling with him but said that he might come in a party with King George V if the Kaiser could be persuaded to invite his English cousin to Berlin. In those circumstances, and providing Asquith and Grey agreed, Churchill said, he would "feel highly honored" to sit down with Tirpitz. Cassel enthusiastically endorsed Ballin's sentiments about the new First Lord:

"His friendly sentiments towards Germany are known to you. I have been acquainted with him since he was quite a young man and he has never made a secret of his admiration of the Kaiser and of the German people. He looks upon the estrangement existing between the two countries as senseless and I am quite sure he would do anything in his power to establish friendly relations.

"The real crux of the situation is that Great Britain regards the enormous increase of the German Navy as a grave menace to her vital interests. This conviction is a deep-rooted one and there are no two opinions in London as to its significance. If it were possible to do something which, without endangering the safety of Germany, would relieve Britain of this nightmare, it is my opinion that people over here would go very far to conciliate German aspirations."

Through Churchill, the Ballin-Cassel proposal that negotiations be reopened by a backdoor route was brought before the British Cabinet. Lloyd George and Churchill warmly supported the unusual idea. In the end, the Cabinet authorized Cassel to go to Berlin to determine whether Ballin was speaking only for himself or whether his views were shared.

On the morning of January 29, 1912, Ballin appeared at the Berlin Castle and asked for an audience with the Emperor. William assumed that his friend was paying a simple birthday visit and was surprised when Ballin told him that Sir Ernest Cassel was in Berlin on a secret mission from the British government and wished to be received at the highest level. In fact, Ballin continued, Sir Ernest had told him that the Cabinet in London had given explicit instructions that he was to evade all diplomatic officials, British and German. William was intrigued and sent for Cassel. When the Englishman arrived, he handed over a document which, he told the Kaiser, had been "prepared with the approval and knowledge of the British Government." The memorandum contained three proposals, which, if accepted by the German government, could lead to a reduction of tension. In the Kaiser's own words, these proposals were, first, "Acceptance of British superiority at sea; no augmentation of the German naval program—a reduction as far as possible of this program"; second, Great Britain would offer "no impediment to our colonial expansion" and "discussion and promotion of our colonial ambitions"; third, the memorandum proposed "mutual declarations that the two powers would not take part in aggressive combinations against each other."

Later, in his memoirs, William claimed that he saw immediately that the "verbal note was aimed at our Naval Law and designed to delay or frustrate it." At the time he was sufficiently interested to telephone Bethmann, who came immediately. He, like the Kaiser, was astonished. Tirpitz was summoned. Cassel requested that, if possible, he be permitted to return to London that night with a preliminary reaction from the German government. The Kaiser agreed. It was decided that the German reply should be written in English "for fear of obscurity and misunderstanding if the note were translated in London." The Chancellor asked the Emperor to draw up the note, "since I knew English best," William recalled. The following scene, described in the Kaiser's words, took place:

"I sat at the writing table in the adjutant's room, the other gentlemen stood around me. I would read a sentence from the [British] note aloud and sketch out an answer, which was, in turn, read aloud. Then criticisms were made right and left; one thought the sentence too complaisant, another too abrupt; it was thereupon remodelled, recast, improved and polished. The Chancellor particularly subjected my grammar and style to much torture, owing to his habit of probing things philosophically. . . . After hours of work the note was finally finished and, having been passed a couple of times from hand to hand and then read aloud by me half a dozen times more, it was signed."

When the group broke up, Bethmann asked Cassel who would come from England for the negotiations. Cassel replied that he did not know, but surmised that it would be a minister, probably Churchill. Cassel, pleased with his reception in Berlin, returned to London carrying the Kaiser's note, which expressed approval of private negotiations and invited an English Cabinet Minister to Berlin. He also carried a long statement from Bethmann-Hollweg about the new Supplementary Navy Law which, the Chancellor declared, the German government was not inclined to modify. Arriving in London, Cassel went straight to Churchill and delivered the statement. "We devoured this document all night long in the Admiralty," Churchill wrote, and in the morning he sent his analysis to Sir Edward Grey: "The spirit may be good, but the facts are grim," the First Lord declared. Britain had expected Germany to continue building two new dreadnoughts a year for the six-year period beginning in 1912, equipping the High Seas Fleet with twelve new capital ships by 1918. The new Navy Law proposed adding a third ship every other year, for a total of fifteen new dreadnoughts by 1918. Against the older formula, the Royal Navy building program had been 4-3-4-3-4-3 over the same period, so that Germany's twelve new ships would have been matched against twenty-one new British dreadnoughts. Now, if the new Navy Law was passed—and Churchill told Grey that passage seemed certain: "even the Socialists are not resisting"—England would have to up her building program to 5-4-5-4-5-4 for a total of twenty-seven new dreadnoughts against the German fifteen. Churchill also noted the creation of a third battle squadron, additions to the personnel of the German Fleet allowing "full commission of 25 battleships" and exposing Britain to "constant danger approximating war conditions." This could be met, he concluded, only by adding £3 million a year to the British Naval Estimates. "This is certainly not dropping the naval challenge." Churchill also noted the German reaction to Britain's offer of helping to promote German colonial expansion: "Cassel says they did not seem to know what they wanted in regard to colonies. They did not seem to be greatly concerned about expansion. 'There were ten large companies in Berlin importing labor *into* Germany.' Overpopulation was not their problem."

When the Cabinet met, it was decided that neither Churchill nor Grey should go to Berlin. Churchill wrote later that "there never was any question of my going . . . nor did I at this time wish to go." Grey did not go for a number of reasons. He had been asked by Asquith to mediate between the coal-mine owners and the strikers, and those negotiations were at a critical point. If the Foreign Secretary went to Berlin, it would be impossible to keep the Anglo-German negotiations private or to downplay the significance of any failure. And, most important to Grey himself, his appearance in Berlin would arouse suspicion and distrust in Paris. The key to

Grey's foreign policy, more significant than any limitation of naval building, was support of France and the Entente.

The minister chosen was Haldane.

Although the British Royal Family had been predominantly German since 1714 when George Louis, Elector of Hanover, mounted the throne as King George I, Ministers of the British Crown never learned to speak German.* The one exception was Richard Burdon Haldane, Asquith's Minister of War and subsequently Lord Chancellor. Haldane spoke German fluently, revered German philosophy, and basked in the pleasures of his long sojourns in German towns and countryside.

There was not a drop of German blood in Richard Burdon Haldane. He was a Scot from Perthshire and Edinburgh, where his father was a solicitor and a fervent Baptist. When he reached university age, he wanted to go to Balliol but his parents fretted over rumors of the dominant influence of the Anglican Church at Oxford. Haldane, with the help of an Edinburgh professor of Greek, persuaded Haldane Senior to permit a course of study in philosophy at the University of Göttingen. At age seventeen, Haldane first arrived in Germany. His first impression on a gray dawn in Göttingen "was to see a woman and a dog drawing along the street a cart containing a man and a calf." His professors were woebegone: they "looked as if they had seen more books than soap or tailors' shops. Most of them are men of about sixty, wearing colored spectacles, broad Tyrolean hats, with dirty, badly shaven faces and their clothes almost tumbling off. They lecture, sometimes in Latin, sometimes in German." Haldane grew his own hair long, grew a mustache, and bathed in the river, which, like the entire town, reeked of tanning. He moved on to the University of Dresden, where he read Kant and Hegel.

Returning to Scotland, Haldane was confronted with a demand by his father that he be baptized. He consented on condition that he be permitted to make a statement afterward. The ceremony concluded, "I rose dripping from the font and, facing the congregation, announced to them that I had consented to go through what had taken place only to allay the anxiety of my parents, but that . . . I could not accept their doctrines and that I regarded what had taken

---

* If they learned a foreign language at all, it was French. In Asquith's Liberal Cabinet, none of the ministers even spoke French, except Churchill, who spoke it with a grandly atrocious accent.

place as the merest external ceremony; and that for the future I had no connection with the church or its teaching or with any other church. I then changed my clothes and walked away from the building. There was much consternation, but nothing was said, probably because there was nothing to say."

In 1877, at twenty-one, Haldane entered chambers in London, reading and drafting papers for a solicitor in Lincoln's Inn. Nothing in the law "seemed difficult in comparison with sifting the books of the German metaphysicians," he recorded in his *Memoirs*. The law became his passion, and he sat up at night in bed reading lawbooks. In 1880, he began his own practice; his fees totaled £31, 10s. In 1881, his income rose to £109; the year after, £160. In 1884, it soared to £1,100. (By 1905, the year before he became Minister of War, Haldane earned over £20,000 annually, although his political duties kept him from full application.) As a young man, he worked in his office until midnight and eschewed vacations. "Of sport and of general society I saw almost nothing in my early days in London," he wrote. "The outcome of this was a certain awkwardness. Moreover, I had no attractive presence . . . and I had a bad voice. These were serious deficiencies for a career at the bar. On the other hand, I could sit down and think systematically, and I had an accurate memory which let slip little of what I had read. . . . I was active and tenacious . . . and was confident, probably to an undue extent, of my power to succeed in whatever I undertook."

Haldane's reputation brought him regularly before the Privy Council and the House of Lords, sitting as judicial bodies. In 1885, at twenty-nine, he entered the House of Commons as Liberal member for East Lothian. The following year, he arranged for his friend and fellow lawyer, H. H. Asquith, to enter Parliament as the member for East Fife.

Haldane was shy around women. He fell in love once, in 1890, at the age of thirty-four. Engagement and "weeks of unbroken happiness" followed. Then, "suddenly, without previous warning, and as a bolt from an unclouded sky, there came to me a note saying that all was over . . . the decision was as irrevocable as it was rapid. . . . Only once or twice again in the course of my life did I see her and then only momentarily and casually. My grief was overwhelming. . . . To this hour, I treasure the memory of those five happy weeks and bless her name. . . . She died in 1897." Haldane remained a bachelor, fond of dogs. He lived with his unmarried sister in London in a tiny house in Queen Anne's Gate and wrote to his mother every day. Beginning in 1898, he began a regular series of annual visits to Weimar during the Easter parliamentary recess. His companion was Professor Hume Brown of Edinburgh University, who was at work on a life of Goethe. Haldane relished these visits to the country of his university years, and the excursions continued even after he became War Minister and traveled incognito as "Mr. Brown."

The purpose of Haldane's visit to Berlin was hidden by an announcement that the War Minister, who was also Chairman of the Royal Commission on the University of London, would be visiting to study developments in German technical education. He carried a message from the Cabinet declaring that "the new German program would entail serious and immediate increase of British naval expenditure . . . [This] would make negotiations difficult if not impossible." Haldane was instructed to suggest that the Germans slow their rate of new construction.

The visit, which came to be called the Haldane Mission, lasted four days. On Thursday, February 8, Haldane arrived on the overnight train at Berlin's Friedrichstrasse Station. Sir Edward Goschen's car took him to the Hotel Bristol near the Embassy. At ten A.M., Goschen came to brief him: Bethmann was coming to the Embassy for lunch at noon and would remain afterward for a private talk. The Chancellor had asked about Haldane's status, public or private, saying that he could not divest himself of his own official position; he had been told that the War Minister was coming on behalf of the Cabinet, but that the talks would be exploratory and that Haldane had no power to make a firm commitment on any point.

At two P.M., after lunch, Bethmann and Haldane met alone. They spoke mostly in German, with Haldane occasionally switching to English to clarify a delicate point and the Chancellor also speaking English to signify his understanding. The first subjects were political. Haldane described English fears over the rise of the German Navy. This was the only obstacle to good relations as "the Morocco question was now out of the way and we had no agreements with France or Russia except those that were in writing and published to the world." Interrupting, the Chancellor asked whether this was really true; Haldane solemnly promised that it was. They talked about Agadir. Bethmann complained about war preparations in the British Fleet and Army during the crisis. Haldane dismissed the complaint by saying that Britain had done only what German officers—General Moltke, for example—would consider as "matters of routine." Bethmann accepted this explanation. The Chancellor brought up the question of neutrality: could England and Germany agree to stay out of any war involving the other? Haldane pointed out that Britain could no more permit France to be crushed while she remained a spectator than Germany could allow England to seize Denmark or attack Austria. Later, speaking of Haldane, Bethmann wrote: "he really was apparently afraid that we would break loose against France if we were sure of the neutrality of England. I replied that the policy of peace which Germany had pursued for more than forty years ought to save her from such a question. If we had planned robber-like attacks, we had the best opportunity during the South African War and the Russo-Japanese War." Haldane acknowledged that England probably would accept a mutual undertaking of neutrality in case the other had to deal with an unprovoked, aggressive attack by a third Great Power. The Chancellor said that one could not easily define "aggression" or "unprovoked attack." Haldane retorted that one "could not define the number of grains it took to make a heap, but one knew a heap when one saw one."

The conversation then turned to the matter of the German Fleet and the new Navy Law. What was the value, Haldane asked, in trying to establish better relations if Germany was going to enlarge her battle fleet and Britain had to respond by increasing hers? If the Germans created a third squadron, Britain would have to counter with five or even six squadrons, perhaps bringing ships now in the Mediterranean back to home waters. The proposal to add a new third ship every other year was even more serious. "We should certainly have to lay down two keels to each one of the newest German additions," Haldane declared. The Chancellor asked whether this would really be the case. Haldane replied that unless it did so, the government would be turned out. Nevertheless, Bethmann said, it was necessary for Germany to create the third squadron, and to do this some additional ships would have to be built. The Chancellor asked Haldane whether he saw a way out of their mutual dilemma. As instructed by the Cabinet, Haldane then proposed a spreading out of the new building program, a reduction of the "tempo." "Perhaps over eight or nine years instead of six?" the Chancellor asked. "Or twelve," said Haldane. Bethmann shook his head doubtfully. "My admirals are very difficult," he said.

Despite obstacles, the two men had talked openly, had identified areas of trouble, and had discussed possible solutions. Bethmann, who had been attempting for two years to bring about an agreement between Germany and England, went off to give the Emperor an optimistic report. Haldane's hopes were just as high. "It was not a case of two diplomats fencing," he declared in his *Memoirs*. "It was two men trying to meet on common ground to accomplish the highest ideal which was possible to mortals." "The atmosphere which resulted was marvellous," he wrote to his mother that night. "The prospect for the moment is very good. I seem to have been inspired by new power."

The Kaiser was affected by this spirit of optimism. The following day, he and Tirpitz were scheduled to sit down with Haldane and, before the British Minister arrived, William wrote to his naval aide, "There is no doubt that in large measure the fate of the Entente, and of Germany, and the whole world depends on today's conversation between Tirpitz and Haldane. It is imperative that Tirpitz realize this. He must work in an open and frank manner without any suspicion and mental reservations. If he succeeds and England and Germany come to an understanding, then I will announce it so that Germany and the whole world will be thankful to him as the man who made peace. Then he will hold a position in the world which no German minister has held since Bismarck."

At noon on Friday, February 9, Haldane went for lunch at the Castle with the Kaiser, the Kaiserin, their daughter Princess Victoria Louise, the Chancellor, and Admiral Tirpitz. After the meal, William produced his famous pink champagne and a silver plate of excellent cigars and read from Goethe's poem "Ilmenau." He invited Haldane and Tirpitz—but not Bethmann—into his private study to discuss the competition in shipbuilding. Because of Admiral Tirpitz, the Emperor explained, the conversation would have to be largely in German. But, he said with a smile, he had found a way to adjust "the balance of power." Leading the two men to a small, narrow table, he placed Haldane in the larger chair at the head of the table, put the Admiral on the visitor's left, and himself sat down on Haldane's right. Once they were seated, the Kaiser leaned over and relit Haldane's cigar. Then began an afternoon of talk, the only occasion in the seventeen years between 1897 and 1914 when Tirpitz, the architect and builder of the High Seas Fleet, ever sat down with a Cabinet Minister of the British government.

William began by saying that, although they were there to discuss naval questions, it was clear that an agreement would benefit both nations and the world. Haldane declared again that for England, the fundamental issue was German shipbuilding. Before any political agreement could be reached, he said, a serious modification of the German building program had to occur; any general political agreement would be "bones without flesh" if the Reich increased its shipbuilding and forced Great Britain to follow at a rate of two keels to one; the British public "would laugh at the agreement and . . . think we had been befooled." Tirpitz proposed a fixed 3 : 2 relationship of fleets (three British battleships for every two German battleships), declaring that Britain's insistence on a Two Power Standard was "hard" for Germany. Politely, Haldane declined, reminding him that England, as an island state, had to be equal at sea to any possible combination of enemies.

Tirpitz pointed out that the 1912 *Novelle* already had been modified: originally he had planned to ask for three new ships a year and had reduced the program to a third ship every other year. These ships, he declared, were essential to creation of the third battle squadron, necessary for the defense of the Empire. "Admiral Tirpitz is a strong and difficult man—a typical Prussian—and he and I fought stiffly," Haldane reported later. "There was perfect politeness but neither of us would move from his position. Under pressure from the Emperor, I got a substantial concession."

The Kaiser, according to Haldane, was "so disturbed" by the impasse and so eager for some agreement to come from the meeting that he applied Bethmann's tactic of the previous day and asked Haldane what he would suggest. Haldane repeated: "Can we not spread out the tempo?," putting off the first of the extra dreadnoughts from 1912 to 1913, and adding the other two in 1916 and 1919 rather than in 1914 and 1916 . To this plan, the Kaiser and Tirpitz eventually agreed; this delay presumably was the "substantial concession" which Haldane later claimed. Even so, Haldane pointed out to the two Germans, no matter when the extra ships were laid down, Britain would lay two new keels for every German keel. The initiative for speeding up or slowing down thus lay with Germany. About five P.M., after almost three hours, the talk came to an end and the Kaiser asked Tirpitz to drive Haldane back to the Hotel Bristol. Once his guest had left, the Emperor sat down and wrote a cheerful note to Ballin: "The third squadron will be asked for and voted, but the building of the three additional units required to complete it will not be started until 1913 and one ship each will be demanded in 1916 and 1919 respectively. Haldane agreed to this and expressed satisfaction. I have made no end of concessions. . . . He [Haldane] was very nice and reasonable. Please remember me to Cassel."

Haldane's day was far from over. He left the Bristol for No. 76 Wilhelmstrasse to call on State Secretary Kiderlen, who had been thoroughly ignored. Haldane spoke to Kiderlen only generally, "for I had the strong impression that the Chancellor did not want him to have a part in the conversation." Subsequently, Haldane went to the

Chancellor's house to dine with Bethmann, Kiderlen, and General Paul von Hindenburg. After dinner, the Chancellor took Haldane aside. Bethmann seemed depressed and said that he had heard "that I was disappointed at the slightness of the slackening in the German building program. I could see that this great, simple man was feeling that his difficulties with his own people were very great." Perhaps, had the Chancellor known, or had Haldane told him then, that the Briton considered the concessions granted by Tirpitz and the Emperor to be "substantial," it might have eased Bethmann's sense of worry. Haldane did not tell him.

Before he slept that night, the British War Minister had one more appointment to keep. At ten P.M. he met the French Ambassador, Jules Cambon, at the British Embassy to brief him on the two days of discussions. Cambon was nervous; the most Germanophile Minister in the British Cabinet was negotiating outside normal diplomatic channels with the three highest figures in the Imperial government. Haldane reassured him: "I said emphatically that we were not going to be disloyal to France or Russia and that the Chancellor understood and agreed." Cambon produced a diplomatic phrasing to describe Haldane's effort: the Minister was trying to create "a détente, rather than an entente."

The following day, Saturday, Haldane heard again, this time from Baron von Stumm of the Foreign Office, that the Chancellor, whom the War Minister was meeting later in the day, was "depressed" by the thought that Haldane believed that no agreement could be made because of the limited German shipbuilding concessions. "The Chancellor," Stumm confided, "was not going to let this agreement—which was the dream of his life—founder because of Tirpitz." Stumm suggested that Bethmann's chances of getting the Emperor to eliminate ships would be much improved if Haldane "took a very strong line to the effect that there must be further naval concessions."

When Haldane met the Chancellor at five P.M., he expressed his doubt that the British Cabinet would be satisfied with a mere spreading out of the new building program. Bethmann declared that the German public expected the third squadron and he must produce it, but that as to the number of new ships and the timing he would do his best. He reiterated his hope that German naval concessions could be linked to a neutrality agreement. Haldane repeated that any political agreement would depend on a shipbuilding agreement. The two men spoke in the friendliest manner. "We sat down at a table with pencils and paper and went on a voyage of discovery," Haldane said later. "At the end . . . he rose and took me by the hand and held it and said that the moment of his life that he had longed for seemed to have come. If we failed, it would be Destiny. But we had, he knew, done all that two men could." "Whether success or failure crowned the effort . . . he would never forget that I had met him with an openness and sympathy for his difficulties." "I got back to the hotel at eight . . . pretty well tired out."

Whatever increased demands Haldane—prompted by Stumm— may have made of the Chancellor in their final meeting, and whatever promises Bethmann may have made to "do his best," there was general agreement that Germany had offered to spread out the building of the new ships to one every third year. When Haldane left Berlin, the Emperor believed that he returned to London satisfied that the German proposal represented a "substantial concession." Bethmann declared, "A promising beginning has been made. It was good to have a chance to speak openly to a member of the British Cabinet."

The War Minister returned to London on Monday, February 12, and attended a meeting of the Cabinet that afternoon. Haldane made his report. The Emperor, he told the Ministers, "had been delightful to me. . . . I am sure he wants peace most genuinely, but he has Germany to deal with." Haldane had no doubt that the Chancellor, too, was sincere in his desire to improve relations. The problem, he said, was that Britons tended to overestimate the power of both the Emperor and the Chancellor. "My impression was that the really decisive influence was that of Admiral von Tirpitz. He has the strongest following throughout Germany." Given Tirpitz' strength and that of the nationalist parties in Germany, Haldane reported, the new Navy Law would be insisted upon. There was even a possibility, he said, that Tirpitz would replace Bethmann as Chancellor. The Cabinet's first reaction was satisfaction and congratulation of Haldane on his conduct of a difficult mission. Grey told Metternich that he was pleased, and a few days later Asquith told the House of Commons that the talks had been "helpful."

This harmony was soon to be broken. Before he left Berlin, Haldane later wrote, "the Emperor . . . handed me with friendly frankness an advance copy of the new [Navy] Bill with permission to show it to my colleagues." The bill was an immensely elaborate technical document and Haldane, lacking expertise, did not read it. Instead, "I put it in my pocket and handed it to the First Lord" at the afternoon Cabinet meeting on the twelfth. At the Admiralty, Churchill and his staff subjected the document to intensive scrutiny, and at the next meeting of the Cabinet, on February 14, Churchill made his report. The new German Navy Bill was much more wide-ranging and threatening than anyone in Britain had imagined. The creation of the third battle squadron and the building of three additional dreadnoughts—the issue on which Haldane had been negotiating—were not what worried the Admiralty. Their concern was focussed, rather, on a vast increase in the number of new destroyers and submarines and, most worrisome of all, a 20 percent increase in active-duty naval personnel, which would make possible "an extraordinary increase in the striking force of ships of all classes immediately available through the year." Fifteen thousand new officers and men, instead of the three thousand to four thousand first estimated, would join the High Seas Fleet. Seventy-two new submarines were to be built; full crews would be provided for 99 of 144 destroyers. With this new manpower, the German Fleet, which had been in large part demobilized in harbor during the winter months, would now be kept at war strength throughout the year. Previously, the Admiralty had calculated that it might have to face seventeen German battleships and four battle cruisers. To meet this threat, the Royal Navy maintained sixteen battleships in home waters, another six in the Atlantic Fleet at Gibraltar three or four steaming days away, and still another six in the Mediterranean Fleet, usually at Malta, nine fast steaming days away. The margin had seemed safe. Now, if the new Navy Bill was enacted, England would face twenty-five battleships, eight battle cruisers, large destroyer flotillas, and packs of submarines, ready year-round to strike. The initial cost of meeting this challenge would be £3 million additional a year, Churchill estimated; the total for six years would be at least £18 million.

The following week, on the twenty-second, Grey and a chastened Haldane met Metternich. The War Minister explained that in Berlin he had understood the strong feeling about the need for a third squadron, but that the increased-personnel plans and the intention to build large numbers of smaller ships had not been mentioned. The Cabinet's feeling, the Ambassador was told, was that German increases would mean bringing more British ships back to home waters, building new ships at ever greater British naval expenditure, and the consequent impossibility of working out any political agreement. Colonial agreements, such as the proposed cession of Zanzibar back to Germany, were clearly out of the question. Metternich, who had been briefed by the Wilhelmstrasse about the Haldane talks, replied that the German government had made substantial concessions regarding the dates of building the three new dreadnoughts and that increases in other ships and naval personnel were outside the scope of current Anglo-German negotiations. Grey said that they would have to be included. "In other words," Metternich observed, "the Cabinet does not agree to the arrangements made by Haldane." "You are quite right," responded Grey.

When Metternich informed Berlin that the British Cabinet was disavowing the terms offered by Haldane, the Kaiser was outraged. Later, he and others in the German government insisted that the War Minister had come representing the Cabinet, armed with full powers, and that his suggestions had been firm offers. Haldane denied this, declaring that he had stated repeatedly in Berlin that his was an exploratory mission with no binding powers and that any tentative agreement he took back to London would be subject to Cabinet examination and approval. To the Kaiser's charge of English bad faith in belatedly objecting to increases in personnel, submarines, and destroyers, Haldane replied that he had not known about them; he had not read the text of the *Novelle;* no one had until he returned to London. Now, quite properly, the Cabinet was reacting to complete knowledge, not the partial information presented to Haldane in Berlin. Bethmann, who understood that Haldane had been an explorer and who already had half expected that the concessions proposed to Haldane would not be enough, was less surprised and less indignant. Tirpitz was not surprised. Convinced from the beginning that the Haldane mission was a trap, intended to block or at least slow down the German building program, he recommended immediate publication of the new Navy Bill and its submission to the Reichstag. "The quicker we publish the *Novelle,* the more we limit the possibility of the English making greater demands on us."

On March 1, Haldane saw Metternich again and repeated his earlier warning that Britain would lay two keels for each additional German capital ship. And, to meet the immediate threat posed by the increases in German naval personnel and fleet readiness, the Admiralty was considering bringing battleships home from the Mediterranean. This news, reported in Berlin, sent the Kaiser into a paroxysm of rage. Without consulting the Chancellor as he was constitutionally required to do, William telegraphed Metternich to warn the British that "I shall consider any transfer of the Mediterranean Squadron into the North Sea as a cause for war." Germany would mobilize and—he added as a practical afterthought—the concessions made to Haldane on the shipbuilding tempo would be withdrawn. When Bethmann heard about William's outburst, he wrote a letter of resignation. Not only was the Emperor ignoring the Chancellor's constitutional right to conduct foreign policy and instruct ambassadors, he was abetting Tirpitz' effort to thwart the entire purpose of his policy: agreement with England. William, caught between two ministers pursuing contradictory policies, had to give ground. Because William did not want Bethmann to go, he gave in temporarily to the Chancellor. Swallowing his anger, he postponed the publication of the Navy Bill and authorized continued negotiations with England.

Bethmann withdrew his resignation and used the reprieve to launch his own diplomatic offensive in London. The Chancellor's goal was to obtain a guarantee of British neutrality should Germany become involved in war. If this could be achieved, he was certain that the Kaiser and even Admiral Tirpitz would pay a price in ships. The Navy Bill, now suspended, could be further modified; the third ship in the new Law, the dreadnought to be built in 1919, might be postponed indefinitely; there might be reductions in the increase in personnel: all this was possible if the British government could propose an acceptable neutrality agreement. The Minister chosen to receive this offer was, again, Haldane. Metternich came to see him on March 12, at Queen Anne's Gate, and that night the War Minister wrote to his mother, "I believe our prayers have been answered and that the good Chancellor has got the better of Tirpitz and his admirals. It appears that after all my mission, which seemed to have been wrecked by a German torpedo, will have the results on which we had set our hopes." Haldane reported the German approach in a memorandum to the Cabinet:

"[Metternich] had a communication from the Chancellor. . . . He gathered from Berlin that if the British Government would offer a suitable political formula, the proposed Fleet Law as it stood would be withdrawn. Some Fleet Law there must be, but one of less magnitude would be introduced. . . . The reduction . . . would be considerable . . . he thought it extended to personnel. He wanted to say that time pressed, as a statement would have to be made almost at once in the Reichstag . . . and the Chancellor wished to be provided with the offer of a formula from us as a reason for not proceeding with his original proposals. I asked whether the formula need go beyond the disclaimer of aggressive intentions and combinations. He indicated that he thought it need not. . . . I said I would see Sir Edward Grey at once."

Grey wrote the formula with Haldane sitting beside him. On March 14, it was approved by the Cabinet and handed to Count Metternich for transmission to Berlin. The statement read:

"England will make no unprovoked attack upon Germany and will pursue no aggressive policy towards her.

"Aggression upon Germany is not the subject and forms no part of any treaty, understanding or combination to which England is now a party, nor will she become a party to anything that has such an object."

When Metternich read the formula, he was worried. He wrote to Grey the same day that unless the word "neutrality" appeared in the draft, he was afraid it would be rejected in Berlin. He suggested adding the sentence "England will therefore observe a benevolent neutrality should war be forced upon Germany." This sentence, with its dire implications for France, Russia, and the future of the Entente, Grey refused to supply. Bethmann read the English formula with dismay, knowing that the English promise "didn't go half far enough"; it could not possibly stand up against the weight of Admiral Tirpitz and the navy party. Metternich was instructed to tell the English that unless there was a guarantee of absolute, unconditional neutrality on Britain's part, the Navy Bill would go before the Reichstag in its original form. On March 16, Metternich received two telegrams from Berlin, asking in the most urgent terms for a reply from the British government. In passing this request along to Grey, the Ambassador mentioned that one reason for the need for haste was the possibility of "a change of personnel in Berlin." "Personnel" meant Bethmann; Grey was being informed that, if no agreement was reached, the Chancellor's resignation was likely. Aware of Bethmann's goodwill and anxious to help him retain power, Grey told Metternich that "as long as he [Bethmann] remained Chancellor, he might rely upon our cooperation with him to preserve the peace of Europe. . . . If this was likely to be of use in personal questions now pending in Berlin, Count Metternich might certainly report it." Metternich transmitted the Foreign Secretary's remark that Bethmann's personality was regarded in England as the single best guarantee of peace. The Kaiser read Metternich's dispatch. Once again, the old fury at English patronizing erupted in William. "I have never in my life heard of an agreement being concluded with reference to one definite statesman and independently of the reigning sovereign," he stormed. "It is clear that Grey has no idea who is master here, namely myself. He dictates to me in advance who is to be my Minister if I am to conclude an agreement with England."

On March 18, Grey confirmed that England would not agree to a pledge of unconditional neutrality as a condition for limiting German shipbuilding. The Emperor, calling on the Chancellor in the Wilhelmstrasse, found Bethmann in a state of collapse and pressed a glass of port wine on him. Bethmann could fight no longer. Grey's refusal to give a pledge of neutrality took from the Chancellor's hand his only weapon against publication of the Navy Bill. Realizing that further negotiations were useless, he informed the Kaiser on March 19 that he no longer opposed the *Novelle*. The Bill was published on March 22 and William left immediately for Vienna, Venice, and Corfu. Grey and Metternich continued to talk, but on April 10 Asquith wrote to Grey that he was "becoming more and more doubtful as to the wisdom of prolonging these discussions with Germany about a formula. Nothing, I believe, will meet her purpose which falls short of a promise on our part of neutrality, a promise we cannot give."

Failure of the naval talks doomed Metternich's ambassadorship. William's marginalia on Metternich's reports and telegrams had become relentlessly negative; the Ambassador was "incorrigible," "flabby," "hopelessly incurable." On May 9, 1902, after a decade in his post, Metternich was recalled, his departure explained as due to poor health. Metternich's replacement was Marschall von Bieberstein, the former State Secretary for Foreign Affairs, who, after leaving the Wilhelmstrasse in 1897, had spent fifteen years as Ambassador to Turkey. Marschall, now sixty-nine, arrived in England, remained a few weeks, and then went home on leave to Germany where, suddenly, he died. Marschall was succeeded by Prince Karl Max von Lichnowsky, an amiable, wealthy Silesian landowner who had had no diplomatic assignment for the previous eight years. To the Kaiser's dismay, Lichnowsky's reports from London on the subject of the alarm created in Britain by the growth of the Germany Navy soon became similar to those of Metternich.

CHAPTER 43

Naval
Estimates and a
"Naval Holiday"

◆

Like many well-born Britons, Winston Churchill regarded Germans as rustic Continental cousins who had been faithful allies in the great wars against Louis XIV and Napoleon. The new German Empire, powerful but primitive, had been guided by Bismarck along paths that did not appear to threaten Great Britain. Britons, aware of Germany's military strength, were confident that it could not touch England, her empire, her world trade, or her wealth. In Churchill's youth and young manhood, Britain's rivals and potential enemies were France and Russia.

Churchill first saw the Kaiser when he was sixteen. His mother's lover Count Kinsky took the Harrow boy to an exhibition at the Crystal Palace where William was the guest of honor. Describing the occasion for his brother Jack, Winston concentrated on the Emperor's spectacular uniform: "a helmet of bright brass surmounted by a white eagle nearly six inches high . . . a polished steel cuirass and perfectly white uniform with high boots." Churchill saw the Kaiser again fifteen years later, in 1906, when as Under Secretary for the Colonies, he was invited to attend German Army maneuvers in Silesia. As a personal guest of the Emperor, Churchill—the German Military Attaché in London informed him—would need a uniform. Winston, who had none, tried to borrow from his brother the plumed hat and leopardskin cloak of the Oxfordshire Hussars. When Jack replied that the plumes were lost and he had turned the leopardskin into a rug six years earlier, Winston borrowed a uniform from his cousin the Duke of Marlborough.

In Silesia, Churchill found the Kaiser still wearing a "white uniform and eagle crested helmet," and sitting on "a magnificent horse . . . surrounded by kings and princes while his legions defiled before him in what seemed an endless procession." Churchill "had about twenty minutes talk with H.I.M. [His Imperial Majesty]. . . . He was very friendly and is certainly a most fascinating personality." Churchill was impressed by the "massive simplicity and force" of the German war machine and wrote to an aunt, "I am very thankful there is a sea between that army and England." Because of the sea, Churchill saw no danger to England from Germany and, as a candidate in 1908, told audiences in Manchester and Dundee that the German threat was a figment of Tory imaginations. In 1909, during the Navy Scare battle in the Cabinet, Churchill sided with Lloyd George and economy against McKenna. In the summer of 1909, Churchill again was invited to observe German Army maneuvers. He was even more impressed: the German Army, he said, is "a terrible engine. It marches sometimes 35 miles a day. It is in number as the sands of the sea." This time, the Emperor was even more cordial: It was " 'My dear Winston' and so on," Churchill wrote to his wife.

Agadir altered Churchill's thinking. "Germany's action at Agadir has put her in the wrong and forced us to consider her claims in the light of her policy and methods," he wrote in a memorandum to himself on Home Office stationery. At the peak of the crisis, he sent Lloyd George a letter filled with urgent military proposals: the British Army to move into Belgium to threaten the German flank; the Fleet to move to its war stations in Scotland. "It is not for . . . Belgium that I would take part in this terrible business," he concluded. "One cause alone could justify our participation—to prevent France from being trampled down and looted by the Prussian Junkers—a disaster ruinous to the world and swiftly fatal to our country."

Once the crisis was over, Churchill—become First Lord of the Admiralty—looked for a way to lessen the rising tension between his country and Germany. The problem was the German Navy. "We knew that a formidable new [German] Navy Law was in preparation and would shortly be declared. If Germany had definitely made up her mind to antagonize Great Britain, we must take up the challenge; but it might be possible by friendly, sincere and intimate con-

versation to avert this perilous development." Churchill heartily
endorsed Sir Ernest Cassel's effort to send a British Cabinet Minister to Berlin to negotiate privately with the Kaiser, Bethmann-
Hollweg, and Tirpitz. "Until Germany dropped the Naval challenge
her policy here would be continually viewed with deepening suspicions and apprehension," Churchill wrote to Cassel on January 7,
1912. "But . . . any slackening on her part would produce an immediate detente with much good will from all England. . . . I
deeply deplore the situation for, as you know, I have never had any
but friendly feelings towards that great nation and her illustrious
sovereign and I regard the antagonism which has developed as in-
sensate. Anything in my power to terminate it, I would gladly do."

Although Churchill favored the Haldane mission, while the
War Minister was in Berlin the First Lord made a speech which,
thanks to its timing and phraseology, seemed unlikely to smooth
Haldane's path. Churchill's address was provoked by the Kaiser's
speech opening the Reichstag. In a London railway station, bound
for Belfast and Glasgow, the First Lord picked up an evening paper.
"One sentence [of William's speech] stood out vividly," Churchill
wrote. "It is my constant duty and care," the Kaiser had said, "to
maintain and strengthen on land and water the power of defense of
the German people, which has no lack of young men fit to bear
arms." Two days later, in Glasgow, Churchill riposted: "This island
has never been and never will be lacking in trained and hardy mariners bred from their boyhood up in the service of the sea." He went
on to spell out the differences between British and German sea
power:

"The purposes of British naval power are essentially defensive.
We have no thoughts . . . of aggression and we attribute no such
thoughts to other great Powers. There is, however, this difference
between the British naval power and the naval power of the great
and friendly Empire—and I trust it may long remain the great and
friendly Empire—of Germany. The British Navy is to us a necessity
and, from some points of view, the German Navy is to them more in
the nature of a luxury. Our naval power involves British existence.
. . . It is the British Navy which makes Great Britain a great power.
But Germany was a great power, respected and honored, all over
the world before she had a single ship."

The German press roared angrily at the description of the German Navy as a "luxury" fleet. Churchill himself recorded that in
Germany "the expression passed angrily from lip to lip." The First
Lord returned from Glasgow to London to find his Cabinet colleagues offended, although Asquith admitted that Churchill had

made "a plain statement of an obvious truth." Churchill was relieved when Haldane, reporting to the Cabinet on his return from
Berlin, said that "far from being a hindrance, the Glasgow speech
had been the greatest possible help. Haldane described how he had
read the operative passages in my speech himself to the Emperor
and von Tirpitz in proof and confirmation of what he had himself
been saying during their previous discussions."

The failure of both the Haldane mission and the subsequent
negotiations aimed at slowing the German tempo saddened Churchill. In April 1912, he expressed this feeling to Cassel: "I suppose it
is difficult for either country to realize how formidable it appears to
the eyes of the other. Certainly it must be almost impossible for
Germany with her splendid armies and warlike population capable
of holding their native soil against all comers, and situated inland
with road and railway communications on every side, to appreciate
the sentiments with which an island state like Britain views the
steady and remorseless development of a rival naval power of the
very highest efficiency. The more we admire the wonderful work
that has been done in the swift creation of German naval strength,
the stronger, the deeper, and the more preoccupying these sentiments become."

The Kaiser had given Haldane the text of the new German
Navy Bill. In May, the *Novelle* passed the Reichstag. It called for a
1920 navy of five battle squadrons, including three squadrons of
dreadnought battleships (twenty-four ships) and eleven dreadnought battle cruisers. The fleet's total personnel would be 101,500.
Whatever his hopes for peace and reduced expenditure, the First
Lord's duty was "to take up the challenge."

On March 18, 1912, Churchill introduced his first Naval Estimates to
the House of Commons. They were largely the work of his predecessor McKenna: four dreadnoughts, eight light cruisers, twenty destroyers, and an unspecified number of submarines. The costs, too,
were McKenna's: £44 million, up £4 million from the previous year.
There was a caveat in the First Lord's speech, but to his listeners it
seemed routine: "These estimates have been framed on the assumption that the existing programs of other naval powers will not be
increased. In the event of such increases, it will be necessary to
present supplementary estimates." This was disingenuous. Before
submitting the Estimates, Churchill already knew that another
power was preparing to add to its existing program. But, as the text
of the new German Supplementary Navy Law had been given in

confidence by the Kaiser to Haldane, the First Lord could not reveal it to the House.

Churchill prepared Parliament and the British public for the inevitable Supplementary Estimates by altering the traditional measure of British naval strength. For decades, Britain had adhered to a self-proclaimed Two Power Standard: the maintenance of a fleet capable of defeating the combined fleets of any two other naval powers. In his March 18 speech, the First Lord formally abandoned the Two Power Standard. Confronting the German challenge, he said, Britain no longer could afford to build against two powers; henceforward, the goal of her construction would be to maintain a 60 percent superiority in dreadnoughts over the single state which menaced her; for every ten battleships in the High Seas Fleet, the Royal Navy must have sixteen. "We must always be ready to meet at our average moment anything that any possible enemy might hurl against us at his selected moment." And this ratio was to be set against the original German Navy Laws without the 1912 Supplement. For every new keel authorized under the still-unpublished *Novelle,* Britain would lay down two. "Nothing, in my opinion," Churchill wrote to Fisher, "would more surely dishearten Germany than the certain proof that as the result of all her present and prospective efforts, she will only be more hopelessly behind in 1920." The First Lord was, forceful, but his speech also contained an original idea whose intent was both pacific and thrifty. Why not lessen the burden of naval armaments on both countries by taking a Naval Holiday?

"Let me make it clear that any retardation or reduction of German construction will, within certain limits, be promptly followed here. . . . Take as an instance . . . the year 1913. In that year . . . Germany will build three capital ships and it will be necessary for us to build five in consequence. Supposing we were both to take a holiday for that year and introduce a blank page into the book of misunderstanding; supposing that Germany were to build no ships that year, she would save herself between six and seven millions sterling. But that is not all. In ordinary circumstances we should not begin our ships until Germany had started hers. The three ships that she did not build would therefore automatically wipe out no fewer than five British potential super-dreadnoughts. That is more than I expect they could hope to do in a brilliant naval action."

It was an unorthodox idea, the suggestion that an armaments race could simply be halted, frozen in time, leaving two powers with precisely the same balance of weaponry. The proposal was not well received in Germany, where the press reminded readers that Churchill was the British Minister who only a few weeks before had denigrated their navy as a "luxury fleet." The Kaiser was cool, sending word to Churchill through Ballin that "such arrangements were possible only between allies."

Meanwhile Churchill's duty was to preserve Britain's naval supremacy. He could take a practical step which did not require either the passage of time (to build new ships) or the approval of a potential foe (mutually, to stop building them): more ships could be called home. Fisher had begun the process in 1904 when he stripped the China and North America squadrons of their battleships and closed down other stations. Now the rest of the battleships would be summoned. The battleships of the Mediterranean Fleet, based at Malta, were pulled back. Four came home; four were left at Gibraltar from where they could steam either way, north toward the Channel and the North Sea or east into the Mediterranean.

The withdrawal from Malta had many levels of significance. Strategically, the decision was based on Fisher's dictum: "We cannot have everything or be strong everywhere. It is futile to be strong in the subsidiary theatre of war and not overwhelmingly supreme in the decisive theatre." The decisive theater was the North Sea. On May 6, 1912, Churchill wrote to Haldane: "We cannot possibly hold the Mediterranean or guarantee any of our interests there until we have obtained a decision in the North Sea. . . . It would be very foolish to lose England in safeguarding Egypt. If we win the big battle in the decisive theatre, we can put everything else straight afterwards. If we lose it, there will not be any afterwards."

The situation in the Mediterranean had changed with the formation of the Entente. France, the traditional foe, was now Britain's partner. The other two naval powers of the inland sea, Italy and Austria, were nominal allies within the Triple Alliance, but their fleets were building against each other. Even if Italy and Austria did combine against Britain, the argument for withdrawal still held. The six obsolescent pre-dreadnoughts of the British Mediterranean Fleet would be no match for the new Austrian and Italian dreadnoughts. To leave these old ships in the Mediterranean, Churchill told the Cabinet on June 26, "would be to expose a British Fleet, equal to nearly one third of our battleship strength and manned by 12,000 of our best officers and seamen, to certain destruction." Indeed it was consideration of the sailors more than of the ships that motivated the withdrawal; the trained seamen of the Mediterranean Fleet were needed to man the new dreadnoughts coming to the Fleet in home waters.

Churchill pressed this argument vigorously. Its discussion was the primary reason for his visit to Malta on board the *Enchantress* in May 1912.* Kitchener, then governing Egypt as Agent-General, hammered the table in opposition. The Mediterranean was the lifeline of the Empire, Kitchener insisted. Removal of the fleet would mean loss of Egypt, Cyprus, and Malta, and the erosion of British power in India, China, and Australasia. Asquith, seeking compromise, promised that some capital ships, battle cruisers if not battleships, would be left in the Mediterranean at Malta.

In July, the discussion shifted to the Committee of Imperial Defence, the Cabinet, and the House of Commons. McKenna, supported by Esher, insisted on keeping battleships in the Mediterranean. Churchill persisted in saying that it should not be done. The Mediterranean was not the lifeline of the Empire, he argued; if necessary, food supplies and other trade could go around the Cape of Good Hope, as they had before the Suez Canal was built. The vital point, he insisted—the critical threat to the future of the Empire— lay not in the Mediterranean but in the North Sea. Eventually, however, Churchill acquiesced in Asquith's promise made to Kitchener at Malta: the old battleships would be withdrawn, but a permanent squadron of four new battle cruisers and four of the latest armored cruisers would go to Malta. The battle cruisers, with their twelve-inch guns, would be a potent deterrent force against the pre-dreadnought Austrian and Italian ships. Should the Austrians venture out of the Adriatic, even Churchill believed that the four *Invincibles* with cruiser support would be more than a match. And, if the battle cruisers got into trouble against slower but more heavily armored enemy ships, they could simply raise speed and slip away. By 1915, the Admiralty hoped, it would have sufficient new construction to ensure security in the North Sea *and* to reenter the Mediterranean with eight modern dreadnoughts.

In arguing for withdrawal, Churchill never took his eye from the primary threat. On July 11, he presented this view to the Committee of Imperial Defence: "The ultimate scale of the German Fleet is of the most formidable character. . . . The whole character of the German Fleet shows that it is designed for aggressive and offensive action of the largest possible character in the North Sea or the North Atlantic. . . . The structure of the German battleships shows clearly that they are intended for attack and for fleet action. . . . I do not pretend to make any suggestion that the Germans would deliver any surprise or sudden attack upon us. It is not for us

---

* It was on this voyage that Churchill and Asquith wooed and won the retired Jacky Fisher in Naples Bay.

to assume that another great nation will fall markedly below the standard of civilisation which we ourselves should be bound by; but we at the Admiralty have got to see, not that they will not do it, but [that] they cannot do it."

In September 1912, as British battleships were leaving the Mediterranean, the French Admiralty announced that the six battleships of the French Atlantic Fleet would be transferred to the Mediterranean. In 1912, France had a formidable but elderly navy of twenty battleships, fourteen of them pre-dreadnoughts and six semi-dreadnoughts (ships of the *Danton* class, with four 12-inch and twelve 9.4-inch guns, similar in armament and armor to the British *Lord Nelsons*). Six of these ships were at Brest. Fourteen were at Toulon, to fulfill the primary mission of France's navy: safeguarding the sea communications between Metropolitan France and the French North African empire, from which flowed food, raw materials, and manpower. The argument for withdrawing the Atlantic ships had a ring similar to the British Admiralty's for withdrawing its Mediterranean battleships: the French Navy was being concentrated in the vital theater; six additional ships would give France superiority over the combined fleets of her two potential opponents, Austria and Italy. Similarly, if left at Brest, the six French pre-dreadnoughts could have been massacred by the modern dreadnoughts of the German High Seas Fleet. The French decision appeared to leave the long French Channel and Atlantic coasts to be defended only by torpedo boats and submarines. A feeling of vulnerability on the part of the citizens of these coasts was urgently communicated to the French Admiralty by their deputies in the Chamber. The response, as discreet as possible, was that an arrangement had been made: the ports and coasts would be defended by the fleet of another, friendly power.

The near-simultaneous realignment of the British and French fleets was too obvious and too convenient to be purely coincidental. Berlin assumed that a bargain had been struck: Britain would guard France's northern coasts while the French looked after British interests in the Mediterranean. In fact, although the French dearly wished for such an arrangement, the British had refused any formal commitment. In the spring of 1912, after the failure of the Haldane mission, French naval authorities began pressing for staff conversations to discuss cooperation in case of war. Churchill had agreed and had himself participated in talks with the Count de Saint-Seine, the French Naval Attaché in London. Nevertheless, the First Lord had warned this French officer that "he must clearly understand that no discussion between military or naval experts could be held to affect in any way the full freedom of action possessed by both countries. On such matters, the Foreign Office would express the view of His Majesty's Government. . . . [The French Naval Attaché] said that he perfectly understood this and quite agreed with it." Having issued this warning, Churchill went on to observe that French interests would be served by creating strength in the Mediterranean equal or superior to that of Austria and Italy combined, an accomplishment both parties knew could be achieved only by transferring the French Atlantic Fleet to Toulon. Having encouraged France's action, Churchill—along with Asquith and Grey—was concerned that France not believe that it possessed a moral argument to compel Great Britain to act. On the eve of the French announcement that the Brest Squadron would move, the First Lord expressed this concern and his own rationalization of the dilemma in a letter to the Prime Minister and the Foreign Secretary:

"The point I am anxious to safeguard is our freedom of choice. . . . That freedom will be sensibly impaired if the French can say that they have denuded their Atlantic seaboard and concentrated in the Mediterranean on the faith of naval arrangements with us. This will not be true. If we did not exist, the French could not make better dispositions. . . . They are not strong enough to face Germany alone, still less to maintain themselves in two theatres. They therefore rightly concentrate their Navy in the Mediterranean where it can be safe and superior and can assure their African communications. Neither is it true that we are relying on France to maintain our position in the Mediterranean. . . . If France did not exist, we should make no other disposition of our forces. . . . Consider how tremendous would be the weapon which France would possess to compel our intervention if she could say, 'On the advice of and by arrangement with your naval authorities we have left our Northern coasts defenceless. We cannot possibly come back in time.' "

French authorities deplored British skittishness about making commitments. The arrangement on fleet dispositions was unilateral, Paul Cambon protested; it left England "free to aid France or not as she liked." Nevertheless, Britain refused to give way. In an exchange of notes on November 22 and 23, Grey and Cambon agreed that discussions between military and naval experts of the two Entente powers did not constitute "an engagement that commits either Government to action in a contingency that has not arisen and may never arise." It was agreed that in a circumstance of grave threat—if either Power had reason to expect a sudden, unprovoked attack by a third Power—the two governments should discuss whether they would act together and, if so, in what manner. At British insistence, it was stated that "the disposition, for instance, of the French and British Fleets respectively at the present moment is not based upon an engagement to cooperate in war." Great Britain appeared to have won. In fact, she had handed to France the "tremendous weapon" which Churchill had predicted.

During the summer of 1912, discussions in the Committee of Imperial Defence, the Cabinet, and Parliament, and conversations with the French, all on the subject of transferring the two fleets, were accompanied by a drumfire of debate in the press and public. "Abandonment of the Mediterranean" was roundly attacked in the Conservative press, by the Navy League, and by a number of prominent people outside government, including Esher, Lord Roberts, and Beresford. "Because of our preoccupation with the North Sea, we have lost our hold upon the Mediterranean, the carotid artery of Empire," proclaimed the *Standard*. The idea of depending on the French Navy to guard the lifeline of Empire "was absolutely repugnant to the mass of Englishmen," declared the *Daily Express*. Indeed, the notion "marked the limits of what a self-respecting people should endure," added the *Globe*. "Rome had to call in the foreigner when her time of decadence approached," said Esher. None of these opponents disputed the importance of British naval supremacy in the North Sea; their contention was that *both* the North Sea and the Mediterranean must be held; the solution was to build more ships. "The choice lies between such increases of Naval Power as will ensure sea command of the Mediterranean . . . or a complete reversal of the traditional policy of Great Britain in regard to her trade routes and military highways to the East," Esher advised the King. The King agreed. Churchill, Grey, and Asquith agreed. The problem was money.

After the war Tirpitz chortled over Britain's withdrawal from the Mediterranean: "In order to estimate the strength of the trump card which our fleet put in the hands of an energetic diplomacy, one must remember that in consequence of the concentration of the English forces which we had caused in the North Sea, the English control of the Mediterranean and Far-Eastern waters had practically ceased." It was difficult to see what use this was to Germany, which had an insignificant squadron in the Far East and a single battle cruiser in the Mediterranean. Churchill, also writing after the war, commented, "The only 'trump card' which Germany secured by this policy was the driving of Britain and France closer together. From the moment that the fleets of Britain and France were disposed in this new way, our common naval interest became very important."

Along with building new British dreadnoughts and shifting existing battleships to home waters, Churchill discovered another way to increase British superiority in the North Sea: Canada, he thought, might be persuaded to build dreadnoughts for the Royal Navy. Logic and precedent were on his side. It was obvious that the rise of the German Navy affected the security and prosperity of the Dominions traditionally shielded by the Royal Navy. Following the 1909 Navy Scare, Australia and New Zealand each had offered to pay for a dreadnought; the following year two battle cruisers named after the two dominions were laid down in British shipyards. In 1911, the Dominion governments agreed that in time of war Dominion ships were "to form an integral part of the British Fleet and remain under the control of the British Admiralty." Canada, up to that point, had made no offer, but with a new Conservative government in power in Ottawa, Churchill decided to ask. To match the new German *Novelle*, Britain needed three new ships. "But," he explained, "if we come forward now all of a sudden and add three new ships, that may have the effect of stimulating the naval competition once more and they would ask us what new factor had occurred which justified or which required this increase in building on our part. If we could say that the new factor was that Canada had decided to take part in the defence of the British Empire, that would be an answer which would involve no invidious comparisons and which would absolve us from going into detailed calculations as to the number of Austrian or German vessels available at any particular moment."

Sir Robert Borden, the Canadian Prime Minister, received the First Lord's proposal favorably. To strengthen his hand in the Canadian Parliament, the British Admiralty prepared a statement on sea power: "Naval supremacy is of two kinds: general and local. General naval supremacy consists in the power to defeat in battle and drive from the seas the strongest hostile navy or combination of hostile navies wherever they may be found. . . . It is the general naval supremacy of Great Britain which is the primary safeguard of the security and interests of the great Dominions of the Crown. . . ."

On December 5, Borden introduced into the Canadian Parliament a Naval Bill asking for £7 million to build three dreadnoughts to be controlled and maintained by the Royal Navy for the common defense of the Empire. The bill created a political storm. The Liberal opposition declared that it perceived no danger to Canada. If the ships were to be built, the opposition said, they should be constructed in Canadian shipyards, manned by Canadian seamen, and controlled by the Canadian government. Churchill pointed out to Borden that no building yards capable of constructing dreadnoughts existed in Canada and that it would cost £15 million to create one. Under such circumstances, the laying of the first keel would wait four years. Invoking this argument, Borden managed to get the bill through the Canadian House in February 1913, but in May it was killed by the Canadian Senate. In November, the Malay States joined Australia and New Zealand by offering to pay for a dreadnought, but no Canadian capital ships were available to the Admiralty at the beginning of the First World War.

Admiral von Tirpitz had always argued that Germany built ships for her own needs without reference to the naval power of other states. Early in 1913, Tirpitz altered this position. In statements to the Reichstag Budget Committee on February 6 and 7, he acknowledged the British First Lord's 60 percent ratio and announced that Germany would abide by it. He did not mention numbers of ships, but put the ratio in terms of battle squadrons: Britain should have eight, Germany five. Tirpitz' speech pleased the English Liberal press, always hopeful that naval spending could be cut. But it had little impact on the British Foreign Secretary or First Lord. Grey, wary that negotiations with Germany could jeopardize the Entente with France, and especially cool after the collapse of the negotiations following the Haldane mission, assumed that Tirpitz' statement reflected the demands made on the Reichstag by the German Army. "What Tirpitz said does not amount to much," Grey said, "and the reason for his saying it is not the love of our beautiful eyes, but the extra fifty millions required for increasing the German Army." Churchill also cautioned his Liberal colleagues to curb their hopes: "We must not try to read into recent German naval declarations a meaning which we should like, but which they do not possess," he told the Commons on March 26, 1913. "If, for instance, I were to say that Admiral Tirpitz had recognized that a British predominance of sixteen to ten dreadnoughts was satisfactory to Germany, that such a preponderance exists almost exactly in the present period [it did], and that in consequence Germany ought not to begin any more capital ships until we did, that might be a logical argument, but it would, I am sure, do a great deal of harm."

In this speech presenting the 1913–1914 Naval Estimates, Chur-

chill renewed his Naval Holiday proposal: "If, for the space of a
year . . . no new ships were built by any nation, in what conceivable manner would the interests of any nation be affected or prejudiced? The proposal . . . involves no alteration in the relative
strength of the navies. It implies no abandonment of any scheme of
naval organization or of naval increase. It is contrary to the system
of no Navy Law. The finances of every country would obtain relief."
Britain would cancel four and Germany two scheduled dreadnoughts, the First Lord pointed out. France, Italy, Austria, and Russia might follow. If his suggestion was rejected, then, he said,
"events will continue to move forward along the path upon which
they have now been set with the result that at every stage the naval
supremacy of the British Empire will be found to be established
upon a more unassailable foundation."

The German Admiralty heard Churchill's proposal with alarm.
The budgetary demands of the German Army had created opposition among taxpayers and in the Reichstag; against this background,
a "Holiday" on naval spending might seem attractive. Arguments
against the plan were marshalled: Great Britain, it was argued,
needed the "Holiday" because her shipbuilding yards were overcrowded and suffering from a shortage of workers; when the "Holiday" was over and building resumed, Britain would have an
advantage because she could build ships more rapidly than Germany; what would happen to the German shipyards and building
workers during the "Holiday" year? Suppose when the "Holiday"
was over and building resumed, the work force had deserted for
other jobs. What about the naval building plans of other powers—
France and Russia—who were Germany's enemies?

A speech in the House of Commons was not a formal British
government proposal, and Tirpitz moved to head off any official
note from the Foreign Office on the subject of a Naval Holiday.
Tirpitz instructed Captain Müller, the German Naval Attaché in
London, how to handle the matter: "Act as though from a naval
standpoint we were not altogether unapproachable and . . . point
out at the same time that the English and the German press have
given the idea an unfavorable, even a contemptuous reception. . . .
In general, you are to treat the matter in as dilatory a manner as
possible and less as a naval than a purely political question. . . .
Talk to Grey about the danger of a naval discussion in the press and
say that Churchill can only harm the tender plant of German-
English detente by his plan of a naval holiday." The German Foreign Ministry fell into line; Prince Karl Lichnowsky, the Ambassador to London, assured Gottlieb von Jagow, the Foreign Minister,

that he would do everything possible to prevent an official British proposal for a Naval Holiday from reaching Berlin. Soon after, he mentioned to Grey that the German government would prefer not to have to deal officially with the First Lord's proposal.

No official proposal was made, but this did not stop Churchill. Again, on October 18, 1913, he returned to his theme. Knowing that the size of the 1914 British Naval Estimates, then in the drafting stage, would shock the Cabinet and country, the First Lord offered his radical alternative: "Next year, we are to lay down four great ships to Germany's two. Now we say, while there is plenty of time, in all friendship and sincerity to our great neighbour Germany: If you will put off beginning your two ships for twelve months from the ordinary date when you would have begun them, we will put off our four ships, in absolute good faith, for exactly the same period. . . . There would be a saving . . . of nearly six millions to Germany and of nearly twelve millions to this country, and the relative strength of the two countries would be absolutely unchanged."

Again, a torrent of criticism, domestic and foreign, descended upon the First Lord. Esher declared that he assumed that "Winston is playing to the Radical gallery . . . as it is inconceivable to me that so clever a fellow should have been silly enough to imagine that he had any chance of obtaining a favourable reply." Other critics pointed out that a holiday limited to capital ships meant that Germany would be able to spend more on submarines and airships. The Paris press protested that if Germany were relieved of the necessity of spending £6 million on her navy, she would pour an additional £6 million into her army. In London, the *Morning Post* advised the First Lord to "take a holiday from speech-making for a year, at least as far as dealing with a reduction of armaments is concerned." In Berlin, Jagow told Goschen that the idea was "utopian and unworkable" and "would throw innumerable men on the pavement." Tirpitz solemnly explained to the Reichstag in February 1914 that the idea was illegal and disorderly: if "construction was [simply] postponed for a year . . . the omission must be made good the following year. This would upset our finances, dislocate work in the shipyards. . . . If on the other hand it was desired permanently to drop the construction of the ships for the holiday year in question, that would mean, since we only undertake the construction of replacement ships, a reduction of our organization as established by law." The Kaiser said little; he told Bethmann-Hollweg that he refused to reopen the "endless, dangerous chapter on the limitation of armaments."

On February 3, 1914, Sir Edward Grey gave a Manchester audience his view on a Naval Holiday and the competition in naval armaments: "It [expenditure on armaments] is really a cosmopolitan matter . . . not a British matter alone. . . . Any large increase in the building program of any great power in Europe has a stimulating effect upon the expenditures in other countries [but] it does not follow that a slackening in the expenditure of one country produces a diminution in the expenditure of others. . . . There is a general impression that there is in Europe an idea that this is a race with some prize to be won at the end of it. It is a most misleading idea, but supposing it exists, consciously or unconciously, it does not follow that if the leading horse slacked off, and that slackening was due to exhaustion, the effect would be a slackening on the part of others. It might be a stimulating one. Whilst British naval expenditure is a great factor in the naval expenditure of Europe, . . . [much of] the increase in expenditure on dreadnoughts . . . is going on without reference to England at all. The ships which Germany is laying down are being laid down under a Naval Law which cannot be altered by anything we can do. . . . If we were to shut down our program altogether and desist from building anything this year . . . I don't think it would cause any alteration in shipbuilding in Europe. . . . Nevertheless, I do think that this dreadnought era is one to be deplored and very wasteful. . . . We are a business country and . . . we are shocked with the sense of the waste of it. . . . As thinking men, we have the foreboding that, in the long run, exceptional expenditure on armaments, carried to an excessive degree, must lead to catastrophe, and may even sink the ship of European prosperity and civilization."

Grey's speech, like Churchill's Naval Holiday proposals, was intended to quiet the restlessness within his party at the level of spending on naval armaments. Every year of the government's existence there had been an increase in the cost of the navy. A program of eight new capital ships had been followed by a program of five capital ships: whatever the numbers, costs soared. Admirals demanded and naval architects designed larger and more expensive ships. *Dreadnought* cost £1,850,000; *Queen Elizabeth* and her sisters each would cost £4 million. The Naval Estimates rose implacably: 1907–1908, £31,250,000; 1908–1909, £32,180,000; 1909–1910, £35,730,000; 1910–1911, £40,420,000; 1911–1912, £44,390,000; 1912–1913, £45,075,000. The total sum was staggering: in six years, the Liberal government had spent or appropriated £229 million on the navy. Some felt that half this sum would have abolished most of England's social imperfections.

Churchill aggravated these Liberal feelings at the Guildhall on November 10, 1913. He announced that because of foreign spending on new ships, the next year's Naval Estimates must rise substantially. Asquith was present and had not been told what Churchill would say. He was "furious"; Lloyd George, also present, called the speech "a piece of madness."

Churchill's statement triggered fresh cries against "bloated" spending on the navy. "When will First Lords and naval experts realize that a financial reserve is one of the most important sinews of war?" asked the *Daily Chronicle*. "If other countries will not join us in the naval holiday, let us take a holiday ourselves," declared a former governor of the Bank of England. Forty Liberal M.P.'s called on the Prime Minister in a body to express their opposition to a further increase in the Naval Estimates. Margot Asquith wrote imperatively to Lloyd George: "Don't let Winston have too much money—it will hurt our party in every way. . . . If one can't be a little economical when all foreign countries are peaceful I don't know *when* one can." Even the First Lord's aunt, Lady Wimbourne, wrote to her nephew, citing the "error of judgement" of "your dear Father" which left him "eating his heart out in years of disappointment." "You are breaking with the traditions of Liberalism in your naval expenditure," she cautioned. "You are in danger of becoming purely a 'Navy man' and losing sight of the far greater job of a great leader of the Liberal party. . . . Nothing is doing the present Government so much harm as this naval expenditure. They will either have to drop you or suffer defeat."

Unionists saw the issue differently. The image of the former apostate was transformed, especially in the eyes of Conservative navalists. They now hailed Churchill as a hero battling the forces of ignorance. *Punch* noted his change in status in a cartoon depicting the First Lord in a sailor suit and behind him a chorus of Tories singing, "You made me love you; I didn't want to do it. . . ."

The public battle was raging when Churchill presented the figures in the new Naval Estimates to the Cabinet on December 5. The total was £50,694,800, up almost £3 million from the previous year. Economies had been made: the First Lord sought only four new dreadnoughts instead of five and only twelve destroyers in place of the previous year's twenty. The increased cost, he explained, came mainly from the rise in costs of construction: "the boom in the shipbuilding trade caused an advance in the price of materials of about 15 percent."

Immediately, the Cabinet plunged into debate. "We had a Cabinet which lasted nearly three hours, two and three quarters of which was occupied by Winston," Asquith wrote to Venetia Stanley at midnight on December 8. The major antagonists were the erstwhile allies Churchill and Lloyd George. As the First Lord raised the Estimates, the Chancellor faced either a deficit or a tax increase. In the Chancellor's view, this was betrayal. "When he [Churchill] went to the Admiralty, I made a bargain with him," Lloyd George told a friend on December 13. "He has not kept it. He has been extravagant." Three days later, at a meeting of the Cabinet, Churchill buttressed his case with detailed facts and figures, item by item. Lloyd George opposed him. There was an exchange of notes across the Cabinet table.

Churchill to Lloyd George:

I consider that you are going back on your word: in trying to drive me out after we had settled and you promised to support the Estimates.

Lloyd George to Churchill:

I agreed to the figure for this year and have stood by it and carried it much to the disappointment of my economical friends. But I told you distinctly I would press for a reduction of a new program with a view to 1915 and I think respectfully you are unnecessarily stubborn. It is only a question of six months postponement of laying down. That cannot endanger our safety.

Churchill to Lloyd George:

No. You said you would *support the Estimates.*

On New Year's Day 1914, the Chancellor gave an interview to the *Daily Chronicle* in which he publicly attacked the Naval Estimates. Anglo-German relations were friendlier than they had been for years; Germany was spending large sums on its army, making it impossible for her to challenge British naval supremacy. Further, the industrial masses of all countries were revolted by the "organized insanity" of the arms race. For these reasons, he was urging that the Naval Estimates be lowered, not increased. In the interview, the Chancellor went beyond policy and administered a personal slap to the First Lord. He reminded readers that Lord Randolph Churchill had resigned rather than agree to "bloated and profligate" Admiralty Estimates. When he read the interview, Churchill, hunting wild boar in France with his friend the Duke of Westminster, wrote to a colleague, "The Chancellor of the Exchequer's interview . . . is a fine illustration of his methods." Churchill fended off the press, saying it was not his policy "to give interviews to newspapers on important subjects of this character while they were still under the consideration of the Cabinet." On this point, most of Lloyd George's colleagues supported Churchill; Asquith called the interview "needless folly"; Grey was "furious . . . and refuses to be placated."

In January 1914, the crisis reached its peak. Churchill told a friend that he had his "back against the wall"; Lloyd George announced that "the Prime Minister must choose between Winston and me." Antagonism was focussed on the issue of four new dreadnoughts or two. Churchill promised the Sea Lords and the navy that "if the declared program of four ships was cut down" he would resign. If the number was reduced below four, the First Lord informed Asquith, "there is no chance whatever of my being able to go on." He wrote to the King that the matter was "vital" and "fundamental." The King agreed: "Without a doubt . . . this year's program of four battleships must be adhered to." Asquith, unwilling to lose either colleague, commanded Lloyd George and Churchill to reach agreement before the next Cabinet meeting. The two old friends met—they still referred to each other as "My dear David" and "My dear Winston"—and the Chancellor suggested a compromise: Churchill would promise that future Naval Estimates would be lower if the current figure were approved. Churchill stiffly refused: "No predecessor of mine had ever been asked or has ever attempted to forecast the Estimates of any but the coming year and I cannot undertake to do so now. . . . While I am responsible, what is necessary will have to be provided. . . . I cannot buy a year of office by a bargain under duress about the estimates of 1915–16."

On January 27, Lloyd George wrote to both the First Lord and the Prime Minister. To Churchill, he said: "My dear Winston . . . Your letter has driven me to despair and I must now decline further negotiations, leaving the issue to be decided by the Prime Minister and the Cabinet. . . . I now thoroughly appreciate your idea of a bargain: it is an argument which binds the Treasury not even to attempt any further economies in the interest of the taxpayer, whilst it does not in the least impose any obligation on the Admiralty not to incur fresh liabilities." To Asquith, the Chancellor wrote: "My

dear Prime Minister, I have laboured in vain to effect an arrangement between Churchill and the critics of his Estimates. . . . I have
utterly failed."

The Cabinet meeting of January 29 was devoted primarily to
the Naval Estimates. Over strong objection from the Chancellor, it
was agreed to spend £52,800,000 and to build four dreadnoughts.
Lloyd George pointed out that this would mean a government deficit of £9,000,000, which would have to be met by new taxation. He
pleaded for a reduction in operating and maintenance costs. After
the meeting, Asquith sent a note to Churchill:

> My dear Winston,
>   Very largely in deference to my appeal, the critical pack (who
> know very well that they have a large body of party opinion
> behind them) have slackened their pursuit. I think that you on
> your side, should . . . show a corresponding disposition and
> throw a baby or two out of the sledge.

Churchill retorted that maintenance costs already had been
"searched and scrubbed . . . as never before. . . . I see absolutely
no hope of further reductions. . . . I do not love this naval expenditure and am grieved to be found in the position of taskmaster. But
I am myself the slave of facts. . . . The sledge is bare of babies and
though the pack may crunch the driver's bones, the winter will not
be ended."

Churchill had the support of the King, the Foreign Secretary,
and, ultimately, of the Prime Minister. Lloyd George knew this. The
night before the Cabinet's final meeting on the subject, he said to
Churchill, "Come to breakfast tomorrow and we shall settle the
matter." Churchill arrived, feeling that later that day one of them
would have to resign. Lloyd George greeted him and said, "Oddly
enough, my wife spoke to me last night about this dreadnought
business. She said, 'You know, my dear, I never interfere in politics,
but they say you are having an argument with that nice Mr. Churchill about building dreadnoughts. Of course I don't understand
these things, but I should have thought it would be better to have
too many rather than too few.' So I have decided to let you build
them. Let's go in to breakfast." '

On March 17, 1914, Churchill presented the last prewar Naval
Estimates to the House of Commons. His speech took two and a
half hours and was described by the *Daily Telegraph* as "the longest
and perhaps also the most weighty and eloquent a speech to which
the House of Commons have listened from a First Lord . . . during

the present generation." The First Lord spoke about the role of the British Navy, the nature of the British Empire, and the danger of war:

"The burden of responsibility laid upon the British Navy is heavy and its weight increases year by year. All the world is building ships. . . . None of these powers need, like us, navies to defend their actual independence or safety. They build them so as to play a part in the world's affairs. It is sport to them. It is life and death to us. . . . Two things have to be considered: First, that our diplomacy depends in great part for its effectiveness upon our naval position, and that our naval strength is the one great balancing force which we can contribute to our own safety and to the peace of the world. Second, we are not a young people with a blank record and a scant inheritance. We have won for ourselves, in times when other powerful nations were paralysed by barbarism or internal war, an exceptional, disproportionate share of the wealth and traffic of the world.

"We have got all we want in territory, but our claim to be left in undisputed enjoyment of vast and splendid possessions, largely acquired by war and largely maintained by force, is one which often seems less reasonable to others than to us. . . .

"We have responsibilities in many quarters today. We are far from being detatched from the problems of Europe . . . the causes which might lead to a general war have not been removed. . . . On the contrary, we are witnessing this year increases of expenditure by Continental Powers in armaments beyond all previous experience. The world is armed as it was never armed before."

The Naval Estimates passed. Four 27,000-ton battleships with 15-inch guns, four light cruisers, and twelve destroyers were authorized. None of these ships had been laid down when war broke out five months later.

CHAPTER 44

"The Anchors Held. . . . We Seemed to Be Safe"

◆

As the Ottoman Empire continued to disintegrate, provinces sloughed away "like pieces falling off an old house." Cyprus in 1878, Tunisia in 1881, Egypt in 1882, Bosnia and Herzegovina in 1908, Tripoli in 1911. Exposure of Turkey's weakness by Italy's wrenching away of Tripoli spurred the ambitions of the small Christian states of the Balkans—Serbia, Montenegro, Greece, Bulgaria—themselves once provinces of the Ottoman Empire. In October 1912, these four powers suddenly attacked European Turkey. The Turkish Army collapsed. By November 3, the Bulgarian Army stood before the walls of Constantinople. On November 8, the Greek Army entered Salonika. On November 28, the Serbs took the port of Durazzo on the Adriatic, providing Serbia with a link to the sea. On December 3, the Turkish government begged the Balkan allies for an armistice.

The Ottoman defeat surprised and dismayed the three Great Powers of Central and Eastern Europe. Germany had been nurturing her relations with Turkey and constructing the Berlin-to-Baghdad Railway. Austria, expecting a quick humbling of the upstart Serbs, instead saw Serbia triumphant on the Adriatic. When Serbian troops entered Durazzo, Austria mobilized 900,000 men and demanded that the Serbs withdraw. If Austria moved against

Serbia, Russia, which had endorsed the formation of the Balkan League and promised to defend its conquests from Turkey, would become involved and European war would be inevitable. Paradoxically, Russia was displeased by the success of Bulgaria; Russia had always intended Constantinople to be occupied by a Russian, not a Bulgarian, army.

Sir Edward Grey, seeking to contain the conflict, proposed a Conference of the Great Powers. The Powers agreed to meet in London, and the Conference opened on December 10, 1912. The Turks were willing to give up what they had lost to Serbia and Greece, but refused to cede Adrianople (now Turkish Edirne), still held by the Turkish Army, to Bulgaria. The Bulgars insisted; the Turks would not yield. In February, the armistice collapsed and a second war began. This time, Adrianople fell to a combined Bulgarian-Serbian army. Again, the Turks sued for peace. Austria insisted that, if the port of Durazzo were not returned to Turkey, it must become independent; it could not remain in Serbian hands. Under Russian pressure, the Serbs gave up Durazzo. On May 30, 1913, the Treaty of London was signed. Adrianople was awarded to Bulgaria, Salonika was given to Greece, and the new state of Albania was created out of Durazzo and the surrounding territory. Peace lasted only one month. On June 29, Bulgaria attacked her former allies, Serbia and Greece, seized Salonika, and defeated the ill-prepared Serbian Army. At this moment, Romania, which had remained neutral in the first two Balkan Wars, fell on Bulgaria's undefended rear. The Romanian Army crossed the Danube and threatened Sofia. The Turks then took advantage of Bulgaria's fresh troubles to emerge from Constantinople and recapture Adrianople. The Kaiser backed his cousin King Carol of Romania; the Tsar was unwilling to support the maverick Tsar Ferdinand of Bulgaria; and the Third Balkan War ended on August 6 with the Treaty of Bucharest. Bulgaria was stripped of most of the gains of her wars against Turkey, Salonika was returned to Greece, and a piece of Bulgarian territory was sliced off and incorporated into Romania.

For Europe, the significance of the three Balkan wars lay less in the backstabbing between allies or the subsequent shifts of territory than in the Great Power decision that little wars should not be allowed to spread. The Conference of London consisted of Grey, who took the Chair, and the Ambassadors to Great Britain of Germany, Austria, Russia, France, and Italy. Sessions, held in St. James's Palace, were informal. "We met in the afternoons, generally about four o'clock," Grey recorded, "and, with a short adjournment to an adjoining room for tea, we continued till six or seven o'clock." Meetings occurred whenever any ambassador wished; many were so boring that Paul Cambon feared the Conference would continue until "there were six skeletons sitting around the table." Nevertheless, useful work was done. When Austria announced that Serbia must give up its gains on the Adriatic and permit an independent Albania, Benckendorff of Russia replied—to the delighted surprise of Mensdorff of Austria—that Russia accepted. There was haggling over villages along the borders. Austria demanded that Montenegro give up the town of Scutari, which it had captured; the Powers supported Austria and discussed methods to induce Montenegro to withdraw. "Eventually," Grey said, "a blend of threat of coercion and the offer of money compensation settled the matter to the satisfaction of Austria, perhaps also to the satisfaction of the King of Montenegro, and this danger to European peace was laid to rest."

In August 1913, after ten months and with the signing of the Treaty of Bucharest, the Conference ended. "There was no formal finish," Grey said. "Nobody went home, we were not photographed in a group; we had no votes of thanks; no valedictory speeches; we just left off meeting. We had not settled anything, not even all the details of Albanian boundaries; but we had served a useful purpose. We had been something to which point after point could be referred; we had been a means of keeping all the six Powers in direct and friendly touch. The mere fact that we were in existence, and that we should have to be broken up before peace was broken, was in itself an appreciable barrier against war. We were a means of gaining time and the longer we remained in being the more reluctance was there for us to disperse. The Governments concerned got used to us and to the habit of making us useful. When we ceased to meet, the present danger to the peace of Europe was over; the things that we did not settle were not threatening that peace; the things that had threatened the relations between the Great Powers in 1912–13 we had deprived of their dangerous features."

Grey modestly described his part in the Conference as "very drab and humdrum," but his prestige soared. It was clear to his confreres and to their governments that Grey was not interested in personal prestige or a triumph for British diplomacy; he worked to preserve the peace of Europe. After the war, Grey noted sadly the hope engendered by the Conference of London and the disappointment of that hope which lay ahead:

"In 1912–13 the current of European affairs was setting towards war. In agreeing to a Conference . . . it was as if we all put out anchors to prevent ourselves from being swept away. The anchors held. Then the current seemed to slacken and the anchors were pulled up. The Conference was allowed to dissolve. We seemed to be safe. In reality it was not so; the set of the current was the same, and in a year's time we were all swept into the cataract of war."

The London Conference had scarcely begun when Alfred von Kiderlen-Waechter died. To replace him, Bethmann-Hollweg summoned from the German Embassy in Rome a diminutive Prussian nobleman primarily known in Berlin for self-effacement and preoccupation with health. Gottlieb von Jagow was a protégé of Bülow. In 1895, when Bülow was ambassador to Italy, he had received a letter from an old regimental comrade, Hermann von Jagow. Jagow's younger brother, Gottlieb, a nervous, puny man in poor health, yearned to be a diplomat. Could Bernhard, his old comrade in arms, find a place for him? Bülow, in the spirit of regimental camaraderie, cleared it with the Foreign Office and invited the young man to join his staff at the Palazzo Caffarelli. Bülow's invitation was "the fulfillment of Gottlieb's wildest dreams and hopes" and the new diplomat reported for duty where, Bülow reported, he was treated "as a son."

When Bülow left Rome for the State Secretaryship in Berlin, his patronage of Gottlieb continued. Jagow was assigned wherever he wanted to go: to Hamburg, to Munich, then back for a prolonged stay in Rome. In 1906, he was summoned for a tour of duty in the Wilhelmstrasse. Jagow promptly went to see Bülow, then Chancellor. Pleading the strain of office work on his delicate health, Jagow asked for a Ministry abroad; Bülow gave him Luxembourg, where work was minimal. In 1909, Bülow suggested him as Ambassador to Italy. The Kaiser was astonished. He and Jagow had been members of the same exclusive student *Corps* at Bonn University; both were entitled to wear the peaked Stürmer cap and black and white ribbon of the elite Borussia *Corps;* bystanders were often surprised to hear the emperor addressing Jagow by the intimate *Du* used between *Corpsbrüder.* But the fraternal relationship had not affected William's low opinion of Jagow. "What?" he said when Bülow proposed to send Jagow to Rome. "Do you really want to send that little squirt out into the world as an ambassador?" Bülow persisted and William agreed. Jagow was ecstatic. "My love for Your Highness will never cease as long as I live," he said to Bülow and joyfully went off to Rome.

Jagow's four years as ambassador were pleasant; thus his summons to Berlin to replace Kiderlen was unwelcome. In the State Secretaryship, he saw hard work combined with innumerable opportunities for failure. No ambassador since Bülow had willingly given up an embassy to take the Wilhelmstrasse and, of the four State Secretaries who preceded Jagow, two had died in office. Accordingly, Jagow resisted his new assignment, arguing that he lacked physical strength and professional ability. In vain. On January 5, 1913, he wrote to Bülow, who was then retired: "Nothing has helped. I am appointed."

At the Wilhelmstrasse, Jagow was the opposite of his predecessor. Kiderlen was large and robust, Jagow small and frail. Kiderlen's behavior fluctuated between warm good humor and coarse rudeness, and he considered his arrangement with Frau Krypke nobody's business but his own. At forty-nine, Jagow was unmarried; he was cool, elitist, and insecure, glancing up furtively to check people's reactions to himself. His purpose, during the eighteen months he held the State Secretaryship before the war, was to maintain the reputation he had achieved in Rome and to accommodate his two masters, the Chancellor and the Kaiser. He attempted no diplomatic initiatives; indeed, Jagow's arrival signified that foreign policy, which had been in Kiderlen's hands until the failure at Agadir, had passed to Bethmann. The Chancellor's ambition was to improve relations with England. On February 7, 1913, only a fortnight after moving into the Wilhelmstrasse, Jagow said in the Reichstag:

"The intimate exchange of opinion which goes on between us and the English Government [Jagow referred to the London Conference] has done a great deal to remove difficulties of many kinds. . . . We have now seen that not only have we points of contact of a sentimental kind with England, but that common interests exist as well. I am no prophet, but I indulge in the hope that, on the ground of common interest which in politics is the most fruitful ground, we can continue to work with England and perhaps reap the harvest. But I must point out to you that we are dealing here with tender plants; we must not destroy them by premature acts or words."

Jagow managed to please the Kaiser. Only a month after the new State Secretary's arrival, William said to Müller, "He's becoming admirably seasoned. The little man says he would be the first to recommend war to His Majesty if anyone tried to dispute Germany's rights in Asia Minor."

German diplomacy, in the years after Agadir, changed tactics. Although the Haldane mission had been rebuffed and Churchill's Naval Holiday proposals turned aside, German policy toward Britain had been, in Churchill's words, "not only correct but considerate.

. . . The personalities who expressed the foreign policy of Germany seemed for the first time to be men to whom we could talk and with whom common action was possible." "The Kaiser was very cautious throughout the Balkan Wars," Bethmann reported, "and remarked to me in November [1912] that 'I shall not march against Paris or Moscow for the sake of Albania or Durazzo.' " William could not prevent himself from issuing snorts of disgust during the Conference about "eunuch-like statesmen" with their "everlasting talk about peace," but on the whole his behavior was temperate, and Anglo-German relations were more cordial than they had been since before the Boer War.

This era of good feelings coincided with the arrival in London of the new German Ambassador, Prince Karl Max Lichnowsky. The Prince, sent to succeed the stricken Marschall von Bieberstein, reached London in November 1912, shortly before the opening of the London Conference. Lichnowsky's wealth and social position set him apart from most German diplomats. He had spent twenty years in the diplomatic corps, serving in Bucharest, London, and Vienna and, for five years (1899–1904), as personnel director at the Wilhelmstrasse. He was responsible for choosing among applicants who wished to enter the service. Lichnowsky's preference was for young men of good family. "I made it a practice to watch the candidate as he entered the room," he explained. "Then I knew pretty well with whom I had to deal." In the internal wars between Bülow and Holstein, Lichnowsky sided with Bülow, under whom he had served in Bucharest. Holstein responded by labelling Lichnowsky "a muddlehead"; Lichnowsky described Holstein as a man "who by his intimates was considered to be not quite normal."

In 1904, Lichnowsky wearied of this squabbling and retired to look after his estates, spending eight years in Silesia surrounded by "flax and turnips, among meadows and horses." To the end of his life, he said, he had no idea why William II suddenly plucked him from country life and sent him to London. When Bethmann, who was not consulted, expressed doubts, the Kaiser grew angry: "I send only *my* ambassador to London, who has *my* confidence, obeys *my* will, fulfills *my* orders with *my* instructions," he told the Chancellor. Once Lichnowsky was installed in the massive German Embassy, he threw open the doors which the reclusive Metternich had kept closed. Invitations to luncheons, dinners, and balls flooded out to London society. The German Ambassador became a regular speaker before British commercial and financial audiences. He stressed the common needs of German and British business and trading interests. He was given the freedom of cities; in June 1914, Oxford University made him an honorary Doctor of Laws.

Lichnowsky's opinions of the English were straightforward:

"The King, although not a genius, is a simple and well-meaning man with sound common sense. . . .

"An Englishman either is a member of society or he would like to be one. . . .

"British gentlemen of both parties have the same education, go to the same colleges and universities, have the same recreations—golf, cricket, lawn tennis, or polo—and spend the weekend in the country. . . .

"The Briton loathes a bore, a schemer, and a prig; he likes a good fellow. . . ."

Lichnowsky never cared for Asquith, whom he described as "a jovial *bon vivant,* fond of the ladies, especially the young and pretty ones . . . partial to cheerful society and good cooking . . . favoring an understanding with Germany, treated all questions with a cheery calm . . ." Nor was Asquith partial to Prince or Princess Lichnowsky, complaining to Venetia Stanley that the Ambassador's voice was "raucous" and "querulous," that an evening with the Lichnowsky couple was "rather trying . . . he is loquacious and inquisitive about trifles . . . she took possession of the piano stool and strummed and drummed infernal patches of tuneless music for the rest of the evening." Margot Asquith, however, liked Princess Lichnowsky and wrote, "In spite of black socks, white boots and her crazy tiaras, I could not but admire her."

Lichnowsky's favorite Englishman was Sir Edward Grey: "The simplicity and honesty of his ways secured him the esteem even of his opponents. . . . His authority was undisputed. . . . On important occasions he used to say, 'I must first bring it before the Cabinet'; but this always agreed with his views." From their first meeting at the Foreign Office on November 14, 1912, the two diplomats worked "hand in hand" to bring their countries closer together. To the annoyance of Berlin, and particularly the Kaiser, who had selected Lichnowsky as "*my* ambassador," the Prince reported to Berlin truths it did not wish to hear. "Sir Edward Grey said that he wished above all that there might be no repetition of . . . 1909 [i.e., the Bosnian Crisis]," the Ambassador reported on the eve of the London Conference. "For he was convinced—and this sentence he twice repeated with special emphasis—that Russia would not a second time beat a retreat but would rather take up arms. . . . If a European war were to arise through Austria's attacking Serbia, and Russia, compelled by public opinion, were to march . . . rather than again put up with a humiliation like that of 1909, thus forcing Germany to come to the aid of Austria, France would inevitably be drawn in *and no one could foretell what further developments might follow* [emphasis Lichnowsky's]. . . . England's policy towards us is one of peace and friendship, but . . . no British Government could reconcile it with the vital interests of the country if it permitted France to be still further weakened. This attitude is based neither on secret treaties nor on the intrigues of Edward VII, nor on the after-effects of the Morocco crisis, but solely on the consideration . . . that after a second collapse of France like that of 1870, the British nation would find itself confronted by one single all-powerful Continental nation, a danger that must be avoided at all costs."

During Lichnowsky's embassy, the long-standing dispute about German penetration of the Middle East via the Berlin-to-Baghdad Railway was settled when Britain withdrew her opposition to the railway. In return for this concession, British traders were granted the same privileges as Germans on all parts of the railway. Control of navigation on the Tigris River and in the Persian Gulf was awarded to Britain. The treaty was initialled on June 15, 1914, and announced by Grey in the House of Commons on June 29, the day after the assassination at Sarajevo.

In April 1914, a shadow fell over Anglo-German relations. Since 1908, the German government, fearful of "encirclement," had worried that Great Britain would extend the ententes with France and Russia to the status of full military alliances. In the spring of 1914, these apprehensions, constantly stirred by rumors of talks between French and British military staffs, were aggravated by reports that Britain and Russia were about to begin naval conversations. The reports were true.

The Russians had wanted a closer military connection with England. They had been rebuffed. In 1912, when Sergei Sazonov, the Russian Foreign Minister, suggested an Anglo-Russian naval understanding, Grey politely ignored the suggestion. In February 1914, Tsar Nicholas II proposed an Anglo-Russian defensive alliance to Sir George Buchanan, the British Ambassador in St. Petersburg. Buchanan replied that Parliament would not permit a peacetime alliance. The Tsar proposed a naval convention similar to the one between England and France. Again, Buchanan demurred. The Russians persisted. In mid-April, King George V, making the first ceremonial visit of his reign, travelled to Paris, capital of Britain's principal Continental partner. Grey accompanied the sovereign; it was the first time the Foreign Secretary had been out of England in nine years of office. The weather was superb; the horse chestnuts were in flower. Grey rode in the procession in a carriage with the French Premier, Domergue, who did not speak English. Grey's French was soon exhausted. They travelled in silence, occasionally waving to the crowds, and Grey had a good chance to study the two French cavalrymen who rode close beside the carriage. One was "swarthy . . . thick-set, sturdy . . . a typical son of the soil. . . . The other was fair, slender, almost frail in body, [with] a sensitive face, suggesting a possible artist or poet. . . . His helmet sat uneasily on him. . . . It brought home to me, as I had never felt it before, what conscription meant. . . . Each of these young men, at the age when life should be developing in different ways . . . must be trained to kill or be killed in defence of his country."

On the last morning of the visit, Grey met the French Foreign Minister at the Quai d'Orsay and was confronted with an urgent request. On behalf of their Russian ally, the French Minister urged Grey to pay heed to the Tsar's plea for a naval convention. Grey took the entreaty home with him for consideration. The strategic issues involved were easily dealt with: the Admiralty did not consider the Russian Fleet a valuable or even a useful potential ally. Most of the Tsar's fleet had been annihilated at Port Arthur or Tsushima, and although the Duma had voted a new five-year program of battleship construction in 1912, these ships still were mostly blueprints. Geography was an additional barrier. "To my mind," Grey said, "it seemed that in a war with Germany, the Russian fleet would not get out of the Baltic and the British fleet would not get into it." Dealing with the diplomatic side of the proposal was more delicate. A flat refusal would offend the Russians by giving the impression that they were not being treated equally with the French. It was important, Grey believed, "to reassure Russia and keep her loyal." In mid-May, on the understanding that there were to be no commitments which could drag Britain into a Continental war, the Cabinet reluctantly assented to secret naval conversations. Benckendorff informed Sazonov in St. Petersburg.

Since 1909, a German spy in the Russian Embassy in London had been reporting to Berlin all of Count Benckendorff's correspondence with Count Sazonov. The spy's report of the impending conversations alarmed the Wilhelmstrasse. German strategists were much less sure than Grey that in wartime a British fleet would not attempt to penetrate the Baltic to support a seaborne Russian invasion of Pomerania. Knowing that many in Britain would be opposed to any closer relationship between England and Russia, the Wilhelmstrasse decided to make public the news its spy had provided, in the hope that the talks might be frustrated before they started. Accordingly, the *Berliner Tageblatt* was given the story, although the source was protected. The London press picked up the *Tageblatt* story, and Grey, to his chagrin, was told that there would be questions in the Commons. On June 11, the Foreign Secretary was asked whether any conversations with a view to a naval agreement had taken place. Grey's reply, true in the narrowest sense, was deliberately misleading: "No such negotiations are in progress and none are likely to be entered upon, as far as I can judge." He went on to promise that the government would not involve itself in talks "which would restrict or hamper the freedom of the Government or of Parliament to decide whether or not Great Britain should participate in a war."

Lichnowsky, kept ignorant by his own government of the spy's activities, was assured that no British military alliance with Russia existed or would be entered into. The Ambassador advised Bethmann that Grey's assurances "left nothing to be desired." The Chancellor, although knowing the truth, played Grey's game and told Lichnowsky that the Foreign Secretary's statement had been "most satisfactory." Jagow told Goschen how pleased he was and that Grey's declaration had come as a "great relief." In St. Petersburg, Sazonov not only buttressed Grey's denial but carried it even further from the truth, telling the German Ambassador that Anglo-Russian naval conversations existed only "in the mind of the *Berliner Tageblatt* and on the moon." The Wilhelmstrasse, concluding that very little was happening and that, in any case, it was preferable to leave their spy in place to continue to monitor events, rather than reveal him and embarrass Grey, let the matter drop.

In fact, very little happened. An eager Captain Volkov, the Russian Naval Attaché in London, had one conversation with Prince Louis of Battenberg, the First Sea Lord. Prince Louis found little to discuss and postponed any further conversations with Russian naval officers until his forthcoming visit to St. Petersburg in August 1914. Benckendorff reported this to Sazonov, adding that Sir Edward Grey wished the talks to go slowly. "He would find it difficult," Benckendorff noted, "to at the same moment issue denials and to negotiate."

In Britain, a sense of calm and security had replaced the alarm of earlier years over the German naval challenge. Churchill's plea for a

Naval Holiday had been rebuffed and building continued on both sides of the North Sea, but the margin of British dreadnought superiority was steadily increasing. In 1909, during the Navy Scare, the British Admiralty ordered eight dreadnoughts to Germany's four. In 1910, the ratio slipped to seven to four, and in 1911, it slipped further, to five to four. But in 1912, the five super-dreadnoughts of the *Queen Elizabeth* class were matched only by the battleship *Kronprinz Wilhelm* and the battlecruiser *Lützow*. In 1913, another five British super-dreadnoughts of the *Revenge* class were ordered, and Germany answered with three ships. In the 1914 Naval Estimates, passed on the eve of the war, the Royal Navy was authorized to build another four dreadnoughts, while the High Seas Fleet was granted only a single new ship. In the aggregate, these numbers—thirty-four British dreadnoughts to eighteen German—substantially exceeded the 16 : 10 margin agreed to by Tirpitz; indeed, it fell only two vessels shy of a superiority of two to one. Addressing the Commons in July 1913, Churchill promised that "the coming months would see the biggest deliveries of warships to the Admiralty in the history of the British Fleet: . . . one torpedo boat a week . . . one light cruiser every thirty days . . . one super-dreadnought every forty-five days."

Tirpitz accepted the 16 : 10 ratio in February 1913 because he had no choice. The reason was cost. In 1913, 170,000 men were added to the peacetime German Army, to bring its total to 870,000. The cost to the taxpayers was an additional £50 million. To add to this sum a demand for more dreadnoughts would be "a great political blunder," Tirpitz wrote to Müller in London. "The bow is overstrung here as much as in England," he explained. Besides, he added gloomily, any increase in German strength would only give Churchill a reason to increase the British program.

Lichnowsky always opposed the dreadnought competition. Soon after arriving in England, he reported to Bethmann: "To me it seems quite obvious that the British Empire, depending as it does on imports from overseas, should regard the protection of its trade routes as indispensable. . . . Great Britain as a world power stands or falls with her predominance at sea. If we ourselves were responsible for the safeguarding of an empire like that of Great Britain, we should without doubt strive to maintain our seapower with the same solicitude as that now shown by the British Ministers." A few months later, the Ambassador endorsed the view of the *Westminster Gazette:* "If Germany succeeds in wresting from England her supremacy at sea, the result will be that the English Channel will practically disappear and that England will be forced to enter into definite military and naval alliances with other Powers."

On April 30, 1913, Lichnowsky first met Winston Churchill at a dinner in honor of the King. The First Lord immediately declared that "the German fleet was the only obstacle to a really intimate understanding between the two countries." Lichnowsky thought Churchill "thoroughly pleasant and genial, but—he wrote to Bethmann—"as he is very vain, and is bent, come what may, on playing a brilliant part, it will be necessary for us to humor his vanity and to avoid doing anything that might make him look ridiculous. I should not feel inclined to overestimate his influence on the Government's foreign policy. Sir Edward Grey and Mr. Asquith . . . regard him as impulsive and flighty." Churchill was indeed determined to play a part. In October 1913, the First Lord told a meeting of Liberal women in Dundee that strengthening the Royal Navy was essential to peace. Britain's naval supremacy, he declared, accounted for the steady improvement in relations with Germany. "It was the feeling of insufficient security and not calm confidence in their own strength which gave rise to irritation between the nations of the earth. If men knew they were secure against any risk of attack, a feeling of calm security spread through the country and it caused freer and better relations with other nations."

Churchill's speech, telegraphed to Berlin, drew enthusiastic applause from the Kaiser, who seized on the First Lord's thesis as a vindication for the German Navy. "What a triumph for Tirpitz!" wrote William II. "Best thanks for the compliment, Winston Churchill! For me and all who with me framed and extended the Navy Law . . . no more brilliant justification could be imagined or expected. . . . A fresh proof of the old theory I have so often maintained that only ruthless, manly, and unaffrighted maintenance of our own interests impresses the English and is at length compelling them to seek a *rapprochement* with us; never the so-called accommodation which they only and invariably take for flabbiness and cowardice. I shall therefore go on ruthlessly and implacably with the execution of the Navy Law down to the smallest detail in spite of all opposition. . . . England comes to us, not in spite of, but because of *my* Imperial Navy!!"

At the end of May 1914, the Admiralty announced that in June major units of the British Fleet would be making ceremonial visits to Baltic ports. Vice Admiral Sir George Warrender would lead the Second Battle Squadron, four of the latest dreadnoughts including

King George V, Ajax, Audacious, and *Centurion,* into Kiel. Rear Admiral Sir David Beatty would take the First Battle Cruiser Squadron, including *Lion, Princess Royal, Queen Mary,* and *New Zealand,* up to Kronstadt, the naval harbor of St. Petersburg.

For a while, it seemed that Winston Churchill also might come to Kiel to meet his counterpart, Admiral Tirpitz, on the deck of a dreadnought. Ballin and Cassel, undeterred by the failure of the Haldane mission two years before, hoped that if the two men got together, the First Lord might persuade the State Secretary to moderate the arms race. Cassel reported that Churchill was excited by the prospect of grappling with Tirpitz. On May 20, Churchill proposed to Grey that he make the visit, suggesting that he might discuss limiting the size of capital ships and reducing concentrations of ships in Home Waters; reopen the question of a Naval Holiday; and banish the secrecy surrounding naval shipbuilding in British and German dockyards. "This policy of secrecy was instituted by the British Admiralty a few years ago with the worst results for us for we have been much less successful in keeping our secrets than the Germans," Churchill wrote to Grey. "We should give naval attachés equal reciprocal facilities to visit the dockyards to see what was going on. This would reduce espionage on both sides which is a continuing cause of suspicion and ill-will." Grey was dubious about a Churchill visit, fearing that more harm than good might result if he unleashed the First Lord on Admiral von Tirpitz. In Berlin, the Kaiser vetoed an invitation unless Asquith first asked for one. If this occurred, the First Lord "would be greeted with pleasure." Grey was unenthusiastic and Asquith did not ask. Churchill did not accompany the battleships to Kiel, although until the last minute a harbor mooring buoy was reserved for the *Enchantress.*

On the early morning of June 23, the gray shapes of the Second Battle Squadron emerged from the mist ten miles off the German Baltic coast. When they entered the port, the mist had evaporated and Kiel Harbor was bathed in sunshine. Yachts and naval launches circled the ships, and the shore was black with spectators. Sir George Warrender and his captains boarded the German flagship, *Friedrich der Grosse,* to be welcomed by Admiral Friedrich von Ingenhol, Commander-in-Chief of the High Seas Fleet.

They went ashore to the Royal Castle, where Prince Henry and Princess Irene greeted them in unaccented English. In the afternoon Prince Henry visited the British flagship, *King George V,* and described her as "the finest ship afloat." The following day, Admiral von Tirpitz arrived from Berlin, hoisted his flag in the battleship *Friedrich Karl,* and invited the English officers to his cabin. Again,

English was spoken, and Tirpitz, sipping champagne, described for his guests the development of the German Navy. That afternoon, all ships in the harbor, British and German, thundered twenty-one-gun salutes as the Kaiser arrived, on board the *Hohenzollern,* which had passed through the Kiel Canal. Airplanes and a zeppelin circled overhead; this ceremony was marred when one of the planes crashed into the sea. Proceeding to its anchorage, the gold and white *Hohenzollern* passed the mammoth *King George V,* whose decks and turrets were lined by sailors in white and by red-jacketed marines. Once the Imperial yacht was anchored a signal fluttered up, inviting all British senior officers aboard. In full-dress uniform, the British admiral and captains climbed the *Hohenzollern*'s accommodation ladder and were received by the enthusiastic Emperor. On June 25, the Kaiser, wearing the uniform of a British Admiral of the Fleet, paid his first and only visit to a British dreadnought. Admiral Warrender served lunch. His guests were led to his private dining room, paneled in mahogany and furnished with comfortable leather chairs and sofas. They ate at small tables set with flowers, and listened to an orchestra playing works by German composers. Warrender gave a speech hailing the spirit of goodfellowship between the British and German fleets. William was in high spirits; he made jokes, poked fun at the top hat of a diplomat present, and asked whether sailors in the British Navy ever swore.

That same day the yacht regatta began. For the rest of the week the harbor and the sea approaches to Kiel were flecked with sails. On Friday the twenty-sixth, the Kaiser invited Warrender, the British Ambassador, Sir Edward Goschen, Prince Henry, and Tirpitz to race with him aboard the *Meteor.* Meanwhile, officers and sailors of the British squadron were fraternizing with German officers and with the townspeople of Kiel. German officers in white waistcoats, with gold braid on their trousers, sat drinking whiskey and soda in the wardrooms of British ships, while young British officers attended tennis matches, tea dances, dinner parties, and balls, where they flirted with German girls. Married English officers were invited to the homes of married German officers. The town of Kiel provided competitive games for English seamen: soccer matches, relay races, tugs of war. Every day, the German Admiralty offered hundreds of free railway passes so that English sailors could visit Berlin and Hamburg. In a somber moment, British and German officers stood bareheaded at the funeral of the pilot killed as the *Hohenzollern* entered the harbor.

There were moments when the fact that the two fleets had been built to fight each other could not be ignored. British officers heard whispers that the Kaiserin and her sons had not come because they so disliked England. German officers who seemed carried away by British goodfellowship found Commander von Müller, the German Naval Attaché in London, at their elbows, hissing urgently; "Be on your guard against the English. England is ready to strike; war is imminent, and the object of this visit is only spying. They want to see how prepared we are. Whatever you do, tell them nothing about our U-boats!" The only evidence of British "spying" was shaky. Fuddled old Lord Brassey, an ardent yachtsman and friend of the Kaiser's, set off for shore one day with a single sailor in a dinghy from his yacht, *Sunbeam,* and found himself inside the U-boat dock of the Kiel building yards, which was closed to civilians. Arrested and kept under guard until identified, he was released in time for dinner. Admiral Warrender offered Admiral von Ingehol and his officers complete freedom of all British ships except for the wireless room and the fire-control section of the conning towers. The German Admiral was forced to refuse, as he could not respond by showing British officers through German ships. When Tirpitz and Ingehol came to lunch on board *King George V,* Warrender repeated his invitation. Tirpitz refused, but Ingehol consented to go inside one of the 13.5-inch gun turrets, which was rotated and the guns elevated for his inspection.

On Sunday, June 28, the Kaiser went racing again aboard the *Meteor.* At two-thirty that afternoon, a telegram arrived in Kiel announcing the assassination of the Archduke Franz Ferdinand. Admiral von Müller, Chief of the Naval Cabinet, ordered a launch and set out to find his master. "We overhauled the *Meteor* sailing on a northerly course with a faint breeze," Müller wrote. "The Kaiser was standing in the stern with his guests, watching the arrival of our launch with some anxiety. I called out to him that I was the bearer of grave news and that I would throw the written message across. But His Majesty insisted upon knowing at once what it was all about so I gave him the message by word of mouth. . . . The Kaiser was very calm and merely asked, 'Would it be better to abandon the race?' "

The character of Kiel Week changed. Flags were lowered to half-mast, and receptions, dinners, and a ball at the Royal Castle were cancelled. Early the next morning, the Kaiser departed, intending to go to Vienna and the Archduke's funeral. Warrender struggled to preserve the spirit of the week. Speaking to a hall filled with sailors from both fleets, he spoke of the friendship between the two countries and called for three cheers for the German Navy. A German admiral called for three cheers for the British Navy. The two admirals shook hands. On the morning of June 30, the British squadron weighed anchor and left the harbor. The signal masts of German warships flew the signal "Pleasant journey." From his flagship, Warrender sent a wireless message back to the German Fleet: "Friends in past and friends forever."

CHAPTER 45

The Coming
of Armageddon:
Berlin

◆

Winston Churchill gave his final peacetime Naval Estimates to the House of Commons on March 17, 1914.
He spoke somberly of the situation in Europe:

"The causes which might lead to a general war have not been
removed and often remind us of their presence. There has not been
the slightest abatement of naval and military preparation. On the
contrary, we are witnessing this year increases of expenditure by
Continental powers on armaments beyond all previous expenditure.
The world is arming as it was never armed before. Every suggestion
for arrest or limitation has so far been ineffectual."

Weapons were accumulating in the armories of states harboring bitter antagonisms. France had waited forty-four years for *revanche*
and the rejoining of Alsace and Lorraine. Russia, defeated in the
Far East in 1905, humiliated in the Balkans in 1908, could not afford
to suffer further abasement; if another challenge were offered by
Austria and Germany, it would be accepted. Austria-Hungary, facing disintegration from within, believed it could save itself by striking down the external source of its difficulties, the Kingdom of
Serbia. The Hapsburg monarchy had Germany's pledge of support.

Germans were ready for war. Britain's gradual adherence to the Triple Entente made more real the nightmare of Encirclement. Britain, for the moment distracted by Ireland, had fears in Europe—primarily of the German Fleet—but few antagonisms. Indeed, her traditional antagonisms with France and Russia had been resolved. Whether, or for what reasons, Britain would fight remained unclear.

In Churchill's words, "the vials of wrath were full."

"I shall not live to see the world war," Bismarck said to Ballin in 1891, "but you will. And it will start in the East."

By the summer of 1914, the Austro-Hungarian Empire had shrunk from the days of Hapsburg magnificence, but it still was larger than any Continental power except Russia. The lands ruled by the Emperor Franz Josef were a patchwork of provinces, races, and nationalities spread across Central Europe and the upper Balkans. Three fifths of the Empire's 40 million people were Slavs—Poles, Czechs, Slovaks, Serbs, Bosnians, Montenegrins—but the Empire was ruled by its two non-Slavic races, the Germanic Austrians and the Magyar Hungarians. The structure of government, a dual monarchy, reflected this arrangement: the Emperor of Austria was also the King of Hungary; Austrians and Magyars controlled the bureaucracy; there was place for the Slavs neither at court nor in the government.

Austria-Hungary's nemesis, a nation of free Slavs, the young, independent Kingdom of Serbia, was set close by the sprawling, multinational empire. Serbia's existence acted as a magnet on the restless populations of Austria's South Slav provinces: Bosnia, Herzegovina, and Montenegro. Inside Serbia and in the South Slav provinces, nationalists longed to break up the Hapsburg Empire and weld the dissident provinces into a single Greater South Slav Kingdom. Belgrade, capital of Serbia, was a center of inflammatory Slav propaganda distributed inside the Empire.

Ultimately, either the Emperor Franz Josef or his heir, the Archduke Franz Ferdinand, would decide how Austria would meet the Serbian challenge. If he lived long enough, it would be the Emperor, but in 1914 Franz Josef was eighty-four. His reign of sixty-six years, the longest in modern Europe, had been marked by a sequence of political defeats and personal calamities. The bald little gentleman with muttonchop whiskers had come to the throne in 1848 as a slim, wavy-haired youth of eighteen. He was still a young man when the northern Italian provinces, Lombardy and Venice, were stripped away. Defeat by Prussia in 1866 led to expulsion of Hapsburg influence in Germany. In 1867, Franz Josef's brother, blond, dreamy Maximilian, briefly installed as Emperor of Mexico, was executed by a firing squad on a Mexican hillside. Franz Josef's only son, rakish Crown Prince Rudolf, killed himself and his mistress in a suicide pact at Mayerling. Franz Josef's wife, Empress Elisabeth, once the most beautiful princess in Europe, withdrew after six years of marriage and wandered Europe for four decades until she was struck down by an anarchist's knife. Franz Josef's response to blows was to tighten his emotions and steel himself for further shocks. Facing political challenge, he vowed to maintain the authority of the Crown and the integrity of the Empire. He had no intention of appeasing the South Slavs by modifying the structure of government and giving them a voice.

This conciliatory course was proposed by Franz Josef's nephew and heir. The Archduke Franz Ferdinand, a ponderous, glowering man with brush-cut hair, had offended his uncle by marrying a Bohemian of insufficient rank, Countess Sophie Chotek. The old Emperor insisted that the Archduke renounce the throne for any children he might have from the marriage; Countess Sophie, wife of the future Emperor, although created a Duchess, was forced in public processions to walk behind the forty-four Hapsburg Archduchesses. Franz Ferdinand himself was restricted to ceremonial functions; he was allowed to inspect army barracks, attend maneuvers, and occasionally to visit provincial capitals. Time was on his side, but he worried that when, eventually, he came to the throne, the disintegration of the Empire would be irreparably advanced. His solution to the problem of nationalist agitation in the South Slav provinces was to reconcile those populations by a radical reconstruction of the structure of the Imperial government: transformation of the Dual Monarchy into a Triad, in which the South Slavs shared power with the Austrians and Magyars. For these views, the Archduke was warmly disliked, especially by the Magyars, who did not relish the thought of diluting their own powerful grip on the Imperial administration.

Meanwhile, another solution for Austria's troubles was growing in popularity: eliminate the source of Slav agitation by crushing Serbia. To the conservative ruling class of the Empire, a preventive war seemed preferable to the kind of decomposition afflicting the Ottoman Empire and more bearable than the protracted negotiations and painful compromises that would be necessary to transform the dual structure into a triad. "Austria," reported the French Ambassador in Vienna on December 13, 1913, "finds herself in an impasse without knowing how she is to escape. . . . People here are becoming accustomed to the idea of a general war as the only possible remedy." The principal advocate of preventive war, General Count Franz Conrad von Hötzendorf, Chief of the General Staff of the Austrian Army, spoke of Serbia as "a dangerous little viper"; he longed to crush the "viper" in its nest. Twice, Austria had mobilized against Serbia, during the Bosnian annexation crisis of 1908–1909 and during the Balkan Wars of 1912–1913. Each time, Conrad had been held back; in 1908, because "at the last moment His Majesty was against it"; in 1912–1913, he complained that he had been "left in the lurch" by Germany.

By 1914, as Conrad knew, the Hapsburg monarchy was too weak to undertake initiatives, military or diplomatic, without assurance of German support. But Conrad also knew that German support must be forthcoming.

The continued existence of Austria-Hungary was vital to the German Empire. Austria was the Reich's only reliable ally. If Austria disintegrated, Germany would face Russia, France, and possibly England alone. In the Wilhelmstrasse, therefore, the preservation of Austria as a Great Power became a cardinal point of German policy. Some German diplomatists worried about this virtually unqualified support for the Hapsburg monarchy. In May 1914, Baron von Tschirschky, the German Ambassador in Vienna, uttered a cry of near despair: "I constantly wonder whether it really pays to bind ourselves so tightly to this phantasm of a state which is cracking in every direction." Tschirschky's cry was ignored. "Our own vital interests demand the preservation of Austria," declared Chancellor von Bethmann-Hollweg.

The Austrian government understood and was prepared to exploit this German predicament. For months, the Kaiser and General von Moltke, Chief of the German General Staff, had given Austria explicit, hearty encouragement to take action against Serbia, even if it meant a German confrontation with Serbia's ally, Russia. On October 26, 1913, the Kaiser had a conversation in Vienna with Count Berchtold, the Austrian Foreign Minister. William began with high-flown talk of the "world historic process," declaring that a war was inevitable in which the Germanic peoples would have to stave off "a mighty impulse of Slavdom." "The Slavs were born to serve and not to rule, and this must be brought home to them," he continued. Specifically, in the case of Serbia, "If His Majesty Francis Joseph demands something, the Serbian Government must yield, and if she does not, then Belgrade will be bombarded and occupied until the will of His Majesty is fulfilled. You may rest assured that I stand behind you and am ready to draw the sword." As he spoke, William moved his hand to the hilt of his sword. The interview concluded with another pledge. "His Majesty ostentatiously used the occasion to assure me that we could absolutely and completely count on him," said Berchtold. "This was the red thread which ran through the utterances of the illustrious Sovereign and when I laid stress on this on taking my departure and thanked him as I left, His Majesty did me the honor to say that whatever came from the Vienna Foreign Office was a command for him."

Moltke had no doubt that war was imminent. He was ready. Like Conrad, he sensed that time was against the Triple Alliance, that the balance of power in Europe was shifting, that Serbia and Russia must be dealt with before the Russian Army was reequipped and the "Slav battering ram" could be driven home. On May 12, 1914, Conrad visited Karlsbad, where Moltke was taking a cure. "General von Moltke expressed the opinion that every delay meant a lessening of our chances," Conrad recorded. The Austrian chief agreed, adding pointedly that "the attitude of Germany in past years has caused us to let many favorable opportunities go by." He asked how long the coming "joint war against Russia and France would last; that is, how long before Germany would be able to turn against Russia with strong forces." Moltke replied, "We hope in six weeks after the beginning of operations to have finished with France, or at least so far as to enable us to direct our principal forces against the East."

Two weeks after the generals met, the Kaiser visited the Archduke Franz Ferdinand at his castle, Konopischt, in Bohemia. The Archduke's garden was famous for its roses and, officially, the German Emperor had come to admire the flowers in bloom. Over two days, William and Franz Ferdinand discussed the dangers posed to the Dual Monarchy and the Triple Alliance by Serbia. They agreed that something must be done. Russia was a factor, but it was the Archduke's opinion that internal difficulties in the Tsar's empire were too great to permit Russia to consider war.

Franz Ferdinand had another appointment at the end of June. He was scheduled to attend army maneuvers in the Bosnian mountains and, as a gesture to the South Slav population, he decided to pay a ceremonial visit to the Bosnian capital, Sarajevo. As a show of goodwill, he asked that the troops normally lining the streets for security during an Imperial visit be dispensed with. Except for a scattering of local policemen, the crowds were to have free access to the Heir to the Throne. On the morning of June 28, Franz Ferdinand, dressed in the pale blue tunic and red-striped black trousers of a cavalry general, with green plumes waving from his cap, sat in the open back seat of the second car, next to his wife, Sophie. Around him on the streets, he saw smiling faces and waving arms. Flags and decorative bright-colored rugs hung from the balconies; his own portrait stared back at him from the windows of shops and houses.

As the procession neared City Hall, the Archduke's chauffeur spotted an object as it was hurled from the crowd. He pressed the accelerator, and a bomb which would have landed in Sophie's lap exploded under the wheels of the car behind. Two officers were wounded and the young bomb-thrower was apprehended by the police. Franz Ferdinand arrived at City Hall shaken and furious. "One comes here for a visit," he shouted, "and is welcomed by bombs." There was an urgent conference. A member of the Archduke's suite asked whether a military guard could be arranged. "Do you think Sarajevo is filled with assassins?" replied the provincial governor.

It was decided to go back through the city by a different route from the one announced. On the way, the driver of the first car, forgetting the alteration, turned into one of the prearranged streets. The Archduke's chauffeur, following behind, was momentarily misled. He started to turn. An official shouted, "That's the wrong way!" At that moment, a slim nineteen-year-old boy stepped forward, aimed a pistol into the car, and fired twice. Sophie sank forward onto her husband's chest. Franz Ferdinand remained sitting upright and for a moment no one noticed that he had been hit. Then the governor, sitting in front, heard him murmur, "Sophie! Sophie! Don't die! Stay alive for our children!" His body sagged and blood from the severed jugular vein in his neck spurted across his uniform. He died almost immediately. Sophie, the Duchess of Hohenberg, died soon after. Fifteen minutes later, both bodies were laid in a room next to the ballroom where waiters were chilling champagne for his reception.

The assassin, Gavrilo Princip, was a native Bosnian, who, on trial, declared that he had acted to "kill an enemy of the South Slavs" and also because the Archduke was "an energetic man who as ruler would have carried through ideas and reforms which stood in our way." Princip was part of a team of youthful assassins, all of whom were Bosnians and thus Austro-Hungarian subjects, belonging to a revolutionary movement whose object was to detach Bosnia and other Slav provinces from the Hapsburg monarchy and incorporate them into a Kingdom of Greater Serbia. They had been provided with six pistols and six bombs taken from the Serbian State Arsenal and smuggled with Serbian help across the frontier. The

Serbian government was not involved, but the plot had been hatched in Belgrade. The organizers were members of a secret society of extreme Serbian nationalists known as the Black Hand.

The assassination horrified Europe. Sympathy lay overwhelmingly with the House of Hapsburg. Scarcely anyone questioned Austria-Hungary's right to impose some form of retribution. Sir Edward Grey, looking back, remembered, "No crime has ever aroused deeper or more general horror throughout Europe. . . . Sympathy for Austria was universal. Both governments and public opinion were ready to support her in any measures, however severe, which she might think it necessary to take for the punishment of the murderer and his accomplices." Despite their shock, most Europeans refused to believe that the assassination would lead to war. War, revolution, and assassination were the normal ingredients of Balkan politics. "Nothing to cause anxiety," announced Le Figaro in Paris. "Terrible shock for the dear old Emperor," King George V noted in his diary.

In Vienna, Franz Josef accepted his nephew's demise with resignation, murmuring, "For me, it is a great worry less." Conrad von Hötzendorf, discreetly ecstatic, hailed the arrival of the long-awaited pretext for preventive war. Now there would be no mere punishment of "the murderer and his accomplices" but the crushing of the "viper," the demolition of the troublesome Serbian state. Count Berchtold, who hitherto had opposed preventive war, changed his mind and demanded that "the Monarchy with unflinching hand . . . tear asunder the threads which its foes are endeavoring to weave into a net above its head." Russia, patron of the Serbs, might object, but Russia could be confronted and forced to back away as she had been in 1909 by Austria's German ally. The key lay in Berlin; an Austrian decision for war must be contingent on Germany's guarantee against Russian intervention. The Emperor was cautious. Conrad came away from an interview with Franz Josef and recorded that the Emperor "does not feel certain of Germany and therefore hesitates to decide." It was essential to learn the German view.

On the morning of July 5, Count Szögyény, the Austrian Ambassador in Berlin, informed the Wilhelmstrasse that he had a personal, handwritten letter from the Emperor Franz Josef to deliver to the Kaiser. William immediately invited Szögyény to lunch with the Kaiserin and himself in Potsdam. The Ambassador arrived at the New Palace at noon, handed the letter to his host, and waited silently while William read it. In shaky script, the eighty-four-year-old Emperor spelled out his interpretation of Sarajevo: "The crime against my nephew is the direct consequence of the agitation carried on by Russian and Serbian Pan-Slavists whose sole aim is to weaken the Triple Alliance and shatter my Empire. The bloody deed was not the work of a single individual but a well-organized plot whose threads extend to Belgrade. Though it may be impossible to prove the complicity of the Serbian Government, there can be no doubt that its policy of uniting all Southern Slavs under the Serbian flag encourages such crimes and that the continuation of this situation is a chronic peril for my House and my territories. My efforts must be directed to isolating Serbia and reducing her size." The letter ended with the question: What would German policy be if Austria decided to "punish . . . this center of criminal agitation in Belgrade?"

William put the letter aside and spoke cautiously. He sympathized with the Emperor, but because of the "serious European complication," he could not answer before discussing it with his Chancellor, he told Szögyény. The Kaiser took the Ambassador in to lunch. When the meal was finished, Szögyény again brought up Franz Josef's letter, pleading the necessity of a reply. This time William's attitude was different. Setting caution aside, he assured the Ambassador that Austria could "rely on Germany's full support." Although constitutionally he still had to consult the Imperial Chancellor, the Kaiser offered his own "opinion that this action must not be long delayed." Indeed—a pleased Szögyény reported by telegram to Berchtold—William declared that "if we [Austria] had really recognized the necessity of warlike action against Serbia, he would regret if we did not make use of the present moment which is all in our favor." As for the possible "serious European complication" which had troubled the Kaiser before lunch, it seemed less serious: "Russia's attitude will no doubt be hostile, but"—the Ambassador reported the Kaiser as saying—"for this he had been prepared for years. Should a war between Austria-Hungary and Russia be unavoidable, we might be convinced that Germany, our old faithful ally, would stand at our side." The risks, William thought, were low: "Russia is in no way prepared for war."

It was a historic moment. The Supreme War Lord of the German Empire, permitting the bellicose side of his nature to take command, had given his ally a blank check to strike down Serbia. If Russia interfered, he accepted the risk of a German war against Russia. And, based on the war plan of his own General Staff, Germany would also fight France.

When the Chancellor was summoned to the New Palace that

afternoon, he endorsed what had been said. "The views of the Kaiser corresponded with my own," he noted in his memoirs. Arriving from Hohenfinow, he found General Erich von Falkenhayn (the Minister of War), two other generals, and a representative of the Navy in attendance on the Kaiser. William read Franz Josef's letter and reported what he had said to Szögyény. No one present objected to this blank check. "The sooner the Austrians make their move against Serbia the better," said General Plessen, a participant, and everyone nodded. All agreed with William's assessment that there was little risk from the Entente Powers: the Tsar would not place himself on the side of "a savage, regicide state"; France would "scarcely let it come to war as it lacked heavy artillery." It seemed so unlikely, so farfetched that Britain might be concerned that England was not even discussed. Nevertheless, Falkenhayn was asked whether, if these calculations proved wrong, the German Army "was ready for all eventualities." The Prussian officer clicked his heels and assured the All Highest, "Certainly, Your Majesty." William wondered aloud whether, in view of the crisis, he should postpone his annual cruise to the Norwegian fjords and whether the High Seas Fleet should sail for its summer exercises in the North Sea. Bethmann urged the Kaiser and the fleet to proceed as planned; sudden cancellations would create alarm in Europe. The following morning, July 6, William saw Admiral Eduard von Capelle, in Tirpitz' absence Acting State Secretary for the Navy, and told him that "he did not believe there would be further military developments." That afternoon the Kaiser left by special train for Kiel, where he boarded the *Hohenzollern* and sailed for Norway.

The same afternoon, Bethmann summoned Count Szögyény and confirmed what the Austrian Ambassador had heard from the Kaiser the day before. "I ascertained that the Imperial Chancellor, like his Imperial Master, considers immediate action on our part as the best solution of our difficulties in the Balkans," Szögyény telegraphed to Berchtold in Vienna. Bethmann reinforced this message by instructing Count Tschirschky, the German Ambassador in Vienna, to inform the Austrian government that "the Emperor Franz Joseph may rest assured that His Majesty [the Kaiser] will faithfully stand by Austria-Hungary as is required by the obligations of his alliance and of ancient friendship."

The clarity and vigor of these German guarantees impressed Vienna. On July 7, after hearing the assurances from Berlin, the Council of Ministers of the Dual Monarchy met to discuss peace or war. Now that the German Kaiser and Chancellor had pledged support and urged quick action, no reason could be found not to settle accounts with Serbia. The Council decided on war, although the Hungarian Premier, Count István Tisza, insisted that diplomatic niceties be observed by preceding the assault with an ultimatum. Grudgingly, the Council agreed, with the proviso that niceties were not to be allowed to stand in the way of action. The Council minutes read: "All present except the Royal Hungarian Premier hold the belief that a purely diplomatic success, even if it ended with a glaring humiliation of Serbia, would be worthless and that therefore such a stringent demand must be addressed to Serbia that will make refusal almost certain, so that the road to a radical solution by means of military action should be opened."

The decision for war, endorsed in Berlin almost before it was made in Vienna, came on July 5, 6, and 7. For the next fifteen days, while the Austrian government drafted its ultimatum to Serbia, Berlin pressed for haste. Jagow, returning on July 9 from his honeymoon, told the Austrian Ambassador in Berlin that "the proposed action against Serbia . . . should be taken without delay." On July 12, Tschirschky called on Berchtold "principally to impress upon the Minister once more, emphatically, that quick action was called for." Day after day, Tschirschky returned to Berchtold, exhorting haste. Germany did not understand why Austria should neglect this opportunity for striking. Threats were hinted: "Germany would consider our further negotiating with Serbia a confession of weakness on our part and this would damage our position in the Triple Alliance and might influence Germany's future policy." The Wilhelmstrasse was distressed to learn that the Emperor Franz Josef refused to mobilize his army until the ultimatum to Serbia had been drafted, sent, and rejected. The German General Staff was chagrined to hear that the Austrian Army required sixteen days to complete mobilization once the Emperor gave the order. By Prussian standards, Austria was going to war frivolously.

Berlin had another concern beyond fear that Austria might lack the will to deliver the blow. It was that the other Powers might find out what was intended and take steps to prevent it by proposals of mediation. Together, Berlin and Vienna met this possibility by constructing an elaborate façade of deception and lies. Summer aided the stratagem: leading officials of the German government were on vacation. Moltke, Chief of the General Staff, was in Karlsbad taking a cure; Tirpitz was taking a holiday in Switzerland; Jagow, who had been honeymooning, returned to Berlin as the War Minister, General von Falkenhayn, departed. Bethmann was said to be studying the stars from the porch of his house in Hohenfinow, although during the month he often travelled secretly to Berlin. The All Highest was cruising beneath the high cliffs and plunging waterfalls of the Norwegian fjords. These absences helped promote the pretext which the Bavarian Minister in Berlin privately reported to his superiors in Munich: "The Imperial [German] administration will, immediately upon presentation of the Austrian ultimatum at Belgrade . . . claim that the Austrian action has been just as much of a surprise to it as to the other Powers, pointing out the fact the Kaiser is on his northern journey and the Chief of the General Staff and the Minister of War are away on leave of absence." Vienna employed the same tactic: throughout the crisis, the Emperor Franz Josef remained at his hunting lodge at Bad Ischl; on July 8, after the decision for war had been made, Berchtold told Conrad, "It would be a good thing if you and the War Minister would go on leave for awhile so as to keep up an appearance that nothing is going on."

During the two weeks in which the Austrian ultimatum was drafted, the German government was kept fully informed. Later, attempting to avoid responsibility for the outbreak of war, the Wilhelmstrasse claimed that it had been unaware of the Note's contents until it was distributed generally to all the Powers. In fact, although Bethmann-Hollweg and Jagow did not read the actual language of the Note until July 23, they knew it was intended not as a basis for negotiations, but as a prelude to war. On July 14, Tschirschky informed Bethmann: "The Note is being composed so that the possibility of its acceptance is practically excluded." This could not, of course, be revealed to the other Powers. To avoid alarming the rest of Europe and to create the impression that Berlin, like other capitals, was wondering how Vienna would respond to Sarajevo, the Wilhelmstrasse deliberately and repeatedly lied to foreign diplomats in Berlin and, through its own ambassadors, to the foreign ministers of other governments. When the British, French, and Russian ambassadors or chargés d'affaires called at the Foreign Office to ask what Germany knew of her ally's intentions, the Wilhelmstrasse soothingly declared that it regarded the situation with tranquillity; were not the Kaiser, the Chancellor, and all the military chiefs on vacation? Accordingly, the British and Russian ambassadors in Berlin also went on vacation. On July 21, Jules Cambon, the French Ambassador, specifically asked Jagow whether he knew anything about the contents of the Austrian Note known to be in preparation. The State Secretary "assured me he knew nothing," Cambon later wrote. To the Russian Chargé, Jagow declared vehemently that he had no foreknowledge of the nature of the Austrian Note. The Austrian government practiced the same deception. On July 18 in St. Petersburg, when Foreign Minister Sergei Sazonov summoned the

Austrian Ambassador and asked for news, the Ambassador "spoke in the most peaceable manner of an entire absence in Austria of an intent to render relations with Serbia more acute. He [the Ambassador] was as gentle as a lamb," Sazonov recorded. Three days later, the Russian Ambassador in Vienna was assured that he too could leave on vacation; the Note to Serbia, he was assured by the Austrian Foreign Ministry, would make no demands which might lead to international complications. Even Italy, Germany's and Austria's Triple Alliance partner, was deceived. Fearing leaks, or worried that the Italians would object—the Triple Alliance was a defensive pact and did not come into play if one of the three allies was itself the aggressor—the Wilhelmstrasse gave the Italian Ambassador no hint of the approaching storm.

Behind this façade, the Austrian ultimatum to Serbia was carefully crafted. Europe knew that something was coming; the Entente Powers counseled moderation. On July 21, Sazonov told Count Pourtalès, the German Ambassador in St. Petersburg, that Russia would do its best to persuade Belgrade to make reasonable amends, but he warned that the Austrian Note must not be an ultimatum. In London the next day, Sir Edward Grey declared that "everything would depend on the form of satisfaction demanded and whether moderation would be exercised." England would exert pressure on Serbia to meet Austria's demands, providing "they are moderate and made reconcilable with the independence of the Serbian nation." Because its demands were anything but moderate, the timing of the Note was crucial. Originally, in response to German pressure for haste, the date had been set for July 18. Then Berchtold remembered that from July 20 to 23 President Raymond Poincaré of France would be in St. Petersburg, making a state visit. The Austrian Foreign Minister decided on caution: "We should consider it unwise to undertake the threatening step in Belgrade at the very time when the peace-loving, reserved Tsar Nicholas and the undeniably cautious Herr Sazonov are under the influence of the two who are always for war, Isvolsky [then Russian Ambassador in Paris] and Poincaré." Accordingly, delivery of the note was timed to coincide with the departure of the French President from the Russian capital: July 23 at five P.M. The ultimatum had a time limit of forty-eight hours and would expire at the same hour on July 25. (Later, to be certain that Poincaré would be at sea, delivery of the note was delayed one hour, until six.)

When the ultimatum was handed over in Belgrade, the Serbs—expecting chastisement but not abasement—were stunned. The note charged that "the murder of Sarajevo was prepared in Belgrade." It contained ten demands, each involving infringement of Serbian sovereignty: All Serbian publications critical of Austria-Hungary must be suppressed. All schoolbooks presenting "propaganda against Austria-Hungary" must be withdrawn. All Serbian government officials, army officers, and schoolteachers holding these views must be dismissed; specific officials and officers named in the note must be arrested. These changes must be monitored inside Serbia by Austrian officials.

The demands were those that a defeated state might expect to receive from a victor. At least one Austrian was candid about the nature and implications of the note. "Russia will never accept it," said the Emperor Franz Josef. "There will be a big war."

Copies of the ultimatum were distributed to the Foreign Ministry in every capital on the morning of July 24. Sir Edward Grey characterized it as "the most formidable document ever addressed from one state to another." In St. Petersburg, Count Sazonov angrily told the Austrian Ambassador, "You are setting fire to Europe!" In the days that followed, a race developed between the Entente Powers, desperately trying to stave off war by establishing a basis for mediation, and the German government, relentlessly pushing Austria to begin the war before these mediation efforts could bear fruit. Seeking room to maneuver, Grey and Sazonov immediately asked that the time limit be extended. The request was rejected. Vienna informed St. Petersburg that Russia seemed to hold the "mistaken idea" that Austria's "Note to the Powers had been sent out with a view to learning their opinion of the case. All we intended was to inform the Powers of our step and thus conform to international etiquette. We consider our action as an affair which concerns exclusively us and Serbia." Berlin grimly approved this approach and demanded war. "Here every delay in the beginning of war operations is regarded as increasing the danger that foreign powers might interfere," telegraphed the Austrian Ambassador in Berlin. All German diplomats steadfastly repeated the falsehood that the Wilhelmstrasse had had no previous knowledge of the contents of the Austrian Note; Jagow said this "very earnestly" to the British Chargé in Berlin.

Unaware that Germany and Austria were determined on war, both England and Russia brought pressure on Serbia to be conciliatory. The Serbs, said Grey, should "give a favorable reply on as many points as possible within the time limit." Sazonov urged Belgrade to make all concessions compatible with the dignity of the nation, and counselled that if war came, Belgrade put aside any idea of armed resistance, allow itself to be occupied, and appeal to the

Powers for protection through mediation. Privately, Sazonov admitted that the Serbs deserved "a lesson." Ultimately, however, the Russian Foreign Minister was not prepared to see Serbian independence abolished. To the German and Austrian ambassadors, he insisted that the issue was an international one and that any Austro-Serbian war could not remain localized. He proposed arbitration, to be placed in the hands of Germany, Italy, Britain, and France; later Tsar Nicholas suggested that the matter be placed before the International Court in The Hague. Russia was willing to accept any compromise which left Serbia with its sovereignty intact. The Serbian government recognized that many of Austria's demands would have to be met. Even before the ultimatum was received, Belgrade had informed the Powers that Serbia "would only be unable to comply with such demands as were inconsistent with the dignity and independence of the Serbian nation." By noon on the twenty-fifth, with only six hours remaining before the ultimatum expired, Serbia informed the British and French ambassadors in Belgrade that it intended to accept Austria's demands with only minor reservations.

When the Serbian reply to Austria's ultimatum was handed to Baron Giesl, the Austrian Minister in Belgrade, it contained submission on every point except one: the demand that Austrian officials be allowed to participate in the judicial inquiry into the plot which had resulted in the Archduke's assassination; this, the Serbs protested, would be a violation of their constitution and of their laws of criminal procedure. Wherever the reply was read, in Europe and in the United States, it was regarded as a remarkable concession to overbearing demands. The Serbs enhanced their submission by offering, if the Austrians agreed, to submit the entire issue either to the Great Powers for arbitration or to the International Court at The Hague. Serbian accommodation, of course, was the last thing desired by Vienna and Berlin. Giesl was handed the Serbian reply at 5:58 P.M. He glanced at it only long enough to note the Serbian refusal to permit Austrian participation in the judicial inquiry. Here were sufficient grounds for war. Giesl reached for his bag, already packed, and boarded the regular six-thirty train which left Belgrade and crossed the Danube into Austrian territory. From there, he telegraphed Vienna. As soon as it was known in Vienna that Giesl had left, the city erupted in celebration. Crowds paraded through the streets, singing patriotic songs. Austria-Hungary was to crush the Serbian "viper."

Diplomatic relations were severed, but war had not been declared. The Entente Powers continued their efforts to mediate. On July 26, Grey sent telegrams to Berlin, Paris, and Rome, proposing a

Four Power Conference in London. France and Italy immediately accepted; the Germans brusquely declined. The Kaiser announced that he would participate only at Austria's express request, which he doubted would be forthcoming "since in vital matters people consult nobody." In Vienna, the British offer was shunned. After the severing of relations with Serbia, Berchtold departed for Bad Ischl to report to the Emperor—and to elude Entente ambassadors anxious to talk of mediation. Austrian officials left behind constantly repeated the official argument that the issue concerned only Austria and Serbia and that "action had been forced on Austria-Hungary."

The Dual Monarchy was resolved on a final reckoning with its neighbor; war had been decided upon and the support of Germany promised. The Austrian government's inability to establish the complicity of the Serbian government in the crime at Sarajevo had become irrelevant. Indeed, Count Berchtold thought it wise to conceal, both from Berlin and from his own Emperor, the report of Herr Wiesner, an official he had dispatched to Sarajevo to investigate the circumstances of the assassination. "There was nothing to prove or even to cause suspicion of the Serbian government's cognizance of the steps leading to the crime," Wiesner had reported.

For three weeks, the Supreme War Lord of the German Empire cruised amidst the natural grandeur of the Norwegian fjords, relaxing by listening to lectures on the American Civil War. William was not absent by choice. Urged by Bethmann to leave Berlin after the historic decision of July 5, the Kaiser was kept away because the Chancellor, seconded by Jagow, felt that the crisis could be better managed without the presence of the excitable Kaiser. On July 18, when the possibility of William's return was raised, Jagow said: "We cannot afford to alarm the world by the premature return of His Majesty." William continued to cruise the waters of the Utenefjord, receiving only scanty information from Berlin, until he learned what was happening:

"While I was on my summer vacation trip . . . I received but meagre news from the Foreign Office and was obliged to rely principally on the Norwegian newspapers from which I received the impression that the situation was growing worse. I telegraphed repeatedly to the Chancellor and the Foreign Office that I considered it advisable to return home, but was asked each time not to interrupt my journey. . . . When . . . I learned from the Norwegian newspapers—*not from Berlin*—of the Austrian ultimatum to

Serbia and immediately after of the Serbian note to Austria, I started upon my return journey without further ado. . . ."

On Monday, July 27, the Kaiser reached Berlin. Bethmann, exhausted and pale, waited on the railway platform. "How did it all happen?" William asked. The Chancellor offered his resignation. "No, you've cooked this broth and now you're going to eat it," the Kaiser informed him. Early the next morning, William read for the first time the text of the Serbian reply to the Austrian ultimatum. He was jubilant. "A brilliant performance for a time limit of only forty-eight hours," he wrote to Jagow. "This is more than one could have expected. A great moral victory for Vienna; with it every reason for war drops away." William ordered the State Secretary to initiate immediate mediation between Austria and Serbia, with Belgrade as a temporary hostage to ensure Serbian good behavior. Jagow and Bethmann were shocked by this Imperial command. Had their master not realized that the purpose of the ultimatum was to ensure rejection and provide grounds for war? Vienna was not interested in "a great moral victory"; she meant to reduce Serbia to vassalage. The Chancellor's reaction was simply to ignore the Kaiser. His instructions that evening to the German Ambassador in Vienna made plain that Tschirschky must "avoid very carefully giving rise to the impression that we wish to hold Austria back." This holding action was not required for long: that evening an Austrian declaration of war was conveyed to Serbia in the form of an open telegram from Count Berchtold to the Serbian Foreign Office. The following morning, July 29, Austrian artillery, across the Danube from Belgrade, opened fire on the Serbian capital.

The Austrian declaration of war and the commencement of hostilities plunged St. Petersburg into gloom. Until that moment, Sazonov had remained conciliatory, sending assurances that he wanted to find a peaceful solution and "was ready to go to the limit in accommodating Austria." He admitted that Austria had grounds for complaint, but he urged that "there must be a way of giving Serbia a deserved lesson while sparing her sovereign rights." Tsar Nicholas II also abhorred the idea of war. Trying to save the peace, resisting pressure from his military staff to order general mobilization, the Tsar reached out to Germany, using the channel of personal appeal to a brother monarch. At one A.M. on the night of July 28–29, after the Austrian declaration of war was sent but before the guns opened fire, Nicholas II telegraphed William II: "Am glad you are back . . . An ignoble war has been declared on a weak country. . . . I beg you in the name of our old friendship to do what you can to stop your allies from going too far." William, reading the Tsar's telegram, noted in the margin: "A confession of his own weakness and an attempt to put the responsibility on my own shoulders . . ." The Kaiser replied to Nicholas that he could not accept the terminology "ignoble war." He accused Serbia of "unscrupulous agitation," an "outrageous crime," and a "dastardly murder."

Nicholas, he trusted, "will doubtless agree with me that we both . . . as well as all Sovereigns, have a common interest in seeing all regicides punished."*

The shelling of Belgrade weakened the chances for European peace. Sazonov was informed as he sat in conference with the Austrian Ambassador; the announcement "transformed" the Foreign Minister, reported his uncomfortable guest. That afternoon, Nicholas II signed a ukase ordering mobilization of four military districts—Moscow, Kiev, Odessa, and Kazan—containing thirteen army corps directed against Austria. The northern districts opposite the German frontier remained unaffected. The Kaiser immediately bombarded the hard-pressed Tsar with bullying telegrams demanding that Russia's partial mobilization be cancelled and warning that "the whole weight of the decision lies solely on your shoulders now, who have to bear the responsibility for . . . involving Europe in the most horrible war she has ever witnessed." On July 29, the German government formally demanded a halt to Russian mobilization, declaring that only an immediate suspension could prevent German mobilization.

Germany now faced the growing likelihood of war with Russia. German policy had been to encourage a localized Balkan war, punish a regicide state, and restore the fortunes of a crumbling ally. Russian intervention had been discounted. The Tsar's army was considered unready and the Kaiser and his advisors had expected Russia to give way, as she had five years earlier in the Bosnian Crisis. The prospect was glittering: localization accomplished; general war avoided; Serbia crushed; Austria reborn; Russia stripped of her status as a Great Power; the balance of power in the Balkans and Europe realigned. Russian mobilization against Austria demolished this dream.

The prospect of a major war did not dishearten German and Austrian generals. On the contrary, Moltke, Conrad, and other mili-

---

* These were the first of the famous "Willy–Nicky" telegrams sent back and forth between Peterhof and Potsdam over three days and nights on the eve of war. All were in English, the common language of the two monarchs.

tary chiefs had long believed that war with Russia was inevitable and that sooner was better; every year the Slav Empire grew in strength. Bethmann no longer opposed this view, but he insisted—since war was imminent—that Russia be forced to mobilize first. The Chancellor worried about appearances in Germany and abroad. Inside the Reich, the socialists might refuse to fight. The sole danger that could rally German workers to the side of the Hohenzollerns was the threat of invasion by Slav hordes. "Russia must ruthlessly be put in the wrong," Bethmann exhorted the Kaiser. The same need to fix blame on Russia affected the two alliance structures in Europe. Both the Triple Alliance and the Dual Alliance were defensive in nature. Italy's adherence to the Triple Alliance, possibly even France's honoring of the Dual Alliance, would stress Who Began the War. The issue would be particularly acute in England. The British, always reluctant to involve themselves in Continental quarrels, would certainly not be interested in a war begun in the Balkans in which Russia appeared to be attacking Germany. All these fruits, at home and abroad, could be gathered if Germany could somehow maneuver Russia into being first to proclaim general mobilization. This became the Chancellor's objective.

Only Bethmann and Lichnowsky were concerned about the British reaction to these events. Germany and Austria had military preponderance on the Continent and the German General Staff had virtually guaranteed victory for the Triple Alliance in a purely European war. But the Chancellor, more prescient than his generals, shrank from a war involving the British Empire. Anything he could do to encourage Britain's natural reluctance to become involved must be tried. The Chancellor's hopes were battered on the evening of July 29, when Lichnowsky telegraphed that he had been summoned that afternoon by Sir Edward Grey. Thoroughly alarmed, the Foreign Secretary had told the German Ambassador that "if war breaks out, it will be the greatest catastrophe the world has ever seen." To prevent war, Grey had proposed that, after occupying Belgrade, Austria halt and submit to mediation by Germany, Italy, France, and Britain. If Austria did not accept, Grey warned, British neutrality could not be counted upon. "The British Government . . . could stand aside as long as the conflict remained confined to Austria and Russia. But if . . . [Germany] and France should be involved, then the situation would immediately be altered and the British Government would . . . find itself forced to make up its mind quickly."

Bethmann was shaken by this telegram. War between Germany and Russia was likely, and the Schlieffen plan called for beginning this war with a swift, overwhelming offensive against Russia's ally, France. If, as Grey threatened, the involvement of France meant the likely intervention of England on France's side, the outcome of the war was far less certain. Bethmann was now at the limit of his own physical endurance. "There is immense commotion in the Wilhelmstrasse. Nobody sleeps," reported the Chancellor's personal assistant. That night Bethmann did not go to bed. At 2:55 A.M., frightened by what he saw coming, he attempted to reverse the course of events in the Balkans. A telegram to Tschirschky informed the Ambassador that if Austria refused mediation, "England will be against us. . . . Under these circumstances, we must urgently and impressively suggest to the . . . Vienna Cabinet the acceptance of mediation." At three A.M. a second frantic telegram went to Tschirschky: "We, of course, are ready to fulfill the obligations of our alliance, but we must decline to be drawn wantonly into a world conflagration by Vienna without having any regard paid to our counsel." Eighteen hours later, the desperate Chancellor telegraphed a third time: "If Vienna declines to give in in any direction . . . it will hardly be possible to place the guilt of the outbreak of war on Russia's shoulders. . . . Vienna will be giving documentary proof that it absolutely wants a war, into which we shall be drawn while Russia remains free of responsibility. This would place us in the eyes of our own people in an untenable situation. Thus we can only urgently advise that Austria accept Grey's proposal."

It was too late. When Tschirschky carried Bethmann's messages to Berchtold, the Austrian Foreign Minister listened silently, then coldly declared that "the restriction of Austrian military operations against Serbia" was "out of the question in view of the feeling in the Army and among the people." On the morning of the thirty-first, Bethmann's call for mediation was discussed by the Austro-Hungarian Cabinet. The German request that Austria submit to mediation was refused by setting three unfulfillable conditions: war against Serbia must be allowed to continue; all Russian mobilization must be stopped; Serbia must unconditionally accept all terms of the Austrian ultimatum. There was bitterness that Berlin, having urged Vienna for weeks to begin the war, should now demand that it be stopped. In the Austrian Cabinet minutes, the source of this reversal was falsely identified: "We had a very doubtful support in the German representative in London. Anything might sooner be expected from Prince Lichnowsky than that he would warmly represent our interests."

Bethmann was becoming desperate. Twisting and turning to escape the implications of what was happening, the Chancellor made an impetuous move to ensure British neutrality. Near midnight on July 29, he summoned the British Ambassador, Sir Edward Goschen, to the Wilhelmstrasse and offered him a bargain. He understood, the Chancellor said, that "Great Britain would never allow France to be crushed." But suppose Germany defeated France in war and then did not "crush" her? Would England remain neutral if the Reich guaranteed in advance the postwar territorial integrity of France and Belgium? (The Chancellor's offer covered only the European homelands; Bethmann refused to promise that Germany would not divide the French and Belgian colonial empires in Africa.) Goschen forwarded the request to London, where it was described by Crowe as "astounding" and rejected by Grey as "dishonorable" and "a disgrace."

While the exhausted Chancellor struggled, the German generals became impatient. The Schlieffen plan did not envisage war against Russia alone, but against both parties to the Dual Alliance, Russia and France. On the Western Front, the distances were shorter, the enemy less numerous, the imponderables fewer. Accordingly, the German war plan called for hurling the bulk of the German Army against France, striving for a knockout blow and the seizure of Paris within six weeks, before the Russian colossus could be mobilized and set into motion. The fact that France had no current quarrel with Germany made no difference; on July 30, Jagow told Sir Edward Goschen that if Germany mobilized, France would be attacked. "He regretted this," Goschen reported to London, "as he knew that France did not desire war, but it would be a military necessity." As the days passed, the German generals worried that the Entente diplomats, with their attempts at mediation in Vienna, and their own Chancellor, with his demands that Russia must mobilize first, would scramble their own fine-tuned plans. Who started the war was of little concern to the generals; their concern was with who would win it. They began to take control.

On Wednesday, July 29, General von Moltke sent a long political memorandum to the Chancellor in which he characterized the Austrian march on Serbia as "a purely private quarrel" undertaken "to burn out with a glowing iron a cancer that has constantly threatened to poison the body of Europe." Because "Russia has placed herself at the side of this criminal nation," a "war which will annihilate for decades the civilization of almost all Europe" was imminent, Moltke continued. Germany had no wish to participate in this war, but to turn her back on Austria would "violate the deep-rooted feelings of fidelity which are among the most beautiful traits of the German character." That afternoon, at a Crown Council in Potsdam, War Minister General von Falkenhayn urged the Kaiser to proclaim "danger of war" (*Kriegsgefahr*). At Bethmann's earnest pleading, William temporarily refused. Disgusted, Moltke sent his own telegram to Vienna, insisting to Conrad that Austria proceed immediately to full mobilization, promising that Germany would follow. On Thursday, July 30, the Emperor Franz Josef proclaimed full mobilization of the Austro-Hungarian Empire. That afternoon at Peterhof, Tsar Nicholas II gave way to pressure from his generals and ordered Russian general mobilization. By nightfall, this news was in Berlin. The German generals demanded a decision about German mobilization. Declaring that he still had not received official word from St. Petersburg, a haggard Bethmann put Moltke and Falkenhayn off for one more night. By noon the next day, he promised, he would give them an answer.

At 11:55 A.M. on Friday, July 31, the official telegram from Pourtalès arrived in the Wilhelmstrasse, where the political and military leaders of the German Empire were assembled. "General mobilization of the [Russian] army and fleet," the telegram reported. "First day of mobilization July 31." For what it was worth, Bethmann had won: the Russians had mobilized first. Together the Chancellor and the War Minister telephoned the Kaiser and asked for a proclamation of *Kriegsgefahr*. William complied. That afternoon, a German ultimatum addressed to St. Petersburg commanded the Tsar to demobilize within twelve hours and to "make us a distinct declaration to that effect." Otherwise Germany would mobilize and declare war. A second ultimatum, more insulting, was sent to Paris: Berlin demanded to know whether France would remain neutral in the coming Russo-German war. If the answer was yes, Germany demanded that France hand over the fortresses of Toul and Verdun as security on her pledge of neutrality. (These great fortress systems anchored France's defenses along her eastern frontier.) Paris was given eighteen hours to reply. Announcement of the German ultimatum to Russia (but not the ultimatum to France) was published in extra editions of Berlin newspapers on the night of July 31 as crowds milled about on the Unter den Linden.

At noon on Saturday, August 1, the German ultimatum to Russia expired without a reply from St. Petersburg. At 12:52 P.M., fifty-two minutes after the expiration of the ultimatum, Count Pourtalès was instructed to call on Count Sazonov and declare that Germany was at war with Russia. At five P.M. the Kaiser signed a decree of general mobilization, and at seven-ten P.M. Count Pourtalès handed Sazonov the German declaration of war. "The curses of the nations will be upon you," Sazonov declared. "We are defending our honor," Pourtalès replied. Then, he stumbled and wept. "So this is the end of my mission," he said. Sazonov patted him on the shoulder and helped him out the door. "Goodbye, goodbye," mumbled the elderly, heartbroken Ambassador.

War had begun in the east, but not in the west. That afternoon, a telegram from London arrived in Berlin. Lichnowsky said that he had spoken to Sir Edward Grey. The Foreign Secretary had asked whether, in response to a promise of French neutrality in a Russo-German war, Germany would refrain from attacking France. On his own authority, Lichnowsky had said yes. William had just signed the general mobilization order and given it to Moltke, who was driving from Potsdam back to Berlin. Excitedly, William sent an aide hurrying after Moltke to bring him back to the New Palace. Before the General arrived, the Kaiser telegraphed his cousin, King George V: "If France offers me neutrality which must be guaranteed by the British fleet and army, I shall of course refrain from attacking France and employ my troops elsewhere. I hope France will not become nervous. The troops on my frontier are in the act of being stopped by telephone and telegraph from crossing into France." The last sentence referred to the sudden cancellation of the 16th Division's planned occupation of Luxembourg as a preliminary to the invasion of France. Bethmann insisted that the army must not cross the border until a reply was received from King George, and William—without consulting Moltke—had commanded his own military aide to telephone the headquarters of the 16th Division and halt the operation.

When Moltke again stood before him, William announced to the astonished General, "Now we can go to war against Russia only. We simply march the whole of our army to the East."

Moltke, witnessing the collapse of his entire war strategy, was "crushed." "Your Majesty, it cannot be done," he pleaded. "The deployment of millions cannot be improvised. If Your Majesty insists on leading the whole army to the East it will not be an army ready for battle but a disorganized mob. . . . These arrangements took a whole year of intricate labor to complete and once settled they cannot be altered."

The Kaiser listened in frustration. "Your uncle would have given me a different answer," he said to Moltke, a reproach, the General wrote later, which "wounded me deeply." Moltke went back to General Staff Headquarters and "burst into tears of abject despair . . . I thought my heart would break." When a staff officer brought him the order officially cancelling the Luxembourg foray, "I threw my pen down on the table and refused to sign. 'Do what you want with this telegram,' I said, 'I will not sign it.' " At eleven that evening, Moltke was back at the palace, where he discovered the Kaiser wearing a military greatcoat over his nightshirt. Another telegram from Lichnowsky had revealed that the Ambassador had misinterpreted Sir Edward Grey's meaning. "A positive proposal by England is, on the whole, not in prospect," Lichnowsky had wired. The Kaiser greeted Moltke stiffly, said, "Now you can do what you like," and went back to bed. Moltke attempted to pull himself together, but never entirely succeeded. "This was my first experience of the war," he wrote later. "I never recovered from the shock of this incident. Something in me broke and I was never the same thereafter."

The German ultimatum to France expired at one P.M. on August 1. At 1:05 P.M. the German Ambassador, Baron von Schoen, inquired at the Quai d'Orsay for France's reply.

He was told coldly that "France would act in accordance with her interests." At three-forty P.M. the French Army and Navy were mobilized. Germany understood that there would be no French neutrality; the Republic would stand by its Russian ally. The German response was automatic: "When the French Cabinet, on our inquiry . . . [replied] that France would act as its own interests required, we had no choice but to declare war on France," said Bethmann.

Four Great Powers were now at war: Germany and Austria versus Russia and France. Italy managed to break free. On July 31, the Italian Council of Ministers voted for neutrality, explaining that neither "the letter nor the spirit of the Triple Alliance oblige . . . [Italy] to take part in a war that does not bear the character of a war of defense." It was obvious to Rome that the war had been precipitated by Austria's attack on Serbia, and the Italian government seized on this. Italy had always been fearful of exposing her long coastline to the British Navy; now, when it seemed possible that Britain would enter the war on the side of the Entente, Italy used the treaty language of the Triple Alliance to escape.

There was a final irony. Even as Germany declared war on Russia—ostensibly because Germany's ally, Austria, was threatened by Russian mobilization—Russian and Austrian diplomats continued to negotiate. On July 27, Austria declared officially that it "does not seek any territorial acquisition in Serbia, and that it has no intention of making any attempt against the integrity of the Kingdom; its sole intention is that of assuring its own tranquillity." Count Sazonov considered this a sufficient basis for talks.

Austria, despite Conrad's strutting, did not want war with Russia. Austria's hope had been that the Tsar would back down; Austria then would be able to proceed against the Serbs. The pace of events in Berlin alarmed Vienna. On August 1, the day Germany was declaring war on Russia, the Austrian Ambassador in St. Petersburg called on Sazonov to continue Austro-Russian negotiations. The difference of interpretation as to what constituted a breach of Serbian sovereignty was discussed; after the meeting the Austrian Ambassador reported to Count von Berchtold that he believed the gap could be bridged. Sazonov meanwhile counselled his visitor that Vienna should not be alarmed by Russian mobilization. "There was no fear that the guns would go off by themselves," said the Russian Foreign Minister, "and . . . the Russian Army . . . was so well-disciplined that the Tsar with one word could make it retire from the frontier." That same morning, the Russian Ambassador in Vienna called on Count von Berchtold. He came, Berchtold noted, "in the most friendly manner . . . he still hoped that it would be possible to settle the question at issue by direct negotiations. . . . [He] took his leave with the remark that between us and Russia there was really only a great misunderstanding."

That evening, August 1, Vienna and St. Petersburg knew of the German declaration of war on Russia. Austro-Russian negotiations could not continue; Austria now had no choice but to follow her ally. During the next five days, while Germany was at war with Russia, Austria, originally the threatened party, remained at peace. A number of stern telegrams arrived from Berlin before, on August 6, Austria-Hungary finally declared war on Russia.

CHAPTER 46

The Coming
of Armageddon:
London

On Friday afternoon, July 24, the British Cabinet met in
the Prime Minister's Room at the House of Commons.
The subject was Ireland. Through the spring, Home Rule, the great
cause and incubus of the Liberal Party, had once again been moving
through Parliament. Debate had focussed on whether the Protestant
counties of Ulster, not wishing to be ruled by a Catholic Parliament
in Dublin, should be entitled to refuse participation in Home Rule.
As passage of the bill became more certain, Ulstermen became
more fiercely agitated. Certain they were about to be betrayed by
Westminster, they had resolved to help themselves. They talked of
setting up a provisional Ulster government; there were active preparations for armed resistance. By summer, 36,000 rifles and three
million rounds of ammunition were in Protestant hands. In their
defiance, the Orangemen had the open encouragement of the British Conservative Party and the quiet complicity of a number of officers of the British Army. These officers, many with roots in the
Anglo-Irish gentry, opposed Home Rule and were unwilling to participate in any military coercion of Ulster. On March 20, the Commander-in-Chief in Ireland had addressed a large group of officers
at the Curragh barracks and found himself confronted with the refusal of the majority of these officers to accept orders to take their

soldiers to Ulster. Rather than fight the Protestant Orangemen, they said they would resign. This near-mutiny had shaken Parliament and the nation. Conservatives accused the Liberal government of sacrificing Ulster; Liberals accused the opposition of encouraging rebellion against the Crown. On July 21, the King had summoned representatives of the interested parties to Buckingham Palace to find a solution. Three days of argument resulted in deadlock and, on July 24, the Conference broke up. These facts, reported in detail to Berlin by German diplomats, helped convince the Wilhelmstrasse that British involvement in Ireland was so great that England need not be taken seriously as a factor in European diplomacy.

That afternoon, the Irish deadlock had been reported to the Cabinet. The meeting was ending, and most members were standing, ready to leave the room, when Sir Edward Grey asked the ministers to remain a few minutes. They resumed their seats. Grey's description of the situation in Central Europe and the Balkans was the first discussion of foreign affairs in more than a month. As he read the Austrian ultimatum to Serbia, preoccupation with Ireland began to fade. Churchill recalled: "[Grey] had been reading or speaking for several minutes before I could disengage my mind from the tedious and bewildering debate which had just closed. . . . Gradually as the phrases and sentences followed one another, impressions of a wholly different character began to form in my mind. . . . The parishes of Fermanagh and Tyrone faded back into the mists and squalls of Ireland and a strange light began immediately, but by perceptible gradations, to fall and grow upon the map of Europe." Grey's words, in his quiet, careful voice, had an impact. That night, in his report to the King, Asquith termed the Austrian ultimatum "the gravest event for many years past in European politics as it may be the prelude to a war in which at least four of the Great Powers may be involved." He wrote to Venetia Stanley, "We are within measurable, or imaginable, distance of a real Armageddon. Happily, there seems to be no reason why we should be anything more than spectators."

Asquith's optimism, as far as England was concerned, was based on recent diplomatic history. Three times in eight years (1905, 1908, and 1911) Europe had approached the brink of war and each time diplomacy had prevailed. In the spring of 1914, the Continent appeared tranquil. Sovereigns and chiefs of state shuttled between each others' capitals, bowing and waving to cheering crowds. Anglo-German relations had reached equilibrium; the naval issue was quiescent; a settlement of the Berlin-to-Baghdad Railway dispute only awaited German signature. The German Ambassador, Prince

Lichnowsky, a partisan of improved relations, was popular in London society. On July 23, the day before Grey informed his Cabinet colleagues of the Austrian ultimatum, Lloyd George had told the House of Commons that relations with Germany were better than they had been for years and that he could predict "substantial economy in naval expenditure." Expanding on this hopeful theme, the Chancellor of the Exchequer announced, "I cannot help thinking that civilisation, which is able to deal with disputes among individuals and small communities at home, and is able to regulate these by means of some sane and well-ordered arbitrament, should be able to extend its operations to the larger sphere of disputes among states."

Even after Sarajevo, the mood in London had not changed. People in Britain reacted as people elsewhere: with horror, with indignation toward the criminals, with sympathy for the elderly Franz Josef. Britons expected the guilty parties to be discovered and punished. Fear of international implications was dispelled by the deliberate atmosphere of calm arranged by the Austrian and German governments. Until July 24, the Foreign Secretary, responsible for monitoring the behavior of other nations, had not mentioned anything to the Cabinet. Grey's silence had not meant ignorance. Lichnowsky returned to London from Berlin on July 6 and gave Grey a hint that, behind the façade, tempers were running high in Berlin and Vienna. The Austrians were determined to have a reckoning with Serbia, he reported, and the Imperial government felt it must support its ally. Grey was understanding. Admitting that Austria had been greatly provoked, the Foreign Secretary declared that "the merits of the dispute between . . . [Austria and Serbia] were not the concern of His Majesty's Government." He would consider the matter "simply and solely from the point of view of the peace of Europe"; here he was "very apprehensive of the view Russia would take." Grey attempted to influence that view, working to persuade St. Petersburg to take a conciliatory attitude toward Austria, but this, he told Lichnowsky on the ninth, would depend heavily on the steps Austria was preparing to take. In general, Grey told the Ambassador, he "saw no reason for taking a pessimistic view of the situation."

Grey's hopefulness, passed along to Berlin, pleased the Wilhelmstrasse. On July 12, the Austrian Ambassador in Berlin telegraphed Vienna: "The German Government believes that it has proof that England would not take part in a war caused by disturbances in the Balkans even if Russia and France were involved in it. . . . England certainly would not expose itself to danger for Serbia or even Russia's sake." Grey made plain to Lichnowsky as well as to the Russians that there were limits to what Britain could approve in Austria's punishment of Serbia. Surely, the Foreign Secretary urged, Vienna did not think of annexing any Serbian territory. Jagow understood and on July 18 telegraphed, "England will not prevent Austria from calling Serbia to account; it is only the destruction of the nation that she would not permit."

Everything depended on the terms of the Austrian note. At two P.M. on July 24, Count von Mensdorff, the Austrian Ambassador in London, handed a copy to Grey. Grey characterized it as "brusque, sudden, and peremptory"; later he amplified this to "the most formidable document that has ever been addressed from one state to another." He took the document with him to that day's Cabinet meeting and, when discussion of Ireland was concluded, informed his colleagues. Returning to the Foreign Office, Grey's first reaction was to ask for an extension of the forty-eight-hour time limit (already down to thirty-one hours by the time the Foreign Secretary received the ultimatum). Coincidentally, in St. Petersburg, Sazonov had had the same reaction and had made the same request. Austria rejected both appeals. Grey then urged the Serbs to be conciliatory and to "give [to Austria] a favorable reply on as many points as possible within the time limit." The Foreign Secretary also proposed a reconvening of the Six Power Conference of London, which had successfully mediated the Balkan upheavals in 1912–1913. The same ambassadors were still in London—Lichnowsky of Germany, Mensdorff of Austria, Imperiale of Italy, Cambon of France, and Benckendorff of Russia—and could be brought together on a few hours' notice. All were personal friends. "If our respective governments would only use us and trust us and give us the chance," Grey wrote, "we could keep the peace of Europe . . . an honourable peace, no vaunting on one side and humiliation on another."

The key to Grey's proposal lay with Germany: if Berlin agreed to mediation, Vienna would have to accept. Accordingly, Grey sounded Lichnowsky first. The Foreign Secretary assumed that the Germans were anxious to calm the Balkan turbulence and prevent war. Grey's assumption seemed to have been sustained on the morning of July 25, when the German Ambassador read him a telegram from the Wilhelmstrasse confirming that Germany had had no previous knowledge of the text of the Austrian ultimatum. Lichnowsky, deliberately left ignorant by Berlin, responded wholeheartedly to Grey's conference proposal. "I see in it the only possibility of avoiding a world war," he telegraphed to Jagow on the afternoon of the twenty-fifth. "Grey will not bestir himself again. . . . Once more, I urgently advise the acceptance of the English proposal."

Hoping for a favorable response from Berlin, Grey delayed sending the proposal to other governments. July 25 was a Saturday and in the early afternoon the Foreign Secretary left London for his fishing cottage in Hampshire. The text of the proposal telegram was left in Sir Arthur Nicolson's hands. At three P.M. Sunday, July 26, the Permanent Under Secretary decided to send out the proposal and to summon the Foreign Secretary back to London. Telegrams over Grey's signature went immediately to the foreign ministers in Paris, Rome, and Berlin. "Ask the Minister for Foreign Affairs if he would be disposed to instruct ambassador here to join with the representatives [of the other invited Powers] and myself to meet in a conference to be held here." If so, "active military operations should be suspended pending results of the conference."

Lichnowsky, supporting Grey's initiative, dispatched three telegrams to Jagow within six hours on the twenty-seventh. His language exhibits frustration and growing panic: "Sir E. Grey had me call on him just now. . . . [He had just read] the Serbian reply to the Austrian note. It appeared to him that Serbia had agreed to the Austrian demands to an extent such as he would never have believed possible. . . . Should Austria fail to be satisfied with this reply . . . it would then be absolutely evident that Austria was only seeking an excuse for crushing Serbia. . . . I found the Minister [Grey] irritated for the first time. He spoke with great seriousness and seemed absolutely to expect that we should successfully make use of our influence to settle the matter. . . . Everybody here is convinced . . . that the key to the situation is to be found in Berlin and that, if peace is seriously desired there, Austria can be restrained from prosecuting—as Sir E. Grey expressed it—a foolhardy policy." And later: "Our entire future relations with England depend on the success of this move by Sir Edward Grey. Should the Minister succeed . . . I will guarantee that our relations with England will remain . . . intimate and confidential. . . . Should Austria's intention of using the present opportunity to overthrow Serbia . . . become more and more apparent, England, I am certain, would place herself unconditionally by the side of France and Russia. . . . If it comes to war under these circumstances, we shall have England against us."

Berlin was unmoved; three weeks of effort by the Reich government had gone into *preventing* other Powers from interfering by mediation. Jagow felt obliged to forward Grey's proposal to Vienna, but he prefaced the English note with his own disclaimer: the German government declared "*in the most decided way that it does not identify itself* with these propositions; that, on the contrary, it advises [Austria] to disregard them, but that it must pass them on to satisfy the English Government." In Berlin, Jagow told Sir Edward Goschen that the proposed conference "would practically amount to a court of arbitration" and could not be considered without Austrian approval. In London, Lichnowsky was instructed to give Sir Edward Grey the same explanation.

On Monday morning, July 27, news of Serbia's submission to the Austrian ultimatum reached London. To Venetia Stanley, Asquith described his reaction: "Serbia has capitulated on the main point, but it is very doubtful if any reservation will be accepted by Austria which is resolved upon a complete and final humiliation. The curious thing is that on many if not most points Austria has a good and Serbia a very bad case, but the Austrians are quite the stupidest people in Europe. . . . It is the most dangerous situation of the last forty years." When the Cabinet met at eleven A.M., Grey reported that Count von Mensdorff had told him that Vienna regarded the Serbian reply as inadequate. He described the Six Power Conference proposal, announcing that France and Italy had accepted immediately; the German reply had not yet arrived. The question of Britain's obligation to maintain Belgian neutrality was raised and the Cabinet agreed to discuss the matter in detail at a subsequent meeting. The First Sea Lord's order not to disperse to the Fleet concentrated at Portland was approved.

When, on Tuesday, July 28, news arrived that Austria had declared war on Serbia, Haldane gave up hope. "The German General Staff is in the saddle," he said. That afternoon, Grey told the House of Commons: "It must be obvious to any person who reflects upon the situation that from the moment the dispute ceases to be one between Austria-Hungary and Serbia and becomes one in which another Great Power is involved, it cannot but end in the greatest catastrophe that has ever befallen the Continent of Europe at one blow. No one can say what would be the limits of the issues that might be raised by such a conflict; the consequences of it, direct and indirect, would be incalculable." Asquith was pessimistic. That night, he and Margot entertained the Churchills and Benckendorffs at dinner. After his guests left, the Prime Minister walked to the Foreign Office, where he found Grey and Haldane. Until one A.M., the three men talked. Asquith's opinion was that "nothing but a miracle could avert war, but still not a British war."

Beginning on Wednesday, July 29, the Cabinet met daily, sometimes twice a day. After the Wednesday meeting, a telegram was sent to all naval, military, and colonial stations warning that war was possible. Grey was instructed to inform the German and French ambassadors that "at this stage we were unable to pledge ourselves in advance, either under all conditions to stand aside, or in any conditions to join in." The Cabinet concluded that a decision regarding a violation of Belgian neutrality, if and when it was made, "will be one of policy rather than of legal obligation."

Disappointed by Berlin's rejection of a Six Power Conference, Grey still had not given up hope of working with Germany. On the afternoon of the twenty-ninth, the Foreign Secretary called in Lichnowsky and said that, if the Wilhelmstrasse would not accept Britain's lead in mediation, Britain would accept a German lead, following any approach Berlin thought feasible. Grey reiterated his belief that Austria had a legitimate grievance against the Serbs and even suggested that Austria might occupy Belgrade to assure compliance with her conditions. Grey believed that an Austro-Serbian war must inevitably escalate into an Austro-Russian war, but even that, he told the Ambassador, would not necessarily concern Great Britain. So long as the conflict was confined to Austria and Russia, England could stand aside, but once Germany and France became involved, the vital interests of England were threatened. Any threat to France's role as a Great Power would bring any English government, Liberal or Conservative, into the war.

Lichnowsky hurriedly sent Grey's remarks off to Berlin. The Ambassador's telegram came to the Kaiser. William's marginalia on this dispatch were remarkable:

The worst and most scandalous piece of English pharisaism that I ever saw! I will never enter into a naval convention with such scoundrels.

Sir E. Grey just sent for me again. The Minister was entirely calm, but very grave, and received me with the words that the situation was continuing to grow more acute. Sazonov had stated that after the declaration of war he will no longer be in a position to negotiate with Austria direct, and had requested them here [in London] to take up the mediation efforts again.

In spite of the Czar's appeal to me!

That sets me out of the running.

Sir E. Grey repeated his suggestion already reported, that we take part in a mediation à quatre, such as we had already accepted in principle. It would seem to him to be a suitable basis for mediation, if Austria, after occupying Belgrade, for example, or other places, should announce her conditions. Should Your Excellency [the dispatch was addressed to Jagow], however, undertake mediation, a prospect I was able early this morning to put before him, this would of course suit him equally well. But mediation seemed now to him to be urgently necessary, if a European catastrophe were not to result.

Good. We have been trying to accomplish this for days, in vain!

Sir E. Grey then said to me that he had a friendly and private communication to make to me, namely, that he did not want our warm personal relations and the intimacy of our talks on all political matters to lead me astray, and he would like to spare himself later the reproach (of) bad faith. The British Government desired now as before to cultivate our previous friendship, and it could stand aside for as long as the conflict remained confined to Austria and Russia. But if we and France should be involved, then the situation would immediately be altered, and the British Government would, under the circumstances, find itself forced to make up its mind quickly. In that event it would not be

Instead of mediation, a serious word to St. Petersburg and Paris, to the effect that England would not help them, would quiet the situation at home.

Aha! The common cheat!

This means, we are to leave Austria in the lurch. Mean and Mephistophelian! Thoroughly English, however.

It remains.

Already made up.

This means they will attack us.

practicable to stand aside and wait for any length of time. "If war breaks out, it will be the greatest catastrophe that the world has ever seen." It was far from his desire to express any kind of threat; he only wanted to protect me from disappointments and

He has shown bad faith all these years just the same, down to the latest speech.

himself from the reproach of bad faith, and had therefore chosen the form of a private explanation.

An absolute failure.

Sir E. Grey added also, that the Government of course had to reckon with public opinion.

We too!

Up to the present it had in general been in favour of Austria, as the justice of a certain satisfaction due her was recognised; but now it was

Newly created! If it wants to, it can turn and direct public opinion, as the press obeys it unconditionally.

beginning to turn completely to the other side, as a result of Austrian stubbornness.

With the aid of the jingo press.

Sir E. Grey said that he believed, if mediation were accepted, that he should be able to secure for Austria every possible satisfaction; there was no longer any question of a humiliating retreat for Austria, as the Serbs would in any case be punished and compelled, with the consent of Russia, to subordinate themselves to Austria's wishes. Thus Austria could obtain guaranties for the future without a war that would jeopardise the peace of Europe.

Once he had finished scribbling in the margins, William took more space and let his feelings flow:

"England reveals herself in her true colours at a moment when she thinks that we are caught in the toils and, so to speak, disposed of! That mean crew of shopkeepers has tried to trick us with dinners and speeches. The boldest deception, the words of the King to Henry for me: 'We shall remain neutral and try to keep out of this as long as possible.' Grey proves the King a liar, and his words to Lichnowsky are the outcome of a guilty conscience, because he feels that he has deceived us. At that, it is as a matter of fact a threat combined with a bluff, in order to separate us from Austria and to prevent us from mobilising, and to shift the responsibility for the war. He knows perfectly well that, if he were to say one single, serious, sharp and warning word at Paris and St Petersburg, and were to warn them to remain neutral, that [sic] both would become quiet at once. But he takes care not to speak the word, and threatens us instead! Common cur! England *alone* bears the responsibility for peace and war, not we any longer! That must be made clear to the world."

Bethmann-Hollweg had a different reaction to Grey's warning that Britain would not allow France to be eliminated as a Great Power. That night—it was still July 29—the Kaiser convened a Crown Council at Potsdam. The Chancellor explained Grey's concern over the future of France and urged that some step be taken to calm British fears and ensure Britain's neutrality. A course was agreed on, and Bethmann hurried back to Berlin. He summoned Sir Edward Goschen. The British Ambassador appeared at the Wilhelmstrasse at one-thirty A.M.; by now it was Thursday, July 30. He listened carefully to the Chancellor and returned to his embassy to send a telegram to London. War involving Germany, France, Austria, and Russia was now almost inevitable, the Chancellor had said. "He [Bethmann] then proceeded to make a strong bid for British neutrality. He said that . . . so far as he was able to judge, the main principle which governed British policy was that Great Britain would never stand by and allow France to be crushed." This was not Germany's aim, Bethmann insisted. To prove it, he promised—on condition of Britain's neutrality—that a victorious Germany would take no territory from a defeated France. Goschen inquired whether this applied to France's colonies in Africa and elsewhere. Bethmann declined to give that assurance. The Chancellor made a similar offer regarding German military operations on Belgian territory: "When the war was over, Belgian integrity would be respected if she had not sided against Germany."

Bethmann's proposal astounded Whitehall. It was not only that Germany was openly revealing her intention of attacking France and probably Belgium. It was the Chancellor's naked suggestion that England cynically betray France on the basis of a German promise. Grey's reaction mingled despair and indignation: "The document made it clear that Bethmann now thought war probable. . . . The proposal meant everlasting dishonour if we accepted it. . . . Did Bethmann not see that he was making an offer that would dishonour us if we agreed to it? What sort of man was it who could not see that? Or did he think so badly of us that he thought we should not see it?"

Grey immediately wrote a reply to Goschen: "His Majesty's Government cannot for a moment entertain the Chancellor's proposal. . . . It would be a disgrace for us to make this bargain with Germany at the expense of France—a disgrace from which the good name of this country would never recover." He walked across to 10 Downing Street with the telegram in his hand. Asquith agreed that they need not wait for Cabinet approval, and the telegram was dispatched. That afternoon, Goschen's telegram, containing the German Chancellor's proposal, and Grey's reply were read to the Cabinet. Grey's decision was approved.

Bethmann had hinted that if war came Germany meant to attack France. Jagow confirmed this to Goschen later on the thirtieth, when he told the British Ambassador that if Germany mobilized, it would be against France as well as Russia. The French government knew what was coming. France's diplomacy since the delivery of the Austrian ultimatum had been hampered by the absence from Paris of both President Poincaré and Foreign Minister René Viviani. Returning from St. Petersburg aboard the battleship *France*, they had cancelled their state visit to Denmark, but arrived back in the capital only on the afternoon of July 29. While France had supported Britain's efforts to establish mediation machinery, she had consistently reassured her Russian ally of her willingness to meet the obligations of the Dual Alliance. Secret military preparations were under way; officers and men excused for the harvest were recalled on the twenty-sixth; French battalions in Morocco were ordered home on the twenty-seventh. On July 28, the French General Staff informed the Russian Military Attaché in Paris of France's "full and active readiness faithfully to execute her responsibilities as an ally."

France, facing the overwhelming threat of the German Army, pleaded with Britain for a commitment to intervene. One of Viviani's first moves on his return to the Quai d'Orsay was to ask Paul Cambon in London to "remind" Sir Edward Grey of the 1912 letters promising that the two Powers would take "joint steps . . . in the event of tension in Europe." On the evening of July 30, President Poincaré summoned Sir Francis Bertie, the British Ambassador to France, and urged Britain to take a stand. "He [Poincaré] is convinced that . . . if His Majesty's Government announce that, in the event of conflict between Germany and France . . . England would come to the aid of France, there would be no war for Germany would at once modify her attitude," Bertie reported. "He is convinced that preservation of peace . . . is in the hands of England." Bertie was obliged to tell the President of the Republic "how difficult it would be for His Majesty's Government to make such an announcement."

Even after Austria declared war and bombarded Belgrade, few in Britain had an inkling that within seven days, England would enter a world war. The man in the street, the majority in the Cabinet and House of Commons still saw the crisis as a distant furor over "Serbian murderers." The Liberal Party in the House of Commons felt that this was a fight between the great Continental alliances and —as Churchill recalled later—that "British participation in a continental struggle would . . . [be] criminal madness." The Cabinet approved the use of Britain's influence to keep the peace and unanimously endorsed Grey's proposal for a Six Power Conference in London. At the same time, the Cabinet also approved the cautionary Admiralty decisions to keep the fleet concentrated at Portland and then to send it to sea. The Cabinet was even willing to authorize Grey's vague warning to the Germans that they should not count absolutely on British neutrality. But it was not willing to give France the guarantee of support for which Poincaré and Cambon were pleading. Within the Cabinet there existed a strong and vocal minority who absolutely opposed British participation in any Continental war. As the probability of war in Europe loomed larger, this group became more active in its determination to keep Great Britain out: the British people wanted peace; the nation had no legal or moral commitments requiring it to go to war. Should the Prime Minister and the Foreign Secretary steer a course toward war, these noninterventionists, including Lloyd George, threatened to resign. Grey's hands were tied. "It was clear to me," he wrote, "that no authority would be obtained from the Cabinet to give the pledge for which France pressed more and more urgently, and that to press the Cabinet for that pledge would be fatal; it would result in the resignation of one group or another and the consequent breakup of the Cabinet altogether."

■ ■ ■

Within the Cabinet, the burden of the crisis fell on Grey. The Foreign Secretary, fifty-two, a widower for nine years, childless, was gradually going blind. In the autumn of 1913, he had been forced to give up squash because of his trouble seeing the ball. By May 1914, his condition had worsened. He was told that he would eventually lose the power of reading. Doctors suggested six months of rest and country life. Grey, who had always worked more from a sense of duty than from love of office, refused. During the absorbing days of July and August, the climax of his career, there were Cabinet meetings once, then twice a day, lasting two or three hours apiece. It was Grey's responsibility to meet and brief foreign ambassadors on the latest developments in British policy. As pressure from France and Germany increased, Cambon and Lichnowsky were constantly at his door, each urgently pleading his country's case. After these interviews, Grey dictated a summary that was telegraphed to British representatives around the world. Communications poured in from British ambassadors in every capital in Europe; Grey was obliged to read and respond with special care to Buchanan in St. Petersburg, Bertie in Paris, and Goschen in Berlin. No matter how tired, Grey could not rest. He was the pivotal figure, not only in the formulation of British foreign policy within the Cabinet but in conducting the diplomacy that would make it work.

Haldane did what he could to help. Grey, at that time, was renting Churchill's house at 33 Eccleston Square (the First Lord was living in a house provided by the Admiralty), but during the crisis he moved in temporarily with Haldane at Queen Anne's Gate. Telegrams and dispatches for the Foreign Secretary were coming in at every hour of the night. So that Grey could get some uninterrupted sleep, Haldane kept a servant sitting up by his door with instructions to bring the dispatch boxes to his bedroom as they arrived and to awaken him. The Lord Chancellor opened the boxes, read the contents, and decided whether the matter was sufficiently urgent to awaken Grey.

Grey sympathized entirely with France and recognized that France had legitimate moral, if not legal, claims on Britain's support. There was no treaty of alliance, but during his nine years of stewardship at the Foreign Office, the bonds between England and France had been woven ever tighter. Grey's feelings were not based on simple Francophilia; he "felt that to stand aside would mean the domination of Germany, the subordination of France and Russia, the isolation of Great Britain. Ultimately, Germany would wield the whole power of the Continent. How would she use it as regards England?" The professional diplomats at the head of the Foreign Office were even more convinced that England must stand by France. Crowe's voice was insistent: "The argument that there is no written bond binding us to France is strictly correct," he wrote in a forceful memorandum for the Foreign Secretary. "There is no contractual obligation. But the Entente has been made, strengthened, put to the test and celebrated in a manner justifying the belief that a moral bond was being forged. The whole policy of the Entente can have no meaning if it does not signify that in a just quarrel England would stand by her friends. This honourable expectation has been raised. We cannot repudiate it without exposing our good name to grave criticism. . . . I feel confident that our duty and our interest will be seen to lie in standing by France in her hour of need. France has not sought the quarrel. It has been forced on her."

In the week before Britain went to war, Grey structured his thoughts around four convictions: First, he believed that a great European war would be an unimaginable catastrophe in destruction of life and national wealth. Once the nations saw this, then, rationally, they must step back from the abyss. Second, he considered that Germany held the key. "Germany was so immensely strong and Austria so dependent on German strength that Germany would have the decisive voice. . . . It was therefore to Germany that we must address ourselves." Third, if, despite everything, war came, the long-range interest of Great Britain demanded that she side with France. If a majority in the Cabinet, Parliament, and the country could not be persuaded to accept his view, then he was prepared to resign. Fourth, in the meantime, while Cabinet, Parliament, and country were coming to grips with these facts and their implications, he must make no pledges on behalf of England that the nation might not fulfill. Better to disappoint by refusing to make a commitment now, than to betray later by reneging.

This struggle came to a head on Friday, July 31. France had received the German ultimatum demanding that she turn over the fortresses of Toul and Verdun as a pledge of neutrality in the coming Russo-German war. The French government was preparing to refuse and to order mobilization.* It was imperative for France to know where

---

* An English appreciation of France's courage came after the war, from Churchill:
   "There was never any chance of France being allowed to escape her ordeal. Even cowardice and dishonour would not have saved her. The Germans had resolved that if

Britain stood. Paul Cambon went to see Sir Edward Grey. The Ambassador's mind was focussed on the massive German troop concentrations on the eastern frontiers of France and Belgium. His task was to extract from Britain the strongest possible commitment. He was aware of the reluctance of the British Cabinet; he knew that Grey had not yet dared to inform Parliament of the existence of the 1912 letters, though the letters clearly spelled out the limited nature of the Anglo-French Entente. But Cambon held two strong cards. One was Grey's conviction that Britain owed loyalty to France. Cambon had to be careful not to push Grey too far; if the Foreign Secretary demanded too much of the Cabinet, was repudiated, and then in consequence resigned, Cambon and France were lost. Grey had advanced in France's direction as far as he could. Cambon's other card was the transfer of the French Fleet to the Mediterranean in 1912, accompanied by an unwritten understanding that the British Fleet would protect France's northern coasts. The 1912 letters specifically stated that this movement of ships was not accompanied by a guarantee of wartime cooperation, but Grey and Churchill both knew that this was what France expected.

Grey's mind was clear; the Cabinet might retreat behind the letters and disavow responsibility, but if it did, he was resolved to resign. Meanwhile, he could only put off the desperate French Ambassador. It was a painful moment: "the very existence of his country as a great nation was at stake and it was vital to France to know what Britain would do," Grey said. But the Foreign Secretary did not dare hold out hopes which might be unjustified. He did not permit himself to "go one inch beyond what the Cabinet had authorized." "The Cabinet thought that for the moment the British Government were unable to guarantee us their intervention," Cambon reported Grey saying. "Public opinion in Britain and the present mood of Parliament would not allow the Government to commit Britain formally at present." Cambon permitted himself to ask whether England "would await the invasion of French territory before intervening"; in that case, he added dryly, "intervention would be too late." He reminded the Foreign Secretary of what Grey already knew: that an isolated Britain, facing a victorious Germany, "would find herself in a state of dependence." Grey could only repeat that the Cabinet could not make a commitment without consulting Parliament. In this respect, he added significantly, "the

---

war came from any cause, they would take and break France forthwith as its first operation. The German military chiefs burned to give the signal, and were sure of the result. She would have begged for mercy in vain. She did not beg."

question of Belgian neutrality could become an important factor and it is probably that point which Parliament will raise first with the Cabinet."

The rallying point for those members of the Cabinet wishing to avoid entanglement in war was that while Britain might have a moral obligation to and a strategic interest in France, the British government was not bound by treaty to come to France's aid. Belgium was different. Since the sixteenth century, England had been unwilling to see the Low Countries in the hands of a Great Power. To keep the Channel coasts out of threatening hands, England had fought Philip II of Spain, Louis XIV, and the Emperor Napoleon. The nation of Belgium had arisen from the ruins of Bonaparte's empire, and in 1839 its perpetual neutrality had been guaranteed by France, Britain, Prussia, and Austria. When war broke out between Prussia and France in 1870, Gladstone made certain that Bismarck understood Britain's commitment to Belgian neutrality. The Prussian Chancellor gave assurances and the army of the elder Moltke advanced into France without trespassing on Belgium. The language of the 1839 treaty was unusual on one point: it gave the signatories the right, but not the duty, of intervention in case of violation. In 1914, as the possibility of German violation loomed, the noninterventionists in the Cabinet clung to this point. Britain, they said, had no obligation to defend Belgium, especially if Belgium itself chose not to fight. If the Belgian Army simply lined the roads while the German Army passed, British troops need not be committed. No one knew what Belgium would do. Even Churchill, keenly aware of the threat posed by a Belgium in German hands, believed that, given a German ultimatum, Belgium would protest formally and then submit.

Each day during this crisis week, the Conservative Party leader, Andrew Bonar Law, came to Grey's room off the Commons Chamber to get the latest news. Bonar Law said that his party's feelings had not yet jelled. He doubted that Conservatives would be overwhelmingly in favor of war unless Belgium was invaded; in that event, he said, the party would be unanimous.

In the Liberal Party, antiwar feelings ran high: "About the same time a very active Liberal member came up to me in the Lobby," Grey wrote, "and told me that he wished me to understand that under no circumstances whatever ought this country to take part in the war, if it came. He spoke in a dictatorial tone, in the manner of a superior addressing a subordinate, whom he thought needed a good talking to. . . . I answered pretty roughly . . . that I hoped we should not be involved in a war, but that it was nonsense to say that there were no circumstances conceivable in which we ought to go to war. 'Under no circumstances,' was the [Member's] retort. 'Suppose Germany violates the neutrality of Belgium?'' [Grey asked]. For a moment he paused, like one who, running at speed, finds himself suddenly confronted with an obstacle unexpected and unforeseen. Then he said with emphasis, 'She won't do it.' 'I don't say she will, but supposing she does,' [Grey persisted.] 'She won't do it,' he repeated confidently, and with that assurance he left me.''

Late on the thirty-first, after Germany had issued its twelve-hour ultimatum to Russia, Grey tried to position Belgium outside the arena of war. In similar dispatches, addressed to both the French and German governments, he asked each for an assurance that Belgian neutrality would be respected provided it was not violated by another Power. France immediately agreed. The German reply was evasive. Jagow told Goschen that he would have to consult the Emperor and the Chancellor before he could answer, and "he rather doubted whether they could answer at all, as any reply they might give could not fail, in the event of war, to have the undesirable effect of disclosing to a certain extent part of their plan of campaign."

Grey's official diplomatic contacts in Berlin were with the Chancellor, Bethmann, and the State Secretary, Jagow. Although disappointed when they rejected his conference proposal, he refused to assign blame. Bethmann remained Chancellor and, said Grey, "the issues of peace and war seemed to depend still more on him than on anyone." Nevertheless, as the days slipped away and no positive signal came from Berlin, Grey began to feel "there were forces other than Bethmann-Hollweg in the seat of authority in Germany. He was not the master of the situation." Grey's fear that Bethmann was losing control was far more justified than the Foreign Secretary could know. The German General Staff was in command; nothing the Chancellor could do, even pleading certain knowledge that violation of Belgium's neutrality would bring England into the war, made any difference. At stake, in the eyes of the generals, was victory or defeat. Only adherence to the carefully sculpted, immensely detailed Schlieffen war plan could guarantee victory. The Schlieffen plan meant attacking France by way of Belgium.

The interlocking gears of the European alliance systems gave events a grim inevitability. Germany was obliged by the terms of her alliance with Austria to support her ally in a war with Russia. France was obliged by the terms of her alliance with Russia to enter any conflict involving Russia and Germany. Germany, thus, had known for twenty years that if she went to war, it would be on two fronts: against Russia and France. Observing the principle of concentration of forces, Count Alfred von Schlieffen, Chief of the German General Staff from 1891 to 1906, decreed that, in a two-front war, "the whole of Germany must throw itself upon one enemy, the strongest, most powerful, most dangerous enemy, and that can only be France." The Russian Army, though larger, was ponderous and ill equipped; Russia could always frustrate victory by retreating, as Kutuzov had done when facing Napoleon. France, the first victim, was to be overwhelmed by the suddenness and power of the German lunge; in 1906, before retiring, Schlieffen allocated seven eighths of the German Army to the west, while one eighth was to fend off the Russians in the east. The French campaign, he estimated, would take six weeks.

The French Army was inferior to the German in numbers, but not in equipment, patriotism, or courage. Dug in behind the massive fortress system constructed along the Franco-German frontier, its flanks anchored in the neutral territory of Belgium in the north and Switzerland in the south, France's army felt confident of holding the Teutons until the Slav steamroller began to crunch down upon the German rear. Schlieffen assessed this and came to an inescapable conclusion: to guarantee speedy victory in the west, he could not allow Belgium to remain neutral. By travelling through Belgium, he could avoid a frontal assault on the French fortresses, envelop the French left flank, rush down on Paris, and destroy the French Army. Accordingly, he allocated sixteen army corps (700,000 men in thirty-four divisions) to the massive right wing of the German Army in the west. This juggernaut was to roll through Belgium. Schlieffen hoped that the Belgian Army of six divisions would not resist and, especially, that it would not destroy the railways and bridges he needed to maintain his tight schedule. If Belgium did fight, she would be annihilated. Schlieffen's plan was never seriously questioned by the Kaiser or the civilian leaders of the Reich. It was adopted and fine-tuned by his successor, Helmuth von Moltke, nephew of the victor of the Franco-Prussian War. Moltke had no qualms: "We must put aside all commonplaces as to the responsibility of the aggressor," he said. "Success alone justifies war."

The average Englishman in the street, the House of Commons,

or the Cabinet had no inkling of the Schlieffen plan. To him, the neutrality of Belgium was fixed and immutable. A breaking of the 1839 treaty and a violation of Belgian neutrality were the only Continental events which might bestir such an Englishman to war. The German generals knew this and did not care. Expecting a short, victorious Continental war, they had taken the likelihood of British belligerency into account and estimated it to be of minimal significance. The size of the British Expeditionary Force—four or six divisions—was well known; should the English choose to place these men in the path of the German juggernaut, they would be ground under along with any Frenchmen or Belgians who got in the way. "The more English the better," Moltke said to Tirpitz, meaning that if the British Army were disposed of in Belgium, he wouldn't have to worry about it turning up elsewhere.* Bethmann abjectly surrendered to the General Staff on invading Belgium. "Military opinion held that a condition of success was passage through Belgium," he wrote after the war. "The offense against Belgium was obvious and the general political consequences of such an offense [i.e., England's reaction] were in no way obscure. . . . General von Moltke was not blind to this consideration, but declared that it was a case of absolute military necessity. I had to accommodate my view to his. . . . It would have been too heavy a burden of responsibility for a civilian authority to have thwarted a military plan that had been elaborated in every detail and declared to be essential."

Moltke remained at his spa in Karlsbad while Austria prepared and delivered her ultimatum. The General was not needed in Berlin because every soldier, bullet, soup kitchen, and railway car had been assigned; meanwhile, his absence from the capital helped create the image of calm which the Wilhelmstrasse was promoting. Once Moltke returned, he began sending memoranda to Jagow and Bethmann. On July 26, he sent Jagow a draft of a German ultimatum, demanding free passage of German troops through Belgium. The demand was excused by saying that Germany had "reliable information" of "France's intention to advance against Germany through Belgian territory." If Belgium did not resist, she was to be offered restoration of independence after the war and possible territorial aggrandizement at the expense of France. If Belgium resisted, she would be treated as an enemy. Jagow prettied up the ultimatum with cushioning phrases (". . . with the deepest regret"; ". . . with

---

* Indeed, so confident was the German General Staff of the minimal impact of the British Expeditionary Force that Moltke advised Tirpitz not to risk any ships trying to prevent the transfer of the BEF to the Continent.

the best of good will") and on July 29 sent it to the German Ambassador in Brussels, instructing him to keep it in his office safe until further notice.

On Sunday, August 2, Moltke sent "some suggestions of a military-political nature" to Jagow. Moltke revealed that he had already drafted a treaty of alliance with Switzerland and sent a copy to the Chief of the Swiss General Staff; all the Wilhelmstrasse had to do, he said, was to ratify the documents. Moltke suggested instigating uprisings against the British in India, Egypt, and South Africa; he urged that Sweden be persuaded to attack Russia in Finland; he proposed that Japan be urged to attack Russia in the Far East. By August 3, Moltke's tone with Jagow became peremptory: "The Belgian Government must be informed on Tuesday, 4 August . . . that to our regret, we shall be forced . . . to put into execution the measures of self-protection against the French menace which we have already described. . . . This communication is a necessity, inasmuch as our troops will already be entering upon Belgian territory early tomorrow morning." On August 4, Moltke ordered the State Secretary to tell Great Britain that "Germany's procedure in Belgium was compelled. . . . This war . . . is a question for Germany not only of her whole national existence and of the continuation of the German Empire created through so many bloody sacrifices, but also of the preservation and maintenance of German civilization and principles as against uncivilized Slavdom. Germany is unable to believe that England will be willing to assist, by becoming an enemy of Germany, in destroying this civilization—a civilization in which English spiritual culture has for ages had so large a share. The decision . . . lies in England's hands." To ensure that everyone in London read his words, Count von Moltke instructed Jagow to send the message *"uncoded."*

On Saturday morning, August 1, when Asquith met the Cabinet, Russia had mobilized; Germany and France were on the brink. The Cabinet was deeply divided on the question of British intervention: some were opposed no matter what the provocation; most were willing to consider it only if Belgian neutrality was threatened. Grey, torn between his sympathies for France and his loyalty to the principle of Cabinet responsibility, wished to move the ministers as far as he could in the direction of France without forcing resignations. Asquith privately supported Grey and was resolved to resign if the

Foreign Secretary departed, but in public he temporized, trying to hold his government together. "Winston very bellicose and demanding immediate mobilization, occupied at least half the time," he wrote to Venetia after the meeting. "Resignations were threatened. Morley declared, 'We should declare now and at once that in no circumstances will we take a hand.' The main controversy pivots upon Belgium and its neutrality. We parted in a fairly amicable mood and are to sit again at 11 tomorrow, Sunday. . . . If we go to war, we shall have a split in the Cabinet. Of course, if Grey went, I should go and then the whole thing would break up."

Maneuvering within the Cabinet, Grey had two goals: maximum support for France and an unconditional guarantee of Belgian neutrality. On Saturday morning, the strength of the antiwar group precluded both. On Saturday afternoon, Cambon reminded Grey through Nicolson that "it was at our request that France had moved her fleets to the Mediterranean, on the understanding that we undertook the protection of her northern and western coasts." Now, failing the protection of the British Fleet, France's Channel and Atlantic coasts lay naked to the High Seas Fleet. Grey promised that he would present the problem to the Cabinet on Sunday morning.

Belgian neutrality was the single issue which created a Cabinet majority, but Germany had not yet directly threatened Belgium. Further, Britain could not be sure that the Belgians would resist a German invasion. Britain could not compel Belgium to fight; neither could Britain go to war to defend a passive Belgium. Indeed, it was the position of the peace group in the British Cabinet that a "simple traverse" of Belgian territory by German troops would not be a cause for British intervention.

On Saturday morning, while the Cabinet was meeting, the men of the City, the managers of British capital and finance, awoke in panic to war's proximity. The Governor of the Bank of England called on Lloyd George to let him know that the City was vehemently opposed to British intervention. Lloyd George later used this episode to refute the accusation that "this was a war intrigued and organized and dictated by financiers for their own purpose." "I saw Money before the war," the Chancellor wrote. "I lived with it for days and did my best to study its nerve, for I knew how much depended on restoring its confidence; and I say that Money was a frightened and trembling thing: Money shivered at the prospect. It is a foolish and ignorant libel to call this a financier's war." Asquith received the same message, not only from bankers and financiers but from cotton men, steel men, and coal men from the north of England. All were "aghast at the bare idea of our plunging into a European conflict, how it would break down the whole system of credit with London at its center, how it would cut up commerce and manufacture . . . ." The Prime Minister hit hard at these critics. The men of the City, he said, "are the greatest ninnies I ever had to tackle. I found them all in a state of funk like old women chattering over teacups in a cathedral town."

Asquith's foresight was as flawed as that of his countrymen. When the crisis arose, he saw no reason why Britain should be more than a spectator to the Continental Armageddon. On July 26, when a visitor mentioned Belgium, Asquith declared, "We have made no pledges to them." As the crisis evolved and magnified within the Cabinet, it became clear that, whatever he did, Asquith would suffer losses. If he supported Grey, then Morley, Burns, and others would go; without Grey, he would go. The key lay with a middle group, who clung to Britain's lack of treaty obligation to France and assumptions that moral obligation could not dictate intervention in a war which was a struggle between the two Continental alliance systems. These men reflected the views of the vast majority of Liberals in the House, the Liberal press, and Liberal voters in the country. Asquith begged his colleagues to compromise; he asked ministers to sleep on their views, to see where adjustments were possible. Meanwhile, he went on with his life. He attended small dinner parties, played bridge, golfed and motored on weekends. His mind was still on Ireland; and on July 30, after the Fleet had gone to Scapa Flow and Grey had rejected the German bid for British neutrality, Asquith still was sitting in the Cabinet Room, a large map of Ulster spread across his lap, trying to make sense of the statistics of population and religion in the six counties. He wrote to Venetia Stanley several times a day, complaining that events were conspiring to keep them apart, and confiding in her every twist of Cabinet argument. It was Venetia he told about getting the King out of bed after midnight on Friday, July 31: Late that evening, Asquith learned that the Kaiser was complaining that his peace efforts were being frustrated by the Tsar's decree of general mobilization. Asquith drafted a personal appeal on the subject from King George to Nicholas II, and at 12:45 A.M. took a taxi to Buckingham Palace to obtain the sovereign's approval. The King awakened, pulled a brown dressing gown over his nightshirt, and came to the Audience Room to meet the Prime Minister and read and sign the proposed appeal. His only change was to begin with "My dear Nicky" and close with "Georgie."*

In the end, Asquith permitted events on the Continent to outpace and influence decisions of the British government. The German ultimatum demanding submission by Belgium within twelve hours forced Britain to choose. Asquith's achievement was that, when the choice was made, Government, Party, and country were united behind him.

On Saturday evening, August 1, Churchill sat in his room at the Admiralty. He still thought that peace had a chance. Not a shot had been fired between the Great Powers; personal telegrams were humming back and forth between the Kaiser and the Tsar. Then came the news that Germany had declared war on Russia:

"I walked across the Horse Guards Parade and entered 10 Downing Street by the garden gate. I found the Prime Minister upstairs in his drawing room; with him were Sir Edward Grey [and] Lord Haldane. . . . I said that I intended instantly to mobilize the Fleet . . . and that I would take full personal responsibility to the Cabinet the next morning. The Prime Minister, who felt himself bound to the Cabinet, said not a single word, but I was clear from his look that he was quite content. As I walked down the steps of Downing Street with Sir Edward Grey, he said to me, 'You should know I have just . . . told Cambon that we shall not allow the German fleet to come into the Channel."

Grey was ahead of himself in making this commitment. On Sunday morning, Grey brought the Cabinet along, urging that "we could not stand the sight of the German Fleet coming down the Channel and, within sight and sound of our shores, bombing the French coast." The majority agreed and Grey was authorized to tell Cambon officially what he had already said the night before: the High Seas Fleet would be held at bay. This was too much for John Burns, who promptly resigned.

Asquith's day had begun when, while he was still at breakfast, Lichnowsky was announced. "He was very emotional," Asquith recorded, "and implored me not to side with France. He said that Germany, with her army cut in two between France and Russia, was far more likely to be crushed than France. He was very agitated,

* The Tsar replied to King George's telegram that he "would gladly have accepted your proposals had not the German ambassador this afternoon presented a note to my government declaring war."

poor man, and wept. I told him that we had no desire to intervene and that it rested largely with Germany to make intervention impossible if she would 1) not invade Belgium, and 2) not send her fleet into the Channel to attack the unprotected north coast of France. He was bitter about the policy of his government in not restraining Austria and seemed quite broken-hearted."

There were two Cabinet meetings on Sunday, August 2, from eleven A.M. to two P.M. and again from six-thirty P.M. to eight-thirty P.M. At the second, the majority of the Cabinet agreed that if Belgian neutrality was violated and Belgium resisted, Britain would enter the war. Ministers could not imagine Belgium fighting valiantly against the invader while appealing in vain to Great Britain. Sunday evening, Grey and Haldane dined together at the Lord Chancellor's house in Queen Anne's Gate. It was evident, Haldane wrote later, "that the country would . . . be unable to keep out of the war. We had arrived at this same conclusion on different grounds. He felt what we owed to France and that our national interest was bound up with her preservation. I thought from my study of the German General Staff that once the German war party had got into the saddle and the sword had been drawn from the scabbard, it would be a war not merely for the overthrow of France and Russia but for the domination of the world. I knew that if we kept out and allowed Germany to get possession even for a time of the northeastern shores of France, our turn would come later and that we should be in the greatest peril, our Navy notwithstanding, and that we might go down without a friend in the world, under a tremendous combination against us." While the two friends talked, a box was brought in to the Foreign Secretary announcing the German ultimatum to Belgium. "Grey asked me what my prescription was," Haldane said. "My answer: Immediate mobilization. He agreed. We decided to go without delay to see the Prime Minister. We found him with some company and took him into another room. . . . Asquith agreed at once. I said to the Prime Minister, who was also War Minister, that as on the next day he would be occupied overwhelmingly with Cabinets and communications to Parliament, he had better write a letter entrusting to me the business of going over to the War Office and in his name, mobilizing my old organization. He agreed."

Within thirty-six hours, the mood in London was transformed. On Saturday morning, a majority of Britons had been resolved that Britain must not become involved in a Continental war. Tens of thousands of Londoners planned to attend a great antiwar demonstration scheduled on Sunday for Trafalgar Square. Then came the news of the threatened German invasion of Belgium. A wave of indignation rolled over the nation, sweeping up the mass of Britons who, although reluctant to fight for France, sprang to the side of neutral Belgium. The Trafalgar Square demonstration evaporated, and on Sunday afternoon, crowds shouting for war with Germany poured into Whitehall, jamming Downing Street. The next morning, Monday, August 3, a Bank Holiday, was a beautiful, cloudless English summer day. The city was packed with excited holiday crowds wanting to participate in the rapidly unfolding historic events. By noon, a dense mass filled Whitehall from Trafalgar Square to the Houses of Parliament; hundreds were buying and waving small Union Jacks, and groups of young men attempted to sing the "Marseillaise."

At eleven A.M. the Cabinet met. During the night, King George had received an appeal from King Albert of the Belgians asking Great Britain to uphold her treaty obligation to defend his nation's neutrality. The German ultimatum and Belgium's decision to oppose the passage of Alexander von Kluck's thirty-four divisions still were unreported in London, but enough was known to galvanize the British Cabinet. Before the meeting, two ministers, Sir John Simon and Lord Beauchamp, resigned, joining Morley and Burns, but there the defections stopped. Lloyd George, the key figure, was moving toward Asquith and Grey. The Cabinet sanctioned mobilization of the British Fleet and Army, although no decision to send the Expeditionary Force to France was made. Discussion of Grey's speech to the Commons that afternoon absorbed the session; the Foreign Secretary reviewed the points he intended to make; the Cabinet assented. As the Cabinet was meeting, Haldane had gone to the War Office. He returned to his old room as Minister of War and summoned the Army Council. "Their breath was somewhat taken away," he wrote, "when I told them that I had come with authority to direct immediate mobilization of the Expeditionary and Territorial forces. . . . I told the generals that the question of whether the Expeditionary Force would actually be dispatched . . . would not be decided until the issue of peace or war had been disposed of by the Cabinet, the Sovereign, and Parliament, but they must be ready."

Grey had begun making notes for his speech to the Commons after the Cabinet meeting on Sunday evening. He did not finish before falling asleep. On Monday morning he was overwhelmed by telegrams. From eleven to two he was with the Cabinet and at two he returned to his room at the Foreign Office. He had one hour before he was to rise in the House. He hoped to use the time to slip away for lunch at Queen Anne's Gate and then work on his notes. It was not to be. Immediately upon returning to the Foreign Office, he was informed that the German Ambassador was waiting to see him. Grey felt he had no choice—"time must be made to see him." "Lichnowsky's first words told me that he had brought nothing from Berlin," but the Ambassador must report to Berlin what was happening in London. What had the Cabinet decided? What was Grey going to say to the House? Would it be a declaration of war? The Foreign Secretary replied that he would not propose a declaration of war but would offer a statement of conditions. What conditions? Lichnowsky asked. Would the neutrality of Belgium be one of them? The Foreign Secretary answered that, much though he wished to satisfy Lichnowsky—"for no man had worked harder to avert war . . . or more genuinely hated this coming war"—he could give no information in advance of his speech. Lichnowsky begged that Belgium neutrality not be named as a casus belli. He knew nothing of the plans of the German General Staff, he said, and he could not believe that they included "a serious violation" of Belgian neutrality. But it might be that Moltke's soldiers would "go through one small corner of Belgium." Grey was convinced that the German Ambassador was telling the truth in his disclaimer of personal knowledge of German military plans. Immensely saddened, hard pressed for time, unable to arrest the onrushing tide of war, Grey spoke to Lichnowsky for half an hour, standing in front of his door. The Ambassador departed. It was the last time the two men saw each other officially.

Just before three, Grey left the Foreign Office to walk to the Houses of Parliament. The crowd in Whitehall was so dense that police had to open a path. Grey found the House of Commons overflowing: the green benches packed with members, shoulder to shoulder; other members sitting in rows of chairs placed four abreast in the Gangway. In the Peers' Gallery, Lord Lansdowne was wedged next to the Archbishop of Canterbury; Lord Curzon, unable to find a seat, stood behind in a doorway. Every seat in the Diplomatic Gallery was taken except two, which attracted attention as if they had been painted orange; they belonged to the German and Austrian ambassadors. Despite the packed hall, the crowd was silent and members were startled when the Chaplain, backing away from the Speaker, stumbled noisily over chairs unexpectedly placed in the aisle behind him.

Grey came onto the floor of the House, wearing a light summer suit and carrying two worn red Foreign Office dispatch boxes. His entry was unobtrusive; he had taken his seat on the Treasury Bench before he was noticed and cheered. From the Press Gallery, his face seemed "extraordinarily pale, with a curious redness, of nights without sleep, too much reading and writing, around the eyes." Lloyd George and Churchill came in together, the Chancellor with dishevelled hair and a face drained of color, the First Lord with his eyes on the floor and a cone of paper twisting perpetually in his hands. The House cheered them both, but the louder acclaim was for Churchill, no longer the Tory renegade, now the man responsible for the British Navy. Asquith came in, his face pink, his hair brilliantly white, and, to further cheers, took his seat before the Dispatch Box.

As he sat waiting to deliver the most important speech of his life, Grey's thoughts went back twenty-eight years to April 1886, when, as a new Member and a new bridegroom, he had watched Gladstone introduce his first Home Rule bill to a crowded House. At the thought of all that had happened in the interim—the death of his wife, the present imminence of war—Grey (he confessed later to a friend) almost broke down. Yet when the Speaker called his name, he remembered later that "I do not recall feeling nervous. At such a moment there could be neither hope of personal success nor fear of personal failure. In a great crisis, a man who has to act or speak stands bare and stripped of choice. He has to do what is in him to do."

At three-ten P.M., Grey rose and began to speak. His words were "grave," "dignified," "clear," and "unadorned," although behind the quiet voice, correspondents noted "suppressed fire" and "a certain terrible indignation." He began with the simple, dreadful truth:

"Mr. Speaker, last week I stated that we were working for peace, not only for this country, but to preserve the peace of Europe. Today it is clear that the peace of Europe cannot be preserved." He asked the House to approach the crisis from the point of view of "British interests, British honour, and British obligations." He gave the history of the military conversations with France. He reminded his listeners that he had always promised that he "would have no secret engagement to spring upon the House" and declared this still to be true. France had a treaty with Russia which was dragging her into war, but "we are not parties to the Franco-Russian alliance and we do not even know the terms of that alliance." Nevertheless, Britain was bound to France, if not by obligation, then by honor and interest. He revealed the naval arrangement by which the French Fleet had been transferred to the Mediterranean, leaving "the northern and western coasts of France absolutely undefended." He reiterated that Britain had made no commitment to defend those coasts. Nevertheless, he said, "my own feeling is that if a foreign fleet, engaged in a war which France had not sought and in which she had not been the aggressor, came down the English Channel and bombarded and battered the unprotected coasts of France, we could not stand aside [cheers broke out in the House] and see the thing going on practically within sight of our eyes, with our arms folded [the cheering mounted in volume], looking on dispassionately, doing nothing!"

Grey clenched his right fist, raised it, and at the word "nothing," slammed it down on the Dispatch Box. The House, observing this unique display of emotion by the Foreign Secretary, exploded with a roar. When the noise subsided, Grey added quietly, "And I believe that would be the feeling of this country."

In the greater roar that followed, Grey knew that he had won the House's approval for the Cabinet's Sunday decision to bar the German Fleet from the English Channel.

If defending the Channel and the coast of France was a matter primarily of honour, defending the independence of Belgium—to which Grey turned next—was a matter of treaty obligation, interest, and honor, all wrapped together. The Foreign Secretary cited the language of those treaties. He addressed the temptations of neutrality: "It may be said, I suppose, that we might stand aside, husband our strength, and that, whatever happened in the course of the war, at the end of it, intervene with effect to put things right and to adjust them to our point of view." This course, Grey warned, would sacrifice both British honor and British interests: "If in a crisis like this we ran away from those obligations of honour and interest as regards the Belgian Treaty, I doubt whether whatever material force we might have at the end of the war would be of very much value in the face of the respect that we should have lost." The theme which had guided Grey's diplomacy during the eight years of his ministry then came to the fore: Britain must not permit "the whole of the west of Europe opposite us . . . falling under the domination of a single power." "Now, Sir, I ask the House from the point of view of British interests, to consider what may be at stake. If France is beaten in a struggle of life and death, beaten to her knees, loses her position as a Great Power, becomes subordinate to the will and power of one greater than herself . . . and if Belgium fell under the same dominating influence, and then Holland and then Denmark . . ." Grey concluded by noting that "the most awful responsibility is resting upon the Government in deciding . . . what to do." He asked for support "not only by the House of Commons, but by the determination and the resolution, the courage and the endurance of the whole country."

Grey's speech achieved its purpose: he prepared a divided British Parliament and public for war. He had spoken for an hour and fifteen minutes, his words punctuated and interrupted often by fervent, hoarse cheers from the Unionist opposition. His own party had been more subdued, reacting with "brooding anxiety" and "sombre acquiescence." Asquith, describing the speech to Venetia Stanley, was only moderately generous: "For the most part conversational in tone with some of Grey's usual ragged ends, but extraordinarily well-reasoned and tactful and really cogent." Lord Hugh Cecil was more acute and more admiring: "Grey's speech was very wonderful —I think in the circumstances one may say the greatest speech delivered in our time. . . . Taking the importance of the occasion, the necessity of persuading many doubtful persons, the extraordinary success it had in that direction, its great dignity, warm emotion, and perfect taste . . . [it was] the greatest example of the art of persuasion that I have ever listened to."

When Grey sat down, speakers arose whose divergent messages evoked contrasting reactions. Bonar Law officially confirmed Unionist support of the government's policy; this was foreknown and the House's approval was warm but predictable. Then came something wholly unexpected: John Redmond, leader of the Irish Nationalists, announced that Ireland was no longer an issue. "I say to the Government that they may withdraw every one of their soldiers from Ireland. The coasts of Ireland will be defended by her armed sons . . . the armed Nationalist Catholics in the South will be only too glad to join the armed Protestant Ulstermen in the North." Members, shouting with joy, leaped to their feet and waved their handkerchiefs. As Redmond later left the hall, Unionist M.P.'s, his implacable foes of a week before, reached to shake his hand. Ramsay MacDonald, leader of the Labour Party, struck a dissident note. Grey's speech, he said, would send "echoes down through history." But, said MacDonald, "I think he is wrong. I think the Government . . . is wrong." Grey had not persuaded him that the country was truly in danger. "There has been no crime committed by statesmen of this character without those statesmen appealing to their nation's honour. We fought the Crimean War because of our honour. We rushed to South Africa because of our honour." The House did not like MacDonald's speech, and showed its displeasure;

next morning, the *Daily Mail* called the speech "incomprehensi-ble."*

The debate was suspended for dinner. When it resumed, Grey, still on the Front Bench, was handed a message from the Belgian Ambassador in London. It announced the German ultimatum to Belgium. The Belgian Council of State had been given twelve hours to make its decision. The Council required only nine hours. Declaring that to accept the German demand would "sacrifice the honor of the nation," Belgium declared itself "firmly resolved to repel by all means in its power every attack upon its rights."

Grey passed the dispatch to the Prime Minister and then to others on the Front Bench. Leaving the House with Grey, Churchill asked the Foreign Secretary, "What happens now?" "Now," replied Grey, "we shall send them an ultimatum to stop the invasion of Belgium within 24 hours." Back in his room, he received the American Ambassador, Walter Page. Did Britain expect Germany to bow to her ultimatum? Page asked. Grey shook his head. "No, of course everybody knows there will be a war." He stopped for a moment, struggling for words. When he resumed, his eyes were filled with tears. "Thus, the efforts of a lifetime go for nothing. I feel like a man who has wasted his life." At dusk that evening, Grey stood with a friend at his window in the Foreign Office, looking down at the lamps being lit in St. James's Park. It was then that the unpoetic Sir Edward Grey uttered the lines which memorably signalled the coming of the First World War. "The lamps are going out all over Europe," he said. "We shall not see them lit again in our lifetime."

At this hour, Germany declared war on France. Excusing the blow that Moltke was about to deliver, Bethmann told the Reichstag that France was at fault. He cited several violations of the German frontier and German airspace: eighty French officers in Prussian uniforms had tried to cross the frontier in twelve motorcars; French aviators had thrown "bombs on the railway at Karlsruhe and Nuremberg." (A subsequent check of German newspapers published in the allegedly bombed areas revealed that both planes and bombs had gone unnoticed.) Jagow, hoping to influence foreign opinion, telegraphed the German ambassadors in London and Rome that "a French physician with the aid of two disguised officers attempted to infect the wells of . . . Metz with cholera bacilli. He [the physician] was shot."

* In 1924, Ramsay MacDonald became the first Labour Prime Minister of Great Britain.

■ ■ ■

On Tuesday morning, August 4, the German Army crossed the Belgian frontier. The British Cabinet met at eleven o'clock to hold what Asquith dryly described as an "interesting" session: "We got the news that the Germans had entered Belgium and had announced . . . that if necessary they would push their way through by force of arms. This simplifies matters, so we sent the Germans an ultimatum to expire at midnight." At two o'clock, Asquith walked to the House to announce the sending of the ultimatum. Again, Whitehall was filled with excited crowds wildly cheering every person going in or out of 10 Downing Street. The Commons took the news of the ultimatum "very calmly and with a good deal of dignity," Asquith reported. This dispassionate style belied the emotions churning beneath. "This whole thing fills me with sadness," he confessed to Venetia Stanley. "We are on the eve of horrible things." Margot saw her husband immediately after his speech when she went to visit him in the Prime Minister's room at the House of Commons:

" 'So it is all up,' I [Margot] said.

"He answered without looking at me:

" 'Yes, it's all up.'

"I sat down beside him with a feeling of numbness in my limbs. . . . Henry sat at his writing table leaning back. . . . What was he thinking of? . . . His sons? . . . would they all have to fight? . . . I got up and leaned my head against his; we could not speak for tears."

Asquith went for an hour's drive by himself. He returned to Downing Street to wait for the expiration of the British ultimatum. The hours passed. Margot looked in on her sleeping children, then joined her husband, who was sitting around the green table in the Cabinet Room with Grey, Haldane, and others, smoking cigarettes. At nine o'clock Lloyd George arrived. No one spoke. Eyes wandered back and forth from the clock to the telephone which linked the Cabinet Room to the Foreign Office. Through the windows, open to the warm night air, came the sound of an immense crowd singing "God Save the King." Against the anthem, the chimes of Big Ben intruded, signalling the approach of the hour. Then— "Boom!"—the first stroke sounded. Every face in the Cabinet Room was white. "Boom! Boom! Boom!"—eleven times the clapper fell against the great bell. When the last stroke fell, Great Britain was at war with Germany.

The Dreadnought Race
1905–1914

◆

BRITISH DREADNOUGHTS

Name of Ship and Class	Program year	Completion date	Displacement tons	Speed (designed) knots	Main armament
Dreadnought	1905–6	12–06	17,900	20.9	10 12-in.
BELLEROPHON CLASS					
Bellerophon	1906–7	2–09	18,600	20.75	10 12-in.
Superb	1906–7	5–09	18,600	20.75	
Teméraire	1906–7	5–09	18,600	20.75	
ST. VINCENT CLASS					
St. Vincent	1907–8	5–09	19,250	21	10 12-in.
Vanguard	1907–8	2–10	19,250	21	
Collingwood	1907–8	4–10	19,250	21	
Neptune	1908–9	1–11	19,900	21	10 12-in.
COLOSSUS CLASS					
Colossus	1909–10	7–11	20,000	21	10 12-in.
Hercules	1909–10	8–11	20,000	21	
ORION CLASS					
Orion	1909–10	1–12	22,500	21	10 13.5-in.
Conqueror	1909–10	11–12	22,500	21	
Monarch	1909–10	3–12	22,500	21	
Thunderer	1909–10	6–12	22,500	21	

KING GEORGE V CLASS

King George V	1910–11	11–12	23,000	21	}10 13.5-in.
Ajax	1910–11	3–13	23,000	21	
Centurion	1910–11	5–13	23,000	21	
Audacious	1910–11	10–13	23,000	21	

IRON DUKE CLASS

Benbow	1911–12	11–14	25,000	21	}10 13.5-in., 12 6-in.
Emperor of India	1911–12	11–14	25,000	21	
Iron Duke	1911–12	3–14	25,000	21	
Marlborough	1911–12	6–14	25,000	21	

QUEEN ELIZABETH CLASS

Queen Elizabeth	1912–13	1–15	27,500	25	}8 15-in., 14 6-in. (16 6-in. in Queen Elizabeth)
Warspite	1912–13	3–15	27,500	25	
Barham	1912–13	10–15	27,500	25	
Valiant	1912–13	2–16	27,500	25	
Malaya	1912–13	2–16	27,500	25	

ROYAL SOVEREIGN CLASS

Royal Sovereign	1913–14	5–16	25,750	21	}8 15-in., 14 6-in.
Royal Oak	1913–14	5–16	25,750	21	
Revenge	1913–14	3–16	25,750	21	
Resolution	1913–14	12–16	25,750	21	
Ramillies	1913–14	9–17	25,750	21	

BRITISH BATTLE CRUISERS

Name of Ship and Class	Program year	Completion date	Displacement tons	Speed (designed) knots	Main armament
INVINCIBLE CLASS					
Invincible	1905–6	3–09	17,250	25.5	}8 12-in.
Inflexible	1905–6	10–08	17,250	25.5	
Indomitable	1905–6	6–08	17,250	25.5	
INDEFATIGABLE CLASS					
Indefatigable	1908–9	4–11	18,750	25.8	}8 12-in.
New Zealand	1909–10	11–12	18,800	25.8	
Australia	1909–10	6–13	18,800	25.8	
LION CLASS					
Lion	1909–10	5–12	26,350	27	}8 13.5-in.
Princess Royal	1909–10	11–12	26,350	27	
Queen Mary	1910–11	8–13	27,000	28	
Tiger	1911–12	10–14	28,500	28	8 13.5-in., 12 6-in.

GERMAN DREADNOUGHTS

Name of Ship and Class	Program year	Completion date	Displacement tons	Speed (designed) knots	Main armament
NASSAU CLASS					
Nassau	1906–7	10–09	18,873	19	
Westfalen	1906–7	11–09	18,873	19	12 11-in., 12 5.9-in.
Rheinland	1907–8	4–10	18,873	19	
Posen	1907–8	5–10	18,873	19	
HELGOLAND CLASS					
Helgoland	1908–9	8–11	22,808	20.5	
Ostfriesland	1908–9	8–11	22,808	20.5	12 12-in., 14 5.9-in.
Thüringen	1908–9	7–11	22,808	20.5	
Oldenburg	1909–10	5–12	22,808	20.5	
KAISER CLASS					
Kaiser	1909–10	8–12	24,724	21	
Friedrich der Grosse	1909–10	10–12	24,724	21	
Kaiserin	1910–11	5–13	24,724	21	10 12-in., 14 5.9-in.
Prinzregent Luitpold	1910–11	8–13	24,724	21	
König Albert	1910–11	7–13	24,724	21	
KÖNIG CLASS					
König	1911–12	8–14	25,796	21	
Grosser Kürfurst	1911–12	8–14	25,796	21	10 12-in., 14 5.9-in.
Markgraf	1911–12	10–14	25,796	21	
Kronprinz Wilhelm	1912–13	11–14	25,796	21	
BAYERN CLASS					
Baden	1913–14	10–16	28,600	22	
Bayern	1913–14	3–16	28,600	22	8 15-in., 16 5.9-in.
Sachsen	1914–15	*	28,800	22	
Württemberg	1914–15	†	28,800	22	

GERMAN BATTLE CRUISERS

Blücher	1906–7	10–09	15,842	24.8	12 8.2-in., 8 5.9-in.
Von der Tann	1907–8	9–10	19,370	24.8	8 11-in., 10 5.9-in.
Moltke	1908–9	9–11	22,979	25.5	10 11-in., 12 5.9-in.
Goeben	1909–10	7–12	22,979	25.5	
Seydlitz	1910–11	5–13	24,988	27	10 11-in., 12 5.9-in.
Lützow	1911–12	8–15	26,741	26.4	8 12-in., 14 5.9-in.
Derfflinger	1911–12	9–14	26,600	25.8	8 12-in., 12 5.9-in.
Hindenburg	1913–14	10–17	26,947	27.5	8 12-in., 14 5.9-in.

*Launched 21 November 1916, but never completed.
†Launched 20 June 1917, but never completed.

ACKNOWLEDGMENTS

In writing this book, I worked in and drew material from the Yale University libraries, the Tulane University Library, the Public Record Office, the British Ministry of Defence Library, and the British Library Newspaper Library. I am grateful to the staffs of these libraries for their efficiency and courtesy.

For their help during the early stages of the book, I am indebted to Robert Gottlieb and Katherine Hourigan. At Random House, I have been fortunate in having available the wise experience and stimulating encouragement of a great editor, Robert Loomis, Harry Evans, Joni Evans, and Carsten Fries also have made my path easier.

From the moment I first described this book to David Godwin of Jonathan Cape, he has reacted with heartwarming enthusiasm. I appreciate also the assistance of his colleagues, Georgina Capel and Jill Black.

In today's world, as giant corporations swallow publishing houses and accountants replace editors in making publishing decisions, authors need skillful, dedicated literary agents. I have Deborah Karl, Andrew Wylie, Gillon Aitken, and Sally Riley, all of whom care deeply about writers and writing. I also have been aided by the timely efforts of Bridget Love and Anna Benn.

Janet Byrne and Judith Karl made up for my inability to master word processing by typing the manuscript. Carmel Wilson provided new photographs at short notice. The Hulton Picture Company in London offered me thousands of tempting picture choices and efficiently provided the ones I selected.

Through the years this book has been in progress, many friends have helped by word of deed. I thank especially Lorna Massie, the late Natalie May, Mary Keeley, Caecelia Davis, Robert and Ina Caro, Thomas Pynchon and Melanie Jackson, Caroline Michel and Matthew Evaqns, Ken Burrows, Gilbert Merritt, Herbert and May Shayne, David Kahn, and Robert Fagles.

My children, Elizabeth Massie, Bob Massie, and Susanna Thomas, have given me support and love; no less has come from Dana Robert and Jim Thomas.

Deborah Karl, daughter of a literary family, has read every line of this book and suggested changes which invariably turned out to be improvements. For her intelligence, her perception, and her devotion, I will always be grateful.

BIBLIOGRAPHY

Albertini, Luigi. *The Origins of the War of 1914*. New York: Oxford University Press: 1953

Askwith, Lord, *Lord James of Hereford*. London: Ernest Benn, 1930

Asquith, Herbert Henry, Earl of Oxford and Asquith. *The Genesis of the War*. London: Cassell, 1923

———. *Fifty Years of Parliament*. 2 vols. Boston: Little, Brown, 1926

———. *Memories and Reflections, 1852–1927*. 2 vols. Boston: Little, Brown, 1928

———. *Letters to Venetia Stanley*. Selected and edited by Michael and Eleanor Brock. Oxford University Press: 1982

Asquith, Margot. *An Autobiography*. 4 vols. New York: George H. Doran, 1920–22

Bacon, Admiral Sir Reginald. *A Naval Scrapbook, 1877–1900*. London: Hutchinson, 1925

———. *The Life of Lord Fisher of Kilverstone*. 2 vols. London: Hodder & Stoughton, 1929

———. *Life of John Rushworth, Earl Jellicoe*. London: Cassell, 1936

———. *From 1900 Onwards*. London: Hutchinson, 1940

Balfour, Michael. *The Kaiser and His Times*. Boston: Houghton Mifflin, 1964

Barkeley, Richard. *The Empress Frederick*. London: Macmillan, 1956

Barker, Dudley. *Prominent Edwardians*. New York: Atheneum, 1969

Barlow, Ima C. *The Agadir Crisis*. Chapel Hill: University of North Carolina Press, 1940

Bassett, Ronald. *Battle Cruisers: A History, 1908–1948*. London: Macmillan, 1981

Battiscombe, Georgina. *Queen Alexandra*. London: Constable, 1969

Bell, Quentin, *Virginia Woolf: A Biography*. 2 vols. London: Hogarth Press, 1972

Beresford, Lord Charles. *Memoirs*. 2 vols. Boston: Little, Brown, 1914

———. *The Betrayal*. London: P. S. King & Son, 1912

Berghahn, Volker L. *Der Tirpitz Plan*. Düsseldorf: Droste Verlag, 1971

———. *Germany and the Approach of War in 1914*. New York: St. Martin's Press, 1973

Bernhardi, General Friedrich von. *Germany and the Next War.* New York: Longmans, Green, 1914

Bernstein, George L. *Liberalism and Liberal Politics in Edwardian England.* Boston: Allen & Unwin, 1986

Bethmann-Hollweg, Theobald von. *Reflections on the World War.* London: Butterworth, 1920

Beyens, Baron. *Germany Before the War.* New York: Thomas Nelson and Sons, 1916

Bigelow, Pulteney. *Prussian Memories 1864–1914.* New York: Putnam's, 1915

Bing, Edward J., ed. *The Secret Letters of the Last Tsar: The Confidential Correspondence Between Nicholas II and His Mother, Dowager Empress Marie Fedorovna.* New York: Longmans, Green, 1938

Bismarck, Otto von. *Bismarck, the Man and the Statesman: Reflections and Reminiscences.* 2 vols. London: Smith, Elder, 1898

———. *New Chapters of Bismarck's Autobiography.* London: Hodder and Stoughton, 1920

Blake, Robert. *Disraeli.* New York: St. Martin's Press, 1967

Blücher, Evelyn. *An English Wife in Berlin.* London: Constable, 1920

Bonham-Carter, Violet. *Winston Churchill: An Intimate Portrait.* New York: Harcourt Brace, 1965

Bradford, Admiral Sir Edward. *Life of Admiral of the Fleet Sir Arthur Knyvet Wilson.* London: John Murray, 1923

Brandenburg, Erich. *From Bismarck to the World War.* New York: Oxford University Press, 1927

Breyer, Siegfried. *Battleships and Battle Cruisers, 1905–1970.* New York: Doubleday, 1973

Bülow, Prince Bernhard von. *Memoirs.* 4 vols. Boston: Little, Brown, 1931–32

Carroll, Malcolm. *Germany and the Great Powers.* New York: Octagon Books, 1975

Cecil, Algernon. *British Foreign Secretaries, 1807–1916.* New York: G. P. Putnam, 1927

Cecil, Lady Gwendolen. *Life of Robert, Marquis of Salisbury.* 4 vols. London: Hodder & Stoughton, 1921–32

Cecil, Lamar. *Albert Ballin: Business and Politics in Imperial Germany.* Princeton, N.J.: Princeton University Press, 1967

———. *The German Diplomatic Service, 1871–1914.* Princeton, N.J.: Princeton University Press, 1976

Chamberlain, Sir Austen. *Down the Years.* London: Cassell, 1935

Chatfield, Admiral of the Fleet Lord. *The Navy and Defence.* London: Heinemann, 1942

Childers, Erskine. *The Riddle of the Sands.* New York: Dover, 1976

Churchill, Randolph S. *Winston S. Churchill: Youth, 1874–1900.* Boston: Houghton Mifflin, 1966

———. *Winston S. Churchill: Young Statesman, 1901–1914.* Boston: Houghton Mifflin, 1967

Churchill, Winston S. *The Story of the Malakand Field Force.* London and New York: Longmans, Green, 1898

———. *The World Crisis, 1911–1918.* 4 vols. New York: Scribner's, 1923–29

———. *A Roving Commission: My Early Life.* New York: Scribner's, 1930

———. *Great Contemporaries.* New York: G. P. Putnam's Sons, 1937

Clarke, I. F. *Voices Prophesying War, 1763–1984.* New York: Oxford University Press, 1966

Cowles, Virginia. *The Kaiser.* New York: Harper & Row, 1963

Crankshaw, Edward. *The Fall of the House of Hapsburg.* New York: Viking, 1963

———. *Bismarck.* New York: Viking, 1981

Cust, Lionel. *King Edward VII and His Court.* London: John Murray, 1930

Dangerfield, George. *The Strange Death of Liberal England.* New York: Capricorn Books, 1961

Davis, Arthur N. *The Kaiser as I Knew Him.* New York: Harper & Brothers, 1918

Dewar, Vice Admiral K.G.B. *The Navy from Within.* London: Gollancz, 1939

Dorling, Taprell. *Men o' War.* London: Phillip Allan, 1929

Dugdale, Blanche E. C. *Arthur James Balfour.* 2 vols. London: Hutchinson, 1939

Dugdale, E. T. S., trans. *German Diplomatic Documents. 1871–1914* (selected translations of *Die grosse Politik*). 4 vols. London: Methuen, 1928

Eckardstein, Baron Hermann von. *Ten Years at the Court of St James, 1895–1905.* London: Butterworth, 1921

Ensor, Robert. *England, 1870–1914.* New York: Oxford University Press, 1936

Escott, T.H.S. *Great Victorians.* New York: Scribner's, 1916

Esher, Viscount Reginald. *The Influence of King Edward and Other Essays.* London: John Murray, 1915

———. *Journals and Letters.* 4 vols. London: Ivor Nicholson and Watson, 1934–38

Eyck, Erich. *Bismarck and the German Empire.* New York: Norton, 1964

Fay, Sidney B. *The Origins of the World War.* 2 vols. New York: Macmillan, 1929

Fischer, Fritz. *Germany's Aims in the First World War.* New York: Norton, 1967

———. *War of Illusions: German Politics from 1911 to 1914.* London: Chatto & Windus, 1975

Fisher, Lord, Admiral of the Fleet. *Memories and Records.* 2 vols. New York: George H. Doran, 1920

———. *Fear God and Dread Nought: Correspondence of Admiral of the Fleet Lord Fisher,* ed. A. J. Marder. 3 vols. London: Jonathan Cape, 1952–59

Fitzmaurice, Lord Edmond. *The Life of Lord Granville.* 2 vols. London: Longmans Green, 1905

Fleming, Peter. *The Siege of Peking.* New York: Harper & Brothers, 1959

Frederick, Empress (Vicky). *Letters of Empress Frederick,* edited by Sir Frederick Ponsonby. London: Macmillan, 1929

Garvin, J. L., and Julian Amery. *The Life of Joseph Chamberlain.* 6 vols. London: Macmillan, 1932–51 [Garvin wrote the first three volumes, Amery the last three]

Geiss, Imanuel. *July 1914: The Outbreak of the First World War: Selected Documents.* New York: Norton, 1974

Gerard, James W. *My Four Years in Germany.* New York: George H. Doran, 1917 [Gerard was U.S. Ambassador to Germany, 1913–1917]

———. *Face to Face with Kaiserism.* London: Hodder & Stoughton, 1918

Gooch, G. P. *History of Modern Europe, 1878–1919.* New York: Henry Holt, 1923

———. *Recent Revelations of European Diplomacy.* New York: Longmans Green, 1928

———. *Before the War: Studies in Diplomacy.* 2 vols. London: Longmans Green, 1926–38

———. *Studies in Diplomacy and Statecraft.* New York: Longmans Green, 1942

———. *Under Six Reigns.* London: Longmans, 1958

Gore, John. *King George V: A Personal Memoir.* London: John Murray, 1941

Goschen, Edward. *Diary, 1900–1914.* London: Royal Historical Society, 1980

Gretton, Vice Admiral Sir Peter. *Winston Churchill and the Royal Navy.* New York: Coward, McCann, 1969

Grey of Fallodon, Viscount. *Twenty-Five Years, 1892–1916.* 2 vols. New York: Frederick A. Stokes, 1925

———. *The Fallodon Papers.* Boston: Houghton Mifflin, 1926

Haldane, Richard Burdon. *An Autobiography.* New York: Doubleday, Doran, 1929

———. *Before the War.* London: Cassell, 1920

Halévy, Elie. *A History of the English People in the Nineteenth Century.* Vol. 5: 1895–1905; vol. 6: 1905–1915. London: Ernest Benn, 1929–34

Haller, Johannes. *Philip Eulenburg: The Kaiser's Friend.* 2 vols. New York: Alfred A. Knopf, 1930

Hamilton, Lord Frederick. *The Vanished Pomps of Yesterday.* New York: George H. Doran, 1921

Hase, Georg von. *Kiel and Jutland.* New York: E. P. Dutton, 1922

Heckstall-Smith, Anthony. *Sacred Cowes.* London: Anthony Blond, 1965

Herwig, Holgar H. *The German Navy Officer Corps, 1890–1918.* New York: Oxford University Press, 1973

———. *Politics of Frustration: The United States in German Naval Planning, 1889–1941,* Boston: Little, Brown, 1976

———. *"Luxury Fleet": The Imperial German Navy.* London: Allen & Unwin, 1980

Hinsley, F. H., ed. *British Foreign Policy under Sir Edward Grey.* New York: Cambridge University Press, 1977

Holstein, Friedrich von. *The Holstein Papers: The Memoirs, Diaries and Correspondence of Friedrich von Holstein.* Edited by Norman Rich and M. H. Fisher. 4 vols. New York: Cambridge University Press, 1955

Hough, Richard. *Louis and Victoria: The Family History of the Mountbattens.* London: Weidenfeld and Nicolson, 1974

Howarth, David. *Trafalgar: The Nelson Touch.* New York: Atheneum, 1969

Hubatsch, Walther. *Die Ära Tirpitz: Studien zur Deutschen Marinepolitik, 1890–1918.* Göttingen: Musterschmidt Verlag, 1955

Huldermann, Bernhard. *Albert Ballin.* London: Cassell, 1922

Hull, Isabel V. *The Entourage of Kaiser Wilhelm II, 1888–1918.* Cambridge University Press, 1982

Humble, Richard. *Before the Dreadnought: The Royal Navy from Nelson to Fisher.* London: MacDonald and Jane's, 1976

Hurd, Archibald, and Henry Castle. *German Seapower: Its Rise, Progress and Economic Basis.* New York: Scribner's, 1913

Hynes, Samuel. *The Edwardian Turn of Mind.* Princeton, N.J.: Princeton University Press, 1968

Jameson, Rear Admiral William. *The Fleet That Jack Built: Nine Men Who Made a Modern Navy.* New York: Harcourt, Brace, 1962

Jane, Fred T. *Jane's Fighting Ships, 1914.* New York: Arco, 1969

Jarausch, Konrad H. *The Enigmatic Chancellor: Bethmann Hollweg and the Hubris of Imperial Germany.* New Haven: Yale University Press, 1973

Jenkins, Roy. *Asquith.* London: Collins, 1964

Keegan, John. *The Price of Admiralty.* New York: Viking, 1988

Kehr, Eckart. *Battleship Building and Party Politics in Germany, 1894–1901.* Chicago: University of Chicago Press, 1973

Kennan, George. *The Decline of Bismarck's European Order.* Princeton, N.J.: Princeton University Press, 1979

Kennedy, A. L. *Salisbury, 1830–1903.* London: John Murray, 1953

Kennedy, Paul. *The Rise of the Anglo-German Antagonism.* London: Allen & Unwin, 1980

———. *The Rise and Fall of British Naval Mastery,* Malabar, Florida: Krieger, 1982

———. *The War Plans of the Great Powers, 1880–1914.* London: Allen & Unwin, 1979

———. *Strategy and Diplomacy, 1870–1945.* London: Fontana, 1984

Kerr, Admiral Mark E. F. *Prince Louis of Battenberg, Admiral of the Fleet.* London: Longmans, Green, 1934

Kühlman, Richard von. *Thoughts on Germany.* London: Macmillan, 1932

Kürenberg, Joachim von. *The Kaiser: A Life of Wilhelm II.* New York: Simon and Schuster, 1955

———. *His Excellency the Spectre: The Life of Fritz von Holstein.* London: Constable, 1933

Lambert, Andrew. *Battleships in Transition: The Creation of the Steam Battlefleet, 1815–1860.* Annapolis: U.S. Naval Institute Press, 1984

Lambi, Ivo N. *The Navy and German Power Politics, 1862–1914.* Boston: Allen & Unwin, 1984

Lee, Sir Sidney. *King Edward VII.* 2 vols. New York: Macmillan, 1925–27

Le Queux, William. *The Invasion of 1910.* London: Eveleigh Nash, 1906

Leslie, Anita. *The Marlborough House Set.* New York: Doubleday, 1973

Lewis, Davis L. *The Race to Fashoda.* New York: Weidenfeld and Nicolson, 1987

Lichnowsky, Prince Karl. *Heading for the Abyss: Reminiscences.* London: Constable, 1928

———. *My Mission to London.* New York: George H. Doran, n.d.

Lloyd George, David. *War Memoirs.* 6 vols. Boston: Little, Brown, 1933–37

Longford, Elizabeth. *Queen Victoria.* New York: Harper & Row, 1964

———. [Pakenham, Elizabeth, later Countess of Longford]. *Jameson's Raid.* London: Weidenfeld and Nicolson, 1960

Ludwig, Emil. *William Hohenzollern.* New York: Putnam, 1926

Mackay, Ruddock. *Fisher of Kilverstone.* New York: Oxford University Press, 1973

Magnus, Sir Philip. *King Edward the Seventh.* New York: E. P. Dutton, 1964

Mahan, Alfred Thayer. *The Influence of Sea Power upon History, 1660–1783.* Boston: Little, Brown, 1895

———. *The Influence of Sea Power Upon the French Revolution and Empire, 1793–1812.* 2 vols. Boston: Little, Brown, 1898

Manchester, William. *The Arms of Krupp.* Boston: Little, Brown, 1964

———. *Winston Churchill: The Last Lion, 1874–1932.* Boston: Little, Brown, 1983

Mansergh, Nicholas. *The Coming of the First World War.* New York: Longmans Green, 1949

Marder, Arthur J. *The Anatomy of British Seapower: A History of British Naval Policy in the Pre-Dreadnought Era, 1880–1905.* New York: Octagon Books, 1976

———. *From the Dreadnought to Scapa Flow: The Royal Navy in the Fisher Era, 1904–1919.* 5 vols. London: Oxford University Press, 1961–65

Marwick, Arthur. *The Deluge: British Society and the First World War.* Boston: Little, Brown, 1960

Maurice, Major General Sir Frederick. *Haldane, 1856–1928.* 2 vols. London: Faber & Faber, 1937–39

Maurois, André. *The Edwardian Era.* New York: Appleton-Century, 1933

Mayer, Arno J. *The Persistence of the Old Regime: Europe to the Great War.* New York: Pantheon, 1981

McKenna, Stephen. *Reginald McKenna, 1863–1943: A Memoir.* London: Eyre & Spottiswoode, 1948

Morgan, Ted. *Churchill: Young Man in a Hurry.* New York: Simon and Schuster, 1982

Morley, John. *The Life of William Ewart Gladstone.* 2 vols. London: Macmillan, 1905

———. *Recollections.* 2 vols. New York: Macmillan, 1917

Morris, James. *Pax Britannica.* New York: Harcourt, Brace, 1968

Morton, Frederic. *A Nervous Splendor: Vienna 1888–1889.* New York: Penguin, 1979

Müller, Admiral Alexander von. *The Kaiser and His Court.* Edited by Walter Gorlitz. New York: Harcourt, Brace, 1959

Munz, Sigmund. *King Edward VII at Marienbad.* London: Hutchinson, 1934

Newton, Lord. *Lord Lansdowne: A Biography.* London: Macmillan, 1929

Nichols, J. Alden. *Germany after Bismarck: The Caprivi Era, 1890–1894.* Cambridge, Mass.: Harvard University Press, 1958

Nicolson, Sir Harold. *Sir Arthur Nicolson: A Study in the Old Diplomacy.* London: Constable, 1930

———. *King George the Fifth: His Life and Reign.* London: Constable, 1952

O'Connor, Richard. *The Spirit Soldiers: A Historical Narrative of the Boxer Rebellion.* New York: G. P. Putnam's Sons, 1973

Padfield, Peter. *Aim Straight: A Biography of Sir Percy Scott.* London: Hodder & Stoughton, 1966

————. *The Battleship Era.* London: Rupert Hart-Davis, 1972

————. *The Great Naval Race.* London: Hart-Davis, MacGinnon, 1974

————. *Rule Britannia: The Victorian and Edwardian Navy.* London: Routledge & Kegan Paul, 1981

Paget, Lady Walburga. *Scenes and Memories.* New York: Scribner's, 1912

Pakenham, Elizabeth: see Longford, Elizabeth

Pakenham, Thomas. *The Boer War.* New York: Random House, 1979

Paléologue, Maurice. *An Ambassador's Memoirs.* 3 vols. New York: Doran, 1925

Parkes, Oscar. *British Battleships, 1860–1950:* A History of Design, Construction and Armament. London: Seely Service, 1957

Pick, F. W. *Searchlight on German Africa.* London: Allen & Unwin, 1939

Pless, Princess Daisy of. *Daisy Princess of Pless.* New York: E. P. Dutton, 1929

————. *Better Left Unsaid.* New York: E. P. Dutton, 1931

Ponsonby, Sir Frederick, ed. *Letters of the Empress Frederick.* London: Macmillan, 1929

————. *Recollections of Three Reigns.* London: Eyre and Spottiswoode, 1951

Pope-Hennessy, James. *Queen Mary.* London: The Reprint Society, 1960

Porter, Cecil. *Not without a Chaperone: Modes and Manners from 1897 to 1914.* London: New English Library, 1972

Reischach, Baron Hugo von. *Under Three Emperors.* London: Constable, 1927

Ritter, Gerhard. *The Sword and the Sceptre: The Problem of Militarism in Germany.* 4 vols. Miami, Fla.: University of Miami Press, 1970

Robertson, Sir Charles Grant. *Bismarck.* New York: Henry Holt, 1919

Röhl, John C. G. *Germany Without Bismarck: The Crisis of Government in the Second Reich, 1890–1900.* London: B. T. Batsford, 1967

———— and Nicholas Sombart. *Kaiser Wilhelm II: New Interpretations.* New York: Cambridge University Press, 1982

Rose, Kenneth. *King George V.* London: Macmillan, 1983

Rotberg, Robert I. *The Founder: Cecil Rhodes and the Pursuit of Power.* New York: Oxford University Press, 1988

Sazanov, Serge. *Fateful Years.* New York: Stokes, 1928

Scheer, Admiral Reinhard. *Germany's High Seas Fleet in the World War.* New York: Peter Smith, 1934

Schmitt, Bernadotte E. *England and Germany, 1740–1914.* Princeton, N.J.: Princeton University Press, 1916

Scott, Admiral Sir Percy. *Fifty Years in the Royal Navy.* New York: George H. Doran, 1919

Spender, J. A. *The Life of the Right Hon. Sir Henry Campbell-Bannerman.* 2 vols. London: Hodder & Stoughton, 1923

————. *Fifty Years of Europe: A Study in Pre-War Documents.* London: Cassell, 1933

————. *The Public Life.* 2 vols. London: Cassell, 1925

———— and Cyril Asquith. *Life of Herbert Henry Asquith, Lord Oxford and Asquith.* 2 vols. London, Hutchinson, 1932

Stamper, C. W. *What I Know, Reminiscences of Five Years Personal Attendance upon His Late Majesty King Edward VII.* London: Mills & Boon, 1913

Steinberg, Jonathan. *Yesterday's Deterrent: Tirpitz and the Birth of the German Battle Fleet.* New York: Macmillan, 1965

Steiner, Zara S. *The Foreign Office and Foreign Policy.* New York: Cambridge University Press, 1969

————. *Britain and the Origins of the First World War.* New York: St. Martin's Press, 1977

Stephen, Adrian. *The Dreadnought Hoax.* London: Chatto & Windus, 1983

Stern, Fritz. *Gold and Iron: Bismarck, Bleichröder and the Building of the German Empire.* New York: Alfred A. Knopf, 1977

Strachey, Lytton. *Queen Victoria.* New York: Harcourt, Brace, 1949

Taylor, A. J. P. *Bismarck: The Man and the Statesman.* New York: Alfred A. Knopf, 1961

———. *Essays in English History.* London: Hamish Hamilton, 1976

Thomas, George M., *The Twelve Days: 24 July to 4 August 1914.* London, Hutchinson, 1964

Tirpitz, Grand Admiral Alfred von. *My Memoirs.* 2 vols. New York: Dodd, Mead, 1919

———. *Politische Dokumente, der Aufbau der deutschen Weltmacht.* 2 vols. Berlin: Cotta, 1924–26

Topham, Anne. *Memories of the Kaiser's Court.* London: Methuen, 1914

Trevelyan, G. M. *Grey of Fallodon.* New York: Longmans Green, 1937

Trotha, Adolf von. *Grossadmiral von Tirpitz: Flottenbau und Reichsgedanke.* Breslau, Germany: Wilh. Gottl. Korn Verlag, 1933

Trotter, Wilfrid Pym. *The Royal Navy in Old Photographs.* London: J. M. Dent & Sons, 1975

Tuchman, Barbara. *The Guns of August.* New York: Macmillan, 1962

———. *The Proud Tower: A Portrait of the World before the War, 1890–1914.* New York: Macmillan, 1966

Victoria. *The Letters of Queen Victoria, 1886–1901.* Edited by George E. Buckle. 3 vols. New York: Longmans Green, 1932

Viktoria Luise, Princess of Prussia. *The Kaiser's Daughter.* Englewood Cliffs, N.J.: Prentice-Hall, 1977

Vizetelly, Henry. *Berlin Under the New Empire.* 2 vols. New York: Greenwood Press, 1968 (first published in 1879)

Waldersee, Count Alfred von. *A Field Marshal's Memoirs.* London: Hutchinson, 1924

Waldeyer-Hartz, Captain Hugo von. *Admiral von Hipper.* London: Rich & Cowan, 1933

Warner, Oliver. *Victory: The Life of Lord Nelson.* Boston: Little, Brown, 1958

Watson, Alfred E. T. *King Edward VII as a Sportsman.* New York: Longmans Green, 1911

Wemyss, Lady Wester. *The Life and Letters of Lord Wester Wemyss, Admiral of the Fleet.* London: Eyre and Spottiswoode, 1935

Wile, Frederic W. *Men around the Kaiser.* Philadelphia: Lippincott, 1913

Wilhelm, Crown Prince of Germany. *Memoirs.* New York: Scribner's, 1922

William II. *My Memoirs, 1878–1918.* London: Cassell, 1922

———. *My Early Life.* New York: George H. Doran, 1926

Williamson, Samuel R., Jr. *The Politics of Grand Strategy: Britain and France Prepare for War, 1904–1914.* Cambridge, Mass.: Harvard University Press, 1969

Willis, Edward F. *Prince Lichnowsky: Ambassador of Peace, 1912–1914.* Berkeley: University of California Press, 1942

Willoughby de Broke, Lord Richard G. V. *The Passing Years.* London: Constable, 1924

Wilson, John. *CB: A Life of Sir Henry Campbell-Bannerman.* London: Constable, 1973

Winton, John. *Jellicoe.* London: Michael Joseph, 1981

Woodward, E. L. *Great Britain and the German Navy.* New York: Oxford University Press, 1935

Young, Kenneth. *Arthur James Balfour.* London: G. Bell, 1963

Zedlitz-Trützschler, Count Robert von. *Twelve Years at the Imperial German Court.* New York: Doran, 1924

NOTES

ABBREVIATIONS USED IN NOTES

BD *British Documents on the Origins of the War, 1898–1914*, ed. G. P. Gooch and Harold Temperley, 11 vols., London, His Majesty's Stationery Office, 1927–38

DGP *Die grosse Politik der europäischen Kabinette, 1871–1914*, 53 vols., Berlin, 1921–27. Cited by document number. Selected translations into English were done by E.T.S. Dugdale. They are citedtogether in the Notes.

FGDN *Fear God and Dread Nought: Correspondence of Admiral of the Fleet Lord Fisher*, ed. A. J. Marder, 3 vols., London, Jonathan Cape, 1952–59

KAUTSKY *Outbreak of the World War*, German Documents Collected by Karl Kautsky, New York, Oxford University Press, 1924

LVS *Letters to Venetia Stanley*, by H. H. Asquith, selected and edited by Michael and Eleanor Brock, New York, Oxford University Press, 1982

PRO Public Record Office, Kew, England

Trafalgar

xv "those far distant, storm-beaten ships": Mahan, *The Influence of Seapower upon the French Revolution and Empire*, 118

xv "No captain can do very wrong": Howarth, 73

Introduction:
Sea Power

xviii "black-browed little Spaniards": *Daily Mail*, June 26, 1897

xviii "The victualing yard": PRO, ADM-179, No. 55

xviii "Chief among the foreigners": *Daily Chronicle*, June 26, 1897

xix "even now, the muzzles": ibid.

xix "by no means conducive": *The Times*, June 26, 1897

xix "Will they stand the wear and tear": *Daily Mail*, June 26, 1897

xx "The United States officers": *Daily Chronicle*, June 26, 1897

xx "Germany has sent us": *Daily Mail*, June 26, 1897

xx "I deeply regret": *Daily News*, June 26, 1897

xxi "a great highway": Mahan, *The Influence of Seapower upon History*, 25

xxii "Give me six hours": Puleston, 117

xxiii "France is, and always will remain": Lady Gwendolen Cecil, IV, 106

xxiii "The countries with which": Paul Kennedy, *Antagonism*, 191

xxiii– "I am just now not reading but
xxiv devouring": Puleston, 159

xxv "It closed the ranks of the Entente": Churchill, *World Crisis*, I, 114–115

xxvii "lest she tread on the toes": *Daily Mail*, June 28, 1897

xxviii "No one looked better": *Daily News*, June 28, 1897

xxix "Perhaps her lawlessness": *The Times*, June 28, 1897

xxix "Admirals just presented": PRO, ADM-179, No. 55

xxx "lines of fire": *Daily Chronicle*, June 28, 1897

xxx "a myriad of brilliant beads": *Daily News*, June 28, 1897

xxx   "a fairy fleet": *Daily Mail,* June
        28, 1897
xxxi "At the stroke of twelve": ibid.

PART I: THE GERMAN CHALLENGE

Chapter 1
Victoria and Bertie

3   "I have a feeling for our dear lit-
       tle Germany": Strachey, 177
4   "An imbecile, a profligate, and a
       buffoon": Longford, 62
4   "What would you like": ibid., 27
4   "You must not touch those":
       ibid., 28
4   "There is no royal road to mu-
       sic": ibid., 31
4   "I am nearer to the throne":
       ibid., 32
5   "I am very young": ibid., 61
5   "the best-hearted, kindest": ibid.,
       66
5   "All dogs like me": ibid., 74
5   "I intend to train myself": ibid.,
       130
5   "Albert's beauty is most strik-
       ing": ibid., 133
5   "delicate   moustachios . . .
       beautifulfigure": ibid.
5   "It is with some emotion": ibid.,
       132
6   "You forget, my dearest Love":
       ibid., 140
6   "ill or not, I NEVER, NEVER": ibid.,
       143
6   "the husband, not the master":
       ibid., 148
6   "We prayed that our little boy":
       Esher, 2
6   "spoke German like their native
       tongue": Lee, I, 17
6   "had been injured by being with
       the Princess Royal": Magnus, 9
6   "What you say of the pride":
       Longford, 271
7   "Luncheon: meat and vegeta-
       bles": ibid., 276
7   "Dress . . . the outward sign":
       Esher, 11
7   "A gentleman does not indulge":
       Lee, I, 49

8   "You may well join": Magnus, 17
8   "I feel very sad about him": ibid.,
       25
8   "You will find Bertie grown up":
       ibid., 27
8   "Bertie has a remarkable social
       talent": ibid.
8   "Bertie's propensity is indescrib-
       able laziness": ibid., 32
8   "I am very sorry": ibid., 28
9   "He was immensely popular":
       ibid., 41
9   "good looks, health": Battis-
       combe, 17
9   "She is a good deal taller": ibid.,
       21
9   "a pearl not to be lost": ibid., 23
10   "Outrageously beautiful": Mag-
       nus, 46
10   "Alix has made an impression":
       ibid., 49
10   "with a heavy heart": ibid., 51
10   "fight a valiant fight": ibid.
10   "I am at a very low ebb": ibid., 52
11   "How am I alive": Longford, 307
11   "Oh, that Boy": Magnus, 52
11   "that *wicked wretches*": Long-
       ford, 315
11   "After a few commonplace re-
       marks": Magnus, 59
11   "I frankly avow": ibid., 60
12   "How beloved Albert": ibid., 62
12   "dear, gentle Alix": ibid., 66
12   "*He* gives you his blessing!":
       ibid., 67
12   "You may think that I like": ibid.
12   "So, my Georgie boy": Nicolson,
       King George V, 42
13   "The Princess had another bad
       night": Battiscombe, 83
13   "I am anxious to repeat":
       Strachey, 303
13   "After '61": Magnus, 77
14   "*anything* of a very confidential
       nature": Longford, 365
14   "The Prince of Wales . . . has
       no right to meddle": Magnus, 166
15   "Freddy, Freddy, you're very
       drunk": ibid., 92
16   "*repulsive,* vulgar, bad and frivo-
       lous": ibid., 120
16   "Bertie and Alix left Windsor to-
       day": ibid., 73

16– "In those heart-rending mo-
17   ments": Longford, 389

17   "and as there are 27 archdukes":
      Magnus, 101

17   "I should like to be your son":
      Longford, 274

18   "The weather is still excellent":
      Morton, 101

18   "could never rid himself": Bü-
      low, IV, 463

18   "stain forever": Lee, I, 250

18   "The country, and all of *us*":
      Longford, 365

18   "You remind me, my dearest
      Mama": Magnus, 197

19   "One day she chanced to look":
      Battiscombe, 209

20   "She has only to say that the P. of
      W. has *never* been fond of read-
      ing": Magnus, 123

20   "The Prince of Wales writes to
      me that there is not much use his
      remaining": ibid., 236

21   "Well, ma'am, as soon as I get
      back": William II, *My Early Life,*
      78

21   "We are not amused": Strachey,
      395

21   "Everyone likes flattery": Long-
      ford, 401

21   "Today, Lord Beaconsfield":
      Strachey, 347

22   "that   *half-mad   firebrand*":
      Magnus, 165

22   "the danger to the country":
      Longford, 518

22   "he speaks to me as if I were a
      public meeting": Strachey, 336

22   "How different, how very differ-
      ent": Longford, f.n. 569

            Chapter 2
         Vicky and Willy

23   "Oh, Madam, it is a Princess":
      Longford, 153

23   "Queen, queen, make them obey
      me": Balfour, 64

24   "Victoria, go and fetch it your-
      self": Longford, 259

24   "Bertie is my caricature":
      Magnus, 28

24   "not to entertain the possibility":
      Empress Frederick, *Letters,* 8

24– "Poor, dear child!": Strachey, 279
25

25   "I think it will kill me": Barkeley,
      60

25   "I am not of a demonstrative na-
      ture": Longford, 269

25   "You ask me . . . what I think":
      Empress Frederick, 10

25   "Endless dark corridors": Paget,
      53

25   "To govern a country": Balfour,
      67

26   "You cannot think how dull":
      Empress Frederick, 16

26   "She delivered judgement": Bal-
      four, 66

26   "She came from a country": ibid.,
      65

26– "Our   darling   grandchild . . .
27   came walking": Empress Freder-
      ick, 24

27   "a clever, dear, good little child":
      Cowles, 29

27   "The poor arm is no better": Em-
      press Frederick, 68

27   "He . . . would be a very pretty
      boy": ibid., 120

27   "My greatest troubles": William
      II, *My Early Life,* 37

28   "the weeping prince": ibid.

28   "the result justified [the]
      method": ibid., 37

28   "Hinzpeter was really a good fel-
      low": Kürenberg, 14

28   "His education will . . . be an
      important task": Lamar Cecil,
      "History as Family Chronicle," in
      Röhl and Sombart, *Kaiser Wil-
      helm II: New Interpretations,* 95

28   "a stern sense of duty": William
      II, *My Early Life,* 31

28– "Willy is a dear": Balfour, 81
29

29   "I am sure you would be
      pleased": Empress Frederick, 119

29   "happy hours spent": William II,
      My Early Life, 20

29   "It is impossible to find two nicer
      boys": Empress Frederick, 168

29   "Willy would be satisfied": ibid.,
      174

30 "the feverish haste and restlessness": William II, *My Early Life*, 158

30 "passionately interested . . . to go to Egypt": ibid., 162

31 "It was so big": ibid., 17

31 "I knew nothing": Bismarck, *The Man and the Statesman*, I, 346

31 "Fritz a furious letter": Empress Frederick, 41

31 "A loyal administration": ibid., 46

32 "Fritz . . . has for the first time in his life": ibid., 43

32 "we are dreadfully alone": ibid.

32 "I feel that I am now every bit as proud": Empress Frederick, 65

32 "To us and to many": ibid., 138

32 "I wonder why Bismarck": ibid., 191

32– "A bottle of champagne": Wil-
33 liam II, *My Early Life*, 95

33 "I really found my family": Lamar Cecil, "History as Family Chronicle," in Röhl and Sombart, *Kaiser Wilhelm II: New Interpretations*, 96

33 "my son, the complete Guards officer": *Holstein Papers*, II, 34

34 "nice but silly": Balfour, 86

34 "For a woman in that position": ibid., 87

34 "Hallelujah Aunts" . . . "blessed set of donkeys": Lamar Cecil, "History as Family Chronicle," in Röhl and Sombart, *Kaiser Wilhelm II: New Interpretations*, 98

34 "the English colony": ibid., 99

34– "a false and intriguing charac-
35 ter": ibid., 100

35 "our state of dependence on England": William II, *My Early Life*, 210

35 "Considering the unripeness": Bismarck, *New Chapters*, 6

35 "My service in the Foreign Office": William II, *My Early Life*, 211

36 "Now Bismarck governs": *Holstein Papers*, II, 202

36 "Have you asked the Crown Princess?": ibid., 195

36 "Everyone agrees": ibid., 164

36 "You have only to look": ibid., 195

36 "knowing her liking for stewed peaches": ibid., 166

36 "My father . . . has a soft heart": Thomas Kohut, "Kaiser Wilhelm II and His Parents," in Röhl and Sombart, *Kaiser Wilhelm II: New Interpretations*, 75

36– "Now I cannot talk to my fa-
37 ther": ibid., 76

37 "The extraordinary impertinence": Balfour, 101

37 "the old hag": *Holstein Papers*, II, 254

37 "William is always much surprised": Balfour, 101

37 "He did not condescend": Empress Frederick, 200

37– "The dream of my life": ibid., 215
38

38 "The doctors determined": Bismarck, *The Man and the Statesman*, II, 331

38 "not more dangerous": William II, *My Early Life*, 284

38 "recovery of my father's voice": ibid., 285

38 "the idea of a knife touching his dear throat": Barkeley, 193

38 "the greatest living authority": *Holstein Papers*, II, 344

39 "fibromatous swelling . . . like any other mortal": William II, *My Early Life*, 285

40 "My arrival gave little pleasure": ibid., 288

40 "You ask how Willy was": Empress Frederick, 256

40 "My father took his sentence": William II, *My Early Life*, 289

40 "To think that I have such a horrid, disgusting illness": Empress Frederick, 260

40 "My darling has got such a fate": Queen Victoria, I, 359

41 "The more failing": Longford, 503

41 "emaciation and the yellow color": William II, *My Early Life*, 294

41 "I thank you": Empress Frederick, 286

41 "At this moment of deep emo-
    tion": Queen Victoria, I, 390

41 "In my entire ministerial career":
    Lamar Cecil, *German Diplomatic
    Service,* 205

41– "My own dear Empress Victo-
42   ria": Longford, 505

42 "What a woman!": ibid., 506

42 "he assured me he would":
    Queen Victoria, I, 405

42 "a jolly little body": *Holstein Pa-
    pers,* I, 142

42 "I don't understand": Bülow, IV,
    618

42 "It was terrible": Queen Victoria,
    I, 408

42– "I soon noticed": William II, *My
43   Early Life,* 300

43 "We are living in sad times": Em-
    press Frederick, 229

43 "The Crown Princess's behavior
    is typical": *Holstein Papers,* II,
    348

43 "the English Princess who is my
    mother": Thomas Kohut, "Kaiser
    Wilhelm II and His Parents," in
    Röhl and Sombart, *Kaiser Wil-
    helm II: New Interpretations,* 79

43– "The decisive interference": Wil-
44   liam II, *My Early Life,* 285

44 "though he fully believed":
    Queen Victoria, I, 377

44– "Am in greatest distress": ibid.,
45   416

45 "I am broken-hearted": ibid., 417

45 "Darling, darling, unhappy
    child": ibid., 507

45 "None of my own sons": ibid.,
    417

45 "Try, my dear Georgy": Magnus,
    202

45 "Colonel Swaine arrived from
    Berlin": Queen Victoria, I, 417

46 "The Queen is extremely glad":
    ibid., 421

46 "Let me ask you to bear with
    poor Mama": ibid., 423

46 "There are many rumors": ibid.,
    424

46 "where I hope to meet": ibid.,
    425

46 "Trust that we shall be very
    cool": ibid., 429

Chapter 3
"Blood and Iron"

49 "not as friends, but as tools, like
    knives and forks": Stern, 231

50 "A Swabian family": Crankshaw,
    Bismarck, 177

50 "he was the clever sophisticated
    son": Taylor, 12

51 "by no means intended": ibid., 18

52 "I asked myself what harm the
    Indians had done me": Crank-
    shaw, *Bismarck,* 21

52 "I have never been able to put up
    with superiors": Taylor, 20

52 "I like piety": ibid., 28

52 "On a night like this": ibid.

53 "We have been saved": ibid., 56

53 "Yes, it is a hot day": Robertson,
    85

53 "It is one of those houses":
    Crankshaw, *Bismarck,* 73

54 "When I have been asked": ibid.,
    87

54 "on ice": Taylor, 43

54 "Bismarck receives no news":
    Crankshaw, *Bismarck,* 103

55 "Hidden in a steep ravine": ibid.,
    123

55 "Were I at all inclined": ibid., 124

56 *"Periculum in mora!"* Eyck, 53

56 "He is here": Taylor, 51

56 "Germany does not look":
    Crankshaw, *Bismarck,* 133

56 "The Prussian monarchy": Rob-
    ertson, 128

56 "Here in the Landtag": Crank-
    shaw, *Bismarck,* 139

57 "Whether the Germans in Hol-
    stein": ibid., 164

59 "Austria was no more wrong":
    Taylor, 87

59 "the thankless task": Robertson,
    212

59 "You know that I was against
    this war": Bismarck, *The Man
    and the Statesman,* II, 52

60 "It is France which has been
    beaten at Sadowa": ibid., 220

60 "If you want war": ibid., 221

61 "with a very, very heavy heart":
    Eyck, 168

61 "The honor and interests of

France": Crankshaw, *Bismarck,* 263

61 "an assurance that he will never": ibid., 267

62 "to the last gaiter button": Robertson, 259

62 "I don't like so many Frenchmen": Taylor, 133

62 "We are no longer looked upon": Crankshaw, *Bismarck,* 299

64 "I'd sooner have had a horse": Taylor, 134

65 "haloed by the iron radiance": Crankshaw, *Bismarck,* 304

65 "His words inspire respect": Robertson, 299

66 "The Emperor is not my monarch": Balfour, 21

66 "The fig leaf of absolutism": ibid., 23

68 "Can't we get into a side street?": Eckardstein, 17

68 "I took office": Taylor, 164

68 "It is not easy to be emperor": ibid., 137

68 "I am bored": ibid., 138

68 "I have the unfortunate nature": ibid., 12

68–69 "Faust complains": ibid.

69 "Far from it, I am all nerves": ibid.

69 "You see, I am sometimes spoiling for a fight": *Holstein Papers,* II, 39

69 "That seems to me to be rudeness": ibid., 52

69 "Oh, he never keeps his friends for long": ibid., I, 126

69 "Part of the trouble": ibid.

69 "I am no orator": Taylor, 198

70 "I never saw Bismarck enter": Bülow, IV, 307

71 "unbearably ugly": Taylor, 112

71 "Simplicity . . . complete lack of adornment": Bülow, I, 27

71 "They eat here always until the walls burst": Crankshaw, *Bismarck,* 386

72 "I have spent the whole night hating": Taylor, 137

72 "This pressure on my brain": Crankshaw, *Bismarck,* 386

72 "The Chancellor has aged": *Holstein Papers,* II, 97

72 "I don't like questions": Taylor, 196

72 "inclination to transgress": *Holstein Papers,* II, 48

73–74 "Herbert's character is unevenly developed": ibid., 199

74 "Even now, the ambassadors seek out Herbert": ibid., 199

74 "The way to loosen Herbert's tongue": ibid.

74 "Both father and son": ibid., 200

74 "eagerness to get rid of Hatzfeldt": ibid., 208

74 "Please do not say anything": Stern, 254

74 "In every great state": Lamar Cecil, *German Diplomatic Service,* 231

75 "I never go to Paris": Robertson, f.n. 482

75 "an emperor who could not talk": Lee, I, 643

75 "These audiences with young Bismarck": Bülow, II, 60

75 "Lately, it almost appears": ibid., 61

75 "Herbert, who is not yet forty": ibid.

75 "You need not praise him": ibid.

Chapter 4
Bismarck's Grand Design

76 "We are satiated": Robertson, 341

76 "You know where a war begins": *Holstein Papers,* I, 92

77 "You forget the importance": Mansergh, 18

77 "We remember that they are waiting for us": ibid., 19

78 "Remember, I forbid you to take Tunis": Robertson, 349

78–79 "If Vienna or London is chosen": Dugdale, I, 61; DGP, II, 175

79 "tying our neat, sea-worthy Prussian frigate": Crankshaw, *Bismarck,* 355

79 "that was worth the bones": Taylor, 167

80 "If I must choose": Crankshaw, *Bismarck*, 355

80 "Never will Prussia forget": Eyck, 188

80 "Prince Bismarck himself states": Crankshaw, *Bismarck*, 373

81 "Bismarck is more necessary than I": Taylor, 188

81 "Those men who have compelled me": Eyck, 265

81 "The most brilliant victories": Stern, 439

82 "Our policy with its criss-cross of commitments": *Holstein Papers*, II, xv

83 "that big Utopian Babbler": Eckardstein, 52

83 "that inhuman exception": E.T.S. Dugdale, I, 151

84 "very pleasant days": ibid., 161; DGP, IV, 38

84 "would be compatible": ibid.; ibid.

84 "England does not need an alliance": ibid., 167; ibid., 47

84 "We are uncommonly grateful": ibid., 168; ibid.

86 "My Lord, we are told": Stern, 411

86 "Neither my colleagues nor I": E.T.S. Dugdale, I, 177; DGP, IV, 63

86 "It is very hard for me": ibid., 179; ibid.

86 "in my presence with Lord Derby": ibid.; ibid.

86 "I replied to the noble Lord": ibid.

86 "why the right to colonize": ibid., 175

87 "So long as they remain": ibid., 176; ibid., 60

87 "Our friendship can be of great help": ibid., 171; ibid., 51

87 "If we fail to push our rights": ibid., 182; ibid., 77

87 "The English . . . have no reason at all": Bülow, I, 556

87 "profit England": E.T.S. Dugdale, I, 190; DGP, IV, 101

87 "produced violent gesticulations": ibid.; ibid.

87 "Herbert Bismarck has come over again": Robertson, 443

88 "Even if you had no colonial aspirations": E.T.S. Dugdale, I, 192; DGP, IV, 103

88 "There is no point in discussing": ibid.

88 "the extension of Germany": Crankshaw, *Bismarck*, 397

88 "they must take care in Berlin": Balfour, 54

88 "lively . . . recollection of the kindness": E.T.S. Dugdale, I, 208; DGP, IV, 132

88 "by your words that our former personal intercourse": ibid., 209; ibid., 133

88 "I value Lord Salisbury's friendship": Eckardstein, 98

88 "Here is Russia": Cowles, 105

88 "I am not a colonialist": Eyck, 272

89 "a German Gladstone ministry": Taylor, 194

89 "the sole object of German colonial policy": Crankshaw, *Bismarck*, 396

89 "When we entered upon our colonial policy": Eyck, 275

90 "I know of no other case": Eckardstein, 133

90 "Meanwhile, we leave it on the table": E.T.S. Dugdale, I, 374; DGP, IV, 405

90 "I see in England": Robertson, 436

90 "We no longer ask for love": Crankshaw, *Bismarck*, 406

92 "The Kaiser is like a balloon": Empress Frederick, 363

92 "too much talk of the Chancellor": Bismarck, *New Chapters*, 102

92 "a rascally young fop": Kennan, 398

94 "to earn money on certain days": Bismarck, *New Chapters*, 105

94 "The employers and shareholders": ibid., 118

95 "the practical aimlessness of the scheme": ibid., 110

95– "the increased expectations": 96 ibid., 113

96 "The waves will mount higher":
    Nichols, 17

96 "They are not my ministers":
    Eyck, 315

97 "cease all direct correspon-
    dence": Röhl, 45

97 "The Chancellor . . . has taken
    sides": Eyck, 317

97 "I am just leaving the political
    deathbed": Robertson, 490

98 "So? I gave the order yesterday":
    Bismarck, *New Chapters,* 166

98 "Well, of course you had him
    thrown out": ibid.

98 "Not even when your sovereign
    commands it?": ibid., 168

98 "How can I rule": Taylor, 246

98 "un garçon mal élevé": Nichols,
    24

99 "I must greatly deplore": Bis-
    marck, *New Chapters,* 178

99 "With deep emotion": Nichols,
    25

99 "I am in better health": Taylor,
    235

99 "I will use it": ibid., 251

99 "I am as miserable": Bülow, IV,
    637

99 "I deeply regret": Queen Victo-
    ria, I, 581

99 "I ask only for sympathy": Rob-
    ertson, 492

99 "I have bid farewell": Taylor, 251

100 "A state funeral": Stern, 457

100 "They can make their minds
    easy": Robertson, 508

100 "so that I will not have to see":
    Taylor, 256

101 "We have not doubted": Nichols,
    197

101 "He has planned an audience":
    ibid., 198

102 "Whatever the Germans may say
    or do": Bülow, I, 391

102 "He stopped when he set foot":
    Robertson, 507

102– "Would it be worthy": Bülow,
  3 IV, 678

103 "to see how long the old man will
    last": Taylor, 264

103 "Very well": Bülow, I, 607

Chapter 5
The New Course: Kaiser William II,
    Caprivi, and Hohenlohe

104 "carries himself well": Morley, I,
    272

104 "If he laughs": Balfour, 138

104– "He was small and . . . hand-
  5 some": Heckstall-Smith, 53

105 "So we are bound together":
    Cowles, 76

105 "Recruits! You have sworn Me
    allegiance": Nichols, 130

105 "There is only one ruler": ibid.,
    106

105 "terrible responsibility to the
    Creator": Bülow, I, 136

105 "enemies of the Empire": Bal-
    four, 159

106 "whether red, black or yellow
    monkeys": Bülow, II, 7

106 "If only I could see the Reichs-
    tag": Balfour, 159

106 "I adore England": ibid., 84

106 "Not one of your ministers":
    Topham, 207

106 "the damned family": Bülow, I,
    544

106 "William the Great": Magnus,
    309

106 "Willy is a bully": ibid., 214

106 "the most brilliant failure in his-
    tory": ibid., 250

106 "an old peacock": Lee, I, 673

106 "He is a Satan": Balfour, 265

107 "as an uncle treats a nephew":
    Queen Victoria, I, 439

107 "discussions of this kind": ibid.,
    440

107 "As regarding the Prince's": ibid.

108 "Most sincerely do I hope": Lee,
    I, 652

108 "How this mistake": Magnus, 212

108 "The whole affair is absolutely
    invented": ibid., 213

108 "I am happy to see": Queen Vic-
    toria, I, 505

108 "Fancy wearing the same uni-
    form": Lee, I, 654

108 "I am now able to feel": Queen
    Victoria, I, 526

108– "A Tsar, an infallible Pope": Em-
  9 press Frederick, 429

109 "William never comes": ibid., 330

109 "Of course, it would be better": Cowles, 101

109 "William is as blind and green": Barkeley, 191

109 "I wish I could put a padlock": Empress Frederick, 434

109 "My mother and I": Queen Victoria, I, 485

109 "this awful lumbago": Empress Frederick, 463

110 "a typical Teuton": Nichols, 31

111 "First, at least one successor": ibid., 34

111 "What kind of a jackass": ibid., 32

111 "I know that I shall be covered with mud": ibid., 33

111 "If anything can lighten for me": ibid., 34

111 "We are getting on well": Lamar Cecil, German Diplomatic Service, 258

111 "after Bismarck, the greatest German": Nichols, 34

111 "to lead the nation back": Röhl, 65

112 "previously, independent statesmen": ibid., 64

112 "take the good wherever": ibid., 65

112 "Caprivi has an absolutely stupid lack": Lamar Cecil, German Diplomatic Service, 259

112 "A horse which has done well": ibid.

113 "would be forced, against his own convictions": Bülow, I, 638

113 "I beg you to tell His Majesty": Nichols, 53

113 "Nothing more satisfactory": ibid., 54

114 "If Bismarck were still at the helm": ibid., 55

114 "Bismarck was able to juggle": Bülow, IV, 55

114 "simple and transparent": Nichols, 58

114 "Well, then, it can't be done": ibid., 56

115 "One thing was said": ibid., 62

115 "I drink to Holy Moscow": Bülow, IV, 639

115 "of the difficulties of my situation": Lamar Cecil, German Diplomatic Service, 257

116 "With a beard like this": Röhl, 72

116 "No, I would not dream of it": ibid., 86

116 "A sensitive old fathead": ibid.

116 "indescribable obstinacy": Lamar Cecil, German Diplomatic Service, 271

116 "One can't get anywhere": Nichols, 356

116 "Caprivi, you get terribly on my nerves": ibid., 357

116 "Your Majesty, I have always": ibid.

117 "For his successor": ibid., 329

117 "My relations with the All Highest": Röhl, 116

117 "Nor would it do any good": ibid., 362

118 "some one closer to me": Nichols, 329

118 "a man neither conservative nor liberal": ibid., 353

118 "I've been trying": Holstein Papers, II, 189

118 "I'm vainly trying": ibid., 209

118 "a quiet man": ibid., 220

118– "The Chancellor will never
19 send": ibid., 221

119 "Age, poor memory, illness": Röhl, 121

119 "his shrunken figure": ibid.

119 "He felt such contempt": Bülow, IV, 467

120 "I am convinced": Röhl, 128

120 "Things are going badly": ibid., 161

120 "Domestic politics make more noise": ibid.

120 "Hohenlohe's back must be stiffened": ibid., 173

120– "In Hohenlohe's great compli-
21 ance": ibid.

121 "make one last, vigorous effort": ibid.

121 "The Holstein of 1888": ibid., 172

121 "I know no constitution": ibid., 213

121 "I felt it was my official responsibility": ibid.

121 "I know that you will do the job well": ibid., 218
121 "If the Kaiser wants": ibid., 229
122 "almost eighty years old": Lamar Cecil, *German Diplomatic Service,* 156

Chapter 6
"The Monster of the Labyrinth"

124 "weak chest": *Holstein Papers,* I, x
124 "tall, erect and unsmiling": ibid., 4
124 "I'd rather be late": ibid., 5
126 "incredibly able intellectually": ibid., II, 261
126 "He is very sensitive": Bülow, III, 126
126 "I see": ibid., IV, 623
126– "You want to know what I
27 think": ibid., 459
127 "I have described this scene": *Holstein Papers,* II, 271
127 "I have sometimes gone beyond": ibid., xvii
127 "For the first time in twenty-five years": ibid., 276
128 "Holstein has once and for all": Bülow, IV, 607
129 "You have been guilty of something": *Holstein Papers,* I, 131
130 "Geheimrat Holstein begs to be excused": Kürenberg, *His Excellency the Spectre,* 59
130 "I hear that I have an excellent official": Lamar Cecil, *German Diplomatic Service,* 263
130 "How often has it happened": Eckardstein, 12
131 "The fellow didn't bow to me": Haller, II, 292
131 "As I perceive you are working . . . against me": ibid., I, 287
131 "If His Majesty does nothing": ibid., 286
131 "His rage was all the more senseless": Bülow, IV, 458
131 "Neither Caprivi, nor Hohenlohe": Haller, II, 297
131 "Holstein's great talents": ibid., I, 354

131– "The situation was made more
32 difficult": Bülow, I, 216
132 "Holstein was like the watchdog": ibid.
132 "In his blind and petty hatred": ibid., 266
132 "Bulow and I": Haller, II, 292
132 "to keep in mind the need": Paul Kennedy, *Antagonism,* 206

Chapter 7
Bülow and *Weltmacht*

135 "The question is not": Paul Kennedy, *Antagonism,* 311
135 "as irresistible as a law of nature": ibid.
136 "One of the conventional lies": Carroll, 350
136 "England is still the state": ibid., 383
136 "Only in war": Padfield, 16
136 "The State is not an Academy of Art": ibid., 18
137 "General Caprivi believed": Röhl, 162
138 "has great tasks to accomplish": Paul Kennedy, "The Kaiser and German *Weltpolitik,*" in Röhl and Sombart, *Kaiser Wilhelm II: New Interpretations,* 158
138 "The German Empire": Carroll, 378
138 "I am the sole arbiter": Lee, II, 136
138 "I am at my very best": Bülow, II, 443
138 "Bülow will be my Bismarck": Lamar Cecil, *German Diplomatic Service,* 288
138 "With me, personal rule": Kathy Lerman, "The Decisive Relationship," in Röhl and Sombart, *Kaiser Wilhelm II: New Interpretations,* 222
138– "Bülow seemed more Latin than
39 German": Mansergh, 78
139 "an eel": Lamar Cecil, *German Diplomatic Service,* 37
139 "an eel is a leech": Balfour, 202
139 "underneath the shiny paint": ibid., 201

139 "He would be quite a fellow": Lamar Cecil, *German Diplomatic Service,* 282

139 "Bernhard makes a secret": ibid.

140 "The closest friend of my life": Bülow, II, 59

140 "My earliest memory of Herbert": ibid.

140 "a beautiful girl": ibid., IV, 17

140 "wavered and swayed": ibid., 207

141 "As I sat next morning": ibid., 555

141 "My father said": ibid., 558

142 "clean-shaven and pasty": *Holstein Papers,* II, 188

142 "When Bulow wants to set": ibid.

142 "A few days ago": ibid., 204

142 "The beauty of it": ibid., 189

142 "her wonderful eyes, black eyes": Bülow, IV, 349

142 "For once in his life": *Holstein Papers,* II, 188

143 "Only if you take the Kaiser": Bülow, I, 5

143 "Ever since his apostasy": ibid., 7

144 "older and weaker": ibid., 10

144 "My dear Bernhard": ibid., 18

144 "to build a fleet": ibid., 19

144 "Now, what about my ships?": ibid., 65

145 "Agreed, agreed": ibid., 68

145 "When one has shared bright days": Lamar Cecil, *German Diplomatic Service,* 281

145 "I adore him": Bülow, I, 161

145 "As a man": Lamar Cecil, *German Diplomatic Service,* 282

145 "He is so *bedeutend*": ibid., 283

146 "leading a contemplative existence": ibid., 288

146 "Build your nest": ibid., 285

146 "An old man full of specters": ibid., 287

146 "The sway of the counselors": ibid.

147 "Would you accept": Bülow, I, 433

147 "Candidly, for me": ibid.

147 "Do accept": ibid., 436

147 "Secretary of State Count Bülow speaking": ibid.

147 "My dear Chancellor": ibid., 443

147 "satisfaction that Chlodwig, the old mummy": ibid., 453

147 "Under Prince Hohenlohe": ibid., 459

147–48 "Holstein . . . suggested": ibid., 454

148 "sobriety, objectivity": ibid.

148 "Bülow gives me his full trust": Lamar Cecil, *German Diplomatic Service,* 294

149 "decades had to pass": ibid., 38

149 "The air is thick": Zedlitz-Trützschler, 104

149 "Whenever, by oversight": ibid., 196

149 "Your light trousers": ibid.

149 "Since I have Bülow": Lerman, "The Decisive Relationship," *Kaiser Wilhelm II: New Interpretations,* 241

Chapter 8
"Ships of My Own"

150 "I had a peculiar passion": William II, *My Early Life,* 229

150 "Osborne is the scene": ibid., 15

150 "I was allowed to play": ibid., 74

150–51 "I often crossed over": ibid., 73

151 "Heavy on the water": ibid., 49

151 "When, as a little boy": Bülow, II, 36

151–52 "Believe me, Your Majesty": ibid., 37

153 "Today's victory": Magnus, 244

153 "a marine Madame Tussaud's": Heckstall-Smith, 44

153–54 "I can recall the portly figure": ibid., 14

155 "Propose abandon race": Eckardstein, 45

156 "old peacock": Lee, I, 673

156 "So, then, you'll soon be off to India": Magnus, 250

156 "the Regatta used to be": Eckardstein, 55

156 "The Boss of Cowes": ibid.

157 "There's no doubt about it": Heckstall-Smith, 53

157 "Half of them": ibid., 52

158 "If the Kaiser steered himself":
Bülow, II, 39
158 "Nevertheless, as we approached
Meteor": Heckstall-Smith, 60

Chapter 9
Tirpitz and the
German Navy Laws

161 "because we do not have a fleet":
Herwig, 12
162 "Who sold his last warship":
ibid., 16
162 "sharp as jagged iron": Tirpitz,
Memoirs, I, 26
162 "Sheer slop!": ibid.
163 "every man and every penny":
Herwig, *Luxury Fleet*, 14
163 "our future is on the water": Balfour, 206
165 "Politics are your affair": Hurd,
200
165 "one is so far from the world":
Steinberg, 150
166 "I was very mediocre": Tirpitz,
Memoirs, I, 2
166 "Between 1864 and 1870": ibid.,
13
166– "Don't they look just like
67 sailors": ibid., 15
167 "like a mechanic": ibid., 47
167 "It was a tossup": ibid., 49
167 "We do not know": ibid., 39
167 "the eleven best years": ibid., 67
167– "Here I have been listening to
68 you": ibid., 62
168 "a crowd of ships": ibid., 68
168 "a high-minded man": ibid., 60
168 "displayed itself in a heterogeneous collection": ibid., 61
169 "Why was Nelson": ibid., 76
169 "like a gramophone record":
Steinberg, 72
169 "a considerable force": ibid., 83
169 "My intentions . . . altered":
ibid., 85
169 "Tirpitz was here": ibid.
170 "not a trace of enthusiasm":
ibid., 86
170 "These are the facts": ibid.
170 "the Kaiser hopes to find": ibid.,
89

170 "was lovely": ibid., 96
170 "Only the present State Secretary": ibid.
170– "He seems to be toying": ibid.,
71 109
171 "and send the bill to the Reichstag": ibid., 112
171 "The Kaiser has no rights": ibid.
171 "Our doom": ibid., 116
171 "to seek out a place": ibid., 103
171 "I relinquished my command":
Tirpitz, *Memoirs*, I, 118
172 Tirpitz' June 1897 memorandum:
Steinberg, 209–221
173 "The Reichstag will never
agree": Hurd, 197
173 "When I became State Secretary": Tirpitz, *Memoirs*, I, 129
173 "but there, money is of no importance": ibid.
173 "Every word of the draft Bill":
ibid., 126
174 "With all the good will in the
world": Steinberg, 140
174– Tirpitz interview with Bismarck:
75 Tirpitz, *Memoirs*, I, 134
175 "he liked the sailors . . . a hole
in the shining coat": ibid., 139
176 "I smiled at them": Hurd, 200
176 "the development of our battle
fleet": Steinberg, 160
176 "We are not thinking": ibid., 164
176 "Our fleet has the function": ibid.
177 "I find the totals": ibid., 171
177 "If the popular assembly allows":
ibid., 160
177 "The present Reichstag": ibid.
178 "I considered it my duty":
Tirpitz, *Memoirs*, I, 143
179 "All peoples": Steinberg, 180
179 "If it is true": ibid., 194
179 "There is, especially on the right
side of this house": ibid., 195
179 "Long live the Kaiser . . . German Emperor, Berlin": ibid., 196
179 "is like the army": ibid., 197
180 "I declare expressly": Hurd, 115
181 preamble to the Second Navy
Law: ibid., 121
182 "the fare was homely": Tirpitz,
Memoirs, I, 210
182 "With his swift comprehension":
ibid., 201

182 "the air of the forest": ibid., 205

183 "I could never discover": ibid., 128

183 "For example": ibid., 204

184 "The naval policy of Germany": Marder, I, 107

184 "The . . . composition of the new German fleet": ibid.

185 "The Admiralty had proof": ibid.

PART II: THE END OF
SPLENDID ISOLATION

Chapter 10
Lord Salisbury

190 "The Queen cannot conclude": Tuchman, Proud Tower, 39

191 "His bitterest detractors": Willoughby de Broke, 186

191 "as if to discover": Young, 100

192 "an almost embarrassing wealth": Asquith, Fifty Years, I, 273

193 "an existence among devils": Gwendolen Cecil, I, 9

193 "I am bullied": ibid., 13

193 "I am obliged": ibid.

193 "Never were two men": ibid., 49

194 "It is the peculiarity of my complaint": ibid., 50

194 "Your prohibition": ibid.

195 "That which is my main expense": ibid., 59

195 "never left cards": ibid., 63

195 "First rate men": ibid., 158

195 "blazing indiscretions": ibid., II, 21

195 "returning to the cold and greasy remains": ibid., I, 71

196 "I dislike and despise": ibid., 96

196 "Ah, Robert, Robert": ibid., 97

196 "My impression": ibid., II, 45

197 "that half-madman": Blake, 605

197 "a Russian agent": ibid., 607

197 "Oh! if the Queen were a man": ibid., 637

197 "much of the trouble": Blake, 577

198 "I do not know": Blake, 746

199 "Der Alte Jude": ibid., 646

199 "Six hours of my day": Gwendolen Cecil, II, 287

199 "He looks ill and sleeps badly": A. L. Kennedy, Old Diplomacy, 37

199 "Prince Bismarck with one hand": Crankshaw, 350

199 "What with deafness": Gwendolen Cecil, II, 287

200 "very agreeable indeed": A. L. Kennedy, Salisbury, 126

200 "laboring oar": Gwendolen Cecil, II, 297

200 "Order of Chastity": A. L. Kennedy, Salisbury, 371

201 "France is . . . England's greatest enemy": Gwendolen Cecil, IV, 106

201 "by sympathy, by interest, by descent": A. L. Kennedy, Salisbury, 67

201 "Nous sommes des poissons": E.T.S. Dugdale, I, 249; DGP, IV, 265

201 "the sea and her chalk cliffs": Bülow, II, 38

201 "England's strength": Queen Victoria, III, 23

201 "Splendid Isolation": Gwendolen Cecil, IV, 86

201–2 "the supremacy of the interests of England": ibid., 89

202 "British foreign policy": Taylor, Essays in English History, 125

202 "A great sleeper": Gwendolen Cecil, II, 16

202 "One subject only": ibid., III, 210

203 "Do whatever you think best": ibid., II, 238

203 "Buccaneers": ibid., III, 208

203 "he had left a madman": ibid., 214

204 "I was told": ibid., 25

204 "Our political arrangements": ibid., IV, 219

204 "left a nasty taste": ibid., II, 15

205 "Hey, diddle diddle": ibid., III, 8

205 "There were evenings": ibid., 6

205 "My father always treats me": ibid., 12

205 "N. has been very hard put to it": ibid., 13

205 "He may be able": ibid.

206 "What a dreadful thing": Queen Victoria, I, 26

206 "triumphant success": ibid., 31

206 "fortune would not be equal": ibid., 34

206 "Every day, I feel the blessing": ibid., III, 37

206 "if not the highest": Tuchman, *Proud Tower,* 9

206 "I will *not* have the Queen worried": Gwendolyn Cecil, III, 190

206 "Always speak the truth to the Queen": ibid., 181

206 "everything": ibid., 182

206 "Lord Salisbury offers this suggestion": Queen Victoria, III, 593

207 "I am too horrified": ibid., 396

207 "Lord Salisbury entirely shares": ibid., 397

207 "Letter received": ibid., I, 443

207– "Sir—In furtherance of the con-
8   versation": ibid., 442

208 "She had an extraordinary knowledge": ibid., III, 186

208 "It appears that his head": ibid., 398

208– "hot-headed, conceited": ibid.,
9   441

209 "He was simply afraid to do so": ibid., 442

209 "an enormous calamity": Gwendolen Cecil, IV, 364

209 "It is a curious Nemesis": Queen Victoria, I, 591

209 "this perfectly useless piece of rock": E.T.S. Dugdale, I, 172; DGP, IV, 53

210 "possession of Heligoland": ibid., II, 37; ibid., VIII, 16

210 "The conditions you enumerate": Queen Victoria, I, 614

210 "Lord Salisbury quite understands": ibid.

210 "Your answer respecting Heligoland": ibid., 615

210 "confidentially": A. L. Kennedy, *Salisbury,* 220

211 "It is wise": Gwendolen Cecil, IV, 367

211 "Lord Salisbury respectfully draws": ibid., 371

211 "Lord Salisbury hopes": ibid.

211 "His Majesty gave the English": Steinberg, 76

212 "William is a little sore": Queen Victoria, II, 547

212 "Your Kaiser seems to forget": Eckardstein, 59

212 "Seeking an outlet": *Holstein Papers,* I, 161

212 "By his boorish behavior": E.T.S. Dugdale, II, 339

Chapter 11
The Jameson Raid
and the Kruger Telegram

213 "I would annex the planets": Elizabeth Pakenham (Longford), 25

213 "the Colossus": Garvin, III, 31

213 "my darling": Rotberg, 14

214 "On one occasion": ibid., 89

214 "younger and more fiery sons": Elizabeth Pakenham (Longford), 22

214 "What have you been doing": ibid., 34

214 "If there be a God": Rotberg, 415

217 "When a community": *The Times*

218 "The nostrils of a racehorse": Elizabeth Pakenham (Longford), 59

218 "The eyes of an affectionate dog": ibid.

218 "a Scotch terrier": ibid.

218 "we drew closely together": Rotberg, 127

219 "All the ideas are Rhodes' ": Elizabeth Pakenham (Longford), 63

219 "Anyone could take the Transvaal": ibid., 62

219 "I'm going": Rotberg, 539

220 "CRISIS IN THE TRANSVAAL": *The Times,* January 1, 1896

220 "The position of thousands of Englishmen": ibid.

220 "There are girls in the gold-reef city": *The Times,* January 11, 1896

220 "an act of war": Elizabeth Pakenham (Longford), 47

220 "a peaceful arrangement": ibid.

220 "If it were supported by us": ibid.

221 "a little nation which was Dutch": William II, *My Memoirs,* 80

221 "If the child is ill": Gooch, *History of Modern Europe,* 215

221 "To threaten us": Balfour, 192; DGP, XI, 7

221 "Our little republic": E.T.S. Dugdale, II, 365

222 "contrary to German interest": ibid., 367; DGP, XI, 4

222 "The status . . . is one": Carroll, 366

222 "We will wash": ibid.

222 "needed no instructions": ibid.

222 "had gone so far": E.T.S. Dugdale, II, 368

222 "absolutely blazing": Balfour, 194

223 "if it had been anyone else": Steinberg, 83

223 "Now suddenly": Lee, I, 725

223 "His Majesty developed": *Holstein Papers,* II, 469

223 " 'That would mean war' ": Lee, I, 721

223 "Oh, no, don't you interfere": *Holstein Papers,* I, 162

223 "I express my sincere congratulations": Lee, I, 722

224 "I express to Your Majesty": ibid.

224 "Nothing that the government has done": Carroll, 372

224 "universal delight": Röhl, 166

224 "tempestuous": Bülow, IV, 665

224 "crude and vehement": ibid.

224 "tore his hair": Eckardstein, 86

224 "England, that rich and placid nation": *Holstein Papers,* I, 160

224 "answered . . . in accordance with German public feeling": Lee, I, 727

224 *"eine Staats-Aktion":* ibid., 722

224 "an expression of the Kaiser's annoyance": *Holstein Papers,* I, 160

224– "The Jameson Raid caused":
25   William II, *My Memoirs,* 80

226 "The nation will never forget": Lee, I, 723

226 "England will concede nothing": *The Times,* leader, January 7, 1896

226 "With respect to the intervention": *The Times,* January 7, 1896

226 "to have an additional squadron": ibid., January 9, 1896

226 "this most gratuitous act": Balfour, 195

226 "Those sharp, cutting answers": Queen Victoria, III, 20

226– "My dear William": Lee, I, 724–
27   25

227 "is entirely suited": ibid., 725

227 "hint to our respectable papers": Queen Victoria, III, 13

227– "Most beloved Grandmama":
28   Lee, I, 725

228 "without enquiring too narrowly": Queen Victoria, III, 20

228 "I should like to hear": Bülow, I, 340

228 "You see, I was a naughty boy": Elizabeth Pakenham (Longford), 99

228 "should probably have joined Jameson": Young, 173

229 "Dr. Jim had personal magnetism": Margot Asquith, III, 26

229 "excess of zeal": Elizabeth Pakenham (Longford), 119

229 "Old Jameson": Rotberg, 523

229 "Neither": ibid., 550

229– "As to one thing": Spender,
30   *Campbell-Bannerman,* I, 198

230 "Do not tell me": Rotberg, 390

230 "Thank goodness": Elizabeth Pakenham (Longford), 256

230 "So little done": ibid., 158

230 "The Jameson Raid": Eckardstein, 85

231 "in his telegram to Kruger": Bülow, IV, 665

231 "England will not forget": ibid., 664

231 "The incident may have its good side": Tirpitz, *Memoirs,* I, 85

231 "the outbreak of hatred": ibid., 86

Chapter 12
"Joe"

232   "The Republic must come": Garvin, I, 152

232   "The Divine Right of Kings": ibid., 467

232   "Lord Salisbury constitutes himself": ibid., 392

232   "a Sicilian bandit": ibid., II, 80

233   "My impression": ibid., I, 467

233   "In that case": ibid.

233   "I would advise him": ibid.

233   "round the garden walks": Morley, *Recollections,* I, 148

234   "swell": ibid., 179

234   "Here in England": Lee, I, 333

234   "it seems almost impossible": Garvin, I, 79

234   "Unfortunately, it wasn't true": ibid., 209

235   "a man who never told the truth": ibid., 227

235   "Radical demagogue": Magnus, 131

235   "His strength in debate": Spender, *The Public Life,* I, 88

235   "watched him and wondered": ibid., 89

235   "a man of obvious mystery": ibid., 86

236   "the Irish people are entitled": Garvin, II, 21

236   "It was mischievous or worse": ibid., 147

236   "To preserve the Union": ibid., I, 140

236   "It was unthinkable": Spender, *The Public Life,* I, 88

236– "Judas, after betraying his Mas-
37   ter": Garvin, II, 480

237   "Traitor!": ibid., 250

237   "no fraternizing": Spender, *The Public Life,* I, 88

237   "Dear lady, welcome home": Garvin, II, 371

237– "Mrs. Chamberlain is very
38   pretty": ibid., 372

238   "Mrs. Chamberlain looked lovely": ibid.

238   "was always ready to discuss politics": A. L. Kennedy, *Salisbury,* 255

238   "She unlocked his heart": Garvin, II, 373

238   "She brought my children nearer": ibid.

238   "must have been dear and refreshing": ibid., 563

238   "proud to call myself a Unionist": Garvin, II, 607

238   "frenzied enthusiasm": ibid., 334

238– "I am an Englishman": ibid., 333
39

239   "Already the weary Titan": Asquith, *Fifty Years,* I, 290

239   "Prince Bismarck has rendered us": Garvin, I, 496

239   "this incarnate representative": ibid.

239   "I don't like to be cheeked": ibid., 497

240   "saw work to be done": ibid., III, 9

240   "I believe that the British race": ibid., 27

240   "It is not enough to occupy": ibid., 19

240   "My dear Salisbury": ibid., 95

240   "an ostentatious order": ibid., 96

240   "The shadow of war": ibid., 179

241   "If the panic": Eckardstein, 93

241   "Chamberlain has rather risen": Garvin, III, 244

241   "two-headed administration": ibid., 203

241   "Chamberlain has Salisbury": ibid., 286

241   "Affairs now are so difficult": Queen Victoria, III, 22

241– "Isolation is much less danger-
42   ous": ibid., 21

242   "public opinion": ibid., 248

242   "I agree with you": ibid., 249

242– "It is not a question": Asquith,
43   *Fifty Years,* I, 290

244   "unquestionably the most energetic": Eckardstein, 103

244   "The English fleet": Garvin, III, 262

244   "would have to show himself": ibid., 257

244   "I admitted": ibid., 260

245   "if I thought that Parliament": ibid.

245   "The Jubilee swindle": ibid., 269

245   "At the same time": ibid., 270
245– "said to me at Homburg": ibid.,
46   276
246   "Mr. Chamberlain . . .": ibid.,
      275
246   "Impossible!": ibid.
246   "I quite agree with you": ibid.,
      279
246   "Since the Crimean War": ibid.,
      282

Chapter 13
Fashoda

247   "His temperature was high": A.
      L. Kennedy, *Salisbury,* 276
248   "Africa was created": Garvin,
      III, 203
248   "Up to ten years ago":
      Gwendolyn Cecil, IV, 225
250   "The question of going forward":
      Queen Victoria, III, 85
250   "My father was much im-
      pressed": A. L. Kennedy, *Salis-
      bury,* 280
251   "the French Embassy in Lon-
      don": Newton, 283
251   "The advance of a French expe-
      dition": A. L. Kennedy, *Salis-
      bury,* 278
251   "an emissary of civilization": BD,
      I, 163
252   "I note your intention": Gooch,
      History of Modern Europe, 289
252   "I have come to resume": A. L.
      Kennedy, *Salisbury,* 286
253   "We are the stronger": ibid., 287
253   "Here is Marchand": Queen Vic-
      toria, III, 287
253   "no title of occupation": A. L.
      Kennedy, *Salisbury,* 290
253   "so long as the French flag flew":
      Queen Victoria, III, 299
253   "Great Britain has been treated":
      A. L. Kennedy, *Old Diplomacy,*
      82
254   "Fashoda is the last straw":
      Marder, *Anatomy,* 331
254   "It seems a deadlock": Queen
      Victoria, III, 289
254   "I deeply sympathize": ibid., 290
254   "Received your cypher": ibid.

254   "We have only arguments":
      Gooch, *Before the War,* I, 96
255   "Not a stone": Queen Victoria,
      III, 298
255   "there would be no humiliation":
      ibid., 304
255   "a French explorer": BD, I, 170
255   "I think a war": Queen Victoria,
      III, 305
255   "very agreeable": ibid., 308
255   "I have received from the French
      ambassador": A. L. Kennedy,
      Old Diplomacy, 83
256   "keeps the French entirely out":
      Queen Victoria, III, 351
256   "I have received news": DGP,
      XIV, ii, 383
256   "had no knowledge": ibid., 385
256   "Poor France": ibid., 409

Chapter 14
Samoa and William's Visit
to Windsor

257   "You ask me": Garvin, III, 246
257   "Last year we offered": E.T.S.
      Dugdale, III, 62; DGP, XIV, ii,
      612
258   "Instead of compliance": Spen-
      der, *Fifty Years,* 184
258   "I suspect": Queen Victoria, III,
      359
258   "said that it was not": ibid.
258– "Dearest Grandmama": ibid.,
59   376
259   "He entirely agrees": ibid., 379
259– "Dear William": ibid., 381
60
260   "wouldn't be dictated to": Eck-
      ardstein, 106
260   "I am waiting daily": ibid.
260   "a document of frothy flum-
      mery": ibid., 111
260   "whether Samoa was the name":
      ibid., 112
260   "What has happened in Samoa":
      E.T.S. Dugdale, III, 57; DGP,
      XIV, 592
260– "What I have preached": ibid.
61
261   "stood alone": Garvin, III, 282

261 "Your government in England":
ibid., 341

261 "abolishes every colonial antagonism": ibid., 342

262 "I AM EQUALLY PLEASED": Queen
Victoria, III, 416

262 "BRAVO!": Bülow, I, 331

262 "Yes, the last few years": Eckardstein, 117

262 "Let him come": ibid.

262 "I AM DÉSOLÉ": Queen Victoria,
III, 389

262 "YOUR HANDICAPS": Eckardstein,
120

262– "It really is enough": ibid.
63

263 "I don't envy": ibid.

263 "the Kaiser could not": ibid., 121

263 "If I go": ibid., 122

263 "I should be awfully glad": ibid.,
123

263 "It was not until": ibid., 124

263 "I hoped": Bülow, I, 355

264 "Beyond any question": ibid.,
364

264 "The entire service": Garvin, III,
500

265 "ruler of the world empire": Bülow, I, 361

265 "From this Tower": ibid., 360

265– "William came to me after tea":
66 Queen Victoria, III, 421

266 "Lord Salisbury has heard": ibid.,
399

266 "but if he was blamed too much":
Bülow, I, 377

266 "the immense harm": Queen
Victoria, III, 423

266 "Joseph Chamberlain was": Bülow, I, 367

266 "an able, energetic, shrewd businessman": ibid., 368

267 "I am the sole master": ibid., 370

267 "with its magnificent park": ibid.,
395

267 "One had only to appear": ibid.

267 "a fat, malicious tom-cat": ibid.,
399

267– "British politicians": ibid., 391
68

268 "The visit . . . has gone off":
ibid., 401

268 "Any far-seeing English statesman": Garvin, III, 507

268 "an incomprehensible blunder":
Eckardstein, 146

268 "a gaucherie": Bülow, I, 385

268 "Count Bülow, whose acquaintance": Eckardstein, 130

269 "Without power": Bülow, I, 415

269 "I will say no more": Eckardstein, 151

269 "the extreme difficulty": ibid.,
144

269 "Chamberlain and Arthur Balfour": Bülow, I, 392

270 "to show a spirit": ibid., 394

Chapter 15
The Boer War
and the Boxer Rebellion

271 "moral and intellectual damages": Thomas Pakenham, 63

271 "A war with the Transvaal":
Garvin, III, 141

271– "Kruger has never": Spender,
72 Asquith, 132

272 "the sands are running low": A.
L. Kennedy, Salisbury, 309

272 "I will tell you one thing":
Gwendolyn Cecil, III, 191

272 "The vast majority": Garvin, III,
513

272 "The South African question":
Eckardstein, 137

272 "the infamous language": A. L.
Kennedy, Salisbury, 313

272 "phenomenal": ibid.

272– "What days of sad news": Lee, I,
73 754

273 "Last year": Queen Victoria, III,
484

273 "I am afraid I am unable": Lee, I,
759

273 "My last paragraph": ibid.

274 "the Kaiser is considering": Eckardstein, 153

274 "Lord Salisbury": ibid., 152

274 the Swiss cheese ultimatum: ibid.,
157

274– "Yet whosoever believes": Gar-
75 vin, III, 516

275 "You have no idea": Lee, I, 770

275 "My armies have driven": Asquith, *Fifty Years,* I, 305

275 "THE DISTURBANCES IN CHINA": *The Times,* June 6, 1900

278 "As to Su Shun": Fleming, 57

278 "Fish in a stewpan": O'Connor, 142

280 "awful sights": Fleming, 94

280 *"Veuillez agréer":* ibid., 118

280 "The face": ibid., 114

281 "Situation desperate": ibid., 132

281 "put to the sword": ibid., 135

281 "impossible to exaggerate": ibid., 137

282 "Lady MacDonald": O'Connor, 296

282 "Peking must be stormed": ibid., 181

282 "Now it is a pleasure": Bülow, I, 417

282 "I never saw him so excited": ibid.

282 "unprecedented in its impudence": ibid.

282 "no business": O'Connor, 181

282 Bülow's description of the "Hun" speech: Bülow, I, 418

282 "I cannot possibly answer": ibid., 419

283 "You struck out the best parts": ibid.

283 "I know you are concerned": ibid., 420

283 "not to endure": DGP, XVI, 76

283 "The strongest corps": E.T.S. Dugdale, III, 130; ibid., 82

283 "I fully agree": ibid.; ibid., 83

284 "How wonderfully": Waldersee, 144

284 "He is extraordinarily restless": ibid., 167

284 "tried to make excuses": ibid., 168

284 "traitor": Bülow, I, 423

285 "It became obvious to me": Waldersee, 209

285 "Naturally, this was": ibid.

285 "betrayed him": Bülow, I, 527

285 "as big a war indemnity": Waldersee, 210

285 "were extraordinarily polite": ibid., 213

285 "farcical" and "absurd": O'Connor, 298

286 "Different staff officers": Waldersee, 249

286 "I rejoice that the French": ibid., 230

286 "They say that the Kaiser": O'Connor, 298

286 "to shoot all the headmen": ibid., 299

286 "exerting a moral influence": Fleming, 253

286 "This is no time": Manchester, *The Arms of Krupp,* 217

286 "It was not a proper position": Eckardstein, 180

287 "seems to desire": O'Connor, 325

287 "At all costs": Eckardstein, 175

Chapter 16
The "Khaki Election" and the
Death of Queen Victoria

288 "the Parliament is in its sixth year": Queen Victoria, III, 586

288 "We all know very well": Asquith, *Fifty Years,* I, 305

289 "A vote for the Liberals": Spender, *Campbell-Bannerman,* I, 291

289 "The elections are wonderfully good": Queen Victoria, III, 603

289 "while marking their ballots": Garvin, III, 605

289 "The stable remains the same": Asquith, *Fifty Years,* II, 3

290 "makes one despair": Amery, IV, 138

290 "his doctors had advocated": Queen Victoria, III, 604

290 "I do very earnestly": ibid., 606

290 "Lord Salisbury thought": ibid., 611

290 "At the time": Churchill, *Great Contemporaries,* 57

291 "Double Duchess": Tuchman, *Proud Tower,* 39

291 "Pray come without fail": Eckardstein, 184

291 "The Colonial Minister": ibid., 185

292 "It is particularly noteworthy":
ibid., 186

292 "You and I": Amery, IV, 146

292 "Better wait": ibid., 147

293 "I was wheeled up to the bed":
Queen Victoria, III, 516

293 "an accomplice of Chamberlain":
Lee, I, 777

293 "It was entirely my own idea":
Longford, 555

294 "Again my old birthday": ibid.,
556

294 "I now rest daily": ibid., 558

294 "The malady appears incurable":
Queen Victoria, III, 576

294 "having been with us," ibid., 580

294 "Oh God!": ibid., 579

295 "He has now been": ibid., 588

295 "The Queen feels": ibid., 592

295 "Your Majesty speaks patheti-
cally": ibid., 594

295 "In May the Queen": Askwith,
261

295 "gloomy and dark": Longford,
558

295 "very poorly and wretched":
Queen Victoria, III, 616

296– Queen Victoria's diary entries:
97 ibid., 618–34

296 "She was thinner": Amery, IV, 7

296 "I am not anxious," ibid., 6

296 "Had a fair night": Queen Victoria, III, 642

296 "as mighty an instrument": Amery, IV, 147

297 "I have duly informed": Newton,
197

297 "prompt recovery": Longford,
561

297 "The last moments": Ponsonby,
82

297 "She was so little": Balfour, 231

298 "William was kindness itself":
Magnus, 272

298 "William's touching and simple
demeanour": ibid.

298 "Let us rather remember": Lee,
II, 526

298 "She was the greatest": Amery,
IV, 8

299 "The Queen is dead, Sir": Lee,
II, 8

299 "see what you can do": Balfour,
231

299 "I hope": Bülow, I, 580

300 "My aunts": ibid., 581

300 "The Kaiser is very tired": ibid.

300 "To crown everything else":
ibid., 582

300 "I am anxious": ibid., 583

301 "Accordingly, I told the Kaiser":
Eckardstein, 189

301 "Baron von Eckardstein tells
me": Amery, IV, 148

301 "Chamberlain's threatened understanding": ibid., 149

301– "Your Majesty is quite right":
2 ibid.

302 "the Russian Emperor": Newton,
199

302 "Russian Grand Duke": ibid.

302 "It is not the British Fleet": Eckardstein, 192

302 "I cannot wobble forever": Amery, IV, 150; DGP, XVI, 295

303 "The military ranks": ibid., 151

303 "I believe there is a Providence":
Cowles

303 "completely under the spell":
Bülow, I, 585

Chapter 17
The End of Anglo-German
Alliance Negotiations

304 "Everything from London": Eckardstein, 202

304 "no desire to burn": Amery, IV,
153

304– "The alliance is moving": Eck-
5 ardstein, 219

305 "out of the hands of Eckardstein": Bülow, I, 591

305 "that person": Amery, IV, 156

305 "unmitigated noodles": Eckardstein, 217

305 "There, what do you": ibid.

305 "hopeless sloppiness": ibid., 202

305 "cleverly managed": ibid., 220

306 "since the liability": BD, II, 68

306 "Nobody here in England": Amery, IV, 157

306 "We ought not": ibid., 160

306– "nations who now criticize":
  7   ibid., 167
308   "the bloodhound of the Trans-
      vaal": Spender, *Fifty Years,* 187
308   "butchers": Amery, IV, 168
308   "for a speech": ibid., 169
308   "there had been no warmer ad-
      vocate": ibid.
308   "The German Army": Bülow, I,
      637
308   "What I have said": Amery, IV,
      173
308   "Mr. Chamberlain is": ibid., 175
308– "You would be interested": ibid.,
  9   176
309   "the temper of the two coun-
      tries": Newton, 207
309   "I hear in the strictest confi-
      dence": E.T.S. Dugdale, III, 171;
      DGP, XVII, 342
309   "It is not the first time": Eckard-
      stein, 288
309   "For a long time at least": ibid.,
      230

Chapter 18
Arthur Balfour

310   "One might as well": A. L. Ken-
      nedy, *Salisbury,* 354
311   "the King's face": Amery, IV,
      448
311   "Joe Chamberlain was": ibid.,
      453
312   "that I was to understand": ibid.,
      V, 67
312   "The country is full": ibid., 71
312   "Arthur hates difficulties": ibid.,
      IV, 464
312   "The difference between Joe and
      me": ibid.
312   "the finest brain": Chamberlain,
      206
313   "the most extraordinary objet
      d'art": Young, xv
313   "To know her slightly": Blanche
      Dugdale, I, 16
313   "Can you tell me": ibid.
313   "a beautiful purity of mind":
      ibid., 21
313   "if he was laughed at": ibid., 20
314   "Pretty Fanny": Young, 13
314   "In these conditions": Blanche
      Dugdale, I, 36
314   "A very good bill": ibid., 37
314   "Ah, when we were young":
      Young, 38
315   "The member for Hertford":
      Blanche Dugdale, I, 45
315   "that very pretty, quaint boy":
      Young, 32
315   "I really delight in him": ibid.
315   "with ill-timed punctuality": ibid.
315   "I saw with intense thankful-
      ness": ibid.
316   "Comatose": Blanche Dugdale, I,
      31
316   "Nearly all the young men":
      Margot Asquith, II, 12
317   "The fact is, Mr. Balfour": ibid.,
      I, 259
317   "You all sit around": Young, 143
317   "Oh, dear": Tuchman, *Proud
      Tower,* 46
317   "exquisite attention": Margot
      Asquith, I, 257
317   "to know intimately": ibid.
317   "I think I should mind": Jenkins,
      79
317   "After an evening": Chamber-
      lain, 217
317   "If he had": Tuchman, *Proud
      Tower,* 52
317   "Who did you say": Blanche
      Dugdale, I, 150
318   "If you think": ibid., 94
318   "drifting with lazy grace":
      Young, 101
318   "a silk-skinned sybarite": ibid.
318   "accidents have occurred":
      Blanche Dugdale, I, 98
318– "failed because he relied":
  19 Young, 105
319   "If necessary, do not hesitate":
      Blanche Dugdale, I, 101
319   "best calculated": ibid.
319   "It is impossible to say": ibid.,
      110
319   "What I have done": ibid., 137
319   "Bloody Balfour": ibid., 113
319   "There are those who talk": ibid.,
      103
320   "jaded palate": ibid., 120
320   "My object is not to bribe": ibid.,
      130

320   "with rather a wry face": Young, 125

320   "formerly as ready": ibid., 130

320   "he had never loved": ibid.

320   "I am very glad": ibid.

320   "I ran up from the station": Blanche Dugdale, I, 166

321   "There is a difference": Margot Asquith, I, 236

321   "My dear Uncle Robert": Blanche Dugdale, I, 187

321   "You ask me about South Africa": Young, 185

321   "Every night I go down to the War Office": Blanche Dugdale, I, 222

321   "Hotel Cecil": ibid., 237

321–22   "this unhappy and persecuted family": ibid., 239

322   "It is better, perhaps": Young, xvii

322   "When I'm at work in politics": ibid., 163

322   "Quite a good fellow": Tuchman, Proud Tower, 49

322–23   "ridiculous," "grotesque": Blanche Dugdale, I, 114

323   "really believe": Tuchman, Proud Tower, 51

323   "Imperishable monuments": Margot Asquith, I, 265

323   "having cooked for him a sparrow": Blanche Dugdale, I, 143

324   "this damned Scottish croquet": Tuchman, Proud Tower, 53

324   "making a raft with his sponge": Blanche Dugdale, I, 144

Chapter 19
Joseph Chamberlain
and Imperial Preference

325   "Colonies are like fruits": Amery, V, 39

326   "either by exemption": Blanche Dugdale, I, 255

327   "It was suggested": ibid., 256

327   "Let us first be quite clear": Amery, V, 119

327–28   "The Cabinet finally resolved": ibid., 121

328   "there was no time to fight": Blanche Dugdale, I, 258

328   "Corn is in a greater degree": ibid., 260

328   "You can burn your leaflets": Jenkins, 136

328–29   "party weapons": Amery, V, 184

329   "a great speech by a great man": Asquith, Fifty Years, II, 11

329   "From that point on": ibid., 10

329   "Chamberlain's views": ibid., 14

329   "for the present": ibid.

329–30   "I should consider": Spender, Campbell-Bannerman, I, 102

330   "I'm not for Free Trade": Young, 124

330   "This reckless, criminal escapade": Amery, V, 193

330   "On the morning of May 16": Jenkins, 137

330   "Tariff Reform has united": Blanche Dugdale, I, 263

331   "Ritchie . . . did not really resign": Ensor, 374

331   "I never heard anything": Blanche Dugdale, I, 270

332   "The Duke, whose mental processes": Spender, Campbell-Bannerman, II, 114

332   "The Duke never read it": Blanche Dugdale, I, 271

333   "dying British industry": Ensor, 375

334   "gladly defer": Jenkins, 139

335   "a Free Trader who sympathized": Spender, Campbell-Bannerman, II, 140

335   "Blenheim Rat," "Blackleg Blueblood": Manchester, Winston Churchill, 361

336   "Some of us were born": ibid., 357

336   "To keep in office": ibid., 359

336   "It is not, on the whole": ibid., 360

Chapter 20
Lord Lansdowne and the
Anglo-French Entente

337   "possibly the greatest gentleman": Barker, 140

337   "The longer I live": ibid., 159

338 "Roberts' appointment": ibid., 153

339 "he must often have seemed": ibid., 154

339 "a dagger": Gooch, *Before the War,* I, 19

339 "would certainly fight": Newton, 220

340 "I congratulate you": Lee, II, 144

340 "At last the noodles": BD, III, 435

340– "I do not think": Gooch, *Before*
41 *the War,* I, 23

341 "naive": Eckardstein, 108

342 "I do not wish to leave this desk": Lee, I, 711

342 "The feeling of all classes": Mansergh, 88

342 "very agreeable and well-informed": Queen Victoria, III, 317

343 "I have the greatest confidence": Gooch, *Before the War,* I, 105

343 "exercises relentlessly": Amery, IV, 194

343 "Delcassé seems to me": ibid., 206

344 "a visit from the King": Spender, *Fifty Years,* 213

344 "quite an informal affair": Lee, II, 223

344 "as officially as possible": ibid.

344 "Vivent les Boers!": ibid., 237

344 "The French don't like us": ibid.

344– "A Divine Providence": ibid.
45

345 "Oh, Mademoiselle": ibid., 238

345 "where I am treated": ibid., 239

345 "Vive le roi": ibid., 240

345 "The visit of King Edward": ibid., 242

345 "So, although the Paris visit": ibid., 243

345 *"Zukunftsmusik":* Woodward, 72

346 "I am in despair": Gwendolyn Cecil, IV, 356

346 "Throughout our conversation": Newton, 281

347 "admit that it was the business": Nicolson, 109

347 "The question comes down": Newton, 281

347 "The Government of the French Republic": Gooch, *Before the War,* I, 43

348 "You expect us to recognize": ibid., 149

348 "The French negotiations": ibid., 47

348 "agreed to afford one another": Spender, *Fifty Years,* 216

349 "If we let ourselves be trampled": E.T.S. Dugdale, III, 221; DGP, XX, 208

350 "If I conclude my agreements": Gooch, *Before the War,* I, 153

Chapter 21
The Morocco Crisis of 1905

352 "Pedicaris alive": Tuchman, *Proud Tower,* 272

353 "grooms, gardeners, electricians": Nicolson, 106

353 "this loose agglomeration": ibid., 83

353 "I do not believe": ibid., 95

353 "in order to secure": Marder, *Anatomy,* 475

354 "when this danger was clear": Woodward, 83

355 "platonic": Nicolson, 116

355 "That is just exactly": E.T.S. Dugdale, III, 224; DGP, XX, 301

355 "a world-wide dominion": Lee, II, 338

355 "if the necessity of a war": Woodward, 82

355 "the earliest possible": Spender, *Fifty Years,* 241

356 "In the face of this chain": Bülow, II, 121

356 "when, as Prince of Prussia": Eckardstein, 126

356 "it was in Germany's interest": Bülow, II, 117

356 "a good thing that France": ibid.

356 "I have been to Asia": ibid., 119

356 "Your Majesty's visit": E.T.S. Dugdale, III, 223; DGP, XX, 262

356 "Tant mieux!": ibid.; ibid.

357 "When the Minister tried to argue": Balfour, 255

358 "all were to be exterminated": Spender, *Fifty Years,* 242

358 "I landed because": Bülow, II, 162

358 "The British generals and admirals": Spender, *Fifty Years,* 243

358 "It is wonderful to think": Balfour, 256

358 "trembling with emotion": Spender, *Fifty Years,* 243

358 "When the news reached me": ibid.

358– "I emphasized again": Bülow, II,
59 127

359 "could not recognize": Bülow, II, 127

359 "about the purpose": Gooch, *Before the War,* I, 249; Mansergh, 94

360 "the most mischievous": Lee, II, 340

360 "This seems a golden opportunity": FGDN, II, 55

361 "We have not, and never had": BD, III, 68

361 "in a friendly manner": Bülow, II, 133

361– "If the Germans find out":
62 Gooch, *Before the War,* I, 176

362 "The Chancellor of the German Empire": Spender, *Fifty Years,* 245

362 "That would mean war": Gooch, *Before the War,* I, 178

362 "the British Navy": Mansergh, 73

362 "Are we in a condition": Gooch, *Before the War,* I, 179

362 "telling me that he had just": Bülow, II, 137

362– "You can't escape me": ibid., 135
63

363 "absolutely insisted": Spender, *Fifty Years,* 245

363 "The fall of Delcassé": ibid.

363 "Delcassé's dismissal": Lee, II, 344

364 "You have seen": Spender, *Fifty Years,* 245

364 "Peaceful, good-humored": Bülow, II, 141

364 "not to linger": Gooch, *History of Modern Europe,* 358

364 "If the Berlin people": Gooch, *Before the War,* I, 261

364 "had a great future behind him": Bülow, II, 221

365 "the most violent": Nicolson, 127

365 "Tell us what you wish": ibid., 128

365 "to securing full guarantees for an open door": ibid., 133

365 "it was not for me": ibid., 134

365 "I felt really insulted": ibid.

365 "He who has the police": Gooch, *Before the War,* I, 262

366 "We are close to a rupture": Nicolson, 137

366 "changeable": ibid.

366 "Tattenbach is again": ibid., 142

366– "This is the third time": ibid., 141
67

367 "epoch-making success": E.T.S. Dugdale, III, 248; DGP, XXI, 312

367 "His Majesty's policy": ibid.; ibid.

367 "did not appear to agree": ibid.; ibid.

367 "The Moroccan Question": ibid., I, 237; ibid., 52

367 "The Entente Cordiale has stood": Mansergh, 100

367– "The treaty may not have given":
68 Bülow, II, 231

368 "I got through a whole series": ibid., 235

368 "was too emotional": ibid., 236

368– "in the most cold-blooded man-
69 ner": ibid., 237

PART III: THE NAVY

Chapter 22
From Sail to Steam

375 "feeling the tropical heat": Bacon, *A Naval Scrapbook,* 21

375 "he had had a headache": ibid., 18

378 "You're a bloomin' Portuguese army": ibid., 80

378 "Now do you 'ear there": Scott, 69

379 "Fanny Adams": ibid., 26

379 "brutes who rejoiced": Humble, 5

381 "Report number of killed": Winton, 25

381 "Many a time": Beresford, I, 25

381– "I am doubtful": ibid.
82

382 "satisfactory knowledge": ibid., 6

382 "Only sometimes, sir": ibid., 5

383 "comparatively lucky": Dewar, 15

384 "suppress independence": ibid., 14

384 "Masthead for the midshipmen": Scott, 27

384– "on a dark night": ibid., 51
85

385 "those old sailing days": ibid., 25

385 "in the evening": ibid.

389 "Although we are living": Humble, 108

390 "I don't feel any water": Beresford, I, 62

390 "Bless me, I forgot": ibid., 49

390 "I did not like the *Defence*": ibid., 41

390 "The retention of masts and sails": Padfield, *The Battleship Era,* 127

391 "Cardinal policy of this country": Marder, *Anatomy,* 105

391 "No doubt the present fleet": Beresford, I, 25

392 "self-perpetuating": Winton, 13

392 "I call the whole system": ibid., 23

392 "On what authority": FGDN, I, 150

393 "As a midshipman": Dewar, 22

394 "I thought we had taken it": Winton, 46

394 "Second division alter course": ibid.

394 "Now we shall see something": ibid.

394 "We shall be very close": ibid.

394 "May I go astern": ibid., 48

395 "It's all my fault": Padfield, *The Battleship Era,* 131

395 "It would be fatal": ibid., 132

396 "The Swell of the Ocean": Bacon, *Scrapbook,* 49

396 "It was customary": Scott, 73

396– "When I went to sea": Dewar, 19
97

397 "Had anyone suggested": Padfield, *The Battleship Era,* 128

397 "It was no wonder": Scott, 73

397 "No one except the Gunnery Lieutenant": Marder, *Scapa Flow,* I, 8

397 "Spread for target practice": Scott, 85

397 "it was considered": Beresford, I, 20

397 "We used to practice": ibid.

397– "Gunners looked along the barrels": ibid.
98

398 "He gave us midshipmen": Scott, 29

398– "absolutely transformed": ibid.
99

399 "had forty-two modern heavy guns": ibid., 62

399 "But the innovation was not liked": ibid., 72

399 "Ship's company of good physique": ibid., 45

399– "contained no reference": ibid.
400

Chapter 23
Jacky Fisher

403 "the son of a Cingalese princess": Fisher, *Memories,* 20

403 "Oriental cunning and duplicity": Marder, *Scapa Flow,* I, 14

403 "an unscrupulous half-Asiatic": ibid.

403 "I entered the Navy": Fisher, *Records,* 25

403 "I have had to fight like hell": FGDN, II, 35

403 "I remember the intense enthusiasm": Mackay, 23

403 The complimentary closes of Fisher's letters are from FGDN, II, 18

403– "I can't bear to read them": FGDN, I, 39
4

404 "Would you kindly leave off": Fisher, *Memories,* 40

404 "spiritual indigestion": FGDN, II, 16

404 "Pretty dull, Sir, this": Fisher, *Memories,* 26

404 "Wouldn't you, Sir, have loved": Bacon, *Fisher,* I, 94

404– "The efficiency of the Fleet":
5   FGDN, I, 150

405 "favoritism": Bacon, *Fisher,* I, 130

405 "if I haul a man up": FGDN, II, 38

405 "pre-historic admirals": Marder, *Scapa Flow,* I, 46

405 "mandarins": FGDN, I, 359

405 "fossils": ibid., 267

405 "Anyone who opposes me, I crush": Marder, *Anatomy,* 394

405 "The Malay": Fisher, *Memories,* 20

405 "The Yellow Peril": Marder, *Anatomy,* 395

405 "that hobgoblin": Mackay, 194

405 "A silly ass": Marder, *Scapa Flow,* I, 17

405 "frightened rabbits": Bacon, *Fisher,* II, 73

405 "deepened his faith in Providence": Marder, *Scapa Flow,* I, 17

406 "My God, Fisher, you must be mad!": FGDN, II, 20

406 "Personally, I hope": ibid., 19

406 "All nations want peace": ibid., I, 125

406 "The French, no doubt": ibid.

406 "On the British Fleet": Fisher, *Records,* 89

406 "Only a congenital idiot": FGDN, I, 166

406 "the suddenness . . . and finality": ibid., 310

406 "The generals may be asses": ibid., 311

407 "We must reconsider": ibid., 179

407 "a wonderful man": ibid., 183

407 "I admire Fisher": Fisher, *Memories,* 182

407 "The German Empire": Lee, II, 333

407 "Jellicoe to be Admiralissimo": FGDN, II, 424

407 "a most magnificent": ibid., I, 17

408 "My dear Jack": ibid., 24

408 "A simple-minded man": Mackay, 3

409 "I heard from my mother": ibid., 73

409 "none of the feelings": FGDN, I, 77

409 "I had happy days": ibid., 18

409 "strange to say": ibid.

409 "I wrote out": ibid., 19

409 "free from defect of speech": ibid.

410 "but I told him I thought": ibid.

410 "The day I joined": Fisher, *Records,* 25

410 "Whenever you took a bit": ibid., 23

411 "about the greatest saint": ibid., 27

411 "He was always teaching me": Mackay, 13

411 "our captain stood on the river bank": Fisher, *Records,* 28

411– "You sank up to your knees":
12   FGDN, I, 28

412 "I never smelt": ibid., 27

412 "and hauled what fellows they could find": ibid., 29

412 "They had not time": ibid., 33

412 "We are all *very, very* sorry": ibid.

412 "Loyal au mort": Fisher, *Records,* 28

412 "Take care of that boy!": ibid., 29

412 "She is such a horrid old tub": FGDN, I, 57

412 "Satanic": Fisher, *Records,* 29

413 "I believe I was the only officer": ibid.

413 "As a sailor, an officer": ibid., 31

413 "The Lords of the Admiralty": FGDN, I, 60

414 "She had a picked crew": Fisher, *Memories,* 149

414 "I never went ashore": ibid., 150

414 "A First Sea Lord told me": Fisher, *Records,* 172

414 "I never can make out why": Fisher, *Memories,* 227

415 "Jack would certainly": Mackay, 40

415 "Splendid": FGDN, II, 365

415 "The mere fact": Mackay, 75

416 "My own most darling Kitty": FGDN, I, 77

416 "I really do not think": ibid., 76

416 "In 17 days": Mackay, 70

415 "Jack would certainly": Mackay, 40

415 "Splendid": FGDN, II, 365

415 "The mere fact": Mackay, 75

416 "My own most darling Kitty": FGDN, I, 77

416 "I really do not think": ibid., 76

416 "In 17 days": Mackay, 70

416 "Dorothy requires cod-liver oil": FGDN, I, 106

416 "Mind, my own darling": ibid., 77

416 "I so often hope": ibid., 81

416 "but, my darling": ibid., 69

416 "I feel my want of French": ibid., 78

416 "Now, my darling, I must say good night": ibid., 72

417 "Every man was provided": Mackay, 94

417 "when we got into heavy weather": Fisher, Memories, 156

417 "his ship is a perfect yacht": Mackay, 108

418 "If you are a gunnery man": FGDN, I, 64

418 "in order to keep": Bacon, Fisher, I, 61

418 "a little man": FGDN, I, 92

418 "were very proud of their captain": Mackay, 135

418 "he attended": ibid., 136

419 "my boy" . . . "the best boy": FGDN, I, 94

419 "As each name was discussed": Fisher, Memories, 158

419 "a wonder": ibid.

419 "A man could crawl": ibid.

419 "took so long to load": Padfield, Rule Britannia, 173

419– "endless inventions": Fisher,
20 Memories, 158

420 "knew not what deck": Parkes, 257

420 "the best ship in the Fleet": Fisher, Records, 204

422 "You need not have": FGDN, I, 106

422 "They've found the range, sir": Beresford, I, 198

422 "the sickness was simply indescribable": FGDN, I, 109

422 "the Admiralty could build": Fisher, Memories, 159

422 "He'll never reach Gibraltar": ibid.

423 "Sir . . . it is our whole wish": Bacon, Fisher, I, 92

423 "I am all right": Mackay, 173

423 "but I was let off with trousers": FGDN, I, 114

424 "I want to introduce Captain Fisher": Bacon, Fisher, I, 91

425 "When all the doctors failed": ibid., 98

425 "beloved Marienbad": ibid.

425 "I got breakfast": Fisher, Records, 47

425 "Every day is happy": FGDN, I, 98

425 "If you are restricted": Fisher, Records, 42

426 "fresh as a daisy": FGDN, I, 129

426 "were husbandeering": ibid.

426 "over-rated" . . . "a fraud": ibid., I, 131

426 "the flood of Americans": ibid.

426 "The Americans swarm": ibid., 133

426 "what the world had to fear": ibid., 189

426 "The Yankees are dead set against us": ibid., 190

426 "about 70 multi-millionaires": Bacon, Fisher, II, 125

426 "Their language . . . English": ibid., 124

427 "that wooden boarding pikes": Fisher, Records, 204

427 "like a hive of bees": ibid., 66

428 "destroyers": FGDN, I, 100

428 "There were no half-measures": ibid., 101

428 "He had a terrific face": ibid., 102

428 "On the other hand": ibid.

428 "Williamson and Paine": ibid.

429 "One ought not to wish for war": ibid., 139

429 "So I did": Fisher, Records, 64

429 "the tip-top appointment": FGDN, I, 139

429 "It is the greatest nonsense": Tuchman, Proud Tower, 239

429– "Imagine a monarch": ibid., 241
30

430 "If you think that war": Marder, Anatomy, 346

430 "by the charm of his manner": ibid.

430 "Such a rush": FGDN, I, 142

430 "detestable and smelly" . . . "a beastly, stuffy": ibid.

431 "The humanizing of war?": Bacon, *Fisher*, I, 121

431 "Look, when I leave The Hague": ibid., 122

431– "England holds": Mackay, 221
32

432 "Thanks to the energetic attitude": Tuchman, *Proud Tower*, 261

Chapter 24
Ut Veniant Omnes

433 *"Renown* . . . should not be": Mackay, 257

434 "I must say your old ship": ibid.

435 "If . . . the whole of the French Fleet": FGDN, I, 166

435 "Preliminary failure in Naval War": ibid., 157

435 "Success in war": ibid., 168

435 "Our frontiers": ibid., 172

435 "five minutes *before*": Fisher, *Records,* 98

435 "General Quarters": Bacon, *Fisher,* I, 129

435 "When Fisher left the ship": ibid.

435 "UT VENIANT OMNES": ibid., 131

435– "As the Commander of one
36 ship": ibid., 130

436 "I am sorry": ibid., 234

436 "I went to a lecture": FGDN, I, 151

437 "It was brought home to them": Bacon, *Fisher,* I, 127

437 "Fisher had a practice": Mackay, 230

437– "It is impossible": Bacon, *Fisher,*
38 I, 128

438 "the efficiency of the Navy": FGDN, I, 150

438 "Fishpond": ibid., II, 36

438 "The new admiral": Mackay, 225

438 "I fancy the new admiral": ibid.

438 "I had not seen Admiral Fisher": ibid.

438– "It is difficult for anyone": ibid.
39

439 "a night attack on Malta": FGDN, I, 155

439 "Woe to the captain": Mackay, 240

439– "sitting in the Superintendant's
40 chair": Bacon, *Fisher,* I, 151

440 "I have burnt": FGDN, I, 151

440 "The other day": ibid., 197

440 "I had a tremendously long day": ibid., 159

440 "Suddenness is the characteristic feature": ibid., 173

440 "In former days": ibid., 165

440– "up and down the quarterdeck":
41 ibid.

441 "the bill to the Admiralty": Mackay, 240

441 "all such splendid men": FGDN, I, 196

441 "The admiral commanding": ibid., 164

441 "Who is going to be hung": ibid., 156

441 "I have the rope around my neck": ibid., 167

441– "In this famous Mediterranean
42 Fleet": ibid.

441 "to encourage the others": ibid., 164

442 "I maintain it to be": ibid., 175

442 "Lord Selborne says 'Trust us' ": ibid., 193

442 "Unless I have the use": ibid., 171

442 "I would sooner have 14 battleships": ibid., 194

442 "[The Admiralty] admit": ibid.

443 "It was splendid for me": ibid., 193

443 "If more destroyers are not obtained": ibid., 156

443 "To steam a fleet at night": Marder, *Anatomy,* 399

443 "serious disappointment": ibid., 400

443 "I must call attention": ibid., 404

443 "His reiterated demands": ibid., 403

443– "The First Sea Lord is a nonen-
44 tity": FGDN, I, 210

444 "Walter Kerr . . . is a slave": ibid., 199

444 "careful never to give away": Bacon, *Fisher,* I, 137

444 "BURN THIS!": FGDN, I, 185 (and throughout Fisher's correspondence)

444 "I can't help it": Mackay, 251

444 "mischievous" . . . "unpleasant prominence": Barker, 37

444– "warmed-over": Mackay, 250
45

445 "It's a place": FGDN, I, 185

445 "You seem to place no trust": ibid., 209

445 "unprecedented": ibid., 187

446 "All has gone exceedingly well": ibid., 207

446 "I believe in the various talks": ibid.

446 "Nearly everything": ibid., 230

446 "Personally, I have always been": ibid., 218

447 "I am 'tabooed' ": ibid., 199

447 "I hear a syndicate": ibid., 216

447 "a few acres of land": Mackay, 253

447 "My dear Admiral": FGDN, I, 222

447 "I think it shows": ibid., 230

448 "I feel very sad": ibid., 238

448 "My object was to keep": Bacon, *Fisher,* I, 161

448 "They began singing": Mackay, 272

448 "like a torpedo boat": ibid.

448 "As usual": FGDN, I, 242

448 "As we passed the ships": Mackay, 272

449 "The Fourth Sea Lord": FGDN, I, 270

449 "You can't get them too young": ibid., 267

449 "Surely we are drawing": Marder, *Scapa Flow,* I, 31

449– "our officers . . . down in the
50   coal hole": FGDN, I, 268

450 "Look here, Brown": ibid., 213

450 "the Mandarins": FGDN, II, 68

450 "the fossils": ibid., I, 67

450 "They look on me": ibid., I, 266

450 "My dear Walker": ibid., 243

450 "I have in my drawer": ibid., 269

450 "I HAVE NO WORK": ibid., 248

450 "On the British Navy": Fisher, *Records,* 248

450 "you may sleep quietly": ibid., 90

450– "The Lord Chief Justice":
51   FGDN, I, 273

451 "Fisher's toys": Marder, *Anatomy,* 559

452 "un-English": ibid., 358

452 "this underhand method": Mackay, 298

452 "the cleverest officer": Marder, *Scapa Flow,* I, 83

452 "The submarine was": Marder, *Anatomy,* 363

452 "exercised an extraordinary . . . influence": ibid., 366

453 "I don't think": ibid., 367

453 "The risks of allowing": ibid., 363

453 "Lord Selborne and all the rest": FGDN, I, 289

453 "The King will never forgive": ibid., 290

453 "The Board will expect me to fulfill": ibid., 288

454 "I was asked the question": Fisher, *Records,* 32

454 "makes my blood boil": FGDN, I, 73

454 "The Regular Army": ibid., 291

454 "A prayer for the War Office": ibid., 300

454 "The military system is rotten": Bacon, *Fisher,* I, 205

454 "the Old Gang": ibid., 212

455 "We have 550 people": FGDN, I, 278

455 "I shall be very disappointed": ibid., 366

455 "My rooms are next the King's": ibid., 286

456 "So I'm all right for Church": ibid., 287

456 "Lord Selborne arrived": ibid.

456 "You must stay till Monday": ibid., 286

456 "I wasn't master": Fisher, *Records,* 37

456 "Sir John, she has been invited": ibid., 38

456 "H.M. has two receptive plates": FGDN, I, 324

457 "Have you seen that halfpenny
     newspaper": Fisher, *Records,* 40
457 "The King came in": Fisher,
     Memories, 26
457 "Anyhow, I am stopping with
     you": Dorling, 221
457 "got the King's nurse": Fisher,
     Records, 40
457– "I had four and a half hours
58   alone": FGDN, I, 327
458 "As I was zero": Fisher, *Records,*
     39

Chapter 25
First Sea Lord

459 "4 days ago": FGDN, I, 316
459 "The die is cast": ibid.
460 "Selborne was so cordial": ibid.,
     324
460 "I am ready for the fray": ibid.,
     325
460 "This fleet of lunatics": Marder,
     Anatomy, 439
460 "no more to be trusted": ibid.
460 "I've been with the Prime Minis-
     ter": FGDN, II, 47
461 "Admiral Sir John Fisher": Mac-
     kay, 335
461 "We never ceased talking":
     FGDN, II, 44
461 "the house that Jack built":
     Marder, *Scapa Flow,* I, 36
463 "too weak to fight": Winton, 102
463 "magnificent on paper": Bacon,
     From 1900 Onward, 107
463 "The first duty of the Navy":
     Marder, *Scapa Flow,* I, 38
463 "with one courageous stroke":
     FGDN, II, 24
464 "It appears necessary to repeat":
     Humble, 192
464 "Bath Chair Flotilla": Bacon,
     From 1900 Onward, 107
465 "No, bless you, Sir": Bacon, ibid.,
     110
465 "the keystone . . . instantly
     ready": FGDN, II, 23
465 "has augmented the fighting
     power": Marder, *Scapa Flow,* I,
     38

466 "which would have disgraced":
     FGDN, I, 362
466 "I don't care if he drinks": Hum-
     ble, 188
466 "Unless retrenchment": Marder,
     Scapa Flow, I, 24
466 "fighting efficiency": FGDN, II,
     124
466 "There is only so much": Marder,
     Scapa Flow, I, 25
466 "amazing array of tumblers":
     ibid.

Chapter 26
The Building of the *Dreadnought*

470 "Selborne has agreed": FGDN, I,
     325
470 "Two governing conditions": D.
     K. Brown, "The Design and Con-
     struction of the Battleship *Dread-
     nought*," Warship, IV, 43
470– "In designing this ship": Parkes,
71   468
471 "when 12 inch guns are fired":
     Marder, *Anatomy,* 531
472 "The fast ship": Parkes, 469
472 "I am an apostle": Fisher, *Memo-
     ries,* 127
473 "no guns be carried": Parkes, 469
473– "It is clearly necessary": FGDN,
74   I, 177
474 "Monsters with short legs":
     Hough, 6
475 "If you fit reciprocating engines":
     Brown, op. cit., 45
475 "were noiseless": Bacon, *From
     1900 Onward,* 96
475 "a glorified snipe marsh": Bacon,
     Fisher, I, 263
475 "Speed is armor": Marder, *Scapa
     Flow,* I, 59
475 "Hitting is the thing": ibid., 62
476 "No holes in the bulkheads":
     Parkes, 470
476 "the extra length": ibid., 471
478 "to infuse her own dauntless":
     The Times, February 12, 1906
478– The account of the launching of
80   the *Dreadnought* is drawn from
     The Times, February 10 and Feb-

ruary 12, 1906; *Daily Chronicle,*
February 12, 1906.

480 "The building and launching":
The Times, February 12, 1906

480 "The *Dreadnought* is a symbol":
ibid.

481 "It was an exciting moment": Bacon, *From 1900 Onward,* 150

482 "The King is greatly pleased":
PRO, ADM 153-19805 and ADM
136—No. 7

482 "He looked very grave and serious": Parkes, 479

483 "a great, white-bellied brute":
Bacon, *From 1900 Onward,* 156

484 "It was far cooler": *The Times,*
August 6, 1907

484 "a cheap swaggerer": Bacon,
From 1900 Onward, 158

484 "the air of mystery": *The Times,*
February 10, 1906

485 "It is hardly too much": ibid.

485 "In my opinion": Marder, *Anatomy,* 540

486 "If there were no natural obstacles": Woodward, 113

486 "paralyzed by the *Dreadnought*":
Marder, *Scapa Flow,* I, 67

487 "The whole British Fleet":
Marder, *Anatomy,* 56

487 "a piece of wanton": ibid.

487 "We said, 'Let there be' ":
Woodward, 105

487 "Putting all one's naval eggs":
Marder, *Anatomy,* 536

488 "I wish to God": Marder, *Scapa
Flow,* I, 70

488 "It should clearly": ibid., 64

489 "When Sir William White suggests": ibid., 69

489 "Knowing as we did": Bacon,
From 1900 Onward, 103

489 "I am afraid it will be rather
hard," Stephen, 40. The story of
the Dreadnought Hoax is also
told in Bell, I, 157–61 and Appendix E

489 "the religious beliefs": ibid., 44

490 "Bunga-Bunga!": ibid., 51

492 "There would be no escape":
FGDN, I, 236

492 "A single fast armored cruiser":
Marder, *Scapa Flow,* I, 55

492 "I on one occasion": FGDN, I,
174

493 "to the world's end": Marder,
Anatomy, 95

494 "of the great Nelsonic idea":
Fisher, *Records,* 222

495 "Vessels of this enormous size":
Parkes, 492

495 "three large armored cruisers":
ibid.

497 "Their speed . . . should have
kept": ibid., 494

Chapter 27
Lord Charles Beresford

498 "One complains": Marder, *Scapa
Flow,* I, 77

498 "Ruthless, Relentless, and Remorseless": ibid., 36

498 "I wish South Africa": FGDN, II,
52

499 "an immense combination":
ibid., 53

499 "Nothing that Sir John Fisher
could say": Mackay, 358

500 "instantly ready for war": Fisher,
FGDN, II, 23

500 "Our only probable enemy":
ibid., 103

501 "As you know": Mackay, 361

501 "Syndicate of Discontent":
FGDN, II, 110

501 "pre-historic fossils": ibid., 35

501 "An attack should always be
met": ibid., 111

501 "Lest I should be exalted":
Barker, 61

502 "Any smart action": Beresford,
II, 559

503 "That white-faced little beggar":
ibid., I, 11

503 "both methods": ibid., 101

504 "his red shirt flung open": ibid.,
164

504 "I was the only person": ibid.,
151

504 "I am an old woman now": ibid.,
152

505 "He is an Irishman": Lee, I, 456

506 "Seeing the difficulty": Beresford, I, 188

506 "Good God!": ibid.

506 "Recall *Condor*": ibid., 189

506 "Arabs were murdering": Beresford, I, 191

507 "I only had to shoot": ibid., 193

507 "I was at work": ibid., 196

507 "With a roar": ibid., 263

507 "my sword rigid": ibid., 266

509 "a coward" . . . "a blackguard": Magnus, 232

509 "The days of duelling": ibid.

510 "I now demand an apology": ibid., 234

510 "Dear Lord Charles Beresford": ibid., 235

510 "I have no desire": ibid., 236

Chapter 28
Fisher Versus Beresford

511 "the British fleet": Beresford, II, 363

511 "We drank much beer": ibid.

512 "He really is very stupid": FGDN, I, 122

512 "*Ramillies* signalmen": Chatfield, 41

513 "Your flagship": ibid.

513 "Beresford did uncommonly well": FGDN, I, 161

513 "He is a first rate officer afloat": ibid., 237

513 "He could do so much good": ibid.

513 "I am very sorry": ibid., 234

513– "There is a good deal": ibid., 237
14

514 "Under the command": Beresford, II, 467

514 "battleships are cheaper": ibid., 484

514 "The Navy, unlike the Army": ibid., 487

514 "As the Emperor was leaving": ibid., 494

515 "The Russian ships were so loaded": ibid., 495

515 "It appeared to me": Marder, *Anatomy*, 440

515 "Lord Nelson's *dictum*": ibid.

515 "a massacre": ibid.

516 "The Service is very sore": Mackay, 359

516 "rotters": FGDN, II, 80

516 "wailing and bemoaning": ibid., 76

516 "What is upsetting": ibid.

516– "It is with extreme reluctance":
17 ibid., 79

517 "extraordinary conduct": ibid.

517 "I thought Lord Tweedmouth": Mackay, 360

518 "I had three hours with Beresford": FGDN, II, 115

518 "Lord Charles Beresford now dictates": ibid., 116

518 "I followed your advice": ibid., 117

518 "My conviction is": ibid.

518– "blow to discipline": ibid., 118
19

519 "All I wish to assure you": ibid., 121

519 "There is not the slightest chance": ibid.

519 "is of itself a match": ibid., 116

519 "looking very like a Roman emperor": Jameson, 89

519 "My principal recollection": Marder, *Scapa Flow*, I, 89

520 "I remember coming up on deck": Scott, 197

520 "my little painted frigate": Jameson, 89

520 "our dangerous lunatic": Marder, *Scapa Flow*, I, 91

520 "We start at scratch": ibid.

520 "a fraud upon the public": FGDN, II, 177

520 "I am most distressed": Mackay, 371

520 "The truth is": ibid.

520– "with the object of disabusing
21 him": ibid., 372

521 "I know him to be ambitious": FGDN, II, 125

522 "It is manifestly impossible": ibid., 178

522 "Improper" . . . "provocative": ibid.

522– The Fisher-Beresford-Tweed-
24 mouth conversations are taken from Bacon, *Fisher*, II, 39, and Marder, *Scapa Flow*, I, 94

524 "I can now make out": Marder, *Scapa Flow,* I, 95

525 "It has come to my notice": ibid., 96

525 "you continue to employ language": ibid.

525 "Like most specialists": Padfield, *Aim Straight,* 171

525 "I would rather go into action": ibid., 162

526 "Paintwork appears": ibid., 164

526 "this signal": ibid., 166

527 "totally opposed to loyalty": ibid., 167

527 "grave disapprobation": ibid., 170

527 "act of insubordination": ibid.

527 "I should like to take": ibid.

527 "There is no doubt": ibid., 177

527 "a traitor": Mackay, 395

528 "Sir J. is in a most nervous state": ibid., 393

528 "He is so bitter": ibid., 399

528 "Sir J. is not well": ibid.

528 "a poisonous woman": FGDN, II, 151

528 "As long as they are": Mackay, 399

528 "She is a terrible looking woman": ibid., 394

528 "The influence of Lady C.": ibid.

528 "that Beresford had the whole Navy": ibid.

528 "the Admiralty fear no inquiry": Marder, *Scapa Flow,* I, 101

529 "There is not a man": Mackay, 394

529 "I am at a loss": Lee, II, 605

529 "My dear William": ibid., 606

530 "about 15 young, unmarried nieces": Magnus, 375

530 "seriously unhinged": ibid., 376

530 "This is very sad": ibid.

530 "youngish man": Mackay, 398

530 "pleasant in manner": ibid.

530 "When I agreed": Magnus, 375

530 "Beresford . . . can do more": FGDN, II, 210

530 "Like a rhinoceros": ibid., 41

531 *"Hell"*: ibid.

531 "In a country like ours": Barker, 69

531 "Keep your hair on": Marder, *Scapa Flow,* I, 100

531 "that I was Jekyll and Hyde": Fisher, *Memories,* 184

531 "was bad for me": FGDN, II, 174

531 "When Your Majesty backed up": Lee, II, 599

531 "Do you know": Fisher, *Memories,* 223

532 "a pack of cowards": Marder, *Scapa Flow,* I, 103

532 "What really amounts": FGDN, II, 177

532 "Either the quarterdeck and silence": ibid., 173

532 "strong objection": FGDN, II, 43

532 "They are all 'blue funkers' ": ibid.

532 "If . . . the Rear Admiral thought": Padfield, *Aim Straight,* 185

532 "A STRANGE OCCURRENCE": ibid.

533 "a gross scandal": ibid.

533 "a sickening tale": ibid.

533 "It can no longer be denied": *The Times,* July 6, 1908

533 "We say frankly": ibid.

533 "alleged dissensions" . . . "unverified rumours": Padfield, *Aim Straight,* 186

533 "Personally . . . I shall never forget": Magnus, 371

533 "My dear Lord Charles Beresford": Lee, II, 600

533 "Make a disturbance": Magnus, 371

533 "Knollys . . . dead on": FGDN, II, 43

534 "For He's a Jolly Good Fellow": Marder, *Scapa Flow,* I, 188

534 "During the whole of my tenure": Bacon, *Fisher,* II, 49

535 "even under pressure": FGDN, II, 247

535 "I shall of course obey": ibid.

536 "I always look": Bacon, *From 1900 Onward,* 124

536 "the King pointed out": Bacon, *Fisher,* II, 113

536 "Lord Charles and Admiral Lambton": Bacon, *From 1900 Onward,* 127

536 "The King has spoken to me": Bacon, *Fisher,* II, 114

537 "the cleverest officer in the Navy": Mackay, 297

537 "Fisher, of course, had no right": Bacon, ibid.

537 "quite violent": Marder, *Scapa Flow,* I, 192

537 "Is the House": FGDN, II, 212

538 "lead to the harmony": Bacon, *Fisher,* II, 53

538 "It was dramatic": Mackay, 413

538 "did not consider it": Marder, *Scapa Flow,* I, 198

539 "We have . . . roped him in": FGDN, II, 249

539 "satisfies in substance": Marder, *Scapa Flow,* I, 198

539 "satisfied . . . there is no such deficiency": ibid., 199

539 "[The committee] feel bound": Bacon, *Fisher,* II, 55

540 "The Committee, by not squashing": FGDN, II, 262

540 "I thought they were great men": ibid., 260

540 "Disgusted": ibid., 267

540 "Asquith 'watered it down' ": ibid.

540 "Will consider most seriously": ibid., 276

540 "a system of espionage": Marder, *Scapa Flow,* I, 203

540 "the mulatto": ibid.

540 "Fear God and Dread Nought": FGDN, II, 278

540– Fisher's decision on his motto:
41 ibid.

541 "SO REALLY SORRY": Marder, *Scapa Flow,* I, 186

541 "had no personal objections": McKenna, 90

541– "Sir Arthur Wilson stands out":
42 ibid.

542– "I do not say": Marder, *Scapa*
43 *Flow,* I, 186

PART IV: BRITAIN AND GERMANY:
POLITICS AND GROWING TENSION,
1906–1910

Chapter 29
Campbell-Bannerman: The Liberals
Return to Power

548 "We will refer it": Spender, *Campbell-Bannerman,* II, 290

548 "I see you are already tired": ibid., I, 62

548 "I sat down timidly": ibid., 100

549 "As to the censure": ibid., 156

549 "Rosebery was one of the ablest": Wilson, 236

549 "in apparent difference": Asquith, *Fifty Years,* I, 278

550 "well-suited to a position": Thomas Pakenham, 534

550 "Campbell-Bannerman's great advantage": Spender, *Campbell-Bannerman,* II, 83

550 "The door has always been open": Asquith, *Fifty Years,* II, 3

550 "a small people": Spender, *Asquith,* I, 135

551 "We . . . held that the war": Jenkins, 114

551 "We are in the right": Wilson, 301

551 "The Boers have committed an aggression": Jenkins, 115

551 "Anti-Joe, but never pro-Kruger": Asquith, *Fifty Years,* I, 303

551 "Master Haldane" . . . "Master Grey": Spender, *Campbell-Bannerman,* I, 342

551 "A vote for the Liberals": ibid., 291

552 "Madame's health": ibid., II, 48

553 "who deserved": ibid.

554 "wholesale burning of farms": Wilson, 348

554 "A phrase often used": Spender, *Campbell-Bannerman,* I, 336

555 "I never said a word": ibid., 337

555 "We have not changed our view": Jenkins, 125

555 "war to the knife—and fork": Asquith, *Fifty Years,* II, 4

555 "I must plough my furrow": ibid., 128

NOTES 957

556 "so straight, so good-tempered": Lee, II, 442
556 "quite sound on foreign politics": ibid.
556 "I lunched with the King": Spender, *Campbell-Bannerman*, II, 174
556 "about half my meals": ibid., 176
556 "The effective management of Irish affairs": Asquith, *Fifty Years*, II, 33
556 "Emphatically and explicitly": ibid., 35
557 "Campbell-Bannerman . . . was genial": Haldane, *Autobiography*, 156
558 "that ingenious person": Margot Asquith, III, 95
558 "a place for which": ibid., 96
558 "The more robust and stronger": Grey, *Twenty-Five Years*, I, 60
558 "all buttoned-up": Spender, *Campbell-Bannerman*, II, 194
558 "I wanted him to know": Grey, *Twenty-Five Years*, I, 61
558 "No surrender!": Haldane, *Autobiography*, 169
559 "I am sure that those": Jenkins, 153
559 "The conditions are in one respect": ibid., 151
559 "with the air of one": Haldane, *Autobiography*, 171
559 "What about the War Office?": ibid., 173
560 "My thoughts have often gone back": Spender, *Campbell-Bannerman*, II, 198
560 "Haldane is always climbing": ibid., 39
560 "We shall see": Haldane, *Autobiography*, 182
560 "Myself he did not like": ibid.
560 "I congratulate you, Sir Henry": Tuchman, *Proud Tower*, 365
561 "Feeling among the horses' heads": Haldane, *Autobiography*, 183
561 "Certainly, sir": ibid.
561 "as a young and blushing virgin": ibid.
561– "The Right Honorable gen-

62 tleman": Spender, *Campbell-Bannerman*, II, 273
562 "In the case of Germany": ibid., 208
562 "The growth of armaments": ibid.
563– "My greatest regret": Asquith, 64 *Memories*, I, 233
564 "Three words made peace": Spender, *Campbell-Bannerman*, I, 351
564 "Henry is a good man": ibid., II, 397
564– "How strange to have spent": 65 ibid., 287
565 "a blazing summer afternoon . . . horses' hooves": Arthur Ponsonby in ibid., 293
565 "I know how great": ibid., 294
565 "seemed to have recovered": ibid., 377
565 "Don't telegraph to 'the King' ": ibid., 384
566 "You are a wonderful colleague": Margot Asquith, III, 136
566 "This is not the last of me": Spender, *Asquith*, I, 196

Chapter 30
The Asquiths, Henry and Margot

567 "simply . . . put the ladder before him": Spender, *Asquith*, I, 22
568 "the best intellectual apparatus": Maurice, 164
568 "Asquith did not originate much": ibid.
568 "We were both rising": Haldane, *Autobiography*, 103
568 "too forensic": Escott, 362
569 "An intelligent, rather good-looking man": Spender, *Asquith*, I, 78
569 "had a conversation with Mr. Asquith": ibid.
569 "A beautiful and simple spirit": Haldane, *Autobiography*, 103
569 "No one would have called her": Jenkins, 30
570 "When I discovered": ibid., 54
570 "She was so different from me": Spender, *Asquith*, I, 98

570 "I was anxious": ibid.

570 "The dinner where I was introduced": Margot Asquith, II, 195

571 "Asquith is the only kind of man": Jenkins, 75

571 "You tell me not to stop": ibid.

571 "Small, rapid, nervous": Margot Asquith, II, 77

571 "I ride better than most people": ibid., 270

571 "I have broken both collarbones": ibid.

571 "I am afraid you resigned": ibid., I, 127

572 "Do look at Miss Tennant!": ibid., 128

572 "I am afraid you have not read": ibid., II, 40

572 "I hear you are going to marry": ibid., I, 251

572 "I will marry you, Peter": ibid., 178

572 "This afternoon as I sat": Jenkins, 81

573 "I was filled with profound misgivings": Spender, *Asquith,* I, 99

573 "wastes her time": Margot Asquith, II, 80

573 "It is not possible": Spender, *Asquith,* I, 96

573 "I fired two shots": Asquith, *Memories,* 309

573– "Supposing I were to give":
74 Spender, *Asquith,* I, 126

574 "An adventure more childishly conceived": Jenkins, 101

574 "Having done by their blundering folly": ibid.

574 "Dr. Jim": Margot Asquith, III, 26

574 "My husband and I": ibid.

574 "No man can lead": Young, 170

574 "war to the knife—and fork": Asquith, *Fifty Years,* II, 4

575 "There is nothing in the world": Spender, *Asquith,* I, 139

575 "to which I can fairly say": ibid., 82

575 "Go and bring the sledgehammer": Tuchman, *Proud Tower,* 371

575 "an inconvenient and dangerous": Lee, II, 582

576 "Asquith was a man who knew": Churchill, *Great Contemporaries,* 113

576 "The first essential": ibid., 117

576 "The Right Honorable Gentleman must wait": Churchill, *Great Contemporaries,* 120

576 "What we have heard today": ibid., 124

577 "In Cabinet, he was": ibid., 116

577 "In his earlier days": Haldane, *Autobiography,* 103

577 "He disliked 'talking shop'": Churchill, *Great Contemporaries,* 116

577 "For many years": Jenkins, 94

577 "No one who has not experienced": ibid.

577 "when my husband became Prime Minister": Margot Asquith, III, 33

577 "I am horribly impatient": LVS, 9

576– "Margot I find rather trying":
77 ibid.

578 "leaving a wake": ibid.

578 "I have sometimes walked up and down": ibid.

578 "It is a grief to me": ibid., 10

578 "a slight weakness": ibid., 471

578 "little harem": ibid., 11

578 "a splendid, virginal, comradely": ibid., 5

578 "talking and laughing": ibid., 532

579 "You have given me": ibid., 553

579 "Your lover—for all time": ibid., 588

579 "Darling—shall I tell you": ibid., 589

579 "No woman should expect": ibid., 12

579 "a woman without refinement": ibid., 13

580 "I'm far too fond": ibid.

580 "Oh . . . if only Venetia would marry": ibid.

580 "Why can't I marry you": ibid., 551

580 "I know quite well": ibid., 557

Chapter 31
Sir Edward Grey
and Liberal Foreign Policy

582   "of pure pleasure": Trevelyan, 17
582   "Sir Edward Grey": ibid., 20
582   "In the clear, cold light": ibid., 37
582   "I believe, however busy": ibid., 32
583   "I cannot think it possible": Grey, *Twenty-Five Years,* I, 19
583   "the fullest and clearest statement": Trevelyan, 62
583–   "There was no pleasure for me":
84   Grey, *Twenty-Five Years,* I, 31
584   "I understand at last": Trevelyan, 57
584   "I . . . said that if we went on": ibid.
584   "The one blow": ibid.
584   "Intensely distasteful": Grey, *Twenty-Five Years,* I, 26
584–   "The cottage became dearer":
85   Trevelyan, 49
585   "that of having everything": Grey, *Twenty-Five Years,* I, 29
585   "an earthly paradise": Grey, *Fallodon Papers,* 128
585   "The angler is by the river": ibid., 132
586   "And now what": ibid., 4
586   "If you will lie on your back": ibid., 28
586   "The greatest of all sport": ibid., 139
586   "one of the great moments": ibid.
586   "in his few intervals indoors": Trevelyan, 41
586   "The memories he amassed": ibid., 40
586–   "the luxuriance of water mead-
87   ows": ibid., 42
587   "I am alone here": ibid., 46
588   "unfriendly act": Grey, *Twenty-Five Years,* I, 19
588   "a feeling of simple pleasure": ibid., 49
588   "Suddenly . . . there came": ibid., 9
588   "The abrupt and rough peremptoriness": ibid., 10
588   "like a noose": ibid., 11

588   "The French were being humiliated": ibid., 51
589   "what the British Government": Wilson, 524
589   "Indications keep trickling in": Grey, *Twenty-Five Years,* I, 115
589   "He put the question": Wilson, 525
589   "I could read French easily": Grey, *Twenty-Five Years,* I, 86
590   "In the event of an attack": Spender, *Campbell-Bannerman,* II, 254
590   "did not attribute": Nicolson, 130
591   "Early in 1906": Grey, *Twenty-Five Years,* I, 91
591   "Conversations such as that": ibid., 92
591–   "My dear Asquith": ibid., 93
92
592   "What really determines": BD, VI, 784
593   "the most unbending determination": ibid., III, Appendix A, 419

Chapter 32
The Anglo-Russian Entente
and the Bosnian Crisis

595   "barbaric, Asiatic, and tyrannical": Empress Frederick, 209
595   "My own opinion": Nicolson, 153
595   "The alternate hectoring and cajolery": ibid.
595–   "on little lacquered feet": ibid.,
96   158
596   "Every day . . . I regret it": Bülow, II, 325
596   "great pleasure . . . In him you have a man": Lee, II, 289. The account of Isvolsky's code is taken from ibid., 326
597   "nothing but good feelings": Gooch, *History of Modern Europe,* 363
598   "New institutions": Lee, II, 567
598   "Isvolsky's former eagerness": Nicolson, 163
598   "He fears, I think": ibid., 185
598–   "I do not wish": Grey, *Twenty-
99   Five Years,* I, 156

599 "beaming with pleasure": BD, IV, 283

599 "the methods of a humane and highly skilled dentist": Nicolson, 175

599 "outside the Russian sphere": ibid.

600 The provisions of the Anglo-Russian Convention are taken from ibid., 325–27

600 "We watch the end of the negotiations": Gooch, *History of Modern Europe,* 396

600– "No one will reproach England":
601 Nicolson, 188

601 "Yes, when taken all round": ibid.

601 "There was no question": ibid., 172

601 "You may call it 'encirclement' ": ibid., 174

601 "An Insult to Our Country": Lee, II, 587

601 "a common murderer": ibid.

601 "hobnobbing": ibid.

601 "The Queen lay on deck": FGDN, II, 180

601 "wasn't actually sick": ibid.

602 "he was more likely to meet": Magnus, 409

602 "is simply like a child": FGDN, II, 181

602 "It's a jolly good thing": Lee, II, 594

602 "What a very nice time": FGDN, II, 183

603 "amiable and chatty": Nicolson, 155

604 "Brazen impudence": Bing, 234

605 "The Whig Statesman": Mansergh, 128

605 "it mattered not to us": Grey, *Twenty-Five Years,* I, 169

605 "it is an essential principle": Churchill, *World Crisis,* I, 35

605 "inopportune": Grey, *Twenty-Five Years,* I, 172

605 "Isvolsky went on to say": ibid., 178

605– "a piece of brigandage": Man-
6 sergh, 127

606 "only at the same time": Grey, *Twenty-Five Years,* I, 185

606 "Our relations with Austria": Woodward, 182

606 "Austria-Hungary behaved": E.T.S. Dugdale, III, 305; DGP, XXVI, 110

606 "The conference won't come off ": DGP, XXVI, 169

606 "duplicitous" . . . "no gentleman": Mansergh, 132

606 "Asquith asked me": Newton, 371

607 "Your Sir Edward Grey": Gooch, *History of Modern Europe,* 418

607 "unless Russia agreed": Spender, *Asquith,* I, 248

607 "We expect a precise answer": DGP, XXVI, 693

607 "with God's help": Spender, *Asquith,* I, 248

607 "Russia's recent conduct": Gooch, *History of Modern Europe,* 423

607 "I solved the Bosnian crisis": Bülow, I, 174

607 "managed the affair excellently": ibid.

607 "taken his stand in shining armor": Spender, *Asquith,* I, 248

607 "Russia was stiff ": Grey, *Twenty-Five Years,* I, 181

608 "I have been assured": ibid., 182

608 "Germany told us": Bing, 236, 239–40

608 "This is *my* war!": Mansergh, 136

Chapter 33
The Navy Scare of 1909

610 "Strategic requirements": Woodward, 98

610 "As you know": McKenna, 65

611 "a preponderance of ten percent": Woodward, 244

612 "a practical certainty": Marder, *Scapa Flow,* I, 154

612– "My dear Grey": McKenna, 71
13

613 "My dear Prime Minister": ibid., 72

613– "I will not dwell": Marder, *Scapa*
14 *Flow,* I, 159

614 "I found the Admiralty's figures": Churchill, *World Crisis*, I,
37

614 "The Admiralty mean to get":
Randolph Churchill, II, 498

614 "What are Winston's reasons":
Marder, *Scapa Flow*, I, 160

614 "The economists are in a state":
McKenna, 79

615 "I think it shows": Marder, *Scapa
Flow*, I, 161

615 "We are placing": McKenna, 82

615 "is rejected either in the Commons": ibid., 81

615 "I do not see how": ibid., 82

616 "nothing less than eight ships":
Marder, *Scapa Flow*, I, 163

616 "No matter what the cost": *The
Times*, March 17, 1909

616 "We want eight": Marder, *Scapa
Flow*, I, 167

616 "Citoyens": ibid.

616– "reincarnation of Marshal Le-
17 Boeuf": ibid.

617 "since Nero fiddled": ibid., 168

617 "In the opinion of this House":
ibid.

617 Grey's speech is taken from
Woodward, 230–34

618 "In the end": Churchill, *World
Crisis*, I, 37

619 "There is no half-way house":
Woodward, 220

620 "According to information":
ibid., 217

621 "I think it would be better": ibid.,
218

621 "We have got to have a margin":
Marder, *Scapa Flow*, I, 164

621 "His Majesty the Kaiser": ibid.,
177

621 "start of building": ibid., 178

622 "How all this scare would vanish": FGDN, II, 235

622 "Until November last": Woodward, 238

622 "Nonsense!": ibid.

622 *"Winston, Churchill, Lloyd,* and
George": FGDN, II, 227

622 "very sore": Marder, *Scapa Flow*,
I, 170

623 "If the Government": ibid., 156

623 "without prejudice": ibid., 171

624 "In the light of what actually happened": Churchill, *World Crisis*,
I, 37

Chapter 34
Invading England

627 "I know of nothing": Marder,
Anatomy, 65

627 "free-booting enterprise": ibid.,
372

627 "The Empire, stripped of its armor": ibid., 377

628 "Unless our Navy": ibid., 378

628 "The only difficulty we see":
ibid., 380

628 "Invasion may be an off-chance":
ibid., 78

628 "A great defensive army": ibid.

628 "Not thirty army corps": ibid.

628 "As to a stronger Regular
Army": ibid.

629 "not an eventuality": *The Times*,
May 12, 1905

629 "I have no hesitation": Hynes, 40

629 "luminous" . . . "quite perfect
in form and language": Tuchman,
Proud Tower, 380

630 "The Navy . . . is the 1st, 2nd,
3rd . . .": Marder, *Anatomy*, 65

630 "I am too busy to waste my
time": Marder, *Scapa Flow*, I, 181

630 "You might as well talk": Fisher,
Records, 91

630 "When the German Emperor":
Tuchman, *Proud Tower*, 380

630 "Refuse to be served": Marwick,
50

631 "envy of England's great Empire": Clarke, 109

631 "this sceptred isle" . . . "this
fortress built by Nature": *Richard
II*, II, I

631 "without losing the perfectly
courteous tone": Clarke, 110

631 "would involve this country":
ibid., 111

632 "The great increase in prosperity": ibid., 113

632 "We might, despite all our precautions": ibid., 112

632 "A couple of thousand men": ibid.

632 "the tube of steel": ibid., 124

633 "The course . . . was about west": Childers, 262

633 "the wind humming into the mainsail" . . . "the persuasive song" . . . "the noble expanse": ibid., 50, 89

633– " 'Here's this huge empire' ":
34 ibid., 80

634 "sun-burnt, brine-burnt": ibid., 99

634 " 'We're a maritime nation' ": ibid., 97

634 "I die full of intense love": ibid., 7

635 "It is not true": ibid.

635 "The pride of these English": Le Queux, 340

635 "too horrible to here describe": ibid., 534

635– "had we adopted his scheme":
36 ibid., 333

636 "the catastrophe that may happen": ibid., opp. p. vi

636 "not keep to remote, one-eyed": Clarke, 145

636– "Most of these men": ibid., 148
37

637 "military men from a foreign nation": ibid., 152

637 "Lord Roberts' repeated statements": Maurice, 256

637– "a strong, aristocratic govern-
38 ment": Le Queux, 542

638 "to be judged by the good sense": Hynes, 42

639 "Bah! What does that matter?": ibid., 47

Chapter 35
The Budget and
the House of Lords

642 "The cure for the House of Lords": quoted in Willoughby de Broke, 256

642 "An obscure and doubtless a useful existence": Dangerfield, 42

642 "We were all out hunting": Willoughby de Broke, 244

643 "the man in the street": Barker, 158

643 "the great Unionist Party": Asquith, *Fifty Years,* II, 44

643 "It is essential": Newton, 353

644 "not the watchdog": Spender, *Campbell-Bannerman,* II, 358

644 "The resources of the House of Commons": Newton, 357

646 "a first class funeral": Asquith, *Fifty Years,* II, 69

646 "slain by the stiletto": Dangerfield, 16

647 "I shall have to rob": Amery, VI, 934

647 "to raise money": Asquith, *Fifty Years,* II, 78

648 "something between incomparable drama": Dangerfield, 22

648 "We sank into a pit": ibid.

648 "Only one stock": Bernstein, 111

648– "A fully equipped duke":
49 Magnus, 430

649 "The question will be asked": ibid.

649 "a swooping robber gull": Asquith, *Fifty Years,* 82

649 "the croakings of a retired raven": ibid., 83

649 "I think my friends": ibid.

649 "firm as a rock": Jenkins, 199

649 "Amendment by the House of Lords": Asquith, *Fifty Years,* 83

649– "an omnipotent House of Com-
50 mons": Willoughby de Broke, 259

650 "a breach of the constitution": Asquith, *Fifty Years,* II, 88

650 "If you gentlemen": Willoughby de Broke, 265

650 "We have got them": Barker, 162

650 "We shall not assume office": Lee, II, 670

651 "if the Lords fail": Asquith, *Fifty Years,* II, 98

651 "I myself do not see": Magnus, 440

651 "Really, it is too bad": Lee, II, 686

652 "till we all nearly screamed": Ponsonby, 255

653 "the head of the British Empire": Bülow, II, 475

653 "My God, he is dying!": Pless, 176

653– The account of King Edward's
55 death is taken from Lee, II, 714–18; Magnus, 455–66; Ponsonby, 270

655 "that horrid Biarritz": Ponsonby, 271

655 "I have lost my best friend": Magnus, 456

655 "The world [is] not the same": Barker, 84

655– "the death of Edward VII": Bü-
56 low, III, 98

656 "the death of the 'Encircler' ": William II, *My Memoirs*, 124

656 "I am deeply grieved": Asquith, *Fifty Years*, II, 100

656 "I felt bewildered": ibid.

656 "The entire royal family": William II, *My Memoirs*, 124

656 The Kaiser's descriptions of the funeral are in ibid., 124, 126

657 "many talks": Spender, *Asquith*, I, 282

657– "Looking into the future": Tuch-
58 man, *Proud Tower*, 392

658 "Yes, sir": Margot Asquith, III, 212

658– "Dear Lord Lansdowne": As-
59 quith, *Fifty Years*, II, 111

659 "Let them make their peers": Dangerfield, 44

659 "invariably objected on principle": Newton, 361

659 "solemn duty to God and country": Tuchman, *Proud Tower*, 396

659– "Even if I am alone": Danger-
60 field, 52

660 "I agree with Lord Lansdowne": Newton, 426

660– The account of the attack on As-
61 quith in the Commons is drawn from Dangerfield, 55–58, and issues of *The Times, The Daily Telegraph, The Daily News,* and *The Daily Chronicle* of July 25, 1911

661 "For God's sake, defend him": Margot Asquith, III, 216

661 "I am not going to degrade myself": Dangerfield, 57

661 "pure bluff": ibid., 63

661 "I have to say": ibid.

661 "boiling with rage": ibid., 65

661 "Traitor!" . . . "Judas!": ibid.

661– "The cataracts, the pines, and the
62 precipices": Tuchman, *Proud Tower,* 402

662 "quite unusually odious": Blanche Dugdale, II, 61

Chapter 36
The Eulenburg Scandal

663 "the internal condition of Germany": Newton, 372

663 "PRUSSIAN COURT SCANDALS": *The Times,* October 24, 1907

663 "It is false and foolish": Balfour, 276

665 "I could never put into words": Haller, I, 10

665 "torment of unfair, narrow-minded, and coarse-natured": ibid., 14

665 "terribly boring": Hull, 50

665 "Her conversation was negligible": ibid.

665 "I enjoy family life little": ibid., 51

665 "My official career": Haller, I, 27

665 "dear Phili": ibid., 30

666 "I shall take care": Bülow, IV, 490

666 "used to enliven our evenings": William II, *My Early Life,* 196

666 "He was one of those": ibid., 197

666 "my bosom friend": Hull, 202

666 "it was like a flood of sunshine": William II, *My Early Life,* 197

667 "has become a radiance": Haller, I, 75

667 "I will lay among my most treasured gifts": ibid., 42

667 "that Prince William": ibid., 41

667 "He was very pale": Röhl, 189

667 "Phil was so excited": Bülow, I, 194

667 "It was very useful": Haller, I, 31

667 "So you are going to be in Bayreuth": ibid.

667 "Your influence on His Majesty": ibid., 73

668 "I would never have dreamed":

Isabel Hull, "Kaiser Wilhelm and the 'Liebenberg Circle,' " in Röhl and Sombart, *Kaiser Wilhelm II: New Interpretations,* 205

668 "If I feel a certain degree": Haller, I, 124

668 "Your letter of today": ibid., 132

669 "The Emperor has never touched me": ibid., 187

669 "would impair my influence": ibid., 218

669 "I agree with you": ibid., 219

669 "I soon fell under the spell": Bülow, IV, 492

669 "The friend who has been": ibid.

669 "I have a great longing": Haller, II, 3

669 "Nothing will ever be able": ibid., 5

669 "in the depths of our souls": ibid., 4

669 "A poor barndoor fowl": ibid., I, 217

669– "I—not as a friend": ibid.
70

670 "We cannot be sufficiently thankful": ibid., I, 87

670 "Bernhard is the most valuable": ibid., II, 6

670 "Bülow will be my Bismarck": ibid., 7

670 "on our boundless love": Röhl, 159

670 "Your Majesty will allow me": ibid., 159

670 "As a personality": Haller, II, 35

670– "You are our dear good sovereign's": ibid., 37
71

671 "One of the best things": ibid., 38

671 "wrinkled, prematurely aged": Röhl, "The Emperor's New Clothels," in Röhl and Sombart, *Kaiser Wilhelm II: New Interpretations,* 43

671 "told me with feverish agitation": Bülow, I, 520

671 "love for his Majesty": ibid., 708

671 "Ten years of uphill work": ibid., 694

671 "sweet, affected piety": Hull, 131

671 "At a certain age": ibid.

671 "men who in their sensitivity": ibid.

671 "As Phili will never come to me": Haller, II, 148

672 "This floating theatre": Bülow, I, 708

672 "My dear Phili": ibid., II, 321

672 "I am now free": Hull, 130

672 "a matter of life and death": Haller, II, 174

672 "exchange pistol shots": ibid.

672 "literally collapsed into his chair": ibid.

672 "for God's sake and the Emperor's": ibid.

672 "Prince Eulenburg having assured me": ibid., 175

673 "I cannot say": ibid.

673 "nothing but good people": Isabel Hull, "Kaiser Wilhelm II and the 'Liebe3nberg Circle,' " in Röhl and Sombart, *Kaiser Wilhelm II: New Interpretations,* 193

673 "unhealthy, late Romantic": ibid.

673 "with unflagging zeal": ibid.

673 "For years": ibid.

673– "Never shall I forget": Crown
74 Prince William, 15

675 "I insist that Philip Eulenburg": Bülow, II, 346

675 "The loss of an old imperial friendship": ibid.

675 "I know myself": ibid.

675 "I was convinced": ibid., 322

675 "Disgusting orgies": *The Times,* October 25, 1907

675 "thought he recognized": ibid.

676 "in the interests of our whole country": Wile, 197

676 "Between that man and me": ibid.

676 "In these painful circumstances": Bülow, II, 347

676 "begging me": ibid., 343

676 "As the highest official": ibid., 344

676 "considered the practices in question": ibid., 349

676– "I have never done anything
77 dirty": Hull, 138

677– "Could you ever have believed":
78 Haller, II, 222

678 "Besides, if anything of the kind": ibid., 242

678 "Harden sent 145 printed accusations": Bülow, III, 30
678 "in the long period of 34 years": Haller, II, 326
678 "Only one thing": Bülow, III, 30
678– "My dear Phili": ibid., 32
79
679 "abnormal instincts": ibid., 31
679 "perilous inclination": ibid.
679 "erotic integrity": ibid., II, 323
679 "An obvious comparison": ibid., III, 33
679 "Prince Eulenberg is not fit": Haller, II, 269
679 "It has been a very difficult year": Balfour, 276
679 "Poor Phili": Hull, 145
679 "absolutely innocent": Isabel Hull, "Kaiser William II and the 'Liebenberg Circle,'" in Röhl and Sombart, *Kaiser Wilhelm II: New Interpretations,* 218

Chapter 37
The *Daily Telegraph* Interview

680 "good sport in the dear old park": Lee, II, 546
680 "My head hit the ground": Bülow, II, 337
681 "bronchitis and acute cough": Lee, II, 554
681 "I cannot say how upset I am": ibid., 555
681 "there is little doubt": BD, VI, 88
681 "The worst of it is": Bülow, II, 338
681 "The German squadron": *The Times,* November 12, 1907
681 "It seems like coming home": ibid.
681 "For a long time": Lee, II, 557
681 "Sunshine and breeze": *The Times,* November 14, 1907
681– "BLUT IST DICKER ALS WASSER": ibid.
82
682 "Sixteen years ago": Lee, II, 558
682 "next to General von Einem": Haldane, *Autobiography,* 221
682 "I said I knew": Haldane, *Before the War,* 48
682 "I will give you the 'gate' ": ibid.

682– "giving us a 'gate' ": ibid., 49
83
683 "I feel myself an intruder": ibid., 50
683 "I wish to express my satisfaction": Gooch, *History of Modern Europe,* 434
683 "It is bound to have": ibid.
683 "the visit of the German Emperor": Jonathan Steinberg, "The Kaiser and the British," in Röhl and Sombart, *Kaiser Wilhelm II: New Interpretations,* 138
683 "Our King makes a better show": Esher, II, 255
683– "The great British people": ibid., 278
84
684 "Overwhelmed with work": Bülow, II, 375
684 "on no account forward it": Spender, *Fifty Years,* 318
684 "Without the slightest suspicion": Bülow, II, 376
684– The précis of the *Daily Telegraph* Interview is drawn from *Holstein Papers,* I, 203–207
85
686 "more than any previous manifestation": Bülow, II, 376
686 "And haven't you learned": ibid., 393
687 "I am not in a position": ibid., 395
687 "To a newcomer like myself": BD, VI, 217
687 "Never before in Prussian history": Jarausch, 59
687– "it will be impossible": ibid.
88
688 "If Your Majesty is displeased": E.T.S. Dugdale, III, 313; DGP, XXIV, 179
688 "He was . . . as he always was": Bülow, II, 397
688 "Go ahead": ibid.
688 "His trustful, childlike attitude": ibid.
689 "The wish that in future": ibid., 404
689 "For the mistake": Gooch, *History of Modern Europe,* 441
689 "Gentlemen, the knowledge": Bülow, II, 409

689 "When, amid a roar of cheering": ibid., 410

689 "In view of the Kaiser's indiscretions": *Holstein Papers,* I, 190

689–90 "We have a population": Cowles, 269

690 "He was longing": Bülow, II, 398

690 "Did you, as people are saying": *Holstein Papers,* I, 190

690 "If you met Kaiser William": Balfour, 291

690 "The two days here": Cowles, 264

690 "in full evening dress": Zedlitz-Trützschler, 252

691 "It is an unusual experience": ibid., 253

691 "Be really kind and gentle": Bülow, II, 420

691 "in such a depressed, pessimistic mood": Jarausch, 60

691 "Uninfluenced by the exaggerations": Bülow, II, 423

691 "grasped my hand": ibid., 424

691 "I've managed": ibid.

691–92 "Must the Emperor abdicate?": ibid., 430

692 "I rushed upstairs": Crown Prince William, 99

692 "The Emperor made no attempt": Cowles, 271

692 "left in the lurch": ibid., 273

692 "I became the scapegoat": Jarausch, 61

692 "You will understand": Balfour, 292

693 "solely and exclusively": Terence Cole, "The Daily Telegraph Affair3," in Röhl and Sombart, *Kaiser Wilhelm II: New Interpretations,* 263

693 "Pharisee!": ibid.

693 "I walked up and down": William II, *My Memoirs,* 117

693 "I could not continue": Bülow, II, 498

693 "shown sufficient energy": ibid., 499

693 "Froben . . . would not have spoken": ibid., 500

693 "Which simply means": ibid., 501

693 "This frank conversation": William II, *My Memoirs,* 117

693 "I've just been having it out": Bülow, II, 502

693 "Have just forgiven Bülow": ibid., 503

693 "How happy I am": ibid.

694 "As a matter of fact": Bülow, II, 575

694 "As far as domestic policy is concerned": ibid.

694 "You leave foreign policy to me": ibid.

694 "I had the peculiar sensation": ibid., 578

695 "I feel even worse": ibid., 592

695 "You mustn't think": ibid.

695 "I decided to acquiesce": William II, *My Memoirs,* 119

695 "This is where": Mansergh, 149

Chapter 38
Naval Talks and Bethmann-Hollweg

697 "no ordinary man": Lee, I, 774

697 "an open mind": Bülow, I, 493

697 "I always felt, with Metternich": Grey, *Twenty-Five Years,* I, 236

698 "every Englishman would spend": Lloyd George, I, 17

698 "Leave it to the police": ibid.

698 "most ready to meet Germany half way": ibid., 19

698 "Such insolent talk": ibid., 17

698 "First-class cheek!": ibid., 18

698 "We should look upon that": ibid., 20

698–99 "Bravo! Metternich!": ibid., 22

699 "the naval question": ibid., 23

699 "This is talk": ibid., 25

699 "This sort of conversation": ibid., 26

699 "The English are afraid": Woodward, 169

700 "will just have to get used to": Balfour, 284

700 "But you must build slower": ibid., 286

700 "then we shall fight": Bülow, II, 358

700 "I looked him straight in the eye": DGP, XXIV, 127–28

700–701 "I beg Your Majesty": Gooch, *Before the War,* I, 268

701 "I must ask Your Excellency": ibid., 270

701 "Our duty is to arm": Woodward, 200

701 "The possibility of preventive war": Marder, *Scapa Flow,* I, 172

701 "The cardinal point": DGP, XXVIII, 18

701 "Feeling that": Bülow, II, 465

702 "our Navy": ibid., 485

702 "Five to six years": Spender, *Fifty Years,* 326

702 "pooh-poohed my fears": Bülow, II, 490

702 "An entente on the Naval Question": ibid., 565

703 "all the qualities": Lamar Cecil, *Ballin,* 122

703 "Bülow's revenge": Jarausch, 68

703 "I do not know": ibid., 11

703– "I cannot believe": ibid., 27
4

704 "late at night": ibid., 28

704 "looked like a summer overcoat": William II, *My Early Life,* 136

704 "This little episode": Jarausch, 35

704 "I spent many happy hours": William II, *My Early Life,* 135

704 "esteem for the diligence": William II, *My Memoirs,* 120

704 "One day I'll make a minister": Jarausch, 40

705 "It disconcerts me": ibid., 53

705 "a man of strong gifts": ibid.

705 "I know him well": ibid., 65

705 "I cannot work with him": ibid.

705 "grave doubts": ibid., 66

705 "Dear Theo": ibid., 70

705 "Only a genius": ibid., 66

705 "Your Excellency is not only": ibid., 60

706 "It was a pleasure for me": William II, *My Memoirs,* 121

706 "He laid down the law": ibid., 127

706 "The idea that he could ally himself": Jarausch, 111

706 "If you cannot avoid": ibid., 111

706– "England had firmly taken": Bethmann-Hollweg, 15
7

707 "I respectfully protest": Bülow, III, 7

707 "Your proposal won't work": Lamar Cecil, *Ballin,* 173

708 "It would be almost incomprehensible": Woodward, 276

708 "I want a good understanding": ibid., 272

708 "The English friendship with France": ibid., 278

709 "siren song": ibid., 284

709 "The appetite of this monster": Marder, *Scapa Flow,* I, 215

709 "I see quite as clearly": Woodward, 284

710 "An indispensable preliminary condition": Marder, *Scapa Flow,* I, 223

710 "England and Germany together": ibid., 224

710 "He reminded me": ibid., 225

710 "I consider any control": Schmitt, 188

PART V: THE ROAD TO ARMAGEDDON

Chapter 39
Agadir

715 "a typical Württemberger": *Holstein Papers,* II, 174

716 "a tool of Holstein": Bülow, IV, 627

716 "Kiderlen was to Holstein": ibid., I, 15

716 "the Oyster-fiend" . . . "the Troubador" . . . *"Spätzle":* ibid., 35

717 "I am to pull": Gooch, "Kiderlen, Man of Agadir," in *Studies in Diplomacy and Statecraft,* 132

718 "a general outburst of hilarity": Bülow, II, 413

718 "Kiderlen's debacle . . . Swabian accent . . . yellow waistcoat": ibid.

718 "Just leave foreign policy to me": ibid., 575

718 "The new Chief": Gooch, "Kiderlen, Man of Agadir," in *Studies in Diplomacy and Statecraft,* 137

718 "Bethmann is a soft nature": ibid., 139

718 "You are putting a louse in the pelt": ibid., 140

719 "Really?" "No, thank God, never!": Lamar Cecil, *German Diplomatic Service,* 167

719 *"Dickkopf"* . . . *"Regenwurm":* ibid., 312

719 "So. Do you think he tells me more?" ibid., 313

719 "the special political interests": Schmitt, 306

720 "exceedingly fertile": Pick, 23

720 "Do not doubt": Jarausch, 120

720 "in Casablanca": Carroll, 645

722 "If you go to Fez": Schmitt, 313

722 "And yet it will not work": Jarausch, 121

722 "Full liberty of action": ibid., 122

723 "exceedingly fertile": Pick, 23

723 "extremely grave difficulties": Jarausch, 121

723 "no one can prevent Morocco": ibid.

723 "Go and see Kiderlen": Gooch, "Kiderlen, Man of Agadir," in *Studies in Diplomacy and Statecraft,* 145

723 "French opinion would not stand for it": ibid.

723 "one could look elsewhere": Schmitt, 315

723 "Bring something back": Gooch, "Kiderlen, Man of Agadir," in *Studies in Diplomacy and Statecraft,* 145

724 "The big space": William II, *My Memoirs,* 138

725 "Dolls' House": Haldane, *Autobiography,* 224

725 "To tell the truth": William II, *My Memoirs,* 141

725 "We will never make war": Carroll, 659

725 "France would bleed": Pick, 15

725 "We will have to take": Jarausch, 122

726 "We cannot leave Morocco": ibid.

726 "During the Kiel Regatta Week": William II, *My Memoirs,* 142

726 "Ships approved": Carroll, 654

726 "Endangered German": Pick, 21

727– "Some German firms": Schmitt,
28 317

728 "Hurrah! A deed!": Carroll, 656

728 "Action at last": ibid.

728 "un joli morceau": Schmitt, 315

728 "We are seizing this region": Carroll, 656

728 "Little by little": Jarausch, 121

728 "serious colonial compensation": ibid., 122

728 "The more silent we are": Carroll, 650

728 "Eh bien?" ibid., 659

729 "The German Government": Schmitt, 318

729 "had not taken any overt step": Grey, *Twenty-Five Years,* I, 215

729 "could not be a disinterested one": ibid., 214

729 "our treaty obligations": ibid.

730 "What is Germany driving at?": Marder, *Scapa Flow,* I, 240

730 "This is a test of strength": Carroll, 667

730 "make some communication": Barlow, 293

730 "long ignorance and silence": ibid.

731 "whether German troops are landed": ibid.

731 "not in a position": Schmitt, 325

731 "I found a different man": Winston Churchill, *World Crisis,* I, 46

731– "When the rude indifference":
32 Lloyd George, I, 40

732 "I was suddenly told": Grey, *Twenty-Five Years,* I, 215

732– The description of Lloyd
33 George's Mansion House speech is drawn from ibid., 216

733 "Lloyd George was closely associated": ibid., 217

733 "Whenever a country occupies": Carroll, 669

733 "The German people refuse": ibid., 670

733 "Hands off!": ibid.

734 "If the English Government had intended": Schmitt, 331

734 "to protect German interests": Grey, *Twenty-Five Years,* I, 218

734 "I observed that I had not": ibid.

734 "I observed that there were no Germans": ibid.

734 "not a man had been landed":
ibid.

734 "That speech had been interrupted": ibid., 220

735 "If, after the many provocations": ibid., 221

735 "had said that it was not consistent": ibid., 222

735 "walking by the fountains": Winston Churchill, *World Crisis,* I, 47

735 "I have just received a communication": ibid., 48

735 "we are dealing with a people":
BD, VII, 625

735 "vanished into the desolate
wastes": Marder, *Scapa Flow,* I,
243

736 "At the end of three days": Barlow, 290

736 "You know the Emperor pretty
well": ibid., 291

736 "Supposing the High Seas Fleet":
Gretton, 37

736 "Practically everybody of importance": Randolph Churchill, II,
515

736 "On the afternoon of July 27":
Winston Churchill, *World Crisis,*
I, 50

737 "exceedingly friendly": Schmitt,
333

737– "Conversations are proceeding":
38 ibid.

738 "Peace or war": Carroll, 672

738 "we are not going to stand":
ibid., 679

738– "The Germans at first": Grey,
39 *Twenty-Five Years,* I, 223

739 "where the fever bacillus and the
sand flea": Carroll, 683

739 "Has the spirit of Prussia perished?": Pick, 32

739 "The last class of reserves": Carroll, 648

739 "If we slink out": ibid., 684

739 "I do not believe": Gooch, "Kiderlen, Man of Agadir," *Studies in
Diplomacy and Statecraft,* 150

740 "The Kaiser was very humble":
Jarausch, 123

740 "Kiderlen informs nobody":
ibid., 122

740 "I am not going to dance attendance": Carroll, 678

740 "We will insist": ibid., 679

740 "Not be satisfied": ibid.

740 "What the devil will happen":
DGP, XXIX, 178

740 "A mon terrible ami": Gooch,
"Kiderlen, Man of Agadir," in
*Studies in Diplomacy and State-
craft,* 155

741 "Almost a fiasco for Germany":
Grey, *Twenty-Five Years,* I, 233

741 "the last nail": Carroll, 692

741 "Without acquiring anything":
ibid., 698

742 "deplorable . . .": Bülow, III, 98

742 "throughout this whole diplomatic campaign": ibid., 99

742 "a considerable increase":
Schmitt, 338

742 "an important dispute with
France": ibid.

742 "We expect no praise": Jarausch,
124

742 "The silence was like that of the
grave": Carroll, 693

742 "Like a flash in the night":
Schmitt, 338

742 "My conscience lets me sleep":
Jarausch, 125

742– "If I had driven toward war":
43 ibid., 126

743 "My dear friend": ibid.

743 "I thought he looked ill": Bülow,
III, 99

Chapter 40
"I Do Believe That
I Am a Glowworm"

746 "I beg your pardon": Haldane,
Autobiography, 227

747 "Our Navy is not worth": Maurice, 288

747 "The fact is": Gretton, 40

747 "puerile and I have dismissed it":
Williamson, 193

747 "In 1911 I had begun to feel":
Haldane, *Autobiography,* 236

748 "By the twentieth day": Bonham-Carter, 184

748   "Are you sure": Randolph Churchill, II, 513
748   "As I entered the drive": Haldane, *Autobiography*, 230
748–49   "He and my father played golf": Bonham-Carter, 188
749   "Mr. Asquith . . . asked me": Winston Churchill, *World Crisis*, I, 67
749   "Hear, O Israel": ibid., 68
749   "it seemed a message": ibid., 69
749–50   "Then he appeared to become": Bonham-Carter, 3
750   "We are all worms": ibid., 4
750   "We seemed to live in a whirl": Manchester, *Winston Churchill*, 112
750   "Mrs Everest it was": Winston Churchill, *A Roving Commission*, 5
751   "a dark, lithe figure": ibid., 4
751   "She had a forehead like a panther's": Margot Asquith, I, 131
751   "in Ireland . . . in a riding habit": Winston Churchill, *A Roving Commission*, 4
751   "The neglect and lack of interest": Randolph Churchill, I, 43
751–52   "Most infants are loved for themselves": Manchester, *Winston Churchill*, 117
752   "I hated this school": Winston Churchill, *A Roving Commission*, 12
752   "In the middle of the room": Randolph Churchill, I, 52
752   "who on heroic occasions": Morley, *Gladstone*, I, 28
752   "I was allowed to learn things": Winston Churchill, *A Roving Commission*, 13
752   "Will you come and see me". Manchester, *Winston Churchill*, 134
753   "I was very disappointed": ibid.
753   "I should have liked to be asked": Winston Churchill, *A Roving Commission*, 15
753   "I found I was unable": ibid.
753   "We were considered such dunces": ibid., 16
753   "Do try to get Papa to come": Randolph Churchill, I, 119

753   "I would go down to you": ibid., 124
753   "I have only read one page": ibid., 156
753–54   "My darling Mummy": ibid.
754   "Darling Mummy: . . . I am so wretched": ibid., 158
754   "he makes as much fuss": ibid., 160
754   "For years I thought my father": Winston Churchill, *A Roving Commission*, 19
754   "Capture seemed certain": ibid., 29
754   "My dear Winston": Randolph Churchill, I, 188
754–55   "While walking along Wish Stream": ibid., 212
756   "At Sandhurst I had a new start": Winston Churchill, *A Roving Commission*, 43
756–57   "It is quite easy, dear Mamma": Randolph Churchill, I, 207
757   "When you have had a boil": ibid., 82
757   "There was no curtain": ibid., 226
757   "gleams of hate": Manchester, *Winston Churchill*, 205
758   "Do remember": Winston Churchill, *A Roving Commission*, 32
758   "All my dreams of comradeship": ibid., 62
758   "a severe mental disease": Randolph Churchill, I, 226
758   "My jacket was wet": Winston Churchill, *A Roving Commission*, 72
758–59   "I was now in the main": ibid., 62
759   "Raise the glorious flag again": ibid., 60
759   "I was now in my twenty-first year": ibid., 62
759   "Found Mamma and Count Kinsky": Randolph Churchill, I, 141
760   "There is nothing more exhilarating": Manchester, *Winston Churchill*, 228
760   "I cannot believe": ibid., 234
760   "palatial bungalow": Winston

Churchill, *A Roving Commission,* 106

760 "The Spanish ships I cannot see": Randolph Churchill, I, 282

761 "If you can get me good letters": ibid., 329

761 "The Himalayas": Winston Churchill, *The Story of Malakand Field Force,* 2

761 "Bright sunlight shining": ibid., 141

761 "about 200 misprints, blunders": ibid., 365

761– "I had never been praised be-
62 fore": Winston Churchill, *A Roving Commission,* 154

762 "My dear Winston": ibid., 155

762 "I had written them": Manchester, *Winston Churchill,* 259

762 "You must work for Egypt": ibid., 263

762 "Oh, how I wish": Randolph Churchill, I, 371

762 "left no wire unpulled": Winston Churchill, *A Roving Commission,* 151

762 "Do not want Churchill": Manchester, *Winston Churchill,* 263

763 "not only for its matter": Winston Churchill, *A Roving Commission,* 164

763 "If there is anything": ibid.

763 "Dear Lord Salisbury": Randolph Churchill, I, 378

763 "filthy tramp": Manchester, *Winston Churchill,* 267

763– Churchill's account of the Battle
64 of Omdurman is taken from *A Roving Commission,* 171–196

764 "Come and see me": Randolph Churchill, I, 407

765 "cloaked from end to end": Manchester, *Winston Churchill,* 298

765 "When one is alone and un-armed": Winston Churchill, *A Roving Commission,* 252

765 "We're not going to let you go": ibid., 258

765 "Englishman 25 years old": Manchester, *Winston Churchill,* 309

766 "I am Winston Bloody Churchill": ibid., 314

766 "the handsomest man in England": Morgan, 138

766 "I suppose you think": Manchester, *Winston Churchill,* 320

766 "The square forehead": ibid., 346

766 "When the young member for Oldham": ibid.

766 "Restless, egotistical, bumptious": ibid., 345

766 "Can my Right Honorable Friend": ibid., 348

767 "If it had not been for me": Magnus, 351

Chapter 41
Churchill at the Admiralty

768 "a poor ambition": Marder, *Scapa Flow,* I, 252

769 "We cannot detect": Morgan, 317

769 "That is because": Bonham-Carter, 190

769 "was to inculcate in myself": Winston Churchill, *World Crisis,* I, 72

770 "had got on too fast": ibid., 87

770 "You seem very young": Morgan, 322

770 "fell desperately in love": FGDN, II, 114

770 "most amusing together": ibid.

771 "My dear Lord Fisher": Randolph Churchill, II, 532

771 "fearfully cut up": Mackay, 432

771 "I had certain main ideas": Winston Churchill, *World Crisis,* I, 77

771 "a veritable volcano": ibid.

771– "But by the Sunday night": ibid.,
72 78

772 "continuous talking": Marder, *Scapa Flow,* I, 264

772 "every sort of news and counsel": Winston Churchill, *World Crisis,* I, 79

772 "The greatest triumph of all": FGDN, II, 418

772 "In two years": ibid., 419

772 "So far every step": ibid., 430

772 "I regret that in regard": ibid., 450

773 "Winston, alas!": Randolph Churchill, II, 565

773 "a Royal Pimp": Manchester, *Winston Churchill,* 440

773 ". . . as regards Winston Churchill": FGDN, II, 459

773 "My dear Fisher": Randolph Churchill, II, 566

774 "Some of us went ashore": Bonham-Carter, 202

774 "Danced on deck": ibid.

774 "I was nearly kidnapped": FGDN, II, 465

774 "WC said the King was always talking": ibid., 464

775 "largely my office": Winston Churchill, *World Crisis,* I, 119

775 "These were great days": ibid., 118

775 "in cramped and oily quarters": Randolph Churchill, II, 552

775 "dancing about the guns": Marder, *Scapa Flow,* I, 253

775 "My young friend yonder": ibid.

775– "W[inston] in glorious form":
76 Bonham-Carter, 210

776 "Winston talks about nothing": Chalmers, 112

776 "You have become a water creature": Randolph Churchill, II, 558

776 "The flags of a dozen admirals": Winston Churchill, *World Crisis,* I, 119

776– "No First Lord in the history of
77 the Navy": Manchester, *Winston Churchill,* 443

777 "He had a yarn": Randolph Churchill, II, 558

777 "Why didn't you lock him up?": Gretton, 76

777 "Do you know your men . . . ?": Marder, *Scapa Flow,* I, 254

777 "None": Bonham-Carter, 217

778 "And what are they?": Manchester, *Winston Churchill,* 443

778 "to help things along": FGDN, II, 418

778 "If, by any misadventure": Marder, *Scapa Flow,* I, 258

779 "Might I ask the First Lord": Morgan, 339

779– "What I ask the Noble Lord to
80 do": ibid., 342

780 "I do hope the whole business": Randolph Churchill, II, 621

781 "there must be some mistake": ibid., 628

781 "Oliver Cromwell was one of the founders": ibid., 629

781 "It seems right": ibid., 631

781 "I bow": ibid.

781 "unworthy of the royal mind": Gretton, 88

782 "No one who has not experienced": Winston Churchill, *World Crisis,* I, 122

782 "To shrink": ibid.

783 "If only we could make a trial gun": ibid., 123

783 "He was steadfast": ibid.

783 "Fancy if they failed": ibid.

783 "everything in the naval world": Randolph Churchill, II, 552

783 "a battle between two great": Manchester, *Winston Churchill,* 443

784 "Speed! Speed!": FGDN, II, 404

784 "The first of all necessities": Winston Churchill, *World Crisis,* I, 140

784 "I do not believe in the wisdom": ibid., 128

784 "The ordeal of coaling ship": ibid., 129

785 "This liquid fuel problem": ibid., 132

785 "lamentable exception": ibid., 131

787 "We were by no means pleased": Winton, 127

788 "a very large number of officers": ibid., 128

788 "I recall vividly": Winston Churchill, *World Crisis,* I, 119

Chapter 42
The Haldane Mission

790 "We all know that blood": Haldane, *Before The War,* 56

790 "fulfilled its purpose": Marder, *Scapa Flow,* I, 273

791 "It readily grants the English": ibid.

791 "The purpose of our naval policy": ibid., 274

791 "He felt that an effort": Winston Churchill, *World Crisis*, I, 94

791 "I felt I should be all the stronger": ibid., 95

795 "Notices on board": Huldermann, 123

796 "and that he would withdraw": ibid., 194

797 "dietary difficulties": Herwig, *Officer Corps*, 43

798 "a quiet unpretentious man": Lamar Cecil, *German Diplomatic Service*, 99

798 "the pairing of a German stallion": Bülow, I, 347

798 "I am no friend of Jews": Lamar Cecil, *German Diplomatic Service*, 99

798 "I heard a few days ago": *Holstein Papers*, II, 80

798 "in no way prejudiced": Bülow, I, 347, 469

798 "the Jewish peril": Lamar Cecil, *Ballin*, 111

798 "Siegfried Meyer": ibid., 109

799 "The essential thing is the throne": ibid., 115

799 "very largely a special preserve": ibid., 123

799 "strengthening of the war fleet": ibid., 151

799– "The fleet is . . . the embodi-
800 ment": ibid., 153

800– "Tirpitz . . . did not wish to ne-
801 gotiate": ibid., 159

801 "Alpha and Omega": ibid., 169

801 "Such a meeting": Huldermann, 151

801 *"his* department . . . *his* specialty": Lamar Cecil, *Ballin*, 173

802 "feel highly honored": Huldermann, 165

802 "His friendly sentiments": ibid.

803 "prepared with the approval": William II, *My Memoirs*, 143

803 "Acceptance of British superiority": Winston Churchill, *World Crisis*, I, 95

803 "verbal note was aimed at our Naval Law": William II, *My Memoirs*, 144

803 "for fear of obscurity": ibid., 145

803 "since I knew English best": ibid.

803 "I sat at the writing table": ibid.

804 "We devoured this document": Winston Churchill, *World Crisis*, I, 95

804 "The spirit may be good": ibid., 96

804 "Even the Socialists are not resisting": ibid.

804 "full commission of 25 battleships": ibid.

804 "This is certainly not dropping": ibid., 97

804 "Cassel says they did not seem": ibid., 96

804 "there never was any question": ibid., 98

805 "was to see a woman and a dog": Haldane, *Autobiography*, 13

805 "looked as if they had seen": Maurice, 17

805– "I rose dripping": Haldane, *Au-
6 tobiography*, 22

806 "seemed difficult in comparison": ibid., 31

806 "Of sport and of general society": ibid., 29

806– "weeks of unbroken happiness":
7 ibid., 117

807 "the new German program": Maurice, 292

807 "the Morocco question was now out of the way": Haldane, *Before the War*, 106

807 "matters of routine": ibid., 107

808 "he really was apparently afraid": Bethmann-Hollweg, 51

808 "could not define": Maurice, 305

808 "We should certainly": ibid., 306

808 "Perhaps over eight or nine years": ibid., 307

808 "My admirals are very difficult": ibid.

808– "It was not a case": ibid., 294
9

809 "The atmosphere which resulted": ibid.

809 "There is no doubt": Marder, *Scapa Flow*, I, 278

809 "The balance of power": Haldane, *Before the War*, 148

809 "bones without flesh": ibid., 109

810 "would laugh at the agreement": BD, VI, 710

810 "hard": Haldane, *Autobiography*, 243

810 "Admiral Tirpitz is a strong and difficult man": Maurice, 295

810 "so disturbed": ibid., 311

810 "Can we not spread out the tempo?": ibid.

810 "The third squadron will be asked for": Huldermann, 175

810 "for I had the strong impression": Maurice, 312

811 "that I was disappointed": ibid., 295

811 "I said emphatically": Maurice, 313

811 "a *détente* rather than an *entente*": Haldane, *Before the War*, 63

811 "depressed": Woodward, 332

811 "The Chancellor": Maurice, 314

811 "We sat down at a table": ibid., 315

811–12 "At the end he rose": ibid., 296

812 "Whether success or failure": ibid., 315

812 "I got back to the hotel": ibid., 297

812 "A promising beginning": Jarausch 2, 128

812 "had been delightful to me": Maurice, 295

812 "My impression was": Haldane, *Before the War*, 67

812 Before I left Berlin: ibid., 110

813 "An extraordinary increase": Winston Churchill, *World Crisis*, I, 102

814 "You are quite right": Huldermann, 179

814 "The quicker we publish": Marder, *Scapa Flow*, I, 280

814 "I shall consider any transfer": Jarausch, 129

815 "I believe our prayers have been answered": Maurice, 298

815 "had a communication from the Chancellor": ibid.

815–16 "England will make": DGP, XXXI, 181

816 "England will therefore observe": ibid.

816 "didn't go half far enough": Jarausch, 130

816 "a change of personnel": BD, VI, 714

816 "as long as he remained": Woodward, 348

816 "I have never in my life": DGP, XXXI, 183

817 "becoming more and more doubtful": BD, VI, 745

Chapter 43
Naval Estimates and a
"Naval Holiday"

818 "a helmet of bright brass": Randolph Churchill, I, 143

819 "white uniform": Manchester, *Winston Churchill*, 424

819 "I am very thankful": ibid.

819 "a terrible engine": ibid., 426

819 "My dear Winston": ibid., 425

819 "Germany's action at Agadir": ibid., 427

819 "It is not for . . . Belgium": Randolph Churchill, II, 513

819–20 "We knew that a formidable new Navy Law": Winston Churchill, *World Crisis*, I, 94

820 "Until Germany dropped": Randolph Churchill, II, 542

820 "One sentence stood out vividly": Winston Churchill, *World Crisis*, I, 99

820 The "Luxury Fleet" speech is drawn from ibid., 100

820 "the expression passed angrily": ibid., 101

821 "a plain statement": Bonham-Carter, 197

821 "far from being a hindrance": Winston Churchill, *World Crisis*, I, 101

821 "I suppose it is difficult": Randolph Churchill, II, 551

821 "These estimates have been framed": Woodward, 368

822 "Let me make it clear": ibid., 369

822 "We must always be ready": FGDN, II, 443

822 "Nothing, in my opinion": Win-

ston Churchill, *World Crisis*, I, 105

822 "Supposing we were both to take a holiday": ibid., I, 109

823 "such arrangements": Winston Churchill, *World Crisis*, I, 109

823 "We cannot have everything": Marder, *Scapa Flow*, I, 289

823 "We cannot possibly hold": Randolph Churchill, II, 570

823 "Would be to expose a British fleet": ibid., 575

823– "The ultimate scale": Marder, 24 *Scapa Flow*, I, 296

826 "he must clearly understand": BD, X, 601

826 "The point I am anxious to safeguard": Winston Churchill, *World Crisis*, I, 112

826 "free to aid France or not": BD, X, ii, 603

826 "an engagement that commits": ibid., 614

827 "The disposition, for instance": Woodward, 382

827 "Because of our preoccupation": Marder, *Scapa Flow*, I, 290

827 "was absolutely repugnant": ibid., 305

827 "marked the limits": ibid.

827 "Rome had to call in": ibid., 290

827 "The choice lies": ibid., 291

827 "In order to estimate": Winston Churchill, *World Crisis*, I, 112

828 "The only 'trump card' ": ibid.

828 "to form an integral part": Woodward, 389

828 "But if we come forward now": Marder, *Scapa Flow*, I, 297

828 "Naval supremacy is of two kinds": Woodward, 391

829 "What Tirpitz said": Marder, *Scapa Flow*, I, 312

829 "We must not try to read": Woodward, 408

830 "If, for the space of a year": ibid., 409

830 "events will continue to move": ibid.

830 "Act as though": ibid., 412

831 "Next year, we are to lay down": ibid., 419

831 "Winston is playing": Marder, *Scapa Flow*, I, 315

831 "take a holiday from speechmaking": ibid.

831 "utopian and unworkable": ibid.

831 "would throw innumerable men": ibid.

831 "construction was postponed for a year": ibid.

831 "endless, dangerous chapter": Woodward, 423

832 "It is really a cosmopolitan matter": ibid., 425

833 "furious": Marder, *Scapa Flow*, I, 316

833 "a piece of madness": ibid.

833 "When will First Lords": ibid.

833 "If other countries will not join us": ibid.

833 "Don't let Winston": Randolph Churchill, II, 636

833 "You are breaking with the tradition": ibid., 645

833 "You made me love you": Marder, *Scapa Flow*, I, 318

833 "the boom in the ship-building trade": Randolph Churchill, II, 637

834 "We had a Cabinet": ibid., 638

834 "When he went to the Admiralty": ibid., 640

834 The Churchill–Lloyd George exchange of notes is in ibid., 642

834 "organized insanity" . . . "bloated and profligate": Marder, *Scapa Flow*, I, 318

835 "The Chancellor of the Exchequer's interview": Randolph Churchill, II, 647

835 "to give interviews": Marder, *Scapa Flow*, I, 319

835 "needless folly": Randolph Churchill, II, 647

835 "furious": ibid., 649

835 "back against the wall": ibid.

835 "the Prime Minister must choose": Marder, *Scapa Flow*, I, 323

835 "if the declared program": Randolph Churchill, II, 646

835 "there is no chance whatever": ibid., 643

835 "vital" . . . "fundamental": ibid., 650

835 "Without a doubt": ibid., 651

835 "No predecessor of mine": ibid., 652

835 "My dear Winston": Marder, *Scapa Flow,* I, 323

835– "My dear Prime Minister": ibid.,
36 324

836 "My dear Winston": Randolph Churchill, II, 659

836 "searched and scrubbed": ibid., 660

836 "Come to breakfast tomorrow": ibid., 662

836– "the longest and perhaps also":
37 Marder, *Scapa Flow,* I, 326

837 Churchill's March 17, 1914, speech is taken from *The Times,* March 18, 1914

Chapter 44
"The Anchors Held. . . .
We Seemed to Be Safe"

839 "We met in the afternoons": Grey, *Twenty-Five Years,* I, 256

840 "there were six skeletons": ibid.

840 "Eventually": ibid., 261

840 "There was no formal finish": ibid., 262

840 "very drab and humdrum": ibid., 263

840– "In 1912–13, the current of Euro-
41 pean affairs": ibid., 267

841 "the fulfillment of Gottlieb's": Bülow, III, 38

841 "What?": ibid., 39

841 "My love for Your Highness": ibid.

842 "Nothing has helped": Lamar Cecil, *German Diplomatic Service,* 318

842 "The intimate exchange of opinion": Woodward, 405

842 "He's becoming admirably seasoned": Lamar Cecil, *German Diplomatic Service,* 319

842– "not only correct but consider-
43 ate": Winston Churchill, *World Crisis,* I, 178

843 "The Kaiser was very cautious": Bethmann-Hollweg, 76; DGP, XXXIII, 302

843 "eunuch-like statesmen": Woodward, 396

843 "I made it a practice": Lichnowsky, 85

843 "a muddlehead": ibid.

843 "who by his intimates": ibid., xix

843 "flax and turnips": ibid., 48

843 "I send only *my* ambassador": Lamar Cecil, *German Diplomatic Service,* 217

844 "The King, although not a genius": Lichnowsky, *My Mission to London,* 66

844 "A jovial *bon vivant*": LVS, 86

844 "querulous" . . . "rather trying": ibid.

844 "In spite of black socks": ibid.

844 "The simplicity and honesty": Lichnowsky, 68

844 "hand in hand": ibid., 159

844– "Sir Edward Grey said": ibid.,
45 167

846 "swarthy . . . thick-set": Grey, *Twenty-Five Years,* I, 270

846 "To my mind": ibid., 274

846 "to reassure Russia": ibid., 276

847 "No such negotiations": ibid., 279

847 "left nothing to be desired": Lamar Cecil, *Ballin,* 203

847 "most satisfactory": Gooch, *History of Modern Europe,* 530

847 "great relief": Grey, *Twenty-Five Years,* I, 283

847 "in the mind of the *Berliner Tageblatt*": Schmitt, 367

847 "He would find it difficult": Gooch, *History of Modern Europe,* 531

848 "the coming months would see": Lichnowsky, 340

848 "a great political blunder": Marder, *Scapa Flow,* I, 430

848 "To me it seems quite obvious": Lichnowsky, 189

848– "If Germany succeeds": ibid., 330
49

849 "the German fleet was the only obstacle": ibid., 336

849 "thoroughly pleasant and genial": ibid.

849 "It was the feeling of insufficient

strength": Spender, *Fifty Years,* 383

849 "What a triumph for Tirpitz!": Woodward, 418

850 "This policy of secrecy": Winston Churchill, *World Crisis,* I, 180

850 "would be greeted with pleasure": Lamar Cecil, *Ballin,* 199

850 "the finest ship afloat": Legge, 334

852 "Be on your guard": Hase, 20

852 "We overhauled the *Meteor*": Müller, 2

853 "Pleasant   journey" . . . "Friends in past": Hase, 39

Chapter 45
The Coming of Armageddon: Berlin

854 "The causes which might lead": *The Times,* March 18, 1914

855 "the vials of wrath": Winston Churchill, *World Crisis,* I, 11

855 "I shall not live": Gooch, *History of Modern Europe,* 557

856– "Austria finds herself": ibid., 516
57

857 "a dangerous little viper": Mansergh, 132

857 "at the last moment": Albertini, I, 562

857 "left in the lurch": Spender, *Fifty Years,* 362

857 "I constantly wonder": ibid., 399

857 "Our own vital interests": Jarausch, 156

857 "world historic process": Spender, *Fifty Years,* 363

857 "The Slavs were born to serve": ibid.

857– "If His Majesty Francis Joseph":
58 ibid., 364

858 "His Majesty ostentatiously used": ibid., 365

858 The account of the Moltke-Conrad conversation is taken from Albertini, I, 561–62

859 "One comes here for a visit": Fay, II, 125

859 "That's the wrong way!": ibid., 126

859 "Sophie! Sophie! Don't die!":

ibid.; dispatch sent to the Foreign Office by Sir Maurice de Bunsen, British Ambassador in Vienna: BD, XI, 15–16

859 "kill an enemy of the South Slavs": Fay, II, 132

859 "an energetic man": ibid.

860 "No crime has ever aroused": Schmitt, 397

860 "Terrible shock": Rose, 167

860 "For me, it is a great worry less": Crankshaw, *The Fall of the House of Hapsburg,* 391

860 "The Monarchy with unflinching hand": Mansergh, 219

860 "does not feel certain of Germany": Geiss, 59

861 "The crime against my nephew": Gooch, *History of Modern Europe,* 533, and Kautsky

861 "serious European complication": Geiss, 76

861 "rely on Germany's full support": ibid.

861 "opinion that this action": ibid., 77

861 "if we had really recognized": ibid.

861 "Russia's attitude": ibid.

861 "Russia is in no way prepared": ibid.

862 "The views of the Kaiser": Bethmann-Hollweg, 119

862 "The sooner the Austrians": Geiss, 71

862 "scarcely let it come to war": Kautsky, No. 49

862 "was ready for all eventualities": Geiss, 71

862 "Certainly, Your Majesty": Bülow, III, 175

862 "he did not believe": Geiss, 72

862 "I ascertained": ibid., 79

862 "The Emperor Franz Joseph may rest assured": ibid., 74

863 "All present except": ibid., 86

863 "principally to impress": ibid., 108

863 "the proposed action against Serbia": ibid., 95

863 "Germany would consider": ibid., 102

864 "The Imperial administration": ibid., 91

864 "It would be a good thing": ibid., 90

864 "The Note is being composed": Kautsky, 113

864 "assured me he knew nothing": Geiss, 154

865 "spoke in the most peaceable manner": ibid., 131

865 "everything would depend": ibid., 138

865 "they are moderate and made reconcilable": ibid., 170

865 "We should consider it unwise": ibid., 117

865 "the murder of Sarajevo": ibid., 143

866 "propaganda against Austria-Hungary": ibid., 145

866 "Russia will never accept it": Gooch, *History of Modern Europe,* 536

866 "the most formidable document": BD, XI, 73

866 "You are setting fire": Geiss, 174

866 "mistaken idea": ibid., 199

866 "Here every delay": ibid., 201

866 "very earnestly": ibid., 213

866 "give a favorable reply": BD, XI, 82

867 "a lesson": Geiss, 242

867 "would only be unable to comply": ibid., 167

868 "since in vital matters": Gooch, *History of Modern Europe,* 537

868 "action had been forced": Schmitt, 416

868 "There was nothing to prove": Gooch, *History of Modern Europe,* 535

868 "We cannot afford to alarm": Geiss, 121

868– "While I was on my summer va-
69 cation": William II, *My Memoirs,* 241

869 "How did it all happen?": Bülow, III, 184

869 "No, you've cooked this broth": ibid.

869 "A brilliant performance": Geiss, 222

869 "avoid very carefully": ibid., 260

869 "was ready to go to the limit": ibid., 241

869 "there must be a way": ibid., 242

869 "Am glad you are back": ibid., 260

870 "A confession of his own weakness": ibid., 261

870 "unscrupulous agitation" . . . "will doubtless agree": ibid.

870 "transformed": ibid., 279

870 "the whole weight of the decision": ibid., 304

871 "Russia must ruthlessly": Jarausch, 169

871 "if war breaks out": Geiss, 289

871 "The British Government could stand aside": ibid.

872 "There is immense commotion": Jarausch, 167

872 "England will be against us": Geiss, 291–92

872 "We, of course, are ready to fulfill": ibid., 293

872 "If Vienna declines": ibid., 305

872 "the restriction of Austrian military operations": ibid., 308

872 "We had a very doubtful support": ibid., 320

873 "Great Britain would never allow": BD, XI, 185

873 "astounding": ibid., 186

873 "dishonorable" . . . "a disgrace": Grey, *Twenty-Five Years,* I, 317

873 "He regretted this": BD, XI, 195

873 "a purely private quarrel" . . . "to burn out with a glowing iron": Geiss, 282

873 "Russia has placed herself": ibid.

873 "violate the deep-rooted feelings": ibid., 284

874 "General mobilization": ibid., 271

874 "make us a distinct declaration": Kautsky, 404

874 "The curses of the nations": Sazonov, 213; Paleologue, I, 48

875 "If France offers me neutrality": Kautsky, No. 575, 451

875 "Now we can go to war": Tuchman, *Guns of August,* 78

875 "Your Majesty, it cannot be done": ibid., 79

875 "Your uncle would have given me": ibid., 80

875 "wounded me deeply": ibid.

875– "burst into tears": ibid., 81
76

876 "A positive proposal by England": ibid.

876 "Now you can do what you like": ibid.

876 "This was my first experience": ibid.

876 "France would act": Kautsky, 448

876 "When the French Cabinet": Bethmann-Hollweg, 145

876 "the letter nor the spirit": Geiss, 344

876 "does not seek any territorial acquisition": ibid., 248

877 "There was no fear": ibid., 341

877 "in the most friendly manner": ibid., 342

Chapter 46
The Coming of Armageddon: London

879 "had been reading": Winston Churchill, World Crisis, I, 193

879 "the gravest event for many years": Spender, Asquith, II, 80

879 "We are within measurable": Asquith, Memories, II, 8

880 "substantial economy": Woodward, Appendix V, 478

880 "I cannot help thinking": ibid., 479

880 "the merits of the dispute": Asquith, Genesis, 187

880 "simply and solely": ibid.

880 "saw no reason": Geiss, 105

880– "The German Government believes": ibid., 110
81

881 "England will not prevent": ibid., 130

881 "brusque, sudden, and peremptory": Grey, Twenty-Five Years, I, 307

881 "the most formidable document": BD, XI, 73

881 "give a favorable reply": ibid., 82

881 "If our respective governments": Grey, Twenty-Five Years, I, 304

881 "I see in it": Geiss, 206

882 "Ask the Minister for Foreign Affairs": BD, XI, 101

882 "Sir E. Grey": Geiss, 238–41

882– "in the most decided way": ibid., 236
83

883 "would practically amount": Grey, Twenty-Five Years, I, 309

883 "Serbia has capitulated": Asquith, Memories, II, 8

883 "The German General Staff": Haldane, Autobiography, 274

883 "It must be obvious": Asquith, Genesis, 188

883 "nothing but a miracle": Jenkins, 325

884 "at this stage": Spender, Asquith, 81

884 "will be one of policy": ibid.

884– Lichnowsky's July 29 telegram
86 with the Kaiser's marginalia is taken from Geiss, 288–90

887 "He then proceeded to make": Grey, Twenty-Five Years, I, 315

887 "When the war was over": ibid.

888 "The document made it clear": ibid., 316

888 "His Majesty's Government cannot": ibid., 317

888 "as he knew France": Geiss, 314

888 "full and active readiness": ibid., 225

889 "joint steps": ibid., 313

889 "He is convinced": ibid., 317

889 "how difficult it would be": ibid.

889 "British participation": Winston Churchill, World Crisis, I, 215

889 "It was clear to me": Grey, Twenty-Five Years, I, 324

890– "felt that to stand aside": ibid., 326
91

891 "The argument": BD, XI, 225

891 "Germany was so immensely strong": Grey, Twenty-Five Years, I, 302

891– "There was never any chance": Winston Churchill, World Crisis, I, 205
92

892 "the very existence of his country": Grey, Twenty-Five Years, I, 328

892 "go one inch beyond": ibid., 329

892 "The Cabinet thought": Geiss, 327

892 "would await the invasion": ibid., 328

892 "would find herself in a state": ibid.

892– "the question of Belgian neutral-
93   ity": ibid., 327

893– "About the same time": Grey,
94   Twenty-Five Years, I, 327

894 "he rather doubted": BD, XI, 234

894 "the issues of peace and war":
     Grey, Twenty-Five Years, I, 312

894 "there were forces": ibid.

895 "the whole of Germany": Tuch-
     man, Guns of August, 19

895 "We must put aside": ibid., 26

896 "The more English the better":
     ibid., 121

896 "Military opinion": Bethmann-
     Hollweg, 147

896 "reliable information": Geiss,
     231

896– "with the deepest regret": ibid.
97

897 "some suggestions": ibid.

897 "The Belgian Government must
     be informed": ibid., 354

897 "Germany's procedure in Bel-
     gium": ibid., 357

897 "uncoded": Kautsky, 567

898 "Winston very bellicose": As-
     quith, Memories, II, 11

898 "it was at our request": BD, XI,
     252

898 "simple traverse": Spender, As-
     quith, II, 90

898 "this was a war intrigued": Lloyd
     George, I, 68

898 "I saw Money": ibid.

899 "aghast at the bare idea": Spen-
     der, Asquith, II, 102

899 "are the greatest ninnies":
     Margot Asquith, IV, 20

899 "We have made no pledges":
     LVS, 114

900 "My dear Nicky": ibid., 140

900 "would gladly": BD, XI, 276

900 "I walked across the Horse
     Guards Parade": Winston Chur-
     chill, World Crisis, I, 217

900 "we could not stand": Grey,
     Twenty-Five Years, II, 1

900– "He was very emotional": As-
901 quith, Memories, II, 11

901 "that the country would . . . be
     unable": Haldane, Autobiogra-
     phy, 274

901 "Grey asked me": ibid., 275

902 "Their breath was somewhat":
     ibid.

903 "time must be made": Grey,
     Twenty-Five Years, II, 13

903 "for no man had worked harder"
     . . . "go through one small cor-
     ner": ibid.

903– The description of the scene in
6   the House of Commons and the
     quotes from Sir Edward Grey's
     speech are taken from August 4,
     1914, editions of The Times, The
     Daily Telegraph, The Daily
     Chronicle, and The Daily News.

906 "For the most part conversa-
     tional": Asquith, Memories, II, 25

906 "Grey's speech was very wonder-
     ful": Trevelyan, 265

907 "sacrifice the honor" . . .
     "firmly resolved": Fay, II, 541

907 "What happens now?": Winston
     Churchill, World Crisis, I, 220

907 "No, of course everybody
     knows": Asquith, Genesis, 213

907 "Thus, the efforts of a lifetime":
     ibid.

907 "The lamps are going out": Grey,
     Twenty-Five Years, II, 20

907 "bombs on the railway": Schmitt,
     461

907 "a French physician": Kautsky,
     508

908 "Interesting" . . . "We got the
     news": LVS, 150

908 "very calmly" . . . "We got
     through all the business": ibid.

908 "This whole thing": ibid.

908 "So it is all up": Margot Asquith,
     IV, 69

INDEX